California
Rules of Court

Federal
District Courts

Volume II – Federal

2022 Edition

Mat #42795578

ISBN 978–1–539–22369–6

PREFACE

Designed for use in the office or courtroom, this pamphlet contains the California federal district rules.

WHAT'S NEW

California Rules of Court, Volume II – Federal District Courts, 2022 Edition, includes rules and associated material governing practice before the California federal district courts. It is current with amendments received through December 1, 2021. For temporary orders and notices relating to COVID–19 and court operations, please see the courts' websites.

CONTACT US

For additional information or research assistance, contact the Reference Attorneys at 1-800-REF-ATTY (1-800-733-2889) or by Live Chat: Access via Westlaw. Contact our U.S. legal editorial department directly with your questions and suggestions by e-mail at editors.us-legal@tr.com.

Thank you for subscribing to this product. Should you have any questions regarding this product please contact Customer Service at 1-800-328-4880 or by fax at 1-800-340-9378. If you would like to inquire about related publications, or to place an order, please contact us at 1-888-728-7677 or visit us at legalsolutions.thomsonreuters.com.

THE PUBLISHER

January 2022

THOMSON REUTERS PROVIEW™

PUBLISHER'S FOREWORD

For the following contents, please refer to the *California Rules of Court, Volume IIA – Federal Bankruptcy Courts, 2022 Edition*:

Federal Rules of Bankruptcy Procedure

United States Bankruptcy Appellate Panel for the Ninth Circuit

United States Bankruptcy Courts of California

TABLE OF CONTENTS

FEDERAL
RULES OF CIVIL PROCEDURE

Including Amendments Effective December 1, 2020

TITLE I. SCOPE OF RULES; FORM OF ACTION

RULE 1. SCOPE AND PURPOSE

These rules govern the procedure in all civil actions and proceedings in the United States district courts, except as stated in Rule 81. They should be construed, administered, and employed by the court and the parties to secure the just, speedy, and inexpensive determination of every action and proceeding.

(Amended December 29, 1948, effective October 20, 1949; February 28, 1966, effective July 1, 1966; April 22, 1993, effective December 1, 1993; April 30, 2007, effective December 1, 2007; April 29, 2015, effective December 1, 2015.)

RULE 2. ONE FORM OF ACTION

There is one form of action—the civil action.

(Amended April 30, 2007, effective December 1, 2007.)

TITLE II. COMMENCING AN ACTION; SERVICE OF PROCESS, PLEADINGS, MOTIONS, AND ORDERS

RULE 3. COMMENCING AN ACTION

A civil action is commenced by filing a complaint with the court.

(Amended April 30, 2007, effective December 1, 2007.)

RULE 4. SUMMONS

(a) Contents; Amendments.

(1) *Contents.* A summons must:

(A) name the court and the parties;

(B) be directed to the defendant;

(C) state the name and address of the plaintiff's attorney or—if unrepresented—of the plaintiff;

(D) state the time within which the defendant must appear and defend;

(E) notify the defendant that a failure to appear and defend will result in a default judgment against the defendant for the relief demanded in the complaint;

(F) be signed by the clerk; and

(G) bear the court's seal.

(2) *Amendments.* The court may permit a summons to be amended.

(b) Issuance. On or after filing the complaint, the plaintiff may present a summons to the clerk for signature and seal. If the summons is properly completed, the clerk must sign, seal, and issue it to the plaintiff for service on the defendant. A summons—or a copy of a summons that is addressed to multiple defendants—must be issued for each defendant to be served.

(c) Service.

(1) *In General.* A summons must be served with a copy of the complaint. The plaintiff is responsible for having the summons and complaint served within the time allowed by Rule 4(m) and must furnish the necessary copies to the person who makes service.

(2) *By Whom.* Any person who is at least 18 years old and not a party may serve a summons and complaint.

(3) *By a Marshal or Someone Specially Appointed.* At the plaintiff's request, the court may order that service be made by a United States marshal or deputy marshal or by a person specially appointed by the court. The court must so order if the plaintiff is authorized to proceed in forma pauperis under 28 U.S.C. § 1915 or as a seaman under 28 U.S.C. § 1916.

(d) Waiving Service.

(1) *Requesting a Waiver.* An individual, corporation, or association that is subject to service under Rule 4(e), (f), or (h) has a duty to avoid unnecessary expenses of serving the summons. The plaintiff may notify such a defendant that an action has been commenced and request that the defendant waive service of a summons. The notice and request must:

   (A) be in writing and be addressed:

      (i) to the individual defendant; or

      (ii) for a defendant subject to service under Rule 4(h), to an officer, a managing or general agent, or any other agent authorized by appointment or by law to receive service of process;

   (B) name the court where the complaint was filed;

   (C) be accompanied by a copy of the complaint, 2 copies of the waiver form appended to this Rule 4, and a prepaid means for returning the form;

   (D) inform the defendant, using the form appended to this Rule 4, of the consequences of waiving and not waiving service;

   (E) state the date when the request is sent;

   (F) give the defendant a reasonable time of at least 30 days after the request was sent—or at least 60 days if sent to the defendant outside any judicial district of the United States—to return the waiver; and

   (G) be sent by first-class mail or other reliable means.

(2) *Failure to Waive.* If a defendant located within the United States fails, without good cause, to sign and return a waiver requested by a plaintiff located within the United States, the court must impose on the defendant:

   (A) the expenses later incurred in making service; and

   (B) the reasonable expenses, including attorney's fees, of any motion required to collect those service expenses.

(3) *Time to Answer After a Waiver.* A defendant who, before being served with process, timely returns a waiver need not serve an answer to the complaint until 60 days after the request was sent—or until 90 days after it was sent to the defendant outside any judicial district of the United States.

(4) *Results of Filing a Waiver.* When the plaintiff files a waiver, proof of service is not required and these rules apply as if a summons and complaint had been served at the time of filing the waiver.

(5) *Jurisdiction and Venue Not Waived.* Waiving service of a summons does not waive any objection to personal jurisdiction or to venue.

(e) Serving an Individual Within a Judicial District of the United States. Unless federal law provides otherwise, an individual—other than a minor, an incompetent person, or a person whose waiver has been filed—may be served in a judicial district of the United States by:

(1) following state law for serving a summons in an action brought in courts of general jurisdiction in the state where the district court is located or where service is made; or

(2) doing any of the following:

   (A) delivering a copy of the summons and of the complaint to the individual personally;

   (B) leaving a copy of each at the individual's dwelling or usual place of abode with someone of suitable age and discretion who resides there; or

   (C) delivering a copy of each to an agent authorized by appointment or by law to receive service of process.

(f) Serving an Individual in a Foreign Country. Unless federal law provides otherwise, an individual—other than a minor, an incompetent person, or a person whose waiver has been filed—may be served at a place not within any judicial district of the United States:

(1) by any internationally agreed means of service that is reasonably calculated to give notice, such as those authorized by the Hague Convention on the Service Abroad of Judicial and Extrajudicial Documents;

(2) if there is no internationally agreed means, or if an international agreement allows but does not specify other means, by a method that is reasonably calculated to give notice:

   (A) as prescribed by the foreign country's law for service in that country in an action in its courts of general jurisdiction;

   (B) as the foreign authority directs in response to a letter rogatory or letter of request; or

   (C) unless prohibited by the foreign country's law, by:

      (i) delivering a copy of the summons and of the complaint to the individual personally; or

      (ii) using any form of mail that the clerk addresses and sends to the individual and that requires a signed receipt; or

(3) by other means not prohibited by international agreement, as the court orders.

(g) Serving a Minor or an Incompetent Person. A minor or an incompetent person in a judicial district of the United States must be served by following state law for serving a summons or like process on such a defendant in an action brought in the courts of general jurisdiction of the state where service is made. A minor or an incompetent person who is not within any judicial district of the United States must be served in the manner prescribed by Rule 4(f)(2)(A), (f)(2)(B), or (f)(3).

(h) Serving a Corporation, Partnership, or Association. Unless federal law provides otherwise or the defendant's waiver has been filed, a domestic or foreign corporation, or a partnership or other unincorporated association that is subject to suit under a common name, must be served:

(1) in a judicial district of the United States:

   (A) in the manner prescribed by Rule 4(e)(1) for serving an individual; or

   (B) by delivering a copy of the summons and of the complaint to an officer, a managing or general agent, or any other agent authorized by appointment or by law to receive service of process and—if the agent is one authorized by statute and the statute so requires—by also mailing a copy of each to the defendant; or

(2) at a place not within any judicial district of the United States, in any manner prescribed by Rule 4(f) for serving an individual, except personal delivery under (f)(2)(C)(i).

(i) Serving the United States and Its Agencies, Corporations, Officers, or Employees.

(1) *United States.* To serve the United States, a party must:

(A)(i) deliver a copy of the summons and of the complaint to the United States attorney for the district where the action is brought—or to an assistant United States attorney or clerical employee whom the United States attorney designates in a writing filed with the court clerk—or

(ii) send a copy of each by registered or certified mail to the civil-process clerk at the United States attorney's office;

(B) send a copy of each by registered or certified mail to the Attorney General of the United States at Washington, D.C.; and

(C) if the action challenges an order of a nonparty agency or officer of the United States, send a copy of each by registered or certified mail to the agency or officer.

(2) *Agency; Corporation; Officer or Employee Sued in an Official Capacity.* To serve a United States agency or corporation, or a United States officer or employee sued only in an official capacity, a party must serve the United States and also send a copy of the summons and of the complaint by registered or certified mail to the agency, corporation, officer, or employee.

(3) *Officer or Employee Sued Individually.* To serve a United States officer or employee sued in an individual capacity for an act or omission occurring in connection with duties performed on the United States' behalf (whether or not the officer or employee is also sued in an official capacity), a party must serve the United States and also serve the officer or employee under Rule 4(e), (f), or (g).

(4) *Extending Time.* The court must allow a party a reasonable time to cure its failure to:

(A) serve a person required to be served under Rule 4(i)(2), if the party has served either the United States attorney or the Attorney General of the United States; or

(B) serve the United States under Rule 4(i)(3), if the party has served the United States officer or employee.

(j) Serving a Foreign, State, or Local Government.

(1) *Foreign State.* A foreign state or its political subdivision, agency, or instrumentality must be served in accordance with 28 U.S.C. § 1608.

(2) *State or Local Government.* A state, a municipal corporation, or any other state-created governmental organization that is subject to suit must be served by:

(A) delivering a copy of the summons and of the complaint to its chief executive officer; or

(B) serving a copy of each in the manner prescribed by that state's law for serving a summons or like process on such a defendant.

(k) Territorial Limits of Effective Service.

(1) *In General.* Serving a summons or filing a waiver of service establishes personal jurisdiction over a defendant:

(A) who is subject to the jurisdiction of a court of general jurisdiction in the state where the district court is located;

(B) who is a party joined under Rule 14 or 19 and is served within a judicial district of the United States and not more than 100 miles from where the summons was issued; or

(C) when authorized by a federal statute.

(2) *Federal Claim Outside State–Court Jurisdiction.* For a claim that arises under federal law, serving a summons or filing a waiver of service establishes personal jurisdiction over a defendant if:

(A) the defendant is not subject to jurisdiction in any state's courts of general jurisdiction; and

(B) exercising jurisdiction is consistent with the United States Constitution and laws.

(*l*) Proving Service.

(1) *Affidavit Required.* Unless service is waived, proof of service must be made to the court. Except for service by a United States marshal or deputy marshal, proof must be by the server's affidavit.

(2) *Service Outside the United States.* Service not within any judicial district of the United States must be proved as follows:

(A) if made under Rule 4(f)(1), as provided in the applicable treaty or convention; or

(B) if made under Rule 4(f)(2) or (f)(3), by a receipt signed by the addressee, or by other evidence satisfying the court that the summons and complaint were delivered to the addressee.

(3) *Validity of Service; Amending Proof.* Failure to prove service does not affect the validity of service. The court may permit proof of service to be amended.

(m) Time Limit for Service. If a defendant is not served within 90 days after the complaint is filed, the court—on motion or on its own after notice to the plaintiff—must dismiss the action without prejudice against that defendant or order that service be made within a specified time. But if the plaintiff shows good cause for the failure, the court must extend the time for service for an appropriate period. This subdivision (m) does not apply to service in a foreign country under Rule 4(f), 4(h)(2), or 4(j)(1), or to service of a notice under Rule 71.1(d)(3)(A).

(n) Asserting Jurisdiction over Property or Assets.

(1) *Federal Law.* The court may assert jurisdiction over property if authorized by a federal statute. Notice to claimants of the property must be given as provided in the statute or by serving a summons under this rule.

(2) *State Law.* On a showing that personal jurisdiction over a defendant cannot be obtained in the district where the action is brought by reasonable efforts to serve a summons under this rule, the court may assert jurisdiction over the defendant's assets found in the district. Jurisdiction is acquired by seizing the assets under the circumstances and in the manner provided by state law in that district.

Rule 4   Notice of a Lawsuit and Request to Waive Service of Summons.

(Caption)

To (*name the defendant or — if the defendant is a corporation, partnership, or association — name an officer or agent authorized to receive service*):

Why are you getting this?

A lawsuit has been filed against you, or the entity you represent, in this court under the number shown above. A copy of the complaint is attached.

This is not a summons, or an official notice from the court. It is a request that, to avoid expenses, you waive formal service of a summons by signing and returning the enclosed waiver. To avoid these expenses, you must return the signed waiver within (*give at least 30 days or at least 60 days if the defendant is outside any judicial district of the United States*) from the date shown below, which is the date this notice was sent. Two copies of the waiver form are enclosed, along with a stamped, self-addressed envelope or other prepaid means for returning one copy. You may keep the other copy.

What happens next?

If you return the signed waiver, I will file it with the court. The action will then proceed as if you had been served on the date the waiver is filed, but no summons will be served on you and you will have 60 days from the date this notice is sent (see the date below) to answer the complaint (or 90 days if this notice is sent to you outside any judicial district of the United States).

If you do not return the signed waiver within the time indicated, I will arrange to have the summons and complaint served on you. And I will ask the court to require you, or the entity you represent, to pay the expenses of making service.

Please read the enclosed statement about the duty to avoid unnecessary expenses.

I certify that this request is being sent to you on the date below.

Date: _____

_____
(Signature of the attorney
or unrepresented party)

_____
(Printed name)

_____
(Address)

_____
(E-mail address)

_____
(Telephone number)

Rule 4   Waiver of the Service of Summons.

(Caption)

To (*name the plaintiff's attorney or the unrepresented plaintiff*):

I have received your request to waive service of a summons in this action along with a copy of the complaint, two copies of this waiver form, and a prepaid means of returning one signed copy of the form to you.

I, or the entity I represent, agree to save the expense of serving a summons and complaint in this case.

I understand that I, or the entity I represent, will keep all defenses or objections to the lawsuit, the court's jurisdiction, and the venue of the action, but that I waive any objections to the absence of a summons or of service.

I also understand that I, or the entity I represent, must file and serve an answer or a motion under Rule 12 within 60 days from_____, the date when this request was sent (or 90 days if it was sent outside the United States). If I fail to do so, a default judgment will be entered against me or the entity I represent.

Date: _____

_____
(Signature of the attorney
or unrepresented party)

_____
(Printed name)

_____
(Address)

_____
(E-mail address)

_____
(Telephone number)

(Attach the following)

Duty to Avoid Unnecessary Expenses of Serving a Summons

Rule 4 of the Federal Rules of Civil Procedure requires certain defendants to cooperate in saving unnecessary expenses of serving a summons and complaint. A defendant who is located in the United States and who fails to return a signed waiver of service requested by a plaintiff located in the United States will be required to pay the expenses of service, unless the defendant shows good cause for the failure.

"Good cause" does not include a belief that the lawsuit is groundless, or that it has been brought in an improper venue, or that the court has no jurisdiction over this matter or over the defendant or the defendant's property.

If the waiver is signed and returned, you can still make these and all other defenses and objections, but you cannot object to the absence of a summons or of service.

If you waive service, then you must, within the time specified on the waiver form, serve an answer or a motion under Rule 12 on the plaintiff and file a copy with the court. By signing and returning the waiver form, you are allowed more time to respond than if a summons had been served.

(Amended January 21, 1963, effective July 1, 1963; February 28, 1966, effective July 1, 1966; April 29, 1980, effective August 1, 1980; amended by Pub.L. 97-462, § 2, January 12, 1983, 96 Stat. 2527, effective 45 days after January 12, 1983; amended March 2, 1987, effective August 1, 1987; April 22, 1993, effective December 1, 1993; April 17, 2000, effective December 1, 2000; April 30, 2007, effective December 1, 2007; April 29, 2015, effective December 1, 2015; April 28, 2016, effective December 1, 2016; April 27, 2017, effective December 1, 2017.)

RULE 4.1 SERVING OTHER PROCESS

(a) In General. Process—other than a summons under Rule 4 or a subpoena under Rule 45—must be served by a United States marshal or deputy marshal or by a person specially appointed for that purpose. It may be served anywhere within the territorial limits of the state where the district court is located and, if authorized by a federal statute, beyond those limits. Proof of service must be made under Rule 4(*l*).

(b) Enforcing Orders: Committing for Civil Contempt. An order committing a person for civil contempt of a decree or injunction issued to enforce federal law may be served and enforced in any district. Any other order in a civil-contempt proceeding may be served only in the state where the issuing court is located or elsewhere in the United States within 100 miles from where the order was issued.

(Adopted April 22, 1993, effective December 1, 1993; amended April 30, 2007, effective December 1, 2007.)

RULE 5. SERVING AND FILING PLEADINGS AND OTHER PAPERS

(a) Service: When Required.

(1) *In General.* Unless these rules provide otherwise, each of the following papers must be served on every party:

(A) an order stating that service is required;

(B) a pleading filed after the original complaint, unless the court orders otherwise under Rule 5(c) because there are numerous defendants;

(C) a discovery paper required to be served on a party, unless the court orders otherwise;

(D) a written motion, except one that may be heard ex parte; and

(E) a written notice, appearance, demand, or offer of judgment, or any similar paper.

(2) *If a Party Fails to Appear.* No service is required on a party who is in default for failing to appear. But a pleading that asserts a new claim for relief against such a party must be served on that party under Rule 4.

(3) *Seizing Property.* If an action is begun by seizing property and no person is or need be named as a defendant, any service required before the filing of an appearance, answer, or claim must be made on the person who had custody or possession of the property when it was seized.

(b) Service: How Made.

(1) *Serving an Attorney.* If a party is represented by an attorney, service under this rule must be made on the attorney unless the court orders service on the party.

(2) *Service in General.* A paper is served under this rule by:

(A) handing it to the person;

(B) leaving it:

(i) at the person's office with a clerk or other person in charge or, if no one is in charge, in a conspicuous place in the office; or

(ii) if the person has no office or the office is closed, at the person's dwelling or usual place of abode with someone of suitable age and discretion who resides there;

(C) mailing it to the person's last known address—in which event service is complete upon mailing;

(D) leaving it with the court clerk if the person has no known address;

(E) sending it to a registered user by filing it with the court's electronic-filing system or sending it by other electronic means that the person consented to in writing—in either of which events service is complete upon filing or sending, but is not effective if the filer or sender learns that it did not reach the person to be served; or

(F) delivering it by any other means that the person consented to in writing—in which event service is complete when the person making service delivers it to the agency designated to make delivery.

(3) *Using Court Facilities.* [Abrogated (Apr. 26, 2018, eff. Dec. 1, 2018.)]

(c) Serving Numerous Defendants.

(1) *In General.* If an action involves an unusually large number of defendants, the court may, on motion or on its own, order that:

(A) defendants' pleadings and replies to them need not be served on other defendants;

(B) any crossclaim, counterclaim, avoidance, or affirmative defense in those pleadings and replies to them will be treated as denied or avoided by all other parties; and

(C) filing any such pleading and serving it on the plaintiff constitutes notice of the pleading to all parties.

(2) *Notifying Parties.* A copy of every such order must be served on the parties as the court directs.

(d) Filing.

(1) *Required Filings; Certificate of Service.*

(A) *Papers after the Complaint.* Any paper after the complaint that is required to be served must be filed no later than a reasonable time after service. But disclosures under Rule 26(a)(1) or (2) and the following discovery requests and responses must not be filed until they are used in the proceeding or the court orders filing:

depositions, interrogatories, requests for documents or tangible things or to permit entry onto land, and requests for admission.

(B) *Certificate of Service.* No certificate of service is required when a paper is served by filing it with the court's electronic-filing system. When a paper that is required to be served is served by other means:

(i) if the paper is filed, a certificate of service must be filed with it or within a reasonable time after service; and

(ii) if the paper is not filed, a certificate of service need not be filed unless filing is required by court order or by local rule.

(2) *Nonelectronic Filing.* A paper not filed electronically is filed by delivering it:

(A) to the clerk; or

(B) to a judge who agrees to accept it for filing, and who must then note the filing date on the paper and promptly send it to the clerk.

(3) *Electronic Filing and Signing.*

(A) *By a Represented Person—Generally Required; Exceptions.* A person represented by an attorney must file electronically, unless nonelectronic filing is allowed by the court for good cause or is allowed or required by local rule.

(B) *By an Unrepresented Person—When Allowed or Required.* A person not represented by an attorney:

(i) may file electronically only if allowed by court order or by local rule; and

(ii) may be required to file electronically only by court order, or by a local rule that includes reasonable exceptions.

(C) *Signing.* A filing made through a person's electronic-filing account and authorized by that person, together with that person's name on a signature block, constitutes the person's signature.

(D) *Same as a Written Paper.* A paper filed electronically is a written paper for purposes of these rules.

(4) *Acceptance by the Clerk.* The clerk must not refuse to file a paper solely because it is not in the form prescribed by these rules or by a local rule or practice.

(Amended January 21, 1963, effective July 1, 1963; March 30, 1970, effective July 1, 1970; April 29, 1980, effective August 1, 1980; March 2, 1987, effective August 1, 1987; April 30, 1991, effective December 1, 1991; April 22, 1993, effective December 1, 1993; April 23, 1996, effective December 1, 1996; April 17, 2000, effective December 1, 2000; April 23, 2001, effective December 1, 2001; April 12, 2006, effective December 1, 2006; April 30, 2007, effective December 1, 2007; April 26, 2018, effective December 1, 2018.)

RULE 5.1 CONSTITUTIONAL CHALLENGE TO A STATUTE—NOTICE, CERTIFICATION, AND INTERVENTION

(a) Notice by a Party. A party that files a pleading, written motion, or other paper drawing into question the constitutionality of a federal or state statute must promptly:

(1) file a notice of constitutional question stating the question and identifying the paper that raises it, if:

(A) a federal statute is questioned and the parties do not include the United States, one of its agencies, or one of its officers or employees in an official capacity; or

(B) a state statute is questioned and the parties do not include the state, one of its agencies, or one of its officers or employees in an official capacity; and

(2) serve the notice and paper on the Attorney General of the United States if a federal statute is questioned—or on the state attorney general if a state statute is questioned—either by certified or registered mail or by sending it to an electronic address designated by the attorney general for this purpose.

(b) Certification by the Court. The court must, under 28 U.S.C. § 2403, certify to the appropriate attorney general that a statute has been questioned.

(c) Intervention; Final Decision on the Merits. Unless the court sets a later time, the attorney general may intervene within 60 days after the notice is filed or after the court certifies the challenge, whichever is earlier. Before the time to intervene expires, the court may reject the constitutional challenge, but may not enter a final judgment holding the statute unconstitutional.

(d) No Forfeiture. A party's failure to file and serve the notice, or the court's failure to certify, does not forfeit a constitutional claim or defense that is otherwise timely asserted.

(Adopted April 12, 2006, effective December 1, 2006; amended April 30, 2007, effective December 1, 2007.)

RULE 5.2 PRIVACY PROTECTION FOR FILINGS MADE WITH THE COURT

(a) Redacted Filings. Unless the court orders otherwise, in an electronic or paper filing with the court that contains an individual's social-security number, taxpayer-identification number, or birth date, the name of an individual known to be a minor, or a financial-account number, a party or nonparty making the filing may include only:

(1) the last four digits of the social-security number and taxpayer-identification number;

(2) the year of the individual's birth;

(3) the minor's initials; and

(4) the last four digits of the financial-account number.

(b) Exemptions from the Redaction Requirement. The redaction requirement does not apply to the following:

(1) a financial-account number that identifies the property allegedly subject to forfeiture in a forfeiture proceeding;

(2) the record of an administrative or agency proceeding;

(3) the official record of a state-court proceeding;

(4) the record of a court or tribunal, if that record was not subject to the redaction requirement when originally filed;

(5) a filing covered by Rule 5.2(c) or (d); and

(6) a pro se filing in an action brought under 28 U.S.C. §§ 2241, 2254, or 2255.

(c) Limitations on Remote Access to Electronic Files; Social–Security Appeals and Immigration Cases. Unless the court orders otherwise, in an action for benefits under the Social Security Act, and in an action or proceeding relating to an order of removal, to relief from removal, or to immigration benefits or detention, access to an electronic file is authorized as follows:

(1) the parties and their attorneys may have remote electronic access to any part of the case file, including the administrative record;

(2) any other person may have electronic access to the full record at the courthouse, but may have remote electronic access only to:

(A) the docket maintained by the court; and

(B) an opinion, order, judgment, or other disposition of the court, but not any other part of the case file or the administrative record.

(d) Filings Made Under Seal. The court may order that a filing be made under seal without redaction. The court may later unseal the filing or order the person who made the filing to file a redacted version for the public record.

(e) Protective Orders. For good cause, the court may by order in a case:

(1) require redaction of additional information; or

(2) limit or prohibit a nonparty's remote electronic access to a document filed with the court.

(f) Option for Additional Unredacted Filing Under Seal. A person making a redacted filing may also file an unredacted copy under seal. The court must retain the unredacted copy as part of the record.

(g) Option for Filing a Reference List. A filing that contains redacted information may be filed together with a reference list that identifies each item of redacted information and specifies an appropriate identifier that uniquely corresponds to each item listed. The list must be filed under seal and may be amended as of right. Any reference in the case to a listed identifier will be construed to refer to the corresponding item of information.

(h) Waiver of Protection of Identifiers. A person waives the protection of Rule 5.2(a) as to the person's own information by filing it without redaction and not under seal.

(Adopted April 30, 2007, effective December 1, 2007.)

RULE 6. COMPUTING AND EXTENDING TIME; TIME FOR MOTION PAPERS

(a) Computing Time. The following rules apply in computing any time period specified in these rules, in any local rule or court order, or in any statute that does not specify a method of computing time.

(1) *Period Stated in Days or a Longer Unit.* When the period is stated in days or a longer unit of time:

(A) exclude the day of the event that triggers the period;

(B) count every day, including intermediate Saturdays, Sundays, and legal holidays; and

(C) include the last day of the period, but if the last day is a Saturday, Sunday, or legal holiday, the period continues to run until the end of the next day that is not a Saturday, Sunday, or legal holiday.

(2) *Period Stated in Hours.* When the period is stated in hours:

(A) begin counting immediately on the occurrence of the event that triggers the period;

(B) count every hour, including hours during intermediate Saturdays, Sundays, and legal holidays; and

(C) if the period would end on a Saturday, Sunday, or legal holiday, the period continues to run until the same time on the next day that is not a Saturday, Sunday, or legal holiday.

(3) *Inaccessibility of the Clerk's Office.* Unless the court orders otherwise, if the clerk's office is inaccessible:

(A) on the last day for filing under Rule 6(a)(1), then the time for filing is extended to the first accessible day that is not a Saturday, Sunday, or legal holiday; or

(B) during the last hour for filing under Rule 6(a)(2), then the time for filing is extended to the same time on the first accessible day that is not a Saturday, Sunday, or legal holiday.

(4) *"Last Day" Defined.* Unless a different time is set by a statute, local rule, or court order, the last day ends:

(A) for electronic filing, at midnight in the court's time zone; and

(B) for filing by other means, when the clerk's office is scheduled to close.

(5) *"Next Day" Defined.* The "next day" is determined by continuing to count forward when the period is measured after an event and backward when measured before an event.

(6) *"Legal Holiday" Defined.* "Legal holiday" means:

(A) the day set aside by statute for observing New Year's Day, Martin Luther King Jr.'s Birthday, Washington's Birthday, Memorial Day, Independence Day, Labor Day, Columbus Day, Veterans' Day, Thanksgiving Day, or Christmas Day;

(B) any day declared a holiday by the President or Congress; and

(C) for periods that are measured after an event, any other day declared a holiday by the state where the district court is located.

(b) Extending Time.

(1) *In General.* When an act may or must be done within a specified time, the court may, for good cause, extend the time:

(A) with or without motion or notice if the court acts, or if a request is made, before the original time or its extension expires; or

(B) on motion made after the time has expired if the party failed to act because of excusable neglect.

(2) *Exceptions.* A court must not extend the time to act under Rules 50(b) and (d), 52(b), 59(b), (d), and (e), and 60(b).

(c) **Motions, Notices of Hearing, and Affidavits.**

(1) *In General.* A written motion and notice of the hearing must be served at least 14 days before the time specified for the hearing, with the following exceptions:

(A) when the motion may be heard ex parte;

(B) when these rules set a different time; or

(C) when a court order—which a party may, for good cause, apply for ex parte—sets a different time.

(2) *Supporting Affidavit.* Any affidavit supporting a motion must be served with the motion. Except as Rule 59(c) provides otherwise, any opposing affidavit must be served at least 7 days before the hearing, unless the court permits service at another time.

(d) **Additional Time After Certain Kinds of Service.** When a party may or must act within a specified time after being served and service is made under Rule 5(b)(2)(C) (mail), (D) (leaving with the clerk), or (F) (other means consented to), 3 days are added after the period would otherwise expire under Rule 6(a).

(Amended December 27, 1946, effective March 19, 1948; January 21, 1963, effective July 1, 1963; February 28, 1966, effective July 1, 1966; December 4, 1967, effective July 1, 1968; March 1, 1971, effective July 1, 1971; April 28, 1983, effective August 1, 1983; April 29, 1985, effective August 1, 1985; March 2, 1987, effective August 1, 1987; April 26, 1999, effective December 1, 1999; April 23, 2001, effective December 1, 2001; April 25, 2005, effective December 1, 2005; April 30, 2007, effective December 1, 2007; March 26, 2009, effective December 1, 2009; April 28, 2016, effective December 1, 2016.)

TITLE III. PLEADINGS AND MOTIONS

RULE 7. PLEADINGS ALLOWED; FORM OF MOTIONS AND OTHER PAPERS

(a) **Pleadings.** Only these pleadings are allowed:

(1) a complaint;

(2) an answer to a complaint;

(3) an answer to a counterclaim designated as a counterclaim;

(4) an answer to a crossclaim;

(5) a third-party complaint;

(6) an answer to a third-party complaint; and

(7) if the court orders one, a reply to an answer.

(b) **Motions and Other Papers.**

(1) *In General.* A request for a court order must be made by motion. The motion must:

(A) be in writing unless made during a hearing or trial;

(B) state with particularity the grounds for seeking the order; and

(C) state the relief sought.

(2) *Form.* The rules governing captions and other matters of form in pleadings apply to motions and other papers.

(Amended December 27, 1946, effective March 19, 1948; January 21, 1963, effective July 1, 1963; April 28, 1983, effective August 1, 1983; April 30, 2007, effective December 1, 2007.)

RULE 7.1 DISCLOSURE STATEMENT

(a) **Who Must File; Contents.** A nongovernmental corporate party must file 2 copies of a disclosure statement that:

(1) identifies any parent corporation and any publicly held corporation owning 10% or more of its stock; or

(2) states that there is no such corporation.

(b) **Time to File; Supplemental Filing.** A party must:

(1) file the disclosure statement with its first appearance, pleading, petition, motion, response, or other request addressed to the court; and

(2) promptly file a supplemental statement if any required information changes.

(Adopted April 29, 2002, effective December 1, 2002; April 30, 2007, effective December 1, 2007.)

RULE 8. GENERAL RULES OF PLEADING

(a) **Claim for Relief.** A pleading that states a claim for relief must contain:

(1) a short and plain statement of the grounds for the court's jurisdiction, unless the court already has jurisdiction and the claim needs no new jurisdictional support;

(2) a short and plain statement of the claim showing that the pleader is entitled to relief; and

(3) a demand for the relief sought, which may include relief in the alternative or different types of relief.

(b) **Defenses; Admissions and Denials.**

(1) *In General.* In responding to a pleading, a party must:

(A) state in short and plain terms its defenses to each claim asserted against it; and

(B) admit or deny the allegations asserted against it by an opposing party.

(2) *Denials—Responding to the Substance.* A denial must fairly respond to the substance of the allegation.

(3) *General and Specific Denials.* A party that intends in good faith to deny all the allegations of a pleading—including the jurisdictional grounds—may do so by a general denial. A party that does not intend to deny all the allegations must either specifically deny designated allegations or generally deny all except those specifically admitted.

(4) *Denying Part of an Allegation.* A party that intends in good faith to deny only part of an allegation must admit the part that is true and deny the rest.

(5) *Lacking Knowledge or Information.* A party that lacks knowledge or information sufficient to form a belief about the truth of an allegation must so state, and the statement has the effect of a denial.

(6) *Effect of Failing to Deny.* An allegation—other than one relating to the amount of damages—is admitted if a responsive pleading is required and the allegation is not denied. If a responsive pleading is not required, an allegation is considered denied or avoided.

(c) Affirmative Defenses.

(1) *In General.* In responding to a pleading, a party must affirmatively state any avoidance or affirmative defense, including:

- accord and satisfaction;
- arbitration and award;
- assumption of risk;
- contributory negligence;
- duress;
- estoppel;
- failure of consideration;
- fraud;
- illegality;
- injury by fellow servant;
- laches;
- license;
- payment;
- release;
- res judicata;
- statute of frauds;
- statute of limitations; and
- waiver.

(2) *Mistaken Designation.* If a party mistakenly designates a defense as a counterclaim, or a counterclaim as a defense, the court must, if justice requires, treat the pleading as though it were correctly designated, and may impose terms for doing so.

(d) Pleading to Be Concise and Direct; Alternative Statements; Inconsistency.

(1) *In General.* Each allegation must be simple, concise, and direct. No technical form is required.

(2) *Alternative Statements of a Claim or Defense.* A party may set out 2 or more statements of a claim or defense alternatively or hypothetically, either in a single count or defense or in separate ones. If a party makes alternative statements, the pleading is sufficient if any one of them is sufficient.

(3) *Inconsistent Claims or Defenses.* A party may state as many separate claims or defenses as it has, regardless of consistency.

(e) Construing Pleadings. Pleadings must be construed so as to do justice.

(Amended February 28, 1966, effective July 1, 1966; March 2, 1987, effective August 1, 1987; April 30, 2007, effective December 1, 2007; April 28, 2010, effective December 1, 2010.)

RULE 9. PLEADING SPECIAL MATTERS

(a) Capacity or Authority to Sue; Legal Existence.

(1) *In General.* Except when required to show that the court has jurisdiction, a pleading need not allege:

(A) a party's capacity to sue or be sued;

(B) a party's authority to sue or be sued in a representative capacity; or

(C) the legal existence of an organized association of persons that is made a party.

(2) *Raising Those Issues.* To raise any of those issues, a party must do so by a specific denial, which must state any supporting facts that are peculiarly within the party's knowledge.

(b) Fraud or Mistake; Conditions of Mind. In alleging fraud or mistake, a party must state with particularity the circumstances constituting fraud or mistake. Malice, intent, knowledge, and other conditions of a person's mind may be alleged generally.

(c) Conditions Precedent. In pleading conditions precedent, it suffices to allege generally that all conditions precedent have occurred or been performed. But when denying that a condition precedent has occurred or been performed, a party must do so with particularity.

(d) Official Document or Act. In pleading an official document or official act, it suffices to allege that the document was legally issued or the act legally done.

(e) Judgment. In pleading a judgment or decision of a domestic or foreign court, a judicial or quasi-judicial tribunal, or a board or officer, it suffices to plead the judgment or decision without showing jurisdiction to render it.

(f) Time and Place. An allegation of time or place is material when testing the sufficiency of a pleading.

(g) Special Damages. If an item of special damage is claimed, it must be specifically stated.

(h) Admiralty or Maritime Claim.

(1) *How Designated.* If a claim for relief is within the admiralty or maritime jurisdiction and also within the court's subject-matter jurisdiction on some other ground, the pleading may designate the claim as an admiralty or maritime claim for purposes of Rules 14(c), 38(e), and 82 and the Supplemental Rules for Admiralty or Maritime Claims and Asset Forfeiture Actions. A claim cognizable only in the admiralty or maritime jurisdiction is an admiralty or maritime claim for those purposes, whether or not so designated.

(2) *Designation for Appeal.* A case that includes an admiralty or maritime claim within this subdivision (h) is an admiralty case within 28 U.S.C. § 1292(a)(3).

(Amended February 28, 1966, effective July 1, 1966; December 4, 1967, effective July 1, 1968; March 30, 1970, effective July 1, 1970; March 2, 1987, effective August 1, 1987; April 11, 1997, effective December 1, 1997; April 12, 2006, effective December 1, 2006; April 30, 2007, effective December 1, 2007.)

RULE 10. FORM OF PLEADINGS

(a) Caption; Names of Parties. Every pleading must have a caption with the court's name, a title, a file number, and a Rule 7(a) designation. The title of the complaint must name all the parties; the title of other pleadings, after naming the first party on each side, may refer generally to other parties.

(b) Paragraphs; Separate Statements. A party must state its claims or defenses in numbered paragraphs, each limited as far as practicable to a single set of circumstances. A later pleading may refer by number to a paragraph in an earlier pleading. If doing so would promote clarity, each claim founded on a separate transaction or occurrence—and each defense other than a denial—must be stated in a separate count or defense.

(c) Adoption by Reference; Exhibits. A statement in a pleading may be adopted by reference elsewhere in the same pleading or in any other pleading or motion. A copy of a written instrument that is an exhibit to a pleading is a part of the pleading for all purposes.

(Amended April 30, 2007, effective December 1, 2007.)

RULE 11. SIGNING PLEADINGS, MOTIONS, AND OTHER PAPERS; REPRESENTATIONS TO THE COURT; SANCTIONS

(a) Signature. Every pleading, written motion, and other paper must be signed by at least one attorney of record in the attorney's name—or by a party personally if the party is unrepresented. The paper must state the signer's address, e-mail address, and telephone number. Unless a rule or statute specifically states otherwise, a pleading need not be verified or accompanied by an affidavit. The court must strike an unsigned paper unless the omission is promptly corrected after being called to the attorney's or party's attention.

(b) Representations to the Court. By presenting to the court a pleading, written motion, or other paper—whether by signing, filing, submitting, or later advocating it—an attorney or unrepresented party certifies that to the best of the person's knowledge, information, and belief, formed after an inquiry reasonable under the circumstances:

(1) it is not being presented for any improper purpose, such as to harass, cause unnecessary delay, or needlessly increase the cost of litigation;

(2) the claims, defenses, and other legal contentions are warranted by existing law or by a nonfrivolous argument for extending, modifying, or reversing existing law or for establishing new law;

(3) the factual contentions have evidentiary support or, if specifically so identified, will likely have evidentiary support after a reasonable opportunity for further investigation or discovery; and

(4) the denials of factual contentions are warranted on the evidence or, if specifically so identified, are reasonably based on belief or a lack of information.

(c) Sanctions.

(1) *In General.* If, after notice and a reasonable opportunity to respond, the court determines that Rule 11(b) has been violated, the court may impose an appropriate sanction on any attorney, law firm, or party that violated the rule or is responsible for the violation. Absent exceptional circumstances, a law firm must be held jointly responsible for a violation committed by its partner, associate, or employee.

(2) *Motion for Sanctions.* A motion for sanctions must be made separately from any other motion and must describe the specific conduct that allegedly violates Rule 11(b). The motion must be served under Rule 5, but it must not be filed or be presented to the court if the challenged paper, claim, defense, contention, or denial is withdrawn or appropriately corrected within 21 days after service or within another time the court sets. If warranted, the court may award to the prevailing party the reasonable expenses, including attorney's fees, incurred for the motion.

(3) *On the Court's Initiative.* On its own, the court may order an attorney, law firm, or party to show cause why conduct specifically described in the order has not violated Rule 11(b).

(4) *Nature of a Sanction.* A sanction imposed under this rule must be limited to what suffices to deter repetition of the conduct or comparable conduct by others similarly situated. The sanction may include nonmonetary directives; an order to pay a penalty into court; or, if imposed on motion and warranted for effective deterrence, an order directing payment to the movant of part or all of the reasonable attorney's fees and other expenses directly resulting from the violation.

(5) *Limitations on Monetary Sanctions.* The court must not impose a monetary sanction:

(A) against a represented party for violating Rule 11(b)(2); or

(B) on its own, unless it issued the show-cause order under Rule 11(c)(3) before voluntary dismissal or settlement of the claims made by or against the party that is, or whose attorneys are, to be sanctioned.

(6) *Requirements for an Order.* An order imposing a sanction must describe the sanctioned conduct and explain the basis for the sanction.

(d) Inapplicability to Discovery. This rule does not apply to disclosures and discovery requests, responses, objections, and motions under Rules 26 through 37.

(Amended April 28, 1983, effective August 1, 1983; March 2, 1987, effective August 1, 1987; April 22, 1993, effective December 1, 1993; April 30, 2007, effective December 1, 2007.)

RULE 12. DEFENSES AND OBJECTIONS: WHEN AND HOW PRESENTED; MOTION FOR JUDGMENT ON THE PLEADINGS; CONSOLIDATING MOTIONS; WAIVING DEFENSES; PRETRIAL HEARING

(a) Time to Serve a Responsive Pleading.

(1) *In General.* Unless another time is specified by this rule or a federal statute, the time for serving a responsive pleading is as follows:

(A) A defendant must serve an answer:

(i) within 21 days after being served with the summons and complaint; or

(ii) if it has timely waived service under Rule 4(d), within 60 days after the request for a waiver was sent, or within 90 days after it was sent to the defendant outside any judicial district of the United States.

(B) A party must serve an answer to a counterclaim or crossclaim within 21 days after being served with the pleading that states the counterclaim or crossclaim.

(C) A party must serve a reply to an answer within 21 days after being served with an order to reply, unless the order specifies a different time.

(2) *United States and Its Agencies, Officers, or Employees Sued in an Official Capacity.* The United States, a United States agency, or a United States officer or employee sued only in an official capacity must serve an answer to a complaint, counterclaim, or crossclaim within 60 days after service on the United States attorney.

(3) *United States Officers or Employees Sued in an Individual Capacity.* A United States officer or employee sued in an individual capacity for an act or omission occurring in connection with duties performed on the United States' behalf must serve an answer to a complaint, counterclaim, or crossclaim within 60 days after service on the officer or employee or service on the United States attorney, whichever is later.

(4) *Effect of a Motion.* Unless the court sets a different time, serving a motion under this rule alters these periods as follows:

(A) if the court denies the motion or postpones its disposition until trial, the responsive pleading must be served within 14 days after notice of the court's action; or

(B) if the court grants a motion for a more definite statement, the responsive pleading must be served within 14 days after the more definite statement is served.

(b) How to Present Defenses. Every defense to a claim for relief in any pleading must be asserted in the responsive pleading if one is required. But a party may assert the following defenses by motion:

(1) lack of subject-matter jurisdiction;

(2) lack of personal jurisdiction;

(3) improper venue;

(4) insufficient process;

(5) insufficient service of process;

(6) failure to state a claim upon which relief can be granted; and

(7) failure to join a party under Rule 19.

A motion asserting any of these defenses must be made before pleading if a responsive pleading is allowed. If a pleading sets out a claim for relief that does not require a responsive pleading, an opposing party may assert at trial any defense to that claim. No defense or objection is waived by joining it with one or more other defenses or objections in a responsive pleading or in a motion.

(c) Motion for Judgment on the Pleadings. After the pleadings are closed—but early enough not to delay trial—a party may move for judgment on the pleadings.

(d) Result of Presenting Matters Outside the Pleadings. If, on a motion under Rule 12(b)(6) or 12(c), matters outside the pleadings are presented to and not excluded by the court, the motion must be treated as one for summary judgment under Rule 56. All parties must be given a reasonable opportunity to present all the material that is pertinent to the motion.

(e) Motion for a More Definite Statement. A party may move for a more definite statement of a pleading to which a responsive pleading is allowed but which is so vague or ambiguous that the party cannot reasonably prepare a response. The motion must be made before filing a responsive pleading and must point out the defects complained of and the details desired. If the court orders a more definite statement and the order is not obeyed within 14 days after notice of the order or within the time the court sets, the court may strike the pleading or issue any other appropriate order.

(f) Motion to Strike. The court may strike from a pleading an insufficient defense or any redundant, immaterial, impertinent, or scandalous matter. The court may act:

(1) on its own; or

(2) on motion made by a party either before responding to the pleading or, if a response is not allowed, within 21 days after being served with the pleading.

(g) Joining Motions.

(1) *Right to Join.* A motion under this rule may be joined with any other motion allowed by this rule.

(2) *Limitation on Further Motions.* Except as provided in Rule 12(h)(2) or (3), a party that makes a motion under this rule must not make another motion under this rule raising a defense or objection that was available to the party but omitted from its earlier motion.

(h) Waiving and Preserving Certain Defenses.

(1) *When Some Are Waived.* A party waives any defense listed in Rule 12(b)(2)-(5) by:

(A) omitting it from a motion in the circumstances described in Rule 12(g)(2); or

(B) failing to either:

(i) make it by motion under this rule; or

(ii) include it in a responsive pleading or in an amendment allowed by Rule 15(a)(1) as a matter of course.

(2) *When to Raise Others.* Failure to state a claim upon which relief can be granted, to join a person required by Rule 19(b), or to state a legal defense to a claim may be raised:

    (A) in any pleading allowed or ordered under Rule 7(a);

    (B) by a motion under Rule 12(c); or

    (C) at trial.

(3) *Lack of Subject–Matter Jurisdiction.* If the court determines at any time that it lacks subject-matter jurisdiction, the court must dismiss the action.

(i) Hearing Before Trial. If a party so moves, any defense listed in Rule 12(b)(1)-(7)—whether made in a pleading or by motion—and a motion under Rule 12(c) must be heard and decided before trial unless the court orders a deferral until trial.

(Amended December 27, 1946, effective March 19, 1948; January 21, 1963, effective July 1, 1963; February 28, 1966, effective July 1, 1966; March 2, 1987, effective August 1, 1987; April 22, 1993, effective December 1, 1993; April 17, 2000, effective December 1, 2000; April 30, 2007, effective December 1, 2007; March 26, 2009, effective December 1, 2009.)

RULE 13. COUNTERCLAIM AND CROSSCLAIM

(a) Compulsory Counterclaim.

(1) *In General.* A pleading must state as a counterclaim any claim that—at the time of its service—the pleader has against an opposing party if the claim:

    (A) arises out of the transaction or occurrence that is the subject matter of the opposing party's claim; and

    (B) does not require adding another party over whom the court cannot acquire jurisdiction.

(2) *Exceptions.* The pleader need not state the claim if:

    (A) when the action was commenced, the claim was the subject of another pending action; or

    (B) the opposing party sued on its claim by attachment or other process that did not establish personal jurisdiction over the pleader on that claim, and the pleader does not assert any counterclaim under this rule.

(b) Permissive Counterclaim. A pleading may state as a counterclaim against an opposing party any claim that is not compulsory.

(c) Relief Sought in a Counterclaim. A counterclaim need not diminish or defeat the recovery sought by the opposing party. It may request relief that exceeds in amount or differs in kind from the relief sought by the opposing party.

(d) Counterclaim Against the United States. These rules do not expand the right to assert a counterclaim—or to claim a credit—against the United States or a United States officer or agency.

(e) Counterclaim Maturing or Acquired After Pleading. The court may permit a party to file a supplemental pleading asserting a counterclaim that matured or was acquired by the party after serving an earlier pleading.

(f) [Abrogated]

(g) Crossclaim Against a Coparty. A pleading may state as a crossclaim any claim by one party against a coparty if the claim arises out of the transaction or occurrence that is the subject matter of the original action or of a counterclaim, or if the claim relates to any property that is the subject matter of the original action. The crossclaim may include a claim that the coparty is or may be liable to the crossclaimant for all or part of a claim asserted in the action against the crossclaimant.

(h) Joining Additional Parties. Rules 19 and 20 govern the addition of a person as a party to a counterclaim or crossclaim.

(i) Separate Trials; Separate Judgments. If the court orders separate trials under Rule 42(b), it may enter judgment on a counterclaim or crossclaim under Rule 54(b) when it has jurisdiction to do so, even if the opposing party's claims have been dismissed or otherwise resolved.

(Amended December 27, 1946, effective March 19, 1948; January 21, 1963, effective July 1, 1963; February 28, 1966, effective July 1, 1966; March 2, 1987, effective August 1, 1987; April 30, 2007, effective December 1, 2007; March 26, 2009, effective December 1, 2009.)

RULE 14. THIRD–PARTY PRACTICE

(a) When a Defending Party May Bring in a Third Party.

(1) *Timing of the Summons and Complaint.* A defending party may, as third-party plaintiff, serve a summons and complaint on a nonparty who is or may be liable to it for all or part of the claim against it. But the third-party plaintiff must, by motion, obtain the court's leave if it files the third-party complaint more than 14 days after serving its original answer.

(2) *Third–Party Defendant's Claims and Defenses.* The person served with the summons and third-party complaint—the "third-party defendant":

    (A) must assert any defense against the third-party plaintiff's claim under Rule 12;

    (B) must assert any counterclaim against the third-party plaintiff under Rule 13(a), and may assert any counterclaim against the third-party plaintiff under Rule 13(b) or any crossclaim against another third-party defendant under Rule 13(g);

    (C) may assert against the plaintiff any defense that the third-party plaintiff has to the plaintiff's claim; and

    (D) may also assert against the plaintiff any claim arising out of the transaction or occurrence that is the subject matter of the plaintiff's claim against the third-party plaintiff.

(3) *Plaintiff's Claims Against a Third–Party Defendant.* The plaintiff may assert against the third-party defendant any claim arising out of the transaction or occurrence that is the subject matter of the plaintiff's claim against the third-party plaintiff. The third-party defendant must then assert any defense under Rule 12 and any counterclaim under Rule 13(a), and may assert any counterclaim under Rule 13(b) or any crossclaim under Rule 13(g).

(4) *Motion to Strike, Sever, or Try Separately.* Any party may move to strike the third-party claim, to sever it, or to try it separately.

(5) *Third–Party Defendant's Claim Against a Nonparty.* A third-party defendant may proceed under this rule against a nonparty who is or may be liable to the third-party defendant for all or part of any claim against it.

(6) *Third–Party Complaint In Rem.* If it is within the admiralty or maritime jurisdiction, a third-party complaint may be in rem. In that event, a reference in this rule to the "summons" includes the warrant of arrest, and a reference to the defendant or third-party plaintiff includes, when appropriate, a person who asserts a right under Supplemental Rule C(6)(a)(i) in the property arrested.

(b) When a Plaintiff May Bring in a Third Party. When a claim is asserted against a plaintiff, the plaintiff may bring in a third party if this rule would allow a defendant to do so.

(c) Admiralty or Maritime Claim.

(1) *Scope of Impleader.* If a plaintiff asserts an admiralty or maritime claim under Rule 9(h), the defendant or a person who asserts a right under Supplemental Rule C(6)(a)(i) may, as a third-party plaintiff, bring in a third-party defendant who may be wholly or partly liable—either to the plaintiff or to the third-party plaintiff—for remedy over, contribution, or otherwise on account of the same transaction, occurrence, or series of transactions or occurrences.

(2) *Defending Against a Demand for Judgment for the Plaintiff.* The third-party plaintiff may demand judgment in the plaintiff's favor against the third-party defendant. In that event, the third-party defendant must defend under Rule 12 against the plaintiff's claim as well as the third-party plaintiff's claim; and the action proceeds as if the plaintiff had sued both the third-party defendant and the third-party plaintiff.

(Amended December 27, 1946, effective March 19, 1948; January 21, 1963, effective July 1, 1963; February 28, 1966, effective July 1, 1966; March 2, 1987, effective August 1, 1987; April 17, 2000, effective December 1, 2000; April 12, 2006, effective December 1, 2006; April 30, 2007, effective December 1, 2007; March 26, 2009, effective December 1, 2009.)

RULE 15. AMENDED AND SUPPLEMENTAL PLEADINGS

(a) Amendments Before Trial.

(1) *Amending as a Matter of Course.* A party may amend its pleading once as a matter of course within:

(A) 21 days after serving it, or

(B) if the pleading is one to which a responsive pleading is required, 21 days after service of a responsive pleading or 21 days after service of a motion under Rule 12(b), (e), or (f), whichever is earlier.

(2) *Other Amendments.* In all other cases, a party may amend its pleading only with the opposing party's written consent or the court's leave. The court should freely give leave when justice so requires.

(3) *Time to Respond.* Unless the court orders otherwise, any required response to an amended pleading must be made within the time remaining to respond to the original pleading or within 14 days after service of the amended pleading, whichever is later.

(b) Amendments During and After Trial.

(1) *Based on an Objection at Trial.* If, at trial, a party objects that evidence is not within the issues raised in the pleadings, the court may permit the pleadings to be amended. The court should freely permit an amendment when doing so will aid in presenting the merits and the objecting party fails to satisfy the court that the evidence would prejudice that party's action or defense on the merits. The court may grant a continuance to enable the objecting party to meet the evidence.

(2) *For Issues Tried by Consent.* When an issue not raised by the pleadings is tried by the parties' express or implied consent, it must be treated in all respects as if raised in the pleadings. A party may move—at any time, even after judgment—to amend the pleadings to conform them to the evidence and to raise an unpleaded issue. But failure to amend does not affect the result of the trial of that issue.

(c) Relation Back of Amendments.

(1) *When an Amendment Relates Back.* An amendment to a pleading relates back to the date of the original pleading when:

(A) the law that provides the applicable statute of limitations allows relation back;

(B) the amendment asserts a claim or defense that arose out of the conduct, transaction, or occurrence set out—or attempted to be set out—in the original pleading; or

(C) the amendment changes the party or the naming of the party against whom a claim is asserted, if Rule 15(c)(1)(B) is satisfied and if, within the period provided by Rule 4(m) for serving the summons and complaint, the party to be brought in by amendment:

(i) received such notice of the action that it will not be prejudiced in defending on the merits; and

(ii) knew or should have known that the action would have been brought against it, but for a mistake concerning the proper party's identity.

(2) *Notice to the United States.* When the United States or a United States officer or agency is added as a defendant by amendment, the notice requirements of Rule 15(c)(1)(C)(i) and (ii) are satisfied if, during the stated period, process was delivered or mailed to the United States attorney or the United States attorney's designee, to the Attorney General of the United States, or to the officer or agency.

(d) Supplemental Pleadings. On motion and reasonable notice, the court may, on just terms, permit a party to serve a supplemental pleading setting out any transaction, occurrence, or event that happened after the date of the pleading to be supplemented. The court may permit supplementation even though the original pleading is defective in stating a claim or defense. The court may order that the opposing party plead to the supplemental pleading within a specified time.

(Amended January 21, 1963, effective July 1, 1963; February 28, 1966, effective July 1, 1966; March 2, 1987, effective August 1, 1987; April 30, 1991, effective December 1, 1991; amended by Pub.L. 102–198, § 11, December 9, 1991, 105 Stat. 1626; amended April 22, 1993, effective December 1, 1993; April 30, 2007, effective December 1, 2007; March 26, 2009, effective December 1, 2009.)

RULE 16. PRETRIAL CONFERENCES; SCHEDULING; MANAGEMENT

(a) Purposes of a Pretrial Conference. In any action, the court may order the attorneys and any unrepresented parties to appear for one or more pretrial conferences for such purposes as:

(1) expediting disposition of the action;

(2) establishing early and continuing control so that the case will not be protracted because of lack of management;

(3) discouraging wasteful pretrial activities;

(4) improving the quality of the trial through more thorough preparation; and

(5) facilitating settlement.

(b) Scheduling.

(1) *Scheduling Order.* Except in categories of actions exempted by local rule, the district judge—or a magistrate judge when authorized by local rule—must issue a scheduling order:

(A) after receiving the parties' report under Rule 26(f); or

(B) after consulting with the parties' attorneys and any unrepresented parties at a scheduling conference.

(2) *Time to Issue.* The judge must issue the scheduling order as soon as practicable, but unless the judge finds good cause for delay, the judge must issue it within the earlier of 90 days after any defendant has been served with the complaint or 60 days after any defendant has appeared.

(3) *Contents of the Order.*

(A) *Required Contents.* The scheduling order must limit the time to join other parties, amend the pleadings, complete discovery, and file motions.

(B) *Permitted Contents.* The scheduling order may:

(i) modify the timing of disclosures under Rules 26(a) and 26(e)(1);

(ii) modify the extent of discovery;

(iii) provide for disclosure, discovery, or preservation of electronically stored information;

(iv) include any agreements the parties reach for asserting claims of privilege or of protection as trial-preparation material after information is produced, including agreements reached under Federal Rule of Evidence 502;

(v) direct that before moving for an order relating to discovery, the movant must request a conference with the court;

(vi) set dates for pretrial conferences and for trial; and

(vii) include other appropriate matters.

(4) *Modifying a Schedule.* A schedule may be modified only for good cause and with the judge's consent.

(c) Attendance and Matters for Consideration at a Pretrial Conference.

(1) *Attendance.* A represented party must authorize at least one of its attorneys to make stipulations and admissions about all matters that can reasonably be anticipated for discussion at a pretrial conference. If appropriate, the court may require that a party or its representative be present or reasonably available by other means to consider possible settlement.

(2) *Matters for Consideration.* At any pretrial conference, the court may consider and take appropriate action on the following matters:

(A) formulating and simplifying the issues, and eliminating frivolous claims or defenses;

(B) amending the pleadings if necessary or desirable;

(C) obtaining admissions and stipulations about facts and documents to avoid unnecessary proof, and ruling in advance on the admissibility of evidence;

(D) avoiding unnecessary proof and cumulative evidence, and limiting the use of testimony under Federal Rule of Evidence 702;

(E) determining the appropriateness and timing of summary adjudication under Rule 56;

(F) controlling and scheduling discovery, including orders affecting disclosures and discovery under Rule 26 and Rules 29 through 37;

(G) identifying witnesses and documents, scheduling the filing and exchange of any pretrial briefs, and setting dates for further conferences and for trial;

(H) referring matters to a magistrate judge or a master;

(I) settling the case and using special procedures to assist in resolving the dispute when authorized by statute or local rule;

(J) determining the form and content of the pretrial order;

(K) disposing of pending motions;

(L) adopting special procedures for managing potentially difficult or protracted actions that may involve complex issues, multiple parties, difficult legal questions, or unusual proof problems;

(M) ordering a separate trial under Rule 42(b) of a claim, counterclaim, crossclaim, third-party claim, or particular issue;

(N) ordering the presentation of evidence early in the trial on a manageable issue that might, on the evidence, be the basis for a judgment as a matter of law under Rule 50(a) or a judgment on partial findings under Rule 52(c);

(O) establishing a reasonable limit on the time allowed to present evidence; and

(P) facilitating in other ways the just, speedy, and inexpensive disposition of the action.

(d) Pretrial Orders. After any conference under this rule, the court should issue an order reciting the action taken. This order controls the course of the action unless the court modifies it.

(e) Final Pretrial Conference and Orders. The court may hold a final pretrial conference to formulate a trial plan, including a plan to facilitate the admission of evidence. The conference must be held as close to the start of trial as is reasonable, and must be attended by at least one attorney who will conduct the trial for each party and by any unrepresented party. The court may modify the order issued after a final pretrial conference only to prevent manifest injustice.

(f) Sanctions.

(1) *In General.* On motion or on its own, the court may issue any just orders, including those authorized by Rule 37(b)(2)(A)(ii)-(vii), if a party or its attorney:

(A) fails to appear at a scheduling or other pretrial conference;

(B) is substantially unprepared to participate—or does not participate in good faith—in the conference; or

(C) fails to obey a scheduling or other pretrial order.

(2) *Imposing Fees and Costs.* Instead of or in addition to any other sanction, the court must order the party, its attorney, or both to pay the reasonable expenses—including attorney's fees—incurred because of any noncompliance with this rule, unless the noncompliance was substantially justified or other circumstances make an award of expenses unjust.

(Amended April 28, 1983, effective August 1, 1983; March 2, 1987, effective August 1, 1987; April 22, 1993, effective December 1, 1993; April 12, 2006, effective December 1, 2006; April 30, 2007, effective December 1, 2007; April 29, 2015, effective December 1, 2015.)

TITLE IV. PARTIES

RULE 17. PLAINTIFF AND DEFENDANT; CAPACITY; PUBLIC OFFICERS

(a) Real Party in Interest.

(1) *Designation in General.* An action must be prosecuted in the name of the real party in interest. The following may sue in their own names without joining the person for whose benefit the action is brought:

(A) an executor;

(B) an administrator;

(C) a guardian;

(D) a bailee;

(E) a trustee of an express trust;

(F) a party with whom or in whose name a contract has been made for another's benefit; and

(G) a party authorized by statute.

(2) *Action in the Name of the United States for Another's Use or Benefit.* When a federal statute so provides, an action for another's use or benefit must be brought in the name of the United States.

(3) *Joinder of the Real Party in Interest.* The court may not dismiss an action for failure to prosecute in the name of the real party in interest until, after an objection, a reasonable time has been allowed for the real party in interest to ratify, join, or be substituted into the action. After ratification, joinder, or substitution, the action proceeds as if it had been originally commenced by the real party in interest.

(b) Capacity to Sue or Be Sued. Capacity to sue or be sued is determined as follows:

(1) for an individual who is not acting in a representative capacity, by the law of the individual's domicile;

(2) for a corporation, by the law under which it was organized; and

(3) for all other parties, by the law of the state where the court is located, except that:

(A) a partnership or other unincorporated association with no such capacity under that state's law may sue or be sued in its common name to enforce a substantive right existing under the United States Constitution or laws; and

(B) 28 U.S.C. §§ 754 and 959(a) govern the capacity of a receiver appointed by a United States court to sue or be sued in a United States court.

(c) Minor or Incompetent Person.

(1) *With a Representative.* The following representatives may sue or defend on behalf of a minor or an incompetent person:

(A) a general guardian;

(B) a committee;

(C) a conservator; or

(D) a like fiduciary.

(2) *Without a Representative.* A minor or an incompetent person who does not have a duly appointed representative may sue by a next friend or by a guardian ad litem. The court must appoint a guardian ad litem—or issue another appropriate order—to protect a minor or incompetent person who is unrepresented in an action.

(d) Public Officer's Title and Name. A public officer who sues or is sued in an official capacity may be designated by official title rather than by name, but the court may order that the officer's name be added.

(Amended December 27, 1946, effective March 19, 1948; December 29, 1948, effective October 20, 1949; February 28, 1966, effective July 1, 1966; March 2, 1987, effective August 1, 1987; April 25, 1988, effective August 1, 1988; amended by Pub.L. 100–690, Title VII, § 7049, November 18, 1988, 102 Stat. 4401 (although amendment by Pub.L. 100–690 could not be executed due to prior amendment by Court order which made the same change effective August 1, 1988); April 30, 2007, effective December 1, 2007.)

RULE 18. JOINDER OF CLAIMS

(a) **In General.** A party asserting a claim, counterclaim, crossclaim, or third-party claim may join, as independent or alternative claims, as many claims as it has against an opposing party.

(b) **Joinder of Contingent Claims.** A party may join two claims even though one of them is contingent on the disposition of the other; but the court may grant relief only in accordance with the parties' relative substantive rights. In particular, a plaintiff may state a claim for money and a claim to set aside a conveyance that is fraudulent as to that plaintiff, without first obtaining a judgment for the money.

(Amended February 28, 1966, effective July 1, 1966; March 2, 1987, effective August 1, 1987; April 30, 2007, effective December 1, 2007.)

RULE 19. REQUIRED JOINDER OF PARTIES

(a) **Persons Required to Be Joined if Feasible.**

(1) *Required Party.* A person who is subject to service of process and whose joinder will not deprive the court of subject-matter jurisdiction must be joined as a party if:

(A) in that person's absence, the court cannot accord complete relief among existing parties; or

(B) that person claims an interest relating to the subject of the action and is so situated that disposing of the action in the person's absence may:

(i) as a practical matter impair or impede the person's ability to protect the interest; or

(ii) leave an existing party subject to a substantial risk of incurring double, multiple, or otherwise inconsistent obligations because of the interest.

(2) *Joinder by Court Order.* If a person has not been joined as required, the court must order that the person be made a party. A person who refuses to join as a plaintiff may be made either a defendant or, in a proper case, an involuntary plaintiff.

(3) *Venue.* If a joined party objects to venue and the joinder would make venue improper, the court must dismiss that party.

(b) **When Joinder Is Not Feasible.** If a person who is required to be joined if feasible cannot be joined, the court must determine whether, in equity and good conscience, the action should proceed among the existing parties or should be dismissed. The factors for the court to consider include:

(1) the extent to which a judgment rendered in the person's absence might prejudice that person or the existing parties;

(2) the extent to which any prejudice could be lessened or avoided by:

(A) protective provisions in the judgment;

(B) shaping the relief; or

(C) other measures;

(3) whether a judgment rendered in the person's absence would be adequate; and

(4) whether the plaintiff would have an adequate remedy if the action were dismissed for nonjoinder.

(c) **Pleading the Reasons for Nonjoinder.** When asserting a claim for relief, a party must state:

(1) the name, if known, of any person who is required to be joined if feasible but is not joined; and

(2) the reasons for not joining that person.

(d) **Exception for Class Actions.** This rule is subject to Rule 23.

(Amended February 28, 1966, effective July 1, 1966; March 2, 1987, effective August 1, 1987; April 30, 2007, effective December 1, 2007.)

RULE 20. PERMISSIVE JOINDER OF PARTIES

(a) **Persons Who May Join or Be Joined.**

(1) *Plaintiffs.* Persons may join in one action as plaintiffs if:

(A) they assert any right to relief jointly, severally, or in the alternative with respect to or arising out of the same transaction, occurrence, or series of transactions or occurrences; and

(B) any question of law or fact common to all plaintiffs will arise in the action.

(2) *Defendants.* Persons—as well as a vessel, cargo, or other property subject to admiralty process in rem—may be joined in one action as defendants if:

(A) any right to relief is asserted against them jointly, severally, or in the alternative with respect to or arising out of the same transaction, occurrence, or series of transactions or occurrences; and

(B) any question of law or fact common to all defendants will arise in the action.

(3) *Extent of Relief.* Neither a plaintiff nor a defendant need be interested in obtaining or defending against all the relief demanded. The court may grant judgment to one or more plaintiffs according to their rights, and against one or more defendants according to their liabilities.

(b) **Protective Measures.** The court may issue orders—including an order for separate trials—to protect a party against embarrassment, delay, expense, or other prejudice that arises from including a person against whom the party asserts no claim and who asserts no claim against the party.

(Amended February 28, 1966, effective July 1, 1966; March 2, 1987, effective August 1, 1987; April 30, 2007, effective December 1, 2007.)

RULE 21. MISJOINDER AND NONJOINDER OF PARTIES

Misjoinder of parties is not a ground for dismissing an action. On motion or on its own, the court may at any time, on just terms, add or drop a party. The court may also sever any claim against a party.

(Amended April 30, 2007, effective December 1, 2007.)

RULE 22. INTERPLEADER

(a) **Grounds.**

(1) *By a Plaintiff.* Persons with claims that may expose a plaintiff to double or multiple liability may be joined as defendants and required to interplead. Joinder for interpleader is proper even though:

(A) the claims of the several claimants, or the titles on which their claims depend, lack a common origin or are adverse and independent rather than identical; or

(B) the plaintiff denies liability in whole or in part to any or all of the claimants.

(2) *By a Defendant.* A defendant exposed to similar liability may seek interpleader through a crossclaim or counterclaim.

(b) Relation to Other Rules and Statutes. This rule supplements—and does not limit—the joinder of parties allowed by Rule 20. The remedy this rule provides is in addition to—and does not supersede or limit—the remedy provided by 28 U.S.C. §§ 1335, 1397, and 2361. An action under those statutes must be conducted under these rules.

(Amended December 29, 1948, effective October 20, 1949; March 2, 1987, effective August 1, 1987; April 30, 2007, effective December 1, 2007.)

RULE 23.   CLASS ACTIONS

(a) Prerequisites. One or more members of a class may sue or be sued as representative parties on behalf of all members only if:

(1) the class is so numerous that joinder of all members is impracticable;

(2) there are questions of law or fact common to the class;

(3) the claims or defenses of the representative parties are typical of the claims or defenses of the class; and

(4) the representative parties will fairly and adequately protect the interests of the class.

(b) Types of Class Actions. A class action may be maintained if Rule 23(a) is satisfied and if:

(1) prosecuting separate actions by or against individual class members would create a risk of:

(A) inconsistent or varying adjudications with respect to individual class members that would establish incompatible standards of conduct for the party opposing the class; or

(B) adjudications with respect to individual class members that, as a practical matter, would be dispositive of the interests of the other members not parties to the individual adjudications or would substantially impair or impede their ability to protect their interests;

(2) the party opposing the class has acted or refused to act on grounds that apply generally to the class, so that final injunctive relief or corresponding declaratory relief is appropriate respecting the class as a whole; or

(3) the court finds that the questions of law or fact common to class members predominate over any questions affecting only individual members, and that a class action is superior to other available methods for fairly and efficiently adjudicating the controversy. The matters pertinent to these findings include:

(A) the class members' interests in individually controlling the prosecution or defense of separate actions;

(B) the extent and nature of any litigation concerning the controversy already begun by or against class members;

(C) the desirability or undesirability of concentrating the litigation of the claims in the particular forum; and

(D) the likely difficulties in managing a class action.

(c) Certification Order; Notice to Class Members; Judgment; Issues Classes; Subclasses.

(1) *Certification Order.*

(A) *Time to Issue.* At an early practicable time after a person sues or is sued as a class representative, the court must determine by order whether to certify the action as a class action.

(B) *Defining the Class; Appointing Class Counsel.* An order that certifies a class action must define the class and the class claims, issues, or defenses, and must appoint class counsel under Rule 23(g).

(C) *Altering or Amending the Order.* An order that grants or denies class certification may be altered or amended before final judgment.

(2) *Notice.*

(A) *For (b)(1) or (b)(2) Classes.* For any class certified under Rule 23(b)(1) or (b)(2), the court may direct appropriate notice to the class.

(B) *For (b)(3) Classes.* For any class certified under Rule 23(b)(3)—or upon ordering notice under Rule 23(e)(1) to a class proposed to be certified for purposes of settlement under Rule 23(b)(3)—the court must direct to class members the best notice that is practicable under the circumstances, including individual notice to all members who can be identified through reasonable effort. The notice may be by one or more of the following: United States mail, electronic means, or other appropriate means.   The notice must clearly and concisely state in plain, easily understood language:

(i) the nature of the action;

(ii) the definition of the class certified;

(iii) the class claims, issues, or defenses;

(iv) that a class member may enter an appearance through an attorney if the member so desires;

(v) that the court will exclude from the class any member who requests exclusion;

(vi) the time and manner for requesting exclusion; and

(vii) the binding effect of a class judgment on members under Rule 23(c)(3).

(3) *Judgment.* Whether or not favorable to the class, the judgment in a class action must:

(A) for any class certified under Rule 23(b)(1) or (b)(2), include and describe those whom the court finds to be class members; and

(B) for any class certified under Rule 23(b)(3), include and specify or describe those to whom the Rule 23(c)(2) notice was directed, who have not requested exclusion, and whom the court finds to be class members.

(4) *Particular Issues.* When appropriate, an action may be brought or maintained as a class action with respect to particular issues.

(5) *Subclasses.* When appropriate, a class may be divided into subclasses that are each treated as a class under this rule.

(d) Conducting the Action.

(1) *In General.* In conducting an action under this rule, the court may issue orders that:

(A) determine the course of proceedings or prescribe measures to prevent undue repetition or complication in presenting evidence or argument;

(B) require—to protect class members and fairly conduct the action—giving appropriate notice to some or all class members of:

    (i) any step in the action;

    (ii) the proposed extent of the judgment; or

    (iii) the members' opportunity to signify whether they consider the representation fair and adequate, to intervene and present claims or defenses, or to otherwise come into the action;

(C) impose conditions on the representative parties or on intervenors;

(D) require that the pleadings be amended to eliminate allegations about representation of absent persons and that the action proceed accordingly; or

(E) deal with similar procedural matters.

(2) *Combining and Amending Orders.* An order under Rule 23(d)(1) may be altered or amended from time to time and may be combined with an order under Rule 16.

(e) Settlement, Voluntary Dismissal, or Compromise. The claims, issues, or defenses of a certified class—or a class proposed to be certified for purposes of settlement—may be settled, voluntarily dismissed, or compromised only with the court's approval. The following procedures apply to a proposed settlement, voluntary dismissal, or compromise:

(1) *Notice to the Class.*

(A) *Information That Parties Must Provide to the Court.* The parties must provide the court with information sufficient to enable it to determine whether to give notice of the proposal to the class.

(B) *Grounds for a Decision to Give Notice.* The court must direct notice in a reasonable manner to all class members who would be bound by the proposal if giving notice is justified by the parties' showing that the court will likely be able to:

    (i) approve the proposal under Rule 23(e)(2); and

    (ii) certify the class for purposes of judgment on the proposal.

(2) *Approval of the Proposal.* If the proposal would bind class members, the court may approve it only after a hearing and only on finding that it is fair, reasonable, and adequate after considering whether:

(A) the class representatives and class counsel have adequately represented the class;

(B) the proposal was negotiated at arm's length;

(C) the relief provided for the class is adequate, taking into account:

    (i) the costs, risks, and delay of trial and appeal;

    (ii) the effectiveness of any proposed method of distributing relief to the class, including the method of processing class-member claims;

    (iii) the terms of any proposed award of attorney's fees, including timing of payment; and

    (iv) any agreement required to be identified under Rule 23(e)(3); and

(D) the proposal treats class members equitably relative to each other.

(3) *Identifying Agreements.* The parties seeking approval must file a statement identifying any agreement made in connection with the proposal.

(4) *New Opportunity to be Excluded.* If the class action was previously certified under Rule 23(b)(3), the court may refuse to approve a settlement unless it affords a new opportunity to request exclusion to individual class members who had an earlier opportunity to request exclusion but did not do so.

(5) *Class–Member Objections.*

(A) *In General.* Any class member may object to the proposal if it requires court approval under this subdivision (e). The objection must state whether it applies only to the objector, to a specific subset of the class, or to the entire class, and also state with specificity the grounds for the objection.

(B) *Court Approval Required for Payment in Connection with an Objection.* Unless approved by the court after a hearing, no payment or other consideration may be provided in connection with:

    (i) forgoing or withdrawing an objection, or

    (ii) forgoing, dismissing, or abandoning an appeal from a judgment approving the proposal.

(C) *Procedure for Approval After an Appeal.* If approval under Rule 23(e)(5)(B) has not been obtained before an appeal is docketed in the court of appeals, the procedure of Rule 62.1 applies while the appeal remains pending.

(f) Appeals. A court of appeals may permit an appeal from an order granting or denying class-action certification under this rule, but not from an order under Rule 23(e)(1). A party must file a petition for permission to appeal with the circuit clerk within 14 days after the order is entered, or within 45 days after the order is entered if any party is the United States, a United States agency, or a United States officer or employee sued for an act or omission occurring in connection with duties performed on the United States' behalf. An appeal does not stay proceedings in the district court unless the district judge or the court of appeals so orders.

(g) Class Counsel.

(1) *Appointing Class Counsel.* Unless a statute provides otherwise, a court that certifies a class must appoint class counsel. In appointing class counsel, the court:

(A) must consider:

(i) the work counsel has done in identifying or investigating potential claims in the action;

(ii) counsel's experience in handling class actions, other complex litigation, and the types of claims asserted in the action;

(iii) counsel's knowledge of the applicable law; and

(iv) the resources that counsel will commit to representing the class;

(B) may consider any other matter pertinent to counsel's ability to fairly and adequately represent the interests of the class;

(C) may order potential class counsel to provide information on any subject pertinent to the appointment and to propose terms for attorney's fees and nontaxable costs;

(D) may include in the appointing order provisions about the award of attorney's fees or nontaxable costs under Rule 23(h); and

(E) may make further orders in connection with the appointment.

(2) *Standard for Appointing Class Counsel.* When one applicant seeks appointment as class counsel, the court may appoint that applicant only if the applicant is adequate under Rule 23(g)(1) and (4). If more than one adequate applicant seeks appointment, the court must appoint the applicant best able to represent the interests of the class.

(3) *Interim Counsel.* The court may designate interim counsel to act on behalf of a putative class before determining whether to certify the action as a class action.

(4) *Duty of Class Counsel.* Class counsel must fairly and adequately represent the interests of the class.

(h) Attorney's Fees and Nontaxable Costs. In a certified class action, the court may award reasonable attorney's fees and nontaxable costs that are authorized by law or by the parties' agreement. The following procedures apply:

(1) A claim for an award must be made by motion under Rule 54(d)(2), subject to the provisions of this subdivision (h), at a time the court sets. Notice of the motion must be served on all parties and, for motions by class counsel, directed to class members in a reasonable manner.

(2) A class member, or a party from whom payment is sought, may object to the motion.

(3) The court may hold a hearing and must find the facts and state its legal conclusions under Rule 52(a).

(4) The court may refer issues related to the amount of the award to a special master or a magistrate judge, as provided in Rule 54(d)(2)(D).

(Amended February 28, 1966, effective July 1, 1966; March 2, 1987, effective August 1, 1987; April 24, 1998, effective December 1, 1998; March 27, 2003, effective December 1, 2003; April 30, 2007, effective December 1, 2007; March 26, 2009, effective December 1, 2009; April 26, 2018, effective December 1, 2018.)

RULE 23.1 DERIVATIVE ACTIONS

(a) Prerequisites. This rule applies when one or more shareholders or members of a corporation or an unincorporated association bring a derivative action to enforce a right that the corporation or association may properly assert but has failed to enforce. The derivative action may not be maintained if it appears that the plaintiff does not fairly and adequately represent the interests of shareholders or members who are similarly situated in enforcing the right of the corporation or association.

(b) Pleading Requirements. The complaint must be verified and must:

(1) allege that the plaintiff was a shareholder or member at the time of the transaction complained of, or that the plaintiff's share or membership later devolved on it by operation of law;

(2) allege that the action is not a collusive one to confer jurisdiction that the court would otherwise lack; and

(3) state with particularity:

(A) any effort by the plaintiff to obtain the desired action from the directors or comparable authority and, if necessary, from the shareholders or members; and

(B) the reasons for not obtaining the action or not making the effort.

(c) Settlement, Dismissal, and Compromise. A derivative action may be settled, voluntarily dismissed, or compromised only with the court's approval. Notice of a proposed settlement, voluntary dismissal, or compromise must be given to shareholders or members in the manner that the court orders.

(Adopted February 28, 1966, effective July 1, 1966; amended March 2, 1987, effective August 1, 1987; April 30, 2007, effective December 1, 2007.)

RULE 23.2 ACTIONS RELATING TO UNINCORPORATED ASSOCIATIONS

This rule applies to an action brought by or against the members of an unincorporated association as a class by naming certain members as representative parties. The action may be maintained only if it appears that those parties will fairly and adequately protect the interests of the association and its members. In conducting the action, the court may issue any appropriate orders corresponding with those in Rule 23(d), and the procedure for settlement, voluntary dismissal, or compromise must correspond with the procedure in Rule 23(e).

(Adopted February 28, 1966, effective July 1, 1966; amended April 30, 2007, effective December 1, 2007.)

RULE 24. INTERVENTION

(a) Intervention of Right. On timely motion, the court must permit anyone to intervene who:

(1) is given an unconditional right to intervene by a federal statute; or

(2) claims an interest relating to the property or transaction that is the subject of the action, and is so situated that disposing of the action may as a practical matter impair or impede the movant's ability to protect its interest, unless existing parties adequately represent that interest.

(b) Permissive Intervention.

(1) *In General.* On timely motion, the court may permit anyone to intervene who:

(A) is given a conditional right to intervene by a federal statute; or

(B) has a claim or defense that shares with the main action a common question of law or fact.

(2) *By a Government Officer or Agency.* On timely motion, the court may permit a federal or state governmental officer or agency to intervene if a party's claim or defense is based on:

(A) a statute or executive order administered by the officer or agency; or

(B) any regulation, order, requirement, or agreement issued or made under the statute or executive order.

(3) *Delay or Prejudice.* In exercising its discretion, the court must consider whether the intervention will unduly delay or prejudice the adjudication of the original parties' rights.

(c) Notice and Pleading Required. A motion to intervene must be served on the parties as provided in Rule 5. The motion must state the grounds for intervention and be accompanied by a pleading that sets out the claim or defense for which intervention is sought.

(Amended December 27, 1946, effective March 19, 1948; December 29, 1948, effective October 20, 1949; January 21, 1963, effective July 1, 1963; February 28, 1966, effective July 1, 1966; March 2, 1987, effective August 1, 1987; April 30, 1991, effective December 1, 1991; April 12, 2006, effective December 1, 2006; April 30, 2007, effective December 1, 2007.)

RULE 25. SUBSTITUTION OF PARTIES

(a) Death.

(1) *Substitution if the Claim Is Not Extinguished.* If a party dies and the claim is not extinguished, the court may order substitution of the proper party. A motion for substitution may be made by any party or by the decedent's successor or representative. If the motion is not made within 90 days after service of a statement noting the death, the action by or against the decedent must be dismissed.

(2) *Continuation Among the Remaining Parties.* After a party's death, if the right sought to be enforced survives only to or against the remaining parties, the action does not abate, but proceeds in favor of or against the remaining parties. The death should be noted on the record.

(3) *Service.* A motion to substitute, together with a notice of hearing, must be served on the parties as provided in Rule 5 and on nonparties as provided in Rule 4. A statement noting death must be served in the same manner. Service may be made in any judicial district.

(b) Incompetency. If a party becomes incompetent, the court may, on motion, permit the action to be continued by or against the party's representative. The motion must be served as provided in Rule 25(a)(3).

(c) Transfer of Interest. If an interest is transferred, the action may be continued by or against the original party unless the court, on motion, orders the transferee to be substituted in the action or joined with the original party. The motion must be served as provided in Rule 25(a)(3).

(d) Public Officers; Death or Separation from Office. An action does not abate when a public officer who is a party in an official capacity dies, resigns, or otherwise ceases to hold office while the action is pending. The officer's successor is automatically substituted as a party. Later proceedings should be in the substituted party's name, but any misnomer not affecting the parties' substantial rights must be disregarded. The court may order substitution at any time, but the absence of such an order does not affect the substitution.

(Amended December 29, 1948, effective October 20, 1949; April 17, 1961, effective July 19, 1961; January 21, 1963, effective July 1, 1963; March 2, 1987, effective August 1, 1987; April 30, 2007, effective December 1, 2007.)

TITLE V. DISCLOSURES AND DISCOVERY

RULE 26. DUTY TO DISCLOSE; GENERAL PROVISIONS GOVERNING DISCOVERY

(a) Required Disclosures.

(1) *Initial Disclosure.*

(A) *In General.* Except as exempted by Rule 26(a)(1)(B) or as otherwise stipulated or ordered by the court, a party must, without awaiting a discovery request, provide to the other parties:

(i) the name and, if known, the address and telephone number of each individual likely to have discoverable information—along with the subjects of that information—that the disclosing party may use to support its claims or defenses, unless the use would be solely for impeachment;

(ii) a copy—or a description by category and location—of all documents, electronically stored information, and tangible things that the disclosing party has in its possession, custody, or control and may use to support its claims or defenses, unless the use would be solely for impeachment;

(iii) a computation of each category of damages claimed by the disclosing party—who must also make available for inspection and copying as under Rule 34 the documents or other evidentiary material, unless privileged or protected from disclosure, on which each computation is based, including materials bearing on the nature and extent of injuries suffered; and

(iv) for inspection and copying as under Rule 34, any insurance agreement under which an insurance business may be liable to satisfy all or part of a possible judgment in the action or to indemnify or reimburse for payments made to satisfy the judgment.

(B) *Proceedings Exempt from Initial Disclosure.* The following proceedings are exempt from initial disclosure:

(i) an action for review on an administrative record;

(ii) a forfeiture action in rem arising from a federal statute;

(iii) a petition for habeas corpus or any other proceeding to challenge a criminal conviction or sentence;

(iv) an action brought without an attorney by a person in the custody of the United States, a state, or a state subdivision;

(v) an action to enforce or quash an administrative summons or subpoena;

(vi) an action by the United States to recover benefit payments;

(vii) an action by the United States to collect on a student loan guaranteed by the United States;

(viii) a proceeding ancillary to a proceeding in another court; and

(ix) an action to enforce an arbitration award.

(C) *Time for Initial Disclosures—In General.* A party must make the initial disclosures at or within 14 days after the parties' Rule 26(f) conference unless a different time is set by stipulation or court order, or unless a party objects during the conference that initial disclosures are not appropriate in this action and states the objection in the proposed discovery plan. In ruling on the objection, the court must determine what disclosures, if any, are to be made and must set the time for disclosure.

(D) *Time for Initial Disclosures—For Parties Served or Joined Later.* A party that is first served or otherwise joined after the Rule 26(f) conference must make the initial disclosures within 30 days after being served or joined, unless a different time is set by stipulation or court order.

(E) *Basis for Initial Disclosure; Unacceptable Excuses.* A party must make its initial disclosures based on the information then reasonably available to it. A party is not excused from making its disclosures because it has not fully investigated the case or because it challenges the sufficiency of another party's disclosures or because another party has not made its disclosures.

(2) *Disclosure of Expert Testimony.*

(A) *In General.* In addition to the disclosures required by Rule 26(a)(1), a party must disclose to the other parties the identity of any witness it may use at trial to present evidence under Federal Rule of Evidence 702, 703, or 705.

(B) *Witnesses Who Must Provide a Written Report.* Unless otherwise stipulated or ordered by the court, this disclosure must be accompanied by a written report—prepared and signed by the witness—if the witness is one retained or specially employed to provide expert testimony in the case or one whose duties as the party's employee regularly involve giving expert testimony. The report must contain:

(i) a complete statement of all opinions the witness will express and the basis and reasons for them;

(ii) the facts or data considered by the witness in forming them;

(iii) any exhibits that will be used to summarize or support them;

(iv) the witness's qualifications, including a list of all publications authored in the previous 10 years;

(v) a list of all other cases in which, during the previous 4 years, the witness testified as an expert at trial or by deposition; and

(vi) a statement of the compensation to be paid for the study and testimony in the case.

(C) *Witnesses Who Do Not Provide a Written Report.* Unless otherwise stipulated or ordered by the court, if the witness is not required to provide a written report, this disclosure must state:

(i) the subject matter on which the witness is expected to present evidence under Federal Rule of Evidence 702, 703, or 705; and

(ii) a summary of the facts and opinions to which the witness is expected to testify.

(D) *Time to Disclose Expert Testimony.* A party must make these disclosures at the times and in the sequence that the court orders. Absent a stipulation or a court order, the disclosures must be made:

(i) at least 90 days before the date set for trial or for the case to be ready for trial; or

(ii) if the evidence is intended solely to contradict or rebut evidence on the same subject matter identified by another party under Rule 26(a)(2)(B) or (C), within 30 days after the other party's disclosure.

(E) *Supplementing the Disclosure.* The parties must supplement these disclosures when required under Rule 26(e).

(3) *Pretrial Disclosures.*

(A) *In General.* In addition to the disclosures required by Rule 26(a)(1) and (2), a party must provide to the other parties and promptly file the following information about the evidence that it may present at trial other than solely for impeachment:

(i) the name and, if not previously provided, the address and telephone number of each witness—separately identifying those the party expects to present and those it may call if the need arises;

    (ii) the designation of those witnesses whose testimony the party expects to present by deposition and, if not taken stenographically, a transcript of the pertinent parts of the deposition; and

    (iii) an identification of each document or other exhibit, including summaries of other evidence—separately identifying those items the party expects to offer and those it may offer if the need arises.

  (B) *Time for Pretrial Disclosures; Objections.* Unless the court orders otherwise, these disclosures must be made at least 30 days before trial. Within 14 days after they are made, unless the court sets a different time, a party may serve and promptly file a list of the following objections: any objections to the use under Rule 32(a) of a deposition designated by another party under Rule 26(a)(3)(A)(ii); and any objection, together with the grounds for it, that may be made to the admissibility of materials identified under Rule 26(a)(3)(A)(iii). An objection not so made—except for one under Federal Rule of Evidence 402 or 403—is waived unless excused by the court for good cause.

  (4) *Form of Disclosures.* Unless the court orders otherwise, all disclosures under Rule 26(a) must be in writing, signed, and served.

(b) Discovery Scope and Limits.

  (1) *Scope in General.* Unless otherwise limited by court order, the scope of discovery is as follows: Parties may obtain discovery regarding any nonprivileged matter that is relevant to any party's claim or defense and proportional to the needs of the case, considering the importance of the issues at stake in the action, the amount in controversy, the parties' relative access to relevant information, the parties' resources, the importance of the discovery in resolving the issues, and whether the burden or expense of the proposed discovery outweighs its likely benefit. Information within this scope of discovery need not be admissible in evidence to be discoverable.

  (2) *Limitations on Frequency and Extent.*

  (A) *When Permitted.* By order, the court may alter the limits in these rules on the number of depositions and interrogatories or on the length of depositions under Rule 30. By order or local rule, the court may also limit the number of requests under Rule 36.

  (B) *Specific Limitations on Electronically Stored Information.* A party need not provide discovery of electronically stored information from sources that the party identifies as not reasonably accessible because of undue burden or cost. On motion to compel discovery or for a protective order, the party from whom discovery is sought must show that the information is not reasonably accessible because of undue burden or cost. If that showing is made, the court may nonetheless order discovery from such sources if the requesting party shows good cause, considering the limitations of Rule 26(b)(2)(C). The court may specify conditions for the discovery.

  (C) *When Required.* On motion or on its own, the court must limit the frequency or extent of discovery otherwise allowed by these rules or by local rule if it determines that:

    (i) the discovery sought is unreasonably cumulative or duplicative, or can be obtained from some other source that is more convenient, less burdensome, or less expensive;

    (ii) the party seeking discovery has had ample opportunity to obtain the information by discovery in the action; or

    (iii) the proposed discovery is outside the scope permitted by Rule 26(b)(1).

  (3) *Trial Preparation: Materials.*

  (A) *Documents and Tangible Things.* Ordinarily, a party may not discover documents and tangible things that are prepared in anticipation of litigation or for trial by or for another party or its representative (including the other party's attorney, consultant, surety, indemnitor, insurer, or agent). But, subject to Rule 26(b)(4), those materials may be discovered if:

    (i) they are otherwise discoverable under Rule 26(b)(1); and

    (ii) the party shows that it has substantial need for the materials to prepare its case and cannot, without undue hardship, obtain their substantial equivalent by other means.

  (B) *Protection Against Disclosure.* If the court orders discovery of those materials, it must protect against disclosure of the mental impressions, conclusions, opinions, or legal theories of a party's attorney or other representative concerning the litigation.

  (C) *Previous Statement.* Any party or other person may, on request and without the required showing, obtain the person's own previous statement about the action or its subject matter. If the request is refused, the person may move for a court order, and Rule 37(a)(5) applies to the award of expenses. A previous statement is either:

    (i) a written statement that the person has signed or otherwise adopted or approved; or

    (ii) a contemporaneous stenographic, mechanical, electrical, or other recording—or a transcription of it—that recites substantially verbatim the person's oral statement.

  (4) *Trial Preparation: Experts.*

  (A) *Deposition of an Expert Who May Testify.* A party may depose any person who has been identified as an expert whose opinions may be presented at trial. If Rule 26(a)(2)(B) requires a report from the expert, the deposition may be conducted only after the report is provided.

  (B) *Trial–Preparation Protection for Draft Reports or Disclosures.* Rules 26(b)(3)(A) and (B) protect drafts of any report or disclosure required under Rule 26(a)(2), regardless of the form in which the draft is recorded.

(C) *Trial–Preparation Protection for Communications Between a Party's Attorney and Expert Witnesses.* Rules 26(b)(3)(A) and (B) protect communications between the party's attorney and any witness required to provide a report under Rule 26(a)(2)(B), regardless of the form of the communications, except to the extent that the communications:

    (i) relate to compensation for the expert's study or testimony;

    (ii) identify facts or data that the party's attorney provided and that the expert considered in forming the opinions to be expressed; or

    (iii) identify assumptions that the party's attorney provided and that the expert relied on in forming the opinions to be expressed.

(D) *Expert Employed Only for Trial Preparation.* Ordinarily, a party may not, by interrogatories or deposition, discover facts known or opinions held by an expert who has been retained or specially employed by another party in anticipation of litigation or to prepare for trial and who is not expected to be called as a witness at trial. But a party may do so only:

    (i) as provided in Rule 35(b); or

    (ii) on showing exceptional circumstances under which it is impracticable for the party to obtain facts or opinions on the same subject by other means.

(E) *Payment.* Unless manifest injustice would result, the court must require that the party seeking discovery:

    (i) pay the expert a reasonable fee for time spent in responding to discovery under Rule 26(b)(4)(A) or (D); and

    (ii) for discovery under (D), also pay the other party a fair portion of the fees and expenses it reasonably incurred in obtaining the expert's facts and opinions.

(5) *Claiming Privilege or Protecting Trial-Preparation Materials.*

(A) *Information Withheld.* When a party withholds information otherwise discoverable by claiming that the information is privileged or subject to protection as trial-preparation material, the party must:

    (i) expressly make the claim; and

    (ii) describe the nature of the documents, communications, or tangible things not produced or disclosed—and do so in a manner that, without revealing information itself privileged or protected, will enable other parties to assess the claim.

(B) *Information Produced.* If information produced in discovery is subject to a claim of privilege or of protection as trial-preparation material, the party making the claim may notify any party that received the information of the claim and the basis for it. After being notified, a party must promptly return, sequester, or destroy the specified information and any copies it has; must not use or disclose the information until the claim is resolved; must take reasonable steps to retrieve the information if the party disclosed it before being notified; and may promptly present the information to the court under seal for a determination of the claim. The producing party must preserve the information until the claim is resolved.

(c) Protective Orders.

(1) *In General.* A party or any person from whom discovery is sought may move for a protective order in the court where the action is pending — or as an alternative on matters relating to a deposition, in the court for the district where the deposition will be taken. The motion must include a certification that the movant has in good faith conferred or attempted to confer with other affected parties in an effort to resolve the dispute without court action. The court may, for good cause, issue an order to protect a party or person from annoyance, embarrassment, oppression, or undue burden or expense, including one or more of the following:

    (A) forbidding the disclosure or discovery;

    (B) specifying terms, including time and place or the allocation of expenses, for the disclosure or discovery;

    (C) prescribing a discovery method other than the one selected by the party seeking discovery;

    (D) forbidding inquiry into certain matters, or limiting the scope of disclosure or discovery to certain matters;

    (E) designating the persons who may be present while the discovery is conducted;

    (F) requiring that a deposition be sealed and opened only on court order;

    (G) requiring that a trade secret or other confidential research, development, or commercial information not be revealed or be revealed only in a specified way; and

    (H) requiring that the parties simultaneously file specified documents or information in sealed envelopes, to be opened as the court directs.

(2) *Ordering Discovery.* If a motion for a protective order is wholly or partly denied, the court may, on just terms, order that any party or person provide or permit discovery.

(3) *Awarding Expenses.* Rule 37(a)(5) applies to the award of expenses.

(d) Timing and Sequence of Discovery.

(1) *Timing.* A party may not seek discovery from any source before the parties have conferred as required by Rule 26(f), except in a proceeding exempted from initial disclosure under Rule 26(a)(1)(B), or when authorized by these rules, by stipulation, or by court order.

(2) *Early Rule 34 Requests.*

    (A) Time to Deliver. More than 21 days after the summons and complaint are served on a party, a request under Rule 34 may be delivered:

        (i) to that party by any other party, and

        (ii) by that party to any plaintiff or to any other party that has been served.

(B) *When Considered Served*. The request is considered to have been served at the first Rule 26(f) conference.

(3) *Sequence*. Unless the parties stipulate or the court orders otherwise for the parties' and witnesses' convenience and in the interests of justice:

    (A) methods of discovery may be used in any sequence; and

    (B) discovery by one party does not require any other party to delay its discovery.

(e) Supplementing Disclosures and Responses.

(1) *In General.* A party who has made a disclosure under Rule 26(a)—or who has responded to an interrogatory, request for production, or request for admission—must supplement or correct its disclosure or response:

    (A) in a timely manner if the party learns that in some material respect the disclosure or response is incomplete or incorrect, and if the additional or corrective information has not otherwise been made known to the other parties during the discovery process or in writing; or

    (B) as ordered by the court.

(2) *Expert Witness.* For an expert whose report must be disclosed under Rule 26(a)(2)(B), the party's duty to supplement extends both to information included in the report and to information given during the expert's deposition. Any additions or changes to this information must be disclosed by the time the party's pretrial disclosures under Rule 26(a)(3) are due.

(f) Conference of the Parties; Planning for Discovery.

(1) *Conference Timing.* Except in a proceeding exempted from initial disclosure under Rule 26(a)(1)(B) or when the court orders otherwise, the parties must confer as soon as practicable—and in any event at least 21 days before a scheduling conference is to be held or a scheduling order is due under Rule 16(b).

(2) *Conference Content; Parties' Responsibilities.* In conferring, the parties must consider the nature and basis of their claims and defenses and the possibilities for promptly settling or resolving the case; make or arrange for the disclosures required by Rule 26(a)(1); discuss any issues about preserving discoverable information; and develop a proposed discovery plan. The attorneys of record and all unrepresented parties that have appeared in the case are jointly responsible for arranging the conference, for attempting in good faith to agree on the proposed discovery plan, and for submitting to the court within 14 days after the conference a written report outlining the plan. The court may order the parties or attorneys to attend the conference in person.

(3) *Discovery Plan.* A discovery plan must state the parties' views and proposals on:

    (A) what changes should be made in the timing, form, or requirement for disclosures under Rule 26(a), including a statement of when initial disclosures were made or will be made;

    (B) the subjects on which discovery may be needed, when discovery should be completed, and whether discovery should be conducted in phases or be limited to or focused on particular issues;

    (C) any issues about disclosure, discovery, or preservation of electronically stored information, including the form or forms in which it should be produced;

    (D) any issues about claims of privilege or of protection as trial-preparation materials, including — if the parties agree on a procedure to assert these claims after production — whether to ask the court to include their agreement in an order under Federal Rule of Evidence 502;

    (E) what changes should be made in the limitations on discovery imposed under these rules or by local rule, and what other limitations should be imposed; and

    (F) any other orders that the court should issue under Rule 26(c) or under Rule 16(b) and (c).

(4) *Expedited Schedule.* If necessary to comply with its expedited schedule for Rule 16(b) conferences, a court may by local rule:

    (A) require the parties' conference to occur less than 21 days before the scheduling conference is held or a scheduling order is due under Rule 16(b); and

    (B) require the written report outlining the discovery plan to be filed less than 14 days after the parties' conference, or excuse the parties from submitting a written report and permit them to report orally on their discovery plan at the Rule 16(b) conference.

(g) Signing Disclosures and Discovery Requests, Responses, and Objections.

(1) *Signature Required; Effect of Signature.* Every disclosure under Rule 26(a)(1) or (a)(3) and every discovery request, response, or objection must be signed by at least one attorney of record in the attorney's own name—or by the party personally, if unrepresented—and must state the signer's address, e-mail address, and telephone number. By signing, an attorney or party certifies that to the best of the person's knowledge, information, and belief formed after a reasonable inquiry:

    (A) with respect to a disclosure, it is complete and correct as of the time it is made; and

    (B) with respect to a discovery request, response, or objection, it is:

        (i) consistent with these rules and warranted by existing law or by a nonfrivolous argument for extending, modifying, or reversing existing law, or for establishing new law;

        (ii) not interposed for any improper purpose, such as to harass, cause unnecessary delay, or needlessly increase the cost of litigation; and

        (iii) neither unreasonable nor unduly burdensome or expensive, considering the needs of the case, prior discovery in the case, the amount in controversy, and the importance of the issues at stake in the action.

(2) *Failure to Sign.* Other parties have no duty to act on an unsigned disclosure, request, response, or objection until it is signed, and the court must strike it unless a signature is promptly supplied after the omission is called to the attorney's or party's attention.

(3) *Sanction for Improper Certification.* If a certification violates this rule without substantial justification, the court, on motion or on its own, must impose an appropriate sanction on the signer, the party on whose behalf the signer was acting, or both. The sanction may include an order to pay the reasonable expenses, including attorney's fees, caused by the violation.

(Amended December 27, 1946, effective March 19, 1948; January 21, 1963, effective July 1, 1963; February 28, 1966, effective July 1, 1966; March 30, 1970, effective July 1, 1970; April 29, 1980, effective August 1, 1980; April 28, 1983, effective August 1, 1983; March 2, 1987, effective August 1, 1987; April 22, 1993, effective December 1, 1993; April 17, 2000, effective December 1, 2000; April 12, 2006, effective December 1, 2006; April 30, 2007, effective December 1, 2007; April 28, 2010, effective December 1, 2010; April 29, 2015, effective December 1, 2015.)

RULE 27.   DEPOSITIONS TO PERPETUATE TESTIMONY

(a) Before an Action Is Filed.

(1) *Petition.* A person who wants to perpetuate testimony about any matter cognizable in a United States court may file a verified petition in the district court for the district where any expected adverse party resides. The petition must ask for an order authorizing the petitioner to depose the named persons in order to perpetuate their testimony. The petition must be titled in the petitioner's name and must show:

(A) that the petitioner expects to be a party to an action cognizable in a United States court but cannot presently bring it or cause it to be brought;

(B) the subject matter of the expected action and the petitioner's interest;

(C) the facts that the petitioner wants to establish by the proposed testimony and the reasons to perpetuate it;

(D) the names or a description of the persons whom the petitioner expects to be adverse parties and their addresses, so far as known; and

(E) the name, address, and expected substance of the testimony of each deponent.

(2) *Notice and Service.* At least 21 days before the hearing date, the petitioner must serve each expected adverse party with a copy of the petition and a notice stating the time and place of the hearing. The notice may be served either inside or outside the district or state in the manner provided in Rule 4. If that service cannot be made with reasonable diligence on an expected adverse party, the court may order service by publication or otherwise. The court must appoint an attorney to represent persons not served in the manner provided in Rule 4 and to cross-examine the deponent if an unserved person is not otherwise represented. If any expected adverse party is a minor or is incompetent, Rule 17(c) applies.

(3) *Order and Examination.* If satisfied that perpetuating the testimony may prevent a failure or delay of justice, the court must issue an order that designates or describes the persons whose depositions may be taken, specifies the subject matter of the examinations, and states whether the depositions will be taken orally or by written interrogatories. The depositions may then be taken under these rules, and the court may issue orders like those authorized by Rules 34 and 35. A reference in these rules to the court where an action is pending means, for purposes of this rule, the court where the petition for the deposition was filed.

(4) *Using the Deposition.* A deposition to perpetuate testimony may be used under Rule 32(a) in any later-filed district-court action involving the same subject matter if the deposition either was taken under these rules or, although not so taken, would be admissible in evidence in the courts of the state where it was taken.

(b) Pending Appeal.

(1) *In General.* The court where a judgment has been rendered may, if an appeal has been taken or may still be taken, permit a party to depose witnesses to perpetuate their testimony for use in the event of further proceedings in that court.

(2) *Motion.* The party who wants to perpetuate testimony may move for leave to take the depositions, on the same notice and service as if the action were pending in the district court. The motion must show:

(A) the name, address, and expected substance of the testimony of each deponent; and

(B) the reasons for perpetuating the testimony.

(3) *Court Order.* If the court finds that perpetuating the testimony may prevent a failure or delay of justice, the court may permit the depositions to be taken and may issue orders like those authorized by Rules 34 and 35. The depositions may be taken and used as any other deposition taken in a pending district-court action.

(c) Perpetuation by an Action. This rule does not limit a court's power to entertain an action to perpetuate testimony.

(Amended December 27, 1946, effective March 19, 1948; December 29, 1948, effective October 20, 1949; March 1, 1971, effective July 1, 1971; March 2, 1987, effective August 1, 1987; April 25, 2005, effective December 1, 2005; April 30, 2007, effective December 1, 2007; March 26, 2009, effective December 1, 2009.)

RULE 28.   PERSONS BEFORE WHOM DEPOSITIONS MAY BE TAKEN

(a) Within the United States.

(1) *In General.* Within the United States or a territory or insular possession subject to United States jurisdiction, a deposition must be taken before:

(A) an officer authorized to administer oaths either by federal law or by the law in the place of examination; or

(B) a person appointed by the court where the action is pending to administer oaths and take testimony.

(2) *Definition of "Officer."* The term "officer" in Rules 30, 31, and 32 includes a person appointed by the court under this rule or designated by the parties under Rule 29(a).

(b) In a Foreign Country.

(1) *In General.* A deposition may be taken in a foreign country:

   (A) under an applicable treaty or convention;

   (B) under a letter of request, whether or not captioned a "letter rogatory";

   (C) on notice, before a person authorized to administer oaths either by federal law or by the law in the place of examination; or

   (D) before a person commissioned by the court to administer any necessary oath and take testimony.

(2) *Issuing a Letter of Request or a Commission.* A letter of request, a commission, or both may be issued:

   (A) on appropriate terms after an application and notice of it; and

   (B) without a showing that taking the deposition in another manner is impracticable or inconvenient.

(3) *Form of a Request, Notice, or Commission.* When a letter of request or any other device is used according to a treaty or convention, it must be captioned in the form prescribed by that treaty or convention. A letter of request may be addressed "To the Appropriate Authority in [name of country]." A deposition notice or a commission must designate by name or descriptive title the person before whom the deposition is to be taken.

(4) *Letter of Request—Admitting Evidence.* Evidence obtained in response to a letter of request need not be excluded merely because it is not a verbatim transcript, because the testimony was not taken under oath, or because of any similar departure from the requirements for depositions taken within the United States.

(c) Disqualification. A deposition must not be taken before a person who is any party's relative, employee, or attorney; who is related to or employed by any party's attorney; or who is financially interested in the action.

(Amended December 27, 1946, effective March 19, 1948; January 21, 1963, effective July 1, 1963; April 29, 1980, effective August 1, 1980; March 2, 1987, effective August 1, 1987; April 22, 1993, effective December 1, 1993; April 30, 2007, effective December 1, 2007.)

RULE 29. STIPULATIONS ABOUT DISCOVERY PROCEDURE

Unless the court orders otherwise, the parties may stipulate that:

(a) a deposition may be taken before any person, at any time or place, on any notice, and in the manner specified—in which event it may be used in the same way as any other deposition; and

(b) other procedures governing or limiting discovery be modified—but a stipulation extending the time for any form of discovery must have court approval if it would interfere with

the time set for completing discovery, for hearing a motion, or for trial.

(Amended March 30, 1970, effective July 1, 1970; April 22, 1993, effective December 1, 1993; April 30, 2007, effective December 1, 2007.)

RULE 30. DEPOSITIONS BY ORAL EXAMINATION

(a) When a Deposition May Be Taken.

(1) *Without Leave.* A party may, by oral questions, depose any person, including a party, without leave of court except as provided in Rule 30(a)(2). The deponent's attendance may be compelled by subpoena under Rule 45.

(2) *With Leave.* A party must obtain leave of court, and the court must grant leave to the extent consistent with Rule 26(b)(1) and (2):

   (A) if the parties have not stipulated to the deposition and:

     (i) the deposition would result in more than 10 depositions being taken under this rule or Rule 31 by the plaintiffs, or by the defendants, or by the third-party defendants;

     (ii) the deponent has already been deposed in the case; or

     (iii) the party seeks to take the deposition before the time specified in Rule 26(d), unless the party certifies in the notice, with supporting facts, that the deponent is expected to leave the United States and be unavailable for examination in this country after that time; or

   (B) if the deponent is confined in prison.

(b) Notice of the Deposition; Other Formal Requirements.

(1) *Notice in General.* A party who wants to depose a person by oral questions must give reasonable written notice to every other party. The notice must state the time and place of the deposition and, if known, the deponent's name and address. If the name is unknown, the notice must provide a general description sufficient to identify the person or the particular class or group to which the person belongs.

(2) *Producing Documents.* If a subpoena duces tecum is to be served on the deponent, the materials designated for production, as set out in the subpoena, must be listed in the notice or in an attachment. The notice to a party deponent may be accompanied by a request under Rule 34 to produce documents and tangible things at the deposition.

(3) *Method of Recording.*

   (A) *Method Stated in the Notice.* The party who notices the deposition must state in the notice the method for recording the testimony. Unless the court orders otherwise, testimony may be recorded by audio, audiovisual, or stenographic means. The noticing party bears the recording costs. Any party may arrange to transcribe a deposition.

(B) *Additional Method.* With prior notice to the deponent and other parties, any party may designate another method for recording the testimony in addition to that specified in the original notice. That party bears the expense of the additional record or transcript unless the court orders otherwise.

(4) *By Remote Means.* The parties may stipulate—or the court may on motion order—that a deposition be taken by telephone or other remote means. For the purpose of this rule and Rules 28(a), 37(a)(2), and 37(b)(1), the deposition takes place where the deponent answers the questions.

(5) *Officer's Duties.*

(A) *Before the Deposition.* Unless the parties stipulate otherwise, a deposition must be conducted before an officer appointed or designated under Rule 28. The officer must begin the deposition with an on-the-record statement that includes:

(i) the officer's name and business address;

(ii) the date, time, and place of the deposition;

(iii) the deponent's name;

(iv) the officer's administration of the oath or affirmation to the deponent; and

(v) the identity of all persons present.

(B) *Conducting the Deposition; Avoiding Distortion.* If the deposition is recorded non-stenographically, the officer must repeat the items in Rule 30(b)(5)(A)(i)-(iii) at the beginning of each unit of the recording medium. The deponent's and attorneys' appearance or demeanor must not be distorted through recording techniques.

(C) *After the Deposition.* At the end of a deposition, the officer must state on the record that the deposition is complete and must set out any stipulations made by the attorneys about custody of the transcript or recording and of the exhibits, or about any other pertinent matters.

(6) *Notice or Subpoena Directed to an Organization.* In its notice or subpoena, a party may name as the deponent a public or private corporation, a partnership, an association, a governmental agency, or other entity and must describe with reasonable particularity the matters for examination. The named organization must designate one or more officers, directors, or managing agents, or designate other persons who consent to testify on its behalf; and it may set out the matters on which each person designated will testify. Before or promptly after the notice or subpoena is served, the serving party and the organization must confer in good faith about the matters for examination. A subpoena must advise a nonparty organization of its duty to confer with the serving party and to designate each person who will testify. The persons designated must testify about information known or reasonably available to the organization. This paragraph (6) does not preclude a deposition by any other procedure allowed by these rules.

(c) Examination and Cross–Examination; Record of the Examination; Objections; Written Questions.

(1) *Examination and Cross–Examination.* The examination and cross-examination of a deponent proceed as they would at trial under the Federal Rules of Evidence, except Rules 103 and 615. After putting the deponent under oath or affirmation, the officer must record the testimony by the method designated under Rule 30(b)(3)(A). The testimony must be recorded by the officer personally or by a person acting in the presence and under the direction of the officer.

(2) *Objections.* An objection at the time of the examination—whether to evidence, to a party's conduct, to the officer's qualifications, to the manner of taking the deposition, or to any other aspect of the deposition—must be noted on the record, but the examination still proceeds; the testimony is taken subject to any objection. An objection must be stated concisely in a nonargumentative and nonsuggestive manner. A person may instruct a deponent not to answer only when necessary to preserve a privilege, to enforce a limitation ordered by the court, or to present a motion under Rule 30(d)(3).

(3) *Participating Through Written Questions.* Instead of participating in the oral examination, a party may serve written questions in a sealed envelope on the party noticing the deposition, who must deliver them to the officer. The officer must ask the deponent those questions and record the answers verbatim.

(d) Duration; Sanction; Motion to Terminate or Limit.

(1) *Duration.* Unless otherwise stipulated or ordered by the court, a deposition is limited to one day of 7 hours. The court must allow additional time consistent with Rule 26(b)(1) and (2) if needed to fairly examine the deponent or if the deponent, another person, or any other circumstance impedes or delays the examination.

(2) *Sanction.* The court may impose an appropriate sanction—including the reasonable expenses and attorney's fees incurred by any party—on a person who impedes, delays, or frustrates the fair examination of the deponent.

(3) *Motion to Terminate or Limit.*

(A) *Grounds.* At any time during a deposition, the deponent or a party may move to terminate or limit it on the ground that it is being conducted in bad faith or in a manner that unreasonably annoys, embarrasses, or oppresses the deponent or party. The motion may be filed in the court where the action is pending or the deposition is being taken. If the objecting deponent or party so demands, the deposition must be suspended for the time necessary to obtain an order.

(B) *Order.* The court may order that the deposition be terminated or may limit its scope and manner as provided in Rule 26(c). If terminated, the deposition may be resumed only by order of the court where the action is pending.

(C) *Award of Expenses.* Rule 37(a)(5) applies to the award of expenses.

(e) Review by the Witness; Changes.

(1) *Review; Statement of Changes.* On request by the deponent or a party before the deposition is completed, the deponent must be allowed 30 days after being notified by the officer that the transcript or recording is available in which:

(A) to review the transcript or recording; and

(B) if there are changes in form or substance, to sign a statement listing the changes and the reasons for making them.

(2) *Changes Indicated in the Officer's Certificate.* The officer must note in the certificate prescribed by Rule 30(f)(1) whether a review was requested and, if so, must attach any changes the deponent makes during the 30–day period.

(f) Certification and Delivery; Exhibits; Copies of the Transcript or Recording; Filing.

(1) *Certification and Delivery.* The officer must certify in writing that the witness was duly sworn and that the deposition accurately records the witness's testimony. The certificate must accompany the record of the deposition. Unless the court orders otherwise, the officer must seal the deposition in an envelope or package bearing the title of the action and marked "Deposition of [witness's name]" and must promptly send it to the attorney who arranged for the transcript or recording. The attorney must store it under conditions that will protect it against loss, destruction, tampering, or deterioration.

(2) *Documents and Tangible Things.*

(A) *Originals and Copies.* Documents and tangible things produced for inspection during a deposition must, on a party's request, be marked for identification and attached to the deposition. Any party may inspect and copy them. But if the person who produced them wants to keep the originals, the person may:

(i) offer copies to be marked, attached to the deposition, and then used as originals—after giving all parties a fair opportunity to verify the copies by comparing them with the originals; or

(ii) give all parties a fair opportunity to inspect and copy the originals after they are marked—in which event the originals may be used as if attached to the deposition.

(B) *Order Regarding the Originals.* Any party may move for an order that the originals be attached to the deposition pending final disposition of the case.

(3) *Copies of the Transcript or Recording.* Unless otherwise stipulated or ordered by the court, the officer must retain the stenographic notes of a deposition taken stenographically or a copy of the recording of a deposition taken by another method. When paid reasonable charges, the officer must furnish a copy of the transcript or recording to any party or the deponent.

(4) *Notice of Filing.* A party who files the deposition must promptly notify all other parties of the filing.

(g) Failure to Attend a Deposition or Serve a Subpoena; Expenses. A party who, expecting a deposition to be taken, attends in person or by an attorney may recover reasonable expenses for attending, including attorney's fees, if the noticing party failed to:

(1) attend and proceed with the deposition; or

(2) serve a subpoena on a nonparty deponent, who consequently did not attend.

(Amended January 21, 1963, effective July 1, 1963; March 30, 1970, effective July 1, 1970; March 1, 1971, effective July 1, 1971; November 20, 1972, effective July 1, 1975; April 29, 1980, effective August 1, 1980; March 2, 1987, effective August 1, 1987; April 22, 1993, effective December 1, 1993; April 17, 2000, effective December 1, 2000; April 30, 2007, effective December 1, 2007; April 29, 2015, effective December 1, 2015; April 27, 2020, effective December 1, 2020.)

RULE 31. DEPOSITIONS BY WRITTEN QUESTIONS

(a) When a Deposition May Be Taken.

(1) *Without Leave.* A party may, by written questions, depose any person, including a party, without leave of court except as provided in Rule 31(a)(2). The deponent's attendance may be compelled by subpoena under Rule 45.

(2) *With Leave.* A party must obtain leave of court, and the court must grant leave to the extent consistent with Rule 26(b)(1) and (2):

(A) if the parties have not stipulated to the deposition and:

(i) the deposition would result in more than 10 depositions being taken under this rule or Rule 30 by the plaintiffs, or by the defendants, or by the third-party defendants;

(ii) the deponent has already been deposed in the case; or

(iii) the party seeks to take a deposition before the time specified in Rule 26(d); or

(B) if the deponent is confined in prison.

(3) *Service; Required Notice.* A party who wants to depose a person by written questions must serve them on every other party, with a notice stating, if known, the deponent's name and address. If the name is unknown, the notice must provide a general description sufficient to identify the person or the particular class or group to which the person belongs. The notice must also state the name or descriptive title and the address of the officer before whom the deposition will be taken.

(4) *Questions Directed to an Organization.* A public or private corporation, a partnership, an association, or a governmental agency may be deposed by written questions in accordance with Rule 30(b)(6).

(5) *Questions from Other Parties.* Any questions to the deponent from other parties must be served on all parties as follows: cross-questions, within 14 days after being served with the notice and direct questions; redirect questions, within 7 days after being served with cross-questions; and recross-questions, within 7 days after being served with redirect questions. The court may, for good cause, extend or shorten these times.

(b) Delivery to the Officer; Officer's Duties. The party who noticed the deposition must deliver to the officer a copy of all the questions served and of the notice. The officer must promptly proceed in the manner provided in Rule 30(c), (e), and (f) to:

   (1) take the deponent's testimony in response to the questions;

   (2) prepare and certify the deposition; and

   (3) send it to the party, attaching a copy of the questions and of the notice.

(c) Notice of Completion or Filing.

   (1) *Completion.* The party who noticed the deposition must notify all other parties when it is completed.

   (2) *Filing.* A party who files the deposition must promptly notify all other parties of the filing.

(Amended March 30, 1970, effective July 1, 1970; March 2, 1987, effective August 1, 1987; April 22, 1993, effective December 1, 1993; April 30, 2007, effective December 1, 2007; April 29, 2015, effective December 1, 2015.)

RULE 32. USING DEPOSITIONS IN COURT PROCEEDINGS

(a) Using Depositions.

   (1) *In General.* At a hearing or trial, all or part of a deposition may be used against a party on these conditions:

     (A) the party was present or represented at the taking of the deposition or had reasonable notice of it;

     (B) it is used to the extent it would be admissible under the Federal Rules of Evidence if the deponent were present and testifying; and

     (C) the use is allowed by Rule 32(a)(2) through (8).

   (2) *Impeachment and Other Uses.* Any party may use a deposition to contradict or impeach the testimony given by the deponent as a witness, or for any other purpose allowed by the Federal Rules of Evidence.

   (3) *Deposition of Party, Agent, or Designee.* An adverse party may use for any purpose the deposition of a party or anyone who, when deposed, was the party's officer, director, managing agent, or designee under Rule 30(b)(6) or 31(a)(4).

   (4) *Unavailable Witness.* A party may use for any purpose the deposition of a witness, whether or not a party, if the court finds:

     (A) that the witness is dead;

     (B) that the witness is more than 100 miles from the place of hearing or trial or is outside the United States, unless it appears that the witness's absence was procured by the party offering the deposition;

     (C) that the witness cannot attend or testify because of age, illness, infirmity, or imprisonment;

     (D) that the party offering the deposition could not procure the witness's attendance by subpoena; or

     (E) on motion and notice, that exceptional circumstances make it desirable—in the interest of justice and with due regard to the importance of live testimony in open court—to permit the deposition to be used.

   (5) *Limitations on Use.*

     (A) *Deposition Taken on Short Notice.* A deposition must not be used against a party who, having received less than 14 days' notice of the deposition, promptly moved for a protective order under Rule 26(c)(1)(B) requesting that it not be taken or be taken at a different time or place—and this motion was still pending when the deposition was taken.

     (B) *Unavailable Deponent; Party Could Not Obtain an Attorney.* A deposition taken without leave of court under the unavailability provision of Rule 30(a)(2)(A)(iii) must not be used against a party who shows that, when served with the notice, it could not, despite diligent efforts, obtain an attorney to represent it at the deposition.

   (6) *Using Part of a Deposition.* If a party offers in evidence only part of a deposition, an adverse party may require the offeror to introduce other parts that in fairness should be considered with the part introduced, and any party may itself introduce any other parts.

   (7) *Substituting a Party.* Substituting a party under Rule 25 does not affect the right to use a deposition previously taken.

   (8) *Deposition Taken in an Earlier Action.* A deposition lawfully taken and, if required, filed in any federal- or state-court action may be used in a later action involving the same subject matter between the same parties, or their representatives or successors in interest, to the same extent as if taken in the later action. A deposition previously taken may also be used as allowed by the Federal Rules of Evidence.

(b) Objections to Admissibility. Subject to Rules 28(b) and 32(d)(3), an objection may be made at a hearing or trial to the admission of any deposition testimony that would be inadmissible if the witness were present and testifying.

(c) Form of Presentation. Unless the court orders otherwise, a party must provide a transcript of any deposition testimony the party offers, but may provide the court with the testimony in nontranscript form as well. On any party's request, deposition testimony offered in a jury trial for any purpose other than impeachment must be presented in nontranscript form, if available, unless the court for good cause orders otherwise.

(d) Waiver of Objections.

   (1) *To the Notice.* An objection to an error or irregularity in a deposition notice is waived unless promptly served in writing on the party giving the notice.

   (2) *To the Officer's Qualification.* An objection based on disqualification of the officer before whom a deposition is to be taken is waived if not made:

     (A) before the deposition begins; or

     (B) promptly after the basis for disqualification becomes known or, with reasonable diligence, could have been known.

   (3) *To the Taking of the Deposition.*

     (A) *Objection to Competence, Relevance, or Materiality.* An objection to a deponent's competence—or to the competence, relevance, or materiality of testimony—is not waived by a failure to make the objection before or during the deposition, unless the ground for it might have been corrected at that time.

(B) *Objection to an Error or Irregularity.* An objection to an error or irregularity at an oral examination is waived if:

(i) it relates to the manner of taking the deposition, the form of a question or answer, the oath or affirmation, a party's conduct, or other matters that might have been corrected at that time; and

(ii) it is not timely made during the deposition.

(C) *Objection to a Written Question.* An objection to the form of a written question under Rule 31 is waived if not served in writing on the party submitting the question within the time for serving responsive questions or, if the question is a recross-question, within 7 days after being served with it.

(4) *To Completing and Returning the Deposition.* An objection to how the officer transcribed the testimony—or prepared, signed, certified, sealed, endorsed, sent, or otherwise dealt with the deposition—is waived unless a motion to suppress is made promptly after the error or irregularity becomes known or, with reasonable diligence, could have been known.

(Amended March 30, 1970, effective July 1, 1970; November 20, 1972, effective July 1, 1975; April 29, 1980, effective August 1, 1980; March 2, 1987, effective August 1, 1987; April 22, 1993, effective December 1, 1993; April 30, 2007, effective December 1, 2007; March 26, 2009, effective December 1, 2009.)

RULE 33. INTERROGATORIES TO PARTIES

(a) In General.

(1) *Number.* Unless otherwise stipulated or ordered by the court, a party may serve on any other party no more than 25 written interrogatories, including all discrete subparts. Leave to serve additional interrogatories may be granted to the extent consistent with Rule 26(b)(1) and (2).

(2) *Scope.* An interrogatory may relate to any matter that may be inquired into under Rule 26(b). An interrogatory is not objectionable merely because it asks for an opinion or contention that relates to fact or the application of law to fact, but the court may order that the interrogatory need not be answered until designated discovery is complete, or until a pretrial conference or some other time.

(b) Answers and Objections.

(1) *Responding Party.* The interrogatories must be answered:

(A) by the party to whom they are directed; or

(B) if that party is a public or private corporation, a partnership, an association, or a governmental agency, by any officer or agent, who must furnish the information available to the party.

(2) *Time to Respond.* The responding party must serve its answers and any objections within 30 days after being served with the interrogatories. A shorter or longer time may be stipulated to under Rule 29 or be ordered by the court.

(3) *Answering Each Interrogatory.* Each interrogatory must, to the extent it is not objected to, be answered separately and fully in writing under oath.

(4) *Objections.* The grounds for objecting to an interrogatory must be stated with specificity. Any ground not stated in a timely objection is waived unless the court, for good cause, excuses the failure.

(5) *Signature.* The person who makes the answers must sign them, and the attorney who objects must sign any objections.

(c) Use. An answer to an interrogatory may be used to the extent allowed by the Federal Rules of Evidence.

(d) Option to Produce Business Records. If the answer to an interrogatory may be determined by examining, auditing, compiling, abstracting, or summarizing a party's business records (including electronically stored information), and if the burden of deriving or ascertaining the answer will be substantially the same for either party, the responding party may answer by:

(1) specifying the records that must be reviewed, in sufficient detail to enable the interrogating party to locate and identify them as readily as the responding party could; and

(2) giving the interrogating party a reasonable opportunity to examine and audit the records and to make copies, compilations, abstracts, or summaries.

(Amended December 27, 1946, effective March 19, 1948; March 30, 1970, effective July 1, 1970; April 29, 1980, effective August 1, 1980; April 22, 1993, effective December 1, 1993; April 12, 2006, effective December 1, 2006; April 30, 2007, effective December 1, 2007; April 29, 2015, effective December 1, 2015.)

RULE 34. PRODUCING DOCUMENTS, ELECTRONICALLY STORED INFORMATION, AND TANGIBLE THINGS, OR ENTERING ONTO LAND, FOR INSPECTION AND OTHER PURPOSES

(a) In General. A party may serve on any other party a request within the scope of Rule 26(b):

(1) to produce and permit the requesting party or its representative to inspect, copy, test, or sample the following items in the responding party's possession, custody, or control:

(A) any designated documents or electronically stored information—including writings, drawings, graphs, charts, photographs, sound recordings, images, and other data or data compilations—stored in any medium from which information can be obtained either directly or, if necessary, after translation by the responding party into a reasonably usable form; or

(B) any designated tangible things; or

(2) to permit entry onto designated land or other property possessed or controlled by the responding party, so that the requesting party may inspect, measure, survey, photograph, test, or sample the property or any designated object or operation on it.

(b) Procedure.

(1) *Contents of the Request.* The request:

(A) must describe with reasonable particularity each item or category of items to be inspected;

(B) must specify a reasonable time, place, and manner for the inspection and for performing the related acts; and

(C) may specify the form or forms in which electronically stored information is to be produced.

(2) *Responses and Objections.*

(A) *Time to Respond.* The party to whom the request is directed must respond in writing within 30 days after being served or — if the request was delivered under Rule 26(d)(2) — within 30 days after the parties' first Rule 26(f) conference. A shorter or longer time may be stipulated to under Rule 29 or be ordered by the court.

(B) *Responding to Each Item.* For each item or category, the response must either state that inspection and related activities will be permitted as requested or state with specificity the grounds for objecting to the request, including the reasons. The responding party may state that it will produce copies of documents or of electronically stored information instead of permitting inspection. The production must then be completed no later than the time for inspection specified in the request or another reasonable time specified in the response.

(C) *Objections.* An objection must state whether any responsive materials are being withheld on the basis of that objection. An objection to part of a request must specify the part and permit inspection of the rest.

(D) *Responding to a Request for Production of Electronically Stored Information.* The response may state an objection to a requested form for producing electronically stored information. If the responding party objects to a requested form—or if no form was specified in the request—the party must state the form or forms it intends to use.

(E) *Producing the Documents or Electronically Stored Information.* Unless otherwise stipulated or ordered by the court, these procedures apply to producing documents or electronically stored information:

(i) A party must produce documents as they are kept in the usual course of business or must organize and label them to correspond to the categories in the request;

(ii) If a request does not specify a form for producing electronically stored information, a party must produce it in a form or forms in which it is ordinarily maintained or in a reasonably usable form or forms; and

(iii) A party need not produce the same electronically stored information in more than one form.

(c) **Nonparties.** As provided in Rule 45, a nonparty may be compelled to produce documents and tangible things or to permit an inspection.

(Amended December 27, 1946, effective March 19, 1948; March 30, 1970, effective July 1, 1970; April 29, 1980, effective August 1, 1980; March 2, 1987, effective August 1, 1987; April 30, 1991, effective December 1, 1991; April 22, 1993, effective December 1, 1993; April 12, 2006, effective December 1, 2006; April 30, 2007, effective December 1, 2007; April 29, 2015, effective December 1, 2015.)

RULE 35. PHYSICAL AND MENTAL EXAMINATIONS

(a) **Order for an Examination.**

(1) *In General.* The court where the action is pending may order a party whose mental or physical condition—including blood group—is in controversy to submit to a physical or mental examination by a suitably licensed or certified examiner. The court has the same authority to order a party to produce for examination a person who is in its custody or under its legal control.

(2) *Motion and Notice; Contents of the Order.* The order:

(A) may be made only on motion for good cause and on notice to all parties and the person to be examined; and

(B) must specify the time, place, manner, conditions, and scope of the examination, as well as the person or persons who will perform it.

(b) **Examiner's Report.**

(1) *Request by the Party or Person Examined.* The party who moved for the examination must, on request, deliver to the requester a copy of the examiner's report, together with like reports of all earlier examinations of the same condition. The request may be made by the party against whom the examination order was issued or by the person examined.

(2) *Contents.* The examiner's report must be in writing and must set out in detail the examiner's findings, including diagnoses, conclusions, and the results of any tests.

(3) *Request by the Moving Party.* After delivering the reports, the party who moved for the examination may request—and is entitled to receive—from the party against whom the examination order was issued like reports of all earlier or later examinations of the same condition. But those reports need not be delivered by the party with custody or control of the person examined if the party shows that it could not obtain them.

(4) *Waiver of Privilege.* By requesting and obtaining the examiner's report, or by deposing the examiner, the party examined waives any privilege it may have—in that action or any other action involving the same controversy—concerning testimony about all examinations of the same condition.

(5) *Failure to Deliver a Report.* The court on motion may order—on just terms—that a party deliver the report of an examination. If the report is not provided, the court may exclude the examiner's testimony at trial.

(6) *Scope.* This subdivision (b) applies also to an examination made by the parties' agreement, unless the agreement states otherwise. This subdivision does not preclude obtaining an examiner's report or deposing an examiner under other rules.

(Amended March 30, 1970, effective July 1, 1970; March 2, 1987, effective August 1, 1987; amended by Pub.L. 100–690, Title VII, § 7047(b), November 18, 1988, 102 Stat. 4401; amended April 30, 1991, effective December 1, 1991; April 30, 2007, effective December 1, 2007.)

RULE 36.   REQUESTS FOR ADMISSION

(a) Scope and Procedure.

(1) *Scope.* A party may serve on any other party a written request to admit, for purposes of the pending action only, the truth of any matters within the scope of Rule 26(b)(1) relating to:

    (A) facts, the application of law to fact, or opinions about either; and

    (B) the genuineness of any described documents.

(2) *Form; Copy of a Document.* Each matter must be separately stated. A request to admit the genuineness of a document must be accompanied by a copy of the document unless it is, or has been, otherwise furnished or made available for inspection and copying.

(3) *Time to Respond; Effect of Not Responding.* A matter is admitted unless, within 30 days after being served, the party to whom the request is directed serves on the requesting party a written answer or objection addressed to the matter and signed by the party or its attorney. A shorter or longer time for responding may be stipulated to under Rule 29 or be ordered by the court.

(4) *Answer.* If a matter is not admitted, the answer must specifically deny it or state in detail why the answering party cannot truthfully admit or deny it. A denial must fairly respond to the substance of the matter; and when good faith requires that a party qualify an answer or deny only a part of a matter, the answer must specify the part admitted and qualify or deny the rest. The answering party may assert lack of knowledge or information as a reason for failing to admit or deny only if the party states that it has made reasonable inquiry and that the information it knows or can readily obtain is insufficient to enable it to admit or deny.

(5) *Objections.* The grounds for objecting to a request must be stated. A party must not object solely on the ground that the request presents a genuine issue for trial.

(6) *Motion Regarding the Sufficiency of an Answer or Objection.* The requesting party may move to determine the sufficiency of an answer or objection. Unless the court finds an objection justified, it must order that an answer be served. On finding that an answer does not comply with this rule, the court may order either that the matter is admitted or that an amended answer be served. The court may defer its final decision until a pretrial conference or a specified time before trial. Rule 37(a)(5) applies to an award of expenses.

(b) Effect of an Admission; Withdrawing or Amending It.
A matter admitted under this rule is conclusively established unless the court, on motion, permits the admission to be withdrawn or amended. Subject to Rule 16(e), the court may permit withdrawal or amendment if it would promote the presentation of the merits of the action and if the court is not persuaded that it would prejudice the requesting party in maintaining or defending the action on the merits. An admis-

sion under this rule is not an admission for any other purpose and cannot be used against the party in any other proceeding.

(Amended December 27, 1946, effective March 19, 1948; March 30, 1970, effective July 1, 1970; March 2, 1987, effective August 1, 1987; April 22, 1993, effective December 1, 1993; April 30, 2007, effective December 1, 2007.)

RULE 37.   FAILURE TO MAKE DISCLOSURES OR TO COOPERATE IN DISCOVERY; SANCTIONS

(a) Motion for an Order Compelling Disclosure or Discovery.

(1) *In General.* On notice to other parties and all affected persons, a party may move for an order compelling disclosure or discovery. The motion must include a certification that the movant has in good faith conferred or attempted to confer with the person or party failing to make disclosure or discovery in an effort to obtain it without court action.

(2) *Appropriate Court.* A motion for an order to a party must be made in the court where the action is pending. A motion for an order to a nonparty must be made in the court where the discovery is or will be taken.

(3) *Specific Motions.*

    (A) *To Compel Disclosure.* If a party fails to make a disclosure required by Rule 26(a), any other party may move to compel disclosure and for appropriate sanctions.

    (B) *To Compel a Discovery Response.* A party seeking discovery may move for an order compelling an answer, designation, production, or inspection. This motion may be made if:

        (i) a deponent fails to answer a question asked under Rule 30 or 31;

        (ii) a corporation or other entity fails to make a designation under Rule 30(b)(6) or 31(a)(4);

        (iii) a party fails to answer an interrogatory submitted under Rule 33; or

        (iv) a party fails to produce documents or fails to respond that inspection will be permitted — or fails to permit inspection — as requested under Rule 34.

    (C) *Related to a Deposition.* When taking an oral deposition, the party asking a question may complete or adjourn the examination before moving for an order.

(4) *Evasive or Incomplete Disclosure, Answer, or Response.* For purposes of this subdivision (a), an evasive or incomplete disclosure, answer, or response must be treated as a failure to disclose, answer, or respond.

(5) *Payment of Expenses; Protective Orders.*

    (A) *If the Motion Is Granted (or Disclosure or Discovery Is Provided After Filing).* If the motion is granted— or if the disclosure or requested discovery is provided after the motion was filed—the court must, after giving an opportunity to be heard, require the party or deponent whose conduct necessitated the motion, the party or attorney advising that conduct, or both to pay the movant's reasonable expenses incurred in making the motion, including attorney's fees. But the court must not order this payment if:

(**i**) the movant filed the motion before attempting in good faith to obtain the disclosure or discovery without court action;

(**ii**) the opposing party's nondisclosure, response, or objection was substantially justified; or

(**iii**) other circumstances make an award of expenses unjust.

(**B**) *If the Motion Is Denied.* If the motion is denied, the court may issue any protective order authorized under Rule 26(c) and must, after giving an opportunity to be heard, require the movant, the attorney filing the motion, or both to pay the party or deponent who opposed the motion its reasonable expenses incurred in opposing the motion, including attorney's fees. But the court must not order this payment if the motion was substantially justified or other circumstances make an award of expenses unjust.

(**C**) *If the Motion Is Granted in Part and Denied in Part.* If the motion is granted in part and denied in part, the court may issue any protective order authorized under Rule 26(c) and may, after giving an opportunity to be heard, apportion the reasonable expenses for the motion.

(**b**) **Failure to Comply with a Court Order.**

(**1**) *Sanctions Sought in the District Where the Deposition Is Taken.* If the court where the discovery is taken orders a deponent to be sworn or to answer a question and the deponent fails to obey, the failure may be treated as contempt of court. If a deposition-related motion is transferred to the court where the action is pending, and that court orders a deponent to be sworn or to answer a question and the deponent fails to obey, the failure may be treated as contempt of either the court where the discovery is taken or the court where the action is pending.

(**2**) *Sanctions Sought in the District Where the Action Is Pending.*

(**A**) *For Not Obeying a Discovery Order.* If a party or a party's officer, director, or managing agent—or a witness designated under Rule 30(b)(6) or 31(a)(4)—fails to obey an order to provide or permit discovery, including an order under Rule 26(f), 35, or 37(a), the court where the action is pending may issue further just orders. They may include the following:

(**i**) directing that the matters embraced in the order or other designated facts be taken as established for purposes of the action, as the prevailing party claims;

(**ii**) prohibiting the disobedient party from supporting or opposing designated claims or defenses, or from introducing designated matters in evidence;

(**iii**) striking pleadings in whole or in part;

(**iv**) staying further proceedings until the order is obeyed;

(**v**) dismissing the action or proceeding in whole or in part;

(**vi**) rendering a default judgment against the disobedient party; or

(**vii**) treating as contempt of court the failure to obey any order except an order to submit to a physical or mental examination.

(**B**) *For Not Producing a Person for Examination.* If a party fails to comply with an order under Rule 35(a) requiring it to produce another person for examination, the court may issue any of the orders listed in Rule 37(b)(2)(A)(i)-(vi), unless the disobedient party shows that it cannot produce the other person.

(**C**) *Payment of Expenses.* Instead of or in addition to the orders above, the court must order the disobedient party, the attorney advising that party, or both to pay the reasonable expenses, including attorney's fees, caused by the failure, unless the failure was substantially justified or other circumstances make an award of expenses unjust.

(**c**) **Failure to Disclose, to Supplement an Earlier Response, or to Admit.**

(**1**) *Failure to Disclose or Supplement.* If a party fails to provide information or identify a witness as required by Rule 26(a) or (e), the party is not allowed to use that information or witness to supply evidence on a motion, at a hearing, or at a trial, unless the failure was substantially justified or is harmless. In addition to or instead of this sanction, the court, on motion and after giving an opportunity to be heard:

(**A**) may order payment of the reasonable expenses, including attorney's fees, caused by the failure;

(**B**) may inform the jury of the party's failure; and

(**C**) may impose other appropriate sanctions, including any of the orders listed in Rule 37(b)(2)(A)(i)-(vi).

(**2**) *Failure to Admit.* If a party fails to admit what is requested under Rule 36 and if the requesting party later proves a document to be genuine or the matter true, the requesting party may move that the party who failed to admit pay the reasonable expenses, including attorney's fees, incurred in making that proof. The court must so order unless:

(**A**) the request was held objectionable under Rule 36(a);

(**B**) the admission sought was of no substantial importance;

(**C**) the party failing to admit had a reasonable ground to believe that it might prevail on the matter; or

(**D**) there was other good reason for the failure to admit.

(**d**) **Party's Failure to Attend Its Own Deposition, Serve Answers to Interrogatories, or Respond to a Request for Inspection.**

(**1**) *In General.*

(**A**) *Motion; Grounds for Sanctions.* The court where the action is pending may, on motion, order sanctions if:

(**i**) a party or a party's officer, director, or managing agent—or a person designated under Rule 30(b)(6) or

31(a)(4)—fails, after being served with proper notice, to appear for that person's deposition; or

    (ii) a party, after being properly served with interrogatories under Rule 33 or a request for inspection under Rule 34, fails to serve its answers, objections, or written response.

(B) *Certification.* A motion for sanctions for failing to answer or respond must include a certification that the movant has in good faith conferred or attempted to confer with the party failing to act in an effort to obtain the answer or response without court action.

(2) *Unacceptable Excuse for Failing to Act.* A failure described in Rule 37(d)(1)(A) is not excused on the ground that the discovery sought was objectionable, unless the party failing to act has a pending motion for a protective order under Rule 26(c).

(3) *Types of Sanctions.* Sanctions may include any of the orders listed in Rule 37(b)(2)(A)(i)-(vi). Instead of or in addition to these sanctions, the court must require the party failing to act, the attorney advising that party, or both to pay the reasonable expenses, including attorney's fees, caused by the failure, unless the failure was substantially justified or other circumstances make an award of expenses unjust.

(e) Failure to Preserve Electronically Stored Information. If electronically stored information that should have been preserved in the anticipation or conduct of litigation is lost because a party failed to take reasonable steps to preserve it, and it cannot be restored or replaced through additional discovery, the court:

    (1) upon finding prejudice to another party from loss of the information, may order measures no greater than necessary to cure the prejudice; or

    (2) only upon finding that the party acted with the intent to deprive another party of the information's use in the litigation may:

        (A) presume that the lost information was unfavorable to the party;

        (B) instruct the jury that it may or must presume the information was unfavorable to the party; or

        (C) dismiss the action or enter a default judgment.

(f) Failure to Participate in Framing a Discovery Plan. If a party or its attorney fails to participate in good faith in developing and submitting a proposed discovery plan as required by Rule 26(f), the court may, after giving an opportunity to be heard, require that party or attorney to pay to any other party the reasonable expenses, including attorney's fees, caused by the failure.

(Amended December 29, 1948, effective October 20, 1949; March 30, 1970, effective July 1, 1970; April 29, 1980, effective August 1, 1980; amended by Pub.L. 96–481, Title II, § 205(a), October 21, 1980, 94 Stat. 2330, effective October 1, 1981; amended March 2, 1987, effective August 1, 1987; April 22, 1993, effective December 1, 1993; April 17, 2000, effective December 1, 2000; April 12, 2006, effective December 1, 2006; April 30, 2007, effective December 1, 2007; April 16, 2013, effective December 1, 2013; April 29, 2015, effective December 1, 2015.)

TITLE VI. TRIALS

RULE 38. RIGHT TO A JURY TRIAL; DEMAND

(a) Right Preserved. The right of trial by jury as declared by the Seventh Amendment to the Constitution—or as provided by a federal statute—is preserved to the parties inviolate.

(b) Demand. On any issue triable of right by a jury, a party may demand a jury trial by:

    (1) serving the other parties with a written demand—which may be included in a pleading—no later than 14 days after the last pleading directed to the issue is served; and

    (2) filing the demand in accordance with Rule 5(d).

(c) Specifying Issues. In its demand, a party may specify the issues that it wishes to have tried by a jury; otherwise, it is considered to have demanded a jury trial on all the issues so triable. If the party has demanded a jury trial on only some issues, any other party may—within 14 days after being served with the demand or within a shorter time ordered by the court—serve a demand for a jury trial on any other or all factual issues triable by jury.

(d) Waiver; Withdrawal. A party waives a jury trial unless its demand is properly served and filed. A proper demand may be withdrawn only if the parties consent.

(e) Admiralty and Maritime Claims. These rules do not create a right to a jury trial on issues in a claim that is an admiralty or maritime claim under Rule 9(h).

(Amended February 28, 1966, effective July 1, 1966; March 2, 1987, effective August 1, 1987; April 22, 1993, effective December 1, 1993; April 30, 2007, effective December 1, 2007; March 26, 2009, effective December 1, 2009.)

RULE 39. TRIAL BY JURY OR BY THE COURT

(a) When a Demand Is Made. When a jury trial has been demanded under Rule 38, the action must be designated on the docket as a jury action. The trial on all issues so demanded must be by jury unless:

    (1) the parties or their attorneys file a stipulation to a nonjury trial or so stipulate on the record; or

    (2) the court, on motion or on its own, finds that on some or all of those issues there is no federal right to a jury trial.

(b) When No Demand Is Made. Issues on which a jury trial is not properly demanded are to be tried by the court. But the court may, on motion, order a jury trial on any issue for which a jury might have been demanded.

(c) Advisory Jury; Jury Trial by Consent. In an action not triable of right by a jury, the court, on motion or on its own:

    (1) may try any issue with an advisory jury; or

(2) may, with the parties' consent, try any issue by a jury whose verdict has the same effect as if a jury trial had been a matter of right, unless the action is against the United States and a federal statute provides for a nonjury trial.

(Amended April 30, 2007, effective December 1, 2007.)

RULE 40. SCHEDULING CASES FOR TRIAL

Each court must provide by rule for scheduling trials. The court must give priority to actions entitled to priority by a federal statute.

(Amended April 30, 2007, effective December 1, 2007.)

RULE 41. DISMISSAL OF ACTIONS

(a) Voluntary Dismissal.

(1) *By the Plaintiff.*

(A) *Without a Court Order.* Subject to Rules 23(e), 23.1(c), 23.2, and 66 and any applicable federal statute, the plaintiff may dismiss an action without a court order by filing:

(i) a notice of dismissal before the opposing party serves either an answer or a motion for summary judgment; or

(ii) a stipulation of dismissal signed by all parties who have appeared.

(B) *Effect.* Unless the notice or stipulation states otherwise, the dismissal is without prejudice. But if the plaintiff previously dismissed any federal- or state-court action based on or including the same claim, a notice of dismissal operates as an adjudication on the merits.

(2) *By Court Order; Effect.* Except as provided in Rule 41(a)(1), an action may be dismissed at the plaintiff's request only by court order, on terms that the court considers proper. If a defendant has pleaded a counterclaim before being served with the plaintiff's motion to dismiss, the action may be dismissed over the defendant's objection only if the counterclaim can remain pending for independent adjudication. Unless the order states otherwise, a dismissal under this paragraph (2) is without prejudice.

(b) Involuntary Dismissal; Effect. If the plaintiff fails to prosecute or to comply with these rules or a court order, a defendant may move to dismiss the action or any claim against it. Unless the dismissal order states otherwise, a dismissal under this subdivision (b) and any dismissal not under this rule—except one for lack of jurisdiction, improper venue, or failure to join a party under Rule 19—operates as an adjudication on the merits.

(c) Dismissing a Counterclaim, Crossclaim, or Third–Party Claim. This rule applies to a dismissal of any counterclaim, crossclaim, or third-party claim. A claimant's voluntary dismissal under Rule 41(a)(1)(A)(i) must be made:

(1) before a responsive pleading is served; or

(2) if there is no responsive pleading, before evidence is introduced at a hearing or trial.

(d) Costs of a Previously Dismissed Action. If a plaintiff who previously dismissed an action in any court files an action based on or including the same claim against the same defendant, the court:

(1) may order the plaintiff to pay all or part of the costs of that previous action; and

(2) may stay the proceedings until the plaintiff has complied.

(Amended December 27, 1946, effective March 19, 1948; January 21, 1963, effective July 1, 1963; February 28, 1966, effective July 1, 1966; December 4, 1967, effective July 1, 1968; March 2, 1987, effective August 1, 1987; April 30, 1991, effective December 1, 1991; April 30, 2007, effective December 1, 2007.)

RULE 42. CONSOLIDATION; SEPARATE TRIALS

(a) Consolidation. If actions before the court involve a common question of law or fact, the court may:

(1) join for hearing or trial any or all matters at issue in the actions;

(2) consolidate the actions; or

(3) issue any other orders to avoid unnecessary cost or delay.

(b) Separate Trials. For convenience, to avoid prejudice, or to expedite and economize, the court may order a separate trial of one or more separate issues, claims, crossclaims, counterclaims, or third-party claims. When ordering a separate trial, the court must preserve any federal right to a jury trial.

(Amended February 28, 1966, effective July 1, 1966; April 30, 2007, effective December 1, 2007.)

RULE 43. TAKING TESTIMONY

(a) In Open Court. At trial, the witnesses' testimony must be taken in open court unless a federal statute, the Federal Rules of Evidence, these rules, or other rules adopted by the Supreme Court provide otherwise. For good cause in compelling circumstances and with appropriate safeguards, the court may permit testimony in open court by contemporaneous transmission from a different location.

(b) Affirmation Instead of an Oath. When these rules require an oath, a solemn affirmation suffices.

(c) Evidence on a Motion. When a motion relies on facts outside the record, the court may hear the matter on affidavits or may hear it wholly or partly on oral testimony or on depositions.

(d) Interpreter. The court may appoint an interpreter of its choosing; fix reasonable compensation to be paid from funds provided by law or by one or more parties; and tax the compensation as costs.

(Amended February 28, 1966, effective July 1, 1966; November 20, 1972, and December 18, 1972, effective July 1, 1975; March 2, 1987, effective August 1, 1987; April 23, 1996, effective December 1, 1996; April 30, 2007, effective December 1, 2007.)

RULE 44. PROVING AN OFFICIAL RECORD

(a) Means of Proving.

(1) *Domestic Record.* Each of the following evidences an official record—or an entry in it—that is otherwise admissible and is kept within the United States, any state, district, or commonwealth, or any territory subject to the administrative or judicial jurisdiction of the United States:

(A) an official publication of the record; or

(B) a copy attested by the officer with legal custody of the record—or by the officer's deputy—and accompanied by a certificate that the officer has custody. The certificate must be made under seal:

(i) by a judge of a court of record in the district or political subdivision where the record is kept; or

(ii) by any public officer with a seal of office and with official duties in the district or political subdivision where the record is kept.

(2) *Foreign Record.*

(A) *In General.* Each of the following evidences a foreign official record—or an entry in it—that is otherwise admissible:

(i) an official publication of the record; or

(ii) the record—or a copy—that is attested by an authorized person and is accompanied either by a final certification of genuineness or by a certification under a treaty or convention to which the United States and the country where the record is located are parties.

(B) *Final Certification of Genuineness.* A final certification must certify the genuineness of the signature and official position of the attester or of any foreign official whose certificate of genuineness relates to the attestation or is in a chain of certificates of genuineness relating to the attestation. A final certification may be made by a secretary of a United States embassy or legation; by a consul general, vice consul, or consular agent of the United States; or by a diplomatic or consular official of the foreign country assigned or accredited to the United States.

(C) *Other Means of Proof.* If all parties have had a reasonable opportunity to investigate a foreign record's authenticity and accuracy, the court may, for good cause, either:

(i) admit an attested copy without final certification; or

(ii) permit the record to be evidenced by an attested summary with or without a final certification.

(b) Lack of a Record. A written statement that a diligent search of designated records revealed no record or entry of a specified tenor is admissible as evidence that the records contain no such record or entry. For domestic records, the statement must be authenticated under Rule 44(a)(1). For foreign records, the statement must comply with (a)(2)(C)(ii).

(c) Other Proof. A party may prove an official record—or an entry or lack of an entry in it—by any other method authorized by law.

(Amended February 28, 1966, effective July 1, 1966; March 2, 1987, effective August 1, 1987; April 30, 1991, effective December 1, 1991; April 30, 2007, effective December 1, 2007.)

RULE 44.1   DETERMINING FOREIGN LAW

A party who intends to raise an issue about a foreign country's law must give notice by a pleading or other writing. In determining foreign law, the court may consider any relevant material or source, including testimony, whether or not submitted by a party or admissible under the Federal Rules of Evidence. The court's determination must be treated as a ruling on a question of law.

(Adopted February 28, 1966, effective July 1, 1966; amended November 20, 1972, effective July 1, 1975; March 2, 1987, effective August 1, 1987; April 30, 2007, effective December 1, 2007.)

RULE 45.   SUBPOENA

(a) In General.

(1) *Form and Contents.*

(A) *Requirements—In General.* Every subpoena must:

(i) state the court from which it issued;

(ii) state the title of the action and its civil-action number;

(iii) command each person to whom it is directed to do the following at a specified time and place: attend and testify; produce designated documents, electronically stored information, or tangible things in that person's possession, custody, or control; or permit the inspection of premises; and

(iv) set out the text of Rule 45(d) and (e).

(B) *Command to Attend a Deposition—Notice of the Recording Method.* A subpoena commanding attendance at a deposition must state the method for recording the testimony.

(C) *Combining or Separating a Command to Produce or to Permit Inspection; Specifying the Form for Electronically Stored Information.* A command to produce documents, electronically stored information, or tangible things or to permit the inspection of premises may be included in a subpoena commanding attendance at a deposition, hearing, or trial, or may be set out in a separate subpoena. A subpoena may specify the form or forms in which electronically stored information is to be produced.

(D) *Command to Produce; Included Obligations.* A command in a subpoena to produce documents, electronically stored information, or tangible things requires the responding person to permit inspection, copying, testing, or sampling of the materials.

(2) *Issuing Court.* A subpoena must issue from the court where the action is pending.

(3) *Issued by Whom.* The clerk must issue a subpoena, signed but otherwise in blank, to a party who requests it. That party must complete it before service. An attorney also may issue and sign a subpoena if the attorney is authorized to practice in the issuing court.

(4) *Notice to Other Parties Before Service.* If the subpoena commands the production of documents, electronically stored information, or tangible things or the inspection

of premises before trial, then before it is served on the person to whom it is directed, a notice and a copy of the subpoena must be served on each party.

(b) Service.

(1) *By Whom and How; Tendering Fees.* Any person who is at least 18 years old and not a party may serve a subpoena. Serving a subpoena requires delivering a copy to the named person and, if the subpoena requires that person's attendance, tendering the fees for 1 day's attendance and the mileage allowed by law. Fees and mileage need not be tendered when the subpoena issues on behalf of the United States or any of its officers or agencies.

(2) *Service in the United States.* A subpoena may be served at any place within the United States.

(3) *Service in a Foreign Country.* 28 U.S.C. § 1783 governs issuing and serving a subpoena directed to a United States national or resident who is in a foreign country.

(4) *Proof of Service.* Proving service, when necessary, requires filing with the issuing court a statement showing the date and manner of service and the names of the persons served. The statement must be certified by the server.

(c) Place of Compliance.

(1) *For a Trial, Hearing, or Deposition.* A subpoena may command a person to attend a trial, hearing, or deposition only as follows:

(A) within 100 miles of where the person resides, is employed, or regularly transacts business in person; or

(B) within the state where the person resides, is employed, or regularly transacts business in person, if the person

(i) is a party or a party's officer; or

(ii) is commanded to attend a trial and would not incur substantial expense.

(2) *For Other Discovery.* A subpoena may command:

(A) production of documents, electronically stored information, or tangible things at a place within 100 miles of where the person resides, is employed, or regularly transacts business in person; and

(B) inspection of premises at the premises to be inspected.

(d) Protecting a Person Subject to a Subpoena; Enforcement.

(1) *Avoiding Undue Burden or Expense; Sanctions.* A party or attorney responsible for issuing and serving a subpoena must take reasonable steps to avoid imposing undue burden or expense on a person subject to the subpoena. The court for the district where compliance is required must enforce this duty and impose an appropriate sanction—which may include lost earnings and reasonable attorney's fees—on a party or attorney who fails to comply.

(2) *Command to Produce Materials or Permit Inspection.*

(A) *Appearance Not Required.* A person commanded to produce documents, electronically stored information, or tangible things, or to permit the inspection of premises, need not appear in person at the place of production or inspection unless also commanded to appear for a deposition, hearing, or trial.

(B) *Objections.* A person commanded to produce documents or tangible things or to permit inspection may serve on the party or attorney designated in the subpoena a written objection to inspecting, copying, testing, or sampling any or all of the materials or to inspecting the premises—or to producing electronically stored information in the form or forms requested. The objection must be served before the earlier of the time specified for compliance or 14 days after the subpoena is served. If an objection is made, the following rules apply:

(i) At any time, on notice to the commanded person, the serving party may move the court for the district where compliance is required for an order compelling production or inspection.

(ii) These acts may be required only as directed in the order, and the order must protect a person who is neither a party nor a party's officer from significant expense resulting from compliance.

(3) *Quashing or Modifying a Subpoena.*

(A) *When Required.* On timely motion, the court for the district where compliance is required must quash or modify a subpoena that:

(i) fails to allow a reasonable time to comply;

(ii) requires a person to comply beyond the geographical limits specified in Rule 45(c);

(iii) requires disclosure of privileged or other protected matter, if no exception or waiver applies; or

(iv) subjects a person to undue burden.

(B) *When Permitted.* To protect a person subject to or affected by a subpoena, the court for the district where compliance is required may, on motion, quash or modify the subpoena if it requires:

(i) disclosing a trade secret or other confidential research, development, or commercial information; or

(ii) disclosing an unretained expert's opinion or information that does not describe specific occurrences in dispute and results from the expert's study that was not requested by a party.

(C) *Specifying Conditions as an Alternative.* In the circumstances described in Rule 45(d)(3)(B), the court may, instead of quashing or modifying a subpoena, order appearance or production under specified conditions if the serving party:

(i) shows a substantial need for the testimony or material that cannot be otherwise met without undue hardship; and

(ii) ensures that the subpoenaed person will be reasonably compensated.

(e) Duties in Responding to a Subpoena.

(1) *Producing Documents or Electronically Stored Information.* These procedures apply to producing documents or electronically stored information:

(A) *Documents.* A person responding to a subpoena to produce documents must produce them as they are kept in the ordinary course of business or must organize and label them to correspond to the categories in the demand.

(B) *Form for Producing Electronically Stored Information Not Specified.* If a subpoena does not specify a form for producing electronically stored information, the person responding must produce it in a form or forms in which it is ordinarily maintained or in a reasonably usable form or forms.

(C) *Electronically Stored Information Produced in Only One Form.* The person responding need not produce the same electronically stored information in more than one form.

(D) *Inaccessible Electronically Stored Information.* The person responding need not provide discovery of electronically stored information from sources that the person identifies as not reasonably accessible because of undue burden or cost. On motion to compel discovery or for a protective order, the person responding must show that the information is not reasonably accessible because of undue burden or cost. If that showing is made, the court may nonetheless order discovery from such sources if the requesting party shows good cause, considering the limitations of Rule 26(b)(2)(C). The court may specify conditions for the discovery.

(2) *Claiming Privilege or Protection.*

(A) *Information Withheld.* A person withholding subpoenaed information under a claim that it is privileged or subject to protection as trial-preparation material must:

(i) expressly make the claim; and

(ii) describe the nature of the withheld documents, communications, or tangible things in a manner that, without revealing information itself privileged or protected, will enable the parties to assess the claim.

(B) *Information Produced.* If information produced in response to a subpoena is subject to a claim of privilege or of protection as trial-preparation material, the person making the claim may notify any party that received the information of the claim and the basis for it. After being notified, a party must promptly return, sequester, or destroy the specified information and any copies it has; must not use or disclose the information until the claim is resolved; must take reasonable steps to retrieve the information if the party disclosed it before being notified; and may promptly present the information under seal to the court for the district where compliance is required for a determination of the claim. The person who produced the information must preserve the information until the claim is resolved.

(f) **Transferring a Subpoena–Related Motion.** When the court where compliance is required did not issue the subpoena, it may transfer a motion under this rule to the issuing court if the person subject to the subpoena consents or if the court finds exceptional circumstances. Then, if the attorney for a person subject to a subpoena is authorized to practice in the court where the motion was made, the attorney may file papers and appear on the motion as an officer of the issuing court. To enforce its order, the issuing court may transfer the order to the court where the motion was made.

(g) **Contempt.** The court for the district where compliance is required—and also, after a motion is transferred, the issuing court—may hold in contempt a person who, having been served, fails without adequate excuse to obey the subpoena or an order related to it.

(Amended December 27, 1946, effective March 19, 1948; December 29, 1948, effective October 20, 1949; March 30, 1970, effective July 1, 1970; April 29, 1980, effective August 1, 1980; April 29, 1985, effective August 1, 1985; March 2, 1987, effective August 1, 1987; April 30, 1991, effective December 1, 1991; April 25, 2005, effective December 1, 2005; April 12, 2006, effective December 1, 2006; April 30, 2007, effective December 1, 2007; April 16, 2013, effective December 1, 2013.)

RULE 46. OBJECTING TO A RULING OR ORDER

A formal exception to a ruling or order is unnecessary. When the ruling or order is requested or made, a party need only state the action that it wants the court to take or objects to, along with the grounds for the request or objection. Failing to object does not prejudice a party who had no opportunity to do so when the ruling or order was made.

(Amended March 2, 1987, effective August 1, 1987; April 30, 2007, effective December 1, 2007.)

RULE 47. SELECTING JURORS

(a) **Examining Jurors.** The court may permit the parties or their attorneys to examine prospective jurors or may itself do so. If the court examines the jurors, it must permit the parties or their attorneys to make any further inquiry it considers proper, or must itself ask any of their additional questions it considers proper.

(b) **Peremptory Challenges.** The court must allow the number of peremptory challenges provided by 28 U.S.C. § 1870.

(c) **Excusing a Juror.** During trial or deliberation, the court may excuse a juror for good cause.

(Amended February 28, 1966, effective July 1, 1966; April 30, 1991, effective December 1, 1991; April 30, 2007, effective December 1, 2007.)

RULE 48. NUMBER OF JURORS; VERDICT; POLLING

(a) **Number of Jurors.** A jury must begin with at least 6 and no more than 12 members, and each juror must participate in the verdict unless excused under Rule 47(c).

(b) **Verdict.** Unless the parties stipulate otherwise, the verdict must be unanimous and must be returned by a jury of at least 6 members.

(c) Polling. After a verdict is returned but before the jury is discharged, the court must on a party's request, or may on its own, poll the jurors individually. If the poll reveals a lack of unanimity or lack of assent by the number of jurors that the parties stipulated to, the court may direct the jury to deliberate further or may order a new trial.

(Amended April 30, 1991, effective December 1, 1991; April 30, 2007, effective December 1, 2007; March 26, 2009, effective December 1, 2009.)

RULE 49. SPECIAL VERDICT; GENERAL VERDICT AND QUESTIONS

(a) Special Verdict.

(1) *In General.* The court may require a jury to return only a special verdict in the form of a special written finding on each issue of fact. The court may do so by:

(A) submitting written questions susceptible of a categorical or other brief answer;

(B) submitting written forms of the special findings that might properly be made under the pleadings and evidence; or

(C) using any other method that the court considers appropriate.

(2) *Instructions.* The court must give the instructions and explanations necessary to enable the jury to make its findings on each submitted issue.

(3) *Issues Not Submitted.* A party waives the right to a jury trial on any issue of fact raised by the pleadings or evidence but not submitted to the jury unless, before the jury retires, the party demands its submission to the jury. If the party does not demand submission, the court may make a finding on the issue. If the court makes no finding, it is considered to have made a finding consistent with its judgment on the special verdict.

(b) General Verdict with Answers to Written Questions.

(1) *In General.* The court may submit to the jury forms for a general verdict, together with written questions on one or more issues of fact that the jury must decide. The court must give the instructions and explanations necessary to enable the jury to render a general verdict and answer the questions in writing, and must direct the jury to do both.

(2) *Verdict and Answers Consistent.* When the general verdict and the answers are consistent, the court must approve, for entry under Rule 58, an appropriate judgment on the verdict and answers.

(3) *Answers Inconsistent with the Verdict.* When the answers are consistent with each other but one or more is inconsistent with the general verdict, the court may:

(A) approve, for entry under Rule 58, an appropriate judgment according to the answers, notwithstanding the general verdict;

(B) direct the jury to further consider its answers and verdict; or

(C) order a new trial.

(4) *Answers Inconsistent with Each Other and the Verdict.* When the answers are inconsistent with each other and one or more is also inconsistent with the general verdict, judgment must not be entered; instead, the court must direct the jury to further consider its answers and verdict, or must order a new trial.

(Amended January 21, 1963, effective July 1, 1963; March 2, 1987, effective August 1, 1987; April 30, 2007, effective December 1, 2007.)

RULE 50. JUDGMENT AS A MATTER OF LAW IN A JURY TRIAL; RELATED MOTION FOR A NEW TRIAL; CONDITIONAL RULING

(a) Judgment as a Matter of Law.

(1) *In General.* If a party has been fully heard on an issue during a jury trial and the court finds that a reasonable jury would not have a legally sufficient evidentiary basis to find for the party on that issue, the court may:

(A) resolve the issue against the party; and

(B) grant a motion for judgment as a matter of law against the party on a claim or defense that, under the controlling law, can be maintained or defeated only with a favorable finding on that issue.

(2) *Motion.* A motion for judgment as a matter of law may be made at any time before the case is submitted to the jury. The motion must specify the judgment sought and the law and facts that entitle the movant to the judgment.

(b) Renewing the Motion After Trial; Alternative Motion for a New Trial. If the court does not grant a motion for judgment as a matter of law made under Rule 50(a), the court is considered to have submitted the action to the jury subject to the court's later deciding the legal questions raised by the motion. No later than 28 days after the entry of judgment—or if the motion addresses a jury issue not decided by a verdict, no later than 28 days after the jury was discharged—the movant may file a renewed motion for judgment as a matter of law and may include an alternative or joint request for a new trial under Rule 59. In ruling on the renewed motion, the court may:

(1) allow judgment on the verdict, if the jury returned a verdict;

(2) order a new trial; or

(3) direct the entry of judgment as a matter of law.

(c) Granting the Renewed Motion; Conditional Ruling on a Motion for a New Trial.

(1) *In General.* If the court grants a renewed motion for judgment as a matter of law, it must also conditionally rule on any motion for a new trial by determining whether a new trial should be granted if the judgment is later vacated or reversed. The court must state the grounds for conditionally granting or denying the motion for a new trial.

(2) *Effect of a Conditional Ruling.* Conditionally granting the motion for a new trial does not affect the judgment's finality; if the judgment is reversed, the new trial must proceed unless the appellate court orders otherwise. If the motion for a new trial is conditionally denied, the appellee may assert error in that denial; if the judgment is reversed, the case must proceed as the appellate court orders.

(d) Time for a Losing Party's New-Trial Motion. Any motion for a new trial under Rule 59 by a party against whom judgment as a matter of law is rendered must be filed no later than 28 days after the entry of the judgment.

(e) Denying the Motion for Judgment as a Matter of Law; Reversal on Appeal. If the court denies the motion for judgment as a matter of law, the prevailing party may, as appellee, assert grounds entitling it to a new trial should the appellate court conclude that the trial court erred in denying the motion. If the appellate court reverses the judgment, it may order a new trial, direct the trial court to determine whether a new trial should be granted, or direct the entry of judgment.

(Amended January 21, 1963, effective July 1, 1963; March 2, 1987, effective August 1, 1987; April 30, 1991, effective December 1, 1991; April 22, 1993, effective December 1, 1993; April 27, 1995, effective December 1, 1995; April 12, 2006, effective December 1, 2006; April 30, 2007, effective December 1, 2007; March 26, 2009, effective December 1, 2009.)

RULE 51. INSTRUCTIONS TO THE JURY; OBJECTIONS; PRESERVING A CLAIM OF ERROR

(a) Requests.

(1) *Before or at the Close of the Evidence.* At the close of the evidence or at any earlier reasonable time that the court orders, a party may file and furnish to every other party written requests for the jury instructions it wants the court to give.

(2) *After the Close of the Evidence.* After the close of the evidence, a party may:

   (A) file requests for instructions on issues that could not reasonably have been anticipated by an earlier time that the court set for requests; and

   (B) with the court's permission, file untimely requests for instructions on any issue.

(b) Instructions. The court:

(1) must inform the parties of its proposed instructions and proposed action on the requests before instructing the jury and before final jury arguments;

(2) must give the parties an opportunity to object on the record and out of the jury's hearing before the instructions and arguments are delivered; and

(3) may instruct the jury at any time before the jury is discharged.

(c) Objections.

(1) *How to Make.* A party who objects to an instruction or the failure to give an instruction must do so on the record, stating distinctly the matter objected to and the grounds for the objection.

(2) *When to Make.* An objection is timely if:

   (A) a party objects at the opportunity provided under Rule 51(b)(2); or

   (B) a party was not informed of an instruction or action on a request before that opportunity to object, and the party objects promptly after learning that the instruction or request will be, or has been, given or refused.

(d) Assigning Error; Plain Error.

(1) *Assigning Error.* A party may assign as error:

   (A) an error in an instruction actually given, if that party properly objected; or

   (B) a failure to give an instruction, if that party properly requested it and—unless the court rejected the request in a definitive ruling on the record—also properly objected.

(2) *Plain Error.* A court may consider a plain error in the instructions that has not been preserved as required by Rule 51(d)(1) if the error affects substantial rights.

(Amended March 2, 1987, effective August 1, 1987; March 27, 2003, effective December 1, 2003; April 30, 2007, effective December 1, 2007.)

RULE 52. FINDINGS AND CONCLUSIONS BY THE COURT; JUDGMENT ON PARTIAL FINDINGS

(a) Findings and Conclusions.

(1) *In General.* In an action tried on the facts without a jury or with an advisory jury, the court must find the facts specially and state its conclusions of law separately. The findings and conclusions may be stated on the record after the close of the evidence or may appear in an opinion or a memorandum of decision filed by the court. Judgment must be entered under Rule 58.

(2) *For an Interlocutory Injunction.* In granting or refusing an interlocutory injunction, the court must similarly state the findings and conclusions that support its action.

(3) *For a Motion.* The court is not required to state findings or conclusions when ruling on a motion under Rule 12 or 56 or, unless these rules provide otherwise, on any other motion.

(4) *Effect of a Master's Findings.* A master's findings, to the extent adopted by the court, must be considered the court's findings.

(5) *Questioning the Evidentiary Support.* A party may later question the sufficiency of the evidence supporting the findings, whether or not the party requested findings, objected to them, moved to amend them, or moved for partial findings.

(6) *Setting Aside the Findings.* Findings of fact, whether based on oral or other evidence, must not be set aside unless clearly erroneous, and the reviewing court must give due regard to the trial court's opportunity to judge the witnesses' credibility.

(b) Amended or Additional Findings. On a party's motion filed no later than 28 days after the entry of judgment, the court may amend its findings—or make additional findings—and may amend the judgment accordingly. The motion may accompany a motion for a new trial under Rule 59.

(c) Judgment on Partial Findings. If a party has been fully heard on an issue during a nonjury trial and the court finds against the party on that issue, the court may enter judgment against the party on a claim or defense that, under the controlling law, can be maintained or defeated only with a favorable finding on that issue. The court may, however, decline to render any judgment until the close of the evidence. A judgment on partial findings must be supported by findings of fact and conclusions of law as required by Rule 52(a).

(Amended December 27, 1946, effective March 19, 1948; January 21, 1963, effective July 1, 1963; April 28, 1983, effective August 1, 1983; April 29, 1985, effective August 1, 1985; April 30, 1991, effective December 1, 1991; April 22, 1993, effective December 1, 1993; April 27, 1995, effective December 1, 1995; April 30, 2007, effective December 1, 2007; March 26, 2009, effective December 1, 2009.)

RULE 53. MASTERS

(a) Appointment.

(1) *Scope.* Unless a statute provides otherwise, a court may appoint a master only to:

(A) perform duties consented to by the parties;

(B) hold trial proceedings and make or recommend findings of fact on issues to be decided without a jury if appointment is warranted by:

(i) some exceptional condition; or

(ii) the need to perform an accounting or resolve a difficult computation of damages; or

(C) address pretrial and posttrial matters that cannot be effectively and timely addressed by an available district judge or magistrate judge of the district.

(2) *Disqualification.* A master must not have a relationship to the parties, attorneys, action, or court that would require disqualification of a judge under 28 U.S.C. § 455, unless the parties, with the court's approval, consent to the appointment after the master discloses any potential grounds for disqualification.

(3) *Possible Expense or Delay.* In appointing a master, the court must consider the fairness of imposing the likely expenses on the parties and must protect against unreasonable expense or delay.

(b) Order Appointing a Master.

(1) *Notice.* Before appointing a master, the court must give the parties notice and an opportunity to be heard. Any party may suggest candidates for appointment.

(2) *Contents.* The appointing order must direct the master to proceed with all reasonable diligence and must state:

(A) the master's duties, including any investigation or enforcement duties, and any limits on the master's authority under Rule 53(c);

(B) the circumstances, if any, in which the master may communicate ex parte with the court or a party;

(C) the nature of the materials to be preserved and filed as the record of the master's activities;

(D) the time limits, method of filing the record, other procedures, and standards for reviewing the master's orders, findings, and recommendations; and

(E) the basis, terms, and procedure for fixing the master's compensation under Rule 53(g).

(3) *Issuing.* The court may issue the order only after:

(A) the master files an affidavit disclosing whether there is any ground for disqualification under 28 U.S.C. § 455; and

(B) if a ground is disclosed, the parties, with the court's approval, waive the disqualification.

(4) *Amending.* The order may be amended at any time after notice to the parties and an opportunity to be heard.

(c) Master's Authority.

(1) *In General.* Unless the appointing order directs otherwise, a master may:

(A) regulate all proceedings;

(B) take all appropriate measures to perform the assigned duties fairly and efficiently; and

(C) if conducting an evidentiary hearing, exercise the appointing court's power to compel, take, and record evidence.

(2) *Sanctions.* The master may by order impose on a party any noncontempt sanction provided by Rule 37 or 45, and may recommend a contempt sanction against a party and sanctions against a nonparty.

(d) Master's Orders. A master who issues an order must file it and promptly serve a copy on each party. The clerk must enter the order on the docket.

(e) Master's Reports. A master must report to the court as required by the appointing order. The master must file the report and promptly serve a copy on each party, unless the court orders otherwise.

(f) Action on the Master's Order, Report, or Recommendations.

(1) *Opportunity for a Hearing; Action in General.* In acting on a master's order, report, or recommendations, the court must give the parties notice and an opportunity to be heard; may receive evidence; and may adopt or affirm, modify, wholly or partly reject or reverse, or resubmit to the master with instructions.

(2) *Time to Object or Move to Adopt or Modify.* A party may file objections to—or a motion to adopt or modify—the master's order, report, or recommendations no later than 21 days after a copy is served, unless the court sets a different time.

(3) *Reviewing Factual Findings.* The court must decide de novo all objections to findings of fact made or recommended by a master, unless the parties, with the court's approval, stipulate that:

(A) the findings will be reviewed for clear error; or

(B) the findings of a master appointed under Rule 53(a)(1)(A) or (C) will be final.

(4) *Reviewing Legal Conclusions.* The court must decide de novo all objections to conclusions of law made or recommended by a master.

(5) *Reviewing Procedural Matters.* Unless the appointing order establishes a different standard of review, the court may set aside a master's ruling on a procedural matter only for an abuse of discretion.

(g) Compensation.

(1) *Fixing Compensation.* Before or after judgment, the court must fix the master's compensation on the basis and terms stated in the appointing order, but the court may set a new basis and terms after giving notice and an opportunity to be heard.

(2) *Payment.* The compensation must be paid either:

(A) by a party or parties; or

(B) from a fund or subject matter of the action within the court's control.

(3) *Allocating Payment.* The court must allocate payment among the parties after considering the nature and amount of the controversy, the parties' means, and the extent to which any party is more responsible than other parties for the reference to a master. An interim allocation may be amended to reflect a decision on the merits.

(h) Appointing a Magistrate Judge. A magistrate judge is subject to this rule only when the order referring a matter to the magistrate judge states that the reference is made under this rule.

(Amended February 28, 1966, effective July 1, 1966; April 28, 1983, effective August 1, 1983; March 2, 1987, effective August 1, 1987; April 30, 1991, effective December 1, 1991; April 22, 1993, effective December 1, 1993; March 27, 2003, effective December 1, 2003; April 30, 2007, effective December 1, 2007; March 26, 2009, effective December 1, 2009.)

TITLE VII. JUDGMENT

RULE 54. JUDGMENT; COSTS

(a) Definition; Form. "Judgment" as used in these rules includes a decree and any order from which an appeal lies. A judgment should not include recitals of pleadings, a master's report, or a record of prior proceedings.

(b) Judgment on Multiple Claims or Involving Multiple Parties. When an action presents more than one claim for relief—whether as a claim, counterclaim, crossclaim, or third-party claim—or when multiple parties are involved, the court may direct entry of a final judgment as to one or more, but fewer than all, claims or parties only if the court expressly determines that there is no just reason for delay. Otherwise, any order or other decision, however designated, that adjudicates fewer than all the claims or the rights and liabilities of fewer than all the parties does not end the action as to any of the claims or parties and may be revised at any time before the entry of a judgment adjudicating all the claims and all the parties' rights and liabilities.

(c) Demand for Judgment; Relief to Be Granted. A default judgment must not differ in kind from, or exceed in amount, what is demanded in the pleadings. Every other final judgment should grant the relief to which each party is entitled, even if the party has not demanded that relief in its pleadings.

(d) Costs; Attorney's Fees.

(1) *Costs Other Than Attorney's Fees.* Unless a federal statute, these rules, or a court order provides otherwise, costs—other than attorney's fees—should be allowed to the prevailing party. But costs against the United States, its officers, and its agencies may be imposed only to the extent allowed by law. The clerk may tax costs on 14 days' notice. On motion served within the next 7 days, the court may review the clerk's action.

(2) *Attorney's Fees.*

(A) *Claim to Be by Motion.* A claim for attorney's fees and related nontaxable expenses must be made by motion unless the substantive law requires those fees to be proved at trial as an element of damages.

(B) *Timing and Contents of the Motion.* Unless a statute or a court order provides otherwise, the motion must:

(i) be filed no later than 14 days after the entry of judgment;

(ii) specify the judgment and the statute, rule, or other grounds entitling the movant to the award;

(iii) state the amount sought or provide a fair estimate of it; and

(iv) disclose, if the court so orders, the terms of any agreement about fees for the services for which the claim is made.

(C) *Proceedings.* Subject to Rule 23(h), the court must, on a party's request, give an opportunity for adversary submissions on the motion in accordance with Rule 43(c) or 78. The court may decide issues of liability for fees before receiving submissions on the value of services. The court must find the facts and state its conclusions of law as provided in Rule 52(a).

(D) *Special Procedures by Local Rule; Reference to a Master or a Magistrate Judge.* By local rule, the court may establish special procedures to resolve fee-related issues without extensive evidentiary hearings. Also, the court may refer issues concerning the value of services to a special master under Rule 53 without regard to the limitations of Rule 53(a)(1), and may refer a motion for attorney's fees to a magistrate judge under Rule 72(b) as if it were a dispositive pretrial matter.

(E) *Exceptions.* Subparagraphs (A)-(D) do not apply to claims for fees and expenses as sanctions for violating these rules or as sanctions under 28 U.S.C. § 1927.

(Amended December 27, 1946, effective March 19, 1948; April 17, 1961, effective July 19, 1961; March 2, 1987, effective August 1, 1987; April 22, 1993, effective December 1, 1993; April 29, 2002, effective December 1, 2002; March 27, 2003, effective December 1, 2003; April 30, 2007, effective December 1, 2007; March 26, 2009, effective December 1, 2009.)

RULE 55. DEFAULT; DEFAULT JUDGMENT

(a) Entering a Default. When a party against whom a judgment for affirmative relief is sought has failed to plead or otherwise defend, and that failure is shown by affidavit or otherwise, the clerk must enter the party's default.

(b) Entering a Default Judgment.

(1) *By the Clerk.* If the plaintiff's claim is for a sum certain or a sum that can be made certain by computation, the clerk—on the plaintiff's request, with an affidavit showing the amount due—must enter judgment for that amount and costs against a defendant who has been defaulted for not appearing and who is neither a minor nor an incompetent person.

(2) *By the Court.* In all other cases, the party must apply to the court for a default judgment. A default judgment may be entered against a minor or incompetent person only if represented by a general guardian, conservator, or other like fiduciary who has appeared. If the party against whom a default judgment is sought has appeared personally or by a representative, that party or its representative must be served with written notice of the application at least 7 days before the hearing. The court may conduct hearings or make referrals—preserving any federal statutory right to a jury trial—when, to enter or effectuate judgment, it needs to:

    (A) conduct an accounting;

    (B) determine the amount of damages;

    (C) establish the truth of any allegation by evidence; or

    (D) investigate any other matter.

(c) Setting Aside a Default or a Default Judgment. The court may set aside an entry of default for good cause, and it may set aside a final default judgment under Rule 60(b).

(d) Judgment Against the United States. A default judgment may be entered against the United States, its officers, or its agencies only if the claimant establishes a claim or right to relief by evidence that satisfies the court.

(Amended March 2, 1987, effective August 1, 1987; April 30, 2007, effective December 1, 2007; March 26, 2009, effective December 1, 2009; April 29, 2015, effective December 1, 2015.)

RULE 56. SUMMARY JUDGMENT

(a) Motion for Summary Judgment or Partial Summary Judgment. A party may move for summary judgment, identifying each claim or defense—or the part of each claim or defense—on which summary judgment is sought. The court shall grant summary judgment if the movant shows that there is no genuine dispute as to any material fact and the movant is entitled to judgment as a matter of law. The court should state on the record the reasons for granting or denying the motion.

(b) Time to File a Motion. Unless a different time is set by local rule or the court orders otherwise, a party may file a motion for summary judgment at any time until 30 days after the close of all discovery.

(c) Procedures.

(1) *Supporting Factual Positions.* A party asserting that a fact cannot be or is genuinely disputed must support the assertion by:

    (A) citing to particular parts of materials in the record, including depositions, documents, electronically stored information, affidavits or declarations, stipulations (including those made for purposes of the motion only), admissions, interrogatory answers, or other materials; or

    (B) showing that the materials cited do not establish the absence or presence of a genuine dispute, or that an adverse party cannot produce admissible evidence to support the fact.

(2) *Objection That a Fact Is Not Supported by Admissible Evidence.* A party may object that the material cited to support or dispute a fact cannot be presented in a form that would be admissible in evidence.

(3) *Materials Not Cited.* The court need consider only the cited materials, but it may consider other materials in the record.

(4) *Affidavits or Declarations.* An affidavit or declaration used to support or oppose a motion must be made on personal knowledge, set out facts that would be admissible in evidence, and show that the affiant or declarant is competent to testify on the matters stated.

(d) When Facts Are Unavailable to the Nonmovant. If a nonmovant shows by affidavit or declaration that, for specified reasons, it cannot present facts essential to justify its opposition, the court may:

    (1) defer considering the motion or deny it;

    (2) allow time to obtain affidavits or declarations or to take discovery; or

    (3) issue any other appropriate order.

(e) Failing to Properly Support or Address a Fact. If a party fails to properly support an assertion of fact or fails to properly address another party's assertion of fact as required by Rule 56(c), the court may:

    (1) give an opportunity to properly support or address the fact;

    (2) consider the fact undisputed for purposes of the motion;

    (3) grant summary judgment if the motion and supporting materials—including the facts considered undisputed—show that the movant is entitled to it; or

    (4) issue any other appropriate order.

(f) Judgment Independent of the Motion. After giving notice and a reasonable time to respond, the court may:

    (1) grant summary judgment for a nonmovant;

    (2) grant the motion on grounds not raised by a party; or

    (3) consider summary judgment on its own after identifying for the parties material facts that may not be genuinely in dispute.

(g) Failing to Grant All the Requested Relief. If the court does not grant all the relief requested by the motion, it may enter an order stating any material fact—including an item of damages or other relief—that is not genuinely in dispute and treating the fact as established in the case.

(h) Affidavit or Declaration Submitted in Bad Faith. If satisfied that an affidavit or declaration under this rule is submitted in bad faith or solely for delay, the court—after notice and a reasonable time to respond—may order the submitting party to pay the other party the reasonable expenses, including attorney's fees, it incurred as a result. An offending party or attorney may also be held in contempt or subjected to other appropriate sanctions.

(Amended December 27, 1946, effective March 19, 1948; January 21, 1963, effective July 1, 1963; March 2, 1987, effective August 1, 1987; April 30, 2007, effective December 1, 2007; March 26, 2009, effective December 1, 2009; April 28, 2010, effective December 1, 2010.)

RULE 57. DECLARATORY JUDGMENT

These rules govern the procedure for obtaining a declaratory judgment under 28 U.S.C. § 2201. Rules 38 and 39 govern a demand for a jury trial. The existence of another adequate remedy does not preclude a declaratory judgment that is otherwise appropriate. The court may order a speedy hearing of a declaratory-judgment action.

(Amended December 29, 1948, effective October 20, 1949; April 30, 2007, effective December 1, 2007.)

RULE 58. ENTERING JUDGMENT

(a) Separate Document. Every judgment and amended judgment must be set out in a separate document, but a separate document is not required for an order disposing of a motion:

(1) for judgment under Rule 50(b);

(2) to amend or make additional findings under Rule 52(b);

(3) for attorney's fees under Rule 54;

(4) for a new trial, or to alter or amend the judgment, under Rule 59; or

(5) for relief under Rule 60.

(b) Entering Judgment.

(1) *Without the Court's Direction.* Subject to Rule 54(b) and unless the court orders otherwise, the clerk must, without awaiting the court's direction, promptly prepare, sign, and enter the judgment when:

(A) the jury returns a general verdict;

(B) the court awards only costs or a sum certain; or

(C) the court denies all relief.

(2) *Court's Approval Required.* Subject to Rule 54(b), the court must promptly approve the form of the judgment, which the clerk must promptly enter, when:

(A) the jury returns a special verdict or a general verdict with answers to written questions; or

(B) the court grants other relief not described in this subdivision (b).

(c) Time of Entry. For purposes of these rules, judgment is entered at the following times:

(1) if a separate document is not required, when the judgment is entered in the civil docket under Rule 79(a); or

(2) if a separate document is required, when the judgment is entered in the civil docket under Rule 79(a) and the earlier of these events occurs:

(A) it is set out in a separate document; or

(B) 150 days have run from the entry in the civil docket.

(d) Request for Entry. A party may request that judgment be set out in a separate document as required by Rule 58(a).

(e) Cost or Fee Awards. Ordinarily, the entry of judgment may not be delayed, nor the time for appeal extended, in order to tax costs or award fees. But if a timely motion for attorney's fees is made under Rule 54(d)(2), the court may act before a notice of appeal has been filed and become effective to order that the motion have the same effect under Federal Rule of Appellate Procedure 4(a)(4) as a timely motion under Rule 59.

(Amended December 27, 1946, effective March 19, 1948; January 21, 1963, effective July 1, 1963; April 22, 1993, effective December 1, 1993; April 29, 2002, effective December 1, 2002; April 30, 2007, effective December 1, 2007.)

RULE 59. NEW TRIAL; ALTERING OR AMENDING A JUDGMENT

(a) In General.

(1) *Grounds for New Trial.* The court may, on motion, grant a new trial on all or some of the issues—and to any party—as follows:

(A) after a jury trial, for any reason for which a new trial has heretofore been granted in an action at law in federal court; or

(B) after a nonjury trial, for any reason for which a rehearing has heretofore been granted in a suit in equity in federal court.

(2) *Further Action After a Nonjury Trial.* After a nonjury trial, the court may, on motion for a new trial, open the judgment if one has been entered, take additional testimony, amend findings of fact and conclusions of law or make new ones, and direct the entry of a new judgment.

(b) Time to File a Motion for a New Trial. A motion for a new trial must be filed no later than 28 days after the entry of judgment.

(c) Time to Serve Affidavits. When a motion for a new trial is based on affidavits, they must be filed with the motion. The opposing party has 14 days after being served to file opposing affidavits. The court may permit reply affidavits.

(d) New Trial on the Court's Initiative or for Reasons Not in the Motion. No later than 28 days after the entry of judgment, the court, on its own, may order a new trial for any reason that would justify granting one on a party's motion. After giving the parties notice and an opportunity to be heard, the court may grant a timely motion for a new trial for a reason not stated in the motion. In either event, the court must specify the reasons in its order.

(e) Motion to Alter or Amend a Judgment. A motion to alter or amend a judgment must be filed no later than 28 days after the entry of the judgment.

(Amended December 27, 1946, effective March 19, 1948; February 28, 1966, effective July 1, 1966; April 27, 1995, effective December 1, 1995; April 30, 2007, effective December 1, 2007; March 26, 2009, effective December 1, 2009.)

RULE 60. RELIEF FROM A JUDGMENT OR ORDER

(a) Corrections Based on Clerical Mistakes; Oversights and Omissions. The court may correct a clerical mistake or a mistake arising from oversight or omission whenever one is found in a judgment, order, or other part of the record. The court may do so on motion or on its own, with or without notice. But after an appeal has been docketed in the appellate court and while it is pending, such a mistake may be corrected only with the appellate court's leave.

(b) Grounds for Relief from a Final Judgment, Order, or Proceeding. On motion and just terms, the court may relieve a party or its legal representative from a final judgment, order, or proceeding for the following reasons:

(1) mistake, inadvertence, surprise, or excusable neglect;

(2) newly discovered evidence that, with reasonable diligence, could not have been discovered in time to move for a new trial under Rule 59(b);

(3) fraud (whether previously called intrinsic or extrinsic), misrepresentation, or misconduct by an opposing party;

(4) the judgment is void;

(5) the judgment has been satisfied, released, or discharged; it is based on an earlier judgment that has been reversed or vacated; or applying it prospectively is no longer equitable; or

(6) any other reason that justifies relief.

(c) Timing and Effect of the Motion.

(1) *Timing.* A motion under Rule 60(b) must be made within a reasonable time—and for reasons (1), (2), and (3) no more than a year after the entry of the judgment or order or the date of the proceeding.

(2) *Effect on Finality.* The motion does not affect the judgment's finality or suspend its operation.

(d) Other Powers to Grant Relief. This rule does not limit a court's power to:

(1) entertain an independent action to relieve a party from a judgment, order, or proceeding;

(2) grant relief under 28 U.S.C. § 1655 to a defendant who was not personally notified of the action; or

(3) set aside a judgment for fraud on the court.

(e) Bills and Writs Abolished. The following are abolished: bills of review, bills in the nature of bills of review, and writs of coram nobis, coram vobis, and audita querela.

(Amended December 27, 1946, effective March 19, 1948; December 29, 1948, effective October 20, 1949; March 2, 1987, effective August 1, 1987; April 30, 2007, effective December 1, 2007.)

RULE 61. HARMLESS ERROR

Unless justice requires otherwise, no error in admitting or excluding evidence—or any other error by the court or a party—is ground for granting a new trial, for setting aside a verdict, or for vacating, modifying, or otherwise disturbing a judgment or order. At every stage of the proceeding, the court must disregard all errors and defects that do not affect any party's substantial rights.

(Amended April 30, 2007, effective December 1, 2007.)

RULE 62. STAY OF PROCEEDINGS TO ENFORCE A JUDGMENT

(a) Automatic Stay. Except as provided in Rule 62(c) and (d), execution on a judgment and proceedings to enforce it are stayed for 30 days after its entry, unless the court orders otherwise.

(b) Stay by Bond or Other Security. At any time after judgment is entered, a party may obtain a stay by providing a bond or other security. The stay takes effect when the court approves the bond or other security and remains in effect for the time specified in the bond or other security.

(c) Stay of an Injunction, Receivership, or Patent Accounting Order. Unless the court orders otherwise, the following are not stayed after being entered, even if an appeal is taken:

(1) an interlocutory or final judgment in an action for an injunction or receivership; or

(2) a judgment or order that directs an accounting in an action for patent infringement.

(d) Injunction Pending an Appeal. While an appeal is pending from an interlocutory order or final judgment that grants, continues, modifies, refuses, dissolves, or refuses to dissolve or modify an injunction, the court may suspend, modify, restore, or grant an injunction on terms for bond or other terms that secure the opposing party's rights. If the judgment appealed from is rendered by a statutory three-judge district court, the order must be made either:

(1) by that court sitting in open session; or

(2) by the assent of all its judges, as evidenced by their signatures.

(e) Stay Without Bond on an Appeal by the United States, Its Officers, or Its Agencies. The court must not require a bond, obligation, or other security from the appellant when granting a stay on an appeal by the United States, its officers, or its agencies or on an appeal directed by a department of the federal government.

(f) Stay in Favor of a Judgment Debtor Under State Law. If a judgment is a lien on the judgment debtor's property under the law of the state where the court is located, the judgment debtor is entitled to the same stay of execution the state court would give.

(g) Appellate Court's Power Not Limited. This rule does not limit the power of the appellate court or one of its judges or justices:

(1) to stay proceedings—or suspend, modify, restore, or grant an injunction—while an appeal is pending; or

(2) to issue an order to preserve the status quo or the effectiveness of the judgment to be entered.

(h) Stay with Multiple Claims or Parties. A court may stay the enforcement of a final judgment entered under Rule 54(b) until it enters a later judgment or judgments, and may prescribe terms necessary to secure the benefit of the stayed judgment for the party in whose favor it was entered.

(Amended December 27, 1946, effective March 19, 1948; December 29, 1948, effective October 20, 1949; April 17, 1961, effective July 19, 1961; March 2, 1987, effective August 1, 1987; April 30, 2007, effective December 1, 2007; March 26, 2009, effective December 1, 2009; April 26, 2018, effective December 1, 2018.)

RULE 62.1 INDICATIVE RULING ON A MOTION FOR RELIEF THAT IS BARRED BY A PENDING APPEAL

(a) Relief Pending Appeal. If a timely motion is made for relief that the court lacks authority to grant because of an appeal that has been docketed and is pending, the court may:

(1) defer considering the motion;

(2) deny the motion; or

(3) state either that it would grant the motion if the court of appeals remands for that purpose or that the motion raises a substantial issue.

(b) Notice to the Court of Appeals. The movant must promptly notify the circuit clerk under Federal Rule of Appellate Procedure 12.1 if the district court states that it would grant the motion or that the motion raises a substantial issue.

(c) Remand. The district court may decide the motion if the court of appeals remands for that purpose.

(Added March 26, 2009, effective December 1, 2009.)

RULE 63. JUDGE'S INABILITY TO PROCEED

If a judge conducting a hearing or trial is unable to proceed, any other judge may proceed upon certifying familiarity with the record and determining that the case may be completed without prejudice to the parties. In a hearing or a nonjury trial, the successor judge must, at a party's request, recall any witness whose testimony is material and disputed and who is available to testify again without undue burden. The successor judge may also recall any other witness.

(Amended March 2, 1987, effective August 1, 1987; April 30, 1991, effective December 1, 1991; April 30, 2007, effective December 1, 2007.)

TITLE VIII. PROVISIONAL AND FINAL REMEDIES

RULE 64. SEIZING A PERSON OR PROPERTY

(a) Remedies Under State Law—In General. At the commencement of and throughout an action, every remedy is available that, under the law of the state where the court is located, provides for seizing a person or property to secure satisfaction of the potential judgment. But a federal statute governs to the extent it applies.

(b) Specific Kinds of Remedies. The remedies available under this rule include the following—however designated and regardless of whether state procedure requires an independent action:

- arrest;
- attachment;
- garnishment;
- replevin;
- sequestration; and
- other corresponding or equivalent remedies.

(Amended April 30, 2007, effective December 1, 2007.)

RULE 65. INJUNCTIONS AND RESTRAINING ORDERS

(a) Preliminary Injunction.

(1) *Notice.* The court may issue a preliminary injunction only on notice to the adverse party.

(2) *Consolidating the Hearing with the Trial on the Merits.* Before or after beginning the hearing on a motion for a preliminary injunction, the court may advance the trial on the merits and consolidate it with the hearing. Even when consolidation is not ordered, evidence that is received on the motion and that would be admissible at trial becomes part of the trial record and need not be repeated at trial. But the court must preserve any party's right to a jury trial.

(b) Temporary Restraining Order.

(1) *Issuing Without Notice.* The court may issue a temporary restraining order without written or oral notice to the adverse party or its attorney only if:

(A) specific facts in an affidavit or a verified complaint clearly show that immediate and irreparable injury, loss, or damage will result to the movant before the adverse party can be heard in opposition; and

(B) the movant's attorney certifies in writing any efforts made to give notice and the reasons why it should not be required.

(2) *Contents; Expiration.* Every temporary restraining order issued without notice must state the date and hour it was issued; describe the injury and state why it is irreparable; state why the order was issued without notice; and be promptly filed in the clerk's office and entered in the record. The order expires at the time after entry—not to exceed 14 days—that the court sets, unless before that time the court, for good cause, extends it for a like period or the adverse party consents to a longer extension. The reasons for an extension must be entered in the record.

(3) *Expediting the Preliminary–Injunction Hearing.* If the order is issued without notice, the motion for a preliminary injunction must be set for hearing at the earliest possible time, taking precedence over all other matters

except hearings on older matters of the same character. At the hearing, the party who obtained the order must proceed with the motion; if the party does not, the court must dissolve the order.

(4) Motion to Dissolve. On 2 days' notice to the party who obtained the order without notice—or on shorter notice set by the court—the adverse party may appear and move to dissolve or modify the order. The court must then hear and decide the motion as promptly as justice requires.

(c) Security. The court may issue a preliminary injunction or a temporary restraining order only if the movant gives security in an amount that the court considers proper to pay the costs and damages sustained by any party found to have been wrongfully enjoined or restrained. The United States, its officers, and its agencies are not required to give security.

(d) Contents and Scope of Every Injunction and Restraining Order.

(1) Contents. Every order granting an injunction and every restraining order must:

    (A) state the reasons why it issued;

    (B) state its terms specifically; and

    (C) describe in reasonable detail—and not by referring to the complaint or other document—the act or acts restrained or required.

(2) Persons Bound. The order binds only the following who receive actual notice of it by personal service or otherwise:

    (A) the parties;

    (B) the parties' officers, agents, servants, employees, and attorneys; and

    (C) other persons who are in active concert or participation with anyone described in Rule 65(d)(2)(A) or (B).

(e) Other Laws Not Modified. These rules do not modify the following:

    (1) any federal statute relating to temporary restraining orders or preliminary injunctions in actions affecting employer and employee;

    (2) 28 U.S.C. § 2361, which relates to preliminary injunctions in actions of interpleader or in the nature of interpleader; or

    (3) 28 U.S.C. § 2284, which relates to actions that must be heard and decided by a three-judge district court.

(f) Copyright Impoundment. This rule applies to copyright-impoundment proceedings.

(Amended December 27, 1946, effective March 19, 1948; December 29, 1948, effective October 20, 1949; February 28, 1966, effective July 1, 1966; March 2, 1987, effective August 1, 1987; April 23, 2001, effective December 1, 2001; April 30, 2007, effective December 1, 2007; March 26, 2009, effective December 1, 2009.)

RULE 65.1 PROCEEDINGS AGAINST A SECURITY PROVIDER

Whenever these rules (including the Supplemental Rules for Admiralty or Maritime Claims and Asset Forfeiture Actions) require or allow a party to give security, and security is given with one or more security providers, each provider submits to the court's jurisdiction and irrevocably appoints the court clerk as its agent for receiving service of any papers that affect its liability on the security. The security provider's liability may be enforced on motion without an independent action. The motion and any notice that the court orders may be served on the court clerk, who must promptly send a copy of each to every security provider whose address is known.

(Adopted February 28, 1966, effective July 1, 1966; amended March 2, 1987, effective August 1, 1987; April 12, 2006, effective December 1, 2006; April 30, 2007, effective December 1, 2007; April 26, 2018, effective December 1, 2018.)

RULE 66. RECEIVERS

These rules govern an action in which the appointment of a receiver is sought or a receiver sues or is sued. But the practice in administering an estate by a receiver or a similar court-appointed officer must accord with the historical practice in federal courts or with a local rule. An action in which a receiver has been appointed may be dismissed only by court order.

(Amended December 27, 1946, effective March 19, 1948; December 29, 1948, effective October 20, 1949; April 30, 2007, effective December 1, 2007.)

RULE 67. DEPOSIT INTO COURT

(a) Depositing Property. If any part of the relief sought is a money judgment or the disposition of a sum of money or some other deliverable thing, a party—on notice to every other party and by leave of court—may deposit with the court all or part of the money or thing, whether or not that party claims any of it. The depositing party must deliver to the clerk a copy of the order permitting deposit.

(b) Investing and Withdrawing Funds. Money paid into court under this rule must be deposited and withdrawn in accordance with 28 U.S.C. §§ 2041 and 2042 and any like statute. The money must be deposited in an interest-bearing account or invested in a court-approved, interest-bearing instrument.

(Amended December 29, 1948, effective October 20, 1949; April 28, 1983, effective August 1, 1983; April 30, 2007, effective December 1, 2007.)

RULE 68. OFFER OF JUDGMENT

(a) Making an Offer; Judgment on an Accepted Offer. At least 14 days before the date set for trial, a party defending against a claim may serve on an opposing party an offer to allow judgment on specified terms, with the costs then accrued. If, within 14 days after being served, the opposing party serves written notice accepting the offer, either party may then file the offer and notice of acceptance, plus proof of service. The clerk must then enter judgment.

(b) Unaccepted Offer. An unaccepted offer is considered withdrawn, but it does not preclude a later offer. Evidence of an unaccepted offer is not admissible except in a proceeding to determine costs.

(c) Offer After Liability is Determined. When one party's liability to another has been determined but the extent of liability remains to be determined by further proceedings, the party held liable may make an offer of judgment. It must be served within a reasonable time—but at least 14 days—before the date set for a hearing to determine the extent of liability.

(d) Paying Costs After an Unaccepted Offer. If the judgment that the offeree finally obtains is not more favorable than the unaccepted offer, the offeree must pay the costs incurred after the offer was made.

(Amended December 27, 1946, effective March 19, 1948; February 28, 1966, effective July 1, 1966; March 2, 1987, effective August 1, 1987; April 30, 2007, effective December 1, 2007; March 26, 2009, effective December 1, 2009.)

RULE 69. EXECUTION

(a) In General.

(1) *Money Judgment; Applicable Procedure.* A money judgment is enforced by a writ of execution, unless the court directs otherwise. The procedure on execution—and in proceedings supplementary to and in aid of judgment or execution—must accord with the procedure of the state where the court is located, but a federal statute governs to the extent it applies.

(2) *Obtaining Discovery.* In aid of the judgment or execution, the judgment creditor or a successor in interest whose interest appears of record may obtain discovery from any person—including the judgment debtor—as provided in these rules or by the procedure of the state where the court is located.

(b) Against Certain Public Officers. When a judgment has been entered against a revenue officer in the circumstances stated in 28 U.S.C. § 2006, or against an officer of Congress in the circumstances stated in 2 U.S.C. § 118,[1] the judgment must be satisfied as those statutes provide.

(Amended December 29, 1948, effective October 20, 1949; March 30, 1970, effective July 1, 1970; March 2, 1987 effective August 1, 1987; April 30, 2007, effective December 1, 2007.)

[1] Now editorially reclassified 2 U.S.C. § 5503.

RULE 70. ENFORCING A JUDGMENT FOR A SPECIFIC ACT

(a) Party's Failure to Act; Ordering Another to Act. If a judgment requires a party to convey land, to deliver a deed or other document, or to perform any other specific act and the party fails to comply within the time specified, the court may order the act to be done—at the disobedient party's expense—by another person appointed by the court. When done, the act has the same effect as if done by the party.

(b) Vesting Title. If the real or personal property is within the district, the court—instead of ordering a conveyance—may enter a judgment divesting any party's title and vesting it in others. That judgment has the effect of a legally executed conveyance.

(c) Obtaining a Writ of Attachment or Sequestration. On application by a party entitled to performance of an act, the clerk must issue a writ of attachment or sequestration against the disobedient party's property to compel obedience.

(d) Obtaining a Writ of Execution or Assistance. On application by a party who obtains a judgment or order for possession, the clerk must issue a writ of execution or assistance.

(e) Holding in Contempt. The court may also hold the disobedient party in contempt.

(Amended April 30, 2007, effective December 1, 2007.)

RULE 71. ENFORCING RELIEF FOR OR AGAINST A NONPARTY

When an order grants relief for a nonparty or may be enforced against a nonparty, the procedure for enforcing the order is the same as for a party.

(Amended March 2, 1987, effective August 1, 1987; April 30, 2007, effective December 1, 2007.)

TITLE IX. SPECIAL PROCEEDINGS

RULE 71.1 CONDEMNING REAL OR PERSONAL PROPERTY

(a) Applicability of Other Rules. These rules govern proceedings to condemn real and personal property by eminent domain, except as this rule provides otherwise.

(b) Joinder of Properties. The plaintiff may join separate pieces of property in a single action, no matter whether they are owned by the same persons or sought for the same use.

(c) Complaint.

(1) *Caption.* The complaint must contain a caption as provided in Rule 10(a). The plaintiff must, however, name as defendants both the property—designated generally by kind, quantity, and location—and at least one owner of some part of or interest in the property.

(2) *Contents.* The complaint must contain a short and plain statement of the following:

(A) the authority for the taking;

(B) the uses for which the property is to be taken;

(C) a description sufficient to identify the property;

(D) the interests to be acquired; and

(E) for each piece of property, a designation of each defendant who has been joined as an owner or owner of an interest in it.

(3) *Parties.* When the action commences, the plaintiff need join as defendants only those persons who have or claim an interest in the property and whose names are then known. But before any hearing on compensation, the plaintiff must add as defendants all those persons who have or claim an interest and whose names have become known or

can be found by a reasonably diligent search of the records, considering both the property's character and value and the interests to be acquired. All others may be made defendants under the designation "Unknown Owners."

(4) *Procedure.* Notice must be served on all defendants as provided in Rule 71.1(d), whether they were named as defendants when the action commenced or were added later. A defendant may answer as provided in Rule 71.1(e). The court, meanwhile, may order any distribution of a deposit that the facts warrant.

(5) *Filing; Additional Copies.* In addition to filing the complaint, the plaintiff must give the clerk at least one copy for the defendants' use and additional copies at the request of the clerk or a defendant.

(d) Process.

(1) *Delivering Notice to the Clerk.* On filing a complaint, the plaintiff must promptly deliver to the clerk joint or several notices directed to the named defendants. When adding defendants, the plaintiff must deliver to the clerk additional notices directed to the new defendants.

(2) *Contents of the Notice.*

(A) *Main Contents.* Each notice must name the court, the title of the action, and the defendant to whom it is directed. It must describe the property sufficiently to identify it, but need not describe any property other than that to be taken from the named defendant. The notice must also state:

(i) that the action is to condemn property;

(ii) the interest to be taken;

(iii) the authority for the taking;

(iv) the uses for which the property is to be taken;

(v) that the defendant may serve an answer on the plaintiff's attorney within 21 days after being served with the notice;

(vi) that the failure to so serve an answer constitutes consent to the taking and to the court's authority to proceed with the action and fix the compensation; and

(vii) that a defendant who does not serve an answer may file a notice of appearance.

(B) *Conclusion.* The notice must conclude with the name, telephone number, and e-mail address of the plaintiff's attorney and an address within the district in which the action is brought where the attorney may be served.

(3) *Serving the Notice.*

(A) *Personal Service.* When a defendant whose address is known resides within the United States or a territory subject to the administrative or judicial jurisdiction of the United States, personal service of the notice (without a copy of the complaint) must be made in accordance with Rule 4.

(B) *Service by Publication.*

(i) A defendant may be served by publication only when the plaintiff's attorney files a certificate stating that the attorney believes the defendant cannot be personally served, because after diligent inquiry within the state where the complaint is filed, the defendant's place of residence is still unknown or, if known, that it is beyond the territorial limits of personal service. Service is then made by publishing the notice—once a week for at least 3 successive weeks—in a newspaper published in the county where the property is located or, if there is no such newspaper, in a newspaper with general circulation where the property is located. Before the last publication, a copy of the notice must also be mailed to every defendant who cannot be personally served but whose place of residence is then known. Unknown owners may be served by publication in the same manner by a notice addressed to "Unknown Owners."

(ii) Service by publication is complete on the date of the last publication. The plaintiff's attorney must prove publication and mailing by a certificate, attach a printed copy of the published notice, and mark on the copy the newspaper's name and the dates of publication.

(4) *Effect of Delivery and Service.* Delivering the notice to the clerk and serving it have the same effect as serving a summons under Rule 4.

(5) *Amending the Notice; Proof of Service and Amending the Proof.* Rule 4(a)(2) governs amending the notice. Rule 4(*l*) governs proof of service and amending it.

(e) Appearance or Answer.

(1) *Notice of Appearance.* A defendant that has no objection or defense to the taking of its property may serve a notice of appearance designating the property in which it claims an interest. The defendant must then be given notice of all later proceedings affecting the defendant.

(2) *Answer.* A defendant that has an objection or defense to the taking must serve an answer within 21 days after being served with the notice. The answer must:

(A) identify the property in which the defendant claims an interest;

(B) state the nature and extent of the interest; and

(C) state all the defendant's objections and defenses to the taking.

(3) *Waiver of Other Objections and Defenses; Evidence on Compensation.* A defendant waives all objections and defenses not stated in its answer. No other pleading or motion asserting an additional objection or defense is allowed. But at the trial on compensation, a defendant—whether or not it has previously appeared or answered—may present evidence on the amount of compensation to be paid and may share in the award.

(f) Amending Pleadings. Without leave of court, the plaintiff may—as often as it wants—amend the complaint at any time before the trial on compensation. But no amendment may be made if it would result in a dismissal inconsistent with Rule 71.1(i)(1) or (2). The plaintiff need not serve a copy of an amendment, but must serve notice of the filing, as provided in Rule 5(b), on every affected party who has appeared and, as provided in Rule 71.1(d), on every affected party who has not appeared. In addition, the plaintiff must give the clerk at least one copy of each amendment for the defendants' use, and additional copies at the request of the clerk or a defendant. A defendant may appear or answer in the time and manner and with the same effect as provided in Rule 71.1(e).

(g) Substituting Parties. If a defendant dies, becomes incompetent, or transfers an interest after being joined, the court may, on motion and notice of hearing, order that the proper party be substituted. Service of the motion and notice on a nonparty must be made as provided in Rule 71.1(d)(3).

(h) Trial of the Issues.

(1) *Issues Other Than Compensation; Compensation.* In an action involving eminent domain under federal law, the court tries all issues, including compensation, except when compensation must be determined:

(A) by any tribunal specially constituted by a federal statute to determine compensation; or

(B) if there is no such tribunal, by a jury when a party demands one within the time to answer or within any additional time the court sets, unless the court appoints a commission.

(2) *Appointing a Commission; Commission's Powers and Report.*

(A) *Reasons for Appointing.* If a party has demanded a jury, the court may instead appoint a three-person commission to determine compensation because of the character, location, or quantity of the property to be condemned or for other just reasons.

(B) *Alternate Commissioners.* The court may appoint up to two additional persons to serve as alternate commissioners to hear the case and replace commissioners who, before a decision is filed, the court finds unable or disqualified to perform their duties. Once the commission renders its final decision, the court must discharge any alternate who has not replaced a commissioner.

(C) *Examining the Prospective Commissioners.* Before making its appointments, the court must advise the parties of the identity and qualifications of each prospective commissioner and alternate, and may permit the parties to examine them. The parties may not suggest appointees, but for good cause may object to a prospective commissioner or alternate.

(D) *Commission's Powers and Report.* A commission has the powers of a master under Rule 53(c). Its action and report are determined by a majority. Rule 53(d), (e), and (f) apply to its action and report.

(i) Dismissal of the Action or a Defendant.

(1) *Dismissing the Action.*

(A) *By the Plaintiff.* If no compensation hearing on a piece of property has begun, and if the plaintiff has not acquired title or a lesser interest or taken possession, the plaintiff may, without a court order, dismiss the action as to that property by filing a notice of dismissal briefly describing the property.

(B) *By Stipulation.* Before a judgment is entered vesting the plaintiff with title or a lesser interest in or possession of property, the plaintiff and affected defen-

dants may, without a court order, dismiss the action in whole or in part by filing a stipulation of dismissal. And if the parties so stipulate, the court may vacate a judgment already entered.

(C) *By Court Order.* At any time before compensation has been determined and paid, the court may, after a motion and hearing, dismiss the action as to a piece of property. But if the plaintiff has already taken title, a lesser interest, or possession as to any part of it, the court must award compensation for the title, lesser interest, or possession taken.

(2) *Dismissing a Defendant.* The court may at any time dismiss a defendant who was unnecessarily or improperly joined.

(3) *Effect.* A dismissal is without prejudice unless otherwise stated in the notice, stipulation, or court order.

(j) Deposit and Its Distribution.

(1) *Deposit.* The plaintiff must deposit with the court any money required by law as a condition to the exercise of eminent domain and may make a deposit when allowed by statute.

(2) *Distribution; Adjusting Distribution.* After a deposit, the court and attorneys must expedite the proceedings so as to distribute the deposit and to determine and pay compensation. If the compensation finally awarded to a defendant exceeds the amount distributed to that defendant, the court must enter judgment against the plaintiff for the deficiency. If the compensation awarded to a defendant is less than the amount distributed to that defendant, the court must enter judgment against that defendant for the overpayment.

(k) Condemnation Under a State's Power of Eminent Domain. This rule governs an action involving eminent domain under state law. But if state law provides for trying an issue by jury—or for trying the issue of compensation by jury or commission or both—that law governs.

(*l*) Costs. Costs are not subject to Rule 54(d).

(Adopted April 30, 1951, effective August 1, 1951; amended January 21, 1963, effective July 1, 1963; April 29, 1985, effective August 1, 1985; March 2, 1987, effective August 1, 1987; April 25, 1988, effective August 1, 1988; amended by Pub.L. 100–690, Title VII, § 7050, November 18, 1988, 102 Stat. 4401 (although amendment by Pub.L. 100–690 could not be executed due to prior amendment by Court order which made the same change effective August 1, 1988); amended April 22, 1993, effective December 1, 1993; March 27, 2003, effective December 1, 2003; April 30, 2007, effective December 1, 2007; March 26, 2009, effective December 1, 2009.)

RULE 72.   MAGISTRATE JUDGES: PRETRIAL ORDER

(a) Nondispositive Matters. When a pretrial matter not dispositive of a party's claim or defense is referred to a magistrate judge to hear and decide, the magistrate judge must promptly conduct the required proceedings and, when appropriate, issue a written order stating the decision. A party may serve and file objections to the order within 14 days after being served with a copy. A party may not assign as error a defect in the order not timely objected to. The district judge in the case must consider timely objections and modify or set aside any part of the order that is clearly erroneous or is contrary to law.

(b) Dispositive Motions and Prisoner Petitions.

(1) *Findings and Recommendations.* A magistrate judge must promptly conduct the required proceedings when assigned, without the parties' consent, to hear a pretrial matter dispositive of a claim or defense or a prisoner petition challenging the conditions of confinement. A record must be made of all evidentiary proceedings and may, at the magistrate judge's discretion, be made of any other proceedings. The magistrate judge must enter a recommended disposition, including, if appropriate, proposed findings of fact. The clerk must promptly mail a copy to each party.

(2) *Objections.* Within 14 days after being served with a copy of the recommended disposition, a party may serve and file specific written objections to the proposed findings and recommendations. A party may respond to another party's objections within 14 days after being served with a copy. Unless the district judge orders otherwise, the objecting party must promptly arrange for transcribing the record, or whatever portions of it the parties agree to or the magistrate judge considers sufficient.

(3) *Resolving Objections.* The district judge must determine de novo any part of the magistrate judge's disposition that has been properly objected to. The district judge may accept, reject, or modify the recommended disposition; receive further evidence; or return the matter to the magistrate judge with instructions.

(Former Rule 72 abrogated December 4, 1967, effective July 1, 1968; new Rule 72 adopted April 28, 1983, effective August 1, 1983; amended April 30, 1991, effective December 1, 1991; April 22, 1993, effective December 1, 1993; April 30, 2007, effective December 1, 2007; March 26, 2009, effective December 1, 2009.)

RULE 73. MAGISTRATE JUDGES: TRIAL BY CONSENT; APPEAL

(a) Trial by Consent. When authorized under 28 U.S.C. § 636(c), a magistrate judge may, if all parties consent, conduct a civil action or proceeding, including a jury or nonjury trial. A record must be made in accordance with 28 U.S.C. § 636(c)(5).

(b) Consent Procedure.

(1) *In General.* When a magistrate judge has been designated to conduct civil actions or proceedings, the clerk must give the parties written notice of their opportunity to consent under 28 U.S.C. § 636(c). To signify their consent, the parties must jointly or separately file a statement consent-

ing to the referral. A district judge or magistrate judge may be informed of a party's response to the clerk's notice only if all parties have consented to the referral.

(2) *Reminding the Parties About Consenting.* A district judge, magistrate judge, or other court official may remind the parties of the magistrate judge's availability, but must also advise them that they are free to withhold consent without adverse substantive consequences.

(3) *Vacating a Referral.* On its own for good cause—or when a party shows extraordinary circumstances—the district judge may vacate a referral to a magistrate judge under this rule.

(c) Appealing a Judgment. In accordance with 28 U.S.C. § 636(c)(3), an appeal from a judgment entered at a magistrate judge's direction may be taken to the court of appeals as would any other appeal from a district-court judgment.

(Former Rule 73 abrogated December 4, 1967, effective July 1, 1968; new Rule 73 adopted April 28, 1983, effective August 1, 1983; amended March 2, 1987, effective August 1, 1987; April 22, 1993, effective December 1, 1993; April 11, 1997, effective December 1, 1997; April 30, 2007, effective December 1, 2007.)

RULE 74. METHOD OF APPEAL FROM MAGISTRATE JUDGE TO DISTRICT JUDGE UNDER TITLE 28, U.S.C. § 636(c)(4) AND RULE 73(d) [ABROGATED]

(Former Rule 74 abrogated December 4, 1967, effective July 1, 1968; new Rule 74 adopted April 28, 1983, effective August 1, 1983; amended April 22, 1993, effective December 1, 1993; abrogated April 11, 1997, effective December 1, 1997; April 30, 2007, effective December 1, 2007.)

RULE 75. PROCEEDINGS ON APPEAL FROM MAGISTRATE JUDGE TO DISTRICT JUDGE UNDER RULE 73(d) [ABROGATED]

(Former Rule 75 abrogated December 4, 1967, effective July 1, 1968; new Rule 75 adopted April 28, 1983, effective August 1, 1983; amended March 2, 1987, effective August 1, 1987; April 22, 1993, effective December 1, 1993; abrogated April 11, 1997, effective December 1, 1997; April 30, 2007, effective December 1, 2007.)

RULE 76. JUDGMENT OF THE DISTRICT JUDGE ON THE APPEAL UNDER RULE 73(d) AND COSTS [ABROGATED]

(Former Rule 76 abrogated December 4, 1967, effective July 1, 1968; new Rule 76 adopted April 28, 1983, effective August 1, 1983; amended April 22, 1993, effective December 1, 1993; abrogated April 11, 1997, effective December 1, 1997; April 30, 2007, effective December 1, 2007.)

TITLE X. DISTRICT COURTS AND CLERKS: CONDUCTING BUSINESS; ISSUING ORDERS

RULE 77. CONDUCTING BUSINESS; CLERK'S AUTHORITY; NOTICE OF AN ORDER OR JUDGMENT

(a) When Court Is Open. Every district court is considered always open for filing any paper, issuing and returning process, making a motion, or entering an order.

(b) Place for Trial and Other Proceedings. Every trial on the merits must be conducted in open court and, so far as convenient, in a regular courtroom. Any other act or proceeding may be done or conducted by a judge in chambers, without the attendance of the clerk or other court official, and anywhere inside or outside the district. But no hearing—other than one ex parte—may be conducted outside the district unless all the affected parties consent.

(c) Clerk's Office Hours; Clerk's Orders.

(1) *Hours.* The clerk's office—with a clerk or deputy on duty—must be open during business hours every day except Saturdays, Sundays, and legal holidays. But a court may, by local rule or order, require that the office be open for specified hours on Saturday or a particular legal holiday other than one listed in Rule 6(a)(6)(A).

(2) *Orders.* Subject to the court's power to suspend, alter, or rescind the clerk's action for good cause, the clerk may:

(A) issue process;

(B) enter a default;

(C) enter a default judgment under Rule 55(b)(1); and

(D) act on any other matter that does not require the court's action.

(d) Serving Notice of an Order or Judgment.

(1) *Service.* Immediately after entering an order or judgment, the clerk must serve notice of the entry, as provided in Rule 5(b), on each party who is not in default for failing to appear. The clerk must record the service on the docket. A party also may serve notice of the entry as provided in Rule 5(b).

(2) *Time to Appeal Not Affected by Lack of Notice.* Lack of notice of the entry does not affect the time for appeal or relieve—or authorize the court to relieve—a party for failing to appeal within the time allowed, except as allowed by Federal Rule of Appellate Procedure (4)(a).

(Amended December 27, 1946, effective March 19, 1948; January 21, 1963, effective July 1, 1963; December 4, 1967, effective July 1, 1968; March 1, 1971, effective July 1, 1971; March 2, 1987, effective August 1, 1987; April 30, 1991, effective December 1, 1991; April 23, 2001, effective December 1, 2001; April 30, 2007, effective December 1, 2007; April 25, 2014, effective December 1, 2014.)

RULE 78. HEARING MOTIONS; SUBMISSION ON BRIEFS

(a) Providing a Regular Schedule for Oral Hearings. A court may establish regular times and places for oral hearings on motions.

(b) Providing for Submission on Briefs. By rule or order, the court may provide for submitting and determining motions on briefs, without oral hearings.

(Amended March 2, 1987, effective August 1, 1987; April 30, 2007, effective December 1, 2007.)

RULE 79. RECORDS KEPT BY THE CLERK

(a) Civil Docket.

(1) *In General.* The clerk must keep a record known as the "civil docket" in the form and manner prescribed by the Director of the Administrative Office of the United States Courts with the approval of the Judicial Conference of the United States. The clerk must enter each civil action in the docket. Actions must be assigned consecutive file numbers, which must be noted in the docket where the first entry of the action is made.

(2) *Items to be Entered.* The following items must be marked with the file number and entered chronologically in the docket:

(A) papers filed with the clerk;

(B) process issued, and proofs of service or other returns showing execution; and

(C) appearances, orders, verdicts, and judgments.

(3) *Contents of Entries; Jury Trial Demanded.* Each entry must briefly show the nature of the paper filed or writ issued, the substance of each proof of service or other return, and the substance and date of entry of each order and judgment. When a jury trial has been properly demanded or ordered, the clerk must enter the word "jury" in the docket.

(b) Civil Judgments and Orders. The clerk must keep a copy of every final judgment and appealable order; of every order affecting title to or a lien on real or personal property; and of any other order that the court directs to be kept. The clerk must keep these in the form and manner prescribed by the Director of the Administrative Office of the United States Courts with the approval of the Judicial Conference of the United States.

(c) Indexes; Calendars. Under the court's direction, the clerk must:

(1) keep indexes of the docket and of the judgments and orders described in Rule 79(b); and

(2) prepare calendars of all actions ready for trial, distinguishing jury trials from nonjury trials.

(d) Other Records. The clerk must keep any other records required by the Director of the Administrative Office of the United States Courts with the approval of the Judicial Conference of the United States.

(Amended December 27, 1946, effective March 19, 1948; December 29, 1948, effective October 20, 1949; January 21, 1963, effective July 1, 1963; April 30, 2007, effective December 1, 2007.)

RULE 80. STENOGRAPHIC TRANSCRIPT AS EVIDENCE

If stenographically reported testimony at a hearing or trial is admissible in evidence at a later trial, the testimony may be proved by a transcript certified by the person who reported it.

(Amended December 27, 1946, effective March 19, 1948; April 30, 2007, effective December 1, 2007.)

TITLE XI. GENERAL PROVISIONS

RULE 81. APPLICABILITY OF THE RULES IN GENERAL; REMOVED ACTIONS

(a) Applicability to Particular Proceedings.

(1) *Prize Proceedings.* These rules do not apply to prize proceedings in admiralty governed by 10 U.S.C. §§ 7651–7681.

(2) *Bankruptcy.* These rules apply to bankruptcy proceedings to the extent provided by the Federal Rules of Bankruptcy Procedure.

(3) *Citizenship.* These rules apply to proceedings for admission to citizenship to the extent that the practice in those proceedings is not specified in federal statutes and has previously conformed to the practice in civil actions. The provisions of 8 U.S.C. § 1451 for service by publication and for answer apply in proceedings to cancel citizenship certificates.

(4) *Special Writs.* These rules apply to proceedings for habeas corpus and for quo warranto to the extent that the practice in those proceedings:

(A) is not specified in a federal statute, the Rules Governing Section 2254 Cases, or the Rules Governing Section 2255 Cases; and

(B) has previously conformed to the practice in civil actions.

(5) *Proceedings Involving a Subpoena.* These rules apply to proceedings to compel testimony or the production of documents through a subpoena issued by a United States officer or agency under a federal statute, except as otherwise provided by statute, by local rule, or by court order in the proceedings.

(6) *Other Proceedings.* These rules, to the extent applicable, govern proceedings under the following laws, except as these laws provide other procedures:

(A) 7 U.S.C. §§ 292, 499g(c), for reviewing an order of the Secretary of Agriculture;

(B) 9 U.S.C., relating to arbitration;

(C) 15 U.S.C. § 522, for reviewing an order of the Secretary of the Interior;

(D) 15 U.S.C. § 715d(c), for reviewing an order denying a certificate of clearance;

(E) 29 U.S.C. §§ 159, 160, for enforcing an order of the National Labor Relations Board;

(F) 33 U.S.C. §§ 918, 921, for enforcing or reviewing a compensation order under the Longshore and Harbor Workers' Compensation Act; and

(G) 45 U.S.C. § 159, for reviewing an arbitration award in a railway-labor dispute.

(b) Scire Facias and Mandamus. The writs of scire facias and mandamus are abolished. Relief previously available through them may be obtained by appropriate action or motion under these rules.

(c) Removed Actions.

(1) *Applicability.* These rules apply to a civil action after it is removed from a state court.

(2) *Further Pleading.* After removal, repleading is unnecessary unless the court orders it. A defendant who did not answer before removal must answer or present other defenses or objections under these rules within the longest of these periods:

(A) 21 days after receiving—through service or otherwise—a copy of the initial pleading stating the claim for relief;

(B) 21 days after being served with the summons for an initial pleading on file at the time of service; or

(C) 7 days after the notice of removal is filed.

(3) *Demand for a Jury Trial.*

(A) *As Affected by State Law.* A party who, before removal, expressly demanded a jury trial in accordance with state law need not renew the demand after removal. If the state law did not require an express demand for a jury trial, a party need not make one after removal unless the court orders the parties to do so within a specified time. The court must so order at a party's request and may so order on its own. A party who fails to make a demand when so ordered waives a jury trial.

(B) *Under Rule 38.* If all necessary pleadings have been served at the time of removal, a party entitled to a jury trial under Rule 38 must be given one if the party serves a demand within 14 days after:

(i) it files a notice of removal; or

(ii) it is served with a notice of removal filed by another party.

(d) Law Applicable.

(1) *"State Law" Defined.* When these rules refer to state law, the term "law" includes the state's statutes and the state's judicial decisions.

(2) *"State" Defined.* The term "state" includes, where appropriate, the District of Columbia and any United States commonwealth or territory.

(3) *"Federal Statute" Defined in the District of Columbia.* In the United States District Court for the District of Columbia, the term "federal statute" includes any Act of Congress that applies locally to the District.

(Amended December 28, 1939, effective April 3, 1941; December 27, 1946, effective March 19, 1948; December 29, 1948, effective October 20, 1949; April 30, 1951, effective August 1, 1951; January 21, 1963, effective July 1, 1963; February 28, 1966, effective July 1, 1966; December 4, 1967, effective July 1, 1968; March 1, 1971, effective July 1, 1971; March 2, 1987, effective August 1, 1987; April 23, 2001, effective December 1, 2001; April 29, 2002, effective December 1, 2002; April 30, 2007, effective December 1, 2007; March 26, 2009, effective December 1, 2009.)

RULE 82. JURISDICTION AND VENUE UNAFFECTED

These rules do not extend or limit the jurisdiction of the district courts or the venue of actions in those courts. An admiralty or maritime claim under Rule 9(h) is governed by 28 U.S.C. § 1390.

(Amended December 29, 1948, effective October 20, 1949; February 28, 1966, effective July 1, 1966; April 23, 2001, effective December 1, 2001; April 30, 2007, effective December 1, 2007; April 28, 2016, effective December 1, 2016.)

RULE 83. RULES BY DISTRICT COURTS; JUDGE'S DIRECTIVES

(a) Local Rules.

(1) *In General.* After giving public notice and an opportunity for comment, a district court, acting by a majority of its district judges, may adopt and amend rules governing its practice. A local rule must be consistent with—but not duplicate—federal statutes and rules adopted under 28 U.S.C. §§ 2072 and 2075, and must conform to any uniform numbering system prescribed by the Judicial Conference of the United States. A local rule takes effect on the date specified by the district court and remains in effect unless amended by the court or abrogated by the judicial council of the circuit. Copies of rules and amendments must, on their adoption, be furnished to the judicial council and the Administrative Office of the United States Courts and be made available to the public.

(2) *Requirement of Form.* A local rule imposing a requirement of form must not be enforced in a way that causes a party to lose any right because of a nonwillful failure to comply.

(b) Procedure When There Is No Controlling Law. A judge may regulate practice in any manner consistent with federal law, rules adopted under 28 U.S.C. §§ 2072 and 2075, and the district's local rules. No sanction or other disadvantage may be imposed for noncompliance with any requirement not in federal law, federal rules, or the local rules unless the alleged violator has been furnished in the particular case with actual notice of the requirement.

(Amended April 29, 1985, effective August 1, 1985; April 27, 1995, effective December 1, 1995; April 30, 2007, effective December 1, 2007.)

RULE 84. FORMS [ABROGATED]

(Amended December 27, 1946, effective March 19, 1948; April 30, 2007, effective December 1, 2007; abrogated April 29, 2015, effective December 1, 2015.)

RULE 85. TITLE

These rules may be cited as the Federal Rules of Civil Procedure.

(Amended April 30, 2007, effective December 1, 2007.)

RULE 86. EFFECTIVE DATES

(a) In General. These rules and any amendments take effect at the time specified by the Supreme Court, subject to 28 U.S.C. § 2074. They govern:

(1) proceedings in an action commenced after their effective date; and

(2) proceedings after that date in an action then pending unless:

(A) the Supreme Court specifies otherwise; or

(B) the court determines that applying them in a particular action would be infeasible or work an injustice.

(b) December 1, 2007 Amendments. If any provision in Rules 1–5.1, 6–73, or 77–86 conflicts with another law, priority in time for the purpose of 28 U.S.C. § 2072(b) is not affected by the amendments taking effect on December 1, 2007.

(Amended December 27, 1946, effective March 19, 1948; December 29, 1948, effective October 20, 1949; April 17, 1961, effective July 19, 1961; January 21, 1963, and March 18, 1963, effective July 1, 1963; April 30, 2007, effective December 1, 2007.)

SUPPLEMENTAL RULES FOR ADMIRALTY OR MARITIME CLAIMS AND ASSET FORFEITURE ACTIONS

RULE A. SCOPE OF RULES

(1) These Supplemental Rules apply to:

(A) the procedure in admiralty and maritime claims within the meaning of Rule 9(h) with respect to the following remedies:

(i) maritime attachment and garnishment,

(ii) actions in rem,

(iii) possessory, petitory, and partition actions, and

(iv) actions for exoneration from or limitation of liability;

(B) forfeiture actions in rem arising from a federal statute; and

(C) the procedure in statutory condemnation proceedings analogous to maritime actions in rem, whether within the admiralty and maritime jurisdiction or not. Except as otherwise provided, references in these Supplemental Rules to actions in rem include such analogous statutory condemnation proceedings.

(2) The Federal Rules of Civil Procedure also apply to the foregoing proceedings except to the extent that they are inconsistent with these Supplemental Rules.

(Added Feb. 28, 1966, eff. July 1, 1966; amended Apr. 12, 2006, eff. Dec. 1, 2006.)

RULE B. IN PERSONAM ACTIONS: ATTACHMENT AND GARNISHMENT

(1) When Available; Complaint, Affidavit, Judicial Authorization, and Process. In an in personam action:

(a) If a defendant is not found within the district when a verified complaint praying for attachment and the affidavit required by Rule B(1)(b) are filed, a verified complaint may contain a prayer for process to attach the defendant's tangible or intangible personal property—up to the amount sued for—in the hands of garnishees named in the process.

(b) The plaintiff or the plaintiff's attorney must sign and file with the complaint an affidavit stating that, to the affiant's knowledge, or on information and belief, the defendant cannot be found within the district. The court must review the complaint and affidavit and, if the conditions of this Rule B appear to exist, enter an order so stating and authorizing process of attachment and garnishment. The clerk may issue supplemental process enforcing the court's order upon application without further court order.

(c) If the plaintiff or the plaintiff's attorney certifies that exigent circumstances make court review impracticable, the clerk must issue the summons and process of attachment and garnishment. The plaintiff has the burden in any post-attachment hearing under Rule E(4)(f) to show that exigent circumstances existed.

(d)(i) If the property is a vessel or tangible property on board a vessel, the summons, process, and any supplemental process must be delivered to the marshal for service.

(ii) If the property is other tangible or intangible property, the summons, process, and any supplemental process must be delivered to a person or organization authorized to serve it, who may be (A) a marshal; (B) someone under contract with the United States; (C) someone specially appointed by the court for that purpose; or, (D) in an action brought by the United States, any officer or employee of the United States.

(e) The plaintiff may invoke state-law remedies under Rule 64 for seizure of person or property for the purpose of securing satisfaction of the judgment.

(2) Notice to Defendant. No default judgment may be entered except upon proof—which may be by affidavit—that:

(a) the complaint, summons, and process of attachment or garnishment have been served on the defendant in a manner authorized by Rule 4;

(b) the plaintiff or the garnishee has mailed to the defendant the complaint, summons, and process of attachment or garnishment, using any form of mail requiring a return receipt; or

(c) the plaintiff or the garnishee has tried diligently to give notice of the action to the defendant but could not do so.

(3) Answer.

(a) By Garnishee. The garnishee shall serve an answer, together with answers to any interrogatories served with the complaint, within 21 days after service of process upon the garnishee. Interrogatories to the garnishee may be served with the complaint without leave of court. If the garnishee refuses or neglects to answer on oath as to the debts, credits, or effects of the defendant in the garnishee's hands, or any interrogatories concerning such debts, credits, and effects that may be propounded by the plaintiff, the court may award compulsory process against the garnishee. If the garnishee admits any debts, credits, or effects, they shall be held in the garnishee's hands or paid into the registry of the court, and shall be held in either case subject to the further order of the court.

(b) By Defendant. The defendant shall serve an answer within 30 days after process has been executed, whether by attachment of property or service on the garnishee.

(Added Feb. 28, 1966, eff. July 1, 1966; amended Apr. 29, 1985, eff. Aug. 1, 1985; Mar. 2, 1987, eff. Aug. 1, 1987; Apr. 17, 2000, eff. Dec. 1, 2000; Apr. 25, 2005, eff. Dec. 1, 2005; Mar. 26, 2009, eff. Dec. 1, 2009.)

RULE C. IN REM ACTIONS: SPECIAL PROVISIONS

(1) When Available. An action in rem may be brought:

(a) To enforce any maritime lien;

(b) Whenever a statute of the United States provides for a maritime action in rem or a proceeding analogous thereto.

Except as otherwise provided by law a party who may proceed in rem may also, or in the alternative, proceed in personam against any person who may be liable.

Statutory provisions exempting vessels or other property owned or possessed by or operated by or for the United States from arrest or seizure are not affected by this rule. When a statute so provides, an action against the United States or an instrumentality thereof may proceed on in rem principles.

(2) Complaint. In an action in rem the complaint must:

(a) be verified;

(b) describe with reasonable particularity the property that is the subject of the action; and

(c) state that the property is within the district or will be within the district while the action is pending.

(3) Judicial Authorization and Process.

(a) Arrest Warrant.

(i) The court must review the complaint and any supporting papers. If the conditions for an in rem action appear to exist, the court must issue an order directing the clerk to issue a warrant for the arrest of the vessel or other property that is the subject of the action.

(ii) If the plaintiff or the plaintiff's attorney certifies that exigent circumstances make court review impracticable, the clerk must promptly issue a summons and a warrant for the arrest of the vessel or other property that is the subject of the action. The plaintiff has the burden in any post-arrest hearing under Rule E(4)(f) to show that exigent circumstances existed.

(b) Service.

(i) If the property that is the subject of the action is a vessel or tangible property on board a vessel, the warrant and any supplemental process must be delivered to the marshal for service.

(ii) If the property that is the subject of the action is other property, tangible or intangible, the warrant and any supplemental process must be delivered to a person or organization authorized to enforce it, who may be: (A) a marshal; (B) someone under contract with the United States; (C) someone specially appointed by the court for that purpose; or, (D) in an action brought by the United States, any officer or employee of the United States.

(c) Deposit in Court. If the property that is the subject of the action consists in whole or in part of freight, the proceeds of property sold, or other intangible property, the clerk must issue—in addition to the warrant—a summons directing any person controlling the property to show cause why it should not be deposited in court to abide the judgment.

(d) Supplemental Process. The clerk may upon application issue supplemental process to enforce the court's order without further court order.

(4) Notice. No notice other than execution of process is required when the property that is the subject of the action has been released under Rule E(5). If the property is not released within 14 days after execution, the plaintiff must promptly—or within the time that the court allows—give public notice of the action and arrest in a newspaper designated by court order and having general circulation in the district, but publication may be terminated if the property is released before publication is completed. The notice must specify the time under Rule C(6) to file a statement of interest in or right against the seized property and to answer. This rule does not affect the notice requirements in an action to foreclose a preferred ship mortgage under 46 U.S.C. §§ 31301 et seq., as amended.

(5) Ancillary Process. In any action in rem in which process has been served as provided by this rule, if any part of the property that is the subject of the action has not been brought within the control of the court because it has been removed or sold, or because it is intangible property in the hands of a person who has not been served with process, the court may, on motion, order any person having possession or control of such property or its proceeds to show cause why it should not be delivered into the custody of the marshal or other person or organization having a warrant for the arrest of the property, or paid into court to abide the judgment; and, after hearing, the court may enter such judgment as law and justice may require.

(6) Responsive Pleading; Interrogatories.

(a) Statement of Interest; Answer. In an action in rem:

(i) a person who asserts a right of possession or any ownership interest in the property that is the subject of the action must file a verified statement of right or interest:

(A) within 14 days after the execution of process, or

(B) within the time that the court allows;

(ii) the statement of right or interest must describe the interest in the property that supports the person's demand for its restitution or right to defend the action;

(iii) an agent, bailee, or attorney must state the authority to file a statement of right or interest on behalf of another; and

(iv) a person who asserts a right of possession or any ownership interest must serve an answer within 21 days after filing the statement of interest or right.

(b) Interrogatories. Interrogatories may be served with the complaint in an in rem action without leave of court. Answers to the interrogatories must be served with the answer to the complaint.

(Added Feb. 28, 1966, eff. July 1, 1966; amended Apr. 29, 1985, eff. Aug. 1, 1985; Mar. 2, 1987, eff. Aug. 1, 1987; Apr. 30, 1991, eff. Dec. 1, 1991; Apr. 17, 2000, eff. Dec. 1, 2000; Apr. 29, 2002, eff. Dec. 1, 2002; Apr. 25, 2005, eff. Dec. 1, 2005; Apr. 12, 2006, eff. Dec. 1, 2006; Apr. 23, 2008, eff. Dec. 1, 2008; Mar. 26, 2009, eff. Dec. 1, 2009.)

RULE D. POSSESSORY, PETITORY, AND PARTITION ACTIONS

In all actions for possession, partition, and to try title maintainable according to the course of the admiralty practice with respect to a vessel, in all actions so maintainable with respect to the possession of cargo or other maritime property, and in all actions by one or more part owners against the others to obtain security for the return of the vessel from any voyage undertaken without their consent, or by one or more part owners against the others to obtain possession of the vessel for any voyage on giving security for its safe return, the process shall be by a warrant of arrest of the vessel, cargo, or other property, and by notice in the manner provided by Rule B(2) to the adverse party or parties.

(Added Feb. 28, 1966, eff. July 1, 1966.)

RULE E. ACTIONS IN REM AND QUASI IN REM: GENERAL PROVISIONS

(1) **Applicability.** Except as otherwise provided, this rule applies to actions in personam with process of maritime attachment and garnishment, actions in rem, and petitory, possessory, and partition actions, supplementing Rules B, C, and D.

(2) **Complaint; Security.**

(a) **Complaint.** In actions to which this rule is applicable the complaint shall state the circumstances from which the claim arises with such particularity that the defendant or claimant will be able, without moving for a more definite statement, to commence an investigation of the facts and to frame a responsive pleading.

(b) **Security for Costs.** Subject to the provisions of Rule 54(d) and of relevant statutes, the court may, on the filing of the complaint or on the appearance of any defendant, claimant, or any other party, or at any later time, require the plaintiff, defendant, claimant, or other party to give security, or additional security, in such sum as the court shall direct to pay all costs and expenses that shall be awarded against the party by any interlocutory order or by the final judgment, or on appeal by any appellate court.

(3) **Process.**

(a) In admiralty and maritime proceedings process in rem or of maritime attachment and garnishment may be served only within the district.

(b) **Issuance and Delivery.** Issuance and delivery of process in rem, or of maritime attachment and garnishment, shall be held in abeyance if the plaintiff so requests.

(4) **Execution of Process; Marshal's Return; Custody of Property; Procedures for Release.**

(a) **In General.** Upon issuance and delivery of the process, or, in the case of summons with process of attachment and garnishment, when it appears that the defendant cannot be found within the district, the marshal or other person or organization having a warrant shall forthwith execute the process in accordance with this subdivision (4), making due and prompt return.

(b) **Tangible Property.** If tangible property is to be attached or arrested, the marshal or other person or organization having the warrant shall take it into the marshal's possession for safe custody. If the character or situation of the property is such that the taking of actual possession is impracticable, the marshal or other person executing the process shall affix a copy thereof to the property in a conspicuous place and leave a copy of the complaint and process with the person having possession or the person's agent. In furtherance of the marshal's custody of any vessel the marshal is authorized to make a written request to the collector of customs not to grant clearance to such vessel until notified by the marshal or deputy marshal or by the clerk that the vessel has been released in accordance with these rules.

(c) **Intangible Property.** If intangible property is to be attached or arrested the marshal or other person or organization having the warrant shall execute the process by leaving with the garnishee or other obligor a copy of the complaint and process requiring the garnishee or other obligor to answer as provided in Rules B(3)(a) and C(6); or the marshal may accept for payment into the registry of the court the amount owed to the extent of the amount claimed by the plaintiff with interest and costs, in which event the garnishee or other obligor shall not be required to answer unless alias process shall be served.

(d) **Directions With Respect to Property in Custody.** The marshal or other person or organization having the warrant may at any time apply to the court for directions with respect to property that has been attached or arrested, and shall give notice of such application to any or all of the parties as the court may direct.

(e) **Expenses of Seizing and Keeping Property; Deposit.** These rules do not alter the provisions of Title 28, U.S.C., § 1921, as amended, relative to the expenses of seizing and keeping property attached or arrested and to the requirement of deposits to cover such expenses.

(f) **Procedure for Release From Arrest or Attachment.** Whenever property is arrested or attached, any person claiming an interest in it shall be entitled to a prompt hearing at which the plaintiff shall be required to show why the arrest or attachment should not be vacated or other relief granted consistent with these rules. This subdivision shall have no application to suits for seamen's wages when process is issued upon a certification of sufficient cause filed pursuant to Title 46, U.S.C. §§ 603 and 604 [2] or to actions by the United States for forfeitures for violation of any statute of the United States.

(5) **Release of Property.**

(a) **Special Bond.** Whenever process of maritime attachment and garnishment or process in rem is issued the execution of such process shall be stayed, or the property released, on the giving of security, to be approved by the court or clerk, or by stipulation of the parties, conditioned to answer the judgment of the court or of any appellate court. The parties may stipulate the amount and nature of such security. In the event of the inability or refusal of the parties so to stipulate the court shall fix the principal sum of the bond or stipulation at an amount sufficient to cover the amount of the plaintiff's claim fairly stated with accrued interest and costs; but the principal sum shall in no event exceed (i) twice the amount of the plaintiff's claim or (ii) the value of the property on due appraisement, whichever is smaller. The bond or stipulation shall be conditioned for the payment of the principal sum and interest thereon at 6 per cent per annum.

(b) General Bond. The owner of any vessel may file a general bond or stipulation, with sufficient surety, to be approved by the court, conditioned to answer the judgment of such court in all or any actions that may be brought thereafter in such court in which the vessel is attached or arrested. Thereupon the execution of all such process against such vessel shall be stayed so long as the amount secured by such bond or stipulation is at least double the aggregate amount claimed by plaintiffs in all actions begun and pending in which such vessel has been attached or arrested. Judgments and remedies may be had on such bond or stipulation as if a special bond or stipulation had been filed in each of such actions. The district court may make necessary orders to carry this rule into effect, particularly as to the giving of proper notice of any action against or attachment of a vessel for which a general bond has been filed. Such bond or stipulation shall be indorsed by the clerk with a minute of the actions wherein process is so stayed. Further security may be required by the court at any time.

If a special bond or stipulation is given in a particular case, the liability on the general bond or stipulation shall cease as to that case.

(c) Release by Consent or Stipulation; Order of Court or Clerk; Costs. Any vessel, cargo, or other property in the custody of the marshal or other person or organization having the warrant may be released forthwith upon the marshal's acceptance and approval of a stipulation, bond, or other security, signed by the party on whose behalf the property is detained or the party's attorney and expressly authorizing such release, if all costs and charges of the court and its officers shall have first been paid. Otherwise no property in the custody of the marshal, other person or organization having the warrant, or other officer of the court shall be released without an order of the court; but such order may be entered as of course by the clerk, upon the giving of approved security as provided by law and these rules, or upon the dismissal or discontinuance of the action; but the marshal or other person or organization having the warrant shall not deliver any property so released until the costs and charges of the officers of the court shall first have been paid.

(d) Possessory, Petitory, and Partition Actions. The foregoing provisions of this subdivision (5) do not apply to petitory, possessory, and partition actions. In such cases the property arrested shall be released only by order of the court, on such terms and conditions and on the giving of such security as the court may require.

(6) Reduction or Impairment of Security. Whenever security is taken the court may, on motion and hearing, for good cause shown, reduce the amount of security given; and if the surety shall be or become insufficient, new or additional sureties may be required on motion and hearing.

(7) Security on Counterclaim.

(a) When a person who has given security for damages in the original action asserts a counterclaim that arises from the transaction or occurrence that is the subject of the original action, a plaintiff for whose benefit the security has been given must give security for damages demanded in the counterclaim unless the court, for cause shown, directs otherwise. Proceedings on the original claim must be stayed until this security is given, unless the court directs otherwise.

(b) The plaintiff is required to give security under Rule E(7)(a) when the United States or its corporate instrumentality counterclaims and would have been required to give security to respond in damages if a private party but is relieved by law from giving security.

(8) Restricted Appearance. An appearance to defend against an admiralty and maritime claim with respect to which there has issued process in rem, or process of attachment and garnishment, may be expressly restricted to the defense of such claim, and in that event is not an appearance for the purposes of any other claim with respect to which such process is not available or has not been served.

(9) Disposition of Property; Sales.

(a) Interlocutory Sales; Delivery.

(i) On application of a party, the marshal, or other person having custody of the property, the court may order all or part of the property sold—with the sales proceeds, or as much of them as will satisfy the judgment, paid into court to await further orders of the court—if:

(A) the attached or arrested property is perishable, or liable to deterioration, decay, or injury by being detained in custody pending the action;

(B) the expense of keeping the property is excessive or disproportionate; or

(C) there is an unreasonable delay in securing release of the property.

(ii) In the circumstances described in Rule E(9)(a)(i), the court, on motion by a defendant or a person filing a statement of interest or right under Rule C(6), may order that the property, rather than being sold, be delivered to the movant upon giving security under these rules.

(b) Sales, Proceeds. All sales of property shall be made by the marshal or a deputy marshal, or by other person or organization having the warrant, or by any other person assigned by the court where the marshal or other person or organization having the warrant is a party in interest; and the proceeds of sale shall be forthwith paid into the registry of the court to be disposed of according to law.

(10) Preservation of Property. When the owner or another person remains in possession of property attached or arrested under the provisions of Rule E(4)(b) that permit execution of process without taking actual possession, the court, on a party's motion or on its own, may enter any order necessary to preserve the property and to prevent its removal.

(Added Feb. 28, 1966, eff. July 1, 1966; amended Apr. 29, 1985, eff. Aug. 1, 1985; Mar. 2, 1987, eff. Aug. 1, 1987; Apr. 30, 1991, eff. Dec. 1, 1991; Apr. 17, 2000, eff. Dec. 1, 2000; Apr. 12, 2006, eff. Dec. 1, 2006.)

2 Repealed by Pub.L. 98–89, § 4(b), Aug. 26, 1983, 97 Stat. 600, section 1 of which enacted Title 46, Shipping.

RULE F. LIMITATION OF LIABILITY

(1) Time for Filing Complaint; Security. Not later than six months after receipt of a claim in writing, any vessel owner may file a complaint in the appropriate district court, as provided in subdivision (9) of this rule, for limitation of liability pursuant to statute. The owner (a) shall deposit with the court, for the benefit of claimants, a sum equal to the amount or value of the owner's interest in the vessel and pending freight, or approved security therefor, and in addition such sums, or approved security therefor, as the court may from time to time fix as necessary to carry out the provisions of the statutes as amended; or (b) at the owner's option shall transfer to a trustee to be appointed by the court, for the benefit of claimants, the owner's interest in the vessel and pending freight, together with such sums, or approved security therefor, as the court may from time to time fix as necessary to carry out the provisions of the statutes as amended. The plaintiff shall also give security for costs and, if the plaintiff elects to give security, for interest at the rate of 6 percent per annum from the date of the security.

(2) Complaint. The complaint shall set forth the facts on the basis of which the right to limit liability is asserted and all facts necessary to enable the court to determine the amount to which the owner's liability shall be limited. The complaint may demand exoneration from as well as limitation of liability. It shall state the voyage if any, on which the demands sought to be limited arose, with the date and place of its termination; the amount of all demands including all unsatisfied liens or claims of lien, in contract or in tort or otherwise, arising on that voyage, so far as known to the plaintiff, and what actions and proceedings, if any, are pending thereon; whether the vessel was damaged, lost, or abandoned, and, if so, when and where; the value of the vessel at the close of the voyage or, in case of wreck, the value of her wreckage, strippings, or proceeds, if any, and where and in whose possession they are; and the amount of any pending freight recovered or recoverable. If the plaintiff elects to transfer the plaintiff's interest in the vessel to a trustee, the complaint must further show any prior paramount liens thereon, and what voyages or trips, if any, she has made since the voyage or trip on which the claims sought to be limited arose, and any existing liens arising upon any such subsequent voyage or trip, with the amounts and causes thereof, and the names and addresses of the lienors, so far as known; and whether the vessel sustained any injury upon or by reason of such subsequent voyage or trip.

(3) Claims Against Owner; Injunction. Upon compliance by the owner with the requirements of subdivision (1) of this rule all claims and proceedings against the owner or the owner's property with respect to the matter in question shall cease. On application of the plaintiff the court shall enjoin the further prosecution of any action or proceeding against the plaintiff or the plaintiff's property with respect to any claim subject to limitation in the action.

(4) Notice to Claimants. Upon the owner's compliance with subdivision (1) of this rule the court shall issue a notice to all persons asserting claims with respect to which the complaint seeks limitation, admonishing them to file their respective claims with the clerk of the court and to serve on the attorneys for the plaintiff a copy thereof on or before a date to be named in the notice. The date so fixed shall not be less than 30 days after issuance of the notice. For cause shown, the court may enlarge the time within which claims may be filed. The notice shall be published in such newspaper or newspapers as the court may direct once a week for four successive weeks prior to the date fixed for the filing of claims. The plaintiff not later than the day of second publication shall also mail a copy of the notice to every person known to have made any claim against the vessel or the plaintiff arising out of the voyage or trip on which the claims sought to be limited arose. In cases involving death a copy of such notice shall be mailed to the decedent at the decedent's last known address, and also to any person who shall be known to have made any claim on account of such death.

(5) Claims and Answer. Claims shall be filed and served on or before the date specified in the notice provided for in subdivision (4) of this rule. Each claim shall specify the facts upon which the claimant relies in support of the claim, the items thereof, and the dates on which the same accrued. If a claimant desires to contest either the right to exoneration from or the right to limitation of liability the claimant shall file and serve an answer to the complaint unless the claim has included an answer.

(6) Information to be Given Claimants. Within 30 days after the date specified in the notice for filing claims, or within such time as the court thereafter may allow, the plaintiff shall mail to the attorney for each claimant (or if the claimant has no attorney to the claimant) a list setting forth (a) the name of each claimant, (b) the name and address of the claimant's attorney (if the claimant is known to have one), (c) the nature of the claim, i.e., whether property loss, property damage, death, personal injury etc., and (d) the amount thereof.

(7) Insufficiency of Fund or Security. Any claimant may by motion demand that the funds deposited in court or the security given by the plaintiff be increased on the ground that they are less than the value of the plaintiff's interest in the vessel and pending freight. Thereupon the court shall cause due appraisement to be made of the value of the plaintiff's interest in the vessel and pending freight; and if the court finds that the deposit or security is either insufficient or excessive it shall order its increase or reduction. In like manner any claimant may demand that the deposit or security be increased on the ground that it is insufficient to carry out the provisions of the statutes relating to claims in respect of loss of life or bodily injury; and, after notice and hearing, the court may similarly order that the deposit or security be increased or reduced.

(8) Objections to Claims: Distribution of Fund. Any interested party may question or controvert any claim without filing an objection thereto. Upon determination of liability the fund deposited or secured, or the proceeds of the vessel and pending freight, shall be divided pro rata, subject to all relevant provisions of law, among the several claimants in proportion to the amounts of their respective claims, duly proved, saving, however, to all parties any priority to which they may be legally entitled.

(9) Venue; Transfer. The complaint shall be filed in any district in which the vessel has been attached or arrested to answer for any claim with respect to which the plaintiff seeks to limit liability; or, if the vessel has not been attached or arrested, then in any district in which the owner has been sued with respect to any such claim. When the vessel has not been attached or arrested to answer the matters aforesaid, and suit has not been commenced against the owner, the proceedings may be had in the district in which the vessel may be, but if the vessel is not within any district and no suit has been commenced in any district, then the complaint may be filed in any district. For the convenience of parties and witnesses, in the interest of justice, the court may transfer the action to any district; if venue is wrongly laid the court shall dismiss or, if it be in the interest of justice, transfer the action to any district in which it could have been brought. If the vessel shall have been sold, the proceeds shall represent the vessel for the purposes of these rules.

(Added Feb. 28, 1966, eff. July 1, 1966; amended Mar. 2, 1987, eff. Aug. 1, 1987.)

RULE G. FORFEITURE ACTIONS IN REM

(1) Scope. This rule governs a forfeiture action in rem arising from a federal statute. To the extent that this rule does not address an issue, Supplemental Rules C and E and the Federal Rules of Civil Procedure also apply.

(2) Complaint. The complaint must:

(a) be verified;

(b) state the grounds for subject-matter jurisdiction, in rem jurisdiction over the defendant property, and venue;

(c) describe the property with reasonable particularity;

(d) if the property is tangible, state its location when any seizure occurred and—if different—its location when the action is filed;

(e) identify the statute under which the forfeiture action is brought; and

(f) state sufficiently detailed facts to support a reasonable belief that the government will be able to meet its burden of proof at trial.

(3) Judicial Authorization and Process.

(a) **Real Property.** If the defendant is real property, the government must proceed under 18 U.S.C. § 985.

(b) **Other Property; Arrest Warrant.** If the defendant is not real property:

(i) the clerk must issue a warrant to arrest the property if it is in the government's possession, custody, or control;

(ii) the court—on finding probable cause—must issue a warrant to arrest the property if it is not in the government's possession, custody, or control and is not subject to a judicial restraining order; and

(iii) a warrant is not necessary if the property is subject to a judicial restraining order.

(c) **Execution of Process.**

(i) The warrant and any supplemental process must be delivered to a person or organization authorized to execute it, who may be: (A) a marshal or any other United States officer or employee; (B) someone under contract with the United States; or (C) someone specially appointed by the court for that purpose.

(ii) The authorized person or organization must execute the warrant and any supplemental process on property in the United States as soon as practicable unless:

(A) the property is in the government's possession, custody, or control; or

(B) the court orders a different time when the complaint is under seal, the action is stayed before the warrant and supplemental process are executed, or the court finds other good cause.

(iii) The warrant and any supplemental process may be executed within the district or, when authorized by statute, outside the district.

(iv) If executing a warrant on property outside the United States is required, the warrant may be transmitted to an appropriate authority for serving process where the property is located.

(4) Notice.

(a) **Notice by Publication.**

(i) **When Publication Is Required.** A judgment of forfeiture may be entered only if the government has published notice of the action within a reasonable time after filing the complaint or at a time the court orders. But notice need not be published if:

(A) the defendant property is worth less than $1,000 and direct notice is sent under Rule G(4)(b) to every person the government can reasonably identify as a potential claimant; or

(B) the court finds that the cost of publication exceeds the property's value and that other means of notice would satisfy due process.

(ii) **Content of the Notice.** Unless the court orders otherwise, the notice must:

(A) describe the property with reasonable particularity;

(B) state the times under Rule G(5) to file a claim and to answer; and

(C) name the government attorney to be served with the claim and answer.

(iii) **Frequency of Publication.** Published notice must appear:

(A) once a week for three consecutive weeks; or

(B) only once if, before the action was filed, notice of nonjudicial forfeiture of the same property was published on an official internet government forfeiture site for at least 30 consecutive days, or in a newspaper of general circulation for three consecutive weeks in a district where publication is authorized under Rule G(4)(a)(iv).

(iv) **Means of Publication.** The government should select from the following options a means of publication reasonably calculated to notify potential claimants of the action:

(A) if the property is in the United States, publication in a newspaper generally circulated in the district where the action is filed, where the property was seized, or where property that was not seized is located;

(B) if the property is outside the United States, publication in a newspaper generally circulated in a district where the action is filed, in a newspaper generally circulated in the country where the property is located, or in legal notices published and generally circulated in the country where the property is located; or

(C) instead of (A) or (B), posting a notice on an official internet government forfeiture site for at least 30 consecutive days.

(b) Notice to Known Potential Claimants.

(i) Direct Notice Required. The government must send notice of the action and a copy of the complaint to any person who reasonably appears to be a potential claimant on the facts known to the government before the end of the time for filing a claim under Rule G(5)(a)(ii)(B).

(ii) Content of the Notice. The notice must state:

(A) the date when the notice is sent;

(B) a deadline for filing a claim, at least 35 days after the notice is sent;

(C) that an answer or a motion under Rule 12 must be filed no later than 21 days after filing the claim; and

(D) the name of the government attorney to be served with the claim and answer.

(iii) Sending Notice.

(A) The notice must be sent by means reasonably calculated to reach the potential claimant.

(B) Notice may be sent to the potential claimant or to the attorney representing the potential claimant with respect to the seizure of the property or in a related investigation, administrative forfeiture proceeding, or criminal case.

(C) Notice sent to a potential claimant who is incarcerated must be sent to the place of incarceration.

(D) Notice to a person arrested in connection with an offense giving rise to the forfeiture who is not incarcerated when notice is sent may be sent to the address that person last gave to the agency that arrested or released the person.

(E) Notice to a person from whom the property was seized who is not incarcerated when notice is sent may be sent to the last address that person gave to the agency that seized the property.

(iv) When Notice Is Sent. Notice by the following means is sent on the date when it is placed in the mail, delivered to a commercial carrier, or sent by electronic mail.

(v) Actual Notice. A potential claimant who had actual notice of a forfeiture action may not oppose or seek relief from forfeiture because of the government's failure to send the required notice.

(5) Responsive Pleadings.

(a) Filing a Claim.

(i) A person who asserts an interest in the defendant property may contest the forfeiture by filing a claim in the court where the action is pending. The claim must:

(A) identify the specific property claimed;

(B) identify the claimant and state the claimant's interest in the property;

(C) be signed by the claimant under penalty of perjury; and

(D) be served on the government attorney designated under Rule G(4)(a)(ii)(C) or (b)(ii)(D).

(ii) Unless the court for good cause sets a different time, the claim must be filed:

(A) by the time stated in a direct notice sent under Rule G(4)(b);

(B) if notice was published but direct notice was not sent to the claimant or the claimant's attorney, no later than 30 days after final publication of newspaper notice or legal notice under Rule G(4)(a) or no later than 60 days after the first day of publication on an official internet government forfeiture site; or

(C) if notice was not published and direct notice was not sent to the claimant or the claimant's attorney:

(1) if the property was in the government's possession, custody, or control when the complaint was filed, no later than 60 days after the filing, not counting any time when the complaint was under seal or when the action was stayed before execution of a warrant issued under Rule G(3)(b); or

(2) if the property was not in the government's possession, custody, or control when the complaint was filed, no later than 60 days after the government complied with 18 U.S.C. § 985(c) as to real property, or 60 days after process was executed on the property under Rule G(3).

(iii) A claim filed by a person asserting an interest as a bailee must identify the bailor, and if filed on the bailor's behalf must state the authority to do so.

(b) Answer. A claimant must serve and file an answer to the complaint or a motion under Rule 12 within 21 days after filing the claim. A claimant waives an objection to in rem jurisdiction or to venue if the objection is not made by motion or stated in the answer.

(6) Special Interrogatories.

(a) Time and Scope. The government may serve special interrogatories limited to the claimant's identity and relationship to the defendant property without the court's leave at any time after the claim is filed and before discovery is closed. But if the claimant serves a motion to dismiss the action, the government must serve the interrogatories within 21 days after the motion is served.

(b) Answers or Objections. Answers or objections to these interrogatories must be served within 21 days after the interrogatories are served.

(c) Government's Response Deferred. The government need not respond to a claimant's motion to dismiss the action under Rule G(8)(b) until 21 days after the claimant has answered these interrogatories.

(7) Preserving, Preventing Criminal Use, and Disposing of Property; Sales.

(a) Preserving and Preventing Criminal Use of Property. When the government does not have actual possession of the defendant property the court, on motion or on its own, may enter any order necessary to preserve the property, to prevent its removal or encumbrance, or to prevent its use in a criminal offense.

(b) Interlocutory Sale or Delivery.

(i) Order to Sell. On motion by a party or a person having custody of the property, the court may order all or part of the property sold if:

(A) the property is perishable or at risk of deterioration, decay, or injury by being detained in custody pending the action;

(B) the expense of keeping the property is excessive or is disproportionate to its fair market value;

(C) the property is subject to a mortgage or to taxes on which the owner is in default; or

(D) the court finds other good cause.

(ii) Who Makes the Sale. A sale must be made by a United States agency that has authority to sell the property, by the agency's contractor, or by any person the court designates.

(iii) Sale Procedures. The sale is governed by 28 U.S.C. §§ 2001, 2002, and 2004, unless all parties, with the court's approval, agree to the sale, aspects of the sale, or different procedures.

(iv) Sale Proceeds. Sale proceeds are a substitute res subject to forfeiture in place of the property that was sold. The proceeds must be held in an interest-bearing account maintained by the United States pending the conclusion of the forfeiture action.

(v) Delivery on a Claimant's Motion. The court may order that the property be delivered to the claimant pending the conclusion of the action if the claimant shows circumstances that would permit sale under Rule G(7)(b)(i) and gives security under these rules.

(c) Disposing of Forfeited Property. Upon entry of a forfeiture judgment, the property or proceeds from selling the property must be disposed of as provided by law.

(8) Motions.

(a) Motion To Suppress Use of the Property as Evidence. If the defendant property was seized, a party with standing to contest the lawfulness of the seizure may move to suppress use of the property as evidence. Suppression does not affect forfeiture of the property based on independently derived evidence.

(b) Motion To Dismiss the Action.

(i) A claimant who establishes standing to contest forfeiture may move to dismiss the action under Rule 12(b).

(ii) In an action governed by 18 U.S.C. § 983(a)(3)(D) the complaint may not be dismissed on the ground that the government did not have adequate evidence at the time the complaint was filed to establish the forfeitability of the property. The sufficiency of the complaint is governed by Rule G(2).

(c) Motion To Strike a Claim or Answer.

(i) At any time before trial, the government may move to strike a claim or answer:

(A) for failing to comply with Rule G(5) or (6), or

(B) because the claimant lacks standing.

(ii) The motion:

(A) must be decided before any motion by the claimant to dismiss the action; and

(B) may be presented as a motion for judgment on the pleadings or as a motion to determine after a hearing or by summary judgment whether the claimant can carry the burden of establishing standing by a preponderance of the evidence.

(d) Petition To Release Property.

(i) If a United States agency or an agency's contractor holds property for judicial or nonjudicial forfeiture under a statute governed by 18 U.S.C. § 983(f), a person who has filed a claim to the property may petition for its release under § 983(f).

(ii) If a petition for release is filed before a judicial forfeiture action is filed against the property, the petition may be filed either in the district where the property was seized or in the district where a warrant to seize the property issued. If a judicial forfeiture action against the property is later filed in another district—or if the government shows that the action will be filed in another district—the petition may be transferred to that district under 28 U.S.C. § 1404.

(e) Excessive Fines. A claimant may seek to mitigate a forfeiture under the Excessive Fines Clause of the Eighth Amendment by motion for summary judgment or by motion made after entry of a forfeiture judgment if:

(i) the claimant has pleaded the defense under Rule 8; and

(ii) the parties have had the opportunity to conduct civil discovery on the defense.

(9) Trial. Trial is to the court unless any party demands trial by jury under Rule 38.

(Added Apr. 12, 2006, eff. Dec. 1, 2006; amended Mar. 26, 2009, eff. Dec. 1, 2009.)

INDEX TO
FEDERAL RULES OF CIVIL PROCEDURE

FEDERAL RULES OF EVIDENCE

Including Amendments Effective December 1, 2020

ARTICLE I. GENERAL PROVISIONS

RULE 101. SCOPE; DEFINITIONS

(a) Scope. These rules apply to proceedings in United States courts. The specific courts and proceedings to which the rules apply, along with exceptions, are set out in Rule 1101.

(b) Definitions. In these rules:

(1) "civil case" means a civil action or proceeding;

(2) "criminal case" includes a criminal proceeding;

(3) "public office" includes a public agency;

(4) "record" includes a memorandum, report, or data compilation;

(5) a "rule prescribed by the Supreme Court" means a rule adopted by the Supreme Court under statutory authority; and

(6) a reference to any kind of written material or any other medium includes electronically stored information.

(Pub.L. 93–595, § 1, Jan. 2, 1975, 88 Stat. 1929; Mar. 2, 1987, eff. Oct. 1, 1987; Apr. 25, 1988, eff. Nov. 1, 1988; Apr. 22, 1993, eff. Dec. 1, 1993; Apr. 26, 2011, eff. Dec. 1, 2011.)

RULE 102. PURPOSE

These rules should be construed so as to administer every proceeding fairly, eliminate unjustifiable expense and delay, and promote the development of evidence law, to the end of ascertaining the truth and securing a just determination.

(Pub.L. 93–595, § 1, Jan. 2, 1975, 88 Stat.1929; Apr. 26, 2011, eff. Dec. 1, 2011.)

RULE 103. RULINGS ON EVIDENCE

(a) Preserving a Claim of Error. A party may claim error in a ruling to admit or exclude evidence only if the error affects a substantial right of the party and:

(1) if the ruling admits evidence, a party, on the record:

(A) timely objects or moves to strike; and

(B) states the specific ground, unless it was apparent from the context; or

(2) if the ruling excludes evidence, a party informs the court of its substance by an offer of proof, unless the substance was apparent from the context.

(b) Not Needing to Renew an Objection or Offer of Proof. Once the court rules definitively on the record—either before or at trial—a party need not renew an objection or offer of proof to preserve a claim of error for appeal.

(c) Court's Statement About the Ruling; Directing an Offer of Proof. The court may make any statement about the character or form of the evidence, the objection made, and the ruling. The court may direct that an offer of proof be made in question-and-answer form.

(d) Preventing the Jury from Hearing Inadmissible Evidence. To the extent practicable, the court must conduct a jury trial so that inadmissible evidence is not suggested to the jury by any means.

(e) Taking Notice of Plain Error. A court may take notice of a plain error affecting a substantial right, even if the claim of error was not properly preserved.

(Pub.L. 93–595, § 1, Jan. 2, 1975, 88 Stat. 1929; Apr. 17, 2000, eff. Dec. 1, 2000; Apr. 26, 2011, eff. Dec. 1, 2011.)

RULE 104. PRELIMINARY QUESTIONS

(a) In General. The court must decide any preliminary question about whether a witness is qualified, a privilege exists, or evidence is admissible. In so deciding, the court is not bound by evidence rules, except those on privilege.

(b) Relevance That Depends on a Fact. When the relevance of evidence depends on whether a fact exists, proof must be introduced sufficient to support a finding that the fact does exist. The court may admit the proposed evidence on the condition that the proof be introduced later.

(c) Conducting a Hearing So That the Jury Cannot Hear It. The court must conduct any hearing on a preliminary question so that the jury cannot hear it if:

(1) the hearing involves the admissibility of a confession;

(2) a defendant in a criminal case is a witness and so requests; or

(3) justice so requires.

(d) Cross–Examining a Defendant in a Criminal Case. By testifying on a preliminary question, a defendant in a criminal case does not become subject to cross-examination on other issues in the case.

(e) Evidence Relevant to Weight and Credibility. This rule does not limit a party's right to introduce before the jury evidence that is relevant to the weight or credibility of other evidence.

(Pub.L. 93–595, § 1, Jan. 2, 1975, 88 Stat.1930; Mar. 2, 1987, eff. Oct. 1, 1987; Apr. 26, 2011, eff. Dec. 1, 2011.)

RULE 105. LIMITING EVIDENCE THAT IS NOT ADMISSIBLE AGAINST OTHER PARTIES OR FOR OTHER PURPOSES

If the court admits evidence that is admissible against a party or for a purpose—but not against another party or for another purpose—the court, on timely request, must restrict the evidence to its proper scope and instruct the jury accordingly.

(Pub.L. 93–595, § 1, Jan. 2, 1975, 88 Stat. 1930; Apr. 26, 2011, eff. Dec. 1, 2011.)

RULE 106. REMAINDER OF OR RELATED WRITINGS OR RECORDED STATEMENTS

If a party introduces all or part of a writing or recorded statement, an adverse party may require the introduction, at that time, of any other part—or any other writing or recorded statement—that in fairness ought to be considered at the same time.

(Pub.L. 93–595, § 1, Jan. 2, 1975, 88 Stat. 1930; Mar. 2, 1987, eff. Oct. 1, 1987; Apr. 26, 2011, eff. Dec. 1, 2011.)

ARTICLE II. JUDICIAL NOTICE

RULE 201. JUDICIAL NOTICE OF ADJUDICATIVE FACTS

(a) Scope. This rule governs judicial notice of an adjudicative fact only, not a legislative fact.

(b) Kinds of Facts That May Be Judicially Noticed. The court may judicially notice a fact that is not subject to reasonable dispute because it:

(1) is generally known within the trial court's territorial jurisdiction; or

(2) can be accurately and readily determined from sources whose accuracy cannot reasonably be questioned.

(c) Taking Notice. The court:

(1) may take judicial notice on its own; or

(2) must take judicial notice if a party requests it and the court is supplied with the necessary information.

(d) Timing. The court may take judicial notice at any stage of the proceeding.

(e) Opportunity to Be Heard. On timely request, a party is entitled to be heard on the propriety of taking judicial notice and the nature of the fact to be noticed. If the court takes judicial notice before notifying a party, the party, on request, is still entitled to be heard.

(f) Instructing the Jury. In a civil case, the court must instruct the jury to accept the noticed fact as conclusive. In a criminal case, the court must instruct the jury that it may or may not accept the noticed fact as conclusive.

(Pub.L. 93–595, § 1, Jan. 2, 1975, 88 Stat. 1930; Apr. 26, 2011, eff. Dec. 1, 2011.)

ARTICLE III. PRESUMPTIONS IN CIVIL CASES

RULE 301. PRESUMPTIONS IN CIVIL CASES GENERALLY

In a civil case, unless a federal statute or these rules provide otherwise, the party against whom a presumption is directed has the burden of producing evidence to rebut the presumption. But this rule does not shift the burden of persuasion, which remains on the party who had it originally.

(Pub.L. 93–595, § 1, Jan. 2, 1975, 88 Stat. 1931; Apr. 26, 2011, eff. Dec. 1, 2011.)

RULE 302. APPLYING STATE LAW TO PRESUMPTIONS IN CIVIL CASES

In a civil case, state law governs the effect of a presumption regarding a claim or defense for which state law supplies the rule of decision.

(Pub.L. 93–595, § 1, Jan. 2, 1975, 88 Stat. 1931; Apr. 26, 2011, eff. Dec. 1, 2011.)

ARTICLE IV. RELEVANCE AND ITS LIMITS

RULE 401. TEST FOR RELEVANT EVIDENCE

Evidence is relevant if:

(a) it has any tendency to make a fact more or less probable than it would be without the evidence; and

(b) the fact is of consequence in determining the action.

(Pub.L. 93–595, § 1, Jan. 2, 1975, 88 Stat.1931; Apr. 26, 2011, eff. Dec. 1, 2011.)

RULE 402. GENERAL ADMISSIBILITY OF RELEVANT EVIDENCE

Relevant evidence is admissible unless any of the following provides otherwise:

- the United States Constitution;
- a federal statute;
- these rules; or
- other rules prescribed by the Supreme Court.

Irrelevant evidence is not admissible.

(Pub.L. 93–595, § 1, Jan. 2, 1975, 88 Stat. 1931; Apr. 26, 2011, eff. Dec. 1, 2011.)

RULE 403. EXCLUDING RELEVANT EVIDENCE FOR PREJUDICE, CONFUSION, WASTE OF TIME, OR OTHER REASONS

The court may exclude relevant evidence if its probative value is substantially outweighed by a danger of one or more of the following: unfair prejudice, confusing the issues, misleading the jury, undue delay, wasting time, or needlessly presenting cumulative evidence.

(Pub.L. 93–595, § 1, Jan. 2, 1975, 88 Stat. 1932; Apr. 26, 2011, eff. Dec. 1, 2011.)

RULE 404. CHARACTER EVIDENCE; OTHER CRIMES, WRONGS OR ACTS

(a) Character Evidence.

(1) Prohibited Uses. Evidence of a person's character or character trait is not admissible to prove that on a particular occasion the person acted in accordance with the character or trait.

(2) Exceptions for a Defendant or Victim in a Criminal Case. The following exceptions apply in a criminal case:

(A) a defendant may offer evidence of the defendant's pertinent trait, and if the evidence is admitted, the prosecutor may offer evidence to rebut it;

(B) subject to the limitations in Rule 412, a defendant may offer evidence of an alleged victim's pertinent trait, and if the evidence is admitted, the prosecutor may:

(i) offer evidence to rebut it; and

(ii) offer evidence of the defendant's same trait; and

(C) in a homicide case, the prosecutor may offer evidence of the alleged victim's trait of peacefulness to rebut evidence that the victim was the first aggressor.

(3) Exceptions for a Witness. Evidence of a witness's character may be admitted under Rules 607, 608, and 609.

(b) Other Crimes, Wrongs, or Acts.

(1) Prohibited Uses. Evidence of any other crime, wrong, or act is not admissible to prove a person's character in order to show that on a particular occasion the person acted in accordance with the character.

(2) Permitted Uses. This evidence may be admissible for another purpose, such as proving motive, opportunity, intent, preparation, plan, knowledge, identity, absence of mistake, or lack of accident.

(3) Notice in a Criminal Case. In a criminal case, the prosecutor must:

(A) provide reasonable notice of any such evidence that the prosecutor intends to offer at trial, so that the defendant has a fair opportunity to meet it;

(B) articulate in the notice the permitted purpose for which the prosecutor intends to offer the evidence and the reasoning that supports the purpose; and

(C) do so in writing before trial—or in any form during trial if the court, for good cause, excuses lack of pretrial notice.

(Pub.L. 93–595, § 1, Jan. 2, 1975, 88 Stat.1932; Mar. 2, 1987, eff. Oct. 1, 1987; Apr. 30, 1991, eff. Dec. 1, 1991; Apr. 17, 2000, eff. Dec. 1, 2000; Apr. 12, 2006, eff. Dec. 1, 2006; Apr. 26, 2011, eff. Dec. 1, 2011; Apr. 27, 2020, eff. Dec. 1, 2020.)

RULE 405. METHODS OF PROVING CHARACTER

(a) By Reputation or Opinion. When evidence of a person's character or character trait is admissible, it may be proved by testimony about the person's reputation or by testimony in the form of an opinion. On cross-examination of the character witness, the court may allow an inquiry into relevant specific instances of the person's conduct.

(b) By Specific Instances of Conduct. When a person's character or character trait is an essential element of a charge, claim, or defense, the character or trait may also be proved by relevant specific instances of the person's conduct.

(Pub.L. 93–595, § 1, Jan. 2, 1975, 88 Stat. 1932; Mar. 2, 1987, eff. Oct. 1, 1987; Apr. 26, 2011, eff. Dec. 1, 2011.)

RULE 406. HABIT; ROUTINE PRACTICE

Evidence of a person's habit or an organization's routine practice may be admitted to prove that on a particular occasion the person or organization acted in accordance with the habit or routine practice. The court may admit this evidence regardless of whether it is corroborated or whether there was an eyewitness.

(Pub.L. 93–595, § 1, Jan. 2, 1975, 88 Stat. 1932; Apr. 26, 2011, eff. Dec. 1, 2011.)

RULE 407. SUBSEQUENT REMEDIAL MEASURES

When measures are taken that would have made an earlier injury or harm less likely to occur, evidence of the subsequent measures is not admissible to prove:

- negligence;
- culpable conduct;
- a defect in a product or its design; or
- a need for a warning or instruction.

But the court may admit this evidence for another purpose, such as impeachment or—if disputed—proving ownership, control, or the feasibility of precautionary measures.

(Pub.L. 93–595, § 1, Jan. 2, 1975, 88 Stat. 1932; Apr. 11, 1997, eff. Dec. 1, 1997; Apr. 26, 2011, eff. Dec. 1, 2011.)

RULE 408. COMPROMISE OFFERS AND NEGOTIATIONS

(a) Prohibited Uses. Evidence of the following is not admissible—on behalf of any party—either to prove or disprove the validity or amount of a disputed claim or to impeach by a prior inconsistent statement or a contradiction:

(1) furnishing, promising, or offering—or accepting, promising to accept, or offering to accept—a valuable consideration in compromising or attempting to compromise the claim; and

(2) conduct or a statement made during compromise negotiations about the claim—except when offered in a criminal case and when the negotiations related to a claim by a public office in the exercise of its regulatory, investigative, or enforcement authority.

(b) Exceptions. The court may admit this evidence for another purpose, such as proving a witness's bias or prejudice, negating a contention of undue delay, or proving an effort to obstruct a criminal investigation or prosecution.

(Pub.L. 93–595, § 1, Jan. 2, 1975, 88 Stat. 1933; Apr. 12, 2006, eff. Dec. 1, 2006; Apr. 26, 2011, eff. Dec. 1, 2011.)

RULE 409. OFFERS TO PAY MEDICAL AND SIMILAR EXPENSES

Evidence of furnishing, promising to pay, or offering to pay medical, hospital, or similar expenses resulting from an injury is not admissible to prove liability for the injury.

(Pub.L. 93–595, § 1, Jan. 2, 1975, 88 Stat.1933; Apr. 26, 2011, eff. Dec. 1, 2011.)

RULE 410. PLEAS, PLEA DISCUSSIONS, AND RELATED STATEMENTS

(a) **Prohibited Uses.** In a civil or criminal case, evidence of the following is not admissible against the defendant who made the plea or participated in the plea discussions:

(1) a guilty plea that was later withdrawn;

(2) a nolo contendere plea;

(3) a statement made during a proceeding on either of those pleas under Federal Rule of Criminal Procedure 11 or a comparable state procedure; or

(4) a statement made during plea discussions with an attorney for the prosecuting authority if the discussions did not result in a guilty plea or they resulted in a later-withdrawn guilty plea.

(b) **Exceptions.** The court may admit a statement described in Rule 410(a)(3) or (4):

(1) in any proceeding in which another statement made during the same plea or plea discussions has been introduced, if in fairness the statements ought to be considered together; or

(2) in a criminal proceeding for perjury or false statement, if the defendant made the statement under oath, on the record, and with counsel present.

(Pub.L. 93–595, § 1, Jan. 2, 1975, 88 Stat. 1933; Pub.L. 94–149, § 1(9), Dec. 12, 1975, 89 Stat. 805; Apr. 30, 1979, eff. Dec. 1, 1980; Apr. 26, 2011, eff. Dec. 1, 2011.)

RULE 411. LIABILITY INSURANCE

Evidence that a person was or was not insured against liability is not admissible to prove whether the person acted negligently or otherwise wrongfully. But the court may admit this evidence for another purpose, such as proving a witness's bias or prejudice or proving agency, ownership, or control.

(Pub.L. 93–595, § 1, Jan. 2, 1975, 88 Stat.1933; Mar. 2, 1987, eff. Oct. 1, 1987; Apr. 26, 2011, eff. Dec. 1, 2011.)

RULE 412. SEX–OFFENSE CASES: THE VICTIM'S SEXUAL BEHAVIOR OR PREDISPOSITION

(a) **Prohibited Uses.** The following evidence is not admissible in a civil or criminal proceeding involving alleged sexual misconduct:

(1) evidence offered to prove that a victim engaged in other sexual behavior; or

(2) evidence offered to prove a victim's sexual predisposition.

(b) **Exceptions.**

(1) **Criminal Cases.** The court may admit the following evidence in a criminal case:

(A) evidence of specific instances of a victim's sexual behavior, if offered to prove that someone other than the defendant was the source of semen, injury, or other physical evidence;

(B) evidence of specific instances of a victim's sexual behavior with respect to the person accused of the sexual misconduct, if offered by the defendant to prove consent or if offered by the prosecutor; and

(C) evidence whose exclusion would violate the defendant's constitutional rights.

(2) **Civil Cases.** In a civil case, the court may admit evidence offered to prove a victim's sexual behavior or sexual predisposition if its probative value substantially outweighs the danger of harm to any victim and of unfair prejudice to any party. The court may admit evidence of a victim's reputation only if the victim has placed it in controversy.

(c) **Procedure to Determine Admissibility.**

(1) **Motion.** If a party intends to offer evidence under Rule 412(b), the party must:

(A) file a motion that specifically describes the evidence and states the purpose for which it is to be offered;

(B) do so at least 14 days before trial unless the court, for good cause, sets a different time;

(C) serve the motion on all parties; and

(D) notify the victim or, when appropriate, the victim's guardian or representative.

(2) **Hearing.** Before admitting evidence under this rule, the court must conduct an in camera hearing and give the victim and parties a right to attend and be heard. Unless the court orders otherwise, the motion, related materials, and the record of the hearing must be and remain sealed.

(d) **Definition of "Victim."** In this rule, "victim" includes an alleged victim.

(Added Pub.L. 95–540, § 2(a), Oct. 28, 1978, 92 Stat. 2046; amended Pub.L. 100–690, Title VII, § 7046(a), Nov. 18, 1988, 102 Stat. 4400; Apr. 29, 1994, eff. Dec. 1, 1994; Pub.L. 103–322, Title IV, § 40141(b), Sept. 13, 1994, 108 Stat. 1919; Apr. 26, 2011, eff. Dec. 1, 2011.)

RULE 413. SIMILAR CRIMES IN SEXUAL–ASSAULT CASES

(a) **Permitted Uses.** In a criminal case in which a defendant is accused of a sexual assault, the court may admit evidence that the defendant committed any other sexual assault. The evidence may be considered on any matter to which it is relevant.

(b) **Disclosure to the Defendant.** If the prosecutor intends to offer this evidence, the prosecutor must disclose it to the defendant, including witnesses' statements or a summary of the expected testimony. The prosecutor must do so at least 15 days before trial or at a later time that the court allows for good cause.

(c) Effect on Other Rules. This rule does not limit the admission or consideration of evidence under any other rule.

(d) Definition of "Sexual Assault." In this rule and Rule 415, "sexual assault" means a crime under federal law or under state law (as "state" is defined in 18 U.S.C. § 513) involving:

    (1) any conduct prohibited by 18 U.S.C. chapter 109A;

    (2) contact, without consent, between any part of the defendant's body—or an object—and another person's genitals or anus;

    (3) contact, without consent, between the defendant's genitals or anus and any part of another person's body;

    (4) deriving sexual pleasure or gratification from inflicting death, bodily injury, or physical pain on another person; or

    (5) an attempt or conspiracy to engage in conduct described in subparagraphs (1)–(4).

(Added Pub.L. 103–322, Title XXXII, § 320935(a), Sept. 13, 1994, 108 Stat. 2136; Apr. 26, 2011, eff. Dec. 1, 2011.)

RULE 414. SIMILAR CRIMES IN CHILD–MOLESTATION CASES

(a) Permitted Uses. In a criminal case in which a defendant is accused of child molestation, the court may admit evidence that the defendant committed any other child molestation. The evidence may be considered on any matter to which it is relevant.

(b) Disclosure to the Defendant. If the prosecutor intends to offer this evidence, the prosecutor must disclose it to the defendant, including witnesses' statements or a summary of the expected testimony. The prosecutor must do so at least 15 days before trial or at a later time that the court allows for good cause.

(c) Effect on Other Rules. This rule does not limit the admission or consideration of evidence under any other rule.

(d) Definition of "Child" and "Child Molestation." In this rule and Rule 415:

    (1) "child" means a person below the age of 14; and

    (2) "child molestation" means a crime under federal law or under state law (as "state" is defined in 18 U.S.C. § 513) involving:

        (A) any conduct prohibited by 18 U.S.C. chapter 109A and committed with a child;

        (B) any conduct prohibited by 18 U.S.C. chapter 110;

        (C) contact between any part of the defendant's body—or an object—and a child's genitals or anus;

        (D) contact between the defendant's genitals or anus and any part of a child's body;

        (E) deriving sexual pleasure or gratification from inflicting death, bodily injury, or physical pain on a child; or

        (F) an attempt or conspiracy to engage in conduct described in subparagraphs (A)–(E).

(Added Pub.L. 103–322, Title XXXII, § 320935(a), Sept. 13, 1994, 108 Stat. 2136; Apr. 26, 2011, eff. Dec. 1, 2011.)

RULE 415. SIMILAR ACTS IN CIVIL CASES INVOLVING SEXUAL ASSAULT OR CHILD MOLESTATION

(a) Permitted Uses. In a civil case involving a claim for relief based on a party's alleged sexual assault or child molestation, the court may admit evidence that the party committed any other sexual assault or child molestation. The evidence may be considered as provided in Rules 413 and 414.

(b) Disclosure to the Opponent. If a party intends to offer this evidence, the party must disclose it to the party against whom it will be offered, including witnesses' statements or a summary of the expected testimony. The party must do so at least 15 days before trial or at a later time that the court allows for good cause.

(c) Effect on Other Rules. This rule does not limit the admission or consideration of evidence under any other rule.

(Added Pub.L. 103–322, Title XXXII, § 320935(a), Sept. 13, 1994, 108 Stat. 2137; Apr. 26, 2011, eff. Dec. 1, 2011.)

ARTICLE V. PRIVILEGES

RULE 501. PRIVILEGE IN GENERAL

The common law—as interpreted by United States courts in the light of reason and experience—governs a claim of privilege unless any of the following provides otherwise:

- the United States Constitution;
- a federal statute; or
- rules prescribed by the Supreme Court.

But in a civil case, state law governs privilege regarding a claim or defense for which state law supplies the rule of decision.

(Pub.L. 93–595, § 1, Jan. 2, 1975, 88 Stat. 1933; Apr. 26, 2011, eff. Dec. 1, 2011.)

RULE 502. ATTORNEY–CLIENT PRIVILEGE AND WORK PRODUCT; LIMITATIONS ON WAIVER

The following provisions apply, in the circumstances set out, to disclosure of a communication or information covered by the attorney-client privilege or work-product protection.

(a) Disclosure Made in a Federal Proceeding or to a Federal Office or Agency; Scope of a Waiver. When the disclosure is made in a federal proceeding or to a federal office or agency and waives the attorney-client privilege or work-product protection, the waiver extends to an undisclosed communication or information in a federal or state proceeding only if:

  (1) the waiver is intentional;

  (2) the disclosed and undisclosed communications or information concern the same subject matter; and

  (3) they ought in fairness to be considered together.

(b) Inadvertent Disclosure. When made in a federal proceeding or to a federal office or agency, the disclosure does not operate as a waiver in a federal or state proceeding if:

  (1) the disclosure is inadvertent;

  (2) the holder of the privilege or protection took reasonable steps to prevent disclosure; and

  (3) the holder promptly took reasonable steps to rectify the error, including (if applicable) following Federal Rule of Civil Procedure 26(b)(5)(B).

(c) Disclosure Made in a State Proceeding. When the disclosure is made in a state proceeding and is not the subject of a state-court order concerning waiver, the disclosure does not operate as a waiver in a federal proceeding if the disclosure:

  (1) would not be a waiver under this rule if it had been made in a federal proceeding; or

  (2) is not a waiver under the law of the state where the disclosure occurred.

(d) Controlling Effect of a Court Order. A federal court may order that the privilege or protection is not waived by disclosure connected with the litigation pending before the court—in which event the disclosure is also not a waiver in any other federal or state proceeding.

(e) Controlling Effect of a Party Agreement. An agreement on the effect of disclosure in a federal proceeding is binding only on the parties to the agreement, unless it is incorporated into a court order.

(f) Controlling Effect of This Rule. Notwithstanding Rules 101 and 1101, this rule applies to state proceedings and to federal court-annexed and federal court-mandated arbitration proceedings, in the circumstances set out in the rule. And notwithstanding Rule 501, this rule applies even if state law provides the rule of decision.

(g) Definitions. In this rule:

  (1) "attorney-client privilege" means the protection that applicable law provides for confidential attorney-client communications; and

  (2) "work-product protection" means the protection that applicable law provides for tangible material (or its intangible equivalent) prepared in anticipation of litigation or for trial.

(Pub.L. 110–322, § 1(a), Sept. 19, 2008, 122 Stat. 3537; Apr. 26, 2011, eff. Dec. 1, 2011.)

ARTICLE VI.   WITNESSES

RULE 601.   COMPETENCY TO TESTIFY IN GENERAL

Every person is competent to be a witness unless these rules provide otherwise. But in a civil case, state law governs the witness's competency regarding a claim or defense for which state law supplies the rule of decision.

(Pub.L. 93–595, § 1, Jan. 2, 1975, 88 Stat.1934; Apr. 26, 2011, eff. Dec. 1, 2011.)

RULE 602.   NEED FOR PERSONAL KNOWLEDGE

A witness may testify to a matter only if evidence is introduced sufficient to support a finding that the witness has personal knowledge of the matter. Evidence to prove personal knowledge may consist of the witness's own testimony. This rule does not apply to a witness's expert testimony under Rule 703.

(Pub.L. 93–595, § 1, Jan. 2, 1975, 88 Stat. 1934; Mar. 2, 1987, eff. Oct. 1, 1987; Apr. 25, 1988, eff. Nov. 1, 1988; Apr. 26, 2011, eff. Dec. 1, 2011.)

RULE 603.   OATH OR AFFIRMATION TO TESTIFY TRUTHFULLY

Before testifying, a witness must give an oath or affirmation to testify truthfully. It must be in a form designed to impress that duty on the witness's conscience.

(Pub.L. 93–595, § 1, Jan. 2, 1975, 88 Stat. 1934; Mar. 2, 1987, eff. Oct. 1, 1987; Apr. 26, 2011, eff. Dec. 1, 2011.)

RULE 604.   INTERPRETER

An interpreter must be qualified and must give an oath or affirmation to make a true translation.

(Pub.L. 93–595, § 1, Jan. 2, 1975, 88 Stat. 1934; Mar. 2, 1987, eff. Oct. 1, 1987; Apr. 26, 2011, eff. Dec. 1, 2011.)

RULE 605.   JUDGE'S COMPETENCY AS A WITNESS

The presiding judge may not testify as a witness at the trial. A party need not object to preserve the issue.

(Pub.L. 93–595, § 1, Jan. 2, 1975, 88 Stat. 1934; Apr. 26, 2011, eff. Dec. 1, 2011.)

RULE 606.   JUROR'S COMPETENCY AS A WITNESS

(a) At the Trial. A juror may not testify as a witness before the other jurors at the trial. If a juror is called to testify, the court must give a party an opportunity to object outside the jury's presence.

(b) During an Inquiry Into the Validity of a Verdict or Indictment.

  (1) **Prohibited Testimony or Other Evidence.** During an inquiry into the validity of a verdict or indictment, a juror may not testify about any statement made or incident that occurred during the jury's deliberations; the effect of anything on that juror's or another juror's vote; or any juror's

mental processes concerning the verdict or indictment. The court may not receive a juror's affidavit or evidence of a juror's statement on these matters.

(2) **Exceptions.** A juror may testify about whether:

(A) extraneous prejudicial information was improperly brought to the jury's attention;

(B) an outside influence was improperly brought to bear on any juror; or

(C) a mistake was made in entering the verdict on the verdict form.

(Pub.L. 93–595, § 1, Jan. 2, 1975, 88 Stat. 1934; Pub.L. 94–149, § 1(10), Dec. 12, 1975, 89 Stat. 805; Mar. 2, 1987, eff. Oct. 1, 1987; Apr. 12, 2006, eff. Dec. 1, 2006; Apr. 26, 2011, eff. Dec. 1, 2011.)

RULE 607. WHO MAY IMPEACH A WITNESS

Any party, including the party that called the witness, may attack the witness's credibility.

(Pub.L. 93–595, § 1, Jan. 2, 1975, 88 Stat.1934; Mar. 2, 1987, eff. Oct. 1, 1987; Apr. 26, 2011, eff. Dec. 1, 2011.)

RULE 608. A WITNESS'S CHARACTER FOR TRUTHFULNESS OR UNTRUTHFULNESS

(a) **Reputation or Opinion Evidence.** A witness's credibility may be attacked or supported by testimony about the witness's reputation for having a character for truthfulness or untruthfulness, or by testimony in the form of an opinion about that character. But evidence of truthful character is admissible only after the witness's character for truthfulness has been attacked.

(b) **Specific Instances of Conduct.** Except for a criminal conviction under Rule 609, extrinsic evidence is not admissible to prove specific instances of a witness's conduct in order to attack or support the witness's character for truthfulness. But the court may, on cross-examination, allow them to be inquired into if they are probative of the character for truthfulness or untruthfulness of:

(1) the witness; or

(2) another witness whose character the witness being cross-examined has testified about.

By testifying on another matter, a witness does not waive any privilege against self-incrimination for testimony that relates only to the witness's character for truthfulness.

(Pub.L. 93–595, § 1, Jan. 2, 1975, 88 Stat.1935; Mar. 2, 1987, eff. Oct. 1, 1987; Apr. 25, 1988, eff. Nov. 1, 1988; Mar. 27, 2003, eff. Dec. 1, 2003; Apr. 26, 2011, eff. Dec. 1, 2011.)

RULE 609. IMPEACHMENT BY EVIDENCE OF A CRIMINAL CONVICTION

(a) **In General.** The following rules apply to attacking a witness's character for truthfulness by evidence of a criminal conviction:

(1) for a crime that, in the convicting jurisdiction, was punishable by death or by imprisonment for more than one year, the evidence:

(A) must be admitted, subject to Rule 403, in a civil case or in a criminal case in which the witness is not a defendant; and

(B) must be admitted in a criminal case in which the witness is a defendant, if the probative value of the evidence outweighs its prejudicial effect to that defendant; and

(2) for any crime regardless of the punishment, the evidence must be admitted if the court can readily determine that establishing the elements of the crime required proving—or the witness's admitting—a dishonest act or false statement.

(b) **Limit on Using the Evidence After 10 Years.** This subdivision (b) applies if more than 10 years have passed since the witness's conviction or release from confinement for it, whichever is later. Evidence of the conviction is admissible only if:

(1) its probative value, supported by specific facts and circumstances, substantially outweighs its prejudicial effect; and

(2) the proponent gives an adverse party reasonable written notice of the intent to use it so that the party has a fair opportunity to contest its use.

(c) **Effect of a Pardon, Annulment, or Certificate of Rehabilitation.** Evidence of a conviction is not admissible if:

(1) the conviction has been the subject of a pardon, annulment, certificate of rehabilitation, or other equivalent procedure based on a finding that the person has been rehabilitated, and the person has not been convicted of a later crime punishable by death or by imprisonment for more than one year; or

(2) the conviction has been the subject of a pardon, annulment, or other equivalent procedure based on a finding of innocence.

(d) **Juvenile Adjudications.** Evidence of a juvenile adjudication is admissible under this rule only if:

(1) it is offered in a criminal case;

(2) the adjudication was of a witness other than the defendant;

(3) an adult's conviction for that offense would be admissible to attack the adult's credibility; and

(4) admitting the evidence is necessary to fairly determine guilt or innocence.

(e) **Pendency of an Appeal.** A conviction that satisfies this rule is admissible even if an appeal is pending. Evidence of the pendency is also admissible.

(Pub.L. 93–595, § 1, Jan. 2, 1975, 88 Stat.1935; Mar. 2, 1987, eff. Oct. 1, 1987; Jan. 26, 1990, eff. Dec. 1, 1990; Apr. 12, 2006, eff. Dec. 1, 2006; Apr. 26, 2011, eff. Dec. 1, 2011.)

RULE 610. RELIGIOUS BELIEFS OR OPINIONS

Evidence of a witness's religious beliefs or opinions is not admissible to attack or support the witness's credibility.

(Pub.L. 93–595, § 1, Jan. 2, 1975, 88 Stat.1936; Mar. 2, 1987, eff. Oct. 1, 1987; Apr. 26, 2011, eff. Dec. 1, 2011.)

RULE 611.   MODE AND ORDER OF EXAMINING WITNESSES AND PRESENTING EVIDENCE

(a) **Control by the Court; Purposes.** The court should exercise reasonable control over the mode and order of examining witnesses and presenting evidence so as to:

(1) make those procedures effective for determining the truth;

(2) avoid wasting time; and

(3) protect witnesses from harassment or undue embarrassment.

(b) **Scope of Cross–Examination.** Cross-examination should not go beyond the subject matter of the direct examination and matters affecting the witness's credibility. The court may allow inquiry into additional matters as if on direct examination.

(c) **Leading Questions.** Leading questions should not be used on direct examination except as necessary to develop the witness's testimony.   Ordinarily, the court should allow leading questions:

(1) on cross-examination; and

(2) when a party calls a hostile witness, an adverse party, or a witness identified with an adverse party.

(Pub.L. 93–595, § 1, Jan. 2, 1975, 88 Stat. 1936; Mar. 2, 1987, eff. Oct. 1, 1987; Apr. 26, 2011, eff. Dec. 1, 2011.)

RULE 612.   WRITING USED TO REFRESH A WITNESS'S MEMORY

(a) **Scope.** This rule gives an adverse party certain options when a witness uses a writing to refresh memory:

(1) while testifying; or

(2) before testifying, if the court decides that justice requires the party to have those options.

(b) **Adverse Party's Options; Deleting Unrelated Matter.** Unless 18 U.S.C. § 3500 provides otherwise in a criminal case, an adverse party is entitled to have the writing produced at the hearing, to inspect it, to cross-examine the witness about it, and to introduce in evidence any portion that relates to the witness's testimony. If the producing party claims that the writing includes unrelated matter, the court must examine the writing in camera, delete any unrelated portion, and order that the rest be delivered to the adverse party. Any portion deleted over objection must be preserved for the record.

(c) **Failure to Produce or Deliver the Writing.** If a writing is not produced or is not delivered as ordered, the court may issue any appropriate order. But if the prosecution does not comply in a criminal case, the court must strike the witness's testimony or—if justice so requires—declare a mistrial.

(Pub.L. 93–595, § 1, Jan. 2, 1975, 88 Stat. 1936; Mar. 2, 1987, eff. Oct. 1, 1987; Apr. 26, 2011, eff. Dec. 1, 2011.)

RULE 613.   WITNESS'S PRIOR STATEMENT

(a) **Showing or Disclosing the Statement During Examination.** When examining a witness about the witness's prior statement, a party need not show it or disclose its contents to the witness. But the party must, on request, show it or disclose its contents to an adverse party's attorney.

(b) **Extrinsic Evidence of a Prior Inconsistent Statement.** Extrinsic evidence of a witness's prior inconsistent statement is admissible only if the witness is given an opportunity to explain or deny the statement and an adverse party is given an opportunity to examine the witness about it, or if justice so requires. This subdivision (b) does not apply to an opposing party's statement under Rule 801(d)(2).

(Pub.L. 93–595, § 1, Jan. 2, 1975, 88 Stat.1936; Mar. 2, 1987, eff. Oct. 1, 1987; Apr. 25, 1988, eff. Nov. 1, 1988; Apr. 26, 2011, eff. Dec. 1, 2011.)

RULE 614.   COURT'S CALLING OR EXAMINING A WITNESS

(a) **Calling.** The court may call a witness on its own or at a party's request. Each party is entitled to cross-examine the witness.

(b) **Examining.** The court may examine a witness regardless of who calls the witness.

(c) **Objections.** A party may object to the court's calling or examining a witness either at that time or at the next opportunity when the jury is not present.

(Pub.L. 93–595, § 1, Jan. 2, 1975, 88 Stat.1937; Apr. 26, 2011, eff. Dec. 1, 2011.)

RULE 615.   EXCLUDING WITNESSES

At a party's request, the court must order witnesses excluded so that they cannot hear other witnesses' testimony. Or the court may do so on its own. But this rule does not authorize excluding:

(a) a party who is a natural person;

(b) an officer or employee of a party that is not a natural person, after being designated as the party's representative by its attorney;

(c) a person whose presence a party shows to be essential to presenting the party's claim or defense; or

(d) a person authorized by statute to be present.

(Pub.L. 93–595, § 1, Jan. 2, 1975, 88 Stat.1937; Mar. 2, 1987, eff. Oct. 1, 1987; Apr. 25, 1988, eff. Nov. 1, 1988; Pub.L. 100–690, Nov. 18, 1988, Title VII, § 7075(a), 102 Stat. 4405; Apr. 24, 1998, eff. Dec. 1, 1998; Apr. 26, 2011, eff. Dec. 1, 2011.)

ARTICLE VII. OPINIONS AND EXPERT TESTIMONY

RULE 701. OPINION TESTIMONY BY LAY WITNESSES

If a witness is not testifying as an expert, testimony in the form of an opinion is limited to one that is:

(a) rationally based on the witness's perception;

(b) helpful to clearly understanding the witness's testimony or to determining a fact in issue; and

(c) not based on scientific, technical, or other specialized knowledge within the scope of Rule 702.

(Pub.L. 93–595, § 1, Jan. 2, 1975, 88 Stat.1937; Mar. 2, 1987, eff. Oct. 1, 1987; Apr. 17, 2000, eff. Dec. 1, 2000; Apr. 26, 2011, eff. Dec. 1, 2011.)

RULE 702. TESTIMONY BY EXPERT WITNESSES

A witness who is qualified as an expert by knowledge, skill, experience, training, or education may testify in the form of an opinion or otherwise if:

(a) the expert's scientific, technical, or other specialized knowledge will help the trier of fact to understand the evidence or to determine a fact in issue;

(b) the testimony is based on sufficient facts or data;

(c) the testimony is the product of reliable principles and methods; and

(d) the expert has reliably applied the principles and methods to the facts of the case.

(Pub.L. 93–595, § 1, Jan. 2, 1975, 88 Stat. 1937; Apr. 17, 2000, eff. Dec. 1, 2000; Apr. 26, 2011, eff. Dec. 1, 2011.)

RULE 703. BASES OF AN EXPERT'S OPINION TESTIMONY

An expert may base an opinion on facts or data in the case that the expert has been made aware of or personally observed. If experts in the particular field would reasonably rely on those kinds of facts or data in forming an opinion on the subject, they need not be admissible for the opinion to be admitted. But if the facts or data would otherwise be inadmissible, the proponent of the opinion may disclose them to the jury only if their probative value in helping the jury evaluate the opinion substantially outweighs their prejudicial effect.

(Pub.L. 93–595, § 1, Jan. 2, 1975, 88 Stat.1937; Mar. 2, 1987, eff. Oct. 1, 1987; Apr. 17, 2000, eff. Dec. 1, 2000; Apr. 26, 2011, eff. Dec. 1, 2011.)

RULE 704. OPINION ON AN ULTIMATE ISSUE

(a) In General—Not Automatically Objectionable. An opinion is not objectionable just because it embraces an ultimate issue.

(b) Exception. In a criminal case, an expert witness must not state an opinion about whether the defendant did or did not have a mental state or condition that constitutes an element of the crime charged or of a defense. Those matters are for the trier of fact alone.

(Pub.L. 93–595, § 1, Jan. 2, 1975, 88 Stat. 1937; Pub.L. 98–473, Title II, § 406, Oct. 12, 1984, 98 Stat. 2067; Apr. 26, 2011, eff. Dec. 1, 2011.)

RULE 705. DISCLOSING THE FACTS OR DATA UNDERLYING AN EXPERT'S OPINION

Unless the court orders otherwise, an expert may state an opinion—and give the reasons for it—without first testifying to the underlying facts or data. But the expert may be required to disclose those facts or data on cross-examination.

(Pub.L. 93–595, § 1, Jan. 2, 1975, 88 Stat. 1938; Mar. 2, 1987, eff. Oct. 1, 1987; Apr. 22, 1993, eff. Dec. 1, 1993; Apr. 26, 2011, eff. Dec. 1, 2011.)

RULE 706. COURT–APPOINTED EXPERT WITNESSES

(a) Appointment Process. On a party's motion or on its own, the court may order the parties to show cause why expert witnesses should not be appointed and may ask the parties to submit nominations. The court may appoint any expert that the parties agree on and any of its own choosing. But the court may only appoint someone who consents to act.

(b) Expert's Role. The court must inform the expert of the expert's duties. The court may do so in writing and have a copy filed with the clerk or may do so orally at a conference in which the parties have an opportunity to participate. The expert:

(1) must advise the parties of any findings the expert makes;

(2) may be deposed by any party;

(3) may be called to testify by the court or any party; and

(4) may be cross-examined by any party, including the party that called the expert.

(c) Compensation. The expert is entitled to a reasonable compensation, as set by the court. The compensation is payable as follows:

(1) in a criminal case or in a civil case involving just compensation under the Fifth Amendment, from any funds that are provided by law; and

(2) in any other civil case, by the parties in the proportion and at the time that the court directs—and the compensation is then charged like other costs.

(d) Disclosing the Appointment to the Jury. The court may authorize disclosure to the jury that the court appointed the expert.

(e) Parties' Choice of Their Own Experts. This rule does not limit a party in calling its own experts.

(Pub.L. 93–595, § 1, Jan. 2, 1975, 88 Stat.1938; Mar. 2, 1987, eff. Oct. 1, 1987; Apr. 26, 2011, eff. Dec. 1, 2011.)

ARTICLE VIII. HEARSAY

RULE 801. DEFINITIONS THAT APPLY TO THIS ARTICLE; EXCLUSIONS FROM HEARSAY

(a) Statement. "Statement" means a person's oral assertion, written assertion, or nonverbal conduct, if the person intended it as an assertion.

(b) Declarant. "Declarant" means the person who made the statement.

(c) Hearsay. "Hearsay" means a statement that:

(1) the declarant does not make while testifying at the current trial or hearing; and

(2) a party offers in evidence to prove the truth of the matter asserted in the statement.

(d) Statements That Are Not Hearsay. A statement that meets the following conditions is not hearsay:

(1) A Declarant–Witness's Prior Statement. The declarant testifies and is subject to cross-examination about a prior statement, and the statement:

(A) is inconsistent with the declarant's testimony and was given under penalty of perjury at a trial, hearing, or other proceeding or in a deposition;

(B) is consistent with the declarant's testimony and is offered:

(i) to rebut an express or implied charge that the declarant recently fabricated it or acted from a recent improper influence or motive in so testifying; or

(ii) to rehabilitate the declarant's credibility as a witness when attacked on another ground; or

(C) identifies a person as someone the declarant perceived earlier.

(2) An Opposing Party's Statement. The statement is offered against an opposing party and:

(A) was made by the party in an individual or representative capacity;

(B) is one the party manifested that it adopted or believed to be true;

(C) was made by a person whom the party authorized to make a statement on the subject;

(D) was made by the party's agent or employee on a matter within the scope of that relationship and while it existed; or

(E) was made by the party's coconspirator during and in furtherance of the conspiracy.

The statement must be considered but does not by itself establish the declarant's authority under (C); the existence or scope of the relationship under (D); or the existence of the conspiracy or participation in it under (E).

(Pub.L. 93–595, § 1, Jan. 2, 1975, 88 Stat.1938; Pub.L. 94–113, § 1, Oct. 16, 1975, 89 Stat. 576; Mar. 2, 1987, eff. Oct. 1, 1987; Apr. 11, 1997, eff. Dec. 1, 1997; Apr. 26, 2011, eff. Dec. 1, 2011; Apr. 25, 2014, eff. Dec. 1, 2014.)

RULE 802. THE RULE AGAINST HEARSAY

Hearsay is not admissible unless any of the following provides otherwise:

- a federal statute;
- these rules; or
- other rules prescribed by the Supreme Court.

(Pub.L. 93–595, § 1, Jan. 2, 1975, 88 Stat. 1939; Apr. 26, 2011, eff. Dec. 1, 2011.)

RULE 803. EXCEPTIONS TO THE RULE AGAINST HEARSAY—REGARDLESS OF WHETHER THE DECLARANT IS AVAILABLE AS A WITNESS

The following are not excluded by the rule against hearsay, regardless of whether the declarant is available as a witness:

(1) Present Sense Impression. A statement describing or explaining an event or condition, made while or immediately after the declarant perceived it.

(2) Excited Utterance. A statement relating to a startling event or condition, made while the declarant was under the stress of excitement that it caused.

(3) Then–Existing Mental, Emotional, or Physical Condition. A statement of the declarant's then-existing state of mind (such as motive, intent, or plan) or emotional, sensory, or physical condition (such as mental feeling, pain, or bodily health), but not including a statement of memory or belief to prove the fact remembered or believed unless it relates to the validity or terms of the declarant's will.

(4) Statement Made for Medical Diagnosis or Treatment. A statement that:

(A) is made for—and is reasonably pertinent to—medical diagnosis or treatment; and

(B) describes medical history; past or present symptoms or sensations; their inception; or their general cause.

(5) Recorded Recollection. A record that:

(A) is on a matter the witness once knew about but now cannot recall well enough to testify fully and accurately;

(B) was made or adopted by the witness when the matter was fresh in the witness's memory; and

(C) accurately reflects the witness's knowledge.

If admitted, the record may be read into evidence but may be received as an exhibit only if offered by an adverse party.

(6) Records of a Regularly Conducted Activity. A record of an act, event, condition, opinion, or diagnosis if:

(A) the record was made at or near the time by—or from information transmitted by—someone with knowledge;

(B) the record was kept in the course of a regularly conducted activity of a business, organization, occupation, or calling, whether or not for profit;

(C) making the record was a regular practice of that activity;

(D) all these conditions are shown by the testimony of the custodian or another qualified witness, or by a certification that complies with Rule 902(11) or (12) or with a statute permitting certification; and

(E) the opponent does not show that the source of information or the method or circumstances of preparation indicate a lack of trustworthiness.

(7) Absence of a Record of a Regularly Conducted Activity. Evidence that a matter is not included in a record described in paragraph (6) if:

(A) the evidence is admitted to prove that the matter did not occur or exist;

(B) a record was regularly kept for a matter of that kind; and

(C) the opponent does not show that the possible source of the information or other circumstances indicate a lack of trustworthiness.

(8) Public Records. A record or statement of a public office if:

(A) it sets out:

(i) the office's activities;

(ii) a matter observed while under a legal duty to report, but not including, in a criminal case, a matter observed by law-enforcement personnel; or

(iii) in a civil case or against the government in a criminal case, factual findings from a legally authorized investigation; and

(B) the opponent does not show that the source of information or other circumstances indicate a lack of trustworthiness.

(9) Public Records of Vital Statistics. A record of a birth, death, or marriage, if reported to a public office in accordance with a legal duty.

(10) Absence of a Public Record. Testimony—or a certification under Rule 902—that a diligent search failed to disclose a public record or statement if:

(A) the testimony or certification is admitted to prove that

(i) the record or statement does not exist; or

(ii) a matter did not occur or exist, if a public office regularly kept a record or statement for a matter of that kind; and

(B) in a criminal case, a prosecutor who intends to offer a certification provides written notice of that intent at least 14 days before trial, and the defendant does not object in writing within 7 days of receiving the notice—unless the court sets a different time for the notice or the objection.

(11) Records of Religious Organizations Concerning Personal or Family History. A statement of birth, legitimacy, ancestry, marriage, divorce, death, relationship by blood or marriage, or similar facts of personal or family history, contained in a regularly kept record of a religious organization.

(12) Certificates of Marriage, Baptism, and Similar Ceremonies. A statement of fact contained in a certificate:

(A) made by a person who is authorized by a religious organization or by law to perform the act certified;

(B) attesting that the person performed a marriage or similar ceremony or administered a sacrament; and

(C) purporting to have been issued at the time of the act or within a reasonable time after it.

(13) Family Records. A statement of fact about personal or family history contained in a family record, such as a Bible, genealogy, chart, engraving on a ring, inscription on a portrait, or engraving on an urn or burial marker.

(14) Records of Documents That Affect an Interest in Property. The record of a document that purports to establish or affect an interest in property if:

(A) the record is admitted to prove the content of the original recorded document, along with its signing and its delivery by each person who purports to have signed it;

(B) the record is kept in a public office; and

(C) a statute authorizes recording documents of that kind in that office.

(15) Statements in Documents That Affect an Interest in Property. A statement contained in a document that purports to establish or affect an interest in property if the matter stated was relevant to the document's purpose—unless later dealings with the property are inconsistent with the truth of the statement or the purport of the document.

(16) Statements in Ancient Documents. A statement in a document that was prepared before January 1, 1998, and whose authenticity is established.

(17) Market Reports and Similar Commercial Publications. Market quotations, lists, directories, or other compilations that are generally relied on by the public or by persons in particular occupations.

(18) Statements in Learned Treatises, Periodicals, or Pamphlets. A statement contained in a treatise, periodical, or pamphlet if:

(A) the statement is called to the attention of an expert witness on cross-examination or relied on by the expert on direct examination; and

(B) the publication is established as a reliable authority by the expert's admission or testimony, by another expert's testimony, or by judicial notice.

If admitted, the statement may be read into evidence but not received as an exhibit.

(19) Reputation Concerning Personal or Family History. A reputation among a person's family by blood, adoption, or marriage—or among a person's associates or in the community—concerning the person's birth, adoption, legitimacy, ancestry, marriage, divorce, death, relationship by blood, adoption, or marriage, or similar facts of personal or family history.

(20) Reputation Concerning Boundaries or General History. A reputation in a community—arising before the controversy—concerning boundaries of land in the community or customs that affect the land, or concerning general historical events important to that community, state, or nation.

(21) Reputation Concerning Character. A reputation among a person's associates or in the community concerning the person's character.

(22) Judgment of a Previous Conviction. Evidence of a final judgment of conviction if:

    (A) the judgment was entered after a trial or guilty plea, but not a nolo contendere plea;

    (B) the conviction was for a crime punishable by death or by imprisonment for more than a year;

    (C) the evidence is admitted to prove any fact essential to the judgment; and

    (D) when offered by the prosecutor in a criminal case for a purpose other than impeachment, the judgment was against the defendant.

The pendency of an appeal may be shown but does not affect admissibility.

(23) Judgments Involving Personal, Family, or General History, or a Boundary. A judgment that is admitted to prove a matter of personal, family, or general history, or boundaries, if the matter:

    (A) was essential to the judgment; and

    (B) could be proved by evidence of reputation.

(24) [Other Exceptions.] [Transferred to Rule 807.]

(Pub.L. 93–595, § 1, Jan. 2, 1975, 88 Stat. 1939; Pub.L. 94–149, § 1(11), Dec. 12, 1975, 89 Stat. 805; Mar. 2, 1987, eff. Oct. 1, 1987; Apr. 11, 1997, eff. Dec. 1, 1997; Apr. 17, 2000, eff. Dec. 1, 2000; Apr. 26, 2011, eff. Dec. 1, 2011; Apr. 13, 2013, eff. Dec. 1, 2013; Apr. 25, 2014, eff. Dec. 1, 2014; Apr. 27, 2017, eff. Dec. 1, 2017.)

RULE 804. EXCEPTIONS TO THE RULE AGAINST HEARSAY—WHEN THE DECLARANT IS UNAVAILABLE AS A WITNESS

(a) Criteria for Being Unavailable. A declarant is considered to be unavailable as a witness if the declarant:

    (1) is exempted from testifying about the subject matter of the declarant's statement because the court rules that a privilege applies;

    (2) refuses to testify about the subject matter despite a court order to do so;

    (3) testifies to not remembering the subject matter;

    (4) cannot be present or testify at the trial or hearing because of death or a then-existing infirmity, physical illness, or mental illness; or

    (5) is absent from the trial or hearing and the statement's proponent has not been able, by process or other reasonable means, to procure:

    (A) the declarant's attendance, in the case of a hearsay exception under Rule 804(b)(1) or (6); or

    (B) the declarant's attendance or testimony, in the case of a hearsay exception under Rule 804(b)(2), (3), or (4).

But this subdivision (a) does not apply if the statement's proponent procured or wrongfully caused the declarant's unavailability as a witness in order to prevent the declarant from attending or testifying.

(b) The Exceptions. The following are not excluded by the rule against hearsay if the declarant is unavailable as a witness:

(1) Former Testimony. Testimony that:

    (A) was given as a witness at a trial, hearing, or lawful deposition, whether given during the current proceeding or a different one; and

    (B) is now offered against a party who had—or, in a civil case, whose predecessor in interest had—an opportunity and similar motive to develop it by direct, cross-, or redirect examination.

(2) Statement Under the Belief of Imminent Death. In a prosecution for homicide or in a civil case, a statement that the declarant, while believing the declarant's death to be imminent, made about its cause or circumstances.

(3) Statement Against Interest. A statement that:

    (A) a reasonable person in the declarant's position would have made only if the person believed it to be true because, when made, it was so contrary to the declarant's proprietary or pecuniary interest or had so great a tendency to invalidate the declarant's claim against someone else or to expose the declarant to civil or criminal liability; and

    (B) is supported by corroborating circumstances that clearly indicate its trustworthiness, if it is offered in a criminal case as one that tends to expose the declarant to criminal liability.

(4) Statement of Personal or Family History. A statement about:

    (A) the declarant's own birth, adoption, legitimacy, ancestry, marriage, divorce, relationship by blood, adoption, or marriage, or similar facts of personal or family history, even though the declarant had no way of acquiring personal knowledge about that fact; or

    (B) another person concerning any of these facts, as well as death, if the declarant was related to the person by blood, adoption, or marriage or was so intimately associated with the person's family that the declarant's information is likely to be accurate.

(5) [Other Exceptions.] [Transferred to Rule 807.]

(6) Statement Offered Against a Party That Wrongfully Caused the Declarant's Unavailability. A statement offered against a party that wrongfully caused—or acquiesced in wrongfully causing—the declarant's unavailability as a witness, and did so intending that result.

(Pub.L. 93–595, § 1, Jan. 2, 1975, 88 Stat. 1942; Pub.L. 94–149, § 1(12), (13), Dec. 12, 1975, 89 Stat. 806; Mar. 2, 1987, eff. Oct. 1, 1987; Pub.L. 100–690, Title VII, § 7075(b), Nov. 18, 1988, 102 Stat. 4405; Apr. 11, 1997, eff. Dec. 1, 1997; Apr. 28, 2010, eff. Dec. 1, 2010; Apr. 26, 2011, eff. Dec. 1, 2011.)

RULE 805. HEARSAY WITHIN HEARSAY

Hearsay within hearsay is not excluded by the rule against hearsay if each part of the combined statements conforms with an exception to the rule.

(Pub.L. 93–595, § 1, Jan. 2, 1975, 88 Stat. 1943; Apr. 26, 2011, eff. Dec. 1, 2011.)

RULE 806. ATTACKING AND SUPPORTING THE DECLARANT'S CREDIBILITY

When a hearsay statement—or a statement described in Rule 801(d)(2)(C), (D), or (E)—has been admitted in evidence, the declarant's credibility may be attacked, and then supported, by any evidence that would be admissible for those purposes if the declarant had testified as a witness. The court may admit evidence of the declarant's inconsistent statement or conduct, regardless of when it occurred or whether the declarant had an opportunity to explain or deny it. If the party against whom the statement was admitted calls the declarant as a witness, the party may examine the declarant on the statement as if on cross-examination.

(Pub.L. 93–595, § 1, Jan. 2, 1975, 88 Stat. 1943; Mar. 2, 1987, eff. Oct. 1, 1987; Apr. 11, 1997, eff. Dec. 1, 1997; Apr. 26, 2011, eff. Dec. 1, 2011.)

RULE 807. RESIDUAL EXCEPTION

(a) In General. Under the following conditions, a hearsay statement is not excluded by the rule against hearsay even if the statement is not admissible under a hearsay exception in Rule 803 or 804:

(1) the statement is supported by sufficient guarantees of trustworthiness—after considering the totality of circumstances under which it was made and evidence, if any, corroborating the statement; and

(2) it is more probative on the point for which it is offered than any other evidence that the proponent can obtain through reasonable efforts.

(b) Notice. The statement is admissible only if the proponent gives an adverse party reasonable notice of the intent to offer the statement—including its substance and the declarant's name—so that the party has a fair opportunity to meet it. The notice must be provided in writing before the trial or hearing—or in any form during the trial or hearing if the court, for good cause, excuses a lack of earlier notice.

(Added Apr. 11, 1997, eff. Dec. 1, 1997; Apr. 26, 2011, eff. Dec. 1, 2011; Apr. 25, 2019, eff. Dec. 1, 2019.)

ARTICLE IX. AUTHENTICATION AND IDENTIFICATION

RULE 901. AUTHENTICATING OR IDENTIFYING EVIDENCE

(a) In General. To satisfy the requirement of authenticating or identifying an item of evidence, the proponent must produce evidence sufficient to support a finding that the item is what the proponent claims it is.

(b) Examples. The following are examples only—not a complete list—of evidence that satisfies the requirement:

(1) Testimony of a Witness with Knowledge. Testimony that an item is what it is claimed to be.

(2) Nonexpert Opinion About Handwriting. A nonexpert's opinion that handwriting is genuine, based on a familiarity with it that was not acquired for the current litigation.

(3) Comparison by an Expert Witness or the Trier of Fact. A comparison with an authenticated specimen by an expert witness or the trier of fact.

(4) Distinctive Characteristics and the Like. The appearance, contents, substance, internal patterns, or other distinctive characteristics of the item, taken together with all the circumstances.

(5) Opinion About a Voice. An opinion identifying a person's voice—whether heard firsthand or through mechanical or electronic transmission or recording—based on hearing the voice at any time under circumstances that connect it with the alleged speaker.

(6) Evidence About a Telephone Conversation. For a telephone conversation, evidence that a call was made to the number assigned at the time to:

(A) a particular person, if circumstances, including self-identification, show that the person answering was the one called; or

(B) a particular business, if the call was made to a business and the call related to business reasonably transacted over the telephone.

(7) Evidence About Public Records. Evidence that:

(A) a document was recorded or filed in a public office as authorized by law; or

(B) a purported public record or statement is from the office where items of this kind are kept.

(8) Evidence About Ancient Documents or Data Compilations. For a document or data compilation, evidence that it:

(A) is in a condition that creates no suspicion about its authenticity;

(B) was in a place where, if authentic, it would likely be; and

(C) is at least 20 years old when offered.

(9) Evidence About a Process or System. Evidence describing a process or system and showing that it produces an accurate result.

(10) Methods Provided by a Statute or Rule. Any method of authentication or identification allowed by a federal statute or a rule prescribed by the Supreme Court.

(Pub.L. 93–595, § 1, Jan. 2, 1975, 88 Stat.1943; Apr. 26, 2011, eff. Dec. 1, 2011.)

RULE 902. EVIDENCE THAT IS SELF–AUTHENTICATING

The following items of evidence are self-authenticating; they require no extrinsic evidence of authenticity in order to be admitted:

(1) Domestic Public Documents That Are Sealed and Signed. A document that bears:

(A) a seal purporting to be that of the United States; any state, district, commonwealth, territory, or insular possession of the United States; the former Panama Canal Zone; the Trust Territory of the Pacific Islands; a political subdivision of any of these entities; or a department, agency, or officer of any entity named above; and

(B) a signature purporting to be an execution or attestation.

(2) Domestic Public Documents That Are Not Sealed but Are Signed and Certified. A document that bears no seal if:

(A) it bears the signature of an officer or employee of an entity named in Rule 902(1)(A); and

(B) another public officer who has a seal and official duties within that same entity certifies under seal—or its equivalent—that the signer has the official capacity and that the signature is genuine.

(3) Foreign Public Documents. A document that purports to be signed or attested by a person who is authorized by a foreign country's law to do so. The document must be accompanied by a final certification that certifies the genuineness of the signature and official position of the signer or attester—or of any foreign official whose certificate of genuineness relates to the signature or attestation or is in a chain of certificates of genuineness relating to the signature or attestation. The certification may be made by a secretary of a United States embassy or legation; by a consul general, vice consul, or consular agent of the United States; or by a diplomatic or consular official of the foreign country assigned or accredited to the United States. If all parties have been given a reasonable opportunity to investigate the document's authenticity and accuracy, the court may, for good cause, either:

(A) order that it be treated as presumptively authentic without final certification; or

(B) allow it to be evidenced by an attested summary with or without final certification.

(4) Certified Copies of Public Records. A copy of an official record—or a copy of a document that was recorded or filed in a public office as authorized by law—if the copy is certified as correct by:

(A) the custodian or another person authorized to make the certification; or

(B) a certificate that complies with Rule 902(1), (2), or (3), a federal statute, or a rule prescribed by the Supreme Court.

(5) Official Publications. A book, pamphlet, or other publication purporting to be issued by a public authority.

(6) Newspapers and Periodicals. Printed material purporting to be a newspaper or periodical.

(7) Trade Inscriptions and the Like. An inscription, sign, tag, or label purporting to have been affixed in the course of business and indicating origin, ownership, or control.

(8) Acknowledged Documents. A document accompanied by a certificate of acknowledgment that is lawfully executed by a notary public or another officer who is authorized to take acknowledgments.

(9) Commercial Paper and Related Documents. Commercial paper, a signature on it, and related documents, to the extent allowed by general commercial law.

(10) Presumptions Under a Federal Statute. A signature, document, or anything else that a federal statute declares to be presumptively or prima facie genuine or authentic.

(11) Certified Domestic Records of a Regularly Conducted Activity. The original or a copy of a domestic record that meets the requirements of Rule 803(6)(A)–(C), as shown by a certification of the custodian or another qualified person that complies with a federal statute or a rule prescribed by the Supreme Court. Before the trial or hearing, the proponent must give an adverse party reasonable written notice of the intent to offer the record—and must make the record and certification available for inspection—so that the party has a fair opportunity to challenge them.

(12) Certified Foreign Records of a Regularly Conducted Activity. In a civil case, the original or a copy of a foreign record that meets the requirements of Rule 902(11), modified as follows: the certification, rather than complying with a federal statute or Supreme Court rule, must be signed in a manner that, if falsely made, would subject the maker to a criminal penalty in the country where the certification is signed. The proponent must also meet the notice requirements of Rule 902(11).

(13) Certified Records Generated by an Electronic Process or System. A record generated by an electronic process or system that produces an accurate result, as shown by a certification of a qualified person that complies with the certification requirements of Rule 902(11) or (12). The proponent must also meet the notice requirements of Rule 902(11).

(14) Certified Data Copied from an Electronic Device, Storage Medium, or File. Data copied from an electronic device, storage medium, or file, if authenticated by a process of digital identification, as shown by a certification of a qualified person that complies with the certification requirements of Rule 902(11) or (12). The proponent also must meet the notice requirements of Rule 902(11).

(Pub.L. 93–595, § 1, Jan. 2, 1975, 88 Stat. 1944; Mar. 2, 1987, eff. Oct. 1, 1987; Apr. 25, 1988, eff. Nov. 1, 1988; Apr. 17, 2000, eff. Dec. 1, 2000; Apr. 26, 2011, eff. Dec. 1, 2011; Apr. 27, 2017, eff. Dec. 1, 2017.)

RULE 903. SUBSCRIBING WITNESS'S TESTIMONY

A subscribing witness's testimony is necessary to authenticate a writing only if required by the law of the jurisdiction that governs its validity.

(Pub.L. 93–595, § 1, Jan. 2, 1975, 88 Stat.1945; Apr. 26, 2011, eff. Dec. 1, 2011.)

ARTICLE X. CONTENTS OF WRITINGS, RECORDINGS, AND PHOTOGRAPHS

RULE 1001. DEFINITIONS THAT APPLY TO THIS ARTICLE

In this article:

(a) A "writing" consists of letters, words, numbers, or their equivalent set down in any form.

(b) A "recording" consists of letters, words, numbers, or their equivalent recorded in any manner.

(c) A "photograph" means a photographic image or its equivalent stored in any form.

(d) An "original" of a writing or recording means the writing or recording itself or any counterpart intended to have the same effect by the person who executed or issued it. For electronically stored information, "original" means any printout—or other output readable by sight—if it accurately reflects the information. An "original" of a photograph includes the negative or a print from it.

(e) A "duplicate" means a counterpart produced by a mechanical, photographic, chemical, electronic, or other equivalent process or technique that accurately reproduces the original.

(Pub.L. 93–595, § 1, Jan. 2, 1975, 88 Stat. 1945; Apr. 26, 2011, eff. Dec. 1, 2011.)

RULE 1002. REQUIREMENT OF THE ORIGINAL

An original writing, recording, or photograph is required in order to prove its content unless these rules or a federal statute provides otherwise.

(Pub.L. 93–595, § 1, Jan. 2, 1975, 88 Stat. 1946; Apr. 26, 2011, eff. Dec. 1, 2011.)

RULE 1003. ADMISSIBILITY OF DUPLICATES

A duplicate is admissible to the same extent as the original unless a genuine question is raised about the original's authenticity or the circumstances make it unfair to admit the duplicate.

(Pub.L. 93–595, § 1, Jan. 2, 1975, 88 Stat. 1946; Apr. 26, 2011, eff. Dec. 1, 2011.)

RULE 1004. ADMISSIBILITY OF OTHER EVIDENCE OF CONTENT

An original is not required and other evidence of the content of a writing, recording, or photograph is admissible if:

(a) all the originals are lost or destroyed, and not by the proponent acting in bad faith;

(b) an original cannot be obtained by any available judicial process;

(c) the party against whom the original would be offered had control of the original; was at that time put on notice, by pleadings or otherwise, that the original would be a subject of proof at the trial or hearing; and fails to produce it at the trial or hearing; or

(d) the writing, recording, or photograph is not closely related to a controlling issue.

(Pub.L. 93–595, § 1, Jan. 2, 1975, 88 Stat. 1946; Mar. 2, 1987, eff. Oct. 1, 1987; Apr. 26, 2011, eff. Dec. 1, 2011.)

RULE 1005. COPIES OF PUBLIC RECORDS TO PROVE CONTENT

The proponent may use a copy to prove the content of an official record—or of a document that was recorded or filed in a public office as authorized by law—if these conditions are met: the record or document is otherwise admissible; and the copy is certified as correct in accordance with Rule 902(4) or is testified to be correct by a witness who has compared it with the original. If no such copy can be obtained by reasonable diligence, then the proponent may use other evidence to prove the content.

(Pub.L. 93–595, § 1, Jan. 2, 1975, 88 Stat. 1946; Apr. 26, 2011, eff. Dec. 1, 2011.)

RULE 1006. SUMMARIES TO PROVE CONTENT

The proponent may use a summary, chart, or calculation to prove the content of voluminous writings, recordings, or photographs that cannot be conveniently examined in court. The proponent must make the originals or duplicates available for examination or copying, or both, by other parties at a reasonable time and place. And the court may order the proponent to produce them in court.

(Pub.L. 93–595, § 1, Jan. 2, 1975, 88 Stat. 1946; Apr. 26, 2011, eff. Dec. 1, 2011.)

RULE 1007. TESTIMONY OR STATEMENT OF A PARTY TO PROVE CONTENT

The proponent may prove the content of a writing, recording, or photograph by the testimony, deposition, or written statement of the party against whom the evidence is offered. The proponent need not account for the original.

(Pub.L. 93–595, § 1, Jan. 2, 1975, 88 Stat. 1947; Mar. 2, 1987, eff. Oct. 1, 1987; Apr. 26, 2011, eff. Dec. 1, 2011.)

RULE 1008. FUNCTIONS OF THE COURT AND JURY

Ordinarily, the court determines whether the proponent has fulfilled the factual conditions for admitting other evidence of the content of a writing, recording, or photograph under Rule 1004 or 1005. But in a jury trial, the jury determines—in accordance with Rule 104(b)—any issue about whether:

(a) an asserted writing, recording, or photograph ever existed;

(b) another one produced at the trial or hearing is the original; or

(c) other evidence of content accurately reflects the content.

(Pub.L. 93–595, § 1, Jan. 2, 1975, 88 Stat. 1947; Apr. 26, 2011, eff. Dec. 1, 2011.)

ARTICLE XI. MISCELLANEOUS RULES

RULE 1101. APPLICABILITY OF THE RULES

(a) **To Courts and Judges.** These rules apply to proceedings before:

- United States district courts;
- United States bankruptcy and magistrate judges;
- United States courts of appeals;
- the United States Court of Federal Claims; and
- the district courts of Guam, the Virgin Islands, and the Northern Mariana Islands.

(b) **To Cases and Proceedings.** These rules apply in:

- civil cases and proceedings, including bankruptcy, admiralty, and maritime cases;
- criminal cases and proceedings; and
- contempt proceedings, except those in which the court may act summarily.

(c) **Rules on Privilege.** The rules on privilege apply to all stages of a case or proceeding.

(d) **Exceptions.** These rules—except for those on privilege—do not apply to the following:

(1) the court's determination, under Rule 104(a), on a preliminary question of fact governing admissibility;

(2) grand-jury proceedings; and

(3) miscellaneous proceedings such as:

- extradition or rendition;
- issuing an arrest warrant, criminal summons, or search warrant;
- a preliminary examination in a criminal case;
- sentencing;
- granting or revoking probation or supervised release; and
- considering whether to release on bail or otherwise.

(e) **Other Statutes and Rules.** A federal statute or a rule prescribed by the Supreme Court may provide for admitting or excluding evidence independently from these rules.

(Pub.L. 93–595, § 1, Jan. 2, 1975, 88 Stat. 1947; Pub.L. 94–149, § 1(14), Dec. 12, 1975, 89 Stat. 806; Pub.L. 95–598, Title II, §§ 251, 252, Nov. 6, 1978, 92 Stat. 2673; Pub.L. 97–164, Title I, § 142, Apr. 2, 1982, 96 Stat. 45; Mar. 2, 1987, eff. Oct. 1, 1987; Apr. 25, 1988, eff. Nov. 1, 1988; Pub.L. 100–690, Title VII, § 7075(c), Nov. 18, 1988, 102 Stat. 4405; Apr. 22, 1993, eff. Dec. 1, 1993; Apr. 26, 2011, eff. Dec. 1, 2011.)

RULE 1102. AMENDMENTS

These rules may be amended as provided in 28 U.S.C. § 2072.

(Pub.L. 93–595, § 1, Jan. 2, 1975, 88 Stat.1948; Apr. 30, 1991, eff. Dec. 1, 1991; Apr. 26, 2011, eff. Dec. 1, 2011.)

RULE 1103. TITLE

These rules may be cited as the Federal Rules of Evidence.

(Pub.L. 93–595, § 1, Jan. 2, 1975, 88 Stat.1948; Apr. 26, 2011, eff. Dec. 1, 2011.)

INDEX TO
FEDERAL RULES OF EVIDENCE

FEDERAL RULES OF APPELLATE PROCEDURE

Including Amendments Effective December 1, 2021

TITLE I.   APPLICABILITY OF RULES

RULE 1.   SCOPE OF RULES; DEFINITION; TITLE

(a) Scope of Rules.

(1) These rules govern procedure in the United States courts of appeals.

(2) When these rules provide for filing a motion or other document in the district court, the procedure must comply with the practice of the district court.

(b) Definition. In these rules, "state" includes the District of Columbia and any United States commonwealth or territory.

(c) Title. These rules are to be known as the Federal Rules of Appellate Procedure.

(As amended Apr. 30, 1979, eff. Aug. 1, 1979; Apr. 25, 1989, eff. Dec. 1, 1989; Apr. 29, 1994, eff. Dec. 1, 1994; Apr. 24, 1998, eff. Dec. 1, 1998; Apr. 29, 2002, eff. Dec. 1, 2002; Apr. 28, 2010, eff. Dec. 1, 2010.)

RULE 2.   SUSPENSION OF RULES

On its own or a party's motion, a court of appeals may—to expedite its decision or for other good cause—suspend any provision of these rules in a particular case and order proceedings as it directs, except as otherwise provided in Rule 26(b).

(As amended Apr. 24, 1998, eff. Dec. 1, 1998.)

TITLE II.   APPEAL FROM A JUDGMENT OR ORDER OF A DISTRICT COURT

RULE 3.   APPEAL AS OF RIGHT—HOW TAKEN

(a) Filing the Notice of Appeal.

(1) An appeal permitted by law as of right from a district court to a court of appeals may be taken only by filing a notice of appeal with the district clerk within the time allowed by Rule 4. At the time of filing, the appellant must furnish the clerk with enough copies of the notice to enable the clerk to comply with Rule 3(d).

(2) An appellant's failure to take any step other than the timely filing of a notice of appeal does not affect the validity of the appeal, but is ground only for the court of appeals to act as it considers appropriate, including dismissing the appeal.

(3) An appeal from a judgment by a magistrate judge in a civil case is taken in the same way as an appeal from any other district court judgment.

(4) An appeal by permission under 28 U.S.C. § 1292(b) or an appeal in a bankruptcy case may be taken only in the manner prescribed by Rules 5 and 6, respectively.

(b) Joint or Consolidated Appeals.

(1) When two or more parties are entitled to appeal from a district-court judgment or order, and their interests make joinder practicable, they may file a joint notice of appeal. They may then proceed on appeal as a single appellant.

(2) When the parties have filed separate timely notices of appeal, the appeals may be joined or consolidated by the court of appeals.

(c) Contents of the Notice of Appeal.

(1) The notice of appeal must:

(A) specify the party or parties taking the appeal by naming each one in the caption or body of the notice, but an attorney representing more than one party may describe those parties with such terms as "all plaintiffs,"

"the defendants," "the plaintiffs A, B, et al.," or "all defendants except X";

(B) designate the judgment—or the appealable order—from which the appeal is taken; and

(C) name the court to which the appeal is taken.

(2) A pro se notice of appeal is considered filed on behalf of the signer and the signer's spouse and minor children (if they are parties), unless the notice clearly indicates otherwise.

(3) In a class action, whether or not the class has been certified, the notice of appeal is sufficient if it names one person qualified to bring the appeal as representative of the class.

(4) The notice of appeal encompasses all orders that, for purposes of appeal, merge into the designated judgment or appealable order. It is not necessary to designate those orders in the notice of appeal.

(5) In a civil case, a notice of appeal encompasses the final judgment, whether or not that judgment is set out in a separate document under Federal Rule of Civil Procedure 58, if the notice designates:

(A) an order that adjudicates all remaining claims and the rights and liabilities of all remaining parties; or

(B) an order described in Rule 4(a)(4)(A).

(6) An appellant may designate only part of a judgment or appealable order by expressly stating that the notice of appeal is so limited. Without such an express statement, specific designations do not limit the scope of the notice of appeal.

(7) An appeal must not be dismissed for informality of form or title of the notice of appeal, for failure to name a party whose intent to appeal is otherwise clear from the notice, or for failure to properly designate the judgment if

the notice of appeal was filed after entry of the judgment and designates an order that merged into that judgment.

(8) Forms 1A and 1B in the Appendix of Forms are suggested forms of notices of appeal.

(d) Serving the Notice of Appeal.

(1) The district clerk must serve notice of the filing of a notice of appeal by sending a copy to each party's counsel of record—excluding the appellant's—or, if a party is proceeding pro se, to the party's last known address. When a defendant in a criminal case appeals, the clerk must also serve a copy of the notice of appeal on the defendant. The clerk must promptly send a copy of the notice of appeal and of the docket entries—and any later docket entries—to the clerk of the court of appeals named in the notice. The district clerk must note, on each copy, the date when the notice of appeal was filed.

(2) If an inmate confined in an institution files a notice of appeal in the manner provided by Rule 4(c), the district clerk must also note the date when the clerk docketed the notice.

(3) The district clerk's failure to serve notice does not affect the validity of the appeal. The clerk must note on the docket the names of the parties to whom the clerk sends copies, with the date of sending. Service is sufficient despite the death of a party or the party's counsel.

(e) Payment of Fees. Upon filing a notice of appeal, the appellant must pay the district clerk all required fees. The district clerk receives the appellate docket fee on behalf of the court of appeals.

(As amended Apr. 30, 1979, eff. Aug. 1, 1979; Mar. 10, 1986, eff. July 1, 1986; Apr. 25, 1989, eff. Dec. 1, 1989; Apr. 22, 1993, eff. Dec. 1, 1993; Apr. 29, 1994, eff. Dec. 1, 1994; Apr. 24, 1998, eff. Dec. 1, 1998; Apr. 25, 2019, eff. Dec. 1, 2019; Apr. 14, 2021, eff. Dec. 1, 2021.)

[RULE 3.1   APPEAL FROM A JUDGMENT OF A MAGISTRATE JUDGE IN A CIVIL CASE (ABROGATED APR. 24, 1998, EFF. DEC. 1, 1998)]

RULE 4.   APPEAL AS OF RIGHT— WHEN TAKEN

(a) Appeal in a Civil Case.

(1) Time for Filing a Notice of Appeal.

(A) In a civil case, except as provided in Rules 4(a)(1)(B), 4(a)(4), and 4(c), the notice of appeal required by Rule 3 must be filed with the district clerk within 30 days after entry of the judgment or order appealed from.

(B) The notice of appeal may be filed by any party within 60 days after entry of the judgment or order appealed from if one of the parties is:

(i) the United States;

(ii) a United States agency;

(iii) a United States officer or employee sued in an official capacity; or

(iv) a current or former United States officer or employee sued in an individual capacity for an act or omission occurring in connection with duties performed on the United States' behalf—including all instances in which the United States represents that person when the judgment or order is entered or files the appeal for that person.

(C) An appeal from an order granting or denying an application for a writ of error coram nobis is an appeal in a civil case for purposes of Rule 4(a).

(2) **Filing Before Entry of Judgment.** A notice of appeal filed after the court announces a decision or order— but before the entry of the judgment or order—is treated as filed on the date of and after the entry.

(3) **Multiple Appeals.** If one party timely files a notice of appeal, any other party may file a notice of appeal within 14 days after the date when the first notice was filed, or within the time otherwise prescribed by this Rule 4(a), whichever period ends later.

(4) **Effect of a Motion on a Notice of Appeal.**

(A) If a party files in the district court any of the following motions under the Federal Rules of Civil Procedure—and does so within the time allowed by those rules—the time to file an appeal runs for all parties from the entry of the order disposing of the last such remaining motion:

(i) for judgment under Rule 50(b);

(ii) to amend or make additional factual findings under Rule 52(b), whether or not granting the motion would alter the judgment;

(iii) for attorney's fees under Rule 54 if the district court extends the time to appeal under Rule 58;

(iv) to alter or amend the judgment under Rule 59;

(v) for a new trial under Rule 59; or

(vi) for relief under Rule 60 if the motion is filed no later than 28 days after the judgment is entered.

(B)(i) If a party files a notice of appeal after the court announces or enters a judgment—but before it disposes of any motion listed in Rule 4(a)(4)(A)—the notice becomes effective to appeal a judgment or order, in whole or in part, when the order disposing of the last such remaining motion is entered.

(ii) A party intending to challenge an order disposing of any motion listed in Rule 4(a)(4)(A), or a judgment's alteration or amendment upon such a motion, must file a notice of appeal, or an amended notice of appeal—in compliance with Rule 3(c)—within the time prescribed by this Rule measured from the entry of the order disposing of the last such remaining motion.

(iii) No additional fee is required to file an amended notice.

(5) **Motion for Extension of Time.**

(A) The district court may extend the time to file a notice of appeal if:

(i) a party so moves no later than 30 days after the time prescribed by this Rule 4(a) expires; and

(ii) regardless of whether its motion is filed before or during the 30 days after the time prescribed by this Rule 4(a) expires, that party shows excusable neglect or good cause.

(B) A motion filed before the expiration of the time prescribed in Rule 4(a)(1) or (3) may be ex parte unless the court requires otherwise. If the motion is filed after the expiration of the prescribed time, notice must be given to the other parties in accordance with local rules.

(C) No extension under this Rule 4(a)(5) may exceed 30 days after the prescribed time or 14 days after the date when the order granting the motion is entered, whichever is later.

(6) Reopening the Time to File an Appeal. The district court may reopen the time to file an appeal for a period of 14 days after the date when its order to reopen is entered, but only if all the following conditions are satisfied:

(A) the court finds that the moving party did not receive notice under Federal Rule of Civil Procedure 77(d) of the entry of the judgment or order sought to be appealed within 21 days after entry;

(B) the motion is filed within 180 days after the judgment or order is entered or within 14 days after the moving party receives notice under Federal Rule of Civil Procedure 77(d) of the entry, whichever is earlier; and

(C) the court finds that no party would be prejudiced.

(7) Entry Defined.

(A) A judgment or order is entered for purposes of this Rule 4(a):

(i) if Federal Rule of Civil Procedure 58(a) does not require a separate document, when the judgment or order is entered in the civil docket under Federal Rule of Civil Procedure 79(a); or

(ii) if Federal Rule of Civil Procedure 58(a) requires a separate document, when the judgment or order is entered in the civil docket under Federal Rule of Civil Procedure 79(a) and when the earlier of these events occurs:

● the judgment or order is set forth on a separate document, or

● 150 days have run from entry of the judgment or order in the civil docket under Federal Rule of Civil Procedure 79(a).

(B) A failure to set forth a judgment or order on a separate document when required by Federal Rule of Civil Procedure 58(a) does not affect the validity of an appeal from that judgment or order.

(b) Appeal in a Criminal Case.

(1) Time for Filing a Notice of Appeal.

(A) In a criminal case, a defendant's notice of appeal must be filed in the district court within 14 days after the later of:

(i) the entry of either the judgment or the order being appealed; or

(ii) the filing of the government's notice of appeal.

(B) When the government is entitled to appeal, its notice of appeal must be filed in the district court within 30 days after the later of:

(i) the entry of the judgment or order being appealed; or

(ii) the filing of a notice of appeal by any defendant.

(2) Filing Before Entry of Judgment. A notice of appeal filed after the court announces a decision, sentence, or order—but before the entry of the judgment or order—is treated as filed on the date of and after the entry.

(3) Effect of a Motion on a Notice of Appeal.

(A) If a defendant timely makes any of the following motions under the Federal Rules of Criminal Procedure, the notice of appeal from a judgment of conviction must be filed within 14 days after the entry of the order disposing of the last such remaining motion, or within 14 days after the entry of the judgment of conviction, whichever period ends later. This provision applies to a timely motion:

(i) for judgment of acquittal under Rule 29;

(ii) for a new trial under Rule 33, but if based on newly discovered evidence, only if the motion is made no later than 14 days after the entry of the judgment; or

(iii) for arrest of judgment under Rule 34.

(B) A notice of appeal filed after the court announces a decision, sentence, or order—but before it disposes of any of the motions referred to in Rule 4(b)(3)(A)—becomes effective upon the later of the following:

(i) the entry of the order disposing of the last such remaining motion; or

(ii) the entry of the judgment of conviction.

(C) A valid notice of appeal is effective—without amendment—to appeal from an order disposing of any of the motions referred to in Rule 4(b)(3)(A).

(4) Motion for Extension of Time. Upon a finding of excusable neglect or good cause, the district court may—before or after the time has expired, with or without motion and notice—extend the time to file a notice of appeal for a period not to exceed 30 days from the expiration of the time otherwise prescribed by this Rule 4(b).

(5) Jurisdiction. The filing of a notice of appeal under this Rule 4(b) does not divest a district court of jurisdiction to correct a sentence under Federal Rule of Criminal Procedure 35(a), nor does the filing of a motion under 35(a) affect the validity of a notice of appeal filed before entry of the order disposing of the motion. The filing of a motion under Federal Rule of Criminal Procedure 35(a) does not suspend the time for filing a notice of appeal from a judgment of conviction.

(6) Entry Defined. A judgment or order is entered for purposes of this Rule 4(b) when it is entered on the criminal docket.

(c) Appeal by an Inmate Confined in an Institution.

(1) If an institution has a system designed for legal mail, an inmate confined there must use that system to receive the benefit of this Rule 4(c)(1). If an inmate files a notice of appeal in either a civil or a criminal case, the notice is timely if it is deposited in the institution's internal mail system on or before the last day for filing and:

    (A) it is accompanied by:

        (i) a declaration in compliance with 28 U.S.C. § 1746—or a notarized statement—setting out the date of deposit and stating that first-class postage is being prepaid; or

        (ii) evidence (such as a postmark or date stamp) showing that the notice was so deposited and that postage was prepaid; or

    (B) the court of appeals exercises its discretion to permit the later filing of a declaration or notarized statement that satisfies Rule 4(c)(1)(A)(i).

(2) If an inmate files the first notice of appeal in a civil case under this Rule 4(c), the 14–day period provided in Rule 4(a)(3) for another party to file a notice of appeal runs from the date when the district court dockets the first notice.

(3) When a defendant in a criminal case files a notice of appeal under this Rule 4(c), the 30–day period for the government to file its notice of appeal runs from the entry of the judgment or order appealed from or from the district court's docketing of the defendant's notice of appeal, whichever is later.

(d) Mistaken Filing in the Court of Appeals. If a notice of appeal in either a civil or a criminal case is mistakenly filed in the court of appeals, the clerk of that court must note on the notice the date when it was received and send it to the district clerk. The notice is then considered filed in the district court on the date so noted.

(As amended Apr. 30, 1979, eff. Aug. 1, 1979; Nov. 18, 1988, Pub.L. 100–690, Title VII, § 7111, 102 Stat. 4419; Apr. 30, 1991, eff. Dec. 1, 1991; Apr. 22, 1993, eff. Dec. 1, 1993; Apr. 27, 1995, eff. Dec. 1, 1995; Apr. 24, 1998, eff. Dec. 1, 1998; Apr. 29, 2002, eff. Dec. 1, 2002; Apr. 25, 2005, eff. Dec. 1, 2005; Mar. 26, 2009, eff. Dec. 1, 2009; Apr. 28, 2010, eff. Dec. 1, 2010; Apr. 26, 2011, eff. Dec. 1, 2011; Apr. 28, 2016, eff. Dec. 1, 2016; Apr. 27, 2017, eff. Dec. 1, 2017.)

RULE 5.   APPEAL BY PERMISSION

(a) Petition for Permission to Appeal.

(1) To request permission to appeal when an appeal is within the court of appeals' discretion, a party must file a petition with the circuit clerk and serve it on all other parties to the district-court action.

(2) The petition must be filed within the time specified by the statute or rule authorizing the appeal or, if no such time is specified, within the time provided by Rule 4(a) for filing a notice of appeal.

(3) If a party cannot petition for appeal unless the district court first enters an order granting permission to do so or stating that the necessary conditions are met, the district court may amend its order, either on its own or in response to a party's motion, to include the required permission or

statement. In that event, the time to petition runs from entry of the amended order.

(b) Contents of the Petition; Answer or Cross–Petition; Oral Argument.

(1) The petition must include the following:

    (A) the facts necessary to understand the question presented;

    (B) the question itself;

    (C) the relief sought;

    (D) the reasons why the appeal should be allowed and is authorized by a statute or rule; and

    (E) an attached copy of:

        (i) the order, decree, or judgment complained of and any related opinion or memorandum, and

        (ii) any order stating the district court's permission to appeal or finding that the necessary conditions are met.

(2) A party may file an answer in opposition or a cross-petition within 10 days after the petition is served.

(3) The petition and answer will be submitted without oral argument unless the court of appeals orders otherwise.

(c) Form of Papers; Number of Copies; Length Limits. All papers must conform to Rule 32(c)(2). An original and 3 copies must be filed unless the court requires a different number by local rule or by order in a particular case. Except by the court's permission, and excluding the accompanying documents required by Rule 5(b)(1)(E):

(1) a paper produced using a computer must not exceed 5,200 words; and

(2) a handwritten or typewritten paper must not exceed 20 pages.

(d) Grant of Permission; Fees; Cost Bond; Filing the Record.

(1) Within 14 days after the entry of the order granting permission to appeal, the appellant must:

    (A) pay the district clerk all required fees; and

    (B) file a cost bond if required under Rule 7.

(2) A notice of appeal need not be filed. The date when the order granting permission to appeal is entered serves as the date of the notice of appeal for calculating time under these rules.

(3) The district clerk must notify the circuit clerk once the petitioner has paid the fees. Upon receiving this notice, the circuit clerk must enter the appeal on the docket. The record must be forwarded and filed in accordance with Rules 11 and 12(c).

(As amended Apr. 30, 1979, eff. Aug. 1, 1979; Apr. 29, 1994, eff. Dec. 1, 1994; Apr. 24, 1998, eff. Dec. 1, 1998; Apr. 29, 2002, eff. Dec. 1, 2002; Mar. 26, 2009, eff. Dec. 1, 2009; Apr. 28, 2016, eff. Dec. 1, 2016; Apr. 25, 2019, eff. Dec. 1, 2019.)

[RULE 5.1 APPEAL BY LEAVE UNDER 28 U.S.C. § 636 (c)(5) (ABROGATED APR. 24, 1998, EFF. DEC. 1, 1998)]

RULE 6. APPEAL IN A BANKRUPTCY CASE

(a) Appeal From a Judgment, Order, or Decree of a District Court Exercising Original Jurisdiction in a Bankruptcy Case. An appeal to a court of appeals from a final judgment, order, or decree of a district court exercising jurisdiction under 28 U.S.C. § 1334 is taken as any other civil appeal under these rules.

(b) Appeal From a Judgment, Order, or Decree of a District Court or Bankruptcy Appellate Panel Exercising Appellate Jurisdiction in a Bankruptcy Case.

(1) Applicability of Other Rules. These rules apply to an appeal to a court of appeals under 28 U.S.C. § 158(d)(1) from a final judgment, order, or decree of a district court or bankruptcy appellate panel exercising appellate jurisdiction under 28 U.S.C. § 158(a) or (b), but with these qualifications:

(A) Rules 4(a)(4), 4(b), 9, 10, 11, 12(c), 13–20, 22–23, and 24(b) do not apply;

(B) the reference in Rule 3(c) to "Forms 1A and 1B in the Appendix of Forms" must be read as a reference to Form 5;

(C) when the appeal is from a bankruptcy appellate panel, "district court," as used in any applicable rule, means "appellate panel"; and

(D) in Rule 12.1, "district court" includes a bankruptcy court or bankruptcy appellate panel.

(2) Additional Rules. In addition to the rules made applicable by Rule 6(b)(1), the following rules apply:

(A) Motion for Rehearing.

(i) If a timely motion for rehearing under Bankruptcy Rule 8022 is filed, the time to appeal for all parties runs from the entry of the order disposing of the motion. A notice of appeal filed after the district court or bankruptcy appellate panel announces or enters a judgment, order, or decree—but before disposition of the motion for rehearing—becomes effective when the order disposing of the motion for rehearing is entered.

(ii) If a party intends to challenge the order disposing of the motion—or the alteration or amendment of a judgment, order, or decree upon the motion—then the party, in compliance with Rules 3(c) and 6(b)(1)(B), must file a notice of appeal or amended notice of appeal. The notice or amended notice must be filed within the time prescribed by Rule 4—excluding Rules 4(a)(4) and 4(b)—measured from the entry of the order disposing of the motion.

(iii) No additional fee is required to file an amended notice.

(B) The Record on Appeal.

(i) Within 14 days after filing the notice of appeal, the appellant must file with the clerk possessing the record assembled in accordance with Bankruptcy Rule 8009—and serve on the appellee—a statement of the issues to be presented on appeal and a designation of the record to be certified and made available to the circuit clerk.

(ii) An appellee who believes that other parts of the record are necessary must, within 14 days after being served with the appellant's designation, file with the clerk and serve on the appellant a designation of additional parts to be included.

(iii) The record on appeal consists of:

● the redesignated record as provided above;

● the proceedings in the district court or bankruptcy appellate panel; and

● a certified copy of the docket entries prepared by the clerk under Rule 3(d).

(C) Making the Record Available.

(i) When the record is complete, the district clerk or bankruptcy-appellate-panel clerk must number the documents constituting the record and promptly make it available to the circuit clerk. If the clerk makes the record available in paper form, the clerk will not send documents of unusual bulk or weight, physical exhibits other than documents, or other parts of the record designated for omission by local rule of the court of appeals, unless directed to do so by a party or the circuit clerk. If unusually bulky or heavy exhibits are to be made available in paper form, a party must arrange with the clerks in advance for their transportation and receipt.

(ii) All parties must do whatever else is necessary to enable the clerk to assemble the record and make it available. When the record is made available in paper form, the court of appeals may provide by rule or order that a certified copy of the docket entries be made available in place of the redesignated record. But any party may request at any time during the pendency of the appeal that the redesignated record be made available.

(D) Filing the Record. When the district clerk or bankruptcy-appellate-panel clerk has made the record available, the circuit clerk must note that fact on the docket. The date noted on the docket serves as the filing date of the record. The circuit clerk must immediately notify all parties of the filing date.

(c) Direct Review by Permission Under 28 U.S.C. § 158(d)(2).

(1) Applicability of Other Rules. These rules apply to a direct appeal by permission under 28 U.S.C. § 158(d)(2), but with these qualifications:

(A) Rules 3–4, 5(a)(3), 6(a), 6(b), 8(a), 8(c), 9–12, 13–20, 22–23, and 24(b) do not apply;

(B) as used in any applicable rule, "district court" or "district clerk" includes—to the extent appropriate—a bankruptcy court or bankruptcy appellate panel or its clerk; and

(C) the reference to "Rules 11 and 12(c)" in Rule 5(d)(3) must be read as a reference to Rules 6(c)(2)(B) and (C).

(2) Additional Rules. In addition, the following rules apply:

(A) The Record on Appeal. Bankruptcy Rule 8009 governs the record on appeal.

(B) Making the Record Available. Bankruptcy Rule 8010 governs completing the record and making it available.

(C) Stays Pending Appeal. Bankruptcy Rule 8007 applies to stays pending appeal.

(D) Duties of the Circuit Clerk. When the bankruptcy clerk has made the record available, the circuit clerk must note that fact on the docket. The date noted on the docket serves as the filing date of the record. The circuit clerk must immediately notify all parties of the filing date.

(E) Filing a Representation Statement. Unless the court of appeals designates another time, within 14 days after entry of the order granting permission to appeal, the attorney who sought permission must file a statement with the circuit clerk naming the parties that the attorney represents on appeal.

(Added Apr. 25, 1989, eff. Dec. 1, 1989; amended Apr. 30, 1991, eff. Dec. 1, 1991; Apr. 22, 1993, eff. Dec. 1, 1993; Apr. 24, 1998, eff. Dec. 1, 1998; Mar. 26, 2009, eff. Dec. 1, 2009; Apr. 25, 2014, eff. Dec. 1, 2014; Apr. 14, 2021, eff. Dec. 1, 2021.)

RULE 7. BOND FOR COSTS ON APPEAL IN A CIVIL CASE

In a civil case, the district court may require an appellant to file a bond or provide other security in any form and amount necessary to ensure payment of costs on appeal. Rule 8(b) applies to a surety on a bond given under this rule.

(As amended Apr. 30, 1979, eff. Aug. 1, 1979; Apr. 24, 1998, eff. Dec. 1, 1998.)

RULE 8. STAY OR INJUNCTION PENDING APPEAL

(a) Motion for Stay.

(1) Initial Motion in the District Court. A party must ordinarily move first in the district court for the following relief:

(A) a stay of the judgment or order of a district court pending appeal;

(B) approval of a bond or other security provided to obtain a stay of judgment; or

(C) an order suspending, modifying, restoring, or granting an injunction while an appeal is pending.

(2) Motion in the Court of Appeals; Conditions on Relief. A motion for the relief mentioned in Rule 8(a)(1) may be made to the court of appeals or to one of its judges.

(A) The motion must:

(i) show that moving first in the district court would be impracticable; or

(ii) state that, a motion having been made, the district court denied the motion or failed to afford the relief requested and state any reasons given by the district court for its action.

(B) The motion must also include:

(i) the reasons for granting the relief requested and the facts relied on;

(ii) originals or copies of affidavits or other sworn statements supporting facts subject to dispute; and

(iii) relevant parts of the record.

(C) The moving party must give reasonable notice of the motion to all parties.

(D) A motion under this Rule 8(a)(2) must be filed with the circuit clerk and normally will be considered by a panel of the court. But in an exceptional case in which time requirements make that procedure impracticable, the motion may be made to and considered by a single judge.

(E) The court may condition relief on a party's filing a bond or other security in the district court.

(b) Proceeding Against a Security Provider. If a party gives security with one or more security providers, each provider submits to the jurisdiction of the district court and irrevocably appoints the district clerk as its agent on whom any papers affecting its liability on the security may be served. On motion, a security provider's liability may be enforced in the district court without the necessity of an independent action. The motion and any notice that the district court prescribes may be served on the district clerk, who must promptly send a copy to each security provider whose address is known.

(c) Stay in a Criminal Case. Rule 38 of the Federal Rules of Criminal Procedure governs a stay in a criminal case.

(As amended Mar. 10, 1986, eff. July 1, 1986; Apr. 27, 1995, eff. Dec. 1, 1995; Apr. 24, 1998, eff. Dec. 1, 1998; Apr. 26, 2018, eff. Dec. 1, 2018.)

RULE 9. RELEASE IN A CRIMINAL CASE

(a) Release Before Judgment of Conviction.

(1) The district court must state in writing, or orally on the record, the reasons for an order regarding the release or detention of a defendant in a criminal case. A party appealing from the order must file with the court of appeals a copy of the district court's order and the court's statement of reasons as soon as practicable after filing the notice of appeal. An appellant who questions the factual basis for the district court's order must file a transcript of the release proceedings or an explanation of why a transcript was not obtained.

(2) After reasonable notice to the appellee, the court of appeals must promptly determine the appeal on the basis of the papers, affidavits, and parts of the record that the parties present or the court requires. Unless the court so orders, briefs need not be filed.

(3) The court of appeals or one of its judges may order the defendant's release pending the disposition of the appeal.

(b) Release After Judgment of Conviction. A party entitled to do so may obtain review of a district-court order regarding release after a judgment of conviction by filing a notice of appeal from that order in the district court, or by filing a motion in the court of appeals if the party has already filed a notice of appeal from the judgment of conviction. Both the order and the review are subject to Rule 9(a). The papers filed by the party seeking review must include a copy of the judgment of conviction.

(c) Criteria for Release. The court must make its decision regarding release in accordance with the applicable provisions of 18 U.S.C. §§ 3142, 3143, and 3145(c).

(As amended Apr. 24, 1972, eff. Oct. 1, 1972; Oct. 12, 1984, Pub.L. 98–473, Title II, § 210, 98 Stat. 1987; Apr. 29, 1994, eff. Dec. 1, 1994; Apr. 24, 1998, eff. Dec. 1, 1998.)

RULE 10.   THE RECORD ON APPEAL

(a) Composition of the Record on Appeal. The following items constitute the record on appeal:

(1) the original papers and exhibits filed in the district court;

(2) the transcript of proceedings, if any; and

(3) a certified copy of the docket entries prepared by the district clerk.

(b) The Transcript of Proceedings.

(1) **Appellant's Duty to Order.** Within 14 days after filing the notice of appeal or entry of an order disposing of the last timely remaining motion of a type specified in Rule 4(a)(4)(A), whichever is later, the appellant must do either of the following:

(A) order from the reporter a transcript of such parts of the proceedings not already on file as the appellant considers necessary, subject to a local rule of the court of appeals and with the following qualifications:

(i) the order must be in writing;

(ii) if the cost of the transcript is to be paid by the United States under the Criminal Justice Act, the order must so state; and

(iii) the appellant must, within the same period, file a copy of the order with the district clerk; or

(B) file a certificate stating that no transcript will be ordered.

(2) **Unsupported Finding or Conclusion.** If the appellant intends to urge on appeal that a finding or conclusion is unsupported by the evidence or is contrary to the evidence, the appellant must include in the record a transcript of all evidence relevant to that finding or conclusion.

(3) **Partial Transcript.** Unless the entire transcript is ordered:

(A) the appellant must—within the 14 days provided in Rule 10(b)(1)—file a statement of the issues that the appellant intends to present on the appeal and must serve on the appellee a copy of both the order or certificate and the statement;

(B) if the appellee considers it necessary to have a transcript of other parts of the proceedings, the appellee must, within 14 days after the service of the order or certificate and the statement of the issues, file and serve on the appellant a designation of additional parts to be ordered; and

(C) unless within 14 days after service of that designation the appellant has ordered all such parts, and has so notified the appellee, the appellee may within the following 14 days either order the parts or move in the district court for an order requiring the appellant to do so.

(4) **Payment.** At the time of ordering, a party must make satisfactory arrangements with the reporter for paying the cost of the transcript.

(c) Statement of the Evidence When the Proceedings Were Not Recorded or When a Transcript Is Unavailable. If the transcript of a hearing or trial is unavailable, the appellant may prepare a statement of the evidence or proceedings from the best available means, including the appellant's recollection. The statement must be served on the appellee, who may serve objections or proposed amendments within 14 days after being served. The statement and any objections or proposed amendments must then be submitted to the district court for settlement and approval. As settled and approved, the statement must be included by the district clerk in the record on appeal.

(d) Agreed Statement as the Record on Appeal. In place of the record on appeal as defined in Rule 10(a), the parties may prepare, sign, and submit to the district court a statement of the case showing how the issues presented by the appeal arose and were decided in the district court. The statement must set forth only those facts averred and proved or sought to be proved that are essential to the court's resolution of the issues. If the statement is truthful, it—together with any additions that the district court may consider necessary to a full presentation of the issues on appeal—must be approved by the district court and must then be certified to the court of appeals as the record on appeal. The district clerk must then send it to the circuit clerk within the time provided by Rule 11. A copy of the agreed statement may be filed in place of the appendix required by Rule 30.

(e) Correction or Modification of the Record.

(1) If any difference arises about whether the record truly discloses what occurred in the district court, the difference must be submitted to and settled by that court and the record conformed accordingly.

(2) If anything material to either party is omitted from or misstated in the record by error or accident, the omission or misstatement may be corrected and a supplemental record may be certified and forwarded:

(A) on stipulation of the parties;

(B) by the district court before or after the record has been forwarded; or

(C) by the court of appeals.

(3) All other questions as to the form and content of the record must be presented to the court of appeals.

(As amended Apr. 30, 1979, eff. Aug. 1, 1979; Mar. 10, 1986, eff. July 1, 1986; Apr. 30, 1991, eff. Dec. 1, 1991; Apr. 22, 1993, eff. Dec. 1, 1993; Apr. 27, 1995, eff. Dec. 1, 1995; Apr. 24, 1998, eff. Dec. 1, 1998; Mar. 26, 2009, eff. Dec. 1, 2009.)

RULE 11. FORWARDING THE RECORD

(a) Appellant's Duty. An appellant filing a notice of appeal must comply with Rule 10(b) and must do whatever else is necessary to enable the clerk to assemble and forward the record. If there are multiple appeals from a judgment or order, the clerk must forward a single record.

(b) Duties of Reporter and District Clerk.

(1) Reporter's Duty to Prepare and File a Transcript. The reporter must prepare and file a transcript as follows:

(A) Upon receiving an order for a transcript, the reporter must enter at the foot of the order the date of its receipt and the expected completion date and send a copy, so endorsed, to the circuit clerk.

(B) If the transcript cannot be completed within 30 days of the reporter's receipt of the order, the reporter may request the circuit clerk to grant additional time to complete it. The clerk must note on the docket the action taken and notify the parties.

(C) When a transcript is complete, the reporter must file it with the district clerk and notify the circuit clerk of the filing.

(D) If the reporter fails to file the transcript on time, the circuit clerk must notify the district judge and do whatever else the court of appeals directs.

(2) District Clerk's Duty to Forward. When the record is complete, the district clerk must number the documents constituting the record and send them promptly to the circuit clerk together with a list of the documents correspondingly numbered and reasonably identified. Unless directed to do so by a party or the circuit clerk, the district clerk will not send to the court of appeals documents of unusual bulk or weight, physical exhibits other than documents, or other parts of the record designated for omission by local rule of the court of appeals. If the exhibits are unusually bulky or heavy, a party must arrange with the clerks in advance for their transportation and receipt.

(c) Retaining the Record Temporarily in the District Court for Use in Preparing the Appeal. The parties may stipulate, or the district court on motion may order, that the district clerk retain the record temporarily for the parties to use in preparing the papers on appeal. In that event the district clerk must certify to the circuit clerk that the record on appeal is complete. Upon receipt of the appellee's brief, or earlier if the court orders or the parties agree, the appellant must request the district clerk to forward the record.

(d) [Abrogated.]

(e) Retaining the Record by Court Order.

(1) The court of appeals may, by order or local rule, provide that a certified copy of the docket entries be for-warded instead of the entire record. But a party may at any time during the appeal request that designated parts of the record be forwarded.

(2) The district court may order the record or some part of it retained if the court needs it while the appeal is pending, subject, however, to call by the court of appeals.

(3) If part or all of the record is ordered retained, the district clerk must send to the court of appeals a copy of the order and the docket entries together with the parts of the original record allowed by the district court and copies of any parts of the record designated by the parties.

(f) Retaining Parts of the Record in the District Court by Stipulation of the Parties. The parties may agree by written stipulation filed in the district court that designated parts of the record be retained in the district court subject to call by the court of appeals or request by a party. The parts of the record so designated remain a part of the record on appeal.

(g) Record for a Preliminary Motion in the Court of Appeals. If, before the record is forwarded, a party makes any of the following motions in the court of appeals:

● for dismissal;

● for release;

● for a stay pending appeal;

● for additional security on the bond on appeal or on a bond or other security provided to obtain a stay of judgment; or

● for any other intermediate order—

the district clerk must send the court of appeals any parts of the record designated by any party.

(As amended Apr. 30, 1979, eff. Aug. 1, 1979; Mar. 10, 1986, eff. July 1, 1986; Apr. 24, 1998, eff. Dec. 1, 1998; Apr. 26, 2018, eff. Dec. 1, 2018.)

RULE 12. DOCKETING THE APPEAL; FILING A REPRESENTATION STATEMENT; FILING THE RECORD

(a) Docketing the Appeal. Upon receiving the copy of the notice of appeal and the docket entries from the district clerk under Rule 3(d), the circuit clerk must docket the appeal under the title of the district-court action and must identify the appellant, adding the appellant's name if necessary.

(b) Filing a Representation Statement. Unless the court of appeals designates another time, the attorney who filed the notice of appeal must, within 14 days after filing the notice, file a statement with the circuit clerk naming the parties that the attorney represents on appeal.

(c) Filing the Record, Partial Record, or Certificate. Upon receiving the record, partial record, or district clerk's certificate as provided in Rule 11, the circuit clerk must file it and immediately notify all parties of the filing date.

(As amended Apr. 30, 1979, eff. Aug. 1, 1979; Mar. 10, 1986, eff. July 1, 1986; Apr. 22, 1993, eff. Dec. 1, 1993; Apr. 24, 1998, eff. Dec. 1, 1998; Mar. 26, 2009, eff. Dec. 1, 2009.)

RULE 12.1 REMAND AFTER AN INDICATIVE RULING BY THE DISTRICT COURT ON A MOTION FOR RELIEF THAT IS BARRED BY A PENDING APPEAL

(a) Notice to the Court of Appeals. If a timely motion is made in the district court for relief that it lacks authority to grant because of an appeal that has been docketed and is pending, the movant must promptly notify the circuit clerk if the district court states either that it would grant the motion or that the motion raises a substantial issue.

(b) Remand After an Indicative Ruling. If the district court states that it would grant the motion or that the motion raises a substantial issue, the court of appeals may remand for further proceedings but retains jurisdiction unless it expressly dismisses the appeal. If the court of appeals remands but retains jurisdiction, the parties must promptly notify the circuit clerk when the district court has decided the motion on remand.

(Added Mar. 26, 2009, eff. Dec. 1, 2009.)

TITLE III. APPEALS FROM THE UNITED STATES TAX COURT

RULE 13. APPEALS FROM THE TAX COURT

(a) Appeal as of Right.

(1) How Obtained; Time for Filing a Notice of Appeal.

(A) An appeal as of right from the United States Tax Court is commenced by filing a notice of appeal with the Tax Court clerk within 90 days after the entry of the Tax Court's decision. At the time of filing, the appellant must furnish the clerk with enough copies of the notice to enable the clerk to comply with Rule 3(d). If one party files a timely notice of appeal, any other party may file a notice of appeal within 120 days after the Tax Court's decision is entered.

(B) If, under Tax Court rules, a party makes a timely motion to vacate or revise the Tax Court's decision, the time to file a notice of appeal runs from the entry of the order disposing of the motion or from the entry of a new decision, whichever is later.

(2) Notice of Appeal; How Filed. The notice of appeal may be filed either at the Tax Court clerk's office in the District of Columbia or by sending it to the clerk. If sent by mail the notice is considered filed on the postmark date, subject to § 7502 of the Internal Revenue Code, as amended, and the applicable regulations.

(3) Contents of the Notice of Appeal; Service; Effect of Filing and Service. Rule 3 prescribes the contents of a notice of appeal, the manner of service, and the effect of its filing and service. Form 2 in the Appendix of Forms is a suggested form of a notice of appeal.

(4) The Record on Appeal; Forwarding; Filing.

(A) Except as otherwise provided under Tax Court rules for the transcript of proceedings, the appeal is governed by the parts of Rules 10, 11, and 12 regarding the record on appeal from a district court, the time and manner of forwarding and filing, and the docketing in the court of appeals.

(B) If an appeal is taken to more than one court of appeals, the original record must be sent to the court named in the first notice of appeal filed. In an appeal to any other court of appeals, the appellant must apply to that other court to make provision for the record.

(b) Appeal by Permission. An appeal by permission is governed by Rule 5.

(As amended Apr. 1, 1979, eff. Aug. 1, 1979; Apr. 29, 1994, eff. Dec. 1, 1994; Apr. 24, 1998, eff. Dec. 1, 1998; Apr. 16, 2013, eff. Dec. 1, 2013; Apr. 25, 2019, eff. Dec. 1, 2019.)

RULE 14. APPLICABILITY OF OTHER RULES TO APPEALS FROM THE TAX COURT

All provisions of these rules, except Rules 4, 6–9, 15–20, and 22–23, apply to appeals from the Tax Court. References in any applicable rule (other than Rule 24(a)) to the district court and district clerk are to be read as referring to the Tax Court and its clerk.

(As amended Apr. 24, 1998, eff. Dec. 1, 1998; Apr. 16, 2013, eff. Dec. 1, 2013.)

TITLE IV. REVIEW OR ENFORCEMENT OF AN ORDER OF AN ADMINISTRATIVE AGENCY, BOARD, COMMISSION, OR OFFICER

RULE 15. REVIEW OR ENFORCEMENT OF AN AGENCY ORDER—HOW OBTAINED; INTERVENTION

(a) Petition for Review; Joint Petition.

(1) Review of an agency order is commenced by filing, within the time prescribed by law, a petition for review with the clerk of a court of appeals authorized to review the agency order. If their interests make joinder practicable, two or more persons may join in a petition to the same court to review the same order.

(2) The petition must:

(A) name each party seeking review either in the caption or the body of the petition—using such terms as "et al.," "petitioners," or "respondents" does not effectively name the parties;

(B) name the agency as a respondent (even though not named in the petition, the United States is a respondent if required by statute); and

(C) specify the order or part thereof to be reviewed.

(3) Form 3 in the Appendix of Forms is a suggested form of a petition for review.

(4) In this rule "agency" includes an agency, board, commission, or officer; "petition for review" includes a petition to enjoin, suspend, modify, or otherwise review, or a notice of appeal, whichever form is indicated by the applicable statute.

(b) Application or Cross–Application to Enforce an Order; Answer; Default.

(1) An application to enforce an agency order must be filed with the clerk of a court of appeals authorized to enforce the order. If a petition is filed to review an agency order that the court may enforce, a party opposing the petition may file a cross-application for enforcement.

(2) Within 21 days after the application for enforcement is filed, the respondent must serve on the applicant an answer to the application and file it with the clerk. If the respondent fails to answer in time, the court will enter judgment for the relief requested.

(3) The application must contain a concise statement of the proceedings in which the order was entered, the facts upon which venue is based, and the relief requested.

(c) Service of the Petition or Application. The circuit clerk must serve a copy of the petition for review, or an application or cross-application to enforce an agency order, on each respondent as prescribed by Rule 3(d), unless a different manner of service is prescribed by statute. At the time of filing, the petitioner must:

(1) serve, or have served, a copy on each party admitted to participate in the agency proceedings, except for the respondents;

(2) file with the clerk a list of those so served; and

(3) give the clerk enough copies of the petition or application to serve each respondent.

(d) Intervention. Unless a statute provides another method, a person who wants to intervene in a proceeding under this rule must file a motion for leave to intervene with the circuit clerk and serve a copy on all parties. The motion—or other notice of intervention authorized by statute—must be filed within 30 days after the petition for review is filed and must contain a concise statement of the interest of the moving party and the grounds for intervention.

(e) Payment of Fees. When filing any separate or joint petition for review in a court of appeals, the petitioner must pay the circuit clerk all required fees.

(As amended Apr. 22, 1993, eff. Dec. 1, 1993; Apr. 24, 1998, eff. Dec. 1, 1998; Mar. 26, 2009, eff. Dec. 1, 2009.)

RULE 15.1 BRIEFS AND ORAL ARGUMENT IN A NATIONAL LABOR RELATIONS BOARD PROCEEDING

In either an enforcement or a review proceeding, a party adverse to the National Labor Relations Board proceeds first on briefing and at oral argument, unless the court orders otherwise.

(Added Mar. 10, 1986, eff. July 1, 1986; amended Apr. 24, 1998, eff. Dec. 1, 1998.)

RULE 16. THE RECORD ON REVIEW OR ENFORCEMENT

(a) Composition of the Record. The record on review or enforcement of an agency order consists of:

(1) the order involved;

(2) any findings or report on which it is based; and

(3) the pleadings, evidence, and other parts of the proceedings before the agency.

(b) Omissions From or Misstatements in the Record. The parties may at any time, by stipulation, supply any omission from the record or correct a misstatement, or the court may so direct. If necessary, the court may direct that a supplemental record be prepared and filed.

(As amended Apr. 24, 1998, eff. Dec. 1, 1998.)

RULE 17. FILING THE RECORD

(a) Agency to File; Time for Filing; Notice of Filing. The agency must file the record with the circuit clerk within 40 days after being served with a petition for review, unless the statute authorizing review provides otherwise, or within 40 days after it files an application for enforcement unless the respondent fails to answer or the court orders otherwise. The court may shorten or extend the time to file the record. The clerk must notify all parties of the date when the record is filed.

(b) Filing—What Constitutes.

(1) The agency must file:

(A) the original or a certified copy of the entire record or parts designated by the parties; or

(B) a certified list adequately describing all documents, transcripts of testimony, exhibits, and other material constituting the record, or describing those parts designated by the parties.

(2) The parties may stipulate in writing that no record or certified list be filed. The date when the stipulation is filed with the circuit clerk is treated as the date when the record is filed.

(3) The agency must retain any portion of the record not filed with the clerk. All parts of the record retained by the agency are a part of the record on review for all purposes and, if the court or a party so requests, must be sent to the court regardless of any prior stipulation.

(As amended Apr. 24, 1998, eff. Dec. 1, 1998.)

RULE 18. STAY PENDING REVIEW

(a) Motion for a Stay.

(1) Initial Motion Before the Agency. A petitioner must ordinarily move first before the agency for a stay pending review of its decision or order.

(2) Motion in the Court of Appeals. A motion for a stay may be made to the court of appeals or one of its judges.

(A) The motion must:

(i) show that moving first before the agency would be impracticable; or

(ii) state that, a motion having been made, the agency denied the motion or failed to afford the relief requested and state any reasons given by the agency for its action.

(B) The motion must also include:

(i) the reasons for granting the relief requested and the facts relied on;

(ii) originals or copies of affidavits or other sworn statements supporting facts subject to dispute; and

(iii) relevant parts of the record.

(C) The moving party must give reasonable notice of the motion to all parties.

(D) The motion must be filed with the circuit clerk and normally will be considered by a panel of the court. But in an exceptional case in which time requirements make that procedure impracticable, the motion may be made to and considered by a single judge.

(b) Bond. The court may condition relief on the filing of a bond or other appropriate security.

(As amended Apr. 24, 1998, eff. Dec. 1, 1998.)

RULE 19. SETTLEMENT OF A JUDGMENT ENFORCING AN AGENCY ORDER IN PART

When the court files an opinion directing entry of judgment enforcing the agency's order in part, the agency must within 14 days file with the clerk and serve on each other party a proposed judgment conforming to the opinion. A party who disagrees with the agency's proposed judgment must within 10 days file with the clerk and serve the agency with a proposed judgment that the party believes conforms to the opinion. The court will settle the judgment and direct entry without further hearing or argument.

(As amended Mar. 10, 1986, eff. July 1, 1986; Apr. 24, 1998, eff. Dec. 1, 1998; Mar. 26, 2009, eff. Dec. 1, 2009.)

RULE 20. APPLICABILITY OF RULES TO THE REVIEW OR ENFORCEMENT OF AN AGENCY ORDER

All provisions of these rules, except Rules 3–14 and 22–23, apply to the review or enforcement of an agency order. In these rules, "appellant" includes a petitioner or applicant, and "appellee" includes a respondent.

(As amended Apr. 24, 1998, eff. Dec. 1, 1998.)

TITLE V. EXTRAORDINARY WRITS

RULE 21. WRITS OF MANDAMUS AND PROHIBITION, AND OTHER EXTRAORDINARY WRITS

(a) Mandamus or Prohibition to a Court: Petition, Filing, Service, and Docketing.

(1) A party petitioning for a writ of mandamus or prohibition directed to a court must file the petition with the circuit clerk and serve it on all parties to the proceeding in the trial court. The party must also provide a copy to the trial-court judge. All parties to the proceeding in the trial court other than the petitioner are respondents for all purposes.

(2)(A) The petition must be titled "In re [name of petitioner]."

(B) The petition must state:

(i) the relief sought;

(ii) the issues presented;

(iii) the facts necessary to understand the issue presented by the petition; and

(iv) the reasons why the writ should issue.

(C) The petition must include a copy of any order or opinion or parts of the record that may be essential to understand the matters set forth in the petition.

(3) Upon receiving the prescribed docket fee, the clerk must docket the petition and submit it to the court.

(b) Denial; Order Directing Answer; Briefs; Precedence.

(1) The court may deny the petition without an answer. Otherwise, it must order the respondent, if any, to answer within a fixed time.

(2) The clerk must serve the order to respond on all persons directed to respond.

(3) Two or more respondents may answer jointly.

(4) The court of appeals may invite or order the trial-court judge to address the petition or may invite an amicus curiae to do so. The trial-court judge may request permission to address the petition but may not do so unless invited or ordered to do so by the court of appeals.

(5) If briefing or oral argument is required, the clerk must advise the parties, and when appropriate, the trial-court judge or amicus curiae.

(6) The proceeding must be given preference over ordinary civil cases.

(7) The circuit clerk must send a copy of the final disposition to the trial-court judge.

(c) Other Extraordinary Writs. An application for an extraordinary writ other than one provided for in Rule 21(a) must be made by filing a petition with the circuit clerk and serving it on the respondents. Proceedings on the application must conform, so far as is practicable, to the procedures prescribed in Rule 21(a) and (b).

(d) Form of Papers; Number of Copies; Length Limits. All papers must conform to Rule 32(c)(2). An original and 3 copies must be filed unless the court requires the filing of a different number by local rule or by order in a particular case. Except by the court's permission, and excluding the accompanying documents required by Rule 21(a)(2)(C):

(1) a paper produced using a computer must not exceed 7,800 words; and

(2) a handwritten or typewritten paper must not exceed 30 pages.

(As amended Apr. 29, 1994, eff. Dec. 1, 1994; Apr. 23, 1996, eff. Dec. 1, 1996; Apr. 24, 1998, eff. Dec. 1, 1998; Apr. 29, 2002, eff. Dec. 1, 2002; Apr. 28, 2016, eff. Dec. 1, 2016; Apr. 25, 2019, eff. Dec. 1, 2019.)

TITLE VI. HABEAS CORPUS; PROCEEDINGS IN FORMA PAUPERIS

RULE 22. HABEAS CORPUS AND SECTION 2255 PROCEEDINGS

(a) Application for the Original Writ. An application for a writ of habeas corpus must be made to the appropriate district court. If made to a circuit judge, the application must be transferred to the appropriate district court. If a district court denies an application made or transferred to it, renewal of the application before a circuit judge is not permitted. The applicant may, under 28 U.S.C. § 2253, appeal to the court of appeals from the district court's order denying the application.

(b) Certificate of Appealability.

(1) In a habeas corpus proceeding in which the detention complained of arises from process issued by a state court, or in a 28 U.S.C. § 2255 proceeding, the applicant cannot take an appeal unless a circuit justice or a circuit or district judge issues a certificate of appealability under 28 U.S.C. § 2253(c). If an applicant files a notice of appeal, the district clerk must send to the court of appeals the certificate (if any) and the statement described in Rule 11(a) of the Rules Governing Proceedings Under 28 U.S.C. § 2254 or § 2255 (if any), along with the notice of appeal and the file of the district-court proceedings. If the district judge has denied the certificate, the applicant may request a circuit judge to issue it.

(2) A request addressed to the court of appeals may be considered by a circuit judge or judges, as the court prescribes. If no express request for a certificate is filed, the notice of appeal constitutes a request addressed to the judges of the court of appeals.

(3) A certificate of appealability is not required when a state or its representative or the United States or its representative appeals.

(As amended Pub.L. 104–132, Title I, § 103, Apr. 24, 1996, 110 Stat. 1218; Apr. 24, 1998, eff. Dec. 1, 1998; Mar. 26, 2009, eff. Dec. 1, 2009.)

RULE 23. CUSTODY OR RELEASE OF A PRISONER IN A HABEAS CORPUS PROCEEDING

(a) Transfer of Custody Pending Review. Pending review of a decision in a habeas corpus proceeding commenced before a court, justice, or judge of the United States for the release of a prisoner, the person having custody of the prisoner must not transfer custody to another unless a transfer is directed in accordance with this rule. When, upon application, a custodian shows the need for a transfer, the court, justice, or judge rendering the decision under review may authorize the transfer and substitute the successor custodian as a party.

(b) Detention or Release Pending Review of Decision Not to Release. While a decision not to release a prisoner is under review, the court or judge rendering the decision, or the court of appeals, or the Supreme Court, or a judge or justice of either court, may order that the prisoner be:

(1) detained in the custody from which release is sought;

(2) detained in other appropriate custody; or

(3) released on personal recognizance, with or without surety.

(c) Release Pending Review of Decision Ordering Release. While a decision ordering the release of a prisoner is under review, the prisoner must—unless the court or judge rendering the decision, or the court of appeals, or the Supreme Court, or a judge or justice of either court orders otherwise—be released on personal recognizance, with or without surety.

(d) Modification of the Initial Order on Custody. An initial order governing the prisoner's custody or release, including any recognizance or surety, continues in effect pending review unless for special reasons shown to the court of appeals or the Supreme Court, or to a judge or justice of either court, the order is modified or an independent order regarding custody, release, or surety is issued.

(As amended Mar. 10, 1986, eff. July 1, 1986; Apr. 24, 1998, eff. Dec. 1, 1998.)

RULE 24. PROCEEDING IN FORMA PAUPERIS

(a) Leave to Proceed In Forma Pauperis.

(1) Motion in the District Court. Except as stated in Rule 24(a)(3), a party to a district-court action who desires to appeal in forma pauperis must file a motion in the district court. The party must attach an affidavit that:

(A) shows in the detail prescribed by Form 4 of the Appendix of Forms the party's inability to pay or to give security for fees and costs;

(B) claims an entitlement to redress; and

(C) states the issues that the party intends to present on appeal.

(2) **Action on the Motion.** If the district court grants the motion, the party may proceed on appeal without prepaying or giving security for fees and costs, unless a statute provides otherwise. If the district court denies the motion, it must state its reasons in writing.

(3) **Prior Approval.** A party who was permitted to proceed in forma pauperis in the district-court action, or who was determined to be financially unable to obtain an adequate defense in a criminal case, may proceed on appeal in forma pauperis without further authorization, unless:

(A) the district court—before or after the notice of appeal is filed—certifies that the appeal is not taken in good faith or finds that the party is not otherwise entitled to proceed in forma pauperis and states in writing its reasons for the certification or finding; or

(B) a statute provides otherwise.

(4) **Notice of District Court's Denial.** The district clerk must immediately notify the parties and the court of appeals when the district court does any of the following:

(A) denies a motion to proceed on appeal in forma pauperis;

(B) certifies that the appeal is not taken in good faith; or

(C) finds that the party is not otherwise entitled to proceed in forma pauperis.

(5) **Motion in the Court of Appeals.** A party may file a motion to proceed on appeal in forma pauperis in the court of appeals within 30 days after service of the notice prescribed in Rule 24(a)(4). The motion must include a copy of the affidavit filed in the district court and the district court's statement of reasons for its action. If no affidavit was filed in the district court, the party must include the affidavit prescribed by Rule 24(a)(1).

(b) **Leave to Proceed In Forma Pauperis on Appeal from the United States Tax Court or on Appeal or Review of an Administrative–Agency Proceeding.** A party may file in the court of appeals a motion for leave to proceed on appeal in forma pauperis with an affidavit prescribed by Rule 24(a)(1):

(1) in an appeal from the United States Tax Court; and

(2) when an appeal or review of a proceeding before an administrative agency, board, commission, or officer proceeds directly in the court of appeals.

(c) **Leave to Use Original Record.** A party allowed to proceed on appeal in forma pauperis may request that the appeal be heard on the original record without reproducing any part.

(As amended Apr. 1, 1979, eff. Aug. 1, 1979; Mar. 10, 1986, eff. July 1, 1986; Apr. 24, 1998, eff. Dec. 1, 1998; Apr. 29, 2002, eff. Dec. 1, 2002; Apr. 16, 2013, eff. Dec. 1, 2013.)

TITLE VII. GENERAL PROVISIONS

RULE 25. FILING AND SERVICE

(a) **Filing.**

(1) **Filing with the Clerk.** A paper required or permitted to be filed in a court of appeals must be filed with the clerk.

(2) **Filing: Method and Timeliness.**

(A) **Nonelectronic Filing.**

(i) **In General.** For a paper not filed electronically, filing may be accomplished by mail addressed to the clerk, but filing is not timely unless the clerk receives the papers within the time fixed for filing.

(ii) **A Brief or Appendix.** A brief or appendix not filed electronically is timely filed, however, if on or before the last day for filing, it is:

• mailed to the clerk by first-class mail, or other class of mail that is at least as expeditious, postage prepaid; or

• dispatched to a third-party commercial carrier for delivery to the clerk within 3 days.

(iii) **Inmate Filing.** If an institution has a system designed for legal mail, an inmate confined there must use that system to receive the benefit of this Rule 25(a)(2)(A)(iii). A paper not filed electronically by an inmate is timely if it is deposited in the institution's internal mail system on or before the last day for filing and:

• it is accompanied by: a declaration in compliance with 28 U.S.C. § 1746—or a notarized statement—setting out the date of deposit and stating that first-class postage is being prepaid; or evidence (such as a postmark or date stamp) showing that the paper was so deposited and that postage was prepaid; or

• the court of appeals exercises its discretion to permit the later filing of a declaration or notarized statement that satisfies Rule 25(a)(2)(A)(iii).

(B) **Electronic Filing and Signing.**

(i) **By a Represented Person—Generally Required; Exceptions.** A person represented by an attorney must file electronically, unless nonelectronic filing is allowed by the court for good cause or is allowed or required by local rule.

(ii) **By an Unrepresented Person—When Allowed or Required.** A person not represented by an attorney:

• may file electronically only if allowed by court order or by local rule; and

- may be required to file electronically only by court order, or by a local rule that includes reasonable exceptions.

   (iii) Signing. A filing made through a person's electronic-filing account and authorized by that person, together with that person's name on a signature block, constitutes the person's signature.

   (iv) Same as a Written Paper. A paper filed electronically is a written paper for purposes of these rules.

(3) Filing a Motion with a Judge. If a motion requests relief that may be granted by a single judge, the judge may permit the motion to be filed with the judge; the judge must note the filing date on the motion and give it to the clerk.

(4) Clerk's Refusal of Documents. The clerk must not refuse to accept for filing any paper presented for that purpose solely because it is not presented in proper form as required by these rules or by any local rule or practice.

(5) Privacy Protection. An appeal in a case whose privacy protection was governed by Federal Rule of Bankruptcy Procedure 9037, Federal Rule of Civil Procedure 5.2, or Federal Rule of Criminal Procedure 49.1 is governed by the same rule on appeal. In all other proceedings, privacy protection is governed by Federal Rule of Civil Procedure 5.2, except that Federal Rule of Criminal Procedure 49.1 governs when an extraordinary writ is sought in a criminal case.

(b) Service of All Papers Required. Unless a rule requires service by the clerk, a party must, at or before the time of filing a paper, serve a copy on the other parties to the appeal or review. Service on a party represented by counsel must be made on the party's counsel.

(c) Manner of Service.

   (1) Nonelectronic service may be any of the following:

     (A) personal, including delivery to a responsible person at the office of counsel;

     (B) by mail; or

     (C) by third-party commercial carrier for delivery within 3 days.

   (2) Electronic service of a paper may be made (A) by sending it to a registered user by filing it with the court's electronic-filing system or (B) by sending it by other electronic means that the person to be served consented to in writing.

   (3) When reasonable considering such factors as the immediacy of the relief sought, distance, and cost, service on a party must be by a manner at least as expeditious as the manner used to file the paper with the court.

   (4) Service by mail or by commercial carrier is complete on mailing or delivery to the carrier. Service by electronic means is complete on filing or sending, unless the party making service is notified that the paper was not received by the party served.

(d) Proof of Service.

   (1) A paper presented for filing must contain either of the following if it was served other than through the court's electronic-filing system:

     (A) an acknowledgment of service by the person served; or

     (B) proof of service consisting of a statement by the person who made service certifying:

       (i) the date and manner of service;

       (ii) the names of the persons served; and

       (iii) their mail or electronic addresses, facsimile numbers, or the addresses of the places of delivery, as appropriate for the manner of service.

   (2) When a brief or appendix is filed by mailing or dispatch in accordance with Rule 25(a)(2)(A)(ii), the proof of service must also state the date and manner by which the document was mailed or dispatched to the clerk.

   (3) Proof of service may appear on or be affixed to the papers filed.

(e) Number of Copies. When these rules require the filing or furnishing of a number of copies, a court may require a different number by local rule or by order in a particular case.

(As amended Mar. 10, 1986, eff. July 1, 1986; Apr. 30, 1991, eff. Dec. 1, 1991; Apr. 22, 1993, eff. Dec. 1, 1993; Apr. 29, 1994, eff. Dec. 1, 1994; Apr. 23, 1996, eff. Dec. 1, 1996; Apr. 24, 1998, eff. Dec. 1, 1998; Apr. 29, 2002, eff. Dec. 1, 2002; Apr. 12, 2006, eff. Dec. 1, 2006; Apr. 30, 2007, eff. Dec. 1, 2007; Mar. 26, 2009, eff. Dec. 1, 2009; Apr. 28, 2016, eff. Dec. 1, 2016; Apr. 26, 2018, eff. Dec. 1, 2018; Apr. 25, 2019, eff. Dec. 1, 2019.)

RULE 26. COMPUTING AND EXTENDING TIME

(a) Computing Time. The following rules apply in computing any time period specified in these rules, in any local rule or court order, or in any statute that does not specify a method of computing time.

(1) Period Stated in Days or a Longer Unit. When the period is stated in days or a longer unit of time:

   (A) exclude the day of the event that triggers the period;

   (B) count every day, including intermediate Saturdays, Sundays, and legal holidays; and

   (C) include the last day of the period, but if the last day is a Saturday, Sunday, or legal holiday, the period continues to run until the end of the next day that is not a Saturday, Sunday, or legal holiday.

(2) Period Stated in Hours. When the period is stated in hours:

   (A) begin counting immediately on the occurrence of the event that triggers the period;

   (B) count every hour, including hours during intermediate Saturdays, Sundays, and legal holidays; and

   (C) if the period would end on a Saturday, Sunday, or legal holiday, the period continues to run until the same time on the next day that is not a Saturday, Sunday, or legal holiday.

(3) Inaccessibility of the Clerk's Office. Unless the court orders otherwise, if the clerk's office is inaccessible:

(A) on the last day for filing under Rule 26(a)(1), then the time for filing is extended to the first accessible day that is not a Saturday, Sunday, or legal holiday; or

(B) during the last hour for filing under Rule 26(a)(2), then the time for filing is extended to the same time on the first accessible day that is not a Saturday, Sunday, or legal holiday.

(4) "Last Day" Defined. Unless a different time is set by a statute, local rule, or court order, the last day ends:

(A) for electronic filing in the district court, at midnight in the court's time zone;

(B) for electronic filing in the court of appeals, at midnight in the time zone of the circuit clerk's principal office;

(C) for filing under Rules 4(c)(1), 25(a)(2)(A)(ii), and 25(a)(2)(A)(iii)—and filing by mail under Rule 13(a)(2)—at the latest time for the method chosen for delivery to the post office, third-party commercial carrier, or prison mailing system; and

(D) for filing by other means, when the clerk's office is scheduled to close.

(5) "Next Day" Defined. The "next day" is determined by continuing to count forward when the period is measured after an event and backward when measured before an event.

(6) "Legal Holiday" Defined. "Legal holiday" means:

(A) the day set aside by statute for observing New Year's Day, Martin Luther King Jr.'s Birthday, Washington's Birthday, Memorial Day, Independence Day, Labor Day, Columbus Day, Veterans' Day, Thanksgiving Day, or Christmas Day;

(B) any day declared a holiday by the President or Congress; and

(C) for periods that are measured after an event, any other day declared a holiday by the state where either of the following is located: the district court that rendered the challenged judgment or order, or the circuit clerk's principal office.

(b) Extending Time. For good cause, the court may extend the time prescribed by these rules or by its order to perform any act, or may permit an act to be done after that time expires. But the court may not extend the time to file:

(1) a notice of appeal (except as authorized in Rule 4) or a petition for permission to appeal; or

(2) a notice of appeal from or a petition to enjoin, set aside, suspend, modify, enforce, or otherwise review an order of an administrative agency, board, commission, or officer of the United States, unless specifically authorized by law.

(c) Additional Time After Certain Kinds of Service. When a party may or must act within a specified time after being served, and the paper is not served electronically on the party or delivered to the party on the date stated in the proof of service, 3 days are added after the period would otherwise expire under Rule 26(a).

(As amended Mar. 1, 1971, eff. July 1, 1971; Mar. 10, 1986, eff. July 1, 1986; Apr. 25, 1989, eff. Dec. 1, 1989; Apr. 30, 1991, eff. Dec. 1, 1991; Apr. 23, 1996, eff. Dec. 1, 1996; Apr. 24, 1998, eff. Dec. 1, 1998; Apr. 29, 2002, eff. Dec. 1, 2002; Apr. 25, 2005, eff. Dec. 1, 2005; Mar. 26, 2009, eff. Dec. 1, 2009; Apr. 28, 2016, eff. Dec. 1, 2016; Apr. 26, 2018, eff. Dec. 1, 2018; Apr. 25, 2019, eff. Dec. 1, 2019.)

RULE 26.1 DISCLOSURE STATEMENT

(a) Nongovernmental Corporations. Any nongovernmental corporation that is a party to a proceeding in a court of appeals must file a statement that identifies any parent corporation and any publicly held corporation that owns 10% or more of its stock or states that there is no such corporation. The same requirement applies to a nongovernmental corporation that seeks to intervene.

(b) Organizational Victims in Criminal Cases. In a criminal case, unless the government shows good cause, it must file a statement that identifies any organizational victim of the alleged criminal activity. If the organizational victim is a corporation, the statement must also disclose the information required by Rule 26.1(a) to the extent it can be obtained through due diligence.

(c) Bankruptcy Cases. In a bankruptcy case, the debtor, the trustee, or, if neither is a party, the appellant must file a statement that:

(1) identifies each debtor not named in the caption; and

(2) for each debtor that is a corporation, discloses the information required by Rule 26.1(a).

(d) Time for Filing; Supplemental Filing. The Rule 26.1 statement must:

(1) be filed with the principal brief or upon filing a motion, response, petition, or answer in the court of appeals, whichever occurs first, unless a local rule requires earlier filing;

(2) be included before the table of contents in the principal brief; and

(3) be supplemented whenever the information required under Rule 26.1 changes.

(e) Number of Copies. If the Rule 26.1 statement is filed before the principal brief, or if a supplemental statement is filed, an original and 3 copies must be filed unless the court requires a different number by local rule or by order in a particular case.

(Added Apr. 25, 1989, eff. Dec. 1, 1989; amended Apr. 30, 1991, eff. Dec. 1, 1991; Apr. 29, 1994, eff. Dec. 1, 1994; Apr. 24, 1998, eff. Dec. 1, 1998; Apr. 29, 2002, eff. Dec. 1, 2002; Apr. 25, 2019, eff. Dec. 1, 2019.)

RULE 27. MOTIONS

(a) In General.

(1) Application for Relief. An application for an order or other relief is made by motion unless these rules prescribe another form. A motion must be in writing unless the court permits otherwise.

(2) Contents of a Motion.

(A) Grounds and Relief Sought. A motion must state with particularity the grounds for the motion, the relief sought, and the legal argument necessary to support it.

(B) Accompanying Documents.

(i) Any affidavit or other paper necessary to support a motion must be served and filed with the motion.

(ii) An affidavit must contain only factual information, not legal argument.

(iii) A motion seeking substantive relief must include a copy of the trial court's opinion or agency's decision as a separate exhibit.

(C) Documents Barred or Not Required.

(i) A separate brief supporting or responding to a motion must not be filed.

(ii) A notice of motion is not required.

(iii) A proposed order is not required.

(3) Response.

(A) Time to File. Any party may file a response to a motion; Rule 27(a)(2) governs its contents. The response must be filed within 10 days after service of the motion unless the court shortens or extends the time. A motion authorized by Rules 8, 9, 18, or 41 may be granted before the 10–day period runs only if the court gives reasonable notice to the parties that it intends to act sooner.

(B) Request for Affirmative Relief. A response may include a motion for affirmative relief. The time to respond to the new motion, and to reply to that response, are governed by Rule 27(a)(3)(A) and (a)(4). The title of the response must alert the court to the request for relief.

(4) Reply to Response. Any reply to a response must be filed within 7 days after service of the response. A reply must not present matters that do not relate to the response.

(b) Disposition of a Motion for a Procedural Order. The court may act on a motion for a procedural order—including a motion under Rule 26(b)—at any time without awaiting a response, and may, by rule or by order in a particular case, authorize its clerk to act on specified types of procedural motions. A party adversely affected by the court's, or the clerk's, action may file a motion to reconsider, vacate, or modify that action. Timely opposition filed after the motion is granted in whole or in part does not constitute a request to reconsider, vacate, or modify the disposition; a motion requesting that relief must be filed.

(c) Power of a Single Judge to Entertain a Motion. A circuit judge may act alone on any motion, but may not dismiss or otherwise determine an appeal or other proceeding. A court of appeals may provide by rule or by order in a particular case that only the court may act on any motion or class of motions. The court may review the action of a single judge.

(d) Form of Papers; Length Limits; Number of Copies.

(1) Format.

(A) Reproduction. A motion, response, or reply may be reproduced by any process that yields a clear black image on light paper. The paper must be opaque and unglazed. Only one side of the paper may be used.

(B) Cover. A cover is not required, but there must be a caption that includes the case number, the name of the court, the title of the case, and a brief descriptive title indicating the purpose of the motion and identifying the party or parties for whom it is filed. If a cover is used, it must be white.

(C) Binding. The document must be bound in any manner that is secure, does not obscure the text, and permits the document to lie reasonably flat when open.

(D) Paper Size, Line Spacing, and Margins. The document must be on 8½ by 11 inch paper. The text must be double-spaced, but quotations more than two lines long may be indented and single-spaced. Headings and footnotes may be single-spaced. Margins must be at least one inch on all four sides. Page numbers may be placed in the margins, but no text may appear there.

(E) Typeface and Type Style. The document must comply with the typeface requirements of Rule 32(a)(5) and the type-style requirements of Rule 32(a)(6).

(2) Length Limits. Except by the court's permission, and excluding the accompanying documents authorized by Rule 27(a)(2)(B):

(A) a motion or response to a motion produced using a computer must not exceed 5,200 words;

(B) a handwritten or typewritten motion or response to a motion must not exceed 20 pages;

(C) a reply produced using a computer must not exceed 2,600 words; and

(D) a handwritten or typewritten reply to a response must not exceed 10 pages.

(3) Number of Copies. An original and 3 copies must be filed unless the court requires a different number by local rule or by order in a particular case.

(e) Oral Argument. A motion will be decided without oral argument unless the court orders otherwise.

(As amended Apr. 1, 1979, eff. Aug. 1, 1979; Apr. 25, 1989, eff. Dec. 1, 1989; Apr. 29, 1994, eff. Dec. 1, 1994; Apr. 24, 1998, eff. Dec. 1, 1998; Apr. 29, 2002, eff. Dec. 1, 2002; Apr. 25, 2005, eff. Dec. 1, 2005; Mar. 26, 2009, eff. Dec. 1, 2009; Apr. 28, 2016, eff. Dec. 1, 2016.)

RULE 28. BRIEFS

(a) Appellant's Brief. The appellant's brief must contain, under appropriate headings and in the order indicated:

(1) a disclosure statement if required by Rule 26.1;

(2) a table of contents, with page references;

(3) a table of authorities—cases (alphabetically arranged), statutes, and other authorities—with references to the pages of the brief where they are cited;

(4) a jurisdictional statement, including:

(A) the basis for the district court's or agency's subject-matter jurisdiction, with citations to applicable statutory provisions and stating relevant facts establishing jurisdiction;

(B) the basis for the court of appeals' jurisdiction, with citations to applicable statutory provisions and stating relevant facts establishing jurisdiction;

(C) the filing dates establishing the timeliness of the appeal or petition for review; and

(D) an assertion that the appeal is from a final order or judgment that disposes of all parties' claims, or information establishing the court of appeals' jurisdiction on some other basis;

(5) a statement of the issues presented for review;

(6) a concise statement of the case setting out the facts relevant to the issues submitted for review, describing the relevant procedural history, and identifying the rulings presented for review, with appropriate references to the record (see Rule 28(e));

(7) a summary of the argument, which must contain a succinct, clear, and accurate statement of the arguments made in the body of the brief, and which must not merely repeat the argument headings;

(8) the argument, which must contain:

(A) appellant's contentions and the reasons for them, with citations to the authorities and parts of the record on which the appellant relies; and

(B) for each issue, a concise statement of the applicable standard of review (which may appear in the discussion of the issue or under a separate heading placed before the discussion of the issues);

(9) a short conclusion stating the precise relief sought; and

(10) the certificate of compliance, if required by Rule 32(g)(1).

(b) Appellee's Brief. The appellee's brief must conform to the requirements of Rule 28(a)(1)–(8) and (10), except that none of the following need appear unless the appellee is dissatisfied with the appellant's statement:

(1) the jurisdictional statement;

(2) the statement of the issues;

(3) the statement of the case; and

(4) the statement of the standard of review.

(c) Reply Brief. The appellant may file a brief in reply to the appellee's brief. Unless the court permits, no further briefs may be filed. A reply brief must contain a table of contents, with page references, and a table of authorities—cases (alphabetically arranged), statutes, and other authorities—with references to the pages of the reply brief where they are cited.

(d) References to Parties. In briefs and at oral argument, counsel should minimize use of the terms "appellant" and "appellee." To make briefs clear, counsel should use the parties' actual names or the designations used in the lower court or agency proceeding, or such descriptive terms as "the employee," "the injured person," "the taxpayer," "the ship," "the stevedore."

(e) References to the Record. References to the parts of the record contained in the appendix filed with the appellant's brief must be to the pages of the appendix. If the appendix is prepared after the briefs are filed, a party referring to the record must follow one of the methods detailed in Rule 30(c). If the original record is used under Rule 30(f) and is not consecutively paginated, or if the brief refers to an unreproduced part of the record, any reference must be to the page of the original document. For example:

- Answer p. 7;
- Motion for Judgment p. 2;
- Transcript p. 231.

Only clear abbreviations may be used. A party referring to evidence whose admissibility is in controversy must cite the pages of the appendix or of the transcript at which the evidence was identified, offered, and received or rejected.

(f) Reproduction of Statutes, Rules, Regulations, etc. If the court's determination of the issues presented requires the study of statutes, rules, regulations, etc., the relevant parts must be set out in the brief or in an addendum at the end, or may be supplied to the court in pamphlet form.

(g) [Reserved]

(h) [Reserved]

(i) Briefs in a Case Involving Multiple Appellants or Appellees. In a case involving more than one appellant or appellee, including consolidated cases, any number of appellants or appellees may join in a brief, and any party may adopt by reference a part of another's brief. Parties may also join in reply briefs.

(j) Citation of Supplemental Authorities. If pertinent and significant authorities come to a party's attention after the party's brief has been filed—or after oral argument but before decision—a party may promptly advise the circuit clerk by letter, with a copy to all other parties, setting forth the citations. The letter must state the reasons for the supplemental citations, referring either to the page of the brief or to a point argued orally. The body of the letter must not exceed 350 words. Any response must be made promptly and must be similarly limited.

(As amended Apr. 30, 1979, eff. Aug. 1, 1979; Mar. 10, 1986, eff. July 1, 1986; Apr. 25, 1989, eff. Dec. 1, 1989; Apr. 30, 1991, eff. Dec. 1, 1991; Apr. 22, 1993, eff. Dec. 1, 1993; Apr. 29, 1994, eff. Dec. 1, 1994; Apr. 24, 1998, eff. Dec. 1, 1998; Apr. 29, 2002, eff. Dec. 1, 2002; Apr. 25, 2005, eff. Dec. 1, 2005; Apr. 16, 2013, eff. Dec. 1, 2013; Apr. 28, 2016, eff. Dec. 1, 2016; Apr. 25, 2019, eff. Dec. 1, 2019.)

RULE 28.1   CROSS–APPEALS

(a) Applicability. This rule applies to a case in which a cross-appeal is filed. Rules 28(a)-(c), 31(a)(1), 32(a)(2), and 32(a)(7)(A)-(B) do not apply to such a case, except as otherwise provided in this rule.

(b) Designation of Appellant. The party who files a notice of appeal first is the appellant for the purposes of this rule and Rules 30 and 34. If notices are filed on the same day, the plaintiff in the proceeding below is the appellant. These designations may be modified by the parties' agreement or by court order.

(c) Briefs. In a case involving a cross-appeal:

(1) Appellant's Principal Brief. The appellant must file a principal brief in the appeal. That brief must comply with Rule 28(a).

(2) Appellee's Principal and Response Brief. The appellee must file a principal brief in the cross-appeal and must, in the same brief, respond to the principal brief in the appeal. That appellee's brief must comply with Rule 28(a), except that the brief need not include a statement of the case unless the appellee is dissatisfied with the appellant's statement.

(3) Appellant's Response and Reply Brief. The appellant must file a brief that responds to the principal brief in the cross-appeal and may, in the same brief, reply to the response in the appeal. That brief must comply with Rule 28(a)(2)–(8) and (10), except that none of the following need appear unless the appellant is dissatisfied with the appellee's statement in the cross-appeal:

(A) the jurisdictional statement;

(B) the statement of the issues;

(C) the statement of the case; and

(D) the statement of the standard of review.

(4) Appellee's Reply Brief. The appellee may file a brief in reply to the response in the cross-appeal. That brief must comply with Rule 28(a)(2)–(3) and (10) and must be limited to the issues presented by the cross-appeal.

(5) No Further Briefs. Unless the court permits, no further briefs may be filed in a case involving a cross-appeal.

(d) Cover. Except for filings by unrepresented parties, the cover of the appellant's principal brief must be blue; the appellee's principal and response brief, red; the appellant's response and reply brief, yellow; the appellee's reply brief, gray; and intervenor's or amicus curiae's brief, green; and any supplemental brief, tan. The front cover of a brief must contain the information required by Rule 32(a)(2).

(e) Length.

(1) Page Limitation. Unless it complies with Rule 28.1(e)(2), the appellant's principal brief must not exceed 30 pages; the appellee's principal and response brief, 35 pages; the appellant's response and reply brief, 30 pages; and the appellee's reply brief, 15 pages.

(2) Type-Volume Limitation.

(A) The appellant's principal brief or the appellant's response and reply brief is acceptable if it:

(i) contains no more than 13,000 words; or

(ii) uses a monospaced face and contains no more than 1,300 lines of text.

(B) The appellee's principal and response brief is acceptable if it:

(i) contains no more than 15,300 words; or

(ii) uses a monospaced face and contains no more than 1,500 lines of text.

(C) The appellee's reply brief is acceptable if it contains no more than half of the type volume specified in Rule 28.1(e)(2)(A).

(f) Time to Serve and File a Brief. Briefs must be served and filed as follows:

(1) the appellant's principal brief, within 40 days after the record is filed;

(2) the appellee's principal and response brief, within 30 days after the appellant's principal brief is served;

(3) the appellant's response and reply brief, within 30 days after the appellee's principal and response brief is served; and

(4) the appellee's reply brief, within 21 days after the appellant's response and reply brief is served, but at least 7 days before argument unless the court, for good cause, allows a later filing.

(As added April 25, 2005, eff. Dec. 1, 2005; amended Mar. 26, 2009, eff. Dec. 1, 2009; Apr. 16, 2013, eff. Dec. 1, 2013; Apr. 28, 2016, eff. Dec. 1, 2016; Apr. 26, 2018, eff. Dec. 1, 2018.)

RULE 29.   BRIEF OF AN AMICUS CURIAE

(a) During Initial Consideration of a Case on the Merits.

(1) Applicability. This Rule 29(a) governs amicus filings during a court's initial consideration of a case on the merits.

(2) When Permitted. The United States or its officer or agency or a state may file an amicus brief without the consent of the parties or leave of court. Any other amicus curiae may file a brief only by leave of court or if the brief states that all parties have consented to its filing, but a court of appeals may prohibit the filing of or may strike an amicus brief that would result in a judge's disqualification.

(3) Motion for Leave to File. The motion must be accompanied by the proposed brief and state:

(A) the movant's interest; and

(B) the reason why an amicus brief is desirable and why the matters asserted are relevant to the disposition of the case.

(4) Contents and Form. An amicus brief must comply with Rule 32. In addition to the requirements of Rule 32, the cover must identify the party or parties supported and indicate whether the brief supports affirmance or reversal. An amicus brief need not comply with Rule 28, but must include the following:

(A) if the amicus curiae is a corporation, a disclosure statement like that required of parties by Rule 26.1;

(B) a table of contents, with page references;

(C) a table of authorities—cases (alphabetically arranged), statutes, and other authorities— with references to the pages of the brief where they are cited;

(D) a concise statement of the identity of the amicus curiae, its interest in the case, and the source of its authority to file;

(E) unless the amicus curiae is one listed in the first sentence of Rule 29(a)(2), a statement that indicates whether:

(i) a party's counsel authored the brief in whole or in part;

(ii) a party or a party's counsel contributed money that was intended to fund preparing or submitting the brief; and

(iii) a person—other than the amicus curiae, its members, or its counsel—contributed money that was intended to fund preparing or submitting the brief and, if so, identifies each such person;

(F) an argument, which may be preceded by a summary and which need not include a statement of the applicable standard of review; and

(G) a certificate of compliance under Rule 32(g)(1), if length is computed using a word or line limit.

(5) Length. Except by the court's permission, an amicus brief may be no more than one-half the maximum length authorized by these rules for a party's principal brief. If the court grants a party permission to file a longer brief, that extension does not affect the length of an amicus brief.

(6) Time for Filing. An amicus curiae must file its brief, accompanied by a motion for filing when necessary, no later than 7 days after the principal brief of the party being supported is filed. An amicus curiae that does not support either party must file its brief no later than 7 days after the appellant's or petitioner's principal brief is filed. A court may grant leave for later filing, specifying the time within which an opposing party may answer.

(7) Reply Brief. Except by the court's permission, an amicus curiae may not file a reply brief.

(8) Oral Argument. An amicus curiae may participate in oral argument only with the court's permission.

(b) During Consideration of Whether to Grant Rehearing.

(1) Applicability. This Rule 29(b) governs amicus filings during a court's consideration of whether to grant panel rehearing or rehearing en banc, unless a local rule or order in a case provides otherwise.

(2) When Permitted. The United States or its officer or agency or a state may file an amicus brief without the consent of the parties or leave of court. Any other amicus curiae may file a brief only by leave of court.

(3) Motion for Leave to File. Rule 29(a)(3) applies to a motion for leave.

(4) Contents, Form, and Length. Rule 29(a)(4) applies to the amicus brief. The brief must not exceed 2,600 words.

(5) Time for Filing. An amicus curiae supporting the petition for rehearing or supporting neither party must file its brief, accompanied by a motion for filing when necessary, no later than 7 days after the petition is filed. An amicus curiae opposing the petition must file its brief, accompanied by a motion for filing when necessary, no later than the date set by the court for the response.

(As amended Apr. 24, 1998, eff. Dec. 1, 1998; Apr. 28, 2010, eff. Dec. 1, 2010; Apr. 28, 2016, eff. Dec. 1, 2016; Apr. 26, 2018, eff. Dec. 1, 2018.)

RULE 30. APPENDIX TO THE BRIEFS

(a) Appellant's Responsibility.

(1) Contents of the Appendix. The appellant must prepare and file an appendix to the briefs containing:

(A) the relevant docket entries in the proceeding below;

(B) the relevant portions of the pleadings, charge, findings, or opinion;

(C) the judgment, order, or decision in question; and

(D) other parts of the record to which the parties wish to direct the court's attention.

(2) Excluded Material. Memoranda of law in the district court should not be included in the appendix unless they have independent relevance. Parts of the record may be relied on by the court or the parties even though not included in the appendix.

(3) Time to File; Number of Copies. Unless filing is deferred under Rule 30(c), the appellant must file 10 copies of the appendix with the brief and must serve one copy on counsel for each party separately represented. An unrepresented party proceeding in forma pauperis must file 4 legible copies with the clerk, and one copy must be served on counsel for each separately represented party. The court may by local rule or by order in a particular case require the filing or service of a different number.

(b) All Parties' Responsibilities.

(1) Determining the Contents of the Appendix. The parties are encouraged to agree on the contents of the appendix. In the absence of an agreement, the appellant must, within 14 days after the record is filed, serve on the appellee a designation of the parts of the record the appellant intends to include in the appendix and a statement of the issues the appellant intends to present for review. The appellee may, within 14 days after receiving the designation, serve on the appellant a designation of additional parts to which it wishes to direct the court's attention. The appellant must include the designated parts in the appendix. The parties must not engage in unnecessary designation of parts of the record, because the entire record is available to the court. This paragraph applies also to a cross-appellant and a cross-appellee.

(2) Costs of Appendix. Unless the parties agree otherwise, the appellant must pay the cost of the appendix. If the appellant considers parts of the record designated by the appellee to be unnecessary, the appellant may advise the appellee, who must then advance the cost of including those parts. The cost of the appendix is a taxable cost. But if any party causes unnecessary parts of the record to be included in the appendix, the court may impose the cost of those parts on that party. Each circuit must, by local rule, provide for sanctions against attorneys who unreasonably and vexatiously increase litigation costs by including unnecessary material in the appendix.

(c) Deferred Appendix.

(1) Deferral Until After Briefs Are Filed. The court may provide by rule for classes of cases or by order in a particular case that preparation of the appendix may be deferred until after the briefs have been filed and that the appendix may be filed 21 days after the appellee's brief is served. Even though the filing of the appendix may be deferred, Rule 30(b) applies; except that a party must designate the parts of the record it wants included in the appendix when it serves its brief, and need not include a statement of the issues presented.

(2) References to the Record.

(A) If the deferred appendix is used, the parties may cite in their briefs the pertinent pages of the record. When the appendix is prepared, the record pages cited in the briefs must be indicated by inserting record page numbers, in brackets, at places in the appendix where those pages of the record appear.

(B) A party who wants to refer directly to pages of the appendix may serve and file copies of the brief within the time required by Rule 31(a), containing appropriate references to pertinent pages of the record. In that event, within 14 days after the appendix is filed, the party must serve and file copies of the brief, containing references to the pages of the appendix in place of or in addition to the references to the pertinent pages of the record. Except for the correction of typographical errors, no other changes may be made to the brief.

(d) Format of the Appendix. The appendix must begin with a table of contents identifying the page at which each part begins. The relevant docket entries must follow the table of contents. Other parts of the record must follow chronologically. When pages from the transcript of proceedings are placed in the appendix, the transcript page numbers must be shown in brackets immediately before the included pages. Omissions in the text of papers or of the transcript must be indicated by asterisks. Immaterial formal matters (captions, subscriptions, acknowledgments, etc.) should be omitted.

(e) Reproduction of Exhibits. Exhibits designated for inclusion in the appendix may be reproduced in a separate volume, or volumes, suitably indexed. Four copies must be filed with the appendix, and one copy must be served on counsel for each separately represented party. If a transcript of a proceeding before an administrative agency, board, commission, or officer was used in a district-court action and has been designated for inclusion in the appendix, the transcript must be placed in the appendix as an exhibit.

(f) Appeal on the Original Record Without an Appendix. The court may, either by rule for all cases or classes of cases or by order in a particular case, dispense with the appendix and permit an appeal to proceed on the original record with any copies of the record, or relevant parts, that the court may order the parties to file.

(As amended Mar. 30, 1970, eff. July 1, 1970; Mar. 10, 1986, eff. July 1, 1986; Apr. 30, 1991, eff. Dec. 1, 1991; Apr. 29, 1994, eff. Dec. 1, 1994; Apr. 24, 1998, eff. Dec. 1, 1998; Mar. 26, 2009, eff. Dec. 1, 2009.)

RULE 31. SERVING AND FILING BRIEFS

(a) Time to Serve and File a Brief.

(1) The appellant must serve and file a brief within 40 days after the record is filed. The appellee must serve and file a brief within 30 days after the appellant's brief is served. The appellant may serve and file a reply brief within 21 days after service of the appellee's brief but a reply brief must be filed at least 7 days before argument, unless the court, for good cause, allows a later filing.

(2) A court of appeals that routinely considers cases on the merits promptly after the briefs are filed may shorten the time to serve and file briefs, either by local rule or by order in a particular case.

(b) Number of Copies. Twenty-five copies of each brief must be filed with the clerk and 2 copies must be served on each unrepresented party and on counsel for each separately represented party. An unrepresented party proceeding in forma pauperis must file 4 legible copies with the clerk, and one copy must be served on each unrepresented party and on counsel for each separately represented party. The court may by local rule or by order in a particular case require the filing or service of a different number.

(c) Consequence of Failure to File. If an appellant fails to file a brief within the time provided by this rule, or within an extended time, an appellee may move to dismiss the appeal. An appellee who fails to file a brief will not be heard at oral argument unless the court grants permission.

(As amended Mar. 30, 1970, eff. July 1, 1970; Mar. 10, 1986, eff. July 1, 1986; Apr. 29, 1994, eff. Dec. 1, 1994; Apr. 24, 1998, eff. Dec. 1, 1998; Apr. 29, 2002, eff. Dec. 1, 2002; Mar. 26, 2009, eff. Dec. 1, 2009; Apr. 26, 2018, eff. Dec. 1, 2018.)

RULE 32. FORM OF BRIEFS, APPENDICES, AND OTHER PAPERS

(a) Form of a Brief.

(1) Reproduction.

(A) A brief may be reproduced by any process that yields a clear black image on light paper. The paper must be opaque and unglazed. Only one side of the paper may be used.

(B) Text must be reproduced with a clarity that equals or exceeds the output of a laser printer.

(C) Photographs, illustrations, and tables may be reproduced by any method that results in a good copy of the original; a glossy finish is acceptable if the original is glossy.

(2) Cover. Except for filings by unrepresented parties, the cover of the appellant's brief must be blue; the appellee's, red; an intervenor's or amicus curiae's, green; any reply brief, gray; and any supplemental brief, tan. The front cover of a brief must contain:

(A) the number of the case centered at the top;

(B) the name of the court;

(C) the title of the case (see Rule 12(a));

(D) the nature of the proceeding (e.g., Appeal, Petition for Review) and the name of the court, agency, or board below;

(E) the title of the brief, identifying the party or parties for whom the brief is filed; and

(F) the name, office address, and telephone number of counsel representing the party for whom the brief is filed.

(3) Binding. The brief must be bound in any manner that is secure, does not obscure the text, and permits the brief to lie reasonably flat when open.

(4) Paper Size, Line Spacing, and Margins. The brief must be on 8½ by 11 inch paper. The text must be double-spaced, but quotations more than two lines long may be indented and single-spaced. Headings and footnotes may be single-spaced. Margins must be at least one inch on all four sides. Page numbers may be placed in the margins, but no text may appear there.

(5) Typeface. Either a proportionally spaced or a mono-spaced face may be used.

(A) A proportionally spaced face must include serifs, but sans-serif type may be used in headings and captions. A proportionally spaced face must be 14–point or larger.

(B) A monospaced face may not contain more than 10½ characters per inch.

(6) Type Styles. A brief must be set in a plain, roman style, although italics or boldface may be used for emphasis. Case names must be italicized or underlined.

(7) Length.

(A) Page Limitation. A principal brief may not exceed 30 pages, or a reply brief 15 pages, unless it complies with Rule 32(a)(7)(B).

(B) Type-Volume Limitation.

(i) A principal brief is acceptable if it:

- contains no more than 13,000 words; or
- uses a monospaced face and contains no more than 1,300 lines of text.

(ii) A reply brief is acceptable if it contains no more than half of the type volume specified in Rule 32(a)(7)(B)(i).

(b) Form of an Appendix. An appendix must comply with Rule 32(a)(1), (2), (3), and (4), with the following exceptions:

(1) The cover of a separately bound appendix must be white.

(2) An appendix may include a legible photocopy of any document found in the record or of a printed judicial or agency decision.

(3) When necessary to facilitate inclusion of odd-sized documents such as technical drawings, an appendix may be a size other than 8½ by 11 inches, and need not lie reasonably flat when opened.

(c) Form of Other Papers.

(1) Motion. The form of a motion is governed by Rule 27(d).

(2) Other Papers. Any other paper, including a petition for panel rehearing and a petition for hearing or rehearing en banc, and any response to such a petition, must be reproduced in the manner prescribed by Rule 32(a), with the following exceptions:

(A) A cover is not necessary if the caption and signature page of the paper together contain the information required by Rule 32(a)(2). If a cover is used, it must be white.

(B) Rule 32(a)(7) does not apply.

(d) Signature. Every brief, motion, or other paper filed with the court must be signed by the party filing the paper or, if the party is represented, by one of the party's attorneys.

(e) Local Variation. Every court of appeals must accept documents that comply with the form requirements of this rule and the length limits set by these rules. By local rule or order in a particular case, a court of appeals may accept documents that do not meet all the form requirements of this rule or the length limits set by these rules.

(f) Items Excluded from Length. In computing any length limit, headings, footnotes, and quotations count toward the limit but the following items do not:

- cover page;
- disclosure statement;
- table of contents;
- table of citations;
- statement regarding oral argument;
- addendum containing statutes, rules, or regulations;
- certificate of counsel;
- signature block;
- proof of service; and
- any item specifically excluded by these rules or by local rule.

(g) Certificate of Compliance.

(1) Briefs and Papers That Require a Certificate. A brief submitted under Rules 28.1(e)(2), 29(b)(4), or 32(a)(7)(B)—and a paper submitted under Rules 5(c)(1), 21(d)(1), 27(d)(2)(A), 27(d)(2)(C), 35(b)(2)(A), or 40(b)(1)—must include a certificate by the attorney, or an unrepresented party, that the document complies with the type-volume limitation. The person preparing the certificate may rely on the word or line count of the word-processing system used to prepare the document. The certificate must state the number of words—or the number of lines of monospaced type—in the document.

(2) Acceptable Form. Form 6 in the Appendix of Forms meets the requirements for a certificate of compliance.

(As amended Apr. 24, 1998, eff. Dec. 1, 1998; Apr. 29, 2002, eff. Dec. 1, 2002; Apr. 25, 2005, eff. Dec. 1, 2005; Apr. 28, 2016, eff. Dec. 1, 2016; Apr. 25, 2019, eff. Dec. 1, 2019.)

RULE 32.1 CITING JUDICIAL DISPOSITIONS

(a) Citation Permitted. A court may not prohibit or restrict the citation of federal judicial opinions, orders, judgments, or other written dispositions that have been:

(i) designated as "unpublished," "not for publication," "non-precedential," "not precedent," or the like; and

(ii) issued on or after January 1, 2007.

(b) Copies Required. If a party cites a federal judicial opinion, order, judgment, or other written disposition that is not available in a publicly accessible electronic database, the party must file and serve a copy of that opinion, order, judgment, or disposition with the brief or other paper in which it is cited.

(Added Apr. 12, 2006, eff. Dec. 1, 2006.)

RULE 33. APPEAL CONFERENCES

The court may direct the attorneys—and, when appropriate, the parties—to participate in one or more conferences to address any matter that may aid in disposing of the proceedings, including simplifying the issues and discussing settlement. A judge or other person designated by the court may preside over the conference, which may be conducted in person or by telephone. Before a settlement conference, the attorneys must consult with their clients and obtain as much authority as feasible to settle the case. The court may, as a result of the conference, enter an order controlling the course of the proceedings or implementing any settlement agreement.

(As amended Apr. 29, 1994, eff. Dec. 1, 1994; Apr. 24, 1998, eff. Dec. 1, 1998.)

RULE 34. ORAL ARGUMENT

(a) In General.

(1) Party's Statement. Any party may file, or a court may require by local rule, a statement explaining why oral argument should, or need not, be permitted.

(2) Standards. Oral argument must be allowed in every case unless a panel of three judges who have examined the briefs and record unanimously agrees that oral argument is unnecessary for any of the following reasons:

(A) the appeal is frivolous;

(B) the dispositive issue or issues have been authoritatively decided; or

(C) the facts and legal arguments are adequately presented in the briefs and record, and the decisional process would not be significantly aided by oral argument.

(b) Notice of Argument; Postponement. The clerk must advise all parties whether oral argument will be scheduled, and, if so, the date, time, and place for it, and the time allowed for each side. A motion to postpone the argument or to allow longer argument must be filed reasonably in advance of the hearing date.

(c) Order and Contents of Argument. The appellant opens and concludes the argument. Counsel must not read at length from briefs, records, or authorities.

(d) Cross-Appeals and Separate Appeals. If there is a cross-appeal, Rule 28.1(b) determines which party is the appellant and which is the appellee for purposes of oral argument. Unless the court directs otherwise, a cross-appeal or separate appeal must be argued when the initial appeal is argued. Separate parties should avoid duplicative argument.

(e) Nonappearance of a Party. If the appellee fails to appear for argument, the court must hear appellant's argument. If the appellant fails to appear for argument, the court may hear the appellee's argument. If neither party appears, the case will be decided on the briefs, unless the court orders otherwise.

(f) Submission on Briefs. The parties may agree to submit a case for decision on the briefs, but the court may direct that the case be argued.

(g) Use of Physical Exhibits at Argument; Removal. Counsel intending to use physical exhibits other than documents at the argument must arrange to place them in the courtroom on the day of the argument before the court convenes. After the argument, counsel must remove the exhibits from the courtroom, unless the court directs otherwise. The clerk may destroy or dispose of the exhibits if counsel does not reclaim them within a reasonable time after the clerk gives notice to remove them.

(As amended Apr. 1, 1979, eff. Aug. 1, 1979; Mar. 10, 1986, eff. July 1, 1986; Apr. 30, 1991, eff. Dec. 1, 1991; Apr. 22, 1993, eff. Dec. 1, 1993; Apr. 24, 1998, eff. Dec. 1, 1998; Apr. 25, 2005, eff. Dec. 1, 2005.)

RULE 35. EN BANC DETERMINATION

(a) When Hearing or Rehearing En Banc May Be Ordered. A majority of the circuit judges who are in regular active service and who are not disqualified may order that an appeal or other proceeding be heard or reheard by the court of appeals en banc. An en banc hearing or rehearing is not favored and ordinarily will not be ordered unless:

(1) en banc consideration is necessary to secure or maintain uniformity of the court's decisions; or

(2) the proceeding involves a question of exceptional importance.

(b) Petition for Hearing or Rehearing En Banc. A party may petition for a hearing or rehearing en banc.

(1) The petition must begin with a statement that either:

(A) the panel decision conflicts with a decision of the United States Supreme Court or of the court to which the petition is addressed (with citation to the conflicting case or cases) and consideration by the full court is therefore necessary to secure and maintain uniformity of the court's decisions; or

(B) the proceeding involves one or more questions of exceptional importance, each of which must be concisely stated; for example, a petition may assert that a proceeding presents a question of exceptional importance if it involves an issue on which the panel decision conflicts with the authoritative decisions of other United States Courts of Appeals that have addressed the issue.

(2) Except by the court's permission:

(A) a petition for an en banc hearing or rehearing produced using a computer must not exceed 3,900 words; and

(B) a handwritten or typewritten petition for an en banc hearing or rehearing must not exceed 15 pages.

(3) For purposes of the limits in Rule 35(b)(2), if a party files both a petition for panel rehearing and a petition for rehearing en banc, they are considered a single document even if they are filed separately, unless separate filing is required by local rule.

(c) Time for Petition for Hearing or Rehearing En Banc. A petition that an appeal be heard initially en banc must be filed by the date when the appellee's brief is due. A petition for a rehearing en banc must be filed within the time prescribed by Rule 40 for filing a petition for rehearing.

(d) Number of Copies. The number of copies to be filed must be prescribed by local rule and may be altered by order in a particular case.

(e) Response. No response may be filed to a petition for an en banc consideration unless the court orders a response. The length limits in Rule 35(b)(2) apply to a response.

(f) Call for a Vote. A vote need not be taken to determine whether the case will be heard or reheard en banc unless a judge calls for a vote.

(As amended Apr. 1, 1979, eff. Aug. 1, 1979; Apr. 29, 1994, eff. Dec. 1, 1994; Apr. 24, 1998, eff. Dec. 1, 1998; Apr. 25, 2005, eff. Dec. 1, 2005; Apr. 28, 2016, eff. Dec. 1, 2016; Apr. 27, 2020, eff. Dec. 1, 2020.)

RULE 36.   ENTRY OF JUDGMENT; NOTICE

(a) Entry. A judgment is entered when it is noted on the docket. The clerk must prepare, sign, and enter the judgment:

(1) after receiving the court's opinion—but if settlement of the judgment's form is required, after final settlement; or

(2) if a judgment is rendered without an opinion, as the court instructs.

(b) Notice. On the date when judgment is entered, the clerk must serve on all parties a copy of the opinion—or the judgment, if no opinion was written—and a notice of the date when the judgment was entered.

(As amended Apr. 24, 1998, eff. Dec. 1, 1998; Apr. 29, 2002, eff. Dec. 1, 2002.)

RULE 37.   INTEREST ON JUDGMENT

(a) When the Court Affirms. Unless the law provides otherwise, if a money judgment in a civil case is affirmed, whatever interest is allowed by law is payable from the date when the district court's judgment was entered.

(b) When the Court Reverses. If the court modifies or reverses a judgment with a direction that a money judgment be entered in the district court, the mandate must contain instructions about the allowance of interest.

(As amended Apr. 24, 1998, eff. Dec. 1, 1998.)

RULE 38.   FRIVOLOUS APPEAL— DAMAGES AND COSTS

If a court of appeals determines that an appeal is frivolous, it may, after a separately filed motion or notice from the court and reasonable opportunity to respond, award just damages and single or double costs to the appellee.

(As amended Apr. 29, 1994, eff. Dec. 1, 1994; Apr. 24, 1998, eff. Dec. 1, 1998.)

RULE 39.   COSTS

(a) Against Whom Assessed. The following rules apply unless the law provides or the court orders otherwise:

(1) if an appeal is dismissed, costs are taxed against the appellant, unless the parties agree otherwise;

(2) if a judgment is affirmed, costs are taxed against the appellant;

(3) if a judgment is reversed, costs are taxed against the appellee;

(4) if a judgment is affirmed in part, reversed in part, modified, or vacated, costs are taxed only as the court orders.

(b) Costs For and Against the United States. Costs for or against the United States, its agency, or officer will be assessed under Rule 39(a) only if authorized by law.

(c) Costs of Copies. Each court of appeals must, by local rule, fix the maximum rate for taxing the cost of producing necessary copies of a brief or appendix, or copies of records authorized by Rule 30(f). The rate must not exceed that generally charged for such work in the area where the clerk's office is located and should encourage economical methods of copying.

(d) Bill of Costs: Objections; Insertion in Mandate.

(1) A party who wants costs taxed must—within 14 days after entry of judgment—file with the circuit clerk and serve an itemized and verified bill of costs.

(2) Objections must be filed within 14 days after service of the bill of costs, unless the court extends the time.

(3) The clerk must prepare and certify an itemized statement of costs for insertion in the mandate, but issuance of the mandate must not be delayed for taxing costs. If the mandate issues before costs are finally determined, the district clerk must—upon the circuit clerk's request—add the statement of costs, or any amendment of it, to the mandate.

(e) Costs on Appeal Taxable in the District Court. The following costs on appeal are taxable in the district court for the benefit of the party entitled to costs under this rule:

(1) the preparation and transmission of the record;

(2) the reporter's transcript, if needed to determine the appeal;

(3) premiums paid for a bond or other security to preserve rights pending appeal; and

(4) the fee for filing the notice of appeal.

(As amended Apr. 30, 1979, eff. Aug. 1, 1979; Mar. 10, 1986, eff. July 1, 1986; Apr. 24, 1998, eff. Dec. 1, 1998; Mar. 26, 2009, eff. Dec. 1, 2009; Apr. 26, 2018, eff. Dec. 1, 2018; Apr. 25, 2019, eff. Dec. 1, 2019.)

RULE 40. PETITION FOR PANEL REHEARING

(a) Time to File; Contents; Response; Action by the Court if Granted.

(1) Time. Unless the time is shortened or extended by order or local rule, a petition for panel rehearing may be filed within 14 days after entry of judgment. But in a civil case, unless an order shortens or extends the time, the petition may be filed by any party within 45 days after entry of judgment if one of the parties is:

(A) the United States;

(B) a United States agency;

(C) a United States officer or employee sued in an official capacity; or

(D) a current or former United States officer or employee sued in an individual capacity for an act or omission occurring in connection with duties performed on the United States' behalf—including all instances in which the United States represents that person when the court of appeals' judgment is entered or files the petition for that person.

(2) Contents. The petition must state with particularity each point of law or fact that the petitioner believes the court has overlooked or misapprehended and must argue in support of the petition. Oral argument is not permitted.

(3) Response. Unless the court requests, no response to a petition for panel rehearing is permitted. Ordinarily, rehearing will not be granted in the absence of such a request. If a response is requested, the requirements of Rule 40(b) apply to the response.

(4) Action by the Court. If a petition for panel rehearing is granted, the court may do any of the following:

(A) make a final disposition of the case without reargument;

(B) restore the case to the calendar for reargument or resubmission; or

(C) issue any other appropriate order.

(b) Form of Petition; Length. The petition must comply in form with Rule 32. Copies must be served and filed as Rule 31 prescribes. Except by the court's permission:

(1) a petition for panel rehearing produced using a computer must not exceed 3,900 words; and

(2) a handwritten or typewritten petition for panel rehearing must not exceed 15 pages.

(As amended Apr. 30, 1979, eff. Aug. 1, 1979; Apr. 29, 1994, eff. Dec. 1, 1994; Apr. 24, 1998, eff. Dec. 1, 1998; Apr. 26, 2011, eff. Dec. 1, 2011; Apr. 28, 2016, eff. Dec. 1, 2016; Apr. 27, 2020, eff. Dec. 1, 2020.)

RULE 41. MANDATE: CONTENTS; ISSUANCE AND EFFECTIVE DATE; STAY

(a) Contents. Unless the court directs that a formal mandate issue, the mandate consists of a certified copy of the judgment, a copy of the court's opinion, if any, and any direction about costs.

(b) When Issued. The court's mandate must issue 7 days after the time to file a petition for rehearing expires, or 7 days after entry of an order denying a timely petition for panel rehearing, petition for rehearing en banc, or motion for stay of mandate, whichever is later. The court may shorten or extend the time by order.

(c) Effective Date. The mandate is effective when issued.

(d) Staying the Mandate Pending a Petition for Certiorari.

(1) Motion to Stay. A party may move to stay the mandate pending the filing of a petition for a writ of certiorari in the Supreme Court. The motion must be served on all parties and must show that the petition would present a substantial question and that there is good cause for a stay.

(2) Duration of Stay; Extensions. The stay must not exceed 90 days, unless:

(A) the period is extended for good cause; or

(B) the party who obtained the stay notifies the circuit clerk in writing within the period of the stay:

(i) that the time for filing a petition has been extended, in which case the stay continues for the extended period; or

(ii) that the petition has been filed, in which case the stay continues until the Supreme Court's final disposition.

(3) Security. The court may require a bond or other security as a condition to granting or continuing a stay of the mandate.

(4) Issuance of Mandate. The court of appeals must issue the mandate immediately on receiving a copy of a Supreme Court order denying the petition, unless extraordinary circumstances exist.

(As amended Apr. 29, 1994, eff. Dec. 1, 1994; Apr. 24, 1998, eff. Dec. 1, 1998; Apr. 29, 2002, eff. Dec. 1, 2002; Mar. 26, 2009, eff. Dec. 1, 2009; Apr. 26, 2018, eff. Dec. 1, 2018.)

RULE 42. VOLUNTARY DISMISSAL

(a) Dismissal in the District Court. Before an appeal has been docketed by the circuit clerk, the district court may dismiss the appeal on the filing of a stipulation signed by all parties or on the appellant's motion with notice to all parties.

(b) Dismissal in the Court of Appeals. The circuit clerk may dismiss a docketed appeal if the parties file a signed dismissal agreement specifying how costs are to be paid and pay any fees that are due. But no mandate or other process may issue without a court order. An appeal may be dismissed on the appellant's motion on terms agreed to by the parties or fixed by the court.

(As amended Apr. 24, 1998, eff. Dec. 1, 1998.)

RULE 43. SUBSTITUTION OF PARTIES

(a) Death of a Party.

(1) After Notice of Appeal Is Filed. If a party dies after a notice of appeal has been filed or while a proceeding is pending in the court of appeals, the decedent's personal representative may be substituted as a party on motion filed with the circuit clerk by the representative or by any party. A party's motion must be served on the representative in accordance with Rule 25. If the decedent has no representative, any party may suggest the death on the record, and the court of appeals may then direct appropriate proceedings.

(2) Before Notice of Appeal Is Filed—Potential Appellant. If a party entitled to appeal dies before filing a notice of appeal, the decedent's personal representative—or, if there is no personal representative, the decedent's attorney of record—may file a notice of appeal within the time prescribed by these rules. After the notice of appeal is filed, substitution must be in accordance with Rule 43(a)(1).

(3) Before Notice of Appeal Is Filed—Potential Appellee. If a party against whom an appeal may be taken dies after entry of a judgment or order in the district court, but before a notice of appeal is filed, an appellant may proceed as if the death had not occurred. After the notice of appeal is filed, substitution must be in accordance with Rule 43(a)(1).

(b) Substitution for a Reason Other Than Death. If a party needs to be substituted for any reason other than death, the procedure prescribed in Rule 43(a) applies.

(c) Public Officer: Identification; Substitution.

(1) Identification of Party. A public officer who is a party to an appeal or other proceeding in an official capacity may be described as a party by the public officer's official title rather than by name. But the court may require the public officer's name to be added.

(2) Automatic Substitution of Officeholder. When a public officer who is a party to an appeal or other proceeding in an official capacity dies, resigns, or otherwise ceases to hold office, the action does not abate. The public officer's successor is automatically substituted as a party. Proceedings following the substitution are to be in the name of the substituted party, but any misnomer that does not affect the substantial rights of the parties may be disregarded. An order of substitution may be entered at any time, but failure to enter an order does not affect the substitution.

(As amended Mar. 10, 1986, eff. July 1, 1986; Apr. 24, 1998, eff. Dec. 1, 1998.)

RULE 44. CASE INVOLVING A CONSTITUTIONAL QUESTION WHEN THE UNITED STATES OR THE RELEVANT STATE IS NOT A PARTY

(a) Constitutional Challenge to Federal Statute. If a party questions the constitutionality of an Act of Congress in a proceeding in which the United States or its agency, officer, or employee is not a party in an official capacity, the questioning party must give written notice to the circuit clerk immediately upon the filing of the record or as soon as the question is raised in the court of appeals. The clerk must then certify that fact to the Attorney General.

(b) Constitutional Challenge to State Statute. If a party questions the constitutionality of a statute of a State in a proceeding in which that State or its agency, officer, or employee is not a party in an official capacity, the questioning party must give written notice to the circuit clerk immediately upon the filing of the record or as soon as the question is raised in the court of appeals. The clerk must then certify that fact to the attorney general of the State.

(As amended Apr. 24, 1998, eff. Dec. 1, 1998; Apr. 29, 2002, eff. Dec. 1, 2002.)

RULE 45. CLERK'S DUTIES

(a) General Provisions.

(1) Qualifications. The circuit clerk must take the oath and post any bond required by law. Neither the clerk nor any deputy clerk may practice as an attorney or counselor in any court while in office.

(2) When Court Is Open. The court of appeals is always open for filing any paper, issuing and returning process, making a motion, and entering an order. The clerk's office with the clerk or a deputy in attendance must be open during business hours on all days except Saturdays, Sundays, and legal holidays. A court may provide by local rule or by order that the clerk's office be open for specified hours on Saturdays or on legal holidays other than New Year's Day, Martin Luther King, Jr.'s Birthday, Washington's Birthday, Memorial Day, Independence Day, Labor Day, Columbus Day, Veterans' Day, Thanksgiving Day, and Christmas Day.

(b) Records.

(1) The Docket. The circuit clerk must maintain a docket and an index of all docketed cases in the manner prescribed by the Director of the Administrative Office of the United States Courts. The clerk must record all papers filed with the clerk and all process, orders, and judgments.

(2) Calendar. Under the court's direction, the clerk must prepare a calendar of cases awaiting argument. In placing cases on the calendar for argument, the clerk must give preference to appeals in criminal cases and to other proceedings and appeals entitled to preference by law.

(3) Other Records. The clerk must keep other books and records required by the Director of the Administrative Office of the United States Courts, with the approval of the Judicial Conference of the United States, or by the court.

(c) Notice of an Order or Judgment. Upon the entry of an order or judgment, the circuit clerk must immediately serve a notice of entry on each party, with a copy of any opinion, and must note the date of service on the docket. Service on a party represented by counsel must be made on counsel.

(d) Custody of Records and Papers. The circuit clerk has custody of the court's records and papers. Unless the court orders or instructs otherwise, the clerk must not permit an original record or paper to be taken from the clerk's office. Upon disposition of the case, original papers constituting the record on appeal or review must be returned to the court or agency from which they were received. The clerk must preserve a copy of any brief, appendix, or other paper that has been filed.

(As amended Mar. 1, 1971, eff. July 1, 1971; Mar. 10, 1986, eff. July 1, 1986; Apr. 24, 1998, eff. Dec. 1, 1998; Apr. 29, 2002, eff. Dec. 1, 2002; Apr. 25, 2005, eff. Dec. 1, 2005.)

RULE 46. ATTORNEYS

(a) Admission to the Bar.

(1) Eligibility. An attorney is eligible for admission to the bar of a court of appeals if that attorney is of good moral and professional character and is admitted to practice before the Supreme Court of the United States, the highest court of a state, another United States court of appeals, or a United States district court (including the district courts for Guam, the Northern Mariana Islands, and the Virgin Islands).

(2) Application. An applicant must file an application for admission, on a form approved by the court that contains the applicant's personal statement showing eligibility for membership. The applicant must subscribe to the following oath or affirmation:

"I, _____, do solemnly swear [or affirm] that I will conduct myself as an attorney and counselor of this court, uprightly and according to law; and that I will support the Constitution of the United States."

(3) Admission Procedures. On written or oral motion of a member of the court's bar, the court will act on the application. An applicant may be admitted by oral motion in open court. But, unless the court orders otherwise, an applicant need not appear before the court to be admitted. Upon admission, an applicant must pay the clerk the fee prescribed by local rule or court order.

(b) Suspension or Disbarment.

(1) Standard. A member of the court's bar is subject to suspension or disbarment by the court if the member:

(A) has been suspended or disbarred from practice in any other court; or

(B) is guilty of conduct unbecoming a member of the court's bar.

(2) Procedure. The member must be given an opportunity to show good cause, within the time prescribed by the court, why the member should not be suspended or disbarred.

(3) Order. The court must enter an appropriate order after the member responds and a hearing is held, if requested, or after the time prescribed for a response expires, if no response is made.

(c) Discipline. A court of appeals may discipline an attorney who practices before it for conduct unbecoming a member of the bar or for failure to comply with any court rule. First, however, the court must afford the attorney reasonable notice, an opportunity to show cause to the contrary, and, if requested, a hearing.

(As amended Mar. 10, 1986, eff. July 1, 1986; Apr. 24, 1998, eff. Dec. 1, 1998.)

RULE 47. LOCAL RULES BY COURTS OF APPEALS

(a) Local Rules.

(1) Each court of appeals acting by a majority of its judges in regular active service may, after giving appropriate public notice and opportunity for comment, make and amend rules governing its practice. A generally applicable direction to parties or lawyers regarding practice before a court must be in a local rule rather than an internal operating procedure or standing order. A local rule must be consistent with—but not duplicative of—Acts of Congress and rules adopted under 28 U.S.C. § 2072 and must conform to any uniform numbering system prescribed by the Judicial Conference of the United States. Each circuit clerk must send the Administrative Office of the United States Courts a copy of each local rule and internal operating procedure when it is promulgated or amended.

(2) A local rule imposing a requirement of form must not be enforced in a manner that causes a party to lose rights because of a nonwillful failure to comply with the requirement.

(b) Procedure When There Is No Controlling Law. A court of appeals may regulate practice in a particular case in any manner consistent with federal law, these rules, and local rules of the circuit. No sanction or other disadvantage may be imposed for noncompliance with any requirement not in federal law, federal rules, or the local circuit rules unless the alleged violator has been furnished in the particular case with actual notice of the requirement.

(As amended Apr. 27, 1995, eff. Dec. 1, 1995; Apr. 24, 1998, eff. Dec. 1, 1998.)

RULE 48. MASTERS

(a) Appointment; Powers. A court of appeals may appoint a special master to hold hearings, if necessary, and to recommend factual findings and disposition in matters ancillary to proceedings in the court. Unless the order referring a matter to a master specifies or limits the master's powers, those powers include, but are not limited to, the following:

(1) regulating all aspects of a hearing;

(2) taking all appropriate action for the efficient performance of the master's duties under the order;

(3) requiring the production of evidence on all matters embraced in the reference; and

(4) administering oaths and examining witnesses and parties.

(b) Compensation. If the master is not a judge or court employee, the court must determine the master's compensation and whether the cost is to be charged to any party.

(As amended Apr. 29, 1994, eff. Dec. 1, 1994; Apr. 24, 1998, eff. Dec. 1, 1998.)

APPENDIX OF FORMS

FORM 1A. NOTICE OF APPEAL TO A COURT OF APPEALS FROM A JUDGMENT OF A DISTRICT COURT

United States District Court for the _____

District of _____

Docket Number _____

_____

A.B., Plaintiff

v.   Notice of Appeal

C.D., Defendant _____

_____ (name all parties taking the appeal)* appeal to the United States Court of Appeals for the _____ Circuit from the final judgment entered on _____ (state the date the judgment was entered).

_____

(s) _____

Attorney for _____

Address: _____

_____

[**Note to inmate filers:** *If you are an inmate confined in an institution and you seek the timing benefit of Fed. R. App. P. 4(c)(1), complete Form 7 (Declaration of Inmate Filing) and file that declaration with this Notice of Appeal.*]

(As amended Apr. 14, 2021, eff. Dec. 1, 2021.)

* See Rule 3(c) for permissible ways of identifying appellants.

FORM 1B. NOTICE OF APPEAL TO A COURT OF APPEALS FROM AN APPEALABLE ORDER OF A DISTRICT COURT

United States District Court for the _____

District of _____

Docket Number _____

_____

A.B., Plaintiff

v.   Notice of Appeal

C.D., Defendant _____

_____ (name all parties taking the appeal)* appeal to the United States Court of Appeals for the _____ Circuit from the order _____ (describe the order) entered on _____ (state the date the order was entered).

_____

(s) _____

    Attorney for _____

    Address: _____

_____

[**Note to inmate filers:** *If you are an inmate confined in an institution and you seek the timing benefit of Fed. R. App. P. 4(c)(1), complete Form 7 (Declaration of Inmate Filing) and file that declaration with this Notice of Appeal.*]

(As amended Apr. 14, 2021, eff. Dec. 1, 2021.)

* See Rule 3(c) for permissible ways of identifying appellants.

FORM 2.   NOTICE OF APPEAL TO A COURT OF APPEALS FROM A DECISION OF THE UNITED STATES TAX COURT

United States Tax Court

Washington, D.C.

Docket No. _____

A.B., Plaintiff
v.
                                                                    Notice of Appeal
Commissioner of
Internal Revenue,
Respondent

_____ (name all parties taking the appeal)* appeal to the United States Court of Appeals for the ___ Circuit from the decision entered on _____ (state the date the decision was entered).

_____

(s) _____

Attorney for _____

Address: _____

(As amended Apr. 22, 1993, eff. Dec. 1, 1993; Mar. 27, 2003, eff. Dec. 1, 2003; Apr. 14, 2021, eff. Dec. 1, 2021.)

1 See Rule 3(c) for permissible ways of identifying appellants.

* See Rule 3(c) for permissible ways of identifying appellants.

FORM 3.   PETITION FOR REVIEW OF ORDER OF AN AGENCY, BOARD, COMMISSION OR OFFICER

United States Court of Appeals for the _____ Circuit

A.B., Petitioner	)	
	)	
v.	)	Petition for Review
XYZ Commission, Respondent	)	

[____ (here name all parties bringing the petition[1]) ____] hereby petition the court for review of the Order of the XYZ Commission (describe the order) entered on _____, 201___.

[(s)]   _____
Attorney for Petitioners
Address:_____

(As amended Apr. 22, 1993, eff. Dec. 1, 1993; Mar. 27, 2003, eff. Dec. 1, 2003.)

[1] See Rule 15.

FORM 4. AFFIDAVIT ACCOMPANYING MOTION FOR PERMISSION TO APPEAL IN FORMA PAUPERIS

UNITED STATES DISTRICT COURT
for the
<_____> DISTRICT OF <_____>

<Name(s) of plaintiff(s)>,	)
Plaintiff(s)	)
v.	)
<Name(s) of defendant(s)>,	) Case No. <Number>
Defendant(s)	)

Affidavit in Support of Motion

I swear or affirm under penalty of perjury that, because of my poverty, I cannot prepay the docket fees of my appeal or post a bond for them. I believe I am entitled to redress. I swear or affirm under penalty of perjury under United States laws that my answers on this form are true and correct. (28 U.S.C. § 1746; 18 U.S.C. § 1621.)

Signed: _____

Instructions

Complete all questions in this application and then sign it. Do not leave any blanks: if the answer to a question is "0," "none," or "not applicable (N/A)," write in that response. If you need more space to answer a question or to explain your answer, attach a separate sheet of paper identified with your name, your case's docket number, and the question number.

Date: _____

My issues on appeal are:

1. *For both you and your spouse estimate the average amount of money received from each of the following sources during the past 12 months. Adjust any amount that was received weekly, biweekly, quarterly, semiannually, or annually to show the monthly rate. Use gross amounts, that is, amounts before any deductions for taxes or otherwise.*

Income source	Average monthly amount during the past 12 months		Amount expected next month	
	You	Spouse	You	Spouse
Employment	$____	$____	$____	$____
Self-employment	$____	$____	$____	$____
Income from real property (such as rental income)	$____	$____	$____	$____
Interest and dividends	$____	$____	$____	$____
Gifts	$____	$____	$____	$____
Alimony	$____	$____	$____	$____
Child support	$____	$____	$____	$____
Retirement (such as social security, pensions, annuities, insurance)	$____	$____	$____	$____
Disability (such as social security, insurance payments)	$____	$____	$____	$____
Unemployment payments	$____	$____	$____	$____
Public-assistance (such as welfare)	$____	$____	$____	$____

Other (specify): _____ $_____ $_____ $_____ $_____

Total monthly income: $_____ $_____ $_____ $_____

2. *List your employment history for the past two years, most recent employer first. (Gross monthly pay is before taxes or other deductions.)*

Employer	**Address**	**Dates of employment**	**Gross monthly pay**
_____	_____	_____	_____
_____	_____	_____	_____
_____	_____	_____	_____

3. *List your spouse's employment history for the past two years, most recent employer first. (Gross monthly pay is before taxes or other deductions.)*

Employer	**Address**	**Dates of employment**	**Gross monthly pay**
_____	_____	_____	_____
_____	_____	_____	_____
_____	_____	_____	_____

4. *How much cash do you and your spouse have? $_____
Below, state any money you or your spouse have in bank accounts or in any other financial institution.*

Financial institution	**Type of account**	**Amount you have**	**Amount your spouse has**
_____	_____	$_____	$_____
_____	_____	$_____	$_____
_____	_____	$_____	$_____

If you are a prisoner seeking to appeal a judgment in a civil action or proceeding, you must attach a statement certified by the appropriate institutional officer showing all receipts, expenditures, and balances during the last six months in your institutional accounts. If you have multiple accounts, perhaps because you have been in multiple institutions, attach one certified statement of each account.

5. *List the assets, and their values, which you own or your spouse owns. Do not list clothing and ordinary household furnishings.*

Home	(Value)	**Other real estate**	(Value)	**Motor vehicle #1**	(Value)
_____		_____		Make & year: _____	
_____		_____		Model: _____	
_____				Registration #: _____	

Motor vehicle #2	(Value)	**Other assets**	(Value)	**Other assets**	(Value)
Make & year: _____		_____		_____	
Model: _____		_____		_____	
Registration #: _____		_____		_____	

6. *State every person, business, or organization owing you or your spouse money, and the amount owed.*

Person owing you or your spouse money	**Amount owed to you**	**Amount owed to your spouse**
_____	_____	_____
_____	_____	_____
_____	_____	_____

7. *State the persons who rely on you or your spouse for support.*

Name [or, if under 18,	**Relationship**	**Age**

initials only]

_____   _____   _____
_____   _____   _____
_____   _____   _____

8. *Estimate the average monthly expenses of you and your family. Show separately the amounts paid by your spouse. Adjust any payments that are made weekly, biweekly, quarterly, semiannually, or annually to show the monthly rate.*

	You	**Your Spouse**
Rent or home-mortgage payment (include lot rented for mobile home)	$_____	$_____
Are real-estate taxes included? ☐ Yes ☐ No		
Is property insurance included? ☐ Yes ☐ No		
Utilities (electricity, heating fuel, water, sewer, and Telephone)	$_____	$_____
Home maintenance (repairs and upkeep)	$_____	$_____
Food	$_____	$_____
Clothing	$_____	$_____
Laundry and dry-cleaning	$_____	$_____
Medical and dental expenses	$_____	$_____
Transportation (not including motor vehicle payments)	$_____	$_____
Recreation, entertainment, newspapers, magazines, etc.	$_____	$_____
Insurance (not deducted from wages or included in mortgage payments)	$_____	$_____
Homeowner's or renter's:	$_____	$_____
Life:	$_____	$_____
Health:	$_____	$_____
Motor Vehicle:	$_____	$_____
Other: _____	$_____	$_____
Taxes (not deducted from wages or included in mortgage payments) (specify): __	$_____	$_____
Installment payments	$_____	$_____
Motor Vehicle:	$_____	$_____
Credit card (name): _____	$_____	$_____
Department store (name): _____	$_____	$_____
Other: _____	$_____	$_____
Alimony, maintenance, and support paid to others	$_____	$_____
Regular expenses for operation of business, profession, or farm (attach detailed statement)	$_____	$_____
Other (specify): _____	$_____	$_____
Total monthly expenses:	$_____	$_____

9. *Do you expect any major changes to your monthly income or expenses or in your assets or liabilities during the next 12 months?*
☐ Yes ☐ No   If yes, describe on an attached sheet.

10. *Have you spent—or will you be spending—any money for expenses or attorney fees in connection with this lawsuit?* ☐ Yes ☐ No
If yes, how much? $_____

11. *Provide any other information that will help explain why you cannot pay the docket fees for your appeal.*

12. *State the city and state of your legal residence.*

Your daytime phone number: (___) _____
Your age: _____ *Your years of schooling:* _____

(As amended Apr. 24, 1998, eff. Dec. 1, 1998; Apr. 28, 2010, eff. Dec. 1, 2010; Apr. 16, 2013, eff. Dec. 1, 2013; Apr. 26, 2018, eff. Dec. 1, 2018.)

FORM 5. NOTICE OF APPEAL TO A COURT OF APPEALS FROM A JUDGMENT OR ORDER OF A DISTRICT COURT OR A BANKRUPTCY APPELLATE PANEL

United States District Court for the ....

District of ....

In re)
)
.............................,)
Debtor)
) File No...........
.............................,)
Plaintiff)
)
v.)
)
.............................,)
Defendant)

Notice of Appeal to
United States Court of Appeals
for the .... Circuit
........................, the plaintiff [or defendant or other party] appeals to the
United States Court of Appeals for the .... Circuit from the
final judgment [or order or decree] of the district court for the district of ....
[or bankruptcy appellate panel of the .... circuit], entered in this case on
........., 20.... [here describe the judgment, order, or decree] ....
 The parties to the judgment [or order or decree] appealed from and the names and
addresses of their respective attorneys are as follows:

Dated ....
Signed ....
Attorney for Appellant

Address: ....
....

[Note to inmate filers: If you are an inmate confined in an institution and you seek the timing benefit of Fed. R. App. P. 4(c)(1), complete Form 7 (Declaration of Inmate Filing) and file that declaration along with this Notice of Appeal.]

(Added Apr. 25, 1989, eff. Dec. 1, 1989; amended Mar. 27, 2003, eff. Dec. 1, 2003; Apr. 28, 2016, eff. Dec. 1, 2016.)

FORM 6. CERTIFICATE OF COMPLIANCE WITH TYPE–VOLUME LIMIT

Certificate of Compliance With Type-Volume Limit, Typeface Requirements, and Type-Style Requirements

1. This document complies with [the type-volume limit of Fed. R. App. P. [*insert Rule citation; e.g., 32(a)(7)(B)*]] [the word limit of Fed. R. App. P. [*insert Rule citation; e.g., 5(c)(1)*]] because, excluding the parts of the document exempted by Fed. R. App. P. 32(f) [and [*insert applicable Rule citation, if any*]]:

☐ this document contains [*state the number of*] words, **or**

☐ this brief uses a monospaced typeface and contains [*state the number of*] lines of text.

2. This document complies with the typeface requirements of Fed. R. App. P. 32(a)(5) and the type-style requirements of Fed. R. App. P. 32(a)(6) because:

☐ this document has been prepared in a proportionally spaced typeface using [*state name and version of word-processing program*] in [*state font size and name of type style*], **or**

☐ this document has been prepared in a monospaced typeface using [*state name and version of word-processing program*] with [*state number of characters per inch and name of type style*].

(s)_____

Attorney for _____

Dated: _____

(Added Apr. 29, 2002, eff. Dec. 1, 2002; amended Apr. 28, 2016, eff. Dec. 1, 2016.)

FORM 7. DECLARATION OF INMATE FILING

_____

[insert name of court; for example,
United States District Court for the District of Minnesota]

_____

A.B., Plaintiff

v.   Case No. _____

C.D., Defendant _____

I am an inmate confined in an institution. Today, _____ *[insert date]*, I am depositing the _____ *[insert title of document; for example, "notice of appeal"]* in this case in the institution's internal mail system. First–class postage is being prepaid either by me or by the institution on my behalf.

I declare under penalty of perjury that the foregoing is true and correct (see 28 U.S.C. § 1746; 18 U.S.C. § 1621).

Sign your name here _____

Signed on _____ *[insert date]*

[Note to inmate filers: *If your institution has a system designed for legal mail, you must use that system in order to receive the timing benefit of Fed. R. App. P. 4(c)(1) or Fed. R. App. P. 25(a)(2)(A)(iii).]*

(Added Apr. 28, 2016, eff. Dec. 1, 2016. As amended Apr. 26, 2018, eff. Dec. 1, 2018.)

APPENDIX

This chart summarizes the length limits stated in the Federal Rules of Appellate Procedure. Please refer to the rules for precise requirements, and bear in mind the following:

- In computing these limits, you can exclude the items listed in Rule 32(f).
- If you use a word limit or a line limit (other than the word limit in Rule 28(j)), you must file the certificate required by Rule 32(g).
- For the limits in Rules 5, 21, 27, 35, and 40:
  - You must use the word limit if you produce your document on a computer; and
  - You must use the page limit if you handwrite your document or type it on a typewriter.
- For the limits in Rules 28.1, 29(a)(5), and 32:
  - You may use the word limit or page limit, regardless of how you produce the document; or
  - You may use the line limit if you type or print your document with a monospaced typeface. A typeface is monospaced when each character occupies the same amount of horizontal space.

	Rule	Document type	Word limit	Page limit	Line limit
Permission to appeal	5(c)	• Petition for permission to appeal • Answer in opposition • Cross–petition	5,200	20	Not applicable
Extraordinary writs	21(d)	• Petition for writ of mandamus or prohibition or other extraordinary writ • Answer	7,800	30	Not applicable
Motions	27(d)(2)	• Motion • Response to a motion	5,200	20	Not applicable
	27(d)(2)	• Reply to a response to a motion	2,600	10	Not applicable
Parties' briefs (where no cross–appeal)	32(a)(7)	• Principal brief	13,000	30	1,300
	32(a)(7)	• Reply brief	6,500	15	650
Parties' briefs (where cross–appeal)	28.1(e)	• Appellant's principal brief • Appellant's response and reply brief	13,000	30	1,300
	28.1(e)	• Appellee's principal and response brief	15,300	35	1,500
	28.1(e)	• Appellee's reply brief	6,500	15	650
Party's supplemental letter	28(j)	• Letter citing supplemental authorities	350	Not applicable	Not applicable
Amicus briefs	29(a)(5)	• Amicus brief during initial consideration of case on merits	One–half the length set by the Appellate Rules for a party's principal brief	One–half the length set by the Appellate Rules for a party's principal brief	One–half the length set by the Appellate Rules for a party's principal brief

	Rule	Document type	Word limit	Page limit	Line limit
	29(b)(4)	• Amicus brief during consideration of whether to grant rehearing	2,600	Not applicable	Not applicable
Rehearing and en banc filings	35(b)(2) & 40(b)	• Petition for hearing en banc • Petition for panel rehearing; petition for rehearing en banc	3,900	15	Not applicable

(Added Apr. 28, 2016, eff. Dec. 1, 2016.)

INDEX TO
FEDERAL RULES OF APPELLATE PROCEDURE

UNITED STATES COURT OF APPEALS
FOR THE
NINTH CIRCUIT

Including Amendments Received Through
December 1, 2021

———

APPENDIX OF FORMS

NINTH CIRCUIT FORMS

GENERAL ORDERS

RULES FOR JUDICIAL–CONDUCT AND JUDICIAL–DISABILITY PROCEEDINGS

ARTICLE I.   GENERAL PROVISIONS

ARTICLE II.   MISCONDUCT AND DISABILITY

ARTICLE III.   INITIATION OF COMPLAINT

ARTICLE IV.   REVIEW OF COMPLAINT BY CHIEF JUDGE

U.S. COURT OF APPEALS

ARTICLE V. INVESTIGATION AND REPORT BY SPECIAL COMMITTEE

Rule 12. Special Committee's Composition.
Rule 13. Conduct of Special–Committee Investigation.
Rule 14. Conduct of Special–Committee Hearings.
Rule 15. Subject Judge's Rights.
Rule 16. Complainant's Rights in Investigation.
Rule 17. Special–Committee Report.

ARTICLE VI. REVIEW BY JUDICIAL COUNCIL

Rule 18. Petition for Review of Chief–Judge Disposition Under Rule 11(c), (d), or (e).
Rule 19. Judicial–Council Disposition of Petition for Review.
Rule 20. Judicial–Council Action Following Appointment of Special Committee.

ARTICLE VII. REVIEW BY COMMITTEE ON JUDICIAL CONDUCT AND DISABILITY

Rule 21. Committee on Judicial Conduct and Disability.
Rule 22. Procedures for Review.

ARTICLE VIII. MISCELLANEOUS RULES

Rule 23. Confidentiality.
Rule 24. Public Availability of Decisions.
Rule 25. Disqualification.
Rule 26. Transfer to Another Judicial Council.
Rule 27. Withdrawal of Complaint or Petition for Review.
Rule 28. Availability of Rules and Forms.
Rule 29. Effective Date.

APPENDIX

Complaint of Judicial Misconduct or Disability.
Guidelines for Judicial Misconduct or Disability Complaints.

PREAMBLE

These local rules of the United States Court of Appeals for the Ninth Circuit are promulgated under the authority of Fed. R. App. P. 2 and 47.

[Effective January 1, 1997. Amended effective December 1, 2009.]

FOREWORD

The Advisory Committee on Rules of Practice and Internal Operating Procedures of the United States Court of Appeals for the Ninth Circuit was appointed by the court in 1984, pursuant to 28 U.S.C. § 2077. The committee first undertook a major restructuring of the Ninth Circuit Rules with the objective of updating the rules to reflect current practice, putting the rules into a simpler format and style, and renumbering the rules to conform to the numbering sequence of the Federal Rules of Appellate Procedure. The purpose of this project was to produce a more readable, easily understandable set of rules in handbook form. The handbook contains the Federal Rules of Appellate Procedure, the Ninth Circuit Rules, and, following certain rules, Circuit Advisory Committee Notes. The committee's role in assisting the Court is more fully defined by 9th Cir. R. 47–2.

Circuit Judges Susan P. Graber and Sandra J. Ikuta currently serve on the committee.

Lawyers serving on the committee include Professor Jennifer Chacón, Davina T. Chen, Xiomara Costello, Kari Hong, Elizabeth Olson White, Professor Elizabeth Porter, Harini P. Raghupathi, Mary-Christine Sungaila, Martha Sheehy, and Todd D. True. The committee is chaired by Professor Jennifer Chacón.

The Court encourages members of the bar to make suggestions for improvements to the rules of Court. Such suggestions should be directed to the Clerk of Court.

Sidney R. Thomas Chief Judge

[Effective January 1, 2005. Amended effective January 1, 2007; July 1, 2007; January 1, 2009; December 1, 2009; July 1, 2013; July 1, 2016; December 1, 2016; December 1, 2018; December 1, 2019.]

COURT STRUCTURE AND PROCEDURES

A. Physical Facilities. The headquarters of the Court are located at 95 Seventh Street, San Francisco, California 94103. The mailing address is P.O. Box 193939, San Francisco, California 94119–3939, and the telephone number is (415) 355–8000. There are divisional clerk's offices in Pasadena, Seattle and Portland.

B. Emergency Telephone Number. The Clerk's Office provides 24–hour telephone service for calls placed to the main Clerk's Office number, (415) 355–8000. Messages left at times other than regular office hours are recorded and monitored on a regular basis by staff attorneys.

The emergency telephone service is to be used only for matters of extreme urgency that must be handled by the Court before the next business day. Callers should make clear the nature of the emergency and the reason why next-business-day treatment is not sufficient.

C. Judges and Supporting Personnel.

(1) *Judges.* The Court has an authorized complement of 29 judgeships. Upon the attainment of senior status, a judge may continue, within statutory limitations, to function as a member of the Court. There are several senior circuit judges who regularly hear cases before the Court.

Although San Francisco is the Court's headquarters, most of the active and senior judges maintain their residence chambers in other cities within the circuit. The residences and chambers of the Court's judges, including its senior judges, are indicated in the listing of judges within these Rules.

The Court has established three regional administrative units to assist the chief judge of the circuit to discharge his administrative responsibilities. They are the Northern, Middle and Southern units. The senior active judge in each unit is designated the administrative judge of the unit.

● The Northern Unit includes the districts of Alaska, Idaho, Montana, Oregon, and Eastern and Western Washington.

- The Middle Unit includes the districts of Arizona, Nevada, Hawaii, Guam, Northern and Eastern California, and the Northern Mariana Islands.
- The Southern Unit includes the districts of Central and Southern California.

Cases arising from the Northern Unit will normally be calendared in Seattle or Portland, from the Middle Unit in San Francisco, and from the Southern Unit in Pasadena. Cases may also be heard in such other places as the Court may designate.

(2) *Appellate Commissioner.* The Appellate Commissioner is an officer appointed by the Court to rule on and to review and make recommendations on a variety of non-dispositive matters, and to serve as a special master as directed by the Court.

(3) *Clerk's Office.* Office hours are from 8:30 a.m. to 5:00 p.m., Monday through Friday, except federal holidays. In addition to the San Francisco office, the Court has permanent, but not full service, Clerk's offices in Seattle, Pasadena, and Portland. Court information, including Court rules, the general orders, calendars and opinions are available on the Court's website at www.ca9.uscourts.gov.

Clerk's office personnel are authorized by Circuit Rule 27-7 to act on certain procedural motions (*see* Circuit Advisory Committee Note to Rule 27-7, infra); are authorized by FRAP 42(b) to handle stipulations for dismissal; and are authorized by Circuit Rule 42-1 to dismiss cases for failure to prosecute.

Inquiries concerning rules and procedures may be directed to the San Francisco, Pasadena, Seattle, or Portland Clerk's office. On matters requiring special handling, counsel may contact the Clerk for information and assistance. It should be emphasized, however, that legal advice will not be given by a judge or any member of the Court staff.

(4) *Office of Staff Attorneys.* The staff attorneys perform a variety of tasks for the Court and work for the entire Court rather than for individual judges.

(a) Inventory. After briefing has been completed, the case management attorneys review the briefs and record in each case in order to identify the primary issues raised in the case and to assign a numerical weight to the case reflecting the relative amount of judge time that likely will have to be spent on the matter.

(b) Research. The research attorneys review briefs and records, research legal issues, and prepare memorandum dispositions for oral presentation to three-judge panels, in cases that are not calendared for oral argument.

(c) Motions. The motions attorneys process all motions, except for procedural motions disposed of by the Clerk, filed in a case prior to assignment of a particular panel for disposition on the merits. The motions attorneys also process emergency motions filed pursuant to Circuit Rules 27-3 and 27-4, and motions for reconsideration of orders filed by motions panels.

(5) *Circuit Court Mediators.* Shortly after a new case is docketed, the Circuit Court Mediators will review the Mediation Questionnaire to determine if a case appears suitable for the Court's settlement program. *See* Circuit Rules 3-4 and

15-2. The Circuit Court Mediators are permanent members of the Court staff. They are experienced appellate practitioners who have had extensive mediation and negotiation training.

(6) *Library.* The staff of the Ninth Circuit library system serve circuit, district, bankruptcy and magistrate judges, as well as staff of other Court units. Services provided include reference and other information services, acquisition of publications for Court libraries and judges' chambers, organization and maintenance of library collections and management of the Circuit library system. The Ninth Circuit library system, headed by the Circuit Librarian, consists of 21 staffed libraries including the headquarters library and 20 branch libraries located throughout the Circuit. The administrative office and the headquarters library are located in San Francisco.

Court libraries may make their collections available to members of the bar and the general public depending on local Court rules. Hours for the headquarters library in San Francisco are Monday through Friday, 9:00 p.m.* to 5:00 p.m. and 8:00 a.m. to 5:00 p.m. during Court week. Information regarding the location and hours of operation for other branch libraries may be obtained by calling the headquarters library reference desk at (415) 355-8650.

(7) *Circuit Executive's Office.* The Circuit Executive's office is the arm of the Circuit's Judicial Council that provides administrative support to appellate, district and bankruptcy judges in the circuit.

D. The Judicial Council. The Judicial Council, established pursuant to 28 U.S.C. § 332, is currently composed of the Chief Judge, four circuit judges, and four district judges. The Council convenes regularly to consider and take required action upon any matter affecting the administration of its own work and that of all federal courts within the circuit, including the consideration of some complaints of judicial misconduct.

E. Court Procedures for Processing and Hearing of Cases.

(1) *Classification of Cases.* After the briefing is completed, the case management attorneys inventory cases in order to weigh them by type, issue, and difficulty. The weight of a case is merely an indication of the relative amount of judicial time that will probably be consumed in disposing of the case. The inventory process enables the Court to balance judges' workloads and hear at a single sitting unrelated appeals involving similar legal issues.

(2) *Designation of Court Calendars.* Under the direction of the Court, the Clerk sets the time and place of court calendars, taking into account, for at least six months in advance, the availability of judges, the number of cases to be calendared, and the places of hearing required or contemplated by statute or policy. The random assignment of judges by computer to particular days or weeks on the calendars is intended to equalize the workload among the judges. At the time of assigning judges to panels, the Clerk does not know which cases ultimately will be allocated to each of the panels.

(3) *Disclosure of Judges on Panels.* The names of the judges on each panel are released to the general public on the Monday of the week preceding argument. At that time, the calendar of cases scheduled for hearing posted on the Court's website is updated to include the names of the judges. This

permits the parties to prepare for oral argument before particular judges. Once the calendar is made public, motions for continuances will rarely be granted.

(4) *Allocation of Cases to Calendars.* Direct criminal appeals receive preference pursuant to FRAP 45(b)(2) and are placed on the first available calendar after briefing is completed. Many other cases are accorded priority by statute or rule. *See* Circuit Rule 34–3. Their place on the court's calendar is a function of both the statutory priority and the length of time the cases have been pending. Pursuant to FRAP 2, the Court also may in its discretion order that any individual case receive expedited treatment.

The Court makes every effort to ensure that calendars are prepared objectively and that no case is given unwarranted preference. The only exception to the rule of random assignment of cases to panels is that a case heard by the Court on a prior appeal may be set before the same panel upon a later appeal. If the panel that originally heard the matter does not specify its intent to retain jurisdiction over any further appeal, the parties may file a motion to have the case heard by the original panel. Matters on remand from the United States Supreme Court are referred to the panel that previously heard the matter.

Normally, court calendars are held each year in the following places:

- 12 in San Francisco (usually the second week of each month),
- 12 in Pasadena (usually the first week of each month),
- 12 in Seattle (usually the first week of each month),
- 6 in Portland,
- 3 in Phoenix;
- 3 in Honolulu; and
- 2 in Anchorage.

Each court calendar usually consists of one week of multiple sittings.

(5) *Selection of Panels.* The Clerk of Court sets the time and place of the calendars. The Clerk utilizes a matrix composed of all active judges and those senior judges who have indicated their availability. The aim is to enable each active judge to sit with every other active and senior judge approximately the same number of times over a two-year period and to assign active judges an equal number of times to each of the locations at which the Court holds hearings.

At present, all panels are composed of no fewer than two members of the Court, at least one of whom is an active judge. Every year, each active judge, except the Chief Judge, is expected to sit on 32 days of oral argument calendars; one oral screening panel; one motions panel; and two certificate of appealability panels. Senior judges are given a choice as to how many cases they desire to hear.

The Court on occasion calls upon district judges to sit on argument panels when there are insufficient circuit judges to constitute a panel. It is Court policy that district judges not participate in the disposition of appeals from their own districts. In addition, the Court attempts to avoid assigning district judges to appeals of cases over which other judges from their district have presided (either on motions or at trial) as visiting judges in other districts.

All active judges and some senior judges serve on a motions panel, whose membership changes monthly.

(6) *Pre–Argument Preparation.* After the cases have been allocated to the panels, the briefs and excerpts of record in each case are distributed to each of the judges scheduled to hear the case. The documents are usually received in the judges' chambers twelve weeks prior to the scheduled time for hearing, and it is the policy of the Court that each judge read all of the briefs prior to oral argument.

(7) *Oral Argument.* The Clerk sends a master calendar notice to all counsel of record about ten weeks prior to the date of oral argument. If counsel finds it impossible to meet the assigned hearing date, a motion for continuance should be filed immediately. Delay in submitting such a motion will militate against the Court's granting the relief requested. Once the identity of the judges are announced, motions for continuance will rarely be granted.

Counsel should inform the Court promptly if the case has become moot, settlement discussions are pending, or relevant precedent has been decided since the briefs were filed.

The Location of Hearing Notice indicates how much time will be allotted to each side for oral argument. If oral argument is allowed, the amount of time, which is within the Court's discretion, generally ranges between 10 and 20 minutes per side. If counsel wishes more time, a motion to that effect must be filed as soon as possible after the notice is received.

Daily court calendars usually commence at 9:00 a.m., Monday through Friday. Counsel are expected to check in with the courtroom deputy at least 30 minutes prior to the start of the calendar. Most arguments are broadcast live via the Court's website at www.ca9.uscourts.gov. Recordings will be available under the Audio and Video heading the day following argument. These recordings do not represent an official record of the proceedings.

(8) *Case Conferences.* At the conclusion of each day's argument, the judges on each panel confer on the cases they have heard. Each judge expresses his or her tentative views and votes in reverse order of seniority. The judges reach a tentative decision regarding the disposition of each case and whether it should be in the form of a published opinion. The presiding judge then assigns each case to a judge for the preparation and submission of a disposition.

[Effective January 1, 2005. Amended effective July 1, 2007; January 1, 2009; December 1, 2009; January 1, 2015; December 1, 2018; December 1, 2019; December 1, 2020; November 1, 2021; December 1, 2021.]

* So in original.

TITLE I. APPLICABILITY OF RULES

FRAP 1. SCOPE OF RULES; DEFINITION; TITLE

[For text of rule, see the Federal Rules of Appellate Procedure]

RULE 1–1. TITLE

The rules of the United States Court of Appeals for the Ninth Circuit are to be known as Circuit Rules.
[Effective January 1, 1997.]

RULE 1–2. SCOPE OF CIRCUIT RULES

In cases where the Federal Rules of Appellate Procedure (FRAP) and the Rules of the United States Court of Appeals for the Ninth Circuit (Circuit Rules) are silent as to a particular matter of appellate practice, any relevant rule of the Supreme Court of the United States shall be applied.

[Effective January 1, 1997.]

FRAP 2. SUSPENSION OF RULES

[For text of rule, see the Federal Rules of Appellate Procedure]

TITLE II. APPEAL FROM A JUDGMENT OR ORDER OF A DISTRICT COURT

FRAP 3. APPEAL AS OF RIGHT—HOW TAKEN

[For text of rule, see the Federal Rules of Appellate Procedure]

RULE 3–1. FILING THE APPEAL

In appeals from the district court, appellant's counsel shall simultaneously submit to the clerk of the district court the notice of appeal, the filing fee, and the appellate docket fee. In appeals from the bankruptcy appellate panel and the Tax Court, the notice of appeal and fees shall be submitted to the Clerk of the court from which the appeal is taken. Petitions for review and applications to enforce federal agency orders, and fees for those petitions and applications, shall be submitted to the Clerk of the Court of Appeals. If the fees are not paid promptly, the Court of Appeals Clerk will dismiss the case after transmitting a warning notice.

The above rules are subject to several exceptions. The docket fee need not be paid upon filing the notice of appeal when: (a) the district court or this Court has granted in forma pauperis or Criminal Justice Act status; (b) an application for in forma pauperis relief or for a certificate of appealability is pending; or (c) the appellant, e.g., the Government, is exempt by statute from paying the fee. Counsel shall advise the Clerk at the time the notice of appeal is filed if one of these conditions exists. (*See* FRAP 24 regarding appeals in forma pauperis.) If a party has filed a petition for permission to appeal pursuant to FRAP 5, the filing fee and docket fee will become due in the district court upon an order of this Court granting permission to appeal. A notice of appeal need not be filed. (*See* FRAP 5.)

[Effective January 1, 1997. Amended effective December 1, 2009.]

RULE 3–2. REPRESENTATION STATEMENT

(a) No FRAP 12(b) Representation Statement is required in: (1) criminal cases; (2) appeals arising from actions filed pursuant to 28 U.S.C. §§ 2241, 2254, and 2255; and (3) appeals filed by pro se appellants.

(b) In all other cases, a party filing an appeal shall attach to the notice a Representation Statement that identifies all parties to the action along with the names, addresses and telephone numbers of their respective counsel, if known.

Cross Reference:

• FRAP 12. Docketing the Appeal; Filing a Representation Statement; Filing the Record, specifically, FRAP 12(b), Filing a Representation Statement.

CIRCUIT ADVISORY COMMITTEE NOTE TO RULE 3–2

The representation statement is critically important and should, to the extent possible, include appellate counsel for all parties, whether or not they were counsel in the lower court. It is used by the Court to determine the contents of the caption, which parties and counsel will be added to the appellate docket, who will receive notice of the appeal and initial schedule, and who will be required or permitted to submit filings in the appeal. When any party or counsel is not accurately listed in the docket, significant problems, such as lack of notice or waiver of arguments, can result. Because the representation statement is filed by appellants (and none is required in pro se or criminal appeals), the Court expects and requires that all parties will carefully review the Court's caption and listing of counsel and parties at the outset of every appeal and will notify the Court immediately of any corrections or updates.

[Effective January 1, 1997. Amended effective December 1, 2020.]

RULE 3–3. PRELIMINARY INJUNCTION APPEALS

(a) Every notice of appeal from an interlocutory order (i) granting, continuing, modifying, refusing or dissolving a preliminary injunction or (ii) refusing to dissolve or modify a preliminary injunction shall bear the caption "PRELIMINARY INJUNCTION APPEAL." Immediately upon filing, the notice of appeal must be transmitted by the district court clerk's office to the Court of Appeals clerk's office.

(b) Within 7 days of filing a notice of appeal from an order specified in subparagraph (a), the parties shall arrange for expedited preparation by the district court reporter of all portions of the official transcript of oral proceedings in the district court which the parties desire to be included in the record on appeal. Unless otherwise established by Court order in a particular case, the following briefing deadlines will apply: Within 28 days of the docketing in the district court of a notice of appeal from an order specified in subparagraph (a), the appellant shall file an opening brief and excerpts of record. Appellee's brief and any supplemental excerpts of record shall be filed within 28 days of service of appellant's opening brief. Appellant may file a brief in reply to appellee's brief within 21 days of service of appellee's brief.

(c) If a party files a motion to expedite the appeal or a motion to grant or stay the injunction pending appeal, the Court, in resolving those motions, may order a schedule for briefing that differs from that described above.

Cross Reference:

- FRAP 8. Stay or Injunction Pending Appeal
- Circuit Rule 27–2. Motions for Stays Pending Appeal
- Circuit Rule 27–3. Emergency Motions
- FRAP 10. The Record on Appeal
- Circuit Rule 10–2. Contents of the Record on Appeal
- Circuit Rule 10–3. Ordering the Reporter's Transcript
- Circuit Rule 30–1. The Excerpts of Record
- FRAP 34. Oral Argument
- Circuit Rule 34–3. Priority Cases

[Effective January 1, 1997. Amended effective December 1, 2002; July 1, 2006; December 1, 2009; June 1, 2017.]

RULE 3–4. MEDIATION QUESTIONNAIRE

(a) The Court encourages the parties in Ninth Circuit civil appeals to engage in mediation. To that end, except as provided in section (b) below, within 7 days of the docketing of a civil appeal, the appellant(s) shall, and the appellee(s) may, complete and submit Form 7, the Ninth Circuit Mediation Questionnaire. The Clerk shall transmit the Mediation Questionnaire to counsel with the time scheduling order. Counsel shall return it according to the instructions contained in the Mediation Questionnaire. The sole purpose of the Mediation Questionnaire is to provide information about new appeals to the Court's Mediation Office.

Appellant's failure to comply with this rule may result in dismissal of the appeal in accordance with Circuit Rule 42–1.

(b) The requirement for filing a Mediation Questionnaire shall not apply to:

(1) an appeal in which the appellant is proceeding without the assistance of counsel;

(2) an appeal from an action filed under 28 U.S.C. §§ 2241, 2254, 2255; and,

(3) petitions for a writ under 28 U.S.C. § 1651.

Cross Reference:

- Circuit Rule 25–5. Electronic Filing, specifically Circuit Rule 25–5(b), documents that may be submitted either electronically or in paper format
- Circuit Rule 15–2. Mediation Questionnaire in Agency Cases
- FRAP 33. Appeal Conferences
- Circuit Rule 33–1. Circuit Mediation Office

[Effective January 1, 1997. Amended effective July 1, 1997; December 1, 2009; July 1, 2013.]

RULE 3–5. PROCEDURE FOR RECALCITRANT WITNESS APPEALS

Every notice of appeal from an order holding a witness in contempt and directing incarceration under 28 U.S.C. § 1826 shall bear the caption "RECALCITRANT WITNESS APPEAL." Immediately upon filing, the notice of appeal must be transmitted by the district court clerk's office to the Court of Appeals clerk's office. It shall also be the responsibility of the appellant to notify directly the motions unit of the Court of Appeals that such a notice of appeal has been filed in the district court. Such notification must be given by telephone (415/355–8000) within 24 hours of the filing of the notice of appeal.

A failure to provide such notice may result in sanctions against counsel imposed by the Court.

Cross Reference:

- FRAP 27. Motions
- Circuit Rule 27–1. Filing of Motions
- Circuit Rule 27–13. Sealed Documents
- Circuit Rule 10–1. Notice of Filing Appeal
- Circuit Rule 25–1. Principal Office of Clerk

CIRCUIT ADVISORY COMMITTEE NOTE TO RULE 3–5

A recalcitrant witness summarily ordered confined pursuant to 28 U.S.C. § 1826(a) is entitled to have the appeal from the order of confinement decided within 30 days after the filing of the notice of appeal. In the interest of obtaining a rapid disposition of the appeal, the Court impresses upon counsel that the record on appeal and briefs must be filed with the Court as soon as possible after the notice of appeal is filed. The Court will establish an expedited schedule for filing the record and briefs and will submit the appeal for decision on an expedited basis. If expedited treatment is sought for an interlocutory appeal, motions for expedition, summary affirmance or reversal, or dismissal may be filed pursuant to Circuit Rule 27–4. A party may file documents using a Doe designation or under seal to avoid disclosure of the identity of the applicant or the subject matter of the grand jury investigation. The party should file an accompanying motion to use such a designation.

[Effective January 1, 1997. Amended effective July 1, 1997; July 1, 2007; December 1, 2009.]

RULE 3–6. SUMMARY DISPOSITION OF CIVIL APPEALS

(a) At any time prior to the completion of briefing in a civil appeal or petition for review, if the Court determines:

(1) that clear error or an intervening court decision or recent legislation requires affirmance, reversal or vacation of the judgment or order appealed from, the grant or denial of a petition for review, or a remand for additional proceedings; or

(2) that it is manifest that the questions on which the decision in the appeal or petition for review depends are so insubstantial as not to justify further proceedings;

the Court may, upon motion of a party, or after affording the parties an opportunity to show cause, issue an appropriate dispositive order.

(b) At any time prior to the disposition of a civil appeal or petition for review if the Court determines that the appeal is not within its jurisdiction, the Court may issue an order dismissing the appeal without notice or further proceedings. *(Eff. 7/95; Rev. 12/1/19)*

[Effective January 1, 1997. Amended effective December 1, 2019.]

FRAP 3.1 APPEAL FROM A JUDGMENT OF A MAGISTRATE JUDGE IN A CIVIL CASE [ABROGATED]

FRAP 4. APPEAL AS OF RIGHT— WHEN TAKEN

[For text of rule, see the Federal Rules of Appellate Procedure]

Cross Reference:
- Circuit Rule 3–5. Procedure for Recalcitrant Witness Appeals
- Circuit Rule 10–2. Contents of the Record on Appeal
- Circuit Rule 27–4. Emergency Criminal Interlocutory Appeals

RULE 4–1. COUNSEL IN CRIMINAL APPEALS

This rule applies to appeals in categories of cases listed in 18 U.S.C. § 3006A.

(a) Continuity of Representation on Appeal. Counsel in criminal cases, whether retained or appointed by the district court, shall ascertain whether the defendant wishes to appeal and file a notice of appeal upon the defendant's request. Retained counsel shall continue to represent the defendant on appeal unless and until counsel is relieved and replaced by substitute counsel or by the defendant pro se in accordance with this rule. If counsel was appointed by the district court pursuant to 18 U.S.C. § 3006A and a notice of appeal has been filed, counsel's appointment automatically shall continue on appeal unless and until counsel is relieved in accordance with this rule.

(b) Application for Indigent Status on Appeal. A person for whom counsel was appointed by the district court under section 3006A of the Criminal Justice Act may appeal to this Court without prepayment of fees and costs or security therefor and without filing the affidavit required by 28 U.S.C. § 1915(a).

If the district court did not appoint counsel, but the defendant or petitioner appears to qualify for appointment of counsel on appeal, retained counsel, or the defendant if the defendant proceeded pro se before the district court, shall file on the client's behalf a financial affidavit (CJA Form 23). If the notice of appeal is filed at the time of sentencing, the motions to proceed on appeal in forma pauperis and for appointment of counsel shall be presented to the district court at that time. If the district court finds that appointment of counsel is warranted, the Court shall appoint the counsel who represented the defendant in district court, a Criminal Justice Act defender, or a panel attorney to represent the defendant or petitioner on appeal. The district court shall require appointed counsel and the court reporter to prepare the appropriate CJA form for preparation of the reporter's transcript. A copy of the order appointing counsel on appeal shall be transmitted forthwith by the Clerk of the district court to the Clerk of this Court. Substitute counsel shall within 14 days of appointment file a notice of appearance in this Court.

If the district court declines to appoint counsel on appeal, and if counsel below believes that the district court erred, counsel shall, within 14 days from the district court's order, file with the Clerk of this Court a motion for appointment of counsel accompanied by a financial affidavit (CJA Form 23).

(c) Withdrawal of Counsel After Filing the Notice of Appeal. A motion to withdraw as counsel on appeal after the filing of the notice of appeal, where counsel is retained in a criminal case or appointed under the Criminal Justice Act, shall be filed with the Clerk of this Court within 21 days after the filing of the notice of appeal and shall be accompanied by a statement of reasons and:

(1) A substitution of counsel which indicates that new counsel has been retained to represent defendant; or

(2) A motion by retained counsel for leave to proceed in forma pauperis and for appointment of counsel under the Criminal Justice Act, supported by a completed financial affidavit (CJA Form 23);

(3) A motion by appointed counsel to be relieved and for appointment of substitute counsel;

(4) A motion by defendant to proceed pro se; or

(5) An affidavit or signed statement from the defendant showing that the defendant has been advised of his or her rights with regard to the appeal and expressly stating that the defendant wishes to dismiss the appeal voluntarily.

Any motion filed pursuant to this section shall be served on defendant; the proof of service shall include defendant's current address.

(6) Alternatively, if after conscientious review of the record appointed counsel believes the appeal is frivolous, on or before the due date for the opening brief, appointed counsel shall file a separate motion to withdraw and an opening brief that identifies anything in the record that might arguably support the appeal, with citations to the record and applicable legal authority. The motion and brief shall be accompanied by proof of service on defendant. *See Anders v. California*, 386 U.S. 738 (1967), and *United States v. Griffy*, 895 F.2d 561 (9th Cir. 1990). The cover of the opening brief shall state that the brief is being filed pursuant to *Anders v. California*. The filing of a motion to withdraw as counsel along with a proposed *Anders* brief serves to vacate the previously established briefing schedule.

To facilitate this Court's independent review of the district court proceedings, counsel shall designate all appropriate reporter's transcripts, including but not limited to complete transcripts for the plea hearing and sentencing hearing, and shall include the transcripts in the excerpts of record. Counsel are advised to consult Circuit Rule 30–1.

When an appointed attorney has properly moved for leave to withdraw pursuant to Anders and has included all appropriate reporter's transcripts, this Court will establish a briefing schedule permitting the defendant to file a pro se supplemental opening brief raising any issues that defendant wishes to present. The order will also direct appellee by a date certain either to file its answering brief or notify the Court by letter that no answering brief will be filed.

(d) Motions for Leave to Proceed Pro Se in Direct Criminal Appeals. The Court will permit defendants in direct criminal appeals to represent themselves if: (1) the defendant's request to proceed pro se and the waiver of the right to counsel are knowing, intelligent and unequivocal; (2) the defendant is apprised of the dangers and disadvantages of self-representation on appeal; and (3) self-representation would not undermine a just and orderly resolution of the appeal. If, after granting leave to proceed pro se the Court finds that appointment of counsel is essential to a just and orderly resolution of the appeal, leave to proceed pro se may be modified or withdrawn.

(e) Post Appeal Proceedings. If the decision of this Court is adverse to the client, in part or in full, counsel, whether appointed or retained, shall, within 14 days after entry of judgment or denial of a petition for rehearing, advise the client of the right to initiate further review by filing a petition for a writ of certiorari in the United States Supreme Court. *See* Sup. Ct. R. 13, 14. If in counsel's considered judgment there are no grounds for seeking Supreme Court review that are non-frivolous and consistent with the standards for filing a petition, *see* Sup. Ct. R. 10, counsel shall further notify the client that counsel intends to move this Court for leave to withdraw as counsel of record if the client insists on filing a petition in violation of Sup. Ct. R. 10.

In cases in which a defendant who had retained counsel or proceeded pro se in this Court wishes to file a petition for writ of certiorari in the United States Supreme Court or wishes to file an opposition to a certiorari petition, and is financially unable to obtain representation for this purpose, this Court will entertain a motion for appointment of counsel within 21 days from judgment or the denial of rehearing. It is the duty of retained counsel to assist the client in preparing and filing a motion for appointment of counsel and a financial affidavit under this subsection.

If requested to do so by the client, appointed or retained counsel shall petition the Supreme Court for certiorari only if in counsel's considered judgment sufficient grounds exist for seeking Supreme Court review. *See* Sup. Ct. R. 10.

Any motion by appointed or retained counsel to withdraw as counsel of record shall be made within 21 days of judgment or the denial of rehearing and shall state the efforts made by counsel to notify the client. A cursory statement of frivolity is not a sufficient basis for withdrawal. *See Austin v. United States*, 513 U.S. 5 (1994) (per curiam); Sup. Ct. R. 10. Within this same period, counsel shall serve a copy of any such motion on the client. If relieved by this Court, counsel shall, within 14 days after such motion is granted, notify the client in writing and, if unable to do so, inform this Court.

Unless counsel is relieved of his or her appointment by this Court, counsel's appointment continues through the resolution of certiorari proceedings and includes providing representation when an opposing party files a petition for certiorari.

(f) Counsel's Claim for Fees and Expenses. An attorney appointed by the Court shall be compensated for services and reimbursed for expenses reasonably incurred as set forth in the Criminal Justice Act. All vouchers claiming compensation for services rendered in this Court under the Criminal Justice Act shall be submitted to the Clerk of this Court no later than 45 days after the final disposition of the case in this Court or after the filing of a petition for certiorari, whichever is later. Subsequent work on the appeal may be claimed on a supplemental voucher. A voucher for work on a petition for a writ of certiorari must be accompanied by a copy of the petition. If a party wishes interim payment, a request for such relief may be filed.

The Clerk shall refer all vouchers, including those requesting payment in excess of the statutory maximum, to the CJA Administrative Attorney for approval of such compensation as the CJA Administrative Attorney deems reasonable and appropriate under the Criminal Justice Act. If the CJA Administrative Attorney concludes that an amount less than that requested by the attorney is appropriate, he or she shall communicate to the attorney the basis for reducing the claim. The CJA Administrative Attorney will offer the attorney an opportunity to respond regarding the propriety and reasonableness of the voucher before approving a reduction in the amount. If the amount requested is reduced, and the attorney seeks reconsideration, the CJA Administrative Attorney shall receive and review the request for reconsideration and may grant it in full or in part. If the CJA Administrative Attorney does not grant a request for reconsideration in full or in part, the request shall be referred to and decided by the Chief Judge or his or her designee.

Whenever the CJA Administrative Attorney certifies payment in excess of the statutory maximum provided by the Criminal Justice Act, the Clerk shall forward the voucher to the Chief Judge's designee for review and approval.

Cross Reference:

- FRAP 42. Voluntary Dismissal
- FRAP 46. Attorneys, specifically, FRAP 46(c), Discipline
- Circuit Rule 27–9. Motions to Dismiss Criminal Appeals, specifically, 27–9.1. Voluntary Dismissals

[Effective January 1, 1997. Amended effective January 1, 1999; January 1, 2001; July 1, 2001; January 1, 2005; July 1, 2006; December 1, 2009; December 1, 2019; March 1, 2021.]

FRAP 5.   APPEAL BY PERMISSION

[For text of rule, see the Federal Rules of Appellate Procedure]

Cross Reference:

- Circuit Rule 39–2. Attorneys Fees and Expenses Under the Equal Access to Justice Act, specifically, 39–2.1. Applications for Fees and 39–2.2. Petitions by Permission

RULE 5–1. CIVIL APPEALS DOCKETING STATEMENT IN APPEALS BY PERMISSION UNDER FED. R. APP. P. 5 [ABROGATED]

RULE 5–2. NUMBER OF COPIES AND LENGTH

(a) **Number of Copies.** The parties must file an original in paper format of a petition, cross-petition, answer, and any supporting papers and appendices filed pursuant to FRAP 5 unless the petition, cross-petition, or answer is submitted via Appellate CM/ECF.

(b) **Length.** Except by permission of the Court, a petition, cross-petition or answer filed under FRAP 5 may not exceed 20 pages. The documents listed at FRAP 5(b)(1)(E) and 32(f) are excluded from the length limit calculation.

Cross Reference:

● Circuit Rule 25–5. Electronic Filing, specifically, Circuit Rule 25–5(b), Documents that may be submitted either electronically or in paper format

● Circuit Rule 32–3. Page/Word Count Conversion Formula for Briefs and Other Documents

[Adopted effective July 1, 2000. Amended effective December 1, 2009; July 1, 2013; December 1, 2016.]

FRAP 5.1 APPEAL BY LEAVE UNDER 28 U.S.C. § 636(c)(5) [ABROGATED]

FRAP 6. APPEAL IN A BANKRUPTCY CASE

[For text of rule, see the Federal Rules of Appellate Procedure]

Cross Reference:

● Circuit Rule 11–4. Retention of Physical Exhibits in the District Court, Transmittal of Clerk's Record on Request, specifically, 11–4.1. Retention of Clerk's Record in the District Court

RULE 6–1. APPEALS FROM FINAL DECISIONS OF THE SUPREME COURT OF THE COMMONWEALTH OF THE NORTHERN MARIANA ISLANDS [ABROGATED]

RULE 6–2. PETITION FOR WRIT OF CERTIORARI TO REVIEW FINAL DECISIONS OF THE SUPREME COURT OF GUAM [ABROGATED]

FRAP 7. BOND FOR COSTS ON APPEAL IN A CIVIL CASE

[For text of rule, see the Federal Rules of Appellate Procedure]

FRAP 8. STAY OR INJUNCTION PENDING APPEAL

[For text of rule, see the Federal Rules of Appellate Procedure]

FRAP 9. RELEASE IN A CRIMINAL CASE

[For text of rule, see the Federal Rules of Appellate Procedure]

RULE 9–1. RELEASE IN CRIMINAL CASES

9–1.1. Release Before Judgment of Conviction.

(a) Every notice of appeal from a release or detention order entered before or at the time of a judgment of conviction shall bear the caption "FRAP 9(a) Appeal." Immediately upon filing, the district court shall transmit the notice of appeal to the Court of Appeals Clerk's Office. Upon filing the notice of appeal, counsel shall contact the Court of Appeals' motions unit to notify the Court that such an appeal has been filed. Unless otherwise directed by the Court, appellant shall file a memorandum of law and facts in support of the appeal within 14 days of filing the notice of appeal. Appellant's memorandum shall be accompanied by the district court's release or detention order and, if the appellant questions the factual basis of the order, a transcript of the district court's bail proceedings. If unable to obtain a transcript of the bail proceedings, the appellant shall state in an affidavit the reasons why the transcript has not been obtained.

(b) Unless otherwise directed by the Court, appellee shall file a response to appellant's memorandum within 10 days of service.

(c) Unless otherwise directed by the Court, appellant may file a reply within 7 days of service of the response. The appeal shall be decided promptly upon the completion of briefing.

9–1.2. Release Pending Appeal.

(a) A motion for bail pending appeal or for revocation of bail pending appeal, made in this Court, shall be accompanied by the district court's bail order, and, if the movant questions the factual basis of the order, a transcript of the proceedings had on the motion for bail made in the district court. If unable to obtain a transcript of the bail proceedings, the movant shall state in an affidavit the reason why the transcript has not been obtained.

(b) A movant for bail pending appeal shall also attach to the motion a certificate of the court reporter containing the name, address, and telephone number of the reporter who will prepare the transcript on appeal and the reporter's verification that the transcript has been ordered and that satisfactory arrangements have been made to pay for it, together with the estimated date of completion of the transcript. A motion for bail which does not comply with part (b) of this rule will be prima facie evidence that the appeal is taken for the purpose of delay within the meaning of 18 U.S.C. § 3143(b).

(c) Unless otherwise directed by the Court, the non-moving party shall file an opposition or statement of non-opposition to all motions for bail or revocation of bail pending appeal of a judgment of conviction within 10 days of service of the motion.

(d) Unless otherwise directed by the Court, the movant may file an optional reply within 7 days of service of the response.

(e) If the appellant is on bail at the time the motion is filed in this Court, that bail will remain in effect until the Court rules on the motion.

Cross Reference:

- Circuit Rule 27–1. Filing of Motions
- Circuit Rule 27–3. Emergency and Urgent Motions

[Effective January 1, 1997. Amended effective January 1, 2001; January 1, 2003; December 1, 2009.]

FRAP 10.   THE RECORD ON APPEAL

[For text of rule, see the Federal Rules of Appellate Procedure]

RULE 10–1.   NOTICE OF FILING APPEAL

When the notice of appeal is filed in the district court, the clerk of the district court shall immediately transmit the notice to the Court of Appeals.

Cross Reference:

- FRAP 3.   Appeal as of Right—How Taken
- Circuit Rule 3–1.   Filing the Appeal

[Effective January 1, 1997. Amended effective December 1, 2009.]

RULE 10–2.   CONTENTS OF THE RECORD ON APPEAL

Pursuant to FRAP 10(a), the complete record on appeal consists of:

(a) the official transcript of oral proceedings before the district court ("transcript"), if there is one; and

(b) the district court clerk's record of original pleadings, exhibits and other papers filed with the district court ("clerk's record").

Cross Reference:

- Circuit Rule 30–1.   The Excerpts of Record

[Effective January 1, 1997. Amended effective December 1, 2009.]

RULE 10–3.   ORDERING THE REPORTER'S TRANSCRIPT

10–3.1.   Civil Appeals.

(a) *Appellant's Initial Notice.* Unless the parties have agreed on which portions of the transcript to order, or appellant intends to order the entire transcript, appellant shall serve appellee with a notice specifying which portions of the transcript appellant intends to order from the court reporter, as well as a statement of the issues the appellant intends to present on appeal. In the alternative, appellant shall serve on appellee a statement indicating that appellant does not intend to order any transcripts. This notice and statement shall be served on appellee within 10 days of the filing of the notice of appeal or within 10 days of the entry of an order disposing of the last timely filed motion of a type specified in FRAP 4(a)(4).

(b) *Appellee's Response.* Within 10 days of the service date of appellant's initial notice, appellee may respond to appellant's initial notice by serving on appellant a list of any additional portions of the transcript that appellee deems necessary to the appeal.

(c) *No Transcripts Necessary.* If the parties agree that no transcripts are necessary, appellant shall file in the district court a notice stating that no transcripts will be ordered, and provide copies of this notice to the court reporter and the Court of Appeals.

(d) *Ordering the Transcript.* Within 30 days of the filing of the notice of appeal, appellant shall file a transcript order in the district court, using the district court's transcript designation form and shall provide a copy of the designation form to the court reporter.

In ordering the transcripts, appellant shall either order all portions of the transcript listed by both appellant and appellee or certify to the district court pursuant to subsection (f) of this rule that the portions listed by appellee in the response to appellant's initial notice are unnecessary.

(e) *Paying for the Transcript.* On or before filing the designation form in the district court, appellant shall make arrangements with the court reporter to pay for the transcripts ordered. The United States Judicial Conference has approved the rates a reporter may charge for the production of the transcript and copies of a transcript. Appellant must pay for the original transcript.

The transcript is considered ordered only after the designation form has been filed in the district court and appellant has made payment arrangements with the court reporter or the district court has deemed the transcripts designated by appellee to be unnecessary and appellee has made financial arrangements. Payment arrangements include obtaining authorization for preparation of the transcript at government expense.

(f) *Paying for Additional Portions of the Transcript.* If appellee notifies appellant that additional portions of the transcript are required pursuant to Circuit Rule 10–3.1(b), appellant shall make arrangements with the court reporter to pay for these additional portions unless appellant certifies that they are unnecessary to the appeal and explains why not.

If such a certificate is filed in the district court, with copies to the court reporter and this Court, the district court shall determine which party shall pay for which portions of the transcript. Appellant may ask the Court of Appeals for an extension of time to make arrangements with the court reporter to pay for the transcripts pending the district court's resolution of the issue.

10–3.2.   Criminal Appeals.

(a) *Early Ordering of the Transcript in Criminal Trials Lasting 10 Days or More.* Where criminal proceedings result in a trial lasting 10 days or more, the district court may authorize the preparation of the transcript for the appeal and payment of the court reporter after the entry of a verdict but before the filing of a notice of appeal. In addition to filing a CJA Form 24 (Authorization and Voucher for Payment of Transcript), in the district court, appointed counsel shall certify to the district court that defendant is aware of the right to appeal, and that the defendant has instructed counsel to appeal regardless of the nature or length of the sentence imposed.

Retained counsel must make a similar certification to the district court along with financial arrangements with the court reporter to pay for the transcripts before obtaining early preparation authorization.

The Court of Appeals waives the reduction on transcript price for transcripts ordered pursuant to this subsection from the date of the initial order to the date the transcripts would otherwise be ordered, i.e., 7 days from the filing of the notice of appeal.

The parties shall comply with all other applicable parts of Circuit Rule 10–3.2(b)–(f).

(b) *Appellant's Initial Notice.* Unless parties have agreed on which portions of the transcript to order or appellant intends to order the entire transcript, appellant shall serve appellee with a notice listing the portions of the transcript appellant will order from the court reporter, as well as a statement of the issues the appellant intends to present on appeal. In the alternative, the appellant shall serve appellee with a statement indicating that no transcripts will be ordered. This notice and statement shall be served on appellee within 7 days of the filing of the notice of appeal or within 7 days of the entry of an order disposing of the last timely filed motion of a type specified in FRAP 4(b).

(c) *Appellee's Response.* Within 7 days of the service of appellant's initial notice, the appellee may serve on the appellant a response specifying what, if any, additional portions of the transcript are necessary to the appeal.

(d) *Ordering the Transcript.* Within 21 days from the filing of the notice of appeal, appellant shall file a transcript order in the district court using the district court's transcript designation form and shall provide a copy of this designation form to the court reporter. Appellant shall order all the portions of the transcript listed by both appellant and appellee, or certify to the district court pursuant to subsection (f) of this rule that the portions of the transcript listed by appellee in the response to appellant's initial notice are unnecessary.

(e) *Paying for the Transcript.* Where appellant is represented by retained counsel, counsel shall make arrangements with the court reporter to pay for the transcripts on or before the day the transcript designation form is filed in the district court. Appellee shall make financial arrangements when the district court has deemed the transcripts designated by appellee to be unnecessary and appellee desires production of those transcripts.

Where the appellant is proceeding in forma pauperis, appellant shall prepare a CJA Voucher Form 24 and submit the voucher to the district court along with the designation form. In either case, failure to make proper arrangements with the court reporter to pay for the ordered transcripts may result in sanctions pursuant to FRAP 46(c).

(f) *Paying for Additional Portions of the Transcript.* If appellee notifies appellant that additional portions of the transcript are required pursuant to Circuit Rule 10–3.2(c), appellant shall make arrangements with the court reporter to pay for these additional portions unless appellant certifies that they are unnecessary to the appeal and explains why not.

If such a certificate is filed in the district court, with copies to the court reporter and this Court, the district court shall determine which party shall pay for which portions of the transcript. Appellant may ask the Court of Appeals for an extension of time to make arrangements with the court reporter to pay for the transcripts pending the district court's resolution of the issue.

CIRCUIT ADVISORY COMMITTEE NOTE TO RULE 10–3

The intent of the requirement of a statement of the issues is to provide the appellee with notice of those transcripts necessary for resolution of the issues to be raised by the appellant on appeal. While failure to comply with this rule may, in the Court's discretion, result in dismissal of the appeal, dismissal is not mandated if the record is otherwise sufficient to permit resolution of the issues on appeal. See *United States v. Alerta*, 96 F.3d 1230, 1233–34 (9th Cir. 1996); *Syncom Capitol Corp. v. Wade*, 924 F.2d 167 (9th Cir. 1991). Similarly, the omission of a given issue from the statement of the issues does not bar appellant from raising that issue in the brief if any transcript portions necessary to support that argument have been prepared.

A party who subsequently determines that the initially designated transcripts are insufficient to address the arguments advanced on appeal may seek leave to file a supplemental transcript designation and, if necessary, to expand the record to include that transcript. [Effective January 1, 1997. Amended effective July 1, 1997; December 1, 2002; December 1, 2009.]

FRAP 11.   FORWARDING THE RECORD

[For text of rule, see the Federal Rules of Appellate Procedure]

RULE 11–1.   FILING THE REPORTER'S TRANSCRIPT

11–1.1.   Time for Filing the Reporter's Transcript. The reporter's transcript shall be filed in the district court within 30 days from the date the Transcript Designation/Ordering Form is filed with the district court, pursuant to the provisions of FRAP 11(b) or in accordance with the scheduling orders issued by the Court for all appeals, whichever is later. Upon motion by a reporter, the Clerk of the Court of Appeals or a designated deputy clerk may grant a reasonable extension of time to file the transcript. The grant of an extension of time does not waive the mandatory fee reduction for the late delivery of transcripts unless such waiver is stated in the order.

11–1.2.   Notice of Reporter Defaults. In the event the reporter fails to prepare the transcripts in accordance with the scheduling order issued by the Court or within an extension of time granted by this Court, appellant shall notify this Court of the need to modify the briefing schedule. Such notice shall be filed within 21 days after the due date for filing of the transcripts. The notice shall indicate when the transcripts were designated, when financial arrangements were made or the voucher was prepared, the dates of hearings for which transcripts have not been prepared and the name of the reporter assigned to those hearings. Prior to submitting any notice, appellant shall contact the court reporter and court reporter supervisor in an effort to cause preparation of the transcripts. The notice shall be accompanied by an affidavit or declaration that describes the contacts appellant has made with the reporter and the supervisor. A copy of the notice and affidavit/declaration shall be served on the court reporter supervisor.

CIRCUIT ADVISORY COMMITTEE NOTE TO RULE 11–1.2

The filing of a motion for an extension of time by a reporter relieves appellant of the requirement to file the notification described in Circuit Rule 11–1.2 as to that reporter.

11–1.3. Form and Content of the Reporter's Transcript. The pages of the transcript shall be consecutively numbered throughout all volumes if all proceedings were reported by one individual. If proceedings were reported by multiple reporters, consecutive numbering is not required. It shall include an index with the names of witnesses, the direct, cross, redirect and other examinations, and exhibit numbers, when offered and received or rejected, as well as instructions and colloquy on instructions. The index shall refer to the number of the volume and the page, shall be cumulative for all volumes, and shall be placed in the first volume. The original set of the transcript shall serve as the copy required by 28 U.S.C. § 753(b).

[Amended effective January 1, 1993; July 1, 1997; July 1, 2006; December 1, 2009; December 1, 2016.]

RULE 11–2. THE CERTIFICATE OF RECORD [ABROGATED]

RULE 11–3. RETENTION OF THE TRANSCRIPT AND CLERK'S RECORD IN THE DISTRICT COURT DURING PREPARATION OF THE BRIEFS [ABROGATED]

RULE 11–4. RETENTION OF PHYSICAL EXHIBITS IN THE DISTRICT COURT, TRANSMITTAL OF CLERK'S RECORD ON REQUEST

11–4.1. Retention of Clerk's Record in the District Court. *[Abrogated 12/1/09]*

11–4.2. Retention of Physical Exhibits in the District Court. For any exhibits not otherwise available on the electronic district court docket, all physical and documentary exhibits in all cases shall be retained in the district court until the mandate issues unless requested by the Court of Appeals. *(Rev. 12/1/09; 6/1/19)*

11–4.3. Transmittal of Reporter's Transcript. *[Abrogated 12/1/09]*

11–4.4. Transmittal of Clerk's Record Upon Requests. When the Court of Appeals at any time requires all or part of the clerk's record, the Clerk of the Court of Appeals will request the record from the district court. The district court clerk shall transmit the record, including agency records lodged or filed with the district court during the district court proceedings, to the Court within 7 days of receiving the request. In appeals from the Bankruptcy Appellate Panel, records will be treated in the same fashion as records on appeal in cases arising from the district court. *(Rev. 12/1/09; Rev. 7/1/13)*

The district court shall within 7 days after a notice of appeal is filed transmit any state court records lodged or filed in 28 U.S.C. § 2254 proceedings to this Court unless the documents are available in the district court's electronic case file or the district court determines that the notice of appeal was prematurely filed. *(New 7/1/13)*

Cross Reference: *(Rev. 12/1/09)*

● Circuit Rule 22–1. Certificate of Appealability (COA) 65, specifically, Circuit Rule 22–1(b)

[Effective January 1, 1997. Amended effective January 1, 2009; December 1, 2009; July 1, 2013; June 1, 2019.]

RULE 11–5. TRANSMITTAL OF THE CLERK'S RECORD AND REPORTER'S TRANSCRIPT AND EXHIBITS IN ALL OTHER CASES [ABROGATED]

RULE 11–6. PREPARATION OF THE CLERK'S RECORD FOR TRANSMITTAL

11–6.1. Preparation of the Clerk's Record for Transmittal. In cases where the clerk's record is to be transmitted to the Court of Appeals pursuant to Circuit Rule 11–4.4 and where the record is not available electronically, the district court clerk shall tab and identify each document by the docket control number assigned when the document was initially entered on the district court docket. The documents shall be assembled in sequence according to filing dates, with a certified copy of the docket entries at the beginning. Papers shall be bound in a volume or volumes with each document individually tabbed showing the number corresponding to the district court docket entry. The docket sheet shall serve as the index.

11–6.2. Number of Copies. *[Abrogated 12/1/09]*

[Effective January 1, 1997. Amended effective December 1, 2009.]

FRAP 12. DOCKETING THE APPEAL; FILING A REPRESENTATION STATEMENT; FILING THE RECORD

[For text of rule, see the Federal Rules of Appellate Procedure]

Cross Reference:

● Circuit Rule 3–1. Filing the Appeal
● Circuit Rule 3–2. Representation Statement
● Circuit Rule 3–4. Mediation Questionnaire

RULE 12–1. NOTICE OF EMERGENCY MOTIONS IN CAPITAL CASES

Upon the filing of a notice of appeal in a capital case in which the district court has denied a stay of execution, the clerk of the district court shall immediately notify the clerk of this Court by telephone of such filing and transmit the notice of appeal by the most expeditious method.

Cross Reference:

● Circuit Rule 22–6. Rules Applicable to all Death Penalty Cases
● Circuit Rule 27–3. Emergency Motions

[Effective January 1, 1997. Amended effective January 1, 1999; December 1, 2009.]

RULE 12–2. REPRESENTATION STATEMENT

Parties filing appeals need file the Representation Statement specified in FRAP 12(b) only as required by Circuit Rule 3–2.

Cross Reference:

● Circuit Rule 3–2. Representation Statement

[Effective July 1, 1994.]

FRAP 12.1. REMAND AFTER AN INDICATIVE RULING BY THE DISTRICT COURT ON A MOTION FOR RELIEF THAT IS BARRED BY A PENDING APPEAL

[For text of rule, see the Federal Rules of Appellate Procedure]

TITLE III. APPEALS FROM THE UNITED STATES TAX COURT

FRAP 13. APPEALS FROM THE TAX COURT

[For text of rule, see the Federal Rules of Appellate Procedure]

RULE 13–1. FILING NOTICE OF APPEAL IN TAX COURT CASES

The content of the notice of appeal and the manner of its filing shall be as prescribed for other civil cases by FRAP 3. Appellants also shall comply with Circuit Rules 3–2 and 3–4.

[Effective January 1, 1997.]

RULE 13–2. EXCERPTS OF RECORD IN TAX COURT CASES

Review of the decisions of the Tax Court shall be in accordance with FRAP 13, except that preparation and filing of the excerpts of record in such cases shall be in accordance with Circuit Rule 30–1. Each reference in Circuit Rule 30–1 to the district court and to the clerk of the district court shall be read as a reference to the Tax Court and to the clerk of the Tax Court, respectively.

[Effective January 1, 1997.]

RULE 13–3. TRANSMISSION OF THE RECORD IN TAX COURT CASES

When the Court of Appeals at any time requires the record, the Clerk will request the record from the tax court. The tax court clerk shall transmit the record to the Court within 14 days of receiving the request.

[Effective January 1, 1997. Amended effective January 1, 2009; December 1, 2009.]

FRAP 14. APPLICABILITY OF OTHER RULES TO APPEALS FROM THE TAX COURT

[For text of rule, see the Federal Rules of Appellate Procedure]

RULE 14–1. APPLICABILITY OF OTHER RULES TO REVIEW DECISIONS OF THE TAX COURT

All provisions of these Circuit Rules are applicable to review of a decision of the Tax Court, except that any Circuit Rules accompanying FRAP 4–9, 15–20, and 22 and 23 are not applicable.

[Effective January 1, 1997.]

TITLE IV. REVIEW OR ENFORCEMENT OF AN ORDER OF AN ADMINISTRATIVE AGENCY, BOARD, COMMISSION, OR OFFICER

FRAP 15. REVIEW OR ENFORCEMENT OF AN AGENCY ORDER—HOW OBTAINED; INTERVENTION

[For text of rule, see the Federal Rules of Appellate Procedure]

RULE 15–1. REVIEW OR ENFORCEMENT OF AGENCY ORDERS

Review of an order of an administrative agency, board, commission or officer (hereinafter "agency") and application for enforcement of an order of an agency shall be governed by FRAP 15. If petitioner or applicant submits the petition or application in paper format, it does not need to supply the Court with the copies required by FRAP 15(c)(3).

Cross Reference:

● Circuit Rule 25–5. Electronic Filing, specifically, Circuit Rule 25–5(b), Documents that may be submitted either electronically or in paper format

[Effective January 1, 1997. Amended effective July 1, 2013.]

RULE 15–2. MEDIATION QUESTIONNAIRE IN AGENCY CASES

(a) The Court encourages the parties in Ninth Circuit agency cases to engage in mediation. To that end, except as provided in section (b) below, within 7 days of the docketing of the petition for review, the petitioner(s) shall, and the respondent(s) may, complete and submit Form 7, the Ninth Circuit Mediation Questionnaire. The Clerk shall transmit the Mediation Questionnaire to counsel with the time scheduling order. Counsel shall return it according to the instructions contained in the Mediation Questionnaire. The sole purpose of the Mediation Questionnaire is to provide information about new petitions to the Court's Mediation Office.

Petitioner's failure to comply with this rule may result in dismissal of the petition in accordance with Circuit Rule 42–1.

(b) The requirement for filing a Mediation Questionnaire shall not apply to:

(1) a petition in which the petitioner is proceeding without the assistance of counsel; and

(2) a petition for review of an order of the Board of Immigration Appeals.

Cross Reference:

- Circuit Rule 3–4. Mediation Questionnaire
- FRAP 33. Appeal Conferences
- Circuit Rule 33–1. Circuit Mediation Office

CIRCUIT ADVISORY COMMITTEE NOTE TO RULE 15–2

Although petitioners challenging Board of Immigration Appeals orders are exempt from the requirement to file Mediation Questionnaires, the parties in these cases are invited to contact the Court Mediation Unit when there is potential for mediation. Petitioners will normally be required to demonstrate eligibility for any requested relief. When making a request for mediation based on applications or circumstances that are not documented in the administrative record, petitioners shall provide supporting documents to the mediators.

[Effective January 1, 1997. Amended effective July 1, 1997; January 1, 2005; December 1, 2009; July 1, 2013.]

RULE 15–3. PROCEDURES FOR REVIEW UNDER THE PACIFIC NORTHWEST ELECTRIC POWER PLANNING AND CONSERVATION ACT

15–3.1. Contents of Petition. A petition for review of a final action or decision of the Bonneville Power Administration (BPA) under the Pacific Northwest Electric Power Planning and Conservation Act ("Northwest Power Act") shall be labeled "Petition for Review under the Northwest Power Act." The petition must state on its face the date of the final action or decision from which review is sought, the title (if one exists), the BPA docket number (if one exists) and the Ninth Circuit docket numbers of any known petitions for review of the same final action or decision.

15–3.2. Consolidation. Petitions for review of the same final action or decision under the Northwest Power Act will be consolidated for briefing and argument. Respondent must file a motion to consolidate all petitions from the same final action or decision within 10 days after the expiration of the time to file petitions for review from that final action or decision unless all the petitions already have been consolidated by the Court or a motion to consolidate all the petitions is pending.

Petitions from related final actions or decisions may be scheduled for hearing before a single panel.

15–3.3. Intervention. Any petitioner in any consolidated case and any party granted leave to intervene in any consolidated case will be deemed to have intervened in all the consolidated cases. Notwithstanding FRAP 15(d), motions to intervene may be filed within 30 days of the expiration of the time to file petitions for review from the final action or decision at issue. A motion to intervene must state on its face the date of the final action or decision from which review is sought, the title (if one exists), the BPA docket number (if one exists) and the Ninth Circuit docket numbers of any known petitions for review of the same final action or decision.

Cross Reference:

- Circuit Rule 1–2. Scope of Circuit Rules

CIRCUIT ADVISORY COMMITTEE NOTE TO RULE 15–3

Parties are encouraged to minimize the number of motions to intervene that they file. A petitioner need not file a motion to intervene in petitions challenging the same BPA final action or decision that its petition challenges. A non-petitioner party seeking intervention may file a single motion to intervene—either in any one of the petitions from the final action or decision at issue or in the consolidated petition. The deadline set forth in FRAP 15(d) to file motions to intervene has been relaxed in these cases in order to make this possible.

[Effective January 1, 1997. Amended effective July 1, 2013.]

RULE 15–4. PETITIONS FOR REVIEW OF BOARD OF IMMIGRATION APPEALS DECISIONS

A petition for review of a Board of Immigration Appeals decision shall state whether petitioner (1) is detained in the custody of the Department of Homeland Security or at liberty and/or (2) has moved the Board of Immigration Appeals to reopen or applied to the district director for an adjustment of status. The petition shall be (1) accompanied by a copy of the Board of Immigration Appeals order being challenged, (2) include the petitioner's alien registration number in the caption and (3) filed as an original in paper format unless submitted via the Appellate Electronic Filing System.

Cross Reference:

- Circuit Rule 25–5. Electronic Filing, specifically, Circuit Rule 25–5(b), Documents that may be submitted either electronically or in paper format

[Effective January 1, 2005. Amended effective December 1, 2009; July 1, 2013; December 1, 2016.]

FRAP 15.1. BRIEFS AND ORAL ARGUMENT IN A NATIONAL LABOR RELATIONS BOARD PROCEEDING

[For text of rule, see the Federal Rules of Appellate Procedure]

FRAP 16. THE RECORD ON REVIEW OR ENFORCEMENT

[For text of rule, see the Federal Rules of Appellate Procedure]

FRAP 17. FILING THE RECORD

[For text of rule, see the Federal Rules of Appellate Procedure]

RULE 17–1. EXCERPTS OF RECORD ON REVIEW OR ENFORCEMENT OF AGENCY ORDERS

Review of agency decisions shall be in accordance with FRAP 17, except that preparation and filing of the Excerpts of Record in such cases shall be in accordance with Circuit Rule 30–1. Each reference in Circuit Rule 30–1 to the district court and to the clerk of the district court shall be read as a reference to the agency. No Excerpts of Record are required in a petition for review of a final order in an immigration case.

[Effective January 1, 1997. Amended effective January 1, 2005; July 1, 2007; December 1, 2009; July 1, 2013; June 1, 2019; December 1, 2019; December 1, 2020.]

RULE 17–2. SANCTIONS FOR FAILURE TO COMPLY WITH CIRCUIT RULE 17–1 [ABROGATED EFFECTIVE DECEMBER 1, 2020]

FRAP 18. STAY PENDING REVIEW

[For text of rule, see the Federal Rules of Appellate Procedure]

Cross Reference:
- Circuit Rule 27–1. Filing of Motions
- Circuit Rule 27–2. Motions for Stays Pending Appeal
- Circuit Rule 27–3. Emergency Motions

FRAP 19. SETTLEMENT OF A JUDGMENT ENFORCING AN AGENCY ORDER IN PART

[For text of rule, see the Federal Rules of Appellate Procedure]

FRAP 20. APPLICABILITY OF RULES TO THE REVIEW OR ENFORCEMENT OF AN AGENCY ORDER

[For text of rule, see the Federal Rules of Appellate Procedure]

RULE 20–1. APPLICABILITY OF OTHER RULES TO REVIEW OF AGENCY DECISIONS

All provisions of these Circuit Rules are applicable to review or enforcement of orders of agencies, except that any Circuit Rules accompanying FRAP 3 through 14, and FRAP 22 and 23 are not applicable. As used in any applicable rule, in proceedings to review or enforce agency orders, the term "appellant" includes a petitioner, the term "appellee" includes a respondent, and the term "appeal" includes a petition for review or enforcement.

[Effective January 1, 1997. Amended effective December 1, 2009.]

TITLE V. EXTRAORDINARY WRITS

FRAP 21. WRITS OF MANDAMUS AND PROHIBITION, AND OTHER EXTRAORDINARY WRITS

[For text of rule, see the Federal Rules of Appellate Procedure]

Cross Reference:
- FRAP 22. Habeas Corpus and Section 2255 Proceedings
- Circuit Rule 27–1. Filing of Motions
- Circuit Rule 27–2. Motions for Stays Pending Appeal
- Circuit Rule 27–3. Emergency Motions

RULE 21–1. EXTRAORDINARY WRITS

Petitions for extraordinary writs shall conform to and be filed in accordance with the provisions of FRAP 21(a).

[Effective January 1, 1997.]

RULE 21–2. FORMAT OF EXTRAORDINARY WRITS AND ANSWERS; NUMBER OF COPIES; LENGTH

(a) Format. Petitions for writs of mandamus, prohibition or other extraordinary relief directed to a district judge, magistrate judge, or bankruptcy judge must bear the title of the appropriate court and may not bear the name of the judge as respondent in the caption. Petitions must include in the caption: the name of each petitioner; the name of the appropriate court as respondent; and the name of each real party in interest. Other petitions for extraordinary writs must include in the caption: the name of each petitioner and the name of each appropriate adverse party below as respondent.

(b) Number of Copies. The parties must file an original in paper format of the petition, an answer, if ordered, and any supporting papers and appendices unless the petition or answer is submitted via the Appellate Electronic Filing System.

(c) Length. Except by permission of the Court, a petition, or answer, if ordered, may not exceed 30 pages. The documents listed at FRAP 21(a)(2)(C) and FRAP 32(f) are excluded from the length limit calculation.

Cross Reference:

- Circuit Rule 25-5. Electronic Filing, specifically, Circuit Rule 25-5(b), Documents that may be submitted either electronically or in paper format.

- Circuit Rule 32-3. Page/Word Count Conversion Formula for Briefs and Other Documents

[Effective January 1, 1997. Amended effective July 1, 2000; January 1, 2005; December 1, 2009; July 1, 2013; December 1, 2016.]

RULE 21-3. CERTIFICATE OF INTERESTED PARTIES

Petitions for writs of mandamus or prohibition, and for other extraordinary writs, shall include the corporate disclosure statement required by FRAP 26.1 and the statement of related cases required by Circuit Rule 28-2.6.

[Effective January 1, 1997.]

RULE 21-4. ANSWERS TO PETITIONS

No answer to such a petition may be filed unless ordered by the Court. Except in emergency cases, the Court will not grant a petition without a response.

Cross Reference:

- FRAP 22. Habeas Corpus and Section 2255 Proceedings
- Circuit Rule 27-1. Filing of Motions
- Circuit Rule 27-2. Motions for Stays Pending Appeal
- Circuit Rule 27-3. Emergency Motions

CIRCUIT ADVISORY COMMITTEE NOTE TO RULES 21-1 TO 21-4

A petition for writ of mandamus, writ of prohibition or other extraordinary relief is processed by the clerk and motions attorneys in the same fashion as a motion. If the panel does not believe that the petition makes a prima facie showing justifying issuance of the writ, it will deny the petition forthwith. That denial is not regarded as a decision on the merits of the claims. In other instances, the panel will direct that an answer and reply may be filed within specified times. The panel may also issue a stay or injunction pending further consideration of the petition. After receipt of the answer and reply, or expiration of the times set therefor, the matter is then forwarded to a new motions panel unless the first panel directs otherwise. The panel may grant or deny the petition or set it for oral argument. If the panel decides to set the petition for argument, it may be calendared before a regular panel of the Court or before the motions panel.

In emergency circumstances, an individual judge may grant temporary relief to permit a motions panel to consider the petition, may decline to act, or may order that an answer be filed. If the judge determines that immediate action on the merits is necessary, the judge will contact the members of the Court currently sitting as a motions panel until two or more judges can consider whether to grant or deny the petition. Except in extreme emergencies, the judges will not grant a petition without calling for an answer to the petition.

[Effective January 1, 1997. Amended effective December 1, 2009; December 1, 2016.]

RULE 21-5. PETITION FOR WRIT OF MANDAMUS PURSUANT TO 18 U.S.C. § 3771(d)(3)

A petition for writ of mandamus filed pursuant to 18 U.S.C. § 3771(d)(3) shall bear the caption "PETITION FOR WRIT OF MANDAMUS PURSUANT TO 18 U.S.C. § 3771(d)(3)." Before filing such a petition, the petitioner's counsel, or the petitioner if appearing pro se, must notify the motions unit of the Court of Appeals that such a petition will be filed, and must make arrangements for the filing and immediate service of the petition on the relevant parties. Such notification must be by telephone (415/355-8020 or 8000). The real party in interest must telephonically notify the Court when it becomes aware of the filing of the petition.

CIRCUIT ADVISORY COMMITTEE NOTE TO RULE 21-5

A failure to notify this Court ahead of time that such a filing is being made will adversely affect this Court's ability to decide any such petition within 72 hours of filing as contemplated by the statute.

Cross Reference:

- Circuit Rule 27-3. Emergency Motions

[Adopted by the Court Executive Committee on an emergency basis, January 27, 2006, subject to final approval by the full Court. Amended effective January 1, 2007; July 1, 2007.]

TITLE VI. HABEAS CORPUS; PROCEEDINGS IN FORMA PAUPERIS

FRAP 22. HABEAS CORPUS AND SECTION 2255 PROCEEDINGS

[For text of rule, see the Federal Rules of Appellate Procedure]

RULE 22-1. CERTIFICATE OF APPEALABILITY (COA)

(a) **General Procedures.** Appeals from the district court's denial of relief in either a 28 U.S.C. § 2254 or a § 2255 proceeding are governed by the procedures set forth in FRAP 4 and 22(b). A request for a certificate of appealability ("COA") must first be considered by the district court. If the district court grants a COA, that court shall state which issue or issues satisfy the standard set forth in 28 U.S.C. § 2253(c)(2). The court of appeals will not act on a request for a COA if the district court has not ruled first. *(Rev. 1/1/04; 12/1/09; 12/1/18)*

(b) **District Court Records.** If the district court denies a COA in full in a § 2254 proceeding and the district court record cannot be accessed electronically, the district court clerk shall forward the entire record to the court of appeals. If the district court denies a COA in full in a § 2255 proceeding and the district court record cannot be accessed electronically, the district court clerk shall forward that portion of the record beginning with the filing of the § 2255 motion. *(Rev. 1/1/04; 12/1/09)*

(c) Grant in Part or in Full by District Court. If the district court grants a COA as to any or all issues, a briefing schedule will be established by the court of appeals at case opening and appellant shall brief only those issues certified or otherwise proceed according to section (e), below. *(Rev. 1/1/04; 3/11/04; 12/1/18)*

(d) Denial in Full by District Court. If the district court denies a COA as to all issues, appellant may file a request for a COA in the court of appeals within 35 days of the filing of a notice of appeal or amended notice of appeal, or the district court's denial of a COA in full, whichever is later. The notice of appeal must be timely filed pursuant to 28 U.S.C. § 2107 and FRAP 4(a), regardless of whether appellant files a request for COA. If appellant does not file a COA request with the court of appeals after the district court denies a COA in full, the court of appeals will deem the notice of appeal to constitute a request for a COA. *(Rev. 1/1/04; 12/1/09; 12/1/18)*

If appellant files a request for a COA with the court of appeals, appellee may, and in capital cases with no pending execution date shall, file a response to the request for a COA within 35 days from service of the COA request. In capital cases where an execution date is scheduled and no stay is in place, appellee shall file a response as soon as practicable after the date appellant's request is served or, if no request is filed, as soon as practicable after the district court's entry of its order denying a COA. *(New 1/1/04; Rev. 12/1/09; 12/1/18)*

If, after the district court has denied a COA in full, the court of appeals also denies a COA in full, appellant, pursuant to Circuit Rule 27-10, may file a motion for reconsideration. *(New 1/1/04; Rev. 12/1/18)*

When the court of appeals grants a COA in part and denies a COA in part, a briefing schedule will be established and no motion for reconsideration will be entertained. Appellant shall brief only those issues certified or otherwise proceed according to section (e), below. *(New 1/1/04; Rev. 12/1/18)*

(e) Briefing Uncertified Issues. Appellants shall brief only issues certified by the district court or the court of appeals, except that, if an appellant concludes during the course of preparing the opening brief, that an uncertified issue should be discussed in the brief, the appellant shall first brief all certified issues under the heading, "Certified Issues," and then, in the same brief, shall discuss any uncertified issues under the heading, "Uncertified Issues." Uncertified issues raised and designated in this manner will be construed as a motion to expand the COA and will be addressed by the merits panel to such extent as it deems appropriate. Except in the extraordinary case, the Court will not permit a longer brief to accommodate the uncertified issues. *(New 1/1/04; Rev. 7/1/16; 12/1/18)*

(f) Response to Uncertified Issues. Appellee may, but need not, address any uncertified issues in its responsive brief. The Court will afford appellee an opportunity to respond before relief is granted on any previously uncertified issue.

Cross Reference: *(New 1/1/04; Rev. 12/1/09)*

● FRAP 27. Motions

● Circuit Rule 11-4. Retention of Physical Exhibits in the District Court, Transmittal of Clerk's Record on Request, specifically, 11-4.2. Retention of Physical Exhibits in the District Court

● Circuit Rule 27-1. Filing of Motions

● FRAP 32. Form of Briefs, Appendices, and Other Papers, specifically, FRAP 32(a)(5)(6)(7)

CIRCUIT ADVISORY COMMITTEE NOTE TO RULE 22-1

The Court may decline to address uncertified issues if they are not raised and designated as required by this Rule. *(Rev. 1/1/04; 12/1/18)*

[Effective January 1, 1997. Amended effective January 1, 1999; January 1, 2004; March 11, 2004; December 1, 2009; July 1, 2016; December 1, 2018.]

RULE 22-2. DIRECT CRIMINAL APPEALS, FIRST PETITIONS, AND STAYS OF EXECUTION: CAPITAL CASES

(a) Assignment. In direct criminal appeals and section 2241, section 2254, and section 2255 appeals which involve judgments of death and finally dispose of the case, the Clerk will assign the appeal to a death penalty panel composed of active judges and senior judges willing to serve on death penalty panels. However, when an execution is scheduled and no stay is in place, the Clerk may select a panel to hear the appeal and any emergency motion whenever in the Clerk's discretion it would be prudent to do so. *(Rev. 12/1/09; 12/1/18)*

(b) Related Civil Proceedings. The Court may apply the provisions of Circuit Rule 22 to any related civil proceedings challenging an execution as being in violation of federal law, including proceedings filed by the prisoner or someone else on his or her behalf.

(c) Duties. Once a case is assigned to a death penalty panel, the panel will handle all matters pertaining to the case, including motions for leave to file a second or successive petition or motion, appeals from authorized second or successive petitions or motions, any related civil proceedings, and remands from the Supreme Court of the United States. When a case is pending before a death penalty en banc court, any additional applications for relief pertaining to that case will be assigned to the panel with responsibility for that case, unless the question presented is such that its decision would resolve an issue then before the en banc court, in which event the additional application will be assigned to the en banc court. The determination as to whether the case is assigned to the panel or the en banc court is made by the Chief Judge in consultation with the concerned panel and the en banc court.

(d) The En Banc Court. The Clerk shall include in the pool of the names of all active judges and the names of those eligible senior judges willing to serve on the en banc court. An eligible senior judge is one who sat on the panel whose decision is subject to review. Judges shall be assigned by random drawing from the pool, and in accordance with Circuit Rule 35-3. Review by the en banc court may include not only orders granting or denying applications for a certificate of appealability and motions to stay or vacate a stay of execution, but may extend to all other issues on appeal. *(Rev. 12/1/09)*

(e) Stays of Execution. Counsel shall communicate with the Clerk of this Court by telephone or email as soon as it becomes evident that emergency relief will be sought from this Court. Any motion for a stay of execution filed before a case has been assigned to a death penalty panel will be presented for decision to a motions panel. Once a death penalty panel has been assigned, that panel then must decide all subsequent matters (unless the case is then before the en banc court).

Any motion for a stay of execution shall be filed electronically and the Clerk will immediately forward the motion to the panel. If an execution is imminent and the death penalty panel has not yet determined whether to grant a stay pending final disposition of the appeal, any judge may issue a temporary stay of a scheduled execution. Any judge or judges who issue a temporary stay of execution shall immediately notify the Clerk and the panel of such action. By majority vote, the panel may vacate such a stay of execution.

A motion for stay of execution shall state whether relief was sought in the district court and, if so, whether all grounds advanced in support thereof in the court of appeals were submitted to the district court and if not, why the matter should not be remanded to the district court or relief denied for that reason. If a majority of the panel votes to deny the stay, it shall enter an order to that effect and, unless impracticable, state the issues presented and the reasons for the denial. If no execution date is set, the ordinary rules for obtaining en banc review of a three-judge panel decision shall apply on a first petition or motion.

When the panel affirms a denial or reverses a grant of a first petition or motion, it shall enter an order staying the mandate pursuant to FRAP 41(b), but any such stay is subject to the limits set forth in FRAP 41(d). If the panel affirms the denial of a first section 2254 petition or section 2255 motion in a capital case and denies a stay of execution, any judge of the Court may request en banc rehearing and issue a temporary stay of execution. *(Rev. 12/1/18)*

[Effective January 1, 1997. Amended effective January 1, 1999; December 1, 2009; December 1, 2018.]

RULE 22–3. APPLICATIONS FOR AUTHORIZATION TO FILE SECOND OR SUCCESSIVE 28 U.S.C. § 2254 PETITION OR § 2255 MOTION— ALL CASES; STAY OF EXECUTION—CAPITAL CASES

(a) Applications. An applicant seeking authorization to file a second or successive 28 U.S.C. § 2254 petition or 28 U.S.C. § 2255 motion in the district court must file an application in the court of appeals demonstrating entitlement to such leave under sections 2254 or 2255. *See* Form 12. An original in paper format of the application must be filed with the Clerk of the court of appeals unless the application is submitted via the Appellate Electronic Filing System. No filing fee is required. If an application for authorization to file a second or successive section 2254 petition or section 2255 motion is mistakenly submitted to the district court, the district court shall refer it to the court of appeals. If an unauthorized second or successive section 2254 petition or section 2255 motion is submitted to the district court, the district court may, in the interests of justice, refer it to the court of appeals. *(Rev. 12/1/09; Rev. 7/1/13; Rev. 7/1/16; Rev. 12/1/18)*

The applicant must:

(1) include Form 12 if submitted by an applicant not represented by counsel;

(2) include the proposed section 2254 petition or section 2255 motion that the applicant seeks to file in the district court;

(3) state as to each claim presented whether it previously has been raised in any state or federal court and, if so, the name of the court and the date of the order disposing of such claim(s); and

(4) state how the requirements of sections 2244(b) or 2255 have been satisfied.

(b) Attachments. If reasonably available to the applicant, the application must include copies of all relevant state court orders and decisions. *(Rev. 12/1/09; Rev. 7/1/16)*

(c) Service.

(1) *Capital Cases:* In capital cases, the applicant must serve a copy of the application, attachments, and proposed section 2254 petition/section 2255 motion on the respondent, and must attach a certificate of service to the application filed with the Court. *(Rev. 7/1/16)*

(2) *Noncapital Cases:* In noncapital cases, service of the application on the respondent is not required. *(New 7/1/16)*

(d) Response.

(1) *Capital Cases:* In capital cases where an execution date is scheduled and no stay is in place, respondent shall respond to the application and file supplemental attachments as soon as practicable. Otherwise, in capital cases, respondent shall respond and file supplemental attachments within 14 days of the date the application is served. *(Rev. 12/1/09)*

(2) *Noncapital Cases:* In noncapital cases, no response is required unless ordered by the Court. Respondent may include supplemental attachments with its response. *(Rev. 7/1/16)*

(e) Decision. The application will be determined by a three-judge panel. In capital cases where an execution date is scheduled and no stay is in place, the Court will grant or deny the application, and state its reasons therefore, as soon as practicable.

(f) Stays of Execution. If an execution date is scheduled and no stay is in place, any judge may, if necessary, enter a stay of execution, *see* Circuit Rule 22–2(e), but the question will be presented to the panel immediately. If the Court grants leave to file a second or successive application, the Court shall stay the applicant's execution pending disposition of the second or successive petition by the district court. *(Rev. 12/1/18)*

Cross Reference:

• Circuit Rule 25–5. Electronic Filing, specifically, Circuit Rule 25–5(b), Documents that may be submitted either electronically or in paper format.

CIRCUIT ADVISORY COMMITTEE NOTE TO RULE 22–3

The district court is required to transfer mistakenly filed applications for authorization to file a second or successive section 2254 petition or 2255 motion. If an applicant files a document that appears to be an unauthorized section 2254 petition or 2255 motion and facially alleges a claim based on a new rule of constitutional law or newly discovered evidence of actual innocence, the district court may transfer the filing to the court of appeals in the interests of justice or, in the alternative, the district court may dismiss the filing without prejudice to the applicant seeking authorization from the court of appeals on Ninth Circuit Form 12.

The rule requires applicants to provide the court of appeals with the proposed petition or motion. Pro se applicants are encouraged to use the form petition or motion adopted by the district court where the applicant anticipates filing the document. *(New 7/1/16)*

[Effective January 1, 1997. Amended effective January 1, 1999; December 1, 2002; December 1, 2009; July 1, 2013; July 1, 2016; December 1, 2018.]

RULE 22–4. APPEALS FROM AUTHORIZED SECOND OR SUCCESSIVE 2254 PETITIONS OR 2255 MOTIONS

This rule applies to appellate proceedings involving the denial of any authorized second or successive ("SOS") section 2254 petition or 2255 motion in capital proceedings. If the district court has denied in full an application for a COA for such an appeal, appellant shall file with the court of appeals a request for a COA. Circuit Rule 22–1 shall apply to the extent not inconsistent with this rule. *(Rev. 12/1/18)*

(a) Necessary Documents. An appellant challenging the denial of an authorized SOS petition or motion and filing a request for a certificate of appealability and/or a stay of execution, shall file with the court of appeals the following documents in an attachment to any COA request:

(1) the original application for permission to file a second or successive section 2254 petition or 2255 motion ("SOS petition") and/or a motion for stay of execution;

(2) all papers filed in the subsequent proceeding in district court;

(3) all orders issued by the district court in the subsequent proceeding;

(4) a copy of all relevant state or federal court opinions or judgments or, if there are no written opinions or judgments, a copy of the relevant portions of the transcripts; and

(5) a copy of the notice of appeal.

If all documents referred to in this provision are not filed, appellant shall state why the documents are unavailable and where they may be obtained. If appellant does not provide the documents, appellee shall provide them or state in any response why they are not available. *(Rev. 12/1/09; 12/1/18)*

(b) Emergency Motions. When the district court has denied an authorized SOS petition or motion and an execution is scheduled and imminent, counsel shall adhere to Circuit Rule 27–3 regarding emergency motions, except to the extent that it may be inconsistent with these rules. Any such motion will be presented to the panel assigned to the case pursuant to Circuit Rule 22–2. *(New 12/1/09; Rev. 12/1/18)*

(c) COA Applications. Where the district court has denied an authorized SOS petition or motion and denied a COA in full, the Clerk shall refer the motion for a COA to the death penalty panel. Oral argument may be held at the request of any member of the panel. Any member of the panel may grant a COA. If the panel votes unanimously to deny a COA in full, it shall enter an order setting forth the issues presented and the reasons why a COA should not issue. A copy of the order shall be circulated by the Clerk to all judges. *(New 12/1/09; Rev. 12/1/18)*

(d) En Banc Review. Any active or senior judge of the Court may request that the en banc court review the panel's order. The request shall be supported by a statement setting forth the requesting judge's reasons why the order should be vacated. If an execution date is scheduled and imminent, the Clerk shall notify the parties when a request for rehearing en banc is made and of the time frame for voting or, if no such request has been made, the Clerk shall notify the parties upon expiration of the period to request en banc rehearing. Such a request for rehearing en banc shall result in en banc review if a majority of active judges votes in favor of en banc review. A judge's failure to vote within the time established by General Order 5.5(b) shall be considered a "yes" vote in favor of en banc review. The en banc coordinator, if time permits, may set a schedule in which other judges may respond to the points made in the request for en banc review. If a majority of active judges votes in favor of en banc review, the Clerk shall notify the parties that the matter will receive en banc review, and identify the members of the en banc court. *(New 12/1/09)*

Any active judge may request a rehearing of the decision of the en banc court by all the active judges of the Court. If no stay is in effect, such judge may issue a temporary stay. The eleven-judge en banc court by majority vote may vacate such a temporary stay, and in that event there will be no stay in effect unless a stay is granted by the full court. *(New 12/1/09)*

(e) Stays of Execution. Where appellant seeks a stay of execution, any motion for stay of execution shall be filed electronically, and the Clerk shall refer any such motion to the death penalty panel. Oral argument may be held at the request of any member of the panel. If a majority of the panel votes to deny the stay, it shall enter an order setting forth the issues presented and the reasons for the denial. *(New 12/1/09; Rev. 12/1/18)*

If the panel denies a stay of execution and the execution date is imminent, any judge of the Court who requests en banc review may issue a temporary stay of execution. That stay shall lapse and be dissolved if a majority of active judges does not vote in favor of en banc review. A judge's failure to vote within the time established by General Order 5.5(b) shall be considered a "yes" vote in favor of en banc review. *(New 12/1/09)*

If the matter receives en banc review, the stay shall remain in effect until the en banc court completes voting on the question of granting a stay. Voting is complete when all available judges have been polled and a majority of the en banc court has voted either to grant or deny a stay. If at the completion of voting, a majority of the en banc court has not voted to grant the stay, there will be no stay in effect unless granted by the full court. *(New 12/1/09)*

If an execution is imminent and the panel has not yet determined whether to grant a stay pending final disposition of the appeal, any judge of the Court may issue a temporary stay of a scheduled execution. Any judge or judges who issue a temporary stay of execution shall immediately notify the Clerk and the panel of such action. By majority vote the panel may vacate such a stay of execution. *(New 12/1/09; Rev. 12/1/18)*

If the relief sought was available in the district court, the motion shall state whether all grounds advanced in support thereof in the court of appeals were submitted to the district court, and, if not, why the matter should not be remanded to the district court or the relief denied for that reason. *(New 12/1/09; Rev. 12/1/18)*

CIRCUIT ADVISORY COMMITTEE NOTE TO RULE 22–4

If a prisoner has been previously granted relief, in whole or in part, a petition or motion challenging a subsequent conviction or sentence shall be considered as a "first petition" or "first motion" and this rule shall not apply. Such a petition or motion will be assigned to the same panel to which the initial petition or motion was assigned. *(Rev. 12/1/09; 1 12/1/18)*

[Effective January 1, 1997. Amended effective January 1, 1999; December 1, 2009; December 1, 2018.]

RULE 22–5. SUBSEQUENT PETITIONS OR MOTIONS; RELATED CIVIL PROCEEDINGS [ABROGATED]

RULE 22–6. RULES APPLICABLE TO ALL DEATH PENALTY CASES

(a) Notice of Emergency Motions. Upon the filing of a notice of appeal where an execution date has been set and the district court has denied a stay of execution, the clerk of the district court shall immediately notify the Clerk of the court of appeals by telephone or email of such filing and electronically transmit the notice of appeal. Counsel shall communicate with the Clerk by telephone or email as soon as it becomes evident that emergency relief will be sought from the court of appeals. *(Rev. 12/1/09; 12/1/18)*

(b) *[Abrogated, see Circuit Rule 32–4, 1/1/99]*

(c) Excerpts of Record. The appellant shall prepare and file excerpts of record in compliance with Circuit Rule 30–1. An appellant unable to obtain all or part of the record shall so notify the court of appeals. In addition to the documents listed in Circuit Rule 30–1.2, excerpts of record shall contain all final orders and rulings of all state courts in appellate and post-conviction proceedings. Excerpts of records shall also include all final orders of the Supreme Court of the United States involving the conviction or sentence.

(d) *[Abrogated 12/1/18]*

[Effective January 1, 1997. Amended effective July 1, 1997; January 1, 1999; December 1, 2009; December 1, 2018.]

FRAP 23. CUSTODY OR RELEASE OF A PRISONER IN A HABEAS CORPUS PROCEEDING

[For text of rule, see the Federal Rules of Appellate Procedure]

RULE 23–1. CUSTODY OF FEDERAL PRISONERS PENDING APPEALS IN PROCEEDINGS TO VACATE SENTENCE

Pending an appeal from the final decision of any court or judge in a proceeding attacking a sentence under 28 U.S.C. § 2255, or an appeal from an order disposing of a motion made under Rules 33 or 35 of the Federal Rules of Criminal Procedure or any other proceeding in which a question of interim release is raised, the detention or release of the prisoner shall be governed by FRAP 23(b), (c) and (d).

[Effective January 1, 1997.]

FRAP 24. PROCEEDING IN FORMA PAUPERIS

[For text of rule, see the Federal Rules of Appellate Procedure]

RULE 24–1. EXCERPTS OF RECORD WAIVER [ABROGATED]

TITLE VII. GENERAL PROVISIONS

FRAP 25. FILING AND SERVICE

[For text of rule, see the Federal Rules of Appellate Procedure]

Cross Reference:
• FRAP 26. Computing and Extending Time, specifically, FRAP 26(c), Additional Time after Service by Mail
• FRAP 40. Petition for Panel Rehearing, specifically, FRAP 40(a), Time for Filing Petition for Rehearing

RULE 25–1. PRINCIPAL OFFICE OF CLERK

The principal office of the Clerk shall be in the United States Court of Appeals, 95 Seventh Street, San Francisco, California.

The duties of the Clerk are set forth in FRAP 45.

[Effective January 1, 1997.]

RULE 25–2. COMMUNICATIONS TO THE COURT

All communications to the Court shall be in writing unless otherwise permitted by these rules. All communications to the Court shall comply with FRAP 32 and shall be filed electronically unless (1) counsel has been granted an exemption from electronic filing under FRAP 25(a)(2)(D); (2) the filer is a pro se party; or (3) the document is excluded from the electronic filing requirement by the Court's orders and/or rules.

If a paper document is to be submitted, the document shall be addressed to the Clerk at the United States Court of Appeals. Documents transmitted via commercial carrier shall be directed to the Court at 95 Seventh Street, San Francisco, CA 94103–1526; documents transmitted via the United States Postal Service shall be directed to Post Office Box 193939, San Francisco, CA 94119–3939.

Parties and counsel shall not submit filings directly to any particular judge.

If adverse weather or other exceptional conditions render the San Francisco Clerk's Office inaccessible, the Court may by special order permit parties to submit paper documents to the Court's divisional offices.

CIRCUIT ADVISORY COMMITTEE NOTE TO RULE 25–2

Litigants are reminded that a commercial carrier's failure to deliver a document within the anticipated interval does not excuse the failure to meet a mandatory and jurisdictional deadline. *Magtanong v. Gonzales*, 494 F.3d 1190, 1191 (9th Cir. 2007).

Notice of Delay: If an appeal or petition has been pending before the Court for any period in excess of those set forth below, the party is encouraged to communicate this fact to the Court. Such notice can be accomplished by a letter to the Clerk identifying the case and the nature of the delay. Generally, such a letter would be appropriate if:

(1) a motion has been pending for longer than 4 months;

(2) the parties have not received notice of oral argument or submission on the briefs within 15 months after the completion of briefing;

(3) a decision on the merits has not been issued within 9 months after submission;

(4) the mandate has not issued within 28 days after the time to file a petition for rehearing has expired; or

(5) a petition for rehearing has been pending for longer than 6 months.

Litigants are advised that the complexity of a given matter may preclude court action within the noted time period.

Cross Reference:
- Circuit Rule 27–1. Filing of Motions
- Circuit Rule 27–2. Motions for Stays Pending Appeal
- Circuit Rule 27–3. Emergency Motions

[Effective January 1, 1997. Amended effective December 1, 2009; March 1, 2021.]

RULE 25–3. FACSIMILE AND E–MAIL FILING

25–3.1. Direct Filing. The Court does not accept for filing documents transmitted by telephone facsimile machine ("fax") or by e-mail, except in extreme emergencies and with advance permission of court personnel. Any party who transmits a document to the Court without authorization may be sanctioned.

Any document transmitted to the Court by fax or e-mail must show service on all other parties by fax, e-mail, or hand delivery, unless another form of service is authorized by the Court.

25–3.2. Third Party Filing. The Court accepts for filing documents transmitted to third parties by fax and subsequently delivered by hand to the Court if the party is exempt from the electronic filing requirement, the document is excluded from the electronic filing requirement by the Court's orders and/or rules, or the party has obtained permission for a third party filing. Documents filed in this fashion must comply with all applicable rules, including requirements for service, number of copies and colors of covers.

The filing party shall designate one copy of the filed document as the "fax original." It shall be of laser quality and shall bear the notation "fax original." Other copies shall not bear that notation.

25–3.3. Electronic Service. [Abrogated].

[Effective January 1, 1997. Amended effective December 1, 2002; December 1, 2009.]

RULE 25–4. CALENDARED CASES

After a case has been scheduled for oral argument, has been argued, is under submission or has been decided, all documents submitted to the Court for filing, including FRAP 28(j) letters, must include the latest of the date of argument, submission or decision. If known, the names of the panel members shall be included. This information shall be included on the initial page and/or cover, if any, immediately below the case number.

[Adopted effective July 1, 2000. Amended effective July 1, 2006; December 1, 2009.]

RULE 25–5. ELECTRONIC FILING

(New Rule 12/1/09, Rev. 7/1/13, 3/23/16; 12/1/18)

(a) Participation. All attorneys and court reporters are required to submit all filings electronically using the Court's Appellate Electronic Filing System unless the Court grants a request to be exempted from the requirement. Filers seeking an exemption must complete the Appellate Electronic Filing System Exemption Form found on the Court's website. If an exempt filer registers for the Appellate Electronic Filing System, that registration will abrogate the exemption. *(Rev. 7/1/13)*

Use of the Appellate Electronic Filing System is voluntary for all parties proceeding without counsel.

If a technical malfunction prevents access to the Appellate Electronic Filing System for a protracted period, the Court by special order may permit paper filings pending restoration of electronic access.

(b) Documents That May Be Submitted Either Electronically or in Paper Format.

(1) Petitions for review of agency orders under FRAP 15(a) and Circuit Rule 15–1;

(2) Applications for enforcement of agency orders under FRAP 15(b) and Circuit Rule 15–1;

(3) Petitions for permission to appeal under FRAP 5 and Circuit Rule 5–2;

(4) Petitions for writs of mandamus or prohibition under FRAP 21 and Circuit Rule 21–1; and

(5) Applications for leave to file second or successive petitions under 28 U.S.C. § 2254 or motions under 28 U.S.C. § 2255 and Circuit Rule 22–3. *(Rev. 7/1/13)*

(c) Deadlines.

(1) *When Permitted.* Electronic filing is permitted at any time other than when precluded by system maintenance. Filings will be processed by the Court during the Court's business hours.

(2) *Timeliness.* An electronic filing successfully completed by 11:59 p.m. Pacific Time will be entered on the Court's docket as of that date. The Court's Appellate Electronic Filing System determines the date and time a filing is completed. If technical failure prevents timely electronic filing of any document, the filing party shall preserve documentation of the failure and seek appropriate relief from the Court.

(d) Technical Requirements. All documents must be submitted in Portable Document Format ("PDF"). The version filed with the Court must be generated from the original word processing file to permit the electronic version of the document to be searched and copied. PDF files created by scanning paper documents are prohibited; however, exhibits submitted as attachments to a document may be scanned and attached if the filer does not possess a word processing file version of the attachment. No single attachment shall exceed 100MB in size. Attachments that exceed that size must be divided into sub-volumes. *(Rev. 7/1/13)*

(e) Signature. Electronic filings shall indicate each signatory by using an "s/" in addition to the typed name of counsel or an unrepresented party. Documents filed on behalf of separately represented parties or multiple pro se parties must indicate one signatory by using an "s/" in addition to the typed name and attest that all other parties on whose behalf the filing is submitted concur in the filing's content.

(f) Service. All filings not submitted through the Appellate Electronic Filing System require a certificate of service or equivalent statement. A sample certificate can be found on the Court's website at Form 25.

(1) *Filings Submitted Electronically That Are Served Electronically.* When a document (other than an original proceeding or petition for review) is submitted electronically, the Appellate Electronic Filing System will automatically notify the other parties and counsel who are registered for electronic filing of the submission; no certificate of service or service of paper copies upon other parties and counsel registered for electronic filing is necessary. Registration for the Appellate Electronic Filing System constitutes consent to electronic service.

(2) *Filings Submitted Electronically That Are Not Served Electronically.* Original proceedings, petitions for review, sealed filings, and any electronically submitted filing in a case involving a pro se litigant or an attorney who is not registered for the Appellate Electronic Filing System must be served pursuant to FRAP 25(c)(1), and must be accompanied by a certificate of service or equivalent statement. A sample certificate can be found on the Court's website at Form 15. Registration for the Appellate Electronic Filing System constitutes consent to service by email.

(g) Court–Issued Documents. Except as otherwise provided by these rules or court order, electronically filed and distributed orders, decrees, and judgments constitute entry on the docket under FRAP 36 and 45(b). Orders also may be issued as "text-only" entries on the docket without an attached document. Such orders are official and binding.

Cross Reference:

- FRAP 25. Filing and Service, specifically, FRAP 25(a)(5), Privacy Protection
- Interim Circuit Rule 27–13. Sealed Documents
- Circuit Rule 22–3. Applications for Authorization to File Second or Successive 28 U.S.C. § 2254 Petition or § 2255 Motion—All Cases; Stay of Execution—Capital Cases, specifically, Circuit Rule 22–3(c)(2), Service in Noncapital Cases

CIRCUIT ADVISORY COMMITTEE NOTE TO RULE 25–5

The parties are reminded of their obligations under FRAP 25(a)(5) to redact personal identifiers.

Additional information regarding the electronic filing and the Appellate Electronic Filing System may be found at the Court's website at www.ca9.uscourts.gov; http://pacer.psc.uscourts.gov; and the informational materials provided to the parties upon the docketing of a case.

Practitioners appointed under the Criminal Justice Act are directed to the Court's website, www.ca9.uscourts.gov/attorneys for information regarding the submission procedures for claims for services and requests related to such services.

When exigent circumstances require submission of an emergency motion under Circuit Rule 27–3 prior to the assignment of an appellate docket number, the moving party shall contact the Motions Attorney Unit at 415–355–8020 to obtain authorization under Circuit Rule 25–3.1 to transmit the motion via facsimile or electronic mail.

[Effective December 1, 2009. Amended effective July 1, 2013; March 23, 2016; December 1, 2018; December 1, 2019.]

FRAP 26. COMPUTING AND EXTENDING TIME

[For text of rule, see the Federal Rules of Appellate Procedure]

RULE 26–1. FILING DEADLINES FOR THE DISTRICTS OF GUAM AND THE NORTHERN MARIANA ISLANDS

Except as provided by order of the Court, or by FRAP 26(b) and 31, all deadlines for filing set forth in FRAP or these rules are extended by 7 days in cases arising from the Districts of Guam and the Northern Mariana Islands when the filing party is not registered for electronic filing.

[Effective January 1, 1997. Amended effective June 1, 2017.]

RULE 26–2. THREE DAY SERVICE ALLOWANCE [ABROGATED EFFECTIVE JUNE 1, 2017]

FRAP 26.1 CORPORATE DISCLOSURE STATEMENT

[For text of rule, see the Federal Rules of Appellate Procedure]

FRAP 27. MOTIONS

[For text of rule, see the Federal Rules of Appellate Procedure]

RULE 27–1.   FILING OF MOTIONS

(1) Form and Length of Motions.

(a) *[Abrogated 7/1/06]*

(b) If electronic filing of the motion, response or reply is not required, the Court requires an original of that filing. The Clerk may direct a party to submit additional paper copies of a motion, response and/or reply when paper copies would aid the Court's review of the motion.

(c) The provisions of FRAP 27(d)(1) otherwise govern the format of motions.

(d) Except by permission of the Court, a motion or a response to a motion may not exceed 20 pages. A reply to a response may not exceed 10 pages. The documents listed at FRAP 27(a)(2)(B) and 32(f) are excluded from the length limit calculation.

(2) Position of Opposing Counsel. If counsel for the moving party learns that a motion is unopposed, counsel shall so advise the Court.

(3) Relief Needed by Date Certain. If a motion requests relief by a date certain to avoid irreparable harm, the motion must specify that date in bold on the caption page. If the requested date is justified in the motion, the Court will make every effort to rule on the motion by that date. *(New 12/1/19)*

Cross Reference:

• Circuit Rule 25–2. Communications to the Court

• Circuit Rule 32–3. Page/Word Count Conversion Formula for Briefs and Other Documents

CIRCUIT ADVISORY COMMITTEE NOTE TO RULE 27–1

(1) Motions Acted on by the Appellate Commissioner. The Appellate Commissioner is an officer appointed by the Court. The Court has delegated broad authority under FRAP 27(b) to the Appellate Commissioner to review a wide variety of motions, e.g., appointment, substitution, and withdrawal of counsel and motions for reinstatement. The Appellate Commissioner may deny a motion for dispositive relief, but may not grant such a request other than those filed under FRAP 42(b).

(2) Motions Acted on by a Single Judge. Under FRAP 27(c), a single judge may grant or deny any motion which by order or rule the Court has not specifically excluded, but a single judge may not dismiss or otherwise effectively determine an appeal or other proceeding. Thus, a single judge may not grant motions for summary disposition, dismissal, or remand. A single judge may grant or deny temporary relief in emergency situations pending full consideration of the motion by a motions panel. In addition, some types of motions may be ruled on by a single judge by virtue of a particular rule or statute.

(3) Motions Acted on by Motions Panels.

(a) Motions Heard by the Motions Panels. The motions panel shall rule on substantive motions, including motions to dismiss, for summary affirmance, and similar motions. The Court has determined that in the interest of uniformity, motions for bail are considered by a three-judge motions panel.

(b) Selection of Motions Panels. Judges are ordinarily assigned to the three-judge motions panel on a rotating basis by the Clerk for a term of one month. A single motions panel is appointed for the entire circuit.

(c) Procedures for Disposition of Motions by the Motions Panel. All three judges of the motions panel participate in ruling on motions that dispose of the appeal. Other substantive motions are presented to two judges; if in agreement, they ordinarily decide the motion. The third judge participates only if

(i) one of the other members of the panel is disqualified or is otherwise unavailable; or

(ii) the other members of the panel disagree on the disposition of a motion or he or she is requested to participate by the other members of the panel.

A motions panel sits in San Francisco for several days each month. If necessary, emergency motions are acted on by telephone. (See Cir. R. 27–3 through 27–4 and Advisory Committee Notes thereto.)

(4) Motions for Clarification, Reconsideration or Modification. Motions for clarification, reconsideration or modification of an order deciding a motion are disfavored by the Court and are rarely granted. The filing of such motions is discouraged. (See Circuit Rule 27–10 as to time limits on filing motions for reconsideration.)

(5) Position of Opposing Counsel. Unless precluded by extreme time urgency, counsel are to make every attempt to contact opposing counsel before filing any motion and to either inform the Court of the position of opposing counsel or provide an explanation regarding the efforts made to obtain that position.

(6) Request to Amend the Briefing Schedule. A party may request modification of the briefing schedule in conjunction with any request for other relief. The request for modification of the briefing schedule should be included in the legend as well as the body of the motion for other relief.

(7) Requests for Judicial Notice. Requests for judicial notice and responses thereto filed during the pendency of the case are retained for review by the panel that will consider the merits of a case. The parties may refer to the materials the request addresses with the understanding that the Court may strike such references and related arguments if it declines to grant the request.

Cross Reference:

• Circuit Rule 25–2. Communications to the Court

• FRAP 32. Form of Briefs, Appendices, and Other Papers, specifically, FRAP 32(c), Form of Other Papers

• Circuit Rule 40–1. Format; Number of Copies

[Effective January 1, 1997. Amended effective January 1, 1999; July 1, 2002; July 1, 2005; January 1, 2006; July 1, 2006; December 1, 2009; December 1, 2016; December 1, 2019.]

RULE 27–2.   MOTIONS FOR STAYS PENDING APPEAL

If a district court stays an order or judgment to permit application to the Court of Appeals for a stay pending appeal, an application for such stay shall be filed in the Court of Appeals within 7 days after issuance of the district court's stay.

Cross Reference:

• Circuit Rule 27–3. Emergency and Urgent Motions

• FRAP 8. Stay or Injunction Pending Appeal

[Effective January 1, 1997. Amended effective December 1, 2009.]

RULE 27–3.   EMERGENCY MOTIONS

If a movant needs relief within 21 days to avoid irreparable harm, the movant must:

(a) make every practicable effort to notify the Court and opposing counsel, and to serve the motion, at the earliest possible time;

(b) clearly state on the caption page of the motion the date by which relief is needed under the legend "Emergency Motion Under Circuit Rule 27–3;" and

(c) submit a Certificate prepared by counsel (or by the unrepresented movant), entitled "Circuit Rule 27–3 Certificate." A sample Certificate is available on the Court's website at Form 16. The Certificate must follow the caption page and must:

(i) contain the names, telephone numbers, e-mail addresses, and office addresses of the attorneys for all parties;

(ii) state the facts showing the existence and nature of the claimed emergency;

(iii) explain why the motion could not have been filed earlier;

(iv) state when and how the movant did or will give notice to, and serve the motion on, counsel for the other parties or on any unrepresented parties, and if known—what the other parties' positions are on the motion; and

(v) explain whether the relief sought in the motion was first sought in the district court or agency, and if not, why the motion should not be remanded or denied.

The motion must otherwise comport with FRAP 27.

Cross Reference:
- FRAP 8. Stay or Injunction Pending Appeal
- FRAP 25. Filing and Service
- Circuit Rule 27–1. Filing of Motions on page 92, specifically Circuit Rule 27–1(3), Relief Needed by Date Certain
- Circuit Rule 27–5. Emergency Motions for Stay of Execution of Sentence of Death

CIRCUIT ADVISORY COMMITTEE NOTE TO RULE 27–3

If irreparable harm will occur within 21 days absent relief, the movant must contact the Court's emergency motions unit via email (emergency@ca9.uscourts.gov) or Telephone (415.355.8020) before or upon filing the motion.

This rule is meant for parties facing significant harm, e.g., imminent removal, not for parties seeking procedural relief, e.g. more time to file a brief.

Cross Reference:
- Circuit Advisory Committee Note to Rule 31–2.2
- Circuit Advisory Committee Note to Rule 32–2

[Effective January 1, 1997. Amended effective July 1, 2000; December 1, 2009; December 1, 2019.]

RULE 27–4. EMERGENCY CRIMINAL INTERLOCUTORY APPEALS

If emergency treatment is sought for an interlocutory criminal appeal, motions for expedition, summary affirmances or reversal, or dismissal may be filed pursuant to Circuit Rule 27–3. To avoid delay in the disposition of such motions, counsel should include with the motion all material that may bear upon the disposition of the appeal, including: information concerning the scheduled trial date; information regarding codefendants; and information concerning other counts contained in the indictment but not in issue.

Cross Reference:
- FRAP 4. Appeal as of Right—When Taken, specifically, FRAP 4(b), Appeals in Criminal Cases
- FRAP 22. Habeas Corpus and Section 2255 Proceedings
- Circuit Rule 22–1. Certificate of Appealability (COA)
- Circuit Rule 22–2. Direct Criminal Appeals, First Petitions, and Stays of Execution: Capital Cases
- Circuit Rule 22–3. Applications for Authorization to File Second or Successive 28 U.S.C. § 2254 Petition or § 2255 Motion—All Cases; Stay of Execution—Capital Cases
- Circuit Rule 25–5. Electronic Filing, specifically, Circuit Rule 25–5(b), Documents that may be submitted either electronically or in paper format
- Circuit Rule 22–5. Subsequent Petitions or Motions; Related Civil Proceedings
- Circuit Rule 22–6. Rules Applicable to all Death Penalty Cases

[Effective January 1, 1997. Amended effective December 1, 2009.]

RULE 27–5. EMERGENCY MOTIONS FOR STAY OF EXECUTION OF SENTENCE OF DEATH [ABROGATED]

RULE 27–6. NO ORAL ARGUMENT UNLESS OTHERWISE ORDERED [ABROGATED]

RULE 27–7. DELEGATION OF AUTHORITY TO ACT ON MOTIONS

The Court may delegate to the Clerk or designated deputy clerks, staff attorneys, appellate commissioners or circuit mediators authority to decide motions filed with the Court. Orders issued pursuant to this section are subject to reconsideration pursuant to Circuit Rule 27–10.

CIRCUIT ADVISORY COMMITTEE NOTE TO RULE 27–7

Procedural Motions. Most non-dispositive procedural motions in appeals or other proceedings that have not yet been calendared are acted on by court staff under the supervision of the clerk, the appellate commissioner, or the chief circuit mediator. Court staff may act on procedural motions whether opposed or unopposed, but if there is any question under the guidelines as to what action should be taken on the motion, it is referred to the appellate commissioner or the chief circuit mediator. Through its General Orders, the Court has delegated authority to act on specific motions and to take other actions on its behalf. See, in particular, General Orders, Appendix A, (which are available on the Court's website).

[Effective January 1; 1997. Amended effective January 1, 2004.]

RULE 27–8. REQUIRED RECITALS IN CRIMINAL AND IMMIGRATION CASES

27–8.1. Criminal Cases. Every motion in a criminal appeal shall recite any previous application for the relief sought and the bail status of the defendant.

27–8.2. Immigration Petitions. Every motion in a petition for review of a decision of the Board of Immigration

Appeals shall recite any previous application for the relief sought and inform the Court if petitioner is detained in the custody of the Department of Homeland Security or at liberty.

[Effective January 1, 1997. Amended effective January 1, 2005; December 1, 2009.]

RULE 27–9. MOTIONS TO DISMISS CRIMINAL APPEALS

27–9.1. Voluntary Dismissals. Motions or stipulations for voluntary dismissals of criminal appeals shall, if made or joined in by counsel for appellant, be accompanied by appellant's written consent thereto, or counsel's explanation of why appellant's consent was not obtained.

Cross Reference:

• FRAP 42. Voluntary Dismissal

27–9.2. Involuntary Dismissals. Motions by appellees for dismissal of criminal appeals, and supporting papers, shall be served upon both appellant and appellant's counsel, if any. If the ground of such motion is failure to prosecute the appeal, appellant's counsel, if any, shall respond within 10 days. If appellant's counsel does not respond, the clerk will notify the appellant of the Court's proposed action.

If the appeal is dismissed for failure to prosecute, the Court may impose sanctions on appellant's counsel. Counsel will be provided with 14 days notice and an opportunity to respond before sanctions are imposed.

[Effective January 1, 1997. Amended effective December 1, 2002; December 1, 2009.]

RULE 27–10. MOTIONS FOR RECONSIDERATION

(a) Filing for Reconsideration.

(1) *Time Limit for Orders That Terminate the Case.* A party seeking further consideration of an order that disposes of the entire case on the merits, terminates a case, or otherwise concludes the proceedings in this Court must comply with the time limits of FRAP 40(a)(1).

(2) *Time Limit for All Other Orders.* Unless the time is shortened or expanded by order of this Court, a motion for clarification, modification or reconsideration of a court order that does not dispose of the entire case on the merits, terminate a case or otherwise conclude proceedings in this Court must be filed within 14 days after entry of the order.

(3) *Required Showing.* A party seeking relief under this rule shall state with particularity the points of law or fact which, in the opinion of the movant, the Court has overlooked or misunderstood. Changes in legal or factual circumstances which may entitle the movant to relief also shall be stated with particularity.

(b) Court Processing.

Motions Panel Orders: A timely motion for clarification, modification, or reconsideration of an order issued by a motions panel shall be decided by that panel. If the case subsequently has been assigned to a merits panel, the motions panel shall contact the merits panel before disposing of the motion. A party may file only one motion for clarification, modification, or reconsideration of a motions panel order. No response to a motion for clarification, modification, or reconsideration of a motions panel's order is permitted unless requested by the Court, but ordinarily the Court will not grant such a motion without requesting a response and, if warranted, a reply. The rule applies to any motion seeking clarification, modification, or reconsideration of a motions panel order, either by the motions panel or by the Court sitting en banc.

Orders Issued Under Circuit Rule 27–7: A motion to reconsider, clarify, or modify an order issued pursuant to Circuit Rule 27–7 by a deputy clerk, staff attorney, circuit mediator, or the appellate commissioner is initially directed to the individual who issued the order or, if appropriate, to his/her successor. The time to respond to such a motion is governed by FRAP 27(a)(3)(A). If that individual is disinclined to grant the requested relief, the motion for reconsideration, clarification, or modification shall be processed as follows:

(1) if the order was issued by a deputy clerk or staff attorney, the motion is referred to an appellate commissioner;

(2) if the order was issued by a circuit mediator, the motion is referred to the chief circuit mediator;

(3) if the order was issued by the appellate commissioner or the chief circuit mediator, the motion is referred to a motions panel.

CIRCUIT ADVISORY COMMITTEE NOTE TO RULE 27–10

Motions for clarification, reconsideration or modification of orders entered by a motions panel are not favored by the Court and should be utilized only where counsel believes that the Court has overlooked or misunderstood a point of law or fact, or where there is a change in legal or factual circumstances after the order which would entitle the movant to relief.

[Adopted effective January 1, 1997. Amended effective July 1, 2000; January 1, 2004; January 1, 2009; December 1, 2009; July 1, 2016; December 1, 2021.]

RULE 27–11. MOTIONS; EFFECT ON SCHEDULE

(a) Motions requesting the types of relief noted below shall stay the schedule for record preparation and briefing pending the Court's disposition of the motion:

(1) dismissal;

(2) transfer to another tribunal;

(3) full remand;

(4) in forma pauperis status in this Court;

(5) production of transcripts at government expense; and

(6) appointment or withdrawal of counsel.

(b) The schedule for record preparation and briefing shall be reset as necessary upon the Court's disposition of the motion. Motions for reconsideration are disfavored and will not stay the schedule unless otherwise ordered by the Court.

[Effective January 1, 1997. Amended effective January 1, 2003.]

RULE 27–12. MOTIONS TO EXPEDITE

Motions to expedite briefing and hearing may be filed and will be granted upon a showing of good cause. "Good cause" includes, but is not limited to, situations in which: (1) an incarcerated criminal defendant contends that the valid guideline term of confinement does not extend beyond 12 months from the filing of the notice of appeal; (2) the projected release date for an incarcerated criminal defendant occurs within 12 months from the filing of the notice of appeal; or (3) in the absence of expedited treatment, irreparable harm may occur or the appeal may become moot. The motion shall set forth the status of transcript preparation and opposing counsel's position or reason why moving counsel has been unable to determine that position. The motion may also include a proposed briefing schedule and date for argument or submission.

A motion pursuant to this rule may include a request for (i) a stay of the order on appeal, or (ii) release of a prisoner pending appeal.

Cross Reference:

- Circuit Rule 27–3. Emergency Motions

[Effective January 1, 1997.]

RULE 27–13. SEALED DOCUMENTS

(a) Introduction. This Court has a strong presumption in favor of public access to documents. Therefore, except as provided in (d) below, the presumption is that every document filed in or by this Court (whether or not the document was sealed in the district court) is in the public record unless this Court orders it to be sealed.

Accordingly, unless a case or document falls within the scope of (d) below, this Court will permit it to be filed under seal only if justified by a motion to seal the document from public view. *See* (e), (f), (g), and (h) below. The Court will not seal a case or a document based solely on the stipulation of the parties.

When an entire case was sealed in district court, the case will be docketed provisionally under seal in this Court, and within 21 days of filing the notice of appeal, a party must file a motion to continue the seal or the seal may be lifted without notice. *See* (g) below. When a document was sealed in the district court, the document will be filed provisionally under seal, and must be accompanied by a notice under subsection (d), a motion to seal under subsection (e), or a notice under subsection (f). The document will remain provisionally sealed until the Court rules on any motion to seal.

Documents in Social Security and Immigration cases, including administrative records, are not filed under seal in this Court. However, remote electronic access to documents is limited by rule to the parties to the case, though the documents will be available for public viewing in the Clerk's Office. *See* Fed. R. Civ. P. 5.2(c); Fed. R. App. P. 25(a)(5). This same rule, however, presumes that the orders and dispositions will be publicly available.

(b) Definitions.

(1) *Sealed Document.* There is no public access via PACER. Once submitted, access to the document is restricted to the Court.

(2) *Sealed Case.* There is no public access via PACER. Access to the docket and all documents filed in the case is restricted to case participants and the Court.

(c) Form of Documents. All documents shall be submitted electronically unless the filer is exempt from the electronic filing requirement. Each document or volume of documents submitted under seal shall include the words "UNDER SEAL" on its cover and/or first page. Any publicly filed redacted version of a sealed document shall include the word "REDACTED" on the cover and/or first page of the document.

Because documents submitted under seal will not be viewable to the parties via the Appellate Electronic Filing System noticing, any notice or motion submitted under seal and any document associated with such notice or motion shall be served on opposing counsel in paper form or, with consent, via email. *See* Circuit Rule 25–5(f)2.

Rather than moving to file the entire excerpts of record under seal, a party shall submit any document(s) it wishes to seal as a separate volume. *See* Circuit Rule 30–1.6(c).

(d) Presentence Reports, Grand Jury Transcripts, and Sealed Filings Mandated by Statute or Procedural Rule. When a statute or procedural rule requires that a brief or other document be filed under seal (*see, e.g.,* 18 U.S.C. § 5038(c), 3509(d); Fed. R. Crim. P. 6(e)), or when a party is filing an original, revised, or amended presentence report, its attachments, and any confidential sentencing memoranda, a motion under subsection (e) is not required.

Instead, the document(s) shall be submitted under seal in accordance with subsection (c), and accompanied by a notice of filing under seal that references this rule and the pertinent statute or procedural rule.

In cases in which any presentence report is referenced in the brief, the party first filing that brief must file under seal the presentence report, the documents attached to the report, and any sentencing memoranda filed under seal in the district court. The report and documents shall be filed on the same day as the brief that references the report and documents, using the presentence report electronic document filing type, without an accompanying notice of filing under seal. These documents shall not be included in the excerpts of record. The party submitting the presentence report and related sealed memoranda shall separately notify the opposing party by email (or first class mail if the opposing party is exempt from electronic filing) of the specific documents submitted, and shall provide a copy upon request.

(e) Motion to Submit a Sealed Document. In the absence of a statutory or procedural requirement as described in (d) above, a party who wishes to submit any document or portion of a document, including a brief, under seal, whether or not it was sealed in the district court, shall file a motion simultaneously with the document. The motion shall explain the specific reasons for this relief and describe the potential for irreparable injury in the absence of such relief. In addition, the motion shall request the least restrictive scope of sealing and be limited in scope to only the specific documents or portion of documents that merit sealing, for example, propose redaction of a single paragraph or limit the request to a portion of a contract. The motion and document will be provisionally sealed pending a ruling on the motion.

Additionally, rather than moving to file the entire excerpts of record under seal, a party shall submit any document(s) that fall within this subsection as a separate volume. *See* subsection (c) above. Where redaction of a document is feasible, the moving party shall highlight in the unredacted document all portions of the document that party is seeking to file under seal.

(f) Notice of Intent to File a Document Publicly That Was the Subject of a Seal Below. If the filing party does not intend to ask that a seal issued by the district court be continued, the party shall file the documents provisionally under seal, along with a notice of intent to file publicly, in order to allow any other party an opportunity to move for appropriate relief within 21 days of the notice. Absent a motion by another party to continue the seal, or a notice pursuant to subsection (d), the provisional seal will be lifted without notice and the documents will be made available to the public.

(g) Motion or Notice to Maintain a Case Under Seal. A party who wants a case that was fully sealed in the district court to remain fully sealed on appeal shall file a motion to continue the seal within 21 days of the filing of the notice of appeal. The motion must explain with specificity why it is necessary for the entire case to be sealed on appeal and why no less restrictive alternatives are available.

When the seal is required by statute or procedural rule, a motion is not required; instead, a party must file a notice that references this rule and the pertinent statute or rule within 21 days of the filing of the notice of appeal.

Absent a motion or notice, the seal may be lifted without notice and the case in full will be made available to the public.

(h) Motions to Unseal. Motions to unseal may be made on any grounds permitted by law. The parties in a civil case may stipulate to the public filing in this Court of a document that was filed under seal in the district court.

(i) Argument. Except as otherwise ordered by the Court, the Court will not close oral argument to the public in any type of case, even when the case itself or the briefs or excerpts of record have been filed under seal. A party seeking a closed hearing shall move for such extraordinary relief at least 14 days prior to the scheduled argument date and explain with specificity why such relief is required and whether any less extraordinary alternative is available.

(j) Dispositions. This Court will presumptively file any disposition publicly, even in cases involving sealed materials. Any party who believes the Court's disposition should be sealed shall file a motion seeking that relief within 28 days of the completion of briefing.

Cross Reference:

• Circuit Rule 25–5. Electronic Filing, specifically Circuit Rule 25–5(f), Service

• Circuit Rule 25–5. Electronic Filing, specifically Circuit Rule 25–5(f)(2), Filings Submitted Electronically That Are Not Served Electronically

CIRCUIT ADVISORY COMMITTEE NOTE TO RULE 27–13

The Court has a strong presumption in favor of public access to Court records in both civil and criminal cases. See The Center for Auto Safety v. Chrysler Group, LLC, 809 F.3d 1092, 1096 (9th Cir. 2016); Oliner v. Kontrabecki, 745 F.3d 1024, 1025–26 (9th Cir. 2014); Seattle Times v. U.S. Dist. Court of Western Washington, 845 F.2d 1513, 1516 (9th Cir. 1988). Motions to file documents under seal are therefore discouraged. Moreover, if the contents of documents originally sealed in the district court have subsequently been disclosed publicly, the Court will be disinclined to maintain the seal.

A motion to seal does not ordinarily change the briefing schedule and any order resolving such a motion will include further instructions for the parties as needed. The Court may defer ruling on the motion until the completion of briefing. If the Court denies a motion to file a document under seal, the Court will ordinarily provide the moving party with an opportunity to withdraw that document and will shield the document from public access during that period.

When the filing of classified documents on an ex parte or sealed basis in a given case is necessary in light of national security issues, the Court will adopt procedures specific to that case.

Cross Reference:

• FRAP 25. Filing and Service, specifically FRAP 25(a)(5), Privacy Protection

• Circuit Advisory Committee Note to Rule 3–5

[Adopted on an Interim Basis effective March 23, 2016. Adopted effective June 1, 2019.]

RULE 27–14. MOTIONS TO TRANSMIT PHYSICAL AND DOCUMENTARY EXHIBITS

If a party asserts that review of an exhibit not currently available on the electronic district court docket is necessary to resolution of an issue on appeal, that party shall move the Court for leave to transmit to the Court a copy or replication of the exhibit. The copy, or photograph or other replication shall not be included with the motion. The Court will defer ruling on the motion until after the completion of briefing. If the exhibit was submitted under seal in the district court, the party moving to transmit the exhibit must also file a notice or motion pursuant to Circuit Rule 27–13. *(Rev. 6/1/19)*

CIRCUIT ADVISORY COMMITTEE NOTE TO RULE 27–14

The parties should be aware that frequently this Court does not have access to trial exhibits because the district courts typically return them to the parties. Therefore, the parties are encouraged during the course of the district court proceedings to file documentary exhibits electronically and, when practicable, to photograph or otherwise electronically replicate physical exhibits in a manner that permits the exhibits' inclusion on the electronic district court docket. The parties may consider including portions of relevant documentary exhibits that were admitted and/or offered and excluded in the excerpts of record. To the extent that the Court finds additional exhibits relevant, the Court may direct the parties to provide the exhibits.

[Effective July 1, 2013. Amended effective June 1, 2019.]

FRAP 28. BRIEFS

*[For text of rule, see the Federal Rules
of Appellate Procedure]*

RULE 28–1. BRIEFS, APPLICABLE RULES

(a) Briefs shall be prepared and filed in accordance with the Federal Rules of Appellate Procedure except as otherwise provided by these rules. *See* FRAP 28, 29, 31 and 32. Briefs not complying with FRAP and these rules may be stricken by the Court.

(b) Parties must not append or incorporate by reference briefs submitted to the district court or agency or this Court in a prior appeal, or refer this Court to such briefs for the arguments on the merits of the appeal.

(c) Appellants proceeding without assistance of counsel may file the informal form briefs provided by the Clerk in lieu of the briefs described in FRAP 28(a) and (c), and need not comply with the technical requirements of FRAP.

Cross Reference:

• FRAP 28. Briefs, specifically, FRAP 28(j), Citation of Supplemental Authorities

CIRCUIT ADVISORY COMMITTEE NOTE TO RULE 28–1 [ABROGATED]

[Effective January 1, 1997. Amended effective July 1, 2000; December 1, 2019.]

RULE 28–2. CONTENTS OF BRIEFS

In addition to the requirements of FRAP 28, briefs shall comply with the following rules:

28–2.1. Certificate as to Interested Parties. [Abrogated]

28–2.2. Statement of Jurisdiction. In a statement preceding the statement of the case in its initial brief, each party shall demonstrate the jurisdiction of the district court or agency and of this Court by stating, in the following order:

(a) The statutory basis of subject matter jurisdiction of the district court or agency;

(b) The basis for claiming that the judgment or order appealed from is final or otherwise appealable, and the statutory basis of jurisdiction of this Court;

(c) The date of entry of the judgment or order appealed from; the date of filing of the notice of appeal or petition for review; and the statute or rule under which it is claimed the appeal is timely.

If the appellee agrees with appellant's statement of one or more of the foregoing matters, it will be sufficient for the appellee to state such agreement under an appropriate heading.

28–2.3. Attorneys Fees. [Abrogated]

28–2.4. Bail / Detention Status.

(a) The opening brief in a criminal appeal shall contain a statement as to the bail status of the defendant. If the defendant is in custody, the projected release date should be included.

(b) The opening brief in a petition for review of a decision of the Board of Immigration Appeals shall state whether petitioner (1) is detained in the custody of the Department of Homeland Security or at liberty and/or (2) has moved the Board of Immigration Appeals to reopen or applied to the district director for an adjustment of status.

28–2.5. Reviewability and Standard of Review. As to each issue, appellant shall state where in the record on appeal the issue was raised and ruled on and identify the applicable standard of review.

In addition, if a ruling complained of on appeal is one to which a party must have objected at trial to preserve a right of review, e.g., a failure to admit or to exclude evidence or the giving of or refusal to give a jury instruction, the party shall state where in the record on appeal the objection and ruling are set forth.

28–2.6. Statement of Related Cases. Each party shall identify in a statement on the last page of its initial brief any known related case pending in this Court. This statement constitutes a certificate of counsel, excluded from the page and word limitations pursuant to FRAP 32(f) and Circuit Rule 32–1(c). As to each such case, the statement shall include the name and Court of Appeals docket number of the related case and describe its relationship to the case being briefed. Cases are deemed related if they:

(a) arise out of the same or consolidated cases in the district court or agency;

(b) raise the same or closely related issues; or

(c) involve the same transaction or event.

If no other cases in this Court are deemed related, no statement is required. The appellee need not include any case identified as related in the appellant's brief.

CIRCUIT ADVISORY COMMITTEE NOTE TO RULE 28–2.6

The purpose of this rule is to alert the parties and the Court to other known cases pending in this Court that might affect how the instant case is managed or decided. This rule does not require counsel to list all known cases raising the same or closely related issues if the list would be lengthy and counsel in good faith believes that listing the cases would not assist the Court or other parties.

28–2.7. Addendum to Briefs.

Statutory. Pertinent constitutional provisions, treaties, statutes, ordinances, regulations or rules must be set forth verbatim and with appropriate citation either (1) following the statement of issues presented for review or (2) in an addendum introduced by a table of contents and bound with the brief or separately; in the latter case, a statement must appear referencing the addendum after the statement of issues. If this material is included in an addendum bound with the brief, the addendum must be separated from the body of the brief (and from any other addendum) by a distinctively colored page. A party need not resubmit material included with a previous brief or addendum; if it is not repeated, a statement must appear under this heading as follows: [e]xcept for the following, all applicable statutes, etc., are contained in the brief or addendum of _____.

Orders Challenged in Immigration Cases. All opening briefs filed in counseled petitions for review of immigration cases must include an addendum comprised of the orders being challenged, including any orders of the immigration court and Board of Immigration Appeals. The addendum shall be bound with the brief, both when it is filed electronically and, when ordered, in hard copies. When paper copies of the brief are ordered, the addendum shall be separated from the brief by a distinctively colored page.

CIRCUIT ADVISORY COMMITTEE NOTE TO RULE 28–2.7

The purpose of the statutory addendum is to provide the Court with convenient access to statutory or other authority that is either specifically at issue or is not already commonly known, not to provide every statute or legal authority that is cited in the brief. For example, when the parties are debating the meaning of a specific clause or portion of a statute, regulation, constitutional provision, or other legal authority, or when they are discussing authority that is not commonly cited, the addenda should include the pertinent provisions of that legal authority. (New 12/1/21)

28–2.8. Record References. Every assertion in the briefs regarding matters in the record, except for undisputed facts offered only for general background, shall be supported by a citation to the Excerpts of Record, unless the filer is exempt from the excerpts requirement.

CIRCUIT ADVISORY COMMITTEE NOTE TO RULE 28–2.8

Because every record-related citation other than undisputed facts offered only for general background shall be supported by the Excerpts of Record, citations directly to the underlying record are otherwise prohibited.

28–2.9. Bankruptcy Appeals. [Abrogated]

[Effective January 1, 1997. Amended effective January 1, 2005. Paragraph 28–2.8 adopted by the Court on an emergency basis, March 22, 2006, subject to further review and consideration by the Advisory Rules Committee. Amended effective July 1, 2007; December 1, 2009; December 1, 2019; December 1, 2020; December 1, 2021.]

RULE 28–3.   LENGTH OF BRIEFS; MOTIONS TO EXCEED PAGE LIMITS [ABROGATED]

(*See* FRAP 32. Form of Briefs, Appendices, and Other Papers, specifically, FRAP 32(a)(7) and Circuit Rule 32. Form of Brief.)

[Abrogated effective January 1996.]

RULE 28–4.   EXTENSIONS OF TIME AND ENLARGEMENTS OF SIZE FOR CONSOLIDATED AND JOINT BRIEFING [ABROGATED]

(*See* Circuit Rule 32–2. Requests to Exceed the Page or Type-Volume Limits.)

[Abrogated effective July 1, 2016.]

RULE 28–5.   MULTIPLE REPLY BRIEFS

A party or group of jointly represented parties is limited to filing a single principal or reply brief, even when responding to multiple briefs by other parties. *(Rev. 6/1/19)*

In the absence of a specifically scheduled due date for the reply brief, the due date for a brief that replies to multiple answering or cross-appeal briefs is calculated from the service date of the last-served answering brief. *(Rev. 1/99)*

Cross Reference: *(New 6/1/19)*

• Circuit Rule 32–2. Requests to Exceed the Page or Type–Volume Limits, specifically, Circuit Rule 32–2(b). Increased word limits for individual briefs responding to multiple briefs

[Effective January 1, 1999. Amended effective June 1, 2019.]

RULE 28–6.   CITATION OF SUPPLEMENTAL AUTHORITIES

The body of a letter filed pursuant to FRAP 28(j) shall not exceed 350 words. If the letter is not required to be filed electronically, litigants shall submit an original of a FRAP 28(j) letter.

CIRCUIT ADVISORY COMMITTEE NOTE TO RULE 28–6

In the interests of promoting full consideration by the Court and fairness to all sides, the parties should file all FRAP 28(j) letters as soon as possible. When practical, the parties are particularly urged to file FRAP 28(j) letters at least 7 days in advance of any scheduled oral argument or within 7 days after notification that the case will be submitted on the briefs.

Cross Reference:

• Circuit Rule 25–4. Calendared Cases

[Effective December 1, 2002. Amended effective July 1, 2006; December 1, 2009.]

FRAP 28.1   CROSS–APPEALS

[For text of rule, see the Federal Rules of Appellate Procedure]

RULE 28.1–1   SEQUENCE, CONTENT, FORM AND LENGTH OF CROSS–APPEAL BRIEFS; CERTIFICATE OF COMPLIANCE

(a) Sequence, Content and Form. The sequence, form and content of briefing are governed by FRAP 28.1(b)—(d) and 32(a)(1), (3), and (4)—(6).

(b) Principal Brief. The length of appellant's principal brief under FRAP 28.1(c)(1) and appellant's response and reply brief under FRAP 28.1 (c)(3) may not exceed 14,000 words.

(c) Principal and Response Brief. The length of appellee's principal and response brief under FRAP 28.1(c)(2) may not exceed 16,500 words.

(d) Reply Brief. The length of appellee's reply brief under FRAP 28.1(c)(4) may not exceed half of the length limit set forth in (b) above.

(e) Exclusions. The materials listed at FRAP 32(f) are excluded from the length limit.

(f) Certificate of Compliance. A brief using a word count length calculation must be accompanied by Form 8 found on the Court's website.

(g) Handwritten or Typewritten Briefs. Handwritten or typewritten briefs filed in cross-appeals may not exceed 50 pages for principal and response/reply briefs; 59 pages for principal/response briefs; and 25 pages for reply briefs.

[Effective December 1, 2016.]

FRAP 29. BRIEF OF AN AMICUS CURIAE

[For text of rule, see the Federal Rules of Appellate Procedure]

RULE 29–1. REPLY BRIEF OF AN AMICUS CURIAE

No reply brief of an amicus curiae will be permitted.

CIRCUIT ADVISORY COMMITTEE NOTE TO RULE 29–1

The filing of multiple amici curiae briefs raising the same points in support of one party is disfavored. Prospective amici are encouraged to file a joint brief. Movants are reminded that the Court will review the amicus curiae brief in conjunction with the briefs submitted by the parties, so that amici briefs should not repeat arguments or factual statements made by the parties.

Amici who wish to join in the arguments or factual statements of a party or other amici are encouraged to file and serve on all parties a short letter so stating in lieu of a brief. If the letter is not required to be filed electronically, the letter shall be provided in an original.

[Effective January 1, 1997. Amended effective December 1, 2009.]

RULE 29–2. BRIEF AMICUS CURIAE SUBMITTED TO SUPPORT OR OPPOSE A PETITION FOR PANEL OR EN BANC REHEARING OR DURING THE PENDENCY OF REHEARING

(a) When Permitted. An amicus curiae may be permitted to file a brief when the Court is considering a petition for panel or en banc rehearing or when the Court has granted rehearing. The United States or its officer or agency, or a State, Territory, Commonwealth, or the District of Columbia may file an amicus curiae brief without the consent of the parties or leave of court. Subject to the provisions of subsection (f) of this rule, any other amicus curiae may file a brief only by leave of court or if the brief states that all parties have consented to its filing.

(b) Motion for Leave to File. The motion must be accompanied by the proposed brief and include the recitals set forth at FRAP 29(a)(3).

(c) Format/Length.

(1) A brief submitted while a petition for rehearing is pending shall be styled as an amicus curiae brief in support of or in opposition to the petition for rehearing or as not supporting either party. A brief submitted during the pendency of panel or en banc rehearing shall be styled as an amicus curiae brief in support of appellant or appellee or as not supporting either party.

(2) A brief submitted while a petition for rehearing is pending may not exceed 15 pages unless it complies with the alternative length limit of 4,200 words. Motions for leave to file a longer brief are strongly disfavored. *(Rev. 12/1/16)*

(3) Unless otherwise ordered by the Court, a brief submitted after the Court has voted to rehear a case en banc may not exceed 25 pages unless it complies with the alternative length limit of 7,000 words. Motions for leave to file a longer brief are strongly disfavored. *(Rev. 7/1/16; Rev 12/1/16)*

(d) Number of Copies.

(1) If a petition for rehearing en banc has been granted and the brief is not required to be submitted electronically, an original and 18 copies of the brief shall be submitted.

(2) For all other briefs described by this rule that are not required to be submitted electronically, an original shall be submitted.

The Clerk may order the submission of paper copies or additional copies of any brief filed pursuant to this rule.

(e) Time for Filing.

(1) *Brief Submitted to Support or Oppose a Petition for Rehearing.* An amicus curiae must serve its brief along with any necessary motion no later than 10 days after the petition or response of the party the amicus wishes to support is filed or is due. An amicus brief that does not support either party must be served along with any necessary motion no later than 10 days after the petition is filed. Motions for extensions of time to file an amicus curiae brief submitted under this rule are disfavored. *(Rev. 12/1/09)*

(2) *Briefs Submitted During the Pendency of Rehearing.* Unless the Court orders otherwise, an amicus curiae supporting the position of the petitioning party or not supporting either party must serve its brief, along with any necessary motion, no later than 21 days after the petition for rehearing is granted. Unless the Court orders otherwise, an amicus curiae supporting the position of the responding party must serve its brief, along with any necessary motion, no later than 35 days after the petition for panel or en banc rehearing is granted. Motions for extensions of time to file an amicus curiae brief submitted under this rule are disfavored. *(Rev. 12/1/09)*

(f) Circulation. Motions for leave to file an amicus curiae brief to support or oppose a petition for panel rehearing are circulated to the panel. Motions for leave to file an amicus curiae brief to support or oppose a petition for en banc rehearing are circulated to all members of the Court. Motions for leave to file an amicus curiae brief during the pendency of en banc rehearing are circulated to the en banc court. *(New 7/1/07)*

Cross Reference:

- FRAP 29. Brief of an Amicus Curiae
- Circuit Rule 25–4. Calendared Cases

CIRCUIT ADVISORY COMMITTEE NOTE TO RULE 29–2

Circuit Rule 29–2 only concerns amicus curiae briefs submitted to support or oppose a petition for panel or en banc rehearing and amicus curiae briefs submitted during the pendency of rehearing. The Court considers the filing of amicus curiae briefs related to petitions for rehearing or en banc review to be appropriate only when the post-disposition deliberations involve novel or particularly complex issues.

FRAP 29(b) permits the timely filing of a non-government entity's amicus curiae brief at this stage only with leave of the Court. Circuit Rule 29–2 also permits such a filing with the consent of all parties, as permitted in FRAP 29(a) for merits briefing. Obtaining such consent relieves the Court of the need to consider a motion. *(Rev. 6/1/19)*

The Court will ordinarily deny motions and disallow stipulations for leave to file an amicus curiae brief where the filing of the brief would result in the recusal of a member of the en banc court. Any member of the Court who would be subject to disqualification in light of the amicus curiae brief may, of course, voluntarily recuse, thereby allowing the filing of the amicus curiae brief. *(New 7/1/07)*

[Effective July 1, 2007. Amended effective December 1, 2009; July 1, 2016; December 1, 2016; June 1, 2019; December 1, 2019.]

RULE 29–3. MOTIONS FOR LEAVE TO FILE AMICUS CURIAE BRIEFS

A motion for leave to file an amicus brief shall state that movant endeavored to obtain the consent of all parties to the filing of the brief before moving the Court for permission to file the proposed brief.

CIRCUIT ADVISORY COMMITTEE NOTE TO RULE 29–3

FRAP 29(a) permits the timely filing of an amicus curiae brief without leave of the Court if all parties consent to the filing of the brief; obtaining such consent relieves the Court of the need to consider a motion.

[Effective January 1, 2012.]

FRAP 30. APPENDIX TO THE BRIEFS

[For text of rule, see the Federal Rules of Appellate Procedure]

RULE 30–1. THE EXCERPTS OF RECORD

30–1.1. Purpose. The Ninth Circuit requires the parties to file Excerpts of Record instead of the Appendix prescribed by FRAP 30. The primary purpose of the excerpts is to compile for the Court all parts of the record, but only those parts of the record, that are relevant and useful to the Court in deciding the appeal.

For purposes of these rules, the terms "Excerpts" and "Excerpts of Record" refer to any type of excerpts submitted by any party, including Supplemental Excerpts and Further Excerpts.

CIRCUIT ADVISORY COMMITTEE NOTE TO RULE 30–1.1

The Excerpts of Record should be a well-organized and accessible compendium of all the documents in the record that are necessary to understand and decide the issues on appeal. Although the Court has access to most of the district court record via PACER, that access is time consuming, and citations to the record serve as a distraction when reading the briefs. The parties should not expect the Court to search through the district court record for the documents that support their arguments on appeal. Therefore, unless a party is exempt from the excerpts-of-record requirement, citations directly to the record are not permitted except for purely background information, such as factual or procedural history, that is undisputed and provided only for general context.

30–1.2. Requirements.

(a) The appellant or petitioner shall submit Excerpts of Record when submitting the opening brief unless the filer is exempt pursuant to Circuit Rule 30–1.3.

(b) The appellee or respondent shall submit Supplemental Excerpts of Record when submitting the answering brief only if the brief refers to documents or portions of documents not included in the initial Excerpts, or if no Excerpts of Record were filed because the appellant or petitioner is exempt pursuant to Circuit Rule 30–1.3.

(c) A non-exempt appellant or petitioner shall submit Further Excerpts of Record when submitting the reply brief only if the brief refers to documents or portions of documents not included in the Excerpts or Supplemental Excerpts.

(d) Any non-exempt party shall submit Supplemental Excerpts of Record when submitting a supplemental brief only if the brief refers to documents or portions of documents not included in any previously filed Excerpts.

(e) All excerpts shall be separate from the brief and submitted electronically at the same time as the brief unless the filing party is exempt from the electronic-filing requirement.

(f) On the same day the excerpts are submitted electronically, the filing party shall serve 1 paper copy of the excerpts on any other party that is not registered for electronic filing, but shall defer submission of paper copies of the excerpts to the Court until directed by the Clerk to do so.

(g) If the filing party is exempt from the electronic-filing requirement, the filing party shall file 3 paper copies of the excerpts at the time the brief is submitted, bound separately from the brief, and serve 1 paper copy on each of the other parties.

(h) Should the Court consider a case en banc, the Clerk will require counsel to submit additional paper copies of the excerpts.

(i) In any petition for review challenging an order of removal in an immigration case, neither party need file Excerpts of Record.

30–1.3. No Excerpts Required for Pro Se Party. A party proceeding without counsel need not file excerpts. If such a party does not file excerpts, counsel for appellee or respondent must file Supplemental Excerpts of Record that contain all of the documents that are cited in the pro se opening brief or otherwise required by Rule 30–1.4, as well as the documents that are cited in the answering brief.

30–1.4. Contents of the Excerpts of Record.

(a) Volume 1 of the Excerpts of Record shall include all decisions being appealed, reviewed, or collaterally challenged, whether oral or written, final or interim. Unless the entire set of excerpts will be submitted in a single volume of no more than 300 pages, Volume 1 of the Excerpts of Record shall not include any other material. This requirement applies to Volume 1 of any Supplemental or Further Excerpts of Record that contain such decisions not included in the initial Excerpts. The documents in the first volume of excerpts ordinarily shall be arranged by file date in reverse chronological order.

(b) Except as provided in subsection (d), additional volumes of any excerpts shall not include any decisions referred to in subsection (a), but shall include all other parts, but only those parts, of the record that are relevant to deciding the appeal. The documents contained in these volumes of excerpts ordinarily shall be arranged in reverse chronological order.

(c) If the excerpts contain the complete trial transcript, the filer may elect to submit the original reporter's transcript as a separate volume(s) of excerpts of no more than 300 pages each, but such volume(s) must be paginated consecutively in accordance with subsection 1.5(c). If documentary trial exhibits, such as written materials and photographs capable of production in PDF format, are relevant to deciding the appeal, they shall be included in the excerpts of record and placed together, either with any separate volume(s) of trial transcripts or at the end of the final volume of unsealed Excerpts of Record (just before the notice of appeal and docket sheet) or, if appropriate, in the final volume of sealed Excerpts. Submission of physical exhibits that are not capable of transmission in PDF format is governed by Circuit Rule 27–14.

(d) When any Excerpts of Record include documents: (1) that are required to be sealed pursuant to statute or rule and submitted under Circuit Rule 27–13(d); or (2) that are being submitted provisionally under seal pursuant to Circuit Rule 27–13(e) or (f); those documents shall be submitted in a separate, final volume(s) of the excerpts. The documents contained in sealed or provisionally sealed volumes ordinarily shall be arranged in reverse chronological order. Pre-sentence reports and related sealed sentencing documents shall not be included in the excerpts, but shall instead be filed using the pre-sentence report filing event. See Circuit Rule 27–13(d).

(e) In social security appeals, the certified administrative record (CAR) shall not be included in the excerpts of record, but shall be submitted by the appellant in its entirety in a separate CAR filing event at the time the opening brief and initial excerpts are filed, unless appellant is exempt from the excerpts requirement, in which case it will be submitted by the appellee at the time the answering brief is filed.

(f) On appeal from a District Court, Bankruptcy Appellate Panel, Bankruptcy Court, or Tax Court case, the notice of appeal and lower court docket sheet shall be included at the end of the last volume in the non-sealed initial Excerpts of Record.

CIRCUIT ADVISORY COMMITTEE NOTE TO RULE 30–1.4

Volume 1 of the Excerpts of Record ordinarily should include:

(a) the judgment or interlocutory order appealed from;

(b) any other orders or rulings, including the text of minute orders (copied into a separate sheet of paper or contained in a separate page from the district court docket sheet), sought to be reviewed;

(c) where an appeal challenges any ruling, order, finding of fact, or conclusion of law, and that ruling, order, finding, or conclusion was delivered orally, that specific portion of the reporter's transcript recording any discussion by court or counsel on which the assignment of error is alleged to rest;

(d) the entire sentencing transcript in any criminal appeal challenging the sentence;

(e) any jury instruction given or refused that presents an issue on appeal; and

(f) any relevant state court decisions in a habeas corpus proceeding.

Circuit Rule 28–2.8 requires every assertion in briefs regarding matters in the record to be supported by a citation to the Excerpts of Record. Excerpts therefore must include, at a minimum, all documents cited by the briefs except for undisputed facts or procedural history offered only for general background.

Legal memoranda and briefs ordinarily are not relevant to the issues on appeal and, therefore, should be excluded from the excerpts. They may be relevant if a party asserts that an issue was waived, forfeited, or not exhausted, to support disputed assertions of procedural history, or in other similar circumstances.

If the briefs cite only certain pages of a long transcript or other document, parties may elect to include only portions of the transcript or document. But the parties should provide enough surrounding pages to provide relevant context and, where a brief raises a sufficiency of the evidence or harmless error argument, the filer ordinarily should include the entire trial transcript.

If the brief is accompanied by a motion to withdraw pursuant to Anders v. California, the initial Excerpts of Record shall include the complete transcripts for the plea hearing or trial and the sentencing hearing. See Circuit Rule 4–1(c)(6).

In criminal cases, the excerpts shall include the final indictment or other charging document.

If the brief raises issues requiring consideration of trial exhibits, whether admitted or excluded, it is counsel's responsibility to provide those exhibits to the Court as part of the excerpts (if they are capable of submission in PDF format) or via separate transmission to the Court pursuant to Circuit Rule 27–14.

The Court prefers excerpts that are organized in reverse chronological order (subject to the provisions relating to the contents of first and sealed volumes), beginning with the most recently filed document or set of documents. For this purpose, transcripts, including trial transcripts, should be placed by hearing date, except that hearings or trials that span multiple dates or sessions should appear in chronological order for that hearing or trial, using the first day of the hearing or trial as the relevant date. Alternative organization of the excerpts is acceptable if better suited to a particular case.

30–1.5. Index and Format.

(a) Except as noted in section (b) below, each set of Excerpts of Record shall be accompanied by a separately bound Table of Contents ("Index Volume") of all documents contained in all numbered volumes of the set, including any separate volumes of trial transcript pursuant to Circuit Rule 30–1.4(c). The Index Volume shall list each document in order, including a citation to where the document may be found in the lower court record, and its location in the volume and page number in the excerpts. When listing the documents in the Index, parties should provide descriptive labels. For example, "Exhibit 12—2018 Deposition of Jeanne Smith" is more helpful than "Exhibit 12 to motion for summary judgment." The individual numbered volumes of excerpts shall no longer include tables of contents.

(b) No volume may exceed 300 pages, including the caption (cover) page. If an entire set of excerpts, including Index and caption page, totals 300 pages or less, they may be submitted together in one single volume.

(c) With the exception of the Index Volume, the pages of each set of excerpts shall be numbered consecutively across all volumes in the set. All pages of each volume shall be included in the consecutive numbering, including but not limited to caption pages, pages used as dividers, blank pages, and certificates of service. The page numbering shall begin with the caption page of the first volume counted as number 1, and every subsequent page across all volumes (including any separate transcript volumes) shall be consecutively numbered. Alternative numbering formats—e.g., using roman numerals or starting each volume with page 1—may not be used. Although caption pages must be included in the consecutive numbering, the page number need not be printed on caption pages. The Index Volume shall be numbered separately when not included in a single volume pursuant to subsection (b).

(d) Each volume must contain a caption (cover) page styled as described in FRAP 32(a), except that the wording "Excerpts of Record" (or "Supplemental Excerpts of Record" or "Further Excerpts of Record") shall be substituted for "Brief." The caption page of each volume, including the index, shall include the volume number ("Volume 2 of 6" or "Index Volume," for example).

(e) The paper copies of all volumes, including the Index Volume and any separate reporter's transcript volumes, shall be bound securely on the left. Paper copies shall be printed on letter-sized light-colored paper with black ink or colored ink where appropriate and the caption pages shall be white. Paper copies of any excerpts may be printed on both sides of the paper, but only if the method of binding allows each volume to lie completely flat when open, such as comb, spiral, coil, or wire binding, and the weight of the paper is sufficient to prevent bleeding through when marked on one side in ink or highlighter.

30–1.6. Citation to the Excerpts of Record. Parties shall cite to the initial Excerpts of Record in the following format: [volume number]–ER–[page number(s)]. If only one volume exists, the volume number shall be omitted. Multi-volume examples: 1–ER–12, 4–ER–874–76. Single-volume example: ER–26–32. The same format applies to Supplemental Excerpts of Record except that "SER" applies rather than "ER." The same format applies to Further Excerpts of Record

except that "FER" applies rather than "ER." Multiple parties on the same side of an appeal who are submitting separate excerpts must include a unique identifier in the citation, such as 1–JonesER–59. Citations to the administrative record in social security cases shall be CAR–[page number].

30–1.7. Prisoner Appeals Without Counsel. In cases involving appeals by prisoners not represented by counsel, the clerk of the district court shall, within 21 days from the receipt of the prisoner's written request, forward to the prisoner copies of the documents comprising the Excerpts of Record so that the prisoner can prepare the briefs on appeal. If the prisoner was granted leave to proceed in forma pauperis at the district court or on appeal, the copies will be produced at no charge to the prisoner.

[Effective January 1, 1997. Amended effective December 1, 2002; July 1, 2003; January 1, 2005; July 1, 2007; December 1, 2009; July 1, 2013; March 23, 2016; December 1, 2019; December 1, 2020.]

RULE 30–2. SANCTIONS FOR FAILURE TO COMPLY WITH CIRCUIT RULE 30–1 [ABROGATED EFFECTIVE DECEMBER 1, 2020]

RULE 30–3. PRISONER APPEALS WITHOUT REPRESENTATION BY COUNSEL

In cases involving appeals by prisoners not represented by counsel, the clerk of the district court shall, within 21 days from the receipt of the prisoner's written request, forward to the prisoner copies of the documents comprising the excerpts of record, so that the prisoner can prepare the briefs on appeal. If the prisoner was granted leave to proceed in forma pauperis at the district court or on appeal, the copies will be produced at no charge to the prisoner. *(Rev. 12/1/09; 6/1/19)*

[Effective January 1, 1997. Amended effective December 1, 2009; June 1, 2019.]

FRAP 31. SERVING AND FILING BRIEFS

[For text of rule, see the Federal Rules of Appellate Procedure]

RULE 31–1. NUMBER OF BRIEFS

Parties submitting a brief electronically shall defer submission of paper copies of the brief until directed by the Clerk to do so, but must serve any unregistered party or exempt counsel with 1 paper copy of the brief on the day that the brief is submitted electronically. Any unregistered party or exempt counsel shall file an original and 6 copies of each brief. If a petition for hearing or rehearing en banc is granted, each party shall file 18 additional copies of its briefs and 10 additional copies of its excerpts of record.

[Effective January 1, 1997. Amended effective January 1, 2005; December 1, 2009; December 1, 2019.]

RULE 31–2. TIME FOR SERVICE AND FILING

31–2.1. Requirement of Timely Filing.

(a) Parties shall observe the briefing schedule set by an order of the Court of Appeals. Specific due dates set by

Court order are not subject to the additional 3–day allowance for service of previous papers by mail set forth in FRAP 26(c). The filing of the appellant's brief before the due date shall not advance the due date for the appellee's brief. If the Court does not set specific due dates for the opening and/or answering brief, the presumptive deadlines of FRAP 31(a) shall apply. However, unless otherwise established by Court order in a particular case, the deadline for filing a reply brief is 21 days from the date of service of the last timely filed answering brief. *(Rev. 12/1/09; 6/1/17)*

(b) *[Abrogated 12/1/09]*

(c) *[Abrogated 1/99]*

31–2.2. Extensions of Time for Filing Briefs.

(a) Streamlined Extensions of Time: If a party has not previously filed a motion for an extension of time to file an opening, answering, reply or cross-appeal brief under subsection (b) of this rule, that party may obtain a single streamlined extension of time to file that brief not to exceed 30 days. The streamlined extension of time is not available:

(1) if a case has been previously expedited;

(2) when a Notice of Oral Argument has issued; or

(3) for any brief filed in a Preliminary Injunction Appeal (Ninth Circuit Rule 3–3), an Incarcerated Recalcitrant Witness Appeal (28 U.S.C. § 1826; Ninth Circuit Rule 3–5) or a Class Action Fairness Act appeal (28 U.S.C. § 1453(c)).

Parties registered for electronic filing may request a streamlined extension of time online via the Appellate Electronic Filing System using the "File Streamlined Request to Extend Time to File Brief" event. A request must be made on or before the brief's due date.

Parties not registered for electronic filing may request a streamlined extension of time by completing Form 13 and placing the form in the mail to the Clerk on or before the brief's due date.

The Clerk will approve requests that comply with the rule and will provide the parties with a new schedule. The Clerk will inform parties not eligible for relief under this subsection as to the appropriate method to obtain relief. *(Rev. 1/1/15)*

(b) Written Motions for Extension of Time to File a Brief: In all other cases, an extension of time may be granted only upon written motion supported by a showing of diligence and substantial need. *(Rev. 1/1/15)*

The motion shall be filed at least 7 days before the expiration of the time prescribed for filing the brief, and shall be accompanied by a declaration stating: *(Rev. 12/1/09)*

(1) when the brief is due;

(2) when the brief was first due;

(3) the length of the requested extension;

(4) the reason an extension is necessary;

(5) movant's representation that movant has exercised diligence and that the brief will be filed within the time requested;

(6) whether any other party separately represented objects to the request, or why the moving party has been unable to determine any such party's position; and

(7) that the court reporter is not in default with regard to any designated transcripts. *(Rev. 12/1/09)*

A conclusory statement as to the press of business does not constitute a showing of diligence and substantial need. *(Rev. 1/96)*

Cross Reference: *(Rev. 12/1/09; Rev. 1/1/15; Rev. 7/1/16)*

• Circuit Rule 11–1. Filing the Reporter's Transcript, specifically, 11–1.2. Notice of Reporter Defaults

• Circuit Rule 27–11. Motions; Effect on Schedule

• Circuit Advisory Committee Note to Rule 32–2 (effect on schedule of motion for leave to file longer brief)

CIRCUIT ADVISORY COMMITTEE NOTE TO RULE 31–2.2

If a party files a motion for a first extension of time to file a brief on or before the due date for the brief, and the Court does not rule on the motion until shortly before the due date, or on or after the due date for the brief, the Court ordinarily will grant some additional time to file the brief even if the Court does not grant the motion in full. Multiple motions for extension of time to file a brief are disfavored, however, and the Court may decline to grant relief if a successive motion fails to demonstrate diligence and substantial need.

If the Court does not act on a motion for extension of time to file a brief before the requested due date, the Court nonetheless expects the moving party to file the brief within the time requested in the motion.

The streamlined extension of time is available only for opening, answering, reply and cross-appeal briefs. A request to extend any other deadline must be made by way of written motion. The streamlined extension of time is intended to be the sole extension of time to file a brief; parties should file a written motion if 30 days is not sufficient time to prepare the brief. If a streamlined extension of time is approved, any further request for an extension of time to file a brief must be made in writing pursuant to Circuit Rule 31–2.2(b). The Clerk's approval of a party's streamlined extension of time to file an initial brief does not prevent that party from obtaining a streamlined extension of time to file a subsequent brief.

The streamlined extension of time replaces the former 14–day telephonic extension of time. *(New 01/01; Rev. 12/1/09; Rev. 1/1/15; Rev. 6/1/19)*

31–2.3. Failure to File Briefs.
If the appellant fails to file a brief within the time allowed by FRAP 31(a) or an extension thereof, the Court may dismiss the appeal pursuant to Circuit Rule 42–1. If appellee does not elect to file a brief, appellee shall notify the Court by letter on or before the due date for the answering brief. Failure to file the brief timely or advise the Court that no brief will be filed will subject counsel to sanctions. *(Rev. 7/93; 12/1/09)*

Cross Reference:

• Circuit Rule 42–1. Dismissal for Failure to Prosecute

[Effective January 1, 1997. Amended effective January 1, 1999; December 1, 2002; December 1, 2009; July 1, 2013; June 1, 2017; June 1, 2019.]

FRAP 32. FORM OF BRIEFS, APPENDICES, AND OTHER PAPERS

[For text of rule, see the Federal Rules of Appellate Procedure]

RULE 32. FORM OF BRIEF [ABROGATED]

(See FRAP 32. Form of Briefs, Appendices, and Other Papers, effective December 1, 1998.)

[Effective January 1, 1997. Abrogated effective January 1, 1999.]

RULE 32-1. LENGTH AND FORM OF BRIEFS, CERTIFICATE OF COMPLIANCE

(a) **Principal Briefs.** The opening and answering briefs filed by appellant and appellee, respectively, may not exceed 14,000 words.

(b) **Reply Brief.** The reply brief filed by appellant may not exceed half of the length set forth in (a) above.

(c) **Exclusions.** The portions of the brief required by FRAP 32(f) are excluded from the length limit calculation.

(d) **Form.** FRAP 32(a)(1)–(6) otherwise governs the brief's form.

(e) **Certificate of Compliance.** A brief using a word count calculation of its length must be accompanied by Form 8, found on the Court's website.

(f) **Handwritten or Typewritten Briefs.** A handwritten or typewritten opening or answering brief may not exceed 50 pages. A handwritten or typewritten reply brief may not exceed 25 pages.

[Effective January 1, 1999. Amended effective December 1, 2002; December 1, 2016.]

RULE 32-2. REQUESTS TO EXCEED THE PAGE OR TYPE-VOLUME LIMITS

(a) **Motions:** The Court disfavors motions to exceed the applicable page or type-volume limits. Except in capital cases, such motions will be granted only upon a showing of diligence and extraordinary and compelling need, such as in a multi-defendant criminal case involving a lengthy trial. A motion for permission to exceed the applicable page or type-volume limits must be filed on or before the brief's due date and must be accompanied by a declaration stating in detail the reasons for the motion.

Any such motions shall be accompanied by a single copy of the brief that the applicant proposes to file and a Form 8 certification as required by Circuit Rule 32-1 as to the word count. The cost of preparing and revising the brief will not be considered by the Court in ruling on the motion.

(b) **When Longer Briefs Are Allowed Automatically:** If no order lengthening the page or type-volume limit has been obtained previously, the Court will allow an extra 5 pages or 1,400 words to separately represented parties that are filing a joint brief. That same longer limit also will be provided to a party or parties that file a single brief answering or replying to either (1) multiple briefs or (2) a longer joint brief filed pursuant to this subsection. Briefs submitted under this subsection must be accompanied by Form 8.

CIRCUIT ADVISORY COMMITTEE NOTE TO RULE 32-2

Motions to exceed the word limit will not be granted absent extraordinary and compelling circumstances. The Court already provides more generous word limits than provided by FRAP and most other Circuits. In almost all cases, the limits provided suffice even for multiple or complex issues. Most overlength briefs could be shorter and unnecessarily burden the Court.

If the Court does not grant a motion for leave to file a longer brief, or grants the motion only in part, the Court ordinarily will provide the party or parties 7 days after the entry of the order to file a compliant brief as directed by the Court. Any order that decides a motion will also make adjustments to the due date(s) for any further briefing.

Rule 32-2(b) encourages separately represented parties to file a joint brief to avoid burdening the Court with repetitive presentations of common facts and issues. The routine lengthening of page or type-volume provided by the rule is intended to accommodate the additional length that may be necessary to permit preparation of a joint brief. A litigant responding to the opposing party's brief as well as an amicus curiae brief filed under FRAP 29(a) is also eligible to file a longer brief automatically.

If a brief that exceeds the usual length limits is submitted by a party or parties ineligible for relief under Rule 32-2(b), the Clerk will reject the brief if it is not accompanied by a motion under Rule 32-2(a).

[Effective January 1, 1999. Amended effective July 1, 2016; July 1, 2016; December 1, 2020.]

RULE 32-3. PAGE/WORD COUNT CONVERSION FORMULA FOR BRIEFS AND OTHER DOCUMENTS

All briefs filed pursuant to court order must conform to the format requirements of FRAP 32(a)(1)–(6).

If an order or rule of this Court sets forth a page limit for a brief or other document, the affected party may comply with the limit by:

(1) filing a monospaced brief of the designated number of pages, or

(2) filing a monospaced or proportionally spaced brief or other document in which the word count divided by 280 does not exceed the designated page limit.

[Effective January 1, 1999. Amended effective December 1, 2016.]

RULE 32-4. BRIEFS AND EXCERPTS OF RECORD IN CAPITAL CASES

Briefs. The requirements of FRAP 32(a)(1)–(6) apply to appeals from district court judgments which finally dispose of a capital case, except that the following type-volume limitation also applies: a principal brief may not exceed 21,000 words and a reply brief may not exceed 9,800 words. The length limit excludes the materials listed at FRAP 32(f). The brief must be accompanied by the Form 8 certificate of compliance.

Excerpts. The appellant shall prepare and file excerpts of record in compliance with Circuit Rule 30-1. An appellant unable to obtain all or parts of the record shall so notify the Court.

In addition to the documents listed in Circuit Rule 30-1.3, excerpts of record in capital cases shall contain all final orders and rulings of all state courts in appellate and post-conviction proceedings. Excerpts of record shall also include all final orders involving the conviction or sentence issued by the Supreme Court of the United States.

[Effective January 1, 1999. Amended effective December 1, 2016.]

RULE 32–5. UNREPRESENTED LITIGANTS

(Abrogated 12/1/16)

Cross Reference:

• Circuit Rule 28–1. Briefs, Applicable Rules

• Circuit Rule 32–1. Length and Form of Briefs, Certificate of Compliance

[Effective January 1, 1999. Amended effective January 1, 2015. Abrogated effective December 1, 2016.]

FRAP 32.1. CITING JUDICIAL DISPOSITIONS

*[For text of rule, see the Federal Rules
of Appellate Procedure]*

FRAP 33. APPEAL CONFERENCES

*[For text of rule, see the Federal Rules
of Appellate Procedure]*

RULE 33–1. CIRCUIT MEDIATION OFFICE

(a) Purpose. The function of the Circuit Mediation Office is to facilitate the voluntary resolution of cases.

(b) Attendance at Mediation Conferences. A judge or circuit mediator may require the attendance of parties, and counsel at a conference or conferences to explore settlement-related issues.

(c) Confidentiality. To encourage efficient and frank settlement discussions, the Court establishes the following rules to achieve strict confidentiality of the mediation process.

(1) The Circuit Mediators will not disclose mediation related communications to the judges or court staff outside the mediation unit.

(2) Documents, e-mail and other correspondence sent only to the Circuit Mediators or to the mediation unit are maintained separately from the court's electronic filing and case management system and are not made part of the public docket.

(3) Should a Circuit Mediator confer separately with any participant in a mediation, those discussions will be maintained in confidence from the other participants in the settlement discussions to the extent that that participant so requests.

(4) Any person, including a Circuit Mediator, who participates in the Circuit Mediation Program must maintain the confidentiality of the settlement process. The confidentiality provisions that follow apply to any communication made at any time in the Ninth Circuit mediation process, including all telephone conferences. Any written or oral communication made by a Circuit Mediator, any party, attorney, or other participant in the settlement discussions:

(A) except as provided in (B), may not be used for any purpose except with the agreement of all parties and the Circuit Mediator; and

(B) may not be disclosed to anyone who is not a participant in the mediation except

(i) disclosure may be made to a client or client representative, an attorney or co-counsel, an insurance representative, or an accountant or other agent of a participant on a need-to-know basis, but only upon receiving assurance from the recipient that the information will be kept confidential;

(ii) disclosure may be made in the context of a subsequent confidential mediation or settlement conference with the agreement of all parties. Consent of the Circuit Mediator is not required.

(5) Written settlement agreements are not confidential except as agreed by the parties.

(6) This rule does not prohibit disclosures that are otherwise required by law.

(d) Binding Determinations by Appellate Commissioner. In the context of a settlement or mediation in a civil appeal, the parties who have otherwise settled the case may stipulate to have one or more issues in the appeal submitted to an appellate commissioner for a binding determination.

CIRCUIT ADVISORY COMMITTEE NOTE TO RULE 33–1

(a) Mediation Conferences. The Circuit Mediation Office is staffed with experienced attorney mediators and is an independent unit in the Court. In any case, the Court may direct that a conference be held, in-person or over the telephone, with counsel, or with counsel and the parties or key personnel. A judge who conducts a settlement conference pursuant to this rule will not participate in the decision on any aspect of the case, except that he or she may vote on whether to take a case en banc. *(Rev. 12/1/09; Rev. 7/1/13)*

Requests by counsel for a conference will be accommodated whenever possible. Parties may request conferences confidentially, either by telephone or by letter directed to the Chief Circuit Mediator. *(Rev. 12/1/09)*

The briefing schedule established by the Clerk's office at the time the appeal is docketed remains in effect unless adjusted by a court mediator to facilitate settlement, or by the Clerk's office pursuant to Circuit Rule 31–2.2. Counsel should discuss settlement with their principals prior to a conference scheduled under this rule. *(Rev. 12/1/09)*

(b) Appeal Case Management Conference. In any case the Court may direct either sua sponte or upon request of a party that a telephone or in-person case management conference be held before an Appellate Commissioner, a senior staff member in the Clerk's office, or a staff attorney. The purpose of a case management conference is to manage the appeal effectively and develop a briefing plan for complex appeals. If a case is selected for a case management conference, counsel shall be notified by order of the date and time of the conference. Case management conferences are held only in exceptional circumstances, such as complex cases involving numerous separately represented litigants or extensive district court/agency proceedings. *(Rev. 1/97)*

(c) Binding Determinations by Appellate Commissioner. Where the parties enter into such a stipulation as set forth at (d) above, the matter may be handled with abbreviated and accelerated briefing and a guaranteed opportunity for in-person or telephonic oral argument before the Appellate Commissioner. The Appellate Commissioner will issue a determination and, if requested, a written statement of reasons. The determination will have no precedential effect and will be final and nonreviewable. Cases will ordinarily be referred to the Appellate Commissioner through the Court's mediation program. In some instances, the Court's pro se unit may also alert parties to the availability of this program. F or further information, please contact the Circuit Mediation Office at (415) 355–7900. *(New 7/1/01; Rev. 7/1/13)*

[Effective January 1, 1997. Amended effective July 1, 2001; December 1, 2009; July 1, 2013.]

FRAP 34. ORAL ARGUMENT

*[For text of rule, see the Federal Rules
of Appellate Procedure]*

RULE 34–1. PLACE OF HEARING

Appeals, applications for original writs, and petitions to review or enforce orders or decisions of administrative agencies may be heard at any session of the Court in the circuit, as designated by the Court. Cases are generally heard in the administrative units where they arise. Petitions to enforce or review orders or decisions of boards, commissions or other administrative bodies shall be heard in the administrative unit in which the person affected by the order or decision is a resident, unless another place of hearing is ordered by the Court.

[Effective January 1, 1997.]

RULE 34–2. CHANGE OF TIME
OR PLACE OF HEARING

No change of the day or place assigned for hearing will be made except by order of the Court for good cause. Only under exceptional circumstances will the Court grant a request to vacate a setting within 14 days of the date set.

[Effective January 1, 1997.]

RULE 34–3. PRIORITY CASES

Any party who believes the case before the Court is entitled to priority in hearing date by virtue of any statute or rule, shall so inform the Clerk in writing no later than the filing of the first brief.

Criminal appeals shall have first priority in hearing or submission date.

Civil appeals in the following categories will receive hearing or submission priority:

(1) Recalcitrant witness appeals brought under 28 U.S.C. § 1826;

(2) Habeas corpus petitions brought under Chapter 153 of Title 28;

(3) Applications for temporary or permanent injunctions;

(4) Appeals alleging deprivation of medical care to the incarcerated or other cruel or unusual punishment;

(5) Appeals entitled to priority on the basis of good cause under 28 U.S.C. § 1657.

Any party who believes the case is entitled to priority in scheduling the date of hearing or submission solely on the basis of good cause under 28 U.S.C. § 1657 shall file a motion for expedition with the clerk at the earliest opportunity.

[Effective January 1, 1997.]

RULE 34–4. CLASSES OF CASES TO
BE SUBMITTED WITHOUT ORAL
ARGUMENT [ABROGATED]

(See FRAP 34(a)(2))

CIRCUIT ADVISORY COMMITTEE
NOTE TO RULE 34–1 TO 34–3

(1) **Appeals Raising the Same Issues.** When other pending cases raise the same legal issues, the Court may advance or defer the hearing of an appeal so that related issues can be heard at the same time. Cases involving the same legal issue are identified during the Court's inventory process. The first panel to whom the issue is submitted has priority. Normally, other panels will enter orders vacating submission and advise counsel of the other pending case when it appears that the first panel's decision is likely to be dispositive of the issue. Panels may also enter orders vacating submission when awaiting the decision of a related case before another court or administrative agency. (Rev. 12/1/09)

(2) **Oral Argument.** Any party to a case may request, or all parties may agree to request, a case be submitted without oral argument. This request or stipulation requires the approval of the panel. Oral argument will not be vacated if any judge on the panel desires that a case be heard. See FRAP 34(f). The Court thoroughly reviews the briefs before oral argument. Counsel therefore should not unnecessarily repeat information and arguments already sufficiently covered in their briefs. Counsel should be completely familiar with the factual record, so as to be prepared to answer relevant questions.

(3) **Disposition.** One judge prepares a draft disposition. The draft is sent to the other two judges for the purpose of obtaining their comments, concurrences, or dissents. Upon adoption of a majority disposition, the author sends it to the Clerk along with any separate concurring or dissenting opinions.

(4) **Mandate.** The mandate of the Court shall issue to the lower tribunal 7 days after expiration of the period to file a petition for rehearing unless the time is shortened or extended by order. (See FRAP 41.) This allows time for filing a petition for rehearing, petition for rehearing en banc, and motion for stay of mandate pending application for writ of certiorari. *(Rev. 12/1/09; Rev. 7/1/16)*

[Effective January 1, 1997. Abrogated effective January 1, 1999.]

FRAP 35. EN BANC DETERMINATION

*[For text of rule, see the Federal Rules
of Appellate Procedure]*

RULE 35–1. PETITION FOR
REHEARING EN BANC

Where a petition for rehearing en banc is made pursuant to FRAP 35(b) in conjunction with a petition for panel rehearing, a reference to the petition for rehearing en banc, as well as to the petition for panel rehearing, shall appear on the cover of the petition.

When the opinion of a panel directly conflicts with an existing opinion by another court of appeals and substantially affects a rule of national application in which there is an overriding need for national uniformity, the existence of such conflict is an appropriate ground for petitioning for rehearing en banc.

[Effective January 1, 1997. Amended effective December 1, 2009.]

RULE 35–2. OPPORTUNITY TO RESPOND

Where a party petitions for hearing or rehearing en banc, the Court will not order a hearing or rehearing en banc without giving the other parties an opportunity to express their views whether hearing or rehearing en banc is appropriate. Where no petition for en banc review is filed, the Court will not ordinarily order a hearing or rehearing en banc without giving counsel an opportunity to respond on the appropriateness of such a hearing.

[Effective January 1, 1997. Amended effective December 1, 2009.]

RULE 35–3. LIMITED EN BANC COURT

The en banc court, for each case or group of related cases taken en banc, shall consist of the Chief Judge of this circuit and 10 additional judges to be drawn by lot from the active judges of the Court. In the absence of the Chief Judge, an 11th active judge shall be drawn by lot, and the most senior active judge on the panel shall preside.

The drawing of the en banc court will be performed by the Clerk or a deputy clerk of the Court in the presence of at least one judge and shall take place on the first working day following the date of the order taking the case or group of related cases en banc.

If a judge whose name is drawn for a particular en banc court is disqualified, recused, or knows that he or she will be unable to sit at the time and place designated for the en banc case or cases, the judge will immediately notify the Chief Judge who will direct the Clerk to draw a replacement judge by lot.

In appropriate cases, the Court may order a rehearing by the full court following a hearing or rehearing en banc.

Cross Reference:

• FRAP 40. Petition for Panel Rehearing

CIRCUIT ADVISORY COMMITTEE
NOTE TO RULE 35–1 TO 35–3

(1) Calculation of Filing Deadline. Litigants are reminded that a petition for rehearing en banc must be received by the clerk in San Francisco on the due date. See FRAP 25(a)(1) and (2)(A) and Circuit Rule 25–2; see also United States v. James, 146 F.3d 1183 (9th Cir. 1998). *(Rev. 12/1/02; 12/1/09; 1/1/12)*

(2) Petition for Rehearing En Banc. When the clerk receives a timely petition for rehearing en banc, copies are sent to all active judges. If the panel grants rehearing it so advises the other members of the Court, and the petition for rehearing en banc is deemed rejected without prejudice to its renewal after the panel completes action on the rehearing. Cases are rarely reheard en banc.

If no petition for rehearing en banc has been submitted and the panel votes to deny rehearing an order to that effect will be prepared and filed.

If a petition for rehearing en banc has been made, any judge may, within 21 days from receipt of the en banc petition, request the panel to make known its recommendation as to en banc consideration. Upon receipt of the panel's recommendation, any judge has 14 days to call for en banc consideration, whereupon a vote will be taken. If no judge requests or gives notice of an intention to request en banc consideration within 21 days of the receipt of the en banc petition, the panel will enter an order denying rehearing and rejecting the petition for rehearing en banc.

Any active judge who is not recused or disqualified and who entered upon active service before the request for an en banc vote is eligible to vote. A judge who takes senior status after a call for a vote may not vote or be drawn to serve on the en banc court. This rule is subject to two exceptions: (1) a judge who takes senior status during the pendency of an en banc case for which the judge has already been chosen as a member of the en banc court may continue to serve on that court until the case is finally disposed of; and (2) a senior judge may elect to be eligible, in the same manner as an active judge, to be selected as a member of the en banc court when it reviews a decision of a panel of which the judge was a member.

The En Banc Coordinator notifies the judges when voting is complete. If the recommendation or request fails of a majority, the En Banc Coordinator notifies the judges and the panel resumes control of the case. The panel then enters an appropriate order denying en banc consideration. The order will not specify the vote tally.

(3) Grant of Rehearing En Banc. When the Court votes to rehear a matter en banc, the Chief Judge will enter an order so indicating. The vote tally is not communicated to the parties. The three-judge panel opinion shall not be cited as precedent by or to this Court or any district court of the Ninth Circuit, except to the extent adopted by the en banc court. *(Rev. 1/1/00)*

After the en banc court is chosen, the judges on the panel decide whether there will be oral argument or additional briefing. If there is to be oral argument, the Chief Judge (or the next senior active judge as the case may be) will enter an order designating the date, time and place of argument. If no oral argument is to be heard, the Chief Judge will designate a date, time, and place for a conference of the en banc court. That date will ordinarily be the submission date of the case. If any issues have been isolated for specific attention, the order may also set forth those issues and additional briefing may be ordered. *(Rev. 1/03; 12/1/09)*

Cross Reference:

• FRAP 32. Form of Briefs, Appendices, and Other Papers on page 133, specifically, FRAP 32(c)(2)

• FRAP 40. Petition for Panel Rehearing on page 159

[Effective January 1, 1997. Amended effective January 1, 2006; July 1, 2007.]

RULE 35–4. FORMAT; NUMBER OF COPIES

(a) Format/Length of Petition and Response. The format and length of a petition for rehearing en banc and any response shall be governed by Circuit Rule 40–1(a).

The petition or response must be accompanied by the completed certificate of compliance found at Form 11.

(b) Number of Copies. If the petition is not required to be filed electronically, a petition for rehearing en banc shall be filed in an original.

[Effective January 1, 1999. Amended effective July 1, 2000; December 1, 2009; December 1, 2021.]

FRAP 36.   ENTRY OF JUDGMENT; NOTICE

*[For text of rule, see the Federal Rules
of Appellate Procedure]*

RULE 36-1.   OPINIONS, MEMORANDA, ORDERS; PUBLICATION

Each written disposition of a matter before this Court shall bear under the number in the caption the designation OPINION, or MEMORANDUM, or ORDER. A written, reasoned disposition of a case or motion which is designated as an opinion under Circuit Rule 36-2 is an OPINION of the Court. It may be an authored opinion or a per curiam opinion. A written, reasoned disposition of a case or a motion which is not intended for publication under Circuit Rule 36-2 is a MEMORANDUM. Any other disposition of a matter before the Court is an ORDER. A memorandum or order shall not identify its author, nor shall it be designated "Per Curiam."

All opinions are published; no memoranda are published; orders are not published except by order of the court. As used in this rule, the term PUBLICATION means to make a disposition available to legal publishing companies to be reported and cited.

[Effective January 1, 1997.]

RULE 36-2.   CRITERIA FOR PUBLICATION

A written, reasoned disposition shall be designated as an OPINION if it:

(a) Establishes, alters, modifies or clarifies a rule of federal law, or

(b) Calls attention to a rule of law that appears to have been generally overlooked, or

(c) Criticizes existing law, or

(d) Involves a legal or factual issue of unique interest or substantial public importance, or

(e) Is a disposition of a case in which there is a published opinion by a lower court or administrative agency, unless the panel determines that publication is unnecessary for clarifying the panel's disposition of the case, or

(f) Is a disposition of a case following a reversal or remand by the United States Supreme Court, or

(g) Is accompanied by a separate concurring or dissenting expression, and the author of such separate expression requests publication of the disposition of the Court and the separate expression.

[Effective January 1, 1997. Amended effective January 1, 2012.]

RULE 36-3.   CITATION OF UNPUBLISHED DISPOSITIONS OR ORDERS

(a) Not Precedent. Unpublished dispositions and orders of this Court are not precedent, except when relevant under the doctrine of law of the case or rules of claim preclusion or issue preclusion.

(b) Citation of Unpublished Dispositions and Orders Issued on or After January 1, 2007. Unpublished dispositions and orders of this Court issued on or after January 1, 2007 may be cited to the courts of this circuit in accordance with FRAP 32.1.

(c) Citation of Unpublished Dispositions and Orders Issued Before January 1, 2007. Unpublished dispositions and orders of this Court issued before January 1, 2007 may not be cited to the courts of this circuit, except in the following circumstances.

(i) They may be cited to this Court or to or by any other court in this circuit when relevant under the doctrine of law of the case or rules of claim preclusion or issue preclusion.

(ii) They may be cited to this Court or by any other courts in this circuit for factual purposes, such as to show double jeopardy, sanctionable conduct, notice, entitlement to attorneys' fees, or the existence of a related case.

(iii) They may be cited to this Court in a request to publish a disposition or order made pursuant to Circuit Rule 36-4, or in a petition for panel rehearing or rehearing en banc, in order to demonstrate the existence of a conflict among opinions, dispositions, or orders.

[Adopted effective July 1, 2000. Amended effective January 1, 2007.]

RULE 36-4.   REQUEST FOR PUBLICATION

Publication of any unpublished disposition may be requested by letter addressed to the Clerk, stating concisely the reasons for publication. Such a request will not be entertained unless received within 60 days of the issuance of this Court's disposition. A copy of the request for publication must be served on the parties to the case. The parties will have 14 days from the date of service to notify the Court of any objections they may have to the publication of the disposition. If such a request is granted, the unpublished disposition will be redesignated an opinion.

[Effective January 1, 1997. Amended effective December 1, 2009.]

RULE 36-5.   ORDERS FOR PUBLICATION

An order may be specially designated for publication by a majority of the judges acting and when so published may be used for any purpose for which an opinion may be used. Such a designation should be indicated when filed with the Clerk by the addition of the words "FOR PUBLICATION" on a separate line.

[Effective January 1, 1997.]

RULE 36-6.   PERIODIC NOTICE TO PUBLISHING COMPANIES [ABROGATED]

CIRCUIT ADVISORY COMMITTEE
NOTE TO RULES 36-1 TO 36-5

The clerk's office is not given advance notice as to when a disposition will be delivered by the judges for filing and, therefore, cannot supply such information to counsel. When a disposition is filed, the Clerk mails or electronically transmits notice of entry of judgment and a copy of the disposition to counsel and the district judge from whom the appeal was taken. All dispositions are public unless ordered sealed by the Court. Once a disposition is filed with the Clerk, anyone may obtain copies of printed decisions by making a written request to the clerk's office, accompanied by a $2.00 fee and self-addressed envelope. Opinions are also available on the day of filing on the Court's website at www.ca9.uscourts.gov and by subscription to the Court's RSS feed at http://www.ca9.uscourts.gov/rss/. Opinions are subject to typographical error. The cooperation of the Bar in calling apparent errors to the attention of the clerk's office is solicited. *(Rev. 12/1/09)*

FRAP 37. INTEREST ON JUDGMENT

[For text of rule, see the Federal Rules of Appellate Procedure]

FRAP 38. FRIVOLOUS APPEAL— DAMAGES AND COSTS

[For text of rule, see the Federal Rules of Appellate Procedure]

FRAP 39. COSTS

[For text of rule, see the Federal Rules of Appellate Procedure]

RULE 39–1. COSTS AND ATTORNEYS FEES ON APPEAL

39–1.1. Bill of Costs. The itemized and verified bill of costs required by FRAP 39(d) shall be submitted on the standard Form 10 provided by this Court. It shall include the following information:

(1) The number of copies of the briefs or excerpts of record reproduced; and

(2) The actual cost per page for each document.

39–1.2. Number of Briefs and Excerpts. Costs will be allowed for the required number of paper copies of briefs and 1 additional copy. Costs will also be allowed for any paper copies of the briefs that the eligible party was required to serve.

If excerpts of record were filed, costs will be allowed for the number of copies of the excerpts of record ordered by the Court to be produced, plus 1 copy for the filer and 1 copy for each party required to be served in paper form.

39–1.3. Cost of Reproduction. In taxing costs for photocopying documents, the clerk shall tax costs at a rate not to exceed 10 cents per page, or at actual cost, whichever is less.

39–1.4. Untimely Filing. Untimely cost bills will be denied unless a motion showing good cause is filed with the bill.

39–1.5. Objection to Bill of Costs. If a response opposing a cost bill is filed, the cost bill shall be treated as a motion under FRAP 27.

The Clerk or a deputy clerk may prepare and enter an order disposing of a cost bill, subject to reconsideration by the Court if exception is filed within 14 days after the entry of the order.

39–1.6. Request for Attorneys Fees.

(a) *Time Limits.* Absent a statutory provision to the contrary, a request for attorneys' fees shall be filed no later than 14 days after the expiration of the period within which a petition for rehearing may be filed, unless a timely petition for rehearing is filed. If a timely petition for rehearing is filed, the request for attorneys fees shall be filed no later than 14 days after the Court's disposition of the petition.

(b) *Contents.* A request for an award of attorneys fees must be supported by a memorandum showing that the party seeking fees is legally entitled to them and must be accompanied by Form 9 or a document that contains substantially the same information, along with:

(1) a detailed itemization of the tasks performed each date and the amount of time spent by each lawyer and paralegal on each task;

(2) a showing that the hourly rates claimed are legally justified; and

(3) an affidavit or declaration attesting to the accuracy of the information. All applications must include a statement that sets forth the application's timeliness. The request must be filed separately from any cost bill.

CIRCUIT ADVISORY COMMITTEE NOTE TO RULES 39–1

Forms for attorneys' fees and cost bills are found at Forms 9 and 10, which are available from the Clerk's Office or may be accessed via the Court's Website (www.ca9.uscourts.gov). *(Rev. 7/1/07; 12/1/18)*

Calculation of Cost Bill Filing Deadline. Litigants are reminded that a cost bill must be received by the Clerk in San Francisco by the due date. See FRAP 25(a)(1) and (2)(A) and Circuit Rule 25–2; but see FRAP 25(a)(2)(C) (document filed by inmate timely if deposited in institution's internal mailing system on or before due date). The deadline is strictly enforced. See Mollura v. Miller, 621 F.2d 334 (9th Cir. 1980). *(New 1/1/05, Rev. 7/1/07)*

Equal Access to Justice Act Applications. Counsel filing applications under 28 U.S.C. § 2412 should carefully review the statutory requirements concerning the timeliness and the contents of the application. In computing the applicable hourly rate under the Equal Access to Justice Act, adjusted for cost-of-living increases, counsel should be aware of the formula set forth in Thangaraja v. Gonzales, 428 F.3d 870, 876–77 (9th Cir. 2005). *(New 7/1/07)*

39–1.7. Opposition to Request for Attorneys Fees. Any party from whom attorneys fees are requested may file an objection to the request. The party seeking fees may file a reply to the objection. The time periods set forth in FRAP 27(a)(3)(A) and (4) for responses and replies to motions govern the intervals for filing an objection to the request and reply to an objection. *(Rev. 7/1/06)*

39–1.8. Request for Transfer. Any party who is or may be eligible for attorneys fees on appeal to this Court may, within the time permitted in Circuit Rule 39–1.6, file a motion to transfer consideration of attorneys fees on appeal to the district court or administrative agency from which the appeal was taken.

39–1.9. Referral to Appellate Commissioner. When the Court has awarded attorneys fees on appeal or on application for extraordinary writ, and a party opposes the amount of attorneys fees requested by the prevailing party, the Court may refer to the Appellate Commissioner the determination of an appropriate amount of attorneys fees.

Within 14 days after the entry of an Appellate Commissioner's order awarding or denying attorneys fees, a party may file a motion for reconsideration. The motion is directed initially to the Appellate Commissioner. If the Appellate Commissioner is disinclined to grant reconsideration, the Appellate Commissioner will refer the motion to the Court.

No response to a motion for reconsideration of a fee order is permitted unless requested by the Appellate Commissioner or the Court, but ordinarily neither the Appellate Commissioner nor the Court will grant reconsideration without requesting a response. *(Rev. 1/97; 12/1/09; 7/1/16)*

Cross Reference:

• Circuit Rule 27–10. Motions for Reconsideration on page 98

[Effective January 1, 1997. Amended effective July 1, 1997; July 1, 2001; December 1, 2002; January 1, 2005; July 1, 2006; July 1, 2007; December 1, 2009; July 1, 2016; December 1, 2019.]

RULE 39–2. ATTORNEYS FEES AND EXPENSES UNDER THE EQUAL ACCESS TO JUSTICE ACT [ABROGATED]

FRAP 40. PETITION FOR PANEL REHEARING

[For text of rule, see the Federal Rules of Appellate Procedure]

RULE 40–1. FORMAT; NUMBER OF COPIES

(a) Format/Length of Petition and Response. The format of a petition for panel rehearing or rehearing en banc and any response is governed by FRAP 32(c)(2). The petition may not exceed 15 pages unless it complies with the alternative length limitation of 4,200 words. A response, when ordered by the Court, must comply with the same length limits as the petition.

If an unrepresented litigant elects to file a form brief pursuant to Circuit Rule 28–1, a petition for panel rehearing or for rehearing en banc need not comply with FRAP 32.

The petition or response must be accompanied by the completed certificate of compliance found at Form 11.

(b) Number of Copies. If the petition is not required to be filed electronically, an original shall be filed.

(c) Copy of Panel Decision. The petition for panel or en banc rehearing shall be accompanied by a copy of the panel's order, memorandum disposition or opinion being challenged.

Cross Reference:

• FRAP 32. Form of Briefs, Appendices, and Other Papers on page 132, specifically, FRAP 32(c)(2)

• Circuit Rule 28–1. Briefs, Applicable Rules on page 107

CIRCUIT ADVISORY COMMITTEE NOTE TO RULE 40–1

Litigants are reminded that a petition for rehearing must be received by the Clerk in San Francisco on the due date. See FRAP

25(a)(1) and (2)(A) and Circuit Rule 25–2; see also United States v. James, 146 F.3d 1183 (9th Cir. 1998).

[Effective January 1, 1999. Amended effective July 1, 2000; July 1, 2006; December 1, 2009; December 1, 2016; December 1, 2021.]

RULE 40–2. PUBLICATION OF PREVIOUSLY UNPUBLISHED DISPOSITION

An order to publish a previously unpublished memorandum disposition in accordance with Circuit Rule 36–4 extends the time to file a petition for rehearing to 14 days after the date of the order of publication or, in all civil cases in which the United States or an agency or officer thereof is a party, 45 days after the date of the order of publication. If the mandate has issued, the petition for rehearing shall be accompanied by a motion to recall the mandate.

[Effective January 1, 1997.]

FRAP 41. MANDATE: CONTENTS; ISSUANCE AND EFFECTIVE DATE; STAY

[For text of rule, see the Federal Rules of Appellate Procedure]

RULE 41–1. STAY OF MANDATE

In the interest of minimizing unnecessary delay in the administration of criminal justice, a motion for stay of mandate pursuant to FRAP 41(d) pending petition to the Supreme Court for certiorari, will not be granted as a matter of course, but will be denied if the Court determines that the petition for certiorari would be frivolous or filed merely for delay.

In other cases, including National Labor Relations Board proceedings, the Court may likewise deny a motion for stay of mandate upon the basis of a similar determination.

CIRCUIT ADVISORY COMMITTEE NOTE TO RULES 41–1

Only in exceptional circumstances will a panel order the mandate to issue immediately upon the filing of a disposition. Such circumstances include cases where a petition for rehearing, or petition for writ of certiorari would be legally frivolous; or where an emergency situation requires that the action of the Court become final and mandate issue at once. The mandate will not be stayed automatically upon the filing of an application to the Supreme Court for writ of certiorari. However, a stay may be granted upon motion.

A motion to stay or recall the mandate will not be routinely granted; it will be denied if the Court determines that the application for certiorari would be frivolous or is made merely for delay. *(Rev. 12/1/09)*

In general, a party has 90 days from the entry of judgment or the denial of a timely petition for rehearing, whichever is later, in which to petition for a writ of certiorari. A circuit court cannot extend this period; application for an extension must be made to the Supreme Court. Counsel should be mindful that the judgment is entered on the day of the Court's decision and not when the mandate — i.e., a certified copy of the judgment — is issued. *(New 1/1/03; Rev. 7/1/16)*

[Effective January 1, 1997. Amended effective December 1, 2009.]

RULE 41–2. TIMING OF MANDATE

In cases disposed of by an order of a motions panel, a mandate will issue 7 days after the time to file a motion for reconsideration expires pursuant to Circuit Rule 27–10, or 7 days after entry of an order denying a timely motion for such relief, whichever is later.

Cross Reference:

- FRAP 35. En Banc Determination, specifically, FRAP 35(c)

- FRAP 40. Petition for Panel Rehearing, specifically, FRAP 40(a)(1)

[Effective January 1, 2004. Amended effective December 1, 2009; December 1, 2016.]

FRAP 42. VOLUNTARY DISMISSAL

[For text of rule, see the Federal Rules of Appellate Procedure]

RULE 42–1. DISMISSAL FOR FAILURE TO PROSECUTE

When an appellant fails to file a timely record, pay the docket fee, file a timely brief, or otherwise comply with rules requiring processing the appeal for hearing, an order may be entered by the clerk dismissing the appeal. In all instances of failure to prosecute an appeal to hearing as required, the Court may take such other action as it deems appropriate, including imposition of disciplinary and monetary sanctions on those responsible for prosecution of the appeal.

[Effective January 1, 1997.]

RULE 42–2. TERMINATION OF BAIL FOLLOWING DISMISSAL

Upon dismissal of an appeal in any case in which an appellant has obtained a release from custody upon a representation that he is appealing the judgment of the district court, the Clerk will notify the appropriate district court that the appeal has been dismissed and that the basis for the continued release on bail or recognizance no longer exists.

[Effective January 1, 1997.]

FRAP 43. SUBSTITUTION OF PARTIES

[For text of rule, see the Federal Rules of Appellate Procedure]

FRAP 44. CASE INVOLVING A CONSTITUTIONAL QUESTION WHEN THE UNITED STATES OR THE RELEVANT STATE IS NOT A PARTY

[For text of rule, see the Federal Rules of Appellate Procedure]

FRAP 45. CLERK'S DUTIES

[For text of rule, see the Federal Rules of Appellate Procedure]

FRAP 46. ATTORNEYS

[For text of rule, see the Federal Rules of Appellate Procedure]

RULE 46–1. ATTORNEYS

46–1.1. Forms for Written Motions. Written motions for admission to the bar of the Court shall be on the form approved by the Court and furnished by the Clerk.

46–1.2. Time for Application. Any attorney who causes a case to be docketed in this Court or who enters an appearance in this Court, and who is not already admitted to the Bar of the Court, shall simultaneously apply for admission.

[Effective January 1, 1997.]

RULE 46–2. ATTORNEY SUSPENSION, DISBARMENT OR OTHER DISCIPLINE

(a) Conduct Subject to Discipline. This Court may impose discipline on any attorney practicing before this Court who engages in conduct violating applicable rules of professional conduct, or who fails to comply with rules or orders of this Court. The discipline may consist of disbarment, suspension, reprimand, counseling, education, a monetary penalty, restitution, or any other action that the Court deems appropriate and just.

(b) Initiation of Disciplinary Proceedings Based on Conduct Before This Court. The Chief Judge or a panel of judges may initiate disciplinary proceedings based on conduct before this Court by issuing an order to show cause under this rule that identifies the basis for imposing discipline.

(c) Reciprocal Discipline. An attorney who practices before this Court shall provide the Clerk of this Court with a copy of any order or other official notification that the attorney has been subjected to suspension or disbarment in another jurisdiction. When this Court learns that a member of the bar of this Court has been disbarred or suspended from the practice of law by any court or other competent authority or resigns during the pendency of disciplinary proceedings, the Clerk shall issue an order to show cause why the attorney should not be suspended or disbarred from practice in this Court.

(d) Response. An attorney against whom an order to show cause is issued shall have 28 days from the date of the order in which to file a response. The attorney may include in the response a request for a hearing pursuant to FRAP 46(c). The failure to request a hearing will be deemed a waiver of any right to a hearing. The failure to file a timely response may result in the imposition of discipline without further notice.

(e) Hearings on Disciplinary Charges. If requested, the Court will hold a hearing on the disciplinary charges, at which the attorney may be represented by counsel. In a matter based on an order to show cause why reciprocal discipline should not be imposed, an appellate commissioner will conduct the hearing. In a matter based on an order to show cause based on conduct before this Court, the Court may refer the matter to an appellate commissioner or other judicial officer to conduct the hearing. In appropriate cases, the Court may appoint an attorney to prosecute charges of misconduct.

(f) Report and Recommendation. If the matter is referred to an appellate commissioner or other judicial officer, that judicial officer shall prepare a report and recommendation. The report and recommendation shall be served on the attorney, and the attorney shall have 21 days from the date of the order within which to file a response. The report and recommendation together with any response shall be presented to a three-judge panel.

(g) Final Disciplinary Action. The final order in a disciplinary proceeding shall be issued by a three-judge panel. If the Court disbars or suspends the attorney, a copy of the final order shall be furnished to the appropriate courts and state disciplinary agencies. If the order imposes a sanction of $1,000 or more, the Court may furnish a copy of the order to the appropriate courts and state disciplinary agencies. If a copy of the final order is distributed to other courts or state disciplinary agencies, the order will inform the attorney of that distribution.

(h) Reinstatement. A suspended or disbarred attorney may file a petition for reinstatement with the Clerk. The petition shall contain a concise statement of the circumstances of the disciplinary proceedings, the discipline imposed by this Court, and the grounds that justify reinstatement of the attorney.

(i) Monetary Sanctions. Nothing in the rule limits the Court's power to impose monetary sanctions as authorized under other existing authority.

CIRCUIT ADVISORY COMMITTEE NOTE TO RULES 46–2

The Court may impose monetary sanctions as follows:

(1) Against a party, its counsel, or both under FRAP 38, where the Court determines that "an appeal is frivolous, it may award just damages and single or double costs to the appellee."

(2) Against a party, its counsel, or both under 28 U.S.C. § 1912, "[w]here a judgment is affirmed by . . . a court of appeals, the Court in its discretion may adjudge to the prevailing party just damages for his delay, and single or double costs."

(3) Under 28 U.S.C. § 1927, where counsel "so multiplies the proceedings in any case unreasonably or vexatiously," counsel "may be required by the Court to satisfy personally the excess costs, expenses and attorneys' fees reasonably incurred because of such conduct."

(4) Abrogated 12/1/20

(5) Under Circuit Rule 42–1, against counsel for "failure to prosecute an appeal to hearing as required by FRAP and the Circuit Rules.

(6) Against counsel for failure to comply with the requirements of FRAP 28 and Circuit Rules 28–1 through 28–3, dealing with the form and content of briefs on appeal. See, e.g., Mitchel v. General Electric Co., 689 F.2d 877 (9th Cir. 1982).

(7) Against counsel for conduct that violates the orders or other instructions of the Court, or for failure to comply with the Federal Rules of Appellate Procedure or any Circuit Rule.

(8) Under the inherent powers of the Court. See, e.g., Chambers v. Nasco, Inc., 501 U.S. 32, 45–50 (1991).

(9) As a form of discipline under FRAP 46(c) and Circuit Rule 46–2, with notice of such sanctions provided to the appropriate courts and state disciplinary agencies when the Court deems such notice to be justified. (Rev. 1/1/02)

[Adopted effective January 1, 2002. Amended effective December 1, 2009; January 1, 2012; December 1, 2020.]

RULE 46–3. CHANGE OF ADDRESS

Changes in the address of counsel and pro se litigants registered for the Appellate Electronic Filing System must be reported by updating their account at: https://pacer.psc.uscourts.gov/pscof/login.jsf. Changes in the address of counsel and pro se litigants who are exempt from or who are not registered for the Appellate Electronic Filing System must be reported to the Clerk of this Court immediately and in writing.

[Effective January 1, 1997. Amended effective December 1, 2009.]

RULE 46–4. PARTICIPATION OF LAW STUDENTS

An eligible law student acting under the supervision of a member of the bar of this Court may appear on behalf of any client in a case before this Court with the written consent of the client if the Requirements for Student Practice before this Court are met. The Requirements for Student Practice are available from the Clerk of Court and on the website at www.ca9.uscourts.gov.

[Effective January 1, 1997. Amended effective January 1, 2005.]

RULE 46–5. RESTRICTIONS ON PRACTICE BY FORMER COURT EMPLOYEES

No former employee of the Court shall participate or assist, by way of representation, consultation, or otherwise, in any case that was pending in the Court during the employee's period of employment. It shall be the responsibility of any former employee, as well as the persons employing or associating with a former employee in the practice of law before this Court, to ensure compliance with this rule.

An attorney who is a former employee may apply to the Court for an exemption. The application must demonstrate that the attorney had no direct or indirect involvement with the case during employment with the Court, and that the attorney was not employed or assigned in the chambers of any judge who participated in the case during the attorney's employment with the Court.

CIRCUIT ADVISORY COMMITTEE NOTE TO RULE 46–5

The rule is intended to avoid the appearance of impropriety if a former court employee were to work on a matter that was pending in the court during the employee's period of employment.

With respect to attorneys employed or assigned in the chambers of any judge, an application for an exemption shall show that the judge did not participate in ruling on any motion or other aspect of the case, including making, responding to, or voting on an en banc call during the employee's period of employment. *(New 7/1/13)*

[Effective January 1, 1997. Amended effective January 1, 2011; July 1, 2013.]

FRAP 47.   LOCAL RULES BY
COURTS OF APPEALS

*[For text of rule, see the Federal Rules
of Appellate Procedure]*

RULE 47–1.   EFFECTIVE DATE OF RULES

Amendments to these rules shall be effective on December 1 or June 1 following their adoption, unless otherwise directed by the Court.

CIRCUIT ADVISORY COMMITTEE NOTE TO RULE 47–1

If members of the bar or public have suggestions for new rules or amendments to the rules, such suggestions should be directed to the Clerk of Court who shall take appropriate action.

[Effective January 1, 1997. Amended effective December 1, 2016.]

RULE 47–2.   ADVISORY COMMITTEE
ON RULES

(a) Function. Pursuant to 28 U.S.C. § 2077(b), the Chief Judge shall appoint an advisory committee on Ninth Circuit Court of Appeals rules and internal operating procedures. The committee shall generally provide a forum for ongoing study of the Court's rules and internal operating procedures, including:

(1) proposing rule changes and commenting on changes proposed by the Court,

(2) considering public comments, including comments from the bar, and

(3) conducting periodic meetings with members of the bar throughout the circuit and reporting back to the committee and the Court the results and any recommendations arising from such meetings.

(b) Membership. The Chief Judge shall appoint three judges, twelve practitioners and one member of a law faculty to serve on the committee for three years. The attorney members shall be selected in a manner that seeks both representation of the various geographic areas in the circuit and the distinct types of litigation considered by the Court. A member of the Lawyer Representatives Coordinating Committee (LRCC) shall be appointed to a two-year term on the Rules committee. That member shall serve as a liaison between the LRCC and Advisory Rules Committee. In addition, if a member of the national Advisory Committee on Appellate Rules is appointed from within the jurisdiction of the Ninth Circuit, that member shall be invited to participate as an ex-officio voting member of the Advisory Rules Committee.

(c) Meetings. The committee shall meet at least once a year and shall have additional meetings as the committee deems appropriate.

[Effective January 1, 1997. Amended effective July 1, 2000.]

FRAP 48.   MASTERS

*[For text of rule, see the Federal Rules
of Appellate Procedure]*

APPENDIX OF FORMS

NINHT CIRCUIT FORMS

FORM 1. NOTICE OF APPEAL FROM A JUDGMENT OR ORDER OF A UNITED STATES DISTRICT COURT

UNITED STATES COURT OF APPEALS
FOR THE NINTH CIRCUIT

Form 1. Notice of Appeal from a Judgment or Order of a United States District Court

Name of U.S. District Court:

U.S. District Court case number:

Date case was first filed in U.S. District Court:

Date of judgment or order you are appealing:

Fee paid for appeal? *(appeal fees are paid at the U.S. District Court)*

⊂ Yes   ⊂ No   ⊂ IFP was granted by U.S. District Court

List all Appellants *(List **each** party filing the appeal. Do not use "et al." or other abbreviations.)*

Is this a cross-appeal? ⊂ Yes   ⊂ No

If Yes, what is the first appeal case number?

Was there a previous appeal in this case?   ⊂ Yes   ⊂ No

If Yes, what is the prior appeal case number?

Your mailing address:

City: State: Zip Code:

Prisoner Inmate or A Number (if applicable):

Signature   **Date**

Complete and file with the attached representation statement in the U.S. District Court

Feedback or questions about this form? Email us at forms@ca9.uscourts.gov

[Effective December 1, 2018.]

FORM 2.   NOTICE OF APPEAL FROM A DECISION
OF THE UNITED STATES TAX COURT
UNITED STATES COURT OF APPEALS
FOR THE NINTH CIRCUIT

Form 2. Notice of Appeal from a Decision of the United States Tax Court

U.S. Tax Court case number:

Date case was first filed in U.S. Tax Court:

Date of judgment or order you are appealing:

Fee paid for appeal? *(appeal fees are paid at the U.S. Tax Court)*   ⊙ Yes   ⊙ No

List all Appellants *(List each party filing the appeal. Do not use "et al." or other abbreviations.)*

Was there a previous appeal in this case?   ⊙ Yes   ⊙ No

If Yes, what is the prior appeal case number?

Your mailing address:

City: State: Zip Code:

Prisoner Inmate or A Number (if applicable):

Signature   **Date**

Complete and file with the attached representation statement in the U.S. Tax Court

Feedback or questions about this form? Email us at forms@ca9.uscourts.gov

[Effective December 1, 2018.]

FORM 3.   PETITION FOR REVIEW OF ORDER OF A FEDERAL AGENCY, BOARD, COMMISSION, OR OFFICER

UNITED STATES COURT OF APPEALS
FOR THE NINTH CIRCUIT

Form 3. Petition for Review of Order of a Federal Agency, Board, Commission, or Officer

Name of Federal Agency, Board, Commission, or Officer:

Date of judgment or order you are challenging:

Fee paid for petition?   ○ Yes   ○ No

List all Petitioners *(List each party filing the petition. Do not use "et al." or other abbreviations.)*

For immigration cases:

    Alien Number(s):

    Is petitioner(s) detained?   ○ Yes   ○ No

    Has petitioner(s) moved the BIA to reopen?   ○ Yes   ○ No

    Has petitioner(s) applied to the district director for an   ○ Yes   ○ No
    adjustment of status?

Have you filed a previous petition for review from this agency? ○ Yes   ○ No

If Yes, what is the prior 9th Circuit case number?

Your mailing address:

City: State: Zip Code:

Prisoner Inmate or A Number (if applicable):

Signature   **Date**

*Complete and file with the attached representation statement and the order being challenged.
See, e.g., Circuit Rule 15-4.*

Feedback or questions about this form? Email us at forms@ca9.uscourts.gov

203

Representation Statement for Petition for Review

Petitioner(s) *(List **each** party filing the petition, do not use "et al." or other abbreviations.)*

Name(s) of party/parties:

Name(s) of counsel (if any):

Address:

Telephone number(s):

Email(s):

Is counsel registered for Electronic Filing in the 9th Circuit?   ☐ Yes   ☐ No

Respondent(s) *(List only the names of parties and counsel (if known) who will oppose you in the petition. List separately represented parties separately.)*

Name(s) of party/parties:

Name(s) of counsel (if any known):

Address:

Telephone number(s):

Email(s):

To list additional parties and/or counsel, attach additional pages as necessary.

Feedback or questions about this form? Email us at *forms@ca9.uscourts.gov*

[Effective December 1, 2018.]

FORM 4. MOTION AND AFFIDAVIT FOR PERMISSION TO PROCEED IN FORMA PAUPERIS
UNITED STATES COURT OF APPEALS
FOR THE NINTH CIRCUIT

Form 4. Motion and Affidavit for Permission to Proceed in Forma Pauperis

Instructions for this form: http://www.ca9.uscourts.gov/forms/form04instructions.pdf

9th Cir. Case Number(s) [   ]

Case Name [   ]

Affidavit in support of motion: I swear under penalty of perjury that I am financially unable to pay the docket and filing fees for my appeal. I believe my appeal has merit. I swear under penalty of perjury under United States laws that my answers on this form are true and correct. 28 U.S.C. § 1746; 18 U.S.C. § 1621.

Signature [   ]   **Date** [   ]

The court may grant a motion to proceed in forma pauperis if you show that you cannot pay the filing fees **and** you have a non-frivolous legal issue on appeal. Please state your issues on appeal. (*attach additional pages if necessary*)

Feedback or questions about this form? Email us at forms@ca9.uscourts.gov

205

1. *For both you and your spouse, estimate the average amount of money received from each of the following sources during the past 12 months. Adjust any amount that was received weekly, biweekly, quarterly, semiannually, or annually to show the monthly rate. Use gross amounts, that is, amounts before any deductions for taxes or otherwise.*

Income Source	Average monthly amount during the past 12 months		Amount expected next month	
	You	Spouse	You	Spouse
Employment	$	$	$	$
Self-Employment	$	$	$	$
Income from real property (such as rental income)	$	$	$	$
Interest and Dividends	$	$	$	$
Gifts	$	$	$	$
Alimony	$	$	$	$
Child Support	$	$	$	$
Retirement (such as social security, pensions, annuities, insurance)	$	$	$	$
Disability (such as social security, insurance payments)	$	$	$	$
Unemployment Payments	$	$	$	$
Public-Assistance (such as welfare)	$	$	$	$
Other (specify)	$	$	$	$
TOTAL MONTHLY INCOME:	$	$	$	$

Feedback or questions about this form? Email us at forms@ca9.uscourts.gov

2. *List your employment history for the past two years, most recent employer first.*
   (Gross monthly pay is before taxes or other deductions.)

Employer	Address	Dates of Employment		Gross Monthly Pay
		From		$
		To		
		From		$
		To		
		From		$
		To		
		From		$
		To		

3. *List your spouse's employment history for the past two years, most recent employer first.*
   (Gross monthly pay is before taxes or other deductions.)

Employer	Address	Dates of Employment		Gross Monthly Pay
		From		$
		To		
		From		$
		To		
		From		$
		To		
		From		$
		To		

Feedback or questions about this form? Email us at forms@ca9.uscourts.gov

4. *How much cash do you and your spouse have?* $ [   ]

Below, state any money you or your spouse have in bank accounts or in any other financial institution.

Financial Institution	Type of Account	Amount You Have	Amount Your Spouse Has
		$	$
		$	$
		$	$
		$	$

If you are a prisoner seeking to appeal a judgment in a civil action or proceeding, you must attach a statement certified by the appropriate institutional officer showing all receipts, expenditures, and balances during the last six months in your institutional accounts. If you have multiple accounts, perhaps because you have been in multiple institutions, attach one certified statement of each account.

5. *List the assets, and their values, which you own or your spouse owns. Do not list clothing and ordinary household furnishing.*

Home	Value	Other Real Estate	Value
	$		$

Motor Vehicle 1: Make & Year	Model	Registration #	Value
			$

Motor Vehicle 2: Make & Year	Model	Registration #	Value
			$

Feedback or questions about this form? Email us at forms@ca9.uscourts.gov

Other Assets	Value
	$
	$
	$

6. *State every person, business, or organization owing you or your spouse money, and the amount owed.*

Person owing you or your spouse	Amount owed to you	Amount owed to your spouse
	$	$
	$	$
	$	$

7. *State the persons who rely on you or your spouse for support. If a dependent is a minor, list only the initials and not the full name.*

Name	Relationship	Age

Feedback or questions about this form? Email us at forms@ca9.uscourts.gov

8. *Estimate the average monthly expenses of you and your family. Show separately the amounts paid by your spouse. Adjust any payments that are made weekly, biweekly, quarterly, semiannually, or annually to show the monthly rate.*

	You	Spouse
Rent or home-mortgage payment (include lot rented for mobile home)	$	$
- Are real estate taxes included? ○ Yes ○ No		
- Is property insurance included? ○ Yes ○ No		
Utilities (electricity, heating fuel, water, sewer, and telephone)	$	$
Home maintenance (repairs and upkeep)	$	$
Food	$	$
Clothing	$	$
Laundry and dry-cleaning	$	$
Medical and dental expenses	$	$
Transportation (not including motor vehicle payments)	$	$
Recreation, entertainment, newspapers, magazines, etc.	$	$
Insurance (not deducted from wages or included in mortgage payments)		
- Homeowner's or renter's	$	$
- Life	$	$
- Health	$	$
- Motor Vehicle	$	$
- Other	$	$
Taxes (not deducted from wages or included in mortgage payments)		
Specify	$	$

Feedback or questions about this form? Email us at forms@ca9.uscourts.gov

		You	Spouse
Installment payments			
- Motor Vehicle		$	$
- Credit Card (name)		$	$
- Department Store (name)		$	$
Alimony, maintenance, and support paid to others		$	$
Regular expenses for the operation of business, profession, or farm (attach detailed statement)		$	$
Other (specify)		$	$
TOTAL MONTHLY EXPENSES		$	$

9. *Do you expect any major changes to your monthly income or expenses or in your assets or liabilities during the next 12 months?* ⃝ Yes ⃝ No

   If Yes, describe on an attached sheet.

10. *Have you spent — or will you be spending — any money for expenses or attorney fees in connection with this lawsuit?* ⃝ Yes ⃝ No

   If Yes, how much? $

11. *Provide any other information that will help explain why you cannot pay the docket fees for your appeal.*

12. *State the city and state of your legal residence.*

City   State

Your daytime phone number (ex., 415-355-8000)

Your age   Your years of schooling

Feedback or questions about this form? Email us at forms@ca9.uscourts.gov

[Effective December 1, 2018.]

FORM 5. NOTICE OF APPEAL FROM A JUDGMENT OR ORDER OF THE BANKRUPTCY APPELLATE PANEL

UNITED STATES COURT OF APPEALS
FOR THE NINTH CIRCUIT

Form 5. Notice of Appeal from a Judgment or Order of the Bankruptcy Appellate Panel

Name of debtor:

Bankruptcy Appellate Panel (BAP) case number:

Date case was first filed in BAP:

Date of judgment or order you are appealing:

Fee paid for appeal?   ○ Yes   ○ No

List all Appellants *(List each party filing the appeal. Do not use "et al." or other abbreviations.)*

Is this a cross-appeal? ○ Yes   ○ No

If Yes, what is the first appeal case number?

Was there a previous appeal in this case?   ○ Yes   ○ No

If Yes, what is the prior appeal case number?

Your mailing address:

City: State: Zip Code:

Prisoner Inmate or A Number (if applicable):

Signature   **Date**

Complete and file with the attached representation statement in the BAP

Feedback or questions about this form? Email us at forms@ca9.uscourts.gov

[Effective December 1, 2018.]

FORM 6.   REPRESENTATION STATEMENT
UNITED STATES COURT OF APPEALS
FOR THE NINTH CIRCUIT
Form 6. Representation Statement

Instructions for this form: http://www.ca9.uscourts.gov/forms/form06instructions.pdf

Appellant(s) *(List **each** party filing the appeal, do not use "et al." or other abbreviations.)*

Name(s) of party/parties:

Name(s) of counsel (if any):

Address:

Telephone number(s):

Email(s):

Is counsel registered for Electronic Filing in the 9th Circuit?   ○ Yes   ○ No

Appellee(s) *(List only the names of parties and counsel who will oppose you on appeal. List separately represented parties separately.)*

Name(s) of party/parties:

Name(s) of counsel (if any):

Address:

Telephone number(s):

Email(s):

To list additional parties and/or counsel, use next page.

Feedback or questions about this form? Email us at forms@ca9.uscourts.gov

Continued list of parties and counsel: *(attach additional pages as necessary)*

Appellants

Name(s) of party/parties:

Name(s) of counsel (if any):

Address:

Telephone number(s):

Email(s):

Is counsel registered for Electronic Filing in the 9th Circuit?   ⊙ Yes   ⊙ No

Appellees

Name(s) of party/parties:

Name(s) of counsel (if any):

Address:

Telephone number(s):

Email(s):

Name(s) of party/parties:

Name(s) of counsel (if any):

Address:

Telephone number(s):

Email(s):

Feedback or questions about this form? Email us at forms@ca9.uscourts.gov

[Effective December 1, 2018.]

FORM 7. MEDIATION QUESTIONNAIRE

UNITED STATES COURT OF APPEALS
FOR THE NINTH CIRCUIT
Form 7. Mediation Questionnaire

Instructions for this form: http://www.ca9.uscourts.gov/forms/form07instructions.pdf

9th Cir. Case Number(s)

Case Name

**Counsel submitting
this form**

**Represented party/
parties**

Briefly describe the dispute that gave rise to this lawsuit.

Feedback or questions about this form? Email us at forms@ca9.uscourts.gov

Briefly describe the result below and the main issues on appeal.

Describe any proceedings remaining below or any related proceedings in other tribunals.

Signature [   ]   **Date** [   ]

(use "s/[typed name]" to sign electronically-filed documents)

Feedback or questions about this form? Email us at forms@ca9.uscourts.gov

[Effective December 1, 2018.]

FORM 8.   CERTIFICATE OF COMPLIANCE FOR BRIEFS

**UNITED STATES COURT OF APPEALS
FOR THE NINTH CIRCUIT**

Form 8. Certificate of Compliance for Briefs

Instructions for this form: http://www.ca9.uscourts.gov/forms/form08instructions.pdf

9th Cir. Case Number(s) [_____]

I am the attorney or self-represented party.

This brief contains [_____] **words**, excluding the items exempted

by Fed. R. App. P. 32(f). The brief's type size and typeface comply with Fed. R.

App. P. 32(a)(5) and (6).

I certify that this brief *(select only one)*:

○ complies with the word limit of Cir. R. 32-1.

○ is a **cross-appeal** brief and complies with the word limit of Cir. R. 28.1-1.

○ is an **amicus** brief and complies with the word limit of Fed. R. App. P.
   29(a)(5), Cir. R. 29-2(c)(2), or Cir. R. 29-2(c)(3).

○ is for a **death penalty** case and complies with the word limit of Cir. R. 32-4.

○ complies with the longer length limit permitted by Cir. R. 32-2(b) because
   (select only one):

   ○ it is a joint brief submitted by separately represented parties;

   ○ a party or parties are filing a single brief in response to multiple briefs; or

   ○ a party or parties are filing a single brief in response to a longer joint brief.

○ complies with the length limit designated by court order dated [_____] .

○ is accompanied by a motion to file a longer brief pursuant to Cir. R. 32-2(a).

Signature [_____] **Date** [_____]

(use "s/[typed name]" to sign electronically-filed documents)

Feedback or questions about this form? Email us at forms@ca9.uscourts.gov

[Adopted effective July 1, 1997. Amended effective January 1, 1999; July 30, 2003; December 1, 2009; July 1, 2016; December 1, 2016; December 1, 2018.]

FORM 9.   APPLICATION FOR ATTORNEYS' FEES UNDER CIRCUIT RULE 39–1.6
UNITED STATES COURT OF APPEALS
FOR THE NINTH CIRCUIT

Form 9. Application for Attorneys' Fees under Circuit Rule 39-1.6

Instructions for this form: http://www.ca9.uscourts.gov/forms/form09instructions.pdf

9th Cir. Case Number(s)

Case Name

For each amount claimed, please attach itemized information indicating service provided, date, hours, and rate.

DESCRIPTION OF SERVICES	Hours	Amount Claimed
Interviews and Conferences		$
Obtaining and Reviewing Records		$
Legal Research		$
Preparing Briefs		$
Preparing for and Attending Oral Argument		$
Other (*specify below*)		$
Total Hours/Compensation Requested:		$

Signature   **Date**

(use "s/[typed name]" to sign electronically-filed documents)

Feedback or questions about this form? Email us at forms@ca9.uscourts.gov

Form 9   *Rev. 01/24/2019*

[Effective July 1, 1998. Amended effective July 1, 2001; September 2, 2008; December 1, 2018; January 24, 2019.]

FORM 10. BILL OF COSTS
UNITED STATES COURT OF APPEALS
FOR THE NINTH CIRCUIT
Form 10. Bill of Costs

Instructions for this form: http://www.ca9.uscourts.gov/forms/form10instructions.pdf

9th Cir. Case Number(s)

Case Name

The Clerk is requested to award costs to (*party name(s)*):

I swear under penalty of perjury that the copies for which costs are requested were actually and necessarily produced, and that the requested costs were actually expended.

Signature   **Date**

(use "s/[typed name]" to sign electronically-filed documents)

COST TAXABLE	REQUESTED *(each column must be completed)*			
DOCUMENTS / FEE PAID	No. of Copies	Pages per Copy	Cost per Page	TOTAL COST
Excerpts of Record*			$	$
Principal Brief(s) *(Opening Brief; Answering Brief; 1st, 2nd , and/or 3rd Brief on Cross-Appeal; Intervenor Brief)*			$	$
Reply Brief / Cross-Appeal Reply Brief			$	$
Supplemental Brief(s)			$	$
Petition for Review Docket Fee / Petition for Writ of Mandamus Docket Fee				$
TOTAL:				$

***Example:** Calculate 4 copies of 3 volumes of excerpts of record that total 500 pages [Vol. 1 (10 pgs.) + Vol. 2 (250 pgs.) + Vol. 3 (240 pgs.)] as:*
No. of Copies: 4; Pages per Copy: 500; Cost per Page: $.10 (or actual cost IF less than $.10);
TOTAL: 4 x 500 x $.10 = $200.

Feedback or questions about this form? Email us at forms@ca9.uscourts.gov

[Effective July 1, 1998. Amended effective January 1, 2005; September 2, 2008; December 1, 2009; December 1, 2018.]

FORM 11. CERTIFICATE OF COMPLIANCE FOR PETITIONS FOR REHEARING OR ANSWERS

UNITED STATES COURT OF APPEALS
FOR THE NINTH CIRCUIT

Form 11. Certificate of Compliance for Petitions for Rehearing or Answers

Instructions for this form: http://www.ca9.uscourts.gov/forms/form11instructions.pdf

9th Cir. Case Number(s) [   ]

I am the attorney or self-represented party.

I certify that pursuant to Circuit Rule 35-4 or 40-1, the attached petition for

panel rehearing/petition for rehearing en banc/answer to petition is (*select one*):

Prepared in a format, typeface, and type style that complies with Fed. R. App.

⊂ P. 32(a)(4)-(6) and **contains the following number of words**: [   ].

(Petitions and answers must not exceed 4,200 words)

OR

⊂ In compliance with Fed. R. App. P. 32(a)(4)-(6) and does not exceed 15 pages.

Signature [   ]   **Date** [   ]

(use "s/[typed name]" to sign electronically-filed documents)

Feedback or questions about this form? Email us at forms@ca9.uscourts.gov

[Adopted effective July 1, 2000. Amended effective July 30, 2003; December 1, 2016; December 1, 2018.]

FORM 12.   APPLICATION FOR LEAVE TO FILE SECOND OR SUCCESSIVE PETITION UNDER 28 U.S.C. § 2254 OR MOTION UNDER 28 U.S.C. § 2255*

UNITED STATES COURT OF APPEALS
FOR THE NINTH CIRCUIT

Form 12. Application for Leave to File Second or Successive Petition under 28 U.S.C. § 2254 or Motion under 28 U.S.C. § 2255

Instructions for this form: http://www.ca9.uscourts.gov/forms/form12instructions.pdf

9th Cir. Case Number *(to be provided by court)* _____

Applicant Name _____

Prisoner Registration Number _____

Address _____

_____

Name of Respondent (Warden) _____

You MUST answer the following questions:

(1) What conviction(s) are you challenging?

_____

_____

(2) In what court(s) were you convicted of these crime(s)?

_____

_____

(3) What was the date of each of your conviction(s) and what is the length of each sentence?

_____

_____

Feedback or questions about this form? Email us at forms@ca9.uscourts.gov

For questions (4) through (10), provide information separately for each of your previous §§ 2254 or 2255 proceedings. Use additional pages if necessary.

(4) Has the judgment of your conviction or sentence been modified or amended? If yes, when and by what court?

_____

_____

(5) With respect to **each** conviction and sentence, have you ever filed a petition or motion for habeas corpus relief in federal court under **28 U.S.C. § 2254** or **§ 2255**?

Yes ☐   No ☐

    (a) In which federal district court did you file a petition or motion?

    _____

    (b) What was the docket number?

    _____

    (c) On what date did you file the petition/motion?

    _____

(6) What grounds were raised in your previous habeas proceeding?
(list all grounds and issues previously raised in that petition/ motion)

_____

_____

_____

(7) Did the district court hold an evidentiary hearing?   Yes ☐   No ☐

Feedback or questions about this form? Email us at forms@ca9.uscourts.gov

(8) How did the district court rule on your petition/motion?

☐ District court **dismissed** petition/motion. If yes, on what grounds?

_____

☐ District court **denied** petition/motion.

☐ District court **granted** relief. If yes, on what claims and what was the relief?

_____

(9) On what date did the district court decide your petition/motion?

_____

(10) Did you file an appeal from that disposition?   Yes ☐   No ☐

(a) What was the docket number of your appeal?

_____

(b) How did the court of appeals decide your appeal?

_____

(11) State concisely each and every ground or issue you wish to raise in your current petition or motion for habeas relief. Summarize briefly the facts supporting each ground or issue.

_____

_____

_____

Feedback or questions about this form? Email us at forms@ca9.uscourts.gov

223

(12) For each ground raised, was it raised in the state courts? If so, what did the state courts rule and when? *(Attach a copy of all relevant state court decisions, if available)*

_____

_____

(13) For each ground/issue raised, was this claim raised in any prior federal petition/motion? *(list each ground separately)*

_____

_____

(14) For each ground/issue raised, does this claim rely on a new rule of constitutional law? *(list each ground separately and give case name and citation for each new rule of law)*

_____

_____

(15) For each ground/issue raised, does this claim rely on newly discovered evidence? What is the evidence and when did you discover it? Why has this newly discovered evidence not been previously available to you? *(list each ground separately)*

_____

_____

_____

Feedback or questions about this form? Email us at forms@ca9.uscourts.gov

224

(16) For each ground/issue raised, does the newly discovered evidence establish your innocence? How?

_____

_____

(17) For each ground/issue raised, does the newly discovered evidence establish a federal constitutional error? Which provision of the Constitution was violated and how?

_____

_____

(18) Provide any other basis for your application not previously stated.

_____

_____

_____

Signature _____ **Date** _____

In capital cases only, proof of service on respondent MUST be attached. A sample proof of service is attached to this form.

Attach proposed section 2254 petition or section 2255 motion to this application.

Mail this form to the court at:
Clerk, U.S. Court of Appeals for the Ninth Circuit, P.O. Box 193939, San Francisco, CA 94119-3939

Feedback or questions about this form? Email us at forms@ca9.uscourts.gov

CERTIFICATE OF SERVICE

Applications for Leave to File Second or Successive 28 U.S.C. §§ 2254/2255 Petitions/Motions

<u>DEATH PENALTY CASES ONLY</u>

Case Name _____ v. _____

I certify that a copy of the application for leave to file a second or successive 28 U.S.C. § 2254 petition or § 2255 motion with any attachments was served, either in person or by mail, on the person listed below.

_____

Signature _____
(Notary NOT required)

Date of Service _____

Name   Address

_____   _____

Feedback or questions about this form? Email us at forms@ca9.uscourts.gov

[Effective July 1, 2002. Amended effective July 30, 2003; July 1, 2016; December 1, 2018.]

* [**Publisher's Note:** For attachment to Form 12, please see Rule 22–3, *ante.*]

FORM 13.   STREAMLINED REQUEST FOR EXTENSION OF TIME TO FILE BRIEF

UNITED STATES COURT OF APPEALS
FOR THE NINTH CIRCUIT
Form 13. Streamlined Request for Extension of Time to File Brief

ATTENTION ELECTRONIC FILERS: DO NOT USE FORM 13
Use Form 13 only if you are not registered for Appellate Electronic Filing.

Electronic filers must make the request by using the electronic document filing type
"Streamlined Request to Extend Time to File Brief," which does not require any form.

Instructions
- Use Form 13 only to request more time to file a **BRIEF**. To request an extension of time to file anything other than a brief, use Form 14.
- You may request a new due date of up to 30 days from your current due date.
- Submit Form 13 on or before your brief's current due date. The clerk will mail you the new briefing schedule.
- Use Form 13 only for your **first** request for an extension of time to file **each** brief. To request any additional extension of time to file the brief or to request a first extension of more than 30 days pursuant to Cir. R. 31-2.2(b), use Form 14.

9th Cir. Case Number(s)

Case Name

Name of each party requesting the extension:

For which brief are you requesting an extension?

○ Opening Brief   ○ First Brief on Cross-Appeal
○ Answering Brief   ○ Second Brief on Cross-Appeal
○ Reply Brief   ○ Third Brief on Cross-Appeal
                      ○ Cross-Appeal Reply Brief

What is your current due date?

What is your requested due date?

Print Name

Signature _____   Date _____

Mail this form on or before your brief's current due date to the court at:
Clerk, U.S. Court of Appeals for the Ninth Circuit, P.O. Box 193939, San Francisco, CA 94119-3939
Feedback or questions about this form? Email us at forms@ca9.uscourts.gov

[Effective January 1, 2013.   Amended effective July 15, 2015;   December 1, 2018.]

FORM 14. MOTION FOR EXTENSION OF TIME

**UNITED STATES COURT OF APPEALS
FOR THE NINTH CIRCUIT**

Form 14. Motion for Extension of Time

Instructions for this form: http://www.ca9.uscourts.gov/forms/form14instructions.pdf

9th Cir. Case Number(s)

Case Name

Requesting Party Name(s)

I am: ○ The party requesting the extension.
          ○ Counsel for the party or parties requesting the extension.

I request an extension of time to file a:

☐ Brief *(you **must** also complete the Declaration on page 3)*
☐ Motion to proceed in forma pauperis
☐ Motion for a certificate of appealability
☐ Response/opposition to a pending motion
☐ Reply to a response/opposition to a pending motion
☐ Motion for reconsideration
☐ Petition for panel/en banc rehearing
☐ Certified Administrative Record
☐ Response to court order dated
☐ Other *(you **must** describe the document)*

The requested new due date is:

I request the extension of time because (**cannot be left blank**):
(attach additional pages if necessary)

Signature   **Date**
(use "s/[typed name]" to sign electronically-filed documents)

Feedback or questions about this form? Email us at forms@ca9.uscourts.gov

---

Recitals in criminal and immigration cases pursuant to Circuit Rule 27-8
Complete this section for criminal or immigration cases.

Previous requests for extension of time to file the document, including any request for a Streamlined Extension of Time under Circuit Rule 31-2.2(a) (*select one*):

       ○ I have **NOT** filed a previous request to extend time to file the document.

       ○ I have previously requested an extension of time to file the document.

           This motion is my [   ] request.
                    (Examples: first, second)

Bail/detention status (*select one*):

       ○ The defendant is incarcerated. The projected release date is: [   ].

       ○ The petitioner is detained.

       ○ The defendant/petitioner in this criminal/immigration case is at liberty.

Signature [   ]   **Date** [   ]
(use "s/[typed name]" to sign electronically-filed documents)

Feedback or questions about this form? Email us at forms@ca9.uscourts.gov

Declaration in support of extension to file brief under Circuit Rule 31-2.2(b)
Complete this section if you are requesting an extension of time to file a brief.

1. I request an extension of time to file the [   ] brief.

   (Examples: opening, answering, reply, first cross-appeal)

2. The brief's current due date is: [   ]

3. The brief's first due date was: [   ]

4. A more detailed explanation of why the extension of time to file the brief is necessary: *(Under Circuit Rule 31-2.2(b), a request for extension of time to file a brief must be "supported by a showing of diligence and substantial need" and a conclusory statement as to the press of business does not constitute such a showing. Attach additional pages if necessary.)*

   [   ]

5. The position of the other party/parties regarding this request is:

   ☐ Unopposed.

   ☐ Opposed by *(name of party/parties opposing this motion)*:

   [   ]

   ☐ Unknown. I am unable to verify the position of the other party/parties because:

   [   ]

6. ☐ The court reporter is not in default with regard to any designated transcripts.

   If the court reporter is in default, please explain:

   [   ]

7. ☐ I have exercised diligence and I will file the brief within the time requested.

I declare under penalty of perjury that the foregoing is true and correct.

Signature [   ] **Date** [   ]

(use "s/[typed name]" to sign electronically-filed documents)

Feedback or questions about this form? Email us at *forms@ca9.uscourts.gov*

[Effective December 1, 2018.]

FORM 15. CERTIFICATE OF SERVICE FOR ELECTRONIC FILING

**UNITED STATES COURT OF APPEALS
FOR THE NINTH CIRCUIT**

Form 15. Certificate of Service for Electronic Filing

Instructions for this form: http://www.ca9.uscourts.gov/forms/form15instructions.pdf

9th Cir. Case Number(s) [   ]

I hereby certify that I electronically filed the foregoing/attached document(s) on this date with the Clerk of the Court for the United States Court of Appeals for the Ninth Circuit using the Appellate Electronic Filing system.

Service on Case Participants Who Are Registered for Electronic Filing:

☐ I certify that I served the foregoing/attached document(s) via email to all registered case participants on this date because it is a sealed filing or is submitted as an original petition or other original proceeding and therefore cannot be served via the Appellate Electronic Filing system.

Service on Case Participants Who Are <u>NOT</u> Registered for Electronic Filing:

☐ I certify that I served the foregoing/attached document(s) on this date by hand delivery, mail, third party commercial carrier for delivery within 3 calendar days, or, having obtained prior consent, by email to the following unregistered case participants *(list each name and mailing/email address)*:

[   ]

Description of Document(s) *(required for all documents)*:

[   ]

Signature [   ] **Date** [   ]

(use "s/[typed name]" to sign electronically-filed documents)

Feedback or questions about this form? Email us at forms@ca9.uscourts.gov

Form 15   *Rev. 12/01/2018*

[Effective December 1, 2018.]

FORM 16. CIRCUIT RULE 27–3 CERTIFICATE FOR EMERGENCY MOTION
UNITED STATES COURT OF APPEALS
FOR THE NINTH CIRCUIT

Form 16. Circuit Rule 27-3 Certificate for Emergency Motion

Instructions for this form: http://www.ca9.uscourts.gov/forms/form16instructions.pdf

9th Cir. Case Number(s) [   ]

Case Name [   ]

I certify the following:

The relief I request in the emergency motion that accompanies this certificate is:

[   ]

Relief is needed no later than *(date)*: [   ]

The following will happen if relief is not granted within the requested time:

[   ]

I could not have filed this motion earlier because:

[   ]

Feedback or questions about this form? Email us at forms@ca9.uscourts.gov

I requested this relief in the district court or other lower court: ○ Yes ○ No

> If not, why not:

I notified 9th Circuit court staff via voicemail or email about the filing of this motion: ○ Yes ○ No

> If not, why not:

I have notified all counsel and any unrepresented party of the filing of this motion:

> On *(date)*:

> By *(method)*:

> Position of other parties:

Name and best contact information for each counsel/party notified:

I declare under penalty of perjury that the foregoing is true.

Signature   **Date**

(use "s/[typed name]" to sign electronically-filed documents)

Feedback or questions about this form? Email us at forms@ca9.uscourts.gov

[Effective December 1, 2018. Amended effective November 21, 2019.]

FORM 17. STATEMENT OF RELATED CASES
PURSUANT TO CIRCUIT RULE 28–2.6
UNITED STATES COURT OF APPEALS
FOR THE NINTH CIRCUIT

Form 17. Statement of Related Cases Pursuant to Circuit Rule 28-2.6

Instructions for this form: http://www.ca9.uscourts.gov/forms/form17instructions.pdf

9th Cir. Case Number(s) [_____]

The undersigned attorney or self-represented party states the following:

○ I am unaware of any related cases currently pending in this court.

○ I am unaware of any related cases currently pending in this court other than the case(s) identified in the initial brief(s) filed by the other party or parties.

○ I am aware of one or more related cases currently pending in this court. The case number and name of each related case and its relationship to this case are:

[   ]

Signature [_____] **Date** [_____]

(use "s/[typed name]" to sign electronically-filed documents)

Feedback or questions about this form? Email us at forms@ca9.uscourts.gov

[Effective December 1, 2018.]

FORM 18. CERTIFICATE FOR PAPER COPY OF ELECTRONIC BRIEF
UNITED STATES COURT OF APPEALS
FOR THE NINTH CIRCUIT
Form 18. Certificate for Paper Copy of Electronic Brief

Instructions for this form: http://www.ca9.uscourts.gov/forms/form18instructions.pdf

9th Cir. Case Number(s)

My name is

I certify that this brief is identical to the version submitted electronically on *(date)*:

Signature   **Date**

(either manual signature or "s/[typed name]" is acceptable)

Feedback or questions about this form? Email us at forms@ca9.uscourts.gov

[Effective December 1, 2018.]

FORM 19.   NOTICE OF SEALING
UNITED STATES COURT OF APPEALS
FOR THE NINTH CIRCUIT
Form 19. Notice of Sealing

Instructions for this form: http://www.ca9.uscourts.gov/forms/form19instructions.pdf

9th Cir. Case Number(s) [   ]

Case Name [   ]

☐ Pursuant to Circuit Rule 27-13(d), the filing of the accompanying document or set of documents under seal is required by a statute or procedural rule.

The applicable statute/rule is:

[   ]

☐ Pursuant to Circuit Rule 27-13(g), maintaining this entire case under seal is mandated by statute or procedural rule.

The applicable statute/rule is:

[   ]

Signature [   ]   **Date** [   ]
(use "s/[typed name]" to sign electronically-filed documents)

Form 19   *Rev. 07/01/2019*

[Effective December 1, 2018.   Amended effective July 1, 2019.]

FORM 20. NOTICE OF INTENT TO UNSEAL
UNITED STATES COURT OF APPEALS
FOR THE NINTH CIRCUIT
Form 20. Notice of Intent to Unseal

Instructions for this form: http://www.ca9.uscourts.gov/forms/form20instructions.pdf

9th Cir. Case Number(s) [   ]

Case Name [   ]

Pursuant to Circuit Rule 27-13(f), I intend to file the following document or set of documents publicly although the document or set of documents were filed under seal in the district court or agency. The document or set of documents filed herewith provisionally under seal are:

[   ]

☐ I understand that unless any other party files a motion to maintain the seal **within 21 days**, these documents will be unsealed without further notice.

Position of the other party or parties, if known:

[   ]

Signature [   ]   **Date** [   ]
(use "s/[typed name]" to sign electronically-filed documents)

Feedback or questions about this form? Email us at forms@ca9.uscourts.gov

Form 20   *Rev. 07/01/2019*

[Effective December 1, 2018. Amended effective July 1, 2019.]

FORM 21. COURT REPORTER MOTION FOR EXTENSION OF TIME TO FILE TRANSCRIPT

UNITED STATES COURT OF APPEALS
FOR THE NINTH CIRCUIT

Form 21. Court Reporter Motion for Extension of Time to File Transcript

Instructions for this form: http://www.ca9.uscourts.gov/forms/form21instructions.pdf

9th Cir. Case Number(s)

Case Name

U.S. District Court for

District Court Case Number(s)

Name of Reporter/Recorder

Proposed new due date:

Explain why you need the extension:

To request a waiver of the fee reduction, you **must** complete the following:

I certify that

(name of district court judge, district court clerk, chief deputy clerk or court reporter supervisor)

has authorized me to represent that I qualify for the waiver of the fee reduction based on good cause shown. I will serve a copy of this motion on the authorizing person.

Signature   **Date**

(use "s/[typed name]" to sign electronically-filed documents)

Feedback or questions about this form? Email us at forms@ca9.uscourts.gov

[Effective December 1, 2018.]

FORM 22. NOTICE OF CHANGE OF ADDRESS
UNITED STATES COURT OF APPEALS
FOR THE NINTH CIRCUIT
Form 22. Notice of Change of Address

ATTENTION ELECTRONIC FILERS: DO NOT USE FORM 22
Electronic filers must use PACER to update their information.
Use Form 22 only if you are **not** registered for Appellate Electronic Filing.

9th Cir. Case Number(s)

Case Name

Full Name(s)

NEW MAILING ADDRESS

Address

City

State/Province/Region   Zip Code

Country (if not USA)

Prisoner Inmate or A Number (if applicable)

Phone Number (if applicable)

Signature   **Date**

Mail this form on or before your brief's current due date to the court at:
Clerk, U.S. Court of Appeals for the Ninth Circuit, P.O. Box 193939, San Francisco, CA 94119-3939

Feedback or questions about this form? Email us at forms@ca9.uscourts.gov

[Effective December 1, 2018.]

FORM 23. FINANCIAL AFFIDAVIT

FINANCIAL AFFIDAVIT
CJA-23 (Rev 3/21)
IN SUPPORT OF REQUEST FOR ATTORNEY, EXPERT, OR OTHER SERVICES WITHOUT PAYMENT OF FEE

IN THE UNITED STATES ☐ DISTRICT COURT ☐ COURT OF APPEALS ☐ OTHER (Specify Below)

IN THE CASE OF
_____ V. _____
FOR _____
AT _____
LOCATION NUMBER

PERSON REPRESENTED (Show your full name)

1 ☐ Defendant - Adult
2 ☐ Defendant - Juvenile
3 ☐ Appellant
4 ☐ Probation Violator
5 ☐ Supervised Release Violator
6 ☐ Habeas Petitioner
7 ☐ 2255 Petitioner
8 ☐ Material Witness
9 ☐ Other (Specify) _____

CHARGE/OFFENSE (Describe if applicable & check box→) ☐ Felony ☐ Misdemeanor

DOCKET NUMBERS
Magistrate Judge
District Court
Court of Appeals

ANSWERS TO QUESTIONS REGARDING ABILITY TO PAY

EMPLOYMENT
Do you have a job? ☐ Yes ☐ No
IF YES, how much do you earn per month? _____
Will you still have a job after this arrest? ☐ Yes ☐ No ☐ Unknown

INCOME & ASSETS

PROPERTY
Do you own any of the following, and if so, what is it worth?
APPROXIMATE VALUE   DESCRIPTION & AMOUNT OWED
Home $_____
Car/Truck/Vehicle $_____
Boat $_____
Stocks/bonds $_____
Other property $_____

CASH & BANK ACCOUNTS
Do you have any cash, or money in savings or checking accounts? ☐ Yes ☐ No
IF YES, give the total approximate amount after monthly expenses $_____

OBLIGATIONS, EXPENSES, & DEBTS
How many people do you financially support? _____

BILLS & DEBTS	MONTHLY EXPENSE	TOTAL DEBT
Housing	$	$
Groceries	$	$
Medical expenses	$	$
Utilities	$	$
Credit cards	$	$
Car/Truck/Vehicle	$	$
Childcare	$	$
Child support	$	$
Insurance	$	$
Loans	$	$
Fines	$	$
Other	$	$

I certify under penalty of perjury that the foregoing is true and correct.

_____
SIGNATURE OF DEFENDANT
(OR PERSON SEEKING REPRESENTATION)   Date _____

[Effective March 2021.]

240

FORM 24.   MOTION FOR APPOINTMENT OF COUNSEL

UNITED STATES COURT OF APPEALS
FOR THE NINTH CIRCUIT
Form 24. Motion for Appointment of Counsel

Instructions for this form: http://www.ca9.uscourts.gov/forms/form24instructions.pdf

9th Cir. Case Number(s) [   ]

Case Name [   ]

Lower Court or Agency Case Number [   ]

1. My name is [   ]

2. I am asking the court to appoint an attorney to help me with this case.

3. My fee status is as follows *(select one)*:

    ○ The district court or this court granted my motion to proceed in forma pauperis.

    ○ I filed a motion to proceed in forma pauperis but the court has not yet ruled on the motion.

    ○ This motion is accompanied by a motion to proceed in forma pauperis.

    ○ I paid the filing fees for this case. However, I cannot afford an attorney for the following reasons:

    [   ]

4. Is this a civil appeal or petition for review?   ○ Yes   ○ No

    If yes, attach an additional page(s) describing the issues on appeal.

My current mailing address

[   ]

City [   ] State [ ] Zip Code [   ]

Prisoner Inmate or A Number (if applicable) [   ]

Signature [   ] **Date** [   ]

Feedback or questions about this form? Email us at forms@ca9.uscourts.gov

[Effective December 1, 2018.]

FORM 25. CERTIFICATE OF SERVICE FOR PAPER FILING
UNITED STATES COURT OF APPEALS
FOR THE NINTH CIRCUIT
Form 25. Certificate of Service for Paper Filing

ATTENTION ELECTRONIC FILERS: DO NOT USE FORM 25
Use Form 25 only if you are **not** registered for Appellate Electronic Filing

Instructions
- You must attach a certificate of service to each document you send to the court and to opposing counsel.
- Include the title of the document you are serving, the name and address of each person you served with a copy of the document, and the date of mailing or hand delivery.
- Sign and date the certificate. You do not need to have the certificate notarized.
- Remember that you must send a copy of **all** documents and attachments to counsel for **each** party to this case.

9th Cir. Case Number(s)

Case Name

I certify that I served on the person(s) listed below, either by mail or hand delivery, a copy of the
and any attachments. *(title of document you are filing, such as Opening Brief, Motion for   , etc.)*

Signature   **Date**

Name	Address	Date Served

Mail this form to the court at:
Clerk, U.S. Court of Appeals for the Ninth Circuit, P.O. Box 193939, San Francisco, CA 94119-3939
Feedback or questions about this form? Email us at forms@ca9.uscourts.gov

[Effective December 1, 2018.]

FORM 26.   NOTICE OF DELAY

UNITED STATES COURT OF APPEALS
FOR THE NINTH CIRCUIT
Form 26. Notice of Delay

Instructions for this form: http://www.ca9.uscourts.gov/forms/form26instructions.pdf

9th Cir. Case Number(s)

Case Name

Name(s) of party or parties filing this notice:

I am notifying the court that this appeal or petition has been pending before the court for a period in excess of that set forth below:

☐ A motion has been pending for longer than 4 months.

☐ The parties have not received notice of oral argument or submission on the briefs within 15 months after the completion of briefing.

☐ A decision on the merits has not been issued within 9 months after submission.

☐ The mandate has not issued within 28 days after the time to file a petition for rehearing has expired.

☐ A petition for rehearing has been pending for longer than 6 months.

☐ Other *(describe the nature of the delay)*:

Signature   **Date**

(use "s/[typed name]" to sign electronically-filed documents)

Feedback or questions about this form? Email us at forms@ca9.uscourts.gov

[Effective December 1, 2018.]

FORM 27. MOTION FOR _____

UNITED STATES COURT OF APPEALS
FOR THE NINTH CIRCUIT

Form 27. Motion for [   ]

Instructions for this form: http://www.ca9.uscourts.gov/forms/form27instructions.pdf

9th Cir. Case Number(s) [   ]

Case Name [   ]

Lower Court or Agency Case Number [   ]

What is your name? [   ]

1. **What** do you want the court to do?

   [   ]

2. **Why** should the court do this? Be specific. Include all relevant facts and law that would persuade the court to grant your request. *(Attach additional pages as necessary. Your motion may not be longer than 20 pages.)*

   [   ]

   Your mailing address:

   [   ]

   City [   ] State [ ] Zip Code [   ]

   Prisoner Inmate or A Number (if applicable) [   ]

Signature [   ] **Date** [   ]

Feedback or questions about this form? Email us at forms@ca9.uscourts.gov

[Effective December 1, 2018.]

FORM 28.   RESPONSE TO MOTION OR COURT ORDER

UNITED STATES COURT OF APPEALS
FOR THE NINTH CIRCUIT
Form 28. Response to Motion or Court Order

Instructions for this form: http://www.ca9.uscourts.gov/forms/form28instructions.pdf

9th Cir. Case Number(s) [   ]

Case Name [   ]

1. What is your name? [   ]
    (For counsel, which party/parties do you represent?)

2. Describe briefly the motion or court order to which you are responding, such as the title of the motion or the type of response requested in the order.

    [   ]

    On what date was the motion or court order filed? [   ]

3. What is your response? Be specific. Include all relevant facts and law that would persuade the court to grant your request. *(Attach additional pages as necessary. Your motion may not be longer than 20 pages.)*

    [   ]

Provide your current mailing address unless registered for electronic filing:

[   ]

City [   ] State [   ] Zip Code [   ]

Prisoner Inmate or A Number (if applicable) [   ]

Signature [   ]   **Date** [   ]

(use "s/[typed name]" to sign electronically-filed documents)

Feedback or questions about this form? Email us at forms@ca9.uscourts.gov

[Effective December 1, 2018.]

245

FORM 29. REQUEST FOR DOCKET SHEET, DOCUMENT, OR RULES
UNITED STATES COURT OF APPEALS
FOR THE NINTH CIRCUIT
Form 29. Request for Docket Sheet, Document, or Rules

Instructions for this form: http://www.ca9.uscourts.gov/forms/form29instructions.pdf

9th Cir. Case Number(s)

Case Name

What are you requesting?

☐ A copy of the Federal Rules of Appellate Procedure and 9th Circuit Rules

☐ A copy of the 9th Circuit docket sheet

☐ A copy of the following document(s) on the 9th Circuit docket:

Date and/or Docket Entry #	Description of Document

Your Name

Your mailing address

City   State   Zip Code

Prisoner Inmate or A Number (if applicable)

Signature   **Date**

Mail this form to the court at:
Clerk, U.S. Court of Appeals for the Ninth Circuit, P.O. Box 193939, San Francisco, CA 94119-3939

Feedback or questions about this form? Email us at forms@ca9.uscourts.gov

[Effective December 1, 2018.]

FORM 30. APPELLATE ELECTRONIC FILING EXEMPTION FORM

UNITED STATES COURT OF APPEALS
FOR THE NINTH CIRCUIT
Form 30. Appellate Electronic Filing Exemption Form

> **ATTENTION SELF-REPRESENTED PARTIES:**
> **DO NOT USE FORM 30**
>
> If you do not have a lawyer, you are automatically exempt from electronic filing.

9th Cir. Case Number(s) [   ]

Case Name [   ]

○ I am a court reporter

○ I am counsel of record for [   ]
(party/parties that you represent)

I hereby request an exemption from the court's requirement that all attorneys and court reporters use Appellate Electronic Filing. I am unable to register for electronic filing because:

[   ]

My name is [   ]

Mailing address [   ]

[   ]

City [   ] State [ ] Zip Code [   ]

Country (if not USA) [   ] Phone [   ]

If approved, I understand that this exemption will apply to all pending and future cases in this court for one calendar year. If I wish to participate in Appellate Electronic Filing in the future, my Appellate Electronic Filing registration will apply to all pending and future cases.

Signature [   ] **Date** [   ]

Mail this form to the court at:
Clerk, U.S. Court of Appeals for the Ninth Circuit, P.O. Box 193939, San Francisco, CA 94119-3939
Feedback or questions about this form? Email us at forms@ca9.uscourts.gov

[Effective December 1, 2018.]

FORM 31. APPLICATION AND OATH FOR ADMISSION

UNITED STATES COURT OF APPEALS
FOR THE NINTH CIRCUIT

Form 31. Application and Oath for Admission

Instructions for this form: http://www.ca9.uscourts.gov/content/atty_instructions.php

PERSONAL INFORMATION

Full Name: [   ]

Last 4 digits of SSN: [   ]   Birth Date: [   ]

Phone: [   ]   Email: [   ]

MAILING ADDRESS (no P.O. Box addresses)

Firm Name or Agency: [   ]

Street Address, incl. Suite/Apt #: [   ]

City: [   ]   State: [   ]   Zip: [   ]

BAR INFORMATION

Federal/State Admissions *(max. 2)*	Status *(active/inactive)*	Admission Date	Bar Number

Answer each question below. If the answer to any of the questions is yes, attach a separate statement providing details.

1. Have you been known by any name other than that appearing on the application?   ◦ Yes ◦ No

2. Have you ever been reprimanded, or suspended or disbarred from practice, before any court or government agency?   ◦ Yes ◦ No

3. Are any actions concerning possible reprimand, suspension, or disbarment currently pending against you?   ◦ Yes ◦ No

4. Are you currently under investigation by any court or government agency?   ◦ Yes ◦ No

Feedback or questions about this form? Email us at forms@ca9.uscourts.gov

SPONSORED MOTION FOR ADMISSION ONLY

To be completed by a sponsor in good standing with the Ninth Circuit Court of Appeals

(Skip to the next section if you were sworn in at a mass bar admission ceremony within the last three (3) months.)

I, [_____], a member in good standing of the
  (full name of sponsor)
Bar of the United States Court of Appeals for the Ninth Circuit hereby move the
admission of [_____] to the Bar of this Court.

I am satisfied that the applicant possesses the qualifications set forth by Federal
Rule of Appellate Procedure 46(a).

Sponsor Signature: [_____]   **Date:** [_____]

Admission Date: [_____]

Phone: [_____]   Email: [_____]

Firm Name or Agency: [_____]

Street Address, incl. Suite/Apt #: [_____]

City: [_____]   State: [_____]   Zip: [_____]

INFORMATION FOR MASS ADMISSION CEREMONY ONLY

Location of Ceremony: [_____]

Date of Ceremony: [_____]

OATH

I, [_____], certify under penalty of perjury
  (TYPE name as you want it to appear on your certificate)
under the laws of the United States of America that the foregoing is true and
correct. I do solemnly swear [or affirm] that I will conduct myself as an attorney
and counselor of this Court, uprightly and according to law; and that I will support
the Constitution of the United States.

Applicant Signature [_____]   **Date** [_____]
(use "s/[typed name]" to sign electronically-filed documents)

Feedback or questions about this form? Email us at forms@ca9.uscourts.gov

[Effective December 1, 2018.]

FORM 32. RESPONSE TO NOTICE OF CASE BEING CONSIDERED FOR ORAL ARGUMENT

UNITED STATES COURT OF APPEALS
FOR THE NINTH CIRCUIT

Form 32. Response to Notice of Case Being Considered for Oral Argument

Instructions for this form: http://www.ca9.uscourts.gov/forms/form32instructions.pdf

9th Cir. Case Number(s) [   ]

Case Name [   ]

Hearing Location (*city*) [   ]

Your Name [   ]

List the sitting dates for the three sitting months you were asked to review:

[   ]

Do you have an unresolvable conflict on any of the above dates? ○ Yes ○ No

If yes, list the specific day(s) and the specific reason(s) you are unavailable:

[   ]

Do you have any other cases pending in this court for which you received a notice of consideration for oral argument during the three sitting months listed above?

○ Yes ○ No

If yes, list the number, name, and hearing city of each of the other case(s):

[   ]

Signature [   ] **Date** [   ]

(use "s/[typed name]" to sign electronically-filed documents)

Feedback or questions about this form? Email us at forms@ca9.uscourts.gov

[Effective December 1, 2018.]

FORM 33.   INMATE DECLARATION OF TIMELY FILING
UNITED STATES COURT OF APPEALS
FOR THE NINTH CIRCUIT
Form 33. Inmate Declaration of Timely Filing

THIS FORM IS ONLY FOR INMATES CONFINED IN AN INSTITUTION

Instructions
- The purpose of this declaration is to inform the court of the date you deposited your filing in the institution's legal mailing system.
- "Inmates" includes those confined in a **jail**, **prison**, or **immigration detention facility**.
- To receive the benefit of Fed. R. App. P. 4(c)(1) or Fed. R. App. P. 25(a)(2)(A)(iii), you must use the institution's system designed for legal mail, and postage must be prepaid.
- You must **also** include a dated certificate of service with the name and address of each person you served with a copy of the document. This is available on Form 25.
- Be sure to sign and date this declaration.

Name of U.S. District Court *(if applicable)* _____

U.S. District Court case number *(if applicable)* _____

Alien number ("A" number) *(if applicable)* _____

9th Cir. Case Number(s) *(if assigned)* _____

Case Name _____

I am an inmate/detainee confined in an institution. On _____ *(date)*,

I deposited the _____

  (title of document you are filing, such as Notice of Appeal, Petition for Review, etc.)

in the institution's legal mail system, with postage prepaid.

I declare under penalty of perjury that the foregoing is true and correct (*see* 28 U.S.C. § 1746; 18 U.S.C. § 1621).

Signature _____   **Date** _____

Feedback or questions about this form? Email us at forms@ca9.uscourts.gov

---

Form 33   *New 12/09/2019*

[Effective December 9, 2019.]

GENERAL ORDERS

Chapter I: GENERAL DEFINITIONS

Terms in these General Orders conform to Title 28 of the United States Code, the Federal Rules of Appellate Procedure ("FRAP"), and the Rules of the United States Court of Appeals for the Ninth Circuit ("Circuit Rules"), unless otherwise indicated. *(Rev. 12/13/10; 9/17/14)*

1.1.   Active Judge—means a circuit judge of this circuit in regular active service.

1.2.   Senior Judge—means a circuit judge of this circuit who has retired from regular active service pursuant to 28 U.S.C. § 371(b) or 28 U.S.C. § 372(a).

1.3.   Member of the Court—means an active judge or a senior judge; in the plural, it means all active judges and senior judges, collectively.

1.4.   Visiting Judge—means any judge or justice of the United States, not a member of the Court, designated, pursuant to 28 U.S.C. §§ 291–96, to act as a member of a panel to hear and decide a case.

1.5.   Judge—without qualification, means an active judge, senior judge, or a visiting judge as the context may require.

a.   *Administrative Judge*—means the most senior eligible active judge willing to serve, not including the Chief Judge, in an administrative unit. Any active judge is eligible to serve as an administrative judge; service is to be in order of seniority, the term of office shall be 3 years. *(Rev. 1/1/07)*

1.6.   Panel—means a division of more than one judge of this Court to which a case or motion is referred for disposition.

1.7.   Disposition—means an opinion, memorandum, or order of the Court, without regard to the distinctions set forth in Circuit Rule 36–1.

1.8.   Appellate Commissioner—means a magistrate judge-level judicial officer appointed by the Court to rule or review and make recommendations on a variety of nondispositive matters, such as applications by appointed counsel for compensation under the Criminal Justice Act and certain motions specified in Chapter Six of these orders, and to serve as special master as directed by the Court. *(Rev. 9/17/14)*

1.9.   Staff Attorney—means an attorney appointed by the Court to assist in the processing of appeals and motions and to perform such other duties as the Court directs.

1.10.   Circuit Mediator—means an attorney employed by the Court to facilitate the settlement of cases and to perform such other duties as the Court directs. *(Rev. 12/13/10)*

1.11.   Administrative Unit. Pursuant to 28 U.S.C. § 41, 3 administrative units are established: the Northern Unit, composed of the districts of Alaska, Idaho, Montana, Oregon, Eastern and Western Washington;

The Middle Unit, composed of the districts of Arizona, Nevada, Hawaii, Guam, Northern Mariana Islands and Northern and Eastern California; and

The Southern Unit, composed of the districts of Central and Southern California.

1.12.   Comeback Cases—means subsequent appeals or petitions from a district court case or agency proceeding involving substantially the same parties and issues from which there previously had been a calendared appeal or petition.

1.13.   Terms Used for Cases, Case Participants, and Dispositive Reliefs. When these General Orders use the term "appeal" without qualification, the intention is to include a petition for review. Therefore, the terms for parties in an appeal (such as appellant and appellee) are intended to correspond to the terms for parties in a petition (such as petitioner and respondent). In addition, the terms for dispositive reliefs used when resolving appeals (such as affirmed and reversed) are intended to correspond to the terms for dispositive reliefs used when resolving petitions (such as denied and granted). *(New 9/17/14)*

Chapter II: FILING & DOCKETING APPEALS

2.1.   Inquiry Regarding Related Matters. *(Abrogated 9/17/14)*

2.2.   Proceedings In Forma Pauperis. With respect to proceedings in this Court in forma pauperis pursuant to 18 U.S.C. § 3006A, 28 U.S.C. § 1915, and FRAP 24, the appointment of counsel by the trial court to represent the defendant shall create a rebuttable presumption of pauper status for the purpose of dispensing with the docket fee in this Court. This presumption may be challenged by the opposing party, or by the Court on its own motion, when it appears that the defendant may not be a pauper. Unless challenged, however, the presumption shall cure, for accounting purposes, any administrative failure by the district court to supply documents in support of pauper status. *(Rev. 9/17/14)*

2.3.   Procedures for Failure to Comply With Deadlines Established by the Court. Circuit Rule 42–1 provides for dismissal if records, docket fees, or appellant's briefs are not timely filed. The Clerk may issue an order to show cause directing the payment of fees or a response with respect to jurisdictional and other issues that may be appropriate for summary disposition. If appellant fails to comply with the order, the Clerk may dismiss the appeal for lack of prosecution; however, a direct criminal appellant shall have a second opportunity to respond. *(Rev. 9/17/14)*

In situations where the failure to prosecute involves the failure to file the brief, the Clerk shall follow these procedures:

a.   *All Civil Appeals, Including All Pro Se and Retained Counsel Habeas Corpus and Criminal Post–Judgment Appeals.* If appellant pro se or appellant's retained or pro bono counsel fails to timely file the opening brief, the Clerk shall dismiss the appeal for failure to prosecute no sooner than 14 days after the brief's due date has passed. *(Rev. 9/17/14)*

b.   *All Direct Criminal Appeals and All Habeas Corpus and Criminal Post–Judgment Appeals in which Appellant is Represented by Counsel Appointed pursuant to the Criminal Justice Act.* If any appellant in a direct criminal appeal or an appellant represented by appointed counsel in a habeas corpus or criminal post-judgment appeal fails to timely file the opening brief, the Clerk shall issue a default order directing appellant to correct the deficiency within 14 days. The default order shall warn that failure to comply timely with the order may result in the imposition of sanctions on counsel, the removal of appointed counsel from the appeal, and/or dismissal of the appeal for failure to prosecute. The default order will further require the United States Attorney or the State Attorney General, within 14 days, to serve the order on appellant individually and to provide proof of service, including appellant's registration number and address, to the Court. The Clerk shall serve the default order on appellant's counsel by overnight mail if counsel is not registered for Appellate ECF.

If the opening brief is submitted along with a motion for relief from default, the Clerk may grant the motion and re-set the remainder of the briefing schedule or refer the motion to an Appellate Commissioner for resolution.

If a motion for extension of time to file the opening brief is filed in response to the default order, the motion will be referred to an Appellate Commissioner for resolution.

If appellant fails to respond to the default order with 14 days of the date of the default order, the matter will be referred to an Appellate Commissioner for further proceedings.

In the event appointed counsel is relieved pursuant to this section, a copy of the order shall be served on the appointing authority. *(Rev. 9/17/14)*

c.   *Direct Criminal Appeals (retained counsel).* *(Abrogated 9/17/14)*

d.   *Direct Criminal Appeals (pro se appellants).* *(Abrogated 9/17/14)*

e.   *Failure to File Answering Brief.* In all cases, if no answering brief is filed, the Clerk shall, no sooner than 14 days after the brief's due date, issue an order that directs appellee either to inform the Clerk by letter that no brief will be filed or to submit the brief along with a motion within 14 days of the date of the order. The Clerk may grant or refer the motion to an Appellate Commissioner, motions panel, or merits panel. If appellee fails to respond to the order, the case will be deemed ready for calendaring on the basis of the opening brief. *(New 9/17/14)*

2.4.   Motions for Reinstatement. Any motion to reinstate an appeal dismissed for want of prosecution shall indicate how the deficiency has been corrected or explain why correction is impossible. *(Rev. 9/17/14)*

Chapter III: CALENDARING

3.1. Time and Place of Court Calendars.

a. *Places of Hearings.* It is policy of the Court that, in general, depending on caseload, there shall be Court calendars each year in the following places: San Francisco; Pasadena; Seattle; Portland; Honolulu; and Anchorage. Court calendars may be set in other locations within the circuit subject to the approval of the Chief Judge. *(Rev. 12/13/10; 9/17/14; 1/11/16)*

b. *Number of Panel Sittings\per Calendar.* Each Court calendar shall consist of as many panel sittings during one or two consecutive weeks as may be deemed appropriate in view of the number of cases ready for hearing, the availability of judges, personnel, and facilities, holidays, and travel-related concerns. *(Rev. 9/17/14; 1/11/16)*

3.2. Assignment of Judges to Calendars. After the time and place of calendars have been established by the Clerk's Office, judges and visiting judges shall be assigned to particular days on the calendars. Except as provided in G.O.3.2.d, the Clerk's Office will use a computer program that is designed to equalize the workload among all judges, randomly assign panels, and take into account the following factors: *(Rev. 1/11/16)*

a. *Composition of Panels.* Except as provided in Circuit Rule 22–2(a) and G.O.3.3.h, oral argument panels will be composed of no fewer than two members of the Court, as defined by G.O.1.3, at least one of whom shall be an active judge at the time the panel is drawn. *(Rev. 1/11/16)*

b. *Assignment of Active Judges.* Every year, the Court will establish the number of panel sitting days required of each active judge. These panel sitting days do not include en banc hearings, motions panels, oral screening panels, three-judge district court cases, certificate of appealability panels, and cases for which a judge's name is drawn by lot. With the approval of the Executive Committee, the Chief Judge may have fewer panel sitting days than other active judges. *(Rev. 12/13/10; 9/17/14)*

c. *Assignment of Senior Judges.* Senior judges may choose the number of panels on which they will serve and are not calendared for hearings away from their home stations unless they are willing. Senior judges who wish to hear cases in particular locations are accommodated to the extent consistent with the other factors listed in this section. However, in order to make the assignment work, they may be required to accept a full load of panel assignments in those locations. Within the context of this subsection "panel" refers to the panel of judges hearing cases in a given location over the course of a sitting. *(Rev. 9/17/14)*

d. *Assignment of Judges to Honolulu and Anchorage Calendars.* Honolulu and Anchorage panels are composed of two willing judges, chosen in the order of when they last served, and one junior judge, if any, who has not yet served. *(New 1/11/16)*

e. *Rotation of Judges.* Insofar as possible, over time, each active judge should sit with every other active and senior judge approximately the same number of times. *(Rev. 1/11/16)*

f. *Parity in Panel Sittings.* Insofar as possible, over time, each active judge should sit on approximately the same number of panels in San Francisco, Pasadena, Seattle, Portland, Honolulu and Anchorage as each of the other active judges. *(Rev. 1/11/16)*

g. *Preferences of Judges.* Insofar as practicable, the wishes of each judge with regard to sitting during particular months and on particular days during any calendar shall be accommodated. *(Rev. 1/11/16)*

h. *Unavailability.* Each member of the Court shall inform the Clerk of Court as far in advance as possible of his or her unavailability for assignment to a calendar. Each member of the Court has the option to exchange days of sitting with another member of the Court upon mutual agreement and with the approval of the Chief Judge. Exchanges of assignments shall normally be accomplished at least 60 days in advance of the hearing week. Although the Clerk's Office may be consulted and must be notified of any exchanges, arrangements for exchanges shall be made by direct contact among the members of the Court.

If, after a matter is under submission to a three-judge panel, a judge becomes unavailable by reason of death, disability, recusal, or retirement from the Court, the remaining two judges may—if in agreement—decide the matter as a quorum pursuant to 28 U.S.C. § 46(d), or shall request the Clerk to draw a replacement judge. If the two judges are not in agreement, the Clerk shall draw a replacement judge. If a replacement judge is requested, the Clerk shall draw a replacement judge from among active judges (and senior judges willing to serve), drawn by lot. Once a replacement judge is designated, the Clerk will advise the parties. *(Rev. 1/11/16; 3/26/19)*

i. *Disqualification or Recusal.* In the event a judge disqualifies or recuses himself or herself before submission, the Clerk shall try to find a replacement by switching cases or judges with panels in the same location. If unsuccessful, the Clerk shall draw a replacement, utilizing a list of active judges randomly drawn by lot as provided in G.O. 3.2.h. In rare instances, argument of the case may be postponed until the next calendar. *(Rev. 12/13/10; Rev. 1/11/16)*

j. *Overburdens.* If a member of the Court falls behind in preparing dispositions, the Chief Judge may determine that the judge should be relieved of further calendar duties until he or she becomes more current. A prima facie case for relieving a judge exists when one or more of the following criteria are met:

(1) 2 or more cases not presently in circulation were assigned to the judge for preparation of a disposition over 9 months earlier;

(2) 5 or more cases not presently in circulation were assigned to the judge for preparation of a disposition over 6 months earlier;

(3) 15 or more cases not presently in circulation were assigned to the judge for preparation of a disposition over 3 months earlier.

The judge may rebut the prima facie case by showing either that within one month or less he or she will no longer meet any of the criteria or that there is good cause for remaining on calendar. The Chief Judge may alternatively assign the judge to fewer panels rather than relieve him or her of all calendar duties.

A judge may also request to be relieved of his or her administrative duties.

Calendar relief is not appropriate to compensate for a judge's increased workload that results from sitting with the district court.

k. *Temporary Calendar Reduction.* Any active judge having completed 7 years of service with the Court may request a one-year reduction to 5 monthly calendars with 3 consecutive months without any calendar duties. The Chief Judge may grant the request if the judge's disposition backlog is reasonably current. Requests shall be granted in order of seniority, but no more than 3 active judges may take such a reduction within a given year. Any judge granted such reduction shall be ineligible for a subsequent grant for 7 years. *(New 9/18/02)*

3.2.1. Selection of Circuit Judge to Serve on Three–Judge District Courts. The Clerk shall select, by random draw from the circuit-wide pool of senior and active judges, a judge to serve on three-judge district courts as required by 28 U.S.C. § 2284.

3.3. Assignment of Cases to Calendars.

a. *Number of Panels Sitting.* *(Abrogated 9/17/14)*

b. *Selection of Cases for Calendars.* Prior to each calendar, the Clerk's Office shall designate the cases that are to be included in the calendar. The Clerk's Office shall identify the judges who have been designated for the panels and, to the extent possible, the districts of any Ninth Circuit district judges who will be sitting on the various panels. *(Rev. 12/13/10; 9/17/14; 1/11/16)*

Cases ready for submission to a panel shall be screened by case management attorneys, who shall designate issues, identify cases with similar issues, and assign a numerical weight to each case. Drawing upon a computerized file of such cases, the Clerk's Office generates a prospective case list using a computer application that takes into account, to the extent possible, the priorities set forth in the following subsection. *(Rev. 1/11/16)*

c. *Priorities.* Generally, cases are selected for calendaring according to the order in which the notices of appeal, petitions, or applications for enforcement were filed, except that priority is given to direct criminal appeals, capital cases, civil appeals having statutory priority, and cases entitled to calendaring priority under Circuit Rule 34–3. Unless petitioner is in the custody of the Department of Homeland Security, petitions for review of orders of the Board of Immigration Appeals are selected for calendaring in the order in which principal briefing is completed. A case may also be advanced in calendaring so that it may be heard at the same time as a case that involves the same legal issues. Capital cases and direct criminal appeals are given priority over all other cases. There is no ordering among civil cases entitled to priority. *(Rev. 1/11/16)*

d. *Assignment of Cases to Panels.* Prior to each calendar, the Clerk's Office shall assign the cases to the panels that will be sitting. The assignments are made using a computer application that takes into account the number of panel sitting days, known recusals and the location and month of oral argument to then randomly assign cases to each sitting panel day. To the extent practicable, each panel sitting day should have cases that add up to the same numerical weight total. The total shall be established by the Court as appropriate for any one panel sitting day. After initial assignment, the Clerk may make adjustments in order to reassign individual cases based on: (1) a judge's conflicts of interest, (2) attorney unavailability and (3) the Court's policy against allocating to a panel on which a district judge is sitting any appeal from that judge's district. Such reassignment will be accomplished by shifting assignment days within the same week or through the drawing of a replacement judge from the list described in G.O. 3.2.h above. *(Rev. 1/11/16)*

e. *Subsequent Proceedings in Calendared Cases.* Once a case has been assigned to a specific panel and the calendar described in G.O. 3.3.d is mailed to the members of the Court, that panel shall have responsibility for all further proceedings in the case, unless it directs otherwise. If it comes to the attention of a motions panel to which a motion for reconsideration has been referred that the case has been assigned to a specific panel, the motions panel shall contact the members of that panel before disposing of the motion. *(Rev. 9/17/14)*

(former f) *Exchange of Assignments.* *(Abrogated 1/11/16)*

f. *Expediting Appeals.* Notwithstanding the foregoing provisions, the Clerk, an Appellate Commissioner, or a motions or screening panel may order that an appeal be expedited for good cause such as those set forth at Circuit Rule 27–12. See also Fed. R. App. P. 2 (Suspension of the Rules). Such a case shall be assigned through the randomized computer calendaring system to the next available panel in the administrative unit where the case would normally be heard and where the panels sitting for that calendar have not yet been assigned their cases. The order directing that a case be expedited may include information about the time and place of the hearing once the next available panel has been determined. *(Rev. 1/11/16)*

g. *Urgent Cases.* The Clerk, the Appellate Commissioner, or a motions or screening panel may determine that extraordinary circumstances require that a case be heard within a specified time period and ordered onto a specific calendar, even though the panels sitting for that calendar have already been assigned their cases. See Fed. R. App. P. 2; Circuit Rule 27–12. Examples of such urgent cases include a case that may become moot in the absence of a decision within a specified time period or a case involving factual circumstances requiring a prompt decision, such as an appeal from a temporary stay. A case designated as an urgent case shall be randomly assigned by the Clerk to a non-recused existing panel, utilizing all panels drawn for the month in which the case must be heard, regardless of geographic location excluding Honolulu and Anchorage (unless the urgent case originates from that location). Absent extraordinary circumstances, the assigned panel shall accept the additional case. The assigned panel may remove another case from its existing calendar to compensate for the assignment of the additional case. If no such panel is available, the Clerk shall draw a panel from the list described in G.O. 3.2.h above. *(New 1/11/16)*

(former h.) *Adding Cases to Calendars.* *(Abrogated 1/11/16)*

h. *Calendaring Policy: Ninth Circuit Only Panels and Emergency Assignments.* Any exceptions to the Court's calendaring policies shall be directed to the Chief Judge. The Chief Judge, in consultation with the Clerk, or a motions or screening panel may determine before a case has been assigned to a panel that a case should only be heard by a panel composed of three members of the Court. This determination may be made because a case is likely to set circuit precedent for a large number of cases, is likely to involve subsequent appeals which would be best heard by the same panel, or is a case of exceptional importance. Such a case shall be calendared according to the usual procedure provided in these General Orders, except that the case shall be assigned to a panel consisting only of members of the Court. In addition, notwithstanding other provisions of this chapter, in exigent circumstances including the death, illness or last minute unavailability or recusal of a judge, when substitution or drawing by lot is impractical, the Chief Judge may direct the Clerk to reassign a case or cases to another judge the Chief Judge determines is available to serve on short notice. *(Rev 1/11/16)*

3.4. Notification of Calendaring of Cases. About fourteen weeks before oral argument, parties are notified of the month that their cases are being considered for oral argument.

About ten weeks before oral argument, parties shall be notified of the time and place of the hearing of their cases.

If a panel decides not to hear oral argument, the parties should be notified at least 14 days before the scheduled hearing date. However, such notices may by necessity be issued any time before the scheduled hearing. *(Rev 1/11/16; 1/13/20)*

3.5. Publication of Calendars. The composition of panels shall be made public on the first working day of the week preceding argument. Calendars shall be posted on the Court's website and in the San Francisco, Pasadena, and Seattle courthouses. Only under exceptional circumstances will the Court consider motions for continuances filed within 14 days of the hearing date. (See Circuit Rule 34–2.) *(Rev. 12/13/10; Rev. 1/11/16)*

3.6. Comeback Cases.

a. *Matters on Remand From the United States Supreme Court.* Matters on remand from the United States Supreme Court will be referred to the last panel that previously heard the matter before the writ of certiorari was granted.

b. *Matters Arising After Remand by an En Banc Court.* Where a new appeal is taken following a remand or other decision by an en banc court, the Clerk's Office shall notify the en banc court that the new appeal is pending, and proceed only after hearing instructions from that en banc court. The en banc court will decide whether to keep the case or to refer it to the three judge panel. The en banc court may elect to refer the case to the three judge panel while retaining jurisdiction over any future en banc proceedings. If the en banc panel so elects, a new en banc court will not be drawn from the eligible pool of judges at the time of future proceedings. *(Rev. 12/10/18; 1/11/16)*

c. *Capital Cases.* Subject to the foregoing provisions, comebacks in capital cases are governed by Circuit Rule 22–2(c), which states, "that once a capital case is assigned to a panel it retains jurisdiction for all future appeals."

d. *Appeals Following Remand or Other Decision in the Same Underlying Case.* When a new appeal is taken to this Court from a district court or agency decision following a remand or other decision by an argument panel, the Clerk's Office will notify the panel that previously heard the case that the new appeal or petition is pending, and will provide a brief description of the issues presented. The prior panel is encouraged to accept a case that predominately involves the interpretation and application of the prior panel decision, except when it is impossible to reconstitute the prior panel. Any motion to assign a new appeal to a prior panel will be referred to the prior panel for decision. A new appeal will be assigned to the prior panel if two of the judges on the prior panel agree to accept the case. If the third judge on the prior panel is unavailable, the Clerk shall draw a replacement, utilizing a list of active judges randomly drawn by lot as provided in G.O. 3.2.h.

3.7. Oral Argument in Pro Bono Project Appeals. If an appeal has been selected for inclusion in the Court's Pro Bono Representation Project and pro bono counsel has been appointed, the panel shall not submit the case on the briefs, but shall hear oral argument unless pro bono counsel withdraws or consents in writing to submission on the briefs.

When a case has been selected for inclusion in the project, the case management attorneys will revise the inventory card to notify the panel that the case should not be submitted on the briefs.

Chapter IV: DISPOSITIONS

4.1. Prevention of Conflicts.

a. *Questions Pending Concurrently Before Two or More Panels.* Whenever an author of a proposed disposition knows that the disposition may decide a question pending concurrently before one or more other panels of the Court, the author shall circulate copies of the proposed disposition to all members of such other panels. The author shall include a memorandum explaining the purpose of the circulation and setting a 14–day time period within which a response, if any, will be expected.

The panel with the earliest originally scheduled oral argument in a case has priority over the disposition of a common legal question pending before two or more panels. A case in oral or written screening is not eligible to have priority. If two or more oral arguments concerning a common legal question are scheduled on the same day, the panel hearing oral argument in the case with the earliest notice of appeal date has priority. If the panel with priority postpones oral argument in the case, refers the case to mediation, elects to forego priority, or does not decide the question in a precedential opinion, then it will no longer have priority over the common legal question. In such an event, the panel will notify the Court as soon as possible, and the next panel with priority will be determined using the same procedure.

If a dispute or uncertainty arises among panels as to priority, or if, for good cause, a panel wishes that, notwithstanding the rules set forth above, the Chief Judge make a decision as to which panel shall be afforded priority over the disposition of a common legal issue pending before two or more panels, priority will be determined by the Chief Judge within fourteen (14) days of the submission of the matter to the Chief Judge by one or more panels.

Within seven (7) days following the notification to the Court by the Chief Judge of a determination concerning priority, any member of the Court may request that the Chief Judge's decision be reviewed by the Court, in which case the determination as to priority will be made by a majority of the non-recused active judges in attendance at the next regularly scheduled Court Meeting, in person, or by electronic media. This provision is intended to provide guidance for internal case processing only, and does not confer a right on any third party. *(Rev. 9/7/16)*

b. *Deferring Submission Pending Decision by Another Court.* Whenever a panel decides to defer or vacate submission pending decision in another case before another court or administrative agency, the panel shall enter an order identifying the case by name and number and the court in which the decision is pending.

4.2. Deciding Cases on Points Not Raised and Argued. If a panel determines to decide a case upon the basis of a significant point not raised by the parties in their briefs, it shall give serious consideration to requesting additional briefing and oral argument before issuing a disposition predicated upon the particular point.

4.3. Writing of Dispositions. An opinion should be written if at least one member of the panel deciding the case specifically determines that a published decision is necessary. *(Rev. 9/17/14)*

4.3.a. Memoranda Dispositions. Unlike an opinion for publication which is designed to clarify the law of the circuit, a memorandum disposition is designed only to provide the parties and the district court with a concise explanation of this Court's decision. Because the parties and the district court are aware of the facts, procedural events and applicable law underlying the dispute, the disposition need recite only such information crucial to the result. Accordingly, all that is necessary is a statement such as the following:

> Defendant's statements were volunteered rather than made in response to police questioning, and were therefore admissible. United States v. Cornejo, 598 F.2d 554, 557 (9th Cir. 1979). AFFIRMED.

(Rev. 12/13/10)

4.4. Suggesting Changes to Draft Dispositions. When a member of a panel suggests a change in a draft disposition to the authoring judge, the judge should, whenever possible, submit proposed language incorporating the suggestion.

4.5. Filing of Dispositions.

a. *Majority, Concurring, and Dissenting Dispositions.* Except for decisions from the bench, the determination of each appeal, administrative review proceeding, and original writ proceeding shall be evidenced by a written disposition concurred in by a majority of the panel assigned to act thereon. The disposition shall indicate the district court or agency and Court of Appeals docket numbers, district judge whose decision is being appealed, date and city of argument, date of submission to the panel, and filing date. The majority disposition shall be certified by one of the members as having been concurred in by such members. Any separate concurring or dissenting disposition shall be certified by the author or by one of the members of the panel as having been prepared by the author thereof. *(Rev. 12/13/10)*

When 2 judges of a panel have concurred in a written disposition but the third judge has neither agreed nor circulated a dissent or concurrence within 60 days after notice of the concurrence and circulation of the proposed disposition in its final form, the author shall submit the disposition to the Clerk and send a copy of the covering memorandum to the third member. Ten days after receipt, the Clerk shall file the disposition with a notation that the third judge may file a separate statement at a later date. The author, with the concurrence of the second judge, may grant the request of the third judge to delay filing for a period of 14 days or for a longer period if the third judge cites extraordinary circumstances or the complexity of the case. *(Rev. 12/13/10)*

b. *Rule 36—Notation on Memoranda Dispositions.* All memoranda dispositions shall contain the following notation:

> This disposition is not appropriate for publication and is not precedent except as provided by Ninth Circuit Rule 36–3.

(Rev. 12/13/10)

c. *Electronic Transmission of Dispositions.* The authoring judge shall transmit the disposition electronically to the Opinions Clerk or the Memoranda Clerk, respectively. *(Rev. 1/1/06; 12/13/10; 9/17/14)*

d. *Temporary Hold.* The authoring judge may request that the Clerk of the Court temporarily withhold filing of an opinion, order, or memorandum disposition. *(Rev. 9/17/14)*

e. *Costs.* In every disposition in a civil or agency case where (1) the judgment is affirmed in part, reversed in part, modified, or vacated; (2) the case is remanded; (3) the panel determines that costs shall be unequally divided among the losing parties; or (4) the panel wishes to depart from the presumptive entitlements set forth at FRAP 39(a)(1)–(3), the disposition shall indicate in its text or in a separate order which party or parties shall bear the costs. See FRAP 39. The Clerk's Office, before filing the disposition, shall determine whether the disposition makes that indication. If the disposition does not indicate which party or parties shall bear the costs, the Clerk's Office immediately shall request that information from the authoring judge, or the presiding judge if the author is not a member of the Court, who will enter an appropriate order.

The authoring judge, or the presiding judge if the author is not a member of the Court, shall also be responsible for motions for reconsideration of the Clerk's orders pertaining to cost bills that are entered under Circuit Rule 39–1.5 and G.O. 6.3.a. The Clerk may refer a motion and proposed order to the authoring judge, or the presiding judge if the author is not a member of the Court, when the motion presents an issue other than technical application of FRAP 39 and Circuit Rule 39–1. *(New 7/1/02; Rev. 9/17/14)*

4.6. Mandate.

a. *Policy Against Issuance of Mandate Forthwith.* FRAP 40 and 41 direct that, following a decision by this Court, the mandate should not issue forthwith, but that time should be allowed after entry of judgment for the filing of a petition for rehearing en banc, or petition for writ of certiorari. Therefore, only in exceptional circumstances should a panel order the issuance of mandate forthwith upon the filing of a disposition. *(Rev. 3/24/04; 9/17/14)*

b. *Exceptions to Policy Against Issuance of Mandate Forthwith.* Exceptional circumstances may include, but are not limited to, instances where it appears from the record that a petition for rehearing en banc, or petition for writ of certiorari would be legally frivolous, where the losing litigant is attempting to defeat a just result by interposing delaying tactics, or where an emergency situation requires that, to effectuate a just result, the action of the Court should become final, and mandate issue, at once. In such a case, the panel may close the disposition with the following language: "No petition for rehearing will be entertained and mandate shall issue forthwith. See Fed. R. App. P. 2." However, such language in the disposition does not prevent a judge from making an en banc call. In a criminal case, the panel may also revoke bail forthwith. *(Rev. 3/24/04; 12/13/10; 9/17/14)*

c. *Stay of Mandate.* A motion for stay of mandate shall be forwarded to the panel. The author, or presiding judge if the author is not a member of the Court, shall dispose of the motion in accordance with the panel's vote on the motion. *(Rev. 3/26/03; 9/17/14)*

d. *Recall of Mandate.* A motion for recall of mandate shall be forwarded to the panel. The author, or the presiding judge if the author is not a member of the Court, shall dispose of the motion in accordance with the panel's vote on the motion. *(New 3/26/03; Rev. 9/17/14)*

Chapter V: EN BANC PROCEDURES

5.1. Definitions and General Provisions.

a. *Definitions*—For purposes of this Chapter:

1. Full Court—means all active judges.

2. En Banc Court—means that number of judges, greater than 3, established by rule of the Court, which shall hear and decide cases taken en banc as provided by statute, rule, or in these General Orders.

3. Judge Eligible to Vote—means any active judge who is not recused or disqualified. Upon entry to active service, a judge may choose to recuse from voting on en banc calls for a transition period specified by the judge. When the transition period expires, the judge will become eligible to vote, including voting on calls in which the voting period has already commenced. Notice of

recusal or disqualification shall be given to the full Court. No senior judge is eligible to vote on whether to take a case en banc. *(Rev. 1/1/04; 9/17/14)*

4. Judge Eligible to Serve on the En Banc Court—means any active or senior judge who is not recused or disqualified and who entered upon active service prior to the date the Court is drawn. Senior judges shall not serve on an en banc court except: (i) a senior judge who was a member of the three-judge panel assigned to the case being heard or reheard en banc may elect to be eligible to be selected as a member of the en banc court. Any senior judge who elects to be eligible shall notify the Clerk's Office prior to the date the panel is drawn; (ii) a senior judge who takes senior status while serving as a member of an en banc court may continue to serve until all matters pending before that en banc court, including remands from the Supreme Court, are finally disposed of. *(Rev. 7/1/03; 3/21/18)*

5. En Banc Coordinator—means an active or senior judge appointed by the Chief Judge to perform the duties set forth in this Chapter.

6. En Banc Call—means a request by a judge or panel that a vote be taken to determine whether a case be heard or reheard by an en banc court.

b. *General Provisions.*

1. *Judicial Participation.* Each judge selected for the en banc court shall make every reasonable effort to sit on the en banc court, but if unable to sit, the judge shall notify the Clerk as promptly as possible, so that the judge may be replaced on the en banc court. If a judge becomes available after notifying the Clerk of inability to sit, that judge shall notify the Clerk of his or her availability and shall sit on the en banc court, unless a replacement judge has already been selected, in which case the replacement judge shall sit on the en banc court. In such event, the originally-selected judge shall be placed back in the pool of judges available to be drawn for service.

If a judge becomes unavailable to sit on the en banc court by reason of death, disability, recusal, or retirement from the Court, a replacement judge shall be selected.

If alternate judges were selected in accordance with Circuit Rule 35–3 at the time the en banc court was originally selected, the replacement judge shall be the designated alternate judge in the order as identified in the original selection process, provided that the alternate judge is available and still eligible to sit on the en banc court pursuant to G.O. 5.1.a.4. If no alternates were drawn, or if there are no drawn alternates available and eligible to serve on the en banc court, then the Clerk shall draw a replacement from the judges eligible to serve on the en banc court in accordance with Circuit Rule 35–3. Once a replacement judge is selected, the Clerk will advise the parties.

All members of the Court, senior and active, and visiting judges who participated in the panel decision, shall be kept informed of en banc proceedings, including all en banc calls, responsive memoranda, and votes, until a case is taken en banc or returned to the panel.

After a case has been taken en banc, only those judges participating in the en banc court shall be included in the distribution of memoranda, proposed opinions, and other communications regarding en banc proceedings. It is permissible for judges on en banc courts to discuss and disclose information concerning such cases with other judges not assigned to the en banc court. *(Rev. 6/23/10; 6/19/19)*

2. Duties of the En Banc Coordinator. The En Banc Coordinator shall supervise the en banc process, including time schedules provided in this Chapter; shall circulate periodic reports on the status of each case under en banc consideration; may, for good cause, extend, suspend, or compress the time schedules provided in this Chapter; may designate another judge to perform all or part of the En Banc Coordinator's duties during the coordinator's absence; may suggest, for any particular case, a modification or suspension of the provisions of this Chapter; and may for good cause suspend en banc proceedings. *(Rev. 7/1/02)*

3. Vote Tallies. The En Banc Coordinator or the Clerk's office will record the en banc votes and circulate the final tally to the Court. Orders rejecting or accepting cases for en banc consideration shall not specify the vote tally. Any judge eligible to vote may direct that his or her dissent from a failure to accept a case for en banc consideration be incorporated in the order. *(Rev. 9/17/14)*

4. **Duties of Panel Members.** The following persons shall be responsible for the distribution of the panel recommendation pursuant to G.O. 5.4.b and for orders denying a petition for rehearing en banc if no timely en banc call is made or if an en banc call fails to receive a majority vote:

(a) The author of a majority disposition, when an active or senior judge of this Court, or

(b) The presiding judge of the panel, when the author is a visiting judge. *(Rev. 9/17/14)*

5. **Computing and Extending Time.** FRAP 26 applies in computing any period of time specified in this Chapter. Until a case is taken en banc or returned to the panel, any request by a judge for an extension of time shall be made in writing or by electronic mail to the En Banc Coordinator with copies to all judges prior to the expiration of the relevant time period. The En Banc Coordinator will ordinarily grant a timely request for an extension of time absent exigent circumstances. A judge who makes an untimely request for an extension of time to request G.O. 5.4.b.1 notice or to call for an en banc vote should confer with the affected panel and attempt to resolve the matter in a collegial manner; however, no untimely request for an extension of time to request G.O. 5.4.b.1 notice or to call for an en banc vote will be granted without the consent of the affected panel. *(Rev. 9/17/14; 10/26/21)*

6. **Notification to En Banc Coordinator.** Judges should direct copies of all en banc correspondence under this Chapter to the En Banc Coordinator and the Clerk of Court or any person the Clerk may designate until a final en banc vote is tallied.

7. **Death Penalty Cases.** En banc procedures in death penalty cases, when a date for execution has been set, are contained in Circuit Rule 22 and shall be supervised by the Capital Case Coordinator.

8. **Stay of Mandate.** Whenever an off-panel judge timely invokes the procedures set forth in this Chapter, the mandate shall automatically be stayed. *(Rev. 10/26/21)*

5.2. Initial Hearing En Banc. Pursuant to Fed. R. App. P. 35(c), a petition requesting that an appeal be heard initially en banc must be filed by the date when the appellee's brief is due. The petition shall be referred to the three-judge panel assigned to the case for resolution. The panel may deny the petition on behalf of the Court or request that the Court vote on whether to hear the case initially en banc.

A three-judge panel may also, *sua sponte*, and in accordance with the rules pertaining to *sua sponte* en banc calls, request a vote on whether a case assigned to that panel should be heard initially en banc. *(Rev. 10/26/21)*

5.3. Amendment of Disposition; Proposal by Judge.

a. *Amendment of Disposition.* If a panel amends its disposition, the panel shall set forth in its amended disposition or separate order: (1) the ruling on the petition for rehearing or petition for rehearing en banc; (2) whether subsequent petitions for rehearing or rehearing en banc may be filed; and (3) the status of any pending petitions for rehearing or rehearing en banc not ruled on. The Clerk's Office shall contact the authoring judge if the amended disposition does not so specify. *(New 7/1/02)*

If a panel substantively amends its disposition, any off-panel judge may, within 7 days of the filing of the amended disposition, notify the panel and the other members of the Court that he or she is considering making an en banc call on the basis of the substantive amendment. Such notification shall extend the time to make an en banc call by 14 days. Thereafter, the provisions of this Chapter relating to a sua sponte en banc calls shall apply. *(New 12/1/02; Rev. 10/26/21)*

b. *Proposal by Judge.* Any active or senior judge may, before an en banc call is made or before the time for calling for en banc expires, propose to the panel that it amend its disposition. Such a request does not suspend en banc procedures. Any proposal to amend shall be accompanied by the text of the proposed amendment.

c. *Modification of Opinion Subject to an En Banc Call.* After an en banc call is made, but prior to the completion of a successful vote on whether the case should be reheard en banc, a panel may modify its opinion in one of two ways:

(1) A panel may withdraw its opinion and issue a new opinion or file a superseding amended opinion. The panel's withdrawal of its opinion or filing of a superseding substantive amended opinion, along with an order permitting the parties to file a new petition for rehearing en banc, moots the en banc call, as well as any pending petition for panel rehearing and petition for

rehearing en banc. Once the panel has filed the new or amended opinion, the parties may file new petitions for panel rehearing or rehearing en banc, and any judge may commence en banc proceedings in accordance with G.O. 5.4.

(2) A panel may propose one or more amendments to its opinion that would be made if the en banc call fails. If the en banc call vote succeeds, then the en banc court takes control of the case. If the en banc call vote fails, then the panel shall proceed under G.O. 5.3.a. and any subsequent en banc call shall also proceed under G.O. 5.3.a. *(New 10/26/21)*

5.4. Rehearing En Banc.

a. *Duties of Clerk.* Upon the filing by a party of a petition for rehearing en banc, the Clerk shall circulate a copy to each active judge and to those senior judges who have requested copies.

b. *Request for Notice of Panel Vote on Petition for Panel Rehearing and Time Within Which Judges Must Act After Notice.*

1. Request for Notice. An off-panel judge may request notice of the panel's vote on a petition for panel rehearing and petition for rehearing en banc within 21 days of the circulation of the last-filed petition for rehearing en banc. In the absence of a timely request for notice, the panel may enter an order denying the petition for rehearing en banc and denying the petition for panel rehearing. *(Rev. 9/17/14)*

2. Circulation of Notice; Vote on Petitions; Proposed Amendments. If a judge timely requests notice pursuant to G.O. 5.4.b.1, the panel shall circulate to all judges notice of its vote on the petitions for panel rehearing and rehearing en banc. If the panel decides to amend its opinion the panel shall notify all judges of its proposed amendments. The panel should respond as soon as possible to the G.O. 5.4b.1 request, but ordinarily within 90 days of the request or the petition for rehearing, whichever is later. *(New 7/1/06)*

A judge may withdraw a request for G.O. 5.4.b.1 notice by notifying the En Banc Coordinator in writing with copies to all judges. The time periods set forth in this Chapter shall be suspended for a period of 7 days following circulation of the notice to enable another judge to pursue en banc consideration. *(New 10/26/21)*

A judge must call for an en banc vote within: (1) 14 days of the date of the panel's distribution of the G.O. 5.4b notice; (2) 21 days after the circulation of the last-filed petition for rehearing en banc; or (3) if a response to the petition for rehearing en banc has been requested, within 14 days after the circulation of the response, whichever is latest. *(Rev. 7/1/02)*

3. Procedure When Only a Petition for Panel Rehearing is Filed. In a case where a party files only a petition for panel rehearing and no petition for rehearing en banc, an off-panel judge may call for en banc within the time limits set forth for sua sponte calls in G.O. 5.4.c.3. Any such call shall act as a request for notice of the panel's vote on the petition for rehearing. Alternatively, an off-panel judge may expressly request notice of the panel's vote on the petition for rehearing, but such a request must also be made within the time limits for sua sponte calls set forth in G.O. 5.4.c.3. The time to call for en banc shall expire 14 days after such notice.

c. *En Banc Calls and Supplemental Briefing.*

1. En Banc Calls. Any judge may call for a vote to rehear a case en banc: (1) in response to notice of the panel's vote that a petition for rehearing en banc be denied and a petition for panel rehearing denied (see G.O. 5.4.b), or (2) sua sponte. The requesting judge shall notify the panel and all other members of the Court of any call, and shall forward a memorandum setting forth reasons: (1) within 14 days of the date of distribution of the call; (2) within 14 days after the circulation of the response to the petition for rehearing en banc; or (3) in the case of sua sponte calls, within 7 days after the circulation of the simultaneous briefing, whichever is latest. *(Rev. 7/1/02)*

2. Supplemental Briefing. When an en banc call is made in a case in which a party has petitioned for en banc consideration and in which no response to the petition has been previously filed, the author of the panel opinion or the Clerk of Court upon request of the En Banc Coordinator, shall ordinarily enter an order directing counsel to file within 21 days of the date of the order a response to the petition for rehearing en banc. The time provided by G.O. 5.5.a in which judges shall circulate memoranda will not start to run until the response is filed or the En Banc Coordinator determines that no response will be filed.

3. Sua Sponte Calls. A judge may sua sponte call for a vote on rehearing en banc within 7 days of the expiration of the time for filing a petition for panel rehearing or rehearing en banc.

This means the sua sponte call must ordinarily be made within 21 days of the filing of the panel's decision in all cases, except civil cases in which the United States is a party. In such cases, the call must ordinarily be made within 52 days of the filing of the panel's decision. See FRAP 40(a). When the panel grants a party an extension of time to file a petition for rehearing or rehearing en banc, the time to make a sua sponte call will extend for 7 days after the petition is due. If a judge makes a sua sponte en banc call when a party has filed a petition for rehearing and rehearing en banc, then the panel or the En Banc Coordinator will order a response to the petition for rehearing and rehearing en banc pursuant to G.O. 5.4.c.2 rather than ordering the parties to file simultaneous supplemental briefing. A judge may also call for en banc within 21 days of the filing of an order directing that a previously unpublished disposition be published. Upon receipt of a timely sua sponte en banc call, the author of the panel opinion or the Clerk of Court upon the request of the En Banc Coordinator shall ordinarily enter an order directing the parties to file simultaneous briefs within 21 days setting forth their respective positions on whether the matter should be reheard en banc. If the En Banc Coordinator orders that no supplemental briefing will be filed, the parties will be notified of the sua sponte en banc call. *(Rev. 7/1/02; 10/4/06; 9/17/14)*

4. Withdrawal of En Banc Calls. A judge may withdraw an en banc call by notifying the En Banc Coordinator in writing with copies to all judges. The time periods set forth in this Chapter shall be suspended for a period of 7 days following circulation of the notice to enable another judge to pursue en banc consideration. *(New 7/1/02; Rev. 10/26/21)*

5.5. Procedure After Supplemental Briefing.

a. *Memoranda.* Any judge may circulate memoranda in response to an en banc call within 21 days after: (1) the conclusion of all supplemental briefing by the parties pursuant to G.O. 5.4.c.2 and .3, or (2) the calling judge's circulation of a memorandum in support of the en banc call, whichever is later. *(Rev. 9/17/14)*

b. *Voting.* When the exchange of memoranda has been completed, the En Banc Coordinator shall notify all active judges to vote. No judge shall circulate further correspondence on the case after that notice. A judge's failure to vote shall be considered a "no" vote. Unless otherwise ordered, each judge shall cast a vote within 7 days of the notice to vote. A judge may change his or her vote if accomplished prior to the expiration of the voting period. Upon the expiration of the voting period, the En Banc Coordinator shall notify the judges of the result and the vote tally. *(Rev. 1/13/20)*

c. *No Majority Favoring En Banc Consideration.* If the call fails to obtain a majority, the panel shall resume control of the case and no further en banc action is required.

d. *Majority Favoring En Banc Consideration.* If a majority of the judges eligible to vote on the en banc call votes in favor of en banc consideration, the Chief Judge shall enter an order taking the case en banc pursuant to Circuit Rule 35–3. The three-judge panel opinion shall not be cited as precedent by or to this Court or any district court of the Ninth Circuit, except to the extent adopted by the en banc court. *(Rev. 1/27/04)*

e. *Recusals.* It is left to the discretion of the individual judge as to whether that judge's recusal is noted in the order either denying or granting en banc review. *(New 10/4/06)*

5.6. Reserved Time. En banc oral arguments and conferences shall normally be scheduled on a quarterly basis in conjunction with Court meetings. A location for each en banc argument will be determined by the Chief Judge in consultation with the Court Executive Committee. Judges are expected to appear in person for en banc hearings. In the event no oral argument is to be heard, the Chief Judge shall designate a date, time, and place for a conference of the en banc court, which ordinarily shall also be the date of submission of the case.

5.7. Assignment of Opinion Writing, Circulation, and Filing of Disposition.

a. *Assignment of Opinion Writing.* After the case has been submitted to the en banc court, the judge senior in service among those voting with the majority shall assign the writing of the majority opinion. In the event more than one judge expresses a minority view, the senior judge among those sharing that view may assign the writing of a dissenting opinion without restricting any judge in the expression of individual views. A judge should not be selected to write a majority or dissenting opinion unless the judge's workload will permit the judge to circulate the opinion within this 45 days.

b. *Circulation of Opinions.*

1. Majority Opinion. Any judge unable to circulate the first draft of the majority opinion within 45 days shall circulate a memorandum to the members of the en banc court stating why the deadline cannot be met. The memorandum should state when the draft opinion will be circulated.

2. Dissenting or Other Separate Opinion. A judge who plans to circulate a dissenting or other separate opinion shall notify the members of the en banc court as soon as possible, but in any event within 14 days after the date of distribution of the draft of the majority opinion. Any dissenting or separate opinion shall be circulated within 30 days after a proposed majority opinion is distributed. Any judge unable to circulate a draft of the dissenting or separate opinion within 30 days after a proposed majority opinion is distributed shall notify the members of the en banc court and state when the dissenting or separate opinion will be circulated. *(Rev. 7/1/06; 9/17/14)*

3. Voting on Opinions. Voting shall conclude within the time established by the Chief Judge or the presiding judge.

c. *Filing of Dispositions.* The author of the majority opinion shall be responsible for coordinating the proposed majority, dissenting, and concurring dispositions, and filing the final dispositions at the appropriate time.

5.8. Rehearing by Full Court.

a. *Petition by a Party.* Upon a timely petition by a party for a rehearing en banc before the full court, the Clerk shall forward a copy thereof to all active judges and any senior judge on the en banc court, and those senior judges who have requested copies. Thereafter, the provisions of this Chapter relating to petitions for rehearing en banc on three-judge panel cases shall apply. *(Rev. 12/13/10)*

b. *Sua Sponte Calls.* If no petition for rehearing en banc before the full court is filed, any judge may, within 7 days after the date such petition was due, request a vote on whether the case should be reheard by the full court. This request shall be accompanied by a memorandum in support of full court consideration. Thereafter, the provisions of this Chapter relating to petitions for rehearing en banc of three-judge panel cases shall apply.

5.9. Stay of Mandate. A motion for stay of mandate in a case decided en banc shall be forwarded to the author of the disposition, who shall dispose of the motion and then send all members of the en banc court a copy of the motion and the disposition of the motion. *(Rev. 3/36/03)*

5.10. Recall of Mandate. A motion for recall of mandate in a case decided en banc shall be forwarded to the members of the en banc court. The authoring judge shall be responsible for entering the order disposing of the motion after polling the members of the en banc court. *(New 3/26/03)*

Chapter VI: MOTIONS & SCREENING CASES

6.1. Definitions. For purposes of these General Orders:

a. *Motion*—means an application to the Court, or a member thereof, for procedural, summary, or discretionary relief. It includes, without limitation, a petition for writ of mandamus or prohibition; a petition for permission to take an interlocutory appeal; an application for stay or application for injunction; an application for permission to file a second or successive habeas corpus petition; an appeal from the grant or denial of bail or change of conditions of bail pending trial; a motion for bail pending appeal; an application for a certificate of appealability; an application for summary affirmance or application for summary reversal; an application for leave to proceed on appeal in forma pauperis or for appointment of counsel; an application for extension of time to take any action required or permitted by law; certain fee vouchers; and Court initiated proceedings, such as disciplinary and dismissal matters. *(Rev. 9/17/14)*

b. *Criminal Motion. (Abrogated 9/17/14)*

c. *Civil Motion. (Abrogated 9/17/14)*

d. *Motions Attorney*—means any staff attorney assigned to the processing of substantive motions for disposition by the Court. *(Rev. 9/17/14)*

e. *(Abrogated 12/13/10)*

f. *Procedural Motion*—means a motion that may be disposed of by the Clerk as specified in detail in Appendix A to these General Orders. *(Rev. 9/17/14)*

g. *Designated Deputy Clerk. (Abrogated 9/17/14)*

h. *Emergency Motion*—means a motion requesting action in 21 days or less, or any other motion which in the Court's judgment requires immediate consideration.

i. *Oral Screening Calendar*—means a calendar consisting of cases deemed suitable for submission without oral argument that are presented orally to a three-judge screening panel.

j. *Written Screening Calendar*—means a calendar consisting of cases deemed suitable for submission without oral argument that are submitted to a three-judge screening panel. *(Rev. 7/1/03)*

k. *COA Calendar*—means a calendar consisting of requests for certificates of appealability and any motions for reconsideration of orders entered by previous COA panels. *(New 7/1/03; Rev. 9/17/14)*

l. *Motions Calendar*—means a calendar consisting of substantive motions and original petitions requiring 2 or 3 judges in cases not assigned to a merits panel. *(New 9/17/14)*

6.2. Assignment of Judges.

a. *Motions and Oral Screening Calendars.* The Court shall appoint, for each month, 2 panels composed of 3 members of the Court to serve on the motions and oral screening calendars, respectively. The motions panel members shall rotate throughout the month as the "lead judge," the "second judge," and the "third judge." Each active judge, except the Chief Judge, shall so serve. The Chief Judge and any senior judge may notify the Clerk that they wish to serve on such panels. Visiting judges shall not serve on motions or oral screening panels. *(Rev. 9/17/14)*

b. *Certificate of Appealability Calendars.* The Court shall appoint 2 judges to serve as the certificate of appealability ("COA") panel. The panel will meet for one day. A new panel will be appointed for each sitting week, depending on judges' availability. All active judges are expected to serve on 2 panels per year. Senior judges may notify the Clerk that they are willing to serve on such panels. Visiting judges shall not be appointed to serve on a COA calendar. *(New 7/1/03; Rev. 9/17/14)*

c. *Written Screening Calendars.* The Court shall also appoint three-judge panels to serve on written screening calendars. The panel may consist entirely of senior judges. Such panels are selected at random by the Clerk's Office at the close of the calendar year, and shall serve together for the succeeding year. Any senior or active judge may notify the Clerk that he/she wishes to serve on the written screening calendar. *(Rev. 9/17/14)*

d. *Scheduling of Motions and Oral Screening Calendars/Procedure Governing Motions Panel Matters.* The monthly motions panels and oral screening panels ("OSP") shall each sit for at least 3 days per month. Judges may opt to serve on the OSP or motions panel during the same month as an oral argument calendar. The panel may readjust the dates of its session. At the beginning of the calendar year, the Clerk shall establish presumptive dates for sessions of the motions and oral screening panels in conjunction with their prospective assignments to oral argument calendars. *(Rev. 7/1/03; 9/25/19)*

Each panel may adjust the structure and dates of its sessions, provided that the panel ensures that: (1) it meets for a length of time sufficient to dispose of those motions or screening cases ready for presentation that month; and, (2) the length of time between panels allows the staff attorneys a sufficient period of time to prepare an adequate calendar; and (3) members of the panel serve for the entire month of their assignment. Exchange of a portion of the panel assignment shall be permitted only under exceptional circumstances.

The presiding judge of each panel should notify the Clerk of any changes in the scheduling of the sessions no later than the second week of the month preceding the scheduled panel assignment.

The procedure governing screening cases is set forth at G.O. 6.5. *(Rev. 9/17/14)*

6.3. Delegation of Authority to Dispose of Motions. The Clerk shall enter the receipt or filing of a motion and transmit it as described below.

a. *Disposition of Motions by the Clerk.* The Clerk may dispose of motions described in and subject to the conditions set forth in FRAP 11(b) and 42(b) and Circuit Rule 39–1.5 and 27–7. The Clerk also may dispose of motions enumerated in Appendix A or may in his or her discretion refer any of those motions to an Appellate Commissioner, circuit mediator, appropriate staff attorney, or a merits panel.

The Clerk may additionally enter orders that deny late requests for costs as untimely, respond to motions for late filing, and otherwise enter orders as set forth at Circuit Rule 39–1.5. Such orders are subject to reconsideration by the authoring judge. *(New 7/1/02; Rev. 12/13/10; 9/17/14)*

b. *Motions in Cases Assigned to Oral Argument Panels.* Except as noted above, all motions in cases that have been calendared for hearing by, or are under submission to, or have otherwise previously been assigned to a merits panel shall be submitted to that panel. The panel may delegate authority to the presiding judge or another judge on the panel to rule on procedural motions. Examples of procedural motions include motions to extend time to file petitions for panel rehearing and rehearing en banc, motions to stay mandate, and motions to file supplemental or amicus briefs. Pursuant to 28 U.S.C. § 2253(c), a request to grant or expand a certificate of appealability may be granted by any one Judge on the assigned panel. *(Rev. 9/17/14; 3/21/18)*

c. *Motions in Cases Assigned to Screening Panels.* All motions filed after the staff attorney has identified a case to be placed on the screening calendar shall be directed to the Office of Staff Attorneys. *(Rev. 9/17/14)*

d. *Procedural Motions Filed During the Pendency of a Substantive Motion.* A procedural motion filed during the pendency of a substantive motion shall be referred to the court unit that is handling the substantive motion. *(Rev. 9/17/14)*

e. *Disposition of Motions by Appellate Commissioner.* The Court authorizes the Chief Judge to delegate to an Appellate Commissioner authority to issue for the Court non-dispositive orders in all appeals and petitions except those that would reverse a decision or order by a district judge or where the following relief is requested:

(1) a stay of a district court judgment,

(2) injunctive relief,

(3) bail,

(4) transcripts pursuant to 28 U.S.C. § 753(f),

(5) certification of a state law question,

(6) a certificate of appealability to appeal,

(7) leave to proceed in forma pauperis where a district court has denied or revoked such leave, *(Rev. 9/17/14)*

(8) reconsideration of an order issued by one or more judges.

Requests for the types of relief listed above shall be presented to a motions panel. If an Appellate Commissioner is inclined to recommend that dispositive action be taken, or that leave to proceed in forma pauperis be denied, or that a motion for appointment of counsel be denied, or that sanctions be granted, the matter shall be presented to a regularly scheduled motions panel. An Appellate Commissioner has authority to deny motions for summary disposition, to dismiss for lack of jurisdiction, and to dismiss for lack of prosecution. An Appellate Commissioner has the discretion to refer any motion to a regularly scheduled motions panel or merits panel in the first instance, regardless of the type of relief requested. In addition, an Appellate Commissioner shall have authority to decide motions for voluntary dismissal and stipulated remand.

The Court also authorizes the Chief Judge to delegate to an Appellate Commissioner motions to proceed pro se by defendants in criminal appeals. Such motions shall be referred directly by the Clerk to an Appellate Commissioner, who shall consider whether the Court should exercise its discretion to allow self-representation under Circuit Rule 4–1(d). An Appellate Commissioner is authorized to hold a hearing in appropriate cases to apprise the defendant of the dangers and disadvantages of self-representation on appeal, to confirm that defendant's request is knowing, intelligent, and unequivocal, and to consider whether self-representation would undermine a just and orderly resolution of the appeal. An Appellate Commissioner shall be authorized to consider such evidence as the Appellate Commissioner deems necessary and to make findings of fact. *(Rev. 12/13/10)*

If defendant decides to withdraw the request to proceed pro se, an Appellate Commissioner is authorized to enter the appropriate order. Otherwise, an Appellate Commissioner shall submit a report and recommendation concerning defendant's motion to a motions panel for further action. *(Rev. 12/13/10; 9/17/14)*

f. *Disposition of Single Judge Motions.* *(Abrogated 9/17/14, see 6.3.b)*

g. *Disposition of Two and Three Judge Motions.*

(1) The following motions may be presented to 2 judges rather than the full panel if only 2 are participating. Any judge participating may vote to grant relief and so order. If all judges present agree that relief will not be granted, they shall so order: *(Rev. 9/17/14)*

   i.   request for certificate of appealability;

   ii.   for leave to proceed in forma pauperis in civil cases;

   iii.   for temporary injunctive relief pending further consideration by the panel; and

   iv.   for transcripts at government expense.

(2) The following motions may be presented to no fewer than 2 judges rather than the full panel if only 2 are present. However, 2 judges must agree in order to either grant or deny the requested relief:

   i.   for injunctive relief pending appeal;

   ii.   petition for permission to appeal pursuant to 28 U.S.C. § 1292(b), Fed. R. Civ. P. 23(f), 28 U.S.C. § 1453, and 28 U.S.C. § 158(d); and *(Rev. 12/13/10)*

   iii.   for reconsideration of an Appellate Commissioner or chief circuit mediator order. *(Rev. 9/17/14)*

Therefore, the third judge must be present for consideration of the above motions if:

   i.   one of the other panel members is disqualified or is otherwise unavailable;

   ii.   the other panel members disagree about the disposition of the motion; or

   iii.   he or she is requested by the other panel members to participate.

(3) Three judges shall participate and decide by majority: *(Rev. 9/17/14)*

   i.   whenever a motion results in the disposition of the case; or

   ii.   the panel chooses to publish its order.

(4) If 2 judges determine that oral argument on a motion is necessary, the panel shall direct the staff attorney to make the necessary arrangements. If one of the judges is recused from consideration of the motion and a three-judge order is desirable, a judge or the staff attorney shall contact the Clerk and have a third judge drawn by lot from the available active judges. *(Rev. 9/17/14)*

(5) If one judge is recused or unavailable to consider a motion requiring the attention of 3 judges, the staff attorney shall contact the Clerk who shall draw a third judge by lot from the available judges. *(Rev. 9/17/14)*

6.4. Emergency Motions.

a. *Assignment to Judges.* Upon the receipt or filing of an emergency motion, the Clerk will notify the merits panel assigned to the case, or in an unassigned case, will notify the motions attorneys. If the motion arises in a potential comeback case, the motions attorneys will contact the previous panel to inquire whether they wish to consider the motion.

In cases that are not assigned to a merits panel, either through the usual calendaring process or as a comeback, the motions attorneys will present emergency motions to the motions panel. In the event one or more judges on the motions panel is unavailable, any substitute judge(s) will be drawn by lot.

Presumptively, the current motions panel will decide all emergency motions in which a response is filed within the sitting month, unless the case has already been assigned to a previous motions panel. If the deadline for filing a response to an emergency motion falls within three business days of the end of the month, the motion will be presented to the following month's motions panel, unless the current month's motions panel orders otherwise.

The default deadline for filing a response to a motion is 10 days. *See* FRAP 27(a)(3). If a shorter or longer response time appears warranted, and the setting of a custom response time could affect which motions panel decides the motion, the motions attorney will consult the current motions panel before setting the response time. Motions to extend time to file a response are not favored and must be approved by the motions panel. *(Rev. 9/25/19)*

b. *Action by Judges.* When relief is requested within 48 hours, judges on motions duty may treat an emergency motion as requesting temporary relief until the motions panel can more fully consider the merits of the motion. A single judge may issue an order granting or denying temporary relief, if no other judge on motions duty is available and the order would not effectively dispose of the motion or the appeal. If the order would in effect decide the motion or appeal, the judge must obtain the concurrence of at least one other judge on the motions panel.

In resolving an emergency motion to grant or stay an injunction pending appeal, the motions panel may set an accelerated briefing schedule for the merits of the appeal, order the case on to the next available argument calendar per General Order 3.3(f) (Expediting Appeals), or order the case on to a specified argument calendar per General Order 3.3(g) (Urgent Cases). If an appeal arising from an application for a temporary or permanent injunction is not formally expedited or designated as urgent, it will still be given priority under Circuit Rule 34–3(c) when it is assigned to a merits panel. *(Rev. 12/13/10; 9/17/14; 9/25/19)*

    c.   *Motions for Stay of Deportation or Removal in Petitions for Review.*

    1.   Temporary Stay. Upon the filing of an initial motion or request for stay of removal or deportation, the order of removal or deportation is temporarily stayed until further order of the Court.

    2.   Supplemental Motion. If the initial motion for stay of removal or deportation fails to discuss the merits of the petition for review or to identify the potential hardships faced by the petitioner due to deportation or removal during the pendency of the petition, petitioner may, within 14 days from the filing of the initial motion, file a supplemental motion for stay. The Court will ordinarily not issue any orders directing or inviting the filing of a supplemental motion.

    3.   Response. The electronic certified administrative record shall be filed with the Court within 35 days from the filing of the petition for review. The respondent shall file its response to the motion for stay within 21 days from the due date of the administrative record. Any dispositive motions respondent seeks to file should be filed at the same time the response is due. *(Revised 3/21/18; Effective 4/1/19)*

    4.   Reply. The petitioner may file a reply to the response within 7 days from service of the response.

    5.   Non–Opposition. If respondent files a notice of non-opposition to the stay motion in lieu of the response provided for in subsection (3) above, the temporary stay shall continue in effect during the pendency of the petition for review or until further order of the Court. If the respondent does not file a response to the stay motion within the time limits set forth in subsection (3), the absence of a timely response will be treated as a notice of non-opposition and will be subject to the terms of this subsection. Respondent may, at any time during the pendency of the petition for review, move to lift the temporary stay. Any such motion to lift the stay, along with any response filed by petitioner within 10 days after service of the motion, will be presented to the next available motions panel for disposition.

    6.   Schedule for Record Preparation and Briefing in All Petitions for Review. A briefing schedule will be established upon the filing of the petition for review. The electronic certified administrative record will be due 35 days from the filing of the petition, rather than the 40 days provided in FRAP 17. The petitioner must serve and file a brief within 60 days after the due date for the record. The respondent must serve and file a brief within 60 days after the petitioner's brief is served. The petitioner may serve and file a reply brief within 21 days after service of the respondent's brief. *(Revised 3/21/18; Effective 4/1/19)*

<u>Note</u>: *Pursuant to this Court's decision in DeLeon v. INS, 115 F.3d 643 (9th Cir. 1997), a final order of deportation or removal is automatically temporarily stayed upon the filing of a motion or request for stay of deportation or removal in a petition for review of such an order. This temporary stay is in effect whether or not the Court issues an order confirming such stay. See id. The Court will not ordinarily issue such an order confirming the stay, although it may issue an order to show cause relating to jurisdictional questions or issues pertaining to the sufficiency of the stay request and/or the payment of fees. With regard to further briefing on the merits of the stay, petitioner may file a supplemental motion within 14 days. See Abbassi v. INS, 143 F.3d 513 (9th Cir. 1998).*

    d.   *Drawing a Merits Panel.* When an emergency motion for stay pending appeal or other similar substantive motion is filed, the Chief Judge, or the Chief Judge's designate, may determine that a merits panel should be immediately drawn and the pending motion be referred to it for resolution. This determination may be made because the case is one: (1) in which the motion and the merits--for the sake of consistency--should be heard by the same panel; (2) in which resolution of the motion may require precedential publication; or (3) that involves issues of exceptional importance. If such a determination is made, the clerk will draw the panel by lot. If a judge who is drawn is unavailable to participate on the panel, or if the clerk cannot timely contact the judge, a replacement judge may be drawn by lot. If the case has been assigned to a motions panel, the motions panel may, in addition to the other options available to it, direct that a merits panel be drawn by lot to hear the motion, as well as the merits.

6.5. Screening Calendars.

a. *Selection and Criteria of Cases for Screening Calendars.* Cases that are eligible for submission without oral argument under FRAP 34(a) may be assigned to screening calendars by the Clerk's Office. Additionally, they should meet all of the following criteria: *(Rev. 9/17/14)*

(1) The result is clear.

(2) The applicable law is established in the Ninth Circuit based on circuit or Supreme Court precedent.

After the Clerk assigns a case to the screening calendar, the Clerk's Office forwards the case materials to the staff attorneys. The staff attorneys then place each screening case on either an oral screening calendar or a written screening calendar. *(Rev. 7/1/02; 7/1/03)*

b. *Oral Screening Panel Presentations.*

1. Disposition of Cases. The staff attorneys shall prepare proposed memorandum dispositions for the cases that they place on the oral screening calendars. An authoring judge will be designated for each case presented to the oral screening panel, and the writing assignment will rotate among the 3 panel members.

The staff attorneys shall orally present the proposed dispositions to the screening panels at periodically scheduled sessions. After the staff attorneys have presented each case, the panel members discuss the proposed disposition and make any necessary revisions. If the 3 panel members unanimously agree with the disposition, the designated authoring judge shall direct the presenting attorney to certify the proposed disposition for filing pursuant to G.O. 6.9. *(Rev. 1/1/00)*

Disposition of cases and/or motions presented at the oral screening panel ordinarily will be by unpublished memorandum or order. If, in the judgment of a panel, a decision warrants publication, the resulting order or opinion shall be included in the daily pre-publication report and specifically flagged as a decision arising from an oral screening panel. *(Rev. 7/1/02; 1/1/07; 9/17/14)*

2. Rejection of Cases. All 3 judges must agree that the case is suitable for the screening program before a case is disposed of by a screening panel. Any one judge may reject a case from screening. Judges normally shall reject any case that does not meet the screening criteria, as outlined above in G.O. 6.5.a. *(Rev. 12/13/10)*

If a case is rejected from screening, it shall be scheduled on the next available argument calendar. The proposed disposition and the rejecting judge's reasons for rejecting the case shall be sent to the Calendar Unit for forwarding to the oral argument panel assigned to the case. *(Rev. 12/13/10)*

3. Petitions for Rehearing. The Clerk shall forward each petition for rehearing in any case disposed of by an oral screening panel to the appropriate staff attorney. If a petition for rehearing en banc is filed in any case disposed of at an oral screening panel, the relevant procedures set forth in Chapter V shall apply. *(Rev. 3/24/04; 9/17/14)*

c. *Written Screening Panels.* When a written screening panel indicates that it is ready for case assignments, staff shall send the requested number of cases taken from the cases designated as those eligible for screening pursuant to G.O. 6.5(a). The authoring judge is responsible for forwarding the written disposition to the Clerk's Office for filing. *(Rev. 7/1/03; 9/17/14)*

1. Rejection by Judges. Any one judge may reject a case from the written screening calendar. Judges shall reject any case that does not meet the screening criteria, as outlined above in G.O. 6.5.a. If a case is rejected, a replacement case will be sent by staff. If a case is rejected from the written screening calendar, it shall be scheduled on the next available argument calendar. The draft disposition, and the rejecting judge's reasons for rejecting the case, along with any bench memorandum, shall be sent to the Calendar Unit for forwarding to the oral argument panel assigned to the case. *(Rev. 7/1/03)*

2. Dispositions. Dispositions ordinarily will be by memorandum. If the panel has not issued a separate order submitting the case, a footnote should be included in the disposition indicating that the panel unanimously agrees that the case should be submitted on the briefs pursuant to FRAP 34(a). *(Rev. 7/1/02; 7/1/03; 9/17/14)*

d. *Written Screening Calendars.* *(Abrogated 3/24/04)*

6.6. Recalcitrant Witness Appeals. Upon receipt of a notice of appeal in which review is sought under 28 U.S.C. § 1826, the Clerk shall docket the appeal and immediately deliver the notice of appeal to the motions unit. A motions attorney shall immediately review the notice of appeal to ascertain whether the appeal properly falls within the purview of 28 U.S.C. § 1826.

If the appeal is within the purview of section 1826, the motions attorney shall immediately notify the presiding judge on the motions panel that is scheduled to sit on the thirtieth day after the notice of appeal was filed. The presiding judge, with the assistance of the motions attorney, shall establish a briefing schedule that will assure that the appeal can be decided within 30 days of the filing of the notice of appeal. That panel shall hear and decide the appeal regardless of whether a motion for extension of time beyond the 30–day period is granted. *(Rev. 9/17/14)*

6.7. Criminal Justice Act Vouchers. All vouchers must be accompanied by one copy of a completed CJA Information Summary Form. As noted in the CJA Information Summary Form, counsel may also submit a detailed explanation along with the form to substantiate the amount requested.

The Clerk shall review each appellate voucher, make computation corrections, make comments concerning the voucher and its compliance with pertinent statutory and administrative guidelines, and send the voucher to an Appellate Commissioner for certification of such compensation as an Appellate Commissioner deems reasonable and appropriate under the Criminal Justice Act.

The Clerk shall inform counsel of the procedures and criteria for requesting compensation. The Chief Judge may designate one or more judges, in addition to the administrative unit judges, to rule on excess CJA fee requests. *(Rev. 9/17/14)*

6.8. Applications for Extraordinary Writs (Exclusive of Habeas Corpus).

a. *General Procedures.* An application for extraordinary writ, whether addressed to an individual judge or to the Court, shall be deemed addressed to the Court. Subject to the following provisions, such an application shall be processed by the Clerk and the staff attorney in the same fashion as a motion referred to a motions panel.

If the panel determines that the writ should not be granted, it shall deny the application forthwith. Such summary denial shall not be regarded as a decision on the merits. Otherwise, the panel shall direct that an answer and reply may be filed within the times fixed by the Court. The panel may also issue a stay or injunction pending further consideration of the application. Further proceedings thereafter shall be had as provided in FRAP 21(b).

After receipt of the answer and reply, or expiration of the times set therefor, the application will be sent to a new motions panel unless the first panel directs otherwise. The panel may grant or deny the application or set it for oral argument. The panel may hear oral argument or direct that the application be calendared in accordance with the provisions set forth in Chapter 3. *(Rev. 9/17/14)*

b. *Emergency Procedures.* *(Abrogated 9/17/14, see G.O. 6.4.a and 6.4.b)*

6.9. Certification of Orders and Memoranda Dispositions. A judge may direct the Clerk, a staff attorney, a circuit mediator, or an Appellate Commissioner to file an order or a memorandum disposition that has been approved by the judge or judges whose name(s) appears therein. In appropriate circumstances, the judge may send confirmation to the Clerk following such certification. Separate written confirmation is not necessary when the judge transmits an order to the Clerk by electronic mail. *(Rev. 1/1/00)*

An Appellate Commissioner may direct the Clerk or a staff attorney to file an order or other document that has been approved by an Appellate Commissioner. *(Rev. 9/17/14)*

6.10. Motions for Clarification and Petitions for Reconsideration or Rehearing. *(Abrogated 7/1/03)*

6.11. Motions for Reconsideration En Banc. Any motion or petition seeking en banc review of an order issued by a motions or oral screening panel shall be processed as a motion for reconsideration en banc. The Clerk shall forward a motion for reconsideration en banc of a motion previously considered by a motions or oral screening panel to the appropriate staff attorney for processing. If the motion was decided by published order or opinion, the motion will be circulated to all active judges. In cases involving judgments of death, the Clerk shall forward all motions for reconsideration en banc to Associates.

The motion shall be referred by the staff attorney to the panel which entered the order in issue. The panel may follow the relevant procedures set forth in Chapter 5 in considering the motion for rehearing en banc, or may reject the suggestion on behalf of the Court. *(Rev. 3/24/04; 12/13/10; 9/17/14)*

Chapter VII: MEDIATION OFFICE

7.1 Purpose and Staffing. The Circuit Mediation Program was established pursuant to FRAP 33 and Circuit Rule 33–1. The goals of the program are to facilitate the voluntary resolution of appeals in order to reduce the Court's workload and to offer parties an alternative to litigation to resolve their disputes.

The circuit mediators are employed by the Court to facilitate the resolution of cases and perform such other duties as the Court directs. They are experienced attorneys who have extensive training and experience in negotiation, mediation and Ninth Circuit practice and procedure. In facilitating the resolution of disputes, the mediators act as adjuncts to the Court and perform a traditional judicial function.

7.2 Authority to Enter Orders. The mediators are certified as deputy clerks and may enter orders as described in Appendix A. They may also issue other procedural orders that facilitate the goals of the program, including orders that require parties (or party representatives with settlement authority), counsel and any other person subject to the jurisdiction of the Court to participate in settlement discussions. These discussions may take place in person, by telephone, or through written communications. Counsel shall be so advised, and discussions shall be arranged in such a manner as to avoid burdensome time and expense requirements upon the parties and attorneys.

A motion or petition for reconsideration, rehearing, modification or clarification of an order entered by a mediator should be referred initially to that mediator. If the mediator declines to reconsider, the motion or petition will be referred to the chief circuit mediator. Orders of the chief circuit mediator are subject to review by a panel of no fewer than 2 judges. *(Rev. 12/13/10)*

7.3 Cases Subject to Mediation. The mediators may act on their own initiative in any matter pending before the Court that has not been assigned to a panel. Where a panel has been assigned, they may act only with the permission and at the direction of the panel. The Mediation Questionnaire is the primary means by which the mediators identify cases for inclusion in the mediation program. Counsel in any matter pending before the Court may contact the mediation office to seek assistance in pursuing the voluntary resolution of a case. Only in extraordinary circumstances and with permission of the chief circuit mediator will the mediators participate in negotiations involving pro se litigants. *(Rev. 12/13/10)*

Any panel may refer a case to the mediation program at any time. Upon referral of a case, the mediator assigned to the case may enter orders related to the mediation function. In cases assigned to a merits panel, the panel may defer or vacate submission pending the outcome of mediation.

7.4 Confidentiality. Mediation confidentiality is governed by Circuit Rule 33–1. The mediation office may adopt additional procedures to protect confidentiality. *(Rev. 9/17/14)*

7.5 Imposition of Sanctions. The chief circuit mediator may enter orders to show cause regarding sanctions to address issues that arise in the mediation program. Sanctions may be appropriate if a participant willfully fails to comply with any properly issued order, including an order to attend a telephone or in-person settlement conference. Any response to the order to show cause shall be referred to the chief circuit mediator, who may discharge it or refer it to an Appellate Commissioner or a panel for further action. *(Rev. 9/17/14)*

7.6 Processing of Selected Cases. The Clerk will refer all FRAP 42(b) motions to the mediation office when the office has conducted or scheduled a conference with the parties. The Clerk will notify the mediation office before assigning to a calendar a case that has been selected for mediation. However, absent an order staying the matter, it will be assigned in the regular course. *(Rev. 12/13/10)*

Chapter VIII: DEATH PENALTY PROCEDURES

8.1. Capital Case Coordinator.

a. *Selection.* The Chief Judge shall appoint an active or senior judge to serve as the Capital Case Coordinator for a particular case or for all capital cases in which an execution date has been set. *(Rev. 3/24/04; 9/17/14)*

b. *Principal Duties.* The Capital Case Coordinator shall:

(1) respond to questions from judges and Court staff regarding death penalty rules and procedures;

(2) *(Abrogated 9/17/14)*

(3) if necessary, establish deadlines for filing dispositions with respect to applications for leave to file second or successive 2254 petitions or 2255 motions or related civil proceedings as defined in Circuit Rule 22–3; *(Rev. 12/13/10)*

(4) establish deadlines for requesting an en banc vote with respect to applications for leave to file second or successive 2254 petitions or 2255 motions or related civil proceedings; *(Rev 3/24/04; 12/13/10)*

(5) establish, in his or her discretion, a period for exchange of memoranda, which either may be a separate period, or may occur contemporaneously with the period established for voting; *(New 3/24/04)*

(6) establish the procedure and time schedule for polling the judges with respect to applications for leave to file second or successive 2254 petitions or 2255 motions or related civil proceedings in which an en banc vote has been requested. The Capital Case Coordinator shall inform the Clerk of the procedure and time schedule. Each judge shall be responsible for informing the Capital Case Coordinator and Clerk how he or she may be contacted; and *(Rev. 12/13/10; 9/17/14)*

(7) direct the Clerk, under appropriate circumstances, to draw a stand-by en banc court to serve in the event that a majority of the eligible non-recused judges votes in favor of rehearing en banc; and *(New 3/24/04; Rev. 9/17/14)*

(8) for good cause under exigent circumstances, suspend the operation of the general orders pertaining to this Chapter. *(New 3/24/04)*

c. *Deadline for Voting.* *(Abrogated 9/17/14)*

8.2. Duties of En Banc Coordinator. When a panel recommends or a judge requests an en banc vote on a first petition or motion as defined in Circuit Rule 22–2 and no execution date has been set, the En Banc Coordinator shall supervise the en banc process in accordance with G.O. 5.1.b.2. *(Rev. 12/13/10)*

8.3. Duties of Chief Judge. The Chief Judge shall supervise the administration of all matters before a death penalty en banc court, except that the Capital Case Coordinator may decide procedural matters not involving an issue before the en banc court. *(Rev. 12/13/10)*

Chapter IX: JUDICIAL PROCEDURES

9.1. Reports by Judges on Cases Under Submission. Each judge shall periodically report to the Chief Judge the number of cases under submission assigned to the reporting judge for the preparation of dispositions, the number of such cases in which dispositions have been written and are in circulation, and the length of time such cases have been under submission and, where applicable, in circulation. Each judge shall also report the number of three-judge district court cases to which the judge has been assigned. The authoring judge shall report orally to the Court concerning the status of cases in which dispositions have not been circulated within 6 months of submission and cases in which dispositions have not been filed within 9 months of submission. Authoring judges shall be notified by the Clerk's Office one month prior to the Court meeting of cases within this category.

9.2. Priorities for Circulation and Consideration of Proposed Dispositions. In non-complex cases, non-precedential memorandum dispositions shall normally be circulated within 7 days of the submission date, precedential published opinions shall normally be circulated within 30 days of the submission date, and dissenting or other separate opinions shall normally be circulated within 14 days after the circulation of the proposed majority opinion.

Judges should normally inform the panel whether they intend to concur or dissent within 7 days after the disposition has been circulated, and shall give priority to responding to circulated proposed dispositions. If concurring, a judge shall transmit editorial suggestions as soon as possible. If a judge is unable to respond within the suggested deadlines, the judge should notify the other members of the panel within the specified time period. *(Rev. 12/11/17)*

9.3.   Delay by Visiting Judges.   If a visiting judge fails to prepare a disposition within 3 months after the preparation thereof is assigned, the presiding member of the panel shall write to the judge and request that he or she prepare and circulate the disposition.   If a visiting judge, sitting with a panel of this Court, fails to act upon a proposed disposition prepared by another member of the panel within one month after such proposed disposition has been transmitted to members of the panel, the presiding member of the panel shall write to the judge and request that he or she act on the matter.

9.4.   Seniority of Visiting Judges.   A visiting judge shall be accorded full seniority in the listing of names in the disposition and in all other respects, except that a member of the Court shall preside at Court sessions and shall assign cases for the preparation of dispositions.

9.5.   Individual Public Expression of Views.   If a member of the Court wishes to express an opinion publicly on pending legislation or other matters in which, because of the nature of the matter, it might be mistakenly assumed that the opinion expressed is that of the Court, it shall be made clear, in expressing such opinion, that the opinion expressed is that of such member only.   Any member so expressing an opinion in writing shall also consider the advisability of sending copies to the other members of the Court.

9.6.   Three–Judge District Court Assignments.   *(Abrogated)*

Chapter X: MEETING OF COURT & EXECUTIVE COMMITTEE

10.1.   Executive Committee of the Court.

a.   *Membership.*   The Executive Committee of the Court shall consist of the Chief Judge, a circuit judge who is eligible to become Chief Judge during the expected tenure of the current Chief Judge and, if there be more than one, the one among them who is designated by the Chief Judge, the 3 administrative unit judges, a senior judge drawn by lot from among those senior judges willing to be considered, and 3 other active judges drawn by lot from among those active judges willing to be considered.   Judges drawn by lot shall serve staggered terms of 3 years.   A judge shall not be eligible to serve again for 2 years following the expiration of his or her term of service on the committee, unless that judge becomes eligible to serve as chief, next in line to be chief, or administrative judge.

Attendance at meetings is required unless excused by the Chief Judge.   Four members shall constitute a quorum.   The Chief Judge shall chair the Executive Committee.   Judges drawn by lot who are also eligible to serve on the Judicial Council shall elect to serve on either the Executive Committee or the Council.   *(Rev. 10/4/06; 9/17/14)*

b.   *Authority.*   The Executive Committee shall have the authority to act for the Court on all administrative matters except:

(1) workload issues, including the number of sittings, size of calendars, and requests for new judgeships;

(2) changes in procedures for deciding cases;

(3) rules;

(4) bankruptcy judge and federal public defender appointments;

(5) major personnel decisions;

(6) major decisions concerning court buildings, space planning and utilization;

(7) those matters the Executive Committee determines are appropriate for de novo discussion by the full Court.

The Executive Committee shall review and may make recommendations to the Court on items 1, 2, 3, 5, 6 and 7.

c.   *Meetings.*   The Executive Committee shall meet 4 to 6 times annually, unless canceled by the Chief Judge.   Special Executive Committee meetings may be called by the Chief Judge at any time, or upon the written request of a majority of the members of the Executive Committee.   *(Rev. 12/13/10)*

d.   *Agendas and Minutes.*   The agenda and minutes of the Executive Committee will be distributed promptly to the full Court.

10.2. Court Meetings.

a. *Time, Place, and Judicial Participation.* Court of appeals meetings shall be held at such times and places as the Chief Judge shall determine. Generally, 4 meetings shall be held each year. Special court meetings may be called by the Chief Judge at any time, and shall be called by the Chief Judge upon the written request of a majority of the active judges. Meetings shall be conducted pursuant to the most recent edition of Roberts Rules of Orders, except to the extent that those rules conflict with statute, applicable court rules, or these General Orders.

All active judges are expected to attend court meetings unless excused by the Chief Judge. A majority of the active judges shall constitute a quorum. Except as otherwise provided by law, senior judges who elect to attend court meetings, unless excused by the Chief Judge, may vote. Those senior judges who do not so elect may not vote, even where permitted by law to do so. *(Rev. 9/17/14)*

b. *Agenda and Non–Agenda Items.*

(i) A written agenda shall be prepared and distributed to each Member of the Court in advance of each court meeting. The agenda items will include any of those items listed in G.O. 10.1.b. 1–7 that are ready for consideration by the Court, any other item referred by the Court Executive Committee or Chief Judge, and any item that a Member of the Court requests that the Chief Judge place on the agenda 14 days prior to the court meeting, or within a reasonable time if circulation of the agenda is delayed. *(Rev. 9/17/14; 9/7/16)*

(ii) *(Abrogated 9/17/14)*

(iii) *(Abrogated 9/7/16)*

c. *Minutes.* Proposed minutes of court meetings shall be distributed to the active judges for correction. Any corrections shall be suggested to the Court Executive within 10 days of the distribution date. Upon the expiration of that period, the minutes shall become final. The final minutes of court meetings shall be distributed to all members of the Court.

10.3. Mail Votes. Between meetings, the Court may act by mail vote. On the request of any active judge, any matter submitted for a mail vote shall be withdrawn and, at the discretion of the Chief Judge, either set for a teleconference meeting or placed on the agenda for the next scheduled court meeting.

Chapter XI: DUTIES of ADMINISTRATIVE UNIT JUDGES

11.1. Duties of the Administrative Unit Judge. The duties of the administrative unit judges are to: *(Rev. 12/13/10)*

(1) Serve as members of the Court Executive Committee.

(2) *(Abrogated 9/17/14)*

(3) On the designation of the Chief Judge, rule on excess CJA fee requests from unit. *(Rev. 9/17/14)*

(4) Be attentive to Court of Appeals support services and facilities within unit (includes reviewing space needs, facility improvements, arrangements for visiting judges chambers, and security), and make recommendations to the Chief Judge. *(Rev. 9/17/14)*

(5) If requested by the Chief Judge, attend installation of district, bankruptcy and magistrate judges (or secure a representative from unit). *(Rev. 9/17/14)*

(6) Represent Court at admission to our bar ceremonies within unit.

(7) Oversee project involving cameras used during circuit court arguments within unit.

(8) Maintain contact with Court of Appeals judges within unit and report on their needs.

(9) Serve as liaison with bar associations within unit and arrange meetings with Lawyer Representatives and Court of Appeals judges.

(10) *(Abrogated 9/17/14)*

(11) *(Abrogated 9/17/14)*

(12) *(Abrogated)*

(13) *(Abrogated 9/17/14)*

(14) *(Abrogated 9/17/14)*

(15) Perform other duties, as requested, by the Chief Judge or the Court.

Chapter XII: MISCELLANEOUS PROVISIONS

12.1.   Seal and Process. *(Abrogated 9/17/14)*

12.2.   Use of Court, Conference, and Robing Rooms. *(Abrogated 9/17/14)*

12.3.   Information Concerning Presentation of Oral Argument. *(Abrogated 9/17/14)*

12.4.   Bar Admission Fees.

a. *Bar Admission Fees.* The admission fee to the bar of this Court is set at $230.00 (effective 11/01/11). The fee is waived for attorneys who are employed by the federal government or community public defender program; such attorneys are conditionally admitted. If the attorney leaves government service but wishes to practice before the Court, that attorney must then satisfy the fee requirement. Court employees are exempt from the admission fee. *(Rev. 9/17/14)*

b. *Expenditures from the Attorney Admission Fund.* All expenditures must be in accordance with the Plan for Administration of the Attorney Admission Fund.

The circuit executive or the Clerk, may authorize expenditures from the Fund for items contained in the approved annual budget and for revolving fund expenditures that do not exceed $1,500 per item. Any single expenditure for a budgeted or revolving fund item exceeding $1,500 requires the additional approval of the Chief Judge or the Chair of the Committee.

The Chief Judge is authorized to approve expenditures from the Fund in any amount within the Chief Judge's annual budget limit. The Chief Judge may delegate this authority to the circuit executive or to the Clerk. See Plan for Administration of Attorney Admission Fund.

12.5.   Discipline of Attorneys Admitted to Practice in This Court. The Clerk shall periodically check the lists forwarded to the Court concerning state disbarments and suspensions against the roll of attorneys practicing before this Court and issue the order described at Circuit Rule 46–2(c). The order shall warn the attorney that failure to respond in a timely fashion will result in removal from the roll of admitted attorneys without further notice. A motions attorney, upon receipt of the response thereto, shall present the matter to a current motions panel for appropriate action pursuant to Circuit Rule 46–2. If the attorney fails to respond to the order to show cause, the Clerk shall order that the attorney be removed from the roll of attorneys eligible to practice before the Court.

If the Court becomes aware of a violation of the applicable rules of professional conduct or a failure to comply with the rules or orders of this Court, or of any other conduct unbecoming a member of its bar, the Court may assign a docket number to the proceedings and take such disciplinary action as it deems necessary pursuant to FRAP 46 and Circuit Rule 46–2. *(Rev. 9/17/14)*

12.6.   Use of General Orders. These General Orders pertain primarily to the Court's internal functioning and therefore do not have standing as rules of the Court. Nevertheless, such orders shall be regarded as public records and shall be available, during office hours, for public inspection at the offices of the Clerk of this Court and all district courts of the circuit. The orders shall also be posted on the Court's website. The Clerk shall provide each member of the Court and visiting judge with a loose-leaf book containing the General Orders. Copies of the General Orders may be purchased, upon request, from the Court of Appeals Clerk's Office in San Francisco. *(Rev. 12/13/10)*

12.7.   Distribution of Briefs, Records, and Exhibits After Use. Since copies of briefs, memoranda, and records, after argument or consideration, may contain comments and notations by the judges, such documents generally are not to be made available to anyone other than Court personnel. However, original Clerk's records, original and any paper copies of reporter's transcripts, and exhibits shall be returned to the district court. *(Rev. 9/17/14)*

12.8.   Prisoner Mail. When mail addressed by the Clerk to a prisoner in a state or federal institution is returned undelivered, the Clerk shall forward the returned mail to the appropriate state or United States Attorney. The Clerk shall include a letter with the returned mail instructing the attorney to use all reasonable means to effect delivery to the prisoner and to submit to the Clerk proof of such efforts and the results thereof within 14 days.

Mail addressed by a prisoner to a member of the Court shall be opened by the Clerk who shall act on any procedural matter as appropriate. All substantive matters shall be forwarded to the Court.

12.9. Sua Sponte Imposition of Sanctions.

a. *Sanctions Imposed Against Counsel or a Party.* Sanctions may be imposed against counsel or a party for conduct that violates the Federal Rules of Appellate Procedure, the Circuit Rules, orders or other instructions of the Court, the rules of professional conduct or responsibility in effect where counsel maintains his or her principal office or as authorized by statute. If sanctions appear to be warranted, the following procedures shall apply.

Any judge or an Appellate Commissioner may issue an order to show cause that directs a litigant to pay a sanction in the amount determined by the Court or to show cause why such sanctions would be unwarranted. The order shall state the grounds for such sanctions, the authority under which such sanctions are authorized, whether the sanction would be imposed against counsel, a party or both, and the date upon which a response shall be filed. Any reply to a response shall be filed within 10 days from service of the response. Upon review of the response and reply, if any, the judge or Appellate Commissioner may discharge the order or may refer the response to the merits panel or motions panel for a determination as to the propriety of sanctions. All dispositions in which orders to show cause have been issued shall specifically address any response or failure to respond to the order. *(Rev. 12/13/10)*

A motions or merits panel may issue an order to show cause that directs a litigant to pay a sanction in the amount determined by the Court or to show cause why such sanctions would be unwarranted. The order shall state the grounds for such sanctions, the authority under which such sanctions are authorized, whether the sanction would be imposed against counsel, a party or both, and the date upon which a response shall be filed. Any reply to a response shall be filed within 10 days from service of the response. Upon review of the response and reply, if any, the panel may deem the order to be discharged or may impose the sanction. *(Rev. 12/13/10)*

Any order relating to the sanction or discipline of any attorney shall be referred to an Appellate Commissioner so that the order can be entered into the Court's internal attorney admissions and discipline database. This includes an order directing counsel to show cause why sanctions should not be imposed; an order discharging such an order to show cause; and an order imposing sanctions or discipline. *(New 3/26/08; Rev. 9/17/14)*

b. *Court Reporter Sanctions.* If a court reporter has failed to prepare previously designated transcripts, and has not responded to a prior warning order, the Clerk may prepare an order to show cause regarding sanctions for an Appellate Commissioner. Copies of the order shall be provided to the chief district judge, appropriate district court personnel, and the reporter regulatory agency. Upon review of the response, an Appellate Commissioner may either discharge the order or refer the response to a merits panel or motions panel for a determination regarding the imposition of sanctions.

When it comes to the attention of a motions panel that a reporter has failed to prepare previously designated transcripts, the panel shall order the reporter to show cause why sanctions should not be imposed or may refer the matter to the Clerk. If the motions panel orders the reporter to show cause, the panel shall review the response and shall either deem the order to be discharged or order the imposition of a fine.

When it comes to the attention of a merits panel that a reporter has failed to prepare previously designated transcripts, the panel shall order the reporter to show cause why sanctions should not be imposed. If the appeal is ordered off the calendar, the panel shall refer the matter to the Clerk. If the merits panel orders the reporter to show cause, the panel shall review the response and shall either deem the order to be discharged or order the imposition of a sanction. *(Rev. 9/17/14)*

12.10. Communication From Other Courts Regarding Cases.

a. *Communications Regarding Dispositions and Extraordinary Writs.* When a district judge, magistrate judge, bankruptcy appellate panel judge or bankruptcy judge is aware of a mistake in a disposition by this Court involving an appeal from that judge's decision, has reason to believe that the affected parties may not point out the mistake, and believes that justice will be disserved if the mistake is not corrected, the judge may bring the mistake to the attention of this Court by way of a letter addressed to the Clerk of Court. The Clerk shall distribute the letter to the members of the panel or as is otherwise appropriate. The judge shall provide copies of the letter to all parties to the appeal. *(Rev. 12/13/10)*

When a district judge, magistrate judge, bankruptcy appellate panel judge or bankruptcy judge wishes to comment on a pending petition for a writ of mandamus or other extraordinary relief that arises out of that judge's cases prior to the entry of an order requiring a response, the judge may send a letter to the Clerk of Court for distribution to the panel that will review the petition. The judge shall provide copies to the parties. *(Rev. 12/13/10)*

b. *Petitions for Rehearing.* When a district judge, magistrate judge, bankruptcy appellate panel judge or bankruptcy judge wishes to comment formally on a filed disposition before the mandate has issued, the judge may send a written communication to the Clerk of Court. The Clerk shall file the communication and distribute it to the panel before whom the petition for rehearing is pending, and, if there is a pending petition for rehearing en banc, to all judges on the Court. The judge shall provide copies of the letter to all parties to the appeal. *(Rev. 12/13/10)*

c. *Closed Cases.* When a district judge, magistrate judge, bankruptcy appellate panel judge or bankruptcy judge wishes to comment formally to the Court of Appeals on a decision or other matter that is no longer pending, the judge shall send a written communication to the Clerk of Court. The Clerk shall distribute the communication to all judges on the Court of Appeals. This does not restrict other informal comments on closed cases which are otherwise permitted. *(Rev. 12/13/10)*

12.11. Suspension of General Orders. Any active judge may request that the Court vote to suspend a provision or provisions of these orders, except to the extent that any suspension would be prohibited by law. The request shall be directed to the Chief Judge. The Chief Judge shall place the matter on the agenda for the next court meeting. If time constraints demand a more immediate resolution of the matter, the Chief Judge shall call for a mail vote. The call shall include a time limit set at the Chief Judge's discretion within which the judges must submit their votes. Any proposed suspension must be approved by the number of votes that equals or exceeds two-thirds of the eligible judges. Any proposed suspension shall state the period for which the suspension will apply.

12.12. Confidentiality. No past or present officer or employee of the Court may divulge or make available information relating to a matter pending before the Court during or prior to the term of that individual's service that is both learned as a result of that individual's official duties and not part of the public records of the Court, unless the disclosure is made:

(a) To a person who is a judge or an officer or employee of the Court at the time the disclosure is made, or was a judge or an officer or employee of the Court at the time the information was obtained;

(b) Pursuant to a statute, rule or order of the Court, or authorization from a judge;

(c) Pursuant to a valid order or subpoena issued by a body competent to issue such an order or subpoena; or

(d) To report an alleged criminal violation to an appropriate law enforcement official.

For the purposes of this section, "information relating to a matter" shall include information:

(a) That is received by the Court pursuant to a protective order or under seal;

(b) Learned in connection with any case which has been or is before the Court which a judge expressly marks "confidential" or states is to be kept confidential pursuant to this section;

(c) That relates to the deliberative processes of the Court in a case that is in the process of being decided or has already been decided. Examples of such information are:

(1) Draft opinions prepared in connection with the preparation by the Court of a final opinion;

(2) Internal memoranda, in draft or final form, prepared in connection with a draft or final opinion or argument of a case before the Court; and

(3) The substance or occurrence of conversations among judges or between a judge and officers or employees of the Court concerning the substance of the case which the Court is in the process of deciding, is about to decide, or has decided.

12.13. Confidentiality and Disposition of Judges' Personal Papers and Property Upon Death. Judges are encouraged to leave instructions concerning the disposition of confidential court documents, personal papers, potential archival material, and in-chambers personal property (collectively, "chambers materials"). In this context, the term "document" includes any means by which communication is stored, including material stored electronically. Examples of potential archival material other than confidential court documents include the judge's commission, honorary recognitions, photographs, and public speeches.

The instructions should provide for appropriate and reasonable measures to protect the confidentiality of internal court communications and documents. Judges are encouraged to consult with the Clerk of Court and court archivist in formulating their instructions and, when formulated, to communicate the instructions concerning disposition of chambers materials to the Clerk of Court.

Judges may elect to leave chambers materials to the Court, an educational, historical society, or other institution, but should condition the gift on safeguarding confidential court communications and documents for a reasonable period of time. In formulating a time restriction, judges should prohibit release of any document that concerns pending cases, including cases that are pending before another court via certiorari, transfer, or remand. Judges should also consider (1) the need for confidentiality of court communications; (2) the confidentiality and privacy interests of colleagues; (3) historians' needs for access; and (4) the public's need for transparency in government. Judges may elect to instruct the court to destroy chambers materials on death, but are encouraged to consult with the Clerk of Court and court archivist to ascertain whether the Court may be interested in preserving specific archival material or personal property not distributed to heirs.

It is the policy of the court that no heir or personal representative shall release documents concerning pending cases to a third party. It is also the policy of the court that no heir or personal representative release confidential court documents or destroy chambers material without first notifying the Clerk of Court and providing reasonable time for the Court to review the proposed release or planned destruction. Judges are encouraged to implement this policy through testamentary or other instructions. *(New 6/17/2015)*

12.14. Purpose and Effect of General Orders These General Orders are meant to guide the internal operations of the court and do not invest any rights in third parties. *(New 9/17/14)*

APPENDIX A. Disposition of Motions by the Clerk

Pursuant to Circuit Rule 27–7, the Court has delegated the authority to decide the following motions to deputized court staff. Unless otherwise noted, a motion can be acted upon by a deputy clerk, staff attorney, circuit mediator or Appellate Commissioner. Orders are subject to reconsideration pursuant to Circuit Rule 27–10.

(1) to file lesser number of paper briefs; *(Rev. 9/17/14)*

(2) to file handwritten or typewritten brief or for exemption from the electronic filing requirement; *(Rev. 12/13/10)*

(3) to consolidate;

(4) to file late amicus brief; *(Rev. 12/13/10)*

(5) to hold oral argument in a specific location;

(6) to substitute party under FRAP 43(a) or (c);

(7) to grant unopposed motions to substitute federal agencies;

(8) to file addendum or appendix;

(9) to transfer records and briefs to new appeal;

(10) to adopt brief;

(11) to stay appellate proceedings (may grant only if based on pending court or agency action and periodic status reports are required; if based on settlement negotiations, may grant only if stay is limited to 6 months);

(12) for withdrawal or substitution of counsel in civil cases, excluding habeas cases; *(Rev. 9/17/14)*

(13) to supplement or correct record or brief; *(Rev. 12/13/10)*

(14) for extension of time;

(15) to file oversized brief;

(16) *(Abrogated 12/13/10)*;

(17) to permit the district court to correct clerical mistake in district court judgment;

(18) to remand in civil cases to enable district court to rule on post-judgment motion (Clerk may grant if unopposed and if movant has complied with FRAP 12.1; Clerk may deny if movant has not complied with FRAP 12.1); *(Rev. 12/13/10)*

(19) to intervene as of right in agency review proceedings;

(20) to strike brief;

(21) to expedite;

(22) to transfer under 28 U.S.C. § 2112(a) (if non-discretionary);

(23) to deny a motion to proceed in forma pauperis as unnecessary when pauper status continues under FRAP 24(a);

(24) to grant a motion to withdraw a previously filed motion;

(25) *(Abrogated 3/23/16)*

(26) to grant, or deny without prejudice to a renewed motion that corrects a defect, appellant's unopposed motion to voluntarily dismiss a case and denying as moot other pending motions; *(Rev. 9/17/14)*

(27) to grant or deny an unopposed motion to voluntarily dismiss a civil appeal or petition for review without prejudice to reinstatement upon the occurrence of stated conditions if the order provides that a motion to reinstate must be filed within 28 days after the occurrence of those; *(Rev. 9/17/14)*

(28) to deny without prejudice to refiling, motions to be relieved as appointed counsel in a criminal appeal when the motion fails to comply with Circuit Rule 4–1(c); *(Rev. 9/17/14)*

(29) to correct the caption or add parties when the motion seeks to remedy a clerical error by this Court.

The Clerk has discretion to refer any of the above motions to an Appellate Commissioner, a circuit mediator, an appropriate staff attorney for presentation to a motions or screening panel, or a merits panel. *(Rev. 9/17/14)*

The Clerk is authorized to enter orders referring to the merits panel motions:

(30) to file an amicus brief;

(31) to grant or to deny oral argument; *(Rev. 9/17/14)*

(32) to set aside waiver of oral argument;

(33) to join in oral argument;

(34) to submit without oral argument;

(35) to take judicial notice;

(36) for imposition of sanctions;

(37) filed after a pattern of frivolous, repetitive motions has been established.

The Clerk may issue for the Court the following orders:

(38) sua sponte order to show cause or to provide information on jurisdiction or summary disposition; *(Rev. 12/13/10)*

(39) sua sponte order to show cause in attorney discipline matter under FRAP 46(b) and to strike from the attorney roll those attorneys who voluntarily resign or who fail to respond to an order to show cause;

(40) order granting National Labor Relations Board's unopposed motion to withdraw application without prejudice, denying as moot other pending motions, and providing for no costs if it appears that none were incurred by appellee or respondent;

(41) order granting National Labor Relations Board's unopposed application for enforcement upon stipulation and denying as moot other pending motions;

(42) order granting National Labor Relations Board's motion for entry of default (unless opposed on grounds other than timely filing of answer) and denying as moot other pending motions;

(43) order denying National Labor Relations Board's motion for entry of default where respondent has timely answered application for enforcement;

(44) *(Abrogated 9/17/14)*

(45) *(Abrogated 9/17/14)*

(46) orders granting timely motions for reinstatement of a civil appeal or petition previously dismissed or remanded without prejudice to reinstatement upon the occurrence of a stated condition or event; *(Rev. 12/13/10)*

(47) order dismissing an appeal for want of prosecution under Circuit Rule 42–1 and dismissing any pending motions as moot;

(48) *[abrogated 12/13/10]*;

(49) *[abrogated 12/13/10]*.

The Clerk has discretion to refer any of the above motions to an Appellate Commissioner, a circuit mediator, an appropriate staff attorney for presentation to a motions or screening panel, or a merits panel. *(Rev. 9/17/14)*

The circuit mediators and staff attorneys shall have the same authority to act on procedural motions as the Clerk, and shall additionally be authorized to issue the following orders for the Court: *(Rev. 9/17/14)*

(50) orders granting unopposed motions for attorney fees;

(51) orders staying appellate proceedings based on pending settlement negotiations for more than 6 months if periodic status reports are required;

(52) orders granting stipulations or unopposed motions to remand cases to administrative agencies (in immigration cases by agreement of the parties the order may include a stay of removal during remand); *(New 1/1/05)*

(53) orders granting stipulations or unopposed motions to remand a case to the district court for consideration, approval and/or implementation of a settlement agreement (remand may be without prejudice to reinstatement upon occurrence of stated condition or event); *(Rev. 12/13/10)*

(54) orders denying untimely petitions for permissive interlocutory appeals; *(Rev. 12/13/10)*

(55) orders denying untimely motions for reconsideration of a motions or oral screening panel order. If the mandate has issued, then the reason for the denial will be because it is untimely and because the mandate has issued. In either case, if the staff attorney believes that the motion for reconsideration, although untimely, deserves review, he/she shall forward the motion to the panel with the customary proposed recommendation); *(Rev. 10/10/07; 9/17/14)*

(56) orders dismissing duplicative notices of appeal when the record is clear that 2 or more appeals have been taken from the same order or judgment; *(Rev. 12/13/10)*

(57) Staff attorneys are authorized to enter orders referring to the merits panel motions: *(Rev. 12/13/10; 9/17/14)*

(a) to dismiss an appeal for lack of jurisdiction that involves legal issues intricately bound up in the merits of the appeal; *(Rev. 12/13/10)*

(b) involving issues pending before an en banc panel; *(Rev. 12/13/10)*

(c) to certify issues to a state court; *(Rev. 12/13/10)*

(d) to withdraw as appointed counsel pursuant to *Anders v. California*, 386 U.S. 738 (1967), in criminal cases and set a due date for a pro se supplemental brief. *(Rev. 12/13/10)*

The mediator or staff attorney has discretion to refer any of the above motions to an Appellate Commissioner or a motions panel. *(Rev. 9/17/14)*

[Effective July 1, 2011. Amended effective November 1, 2011; September 17, 2014; June 17, 2015; August 25, 2015; January 11, 2016; March 23, 2016; September 7, 2016; December 11, 2017; March 21, 2018; March 26, 2019; April 1, 2019; June 19, 2019; September 25, 2019; January 13, 2020; October 26, 2021.]

ADMINISTRATIVE ORDER REGARDING THE FILING, SERVICE, AND MANAGEMENT OF HIGHLY SENSITIVE DOCUMENTS (HSDs)

Following a security audit of CM/ECF by the Department of Homeland Security, the Secretary of the Judicial Conference issued a policy directive that all federal courts start accepting highly sensitive documents (HSDs) for filing only in paper form or via a secure electronic device, and that courts store HSDs in a secure paper filing system or on a secure, standalone computer system not connected to any network. Implementation is left to each court. This administrative order establishes initial procedures to identify and ensure the security of HSDs. Modifications may be made by further administrative order or by adoption of General or Special Orders or rule changes.

A. General Principles. The presumption in favor of public access to court documents remains intact, and this court's procedures for filing sealed documents electronically (Circuit Rule 27–13) are unchanged. By this Order, the court creates a new level of protection for HSDs.

In this Circuit, HSDs are defined as: Unclassified sealed documents involving: foreign sovereign interests; criminal activity related to cybersecurity, intellectual property, or trade secrets; terrorism; investigation of public officials; potential negative impact on national security or foreign relations of the United States; and sensitive commercial information likely to be of interest to foreign powers.

The following types of documents have restricted access under Circuit Rule 27–13, but generally will not qualify as HSDs: (1) presentence reports and related documents; (2) pleadings related to cooperation in most criminal cases; (3) social security administrative records; (4) immigration administrative records; and (5) most sealed documents in civil cases.

Classified documents will continue to be handled in accordance with existing statutes and procedures.

B. HSD Designation by Originating Court or Agency Required. If an originating court or agency designates a document as HSD, the document will retain that designation on appeal absent an order of this court to the contrary. No motion is required. If an originating court or agency maintains a document electronically (because it is not designated as an HSD), this court will presumptively do the same. Any request to re-designate sealed documents currently residing on CM/ECF as HSDs should therefore be directed to the originating court or agency in the first instance.

C. Documents Not Part of the Originating Court or Agency Record. In the rare circumstance when a party wishes to submit to the court of appeals a document that is not part of the originating court or agency record, and seeks to have that document designated as HSD, the party must submit a motion that satisfies the sealing requirements in Circuit Rule 27–13, and specifically addresses: (a) why the court of appeals should accept documents that are not part of the originating court or agency record, (b) how the documents fall within the definition of HSD, and (c) what potential irreparable injury the United States will face if the documents are not treated as HSDs.

D. Transmission of HSD Material.

(1) HSDs and related motions must be transmitted to this court in (a) paper format or (b) as an electronic copy on a secure electronic device.

(2) Any electronic copy must be submitted on a Windows compatible USB flash drive, DVD, CD, or portable hard drive that is labeled with the case number and the date it was presented to the Clerk's Office. Materials must be in a familiar file format that can be accessed using commonly available software and must use a naming convention that clearly identifies each individual file.

(3) Paper and electronic copies must be sealed in an interior envelope marked "HIGHLY SENSITIVE DOCUMENT." The outside of the envelope must state the case number and name, the type of filing, and the HSD designation in the district court or agency.

E. Service. The filing party must serve the HSD on the other party by personal delivery, mail, or third-party carrier, as specified by Fed. R. App. P. 25(c)(1)(A)–(C). A certificate of service should be included with the HSD submission in paper or electronic format.

F. Questions About HSD Filing Procedures. Any questions about how to proceed under this Administrative Order should be directed to the Clerk's Office at HSD@ca9.uscourts.gov.

[Dated: January 16, 2021.]

RULES FOR JUDICIAL–CONDUCT
AND JUDICIAL–DISABILITY PROCEEDINGS

PREFACE

These Rules were promulgated by the Judicial Conference of the United States, after public comment, pursuant to 28 U.S.C. §§ 331 and 358, to establish standards and procedures for addressing complaints filed by complainants or identified by chief judges under the Judicial Conduct and Disability Act, 28 U.S.C. §§ 351–364.

[Adopted March 11, 2008, effective April 10, 2008.]

ARTICLE I.   GENERAL PROVISIONS
RULE 1.   SCOPE AND COVERED JUDGES

(a) **Scope.** These Rules govern proceedings under the Judicial Conduct and Disability Act (Act), 28 U.S.C. §§ 351–364, to determine whether a covered judge has engaged in conduct prejudicial to the effective and expeditious administration of the business of the courts or is unable to discharge the duties of office because of mental or physical disability.

(b) **Covered Judge.** A covered judge is defined under the Act and is limited to judges of United States courts of appeals, judges of United States district courts, judges of United States bankruptcy courts, United States magistrate judges, and judges of the courts specified in 28 U.S.C. § 363.

[Adopted March 11, 2008, effective April 10, 2008. Amended effective September 17, 2015; March 12, 2019.]

Commentary on Rule 1

In September 2006, the Judicial Conduct and Disability Act Study Committee ("Breyer Committee"), appointed in 2004 by Chief Justice Rehnquist, presented a report ("Breyer Committee Report"), 239 F.R.D. 116 (Sept. 2006), to Chief Justice Roberts that evaluated implementation of the Judicial Conduct and Disability Act of 1980, 28 U.S.C. §§ 351–364. The Breyer Committee had been formed in response to criticism from the public and Congress regarding the effectiveness of the Act's implementation. The Executive Committee of the Judicial Conference directed its Committee on Judicial Conduct and Disability to consider the Breyer Committee's recommendations and to report on their implementation to the Conference.

The Breyer Committee found that it could not evaluate implementation of the Act without establishing interpretive standards, Breyer Committee Report, 239 F.R.D. at 132, and that a major problem faced by chief judges in implementing the Act was the lack of authoritative interpretive standards. *Id.* at 212–15. The Breyer Committee then established standards to guide its evaluation, some of which were new formulations and some of which were taken from the "Illustrative Rules Governing Complaints of Judicial Misconduct and Disability," discussed below. The principal standards used by the Breyer Committee are in Appendix E of its Report. *Id.* at 238.

Based on the Breyer Committee's findings, the Committee on Judicial Conduct and Disability concluded that there was a need for the Judicial Conference to exercise its power under Section 358 of the Act to fashion standards guiding the various officers and bodies that must exercise responsibility under the Act. To that end, the Committee on Judicial Conduct and Disability proposed rules based largely on Appendix E of the Breyer Committee Report and the Illustrative Rules.

The Illustrative Rules were originally prepared in 1986 by the Special Committee of the Conference of Chief Judges of the United States Courts of Appeals, and were subsequently revised and amended, most recently in 2000, by the predecessor to the Committee on Judicial Conduct and Disability. The Illustrative Rules were adopted, with minor variations, by circuit judicial councils, to govern complaints under the Judicial Conduct and Disability Act.

After being submitted for public comment pursuant to 28 U.S.C. § 358(c), the Judicial Conference promulgated the present Rules on March 11, 2008. They were amended on September 17, 2015, and again on March 12, 2019.

The definition of a covered judge tracks the Judicial Conduct and Disability Act. *See* 28 U.S.C. § 351(d)(1) (defining the term "judge" as "a circuit judge, district judge, bankruptcy judge, or magistrate judge"). As long as the subject of a complaint retains the judicial office and remains a covered judge as defined in Rule 1(b), a complaint must be addressed. *Id.*; 28 U.S.C. §§ 371(b); 372(a).

Rules 8(c) and (d) address the procedures for processing a complaint involving allegations against a person *not* covered by the Act, such as other court personnel, or against both a covered judge and a noncovered person.

Court employees seeking to report, or file a claim related to, misconduct or the denial of rights granted under their Employment Dispute Resolution (EDR) plan by other court personnel may wish to consult the Model EDR Plan and the EDR plan for the relevant court, among other resources. *See* Guide to Judiciary Policy, Vol. 12, appx. 2B.

RULE 2. CONSTRUCTION AND EFFECT

(a) Generally. These Rules are mandatory; they supersede any conflicting judicial-council rules. Judicial councils may promulgate additional rules to implement the Act as long as those rules do not conflict with these Rules.

(b) Exception. A Rule will not apply if, when performing duties authorized by the Act, a chief judge, a special committee, a judicial council, the Committee on Judicial Conduct and Disability, or the Judicial Conference expressly finds that exceptional circumstances render application of that Rule in a particular proceeding manifestly unjust or contrary to the purposes of the Act or these Rules.

[Adopted March 11, 2008, effective April 10, 2008. Amended effective September 17, 2015; March 12, 2019.]

Commentary on Rule 2

Unlike the Illustrative Rules, these Rules provide mandatory and nationally uniform provisions governing the substantive and procedural aspects of misconduct and disability proceedings under the Act. The mandatory nature of these Rules is authorized by 28 U.S.C. § 358(a) and (c). Judicial councils retain the power to promulgate rules consistent with these Rules. For example, a local rule may authorize the electronic distribution of materials pursuant to Rule 8(b).

Rule 2(b) recognizes that unforeseen and exceptional circumstances may call for a different approach in particular cases.

RULE 3. GENERAL DEFINITIONS

The following general definitions apply to these Rules. Cognizable misconduct and disability are defined in Rule 4.

(a) Chief Judge. "Chief judge" means the chief judge of a United States court of appeals, of the United States Court of International Trade, or of the United States Court of Federal Claims.

(b) Circuit Clerk. "Circuit clerk" means a clerk of a United States court of appeals, the clerk of the United States Court of International Trade, the clerk of the United States Court of Federal Claims, or the circuit executive of the United States Court of Appeals for the Federal Circuit.

(c) Complaint. A "complaint" is:

(1) a document that, in accordance with Rule 6, is filed by, or on behalf of, any person, including a document filed by an organization; or

(2) information from any source, other than a document described in (c)(1), that gives a chief judge probable cause to believe that a covered judge, as defined in Rule 1(b), has engaged in misconduct or may have a disability, whether or not the information is framed as or is intended to be an allegation of misconduct or disability.

(d) Court of Appeals, District Court, and District Judge. "Court of appeals," "district court," and "district judge," where appropriate, include the United States Court of Federal Claims, the United States Court of International Trade, and the judges thereof.

(e) Judicial Council and Circuit. "Judicial council" and "circuit," where appropriate, include any courts designated in 28 U.S.C. § 363.

(f) Judicial Employee. "Judicial Employee" includes judicial assistants, law clerks, and other court employees, including unpaid staff, such as interns, externs, and other volunteer employees.

(g) Magistrate Judge. "Magistrate judge," where appropriate, includes a special master appointed by the Court of Federal Claims under 42 U.S.C. § 300aa–12(c).

(h) Subject Judge. "Subject judge" means a covered judge, as described in Rule 1(b), who is the subject of a complaint.

[Adopted March 11, 2008, effective April 10, 2008. Amended effective September 17, 2015; March 12, 2019.]

Commentary on Rule 3

Rule 3 is derived and adapted from the Breyer Committee Report and the Illustrative Rules.

Unless otherwise specified or the context otherwise indicates, the term "complaint" is used in these Rules to refer both to complaints identified by a chief judge under Rule 5 and to complaints filed by a complainant under Rule 6.

Under the Act, a "complaint" may be filed by "any person" or "identified" by a chief judge. *See* 28 U.S.C. § 351(a), (b). Under Rule 3(c)(1), a complaint may be submitted by, or on behalf of, any person, including a document filed by an organization. Traditional standing requirements do not apply. Individuals or organizations may file a complaint even if they have not been directly injured or aggrieved.

Generally, the word "complaint" brings to mind the commencement of an adversary proceeding in which the contending parties are left to present the evidence and legal arguments, and judges play the role of an essentially passive arbiter. The Act, however, establishes an administrative, inquisitorial process. For example, even absent a complaint filed by a complainant under Rule 6, chief judges are expected in some circumstances to trigger the process—"identify a complaint," *see* 28 U.S.C. § 351(b) and Rule 5—and conduct an investigation without becoming a party. *See* 28 U.S.C. § 352(a); Breyer Committee Report, 239 F.R.D. at 214; Illustrative Rule 2(j). Where the complainant reveals information of misconduct or disability but does not claim it as such, the chief judge is not limited to the "four corners of the complaint" and should proceed under Rule 5 to determine whether identification of a complaint is appropriate. *See* Breyer Committee Report, 239 F.R.D. at 183–84.

An allegation of misconduct or disability filed under Rule 6 is a "complaint," and the Rule so provides in subsection (c)(1). However, both the nature of the process and the use of the term "identify" suggest that the word "complaint" covers more than a document formally triggering the process. The process relies on chief judges considering known information and triggering the process when appropriate. "Identifying" a "complaint," therefore, is best understood as the chief judge's concluding that information known to the judge constitutes probable cause to believe that misconduct occurred or a disability exists, whether or not the information is framed as, or intended to be, an accusation. This definition is codified in subsection (c)(2).

The remaining subsections of Rule 3 provide technical definitions clarifying the application of the Rules.

ARTICLE II. MISCONDUCT AND DISABILITY
RULE 4. MISCONDUCT AND DISABILITY DEFINITIONS

(a) Misconduct Generally. Cognizable Misconduct is conduct prejudicial to the effective and expeditious administration of the business of the courts. Cognizable misconduct includes, but is not limited to, the following:

(1) Violation of Specific Standards of Judicial Conduct. Cognizable misconduct includes:

(A) using the judge's office to obtain special treatment for friends or relatives;

(B) accepting bribes, gifts, or other personal favors related to the judicial office;

(C) engaging in improper ex parte communications with parties or counsel for one side in a case;

(D) engaging in partisan political activity or making inappropriately partisan statements;

(E) soliciting funds for organizations; or

(F) violating rules or standards pertaining to restrictions on outside income or knowingly violating requirements for financial disclosure.

(2) *Abusive or Harassing Behavior.* Cognizable misconduct includes:

(A) engaging in unwanted, offensive, or abusive sexual conduct, including sexual harassment or assault;

(B) treating litigants, attorneys, judicial employees, or others in a demonstrably egregious and hostile manner; or

(C) creating a hostile work environment for judicial employees.

(3) *Discrimination.* Cognizable misconduct includes intentional discrimination on the basis of race, color, sex, gender, gender identity, pregnancy, sexual orientation, religion, national origin, age, or disability;

(4) *Retaliation.* Cognizable misconduct includes retaliating against complainants, witnesses, judicial employees, or others for participating in this complaint process, or for reporting or disclosing judicial misconduct or disability;

(5) *Interference or Failure to Comply With the Complaint Process.* Cognizable misconduct includes refusing, without good cause shown, to cooperate in the investigation of a complaint or enforcement of a decision rendered under these Rules; or

(6) *Failure to Report or Disclose.* Cognizable misconduct includes failing to call to the attention of the relevant chief district judge or chief circuit judge any reliable information reasonably likely to constitute judicial misconduct or disability.

A judge who receives such reliable information shall respect a request for confidentiality but shall nonetheless disclose the information to the relevant chief district judge or chief circuit judge, who shall also treat the information as confidential. Certain reliable information may be protected from disclosure by statute or rule. A judge's assurance of confidentiality must yield when there is reliable information of misconduct or disability that threatens the safety or security of any person or that is serious or egregious such that it threatens the integrity and proper functioning of the judiciary.

A person reporting information of misconduct or disability must be informed at the outset of a judge's responsibility to disclose such information to the relevant chief district judge or chief circuit judge.

Reliable information reasonably likely to constitute judicial misconduct or disability related to a chief circuit judge should be called to the attention of the next most-senior active circuit judge. Such information related to a chief district judge should be called to the attention of the chief circuit judge.

(7) *Conduct Outside the Performance of Official Duties.* Cognizable misconduct includes conduct occurring outside the performance of official duties if the conduct is reasonably likely to have a prejudicial effect on the administration of the business of the courts, including a substantial and widespread lowering of public confidence in the courts among reasonable people.

(b) Conduct Not Constituting Cognizable Misconduct.

(1) *Allegations Related to the Merits of a Decision or Procedural Ruling.* Cognizable misconduct does not include an allegation that calls into question the correctness of a judge's ruling, including a failure to recuse.

If the decision or ruling is alleged to be the result of an improper motive, *e.g.*, a bribe, ex parte contact, racial or ethnic bias, or improper conduct in rendering a decision or ruling, such as personally derogatory remarks irrelevant to the issues, the complaint is not cognizable to the extent that it calls into question the merits of the decision.

(2) *Allegations About Delay.* Cognizable misconduct does not include an allegation about delay in rendering a decision or ruling, unless the allegation concerns an improper motive in delaying a particular decision or habitual delay in a significant number of unrelated cases.

(c) Disability. Disability is a temporary or permanent impairment, physical or mental, rendering a judge unable to discharge the duties of the particular judicial office. Examples of disability include substance abuse, the inability to stay awake during court proceedings, or impairment of cognitive abilities that renders the judge unable to function effectively.

[Adopted March 11, 2008, effective April 10, 2008. Amended effective March 12, 2019.]

Commentary on Rule 4

The phrase "prejudicial to the effective and expeditious administration of the business of the courts" is not subject to precise definition, and subsection (a) therefore provides some specific examples. 28 U.S.C. § 351(a). The Code of Conduct for United States Judges sets forth behavioral guidelines for judges. While the Code's Canons are instructive, ultimately the responsibility for determining what constitutes cognizable misconduct is determined by the Act and these Rules, as interpreted and applied by judicial councils, subject to review and limitations prescribed by the Act and these Rules. *See also* Rule 24 (Public Availability of Decisions).

Even where specific, mandatory rules exist—for example, governing the receipt of gifts by judges, outside earned income, and financial disclosure obligations—the distinction between the misconduct statute and these specific, mandatory rules must be borne in mind. For example, an inadvertent, minor violation of any one of these rules, promptly remedied when called to the attention of the judge, might still be a violation but might not rise to the level of misconduct under the Act. By contrast, a pattern of such violations of the Code might well rise to the level of misconduct.

Rule 4(a)(2)(A) provides expressly that unwanted, offensive, or abusive sexual conduct by a judge, including sexual harassment or assault, constitutes cognizable misconduct. The Rule recognizes that anyone can be a victim of unwanted, offensive, or abusive sexual conduct, regardless of their sex and of the sex of the judge engaging in the misconduct.

Under Rule 4(a)(4), a judge's efforts to retaliate against any person for reporting or disclosing misconduct, or otherwise participating in the complaint process constitute cognizable misconduct. The Rule makes the prohibition against retaliation explicit in the interest of promoting public confidence in the complaint process.

Rules 4(a)(2), (3), and (4) reflect the judiciary's commitment to maintaining a work environment in which all judicial employees are treated with dignity, fairness, and respect, and are free from harassment, discrimination, and retaliation. *See* Code of Conduct for United States Judges, Canon 3A(3) cmt. ("The duty to be respectful includes the responsibility to avoid comment or behavior that could reasonably be interpreted as harassment, prejudice or bias.").

Rule 4(a)(5) provides that a judge's refusal, without good cause shown, to cooperate in the investigation of a complaint or enforcement of a decision rendered under these Rules constitutes cognizable misconduct. While the exercise of rights under the Fifth Amendment to the Constitution would constitute good cause under Rule 4(a)(5), given the fact-specific nature of the inquiry, it is not possible to otherwise anticipate all circumstances that might also constitute good cause. The Commentary on Rule 13 provides additional discussion regarding Rule 4(a)(5). The Rules contemplate that judicial councils will not consider commencing proceedings under Rule 4(a)(5) except as necessary after other means to acquire the information or enforce a decision have been tried or have proven futile.

All judges have a duty to bring to the attention of the relevant chief district judge or chief circuit judge reliable information reasonably likely to constitute judicial misconduct or disability. *See* Rule 4(a)(6). This duty is included within every judge's obligation to assist in addressing allegations of misconduct or disability and to take appropriate action as necessary. Public confidence in the integrity and impartiality of the judiciary is promoted when judges take appropriate action based on reliable information of likely misconduct. Appropriate action depends on the circumstances, but the overarching goal of such action should be to prevent harm to those affected by the misconduct and to prevent recurrence. *See* Code of Conduct for United States Judges, Canon 3B(6) & cmt. These Rules incorporate those principles while allowing for appropriate, expeditious, fair, and effective resolutions of all such complaints.

The formal procedures outlined in these Rules are intended to address serious issues of judicial misconduct and disability. By statute and rule, the chief circuit judge administers the misconduct and disability complaint process, including the authority to investigate an allegation and, if warranted, to identify a formal complaint. *See* Rule 5. Disclosures made to or otherwise brought to the attention of the appropriate chief district judge of reliable information of misconduct or disability that threatens the safety or security of any person or that is serious or egregious such that it threatens the integrity and proper functioning of the judiciary warrant communication to and consultation with the chief circuit judge in light of the chief circuit judge's statutory responsibility for overseeing any required final action.

In practice, however, not all allegations of misconduct or disability will warrant resort to the formal procedures outlined in these Rules because they appear likely to yield to effective, prompt resolution through informal corrective action. In such cases, allegations may initially be addressed to the chief district judge or the chief circuit judge to determine whether informal corrective action will suffice and to initiate such steps as promptly as is reasonable under the circumstances.

A person who seeks to report information of misconduct or disability on a confidential or anonymous basis may proceed through various alternative avenues within the judiciary, including the Office of Judicial Integrity and/or comparable offices within the circuits.

Rule 4(a)(7) reflects that an allegation can meet the statutory standard for misconduct even though the judge's alleged conduct did not occur in the course of the performance of official duties. Furthermore, some conduct specified in Rule 4(a)(1) through 4(a)(6), or not specified within these Rules, might constitute misconduct occurring outside the performance of official duties. The Code of Conduct for United States Judges expressly covers a wide range of extra-official activities, and some of these activities may constitute misconduct under the Act and these Rules. For example, allegations that a judge solicited funds for a charity or other organization or participated in a partisan political event are cognizable under the Act even though they did not occur in the course of the performance of the judge's official duties.

Rule 4(b)(1) tracks the Act, 28 U.S.C. § 352(b)(1)(A)(ii), in excluding from the definition of misconduct allegations "[d]irectly related to the merits of a decision or procedural ruling." This exclusion preserves the independence of judges in the exercise of judicial authority by ensuring that the complaint procedure is not used to collaterally call into question the substance of a judge's decision or procedural ruling. Any allegation that calls into question the correctness of an official decision or procedural ruling of a judge—without more—is merits-related. The phrase "decision or procedural ruling" is not limited to rulings issued in deciding Article III cases or controversies. Thus, a complaint challenging the correctness of a chief judge's determination to dismiss a prior misconduct complaint would be properly dismissed as merits-related—in other words, as challenging the substance of the judge's administrative determination to dismiss the complaint—even though it does not concern the judge's rulings in Article III litigation. Similarly, an allegation that a judge incorrectly declined to approve a Criminal Justice Act voucher is merits-related under this standard.

Conversely, an allegation that a judge conspired with a prosecutor to make a particular ruling is not merits-related, even though it "relates" to a ruling in a colloquial sense. Such an allegation attacks the propriety of conspiring with the prosecutor and goes beyond a challenge to the correctness—"the merits"—of the ruling itself.

An allegation that a judge ruled against the complainant because the complainant is a member of a particular racial or ethnic group, or because the judge dislikes the complainant personally, is also not merits-related. Such an allegation attacks the propriety of arriving at rulings with an illicit or improper motive. Similarly, an allegation that a judge used an inappropriate term to refer to a class of people is not merits-related even if the judge used it on the bench or in an opinion; the correctness of the judge's rulings is not at stake. An allegation that a judge treated litigants, attorneys, judicial employees, or others in a demonstrably egregious and hostile manner is also not merits-related.

The existence of an appellate remedy is usually irrelevant to whether an allegation is merits-related. The merits-related ground for dismissal exists to protect judges' independence in making rulings, not to protect or promote the appellate process. A complaint alleging an incorrect ruling is merits-related even though the complainant has no recourse from that ruling. By the same token, an allegation that is otherwise cognizable under the Act should not be dismissed merely because an appellate remedy appears to exist (for example, vacating a ruling that resulted from an improper ex parte communication). However, there may be occasions when appellate and misconduct proceedings overlap, and consideration and disposition of a complaint under these Rules may be properly deferred by the chief judge until the appellate proceedings are concluded to avoid inconsistent decisions.

Because of the special need to protect judges' independence in deciding what to say in an opinion or ruling, a somewhat different standard applies to determine the merits-relatedness of a non-frivolous allegation that a judge's language in a ruling reflected an improper motive. If the judge's language was relevant to the case at hand — for example, a statement that a claim is legally or factually "frivolous"—then the judge's choice of language is presumptively merits-related and excluded, absent evidence apart from the ruling itself suggesting an improper motive. If, on the other hand, the challenged language does not seem relevant on its face, then an additional inquiry under Rule 11(b) is necessary.

With regard to Rule 4(b)(2), a complaint of delay in a single case is excluded as merits-related. Such an allegation may be said to challenge the correctness of an official action of the judge, *i.e.*, assigning a low priority to deciding the particular case. But, an allegation of a habitual pattern of delay in a significant number of unrelated cases, or an allegation of deliberate delay in a single case arising out of an improper motive, is not merits-related.

Rule 4(c) relates to disability and provides only the most general definition, recognizing that a fact-specific approach is the only one available. A mental disability could involve cognitive impairment or any psychiatric or psychological condition that renders the judge unable to discharge the duties of office. Such duties may include those that are administrative. If, for example, the judge is a chief judge, the judicial council, fulfilling its obligation under 28 U.S.C. § 332(d)(1) to make "necessary and appropriate orders for the effective and expeditious administration of justice," may find, under 28 U.S.C. § 45(d) or § 136(e), that the judge is "temporarily unable to perform" his or her chief-judge duties. In that event, an appropriate remedy could involve, under Rule 20(b)(1)(D)(vii), temporary reassignment of chief-judge duties to the next judge statutorily eligible to perform them.

Confidentiality as referenced elsewhere in these Rules is directed toward protecting the fairness and thoroughness of the process by which a complaint is filed or initiated, investigated (in specific circumstances), and ultimately resolved, as specified under these Rules. Nothing in these Rules concerning the confidentiality of the complaint process or the Code of Conduct for Judicial Employees concerning use or disclosure of confidential information received in the course of official duties prevents judicial employees from reporting or disclosing misconduct or disability. *See* Rule 23(c).

ARTICLE III. INITIATION OF COMPLAINT

Rule 5. IDENTIFICATION OF COMPLAINT

(a) Identification. When a chief judge has information constituting reasonable grounds for inquiry into whether a covered judge has engaged in misconduct or has a disability, the chief judge may conduct an inquiry, as he or she deems appropriate, into the accuracy of the information even if no related complaint has been filed. A chief judge who finds probable cause to believe that misconduct has occurred or that a disability exists may seek an informal resolution that he or she finds satisfactory. If no informal resolution is achieved or is feasible, the chief judge may identify a complaint and, by written order stating the reasons, begin the review provided in Rule 11. If the evidence of misconduct is clear and convincing and no informal resolution is achieved or is feasible, the chief judge must identify a complaint. A chief judge must not decline to identify a complaint merely because the person making the allegation has not filed a complaint under Rule 6. This Rule is subject to Rule 7.

(b) Submission Not Fully Complying With Rule 6. A legible submission in substantial but not full compliance with Rule 6 must be considered as possible grounds for the identification of a complaint under Rule 5(a).

[Adopted March 11, 2008, effective April 10, 2008. Amended effective September 17, 2015; March 12, 2019.]

Commentary on Rule 5

This Rule is adapted from the Breyer Committee Report, 239 F.R.D. at 245–46.

The Act authorizes a chief judge, by written order stating reasons, to identify a complaint and thereby dispense with the filing of a written complaint. *See* 28 U.S.C. § 351(b). Under Rule 5, when a chief judge becomes aware of information constituting reasonable grounds to inquire into possible misconduct or disability on the part of a covered judge, and no formal complaint has been filed, the chief judge has the power in his or her discretion to begin an appropriate inquiry. A chief judge's decision whether to informally seek a resolution and/or to identify a complaint is guided by the results of that inquiry. If the chief judge concludes that there is probable cause to believe that misconduct has occurred or a disability exists, the chief judge may seek an informal resolution, if feasible, and if failing in that, may identify a complaint. Discretion is accorded largely for the reasons police officers and prosecutors have discretion in making arrests or bringing charges. The matter may be trivial and isolated, based on marginal evidence, or otherwise highly unlikely to lead to a misconduct or disability finding. On the other hand, if the inquiry leads the chief judge to conclude that there is clear and convincing evidence of misconduct or a disability, and no satisfactory informal resolution has been achieved or is feasible, the chief judge is required to identify a complaint.

An informal resolution is one agreed to by the subject judge and found satisfactory by the chief judge. Because an informal resolution under Rule 5 reached before a complaint is filed under Rule 6 will generally cause a subsequent Rule 6 complaint alleging the identical matter to be concluded, *see* Rule 11(d), the chief judge must be sure that the resolution is fully appropriate before endorsing it. In doing so, the chief judge must balance the seriousness of the matter against the particular judge's alacrity in addressing the issue. The availability of this procedure should encourage attempts at swift remedial action before a formal complaint is filed.

When a chief judge identifies a complaint, a written order stating the reasons for the identification must be provided; this begins the process articulated in Rule 11. Rule 11 provides that once a chief judge has identified a complaint, the chief judge, subject to the disqualification provisions of Rule 25, will perform, with respect to that complaint, all functions assigned to the chief judge for the determination of complaints filed by a complainant.

In high-visibility situations, it may be desirable for a chief judge to identify a complaint without first seeking an informal resolution (and then, if the circumstances warrant, dismiss or conclude the identified complaint without appointment of a special committee) in order to assure the public that the allegations have not been ignored.

A chief judge's decision not to identify a complaint under Rule 5 is not appealable and is subject to Rule 4(b)(1), which excludes merits-related complaints from the definition of misconduct.

A chief judge may not decline to identify a complaint solely on the basis that the unfiled allegations could be raised by one or more persons in a filed complaint, but none of these persons has opted to do so.

Subsection (a) concludes by stating that this Rule is "subject to Rule 7." This is intended to establish that only (i) the chief judge of the home circuit of a potential subject judge, or (ii) the chief judge of a circuit in which misconduct is alleged to have occurred in the course of official business while the potential subject judge was sitting by designation, shall have the power or a duty under this Rule to identify a complaint.

Subsection (b) provides that submissions that do not comply with the requirements of Rule 6(d) must be considered under Rule 5(a). For instance, if a complaint has been filed but the form submitted is unsigned, or the truth of the statements therein are not verified in writing under penalty of perjury, then a chief judge must nevertheless consider the allegations as known information and as a possible basis for the identification of a complaint under the process described in Rule 5(a).

RULE 6.   FILING OF COMPLAINT

(a) Form. A complainant may use the form reproduced in the Appendix to these Rules or a form designated by the rules of the judicial council in the circuit in which the complaint is filed. A complaint form is also available on each court of appeals' website or may be obtained from the circuit clerk or any district court or bankruptcy court within the circuit. A form is not necessary to file a complaint, but the complaint must be written and must include the information described in (b).

(b) Brief Statement of Facts. A complaint must contain a concise statement that details the specific facts on which the claim of misconduct or disability is based. The statement of facts should include a description of:

(1) what happened;

(2) when and where the relevant events happened;

(3) any information that would help an investigator check the facts; and

(4) for an allegation of disability, any additional facts that form the basis of that allegation.

(c) Legibility. A complaint should be typewritten if possible. If not typewritten, it must be legible. An illegible complaint will be returned to the complainant with a request to resubmit it in legible form. If a resubmitted complaint is still illegible, it will not be accepted for filing.

(d) Complainant's Address and Signature; Verification. The complainant must provide a contact address and sign the complaint. The truth of the statements made in the complaint must be verified in writing under penalty of perjury. If any of these requirements are not met, the submission will be accepted, but it will be reviewed under only Rule 5(b).

(e) Number of Copies; Envelope Marking. The complainant shall provide the number of copies of the complaint required by local rule. Each copy should be in an envelope marked "Complaint of Misconduct" or "Complaint of Disability." The envelope must not show the name of any subject judge.

[Adopted March 11, 2008, effective April 10, 2008. Amended effective September 17, 2015; March 12, 2019.]

Commentary on Rule 6

The Rule is adapted from the Illustrative Rules and is largely self-explanatory. As discussed in the Commentary on Rule 4 and in Rule 23(c), confidentiality as referenced elsewhere in these Rules does not prevent judicial employees from reporting or disclosing misconduct or disability.

RULE 7.   WHERE TO INITIATE COMPLAINT

(a) Where to File. Except as provided in (b),

(1) a complaint against a judge of a United States court of appeals, a United States district court, a United States bankruptcy court, or a United States magistrate judge must be filed with the circuit clerk in the jurisdiction in which the subject judge holds office.

(2) a complaint against a judge of the United States Court of International Trade or the United States Court of Federal Claims must be filed with the respective clerk of that court.

(3) a complaint against a judge of the United States Court of Appeals for the Federal Circuit must be filed with the circuit executive of that court.

(b) Misconduct in Another Circuit; Transfer. If a complaint alleges misconduct in the course of official business while the subject judge was sitting on a court by designation under 28 U.S.C. §§ 291–293 and 294(d), the complaint may be filed or identified with the circuit clerk of that circuit or of the subject judge's home circuit. The proceeding will continue in the circuit of the first-filed or first-identified complaint. The judicial council of the circuit where the complaint was first filed or first identified may transfer the complaint to the subject judge's home circuit or to the circuit where the alleged misconduct occurred, as the case may be.

[Adopted March 11, 2008, effective April 10, 2008. Amended effective September 17, 2015.]

Commentary on Rule 7

Title 28 U.S.C. § 351 states that complaints are to be filed with "the clerk of the court of appeals for the circuit." However, in many circuits, this role is filled by circuit executives. Accordingly, the term "circuit clerk," as defined in Rule 3(b) and used throughout these Rules, applies to circuit executives.

Section 351 uses the term "the circuit" in a way that suggests that either the home circuit of the subject judge or the circuit in which misconduct is alleged to have occurred is the proper venue for complaints. With an exception for judges sitting by designation, the Rule requires the filing or identification of a misconduct or disability complaint in the circuit in which the judge holds office, largely based on the administrative perspective of the Act. Given the Act's emphasis on the future conduct of the business of the courts, the circuit in which the judge holds office is the appropriate forum because that circuit is likely best able to influence a judge's future behavior in constructive ways.

However, when judges sit by designation, the non-home circuit has a strong interest in redressing misconduct in the course of official business, and where allegations also involve a member of the bar—ex parte contact between an attorney and a judge, for example—it may often be desirable to have the judicial and bar misconduct proceedings take place in the same venue. Rule 7(b), therefore, allows transfer to, or filing or identification of a complaint in, the non-home circuit. The proceeding may be transferred by the judicial council of the filing or identified circuit to the other circuit.

RULE 8.   ACTION BY CIRCUIT CLERK

(a) Receipt of Complaint. Upon receiving a complaint against a judge filed under Rule 6 or identified under Rule 5, the circuit clerk must open a file, assign a docket number according to a uniform numbering scheme promulgated by the Committee on Judicial Conduct and Disability, and acknowledge the complaint's receipt.

(b) Distribution of Copies. The circuit clerk must promptly send copies of a complaint filed under Rule 6 to the chief judge or, where the chief judge is disqualified from considering a complaint, to the judge authorized to act as chief judge under Rule 25(f), and copies of complaints filed under Rule 6 or identified under Rule 5 to each subject judge. The circuit clerk must retain the original complaint. Any further distribution should be as provided by local rule.

(c) Complaint Against Noncovered Person. If the circuit clerk receives a complaint about a person not holding an office described in Rule 1(b), the clerk must not accept the complaint under these Rules.

(d) Complaint Against Judge and Another Noncovered Person. If the circuit clerk receives a complaint about a judge described in Rule 1(b) and a person not holding an office described in Rule 1(b), the clerk must accept the complaint under these Rules only with regard to the judge and must so inform the complainant.

[Adopted March 11, 2008, effective April 10, 2008. Amended effective September 17, 2015; March 12, 2019.]

Commentary on Rule 8

This Rule is adapted from the Illustrative Rules and is largely self-explanatory.

The uniform docketing scheme described in subsection (a) should take into account potential problems associated with a complaint that names multiple judges. One solution may be to provide separate docket numbers for each subject judge. Separate docket numbers would help avoid difficulties in tracking cases, particularly if a complaint is dismissed with respect to some, but not all of the named judges.

Complaints against noncovered persons are not to be accepted for processing under these Rules but may, of course, be accepted under other circuit rules or procedures for grievances.

RULE 9.   TIME FOR FILING OR IDENTIFYING COMPLAINT

A complaint may be filed or identified at any time. If the passage of time has made an accurate and fair investigation of a complaint impracticable, the complaint must be dismissed under Rule 11(c)(1)(E).

[Adopted March 11, 2008, effective April 10, 2008. Amended effective September 17, 2015.]

Commentary on Rule 9

This Rule is adapted from the Act, 28 U.S.C. §§ 351, 352(b)(1)(A)(iii), and the Illustrative Rules.

RULE 10.   ABUSE OF COMPLAINT PROCEDURE

(a) Abusive Complaints. A complainant who has filed repetitive, harassing, or frivolous complaints, or has otherwise abused the complaint procedure, may be restricted from filing further complaints. After giving the complainant an opportunity to show cause in writing why his or her right to file further complaints should not be limited, the judicial council may prohibit, restrict, or impose conditions on the complainant's use of the complaint procedure. Upon written request of the complainant, the judicial council may revise or withdraw any prohibition, restriction, or condition previously imposed.

(b) Orchestrated Complaints. When many essentially identical complaints from different complainants are received and appear to be part of an orchestrated campaign, the chief judge may recommend that the judicial council issue a written order instructing the circuit clerk to accept only a certain number of such complaints for filing and to refuse to accept additional complaints. The circuit clerk must send a copy of any such order to anyone whose complaint was not accepted.

[Adopted March 11, 2008, effective April 10, 2008. Amended effective September 17, 2015.]

Commentary on Rule 10

This Rule is adapted from the Illustrative Rules.

Rule 10(a) provides a mechanism for a judicial council to restrict the filing of further complaints by a single complainant who has abused the complaint procedure. In some instances, however, the complaint procedure may be abused in a manner for which the remedy provided in Rule 10(a) may not be appropriate. For example, some circuits have been inundated with submissions of dozens or hundreds of essentially identical complaints against the same judge or judges, all submitted by different complainants. In many of these instances, persons with grievances against a particular judge or judges used the Internet or other technology to orchestrate mass complaint-filing campaigns against them. If each complaint submitted as part of such a campaign were accepted for filing and processed according to these Rules, there would be a serious drain on court resources without any benefit to the adjudication of the underlying merits.

A judicial council may, therefore, respond to such mass filings under Rule 10(b) by declining to accept repetitive complaints for filing, regardless of the fact that the complaints are nominally submitted by different complainants. When the first complaint or complaints have been dismissed on the merits, and when further, essentially identical submissions follow, the judicial council may issue a second order noting that these are identical or repetitive complaints, directing the circuit clerk not to accept these complaints or any further such complaints for filing, and directing the clerk to send each putative complainant copies of both orders.

ARTICLE IV.   REVIEW OF COMPLAINT BY CHIEF JUDGE
RULE 11.   CHIEF JUDGE'S REVIEW

(a) Purpose of Chief Judge's Review. When a complaint is identified by the chief judge or is filed, the chief judge must review it unless the chief judge is disqualified under Rule 25, in which case the most senior active circuit judge not disqualified will review the complaint. If a complaint contains information constituting evidence of misconduct or disability, but the complainant does not claim it as such, the chief judge must treat the complaint as if it did allege misconduct or disability and give notice to the subject judge. After reviewing a complaint, the chief judge must determine whether it should be:

(1) dismissed;

(2) concluded on the ground that voluntary corrective action has been taken;

(3) concluded because intervening events have made action on the complaint no longer necessary; or

(4) referred to a special committee.

(b) Chief Judge's Inquiry. In determining what action to take under Rule 11(a), the chief judge may conduct a limited inquiry. The chief judge, or a designee, may communicate orally or in writing with the complainant, the subject judge, and any others who may have knowledge of the matter, and may obtain and review transcripts and other relevant documents. In conducting the inquiry, the chief judge must not determine any reasonably disputed issue. Any such determination must be left to a special committee appointed under Rule 11(f) and to the judicial council that considers the committee's report.

(c) Dismissal.

(1) *Permissible grounds.* A complaint may be dismissed in whole or in part to the extent that the chief judge concludes that the complaint:

(A) alleges conduct that, even if true, is not prejudicial to the effective and expeditious administration of the business of the courts and does not indicate a mental or physical disability resulting in the inability to discharge the duties of judicial office;

(B) is directly related to the merits of a decision or procedural ruling;

(C) is frivolous;

(D) is based on allegations lacking sufficient evidence to raise an inference that misconduct has occurred or that a disability exists;

(E) is based on allegations that are incapable of being established through investigation;

(F) has been filed in the wrong circuit under Rule 7; or

(G) is otherwise not appropriate for consideration under the Act.

(2) *Impermissible Grounds.* A complaint must not be dismissed solely because it repeats allegations of a previously dismissed complaint if it also contains material information not previously considered and does not constitute harassment of the subject judge.

(d) Corrective Action. The chief judge may conclude a complaint proceeding in whole or in part if:

(1) an informal resolution under Rule 5 satisfactory to the chief judge was reached before the complaint was filed under Rule 6; or

(2) the chief judge determines that the subject judge has taken appropriate voluntary corrective action that acknowledges and remedies the problems raised by the complaint.

(e) Intervening Events. The chief judge may conclude a complaint proceeding in whole or in part upon determining that intervening events render some or all of the allegations moot or make remedial action impossible as to the subject judge.

(f) Appointment of Special Committee. If some or all of a complaint is not dismissed or concluded, the chief judge must promptly appoint a special committee to investigate the complaint or any relevant portion of it and to make recommendations to the judicial council. Before appointing a special committee, the chief judge must invite the subject judge to respond to the complaint either orally or in writing if the judge was not given an opportunity during the limited inquiry. In the chief judge's discretion, separate complaints may be joined and assigned to a single special committee. Similarly, a single complaint about more than one judge may be severed and more than one special committee appointed.

(g) Notice of Chief Judge's Action; Petition for Review.

(1) *When Chief Judge Appoints Special Committee.* If the chief judge appoints a special committee, the chief judge must notify the complainant and the subject judge that the matter has been referred to a committee, notify the complainant of a complainant's rights under Rule 16, and identify the members of the committee. A copy of the order appointing the special committee must be sent to the Committee on Judicial Conduct and Disability.

(2) *When Chief Judge Disposes of Complaint Without Appointing Special Committee.* If the chief judge disposes of a complaint under Rule 11(c), (d), or (e), the chief judge must prepare a supporting memorandum that sets forth the reasons for the disposition. If the complaint was initiated by identification under Rule 5, the memorandum must so indicate. Except as authorized by 28 U.S.C. § 360, the memorandum must not include the name of the complainant or of the subject judge. The order and memoranda incorporated by reference in the order must be promptly sent to the complainant, the subject judge, and the Committee on Judicial Conduct and Disability.

(3) *Right to Petition for Review.* If the chief judge disposes of a complaint under Rule 11(c), (d), or (e), the complainant and the subject judge must be notified of the right to petition the judicial council for review of the disposition, as provided in Rule 18. If the chief judge so disposes of a complaint that was identified under Rule 5 or filed by its subject judge, the chief judge must transmit the order and memoranda incorporated by reference in the order to the judicial council for review in accordance with Rule 19. In the event of such a transmission, the subject judge may make a written submission to the judicial council but will have no further right of review except as allowed under Rule 21(b)(1)(B). When a disposition is to be reviewed by the judicial council, the chief judge must promptly transmit all materials obtained in connection with the inquiry under Rule 11(b) to the circuit clerk for transmittal to the council.

(h) Public Availability of Chief Judge's Decision. The chief judge's decision must be made public to the extent, at the time, and in the manner provided in Rule 24.

[Adopted March 11, 2008, effective April 10, 2008. Amended effective September 17, 2015; March 12, 2019.]

Commentary on Rule 11

This Rule describes complaint-review actions available either to the chief judge or, where that judge is the subject judge or is otherwise disqualified under Rule 25, such as where the complaint is filed against the chief judge, to the judge designated under Rule 25(f) to perform the chief judge's duties under these Rules. Subsection (a) of this Rule provides that where a complaint has been filed under Rule 6, the ordinary doctrines of waiver do not apply. The chief judge must identify as a complaint any misconduct or disability issues raised by the factual allegations of the complaint even if the complainant makes no such claim with regard to those issues. For example, an allegation limited to misconduct in fact-finding that mentions periods during a trial when the judge was asleep must be treated as a complaint regarding disability. A formal order giving notice of the expanded scope of the proceeding must be given to the subject judge.

Subsection (b) describes the nature of the chief judge's inquiry. It is based largely on the Breyer Committee Report, 239 F.R.D. at 243–45. The Act states that dismissal is appropriate "when a limited inquiry . . . demonstrates that the allegations in the complaint lack any factual foundation or are conclusively refuted by objective evidence." 28 U.S.C. § 352(b)(1)(B). At the same time, however, Section 352(a) states that "[t]he chief judge shall not undertake to make findings of fact about any matter that is reasonably in dispute." These two statutory standards should be read together so that a matter is not "reasonably" in dispute if a limited inquiry shows that the allegations do not constitute misconduct or disability, that they lack any reliable factual foundation, or that they are conclusively refuted by objective evidence.

In conducting a limited inquiry under subsection (b), the chief judge must avoid determinations of reasonably disputed issues, including reasonably disputed issues as to whether the facts alleged constitute misconduct or disability, which are ordinarily left to the judicial council and its special committee. An allegation of fact is ordinarily not "refuted" simply because the subject judge denies it. The limited inquiry must reveal something more in the way of refutation before it is appropriate to dismiss a complaint that is otherwise cognizable. If it is the complainant's word against the subject judge's—in other words, there is simply no other significant evidence of what happened or of the complainant's unreliability—then there must be a special-committee investigation. Such a credibility issue is a matter "reasonably in dispute" within the meaning of the Act.

However, dismissal following a limited inquiry may occur when a complaint refers to transcripts or to witnesses and the chief judge determines that the transcripts and witnesses all support the subject judge. Breyer Committee Report, 239 F.R.D. at 243. For example, consider a complaint alleging that the subject judge said X, and the complaint mentions, or it is independently clear, that five people may have heard what the judge said. Id. The chief judge is told by the subject judge and one witness that the judge did not say X, and the chief judge dismisses the complaint without questioning the other four possible witnesses. Id. In this example, the matter remains reasonably in dispute. If all five witnesses say the subject judge did not say X, dismissal is appropriate, but if potential witnesses who are reasonably accessible have not been questioned, then the matter remains reasonably in dispute. Id.

Similarly, under subsection (c)(1)(A), if it is clear that the conduct or disability alleged, even if true, is not cognizable under these Rules, the complaint should be dismissed. If that issue is reasonably in dispute, however, dismissal under subsection (c)(1)(A) is inappropriate.

Essentially, the standard articulated in subsection (b) is that used to decide motions for summary judgment pursuant to Fed. R. Civ. P. 56. Genuine issues of material fact are not resolved at the summary judgment stage. A material fact is one that "might affect the outcome of the suit under the governing law," and a dispute is "genuine" if "the evidence is such that a reasonable jury could return a verdict for the nonmoving party." *Anderson v. Liberty Lobby*, 477 U.S. 242, 248 (1986). Similarly, the chief judge may not resolve a genuine issue concerning a material fact or the existence of misconduct or a disability when conducting a limited inquiry pursuant to subsection (b).

Subsection (c) describes the grounds on which a complaint may be dismissed. These are adapted from the Act, 28 U.S.C. § 352(b), and the Breyer Committee Report, 239 F.R.D. at 239–45. Subsection (c)(1)(A) permits dismissal of an allegation that, even if true, does not constitute misconduct or disability under the statutory standard. The proper standards are set out in Rule 4 and discussed in the Commentary on that Rule. Subsection (c)(1)(B) permits dismissal of complaints related to the merits of a decision by a subject judge; this standard is also governed by Rule 4 and its accompanying Commentary.

Subsections (c)(1)(C)–(E) implement the statute by allowing dismissal of complaints that are "frivolous, lacking sufficient evidence to raise an inference that misconduct has occurred, or containing allegations which are incapable of being established through investigation." 28 U.S.C. § 352(b)(1)(A)(iii).

Dismissal of a complaint as "frivolous" under Rule 11(c)(1)(C) will generally occur without any inquiry beyond the face of the complaint. For instance, when the allegations are facially incredible or so lacking in indicia of reliability that no further inquiry is warranted, dismissal under this subsection is appropriate.

A complaint warranting dismissal under Rule 11(c)(1)(D) is illustrated by the following example. Consider a complainant who alleges an impropriety and asserts that he knows of it because it was observed and reported to him by a person who is identified. The subject judge denies that the event occurred. When contacted, the source also denies it. In such a case, the chief judge's proper course of action may turn on whether the source had any role in the allegedly improper conduct. If the complaint was based on a lawyer's statement that he or she had an improper ex parte contact with a judge, the lawyer's denial of the impropriety might not be taken as wholly persuasive, and it would be appropriate to conclude that a real factual issue is raised. On the other hand, if the complaint quoted a disinterested third party and that disinterested party denied that the statement had been made, there would be no value in opening a formal investigation. In such a case, it would be appropriate to dismiss the complaint under Rule 11(c)(1)(D).

Rule 11(c)(1)(E) is intended, among other things, to cover situations when no evidence is offered or identified, or when the only identified source is unavailable. Breyer Committee Report, 239 F.R.D. at 243. For example, a complaint alleges that an unnamed attorney told the complainant that the subject judge did X. Id. The subject judge denies it. The chief judge requests that the complainant (who does not purport to have observed the subject judge do X) identify the unnamed witness, or that the unnamed witness come forward so that the chief judge can learn the unnamed witness's account. Id. The complainant responds that he has spoken with the unnamed witness, that the unnamed witness is an attorney who practices in federal court, and that the unnamed witness is unwilling to be identified or to come forward. Id. at 243–44. The allegation is then properly dismissed as containing allegations that are incapable of being established through investigation. Id.

If, however, the situation involves a reasonable dispute over credibility, the matter should proceed. For example, the complainant alleges an impropriety and alleges that he or she observed it and that there were no other witnesses; the subject judge denies that the event occurred. Unless the complainant's allegations are facially incredible or so lacking indicia of reliability as to warrant dismissal under Rule 11(c)(1)(C), a special committee must be appointed because there is a material factual question that is reasonably in dispute.

Dismissal is also appropriate when a complaint is filed so long after an alleged event that memory loss, death, or changes to unknown residences prevent a proper investigation.

Subsection (c)(2) indicates that the investigative nature of the process prevents the application of claim preclusion principles where new and material evidence becomes available. However, it also recognizes that at some point a renewed investigation may constitute harassment of the subject judge and should not be undertaken, depending of course on the seriousness of the issues and the weight of the new evidence.

Rule 11(d) implements the Act's provision for dismissal if voluntary appropriate corrective action has been taken. It is largely adapted from the Breyer Committee Report, 239 F.R.D. at 244–45. The Act authorizes the chief judge to conclude the complaint proceedings if "appropriate corrective action has been taken." 28 U.S.C. § 352(b)(2). Under the Rule, action taken after a complaint is filed is "appropriate" when it acknowledges and remedies the problem raised by the complaint. Breyer Committee Report, 239 F.R.D. at 244. Because the Act deals with the conduct of judges, the emphasis is on correction of the judicial conduct that was the subject of the complaint. *Id.* Terminating a complaint based on corrective action is premised on the implicit understanding that voluntary self-correction or redress of misconduct or a disability may be preferable to sanctions. *Id.* The chief judge may facilitate this process by giving the subject judge an objective view of the appearance of the judicial conduct in question and by suggesting appropriate corrective measures. *Id.* Moreover, when corrective action is taken under Rule 5 satisfactory to the chief judge before a complaint is filed, that informal resolution will be sufficient to conclude a subsequent complaint based on identical conduct.

"Corrective action" must be voluntary action taken by the subject judge. Breyer Committee Report, 239 F.R.D. at 244. A remedial action directed by the chief judge or by an appellate court without the participation of the subject judge in formulating the directive or without the subject judge's subsequent agreement to such action does not constitute the requisite voluntary corrective action. *Id.* Neither the chief judge nor an appellate court has authority under the Act to impose a formal remedy or sanction; only the judicial council can impose a formal remedy or sanction under 28 U.S.C. § 354(a)(2). *Id.* Compliance with a previous judicial-council order may serve as corrective action allowing conclusion of a later complaint about the same behavior. *Id.*

Where a subject judge's conduct has resulted in identifiable, particularized harm to the complainant or another individual, appropriate corrective action should include steps taken by that judge to acknowledge and redress the harm, if possible, such as by an apology, recusal from a case, or a pledge to refrain from similar conduct in the future. *Id.* While the Act is generally forward-looking, any corrective action should, to the extent possible, serve to correct a specific harm to an individual, if such harm can reasonably be remedied. *Id.* In some cases, corrective action may not be "appropriate" to justify conclusion of a complaint unless the complainant or other individual harmed is meaningfully apprised of the nature of the corrective action in the chief judge's order, in a direct communication from the subject judge, or otherwise. *Id.*

Voluntary corrective action should be proportionate to any plausible allegations of misconduct in a complaint. The form of corrective action should also be proportionate to any sanctions that the judicial council might impose under Rule 20(b), such as a private or public reprimand or a change in case assignments. Breyer Committee Report, 239 F.R.D at 244–45. In other words, minor corrective action will not suffice to dispose of a serious matter. *Id.*

Rule 11(e) implements Section 352(b)(2) of the Act, which permits the chief judge to "conclude the proceeding," if "action on the complaint is no longer necessary because of intervening events," such as a resignation from judicial office. Ordinarily, stepping down from an administrative post such as chief judge, judicial-council member, or court-committee chair does not constitute an event rendering unnecessary any further action on a complaint alleging judicial misconduct. Breyer Committee Report, 239 F.R.D. at 245. As long as the subject of a complaint retains the judicial office and remains a covered judge as defined in Rule 1(b), a complaint must be addressed. *Id.*; 28 U.S.C. §§ 371(b); 372(a).

Concluding a complaint proceeding, by either the judicial council of the subject judge or the judicial council to which a complaint proceeding has been transferred, precludes remedial action under the Act and these Rules as to the subject judge. But the Judicial Conference and the judicial council of the subject judge have ample authority to assess potential institutional issues related to the complaint as part of their respective responsibilities to promote "the expeditious conduct of court business," 28 U.S.C. § 331, and to "make all necessary and appropriate orders for the effective administration of justice within [each] circuit." *Id.* at § 332(d)(1). Such an assessment might include an analysis of what conditions may have enabled misconduct or prevented its discovery, and what precautionary or curative steps could be undertaken to prevent its recurrence. The judicial council may request that the Committee on Judicial Conduct and Disability transmit its order to relevant Congressional entities.

If a complaint is not disposed of pursuant to Rule 11(c), (d), or (e), a special committee must be appointed. Rule 11(f) states that a subject judge must be invited to respond to the complaint before a special committee is appointed, if no earlier response was invited.

Subject judges receive copies of complaints at the same time that they are referred to the chief judge, and they are free to volunteer responses to them. Under Rule 11(b), the chief judge may request a response if it is thought necessary. However, many complaints are clear candidates for dismissal even if their allegations are accepted as true, and there is no need for the subject judge to devote time to a defense.

The Act requires that the order dismissing a complaint or concluding a proceeding contain a statement of reasons and that a copy of the order be sent to the complainant. 28 U.S.C. § 352(b). Rule 24, dealing with availability of information to the public, contemplates that the order will be made public, usually without disclosing the names of the complainant or the subject judge. If desired for administrative purposes, more identifying information can be included in a non-public version of the order.

When a complaint is disposed of by the chief judge, the statutory purposes are best served by providing the complainant with a full, particularized, but concise explanation, giving reasons for the conclusions reached. *See also* Commentary on Rule 24 (dealing with public availability).

Rule 11(g) provides that the complainant and the subject judge must be notified, in the case of a disposition by the chief judge, of the right to petition the judicial council for review. Because an identified complaint has no "complainant" to petition for review, the chief judge's dispositive order on such a complaint will be transmitted to the judicial council for review. The same will apply where a complaint was filed by its subject judge. A copy of the chief judge's order, and memoranda incorporated by reference in the order, disposing of a complaint must be sent by the circuit clerk to the Committee on Judicial Conduct and Disability.

ARTICLE V. INVESTIGATION AND REPORT BY SPECIAL COMMITTEE
RULE 12. SPECIAL COMMITTEE'S COMPOSITION

(a) **Membership.** Except as provided in (e), a special committee appointed under Rule 11(f) must consist of the chief judge and equal numbers of circuit and district judges. These judges may include senior judges. If a complaint is about a district judge, bankruptcy judge, or magistrate judge, then, when possible, the district-judge members of the special committee must be from districts other than the district of the subject judge. For the courts named in 28 U.S.C. § 363, the special committee must be selected from the judges serving on the subject judge's court.

(b) **Presiding Officer.** When appointing the special committee, the chief judge may serve as the presiding officer or else must designate a committee member as the presiding officer.

(c) **Bankruptcy Judge or Magistrate Judge as Adviser.** If the subject judge is a bankruptcy judge or magistrate judge, he or she may, within 14 days after being notified of the special committee's appointment, ask the chief judge to designate as a committee adviser another bankruptcy judge or magistrate judge, as the case may be. The chief judge must grant such a request but may otherwise use discretion in naming the adviser. Unless the adviser is a Court of Federal Claims special master appointed under 42 U.S.C. § 300aa–12(c), the adviser must be from a district other than the district of the subject bankruptcy judge or subject magistrate judge. The adviser cannot vote but has the other privileges of a special-committee member.

(d) **Provision of Documents.** The chief judge must certify to each other member of the special committee and to any adviser copies of the complaint and statement of facts, in whole or relevant part, and any other relevant documents on file.

(e) **Continuing Qualification of Special–Committee Member.** A member of a special committee may continue to serve on the committee even though the member relinquishes the position of chief judge, active circuit judge, or active district judge, as the case may be, but only if the member continues to hold office under Article III, Section 1, of the Constitution of the United States, or under 28 U.S.C. § 171.

(f) **Inability of Special–Committee Member to Complete Service.** If a member of a special committee can no longer serve because of death, disability, disqualification, resignation, retirement from office, or other reason, the chief judge must decide whether to appoint a replacement member, either a circuit or district judge as needed under (a). No special committee appointed under these Rules may function with only a single member, and the votes of a two-member committee must be unanimous.

(g) **Voting.** All actions by a special committee must be by vote of a majority of all members of the committee.

[Adopted March 11, 2008, effective April 10, 2008. Amended effective September 17, 2015; March 12, 2019.]

Commentary on Rule 12

This Rule is adapted from the Act and the Illustrative Rules.

Rule 12 leaves the size of a special committee flexible, to be determined on a case-by-case basis. The question the size of a special committee is one that should be weighed with care in view of the potential for consuming the members' time; a large committee should be appointed only if there is a special reason to do so. Rule 12(a) acknowledges the common practice of including senior judges in the membership of a special committee.

Although the Act requires that the chief judge be a member of each special committee, 28 U.S.C. § 353(a)(1), it does not require that the chief judge preside. Accordingly, Rule 12(b) provides that if the chief judge does not preside, he or she must designate another member of the special committee as the presiding officer.

Rule 12(c) provides that the chief judge must appoint a bankruptcy judge or magistrate judge as an adviser to a special committee at the request of a bankruptcy or magistrate subject judge. Subsection (c) also provides that the adviser will have all the privileges of a member of the special committee except a vote. The adviser, therefore, may participate in all deliberations of the special committee, question witnesses at hearings, and write a separate statement to accompany the committee's report to the judicial council.

Rule 12(e) provides that a member of a special committee who remains an Article III judge may continue to serve on the committee even though the member's status otherwise changes. Thus, a special committee that originally consisted of the chief judge and an equal number of circuit and district judges, as required by the law, may continue to function even though changes of status alter that composition. This provision reflects the belief that stability of membership will contribute to the quality of the work of such committees.

Stability of membership is also the principal concern animating Rule 12(f), which deals with the case in which a special committee loses a member before its work is complete. The Rule permits the chief judge to determine whether a replacement member should be appointed. Generally, appointment of a replacement member is desirable in these situations unless the special committee has conducted evidentiary hearings before the vacancy occurs. However, cases may arise in which a special committee is in the late stages of its work, and in which it would be difficult for a new member to play a meaningful role. The Rule also preserves the collegial character of the special-committee process by prohibiting a single surviving member from serving as a committee and by providing that a committee of two surviving members will, in essence, operate under a unanimity rule.

Rule 12(g) provides that actions of a special committee must be by vote of a majority of all the members. All the members of a special committee should participate in committee decisions. In that circumstance, it seems reasonable to require that special-committee decisions be made by a majority of the membership, rather than a majority of some smaller quorum.

RULE 13.   CONDUCT OF SPECIAL–COMMITTEE INVESTIGATION

(a) **Extent and Methods of Special–Committee Investigation.** A special committee should determine the appropriate extent and methods of its investigation in light of the allegations in the complaint and the committee's preliminary inquiry. In investigating the alleged misconduct or disability, the special committee should take steps to determine the full scope of the potential misconduct or disability, including whether a pattern of misconduct or a broader disability exists. The investigation may include use of appropriate experts or other professionals. If, in the course of the investigation, the special committee has cause to believe that the subject judge may have engaged in misconduct or has a disability that is beyond the specific pending complaint, the committee must refer the new matter to the chief judge for a determination of whether action under Rule 5 or Rule 11 is necessary before the committee's investigation is expanded to include the new matter.

(b) **Criminal Conduct.** If the special committee's investigation concerns conduct that may be a crime, the committee must consult with the appropriate prosecutorial authorities to the extent permitted by the Act to avoid compromising any criminal investigation. The special committee has final authority over the timing and extent of its investigation and the formulation of its recommendations.

(c) **Staff.** The special committee may arrange for staff assistance to conduct the investigation. It may use existing staff of the judiciary or may hire special staff through the Director of the Administrative Office of the United States Courts.

(d) **Delegation of Subpoena Power; Contempt.** The chief judge may delegate the authority to exercise the subpoena powers of the special committee. The judicial council or special committee may institute a contempt proceeding under 28 U.S.C. § 332(d) against anyone who fails to comply with a subpoena.

[Adopted March 11, 2008, effective April 10, 2008. Amended effective September 17, 2015; March 12, 2019.]

Commentary on Rule 13

This Rule is adapted from the Illustrative Rules.

Rule 13, as well as Rules 14, 15, and 16, are concerned with the way in which the special committee carries out its mission. They reflect the view that the special committee has two roles that are separated in ordinary litigation. First, the special committee has an investigative role of the kind that is characteristically left to executive branch agencies or discovery by civil litigants. 28 U.S.C. § 353(c). Second, it has a formalized fact-finding and recommendation-of-disposition role that is characteristically left to juries, judges, or arbitrators. *Id.* Rule 13 generally governs the investigative stage. Even though the same body has responsibility for both roles under the Act, it is important to distinguish between them in order to ensure that appropriate rights are afforded at appropriate times to the subject judge.

Rule 13(a) includes a provision making clear that the special committee may choose to consult appropriate experts or other professionals if it determines that such a consultation is warranted. If, for example, the special committee has cause to believe that the subject judge may be unable to discharge all of the duties of office by reason of mental or physical disability, the committee could ask the subject judge to respond to inquiries and, if necessary, request the judge to undergo a medical or psychological examination. In advance of any such examination, the special committee may enter into an agreement with the subject judge as to the scope and use that may be made of the examination results. In addition or in the alternative, the special committee may ask to review existing records, including medical records.

The extent of the subject judge's cooperation in the investigation may be taken into account in the consideration of the underlying complaint. If, for example, the subject judge impedes reasonable efforts to confirm or disconfirm the presence of a disability, the special committee may still consider whether the conduct alleged in the complaint and confirmed in the investigation constitutes disability. The same would be true of a complaint alleging misconduct.

The special committee may also consider whether such a judge might be in violation of his or her duty to cooperate in an investigation under these Rules, a duty rooted not only in the Act's definition of misconduct but also in the Code of Conduct for United States Judges, which emphasizes the need to maintain public confidence in the judiciary, *see* Canon 2(A) and Canon 1 cmt., and requires judges to "facilitate the performance of the administrative responsibilities of other judges and court personnel," Canon 3(B)(1). If the special committee finds a breach of the duty to cooperate and believes that the breach may amount to misconduct under Rule 4(a)(5), it should determine, under the final sentence of Rule 13(a), whether that possibility should be referred to the chief judge for consideration of action under Rule 5 or Rule 11. *See also* Commentary on Rule 4.

One of the difficult questions that can arise is the relationship between proceedings under the Act and criminal investigations. Rule 13(b) assigns responsibility for coordination to the special committee in cases in which criminal conduct is suspected, but gives the committee the authority to determine the appropriate pace of its activity in light of any criminal investigation.

Title 28 U.S.C. § 356(a) provides that a special committee will have full subpoena powers as provided in 28 U.S.C. § 332(d). Section 332(d)(1) provides that subpoenas will be issued on behalf of a judicial council by the circuit clerk "at the direction of the chief judge of the circuit or his designee." Rule 13(d) contemplates that, where the chief judge designates someone else as presiding officer of the special committee, the presiding officer also be delegated the authority to direct the circuit clerk to issue subpoenas related to committee proceedings. That is not intended to imply, however, that the decision to use the subpoena power is exercisable by the presiding officer alone. *See* Rule 12(g).

RULE 14.   CONDUCT OF SPECIAL–COMMITTEE HEARINGS

(a) **Purpose of Hearings.** The special committee may hold hearings to take testimony and receive other evidence, to hear argument, or both. If the special committee is investigating allegations against more than one judge, it may hold joint or separate hearings.

(b) **Special–Committee Evidence.** Subject to Rule 15, the special committee must obtain material, nonredundant evidence in the form it considers appropriate. In the special committee's discretion, evidence may be obtained by committee members, staff, or both. Witnesses offering testimonial evidence may include the complainant and the subject judge.

(c) **Counsel for Witnesses.** The subject judge has the right to counsel. The special committee has discretion to decide whether other witnesses may have counsel present when they testify.

(d) **Witness Fees.** Witness fees must be paid as provided in 28 U.S.C. § 1821.

(e) **Oath.** All testimony taken at a hearing must be given under oath or affirmation.

(f) **Rules of Evidence.** The Federal Rules of Evidence do not apply to special-committee hearings.

(g) **Record and Transcript.** A record and transcript must be made of all hearings.

[Adopted March 11, 2008, effective April 10, 2008. Amended effective September 17, 2015.]

Commentary on Rule 14

This Rule is adapted from the Act, 28 U.S.C. § 353, and the Illustrative Rules.

Rule 14 is concerned with the conduct of fact-finding hearings. Special–committee hearings will normally be held only after the investigative work has been completed and the committee has concluded that there is sufficient evidence to warrant a formal fact-finding proceeding. Special–committee proceedings are primarily inquisitorial rather than adversarial. Accordingly, the Federal Rules of Evidence do not apply to such hearings. Inevitably, a hearing will have something of an adversary character. Nevertheless, that tendency should be moderated to the extent possible. Even though a proceeding will commonly have investigative and hearing stages, special-committee members should not regard themselves as prosecutors one day and judges the next. Their duty—and that of their staff—is at all times to be impartial seekers of the truth.

Rule 14(b) contemplates that material evidence will be obtained by the special committee and presented in the form of affidavits, live testimony, etc. Staff or others who are organizing the hearings should regard it as their role to present evidence representing the entire picture. With respect to testimonial evidence, the subject judge should normally be called as a special-committee witness. Cases may arise in which the subject judge will not testify voluntarily. In such cases, subpoena powers are available, subject to the normal testimonial privileges. Although Rule 15(c) recognizes the subject judge's statutory right to call witnesses on his or her own behalf, exercise of this right should not usually be necessary.

RULE 15.   SUBJECT JUDGE'S RIGHTS

(a) Notice.

(1) *Generally.* The subject judge must receive written notice of:

(A) the appointment of a special committee under Rule 11(f);

(B) the expansion of the scope of an investigation under Rule 13(a);

(C) any hearing under Rule 14, including its purposes, the names of any witnesses the special committee intends to call, and the text of any statements that have been taken from those witnesses.

(2) *Suggestion of Additional Witnesses.* The subject judge may suggest additional witnesses to the special committee.

(b) Special–Committee Report. The subject judge must be sent a copy of the special committee's report when it is filed with the judicial council.

(c) Presentation of Evidence. At any hearing held under Rule 14, the subject judge has the right to present evidence, to compel the attendance of witnesses, and to compel the production of documents. At the request of the subject judge, the chief judge or the judge's designee must direct the circuit clerk to issue a subpoena to a witness under 28 U.S.C. § 332(d)(1). The subject judge must be given the opportunity to cross-examine special-committee witnesses, in person or by counsel.

(d) Presentation of Argument. The subject judge may submit written argument to the special committee and must be given a reasonable opportunity to present oral argument at an appropriate stage of the investigation.

(e) Attendance at Hearings. The subject judge has the right to attend any hearing held under Rule 14 and to receive copies of the transcript, of any documents introduced, and of any written arguments submitted by the complainant to the special committee.

(f) Representation by Counsel. The subject judge may choose to be represented by counsel in the exercise of any right enumerated in this Rule. As provided in Rule 20(e), the United States may bear the costs of the representation.

[Adopted March 11, 2008, effective April 10, 2008. Amended effective September 17, 2015; March 12, 2019.]

Commentary on Rule 15

This Rule is adapted from the Act and the Illustrative Rules.

The Act states that these Rules must contain provisions requiring that "the judge whose conduct is the subject of a complaint . . . be afforded an opportunity to appear (in person or by counsel) at proceedings conducted by the investigating panel, to present oral and documentary evidence, to compel the attendance of witnesses or the production of documents, to cross-examine witnesses, and to present argument orally or in writing." 28 U.S.C. § 358(b)(2). To implement this provision, Rule 15(e) gives the subject judge the right to attend any hearing held for the purpose of receiving evidence of record or hearing argument under Rule 14.

The Act does not require that the subject judge be permitted to attend all proceedings of the special committee. Accordingly, the Rules do not give a right to attend other proceedings—for example, meetings at which the special committee is engaged in investigative activity, such as interviewing persons to learn whether they ought to be called as witnesses or examining for relevance purposes documents delivered pursuant to a subpoena duces tecum, or meetings in which the committee is deliberating on the evidence or its recommendations.

RULE 16.   COMPLAINANT'S RIGHTS IN INVESTIGATION

(a) Notice. The complainant must receive written notice of the investigation as provided in Rule 11(g)(1). When the special committee's report to the judicial council is filed, the complainant must be notified of the filing. The judicial council may, in its discretion, provide a copy of the report of a special committee to the complainant.

(b) Opportunity to Provide Evidence. If the complainant knows of relevant evidence not already before the special committee, the complainant may briefly explain in writing the basis of that knowledge and the nature of that evidence. If the special committee determines that the complainant has information not already known to the committee that would assist in the committee's investigation, a representative of the committee must interview the complainant.

(c) Presentation of Argument. The complainant may submit written argument to the special committee. In its discretion, the special committee may permit the complainant to offer oral argument.

(d) Representation by Counsel. A complainant may submit written argument through counsel and, if permitted to offer oral argument, may do so through counsel.

[Adopted March 11, 2008, effective April 10, 2008. Amended effective September 17, 2015; March 12, 2019.]

Commentary on Rule 16

This Rule is adapted from the Act and the Illustrative Rules.

In accordance with the view of the process as fundamentally administrative and inquisitorial, these Rules do not give the complainant the rights of a party to litigation and leave the complainant's role largely to the discretion of the special committee. However, Rule 16(b) gives the complainant the prerogative to make a brief written submission showing that he or she is aware of relevant evidence not already known to the special committee. (Such a submission may precede any written or oral argument the complainant provides under Rule 16(c), or it may accompany that argument.) If the special committee determines, independently or from the complainant's submission, that the complainant has information that would assist the committee in its investigation, the complainant must be interviewed by a representative of the committee. Such an interview may be in person or by telephone, and the representative of the special committee may be either a member or staff.

Rule 16 does not contemplate that the complainant will ordinarily be permitted to attend proceedings of the special committee except when testifying or presenting oral argument. A special committee may exercise its discretion to permit the complainant to be present at its proceedings, or to permit the complainant, individually or through counsel, to participate in the examination or cross-examination of witnesses.

The Act authorizes an exception to the normal confidentiality provisions where the judicial council in its discretion provides a copy of the report of the special committee to the complainant and to the subject judge. 28 U.S.C. § 360(a)(1). However, the Rules do not entitle the complainant to a copy of the special committee's report.

RULE 17.   SPECIAL–COMMITTEE REPORT

The special committee must file with the judicial council a comprehensive report of its investigation, including findings and recommendations for council action. The report must be accompanied by a statement of the vote by which it was adopted, any separate or dissenting statements of special-committee members, and the record of any hearings held under Rule 14. In addition to being sent to the subject judge under Rule 15(b), a copy of the report and any accompanying statements and documents must be sent to the Committee on Judicial Conduct and Disability.

[Adopted March 11, 2008, effective April 10, 2008. Amended effective September 17, 2015; March 12, 2019.]

Commentary on Rule 17

This Rule is adapted from the Illustrative Rules and is self-explanatory. The provision for sending a copy of the special-committee report and accompanying statements and documents to the Committee on Judicial Conduct and Disability was new at the time the Judicial Conference promulgated the Rules for Judicial–Conduct and Judicial–Disability Proceedings in 2008.

ARTICLE VI.   REVIEW BY JUDICIAL COUNCIL
RULE 18.   PETITION FOR REVIEW OF CHIEF–JUDGE DISPOSITION UNDER RULE 11(c), (d), OR (e)

(a) Petition for Review. After the chief judge issues an order under Rule 11(c), (d), or (e), the complainant or the subject judge may petition the judicial council of the circuit to review the order. By rules promulgated under 28 U.S.C. § 358, the judicial council may refer a petition for review filed under this Rule to a panel of no fewer than five members of the council, at least two of whom must be district judges.

(b) When to File; Form; Where to File. A petition for review must be filed in the office of the circuit clerk within 42 days after the date of the chief judge's order. The petition for review should be in letter form, addressed to the circuit clerk, and in an envelope marked "Misconduct Petition" or "Disability Petition." The name of the subject judge must not be shown on the envelope. The petition for review should be typewritten or otherwise legible. It should begin with "I hereby petition the judicial council for review of . . ." and state the reasons why the petition should be granted. It must be signed.

(c) Receipt and Distribution of Petition. A circuit clerk who receives a petition for review filed in accordance with this Rule must:

(1) acknowledge its receipt and send a copy to the complainant or subject judge, as the case may be;

(2) promptly distribute to each member of the judicial council, or its relevant panel, except for any member disqualified under Rule 25, or make available in the manner provided by local rule, the following materials:

(A) copies of the complaint;

(B) all materials obtained by the chief judge in connection with the inquiry;

(C) the chief judge's order disposing of the complaint;

(D) any memorandum in support of the chief judge's order;

(E) the petition for review; and

(F) an appropriate ballot; and

(3) send the petition for review to the Committee on Judicial Conduct and Disability. Unless the Committee on Judicial Conduct and Disability requests them, the circuit clerk will not send copies of the materials obtained by the chief judge.

(d) Untimely Petition. The circuit clerk must refuse to accept a petition that is received after the time allowed in (b).

(e) Timely Petition Not in Proper Form. When the circuit clerk receives a petition for review filed within the time allowed but in a form that is improper to a degree that would substantially impair its consideration by the judicial council—such as a document that is ambiguous about whether it is intended to be a petition for review — the circuit clerk must acknowledge its receipt, call the filer's attention to the deficiencies, and give the filer the opportunity to correct the deficiencies within the original time allowed for filing the petition or within 21 days after the date on which a notice of the deficiencies was sent to the complainant, whichever is later. If the deficiencies are corrected within the time allowed, the circuit clerk will proceed according to paragraphs (a) and (c) of this Rule. If the deficiencies are not corrected, the circuit clerk must reject the petition.

[Adopted March 11, 2008, effective April 10, 2008. Amended effective September 17, 2015; March 12, 2019.]

Commentary on Rule 18

Rule 18 is adapted largely from the Illustrative Rules.

Subsection (a) permits the subject judge, as well as the complainant, to petition for review of the chief judge's order dismissing a complaint under Rule 11(c), or concluding that appropriate corrective action or intervening events have remedied or mooted the problems raised by the complaint pursuant to Rule 11(d) or (e). Although the subject judge may ostensibly be vindicated by the dismissal or conclusion of a complaint, the chief judge's order may include language disagreeable to the subject judge. For example, an order may dismiss a complaint, but state that the subject judge did in fact engage in misconduct. Accordingly, a subject judge may wish to object to the content of the order and is given the opportunity to petition the judicial council of the circuit for review.

Subsection (b) contains a time limit of 42 days to file a petition for review. It is important to establish a time limit on petitions for review of chief judges' dispositions in order to provide finality to the process. If the complaint requires an investigation, the investigation should proceed; if it does not, the subject judge should know that the matter is closed.

The standards for timely filing under the Federal Rules of Appellate Procedure should be applied to petitions for review. *See* Fed. R. App. P. 25(a)(2)(A), (C).

Rule 18(e) provides for an automatic extension of the time limit imposed under subsection (b) if a person files a petition that is rejected for failure to comply with formal requirements.

RULE 19.   JUDICIAL–COUNCIL DISPOSITION OF PETITION FOR REVIEW

(a) Rights of Subject Judge.   At any time after a complainant files a petition for review, the subject judge may file a written response with the circuit clerk. The circuit clerk must promptly distribute copies of the response to each member of the judicial council or of the relevant panel, unless that member is disqualified under Rule 25. Copies must also be distributed to the chief judge, to the complainant, and to the Committee on Judicial Conduct and Disability. The subject judge must not otherwise communicate with individual judicial-council members about the matter. The subject judge must be given copies of any communications to the judicial council from the complainant.

(b) Judicial–Council Action.   After considering a petition for review and the materials before it, the judicial council may:

(1) affirm the chief judge's disposition by denying the petition;

(2) return the matter to the chief judge with directions to conduct a further inquiry under Rule 11(b) or to identify a complaint under Rule 5;

(3) return the matter to the chief judge with directions to appoint a special committee under Rule 11(f); or

(4) in exceptional circumstances, take other appropriate action.

(c) Notice of Judicial–Council Decision.   Copies of the judicial council's order, together with memoranda incorporated by reference in the order and separate concurring or dissenting statements, must be given to the complainant, the subject judge, and the Committee on Judicial Conduct and Disability.

(d) Memorandum of Judicial–Council Decision.   If the judicial council's order affirms the chief judge's disposition, a supporting memorandum must be prepared only if the council concludes that there is a need to supplement the chief judge's explanation. A memorandum supporting a judicial-council order must not include the name of the complainant or the subject judge.

(e) Review of Judicial–Council Decision.   If the judicial council's decision is adverse to the petitioner, and if no member of the council dissented, the complainant must be notified that he or she has no right to seek review of the decision. If there was a dissent, the petitioner must be informed that he or she can file a petition for review under Rule 21(b).

(f) Public Availability of Judicial–Council Decision.   Materials related to the judicial council's decision must be made public to the extent, at the time, and in the manner set forth in Rule 24.

[Adopted March 11, 2008, effective April 10, 2008. Amended effective September 17, 2015; March 12, 2019.]

Commentary on Rule 19

This Rule is adapted largely from the Act and is self-explanatory.

The judicial council should ordinarily review the decision of the chief judge on the merits, treating the petition for review for all practical purposes as an appeal. The judicial council may respond to a petition for review by affirming the chief judge's order, remanding the matter, or, in exceptional cases, taking other appropriate action.

Under Rule 19(b), after considering a petition for review and the materials before it, a judicial council may return a matter to the chief judge to take various actions, including conducting further inquiry under Rule 11(b), identifying a complaint under Rule 5, or appointing a special committee under Rule 11(f).

A petition for review of a judicial council's decision under this Rule may be filed in any matter in which one or more members of the council dissented from the order. *See* Rule 21(b).

RULE 20. JUDICIAL–COUNCIL ACTION FOLLOWING APPOINTMENT OF SPECIAL COMMITTEE

(a) **Subject Judge's Rights.** Within 21 days after the filing of the report of a special committee, the subject judge may send a written response to the members of the judicial council. The subject judge must also be given an opportunity to present argument, personally or through counsel, written or oral, as determined by the judicial council. The subject judge must not otherwise communicate with judicial-council members about the matter.

(b) **Judicial–Council Action.**

(1) *Discretionary Actions.* Subject to the subject judge's rights set forth in subsection (a), the judicial council may:

(A) dismiss the complaint because:

(i) even if the claim is true, the claimed conduct is not conduct prejudicial to the effective and expeditious administration of the business of the courts and does not indicate a mental or physical disability resulting in inability to discharge the duties of office;

(ii) the complaint is directly related to the merits of a decision or procedural ruling;

(iii) the facts on which the complaint is based have not been established; or

(iv) the complaint is otherwise not appropriate for consideration under 28 U.S.C. §§ 351–364.

(B) conclude the proceeding because appropriate corrective action has been taken or intervening events have made the proceeding unnecessary.

(C) refer the complaint to the Judicial Conference with the judicial council's recommendations for action.

(D) take remedial action to ensure the effective and expeditious administration of the business of the courts, including:

(i) censuring or reprimanding the subject judge, either by private communication or by public announcement;

(ii) ordering that no new cases be assigned to the subject judge for a limited, fixed period;

(iii) in the case of a magistrate judge, ordering the chief judge of the district court to take action specified by the council, including the initiation of removal proceedings under 28 U.S.C. § 631(i) or 42 U.S.C. § 300aa–12(c)(2);

(iv) in the case of a bankruptcy judge, removing the judge from office under 28 U.S.C. § 152(e);

(v) in the case of a circuit or district judge, requesting the judge to retire voluntarily with the provision (if necessary) that ordinary length-of-service requirements be waived;

(vi) in the case of a circuit or district judge who is eligible to retire but does not do so, certifying the disability of the judge under 28 U.S.C. § 372(b) so that an additional judge may be appointed; and

(vii) in the case of a circuit chief judge or district chief judge, finding that the judge is temporarily unable to perform chief-judge duties, with the result that those duties devolve to the next eligible judge in accordance with 28 U.S.C. § 45(d) or § 136(e).

(E) take any combination of actions described in (b)(1)(A)—(D) of this Rule that is within its power.

(2) *Mandatory Actions.* A judicial council must refer a complaint to the Judicial Conference if the council determines that a circuit judge or district judge may have engaged in conduct that:

(A) might constitute ground for impeachment; or

(B) in the interest of justice, is not amenable to resolution by the judicial council.

(c) **Inadequate Basis for Decision.** If the judicial council finds that a special committee's report, recommendations, and record provide an inadequate basis for decision, it may return the matter to the committee for further investigation and a new report, or it may conduct further investigation. If the judicial council decides to conduct further investigation, the subject judge must be given adequate prior notice in writing of that decision and of the general scope and purpose of the additional investigation. The judicial council's conduct of the additional investigation must generally accord with the procedures and powers set forth in Rules 13 through 16 for the conduct of an investigation by a special committee.

(d) Judicial–Council Vote. Judicial–council action must be taken by a majority of those members of the council who are not disqualified. A decision to remove a bankruptcy judge from office requires a majority vote of all the members of the judicial council.

(e) Recommendation for Fee Reimbursement. If the complaint has been finally dismissed or concluded under (b)(1)(A) or (B) of this Rule, and if the subject judge so requests, the judicial council may recommend that the Director of the Administrative Office use funds appropriated to the judiciary to reimburse the judge for reasonable expenses incurred during the investigation, when those expenses would not have been incurred but for the requirements of the Act and these Rules. Reasonable expenses include attorneys' fees and expenses related to a successful defense or prosecution of a proceeding under Rule 21(a) or (b).

(f) Judicial–Council Order. Judicial–council action must be by written order. Unless the judicial council finds that extraordinary reasons would make it contrary to the interests of justice, the order must be accompanied by a memorandum setting forth the factual determinations on which it is based and the reasons for the council action. Such a memorandum may incorporate all or part of any underlying special-committee report. If the complaint was initiated by identification under Rule 5, the memorandum must so indicate. The order and memoranda incorporated by reference in the order must be provided to the complainant, the subject judge, and the Committee on Judicial Conduct and Disability. The complainant and the subject judge must be notified of any right to review of the judicial council's decision as provided in Rule 21(b). If the complaint was identified under Rule 5 or filed by its subject judge, the judicial council must transmit the order and memoranda incorporated by reference in the order to the Committee on Judicial Conduct and Disability for review in accordance with Rule 21. In the event of such a transmission, the subject judge may make a written submission to the Committee on Judicial Conduct and Disability but will have no further right of review.

[Adopted March 11, 2008, effective April 10, 2008. Amended effective September 17, 2015; March 12, 2019.]

Commentary on Rule 20

This Rule is largely adapted from the Illustrative Rules.

Rule 20(a) provides that within 21 days after the filing of the report of a special committee, the subject judge may address a written response to all of the members of the judicial council. The subject judge must also be given an opportunity to present argument to the judicial council, personally or through counsel, or both, at the direction of the council. Whether that argument is written or oral would be for the judicial council to determine. The subject judge may not otherwise communicate with judicial-council members about the matter.

Rule 20(b)(1)(B) allows a judicial council to conclude a proceeding where appropriate corrective action has been taken or intervening events have made the proceeding unnecessary. This provision tracks Rules 11(d) and (e), which provide for similar action by the chief judge. As with Rule 11(d), appropriate corrective action must acknowledge and remedy the problem raised by the complaint. *See* Breyer Committee Report, 239 F.R.D. at 244. And similar to Rule 11(e), although "action on the complaint is no longer necessary because of intervening events," the Judicial Conference and the judicial council of the subject judge may nonetheless be able to take action on potential institutional issues related to the complaint (such as an analysis of what conditions may have enabled misconduct or prevented its discovery, and what precautionary or curative steps could be undertaken to prevent its recurrence). 28 U.S.C. § 352(b)(2).

Rule 20(b)(1)(D) recites the remedial actions enumerated in 28 U.S.C. § 354(a)(2) while making clear that this list is not exhaustive. A judicial council may consider lesser remedies. Some remedies may be unique to senior judges, whose caseloads can be modified by agreement or through statutory designation and certification processes.

Under 28 U.S.C. §§ 45(d) and 136(e), which provide for succession where "a chief judge is temporarily unable to perform his duties as such," the determination whether such an inability exists is not expressly reserved to the chief judge. Nor, indeed, is it assigned to any particular judge or court-governance body. Clearly, however, a chief judge's inability to function as chief could implicate "the effective and expeditious administration of justice," which the judicial council of the circuit must, under 28 U.S.C. § 332(d)(1), "make all necessary and appropriate orders" to secure. For this reason, such reassignment is among a judicial council's remedial options, as subsection (b)(1)(D)(vii) makes clear. Consistent with 28 U.S.C. §§ 45(d) and 136(e), however, any reassignment of chief-judge duties must not outlast the subject judge's inability to perform them. Nor can such reassignment result in any extension of the subject judge's term as chief judge.

Rule 20(c) provides that a judicial council may return a matter to a special committee to augment its findings and report of its investigation to include additional areas of inquiry and investigation to allow the judicial council to reach a complete and fully informed judgment. Rule 20(c) also provides that if the judicial council decides to conduct an additional investigation, the subject judge must be given adequate prior notice in writing of that decision and of the general scope and purpose of the additional investigation. The conduct of the investigation will be generally in accordance with the procedures set forth in Rules 13 through 16 for the conduct of an investigation by a special committee. However, if hearings are held, the judicial council may limit testimony or the presentation of evidence to avoid unnecessary repetition of testimony and evidence before the special committee.

Rule 20(d) provides that judicial-council action must be taken by a majority of those members of the council who are not disqualified, except that a decision to remove a bankruptcy judge from office requires a majority of all the members of the council as required by 28 U.S.C. § 152(e). However, it is inappropriate to apply a similar rule to the less severe actions that a judicial council may take under the Act. If some members of the judicial council are disqualified in the matter, their disqualification should not be given the effect of a vote against council action.

With regard to Rule 20(e), the judicial council, on the request of the subject judge, may recommend to the Director of the Administrative Office that the subject judge be reimbursed for reasonable expenses incurred, including attorneys' fees. The judicial council has the authority to recommend such reimbursement where, after investigation by a special committee, the complaint has been finally dismissed or concluded under subsection (b)(1)(A) or (B) of this Rule. It is contemplated that such reimbursement may be provided for the successful prosecution or defense of a proceeding under Rule 21(a) or (b), in other words, one that results in a Rule 20(b)(1)(A) or (B) dismissal or conclusion.

Rule 20(f) requires that judicial-council action be by order and, normally, that it be supported with a memorandum of factual determinations and reasons. Notice of the action must be given to the complainant and the subject judge, and must include notice of any right to petition for review of the judicial council's decision under Rule 21(b). Because an identified complaint has no "complainant" to petition for review, a judicial council's dispositive order on an identified complaint on which a special committee has been appointed must be transmitted to the Committee on Judicial Conduct and Disability for review. The same will apply where a complaint was filed by its subject judge.

ARTICLE VII.   REVIEW BY COMMITTEE ON JUDICIAL CONDUCT AND DISABILITY

RULE 21.   COMMITTEE ON JUDICIAL CONDUCT AND DISABILITY

(a) **Committee Review.** The Committee on Judicial Conduct and Disability, consisting of seven members, considers and disposes of all petitions for review under (b) of this Rule, in conformity with the Committee's jurisdictional statement. Its review of judicial-council orders is for errors of law, clear errors of fact, or abuse of discretion. Its disposition of petitions for review is ordinarily final. The Judicial Conference may, in its sole discretion, review any such Committee decision, but a complainant or subject judge does not have a right to this review.

(b) **Reviewable Matters.**

(1) *Upon Petition.* A complainant or subject judge may petition the Committee for review of a judicial-council order entered in accordance with:

(A) Rule 20(b)(1)(A), (B), (D), or (E); or

(B) Rule 19(b)(1) or (4) if one or more members of the judicial council dissented from the order.

(2) *Upon Committee's Initiative.* At its initiative and in its sole discretion, the Committee may review any judicial-council order entered under Rule 19(b)(1) or (4), but only to determine whether a special committee should be appointed. Before undertaking the review, the Committee must invite that judicial council to explain why it believes the appointment of a special committee is unnecessary, unless the reasons are clearly stated in the council's order denying the petition for review. If the Committee believes that it would benefit from a submission by the subject judge, it may issue an appropriate request. If the Committee determines that a special committee should be appointed, the Committee must issue a written decision giving its reasons.

(c) **Committee Vote.** Any member of the Committee from the same circuit as the subject judge is disqualified from considering or voting on a petition for review related to that subject judge. Committee decisions under (b) of this Rule must be by majority vote of the qualified Committee members. Those members hearing the petition for review should serve in that capacity until final disposition of the petition, whether or not their term of committee membership has ended. If only six members are qualified to consider a petition for review, the Chief Justice shall select an additional judge to join the qualified members to consider the petition. If four or fewer members are qualified to consider a petition for review, the Chief Justice shall select a panel of five judges, including the qualified Committee members, to consider it.

(d) Additional Investigation. Except in extraordinary circumstances, the Committee will not conduct an additional investigation. The Committee may return the matter to the judicial council with directions to undertake an additional investigation. If the Committee conducts an additional investigation, it will exercise the powers of the Judicial Conference under 28 U.S.C. § 331.

(e) Oral Argument; Personal Appearance. There is ordinarily no oral argument or personal appearance before the Committee. In its discretion, the Committee may permit written submissions.

(f) Committee Decision. A Committee decision under this Rule must be transmitted promptly to the Judicial Conference. Other distribution will be by the Administrative Office at the direction of the Committee chair.

(g) Finality. All orders of the Judicial Conference or of the Committee (when the Conference does not exercise its power of review) are final.

[Adopted March 11, 2008, effective April 10, 2008. Amended effective September 17, 2015.]

Commentary on Rule 21

This Rule is largely self-explanatory.

Rule 21(a) is intended to clarify that the delegation of power to the Committee on Judicial Conduct and Disability to dispose of petitions for review does not preclude review of such dispositions by the Judicial Conference. However, there is no right to such review in any party.

Rules 21(b)(1)(B) and (b)(2) are intended to fill a jurisdictional gap as to review of a dismissal or a conclusion of a complaint under Rule 19(b)(1) or (4). Where one or more members of a judicial council reviewing a petition have dissented, the complainant or the subject judge has the right to petition for review by the Committee. Under Rule 21(b)(2), the Committee may review such a dismissal or conclusion in its sole discretion, whether or not a dissent occurred, and only as to the appointment of a special committee. Any review under Rule 21(b)(2) will be conducted as soon as practicable after the dismissal or conclusion at issue. No party has a right to such review, and such review will be rare.

Rule 21(c) provides for review only by Committee members from circuits other than that of the subject judge. The Rule provides that every petition for review must be considered and voted on by at least five, and if possible by seven, qualified Committee members to avoid the possibility of tie votes. If six, or four or fewer, members are qualified, the Chief Justice shall appoint other judges to join the qualified members to consider the petition for review. To the extent possible, the judges whom the Chief Justice selects to join the qualified members should be drawn from among former members of the Committee.

Under this Rule, all Committee decisions are final in that they are unreviewable unless the Judicial Conference, in its discretion, decides to review a decision. Committee decisions, however, do not necessarily constitute final action on a complaint for purposes of Rule 24.

RULE 22.   PROCEDURES FOR REVIEW

(a) Filing Petition for Review. A petition for review of a judicial-council decision on a reviewable matter, as defined in Rule 21(b)(1), may be filed by sending a brief written statement to the Committee on Judicial Conduct and Disability at JCD_PetitionforReview@ao.uscourts.gov or to:

> Judicial Conference Committee on Judicial Conduct and Disability
> Attn: Office of the General Counsel
> Administrative Office of the United States Courts
> One Columbus Circle, NE
> Washington, D.C. 20544

The Administrative Office will send a copy of the petition for review to the complainant or the subject judge, as the case may be.

(b) Form and Contents of Petition. No particular form is required. The petition for review must contain a short statement of the basic facts underlying the complaint, the history of its consideration before the appropriate judicial council, a copy of the council's decision, and the grounds on which the petitioner seeks review. The petition for review must specify the date and docket number of the judicial-council order for which review is sought. The petitioner may attach any documents or correspondence arising in the course of the proceeding before the judicial council or its special committee. A petition for review should not normally exceed 20 pages plus necessary attachments. A petition for review must be signed by the petitioner or his or her attorney.

(c) Time. A petition for review must be submitted within 42 days after the date of the order for which review is sought.

(d) Action on Receipt of Petition. When a petition for review of a judicial-council decision on a reviewable matter, as defined in Rule 21(b)(1), is submitted in accordance with this Rule, the Administrative Office shall acknowledge its receipt, notify the chair of the Committee on Judicial Conduct and Disability, and distribute the petition to the members of the Committee for their deliberation.

[Adopted March 11, 2008, effective April 10, 2008. Amended effective September 17, 2015; March 12, 2019.]

Commentary on Rule 22

Rule 22 is self-explanatory.

ARTICLE VIII. MISCELLANEOUS RULES
RULE 23. CONFIDENTIALITY

(a) Confidentiality Generally. Confidentiality under these Rules is intended to protect the fairness and thoroughness of the process by which a complaint is filed or initiated, investigated (in specific circumstances), and ultimately resolved, as specified under these Rules.

(b) Confidentiality in the Complaint Process.

(1) *General Rule.* The consideration of a complaint by a chief judge, a special committee, a judicial council, or the Committee on Judicial Conduct and Disability is confidential. Information about this consideration must not be publicly disclosed by any judge or judicial employee, or by any person who records or transcribes testimony except as allowed by these Rules. A chief judge, a judicial council, or the Committee on Judicial Conduct and Disability may disclose the existence of a proceeding under these Rules when necessary or appropriate to maintain public confidence in the judiciary's ability to redress misconduct or disability.

(2) *Files.* All files related to a complaint must be separately maintained with appropriate security precautions to ensure confidentiality.

(3) *Disclosure in Decisions.* Except as otherwise provided in Rule 24, written decisions of a chief judge, a judicial council, or the Committee on Judicial Conduct and Disability, and dissenting opinions or separate statements of members of a council or the Committee may contain information and exhibits that the authors consider appropriate for inclusion, and the information and exhibits may be made public.

(4) *Availability to Judicial Conference.* On request of the Judicial Conference or its Committee on Judicial Conduct and Disability, the circuit clerk must furnish any requested records related to a complaint. For auditing purposes, the circuit clerk must provide access to the Committee on Judicial Conduct and Disability to records of proceedings under the Act at the site where the records are kept.

(5) *Availability to District Court.* If the judicial council directs the initiation of proceedings for removal of a magistrate judge under Rule 20(b)(1)(D)(iii), the circuit clerk must provide to the chief judge of the district court copies of the report of the special committee and any other documents and records that were before the council at the time of its decision. On request of the chief judge of the district court, the judicial council may authorize release to that chief judge of any other records relating to the investigation.

(6) *Impeachment Proceedings.* If the Judicial Conference determines that consideration of impeachment may be warranted, it must transmit the record of all relevant proceedings to the Speaker of the House of Representatives.

(7) *Subject Judge's Consent.* If both the subject judge and the chief judge consent in writing, any materials from the files may be disclosed to any person. In any such disclosure, the chief judge may require that the identity of the complainant, or of witnesses in an investigation conducted under these Rules, not be revealed.

(8) *Disclosure in Special Circumstances.* The Judicial Conference, its Committee on Judicial Conduct and Disability, a judicial council, or a chief judge may authorize disclosure of information about the consideration of a complaint, including the papers, documents, and transcripts relating to the investigation, to the extent that disclosure is justified by special circumstances and is not

prohibited by the Act. For example, disclosure may be made to judicial researchers engaged in the study or evaluation of experience under the Act and related modes of judicial discipline, but only where the study or evaluation has been specifically approved by the Judicial Conference or by the Committee on Judicial Conduct and Disability. Appropriate steps must be taken to protect the identities of the subject judge, the complainant, and witnesses from public disclosure. Other appropriate safeguards to protect against the dissemination of confidential information may be imposed.

(9) *Disclosure of Identity by Subject Judge.* Nothing in this Rule precludes the subject judge from acknowledging that he or she is the judge referred to in documents made public under Rule 24.

(10) *Assistance and Consultation.* Nothing in this Rule prohibits a chief judge, a special committee, a judicial council, or the Judicial Conference or its Committee on Judicial Conduct and Disability, in the performance of any function authorized under the Act or these Rules, from seeking the help of qualified staff or experts or from consulting other judges who may be helpful regarding the performance of that function.

(c) Disclosure of Misconduct and Disability. Nothing in these Rules and Commentary concerning the confidentiality of the complaint process, or in the Code of Conduct for Judicial Employees concerning the use or disclosure of confidential information received in the course of official duties, prevents a judicial employee from reporting or disclosing misconduct or disability.

[Adopted March 11, 2008, effective April 10, 2008. Amended effective September 17, 2015; March 12, 2019.]

Commentary on Rule 23

Rule 23 was adapted from the Illustrative Rules.

The Act applies a rule of confidentiality to "papers, documents, and records of proceedings related to investigations conducted under this chapter" and states that they may not be disclosed "by any person in any proceeding," with enumerated exceptions. 28 U.S.C. § 360(a). Three questions arise: Who is bound by the confidentiality rule, what proceedings are subject to the rule, and who is within the circle of people who may have access to information without breaching the rule?

With regard to the first question, Rule 23(b)(1) provides that judges, employees of the judiciary, and those persons involved in recording proceedings and preparing transcripts are obliged to respect the confidentiality requirement. This of course includes subject judges who do not consent to identification under Rule 23(b)(9).

With regard to the second question, Rule 23(b)(1) applies the rule of confidentiality broadly to consideration of a complaint at any stage.

With regard to the third question, there is no barrier of confidentiality among a chief judge, a judicial council, the Judicial Conference, and the Committee on Judicial Conduct and Disability. Each may have access to any of the confidential records for use in their consideration of a referred matter, a petition for review, or monitoring the administration of the Act. A district court may have similar access if the judicial council orders the district court to initiate proceedings to remove a magistrate judge from office, and Rule 23(b)(5) so provides.

In extraordinary circumstances, a chief judge, a judicial council, or the Committee on Judicial Conduct and Disability may disclose the existence of a proceeding under these Rules. The disclosure of such information in high-visibility or controversial cases is to reassure the public that the judiciary is capable of redressing judicial misconduct or disability. Moreover, the confidentiality requirement does not prevent a chief judge from "communicat[ing] orally or in writing with . . . [persons] who may have knowledge of the matter," as part of a limited inquiry conducted by the chief judge under Rule 11(b).

Rule 23 recognizes that there must be some exceptions to the Act's confidentiality requirement. For example, the Act requires that certain orders and the reasons for them must be made public. 28 U.S.C. § 360(b). Rule 23(b)(3) makes it explicit that written decisions, as well as dissenting opinions and separate statements, may contain references to information that would otherwise be confidential and that such information may be made public. However, subsection (b)(3) is subject to Rule 24(a), which provides the general rule regarding the public availability of decisions. For example, the name of a subject judge cannot be made public in a decision if disclosure of the name is prohibited by that Rule.

The Act makes clear that there is a barrier of confidentiality between the judicial branch and the legislative branch. It provides that material may be disclosed to Congress only if it is believed necessary to an impeachment investigation or trial of a judge. 28 U.S.C. § 360(a)(2). Accordingly, Section 355(b) of the Act requires the Judicial Conference to transmit the record of a proceeding to the House of Representatives if the Conference believes that impeachment of a subject judge may be appropriate. Rule 23(b)(6) implements this requirement.

The Act provides that confidential materials may be disclosed if authorized in writing by the subject judge and by the chief judge. 28 U.S.C. § 360(a)(3). Rule 23(b)(7) implements this requirement. Once the subject judge has consented to the disclosure of confidential materials related to a complaint, the chief judge ordinarily will refuse consent only to the extent necessary to protect the confidentiality interests of the complainant or of witnesses who have testified in investigatory proceedings or who have provided information in response to a limited inquiry undertaken pursuant to Rule 11. It will generally be necessary, therefore, for the chief judge to require that the identities of the complainant or of such witnesses, as well as any identifying information, be shielded in any materials disclosed, except insofar as the chief judge has secured the consent of the complainant or of a particular witness to disclosure, or there is a demonstrated need for disclosure of the information that, in the judgment of the chief judge, outweighs the confidentiality interest of the complainant or of a particular witness (as may be the case where the complainant is delusional or where the complainant or a particular witness has already demonstrated a lack of concern about maintaining the confidentiality of the proceedings).

Rule 23(b)(8) permits disclosure of additional information in circumstances not enumerated. For example, disclosure may be appropriate to permit prosecution for perjury based on testimony given before a special committee, where a special committee discovers evidence of a judge's criminal conduct, to permit disciplinary action by a bar association or other licensing body, or in other appropriate circumstances.

Under subsection (b)(8), where a complainant or other person has publicly released information regarding the existence of a complaint proceeding, the Judicial Conference, the Committee on Judicial Conduct and Disability, a judicial council, or a chief judge may authorize the disclosure of information about the consideration of the complaint, including orders and other materials related to the complaint proceeding, in the interest of assuring the public that the judiciary is acting effectively and expeditiously in addressing the relevant complaint proceeding.

Subsection (b)(8) also permits the authorization of disclosure of information about the consideration of a complaint, including the papers, documents, and transcripts relating to the investigation, to judicial researchers engaged in the study or evaluation of experience under the Act and related modes of judicial discipline. The Rule envisions disclosure of information from the official record of a complaint proceeding to a limited category of persons for appropriately authorized research purposes only, and with appropriate safeguards to protect individual identities in any published research results. In authorizing disclosure, a judicial council may refuse to release particular materials when such release would be contrary to the interests of justice, or when those materials constitute purely internal communications. The Rule does not envision disclosure of purely internal communications between judges and their colleagues and staff.

Under Rule 23(b)(10), any of the specified judges or entities performing a function authorized under these Rules may seek expert or staff assistance or may consult with other judges who may be helpful regarding performance of that function; the confidentiality requirement does not preclude this. A chief judge, for example, may properly seek the advice and assistance of another judge who the chief judge deems to be in the best position to communicate with the subject judge in an attempt to bring about corrective action. As another example, a new chief judge may wish to confer with a predecessor to learn how similar complaints have been handled. In consulting with other judges, of course, a chief judge should disclose information regarding the complaint only to the extent the chief judge deems necessary under the circumstances.

Rule 23(c) provides that confidentiality as referenced in these Rules and Commentary is directed toward protecting the fairness and thoroughness of the process by which a complaint is filed or initiated, investigated (in specific circumstances), and ultimately resolved, as specified under these Rules. Nothing in these Rules concerning the confidentiality of the complaint process or the Code of Conduct for Judicial Employees concerning use or disclosure of confidential information received in the course of official duties prevents judicial employees from reporting or disclosing misconduct or disability.

Judges should bring such matters to the attention of the relevant chief district judge or chief circuit judge in accordance with Rule 4(a)(6). Judges should be mindful of Canon 3(B)(6) of the Code of Conduct for United States Judges, which provides in part that a judge "should take appropriate action upon receipt of reliable information indicating the likelihood that a judge's conduct contravened the Code."

RULE 24. PUBLIC AVAILABILITY OF DECISIONS

(a) General Rule; Specific Cases. When final action has been taken on a complaint and it is no longer subject to review as of right, all orders entered by the chief judge and judicial council, including memoranda incorporated by reference in those orders and any dissenting opinions or separate statements by members of the judicial council, must be made public, with the following exceptions:

(1) if the complaint is finally dismissed under Rule 11(c) without the appointment of a special committee, or if it is concluded under Rule 11(d) because of voluntary corrective action, the publicly available materials generally should not disclose the name of the subject judge without his or her consent.

(2) if the complaint is concluded because of intervening events, or dismissed at any time after a special committee is appointed, the judicial council must determine whether the name of the subject judge should be disclosed.

(3) if the complaint is finally disposed of by a privately communicated censure or reprimand, the publicly available materials must not disclose either the name of the subject judge or the text of the reprimand.

(4) if the complaint is finally disposed of under Rule 20(b)(1)(D) by any remedial action other than private censure or reprimand, the text of the dispositive order must be included in the materials made public, and the name of the subject judge must be disclosed.

(5) the name of the complainant must not be disclosed in materials made public under this Rule unless the chief judge or the judicial council orders disclosure.

(b) Manner of Making Public. The orders described in (a) must be made public by placing the orders on the court's public website and by placing them in a publicly accessible file in the office of the circuit clerk. If the orders appear to have precedential value, the chief judge may cause them to be published. In addition, the Committee on Judicial Conduct and Disability will make available on the judiciary's website, www.uscourts.gov, selected illustrative orders described in paragraph (a), appropriately redacted, to provide additional information to the public on how complaints are addressed under the Act.

(c) Orders of Committee on Judicial Conduct and Disability. Orders of the Committee on Judicial Conduct and Disability constituting final action in a complaint proceeding arising from a particular circuit will be made available to the public in the office of the circuit clerk of the relevant court of appeals. The Committee on Judicial Conduct and Disability will also make such orders available on the judiciary's website, www.uscourts.gov. When authorized by the Committee on Judicial Conduct and Disability, other orders related to complaint proceedings will similarly be made available.

(d) Complaints Referred to Judicial Conference. If a complaint is referred to the Judicial Conference under Rule 20(b)(1)(C) or 20(b)(2), materials relating to the complaint will be made public only if ordered by the Judicial Conference.

[Adopted March 11, 2008, effective April 10, 2008. Amended effective September 17, 2015; March 12, 2019.]

Commentary on Rule 24

Rule 24 is adapted from the Illustrative Rules and the recommendations of the Breyer Committee.

The Act requires the circuits to make available only written orders of a judicial council or the Judicial Conference imposing some form of sanction. 28 U.S.C. § 360(b). The Judicial Conference, however, has long recognized the desirability of public availability of a broader range of orders and other materials. In 1994, the Judicial Conference "urge[d] all circuits and courts covered by the Act to submit to the West Publishing Company, for publication in Federal Reporter 3d, and to Lexis all orders issued pursuant to [the Act] that are deemed by the issuing circuit or court to have significant precedential value to other circuits and courts covered by the Act." Report of the Proceedings of the Judicial Conference of the United States, Mar. 1994, at 28. Following this recommendation, the 2000 revision of the Illustrative Rules contained a public availability provision very similar to Rule 24. In 2002, the Judicial Conference again voted to encourage the circuits "to submit non-routine public orders disposing of complaints of judicial misconduct or disability for publication by on-line and print services." Report of the Proceedings of the Judicial Conference of the United States, Sept. 2002, at 58. The Breyer Committee Report further emphasized that "[p]osting such orders on the judicial branch's public website would not only benefit judges directly, it would also encourage scholarly commentary and analysis of the orders." Breyer Committee Report, 239 F.R.D. at 216. With these considerations in mind, Rule 24 provides for public availability of a wide range of materials.

Rule 24 provides for public availability of orders of a chief judge, a judicial council, and the Committee on Judicial Conduct and Disability, as well as the texts of memoranda incorporated by reference in those orders, together with any dissenting opinions or separate statements by members of the judicial council. No memoranda other than those incorporated by reference in those orders shall be disclosed. However, these orders and memoranda are to be made public only when final action on the complaint has been taken and any right of review has been exhausted. The provision that decisions will be made public only after final action has been taken is designed in part to avoid public disclosure of the existence of pending proceedings. Whether the name of the subject judge is disclosed will then depend on the nature of the final action. If the final action is an order predicated on a finding of misconduct or disability (other than a privately communicated censure or reprimand) the name of the subject judge must be made public. If the final action is dismissal of the complaint, the name of the subject judge must not be disclosed. Rule 24(a)(1) provides that where a proceeding is concluded under Rule 11(d) by the chief judge on the basis of voluntary corrective action, the name of the subject judge must not be disclosed. Shielding the name of the subject judge in this circumstance should encourage informal disposition.

If a complaint is dismissed as moot, or because intervening events have made action on the complaint unnecessary, after appointment of a special committee, Rule 24(a)(2) allows the judicial council to determine whether the subject judge will be identified. In such a case, no final decision has been rendered on the merits, but it may be in the public interest—particularly if a judicial officer resigns in the course of an investigation—to make the identity of the subject judge known.

Once a special committee has been appointed, and a proceeding is concluded by the full judicial council on the basis of a remedial order of the council, Rule 24(a)(4) provides for disclosure of the name of the subject judge.

Rule 24(a)(5) provides that the identity of the complainant will be disclosed only if the chief judge so orders. Identifying the complainant when the subject judge is not identified would increase the likelihood that the identity of the subject judge would become publicly known, thus circumventing the policy of nondisclosure. It may not always be practicable to shield the complainant's identity while making public disclosure of the judicial council's order and supporting memoranda; in some circumstances, moreover, the complainant may consent to public identification.

Rule 24(b) makes clear that circuits must post on their external websites all orders required to be made public under Rule 24(a).

Matters involving orders issued following a special-committee investigation often involve highly sensitive situations, and it is important that judicial councils have every opportunity to reach a correct and just outcome. This would include the ability to reach informal resolution before a subject judge's identity must be released. But there must also come a point of procedural finality. The date of finality—and thus the time at which other safeguards and rules such as the publication requirement are triggered—is the date on which the judicial council issues a Final Order. *See In re Complaint of Judicial Misconduct*, 751 F.3d 611, 617 (2014) (requiring publication of a judicial-council order "[e]ven though the period for review had not yet elapsed" and concluding that "the order was a final decision because the Council had adjudicated the matter on the merits after having received a report from a special investigating committee"). As determined in the cited case, modifications of this kind to a final order are subject to review by the Committee on Judicial Conduct and Disability.

Rule 24 is adapted from the Illustrative Rules and the recommendations of the Breyer Committee.

The Act requires the circuits to make available only written orders of a judicial council or the Judicial Conference imposing some form of sanction. 28 U.S.C. § 360(b). The Judicial Conference, however, has long recognized the desirability of public availability of a broader range of orders and other materials. In 1994, the Judicial Conference "urge[d] all circuits and courts covered by the Act to submit to the West Publishing Company, for publication in Federal Reporter 3d, and to Lexis all orders issued pursuant to [the Act] that are deemed by the issuing circuit or court to have significant precedential value to other circuits and courts covered by the Act." Report of the Proceedings of the Judicial Conference of the United States, Mar. 1994, at 28. Following this recommendation, the 2000 revision of the Illustrative Rules contained a public availability provision very similar to Rule 24. In 2002, the Judicial Conference again voted to encourage the circuits "to submit non-routine public orders disposing of complaints of judicial misconduct or disability for publication by on-line and print services." Report of the Proceedings of the Judicial Conference of the United States, Sept. 2002, at 58. The Breyer Committee Report further emphasized that "[p]osting such orders on the judicial branch's public website would not only benefit judges directly, it would also encourage scholarly commentary and analysis of the orders." Breyer Committee Report, 239 F.R.D. at 216. With these considerations in mind, Rule 24 provides for public availability of a wide range of materials.

Rule 24 provides for public availability of orders of a chief judge, a judicial council, and the Committee on Judicial Conduct and Disability, as well as the texts of memoranda incorporated by reference in those orders, together with any dissenting opinions or separate statements by members of the judicial council. No memoranda other than those incorporated by reference in those orders shall be disclosed. However, these orders and memoranda are to be made public only when final action on the complaint has been taken and any right of review has been exhausted. The provision that decisions will be made public only after final action has been taken is designed in part to avoid public disclosure of the existence of pending proceedings. Whether the name of the subject judge is disclosed will then depend on the nature of the final action. If the final action is an order predicated on a finding of misconduct or disability (other than a privately communicated censure or reprimand) the name of the subject judge must be made public. If the final action is dismissal of the complaint, the name of the subject judge must not be disclosed. Rule 24(a)(1) provides that where a proceeding is concluded under Rule 11(d) by the chief judge on the basis of voluntary corrective action, the name of the subject judge generally should not be disclosed, except where the complainant or another person has disclosed the existence of a complaint proceeding to the public. Shielding the name of the subject judge in this circumstance should encourage informal disposition.

If a complaint is dismissed as moot, or because intervening events have made action on the complaint unnecessary, after appointment of a special committee, Rule 24(a)(2) allows the judicial council to determine whether the subject judge will be identified. In such a case, no final decision has been rendered on the merits, but it may be in the public interest—particularly if a judicial officer resigns in the course of an investigation — to make the identity of the subject judge known.

Once a special committee has been appointed, and a proceeding is concluded by the full judicial council on the basis of a remedial order of the council, Rule 24(a)(4) provides for disclosure of the name of the subject judge.

Rule 24(a)(5) provides that the identity of the complainant will be disclosed only if the chief judge so orders. Identifying the complainant when the subject judge is not identified would increase the likelihood that the identity of the subject judge would become publicly known, thus circumventing the policy of nondisclosure. It may not always be practicable to shield the complainant's identity while making public disclosure of the judicial council's order and supporting memoranda; in some circumstances, moreover, the complainant may consent to public identification.

Rule 24(b) makes clear that circuits must post on their external websites all orders required to be made public under Rule 24(a). The judiciary will seek ways to make decisions on complaints filed in their courts more readily accessible to the public through searchable electronic indices.

Matters involving orders issued following a special-committee investigation often involve highly sensitive situations, and it is important that judicial councils have every opportunity to reach a correct and just outcome. This would include the ability to reach informal resolution before a subject judge's identity must be released. But there must also come a point of procedural finality. The date of finality—and thus the time at which other safeguards and rules such as the publication requirement are triggered—is the date on which the judicial council issues a Final Order. *See In re Complaint of Judicial Misconduct*, 751 F.3d 611, 617 (2014) (requiring publication of a judicial council order "[e]ven though the period for review had not yet elapsed" and concluding that "the order was a final decision because the Council had adjudicated the matter on the merits after having received a report from a special investigating committee"). As determined in the cited case, modifications of this kind to a final order are subject to review by the Committee on Judicial Conduct and Disability.

RULE 25. DISQUALIFICATION

(a) General Rule. Any judge is disqualified from participating in any proceeding under these Rules if the judge concludes that circumstances warrant disqualification. If a complaint is filed by a judge, that judge is disqualified from participating in any consideration of the complaint except to the extent that these Rules provide for a complainant's participation. A chief judge who has identified a complaint under Rule 5 is not automatically disqualified from considering the complaint.

(b) Subject Judge. A subject judge, including a chief judge, is disqualified from considering a complaint except to the extent that these Rules provide for participation by a subject judge.

(c) Chief Judge Disqualified From Considering Petition for Review of Chief Judge's Order. If a petition for review of the chief judge's order entered under Rule 11(c), (d), or (e) is filed with the judicial council in accordance with Rule 18, the chief judge is disqualified from participating in the council's consideration of the petition.

(d) Member of Special Committee Not Disqualified. A member of the judicial council who serves on a special committee, including the chief judge, is not disqualified from participating in council consideration of the committee's report.

(e) Subject Judge's Disqualification After Appointment of Special Committee. Upon appointment of a special committee, the subject judge is disqualified from participating in the identification or consideration of any complaint, related or unrelated to the pending matter, under the Act or these Rules. The disqualification continues until all proceedings on the complaint against the subject judge are finally terminated with no further right of review.

(f) Substitute for Disqualified Chief Judge. If the chief judge is disqualified from performing duties that the Act and these Rules assign to a chief judge (including where a complaint is filed against a chief judge), those duties must be assigned to the most-senior active circuit judge not disqualified. If all circuit judges in regular active service are disqualified, the judicial council may determine whether to request a transfer under Rule 26, or, in the interest of sound judicial administration, to permit the chief judge to dispose of the complaint on the merits. Members of the judicial council who are named in the complaint may participate in this determination if necessary to obtain a quorum of the council.

(g) Judicial–Council Action When Multiple Judges Disqualified. Notwithstanding any other provision in these Rules to the contrary,

(1) a member of the judicial council who is a subject judge may participate in its disposition if:

(A) participation by one or more subject judges is necessary to obtain a quorum of the judicial council;

(B) the judicial council finds that the lack of a quorum is due to the naming of one or more judges in the complaint for the purpose of disqualifying that judge or those judges, or to the naming of one or more judges based on their participation in a decision excluded from the definition of misconduct under Rule 4(b); and

(C) the judicial council votes that it is necessary, appropriate, and in the interest of sound judicial administration that one or more subject judges be eligible to act.

(2) otherwise disqualified members may participate in votes taken under (g)(1)(B) and (g)(1)(C).

(h) Disqualification of Members of Committee on Judicial Conduct and Disability. No member of the Committee on Judicial Conduct and Disability is disqualified from participating in any proceeding under the Act or these Rules because of consultations with a chief judge, a member of a special committee, or a member of a judicial council about the interpretation or application of the Act or these Rules, unless the member believes that the consultation would prevent fair-minded participation.

[Adopted March 11, 2008, effective April 10, 2008. Amended effective September 17, 2015; March 12, 2019.]

Commentary on Rule 25

Rule 25 is adapted from the Illustrative Rules.

Subsection (a) provides the general rule for disqualification. Of course, a judge is not disqualified simply because the subject judge is on the same court. However, this subsection recognizes that there may be cases in which an appearance of bias or prejudice is created by circumstances other than an association with the subject judge as a colleague. For example, a judge may have a familial relationship with a complainant or subject judge. When such circumstances exist, a judge may, in his or her discretion, conclude that disqualification is warranted.

Subsection (e) makes it clear that the disqualification of the subject judge relates only to the subject judge's participation in any proceeding arising under the Act or these Rules. For example, the subject judge cannot initiate complaints by identification, conduct limited inquiries, or choose between dismissal and special-committee investigation as the threshold disposition of a complaint. Likewise, the subject judge cannot participate in any proceeding arising under the Act or these Rules as a member of any special committee, the judicial council of the circuit, the Judicial Conference, or the Committee on Judicial Conduct and Disability. The Illustrative Rule, based on Section 359(a) of the Act, is ambiguous and could be read to disqualify a subject judge from service of any kind on each of the bodies mentioned. This is undoubtedly not the intent of the Act; such a disqualification would be anomalous in light of the Act's allowing a subject judge to continue to decide cases and to continue to exercise the powers of chief circuit or district judge. It would also create a substantial deterrence to the appointment of special committees, particularly where a special committee is needed solely because the chief judge may not decide matters of credibility in his or her review under Rule 11.

While a subject judge is barred by Rule 25(b) from participating in the disposition of the complaint in which he or she is named, Rule 25(e) recognizes that participation in proceedings arising under the Act or these Rules by a judge who is the subject of a special committee investigation may lead to an appearance of self-interest in creating substantive and procedural precedents governing such proceedings. Rule 25(e) bars such participation.

Under the Act, a complaint against the chief judge is to be handled by "that circuit judge in regular active service next senior in date of commission." 28 U.S.C. § 351(c). Rule 25(f) provides that seniority among judges other than the chief judge is to be determined by date of commission, with the result that complaints against the chief judge may be routed to a former chief judge or other judge who was appointed earlier than the chief judge. The Rules do not purport to prescribe who is to preside over meetings of the judicial council. Consequently, where the presiding member of the judicial council is disqualified from participating under these Rules, the order of precedence prescribed by Rule 25(f) for performing "duties that the Act and these Rules assign to a chief judge" does not apply to determine the acting presiding member of the council. That is a matter left to the internal rules or operating practices of each judicial council. In most cases the most senior active circuit judge who is a member of the judicial council and who is not disqualified will preside.

Sometimes a single complaint is filed against a large group of judges. If the normal disqualification rules are observed in such a case, no court of appeals judge can serve as acting chief judge of the circuit, and the judicial council will be without appellate members. Where the complaint is against all circuit and district judges, under normal rules no member of the judicial council can perform the duties assigned to the council under the statute.

A similar problem is created by successive complaints arising out of the same underlying grievance. For example, a complainant files a complaint against a district judge based on alleged misconduct, and the complaint is dismissed by the chief judge under the statute. The complainant may then file a complaint against the chief judge for dismissing the first complaint, and when that complaint is dismissed by the next senior judge, still a third complaint may be filed. The threat is that the complainant will bump down the seniority ladder until, once again, there is no member of the court of appeals who can serve as acting chief judge for the purpose of the next complaint. Similarly, complaints involving the merits of litigation may involve a series of decisions in which many judges participated or in which a rehearing en banc was denied by the court of appeals, and the complaint may name a majority of the judicial council as subject judges.

In recognition that these multiple-judge complaints are virtually always meritless, the judicial council is given discretion to determine: (1) whether it is necessary, appropriate, and in the interest of sound judicial administration to permit the chief judge to dispose of a complaint where it would otherwise be impossible for any active circuit judge in the circuit to act, and (2) whether it is necessary, appropriate, and in the interest of sound judicial administration, after appropriate findings as to need and justification are made, to permit subject judges of the judicial council to participate in the disposition of a petition for review where it would otherwise be impossible to obtain a quorum.

Applying a rule of necessity in these situations is consistent with the appearance of justice. *See, e.g., In re Complaint of Doe,* 2 F.3d 308 (8th Cir. Jud. Council 1993) (invoking the rule of necessity); *In re Complaint of Judicial Misconduct,* No. 91–80464 (9th Cir. Jud. Council 1992) (same). There is no unfairness in permitting the chief judge to dispose of a patently insubstantial complaint that names all active circuit judges in the circuit.

Similarly, there is no unfairness in permitting subject judges, in these circumstances, to participate in the review of the chief judge's dismissal of an insubstantial complaint. The remaining option is to assign the matter to another body. Among other alternatives, the judicial council may request a transfer of the petition under Rule 26. Given the administrative inconvenience and delay involved in these alternatives, it is desirable to request a transfer only if the judicial council determines that the petition for review is substantial enough to warrant such action.

In the unlikely event that a quorum of the judicial council cannot be obtained to consider the report of a special committee, it would normally be necessary to request a transfer under Rule 26.

Rule 25(h) recognizes that the jurisdictional statement of the Committee on Judicial Conduct and Disability contemplates consultation between members of the Committee and judicial participants in proceedings under the Act and these Rules. Such consultation should not automatically preclude participation by a member in that proceeding.

RULE 26. TRANSFER TO ANOTHER JUDICIAL COUNCIL

In exceptional circumstances, a chief judge or a judicial council may ask the Chief Justice to transfer a proceeding based on a complaint identified under Rule 5 or filed under Rule 6 to the judicial council of another circuit. The request for a transfer may be made at any stage of the proceeding before a reference to the Judicial Conference under Rule 20(b)(1)(C) or 20(b)(2) or a petition for review is filed under Rule 22. Upon receiving such a request, the Chief Justice may refuse the request or select the transferee judicial council, which may then exercise the powers of a judicial council under these Rules.

[Adopted March 11, 2008, effective April 10, 2008. Amended effective September 17, 2015; March 12, 2019.]

Commentary on Rule 26

Rule 26 implements the Breyer Committee's recommended use of transfers. Breyer Committee Report, 239 F.R.D. at 214–15.

Rule 26 authorizes the transfer of a complaint proceeding to another judicial council selected by the Chief Justice. Such transfers may be appropriate, for example, in the case of a serious complaint where there are multiple disqualifications among the original judicial council, where the issues are highly visible and a local disposition may weaken public confidence in the process, where internal tensions arising in the council as a result of the complaint render disposition by a less involved council appropriate, or where a complaint calls into question policies or governance of the home court of appeals. The power to effect a transfer is lodged in the Chief Justice to avoid disputes in a judicial council over where to transfer a sensitive matter and to ensure that the transferee council accepts the matter.

Upon receipt of a transferred proceeding, the transferee judicial council shall determine the proper stage at which to begin consideration of the complaint — for example, reference to the transferee chief judge, appointment of a special committee, etc.

RULE 27. WITHDRAWAL OF COMPLAINT OR PETITION FOR REVIEW

(a) Complaint Pending Before Chief Judge. With the chief judge's consent, the complainant may withdraw a complaint that is before the chief judge for a decision under Rule 11. The withdrawal of a complaint will not prevent the chief judge from identifying or having to identify a complaint under Rule 5 based on the withdrawn complaint.

(b) Complaint Pending Before Special Committee or Judicial Council. After a complaint has been referred to the special committee for investigation and before the committee files its report, the complainant may withdraw the complaint only with the consent of both the subject judge and either the special committee or the judicial council.

(c) Petition for Review. A petition for review addressed to the judicial council under Rule 18, or the Committee on Judicial Conduct and Disability under Rule 22, may be withdrawn if no action on the petition has been taken.

[Adopted March 11, 2008, effective April 10, 2008. Amended effective September 17, 2015.]

Commentary on Rule 27

Rule 27 is adapted from the Illustrative Rules and treats the complaint proceeding, once begun, as a matter of public business rather than as the property of the complainant. Accordingly, the chief judge or the judicial council remains responsible for addressing any complaint under the Act, even a complaint that has been formally withdrawn by the complainant.

Under subsection (a), a complaint pending before the chief judge may be withdrawn if the chief judge consents. Where the complaint clearly lacked merit, the chief judge may accordingly be saved the burden of preparing a formal order and supporting memorandum. However, the chief judge may, or be obligated under Rule 5, to identify a complaint based on allegations in a withdrawn complaint.

If the chief judge appoints a special committee, Rule 27(b) provides that the complaint may be withdrawn only with the consent of both the body before which it is pending (the special committee or the judicial council) and the subject judge. Once a complaint has reached the stage of appointment of a special committee, a resolution of the issues may be necessary to preserve public confidence. Moreover, the subject judge is given the right to insist that the matter be resolved on the merits, thereby eliminating any ambiguity that might remain if the proceeding were terminated by withdrawal of the complaint.

With regard to all petitions for review, Rule 27(c) grants the petitioner unrestricted authority to withdraw the petition. It is thought that the public's interest in the proceeding is adequately protected, because there will necessarily have been a decision by the chief judge and often by the judicial council as well in such a case.

RULE 28. AVAILABILITY OF RULES AND FORMS

These Rules and copies of the complaint form as provided in Rule 6(a) must be available without charge in the office of the circuit clerk of each court of appeals, district court, bankruptcy court, or other federal court whose judges are subject to the Act. Each court must also make these Rules, the complaint form, and complaint-filing instructions available on the court's website, or provide an Internet link to these items on the appropriate court of appeals website or on www.uscourts.gov.

[Adopted March 11, 2008, effective April 10, 2008. Amended effective September 17, 2015.]

RULE 29. EFFECTIVE DATE

These Rules will become effective after promulgation by the Judicial Conference of the United States.

[Adopted March 11, 2008, effective April 10, 2008. Amended effective March 12, 2019.]

APPENDIX

COMPLAINT OF JUDICIAL MISCONDUCT OR DISABILITY

Judicial Council of the Ninth Circuit

COMPLAINT OF JUDICIAL MISCONDUCT OR DISABILITY

To begin the complaint process, complete this form and prepare the brief statement of facts described in item 5 (below). The RULES FOR JUDICIAL-CONDUCT AND JUDICIAL-DISABILITY PROCEEDINGS, adopted by the Judicial Conference of the United States, contain information on what to include in a complaint (Rule 6), where to file a complaint (Rule 7), and other important matters. The Ninth Circuit Judicial Council also adopted local misconduct rules. The rules are available in federal court clerks' offices, on individual federal courts' Web sites, and on www.uscourts.gov, and https://www.ca9.uscourts.gov/misconduct/judicial_misconduct.php.

Your complaint (this form and the statement of facts) should be typewritten and must be legible. Under the Ninth Circuit's local misconduct rules, you are required to file five copies of your misconduct complaint and exhibits, plus one copy for each additional judge if more than one subject judge is named in your complaint. Enclose your complaint in an envelope marked "COMPLAINT OF MISCONDUCT" or "COMPLAINT OF DISABILITY" and submit it to the appropriate clerk of court. **Do not put the name of any judge on the envelope.**

1.   Name of Complainant: _____

      Contact Address: _____

                              _____

      Daytime telephone: (__) _____

2.   Name(s) of Judge(s):   _____

      Court: _____

3.   Does this complaint concern the behavior of the judge(s) in a particular lawsuit or lawsuits?

          [   ] Yes   [   ] No

      If "yes," give the following information about each lawsuit:

      Court: _____

      Case Number: _____

      Docket number of any appeal to the _____ Circuit: _____

      Are (were) you a party or lawyer in the lawsuit?

      [   ] Party   [   ] Lawyer   [   ] Neither

Page 1 of 3

If you are (were) a party and have (had) a lawyer, give the lawyer's name, address, and telephone number:

_____

_____

_____

4. Have you filed any lawsuits against the judge?

   [   ] Yes   [   ] No

   If "yes," give the following information about each such lawsuit:

   Court: _____

   Case Number: _____

   Present status of lawsuit: _____

   Name, address, and telephone number of your lawyer for the lawsuit against the judge:

   _____

   _____

   _____

   Court to which any appeal has been taken in the lawsuit against the judge:

   _____

   Docket number of the appeal: _____

   Present status of the appeal: _____

5. **Brief Statement of Facts.** Attach a brief statement of the specific facts on which the claim of judicial misconduct or disability is based. Include what happened, when and where it happened, and any information that would help an investigator check the facts. If the complaint alleges judicial disability, also include any additional facts that form the basis of that allegation. Local Rule 6.1(b) provides that your statement of facts must not be longer than five pages (five sides), or 1,200 words, whichever is less.

   You must provide objectively verifiable proof such as the names of witnesses or recorded documents or transcripts to support your allegations. Adverse rulings do not support misconduct allegations, as the appropriate forum for an argument that a judge erred is the appellate court. Thus, you need not include copies of your filings in the underlying case or the judge's orders because even if a review of those documents is necessary, the documents are accessible via PACER. Excess or irrelevant documentation will be returned to the complainant.

Page 2 of 3

316

6.   **Acknowledgment, declaration and signature:**

In the space provided below, please write the following statement: "I understand that even if I successfully prove that the judge engaged in misconduct or is disabled, this procedure cannot change the outcome of the underlying case." (If this statement is not written, your complaint will not be processed and will be returned to you.)

_____
_____
_____

I declare under penalty of perjury that the statements made in this complaint are true and correct to the best of my knowledge.

(Signature)_____   (Date)_____

Page 3 of 3

317

GUIDELINES FOR JUDICIAL MISCONDUCT OR DISABILITY COMPLAINTS

Congress has created a procedure that permits any person to file a complaint in the courts about the behavior of federal judges—but not about the decisions federal judges make in deciding cases. Above is a link to the Judicial Conference of the United States' Judicial–Conduct Rules that explain what may be complained about, who may be complained about, where to file a complaint, and how the complaint will be processed. You must comply with these rules, or we may reject your complaint without considering your arguments.

Almost all complaints in recent years have been dismissed because they do not follow the law about such complaints. The law says that complaints about judges' decisions and complaints with no evidence to support them must be dismissed. If you are a litigant in a case and believe the judge made a wrong decision—even a very wrong decision—you may not use this procedure to complain about the decision. An attorney can explain the rights you have as a litigant to seek review of a judicial decision.

Please note the following to avoid the rejection or summary dismissal of your complaint:

- You must either use the Ninth Circuit complaint form [link above], or shall identify all subject judge(s) on the first page of your complaint. Ninth Circuit Local Rule 6.1(a)

- You must submit a statement of facts in support of your claims that is no more five pages (five sides), or 1,200 words, whichever is less, unless the Chief Judge grants permission for additional pages. You must submit your complaint on standard 8.5x11 size paper. Ninth Circuit Local Rule 6.1(b)

- You must provide concrete proof to support your claims of misconduct. For example, we will dismiss your complaint if you try to argue that a judge was biased or disabled, but the only evidence you provide is the ruling against you or your guess about what went on in the judge's mind. No. 08–90172 (In re Complaint of Judicial Misconduct, 569 F.3d 1093, 1093 (9th Cir. Jud. Council 2009)

- You may not request that the Chief Judge or Judicial Council take action in an underlying case. The Judicial Council only has power over administrative matters and is not a court. For example, you cannot use this misconduct procedure to request that the Chief Judge or the Judicial Council vacate an underlying order, force a judge to recuse himself, award damages, or grant any kind of relief that you would ask for from a court. No. 08–90066+ (In re Complaint of Judicial Misconduct, 567 F.3d 429 (9th Cir. Jud. Council 2009)

- Just because you file a misconduct complaint, a judge need not recuse or stay your case, nor will a new judge be assigned to your underlying case. No. 08–90026 (In re Complaint of Judicial Misconduct, 583 F.3d 599 (9th Cir. Jud. Council 2009)

- You can only file a misconduct complaint against federal judges. You cannot use this procedure to complain about court staff, opposing parties or opposing counsel. No. 08–90066+ (In re Complaint of Judicial Misconduct, 567 F.3d 429 (9th Cir. Jud. Council 2009)

- You may be restricted from filing further misconduct complaints if you abuse this procedure. No. 07–89142 (In re Complaint of Judicial Misconduct, 552 F.3d 1146 (9th Cir. Jud. Council 2009))

Local Rules for Misconduct Proceedings

The Ninth Circuit Judicial Council adopted the following local rules for misconduct proceedings:

Local Rule 6.1(a): Name of Subject Judge. Complainant must either use the form appended to the local rules, or shall identify any and all subject judge(s) on the first page of the complaint. If complainant fails to so identify the subject judge(s), the complaint will be returned to complainant with a request to do so.

Local Rule 6.1(b): Page Limit. The statement of facts must not be longer than five pages (five sides), or 1,200 words, whichever is less. The complaint must be submitted on standard 8.5 × 11 size paper. A complainant may petition the Chief Judge for permission to submit additional pages if extraordinary circumstances exist, and the Chief Judge may delegate the consideration of these requests to the Circuit Executive.

Local Rule 6.1(d): Acknowledgment. The complaint must include the following written acknowledgment: "I understand that even if I successfully prove that the judge engaged in misconduct or is disabled, this procedure cannot change the outcome of the underlying case." Complainant may either write this acknowledgment in the space provided in Section 6 of the complaint form, or complainant must write out the acknowledgment on the first page of the complaint. If complainant fails to write out the acknowledgment, the complaint will be returned to complainant with a request to do so.

Local Rule 6.1(e): Number of Copies. The complainant must file an original and one copy of (1) the complaint form, (2) the statement of facts, and (3) any documents submitted.

Local Rule 18.1(b): Page Limit and Number of Copies. A petition for review must not be longer than five pages (five sides), or 1,200 words, whichever is less. A complainant may petition the Chief Judge for permission to submit additional pages if extraordinary circumstances exist, and the Chief Judge may delegate the consideration of these requests to the Circuit Executive. The complainant must file an original and one copy of the petition for review, along with a copy of the original complaint.

[Effective February 25, 2010. Amended effective March 12, 2019.]

INDEX TO UNITED STATES COURT OF APPEALS
FOR THE NINTH CIRCUIT

UNITED STATES DISTRICT COURT
FOR THE EASTERN DISTRICT OF CALIFORNIA

Including Amendments Received Through
December 1, 2021

GENERAL RULES

RULE 100. TITLE—CONSTRUCTION— NUMBERING (Fed. R. Civ. P. 1)

(a) Title. These are the Local Rules of Practice for the United States District Court, Eastern District of California. They may be cited as "L.R."

(b) Numbering. When a Local Rule is a general, civil, or magistrate judges' Rule, the Rule number appears without designation; when criminal, the abbreviation "Crim" prefaces the Rule number to distinguish it. Admiralty and In Rem Rules are prefaced by the letter "A."*

(c) Construction. These Local Rules are adopted pursuant to 28 U.S.C. § 2071, Fed. R. Civ. P. 83, and Fed. R. Crim. P. 57. They are intended to supplement and shall be construed and administered consistently with and subordinately to the United States Constitution; federal statutes; the Federal Rules of Civil Procedure, including the Supplemental Rules for Admiralty or Maritime Claims and Asset Forfeiture Actions (Supplemental Rules); the Federal Rules of Criminal Procedure; the Federal Rules of Appellate Procedure; and the Rules Governing Section 2254 Cases in the United States District Courts.

(d) Applicability. Local Rules 100 through 199 and 300 through 399 govern proceedings in all actions in the United States District Court for the Eastern District of California to the extent not inconsistent with other Rules more specifically applicable to the particular action. Local Rules 200 through 299 govern proceedings in civil actions only, while Local Rules 400 through 499 are limited in application to criminal actions. Local Rules 500 through 599 are the Admiralty and In Rem Rules for the Eastern District of California.

(e) Effective Date. These Local Rules are effective on December 1, 2009, and shall govern all actions then pending or commenced thereafter. Where justice requires, the Court may order that an action pending before that date be governed by the practice of the Court before the adoption of these Local Rules.

(f) Electronic Filing Rules. These Local Rules include the requirements and procedures for electronic filing, service, and retention of documents. The Clerk shall maintain on the Court's website a comprehensive electronic filing user's manual that contains the procedures applicable to electronic filing. The Clerk shall notify the membership of the Bar of this Court and other attorneys authorized to practice in this Court of changes to electronic filing procedures by the most appropriate means.

[Effective December 1, 2009.]

* [**Publisher's Note:** So in original.]

RULE 101. DEFINITIONS (Fed. R. Civ. P. 1)

For purposes of these Rules, unless the context otherwise requires, the terms below are defined as follows:

"Action" means a case, proceeding, or matter.

"Affidavit" includes a declaration prepared in accordance with federal law. *See* 28 U.S.C. § 1746.

"Attorney" refers to a member of the Bar of this Court, licensed to practice law by the State of California or a member of the bar in another state authorized to practice in this Court unless inconsistent with the purpose and intent of a particular Rule. Compare "attorney" with "counsel." *See* L.R. 183.

"Attorney's Signature" includes either a handwritten signature or an electronic signature.

"Briefs" include memoranda, points and authorities, and other written arguments, or compilations of authorities.

"Chief Judge" means the Chief Judge of the District appointed pursuant to 28 U.S.C. § 136.

"Clerk" means the Clerk of the District Court appointed pursuant to 28 U.S.C. § 751, or a duly authorized deputy clerk, as the case may be.

"CM/ECF" is the Case Management / Electronic Case Files docketing and file system implemented by the Eastern District of California. Districts implementing CM/ECF electronically manage their case files, i.e., the case files are stored in a data base and not in paper (CM), and filings in court are performed, to the extent possible, electronically in lieu of paper (ECF).

"Complaint" includes any complaint, petition, counterclaim, cross-claim, claim for relief under Fed. R. Civ. P. 14, or other claim for affirmative relief.

"Consent to Service" is the authorization by an attorney or party to accept service during the course of an action by electronic means pursuant to Fed. R. Civ. P. 5(b)(2)(E) and Fed. R. Crim. P. 49. *See* L.R. 135(g).

"Conventional Filing" is the filing of a document with the Clerk of Court in paper format. Documents filed conventionally may be filed via mail or in person. Parties that require a conventionally-filed document to be conformed and returned must submit one additional legible conformed copy, and if mailed, a postage paid return envelope. If a postage paid envelope is not received, documents cannot be returned.

"Conventional Service" is service during the course of an action accomplished pursuant to Fed. R. Civ. P. 5(b)(2)(A)–(D) and Fed. R. Crim. P. 49.

"Courtesy Paper Copy" is a document submitted in paper format to the Clerk for delivery to chambers when an electronic filing exceeds 25 pages or an exhibit or attachment exceeds 50 pages. The courtesy paper copy must be prominently labeled COURTESY COPY in the upper right corner of the first page. *See* L.R. 133(f).

"Counsel" refers to an attorney and/or a party acting in propria persona or pro se. *See* L.R. 183.

"Court" means the Judge and/or Magistrate Judge to whom an action has been assigned or before whom an action is being conducted.

"Courtroom Deputy Clerk" means the deputy clerk assigned to the particular Judge or Magistrate Judge to whom an action has been assigned or the Judge or Magistrate Judge before whom an action or a part thereof is being conducted.

"Days" are calculated pursuant to Fed. R. Civ. P. 6 and Fed. R. Crim. P. 45, for the purposes of these Local Rules.

"Defendant" includes any party against whom a complaint, petition, counterclaim, cross-claim, claim for relief under Fed. R. Civ. P. 14, indictment, information, violation notice, citation, or any other claim for affirmative relief is made.

"Direct Electronic Filing" means the filing of a document in electronic format via the Internet through the Court's ECF system.

"ECF System" means the Electronic Case Files system used by the Court, also referred to as CM/ECF, that allows for the filing and service of documents in .pdf format.

"E–Filing Registration" means registering with the United States District Court for the Eastern District of California to file documents electronically through ECF, distinct from PACER registration; e–filing registration also acts as a consent to service by electronic means during the course of an action unless the attorney opts out. *See* L.R. 135(g).

"Electronic Case Files" are the official records of each case file kept by the Court in electronic format.

"Electronic Filing" means the filing of documents in .pdf format through the Court's ECF system or submitted to the Clerk in electronic format on portable electronic media.

"Electronic Signature" is the signature on an electronically-filed document, constituting a combination of (1) the person's representative signature, "/s/—Name" or a facsimile personalized signature on the signature line of the document, coupled with (2) the successful electronic filing of that document through use of the person's login and password. Alternatively, when a document is submitted to the Clerk on portable electronic media, signatures shall appear either as a facsimile of the original (in a scanned document placed on portable electronic media), or on a separate, scanned signature page if the document was published to .pdf and then placed on portable electronic media. In the latter situation, the docket shall reflect submission of the signature page.

"Email Box" means the email box assigned to each respective Judge or Magistrate Judge as listed on the Court's website used exclusively for transmission of emailed documents pertinent to court proceedings.

"En banc" means the several Judges or Magistrate Judges acting as a group or sitting en banc.

"Fed. R. App. P." means the Federal Rules of Appellate Procedure.

"Fed. R. Civ. P." means the Federal Rules of Civil Procedure.

"Fed. R. Crim. P." means the Federal Rules of Criminal Procedure.

"Filed" means delivered into the custody of the Clerk and accepted by the Clerk for inclusion in the official records of the action. Documents are filed for purposes of these Rules whether they are conventionally filed in paper or electronically filed, so long as the manner of filing is as provided for in these Rules or by order of the Court. *See generally* L.R. 133.

"General Duty Judge" means the Judge in Sacramento appointed by the Chief Judge to perform the following duties in Sacramento:

(a) Preside over naturalization ceremonies (or arrange for a substitute Judge or Magistrate Judge), and hear contested applications for citizenship;

(b) Select and impanel Grand Juries and preside over matters before the Grand Jury, including release and substitution of jurors and alternates, motions to compel testimony and production of records, bank secrecy and other protective orders, issuance of subpoenas and motions to disclose or quash, receipt and safekeeping of confidential materials such as those submitted to the Court pursuant to Fed. R. Crim. P. 6(e)(3)(B);

(c) Preside over attorney admissions;

(d) Assume and discharge the duties of a United States Magistrate Judge when the need arises; and

(e) Preside over such other miscellaneous matters as may from time to time be designated by the Chief Judge.

"General Order" means an order entered or adopted by the Chief Judge or by the Judges en banc relating to internal court administration. *See* L.R. 102(a).

"Judge" means a United States District Judge.

"Lodged" means delivered to the Clerk or to the courtroom deputy clerk for inclusion in the official records of the action. Lodged documents are not normally part of a record on appeal.

"Magistrate Judge" means a United States Magistrate Judge appointed pursuant to 28 U.S.C. § 631.

"Magistrate Judge Actions" are all criminal complaints, initial Rule 40 appearances or class B and C misdemeanors also known as "Petty Offense Actions," and all other actions opened as "mj" actions.

"Miscellaneous Case/Action" is a number assigned to an ancillary or supplementary proceeding not defined as a civil or criminal action.

"Motion" means a motion, application, petition, or other request made to the Court for an order or other judicial activity.

"Notice of Electronic Filing" is a notice generated in ECF that notifies parties that a document has been filed.

"Order" means any directive by the Court other than a judgment, including oral, telephonic, written, and electronic directives.

"PACER," short for Public Access to Court Electronic Records, is a system maintained by the Administrative Office of the United States Courts for access to court electronic records. Registration to this system is required to access documents filed in ECF.

"PACER Registration" is a separate requirement for e-filing along with e-filing registration. PACER registration allows users to view documents through the PACER (Public Access to Court Electronic Records) System, http://pacer.psc. uscourts.gov. *See* L.R. 135(g)(3).

".PDF" or "Portable Document Format" is the required format for documents filed through the ECF system. Documents may be converted to .pdf format through .PDF software.

".PDF Software" is the software needed to convert word processor or scanned documents to .pdf format.

"Plaintiff" includes any party who files a complaint, petition, cross-claim, claim for relief under Fed. R. Civ. P. 14, or any other claim for affirmative relief.

"Pretrial Conference" means the final pretrial conference as defined in Fed. R. Civ. P. 16(e). *See* L.R. 282.

"Prisoner Actions" are actions brought in propria persona by a person in custody who is seeking habeas corpus relief (28 U.S.C. § 2241 et seq.) or any relief authorized by 42 U.S.C. § 1981 et seq., or actions pursuant to *Bivens* or the Federal Tort Claims Act.

"Pro Se Action" means an action in which all the plaintiffs or all the defendants are proceeding in propria persona. In these Rules, "pro se" and "in propria persona" are used interchangeably.

"Received" means accepted by the Clerk for physical inclusion in the Court's records but not suitable for filing as part of the official record in the action, *e.g.*, copies of correspondence between the parties, letters to the Court not suitable for filing, and other miscellaneous documents. Received documents are not normally part of a record on appeal.

"Removed Case" means an action removed from state court to federal court pursuant to 28 U.S.C. § 1441 et seq. Removed cases are initiated pursuant to the CM/ECF procedures in the same fashion as any other civil action. The appropriate state court file records, *see* 28 U.S.C. §§ 1446(a), 1447(b), should be filed electronically or as otherwise provided herein. *See* L.R. 133.

"Serve" includes service of process, personal and mailed service during the course of the action by conventional filers, and the service of documents by electronic filers during the course of the action effected through the CM/ECF System and communicated by the Notice of Electronic Filing. *See* Fed. R. Civ. P. 4, 4.1, 5; Fed. R. Crim. P. 49, L.R. 135.

"Signature" refers to either a handwritten signature on a paper document or an electronic signature. A signature on a document submitted to the Clerk on portable electronic media shall appear either as a facsimile of the original in a scanned document, or on a separate, scanned signature page if the document was published to .pdf. *See* L.R. 131.

"Status Conference" means any pretrial, scheduling, or discovery conference excepting the final pretrial conference as defined in Fed. R. Civ. P. 16(e). *See* L.R. 240.

"Text Only Order" refers to an order issued by the Court without an attached electronic document. The order appears as a docket entry with the words "Text Entry Only." *See* L.R. 137.

"Weapon" means any instrument intended to be used for attack or defense, including but not limited to firearms and knives. *See* L.R. 103.

[Effective December 1, 2009. Amended effective October 1, 2013.]

RULE 102. SCOPE AND AVAILABILITY OF LOCAL RULES (Fed. R. Civ. P. 1)

(a) Scope. These Rules govern all actions in the United States District Court for the Eastern District of California, the boundaries of which are set forth in 28 U.S.C. § 84. Outside the scope of these Rules are matters relating to internal court administration that, in the discretion of the Court en banc, may be accomplished through the use of General Orders, provided, however, that no matter appropriate for inclusion in these Rules shall be treated by General Order. No party or attorney shall be bound by any General Order.

(b) Availability of Local Rules. The Clerk shall maintain updated Rules in .pdf format available for downloading on the Court's website: www.caed.uscourts.gov.

(c) Notice After Adoption. Immediately upon the adoption of these Rules or any change in these Rules, copies of the new and revised Rules shall be provided to such publications and persons as the Chief Judge deems appropriate. The Clerk shall promptly notify the Judicial Council and the Administrative Office of the United States Courts, all county law libraries in the Eastern District of California and other law libraries maintained by the State or by law schools in the Eastern District of California. Copies shall be distributed in a manner calculated to ensure maximum notification to those practicing in the Eastern District of California. A notice shall be posted prominently in the Clerk's Offices and on the Court's website.

(d) Procedures Outside the Rules. Unless contrary to law, the Court in its discretion may make such orders supplementary or contrary to the provisions of these Rules as it may deem appropriate and in the interests of justice and case management under Fed. R. Civ. P. 16 or Fed. R. Crim. P. 17.1 in a special circumstance.

[Effective December 1, 2009.]

RULE 103. POLICY REGARDING WEAPONS IN THE COURTHOUSE AND COURTROOMS (Fed. R. Civ. P. 83)

(a) Prohibition on Unauthorized Weapons. Only duly authorized law enforcement officers are allowed to carry weapons in the United States Courthouses or any building housing a Court of the United States within the Eastern District of California. Only the United States Marshal, deputy marshals, and court security officers are authorized to carry weapons within the confines of the courtrooms, secured judicial corridors, and chambers of the Judges, Magistrate Judges, and Bankruptcy Judges. The United States Marshal is ordered to provide appropriate security to ensure against the introduction of unauthorized weapons or other dangerous weapons into the United States Courthouses, courtrooms, or any building housing a Court of the United States and/or any grounds appurtenant to such building within the Eastern District of California.

(b) Authorization for Weapon Possession. In high security situations, or when the United States Marshal otherwise deems it appropriate, the United States Marshal may authorize a duly authorized law enforcement officer to carry a weapon in the courtroom, provided the law enforcement officer wears an identification badge issued by the United States Marshal. Law enforcement officers so authorized to carry weapons within the courtroom shall immediately identify themselves to every United States Marshal and/or court security officer on duty within that courtroom.

(c) Use of Weapons in Evidence. Before any weapon is introduced as evidence in a court proceeding, said weapon shall first be rendered inoperable to the satisfaction of the United States Marshal and appropriately marked as evidence. In all actions in which a weapon is to be introduced as evidence, that fact shall be made known to the United States Marshal and/or court security officer on duty before the introduction of the weapon into the courtroom. At that time and place, the weapon shall be inspected by the United States Marshal and/or court security officer to ensure that it is in fact inoperable.

[Effective December 1, 2009.]

RULE 110. SANCTIONS FOR NONCOMPLIANCE WITH RULES (Fed. R. Civ. P. 11)

Failure of counsel or of a party to comply with these Rules or with any order of the Court may be grounds for imposition by the Court of any and all sanctions authorized by statute or Rule or within the inherent power of the Court.

[Effective December 1, 2009.]

RULE 120. SESSIONS OF COURT— INTRADISTRICT VENUE (Fed. R. Civ. P. 3)

(a) Sacramento and Fresno. Court shall be in continuous session at Sacramento and Fresno. See 28 U.S.C. §§ 84, 132 et seq. The Court maintains libraries in Sacramento and Fresno which are open to attorneys admitted to practice in this Court and to persons appearing in propria persona in this Court, who may use the libraries in accordance with such General Orders as the Court may adopt. Persons using the libraries are directed to refrain from requesting legal advice.

(b) Other Regular Sessions. The Magistrate Judges also hold regular sessions in Bakersfield, Redding and Yosemite National Park.

(c) Other Sessions. Sessions of court may also be held at other places in the District as the Court requires.

(d) Commencement of Actions. All civil and criminal actions and proceedings of every nature and kind cognizable in the United States District Court for the Eastern District of California arising in Calaveras, Fresno, Inyo, Kern, Kings, Madera, Mariposa, Merced, Stanislaus, Tulare, and Tuolumne counties shall be commenced in the United States District Court sitting in Fresno, California, and in Bakersfield, California, Yosemite National Park, or other designated places within those counties as the Court shall designate when appropriate

for Magistrate Judge criminal proceedings. All civil and criminal actions and proceedings of every nature and kind cognizable in the United States District Court for the Eastern District of California arising in Alpine, Amador, Butte, Colusa, El Dorado, Glenn, Lassen, Modoc, Mono, Nevada, Placer, Plumas, Sacramento, San Joaquin, Shasta, Sierra, Siskiyou, Solano, Sutter, Tehama, Trinity, Yolo, and Yuba counties shall be commenced in the United States District Court sitting Sacramento, California, and in Redding, California, or other designated places within those counties as the Court shall designate when appropriate for Magistrate Judge criminal proceedings.

(e) Assignment of Actions. All actions will be assigned in accordance with the Assignment Plan approved by the Court en banc and reproduced as Appendix A to these Rules.

(f) Transfer. Whenever in any action the Court finds upon its own motion, motion of any party, or stipulation that the action has not been commenced in the proper court in accordance with this Rule, or for other good cause, the Court may transfer the action to another venue within the District.

(g) General Duty Judge. The Chief Judge shall, from time to time, appoint a General Duty Judge. See L.R. 101.

[Effective December 1, 2009.]

RULE 121. THE CLERK OF THE DISTRICT COURT (Fed. R. Civ. P. 77)

(a) Locations. The Clerk of the District Court shall maintain offices at 501 "I" Street, Sacramento, California 95814, where the records of the United States District Court sitting in Sacramento shall be kept, and offices at 2500 Tulare Street, Fresno, California 93721, where the records of the United States District Court sitting in Fresno shall be kept.

(b) Office Hours. The regular office hours of the Clerk at Sacramento and Fresno shall be from 9:00 a.m. to 4:00 p.m. each day except Saturdays, Sundays, legal holidays, and such other times so ordered by the Chief Judge. See Fed. R. Civ. P. 77; Fed. R. Crim. P. 56.

(c) Advance Payment of Fees. Except as required by law, or as otherwise directed by the Court, the Clerk shall not file any paper, issue any process, or render any other service for which a fee is prescribed by statute or by the Judicial Conference of the United States unless the fee is prepaid. See 28 U.S.C. § 1914 et seq.

(d) Civil Complaint—Filing Procedures for Attorneys. Complaint filings by attorneys in civil actions (including prisoner, habeas corpus, in forma pauperis, and removal) shall be performed electronically. Detailed procedures are prescribed on the Court's website. See also L.R. 133.

(e) Initial Action Filing Procedures—Death Penalty Habeas Corpus. Whatever the manner of their filing, death penalty habeas corpus initial filings shall be assigned to a Judge and, in Sacramento, to a Magistrate Judge, immediately and communicated to the assigned Judge and Magistrate Judge immediately.

(f) Initial Action Filing Procedures—Miscellaneous Actions in General. With the sole exception of grand jury proceedings and miscellaneous actions filed by pro se plaintiffs, all documents submitted for filing in a miscellaneous proceeding, no matter when the action was originally commenced, shall be filed in accordance with the provisions governing civil actions in general. Grand jury proceedings should be submitted for filing by the United States Attorney in original paper format. These documents will be scanned into .pdf format by the Clerk and, except where authorized to be publicly available, shall be kept on a secure part of the Court's servers. All grand jury paper documents shall be returned to the United States Attorney.

[Effective December 1, 2009.]

RULE 122. AUTHORITY OF ASSIGNED JUDGES AND MAGISTRATE JUDGES IN EMERGENCIES (Fed. R. Civ. P. 63)

The Judge assigned to an action, or the Magistrate Judge when authorized, shall preside over the trial and determine all motions or other matters in that action, except as otherwise provided in Fed. R. Civ. P. 63 and Fed. R. Crim. P. 25, or as otherwise ordered, or in cases of emergency. In the event of an emergency requiring prompt action, if the assigned Judge or Magistrate Judge is unavailable, the matter shall be presented to the Clerk for temporary assignment to another available Judge or Magistrate Judge, if necessary. In such instance, it shall be the responsibility of counsel presenting the matter to provide the Judge or Magistrate Judge to whom the matter is presented with a detailed explanation of the necessity for the application's being handled on an emergency basis. The matter shall be returned to the calendar of the unavailable assigned Judge or Magistrate Judge upon the resolution of the matter, unless the matter is transferred pursuant to these Rules.

[Effective December 1, 2009.]

RULE 123. RELATED CASES (Fed. R. Civ. P. 83)

(a) **Definition of Related Cases.** An action is related to another action within the meaning of this Rule when

(1) both actions involve the same parties and are based on the same or a similar claim;

(2) both actions involve the same property, transaction, or event;

(3) both actions involve similar questions of fact and the same question of law and their assignment to the same Judge or Magistrate Judge is likely to effect a substantial savings of judicial effort, either because the same result should follow in both actions or otherwise; or

(4) for any other reasons, it would entail substantial duplication of labor if the actions were heard by different Judges or Magistrate Judges.

(b) **Duties of Counsel.** Counsel who has reason to believe that an action on file or about to be filed may be related to another action on file (whether or not dismissed or otherwise terminated) shall promptly file in each action and serve on all parties in each action a Notice of Related Cases. This notice shall set forth the title and number of each possibly related

action, together with a brief statement of their relationship and the reasons why assignment to a single Judge and/or Magistrate Judge is likely to effect a savings of judicial effort and other economies. The Clerk shall notify the Judges and Magistrate Judges to whom the actions are assigned promptly of such filing.

(c) **Reassignment.** Following the filing of a Notice of Related Cases, the Chief Judge or a Judge designated by the Chief Judge may, by special order, reassign either action to any Judge or Magistrate Judge sitting in the Eastern District of California as the situation may dictate. If the Judge to whom the action with the lower or lowest number has been assigned determines that assignment of the actions to a single Judge is likely to effect a savings of judicial effort or other economies, that Judge is authorized to enter an order reassigning all higher numbered related actions to himself or herself.

(d) **Refiling.** An action may not be dismissed and thereafter refiled for the purpose of obtaining a different Judge or Magistrate Judge. If an action is dismissed and it, or one essentially the same, is refiled, it shall be assigned to the same Judge and Magistrate Judge. It is the duty of all counsel appearing therein to bring the facts of the refiling to the attention of the Clerk pursuant to this Rule. See L.R. 110.

(e) **Habeas Corpus Petitions.** Related habeas corpus petitions are governed by L.R. 190(d) or L.R. 191(f)(5) as the case may be.

(f) **Petition for Violation of Probation or Supervised Release.** Where a Notice of Related Cases is filed suggesting that a petition for probation action and/or violation of the terms of supervised release should be related to a new indictment, and the basis of the probation petition or alleged supervised release violation is the conduct underlying the new indictment, the two actions shall be related and the Judge or Magistrate Judge assigned to the new criminal action shall also be assigned the earlier action, unless the original sentencing judge desires to retain the first action, in which circumstance both actions shall be assigned to the original sentencing judge.

[Effective December 1, 2009.]

RULE 130. GENERAL FORMAT OF DOCUMENTS (Fed. R. Civ. P. 7)

(a) **Electronically–Filed Documents.** Documents electronically filed shall be created and formatted to comply, in appearance and presentation both in an electronic format and when printed, with the requirements for conventionally-filed paper documents.

(b) **Conventionally–Filed Documents and Courtesy Copies.** All documents presented for conventional filing or lodging and the chambers courtesy copies shall be on white, unglazed opaque paper of good quality with numbered lines in the left margin, 8–1/2″ × 11″ in size, and shall be flat, unfolded (except where necessary for presentation of exhibits), firmly bound at the top left corner, pre-punched with two (2) holes (approximately 1/4″ diameter) centered 2–3/4″ apart, 1/2″ to 5/8″ from the top edge of the document, and shall comply with all other applicable provisions of these Rules. Matters contained thereon shall be presented by typewriting, printing, photographic or offset reproduction, or other clearly legible process, without erasures or interlining that materially defaces the document, and shall appear on one side of each sheet only.

(c) Spacing. Documents shall be double-spaced except for the identification of counsel, title of the action, category headings, footnotes, quotations, exhibits and descriptions of real property. Quotations of more than fifty (50) words shall be indented.

(d) Numbering. Each page shall be numbered consecutively at the bottom and shall provide a brief description of the document on the same line.

[Effective December 1, 2009.]

RULE 131. COUNSEL IDENTIFICATION AND SIGNATURES (Fed. R. Civ. P. 7)

(a) Counsel Identification. The name, address, telephone number, and the California State Bar membership number of all attorneys, or, if in propria persona, the name, address, and telephone number of the party, and the specific identification of each party represented by name and interest in the litigation (e.g., plaintiff Smith, defendant Jones) shall appear in the upper left-hand corner of the first page of each document presented for filing, except that in the instance of multi-party representation reference may be made to the signature page for the complete list of parties represented. Attorneys for service shall be designated in accordance with L.R. 180. See Fed. R. Civ. P. 11; L.R. 180, 182; Cal. Rules of Court 2.111.

(b) Signatures Generally. All pleadings and non-evidentiary documents shall be signed by the individual attorney for the party presenting them, or by the party involved if that party is appearing in propria persona. Affidavits and certifications shall be signed by the person executing the document. The name of the person signing the document shall be typed or printed underneath the signature. See Fed. R. Civ. P. 11. If a document is submitted to the Clerk via portable electronic media, signatures shall appear either as a facsimile of the original (in a scanned document placed on portable electronic media), or on a separate, scanned signature page if the document was published to .pdf and then placed on portable electronic media. In the latter situation, the docket shall reflect the submission of the signature page.

(c) Attorney Signatures. Anything filed using an attorney's name, login, and password will be deemed to have been signed by that attorney for all purposes, including Fed. R. Civ. P. 11. For example, for the attorney whose login and password is being used, it is sufficient to indicate a signature as in the following example: "/s/ John M. Barrister, Esquire."

(d) Misuse of Attorney's Electronic Signature. Any person challenging the authenticity of an electronically-filed document or placement of the attorney's signature on that document must file an objection and request that the document be stricken within twenty-one (21) days of receiving the Notice of Electronic Filing, or at a later time for good cause shown by an attorney exercising due diligence. Attorneys are responsible for, and must take care to ensure, the validity of their signatures.

(e) Documents Requiring Signatures of Multiple Counsel. Documents that are normally signed by more than one counsel, whether the counsel represent the same party or different parties, may be prepared by obtaining approval from any other counsel to state that the other counsel has authorized submission of the document on that counsel's behalf. Submitting counsel shall place the other counsel's signature on the electronic filing by using "/s/ counsel's name (as authorized on [date])." Alternatively, one counsel may obtain the original signatures from all counsel who are filing the document, scan the signature page(s) only and file the signature page(s) as an attachment to the document with an explanatory statement on the signature page of the filed document.

(f) Non–Attorney's Electronic Signature. Documents that are required to be signed by a person who is not the attorney of record in a particular action (verified pleadings, affidavits, papers authorized to be filed electronically by persons in pro per, etc.), may be submitted in electronic format bearing a "/s/" and the person's name on the signature line along with a statement that counsel has a signed original, e.g., "/s/ John Doe (original signature retained by attorney Mary Roe)." It is counsel's duty to maintain this original signature for one year after the exhaustion of all appeals. This procedure may also be followed when a hybrid electronic/paper document is filed, i.e., the conventionally served document may also contain an annotated signature in lieu of the original.

(g) Misuse of Non–Attorney's Electronic Signature. A non-filing signatory, party, or attorney who disputes the authenticity of an electronically-filed document with a non-attorney signature must file an objection and request that the document be stricken within twenty-one (21) days of receiving the Notice of Electronic Filing or a copy of the document, whichever first occurs, unless good cause exists for a later contest of the signature by a person exercising due diligence.

(h) Electronic Signatures on Certain Documents in Criminal Actions. Several documents in criminal actions require the signature of a non-attorney, such as a grand jury foreperson, a defendant, a third-party custodian, a United States Marshal, an officer from Pretrial Services or Probation, or some other federal officer or agent. Unless the procedure in L.R. 131(f) is followed, the Clerk will scan these documents, upload them to the CM/ECF system, and except as otherwise provided by administrative procedures, discard the paper documents. The electronically-filed document as it is maintained on the Court's servers shall constitute the official version of that record.

[Effective December 1, 2009.]

RULE 132. NOTICE OF CLAIM OF UNCONSTITUTIONALITY (Fed. R. Civ. P. 5.1)

(a) Notice of Claim of Unconstitutionality of Federal Law. If, at any time in an action to which neither the United States nor any of its officers, agencies, or employees is a party, any party draws in issue the constitutionality of a federal administrative regulation of general applicability, that party shall immediately file a notice identifying the regulation in issue and setting forth in what respects its constitutionality is questioned. Thereupon, or sua sponte, the Court shall serve a copy of the notice on the United States Attorney General, on the United States Attorney, and on all other parties. If the party required to file and serve the notice fails to do so, every other party shall file and serve such a notice, provided that, as soon as a notice is filed and served, all other parties are relieved of this obligation. Cf. 28 U.S.C. § 2403(a) (requirement re Acts of Congress); Fed. R. Civ. P. 5.1.

(b) Notice of Claim of Unconstitutionality of State Law. If, at any time in an action to which neither a State nor any of its officers, agencies, or employees is a party, any party draws in issue the constitutionality of any state administrative regulation of general applicability, that party shall immediately file a notice identifying the regulation in issue and setting forth in what respects its constitutionality is questioned. Thereupon, or sua sponte, the Court shall serve a copy of that notice on the Attorney General of the State and on all other parties. If the party required to file and serve such a notice fails to do so, every other party shall file and serve such notice, provided that as soon as a notice is filed and served, all other parties are relieved of this obligation. Cf. 28 U.S.C. § 2403(b) (requirement re state statutes); Fed. R. Civ. P. 5.1.

[Effective December 1, 2009.]

RULE 133. FILING AND CONTENTS OF DOCUMENTS (Fed. R. Civ. P. 5)

(a) Electronic Filing. The Eastern District of California is an electronic case management/filing district (CM/ECF). Unless excused by the Court or by the electronic filing procedures set forth in these Rules, attorneys shall file all documents electronically pursuant to those Rules. All complaints, and subsequent motions, pleadings, briefs, exhibits, and all other documents in an action shall be electronically filed except as otherwise provided by these Rules. Pro se parties shall file and serve paper documents as provided in these Rules. After a pro se party files a paper document, the Clerk will transform the paper filing into an electronic record and ultimately discard the paper filing.

(b) Exceptions.

(1) *Attorney Exceptions.* In exceptional circumstances and for specific documents, an attorney may apply for permission to file documents in paper format. See L.R. 133(b)(3). The decision to permit paper filing is in the sole discretion of the assigned Judge or Magistrate Judge. Any request to file paper documents must be made no less than seven (7) days before the date the documents would otherwise be due to be filed. Permission to file paper documents may be revoked at any time. Paper filings will be scanned, and the electronic format will become the official court record unless otherwise ordered by the assigned Judge or Magistrate Judge. The paper filing will ultimately be discarded.

(2) *Pro Se Party Exception.* Any person appearing pro se may **not** utilize electronic filing except with the permission of the assigned Judge or Magistrate Judge. See L.R. 133(b)(3). All pro se parties shall file and serve paper documents as

required by applicable Federal Rules of Civil or Criminal Procedure or by these Rules.

(3) *Form of Requests.* Requests to use paper or electronic filing as exceptions from these Rules shall be submitted as stipulations as provided in L.R. 143 or, if a stipulation cannot be had, as written motions setting out an explanation of reasons for the exception. Points and authorities are not required, and no argument or hearing will normally be held. Requests may also be made in scheduling conference and pretrial conference statements when the need can be foreseen.

(4) *Grand Jury Exception.* Grand jury proceedings shall be submitted for filing by the United States Attorney in paper format. These documents will be scanned into .pdf format by the Clerk and, unless authorized to be publicly available, shall be kept under seal. All paper documents shall be returned to the United States Attorney.

(5) *Exception for Certain Other Criminal Documents.* See L.R. 131(h).

(c) Controlling Procedures. Whenever, in these Rules, reference is made to filing or service of a document, the reference shall include filing and serving documents electronically in conformity with these Rules. If these Rules require paper filings or service for certain persons or circumstances, then conventional filing and service procedures shall control to that extent.

(d) Paper Documents.

(1) *Delivery of Paper Documents to the Clerk.* Except as expressly authorized in advance by the Court, all paper documents presented for filing or lodging shall be delivered to the Clerk who will, when appropriate, deliver the documents to the Judge or Magistrate Judge after docketing. Original documents to be filed or lodged shall not be mailed to chambers. If a particular document is to be brought to the immediate attention of the Judge or Magistrate Judge assigned to the action, a copy may be mailed or otherwise delivered to the chambers, but the original shall be presented to the Clerk. See Fed. R. Civ. P. 5; L.R. 121(b). All documents delivered to the Clerk for filing or lodging in a pending action should be presented to the Clerk at the office where the action is pending. See L.R. 120, 121. However, unless otherwise ordered by the Court, documents filed at an incorrect office will be accepted by that office.

(2) *Filing of Multiple Copies of Paper Documents.* One additional legible conformed copy of all paper documents to be filed or lodged shall be delivered to the Clerk, for the Court's use, except that in actions to be heard by a District Court composed of three Judges, three additional legible conformed copies of each brief and supporting documents shall be delivered to the Clerk.

(3) *Handling of Improper Paper Documents.* The Clerk will not refuse to file a paper document that is submitted for filing in a pending action on account of improper formatting. The Clerk will scan it and, if improperly filed, notify the Court that the document was filed in an improper format. An order to show cause (OSC) may be issued in appropriate actions regarding an attorney's disregard for the requirement to utilize electronic filing or other violations of these electronic filing procedures. See L.R. 110.

(e) Facsimile Documents.

(1) *Facsimile as Original Document.* For purposes of this Rule, the image of the original manual signature appearing on a facsimile (fax) copy filed pursuant to this Rule shall constitute an original signature for all court purposes. The document, which itself may be in whole or in part a fax copy, must be marked "original" before submission to the Clerk for filing.

(2) *Retention of Actual Original.* The originator of the document, or in the case of an affidavit or certification, the presenting attorney or party, must maintain the document containing the original manual signature until the conclusion of the action, including any appeal and remand after appeal. In the event there are multiple signatories to a document, the filing party or attorney shall retain the originally signed document(s).

(3) *Filing of Actual Original.* The Court may require that the document containing the original manual signature be filed.

(4) *No Direct Fax to Clerk or Chambers.* This Rule does not provide for documents to be transmitted via fax directly to the Clerk. Documents directly faxed to the Clerk or to a chambers of the Court will not be filed, lodged, received, returned, or acknowledged, absent an express order of the Court.

(f) Chambers Courtesy Paper Copies. A person who electronically files any document (excluding attachments or exhibits) in excess of 25 pages must also provide a courtesy paper copy of the document to the appropriate chambers. A person who electronically files attachments or exhibits that total in excess of 50 pages must also provide a paper courtesy copy of those attachments or exhibits to chambers by delivering it to the Clerk. The courtesy copy must be mailed or otherwise sent to the pertinent courtroom deputy clerk no later than the next business day following the electronic filing. *All courtesy copies shall be prominently labeled as such in capital letters on the face sheet of the courtesy copy.* Chambers have no obligation to retain the courtesy copies. See also L.R. 130(b).

(g) Caption and Title. Following the counsel identification and commencing on the eighth line of the initial page of each document (except where additional space is required for identification), there shall appear: (1) the title of the Court, (2) the title of the action, (3) the file number of the action, followed by the initials of the Judge and Magistrate Judge to whom it is currently assigned, (4) a title describing the document, (5) immediately below the case number and title of the document, a statement of the date, time, and name of the Judge or Magistrate Judge for any scheduled hearing, and (6) any other matter required by these Rules.

(h) Reference to Parties. If there are more than two parties, including intervenors or amici, references to all parties shall include the name (which may be abbreviated) of the particular party or parties to whom reference is made.

(i) Citations.

(1) *Federal Citations.* Citations to federal decisions shall be to the United States Supreme Court Reports, Federal Reports, Federal Supplement, or Federal Rules Decisions, if so reported, and shall indicate the court and year of decision.

Citations to federal statutes shall be to the United States Code, if so codified. Citations to federal administrative rules shall be to the Code of Federal Regulations, if so codified, or to the Federal Register, if published therein.

(2) *State Citations.* Citations to California decisions shall be to the official California Reports. Citations to other state cases shall be to the National Reporter System, showing state and year of decision. Other parallel citations may be added.

(3) *Unreported, Uncodified Citations.*

(i) General Requirement. If case, statutory, or regulatory authority is relied upon that has not been reported, published or codified in any of the foregoing references, and that is not available through Westlaw/Lexis, a copy of that authority shall be appended to the brief or other document in which the authority is cited. This requirement shall include, but not be limited to, the Statutes at Large, the Public Laws of the United States, the California Administrative Code, administrative regulations not contained in the Code of Federal Regulations or the Federal Register, and decisions and other matters published in specialized reporter services.

(ii) Incarcerated Pro Se Parties. In any action wherein a party is incarcerated and appearing pro se, that party shall be served with a paper copy of the case, statutory, or regulatory authority cited by the filing party that has not been reported as set forth in (1) and (2) above, regardless of its availability in Westlaw/Lexis, as well as a paper copy of that authority otherwise required to be appended in 3(i) above. No copy of the authority available in Westlaw/Lexis shall be filed with the court.

(j) Depositions. Depositions shall not be filed through CM/ECF. Before or upon the filing of a document making reference to a deposition, counsel relying on the deposition shall ensure that a courtesy hard copy of the entire deposition so relied upon has been submitted to the Clerk for use in chambers. Alternatively, counsel relying on a deposition may submit an electronic copy of the deposition in lieu of the courtesy paper copy to the email box of the Judge or Magistrate Judge and concurrently email or otherwise transmit the deposition to all other parties. Neither hard copy nor electronic copy of the entire deposition will become part of the official record of the action absent order of the Court. Pertinent portions of the deposition intended to become part of the official record shall be submitted as exhibits in support of a motion or otherwise. See L.R. 250.1(a).

(k) Tables. Briefs exceeding fifteen (15) pages in length shall be accompanied by an indexed table of contents related to the headings or subheadings and by an indexed table of statutes, rules, ordinances, cases, and other authorities cited.

[Effective December 1, 2009. Amended effective July 1, 2011; September 20, 2012.]

RULE 134. TIME OF FILING (Fed. R. Civ. P. 5)

(a) Filing Complete. Emailing a document to the Clerk or to the Court (as opposed to electronic filing in CM/ECF) shall not constitute "filing" of the document. Except as noted in L.R. 121 for the filing of initial documents, a document filed electronically shall not be considered filed for purposes of these Rules or the Federal Rules of Civil or Criminal Procedure until the filing counsel receives a system-generated "Notice of Electronic Filing." See L.R. 135. Paper filings, when permitted or required by these procedures, shall be complete upon presentation to the Clerk.

(b) Time of Filing. A document will generally be deemed filed on a particular day if filed before midnight (Pacific Time) on that business day. However, if the time of day at which the document is filed is of the essence, the Court may order that the document be filed by a time certain. Filings via CM/ECF may be made twenty-four hours a day, but portable electronic media may be submitted over the counter at the Clerk's Office only during Clerk's Office business hours. See 77–121(b).

(c) Technical Failures. The Clerk shall deem the CM/ECF site to be subject to a technical failure on a given day if the site is unable to accept filings continuously or intermittently over the course of any period of time greater than two hours after 2:00 p.m. on a given day. Known systems outages will be posted on the website, if possible. CDs or other electronic media may be filed during a time of technical failure.

(1) *Untimely Filings Due to CM/ECF Failure.* A party may file on the next business day following the technical failure that is announced on the Court's website. If the technical failure is not so announced on the Court's website, then the party must file the document as promptly as possible and seek appropriate relief from the Court.

(2) *Service Required Despite Court's Technical Failure.* If filing is impossible due to the CM/ECF failure, counsel shall timely serve the document directly on all counsel in the action by email, overnight delivery, or other expeditious means appropriate to the circumstances.

(3) *Failure at the Sender.* Problems on the filer's end, such as phone line problems, problems with the filer's Internet Service Provider (ISP), or hardware or software problems, will not constitute a technical failure under these procedures nor excuse an untimely filing. A filer subject to mandatory electronic filing who cannot directly file a document electronically because of a technical problem on the filer's end must file the document electronically from another computer or in portable electronic format at the Clerk's Office. If electronic filing is not possible in any form, the party may file a paper document, shall annotate on the cover page that electronic filing was not possible because of technical reasons, and shall file electronically as soon as possible.

(d) After–Hours Filed Documents. Generally, documents, including motions for temporary restraining orders, filed electronically after normal business hours of the Clerk's Office will not be reviewed by the Court until the next business day, at the earliest.

[Effective December 1, 2009. Amended effective July 1, 2011.]

RULE 135. SERVICE OF DOCUMENTS DURING ACTION (Fed. R. Civ. P. 5)

(a) Service of Electronic Documents. "Service" as utilized in these Rules includes electronic service as set forth in the CM/ECF procedures in these Rules. "Notice of Electronic Filing" is a notice automatically generated by CM/ECF at the time a document is filed with the system. When counsel have consented to electronic service, see L.R. 135(g), this Notice will constitute automatic service of the document on all others who have consented. This Notice will set forth the time of filing, the name of the parties and attorney(s) filing the document, the type of document, the text of the docket entry, the name of the parties and/or attorney(s) receiving the notice, and an electronic link (hyperlink) to the filed document that allows recipients to retrieve the document automatically. Service via this electronic Notice constitutes service pursuant to Fed. R. Civ. P. 5(b)(2)(E) and Fed. R. Crim. P. 49.

(b) Conventional Service. If persons are not registered for the CM/ECF system, e.g., prisoners or pro se parties, or have not consented to receive electronic service, the Notice will identify the persons who were not electronically served. Persons who were not electronically served must be conventionally served. Persons who are unregistered or do not consent may not rely on electronic service and must serve documents conventionally as otherwise provided by the Rules. Counsel shall serve these persons in accordance with the appropriate Federal Rules of Procedure.

(c) Proof of Service for Paper Documents. When service of any pleading, notice, motion, or other document required to be served is made, proof of such service shall be endorsed upon or affixed to the original of the document when it is lodged or filed. Except for ex parte matters, a paper document shall not be submitted for filing unless it is accompanied by a proof of service. Proof of service shall be under penalty of perjury and shall include the date, manner and place of service.

(d) Service Upon All Parties. Unless a party expressly waives service, copies of all documents submitted to the Court shall be served upon all parties to the action, except that no service need be made upon parties held in default for failure to appear unless the document involved asserts new or additional claims for relief against such defaulting parties. See Fed. R. Civ. P. 5(a).

(e) Service Upon Pro Se Party. Service of all documents authorized to be served in accordance with Fed. R. Civ. P. 5 or Fed. R. Crim. P. 49 shall be complete when served upon a party appearing in propria persona. See also Fed. R. Civ. P. 4.1.

(f) Service Upon Attorney. Service of all documents authorized to be served in accordance with Fed. R. Civ. P. 5 or Fed. R. Crim. P. 49 shall be complete when served upon the attorney for the party, if the party has appeared and is represented by an attorney. When an attorney represents multiple parties, service of one copy of the document upon that attorney shall constitute service upon all parties represented by that attorney, unless the Court otherwise orders. Where multiple attorneys represent the same party or parties, service shall be made upon all such attorneys, unless the Court otherwise orders. See also Fed. R. Civ. P. 4.1.

(g) Attorney Registration for Electronic Filing. All attorneys who wish to file documents in the Eastern District of

California must be admitted to practice or admitted to appear pro hac vice. Admission to practice in the Eastern District of California includes the requirement that the attorney complete an e-filing registration form and receive a username and password. Completion of the registration form will permit electronic filing of documents and, unless an attorney opts out, will authorize acceptance of service by electronic means. To do this, an attorney must have a valid internet email address. After registration, attorneys will receive a unique user name and password. Registration enables an attorney to file documents electronically. The court registration name and password, when utilized for the electronic filing of documents, will serve as the party's signature for Fed. R. Civ. P. 11 purposes. See also L.R. 131. In conjunction with the court filing registration requirement, registration for PACER, see L.R. 135(g)(3), is also mandated in order to permit access to images of documents maintained within court electronic records.

(1) *Consent to Service.* Unless an attorney opts out by designating such on the registration form, registration as a filing user constitutes: (1) consent to receive service electronically pursuant to Fed. R. Civ. P. 5(b)(2)(E) and Fed. R. Crim. P. 49 and waiver of the right to receive service by any other means; and (2) consent to making electronic service pursuant to Fed. R. Civ. P. 5(b)(2)(E) and Fed. R. Crim. P. 49 and waiver of the right to make service by any other means. This consent pertinent to Fed. R. Civ. P. 5 does **not** affect service of a summons and complaint pursuant to Fed. R. Civ. P. 4, i.e., there is no electronic service of a complaint. The foregoing waiver of service and notice applies to notice of the entry of an order or judgment. Service by electronic means is complete upon transmission of the Notice of Electronic Filing.

(2) *Court Preference.* Although the Eastern District of California does not require attorneys to serve and/or accept service of documents by electronic means, the Court **strongly encourages** the use of this practice.

(3) *PACER Registration Required.* Documents already on the Court's servers are accessed through the Public Access to Court Electronic Records ("PACER") Service Center. A PACER login is required in order to utilize CM/ECF to review documents, *in addition to*, the password issued by the Court for filing purposes. To register for PACER, a user must complete the online form or submit a registration form, available on the PACER website (http://pacer.psc.uscourts.gov).

(4) *Credit Card Payment.* All fees related to electronically-filed documents, e.g., complaint, should be paid by use of a credit card on the Court's secure servers. If credit card payment cannot be made, fees may be paid by check or money order; however, when payment of fees is required, the document will not be filed until payment is tendered.

[Effective December 1, 2009.]

RULE 136. (FED. R. CIV. P. 6) [DELETED EFFECTIVE DECEMBER 1, 2009]

RULE 137. REDUCTION OF ORDERS TO WRITING—SERVICE OF ORDERS
(Fed. R. Civ. P. 5)

(a) **Reduction of Orders to Writing.** Subject to Fed. R. Civ. P. 58 and unless the Court otherwise directs or permits, whenever the Court makes an oral order (except intermediate orders in the course of a hearing), the prevailing party shall serve upon all other parties and lodge a proposed written order embodying all provisions of the orally-announced order. Unless all counsel have approved the order as to form, counsel preparing the order shall serve it on all other parties and wait seven (7) days before lodging the proposed order. Counsel submitting a proposed order to the Court shall provide a certificate reflecting service and expiration of the seven (7) days. Counsel not preparing the order shall have seven (7) days after service of a copy of the proposed order within which to apply to the Court for correction or modification of the proposed order to reflect accurately the ruling of the Court or to submit an alternative order. If the proposed order is approved by the Court, it shall be signed and filed.

(b) **Electronically–Lodged Proposed Orders.** When a proposed order is electronically submitted to the Court, the person proposing the order must submit it via CM/ECF, thereby effecting service on all other parties. Except in situations in which a proposed order is contained in a stipulation, electronically-submitted proposed orders may not be combined into a motion or request. In addition to filing the proposed order electronically in .pdf format, the proposing person must also submit by email a separate proposed order in Word format to the appropriate Judge or Magistrate Judge's email box listed on the Court's website. The email subject line must contain the words "proposed order" as well as the case number. Counsel should not include table/cell formatting in the date and signature portions of proposed orders. Use of table/cell formatting in the date and signature portions of proposed orders may cause the document(s) to be returned unsigned and/or unprocessed.

In all cases involving submission of a proposed order, simply emailing the word processing document to the Judge or Magistrate Judge's email box does **not** constitute the proper submission of that proposed order with the Court. Conversely, simply submitting a .pdf version of the proposed order via CM/ECF does **not** constitute proper submission of the proposed order. **Both** the submission of the .pdf version and the submission via email to the email box of the assigned Judge or Magistrate Judge must be accomplished.

(c) **Documents Requiring Leave of Court.** If filing a document requires leave of court, such as an amended complaint after the time to amend as a matter of course has expired, counsel shall attach the document proposed to be filed as an exhibit to moving papers seeking such leave and lodge a proposed order as required by these Rules. If the Court grants the motion, counsel shall file and serve the document in accordance with these Rules and the Federal Rules of Civil and Criminal Procedure.

(d) **Order Processing.** Orders will be generated by chambers and converted to .pdf, or generated in .pdf format in CM/ECF. The assigned Judge, Magistrate Judge, or their designee will electronically file all signed orders. Any order signed electronically has the same force and effect as if the Judge or Magistrate Judge had signed a paper copy of the order and it had been entered on the docket conventionally.

(e) Routine Orders. The Court may grant routine orders by a text-only entry upon the docket. In such cases, no .pdf document will issue; the text-only entry shall constitute the Court's only order on the matter. The System will generate a "Notice of Electronic Filing" as described in these procedures for purposes of electronic service, and the Clerk will effect conventional service if required.

(f) Service. Copies of all written orders signed and filed by the Court conventionally or electronically, whether drafted by counsel or by the Court, shall be served forthwith by the Clerk on all counsel who have appeared in the action. A certificate of service by the Clerk shall accompany the order as served and shall be attached to the order as filed.

[Effective December 1, 2009. Amended effective October 1, 2013.]

RULE 138. FILES AND RECORDS—EXHIBITS (Fed. R. Civ. P. 39)

(a)(1) *Official Court Record.* Except as provided by these Rules, the official court record in all actions filed after January 3, 2005 is the electronic case file. For cases filed before January 3, 2005, all documents filed up to January 3, 2005 will be maintained in paper format; all documents filed after January 3, 2005 will be maintained in electronic format. The official court record in these actions is paper up to January 3, 2005 and electronic thereafter. After January 3, 2005, the official record shall include paper documents permitted by these Rules. When paper filings are authorized, the Court may order that the paper filings be maintained indefinitely by the Clerk until archival and may also order that the paper file created be the official record of the Court.

(a)(2) *Custody and Withdrawal of the Official Case Record.* All electronic and paper files and records of the Court shall remain in the custody of the Clerk. No file and no record, paper, or item belonging to the files of the Court shall be taken from the custody of the Clerk without a special order of the Court and a receipt given by the party obtaining it, describing it and the date of its receipt, except as otherwise provided by this Rule. Retention of sealed paper documents shall be governed by the sealed documents procedures. See L.R. 141.

(b) Administrative Records. Due to the usual size of administrative records, attorneys shall, if possible, submit the administrative record in electronic format with a mandatory courtesy copy in paper for the assigned Judge or Magistrate Judge. If there is no electronic record, the Clerk will accept for filing a certified paper copy accompanied by an electronic "Notice of Filing in Paper Format." The administrative record will be maintained in paper format and returned to the submitting attorney at the conclusion of the action, if no appeal is filed, and after appeal or further proceedings in the district court as appropriate. Administrative record or trial transcript procedures for Social Security or habeas corpus actions are set forth in L.R. 190(f), 191(i), and 206(c). Pro se parties shall submit the administrative records in paper if they have the obligation to file the administrative records.

(c)(1) *Pretrial/Post–trial Exhibits and Affidavits; Size Guidelines for Electronic Format.* Unless otherwise permitted or required to be filed in paper format by these Rules, all pretrial exhibits and affidavits must be submitted in electronic format. While there is no presumptive page limit on exhibits that may be submitted to the Court in electronic format, voluminous scanned attachments and exhibits may have to be divided into separate attachments. Current size limits for documents submitted through CM/ECF can be found through the Court Information link on the Court's CM/ECF Welcome Page: https://ecf.caed.uscourts.gov/cgi–bin/CourtInfo.pl.

(c)(2) *Scanning Exhibits.* Absent special circumstances, exhibits that are black and white documents should be scanned in black and white with a scanner configured at 300 dots per inch (dpi), if possible. (Higher resolutions take too much electronic file space and are slower to load/upload, while lower resolutions will provide a poor quality document). Documents in color in their original form, such as color photographs, may be scanned in color and submitted. The filing counsel shall verify the readability of scanned documents before filing them electronically. Parties who anticipate filing many exhibits in color should seek special procedures for filing at the time of a scheduling conference or from the Court at reasonable time before the due date of the filing. These procedures could include an exemption from the usual electronic size of a filed document or filing in paper.

(c)(3) *Retention of Scanned Documents.* Originals of documents requiring scanning that are filed electronically must be retained by the filing counsel and made available, upon request, to the Court and other parties, for at least one year after final judgment and completion of all appeals. If law, including state law concerning attorney practice, or the needs of the action require further retention, filing counsel shall retain the originals for the necessary period.

(d) Pretrial/Post–Trial Exhibits; Conventional (Paper) Submission. Pro se parties may only file paper documents and need not seek permission to do so. If an attorney, for exceptional circumstances, believes submission of exhibits must be in paper format, the attorney must apply to the Court for an exemption from the requirement for electronic submission. Any such application must be filed no less than seven (7) days before the date the filing is due. When exhibits are submitted in paper format, the party shall file and serve the exhibits and also electronically file, a one page .pdf document entitled "Notice of Attachment" referencing the electronically-filed pleading, motion or other document pertinent to the Notice and stating that exhibits are being submitted in paper. The Notice shall specify the date of the order permitting filing in paper to enable the docket to reflect that documents are being held as ordered with the Clerk in paper format. The party shall also file a CD or other appropriate media containing the filed exhibits for the Clerk's use. Unless the Court orders otherwise, no court file containing the paper exhibits shall be maintained, and the exhibits shall be placed in the chronological paper file and discarded after a one year period.

(e) Trial Exhibits. Exhibits offered or admitted at trial will not be scanned or received electronically unless ordered by the Court.

(f) Custody of Exhibits. All exhibits, including models and diagrams marked for identification or introduced in evidence, upon the hearing of any action or motion, shall be delivered to the Clerk, who shall keep custody of the same, except as otherwise ordered by the Court. All exhibits received in evidence that are in the nature of narcotic drugs, legal or counterfeit money, firearms or contraband of any kind shall be entrusted to the custody of the arresting or investigative agency of the Government pending disposition of the action and for any appeal period thereafter.

(g) Withdrawal of Civil Exhibits. In a civil action, after judgment has become final or upon the filing of a stipulation of the parties waiving the right of appeal, rehearing and a new trial, any party may withdraw any evidentiary exhibit originally produced by that party unless some other person files and serves on all other parties prior notice of a claim or entitlement to the exhibit, in which case the Clerk shall not deliver the exhibit, except with the written consent of all claimants, until the Court has determined the identity of the person entitled thereto.

(h) Withdrawal of Criminal Exhibits. Absent a stipulation of all parties, see L.R. 143, the Clerk shall maintain all exhibits during the pendency of the criminal trial and all appeals unless otherwise provided in these Rules. Following the spreading of mandate, the Clerk shall notify all parties of the availability of the exhibit for repossession by the party offering the exhibit in the absence of objection by another party. If no objection is lodged within twenty-eight (28) days, the Clerk may return the exhibit to the party offering it on request.

(i) Disposition of Unclaimed Exhibits. If exhibits are not re-claimed within sixty (60) days after notice to the parties to claim the same, the Clerk may dispose of them as the Clerk may deem fit.

(j) Substitution of Copies. Unless there is a specific reason why original exhibits should be retained, the assigned Judge or Magistrate Judge may, upon stipulation or motion, order them returned to the party to whom they belong upon the filing of a copy certified by the Clerk or approved by counsel for all parties concerned.

(k) Electronic and Mailed Correspondence. Non–case related correspondence is not governed by these Rules. Appropriate case-related correspondence shall be transmitted to the email address or conventional mail address of the pertinent courtroom deputy clerk. The assigned Judge or Magistrate Judge to whom the correspondence is addressed will determine whether such correspondence should be filed.

(*l*) Submission of Audio and Video Files on Portable Media. All audio and video files are required to be submitted electronically in one of the formats listed on the Electronic Evidence Submission page on the Court's Website www.caed.uscourts.gov. Submissions must be made on either a Compact Disk (CD), Digital Video Disk (DVD), or USB (Universal Serial Bus) Flash Drive. All other formats requiring proprietary programs to view electronic files will not be accepted. Media submitted to the Court must be labeled, contain files for submission only and be free of damage.

[Effective December 1, 2009. Amended effective July 1, 2011; February 1, 2019.]

RULE 140. PRIVACY CONCERNS AND REDACTION (Fed. R. Civ. P. 5.2) (Fed. R. Crim. P. 49.1)

(a) Privacy in General. Except as set forth below, pursuant to the Judicial Conference Policy on Privacy and Electronic Access to Case Files, and the E–Government Act of 2002, Pub. L. No. 107–347, effective April 16, 2003, when filing documents, counsel and the Court shall omit or, where reference is necessary, partially redact the following personal data identifiers from all pleadings, documents, and exhibits, whether filed electronically or on paper, unless the Court orders otherwise:

(i) Minors' names: In criminal actions, use the minors' initials; in civil actions use initials when federal or state law *require* the use of initials, or when the specific identity of the minor is not necessary to the action or individual document;

(ii) Financial account numbers: Identify the name or type of account and the financial institution where maintained, but use only the last four numbers of the account number;

(iii) Social Security numbers: Use only the last four numbers;

(iv) Dates of birth: Use only the year;

(v) Home addresses in criminal actions only; use only the city and state; and

(vi) All other circumstances: Redact when federal law *requires* redaction.

(b) Order Required for Other Redactions. No other redactions are permitted unless the Court has authorized the redaction. Counsel has the responsibility to be cognizant of federal privacy law and, when appropriate, state privacy law. Moreover, counsel should recognize proprietary or trade secret information that is protected from dissemination by law. When counsel seeks to submit protected information, a protective order or order authorizing redaction should be sought. A party that makes a redacted filing may also file an unredacted copy under seal if the Court so orders. The unredacted copy will be retained by the Court under seal as part of the record.

(c) Reference List for Redacted Documents. If the Court so orders, a filing that contains redacted information may be filed together with a reference list that identifies each item of redacted information and specifies an appropriate identifier that uniquely corresponds to each item of redacted information listed. The reference list must be filed under seal and may be amended as of right. All references in the action to the identifiers included in the reference list will be construed to refer to the corresponding items of information.

(d) Submission of Unredacted Documents. Pursuant to the terms of a protective order or applicable law, counsel may seek to submit an unredacted document containing protected information for review by the Court. In such an event, counsel is required to file a motion to file the document under seal. See L.R. 141. If the Court grants the motion, counsel shall then submit the unredacted paper document to the Clerk for review by the Court. The paper document must have a cover page with the caption and number of the action and a prominent designation stating the following: "Document filed under seal."

(e) No Sua Sponte Sealing or Redaction. Neither the Clerk nor the Court will review filed documents for compliance with privacy or other protective law, nor will the Court as a matter of course seal on its own motion documents containing personal data identifiers, or redact documents, whether filed electronically or on paper. No procedure set forth herein will excuse a violation of privacy or other law by counsel or party.

(f) Redaction Exceptions. Filings of administrative transcripts, see L.R. 138(b), need not be redacted to comply with this Rule. Filings of official records of a state court proceeding in an action removed to federal court need not be redacted. In a civil or criminal forfeiture proceeding, financial account numbers that identify the property alleged to be subject to forfeiture need not be redacted. See L.R. 570.

[Effective December 1, 2009.]

RULE 141. SEALING OF DOCUMENTS (Fed. R. Civ. P. 5.2, 26) (Fed. R. Crim. P. 49, 49.1)

(a) Sealing Documents: General Principles. Documents may be sealed only by written order of the Court, upon the showing required by applicable law. To ensure that documents are properly sealed, specific requests to seal must be made even if an existing protective order, statute, or rule requires or permits the sealing of the document. Notice that a request to seal has been made will typically be filed in the publicly available case file. Unless the Court orders otherwise, court orders sealing documents will also be filed in the publicly available case file and will not reveal the sealed information. Access to all documents filed under seal will be restricted to the Court and authorized court personnel.

(b) Requests to Seal. If a party seeks to seal documents, the party shall submit, in the manner prescribed below, a "Notice of Request to Seal Documents," a "Request to Seal Documents," a proposed order, and all documents covered by the request.

Except in pre-indictment criminal investigations in which sealing is sought, the "Notice of Request to Seal Documents" shall be filed electronically, or for non-electronic filers, shall be submitted on paper to the Clerk for filing by hand delivery, by same-day or overnight delivery service provided by a courier, or by U.S. Mail, and shall be served on all parties. The Notice shall describe generally the documents sought to be sealed, the basis for sealing, the manner in which the "Request to Seal Documents," proposed order, and the documents themselves were submitted to the Court, and whether the Request, proposed order, and documents were served on all other parties.

Except in criminal pre-indictment matters, the "Request to Seal Documents," the proposed order, and all documents covered by the Request shall be either (1) e-mailed to the appropriate Judge or Magistrate Judge's proposed orders e-mail box listed on the Court's website, with the e-mail subject line including the case number and the statement: "Request to Seal Documents"; or (2) submitted on paper to the Clerk by hand delivery, by same-day or overnight courier, or by U.S. Mail; the envelope containing the Request, proposed order

and documents shall state in a prominent manner "Request to Seal Documents." If the Request, proposed order, and documents are delivered to the Clerk, the party seeking sealing shall submit a self-addressed, stamped envelope for return of the documents. In either case, the Request, proposed order, and submitted documents shall not be filed at this time.

Except in matters in which it is clearly appropriate not to serve the "Request to Seal Documents," proposed order, and/or documents upon the parties, which would include criminal pre-indictment matters, all Requests, proposed orders, and submitted documents shall be served on all parties on or before the day they are submitted to the Court. See L.R. 135.

The "Request to Seal Documents" shall set forth the statutory or other authority for sealing, the requested duration, the identity, by name or category, of persons to be permitted access to the documents, and all other relevant information. If the Request, proposed order, and/or documents covered by the Request were submitted without service upon one or more other parties, the Request also shall set forth the basis for excluding any party from service. The documents for which sealing is requested shall be paginated consecutively so that they may be identified without reference to their content, and the total number of submitted pages shall be stated in the request.

In pre-indictment criminal investigations, unless otherwise ordered, instead of filing a "Notice of Request to Seal Documents," government counsel shall submit to the Court, with the "Request to Seal Documents," proposed order, and documents proposed for sealing, a second proposed order sanitized of any identifying information, indicating in the caption that attached documents have been approved for filing under seal, with the understanding that the sanitized order will be filed in the publicly available case file.

(c) Oppositions to Sealing Requests. Except in criminal pre-indictment matters, and unless otherwise ordered by the Court, a party may submit an opposition to the "Request to Seal Documents" within three days of the date of service of the "Notice of Request to Seal Documents." The opposition shall be either: (1) e-mailed to the appropriate Judge or Magistrate Judge's proposed orders e-mail box listed on the Court's website, with the e-mail subject line including the case number and statement: "Opposition to Request to Seal Documents"; or (2) submitted on paper to the Clerk by hand delivery, by same-day or overnight courier, in an envelope stating in a prominent manner "Opposition to Request to Seal Documents." The Opposition shall be served on the party or parties requesting sealing and on any other party served with the "Request to Seal Documents." The Opposition shall not be filed at this time.

(d) Orders on Sealing Requests. Unless the Court orders otherwise, following review of a "Request to Seal Documents," the documents sought to be sealed, and any opposition to the Request, the Court will file in the publicly available case file an order granting or denying the Request. The order shall identify the documents for which sealing has been granted or denied by page number without revealing their contents. The Court may file a more detailed ruling under seal. The publicly filed order or the docket shall include a notation that a sealed order has been filed.

(e) Disposition of Documents. Upon issuance of an order on a sealing request and unless the Court has ordered otherwise, the Clerk will file under seal the request, proposed order, and any opposition. Disposition of the documents covered by the request to seal depends on whether the request is denied or granted.

(1) *Denial.* If a Request is denied in full or in part, the Clerk will return to the submitting party the documents for which sealing has been denied.

(2) *Grant.* If a Request is granted in full or in part, the disposition of documents to be sealed depends upon whether the requesting party is authorized to file electronically.

(i) Electronic Filer. If the requesting party is authorized to file electronically, then counsel for the requesting party shall either e-mail to the Clerk, at the e-mail address for sealed documents listed on the Court's website, an electronic copy of the documents covered by the sealing order, in .pdf format as an attachment, or submit to the Clerk by hand-delivery, U.S. mail, or same-day or overnight courier, a CD containing a copy of the documents in .pdf format. If submitted by e-mail, the subject line of the e-mail shall include the case number and the body of the e-mail shall identify the order authorizing the sealing of the attached documents. If submitted by hand, U.S. mail, or courier, the envelope containing the CD shall state in a prominent manner: "Sealed Documents" and shall identify the order authorizing sealing. The Clerk will file the documents under seal and will then return to the submitting party any documents submitted by hand, U.S. mail, or courier and any CD.

(ii) Non–Electronic Filer. If the requesting party is not authorized to file electronically, the Court will transmit to the Clerk the documents to be sealed along with the order authorizing sealing. The Clerk will scan the documents to be sealed and file them under seal. The Clerk will then return the documents to the submitting party.

(f) Unsealing Documents. Upon the motion of any person, or upon the Court's own motion, the Court may, upon a finding of good cause or consistent with applicable law, order documents unsealed. See Fed. R. Civ. P. 5.2, Fed. R. Crim. P. 49.1.

[Effective December 1, 2009. Amended effective June 1, 2010.]

RULE 141.1   ORDERS PROTECTING CONFIDENTIAL INFORMATION
(Fed. R. Civ. P. 26)

(a) Presumption of Public Access; Limits to Protection.

(1) All information provided to the Court in a specific action is presumptively public, but may be sealed in conformance with L.R. 141. Confidential information exchanged through discovery, contained in documents to be filed in an action, or presented at a hearing or trial otherwise may be protected by seeking a protective order as described herein.

(2) A protective order is entered without prejudice to any rulings made in a different lawsuit or dispute, and the determination in an action in this Court does not bind other courts.

(b) Mechanics of Obtaining a Protective Order.

(1) *Non–Trial Civil and Criminal Protective Orders.* Either the person possessing or the party seeking information to be protected may move the Court for a protective order pursuant to L.R. 230, 251, or 430.1 or may submit a proposed stipulated protective order signed by all parties and the person possessing the information in accordance with L.R. 143. See L.R. 302(c)(2). A protective order issued prior to trial does not affect the admission of evidence at trial unless the order specifically so states.

(2) *Protective Order for Civil Trial.* A party seeking a protective order relating to the admission of evidence at trial shall submit a stipulation or request with the party's pretrial statement. A non-party seeking a protective order for trial shall submit a motion at or before the time for filing pretrial statements or promptly following discovery of the need for the order. See L.R. 230, 281, 282.

(3) *Protective Order for Criminal Trial.* Before the trial confirmation hearing in a felony or Class A misdemeanor case, either the person possessing or the party seeking information to be protected may move the Court for a protective order pursuant to L.R. 430.1 or may submit a proposed stipulated protective order signed by all parties and the person possessing the information in accordance with L.R. 143. In any other criminal action, a motion or proposed stipulated protective order shall be filed at least fourteen (14) days prior to trial. See L.R. 450.

(c) Requirements of a Proposed Protective Order. All stipulations and motions seeking the entry of a protective order shall be accompanied by a proposed form of order. Every proposed protective order shall contain the following provisions:

(1) A description of the types of information eligible for protection under the order, with the description provided in general terms sufficient to reveal the nature of the information (e.g., customer list, formula for soda, diary of a troubled child);

(2) A showing of particularized need for protection as to each category of information proposed to be covered by the order; and

(3) A showing as to why the need for protection should be addressed by a court order, as opposed to a private agreement between or among the parties.

(d) Hearing on Civil or Criminal Protective Orders. The Court may order that the person for whose benefit a protective order is sought shall attend a hearing, in camera or in open court, to discuss the necessity for the protective order.

(e) Filing Documents Subject to Protective Order. Documents that are the subject of a protective order may be filed under seal only if a sealing order is first obtained in compliance with L.R. 141.

(f) Closed Actions. Once the Clerk has closed an action, unless otherwise ordered, the Court will not retain jurisdiction over enforcement of the terms of any protective order filed in that action.

[Effective June 1, 2010.]

RULE 142. AFFIDAVITS (Fed. R. Civ. P. 43)

(a) **Requirements.** An affidavit, see L.R. 101, submitted in support of any motion shall

(1) identify the affiant, the party or parties on whose behalf it is submitted, and the motion to which it pertains, see L.R. 133(h);

(2) be served on all other parties and filed with the motion, opposition or reply to which it relates, unless accompanied by an affidavit of counsel purporting to show good cause for the separate filing thereof; and

(3) identify, authenticate, and attach documents and exhibits offered in support of or in opposition to the motion, unless such documents and exhibits are already in the record and specifically referred to in the motion or opposition.

(b) **Affidavits Referencing Depositions.** When deposition testimony is referenced in or appended to an affidavit, the party filing the affidavit shall comply with L.R. 133(j).

[Effective December 1, 2009.]

RULE 143. STIPULATIONS (Fed. R. Civ. P. 83)

(a) **Form.** Except stipulations entered into during the course of a deposition and set forth in the transcript thereof, stipulations shall be

(1) in writing, signed by all attorneys or pro se parties who have appeared in the action and are affected by the stipulation, except as otherwise required by Fed. R. Civ. P. 41(a)(1)(A), and filed;

(2) made in open court and noted by the courtroom deputy clerk upon the minutes or by the court reporter in the notes; or

(3) recited in a pretrial or other court order.

Stipulations not in conformity with these requirements will not be recognized unless necessary to prevent manifest injustice.

(b) **Order.** Stipulations are not effective unless approved by the Court, except as otherwise provided in these Rules or in the Federal Rules of Civil, Criminal, or Appellate Procedure. A proposed order shall be submitted with a written stipulation and may consist of an endorsement on the stipulation of the words, **"IT IS SO ORDERED,"** with spaces designated for the date and signature of the Judge or Magistrate Judge. See L.R. 137.

[Effective December 1, 2009.]

RULE 144. EXTENDING AND SHORTENING TIME (Fed. R. Civ. P. 6)

(a) **Extensions on Stipulation.** Unless the filing date has been set by order of the Court, an initial stipulation extending time for no more than twenty-eight (28) days to respond to a complaint, cross-claim or counterclaim, or to respond to interrogatories, requests for admissions, or requests for production of documents may be filed without approval of the Court if the stipulation is signed on behalf of all parties who have appeared in the action and are affected by the stipulation. All other extensions of time must be approved by the Court. No open extensions of time by stipulation of the parties will be recognized.

(b) **Contents of Application for Extension.** All motions for extensions of time shall set forth the total period of extensions already obtained by the parties as to the particular matters for which the extension is sought.

(c) **Initial Ex Parte Extension.** The Court may, in its discretion, grant an initial extension ex parte upon the affidavit of counsel that a stipulation extending time cannot reasonably be obtained, explaining the reasons why such a stipulation cannot be obtained and the reasons why the extension is necessary. Except for one such initial extension, ex parte applications for extension of time are not ordinarily granted.

(d) **Time for Requesting Extensions.** Counsel shall seek to obtain a necessary extension from the Court or from other counsel or parties in an action as soon as the need for an extension becomes apparent. Requests for Court-approved extensions brought on the required filing date for the pleading or other document are looked upon with disfavor.

(e) **Shortening Time.** Applications to shorten time shall set forth by affidavit of counsel the circumstances claimed to justify the issuance of an order shortening time. Ex parte applications to shorten time will not be granted except upon affidavit of counsel showing a satisfactory explanation for the need for the issuance of such an order and for the failure of counsel to obtain a stipulation for the issuance of such an order from other counsel or parties in the action. Stipulations for the issuance of an order shortening time require the approval of the Judge or Magistrate Judge on whose calendar the matter is to be heard before such stipulations are given effect. Any proposed order shortening time shall include blanks for the Court to designate a time and date for the hearing and for the filing of any response to the motion.

[Effective December 1, 2009.]

RULE 145. APPEALS FROM BANKRUPTCY COURT (Fed. R. Civ. P. 83)

(a) **Motion for Leave to Appeal from Bankruptcy Court.** All motions for leave to file an interlocutory appeal from the Bankruptcy Court to the District Court shall comply with Bankruptcy Rule 8003(a) and be addressed to the District Court. Compliance with Rule 8003(a)(3) requires a concise statement of (1) why the appeal is meritorious, and (2) why interlocutory review is appropriate. The appropriateness of interlocutory appeal should address: (a) whether further proceedings in the Bankruptcy Court will affect the scope of the order to be reviewed; (b) whether the order determines and seriously affects substantive rights; and (c) whether the denial of immediate review will cause irreparable harm to appellant.

(b) **Determination of Reviewability.** If a notice of appeal is filed from a judgment, order or decree of the Bankruptcy Court without a motion for leave to appeal, the District Court may partially remand the matter to the Bankruptcy Court for a recommendation concerning the finality of the subject judgment, order or decree. If the Bankruptcy Court advises the District Court that the subject judgment, order or decree is not final but interlocutory, the Bankruptcy Court shall make a recommendation to the District Court whether leave to appeal should be granted. In aid of the Bankruptcy Court's determination on such recommendations, the Bankruptcy Court may order the parties to the appeal to file briefs in support of finality or leave.

[Effective December 1, 2009.]

RULE 146.　APPEALS TO THE NINTH CIRCUIT (Fed. R. Civ. P. 83)

Electronic filers shall file a Notice of Appeal electronically. It is not necessary to provide the Court with paper copies of the notice for service on the other parties. The electronic notice generated by the system will constitute the copy the Clerk is required to serve under Fed. R. App. P. 3(d). Conventional filing and service shall be made upon, and by, pro se parties unless authorized by the Court to file electronically.

[Effective December 1, 2009.]

RULE 150.　DEPOSITS OF REGISTRY FUNDS (Fed. R. Civ. P. 67)

(a) Deposits. Specific leave of court is required before making a deposit into the registry of the Court. Leave of court may be requested by stipulation of all parties who have appeared or by motion set on the regular calendar of the assigned Magistrate Judge not less than seven (7) days from the date of filing and service. A copy of a proposed order shall be delivered promptly to the Court's financial unit for inspection pursuant to (d). See L.R. 302(c)(6).

(b) Placement of Deposit. In any instance in which money is deposited into the registry of the Court, the deposit shall be placed in an interest-bearing account at such financial institutions as the Court may, by General Order, have designated as qualifying for the making of such deposits of registry funds. All matters relating to the creation and administration of such account or accounts shall be governed by General Order.

(c) Placement of Interpleader Deposit. Interpleader funds deposited under 28 U.S.C. § 1335 meet the IRS definition of a "Disputed Ownership Fund" (DOF), a taxable entity that requires tax administration. Unless otherwise ordered by the Court, interpleader funds shall be deposited in the DOF established at such financial institution as the Court may, by General Order, have designated as qualifying for the making of such deposits and shall be deposited into one account. All matters relating to the creation and administration of such DOF account or accounts shall be governed by General Order.

(d) Order for Deposit or Disbursement—Interest–Bearing Account. Whenever a party seeks a court order for money to be deposited in, or disbursed from, an interest-bearing account, the party shall email a copy of the proposed order to the Court's financial unit, at financial@caed.uscourts.gov, which will inspect the proposed order for proper form and content and compliance with the Rule before signature by the Court.

(e) Order for Disbursement of Registry Funds. At such time as registry funds are to be disbursed, an order directing the Clerk, which must be clearly entitled "Order to Disburse Funds," shall be presented to the presiding judge before whom the action is pending for approval and signature. The order must indicate which parties are entitled to principal and any accrued interest. It must also contain the name and mailing address of the party entitled to said funds, unless forbidden elsewhere in this Court's local rules, in which case the information may be redacted and/or provided directly to the Court's financial office. Funds will only be disbursed after the time for appeal has expired, or upon written stipulation by all parties approved by the court. A copy of the proposed disbursement order shall be delivered promptly to the Court's financial unit for inspection pursuant to (d).

(f) Registry Fund Fees. All funds invested in the court's registry will be assessed a registry fee. All matters relating to fees and taxes shall be governed by General Order.

[Effective December 1, 2009. Amended effective April 1, 2017.]

RULE 151.　SECURITY (Fed. R. Civ. P. 65.1)

(a) Scope of Rule. Whenever a security, bond, or undertaking is required by federal statute, the Federal Rules of Civil, Criminal or Appellate Procedure, or by order of the Court, and the form or amount thereof is not otherwise specified by statute, rule, or order, the amount and form shall be as provided by this Rule. See 18 U.S.C. § 3141 et seq., 31 U.S.C. § 9301 et seq.; Fed. R. App. P. 7, 8; Fed. R. Civ. P. 65, 65.1; Fed. R. Crim. P. 46.

(b) Security for Costs. On its own motion or on motion of a party, the Court may at any time order a party to give a security, bond, or undertaking in such amount as the Court may determine to be appropriate. The provisions of Title 3A, part 2, of the California Code of Civil Procedure, relating to vexatious litigants, are hereby adopted as a procedural Rule of this Court on the basis of which the Court may order the giving of a security, bond, or undertaking, although the power of the Court shall not be limited thereby.

(c) Bond for Writ of Attachment. See Cal. Civ. Proc. Code § 481.010 et seq.

(d) Supersedeas Bond. When required, a supersedeas bond shall be 125 percent of the amount of the judgment unless the Court otherwise orders. See Fed. R. Civ. P. 62.

(e) Form of Bond. A security, bond, or undertaking shall be given, signed and acknowledged by the party offering it and by that party's surety. Every security, bond, undertaking, or deposit instrument shall state the conditions of the obligation and shall contain a provision expressly subjecting it to all applicable federal law.

(f) Corporate Surety. No security, bond, or undertaking with corporate surety shall be accepted unless the corporate surety is in compliance with the provisions of 31 U.S.C. §§ 9304–06, and there is, either attached to the face of the security, bond, or undertaking or on file with the Clerk, a duly authenticated power of attorney appointing the agents or officers executing such obligation to act on behalf of the corporate surety.

(g) Personal Surety. No security, bond, or undertaking with personal surety in a civil matter shall be accepted unless it is accompanied by affidavits in the form prescribed by sections 995.510 and 995.520 of the California Code of Civil Procedure. No Clerk, Marshal or deputy marshal, member of the Bar, or other officer or employee of the Court will be accepted as surety in this Court, absent express Court approval. The Court may, in its discretion, require that more than one personal surety be obligated on the security, bond, or undertaking.

(h) Cash, Negotiable Bonds of the United States. In lieu of corporate or personal surety, a party may deposit with the Clerk the required amount of lawful money or negotiable bonds of the United States accompanied by a written instrument, to be approved by the Court, executed and acknowledged by the party, setting forth the conditions upon which the deposit is made, and the fact that the Clerk may collect or sell the obligations and apply the proceeds, or the cash deposited, in the case of default as provided in the bond. Where the true owner is other than the party making the deposit, the instrument shall so state and shall be executed and acknowledged by the true owner. Upon exoneration of the deposit, it shall be returned by the Clerk to the depositor or, if the depositor is other than the true owner, then to the true owner.

(i) Personal and Real Property Bonds. If personal property is provided as security, it shall be accompanied by a security agreement and a financing statement, executed in conformity with the California Commercial Code. If real property is provided as security, a trust deed naming the Clerk as beneficiary and describing the property shall be deposited with the Clerk.

(j) Required Affidavit of Ownership. Any deposit of money or documents evidencing ownership of property shall be accompanied by an affidavit (accompanied by preliminary title report, litigation guarantee, or abstract from a title company, in the case of real property) that the property is unencumbered, or if encumbered, is encumbered in an amount specified, and that the property is of a specified value (assessed value, in the case of real property). See 31 U.S.C. § 9303; L.R. 150.

(k) Submission to Jurisdiction—Agent for Service of Process. Notwithstanding any provision of a security agreement to the contrary, all sureties or depositors of security subject themselves to the jurisdiction of this Court, irrevocably appoint the Clerk as their agent on whom any papers affecting their liability may be served, and consent that their liability shall be joint and several, that judgment may be entered against them in accordance with this obligation simultaneously with judgment against their principals, and that execution may therefore issue against their property. Notwithstanding appointment of the Clerk as agent for service of process, any person seeking judgment against any surety or depositor shall make a good faith effort to give actual notice to the surety or depositor of all actions or motions by which judgment is sought against the surety or depositor.

(*l*) Further Security or Justification of Personal Sureties. Upon reasonable notice to the party presenting the security, any other party for whose benefit it is presented may apply to the Court at any time for further or different security or for an order requiring personal sureties to establish the facts supporting their affidavits under sections 995.510 and 995.520 of the California Code of Civil Procedure.
[Effective December 1, 2009.]

RULE 159. NOTICE OF FILING OF BANKRUPTCY (Fed. R. Civ. P. 16)

When a party files a bankruptcy petition, or an involuntary proceeding is commenced against a party, the party shall file a "Notice of Bankruptcy Proceeding" in the action within seven (7) days after the filing of the petition. The Notice must identify the filing party, the date of the filing, the bankruptcy case number, the court where the filing occurred, and set forth the party's position regarding whether the action is subject to the automatic stay of 11 U.S.C. § 362. If the filing party has not filed the required Notice and another party learns of the bankruptcy filing, that party must file the Notice within seven (7) days of learning of the bankruptcy filing.
[Effective October 1, 2013.]

RULE 160. NOTICE OF SETTLEMENT OR OTHER DISPOSITION (Fed. R. Civ. P. 16)

(a) Notice. When an action has been settled or otherwise resolved by agreement of the parties, or when any motion seeking general or interim relief has been resolved by agreement outside of Court, and whether the action is pending in the District Court or is before an appellate court, it is the duty of counsel to immediately file a notice of settlement or resolution. See L.R. 272.

(b) Dispositional Documents. Upon such notification of disposition or resolution of an action or motion, the Court shall fix a date upon which the documents disposing of the action or motion must be filed, which date shall not be more than twenty-one (21) days from the date of said notification, absent good cause. The Court may, on good cause shown, extend the time for filing the dispositional papers. A failure to file dispositional papers on the date prescribed by the Court may be grounds for sanctions. See L.R. 272.
[Effective December 1, 2009. Amended effective September 20, 2012.]

RULE 161. GRAND AND PETIT TRIAL JURORS (Fed. R. Civ. P. 47)

The Plan for the Random Selection of Grand and Petit Trial Jurors, approved by this Court and the reviewing panel pursuant to the Jury Selection and Service Act of 1968 (Public Law 90–274) and filed in the Office of the Clerk governs the management of the jury selection process.
[Effective December 1, 2009.]

RULE 162.1 EXAMINATION AND CHALLENGES OF TRIAL JURY—CIVIL AND CRIMINAL (Fed. R. Civ. P. 47)

(a) Examination of Jurors. Examination of prospective jurors shall be by the Court subject to supplementation by counsel as provided by Fed. R. Civ. P. 47 and Fed. R. Crim. P. 24. Not less than seven (7) days before commencement of the trial, unless otherwise ordered, counsel shall file, and serve any requested questions for voir dire examination touching upon unique or unusual aspects of the action. These requests may be reasonably supplemented by oral requests during voir dire examination to remedy omissions, to clarify, or to pursue lines of inquiry suggested by answers.

(b) Procedure. Counsel shall consult with the courtroom deputy clerk of the assigned Judge or Magistrate Judge for procedures utilized by that Judge in the selection of a jury and in the exercise of peremptory challenges. See 28 U.S.C. § 1870; Fed. R. Civ. P. 47(b).

[Effective December 1, 2009.]

RULE 162.2 IMPANELMENT OF TRIAL JURY— CIVIL AND CRIMINAL (Fed. R. Civ. P. 48)

(a) Number of Jurors. Whenever a jury is demanded in civil actions, trial of the action shall be before a jury consisting of no fewer than six and no more than twelve members. See Fed. R. Civ. P. 48. Unless waived by the defendant in writing and in the presence of the Court, all criminal trials shall be before a jury consisting of twelve members, plus such alternates as may be impaneled.

(b) Procedure. Counsel shall consult with the courtroom deputy clerk of the assigned Judge or Magistrate Judge for procedures utilized by that Judge in the impanelment of a jury.

[Effective December 1, 2009.]

RULE 163. JURY INSTRUCTIONS AND VERDICTS—CIVIL AND CRIMINAL ACTIONS (Fed. R. Civ. P. 51)

(a) Filing. Unless the Court otherwise orders or permits, requested jury instructions in all actions shall be filed and copies served on all parties at the opening of the trial. Instructions thereafter presented may be deemed not to have been properly requested unless (1) the necessity for the request arose in the course of trial and could not reasonably have been anticipated before trial from the pleadings, discovery or nature of the action and (2) the request is presented as promptly as possible. See Fed. R. Civ. P. 51; Fed. R. Crim. P. 30.

(b) Form and Number.

(1) *Electronic Filers.* Two copies of the instructions shall be submitted. One copy shall be electronically filed as a .pdf document and shall contain each instruction on a separate page, numbered and identified as to the party presenting it. Each instruction shall cite the decision, statute, ordinance, regulation, or other authority supporting the proposition stated in the instruction. The second copy (jury copy) shall comply with (b)(4) and shall be submitted by e-mail to the appropriate e-mail address as listed on the Court's website in Word format. See L.R. 137(b).

(2) *Conventional Filers.* Two (2) copies of the instructions shall be filed on 8–1/2″ × 11″ paper. The first copy shall

contain each instruction on a separate page, numbered and identified as to the party presenting it. Each instruction shall cite the decision, statute, ordinance, regulation, or other authority supporting the proposition stated in the instruction. The second copy (jury copy) shall comply with (b)(4).

(3) *Cover Sheet.* The cover sheet on each set of instructions shall contain the appropriate caption (title, Court and cause) and an identification of the party presenting the instructions.

(4) *Jury Copies.* As the jury copy may be duplicated and given to the jury, the individual instructions shall be unnumbered and unidentified as to the party presenting them and shall contain no citation to the authority supporting the proposition stated in the instruction.

(c) Content. Each requested instruction shall be (as far as possible) free of legal jargon, understandable, concise, impartial, and free from argument. All requested instructions on a single subject shall be grouped together when submitted to the Court. All instructions intended as alternates shall be so designated.

(d) Standard Instructions. When the instructions are derived from the Ninth Circuit Pattern Jury Instructions, California Jury Instructions—Civil (CACI), California Jury Instructions—Civil (BAJI), California Jury Instructions— Criminal (CALJIC) or Federal Jury Practice and Instructions (Civil and Criminal), or other source of standard instructions, the source shall be from the latest edition provided. If a standard instruction is altered by omissions, additions, or modifications by counsel (other than substitution of the parties' names for "plaintiff" and "defendant"), the modification shall be specifically noted and explained on the file copy.

(e) Verdict and Special Interrogatories. The jury instructions shall be accompanied by a form or forms of verdict. Requests for special verdicts or interrogatories to be answered in connection with a general verdict shall also accompany the instructions.

(f) Conference—Objections. The Court will set a time for a conference with counsel for the purpose of settling instructions. Unless the Court orders otherwise, counsel shall be prepared at that time to object to any instructions and to support any objection with citation to authority. Upon the settling of the instructions, and before counsel's final argument to the jury, the Court will hold a hearing on the record and outside the presence of the jury for the purpose of permitting counsel to voice any objections concerning the instructions.

[Effective December 1, 2009. Amended effective October 1, 2013.]

RULE 170. COURT REPORTERS AND COURT RECORDERS (Fed. R. Civ. P. 80)

Official reporting in the Eastern District of California is governed by 28 U.S.C. § 753 and by such fee schedules and regulations promulgated by the Administrative Office of the United States Courts, General Orders, or other regulations as may from time to time be filed with the Clerk. Copies of such documents may be obtained from the Clerk. Each reporter shall be responsible for maintaining all records of reported proceedings before the Judge or Magistrate Judge to whom the reporter is assigned. When court proceedings are recorded, the official court recorder shall be responsible for maintaining the recordings.

[Effective December 1, 2009.]

RULE 171. PUBLICATION (Fed. R. Civ. P. 83)

There is no official newspaper for the Eastern District of California. In each instance in which publication of any document, notice, or other matter is required or permitted, the Court shall designate by order the appropriate newspaper or other vehicle for publication. In seeking such designation, counsel shall file a motion proposing the place and manner of publication, setting forth such information as the language to be published, the frequency of publication, the reasons underlying selection of the proposed vehicle of publication, and all other relevant matters.

[Effective December 1, 2009.]

RULE 173. PHOTOGRAPHING, RECORDING OR BROADCASTING OF JUDICIAL PROCEEDINGS (Fed. R. Civ. P. 83)

(a) **Prohibitions Imposed.** All forms, means, and manner of taking photographs, tape recordings, broadcasting, or televising are prohibited in all courtrooms and the corridors adjacent thereto in the United States Courthouse Buildings during the course of, or in connection with, any judicial proceedings, whether the Court is actually in session or not.

(b) **Permissible Reproduction.** This Rule shall not prohibit recordings by a court reporter; provided, however, no court reporter or other person shall use or permit to be used any part of any recording of a court proceeding on, or in connection with, any radio or television broadcast of any kind. The Court may, in appropriate circumstances, permit photographs to be taken or recordings to be made under such conditions as may be imposed.

[Effective December 1, 2009.]

RULE 180. ATTORNEYS (Fed. R. Civ. P. 83)

(a) **Admission to the Bar of This Court.** Admission to and continuing membership in the Bar of this Court are limited to attorneys who are active members in good standing of the State Bar of California.

(1) *Petition for Admission.* Each applicant for admission shall present to the Clerk an affidavit petitioning for admission, stating both residence and office addresses, the courts in which the applicant has been admitted to practice, the respective dates of admissions to those courts, whether the applicant is active and in good standing in each, and whether the applicant has been or is being subjected to any disciplinary proceedings. Forms will be furnished by the Clerk and shall be available on the Court's website.

(2) *Proof of Bar Membership.* The petition shall be accompanied by a certificate of standing from the State Bar of California or a printout from the State Bar of California website that provides that the applicant is an active member of the State Bar of California and shall include the State Bar number.

(3) *Oath and Prescribed Fee.* Upon qualification the applicant may be admitted, upon oral motion or without appearing, by signing the prescribed oath and paying the prescribed fee, together with any required assessment, which the Clerk shall place as directed by law with any excess credited to the Court's Nonappropriated Fund.

(b) **Practice in This Court.** Except as otherwise provided herein, only members of the Bar of this Court shall practice in this Court.

(1) *Attorneys for the United States.* An attorney who is not eligible for admission under (a), but who is a member in good standing of and eligible to practice before, the Bar of any United States Court or of the highest Court of any State, or of any Territory or Insular Possession of the United States, may practice in this Court in any matter in which the attorney is employed or retained by the United States or its agencies. Attorneys so permitted to practice in this Court are subject to the jurisdiction of this Court with respect to their conduct to the same extent as members of the Bar of this Court.

(2) *Attorneys Pro Hac Vice.* An attorney who is a member in good standing of, and eligible to practice before, the Bar of any United States Court or of the highest Court of any State, or of any Territory or Insular Possession of the United States, and who has been retained to appear in this Court may, upon application and in the discretion of the Court, be permitted to appear and participate in a particular case. Unless authorized by the Constitution of the United States or an Act of Congress, an attorney is not eligible to practice pursuant to (b)(2) if any one or more of the following apply: (i) the attorney resides in California, (ii) the attorney is regularly employed in California, or (iii) the attorney is regularly engaged in professional activities in California.

(i) **Application.** The pro hac vice application shall be electronically presented to the Clerk and shall state under penalty of perjury (i) the attorney's residence and office addresses, (ii) by what courts the attorney has been admitted to practice and the dates of admissions, (iii) a certificate of good standing from the court in the attorney's state of primary practice, (iv) that the attorney is not currently suspended or disbarred in any court, and (v) if the attorney has concurrently or within the year preceding the current application made any other pro hac vice applications to this Court, the title and number of each action in which such application was made, the date of each application, and whether each application was granted.

(ii) **Designee.** The attorney shall also designate in the application a member of the Bar of this Court with whom the Court and opposing counsel may readily communicate regarding that attorney's conduct of the action and upon whom service shall be made. The attorney shall submit with such application the name, address, telephone number, and consent of such designee.

(iii) **Prescribed Fee.** The pro hac vice application shall also be accompanied by payment to the Clerk of any prescribed fee, together with any required assessment which the Clerk shall place as directed by law with any excess credited to the Court's Nonappropriated Fund. If the pro hac vice application is denied, the Court may refund any or all of the fee or assessment paid by the attorney.

(iv) Subject to Jurisdiction. If the application is granted, the attorney is subject to the jurisdiction of the Court with respect to conduct to the same extent as a member of the Bar of this Court.

(3) *Certified Students.* See L.R. 181.

(4) *Designated Officers, Agents or Employees.*

(A) An officer, agent or employee of a federal agency or department may practice before the Magistrate Judges on criminal matters in this Court, whether or not that officer, agent, or employee is an attorney, if that officer, agent or employee:

(i) has been assigned by the employing federal agency or department to appear as a prosecutor on its behalf;

(ii) has received four or more hours training from the United States Attorney's Office in the preceding twenty-four (24) months;

(iii) has filed a designation in accordance with (B); and

(iv) is supervised by the United States Attorney's Office. Supervision by the United States Attorney's Office means that employees of that Office are available to answer questions of any such officer, agent, or employee.

(B) Designations shall be filed on a form provided by the Clerk that shall include a verification that the officer, agent, or employee has satisfied the requirements of this Rule. A designation is effective for twenty-four (24) months. The officer, agent, or employee shall file the designation either in Fresno, if the officer, agent, or employee anticipates appearing only before Magistrate Judges at locations in the counties specifically enumerated in L.R. 120(b), or in Sacramento in all other circumstances. After filing the designation in any calendar year, the officer, agent, or employee shall not appear before any particular Magistrate Judge without providing a copy of the designation to that Magistrate Judge.

(C) Officers, agents and employees so permitted to practice in this Court are subject to the jurisdiction of this Court with respect to their conduct to the same extent as members of the Bar of this Court.

(5) *RIHC and RLSA Attorneys.* An attorney who is currently designated by the State Bar of California as Registered In–House Counsel (RIHC) or as a Registered Legal Services Attorney (RLSA) may petition the Court to practice by completing the petition for admission, supplying the proof of bar membership, and providing the oath and prescribed fee under (a). Any attorney allowed to practice in the Eastern District of California under this section may only practice as long as the attorney is designated as an RIHC or RLSA by the State Bar of California.

(c) Notice of Change in Status. An attorney who is a member of the Bar of this Court or who has been permitted to practice in this Court under (b) shall promptly notify the Court of any change in status in any other jurisdiction that would make the attorney ineligible for membership in the Bar of this Court or ineligible to practice in this Court. In the event an attorney appearing in this Court under (b) is no longer eligible to practice in any other jurisdiction by reason of suspension for nonpayment of fees or enrollment as an inactive member, the attorney shall forthwith be suspended from practice before this Court without any order of Court until becoming eligible to practice in another jurisdiction.

(d) Penalty for Unauthorized Practice. The Court may order any person who practices before it in violation of this Rule to pay an appropriate penalty that the Clerk shall credit to the Court's Nonappropriated Fund. Payment of such sum shall be an additional condition of admission or reinstatement to the Bar of this Court or to practice in this Court.

(e) Standards of Professional Conduct. Every member of the Bar of this Court, and any attorney permitted to practice in this Court under (b), shall become familiar with and comply with the standards of professional conduct required of members of the State Bar of California and contained in the State Bar Act, the Rules of Professional Conduct of the State Bar of California, and court decisions applicable thereto, which are hereby adopted as standards of professional conduct in this Court. In the absence of an applicable standard therein, the Model Rules of Professional Conduct of the American Bar Association may be considered guidance. No attorney admitted to practice before this Court shall engage in any conduct that degrades or impugns the integrity of the Court or in any manner interferes with the administration of justice.

(f) Attorney Registration for Electronic Filing. All attorneys who wish to file documents in the Eastern District of California must be admitted to practice or admitted to appear pro hac vice. They must also complete an e-filing registration as prescribed in L.R. 135.

[Effective December 1, 2009. Amended effective January 1, 2015; February 1, 2019.]

RULE 181. CERTIFIED STUDENTS
(Fed. R. Civ. P. 83)

(a) Definitions.

(1) "Certified Student" means a law student who has been certified by the Clerk pursuant to this Rule.

(2) "Dean" means the Dean or the Dean's specially designated representative at the law school in which the student is enrolled or from which the student has graduated.

(3) "Supervising Attorney" means an attorney admitted to the Bar of this Court who satisfies the requirements of (e).

(4) "Accredited law school" means a law school accredited by the State Bar of California or the American Bar Association. Upon application and a showing of good cause therefor, the Chief Judge shall have sole discretion to determine that a student from a law school not qualifying under the foregoing accreditation requirement may be a Certified Student under this Rule.

(b) Eligibility for Certification. To engage in the activities permitted under this Rule, a Certified Student must:

(1) either have successfully completed one year of full-time studies at an accredited law school or have passed the First Year Law Student's Examination;

(2) be currently enrolled in an accredited law school in good academic standing, subject to the normal hiatus between quarters or semesters, or have graduated from an accredited law school but subject to the limitations of (g)(4);

(3) either have successfully completed or be currently enrolled in academic courses that provide training in both evidence and civil procedure, unless otherwise specifically ordered by the Chief Judge upon application on good cause shown;

(4) have submitted an Application for Certification to the Clerk; and

(5) have received a Notice of Certification from the Clerk.

(c) Application for Certification. Law students shall apply for certification on a form to be furnished by and filed with the Clerk accompanied by the prescribed filing fee. Applications for Certification shall provide for signatures and attestations as follows:

(1) Law students shall attest that—

(A) they have read, are familiar with, and will abide by the Rules of Professional Conduct of the State Bar of California and these Rules;

(B) they meet all the requirements of (b)(1), (2), and (3), or anticipate satisfaction of those requirements in the normal course of events; and

(C) they shall immediately notify the Clerk upon failing to meet the requirements of (b)(1) or upon ceasing to meet the requirements of (b)(2).

(2) Deans shall attest that—

(A) they are the Deans or have been specifically designated by the Dean to administer the law school's practical training program;

(B) the named law students meet the requirements of (b)(1), (2) and (3) or satisfaction of those requirements is anticipated in the normal course of events; and

(C) they have no knowledge of facts or information that might disqualify the law students from participation in the activities permitted by this Rule.

(3) Supervising Attorneys shall specify the period during which they will be responsible for and will supervise the law student and shall attest that each Supervising Attorney—

(A) meets the requirements of (e)(1), and

(B) has read, is familiar with, and will abide by and will assume full responsibility under the requirements of (e)(2) through (8).

(d) Permitted Activities.

(1) A Certified Student may engage in the activities permitted hereunder only if the client on whose behalf the student is to act has approved in writing on a Consent Form available from the Clerk the performance of such acts by such Certified Student. The term "client" shall mean the individual client, the corporate officer or other similar individual authorized to act on behalf of a nongovernmental entity, or the government attorney or other appropriate legal officer authorized to act on behalf of a government agency, as the case may be.

(2) Except as permitted in (d)(3), a Certified Student may engage in the following activities on behalf of a nongovernmental client only with the approval and under the direct and immediate supervision and in the personal presence of the Supervising Attorney or the Supervising Attorney's designee:

(A) appearing at or taking depositions on behalf of the client; and

(B) appearing on behalf of the client in any trial, hearing, or other proceeding before any Judge, Magistrate Judge, or special master of the United States District Court for the Eastern District of California, but only to the extent approved by such Judge, Magistrate Judge, or special master.

(3) A Certified Student may appear in any action on behalf of a government agency or on behalf of the Office of the Federal Defender in the prosecution or defense of misdemeanors, but only subject to approval by the Judge or Magistrate Judge presiding at the hearing or trial in such action, without the personal appearance of the Supervising Attorney, but only if the Supervising Attorney or the Supervising Attorney's designee shall be available by telephone or otherwise to advise the Certified Student.

(4) A Certified Student may engage in the following acts on behalf of a government agency as a representative of that agency without the personal appearance of the Supervising Attorney, but only if the Supervising Attorney or the Supervising Attorney's designee is available by telephone or otherwise to advise the Certified Student:

(A) appearing at or taking depositions on behalf of the agency;

(B) appearing on behalf of the agency in any noncriminal trial hearing, or other proceeding, before any Judge, Magistrate Judge, or special master of the United States District Court for the Eastern District of California, but only to the extent approved by such Judge, Magistrate Judge, or special master;

(C) appearing in any proceeding in actions brought under Title 42 of the United States Code to review a final decision of the Commissioner of Social Security;

(D) appearing in any proceeding in actions brought to enforce Internal Revenue Service summonses filed pursuant to 26 U.S.C. §§ 7402(b) and 7604(a), and/or actions to quash administrative summonses filed pursuant to 26 U.S.C. § 7609(b)(2);

(E) appearing in any proceeding in actions to enforce collection on promissory notes involving federally insured loans and direct federal loans in which the prayer for relief is less than $25,000;

(F) appearing in any proceeding in actions to enforce cease and desist orders issued by the National Labor Relations Board;

(G) appearing in any proceeding in actions to enforce civil penalties assessed under 46 U.S.C. §§ 2302, 4311(d), and/or 12309(c); and

(H) appearing in any proceeding in petitions for writs, or actions seeking relief under the Federal Civil Rights Act by incarcerated persons acting in propria persona.

(5) In all instances in which, under these Rules, a Certified Student is permitted to appear in any trial, hearing, or other proceeding before any Judge, Magistrate Judge, or special master of the United States District Court for the Eastern District of California, the Certified Student shall, as a condition to such appearance, cause the filing of the Consent Form or present the Consent Form for filing to the Judge, Magistrate Judge, or special master.

(6) Certified Students whose Supervising Attorneys are not governmental attorneys or attorneys acting full-time on behalf of the Office of the Federal Defender shall satisfy not only the requirements of this Rule, but also the requirements imposed by the State Bar of California Rules Governing the Practical Training of Law Students, as those Rules may be amended from time to time.

(7) Nothing in this Rule shall prevent a student, certified or uncertified, from performing any advisory or representational activity that a person who is not admitted to practice before the United States District Court for the Eastern District of California could lawfully perform.

(e) Supervising Attorney. The Supervising Attorney shall:

(1) be admitted to practice before the United States District Court for the Eastern District of California;

(2) supervise no more than twelve (12) Certified Students concurrently, provided, however, that this limitation on supervision may be modified by the Chief Judge upon application and showing of good cause therefor;

(3) assume personal professional responsibility for any work performed by the Certified Student while under the attorney's supervision;

(4) assist and counsel with the Certified Student in the activities permitted under this Rule and review such activities with the Certified Student;

(5) read, approve, and sign any pleadings, briefs or other papers prepared by the Certified Student before the filing thereof, provided, however, that this requirement shall not apply to (i) amendments to accusatory pleadings; (ii) papers other than pleadings and briefs filed by a Certified Student whose Supervising Attorney is a member of the United States Attorney's Office; (iii) papers other than pleadings and briefs filed by a Certified Student whose Supervising Attorney is a member of the Federal Defender's Office; or (iv) pleadings and briefs filed in a Magistrate Judge's Court in a county other than Sacramento or Fresno by a Certified Student whose Supervising Attorney is a member of the United States Attorney's Office and whose Supervising Attorney has approved the pleading or brief after hearing it read over the telephone and authorizing the filing thereof;

(6) provide the required supervision of the Certified Student for the activities listed in this Rule;

(7) assign full responsibility for supervision to another designated attorney qualified to serve as a Supervising Attorney under this Rule in any instance in which the Supervising Attorney is to be unavailable; and

(8) notify the Clerk promptly in writing whenever the attorney's supervision of the Certified Student will cease without a written substitution of another qualified Supervising Attorney being filed.

(f) Use of the Designation "Certified Student." A Certified Student may be designated as such on pleadings, briefs, letters on the Supervising Attorney's letterhead, and other documents on which the Certified Student has worked with or under the supervision and direction of the Supervising Attorney, by placing the Certified Student's name thereon with the words "Certified Student" immediately thereunder.

(g) Duration of Certification. Certification shall commence with the issuance by the Clerk of a Notice of Certification and shall remain in effect for the period specified in the Notice of Certification unless sooner terminated by the earliest of the following occurrences, absent relief from such termination granted by the Chief Judge:

(1) the Supervising Attorney terminates supervision of the Certified Student without a written substitution of another qualified Supervising Attorney on a form provided by and filed with the Clerk;

(2) the Certified Student ceases to be enrolled in an accredited law school before graduation therefrom, excepting the normal hiatus between quarters or semesters;

(3) the Dean notifies the Clerk that the Certified Student should be disqualified from participation in the activities permitted by this Rule;

(4) the Certified Student fails to take or is notified of a failure to pass the first California General Bar Examination after the Certified Student's graduation from law school; or

(5) certification is withdrawn by the Chief Judge.

Upon the happening of any of the occurrences listed in (1), (3) or (5), the Clerk shall send Notice of Withdrawal of Certification to the Certified Student, the Supervising Attorney, and the Dean, which Notice shall set forth the reasons for the termination of Certified Student status.

(h) Rights Upon Withdrawal of Certification. If certification is withdrawn under (g)(3) or (5), the termination shall be effective fourteen (14) days from the date on which the Clerk transmits the Notice of Withdrawal of Certification. Upon receipt of such Notice, the Certified Student may present a request for a stay of the termination pending hearing, which the Chief Judge may allow only upon good cause shown. The Certified Student may contest the termination by a request to the Chief Judge, presented within fourteen (14) days of the transmission of the Notice of Withdrawal of Certification, for a hearing to show cause why certification should not be terminated. Hearing on such request shall be commenced within twenty-one (21) days following receipt of such request, unless the time for such hearing be extended by the Chief Judge upon a showing of good cause. The Chief Judge may assign responsibility for the conduct of the proceedings under this subsection to any Judge.

[Effective December 1, 2009.]

RULE 182. ATTORNEYS—APPEARANCE AND WITHDRAWAL (Fed. R. Civ. P. 83)

(a) Appearance as Attorney of Record.

(1) *Appearance Required.* Except as permitted in (b) and except as the Court may allow a courtesy appearance in

criminal actions, no attorney may participate in any action unless the attorney has appeared as an attorney of record. A single client may be represented by more than one attorney of record to the extent authorized by the applicable Rules of Professional Conduct.

(2) *Manner of Making Appearance.* Appearance as an attorney of record is made (i) by signing and filing an initial document, see L.R. 131(a); (ii) by causing the attorney's name to be listed in the upper left hand corner of the first page of the initial document; (iii) by physically appearing at a court hearing in the matter, formally stating the appearance on the record, and then signing and filing a confirmation of appearance within seven (7) days; or (iv) by filing and serving on all parties a substitution of attorneys as provided in (g).

(b) **Attorneys Within Organizations.** Appearances as an attorney of record shall not be made in the name of a law firm, organization, public entity, agency, or department. See Fed. R. Civ. P. 11. When an attorney is employed or retained by a law firm, organization, public entity, agency, or department, however, the attorney may participate in an action, without filing a substitution of attorneys, if another person employed or retained by the same law firm, organization, public entity, agency, or department is attorney of record in the action.

(c) **Counsel for Service.**

(1) *Designation of Counsel for Service.* When multiple attorneys from a single law firm, organization, public entity, agency, or department are listed in the upper left hand corner of the first page of each filed document, see L.R. 131(a), one of the listed attorneys shall be designated as counsel for service. That designation shall be accomplished by so designating in the counsel identification in the upper left hand corner of the first page of the initial document or by filing and serving a document entitled "Designation of Counsel for Service," which will state the name, address, and telephone number of the designated counsel for service and will be signed by that counsel. The Clerk will serve court orders on the designated counsel for service. See L.R. 137(f). The identity of counsel for service in a particular action may be changed by filing and serving on all parties a document entitled "Change in Designation of Counsel for Service" stating the name, address, and telephone number of new and old counsel for service, identifying new counsel for service and bearing the signature of the new counsel for service.

(2) *Service in the Absence of a Designation.* If no designation of counsel for service has been made in a particular instance, the Clerk may select the attorney for service from the listing in the upper left hand corner of the first page of the initial filed document or from the signature block.

(d) **Withdrawal.** Unless otherwise provided herein, an attorney who has appeared may not withdraw leaving the client in propria persona without leave of court upon noticed motion and notice to the client and all other parties who have appeared. The attorney shall provide an affidavit stating the current or last known address or addresses of the client and the efforts made to notify the client of the motion to withdraw. Withdrawal as attorney is governed by the Rules of Profes-

sional Conduct of the State Bar of California, and the attorney shall conform to the requirements of those Rules. The authority and duty of the attorney of record shall continue until relieved by order of the Court issued hereunder. Leave to withdraw may be granted subject to such appropriate conditions as the Court deems fit.

(e) **Withdrawal Following Limited Appearance.** Any attorney who has appeared on behalf of a party in an action solely for the purpose of contesting an application for a temporary restraining order or other preliminary injunctive relief may withdraw from that action within fourteen (14) days after making that appearance, or at such other time as the Court may determine, by filing a notice and affidavit that the attorney is no longer counsel of record for the party. Such application shall establish that the attorney has returned all documents and other items received in connection with the action and shall set forth the last known address and telephone number of the party.

(f) **Change of Address.** Each appearing attorney and pro se party is under a continuing duty to notify the Clerk and all other parties of any change of address or telephone number of the attorney or the pro se party. Absent such notice, service of documents at the prior address of the attorney or pro se party shall be fully effective. Separate notice shall be filed and served on all parties in each action in which an appearance has been made.

(g) **Substitution of Attorneys.** An attorney who has appeared in an action may substitute another attorney and thereby withdraw from the action by submitting a substitution of attorneys that shall set forth the full name and address of the new individual attorney and shall be signed by the withdrawing attorney, the new attorney, and the client. All substitutions of attorneys shall require the approval of the Court, and the words "IT IS SO ORDERED" with spaces designated for the date and signature of the Judge affixed at the end of each substitution of attorneys.

(h) **Local Co–Counsel.** A Judge to whom an action is assigned has discretion in that action, and upon notice, to require an attorney appearing in this Court who maintains an office outside this District to designate a member of the Bar of this Court who does maintain an office within this District as co-counsel with the authority to act as attorney of record for all purposes. In such a case, the attorney shall file with such designation the address, telephone number and consent of the designee.

(i) **Formal Notice of Association of Counsel.** Any attorney not substituted in as counsel of record under (g) and not authorized to participate under other provisions in this Rule must file a notice of association, signed by an attorney of record and the associating attorney, and served on all parties.

[Effective December 1, 2009.]

RULE 183.   PERSONS APPEARING IN PROPRIA PERSONA (Fed. R. Civ. P. 83)

(a) **Rules Governing Appearance.** Any individual who is representing himself or herself without an attorney must appear personally or by courtesy appearance by an attorney admitted to the Bar of this Court and may not delegate that duty to any other individual, including husband or wife, or any other party on the same side appearing without an attorney. Any individual representing himself or herself without an attorney is bound by the Federal Rules of Civil or Criminal Procedure, these Rules, and all other applicable law. All obligations placed on "counsel" by these Rules apply to individuals appearing in propria persona. Failure to comply therewith may be ground for dismissal, judgment by default, or any other sanction appropriate under these Rules. A corporation or other entity may appear only by an attorney.

(b) Address Changes. A party appearing in propria persona shall keep the Court and opposing parties advised as to his or her current address. If mail directed to a plaintiff in propria persona by the Clerk is returned by the U.S. Postal Service, and if such plaintiff fails to notify the Court and opposing parties within sixty-three (63) days thereafter of a current address, the Court may dismiss the action without prejudice for failure to prosecute.

(c) Pro Se Party Exceptions to Electronic Filing. Pro se parties are exempted from the requirement of filing documents electronically. Pro se parties must file documents conventionally, and any person appearing pro se may use electronic filing only with the permission of the assigned Judge. See L.R. 133.

[Effective December 1, 2009.]

RULE 184. DISCIPLINARY PROCEEDINGS AGAINST ATTORNEYS (Fed. R. Civ. P. 83)

(a) Discipline. In the event any attorney subject to these Rules engages in conduct that may warrant discipline or other sanctions, any Judge or Magistrate Judge may initiate proceedings for contempt under 18 U.S.C. § 401 or Fed. R. Crim. P. 42, or may, after reasonable notice and opportunity to show cause to the contrary, take any other appropriate disciplinary action against the attorney. In addition to or in lieu of the foregoing, the Judge or Magistrate Judge may refer the matter to the disciplinary body of any Court before which the attorney has been admitted to practice.

(b) Notice of Change in Status. An attorney who is a member of the Bar of this Court or who has been permitted to practice in this Court shall promptly notify the Court of any disciplinary action or any change in status in any jurisdiction that would make the attorney ineligible for membership in the Bar of this Court or ineligible to practice in this Court. If an attorney's status so changes with respect to eligibility, the attorney shall forthwith be suspended from practice before this Court without any order of Court until becoming eligible to practice. Upon written motion to the Chief Judge, an attorney shall be afforded an opportunity to show cause why the attorney should not be suspended or disbarred from practice in this Court.

(c) Penalty for Unauthorized Practice. The Court may order any person who practices before it in violation of this Rule to pay an appropriate penalty that the Clerk shall credit to the Court's Nonappropriated Fund. Payment of such sum

shall be an additional condition of admission or reinstatement to the Bar of this Court or to practice in this Court.

[Effective December 1, 2009.]

RULE 190. PETITIONS FOR HABEAS CORPUS AND MOTIONS PURSUANT TO 28 U.S.C. §§ 2254 & 2255 (Fed. R. Civ. P. 81)

(a) Scope of This Rule. All petitions for writs of habeas corpus pursuant to 28 U.S.C. § 2254 and motions filed pursuant to 28 U.S.C. § 2255 shall be subject to the provisions of this Rule unless otherwise ordered by the Court.

(b) Form of Petitions and Motions. The petition or motion shall be signed under penalty of perjury, and, if presented in propria persona, upon the form and in accordance with the instructions approved by the Court. Copies of the forms and instructions shall be supplied by the Clerk upon request. In the event a petition or motion is submitted that is not in the proper form, the Clerk shall forthwith transmit the proper form and instructions to the person submitting the petition or making the motion.

(c) Filing. Petitions and motions shall be addressed to the Clerk of the United States District Court for the Eastern District of California, 501 "I" Street, Sacramento, California 95814, or 2500 Tulare Street, Fresno, California 93721, according to L.R. 120(b). No petition or motion shall be addressed to an individual Judge or Magistrate Judge.

(d) Assignment. Petitions and motions shall be assigned by the Clerk pursuant to L.R. 122, provided that motions under 28 U.S.C. § 2255 shall, if possible, be assigned to the sentencing Judge or Magistrate Judge. If, in the same matter in this Court, the petitioner has previously filed a petition for relief or for a stay of enforcement, the new petition shall be assigned to the Judge or Magistrate Judge who considered the prior matter.

(e) Contents.

(1) All petitions by state prisoners shall state with specificity that all issues raised in the petition, either

(A) have been raised before all state tribunals in which the issues could be heard, to the exhaustion of petitioner's state remedies; or

(B) have not been raised before all state tribunals in which the issues could be heard, in which case the petition shall also set forth all facts which justify the failure to exhaust state remedies.

(2) All petitions shall state whether or not petitioner has previously sought relief arising out of the same matter from this Court or any other federal court, together with the ruling and reasons given for denial of relief.

(f) State Court Habeas Transcripts. Due to the size of state court records, the Attorney General should, if possible, file habeas corpus transcripts and other state court records in electronic format along with a mandatory courtesy copy for chambers in paper. If the Attorney General cannot provide an electronic copy, a certified paper copy shall be filed concurrently with electronic filing of a Notice of Filing in Paper Format. These state court records will be returned to the

Attorney General at the conclusion of the action, if no appeal is filed, and after appeal or further proceedings in the district court as appropriate. If the Attorney General and the Clerk agree, the state court records may be discarded by the Clerk.

(g) Where Relief Is Granted. If relief is granted on a petition of a state prisoner, or if any stay of execution of state court judgment is issued by the Court, the Clerk shall forthwith notify the state authority having jurisdiction over the prisoner of the action taken.

[Effective December 1, 2009.]

RULE 191. SPECIAL REQUIREMENTS FOR HABEAS CORPUS PETITIONS INVOLVING THE DEATH PENALTY (Fed. R. Civ. P. 81)

(a) Applicability. This Rule shall govern the procedures for a first petition for a writ of habeas corpus filed pursuant to 28 U.S.C. § 2254 in which a petitioner seeks relief from a judgment imposing the penalty of death. A subsequent filing relating to a particular petition may be deemed a first petition under these Rules if the original filing was not dismissed on the merits. The application of this Rule may be modified by the Judge or Magistrate Judge to whom the petition is assigned. *See* Rule 102(d), supra.

(b) Notices From California Attorney General. The California Attorney General is requested to notify the Chief Judge and Clerk, within seven (7) days, whenever an execution date is set. The Chief Judge, or a designate, will request a semi-annual report from the Attorney General's Office that includes the following categories: (1) all scheduled executions in California; (2) all capital cases pending on direct appeal before the California Supreme Court; (3) all capital cases pending before the California Supreme Court on habeas corpus: (4) all capital cases affirmed by the California Supreme Court on direct appeal since the last report; (5) all capital cases denied by the California Supreme Court on habeas corpus since the last report; and (6) until December 31, 2010, all capital cases affirmed on direct appeal by the California Supreme Court.

(c) Attorney Representation. Each indigent petitioner shall be represented by an attorney unless petitioner has clearly elected to proceed pro se. In the event a petitioner seeks to proceed pro se, the Court will conduct a hearing to determine whether the petitioner's election is appropriate under applicable legal standards. Unless petitioner is represented by a retained attorney, an attorney shall be appointed in every case as soon as possible. A Selection Board appointed by the Chief Judge will certify attorneys qualified for appointment in death penalty cases. The Selection Board consists of a lawyer representative from: (1) The Capital Habeas Unit of the Office of the Federal Defender; (2) the California Appellate Project; (3) the Habeas Corpus Resource Center; (4) the State Public Defender; and (5) a member of the State Bar. If the Selection Board agrees, preference will be given to counsel who represented petitioner on state habeas corpus, except when state habeas counsel also actively represented petitioner on direct appeal. Appointment and compensation of a second attorney shall be governed by Section 2.11 of Volume VII of the Guide to Judiciary Policies and Proce-

dures, Appointment of Counsel in Criminal Cases. Having appointed counsel to represent the petitioner, the Court generally will not consider pro se documents about the presentation of his or her case. However, the Court generally will consider pro se motions concerning petitioner's representation by appointed counsel.

(d) Budgeting and Case Management. The Judicial Council of the Ninth Circuit has mandated up-front budgeting in all pending capital habeas cases in which CJA counsel have been appointed. To assist in the budgeting and case management process, the Judicial Council routinely publishes updates of a CJA Capital Habeas Costs Policy. The Costs Policy is posted on the public internet site for the Eastern District of California, both the Sacramento and Fresno Divisions.

(e) Filing. Petitions shall be filed in accordance with Local Rule 190. All initial filings, whether a petition, request for stay and appointment of counsel, or other document, (1) shall state whether petitioner has previously sought relief arising out of the same matter from this Court or any other federal court, together with the ruling and reasons given for denial of relief; and (2) shall set forth any scheduled execution date. All filings shall contain the wording in full caps and underscored "DEATH PENALTY CASE" directly under the case number. No filing fee is required.

(f) Transfer of Venue. Subject to the provisions of 28 U.S.C. § 2241(d), it is the policy of this Court that a petition should be heard in the District in which petitioner was convicted rather than in the District of petitioner's present confinement. If an order for the transfer of venue is made, the Judge may order a stay of execution to continue until such time as the transferee court acts upon the petition or the order of stay. All actions shall be commenced in accordance with Local Rule 120.

(g) Stays of Execution.

(1) *Temporary Stay for Appointment of an Attorney.* When the attorney in state court proceedings withdraws at the conclusion of the state court proceedings or is otherwise not available or qualified to proceed, an indigent petitioner acting pro se, or a member of the Selection Board acting on petitioner's behalf, may file an application for appointment of an attorney and for a temporary stay of execution. Upon the filing of this application, the Court may, in its discretion, issue a temporary stay of execution and refer the case to the Selection Board for recommendation of counsel. The temporary stay will remain in effect until ninety (90) days after counsel is appointed.

(2) *Stay Pending Final Disposition.* Upon the filing of a habeas corpus petition, unless the petition is patently frivolous, the Court may, in its discretion, issue a stay of execution pending final disposition of the matter. When an execution date is set and a non-frivolous petition is pending, the Court will issue a stay of execution.

(3) *Stay Pending Appeal.* If the petition is denied, the Court will consider an application for a stay of execution to continue in effect until the Court of Appeals has the opportunity to issue a stay.

(h) Procedures for Considering the Petition. Absent summary dismissal of the petition under Rule 4 of the Rules Governing § 2254 cases, the following schedule and procedures shall apply subject to modification by the Court. Requests for enlargement of any time period in this Rule shall comply with the applicable Local Rules of the Court. *See* L.R. 144.

(1) Respondent shall as soon as possible, but in any event on or before forty-five (45) days from the date of service of the order appointing counsel, lodge with the Clerk the following: (A) transcripts of the state trial court proceedings; (B) appellant's and respondent's briefs on direct appeal to the California Supreme Court, and the opinion or orders of that Court; and (C) petitioner's and respondent's briefs in any state court habeas corpus proceedings, and all opinions, orders and transcripts of such proceedings. Lodged materials are to be marked and numbered so that they can be uniformly cited. Respondent shall file an index of the lodged materials listed above. If any items identified in paragraphs (A) through (C) above are not available, respondent shall state when, if at all, such missing material can be filed.

(2) If counsel for petitioner claims that respondent has not complied with paragraph (1), or if counsel for petitioner does not have copies of all the documents identified in the filed index of lodged documents, counsel for petitioner shall file a notice to that effect with the Court. Copies of any missing documents will be provided to counsel for petitioner by the Court.

(3) These state court records will be returned to the respondent when all federal proceedings are complete, or if the respondent and the Court agree, the records will be discarded by the Court.

(4) The petition shall conform to the requirements of Rule 2 of the Rules Governing § 2254 Cases. The answer and any traverse shall conform to the requirements of Rule 5 of the Rules Governing § 2254 Cases.

(5) Formal discovery requires leave of the Court. *See* Rule 6 of the Rules Governing § 2254 Cases. Investigation, or informal discovery between the parties by agreement, does not require leave of the Court.

(6) The Court will order an answer, merits briefing, and briefing of a motion for an evidentiary hearing according to a case management plan developed for each individual case.

(i) Evidentiary Hearing. If an evidentiary hearing is held, the parties may request the preparation of a transcript of the hearing, to be provided to petitioner and respondent for use in briefing and post-hearing argument.

(j) Final Dispositive Orders. Consistent with Rule 11 of the Rules Governing § 2254 Cases, and unless further input is solicited from the parties, the Court will issue or deny a certificate of appealability (COA) when it enters its final order adverse to the petitioner. See 28 U.S.C. § 2253(c)(2). If the petitioner moves for reconsideration of the denial of a COA, the motion does not extend the time within which to appeal.

[Effective December 1, 2009. Amended effective July 1, 2011.]

CIVIL RULES

RULE 200. DESIGNATION OF CATEGORY OF ACTION (Fed. R. Civ. P. 3)

Every complaint, amended complaint, or other document initiating a civil action shall be accompanied by a completed civil cover sheet, on a form available from the Clerk and on the Court's website.

This requirement is solely for administrative purposes, and matters appearing only on the civil cover sheet have no cognizable effect in the action.

[Effective December 1, 2009.]

RULE 201. DEMAND FOR JURY TRIAL (Fed. R. Civ. P. 38)

Where demand is made for a jury trial, it shall appear immediately following the title of the complaint or answer containing the demand, or on such other document as may be permitted by Fed. R. Civ. P. 38(b).

Any notation on the civil cover sheet, as described in L.R. 200, concerning whether a jury trial is or is not demanded, shall not constitute a demand for a jury trial under these Rules.

[Effective December 1, 2009.]

RULE 202. MINORS AND INCOMPETENTS (Fed. R. Civ. P. 17)

(a) Appointment of Representative or Guardian. Upon commencement of an action or upon initial appearance in defense of an action by or on behalf of a minor or incompetent person, the attorney representing the minor or incompetent person shall present (1) appropriate evidence of the appointment of a representative for the minor or incompetent person under state law, or, (2) a motion for the appointment of a guardian ad litem by the Court, or, (3) a showing satisfactory to the Court that no such appointment is necessary to ensure adequate representation of the minor or incompetent person. *See* Fed. R. Civ. P. 17(c).

(b) Settlement. No claim by or against a minor or incompetent person may be settled or compromised absent an order by the Court approving the settlement or compromise.

(1) *Initial State Court Approval.* In actions in which the minor or incompetent is represented by an appointed representative pursuant to appropriate state law, excepting only those actions in which the United States courts have exclusive jurisdiction, the settlement or compromise shall first be approved by the state court having jurisdiction over the personal representative. Following such approval, a copy of the order and all supporting and opposing documents filed in connection therewith shall be filed in the District Court with a copy to all parties and to the Judge or Magistrate Judge who may either approve the settlement or compromise without hearing or calendar the matter for hearing.

(2) *Approval in All Other Actions.* In all other actions, the motion for approval of a proposed settlement or compromise shall be filed and calendared pursuant to L.R. 230. The application shall disclose, among other things, the age and sex of the minor or incompetent, the nature of the causes of action to be settled or compromised, the facts and circumstances out of which the causes of action arose, including the time, place and persons involved, the manner in which the compromise amount or other consideration was determined, including such additional information as may be required to enable the Court to determine the fairness of the settlement or compromise, and, if a personal injury claim, the nature and extent of the injury with sufficient particularity to inform the Court whether the injury is temporary or permanent. If reports of physicians or other similar experts have been prepared, such reports shall be provided to the Court. The Court may also require the filing of experts' reports when none have previously been prepared or additional experts' reports if appropriate under the circumstances. Reports protected by an evidentiary privilege may be submitted in a sealed condition to be reviewed only by the Court *in camera*, with notice of such submission to all parties.

(c) Disclosure of Attorney's Interest. When the minor or incompetent is represented by an attorney, it shall be disclosed to the Court by whom and the terms under which the attorney was employed; whether the attorney became involved in the application at the instance of the party against whom the causes of action are asserted, directly or indirectly; whether the attorney stands in any relationship to that party; and whether the attorney has received or expects to receive any compensation, from whom, and the amount.

(d) Attendance at Hearing. Upon the hearing of the application, the representative compromising the claim on behalf of the minor or incompetent, and the minor or incompetent shall be in attendance unless, for good cause shown, the Court excuses their personal attendance. The Court may require the testimony of any appropriate expert, as well as the submission of other evidence relating to the application.

(e) Payment of Judgment. Whenever money or property is recovered on behalf of a minor or incompetent person, the money or property will be (1) disbursed to the representative pursuant to state law upon a showing that the representative is duly qualified under state law, (2) disbursed otherwise pursuant to state law, or (3) disbursed pursuant to such other order as the Court deems proper for the protection of the minor or incompetent person.

(f) Interim Disbursements. Applications for orders authorizing interim disbursements shall be heard by the appropriate state court judge or by the assigned Magistrate Judge. *See* L.R. 302(c)(14). In the event of a hearing by a state court judge concerning interim disbursements, a copy of the order shall be filed with a copy to the Magistrate Judge and shall be reviewed by the Magistrate Judge in accordance with (b)(1).

[Effective December 1, 2009. Amended effective October 1, 2013.]

RULE 203. NOTICE OF REQUIREMENT OF THREE–JUDGE COURT (Fed. R. Civ. P. 24)

Whenever any action is required by Act of Congress to be heard and determined by a District Court of three Judges, the plaintiff shall immediately file a notice to this effect and serve a copy on all other parties. If the plaintiff fails to do so, every other party shall file and serve such notice provided that, as soon as a notice is filed and served, all other parties are relieved of this obligation. See 28 U.S.C. § 2284 governing the filing of papers in actions heard by a three-judge court.

[Effective December 1, 2009.]

RULE 204. ALLEGATIONS OF JURISDICTION (Fed. R. Civ. P. 8)

When an affirmative allegation of jurisdiction is required pursuant to Fed. R. Civ. P. 8(a)(1), it (i) shall appear as the first allegation of any complaint, petition, counterclaim, cross-claim, or third party claim; (ii) shall be styled "Jurisdiction"; (iii) shall state the claimed statutory or other basis of federal jurisdiction; and (iv) shall state the facts supporting such jurisdictional claim.

[Effective December 1, 2009.]

RULE 205. SPECIAL RULE FOR CLASS ACTIONS (Fed. R. Civ. P. 23)

In any action sought to be maintained as a class action:

(1) Determination. Within such time as the Court may direct pursuant to order issued under Fed. R. Civ. P. 16(d), the plaintiff shall move for a determination under Fed. R. Civ. P. 23 whether the action is to be maintained as a class action. In ruling on the motion, the Court may allow or conditionally allow the action to be so maintained, may disallow and strike the class action allegations, or may order postponement of the determination pending discovery or such other preliminary procedures as appear appropriate and necessary.

(2) Counterclaims or Cross–Claims. The foregoing provisions shall apply, with appropriate adaptations, to any counterclaim or cross-claim alleged to be brought for or against a class.

(3) Notice of Petition for Permissive Appeal Pursuant to F. R. Civ. P. 23(f). When, pursuant to F. R. Civ. P. 23(f), a party files a petition in the Court of Appeals, requesting permission to appeal an order granting or denying class-certification, the party shall file a "Notice of Petition for Permission to Appeal Pursuant to Fed. R. Civ. P. 23(f)" in the district court within seven (7) days. The Notice must identify the filing party, the court of appeals case number, date of the filing, the party's position regarding the effect of the permissive appeal and whether the party will be requesting a stay.

[Effective December 1, 2009. Amended effective October 1, 2013.]

RULE 206. SPECIAL RULE FOR SOCIAL SECURITY AND BLACK LUNG ACTIONS (Fed. R. Civ. P. 8)

(a) Pleadings. Complaints under Titles II, XVI, and XVIII of the Social Security Act, 42 U.S.C. §§ 405(g), 1383(c)(3), and/or 1395ff, or under Part B, Title N, of the Federal Coal Mine Health and Safety Act of 1969, shall contain the following information in addition to the matters otherwise required by the Federal Rules of Civil Procedure and these Rules:

(1) In actions involving claims for retirement, survivors, disability, health insurance and black lung benefits, the last four digits of the social security number of the worker on whose wage record the application for benefits was filed (who may or may not be the plaintiff); or

(2) In actions involving claims for supplemental security income benefits, the last four digits of the social security number of the plaintiff.

Plaintiff shall disclose privately to defendant within seven (7) days after a request for the full social security number of the worker or plaintiff, as the case may be.

(b) Administrative Transcripts in Social Security Actions. See L.R. 138(b).

(c) Privacy Issues in Social Security Actions. Except for court orders and proposed findings and recommendations, Internet access to the individual documents will be limited to attorneys of record, persons authorized by the Court, and court staff. Docket sheets, court orders and proposed findings and recommendations, however, will be available over the Internet to non-parties. Pro se parties and non-parties will continue to have direct access to the documents on file with the Clerk. See L.R. 140(a).

[Effective December 1, 2009.]

RULE 210. SERVICE OF PROCESS AND RETURN OF SERVICE (Fed. R. Civ. P. 4)

(a) Issuance of Summons. Summons may be prepared by counsel for issuance by the Clerk in actions using conventional filing. The Clerk will prepare and transmit the summons electronically to counsel for plaintiffs that are electronic filers.

(b) Proof of Service of Process. If service of process is not waived, proof of service of process shall be made by acknowledgment of the party served or by affidavit of the person serving such process. Such proof of service shall be filed and served on all parties who have been served or who have appeared in the action as of the time of filing the proof of service, as soon as possible after service has been completed and, in any event, before any action based upon the service is requested or taken by the Court or is taken by a party in reliance on proper service. Such proof of service shall show the date, place, and manner of the service. When service is made by personal delivery, it shall show the hour, the particular address or vicinity at which service was made, the name and address of the person served, and the name and address of the person making the service. See Fed. R. Civ. P. 4(l).

(c) Filing of Waiver of Service. If the defendant has waived service of process, the plaintiff shall file the waiver of service as soon as possible after receiving the waiver and, in any event, before any action based upon the waiver of service is requested or taken by the Court or is taken by a party in reliance on proper service or a waiver thereof. See Fed. R. Civ. P. 4(d)(4).

(d) Service of Process Required. Counsel for plaintiff shall effect service of process on the defendant. See Fed. R. Civ. P. 4. Electronic filing does not affect this requirement.

(e) Service of Other Process. See Fed. R. Civ. P. 4.1.

[Effective December 1, 2009.]

RULE 220. CHANGED PLEADINGS (Fed. R. Civ. P. 15)

As used in this Rule, the term "changed pleadings" shall refer to amended and supplemental pleadings permitted and filed pursuant to Fed. R. Civ. P. 15.

Unless prior approval to the contrary is obtained from the Court, every pleading to which an amendment or supplement is permitted as a matter of right or has been allowed by court order shall be retyped and filed so that it is complete in itself without reference to the prior or superseded pleading. No pleading shall be deemed amended or supplemented until this Rule has been complied with. All changed pleadings shall contain copies of all exhibits referred to in the changed pleading. Permission may be obtained from the Court, if desired, for the removal of any exhibit or exhibits attached to a superseded pleading, in order that the same may be attached to the changed pleading.

[Effective December 1, 2009.]

RULE 230. CIVIL MOTION CALENDAR AND PROCEDURE (Fed. R. Civ. P. 78)

(a) Motion Calendar. Each Judge or Magistrate Judge maintains an individual motion calendar. Information as to the times and dates for each motion calendar may be obtained from the Clerk or the courtroom deputy clerk for the assigned Judge or Magistrate Judge.

(b) Notice, Motion, Brief and Evidence. Except as otherwise provided in these Rules or as ordered or allowed by the Court, all motions shall be noticed on the motion calendar of the assigned Judge or Magistrate Judge. The moving party shall file a notice of motion, motion, accompanying briefs, affidavits, if appropriate, and copies of all documentary evidence that the moving party intends to submit in support of the motion. The matter shall be set for hearing on the motion calendar of the Judge or Magistrate Judge to whom the action has been assigned or before whom the motion is to be heard not less than twenty-eight (28) days after service and filing of the motion. Motions defectively noticed shall be filed, but not set for hearing; the Clerk shall immediately notify the moving party of the defective notice and of the next available dates and times for proper notice, and the moving party shall file and serve a new notice of motion setting forth a proper time and date. See L.R. 135.

(c) Opposition and Non–Opposition. Opposition, if any, to the granting of the motion shall be in writing and shall be filed and served not less than fourteen (14) days preceding the noticed (or continued) hearing date. A responding party who has no opposition to the granting of the motion shall serve and file a statement to that effect, specifically designating the motion in question. No party will be entitled to be heard in opposition to a motion at oral arguments if opposition to the motion has not been timely filed by that party. See L.R. 135. A failure to file a timely opposition may also be construed by the Court as a non-opposition to the motion.

(d) Reply. Not less than seven (7) days preceding the date of hearing, the moving party may serve and file a reply to any opposition filed by a responding party.

(e) Related or Counter–Motions. Any counter-motion or other motion that a party may desire to make that is related to the general subject matter of the original motion shall be served and filed in the manner and on the date prescribed for the filing of opposition. If a counter-motion or other related motion is filed, the Court may continue the hearing on the original and all related motions so as to give all parties reasonable opportunity to serve and file oppositions and replies to all pending motions.

(f) Continuances. Requests for continuances of hearings on the motion calendar, upon stipulation or otherwise, shall be made to the Judge or Magistrate Judge on whose calendar the matter is set, at least seven (7) days before the scheduled hearing date. All stipulations for continuance shall be submitted for approval to the Court. See L.R. 143, 144.

(g) Hearing and Oral Argument. Upon the call of the motion, the Court will hear appropriate and reasonable oral argument. Alternatively, the motion may be submitted upon the record and briefs on file if the parties stipulate thereto, or if the Court so orders, subject to the power of the Court to reopen the matter for further briefs or oral arguments or both. Any party that believes that extended oral argument, more than 10 minutes per side or 20 minutes in the aggregate, will be required shall notify the courtroom deputy clerk so that the hearing may be rescheduled if deemed appropriate by the Court.

(h) Use of Affidavits. Factual contentions involved in pretrial motions shall be initially presented and heard upon affidavits, except that the Court may in its discretion require or allow oral examination of witnesses. See L.R. 142.

(i) Failure to Appear. Absent notice of intent to submit the matter on the briefs, failure to appear may be deemed withdrawal of the motion or of opposition to the motion, in the discretion of the Court, or may result in the imposition of sanctions.

(j) Applications for Reconsideration. Whenever any motion has been granted or denied in whole or in part, and a subsequent motion for reconsideration is made upon the same or any alleged different set of facts, counsel shall present to the Judge or Magistrate Judge to whom such subsequent motion is made an affidavit or brief, as appropriate, setting forth the material facts and circumstances surrounding each motion for which reconsideration is sought, including:

(1) when and to what Judge or Magistrate Judge the prior motion was made;

(2) what ruling, decision, or order was made thereon;

(3) what new or different facts or circumstances are claimed to exist which did not exist or were not shown upon such prior motion, or what other grounds exist for the motion; and

(4) why the facts or circumstances were not shown at the time of the prior motion.

(k) Motions Before a Magistrate Judge. Only those motions in matters specified in L.R. 302 and 303 shall be noticed, briefed, and argued before a Magistrate Judge. All other motions shall be noticed, briefed and argued before a Judge.

(*l*) Motions in Prisoner Actions. All motions, except motions to dismiss for lack of prosecution, filed in actions wherein one party is incarcerated and proceeding in propria persona, shall be submitted upon the record without oral argument unless otherwise ordered by the Court. Such motions need not be noticed on the motion calendar. Opposition, if any, to the granting of the motion shall be served and filed by the responding party not more than twenty-one (21) days after the date of service of the motion. A responding party who has no opposition to the granting of the motion shall serve and file a statement to that effect, specifically designating the motion in question. Failure of the responding party to file an opposition or to file a statement of no opposition may be deemed a waiver of any opposition to the granting of the motion and may result in the imposition of sanctions. The moving party may, not more than seven (7) days after the opposition has been filed in CM/ECF, serve and file a reply to the opposition. All such motions will be deemed submitted when the time to reply has expired.

[Effective December 1, 2009. Amended effective February 19, 2013; February 1, 2019.]

RULE 231. TEMPORARY RESTRAINING ORDER—PRELIMINARY INJUNCTION
(Fed. R. Civ. P. 65)

(a) Temporary Restraining Orders. Except in the most extraordinary of circumstances, no temporary restraining order shall be granted in the absence of actual notice to the affected party and/or counsel, by telephone or other means, or a sufficient showing of efforts made to provide notice. See Fed. R. Civ. P. 65(b). Appropriate notice would inform the affected party and/or counsel of the intention to seek a temporary restraining order, the date and time for hearing to be requested of the Court, and the nature of the relief to be requested. Once a specific time and location has been set by the Court, the moving party shall promptly give additional notice of the time and location of the hearing.

(b) Timing of Motion. In considering a motion for a temporary restraining order, the Court will consider whether the applicant could have sought relief by motion for preliminary injunction at an earlier date without the necessity for seeking last-minute relief by motion for temporary restraining order. Should the Court find that the applicant unduly delayed in seeking injunctive relief, the Court may conclude that the delay constitutes laches or contradicts the applicant's

allegations of irreparable injury and may deny the motion solely on either ground.

(c) Documents to Be Filed. No hearing on a temporary restraining order will normally be set unless the following documents are provided to the Court and, unless impossible under the circumstances, to the affected parties or their counsel:

(1) a complaint;

(2) a motion for temporary restraining order;

(3) a brief on all relevant legal issues presented by the motion;

(4) an affidavit in support of the existence of an irreparable injury;

(5) an affidavit detailing the notice or efforts to effect notice to the affected parties or counsel or showing good cause why notice should not be given, see L.R. 142;

(6) a proposed temporary restraining order with a provision for a bond, see L.R. 151;

(7) a proposed order with blanks for fixing the time and date for hearing a motion for preliminary injunction, the date for the filing of responsive papers, the amount of the bond, if any, and the date and hour of issuance, see L.R. 137; and

(8) in all instances in which a temporary restraining order is requested ex parte, the proposed order shall further notify the affected party of the right to apply to the Court for modification or dissolution on two (2) days' notice or such shorter notice as the Court may allow. See Fed. R. Civ. P. 65(b).

(d) Preliminary Injunction.

(1) *Notice.* See L.R. 144, 230.

(2) *Accompanying Documents.* All motions for preliminary injunction shall be accompanied by (i) briefs on all relevant legal issues to be presented by the motion, (ii) affidavits in support of the motion, including affidavits on the question of irreparable injury, and (iii) a proposed order with a provision for a bond. See L.R. 230, 151.

(3) *Required Information.* All parties shall inform the Court in their briefs of the following: (i) whether they desire to present oral testimony at the hearing, and (ii) an estimate of the amount of time they anticipate will be required for the hearing. The parties shall inform the Court and all other parties immediately upon learning of a change in the need for a preliminary injunction, the length of time the hearing will require, or other similar information.

(e) Modification or Dissolution. When a preliminary injunction or temporary restraining order has been issued, the affected party may apply to the Court for modification or dissolution of the injunction or order. Such motion shall normally be accompanied by a brief on all relevant legal issues to be presented in its support and affidavits supporting modification or dissolution and detailing the notice to or efforts to notify the affected party or counsel.

(f) Actions Involving Real Property. A motion for a preliminary injunction or a temporary restraining order to limit picketing, restrain real property encroachments, or protect easements shall depict by drawings, plot plans, photographs, or other appropriate means, or shall describe in detail the premises involved, including, if applicable, the length and width of the frontage on a street or alley, the width of sidewalks, and the number, size, and location of entrances.

[Effective December 1, 2009.]

RULE 232. RECEIVERS (Fed. R. Civ. P. 66)

(a) Definitions. For purposes of this Rule:

(1) "temporary receiver" shall mean a receiver appointed without notice or on less than the notice provided in L.R. 230 to the party sought to be subjected to the receivership, and

(2) "receiver" shall mean any receiver appointed after the giving of either (i) at least the notice of hearing upon the motion for appointment of receiver required by L.R. 230, or (ii) such lesser notice of hearing on the motion as may be agreed to by the party sought to be subjected to the receivership and the Court.

(b) Notice: Temporary Receiver. A temporary receiver shall not be appointed without notice to the party sought to be subjected to receivership except upon an appropriate showing of necessity and immediacy of potential harm. If a temporary receiver is appointed ex parte, the party seeking and securing such appointment shall give notice forthwith of the temporary receiver's appointment, any terms and conditions pertaining thereto, and the date calendared for subsequent hearing on the question of continuance of the receivership.

(c) Continuance of Receivership. Upon appointment of a temporary receiver, the Court shall calendar a hearing on the continuation of the receivership. The determination whether to continue the receivership shall be made as set forth in (d), and no weight shall be given to the fact that a temporary receiver was appointed.

(d) Appointment of a Receiver. A receiver may be appointed upon the notice set forth in (a)(2). Motions for appointment of a receiver need not be preceded by a motion for appointment of a temporary receiver.

(e) Reports of Receivers.

(1) Unless otherwise ordered by the Court, at least one (1) day before the hearing provided in (c), the temporary receiver shall file and personally serve a summary report of the temporary receivership.

(2) At such time as the Court may direct, and at least once a year, a receiver shall file and serve a report that shall be heard with notice to all parties in accordance with L.R. 230. The report shall contain (i) a summary of the operations of the receiver, (ii) an inventory of all the assets and their value, (iii) a schedule of all the receiver's receipts and disbursements, (iv) the receiver's recommendations for a continuation or discontinuation of the receivership and the reasons therefor, and (v) such other matters as the Court may direct. At the hearing, the Court shall approve or disapprove the receiver's report and determine whether the receivership shall be continued.

(f) Notice of Hearings. Unless the Court otherwise orders, L.R. 230 shall apply to all motions by the receiver.

(g) Employment and Compensation of Attorneys, Accountants, and Investigators. A receiver shall not employ an attorney, accountant, or investigator without first obtaining an order of the Court authorizing such employment, which order may set forth a tentative basis for computation of compensation. The actual compensation of such persons shall subsequently be fixed by the Court, after hearing, upon the applicant's affidavit setting forth in reasonable detail the nature of the services and the existence of any agreements concerning the amount of compensation to be paid.

(h) Deposit of Funds. A receiver shall deposit all funds received in a depository designated by the Court, entitled "Receiver's Account" together with the name and number of the action. See L.R. 150.

(i) Undertaking of Receiver. A receiver shall not act until a sufficient undertaking as determined by the Court is filed. See L.R. 151.

[Effective December 1, 2009.]

RULE 240. STATUS CONFERENCE
(Fed. R. Civ. P. 16)

(a) Conference. After an action has been filed, the assigned Judge or Magistrate Judge shall order the holding of one or more status conferences for the purpose of entering a pretrial scheduling order, and further status conferences may be held at any time thereafter, with or without the request of any party. See Fed. R. Civ. P. 16. All parties receiving notice of any status conference shall appear in person or by attorney, shall be prepared to discuss such subjects as may be specified in the order noticing the conference, and shall have authority to enter into stipulations and to make admissions regarding all matters that the participants may reasonably anticipate may be discussed. Such subjects may include:

(1) service of process on parties not yet served;

(2) jurisdiction and venue;

(3) whether the action is required to be heard by a District Court composed of three Judges, see L.R. 203, or whether the action draws in issue the constitutionality of a statute or regulation under circumstances requiring notice as set forth in 28 U.S.C. § 2403, Fed. R. Civ. P. 5.1 or L.R. 132;

(4) joinder of additional parties and amendment of pleadings;

(5) the formulation and simplification of the issues, including elimination of frivolous claims and defenses;

(6) the appropriateness of any variance from the usual filing and service requirements applicable to the action;

(7) the disposition of pending motions, the timing of a motion for class certification, see L.R. 205, the appropriateness and timing of summary adjudication under Fed. R. Civ. P. 56, and other anticipated motions;

(8) propriety of initial disclosures as contemplated by Fed. R. Civ. P. 26(a)(1); results of the initial discovery conference; anticipated or outstanding discovery, including the necessity for relief from discovery limits; and the control and scheduling of discovery, including deferral of discovery whether to hold

further discovery conferences, and other orders affecting discovery pursuant to Fed. R. Civ. P. 26 and 29 through 37;

(9) the avoidance of unnecessary proof and of cumulative evidence, and limitations or restrictions on the use of testimony under Fed. R. Evid. 702;

(10) the possibility of obtaining admissions of fact and of documents that will avoid unnecessary proof, stipulations regarding the authenticity of documents, and advance rulings from the Court on the admissibility of evidence;

(11) further proceedings, including setting dates for further conferences, for the completion of motions and discovery and for pretrial and trial; the appropriateness of an order adopting a plan for disclosure of experts under Fed. R. Civ. P. 26(a)(2), Cal. Civ. Proc. Code § 2034.210 et seq., or an alternative plan; and the appropriateness of an order establishing a reasonable limit on the time allowed for presenting evidence;

(12) modification of the standard pretrial procedures specified by these Rules because of the relative simplicity or complexity of the action;

(13) the appropriateness of an order for a separate trial pursuant to Fed. R. Civ. P. 42(b) with respect to a claim, counterclaim, cross-claim, or third-party claim, or affirmative defense, or with respect to any particular issue in the action;

(14) the appropriateness of an order directing a party or parties to present evidence early in the trial with respect to a manageable issue that could, on the evidence, be the basis for a judgment as a matter of law under Fed. R. Civ. P. 50(a) or a judgment on partial findings under Fed. R. Civ. P. 52(c);

(15) appropriateness of special procedures such as reference to a special master or Magistrate Judge or the Judicial Panel on Multidistrict Litigation, or application of the Manual for Complex Litigation;

(16) the prospects for settlement and the use of special procedures to assist in resolving the dispute when authorized by statute or these Rules, provided, however, that counsel shall not, in the absence of a written stipulation, reveal any offers made or rejected during settlement negotiations, and counsel shall specify whether they will stipulate to the trial Judge acting as settlement judge and waive any disqualification by virtue thereof;

(17) the appropriateness of alternate dispute resolution, such as this District's Voluntary Dispute Resolution Program (VDRP), or any other alternative dispute resolution procedure; and

(18) any other matters that may facilitate the just, speedy and inexpensive determination of the action.

(b) Reports. Except in those types of actions specifically exempted from initial disclosure by Fed. R. Civ. P. 26(a)(1)(B), the parties must submit reports to the Court concerning their proposed discovery plan within fourteen (14) days after their discovery conference. The Court may require the submission of preconference reports on some or all of the foregoing subjects. See also L.R. 271(d)(2).

(c) Exceptions to Mandatory Scheduling Order Requirement. The following categories of civil actions are excepted from the mandatory scheduling order requirement set forth in Fed. R. Civ. P. 16(b):

(1) actions brought under Title 42 of the United States Code to review a final decision of the Commissioner of Social Security;

(2) actions brought to enforce Internal Revenue Service summonses filed pursuant to 26 U.S.C. §§ 7402(b) and 7604(a), and actions to quash administrative summonses filed pursuant to 26 U.S.C. § 7609(b)(2);

(3) actions for writs of entry in connection with the enforcement of Internal Revenue Service tax liens;

(4) actions to enforce collection on promissory notes involving federally insured loans and direct federal loans in which the prayer for relief is less than $25,000;

(5) actions to enforce cease and desist orders issued by the National Labor Relations Board;

(6) actions to enforce arbitration awards;

(7) actions under 46 U.S.C. §§ 2302, 4311(d) and 12309(c);

(8) prisoner actions as defined in L.R. 101;

(9) petitions for writs of habeas corpus by incarcerated persons;

(10) extradition proceedings;

(11) discovery disputes originating from out-of-district actions;

(12) civil commitment proceedings; and

(13) Federal Debt Collection proceedings.

[Effective December 1, 2009. Amended effective February 1, 2019.]

RULE 250.1 DEPOSITIONS (Fed. R. Civ. P. 30)

(a) Filing of Depositions. Depositions taken orally or by written question, whether duces tecum or not, subpoenas and notices therefor, proofs of service thereof, if any, and related documents shall not be filed unless and until there is a proceeding in which the document or proof of service is at issue. Before or upon the filing of a document making reference to a deposition, counsel shall comply with L.R. 133(j).

(b) Custody and Maintenance of Deposition Transcripts. Counsel noticing a deposition is responsible to obtain the original deposition transcript or audio or video tape record from the deposition reporter, see Fed. R. Civ. P. 30(f), and to retain it under conditions suitable to protect it from loss, destruction or tampering until the earlier of (1) the date it is filed in accordance with L.R. 133(j) and 250.1(a), or (2) one year after the judgment has become final or other final disposition of the action. Before that date, for good cause, any party or intervenor may move the Court for an order prohibiting the destruction of a transcript or record permitted hereunder or otherwise directing the custody and maintenance of the transcript or record.

[Effective December 1, 2009.]

RULE 250.2 INTERROGATORIES
(Fed. R. Civ. P. 33)

(a) Interrogatories. Interrogatories shall be so arranged that after each separate question there shall appear a blank space reasonably calculated to enable the answering party to insert the answers and/or objections. The answering party shall answer or object within the spaces provided or, if unable to do so, shall retype the interrogatories along with the answers and/or objections.

(b) Objections. Each objection to any interrogatory shall include a statement of reasons and, if appropriate, citation to relevant authority. See Fed. R. Civ. P. 33(b)(4).

(c) Filing of Interrogatories. Interrogatories, responses, and proofs of service thereof shall not be filed unless and until there is a proceeding in which the interrogatories or proof of service is at issue. When required in a proceeding, only that part of the set of interrogatories and answers that is in issue shall be filed.

[Effective December 1, 2009.]

RULE 250.3 PRODUCTION OF DOCUMENTS
(Fed. R. Civ. P. 34)

(a) Requests for Production. Responses to requests for production shall set forth each request in full before each response.

(b) Objections. Each objection to any request for production shall include a statement of reasons and, if appropriate, citation to relevant authority. See Fed. R. Civ. P. 33(b)(2)(C).

(c) Filing of Requests for Production. Requests for production, responses and proofs of service thereof shall not be filed unless and until there is a proceeding in which the request, response, or proof of service is at issue. When required in a proceeding, only that part of the request for production, response or proof of service that is in issue shall be filed.

[Effective December 1, 2009.]

RULE 250.4 REQUESTS FOR ADMISSION
(Fed. R. Civ. P. 36)

(a) Requests for Admission. Responses to requests for admission shall set forth each request in full before each response.

(b) Objections. Each objection to any request for admission shall include a statement of reasons and, if appropriate, citation to relevant authority. See Fed. R. Civ. P. 36(a)(5).

(c) Filing of Requests for Admission. Requests for admission, responses, and proofs of service thereof shall not be filed unless and until there is a proceeding in which the document or proof of service is at issue. When required in a proceeding, only that part of the request for admission and response that is in issue shall be filed.

[Effective December 1, 2009.]

RULE 250.5 SUBPOENAS DUCES TECUM (Fed. R. Civ. P. 45)

(a) Subpoenas Duces Tecum. Responses to subpoenas duces tecum shall identify each category in the subpoena duces tecum as to which no documents are produced because no documents exist in the possession of the person subpoenaed and shall comply with Fed. R. Civ. P. 45(d)(2).

(b) Objections. Each objection to any subpoenas duces tecum shall include a statement of reasons and, if appropriate, citation to relevant authority. See Fed. R. Civ. P. 45(c)(2)(B).

(c) Service of Subpoenas Duces Tecum. Subpoenas duces tecum directed to parties or non-parties shall be served on all parties to the action and on the non-party. Fed. R. Civ. P. 45.

(d) Filing of Subpoenas Duces Tecum. Subpoenas duces tecum, responses, and proofs of service thereof shall not be filed unless and until there is a proceeding in which the request, response, or proof of service is at issue. When required in a proceeding, only that part of the subpoena duces tecum, response, or proof of service that is in issue shall be filed.

[Effective December 1, 2009.]

RULE 251. MOTIONS DEALING WITH DISCOVERY MATTERS (Fed. R. Civ. P. 37)

(a) Hearing Regarding Discovery Disagreements. Except as provided in (e), a hearing of a motion pursuant to Fed. R. Civ. P. 26 through 37 and 45, including any motion to exceed discovery limitations or motion for protective order, may be had by the filing and service of a notice of motion and motion scheduling the hearing date on the appropriate calendar at least twenty-one (21) days from the date of filing and service. No other documents need be filed at this time. The hearing may be dropped from the calendar without prejudice if the Joint Statement re Discovery Disagreement or an affidavit as set forth below is not filed at least seven (7) days before the scheduled hearing date. If the notice of motion and motion are filed concurrently with the Joint Statement, the motion shall be placed on the next regularly scheduled calendar for the Magistrate Judge or Judge hearing the motion at least seven (7) days thereafter.

(b) Requirement of Conferring. Except as hereinafter set forth, a motion made pursuant to Fed. R. Civ. P. 26 through 37 and 45, including any motion to exceed discovery limitations or motion for protective order, shall not be heard unless (1) the parties have conferred and attempted to resolve their differences, and (2) the parties have set forth their differences and the bases therefor in a Joint Statement re Discovery Disagreement. Counsel for all interested parties shall confer in advance of the filing of the motion or in advance of the hearing of the motion in a good faith effort to resolve the differences that are the subject of the motion. Counsel for the moving party or prospective moving party shall be responsible for arranging the conference, which shall be held at a time and place and in a manner mutually convenient to counsel.

(c) Joint Statement re Discovery Disagreement. If the moving party is still dissatisfied after the conference of counsel, that party shall draft and file a document entitled "Joint Statement re Discovery Disagreement." All parties who are concerned with the discovery motion shall assist in the preparation of, and shall sign, the Joint Statement, which shall specify with particularity the following matters:

(1) The details of the conference or conferences;

(2) A statement of the nature of the action and its factual disputes insofar as they are pertinent to the matters to be decided and the issues to be determined at the hearing; and

(3) The contentions of each party as to each contested issue, including a memorandum of each party's respective arguments concerning the issues in dispute and the legal authorities in support thereof.

Each specific interrogatory, deposition question or other item objected to, or concerning which a protective order is sought, and the objection thereto, shall be reproduced in full. The respective arguments and supporting authorities of the parties shall be set forth immediately following each such objection. When an objection is raised to a number of items or a general protective order is sought that is related to a number of specific items, the arguments and briefing need not be repeated. If a protective order is sought that is unrelated to specific, individual items, repetition of the original discovery document is not required. All arguments and briefing that would otherwise be included in a memorandum of points and authorities supporting or opposing the motion shall be included in this joint statement, and no separate briefing shall be filed.

(d) Failure to Meet or Obtain Joint Statement. If counsel for the moving party is unable, after a good faith effort, to secure the cooperation of counsel for the opposing party in arranging the required conference, or in preparing and executing the required joint statement, counsel for the moving party may file and serve an affidavit so stating, setting forth the nature and extent of counsel's efforts to arrange the required conference or procure the required joint statement, the opposing counsel's responses or refusals to respond to those efforts, the issues to be determined at the hearing, and the moving party's contentions with regard to the issues, including any briefing in respect thereto. Refusal of any counsel to participate in a discovery conference, or refusal without good cause to execute the required joint statement, shall be grounds, in the discretion of the Court, for entry of an order adverse to the party represented by counsel so refusing or adverse to counsel. *See* L.R. 110.

(e) Exceptions From Required Joint Statement re Discovery Disagreement. The foregoing requirement for a Joint Statement re Discovery Disagreement shall not apply to the following situations: (1) when there has been a complete and total failure to respond to a discovery request or order, or (2) when the only relief sought by the motion is the imposition of sanctions. In either instance, the aggrieved party may bring a motion for relief for hearing on fourteen (14) days notice. The responding party shall file a response thereto not later than seven (7) days before the hearing date. The moving party may file and serve a reply thereto not less than two (2) court days before the hearing date. L.R. 135.

(f) Notice Provisions. By reason of the notice provisions set forth in (a) and (e), the provisions of L.R. 230 shall not apply to motions and hearings dealing with discovery matters.

[Effective December 1, 2009. Amended effective January 1, 2015.]

RULE 260. MOTIONS FOR SUMMARY JUDGMENT OR SUMMARY ADJUDICATION (Fed. R. Civ. P. 56)

(a) Motions for Summary Judgment or Summary Adjudication. Each motion for summary judgment or summary adjudication shall be accompanied by a "Statement of Undisputed Facts" that shall enumerate discretely each of the specific material facts relied upon in support of the motion and cite the particular portions of any pleading, affidavit, deposition, interrogatory answer, admission, or other document relied upon to establish that fact. The moving party shall be responsible for the filing of all evidentiary documents cited in the moving papers. See L.R. 133(j).

(b) Opposition. Any party opposing a motion for summary judgment or summary adjudication shall reproduce the itemized facts in the Statement of Undisputed Facts and admit those facts that are undisputed and deny those that are disputed, including with each denial a citation to the particular portions of any pleading, affidavit, deposition, interrogatory answer, admission, or other document relied upon in support of that denial. The opposing party may also file a concise "Statement of Disputed Facts," and the source thereof in the record, of all additional material facts as to which there is a genuine issue precluding summary judgment or adjudication. The opposing party shall be responsible for the filing of all evidentiary documents cited in the opposing papers. See L.R. 133(j). If a need for discovery is asserted as a basis for denial of the motion, the party opposing the motion shall provide a specification of the particular facts on which discovery is to be had or the issues on which discovery is necessary.

(c) Stipulated Facts. All interested parties may jointly file a stipulation setting forth a statement of stipulated facts to which all interested parties agree. As to any stipulated facts, the parties so stipulating may state that their stipulations are entered into only for the purposes of the motion for summary judgment and are not intended to be otherwise binding.

(d) Use of Affidavits. See Fed. R. Civ. P. 56(e); L.R. 142.

(e) Use of Depositions. See L.R. 133(j), 250.1.

(f) Summary Adjudication. This Rule shall apply to motions for orders specifying material facts that appear without substantial controversy pursuant to Fed. R. Civ. P. 56(d), except that the proposed "Statement of Undisputed Facts" and the "Statement of Disputed Facts" shall be limited to the facts that the moving party asserts are without substantial controversy and the facts the opposing party contends are in dispute.

[Effective December 1, 2009.]

RULE 270. COURT SETTLEMENT CONFERENCES (Fed. R. Civ. P. 16)

(a) Setting of Settlement Conferences. A settlement conference shall be held in all actions unless otherwise ordered by the Court on objection of a party or for other good cause. Counsel shall notify the Court when the settlement conference is set if the litigation is unusual or complex and if there is a need to provide for additional time or special arrangements to ensure that the settlement conference will be meaningful.

(b) Settlement Conferences Before the Assigned Trial Judge or Assigned Magistrate Judge. Unless all the parties affirmatively request that the assigned trial Judge participate in the conference and waive in writing any claim of disqualification on that basis to act as the trial Judge in the action thereafter, the assigned trial Judge shall not conduct the settlement conference. See L.R. 240(a)(16). If the assigned Magistrate Judge is not the trial Judge, this Rule does not prohibit the assigned Magistrate Judge from conducting the conference, in his or her discretion, except that, at the time the settlement conference is scheduled or as otherwise ordered by the Court, any party may request that the conference not be conducted by the assigned Magistrate Judge.

(c) Settlement Conference Statements. Unless otherwise ordered by the Court, the submission of settlement conference statements before the conference is optional. Statements submitted before the conference are reviewed in preparation for the conference and may assist in achieving the goals of the conference; they should be drafted with that purpose in mind.

(d) Confidentiality of Settlement Conference Statements. Settlement conference statements shall not be disclosed to the Judge or Magistrate Judge assigned to try the action unless the parties have agreed, and the Judge or Magistrate Judge has approved, that such Judge or Magistrate Judge will preside at the settlement conference. Settlement conference statements may be e-mailed in .pdf format directly to the courtroom deputy clerk of the Judge or Magistrate Judge before whom the settlement conference is to be held or may be submitted in paper directly to chambers. If the statement is confidential, it must be clearly captioned to reveal its confidential character. If a party is submitting a confidential settlement conference statement, the party must file a one page document entitled "Notice of Submission of Confidential Settlement Conference Statement." That filing, if done electronically, will thereby effect service of this notice on all other parties. If the notice is filed conventionally, the filing party must serve all other parties. The parties may agree, or not, to serve each other with the settlement statements.

(e) Return of Settlement Conference Statements. At the completion of the settlement conference, the Judge or Magistrate Judge before whom the settlement conference is held shall return the statements to the respective parties who submitted them or otherwise dispose of them. Settlement conference statements shall not be filed or made a part of the Court's records.

(f) Participation of a Principal.

(1) *United States Not a Party.* In actions in which the United States is not a party, and unless specifically permitted otherwise by the Judge or Magistrate Judge conducting the settlement conference, counsel shall be accompanied in person by a person capable of disposition, or shall be fully authorized to settle the matter at the settlement conference on any terms. When settlement must be approved by a vote of a party's governing body, unless specifically permitted otherwise by the Judge or Magistrate Judge conducting the settlement conference, counsel shall be designated or shall be accompanied in person by a representative designated by the body who shall have learned the body's preconference disposition relative to settlement.

(2) *United States a Party.* In actions in which the United States is a party, the attorney for the United States shall obtain the approval of the United States Attorney to compromise any matter within the authority delegated to the United States Attorney by rule or regulation of the Attorney General. If such delegated authority to approve a compromise settlement is limited by the opposition of another federal agency, a responsible and knowledgeable representative of such agency shall attend the conference. In other actions in which the approval of officials of the Department of Justice in Washington, D.C. is required for a compromise settlement, the attorney for the United States shall, before the settlement conference, attempt to confer with such officials, or their appropriate representatives, to determine the terms and conditions upon which a compromise settlement would be approved. If a tentative compromise settlement that is within such terms and conditions is agreed to at the conference, the attorney for the United States shall promptly recommend it to and seek the required approval of the appropriate official.

[Effective December 1, 2009. Amended effective February 1, 2019.]

RULE 271. VOLUNTARY DISPUTE RESOLUTION PROGRAM (Fed. R. Civ. P. 16)

(a) Purpose and Scope.

(1) *Purpose.* Pursuant to 28 U.S.C. § 651 et seq., and in recognition of the economic burdens and delay in the resolution of disputes that can be imposed by full, formal litigation, this Rule governs the referral of certain actions to the Voluntary Dispute Resolution Program ("VDRP") at the election of parties.

It is the Court's intention that the VDRP shall allow the participants to take advantage of a wide variety of alternative dispute resolution methods. These methods may include, but are not limited to, mediation, negotiation, early neutral evaluation, and settlement facilitation. The specific method or methods employed will be determined by the Neutral and the parties and may vary from matter to matter.

(2) *Scope.* This Rule presumptively applies to all civil actions except (i) prisoner petitions and actions, including habeas corpus petitions, (ii) actions in which one of the parties is appearing pro se, (iii) voting rights actions, (iv) social security actions, (v) deportation actions, (vi) Freedom of Information Act actions, and (vii) actions involving the constitutionality of federal, state or local statutes or ordinances. The fact that an

action falls in a category that is exempt from presumptive applicability of this Rule neither (1) precludes the parties to such an action from agreeing to participate in an Alternative Dispute Resolution ("ADR") process, nor (2) deprives the Court of authority to compel participation in an appropriate ADR proceeding.

(3) *Parties Retain the Option of Securing ADR Services Outside the Program Sponsored by the Court.* Nothing in this Rule precludes the parties from agreeing to seek ADR services outside the VDRP. ADR proceedings conducted outside this Rule, however, will not be subject to the provisions of this Rule unless the parties stipulate to adopt one or more provisions to govern their ADR proceedings.

(b) Program Administration.

(1) *ADR Judge.*

(A) Appointment. The Chief Judge shall appoint one or more Judges or Magistrate Judges to serve as the ADR Judge of this Court. When necessary or appropriate, including but not limited to instances when the designated ADR Judge is the assigned Judge or Magistrate Judge for a particular action, the Chief Judge shall appoint another Judge or Magistrate Judge to perform the duties of ADR Judge temporarily.

(B) Duties. The ADR Judge shall serve as the primary liaison between the Court and the VDRP staff, consulting with that staff on matters of policy, program design and evaluation, education, training, and administration. The ADR Judge shall rule on all disputes resulting from a party's request to be excused from appearing in person at any VDRP proceeding and shall hear and determine all complaints alleging violations of this Rule.

(2) *VDRP Administrator.* The VDRP Administrator shall be responsible for implementing, administering, overseeing, and evaluating the VDRP and procedures covered by this Rule. These responsibilities shall extend to educating parties, lawyers, Judges, and court staff about the VDRP and its rules. In addition, the VDRP Administrator shall ensure that appropriate systems are maintained for recruiting, screening, and training Neutrals, as well as for maintaining on an ongoing basis the Neutrals' ability to provide role-appropriate and effective services to the parties.

(3) *Rules and Materials Available.* The Clerk shall make pertinent rules and explanatory materials available to the parties.

(4) *Parties May Request Referral to the VDRP at Any Time.* Notwithstanding any other provision of this Rule, parties, individually or in any combination, including parties to a counterclaim, cross-action, or third-party action, may ask the assigned Judge or Magistrate Judge, at any stage in the proceedings, to refer the action, in whole or in part, to the VDRP. The Court may enter an order of reference only if all parties voluntarily agree to the proposed reference. For the purposes of this Rule, the phrase "all parties" means all parties to an action or, in a complex action in which counterclaims, cross-actions, or third-party actions are pending, all parties to a discrete sub-part of the complex action. The decision whether to enter an order of reference is within the

Court's discretion and includes the considerations set forth in (i)(3) and (4).

(c) Referral to the VDRP.

(1) *Notice of Availability.* The Clerk shall provide a notice of the availability of the VDRP with a citation to this Rule to all plaintiffs upon the filing of the complaint or to defendants upon a removal. The notice will order the plaintiff to provide all other parties with copies of the notice at the time service is effected or, for parties already served, no more than fourteen (14) days after plaintiff receives the notice from the Court. After filing of the original complaint or a removal action, any party who causes a new party to be joined in the action shall promptly serve a copy of the notice on the new party.

(2) *Authority of Assigned Judge and Magistrate Judge.* As part of the status or scheduling conference or otherwise, the assigned Judge or Magistrate Judge may inform the parties of the availability of the VDRP. See L.R. 240(a)(17). In general, actions may not be assigned to the VDRP over the objection of a party. Nevertheless, when a complex action including counterclaims, cross-actions or third-party actions are pending, the Court may assign discrete sub-parts of the complex action to the VDRP if all parties to the sub-part agree to reference to the VDRP and the party objecting to the VDRP is not a party to the sub-part of the complaint, counterclaim, cross-action, or third-party action to be assigned to the VDRP.

(3) *Request by the Parties.* Parties may request referral to the VDRP by filing a Stipulation and Order reflecting the agreement of all parties to submit the action to the VDRP pursuant to this Rule. See L.R. 143; 271(i).

(d) VDRP Selection Process.

(1) *The Parties' Duty to Consider VDRP and Confer.* In accordance with L.R. 240(a)(17), unless otherwise ordered, in every action to which this Rule applies, the parties must confer about—

(A) whether the parties are willing to participate in the VDRP; and

(B) when the VDRP session, if any, should be held.

(2) *The Parties' Duty to Report.* The parties must report in their status conference report their shared or separate views about referral to the VDRP and when the VDRP session, if any, should occur. In these reports or statements, counsel must represent that they understand and have explained to their clients the VDRP rules and process and that, with their assistance, their clients have carefully considered whether their action might benefit from participation in the VDRP. If all parties stipulate to using the VDRP, these reports or statements must be accompanied by a Stipulation and Order for VDRP Referral in conformity with (i).

(e) Panels of Neutrals; Selection of Neutrals.

(1) *Panels of Neutrals.* The VDRP Administrator shall ensure that a panel is maintained of persons who are trained and otherwise qualified to serve as Neutrals for the VDRP. Only persons who agree to serve on the terms set forth in this Rule and in any pertinent General Orders, and whose background, training, and skills satisfy the requirements that the Court establishes for the VDRP, shall be admitted to and remain as members of the panel.

(2) *Parties to Confer About Selection of Neutral and Confirm Neutral's Availability.* Unless otherwise ordered, the parties may confer about and attempt to agree on a Neutral at the same time they confer under (d)(1)(A), for the purposes of discussing the appropriateness of the VDRP in the particular action and suggesting the time frame in which the VDRP session should be held. If authorized by the assigned Judge, the parties may nominate a Neutral who is not on the Court-approved panel. Before nominating a Neutral, the individual must have confirmed his or her availability and willingness to serve within the time frame they propose.

(3) *Selection by the Parties or Randomly by the Clerk.* Upon the filing of a Stipulation and Order for VDRP Referral, the assigned Judge or Magistrate Judge or the VDRP Administrator may assign a Neutral, or the VDRP Administrator may supply to the parties a list of not more than three (3) potential Neutrals, from which list the parties shall agree upon one. If the identity of the Neutral is by selection of the parties, counsel for the party first asserting jurisdiction in the Court shall report the selection of the parties, in writing, to the VDRP Administrator within fourteen (14) days following service of the list by the VDRP Administrator. If the parties are unable to agree upon a Neutral or fail to communicate their agreement to the VDRP Administrator, the VDRP Administrator may designate a Neutral drawn randomly from the panel of Neutrals to be the Neutral assigned to the action and shall notify the parties and the Neutral of that designation. The Neutral shall notify the VDRP Administrator within fourteen (14) days from notification of selection whether he or she is able and willing to serve as Neutral for the action, or whether he or she is unable or unwilling to serve as Neutral for that action. If a selected Neutral is unable or unwilling to serve, the VDRP Administrator shall select and notify another Neutral. When a Neutral has agreed to serve, the VDRP Administrator shall send notice to the Neutral and the parties of the selection.

(4) *Documents Provided to the Neutral.* Promptly after the Neutral is designated, the VDRP Administrator shall provide her or him with a copy of

(A) the Stipulation and Order for VDRP Referral;

(B) each party's most recent pleading; and

(C) any other order or document from the court file that sets forth requirements or stipulations related to the VDRP proceedings.

(f) Disqualification of Neutrals.

(1) *Applicable Standards.* No person may serve as a Neutral in a VDRP proceeding under this Rule in violation of

(A) the standards set forth in 28 U.S.C. § 455;

(B) any applicable standard of professional responsibility or rule of professional conduct; or

(C) any additional standards adopted by the Court.

(2) *Mandatory Disqualification and Notice of Recusal.* A prospective Neutral who discovers a circumstance requiring disqualification shall immediately submit to the parties and to the VDRP Administrator a written notice of recusal. The parties may not waive a basis for disqualification that is described in 28 U.S.C. § 455(b).

(3) *Disclosure and Waiver of Non–Mandatory Grounds for Disqualification.* If a prospective Neutral discovers a circumstance that would not compel disqualification under rules of professional conduct or under 28 U.S.C. § 455(b), but that might be covered by 28 U.S.C. § 455(a) (impartiality might reasonably be questioned), the Neutral must promptly disclose that circumstance in writing to all counsel and the VDRP Administrator. A party may waive a possible basis for disqualification that is premised only on 28 U.S.C. § 455(a), but any such waiver must be in writing and delivered to the VDRP Administrator within fourteen (14) days of the party's receiving notice of the possible basis for disqualification. See L.R. 102(d).

(g) Compensation of Neutrals. Neutrals shall serve without compensation.

(h) Immunity of Neutrals. All persons serving as Neutrals under this Rule are deemed to be performing quasi-judicial functions and shall be immune to the extent provided by 28 U.S.C. § 655(c) and applicable authorities.

(i) Stipulation and Order for VDRP Referral.

(1) *File With Status Conference Report.* If all parties stipulate to using the VDRP, pursuant to (d), counsel must file with their Status Conference Reports pursuant to L.R. 240(a)(17), or with statements they file separately to comply with this Rule, a Stipulation and Order for VDRP Referral.

(2) *Contents of Stipulation and Order.* The Stipulation and Order for VDRP Referral must:

(A) specify the time frame within which the parties propose the VDRP process will be completed and the date by which the Neutral must file confirmation of that completion;

(B) suggest and explain any modifications or additions to the case management plan that would be advisable because of the reference to the VDRP; and

(C) describe any pretrial activity, e.g., specified discovery or motions, that shall be completed before the VDRP session is held or that shall be stayed until the VDRP session is concluded.

(3) *Protection Against Unreasonable Delay.* In fixing deadlines in its Order of VDRP Referral, the Court will assure that the time allotted for completing the VDRP process is no more than is appropriate and that the referral does not cause unreasonable delay in case development, in hearing motions, or in commencing trial.

(4) *Assigned Judge's Continuing Responsibility for Case Management.* Neither the parties' agreement to participate in the VDRP nor the Court's referral of an action to the VDRP shall reduce the assigned Judge's power and responsibility to maintain overall management control of an action before, during, and after the pendency of the VDRP process.

(j) Communications by Neutral Before the VDRP Session. Promptly after being appointed to serve in an action, the Neutral may hold a brief joint telephone conference with all counsel involved in the VDRP, or may communicate in writing with all counsel involved in the VDRP, to discuss:

(1) fixing a convenient date and place for the VDRP session (the session shall be held as soon as reasonably possible, but no more than ninety-one (91) days after the Neutral is selected, unless otherwise ordered by the Court);

(2) the type of session desired by the parties (i.e. settlement conference, evaluation, or other dispute resolution process) and the procedures that will be following during the session;

(3) who shall attend the session on behalf of each party;

(4) what material or exhibits should be provided to the Neutral before the session or brought by the parties to the session;

(5) any issues or matters that it would be especially helpful to have the parties address in their written pre-session statements; and

(6) any other matters that might enhance the utility of the VDRP proceeding.

(k) Written VDRP Statements.

(1) *Service Deadline.* Unless otherwise directed by the Neutral, at least seven (7) days before the VDRP session, each party shall submit directly to the Neutral and serve on all other parties a written VDRP statement not to exceed ten (10) pages. Statements shall not be filed, and the assigned Judge or Magistrate Judge shall not have access to them.

(2) *The Content of the Statements.* Unless otherwise directed by the Neutral, each statement must:

(A) give a brief statement of the facts;

(B) identify the pertinent principles of law;

(C) identify the significant legal and factual issues that are in dispute;

(D) identify any legal or factual issues whose early resolution might reduce the scope of the dispute or contribute significantly to the productivity of settlement discussions;

(E) identify by name and role with respect to the litigation and the parties the person(s) in addition to counsel who will attend the session as representatives of the party filing the statement with decision-making authority; and

(F) identify or attach particular document(s) or other physical evidence, if any, central to an understanding of the dispute and an appreciation of the merits of each party's case.

(*l*) Attendance at the VDRP Session.

(1) *In Person Attendance.* All parties and their lead counsel, having authority to settle and to adjust pre-existing settlement authority if necessary, are required to attend the VDRP session in person unless excused under (*l*)(2). Insurer representatives also are required to attend in person, unless excused, if their agreement would be necessary to achieve a settlement.

(A) Corporations and Other Non–Governmental Entities. A corporation or other non-governmental entity satisfies this attendance requirement if represented by a person who has, to the greatest extent possible, authority to settle, and who is knowledgeable about the facts of the action and the corporation's or non-governmental entity's position in the action.

(B) Governmental Entities. A governmental entity satisfies this attendance requirement if represented by a person who has, to the greatest extent possible, authority to settle, and who is knowledgeable about the facts of the action, the governmental entity's position in the action, and the procedures and policies under which the governmental entity can enter into, finalize, and perform settlements.

(2) *Requests to Be Relieved of Duty to Appear in Person.*

(A) Duty to Confer. No one may ask the Neutral to be relieved of the duty to attend a VDRP session in person, unless that person first has conferred about the matter with the other parties who will be participating in the session.

(B) Standard. A person may be excused from attending a VDRP session in person only on a showing that personal attendance would impose a serious and unjustifiable hardship.

(3) *Participation by Telephone When Appearance in Person Is Excused.* Every person who is excused from attending a VDRP session in person must be available to participate by telephone, unless otherwise directed by the Neutral.

(m) Confidentiality of VDRP Proceedings.

(1) *Generally Applicable Provision.* Except as provided in this Rule, and except as otherwise required by law or as stipulated in writing by all parties and the Neutral, all communications made in connection with any VDRP proceeding under this Rule shall be privileged and confidential to the fullest extent provided by applicable law.

(2) *Limitations on Communication With Assigned Judge or Magistrate Judge.* No person may disclose to the assigned Judge or Magistrate Judge any communication made, position taken, or opinion formed by any party or Neutral in connection with any VDRP proceeding under this Rule except as otherwise:

(A) stipulated in writing by all parties and the Neutral;

(B) provided in this Rule; or

(C) ordered by the Court—after application of pertinent legal tests that are appropriately sensitive to the interests underlying VDRP confidentiality—in connection with a proceeding to determine:

(i) whether, a signed writing or otherwise sufficient evidence is produced that appears to constitute a binding agreement, the parties entered an enforceable settlement contract at the end of the VDRP session, or

(ii) whether a person violated a legal norm, rule, court order, or ethical duty during or in connection with the VDRP session.

(3) *Authorized Studies and Assessments of Program.* Nothing in this Rule shall be construed to prevent any participant or Neutral in a VDRP proceeding from responding to an appropriate request for information duly made by persons authorized by the Court to monitor or evaluate any aspect of the VDRP or to enforce any provision of the Rule. The identity of the sources of such information provided for purposes of monitoring or evaluating the VDRP shall be appropriately protected.

(n) Neutral's VDRP Completion Report.

(1) *Timing and Limited Content.* By the deadline fixed in the Stipulation and Order for VDRP Referral, or, if no such deadline was fixed, no later than fourteen (14) days after the VDRP session has been concluded, the Neutral shall submit to the VDRP Administrator (copying all parties) the Neutral's VDRP Completion Report that reports only the date on which the parties completed the VDRP process.

(2) *Prohibition on Disclosure of Confidential Communications or Neutral's Opinions.* Except as otherwise provided in this Rule, the Neutral's VDRP Completion Report must not disclose to the assigned Judge any confidential communication or any opinions or thoughts the Neutral might have about the merits of the action, about how the action should be managed, or about the character of any party's participation in the VDRP proceeding. The Neutral may communicate an alleged abuse of the VDRP process to the ADR Judge.

(o) Parties' Joint VDRP Completion Report.

(1) *Completion Report.* By the deadline fixed in the Stipulation and Order for VDRP Referral, or, if no such deadline was fixed, no later than fourteen (14) days after the VDRP session has been concluded, the parties must jointly file the Parties' Joint VDRP Completion Report in which they report to the assigned Judge or Magistrate Judge:

(A) whether the action in its entirety was resolved or settled during the VDRP session, and if so, when a request for dismissal will be filed;

(B) if the action in its entirety was not resolved or settled, whether any resolution, stipulation, or agreement was reached on any part of the action, including but not limited to any stipulation or agreement regarding facts, issues, procedures, or claims; and

(C) the current status of the action, including an update, as appropriate, on the subjects set forth in L.R. 240.

(2) *Dismissal.* Where appropriate, a Dismissal or Stipulation and Order for dismissal of the action, pursuant to Fed. R. Civ. P. 41, may be filed in lieu of the Parties' Joint VDRP Completion Report if the Dismissal or Stipulation and Order for dismissal is filed within fourteen (14) days after completion of the VDRP session.

(p) Violations of This Local Rule.

(1) *Complaints Alleging Material Violations.* A complaint alleging that any person or party has materially violated this Rule must be presented in writing directly to the ADR Judge or a Judge who has been designated by the Chief Judge to hear the matter and to whom the underlying action is not assigned (the "designated Judge"). Copies of any such complaint must be sent to all counsel and the Neutral at the time they are presented to the ADR Judge or designated Judge. Any such complaint must be accompanied by a competent affidavit, must not be filed or lodged, and must not be presented to the Judge or Magistrate Judge to whom the underlying action is assigned for litigation.

(2) *Proceedings in Response to Complaint.* Upon receipt of an appropriately presented and supported complaint of material violation, the ADR Judge or designated Judge shall determine whether the matter warrants further proceedings and

shall so notify the parties and the person complaining. If further proceedings are warranted, the ADR Judge or designated Judge may issue an order to show cause why sanctions should not be imposed. Any such proceeding shall be conducted on the record, and the ADR Judge or designated Judge shall have the discretion as to whether the proceedings should be under seal. The ADR Judge or designated Judge shall afford all interested persons an opportunity to be heard before deciding whether to impose or recommend a sanction.

[Effective December 1, 2009.]

RULE 272. NOTICE OF SETTLEMENT
(Fed. R. Civ. P. 16)

(a) General Rule. See L.R. 160.

(b) Sanctions. If for any reason attributable to counsel or parties, including settlement, the Court is unable to commence a jury trial as scheduled when a panel of prospective jurors has reported for voir dire, the Court may assess against counsel or parties responsible all or part of the cost of the panel. See L.R. 110.

[Effective December 1, 2009.]

RULE 280. DILIGENCE—SETTING FOR PRETRIAL CONFERENCE OR FOR TRIAL (Fed. R. Civ. P. 40)

(a) Counsel's Duty of Diligence. All counsel shall proceed with reasonable diligence to take all steps necessary to bring an action to issue and readiness for pretrial conference and trial. The action shall be ready for trial on the date set by the Court.

(b) Motion to Set for Pretrial Conference and/or Trial. Although ordinarily it is expected that the pretrial conference will be set at a status conference, any party who is ready to proceed to pretrial conference and trial may serve and file a motion to have the action set for pretrial conference or trial or both. The motion shall be accompanied by a Certificate of Readiness stating:

(1) The action is at issue as to all parties.

(2) The party has completed all desired depositions, other discovery, and pretrial motions, except specified discovery or motions, if any. Reasons for any exceptions shall be given, together with the date of anticipated completion thereof.

(3) The party has met all obligations with respect to deposition and discovery requests or motions of other parties.

(4) The party is ready for pretrial conference and trial.

(c) Opposition and Reply re Motion to Set. Opposition to a motion to set an action for pretrial conference or trial and any reply shall be filed in accordance with L.R. 230. Opposition shall state with specificity the reasons for opposing the motion.

(d) Notice. The Clerk shall serve notice of every order setting an action for pretrial conference or trial on all counsel, whether made pursuant to motion or sua sponte.

[Effective December 1, 2009.]

RULE 281. PRETRIAL STATEMENTS
(Fed. R. Civ. P. 16)

(a) Time for Filing. As required by the pretrial (scheduling) order in the action, counsel shall file either separate pretrial statements or a joint pretrial statement as follows:

(1) *Separate Statements.* Not less than fourteen (14) days before the date set by the Court for the holding of the final pretrial conference, counsel for the plaintiff shall serve and file a pretrial statement in the form prescribed herein. Not less than seven (7) days before the date set for the holding of the pretrial conference, counsel for all other parties shall serve on all parties and file pretrial statements that may adopt by reference any or all of the matters set forth in the plaintiff's pretrial statement.

(2) *Joint Statements.* Not less than seven (7) days before the date set by the Court for the holding of the final pretrial conference, or such other time as the Court may order, counsel for all parties shall file a joint pretrial statement in the form prescribed herein or in such other form as the Court may prescribe.

(3) *Word Processed Copy.* Electronic filers shall also concurrently submit an electronic copy of their statement in Word format following the procedures for proposed orders. *See* L.R. 137(b).

(b) Form, Contents. The pretrial statement shall state the name of the party or parties on whose behalf it is presented and set forth the nature of the action and the following matters, under the following captions and in the following order:

(1) *Jurisdiction—Venue.* The factual and statutory basis of federal jurisdiction and venue and whether there is any dispute concerning jurisdiction or venue.

(2) *Jury—Non-Jury.* Whether the party has demanded a jury trial of all or any of the issues or, if not, whether a demand for jury trial made by any other party is conceded or contested.

(3) *Undisputed Facts.* A plain, concise statement of the facts that are undisputed.

(4) *Disputed Factual Issues.* A plain, concise statement of each fact (and any related essential facts) that the party claims or concedes to be in dispute.

(5) *Disputed Evidentiary Issues.* A plain, concise summary of any reasonably anticipated disputes concerning admissibility of live and deposition testimony, physical and demonstrative evidence and the use of special technology at trial, including computer animation, video discs, and other high technology, and a statement whether each such dispute should be resolved by motion in limine, briefed in the trial brief, or addressed in some other manner.

(6) *Special Factual Information in Certain Actions.* In addition to the facts and issues described in (3) through (5), the following special information with respect to the following types of actions shall be specified within either the disputed or undisputed facts sections as appropriate:

(i) In eminent domain actions:

(A) As to each parcel involved, its designation, general description, location, and size; the interest taken; the names of persons claiming an interest therein and the interests claimed; whether an order of possession has been issued; each objection or defense to the taking, if any; and the claimed market value of the interest taken at the time of the taking.

(B) Whether consolidation of trial with other actions would be practicable or desirable.

(C) Suggested procedures for a mutual exchange of lists of comparable sales to be relied upon by the valuation experts, such lists to include for each transaction, to the extent known, the names of the parties, the date of transaction, amount of consideration, location of property, and recording date.

(D) Whether evidence of value other than comparable sales is to be relied upon and, if so, the method of valuation and the authority for its use.

(ii) In patent actions:

(A) The name, number, filing, and issue date of the patent or patents involved.

(B) The names of all persons claiming a present interest in each patent.

(C) An abstract of each patent sufficient to permit determination of the nature and essence of the technical disclosure of the application. An abstract in keeping with that called for in Patent Office Rule 1.72(b) shall be deemed sufficient. *See* 37 C.F.R. § 1.72.

(D) A statement of the facts relied upon to support any charge of infringement.

(E) Where invalidity of a patent has been asserted as a defense, any and all prior art (patents, publications, and public uses) pleaded in the answer or noticed pursuant to 35 U.S.C. § 282, in relation to the defense invoked, whether the defense be 35 U.S.C. § 102 or 35 U.S.C. § 103.

(F) An explanation of any interparty tests that have been conducted and a request for such interparty tests as should be ordered before setting for trial.

(iii) In actions involving contracts:

(A) The parties' respective versions of the terms of the contract.

(B) Whether the contract and any modifications or collateral agreements were written or oral or both, specifying any document, letter, or other writing relied upon by date and parties, and indicating any oral agreement relied upon by date, place, and parties.

(C) Any misrepresentation of fact, mistake, or other matter affecting validity.

(D) Any breach of contract.

(E) Any waiver or estoppel.

(F) The relief sought (rescission, restitution, damages for breach, specific performance, etc.).

(G) The measure of restitution or damages and an itemized statement of the elements thereof.

(iv) In tort actions for personal injury, wrongful death or property damage:

(A) The date, place, and general nature of the incident; the particular acts, omissions, or conditions constituting the basis for liability; the particular acts, omissions or conditions constituting the basis of any defense; any statute, ordinance, or regulation violated by either party; the applicability of the doctrine of strict liability or res ipsa loquitur.

(B) Each plaintiff's age; injuries sustained; any prior injury or condition worsened; periods of hospitalization; medical expenses and estimated future medical expenses; the period of total and/or partial disability; annual, monthly, or weekly earnings before the incident; earnings loss to date and estimated diminution of future earnings power; property damage; general damages; punitive damages.

(C) In wrongful death actions: the names and ages of dependents; the annual, monthly, or weekly contribution of decedent to dependents before death; the physical condition, education, and training of decedent at the time of death.

(7) *Relief Sought.* The elements of monetary damage, if any, and the specific nature of any other relief sought.

(8) *Points of Law.* A statement of the legal theory or theories of recovery or of defense and of any points of law (substantive or procedural) that are or may reasonably be expected to be in controversy, citing the pertinent statutes, ordinances, regulations, cases, and other authorities relied upon. Extended legal argument is not required in the pretrial statement.

(9) *Abandoned Issues.* A statement of all issues raised by the pleadings that have been abandoned, including, for example, claims for relief and affirmative defenses.

(10) *Witnesses.* A list (names and addresses) of all prospective witnesses, whether offered in person or by deposition or interrogatory, designating those who are expert witnesses. Only witnesses so listed will be permitted to testify at the trial, except as may be otherwise provided in the pretrial order.

(11) *Exhibits—Schedules and Summaries.* A list of documents or other exhibits that the party expects to offer at trial. Only exhibits so listed will be permitted to be offered at trial except as may be otherwise provided in the pretrial order.

(12) *Discovery Documents.* A list of all portions of depositions, answers to interrogatories, and responses to requests for admission that the party expects to offer at trial.

(13) *Further Discovery or Motions.* Any requests for further discovery or pretrial motions. Where discovery and/or law and motion has been terminated by a Court order, counsel shall set forth the grounds for relief from that order and why a motion to be relieved was not made before the date ordered in the status conference for termination. Motions for relief at pretrial are not favored and will ordinarily be denied unless the moving party makes a strong showing.

(14) *Stipulations.* Any stipulations requested or offered for pretrial or trial purposes.

(15) *Amendments—Dismissals.* Any requested amendments to pleadings, dismissals, additions or substitutions of parties, or dispositions as to defaulting parties.

(16) *Settlement Negotiations.* A statement whether settlement negotiations between parties and/or a court settlement conference under L.R. 270 would be helpful.

(17) *Agreed Statements.* A statement whether presentation of all or part of the action upon an Agreed Statement of Facts is feasible and advisable.

(18) *Separate Trial of Issues.* A statement whether separate trial of any of the issues is feasible and advisable.

(19) *Impartial Experts—Limitation of Experts.* A statement whether appointment by the Court of impartial expert witnesses or limitation of the number of expert witnesses is advisable.

(20) *Attorneys' Fees.* A statement whether attorneys' fees are sought and the time and manner in which they are to be ascertained. *See* L.R. 293.

(21) *Trial Exhibits.* Any special handling of trial exhibits and a statement of advisability of court retention of exhibits pending appeal decision. *See* L.R. 138(e).

(22) *Trial Protective Order.* Whether a trial protective order will be sought pursuant to L.R. 141.1(b)(2).

(23) *Miscellaneous.* Any other appropriate comments, suggestions, or information that might aid in the disposition of the action, including references to any matters set forth in Fed. R. Civ. P. 16(c).

(c) Claims of Privilege. If any privilege against disclosure is claimed with respect to any statement required by this Rule and the validity of the claim has not yet been determined, a party may omit such statement and include instead a statement of such claim of privilege and the grounds therefor.

(d) Fed. R. Civ. P. 26(a)(3) Disclosures. The foregoing disclosures satisfy the requirements of Fed. R. Civ. P. 26(a)(3).

[Effective December 1, 2009. Amended effective June 1, 2010; October 1, 2013.]

RULE 282. PRETRIAL CONFERENCE
(Fed. R. Civ. P. 16)

The agenda for the pretrial conference shall include discussion of the following:

(1) The items set forth in the pretrial statements filed pursuant to L.R. 281 and the matters set forth in Fed. R. Civ. P. 16(c).

(2) The filing of trial briefs on designated points of law likely to be presented at trial. See L.R. 285.

(3) The procedures for voir dire and the filing of proposed voir dire questions and proposed jury instructions. See L.R. 163.

(4) The filing and exchange of lists of documentary and other exhibits, summaries, schedules, and other illustrative exhibits to be offered at trial, statements waiving or reserving objections to the exhibits listed by other parties, and the marking and indexing of exhibits.

(5) The filing of statements designating portions of depositions, admissions and answers to interrogatories that the respective parties intend to offer at the trial (except portions to be used only for impeachment or rebuttal).

(6) The inspection of originals of listed exhibits and of reports of experts who will be called as witnesses. See L.R. 281.

(7) The filing of proposed findings of fact and conclusions of law.

All of the foregoing agenda items shall be subject to any appropriate claims of privilege from disclosure. See L.R. 281(c).

[Effective December 1, 2009.]

RULE 283. PRETRIAL ORDER
(Fed. R. Civ. P. 16)

(a) **Preparation of Pretrial Order.** The Court, or a party if so directed by the Court, shall prepare a proposed pretrial order, serve a copy thereof on all parties, and lodge the original. See L.R. 137. If directed by the Court, a party shall do so within fourteen (14) days after the pretrial conference. Any party upon whom the proposed pretrial order is served may, within the time permitted in the proposed pretrial order, submit objections to the proposed pretrial order and, in so doing, shall set forth the basis of the objections and any changes to be made in the proposed pretrial order.

(b) **Contents of Pretrial Order.** All pretrial orders shall recite the appearances and representations (and any non-appearances) at the pretrial conference and the action taken by the Court and agreements made by the parties with respect to each of the items discussed at the conference, except that parties shall not refer to settlement negotiations. All pretrial orders shall conclude by setting the date for the trial and stating the Court's estimate of the number of court days required for the trial.

(c) **Pretrial Order to Control.** See Fed. R. Civ. P. 16.

[Effective December 1, 2009.]

RULE 285. TRIAL BRIEFS (Fed. R. Civ. P. 16)

(a) **Opening Briefs.** Counsel for each party shall file and serve on all other parties within the time set by the Court but not less than fourteen (14) days before trial a brief setting forth:

(1) a short statement of facts;

(2) all admissions and stipulations not recited in the pretrial order; and

(3) a summary of points of law, including reasonably anticipated disputes concerning admissibility of evidence, legal arguments, and citations of authority in support thereof.

(b) **Responding Briefs.** Although not required to do so, opposing counsel may file and serve on all other parties an answering brief within the time set by the Court but not less than seven (7) days before trial; provided, however, that as to any evidentiary questions raised in a trial brief by one party and not also addressed in the opposing party's opening brief, a

brief shall be filed and served by the opposing party on those questions at least seven (7) days before trial.

[Effective December 1, 2009.]

RULE 290. SETTLEMENT OF FINDINGS OF FACT AND CONCLUSIONS OF LAW (Fed. R. Civ. P. 52)

(a) **Preparation of Proposed Findings of Fact, Conclusions of Law.** After a ruling requiring preparation of findings of fact and conclusions of law, the prevailing party shall, unless otherwise directed by the Court, prepare proposed findings of fact and conclusions of law.

(b) **Procedure.** Proposed findings and conclusions that are signed and approved as to form by all parties shall be lodged with the Clerk who shall immediately present them to the Court. Alternatively, counsel shall follow the procedure for proposed orders. See L.R. 137.

(c) **Disapproval.** Any party who disapproves the form of proposed findings and conclusions shall, within seven (7) days after service of a copy thereof, file and serve a notice of disapproval, together with reasons therefor, and lodge and serve a proposed modification thereof.

[Effective December 1, 2009.]

RULE 291.1 POST–TRIAL MOTIONS FOR JUDGMENT AS A MATTER OF LAW (Fed. R. Civ. P. 50)

Motions for judgment as a matter of law shall state with specific references to relevant portions of any existing record and to any supporting affidavits: (1) the particular errors of law claimed, (2) if a ground is insufficiency of the evidence, the particulars thereof, and (3) if a ground is newly discovered evidence, the particulars thereof, together with a full, complete description of the facts relating to the discovery of such evidence and the movant's diligence in connection therewith. A motion for judgment as a matter of law and any opposition thereto shall be supported by briefs. Except as otherwise provided in this Rule or in the Federal Rules of Civil Procedure, L.R. 230 shall apply to motions for judgment as a matter of law. See Fed. R. Civ. P. 50.

[Effective December 1, 2009.]

RULE 291.2 MOTIONS FOR NEW TRIAL (Fed. R. Civ. P. 59)

Motions for new trial shall state with specific references to relevant portions of any existing record and to any supporting affidavits: (1) the particular errors of law claimed, (2) if a ground is insufficiency of the evidence, the particulars thereof, and (3) if a ground is newly discovered evidence, the particulars thereof, together with a full, complete description of the facts relating to the discovery of such evidence and the movant's diligence in connection therewith. A motion for new trial and any opposition thereto shall be supported by briefs. Except as otherwise provided in this Rule or in the Federal

Rules of Civil Procedure, L.R. 230 shall apply to motions for new trial.

[Effective December 1, 2009.]

RULE 292. COSTS (Fed. R. Civ. P. 54)

(a) Rules for Taxing Costs. Costs shall be taxed in conformity with the provisions of 28 U.S.C. § 1920, and such other provisions of law as may be applicable.

(b) Filing of Cost Bill. Within fourteen (14) days after entry of judgment or order under which costs may be claimed, the prevailing party may serve on all other parties and file a bill of costs conforming to 28 U.S.C. § 1924. The cost bill shall itemize the costs claimed and shall be supported by a memorandum of costs and an affidavit of counsel that the costs claimed are allowable by law, are correctly stated, and were necessarily incurred. Cost bill forms shall be available from the Clerk upon request or on the Court's website.

(c) Objections. The party against whom costs are claimed may, within seven (7) days from date of service, file specific objections to claimed items with a statement of grounds for objection.

(d) Taxing Costs. If no objection is filed, the Clerk shall proceed to tax and enter costs. If objections are filed, they should state specific objections to claimed items with a statement of grounds thereof. The Clerk may require and consider further affidavits as necessary to determine allowable costs. The parties may request a hearing, in person or by telephone conference call, and the Clerk shall schedule the hearing as needed. Upon the taxation and entry of costs the Clerk shall serve notice thereof to all parties.

(e) Review. On motion filed and served within seven (7) days after notice of the taxing of costs has been served, the action of the Clerk may be reviewed by the Court as provided in Fed. R. Civ. P. 54(d). See L.R. 230.

(f) Items Taxable. Items taxable as costs include the following:

(1) Clerk's fees (28 U.S.C. §§ 1914, 1920(1));

(2) Marshal's fees and fees for service by a person other than the Marshal under Fed. R. Civ. P. 4 to the extent they do not exceed the amount allowable for the same service by the Marshal (28 U.S.C. §§ 1920(1), 1921);

(3) Court reporter's fees (28 U.S.C. § 1920(2));

(4) Docket fees (28 U.S.C. §§ 1920(5), 1923);

(5) Fees for exemplification and copies of papers necessarily obtained for use in the action (28 U.S.C. § 1920(4));

(6) Fees to masters, receivers, and commissioners (Fed. R. Civ. P. 53(a));

(7) Premiums on undertaking bonds or security required by law or by order of the Court or necessarily incurred by a party to secure a right accorded in the action;

(8) Per diem, mileage and subsistence for witnesses (28 U.S.C. § 1821);

(9) Compensation of Court-appointed experts, compensation for interpreters, and salaries, fees, expenses, and costs of special interpretation services (28 U.S.C. §§ 1828, 1920(6));

(10) Costs on appeal taxable in the District Court pursuant to Fed. R. App. P. 39(e); and

(11) Other items allowed by any statute or rule or by the Court in the interest of justice.

(g) Reimbursement of Pro Bono Costs. Costs shall be reimbursed to pro bono counsel representing pro se civil litigants in accordance with the rules and procedures set forth in General Order 510.

[Effective December 1, 2009. Amended effective March 8, 2012.]

RULE 293. AWARDS OF ATTORNEYS' FEES (Fed. R. Civ. P. 54)

(a) Time for Application. Motions for awards of attorneys' fees to prevailing parties pursuant to statute shall be filed not later than twenty-eight (28) days after entry of final judgment. Such motions are governed by L.R. 230 for notice, opposition, reply, and decision. See also Fed. R. Civ. P. 54(d), 58.

(b) Matters to Be Shown. All motions for awards of attorneys' fees pursuant to statute shall, at a minimum, include an affidavit showing:

(1) that the moving party was a prevailing party, in whole or in part, in the subject action, and, if the party prevailed only in part, the specific basis on which the moving party claims to be a prevailing party;

(2) that the moving party is eligible to receive an award of attorneys' fees, and the basis of such eligibility;

(3) the amount of attorneys' fees sought;

(4) the information pertaining to each of the criteria set forth in (c); and

(5) such other matters as are required under the statute under which the fee award is claimed.

(c) Criteria for Award. In fixing an award of attorneys' fees in those actions in which such an award is appropriate, the Court will consider the following criteria:

(1) the time and labor required of the attorney(s);

(2) the novelty and difficulty of the questions presented;

(3) the skill required to perform the legal service properly;

(4) the preclusion of other employment by the attorney(s) because of the acceptance of the action;

(5) the customary fee charged in matters of the type involved;

(6) whether the fee contracted between the attorney and the client is fixed or contingent;

(7) any time limitations imposed by the client or the circumstances;

(8) the amount of money, or the value of the rights involved, and the results obtained;

(9) the experience, reputation, and ability of the attorney(s);

(10) the "undesirability" of the action;

(11) the nature and length of the professional relationship between the attorney and the client;

(12) awards in similar actions; and

(13) such other matters as the Court may deem appropriate under the circumstances.

[Effective December 1, 2009.]

MAGISTRATE JUDGES' RULES

RULE 300. SCOPE OF MAGISTRATE JUDGES' RULES—GENERAL AUTHORITY (Fed. R. Civ. P. 72)

(a) **General Applicability.** Local Rules 300 through 399 govern the discharge of duties by the United States Magistrate Judges in the Eastern District of California in all actions. The Rules are promulgated pursuant to 28 U.S.C. § 636(b)(4) and are intended to amplify the provisions of Chapter 43 of Title 28 of the United States Code and the Federal Rules of Civil and Criminal Procedure (including the Supplemental Rules for Admiralty or Maritime Claims and Asset Forfeiture Actions). Proceedings before Magistrate Judges are also governed by L.R. 100 through 199 and such other Rules as may be applicable to the particular action.

(b) **Definitions.** As used in these Magistrate Judges' Rules:

(1) "Magistrate Judge" means both the full-time Magistrate Judges and the part-time Magistrate Judges sitting in the Eastern District of California.

(2) "General pretrial matters" means all pretrial matters as to which the standard of review is the "clearly erroneous or contrary to law" standard set forth in 28 U.S.C. § 636(b)(1)(A). See Fed. R. Civ. P. 72(a).

(3) "Excepted pretrial matters" means all pretrial matters as to which de novo review by a Judge is available. See Fed. R. Civ. P. 72(b).

[Effective December 1, 2009.]

RULE 301. TRIALS BY CONSENT (Fed. R. Civ. P. 73)

Upon the consent of all appearing parties, the Magistrate Judges are specially designated to conduct any and all proceedings in any civil action, including the conduct of jury or nonjury trials, and to order the entry of final judgments, in accordance with Fed. R. Civ. P. 73 and 28 U.S.C. § 636(a)(5) and (c). In such actions, L.R. 303 and 304 shall be inapplicable.

[Effective December 1, 2009.]

RULE 302. DUTIES TO BE PERFORMED BY MAGISTRATE JUDGES (Fed. R. Civ. P. 72)

(a) **General.** It is the intent of this Rule that Magistrate Judges perform all duties permitted by 28 U.S.C. § 636(a), (b)(1)(A), or other law where the standard of review of the Magistrate Judge's decision is clearly erroneous or contrary to law. Specific duties are enumerated in (b) and (c); however, those described duties are not to be considered a limitation of this general grant.

Magistrate Judges will perform the duties described in 28 U.S.C. § 636(b)(1)(B) and Fed. R. Civ. P. 53 upon specific designation of a District Judge or by designation in (b) and (c).

(b) **Duties to Be Performed in Criminal Matters by a Magistrate Judge Pursuant to 28 U.S.C. § 636(a), (b)(1)(A), (b)(1)(B), (b)(3), or Other Law.**

(1) All pretrial matters in felony criminal actions except motions to suppress evidence, motions to quash or dismiss an indictment or information, motions to discover the identity of an informant, motions for severance, and entry of pleas of guilty;

(2) Preliminary proceedings in felony probation or supervised release revocation actions;

(3) All pretrial, trial, and post-trial matters in any misdemeanor action (including petty offenses and infractions), see Fed. R. Crim. P. 58; L.R. 421;

(4) Supervision of proceedings conducted pursuant to letters rogatory or letters of request;

(5) Receipt of indictments returned by the grand jury in accordance with Fed. R. Crim. P. 6(e)(4), 6(f);

(6) Conduct of all proceedings contemplated by Fed. R. Crim. P. 1, 3, 4, 5, 5.1, 9, 40, 41, except Rule 41(e) post–indictment/information motions and Rule 41(f) motions in felony actions made at any time; included within this grant are applications for mobile tracking devices (18 U.S.C. § 3117), pen registers or trap and trace devices (18 U.S.C. § 3121 et seq.), applications for retrieval of electronic communications records (18 U.S.C. § 2701 et seq.), and applications for disclosure of tax return information (26 U.S.C. § 6103);

(7) Motions to exonerate bail;

(8) Extradition proceedings, 18 U.S.C. § 3181 et seq.;

(9) Upon specific designation of a Judge and consent of the parties, jury voir dire in criminal actions.

(c) **Duties to Be Performed in Civil Matters by a Magistrate Judge Pursuant to 28 U.S.C. § 636(a), (b)(1)(A), (b)(1)(B), (b)(3), or Other Law.**

(1) All discovery motions, including Fed. R. Civ. P. 37 motions, and supervision of proceedings conducted pursuant to letters rogatory or letters of request; all stipulations and motions relating to protective orders and sealing documents submitted or filed for hearing before discovery cutoff;

(2) Supervision of proceedings conducted pursuant to letters rogatory or letters of request;

(3) All pretrial motions pursuant to the Supplemental Rules for Admiralty or Maritime Claims and Asset Forfeiture Actions, except a motion for injunctive relief, for judgment on the pleadings, for summary judgment, to dismiss for failure to state a claim upon which relief can be granted, and to dismiss an action involuntarily;

(4) Review of petitions in civil commitment proceedings under Title III of the Narcotic Addict Rehabilitation Act;

(5) Proceedings under 46 U.S.C. §§ 2302, 4311(d), and 12309(c);

(6) All motions for specific leave of court for the making of deposits into the registry of the Court, and all motions for

orders providing for special placement of deposits, see L.R. 150;

(7) All motions brought pursuant to the Federal Debt Collections Procedures Act of 1990, 28 U.S.C. § 3001 et seq.;

(8) Applications for writs of entry in connection with the enforcement of Internal Revenue Service tax liens;

(9) Petitions to enforce Internal Revenue Service summonses filed pursuant to 26 U.S.C. §§ 7402(b) and 7604(a);

(10) Petitions to quash administrative summonses filed pursuant to 26 U.S.C. § 7609(b)(2);

(11) Examinations of judgment debtors in accordance with Fed. R. Civ. P.69;

(12) Settlement conferences as may be calendared;

(13) In Fresno, all pretrial scheduling conferences and the final pretrial conference;

(14) All applications for interim disbursement under L.R. 202(f);

(15) Actions brought under Title 42 of the United States Code to review a final decision of the Commissioner of Social Security, including dispositive and non-dispositive motions and matters;

(16) Actions involving federally insured student loans, 20 U.S.C. § 1071 et seq., including dispositive and non-dispositive motions and matters;

(17) Actions brought by a person in custody who is seeking habeas corpus relief (28 U.S.C. § 2241 et seq.), or any relief authorized by 42 U.S.C. § 1981 et seq., *Bivens* or the Federal Tort Claims Act including dispositive and non-dispositive motions and matters;

(18) Upon specific designation of a Judge, jury verdicts in civil actions;

(19) Motions for entry of default judgment under Fed. R. Civ. P. 55(b)(2);

(20) Enforcement of L.R. 271 as provided in L.R. 271(i);

(21) In Sacramento, all actions in which all the plaintiffs or defendants are proceeding in propria persona, including dispositive and non-dispositive motions and matters. Actions initially assigned to a Magistrate Judge under this paragraph shall be referred back to the assigned Judge if a party appearing in propria persona is later represented by an attorney appearing in accordance with L.R. 180.

(d) Retention by a District Judge. Notwithstanding any other provision of this Rule, a Judge may retain any matter otherwise routinely referred to a Magistrate Judge. Applications for retention of such matters, however, are looked upon with disfavor and granted only in unusual and compelling circumstances.

[Effective December 1, 2009. Amended effective February 1, 2019.]

RULE 303. ROLE OF MAGISTRATE JUDGE AND PROCEDURE FOR RESOLVING GENERAL PRETRIAL MATTERS IN CRIMINAL AND CIVIL ACTIONS (Fed. R. Civ. P. 72)

(a) Determination. In accordance with 28 U.S.C. § 636(b)(1), a Magistrate Judge shall hear, conduct such evidentiary hearings as are appropriate in, and determine all general pretrial matters referred in accordance with L.R. 302. Rulings of the Magistrate Judge shall be in writing with a statement of the reasons therefor and shall be filed and served on all parties.

(b) Finality. Rulings by Magistrate Judges pursuant to this Rule shall be final if no reconsideration thereof is sought from the Court within fourteen (14) days calculated from the date of service of the ruling on the parties, unless a different time is prescribed by the Magistrate Judge or the Judge.

(c) Reconsideration by a District Judge. A party seeking reconsideration of the Magistrate Judge's ruling shall file a request for reconsideration by a Judge and serve the Magistrate Judge and all parties. Such request shall specifically designate the ruling, or part thereof, objected to and the basis for that objection. This request shall be captioned "Request for Reconsideration by the District Court of Magistrate Judge's Ruling."

(d) Opposition. Opposition to the request shall be served and filed within seven (7) days after service of the request.

(e) Notice and Argument. The timing requirements of L.R. 230 have no application to requests for reconsideration under this Rule. The request shall be referred to the assigned Judge automatically by the Clerk, promptly following the date for filing opposition, without the necessity of a specific motion for such reference by the parties. Unless otherwise ordered, requests in criminal actions shall be calendared and heard at the trial confirmation. No oral argument shall be allowed in the usual civil action unless the assigned Judge specifically calendars such argument, either on request of a party or sua sponte.

(f) Standard of Review. The standard that the assigned Judge shall use in all such requests is the "clearly erroneous or contrary to law" standard set forth in 28 U.S.C. § 636(b)(1)(A). See Fed. R. Civ. P. 72(a).

(g) The assigned Judge may also reconsider any matter at any time sua sponte.

[Effective December 1, 2009.]

RULE 304. MAGISTRATE JUDGES' AUTHORITY IN EXCEPTED PRETRIAL MATTERS (Fed. R. Civ. P. 72)

(a) Determination. In accordance with 28 U.S.C. § 636(b)(1)(B) and (C), the Magistrate Judges shall hear, conduct such evidentiary hearings as are appropriate in, and submit to the assigned Judge proposed findings of fact and recommendations for the disposition of excepted pretrial motions referred in accordance with L.R. 302. The Magistrate

Judge shall file the proposed findings and recommendations and shall serve all parties.

(b) Objections. Within fourteen (14) days after service of the proposed findings and recommendations on the parties, unless a different time is prescribed by the Court, any party may file, and serve on all parties, objections to such proposed findings and/or recommendations to which objection is made and the basis for the objection.

(c) Transcripts. If objection is made to a proposed finding or recommendation based upon a ruling made during the course of any evidentiary hearing, which ruling has not otherwise been reduced to writing, the party making such objection shall so indicate at the time of filing objections and shall forthwith cause a transcript of all relevant portions of the record to be prepared and filed.

(d) Response. Responses to objections shall be filed, and served on all parties, within fourteen (14) days after service of the objections.

(e) Notice and Argument. The timing requirements of L.R. 230 have no application to objections to proposed findings and recommendations under this Rule. No separate notice is required. The objections shall be referred to the assigned Judge automatically by the Clerk, promptly following the date for filing opposition, without the necessity of a specific motion for such reference by the parties. Unless otherwise ordered, requests in criminal actions shall be calendared by the courtroom deputy clerk upon request of any party filed with that party's objections or opposition thereto or upon the direction of the assigned Judge.

(f) Review. See Fed. R. Civ. P. 72(b).

[Effective December 1, 2009. Amended, effective June 1, 2010.]

RULE 305. PROCEDURES FOR THE DISPOSITION OF CIVIL ACTIONS ON CONSENT OF THE PARTIES (Fed. R. Civ. P. 73)

(a) Notice of Option. The Clerk shall notify the parties in all civil actions that they may consent to have a Magistrate Judge conduct any and all proceedings in the action and order the entry of a final judgment. Such notice shall be handed or transmitted by the Clerk to the plaintiff at the time the action is filed, and to the removing defendant at the time of removal, and the plaintiff or defendant shall transmit the notice to all other parties as an attachment to copies of the complaint and summons, or the removal documents, when served. See also 28 U.S.C. § 636(c). The Court may, at appropriate times, inform the parties of the options available under section 636(c). All such communication shall comply with the requirement of section 636(c)(2).

(b) Reference to Magistrate Judge. After all necessary consents have been obtained, the Clerk shall transmit the file in the action to the assigned Judge, for review, approval by the Judge and Magistrate Judge, and referral. Notwithstanding the consent of all parties, the Judge or Magistrate Judge may reject the referral. Once an action has been referred to a Magistrate Judge, that Magistrate Judge shall have authority to conduct all proceedings referred to the Magistrate Judge, including, if appropriate, authority to enter a final judgment in the action. See Fed. R. Civ. P. 73(a).

(c) Appeal to the Court of Appeals. Upon the entry of final judgment in any action disposed of by a Magistrate Judge on consent of the parties under the authority of 28 U.S.C. § 636(c) and these Rules, an aggrieved party may appeal directly to the United States Court of Appeals for the Ninth Circuit in the same manner as governs appeals from any other final judgment of the Court. See Fed. R. Civ. P. 73(c).

[Effective December 1, 2009.]

CRIMINAL RULES

RULE 400. GENERAL RULES APPLICABLE IN CRIMINAL ACTIONS, ELECTRONIC FILING AND PLAN FOR PROMPT DISPOSITION OF CRIMINAL ACTIONS (Fed. R. Crim. P. 50)

(a) Applicability of General Rules. Local Rules 100 to 199 and 300 to 399 are fully applicable in criminal actions in the absence of a specific Criminal Rule directly on point.

(b) Filings in Criminal Actions in General. Criminal Proceedings are defined as all felony and class–A misdemeanor actions that are opened as "cr" actions by the District Court. In general, all documents submitted for filing in this district by attorneys in a criminal proceeding on or after January 3, 2005 shall be filed electronically. See L.R. 135. Pro se defendants must file and serve conventionally in accord with applicable Rules unless specifically authorized to file electronically. See L.R. 133.

(c) Filings in Magistrate Judge Criminal Actions in General. Magistrate Judge Criminal Actions are defined as all complaints, initial Rule 40 appearances or class B and C misdemeanors also known as "Petty Offense Actions," and all other actions where a "mj" action is opened. In general, except for filings by pro se defendants, all documents submitted for filing after January 3, 2005 shall be submitted in electronic format. See L.R. 135.

(d) Exemption From Electronic Filing for CVB Actions. Until the District Court is responsible for transmitting statistics in actions generated via the Central Violations Bureau (CVB), and maintained as CVB actions, such actions are exempt from CM/ECF.

(e) Mandatory Exceptions From Electronic Filing in Criminal Actions. Due to their unique nature, the following documents shall be filed in paper format and scanned into electronic format by the Clerk:

(1) Indictments / Informations;

(2) Arrest Warrants issued by a Judge or Magistrate Judge;

(3) Search Warrants and accompanying documents;

(4) Seizure Warrants and accompanying documents;

(5) Pen Register authorizations and like documents;

(6) Criminal Complaints and accompanying documents;

(7) Rule 5(c)(3) / 20 documents;

(8) Writs ad testificandum and prosequendum; and

(9) Wiretap proceedings.

(f) Filings in Juvenile Actions. Documents in juvenile delinquency matters shall not be filed electronically.

(g) Adoption of Plan for Prompt Disposition of Criminal Actions. Pursuant to the requirements of Fed. R. Crim. P. 50(b), the Speedy Trial Act of 1974 (18 U.S.C. §§ 3161–74), and the Federal Juvenile Delinquency Act (18 U.S.C. §§ 5036–37), the Court en banc has adopted a local plan establishing time limits and procedures for the prompt disposition of criminal actions. The Local Plan provides that "a copy of Section II shall be made available to practicing members of the Bar."

(h) Availability of Plan. Counsel may obtain a copy of Section II from the Clerk and also on the court website. Counsel in criminal actions shall acquaint themselves with Section II of the Local Plan.

[Effective December 1, 2009.]

RULE 401. SHACKLING OF IN–CUSTODY DEFENDANTS (Fed. R. Crim. P. 43)

(a) Applicability. This Rule is applicable to the shackling, when advisable, of in custody defendants during criminal court proceedings convened in the Sacramento and the Fresno Courthouses.

(b) Definitions.

(1) "Crime of Violence" means:

(A) an offense that has as an element of the offense the use, attempted use, or threatened use of physical force against the person or property of another;

(B) any other offense that is a felony and that, by its nature, involves a substantial risk that physical force against the person or property of another may be used in the course of committing the offense.

(2) "Fully Shackled" means leg restraints (including waist chains), and handcuffs.

(3) "Long Cause Proceeding" means a proceeding that is expected to last at least 30 minutes, such as an evidentiary hearing.

(c) Shackling at Initial Appearance.

(1) *Single Defendant Actions.*

(A) Prior to the commencement of initial appearances, the Marshal shall make an individualized shackling recommendation for each prisoner. In connection with this recommendation, the Marshal shall complete a written form (Prisoner Restraint Level Form) giving the recommendation regarding the level of restraint necessary, if any.

(B) Once the Prisoner Restraint Level Form is completed by the Marshal, and as soon as practicable, it shall be given to the Judge or Magistrate Judge presiding over the initial proceeding. The Court may review the information on the Form, a Pre–Trial Service report, and any other information pertinent to shackling. The Court shall then annotate on the form its determination regarding the appropriate restraint level. Unless it is not feasible, the Form shall be distributed to the defendant's attorney and the Assistant United States Attorney prior to hearing.

(C) The attorney for either party may request that the Court modify its restraint level determination for the initial proceeding. At the end of the initial proceeding, the deputy courtroom clerk shall annotate the Court's final restraint level determination in the minutes.

(D) When making a determination on restraints, the Court shall, where information is reasonably available, consider the following as it may weigh in favor of, or against, imposition of restraints:

(i) The nature and circumstances of the offense charged, including whether the offense is a crime of violence, a federal crime of terrorism, or involves a firearm, explosive, or destructive device;

(ii) The weight of the evidence against the in custody defendant;

(iii) The history and characteristics of the in custody defendant, including: the in custody defendant's character, physical and mental condition, past conduct, history relating to drug or alcohol abuse, criminal history, and record concerning appearance at court proceedings; and whether, at the time of the current offense or arrest, the in custody defendant was on probation, on parole, or on other release pending trial, sentencing, appeal, or completion of sentence for an offense under federal, state, or local law;

(iv) Circumstances of the defendant's arrest, including but not limited to, voluntary surrender, or flight to avoid apprehension, resistance upon arrest, other indicia of possible flight.

(2) *Multiple Defendant Actions.* In an action where multiple defendants are charged, and it is likely that the action will require an appearance by multiple defendants at any proceeding, the Court shall consider the following in determining restraint levels:

(A) Those factors described in (c)(1)(D) above;

(B) The number of defendants in the action;

(C) The Marshal staffing actually available to counteract any disruption or other untoward behavior;

(D) The logistical disruption which might entail in having numerous defendants with varied restraint levels.

The Prisoner Restraint Form procedure set forth in (c)(1)(A)–(C) above shall be employed in a multiple defendant action. A determination shall be made for each defendant.

(d) **Subsequent Proceedings.** The Court's determination of shackling status made at the initial appearance shall continue in effect unless changed circumstances warrant a different restraint level, or a Judge determines on de novo review that a different restraint level is appropriate, giving the affected parties an opportunity to be heard. Any party may request that the court change the restraint level. Nothing herein alters the inherent power of the Judge to order up to full and immediate shackling if such an order is necessary, in the discretion of the Judge, to ensure the safety of all people in the courtroom. After the implementation of such an order, the affected parties will be afforded the opportunity to be heard within a time reasonably proximate to the shackling.

(e) **Multiple Actions Proceedings.** Notwithstanding any other provision of this Rule, in a proceeding in which multiple defendants in different actions are present in the courtroom at the same time, a Judge may direct, prior to the commencement of the proceeding, that all in custody defendants be restrained at the level the Judge believes appropriate. Any party may be heard to argue a different restraint level at the time that party's case is heard.

(f) **Unshackling of Writing Hand.** When an in custody defendant is fully shackled:

(1) At Rule 11 proceedings, the in custody defendant shall be permitted the unshackled use of the defendant's writing hand, unless the Marshal recommends full shackling for particularized reasons, and the Court adopts the recommendation.

(2) In long cause proceedings, the in custody defendant shall be permitted the unshackled use of the defendant's writing hand, unless the Marshal recommends full shackling for particularized reasons, and the Court adopts the recommendation. The in custody defendant shall remain seated at the defense table, except when giving testimony.

(g) **Jury Proceedings.** This Rule does not apply to trial proceedings at which a jury is being chosen or has been impaneled.

[Effective December 1, 2009. Amended, effective March 3, 2010.]

RULE 403. COURT INTERPRETER SERVICES IN CRIMINAL ACTIONS (Fed. R. Crim. P. 5)

(a) **Courtroom Proceedings.** Regardless of the presence of a private interpreter, only official, judicially-designated interpreters may interpret official courtroom proceedings in criminal actions, except as provided in 28 U.S.C. § 1827(f)(1).

(b) **Staff Interpreter.** Pursuant to 28 U.S.C. § 1827(c), the Court employs a staff court interpreter in both Sacramento and Fresno, who is responsible for securing the services of qualified interpreters.

(c) **Notice of Need for Interpreter Services.** Defense counsel in criminal actions shall promptly determine whether they will need interpreter services for any defendants or defense witnesses at future court proceedings and shall timely notify the staff court interpreter that an interpreter is needed. It may take up to one week to arrange for interpreter services in languages other than Spanish, and three court days for Spanish interpreter services. Notification of the need for interpreter services should include identification of the language required, any dialect, and any additional information that could assist the staff court interpreter. As to interpreters for Government witnesses, *see* 28 U.S.C. § 1827.

(d) **Notice of Continuation or Cancellation of Interpreter Services.** If a scheduled court proceeding is cancelled or rescheduled, counsel shall promptly notify the staff court interpreter of the cancellation or continuation at least two court days prior to the scheduled hearing.

(e) **Sanctions.** Unjustified failure to timely notify the staff court interpreters of the need for an interpreter or of a cancelled or rescheduled hearing may result in sanctions, including an order to pay the cost of interpreter services.

[Effective December 1, 2009. Amended effective February 19, 2013; October 1, 2013; January 1, 2015.]

RULE 410. FIXED SUMS PAYABLE IN LIEU OF APPEARANCE (Fed. R. Crim. P. 46)

This Court has provided by General Order for the payment of a fixed sum in suitable misdemeanor actions in lieu of appearance. Acceptance and payment of such fixed sum shall terminate the action; however, a Magistrate Judge may fix a higher amount in the event that payment of the fixed sum is not timely made or otherwise under conditions set forth by General Order so long as the fixed sum does not exceed the maximum authorized fine.

Copies of General Orders referenced in this Rule are available on request from the Clerk and on the Court's website.

[Effective December 1, 2009.]

RULE 420. REFERRAL OF MISDEMEANORS TO MAGISTRATE JUDGES (Fed. R. Crim. P. 58)

(a) **Referral to a Magistrate Judge.** All citations, violation notices, complaints, informations or indictments charging misdemeanors shall be referred by the Clerk directly to the appropriate Magistrate Judge. See L.R. 302(b)(3).

(b) **Court Reporters.** A party requesting a court reporter for the hearing or trial of a misdemeanor must make such request sufficiently before trial to ensure the presence of a court reporter.

[Effective December 1, 2009.]

RULE 421. DISPOSITION OF MISDEMEANOR ACTIONS (Fed. R. Crim. P. 58)

(a) **Authorization.** Each Magistrate Judge is designated to try persons accused of misdemeanors and petty offenses and to sentence such persons upon conviction. See L.R. 302(b)(2).

(b) **Pretrial and Post–Trial Matters.** Except as set forth herein, the Magistrate Judge to whom a misdemeanor or petty offense action is assigned shall have the authority to hear and dispose of all pretrial or post-trial matters arising in that action.

(c) **Jury Trials.** When a defendant requests a jury trial in an action pending before a Magistrate Judge in Bakersfield, Redding, or Yosemite National Park the Magistrate Judge may set the matter for trial in Sacramento or Fresno or may transfer the action to Sacramento or Fresno for trial. See L.R. 120(d).

(d) **Presentence Reports.** Each Magistrate Judge is authorized to direct the Probation Office to conduct a presentence investigation and to render a report as provided in Fed. R. Crim. P. 32 and L.R. 460. Such requests by Magistrate Judges in misdemeanor petty offense actions shall be limited to those actions in which the Magistrate Judge determines that exceptional circumstances exist. See L.R. 460.

[Effective December 1, 2009.]

RULE 422. APPEAL FROM CONVICTION BY A MAGISTRATE JUDGE (Fed. R. Crim. P. 58)

(a) **Notice of Appeal.** A defendant who has been convicted in a trial by a Magistrate Judge may appeal to a District Judge by proceeding in accordance with Fed. R. Crim. P. 58(g)(2).

(b) **Record.** Within fourteen (14) days after filing the notice of appeal the appellant shall order the official transcript as prescribed by Fed. R. App. P. 10(b), or file a certificate stating that no transcript will be ordered.

(c) **Assignment to a District Judge.** The Clerk shall assign the appeal to a Judge in the same manner as any indictment or felony information. See L.R. 120, Appendix A.

(d) **Notice of Hearing.** After assignment, the Clerk shall promptly notify the parties of the date and time set for oral argument which shall not be less than sixty-three (63) nor more than ninety-one (91) days after the date of the notice. An earlier date may be set upon joint application of the parties to the assigned Judge.

(e) **Time for Serving and Filing Briefs.** Appellant's brief shall be served and filed within twenty-one (21) days after the filing of the transcript or certificate stating that no transcript will be ordered. Appellee's brief shall be served and filed within twenty-one (21) days after the filing and service of the appellant's brief. See L.R. 135. Appellant may serve and file a reply brief within seven (7) days after service of the appellee's brief. These periods may be altered by the assigned Judge upon application of the parties or sua sponte. See L.R. 144.

[Effective December 1, 2009. Amended effective February 1, 2019.]

RULE 423. REFERRAL OF CLASS A MISDEMEANORS TO THE DISTRICT COURT (Fed. R. Crim. P. 58)

The following procedure shall be observed in each instance in which a defendant charged with a misdemeanor elects to be tried by a Judge pursuant to 18 U.S.C. § 3401:

(a) **Right to Trial Before Judge or Magistrate Judge.** At the time of arraignment and bail setting in Class A misdemeanor actions, the Magistrate Judge will explain the defendant's right to trial by Magistrate Judge or Judge. If the defendant declines to be tried by a Magistrate Judge, the Magistrate Judge shall order the defendant to appear before a Judge at the date and time directed by the Clerk pursuant to summons.

(b) **Election to Trial Before District Judge.** Upon a defendant's election to trial before a Judge, the Magistrate Judge shall forthwith inform the United States Attorney by written notice of the pendency of the action and the defendant's election, providing the United States Attorney copies of all documents theretofore filed in the action. The Magistrate Judge's responsibility in the action under L.R. 420, 421 and 422 shall thereupon terminate, but the Magistrate Judge may entertain a motion from the United States Attorney to dismiss the charged offense.

(c) Options Available to United States Attorney. Upon a defendant's election to trial before a Judge, the United States Attorney has discretion to determine whether the action shall proceed. The United States Attorney may file an information against the defendant. Upon election not to prosecute the action, the United States Attorney shall move the Magistrate Judge for dismissal and exoneration of bail, if bail has been posted. If the United States Attorney does not commence proceedings on the action or dismiss it within ninety-one (91) days after service of notice by the Magistrate Judge that the defendant has elected to be tried by a Judge, then the charge against the defendant shall be dismissed with prejudice on motion of the Court or the defendant.

(d) Defendants in Custody. If the defendant electing trial before a Judge is in custody, the Magistrate Judge shall immediately notify the United States Attorney by telephone of the election and shall order the transportation of the defendant to the appropriate facility unless released from custody.

[Effective December 1, 2009.]

RULE 430.1 CRIMINAL MOTIONS AND PROCEDURES (Fed. R. Crim. P. 12)

(a) Motion Calendar. Each Judge and Magistrate Judge will maintain an individual motion calendar. Information as to the times and dates for calling each motion calendar may be obtained from the Clerk or the courtroom deputy clerk for the assigned Judge or Magistrate Judge.

(b) Motion Procedures. Entries of pleas of guilty and motions to quash or dismiss an information or indictment, to suppress evidence, to sever, and to discover the identity of informants shall be heard by the assigned Judge. See L.R. 302(b)(1). All other pretrial matters in criminal actions shall be heard by the Magistrate Judge, L.R. 302(b)(1), unless the assigned Judge elects to hear some or all of such matters in individual actions. See L.R. 302(d). Motions to be heard by the Magistrate Judge shall be filed separately from those to be heard by the Judge. Motions and accompanying documents shall conform to the requirements of the Federal Rules of Criminal Procedure and these Rules. See, e.g., Fed. R. Crim. P. 47, 49; L.R. 130, 131, 132, 134.

(c) Notice. Except as otherwise provided in these Rules or as ordered or allowed by the Court, all motions shall be noticed on the motion calendar of the assigned Judge or Magistrate Judge as may be appropriate depending on the character of the motion and the orders of the Court. The moving party shall file a notice of motion, motion, accompanying brief, affidavits, if appropriate, and copies of all documentary evidence that the moving party intends to submit in support of the motion. All pretrial motions shall be filed within twenty-one (21) days after arraignment unless a different time is specifically prescribed by the Court. The moving party shall notice all pretrial motions for hearing on the regularly scheduled calendar of the assigned Judge or Magistrate Judge not less than fourteen (14) days after the filing of the motion, and at least seven (7) days before the date of trial confirmation if that date has been established. See L.R. 135.

(d) Opposition. The responding party shall file and serve an opposition brief and any accompanying affidavits or documentary evidence on all other parties within seven (7) days. A responding party who has no opposition to the granting of the motion shall serve and file a statement to that effect, specifically designating the motion in question. No party will be entitled to be heard in opposition to a motion at oral argument if that party has not timely filed an opposition to the motion. See L.R. 135.

(e) Reply. The moving party may file and serve a reply brief within three (3) days following service of the opposition. The moving party controls the initial filing date of the motion and the amount of time available between the filing of the motion and the trial confirmation date, and will not be heard to complain that time for the reply brief was cut short due to the late filing of the motion.

(f) Extensions of Time. If a party is unable to comply with the foregoing schedule for the filing of motions, that party shall move the assigned Magistrate Judge for an extension of time specifically setting forth the basis for the requested extension. See L.R. 144. Such motion shall be made as soon as practicable but, in any event, not later than the last date set by the Court for the filing of motions.

(g) Calculation of Time Periods. The time periods fixed by this Rule shall supersede the time periods for service of notices of motion, affidavits, and other documents prescribed in Fed. R. Crim. P. 47.

(h) Evidentiary Hearings. The notice of all motions and each response or opposition thereto shall contain a statement whether an evidentiary hearing is requested and an estimate of the time required for the presentation of evidence and/or arguments. The reply brief shall contain a re-estimate of the time or a statement that the original estimate is unchanged. *Counsel shall comply with L.R. 403 as to witnesses or parties requiring interpreter services.*

(i) Motions for Reconsideration. Whenever any motion has been granted or denied in whole or in part, and a subsequent motion for reconsideration is made upon the same or any alleged different set of facts, see L.R. 303, it shall be the duty of counsel to present to the Judge or Magistrate Judge to whom such subsequent motion is made an affidavit or brief, as appropriate, setting forth the material facts and circumstances surrounding each motion for which reconsideration is sought, including:

(1) when and to what Judge or Magistrate Judge the prior motion was made;

(2) what ruling, decision or order was made thereon; and

(3) what new or different facts or circumstances are claimed to exist that did not exist or were not shown upon such prior motion or what other grounds exist for the motion.

(j) Appeal From Magistrate Judge's Rulings. An appeal from a final decision of the Magistrate Judge shall be served and filed within fourteen (14) days after service of the Magistrate Judge's decision concurrently with the required filing fee. See generally L.R. 303, 304. To the extent appropriate, the brief supporting the appeal shall contain the information prescribed in (i).

[Effective December 1, 2009.]

RULE 430.2 CRIMINAL TRIAL SETTING PROCEDURES (Fed. R. Crim. P. 17.1)

(a) Trial, Trial Confirmation Dates. Except as otherwise provided in this Rule, the Magistrate Judge shall assign the trial, trial confirmation, and/or pretrial conference dates at the time the defendant is arraigned. Each criminal action to be tried before a Judge shall be set for trial, and for trial confirmation and/or pretrial conference, in such manner and in accordance with such scheduling practices as the assigned Judge may prescribe.

(b) Complex Actions. Any party who believes the criminal action is unusual or complex within the meaning of 18 U.S.C. § 3161 shall so inform the Magistrate Judge at the time of arraignment. If the Magistrate Judge determines that the action is unusual or complex, the action shall be placed on the assigned Judge's next available criminal motion calendar for a status conference.

(c) Shortening and Extending Time. See L.R. 144.

[Effective December 1, 2009.]

RULE 440. PRETRIAL DISCOVERY AND INSPECTION (Fed. R. Crim. P. 16)

(a) Initial Disclosure. Upon request of the defendant and unless otherwise ordered by the Court, all discovery required by Fed. R. Crim. P. 16(a)(1)(A), (B), (C), (D), (E) and (G) to be provided by the Government shall be provided in the manner set forth in the Rule within fourteen (14) days from the date of arraignment.

(b) Discovery of Reports. All discovery of reports of examination or tests, as provided for in Fed. R. Crim. P. 16(a)(1)(F), shall, when in possession of government counsel, be made in conformance with the preceding paragraph, and when not in government counsel's possession, as soon as reasonably possible after the expiration of the fourteen (14) day period. In no event shall the Government fail to disclose such reports at least seven (7) days before the trial confirmation/pretrial conference.

(c) Discovery From Defendant. Unless otherwise ordered by the Court, all discovery required by Fed. R. Crim. P. 16(b) to be provided by the defendant shall be provided within twenty-one (21) days from the request for such discovery.

(d) Continuing Duty. The duty of the Government and the defendant to provide discovery under this Rule is a continuing one. Upon failure to provide discovery and inspection as required by this Rule, the Government or the defendant or counsel may be subject to sanctions as set forth in L.R. 110.

[Effective December 1, 2009.]

RULE 450. TRIAL CONFIRMATION (Fed. R. Crim. P. 17.1)

A trial confirmation hearing shall be calendared in each criminal action on a date approximately two (2) weeks before the scheduled trial date. The following persons shall appear at the trial confirmation hearing: the defendant, the defen-

dant's attorney, if any, and a prosecutor from the United States Attorney's Office who is familiar with the facts and has authority to take action. Before the trial confirmation hearing, the defendant's attorney or the pro se defendant shall have completed all work necessary for a determination of whether the defendant will go to trial or plead guilty. All defendants who elect to plead guilty shall be prepared to plead guilty before or at the trial confirmation hearing. See L.R. 160.

[Effective December 1, 2009.]

RULE 460. DISCLOSURE OF PRESENTENCE REPORTS, PRETRIAL SERVICES REPORTS AND RELATED RECORDS (Fed. R. Crim. P. 32, 18 U.S.C. § 3153(c))

(a) Confidential Character of Presentence Reports, Pretrial Services Reports, and Related Records. The presentence reports, pretrial services reports, violation reports, and related documents are confidential records of the United States District Court. Unless further disclosure is expressly authorized by order of the Court or this rule, such records shall be disclosed only to the Court, court personnel, the defendant, the defendant's counsel, the defense investigator, if any, and the United States Attorney's Office in connection with the sentencing, detention/release, or violation hearing.

(b) Requests for Disclosure. Any applicant seeking an order authorizing further disclosure of a presentence report or pretrial services report maintained by the probation or pretrial services offices shall file a written petition to the Court establishing with particularity the need for specific information in the records. Requests for disclosure made to probation or pretrial services officers are improper. Except as provided in (c) below, no further disclosure shall be made except upon an order issued by the Court.

(c) Exceptions. Nothing in this rule is intended to prohibit probation or pretrial services from disclosing records without court order as is authorized by statute, regulation, or formalized national policy.

(d) Availability of Proposed Presentence Report. A copy of the probation officer's proposed presentence report, including the probation officer's recommendations, shall be made available to the United States Attorney's Office and to defense counsel not less than thirty-five (35) days before the date set for sentencing hearing.

(e) Objections to the Report. Defense counsel shall discuss the presentence report with the defendant. Not less than twenty-eight (28) days before the date set for the sentencing hearing, counsel for defendant and the Government shall each deliver to the probation officer and exchange with each other a written statement of all objections they have to statements of material fact, sentencing classifications, sentencing guideline ranges, and policy statements contained in or omitted from the presentence report. After receipt of the objections, the probation officer shall conduct any further investigation and make any necessary revisions to the presentence report.

(f) Submission to the Court. Not less than twenty-one (21) days before the date set for the sentencing hearing, the probation officer shall submit the presentence report, including recommendations, to the sentencing Judge and make it available to counsel for the defendant and the Government. If the presentence report has not been revised, counsel may be so notified and not given a new report.

(g) Formal Objections to Report. Not less than fourteen (14) days before the sentencing hearing, counsel for the defendant and the Government shall each file and serve on each other and the probation officer, a concise memorandum of all objections and facts in dispute to be resolved by the Court. This memorandum must specifically identify each item in the report which is challenged as inaccurate or untrue, must set forth the remedy sought (i.e., specified findings or the Court's agreement to disregard the disputed information), and must set forth the reason that the contested information will affect the sentencing guideline, departure or adjustment in the particular action. This requirement is not satisfied by submission of the written objections to the probation officer as set forth in (d).

(h) Limitation on Objections. Except for good cause shown, no objections may be made to the presentence report other than those previously submitted to the probation officer pursuant to (d) and those relating to information contained in the presentence report that was not contained in the proposed presentence report.

(i) Resolution of Disputes. Except with regard to objections not yet resolved, the Court may accept the presentence report as accurate. In resolving any disputes concerning the report, the Court may consider any relevant information having sufficient indicia of reliability.

(j) Sentencing Proceedings. At the time set for imposition of sentence, if there are no material items in dispute, the Court may proceed with the imposition of sentence. If any material dispute remains with respect to the presentence report, the Court shall afford the parties adequate opportunity to present arguments and information on the matter. If the Court determines that the matter cannot be resolved without an evidentiary hearing, the action may be continued for a reasonable period if necessary to enable the parties to secure

the attendance of witnesses and the production of documents at the hearing.

[Effective December 1, 2009. Amended effective February 19, 2013; October 1, 2013; February 1, 2019.]

RULE 461. DISCLOSURE OF OTHER PROBATION OR PRETRIAL SERVICES RECORDS
(Fed. R. Crim. P. 32, 18 U.S.C. § 3153(c))

(a) Confidential Character of Probation or Pretrial Services Records. Probation or pretrial services records, maintained by the probation and pretrial services offices, are confidential records of the United States District Court. Such records shall be disclosed only to the Court, unless further disclosure is authorized by order of the Court or this rule.

(b) Requests for Disclosure. Any applicant seeking an order authorizing further disclosure of confidential records maintained by the probation or pretrial services offices shall file a written petition to the Court establishing with particularity the need for specific information in the records. Requests for disclosure made to probation or pretrial services officers are improper. Except as provided in (c) below, no disclosure shall be made except upon an order issued by the Court.

(c) Exceptions. Nothing in this rule is intended to prohibit probation or pretrial services from disclosing records without court order as is authorized by statute, regulation, or formalized national policy.

[Effective December 1, 2009. Amended effective February 19, 2013.]

RULE 480. RULE 35 MOTIONS—SERVICE
(Fed. R. Crim. P. 35)

Motions and supporting documents filed pursuant to Fed. R. Crim. P. 35 shall be served on opposing counsel and the United States Probation Department. See L.R. 135(c). In calendaring and responding to a motion under Fed. R. Crim. P. 35, counsel shall specify whether oral argument is desired. Failure to request oral argument shall result in submission on the written record.

[Effective December 1, 2009.]

ADMIRALTY AND IN REM RULES

RULE 500. TITLE AND SCOPE OF RULES

(a) Title. These are the Local Admiralty and In Rem Rules for the United States District Court for the Eastern District of California.

(b) Applicability. These Local Admiralty and In Rem Rules apply to maritime and admiralty proceedings as defined in Supplemental Rule A of the Supplemental Rules for Admiralty or Maritime Claims and Asset Forfeiture Actions (Supplemental Rules) and to all in rem and quasi in rem proceedings referenced in Supplemental Rule A pending or filed in the United States District Court for the Eastern District of California. Local Rules 100 through 399 also apply to all civil actions, including maritime and admiralty proceedings and in rem proceedings. See L.R. 100(b).

(c) Inconsistency With Other Local Rules. If a general, civil, criminal, or magistrate judges' Local Rule is inconsistent with one of these Local Rules 500 through 599, these Rules shall control all proceedings within the scope of Supplemental Rule A. L.R. 151 shall have no application to proceedings governed by the Supplemental Rules and these Local Admiralty and In Rem Rules.

(d) Supplemental Rule G governs civil forfeiture actions.

[Effective December 1, 2009.]

RULE 501. THE UNITED STATES MARSHAL

(a) Locations. The United States Marshal for the Eastern District of California maintains permanent offices at 501 "I" Street, Sacramento, California 95814, and at the United States Courthouse, 2500 Tulare Street, Fresno, California 93721.

(b) Office Hours. The regular office hours of the Marshal at Sacramento and Fresno are from 8:00 a.m. to 4:30 p.m. each day except Saturdays, Sundays, and holidays.

(c) Emergency Telephone. In emergencies, the United States Marshal may be reached by telephone 24 hours a day at (916) 930–2030 in Sacramento and (559) 487–5600 in Fresno.

(d) Meaning of "Marshal." When used throughout these Local Admiralty and In Rem Rules, unless otherwise specified, the term "Marshal" means the United States Marshal appointed pursuant to 28 U.S.C. § 561, or a duly appointed deputy marshal, as the case may be.

[Effective December 1, 2009.]

RULE 510. COMPLAINTS, ALLEGATIONS AND ACCOMPANYING AFFIDAVIT

(a) Caption. Every complaint filed as a Fed. R. Civ. P. 9(h) action shall set forth "In Admiralty" following the designation of the Court, in addition to the statement, if any, contained in the body of the complaint pursuant to Fed. R. Civ. P. 9(h). If the complaint contains one or more causes of action at law, it shall set forth "At Law and In Admiralty."

(b) Mandatory Allegations. Every complaint in actions under Supplemental Rule B and C shall state the dollar amount of the debt, damages, or salvage for which the action is brought. This dollar amount shall also be stated in the process, together with a description of the nature of any other items of damage including any unliquidated items claimed, such as attorneys' fees. The defendant or claimant may post bond pursuant to Supplemental Rule E(5) based on such allegations. See L.R. 151, 523.

(c) Mandatory Allegations in Salvage Actions. In salvage actions, the complaint shall state to the extent known or the estimated dollar value of the hull, cargo, freight, and other property salved, the dollar amount claimed, and the names of the principal salvers, and shall state that the action is instituted in their behalf and in behalf of all other persons interested or associated with them.

(d) Affidavit Showing Defendant's Absence. The affidavit accompanying the complaint as required by Supplemental Rule B shall state with particularity the efforts made to obtain in personam jurisdiction over the defendant within the District. The phrase "not found within the district" in Supplemental Rule B(1) means that, in an in personam action, the defendant cannot be served with the summons and complaint as provided in Fed. R. Civ. P. 4.

[Effective December 1, 2009.]

RULE 512. PROCESS GENERALLY

(a) Issuance of Summons. See L.R. 210(a).

(b) Proof of Service. See L.R. 210(b).

(c) Judicial Authorization for Arrest, Attachment or Garnishment. See Supplemental Rules B(1), C(3). Unless otherwise ordered, the review of complaints and accompanying papers provided for in Supplemental Rules B(1) and C(3) is conducted in the absence of the affiant party or attorney. The plaintiff shall lodge a form of order that, upon signature by the Court, will direct the arrest, attachment or garnishment. See L.R. 137(b).

(d) Issuance of Authorization by the Clerk. Process may be issued by the Clerk only when a plaintiff or attorney certifies by affidavit filed with the Clerk that specified exigent circumstances make review by the Court impracticable, but no such process shall be issued until every effort to secure judicial review has been pursued, including conducting a hearing by telephone conference.

(e) Use of State Procedures. When the plaintiff invokes a state procedure in order to attach or garnish under Fed. R. Civ. P. 4(n), the process of attachment or garnishment shall so state.

(f) Instructions to Marshal. If service of process is to be effected by the Marshal, see Supplemental Rules C(3) and E(4), the party who requires service shall state in writing that party's instructions to the Marshal on appropriate forms available from the Marshal's Office specifying information necessary to effect service. If the party does not wish the process to be served at the time of giving instructions, the party shall request that service of process be held in abeyance. In such a case, the Marshal has no responsibility to ensure that process is served at a later date absent further instruction.

(g) Seizure of Property Already in Custody of the United States. When property in the custody of an officer or employee of the United States is to be arrested or attached, the person effecting service shall deliver a copy of the complaint and warrant for arrest, order of the Court, or summons and process of attachment, to such officer or employee or, if such officer or employee is not found within the District, then to the custodian of the property within the District. The person effecting service shall notify such officer, employee, or custodian not to relinquish the property from custody until ordered to do so by the Court.

[Effective December 1, 2009.]

RULE 513. PROMPT HEARING FOLLOWING ARREST, ATTACHMENT OR GARNISHMENT

Whenever property is arrested, attached, or garnished, any person claiming an interest in the property shall be entitled to a prompt hearing before the Court on written notice to the party bringing the arrest, attachment, or garnishment and to all other parties who have appeared in the action. The hearing shall be noticed and scheduled as is a hearing on a request for temporary restraining order. See L.R. 231. At the hearing, the party that obtained the arrest, attachment, or garnishment shall show cause why the arrest, attachment, or garnishment order should not be vacated forthwith and other appropriate relief granted. See Supplemental Rules B(1), C(3), and E(4)(f). This Rule shall not apply to those actions excepted in Supplemental Rule E(4)(f).

[Effective December 1, 2009.]

RULE 520. SECURITY FOR COSTS

(a) Security for Costs in Supplemental Rule E Actions. In an action governed by Supplemental Rule E, a party may serve on all parties and file a motion for an order requiring the posting of security for costs or for an increase in the amount of security for costs previously posted. See L.R. 144, 230.

(b) Security for Costs in Supplemental Rule F Actions. The amount of the security for costs required by Supplemental Rule F(1) shall be $1000 unless a different amount is specifically set by the Court. Unless otherwise ordered by the Court, the security for costs may be combined with the security for value and interest, if such security is posted.

(c) Time of Posting Security. The $1000 security for costs required by Supplemental Rule F(1) and L.R. 520(b) shall be posted before issuance of process and service of the complaint. Any party ordered to post security for costs in a Supplemental Rule E action or additional security in an action under Supplemental Rules E or F shall do so within seven (7) days after service of the order requiring its posting, unless a different time is specified by the Court.

(d) Election to Make Deposit in Lieu of Bond. See L.R. 150, 151.

(e) Sanction for Failure to Post Security. A party that fails to post security as required or as ordered may not participate further in the action except to seek relief from this Rule.

[Effective December 1, 2009.]

RULE 521. DEPOSITS OF MARSHAL'S FEES AND EXPENSES

(a) Deposit Required Before Seizure. A party who seeks arrest, attachment, or garnishment of property in an action governed by Supplemental Rule E shall deposit with the Marshal the sum estimated by the Marshal to be sufficient to pay the fees and expenses of arresting and keeping the property for at least fourteen (14) days. The Marshal is not required to execute process of arrest, attachment, or garnishment until such deposit is made. See 28 U.S.C. § 1921.

(b) Additional Deposits Required After Seizure. A party who has caused the Marshal to arrest, attach, or garnish property shall advance additional sums from time to time as required by the Marshal to pay the fees and expenses of the Marshal until the property is released or disposed of as provided in Supplemental Rule E.

(c) Sanction for Failure to Make Deposit. Any party who fails to make a deposit when required by the Marshal may not participate further in the action except to seek relief from this Rule.

[Effective December 1, 2009.]

RULE 522. INTERVENORS' CLAIMS

(a) Presentation of Claims. When a vessel or other property has been arrested, attached, or garnished, and is in the custody of the Marshal or a substitute custodian, anyone other than the party obtaining the original arrest, attachment, or garnishment who has a claim against the vessel or other property shall present that claim by filing a complaint in intervention, rather than an original complaint, unless otherwise ordered by the Court.

(b) Intervenor's Arrest, Attachment, or Garnishment. Upon satisfaction of Fed. R. Civ. P. 24, the intervenor may deliver a conformed copy of the complaint in intervention to the Marshal who shall deliver it to the custodian of the vessel or other property. In such a case, the intervenor shall thereafter be subject to the rights and obligations of a party originally arresting, attaching, or garnishing the vessel or other property, and the vessel or other property shall stand arrested, attached, or garnished by the intervenor as well as by the original arresting, attaching, or garnishing party. The intervenor in such a case shall not be required to advance a security deposit to the Marshal as was required of the original arresting, attaching, or garnishing party under L.R. 521.

(c) Sharing of Marshal's Fees and Expenses. An intervenor who has delivered a conformed copy of the complaint in intervention to the Marshal shall owe a debt to the originally arresting, attaching, or garnishing party that is enforceable on motion, consisting of the intervenor's share of the Marshal's fees and expenses in the proportion that the intervenor's claim bears to the sum of all the claims on which the vessel or other property has been arrested, attached, or garnished.

(d) Intervenor's Obligation Upon Vacation of the Arrest, Attachment, or Garnishment by the Original Party. If the originally arresting, attaching, or garnishing party permits vacation of the arrest, attachment, or garnishment, an intervenor who has delivered conformed copies of a complaint in intervention to the Marshal shall bear responsibility for the fees and expenses and shall deposit the sum estimated by the Marshal to be sufficient to pay fees and expenses for ten (10) days within thirty-six (36) hours after notice from the Marshal requiring such deposit. Such notice may be given as soon as the Marshal learns that the originally arresting, attaching, or garnishing party intends to permit vacation of the arrest, attachment, or garnishment, and an intervenor's deposit received before the funds of the originally arresting, attaching, or garnishing party are exhausted will be held for use upon exhaustion of such funds. If more than one complaint in intervention has been delivered to the Marshal, the intervenors shall step into the position of the originally arresting, attaching, or garnishing party as provided herein in order of the delivery of their complaints in intervention to the Marshal. On the sharing of Marshal's fees and expenses among intervenors, see L.R. 522(c).

[Effective December 1, 2009.]

RULE 523. UNDERTAKINGS IN LIEU OF ARREST

If, before or after commencement of the action, all parties accept a written undertaking to respond on behalf of the vessel or other property sued in return for forgoing the arrest or stipulating to the release of the vessel or other property, the undertaking shall be filed and shall become a party in place of the vessel or other property sued and be deemed referred to under the name of the vessel or other property in any pleading, order, or judgment in the action.

[Effective December 1, 2009.]

RULE 530. PUBLICATION OF NOTICE OF ACTION AND ARREST

(a) Content of Notice. The notice required by Supplemental Rule C(4) shall be published once in accordance with L.R. 171. See L.R. 580. The notice shall contain the following:

(1) The court, title, and number of the action;

(2) The date of the arrest;

(3) The identity of the property arrested;

(4) The name, address, and telephone number of the attorney for the plaintiff or the plaintiff if appearing in propria persona;

(5) A statement that claims of persons entitled to possession or claiming an interest pursuant to Supplemental Rule C(6) must be filed and served on the attorney for the plaintiff or the plaintiff if appearing in propria persona in accordance with and within the time specified in Supplemental Rule C(6) following the date of publication;

(6) A statement that (i) answers to the complaint must be filed and served in accordance with and within the time specified in Supplemental Rule C(6) following the date of publication and (ii) default may be entered and condemnation ordered in the absence thereof;

(7) A statement that motions for intervention under Fed. R. Civ. P. 24 by persons claiming maritime liens or other interests shall be filed and served on the attorney for the plaintiff or the plaintiff if appearing in propria persona in accordance with and within the time specified in Supplemental Rule C(6) for filing a claim following the date of publication;

(8) The name, address, and telephone number of the Marshal; and

(9) Such other information as the Court may order.

(b) Filing of Proof of Publication. Plaintiff shall cause to be filed no later than twenty-eight (28) days after the date of publication sworn proof of publication by or on behalf of the publisher of the newspaper in which notice was published, together with a copy of the proof of publication or reproduction thereof.

[Effective December 1, 2009.]

RULE 540. DEFAULT IN ACTIONS IN REM

(a) Notice Required. A party seeking a default judgment in an action in rem shall show to the satisfaction of the Court that due notice of the action and arrest of the property has been given:

(1) By publication, see L.R. 530;

(2) By personal service on the person having custody of the property;

(3) If the property is in the hands of a law enforcement officer, by personal service on the person having custody before its possession by law enforcement agency or officer; and

(4) By personal service or by certified mail, return receipt requested, to every other person who has not appeared in the action and is known to have an interest in the property; provided, however, that failure to give actual notice to such other person may be excused upon a satisfactory showing of diligent efforts to give such notice without success.

(b) Notice to Persons With Recorded Interests. In providing the notice required by the foregoing (a)(3), the plaintiff shall satisfy the following requirements, provided, however, that such satisfaction shall not limit the obligation to give notice to any other persons known to have an interest.

(1) If the defendant property is a vessel documented under the laws of the United States, the party must obtain a current certificate of ownership from the United States Coast Guard and give notice to all persons named therein.

(2) If the defendant property is a vessel with an identifying number, the party must obtain information from the issuing authority and give notice to the persons named in the records of such authority.

(3) If the defendant property is of such character that there exists a registry of recorded property interests and/or security

interests in the property (whether governmental or private), the party must obtain information from each such registry and give notice to the persons named in the records of each such registry.

(c) Evidence of Search for Recorded Interests. As part of the motion for default judgment, the moving party shall provide to the Court a copy of the United States Coast Guard certificate of ownership, any numbering identification obtained from any issuing authority, and/or the information obtained from the private and/or governmental registries.

(d) Motion for Default Judgment. Upon a showing that no one has appeared to claim the property and give security, and that due notice of the action and arrest of the property has been given, a party may move for judgment at any time after the time for answer has expired. See L.R. 302(c)(19). If no one has appeared, the party may have an ex parte hearing before the Court and judgment without further notice. If any person has appeared and does not join in the motion for judgment, such person shall be given seven (7) days notice of the motion; provided, however, that the Court can extend or shorten the time of the required notice on good cause. See L.R. 144.

[Effective December 1, 2009.]

RULE 550. CUSTODY OF PROPERTY

(a) Safekeeping of Property When Seized. When a vessel, cargo, or other property is seized, the Marshal shall take custody and arrange for adequate and necessary security for its safekeeping which may include, in the Marshal's discretion, the placing of keepers on or near the vessel. The Court may order the appointment of a facility or person as substitute custodian of the property in lieu of the Marshal on motion of any party or on its own motion. See L.R. 550(c).

(b) Cargo Handling, Repairs and Movement of the Vessel. Upon arrest or attachment of the vessel, no cargo handling, repairs, or movement of the vessel may be made without a court order. The applicant for such an order shall give notice to the Marshal and to all parties who have appeared before the application for such order, and the certificate of service of such notice shall be filed before application is made to the Court. For good cause shown, and upon proof of adequate insurance coverage to indemnify for any liability, the Court may direct the Marshal to allow the conduct of cargo handling, repairs, movement of the vessel, or other operations on a vessel under arrest or attachment. Neither the United States nor the Marshal shall be liable for the consequence of the undertaking or continuation of any such activities during the arrest or attachment.

(c) Motion for Change in Arrangements. After a vessel, cargo, or other property has been taken into custody by the Marshal, any party then appearing may move the Court to dispense with keepers or to remove or place the vessel, cargo, or other property at a specified facility, to designate a substitute custodian, or for similar relief. The applicant for such an order shall obtain a hearing date from the courtroom deputy clerk for the assigned Judge or Magistrate Judge and thereupon give notice of the motion to the Marshal and to all parties who have appeared. The moving papers shall establish the suitability of the substitute custodian and the existence of adequate insurance. At the hearing of the motion, the Court will determine whether such a facility or substitute custodian is capable of and will safely keep the vessel, cargo, or other property. No hearing date need be obtained for an order to be made concurrently with the order authorizing the Marshal to take the vessel, cargo, or other property into custody if the moving papers for that authority and for the substitute custodian are filed concurrently, satisfy the requirements stated herein and expressly declare in the caption that no hearing is requested.

(d) Insurance. The Marshal may order insurance to protect the Marshal, any deputy Marshal, keepers and substitute custodians from liability assumed in arresting and holding the vessel, cargo, or other property and performing whatever services are undertaken to protect the vessel, cargo, or other property and maintain the Court's custody. The party applying for arrest of the vessel, cargo, or other property shall reimburse the Marshal for premiums paid for the insurance and shall be an additional insured on the policy. The party applying for removal of the vessel, cargo, or other property to another location, for designation of a substitute custodian or for other relief that will require an additional premium shall reimburse the Marshal therefor. The premiums charged for the liability insurance are taxable as administrative costs while the vessel, cargo, or other property is in the custody of the Court.

(e) Claims by Suppliers for Payment of Charges. A person who furnishes services or supplies to a vessel, cargo, or other property in custody who has not been paid and claims the right to payment as an expense of administration shall submit an invoice to the Court for approval in the form of a verified claim at any time before the vessel, cargo, or other property is released or sold. The supplier must serve copies of the claim on the Marshal, substitute custodian if one has been appointed, and all parties appearing in the action. The Court may consider the claims individually or schedule a single hearing for all claims against the property.

[Effective December 1, 2009.]

RULE 560. APPRAISAL

(a) Order for Appraisal. An order for appraisal of property so that security may be given or altered will be entered by the Clerk at the written request of any interested party. If the parties do not agree in writing on the selection of the appraiser, the Court will appoint the appraiser.

(b) Appraiser's Oath. The appraiser shall be sworn to the faithful and impartial discharge of duties before any federal or state officer authorized by law to administer oaths, and a copy of the oath shall be filed.

(c) Appraisal. The appraiser shall give two (2) court days personal notice or one (1) day other notice plus the three (3) days for service of notice of the time and place of making the appraisal to the parties who have appeared in the action. The appraiser shall file the appraisal in writing as soon as it is completed and shall serve it on all parties. See L.R. 135.

(d) Cost of Appraisal. Absent stipulation of the parties or order of the Court to the contrary, the appraiser shall be paid by the party requesting the appraisal. Appraiser's fees shall thereafter be taxed as the Court orders.

[Effective December 1, 2009.]

RULE 570. SALE OF PROPERTY

(a) Notice. Unless otherwise ordered upon a showing of urgency, impracticality or other good cause, or as provided by law, notice of the sale of property in an action in rem shall be published daily in accordance with L.R. 171 for a period of four (4) days before the date of sale. See L.R. 580.

(b) Payment of Bid. The person whose bid is accepted shall immediately pay the Marshal for deposit into the Court's registry either the full purchase price if the bid is no more than $1000 or a deposit of $1000 or 10 percent of the bid, whichever is greater, if the bid exceeds $1000. The bidder shall pay the balance of the purchase price within three (3) court days following the sale. If an objection to the sale is filed within that time, the bidder is excused from paying the balance of the purchase price until three (3) court days after the sale is confirmed. Payments to the Marshal shall be in cash, certified check or cashier's check. The Court may specify different terms in any order of sale.

(c) Penalty for Late Payment of Balance. A successful bidder who fails to pay the balance of the bid within the time allowed under these Rules or a different time specified by the Court shall also pay the Marshal the costs of keeping the property from the date payment of the balance was due to the date the bidder pays the balance and takes delivery of the property. Unless otherwise ordered by the Court, the Marshal shall refuse to release the property until this additional charge is paid.

(d) Penalty for Default in Payment of Balance. A successful bidder who fails to pay the balance of the bid within the time allowed is in default, and the Court may at any time thereafter order a sale to the second highest bidder or order a new sale as appropriate. Any sum deposited by the bidder in default shall be forfeited and applied to pay any additional costs incurred by the Marshal by reason of the forfeiture and default, including costs incident to resale. The balance of the deposit, if any, shall be retained in the registry subject to further order of the Court, and the Court shall be given notice of its existence whenever the registry deposits are reviewed.

(e) Report of Sale by the Marshal. At the conclusion of the sale and no later than one (1) court day before payment of the balance is due, the Marshal shall forthwith file a report of the fact of sale, the date thereof, the price obtained, the name and address of the successful bidder, and any other pertinent information.

(f) Time and Procedure for Objection to Sale. An interested person may object to the sale by filing an objection within three (3) days following the sale, serving the objection on all parties, the successful bidder and the Marshal, and depositing a sum with the Marshal that is sufficient to pay the expense of keeping the property for at least six (6) court days. Service shall be in person or by an appropriate overnight delivery method calculated to ensure delivery to the recipient

within thirty (30) hours of transmittal. Payment of the required deposit to the Marshal shall be in cash, certified check, or cashier's check. The written objection must be endorsed by the Marshal with an acknowledgment of receipt before filing.

(g) Confirmation of Sale Without Motion. A sale shall stand confirmed as of course without any affirmative action by the Court unless (1) objection is filed within the time allowed under these Rules, or (2) the purchaser is in default for failure to pay the balance due the Marshal. The purchaser in a sale so confirmed as of course shall present a form of order reflecting the confirmation of the sale for entry by the Clerk on or after the fifth day following the sale. The Marshal shall transfer title to the purchaser upon presentation of such order signed by the Clerk.

(h) Confirmation of Sale on Motion. If an objection has been filed or if the successful bidder is in default, the Marshal, the objector, the successful bidder, or a party may move the Court for relief. The motion will be heard summarily by the Court. The person seeking a hearing on such motion shall apply to the Court for an order fixing the date and time of the hearing and directing the manner of giving notice and shall give notice of the motion to the Marshal, all parties, the successful bidder and the objector. The Court may confirm the sale, order a new sale, or grant such other relief as justice requires.

(i) Disposition of Deposits.

(1) *Objection Sustained.* If an objection is sustained, sums deposited by the successful bidder will be returned to the bidder forthwith. The sum deposited by the objector will be applied to pay the fees and expenses incurred by the Marshal in keeping the property until it is resold, and any balance remaining shall be returned to the objector. The objector will be reimbursed for the expense of keeping the property from the proceeds of a subsequent sale.

(2) *Objection Overruled.* If the objection is overruled, the sum deposited by the objector will be applied to pay the expense of keeping the property from the day the objection was filed until the day the sale is confirmed, and any balance remaining will be returned to the objector forthwith.

(j) Title to Property Sold. Failure of a party to give the required notice of the action and arrest of the vessel, cargo or other property or required notice of the sale may afford grounds for objecting to the sale but does not affect the title of a bona fide purchaser of the property without notice of the failure.

[Effective December 1, 2009.]

RULE 580. PUBLICATION OF NOTICES

Every notice required to be published in a newspaper by any statute of the United States or any Rule applying to admiralty and maritime proceedings, including the Supplemental Rules for Certain Admiralty and Maritime Claims and these Local Rules, shall be published in accordance with L.R. 171.

[Effective December 1, 2009.]

RULE 590.   RATE OF PREJUDGMENT
INTEREST ALLOWED

Unless the Court directs otherwise, an award of prejudgment interest shall be computed at the rate authorized in 28 U.S.C. § 1961, providing for interest on judgments.

[Effective December 1, 2009.]

APPENDIX A. AUTOMATED CASE ASSIGNMENT PLAN

(a) Purpose. This Assignment Plan is adopted to set forth a method whereby actions are assigned in this District, in accordance with the provisions of 28 U.S.C. § 137. Civil and criminal actions shall be assigned at random by means of an Automated Case Assignment System. All proceedings hereunder shall be under the supervision of the Clerk.

(b) Assignment of Civil Actions. Upon the filing of the initial complaint or other document first filed in a civil action, the Clerk shall assign a case number which shall be consecutive and prefixed by a the number "1:" denoting Fresno or "2:" denoting Sacramento, a filing year (the last two digits of the year in which the action is filed), followed by a "-cv-" and the next available case number available. Example: 1:05–cv–00205.

(c) Assignment of Criminal Actions. Upon the filing of the indictment, information, or other first document in a criminal action, the Clerk shall mark as provided in (b) except that "-cr-" will be used instead of "-cv-."

(d) Assignment of Miscellaneous Actions. Upon the filing of the first document in any action other than a civil action or a criminal action, the Clerk shall mark it as provided in (b)(1) and (2), except that "mc" will be used instead of "cv."

(e) Assignment Procedure. The Clerk shall assign actions to a Judge sitting in Sacramento or Fresno, where the action is filed, in the following manner:

(1) There shall be a separate category for each of the following types of actions:

A. Fresno Civil:
1. Frs DJ Civ (Civil)
2. Frs DJ Civ (Death Penalty)
3. Frs DJ Civ (Prisoner Civil Rights)
4. Frs DJ Civ (Prisoner Habeas Corpus)
5. Frs MJ Civ (Civil)
6. Frs MJ Civ (Prisoner Civil Rights)
7. Frs MJ Civ (Prisoner Habeas Corpus)
8. Frs MJ Civ (Social Security)
9. Frs MJ FP (In Forma Pauperis)
10. Frs MJ MC (Miscellaneous)

B. Fresno Criminal:
1. Frs DJ Cr (01 Defendant)
2. Frs DJ Cr (02–04 Defendants)
3. Frs DJ Cr (05–07 Defendants)
4. Frs DJ Cr (8+ Defendants)
5. Frs DJ Mc (Pre–Indictment Criminal)
5. Frs MJ (Mag Case/Petty Offense)
6. Frs MJ Cr (Misdemeanor)
7. Frs MJ SW (Search Warrant)

C. Sacramento Civil:
1. Sac All St (Settlement Conf)
2. Sac DJ (Emergency / TRO)
3. Sac DJ Civ (Bankruptcy)
4. Sac DJ Civ (Civil Rights)
5. Sac DJ Civ (Contract)
6. Sac DJ Civ (Death Penalty)

7. Sac DJ Civ (Federal Tax Suits)

8. Sac DJ Civ (Forfeiture/Penalty)

9. Sac DJ Civ (Labor)

10. Sac DJ Civ (Other Statutes)

11. Sac DJ Civ (Personal Injury)

12. Sac DJ Civ (Personal Property)

13. Sac DJ Civ (Prisoner Petitions)

14. Sac DJ Civ (Pro Se)

15. Sac DJ Civ (Property Rights)

16. Sac DJ Civ (Real Property)

17. Sac DJ Civ (Social Security)

18. Sac DJ Civ (Unassigned Presider)

19. Sac DJ Mc (Miscellaneous)

20. Sac MJ Civ (Civil)

21. Sac MJ Civ (Death Penalty)

22. Sac MJ Civ (Prisoner Civil Rights)

23. Sac MJ Civ (Prisoner Habeas Corpus)

24. Sac MJ Civ (Pro Se)

25. Sac MJ Civ (Social Security)

26. Sac MJ Mc (Miscellaneous)

27. Sac MJ St (Settlement Conference)

D. Sacramento Criminal:

1. Sac DJ Cr (01–05 Defendants)

2. Sac DJ Cr (06–10 Defendants)

3. Sac DJ Cr (11 + Defendants)

4. Sac DJ Cr (Appeals from MJ)

5. Sac DJ SW (Wire Tap)

6. Sac MJ (Mag Case/Petty Offense)

7. Sac MJ Cr (Misdemeanor)

8. Sac MJ SW (Search Warrant)

E. Bakersfield Criminal:

1. Bak MJ (Mag Case/Petty Offense)

2. Bak MJ Cr (Misdemeanor)

F. Redding Criminal:

1. Red MJ (Mag Case/Petty Offense)

2. Red MJ Cr (Misdemeanor)

3. Red MJ SW (Search Warrant)

G. Yosemite Criminal:

1. Yos MJ (Mag Case/Petty Offense)

2. Yos MJ Cr (Misdemeanor)

(2) Each category or "deck" shall contain a number of "cards" signifying the name of each active Judge. The number of cards for each Judge shall be equal, except as may from time to time be determined by the Court.

(3) The "deck of cards" shall be automatically shuffled by the computer at the time the categories are filled and each time an assignment is made, so that the sequence of the Judge's names shall be random and secret.

(4) When the initial document is presented for filing and has been marked pursuant to (b), (c), or (d), the Clerk shall draw a Judge from the applicable category in the Automated Case Assignment System on the computer.

(5) Thereafter the Clerk shall proceed by assigning the initials of the assigned Judge and Magistrate Judge, immediately after the case number placed on the document pursuant to (b), (c), and (d). All subsequent papers filed in the action shall bear the designation "1:" or "2:" followed by the year, case type "-cv-," "-cr-," or "-mc-" and the case number, followed by the initials of the assigned Judge or Judge and Magistrate Judge, e.g., **"1:05–cr–00200–ABC" or "2:05–cv–0700–ABC– DEF."**

(6) The assignment of each action shall be completed as each initial document is presented for filing and before the processing of the next action is begun.

(7) In emergency situations (in Sacramento) when counsel deems prompt action necessary and if the assigned Judge is absent or otherwise unable to hear the matter in time, the Clerk shall draw the name of another Judge in the manner hereinabove described from the category "Emergency Applications." The matter shall be returned to the calendar of the unavailable assigned Judge upon completion of the hearing on the emergency application unless the matter is transferred pursuant to these Rules.

(f) Reassignments. No action, once assigned, shall be reassigned to any other Judge except as hereinafter provided:

(1) Actions may be reassigned between Judges on order signed by the transferring and accepting Judges as approved by the Court.

(2) Actions may be assigned and reassigned by order of the Court to effectuate the related case rule. See L.R. 123.

(3) In the event the Judge to whom an action has been assigned files therein a statement of disqualification or is disqualified, the Court may make an order directing the Clerk to draw again for reassignment of the action to another Judge and to replace the name of the disqualified Judge in the Automated Case Assignment System.

(4) With the approval of the Court en banc, the Chief Judge may make such other assignments, reassignments or related orders as are conducive to the equitable division and just, efficient and economical determination of the business of the Court.

(5) At the time of each reassignment the Clerk shall make such appropriate adjustment in the Automated Case Assignment System as is necessary to balance the equal number of "cards" in each assignment category.

(g) Visiting Judges. Whenever a Judge has been assigned to serve as a visiting Judge in this Court, the Chief Judge shall, before the arrival of such Judge, make an order transferring to the visiting Judge from the other Judges those actions designated by them as available for transfer. Selection of actions for this purpose shall be made upon a basis equitable among all the Judges and after consultation with them.

(h) Review of Assignments. A Judge may request the Chief Judge to review an assignment or reassignment. If the Chief Judge requests such review, the Chief Judge shall designate another Judge to serve on the hearing of such request. A Judge affected by a ruling may have the ruling reviewed by the Court en banc.

(i) Assignment Reports.

(1) The Clerk shall maintain assignments in the Automated Case Assignment System which shall contain an account of all actions assigned to each of the Judges or to any visiting Judge and all reassignments among Judges.

(2) At the end of each month, the Clerk will prepare from the foregoing records for the Chief Judge (copy to each Judge) a report showing the number of actions assigned to and pending before each Judge and such other information as the Chief Judge may direct.

(j) Social Security Actions. Notwithstanding any other provision in Appendix A, Social Security individual benefits review actions brought in Sacramento under 42 U.S.C. §§ 405(g), 1383(c)(3), and/or 1395ff, shall be assigned as follows:

(1) When initially assigned, the action shall be randomly assigned to a Magistrate Judge only. The parties shall forthwith be informed of their right to consent to proceed before a Magistrate Judge pursuant to 28 U.S.C. § 636(c). Such notice shall be handed or transmitted by the Clerk to the plaintiff at the time the action is filed, and the plaintiff shall transmit the notice to all other parties as an attachment to copies of the complaint and summons, when served. The form entitled Consent to Assignment or Request for Reassignment shall be returned to the Clerk within ninety (90) days from the date the action was filed.

(2) If all executed Consent to Assignment or Request for Reassignment forms have not been returned within ninety (90) days, parties will be ordered to show cause why the forms have not been returned to the Clerk.

(3) If any party requests reassignment to a United States District Judge, the Clerk will randomly assign a District Judge to hear the action. In the absence of a future consent by all parties, the action shall be adjudicated pursuant to 28 U.S.C. § 636(b)(1)(A) and (b)(3); L.R. 302(c)(15).

(k) Prisoner Civil Rights and Habeas Corpus Actions. Notwithstanding any other provision in Appendix A, actions encompassed by L.R. 302(c)(17) (generally actions brought by a person in state custody for habeas corpus relief or whether in state or federal custody pursuant to 42 U.S.C. § 1981 et seq. or its federal *Bivens* equivalent) shall be assigned as follows:

(1) When initially assigned, the action shall be randomly assigned to a Magistrate Judge only. The parties shall be given notice of their right to proceed before a Magistrate Judge pursuant to 28 U.S.C. § 636(c). Such notice shall be transmitted by the Clerk to the plaintiff/petitioner as soon as practicable after the filing of the complaint. Respondents in habeas corpus actions shall be given notice at the time the petition is transmitted to the appropriate government attorney. Defendants in civil rights actions shall be given notice when an order to serve defendants is issued. Notice shall include a form entitled "Consent to Assignment or Request for Reassignment," and the form shall be returned no later than thirty (30) days after receipt of the consent notice referenced above.

(2) If executed Consent to Assignment or Request for Reassignment forms have not been returned as required by (1) above, the parties may be ordered to show cause why the forms have not been returned to the Clerk.

(3) If any party requests reassignment to a United States District Judge, the Clerk shall randomly assign a District Judge as presiding judge. In the absence of a future consent by all parties, the action shall be adjudicated pursuant to 28 U.S.C. § 636(b)(1)(A) and (b)(3); L.R. 302(c)(17). Actions in which all parties have consented pursuant to 28 U.S.C. § 636(c) shall remained assigned to the Magistrate Judge only.

(*l*) Direct Assignments. Notwithstanding any other provision in Appendix A, the Judges of this Court have agreed that the following actions shall be directly assigned as follows.

(1) Criminal actions arising from a wire tap search warrant shall be directly assigned to the Judge who was assigned the wire tap search warrant.

(2) Civil forfeiture actions arising from a criminal action shall be directly assigned to the Judge who was assigned to the criminal action. If the civil forfeiture action is filed prior to the criminal action, the Judge initially assigned the civil forfeiture action shall be directly assigned to the criminal action.

(3) All civil actions initiated by non-prisoner plaintiffs from Butte, Lassen, Modoc, Plumas, Shasta, Siskiyou, Tehama, and Trinity counties shall be directly assigned to the Magistrate Judge sitting in Redding. The direct assignment of these cases would be for those purposes anticipated by these Rules, including resolution of discovery disputes, conducting of settlement conferences, and holding jury trials with consent of the parties.

(4) All civil actions where defendants reside in Inyo and Kern counties shall be directly assigned to the Magistrate Judge sitting in Bakersfield. The direct assignment of these cases would be for those purposes anticipated by these Rules including resolution of discovery disputes, conducting of settlement conferences, and holding jury trials with consent of the parties.

[Effective December 1, 2009. Amended effective February 1, 2019.]

ELECTRONIC CASE FILING

Effective May 15, 2008, the Eastern District of California, in accordance with Judicial Conference Policy and amendments to Federal Rule of Civil Procedure 5.2 and Federal Rule of Criminal Procedure 49.1 will implement the following policy regarding official court transcripts:

1. A transcript provided to the court by a court reporter or transcriber will be available at the Clerk's Office, for inspection only, for a period of 90 days after it is filed.

2. During the 90–day period, a copy of the transcript may be obtained from the court reporter or transcriber at the rate established by the Judicial Conference. The transcript will be available at the public terminal at the Courthouse and remotely electronically available to any attorneys of record who have purchased a copy from the court reporter.

3. After the 90–day period has ended, the transcript will be available for copying in the Clerk's Office and for download through PACER.

Note: This policy applies to transcripts of events taking place in the court's courtrooms, not depositions taken outside of court or proceedings of state courts or other jurisdictions.

This policy establishes a procedure for counsel to request the redaction from the transcript of specific personal data identifiers before the transcript is made electronically available to the general public.

Counsel are strongly urged to share this notice with their clients so that an informed decision about the inclusion of certain materials may be made. **The responsibility for redacting personal identifiers rests solely with counsel and the parties.** Neither the Clerk nor the Court Reporter will review transcripts for compliance with this policy.

Notice of Intent to Redact:

Within five (5) business days of the filing of an official court transcript, each party wishing to redact a transcript must inform the court by filing a Notice of Intent to Redact (form available on our website).

Redaction Request:

If a redaction is requested, counsel **must** submit **to the court reporter** a Redaction Request (form available on our website) <u>within 21 days from the filing of the transcript</u>, indicating where the personal identifiers appear in the transcript by page and line and how they are to be redacted. Note: This procedure is limited to the redaction of the specific personal data identifiers listed below:

- social security numbers to the last four digits;
- financial account numbers to the last four digits;
- dates of birth to the year;
- names of minor children to the initials; and
- home addresses to the city and state.

If an attorney files a Notice of Intent to Redact but fails to timely file a Redaction Request or Motion to Extend Time, no redactions will be made and the original transcript will be remotely publicly available after 90 days.

Requests for Additional Redactions:

If counsel would like to request further redactions, in addition to those personal identifiers listed above, counsel must move the Court by filing a separate Motion for Redaction of Electronic Transcript. Until the Court has ruled on any such motion, the transcript will not be electronically available, even if the 90–day restriction period has ended.

Remote Public Access to Transcripts:

If a redacted transcript is filed with the Court, that redacted transcript will be remotely electronically available through PACER after 90 calendar days from the date of filing of the original transcript and the original transcript will never be made publicly available. If the original transcript is filed without redaction, that original transcript will be remotely electronically available through PACER after 90 calendar days.

CJA Panel Attorneys:

An attorney who is serving as appointed "standby" counsel for a pro se litigant must review the transcript as if the pro se party were his/her client. If an attorney represents a client pursuant to the Criminal Justice Act (CJA), including serving as standby counsel, the attorney conducting the review of the transcript is entitled to compensation under the CJA for functions reasonably performed to fulfill the obligation and for reimbursement of related reasonable expenses.

PACER Fees:

PACER fees will be applied both during and after the 90–day restriction period. Charges will not be capped at 30 pages as they are for other court documents, but will rather accrue for the entire transcript. The user will incur PACER charges for each time the transcript is accessed even though he/she may have purchased it from the court reporter and obtained remote access through CM/ECF. There is no "free look" for transcripts.

ATTORNEY NAME, BAR #

LAW FIRM

ADDRESS

CITY, STATE, ZIP

PHONE NUMBER

E–MAIL

IN THE UNITED STATES DISTRICT COURT
FOR THE EASTERN DISTRICT OF CALIFORNIA

Plaintiff(s),	No.
vs.	
Defendant(s).	**NOTICE OF INTENT**
	TO REQUEST REDACTION

_____/

Notice is hereby given that [PARTY NAME] intends to file a Redaction Request. The Redaction Request will be filed with the Court Reporter / Transcriber within 21 days from the filing of the transcript.

Date:

/s/–

ATTORNEY NAME, BAR #

LAW FIRM

ADDRESS

CITY, STATE, ZIP

PHONE NUMBER

E–MAIL

**IN THE UNITED STATES DISTRICT COURT
FOR THE EASTERN DISTRICT OF CALIFORNIA**

,

       Plaintiff(s),   No.

vs.

     ,   **REDACTION REQUEST** [1]

       Defendant(s).

_____/

Now comes by counsel for [PARTY NAME] and gives this Redaction Request. The Redaction Policy requires redaction of the following personal identifiers from the transcripts made electronically available:

- Social Security numbers to the last four digits,
- Financial account numbers to the last four digits,
- Dates of birth to the year,
- Names of minor children to the initials, and
- Home addresses to the city and state.

It is requested that consistent with the Policy, the following information be redacted prior to the transcript being made remotely electronically available:

Document # of Transcript	Page	Line(s)	Identifier (Example: SSN 009–09–9999)	Redaction Requested (Example: SSN XXX–XX–9999)

The undersigned understands that redactions other than the personal identifiers listed in the Policy requires a separate Motion for Additional Redactions be filed with the court within 21 days of the filing of the transcript and requires court approval.

Date:

                                       /s/–

[1] **NOTE:** *This Redaction Request should be filed directly with the Court Reporter and __NOT__ with the court.*

JURY PLAN

CHAPTER ONE. GENERAL MATTERS

Section 1.01 Authority. The United States District Court for the Eastern District of California adopts this Juror Management Plan in accordance with the provisions of the Jury Selection and Service Act of 1968 (Public Law 90–274), as amended and codified in 28 U.S.C. § 1861 *et seq.*

Section 1.02 Application. This Plan will take effect after approval by a reviewing panel of the United States Court of Appeals for the Ninth Circuit pursuant to 28 U.S.C. § 1863(a). The prior Jury Plan will be superseded as of the effective date of this revised Plan.

Section 1.03 Juror Management Defined. For purposes of this Plan, the phrase *juror management* will be deemed to include all activities associated with the master and qualified jury wheels relating to the selection, qualification, and service of grand and petit jurors.

Section 1.04 Policy. It is the policy of the Court that all litigants in this Court, entitled to trial by jury, shall have the right to grand and petit juries selected at random from a fair cross section of the community in the district or division in which the Court convenes, and that all U.S. Citizens residing within the District shall have the opportunity to be considered for service on grand and petit juries, and shall have an obligation to serve as jurors when summoned for that purpose. No U.S. Citizen shall be excluded from service as a grand or petit juror because of race, color, religion, sex, national origin, or economic status.

Section 1.05 Management Responsibilities. In accordance with 28 U.S.C. § 1863(b)(1), the Clerk of Court will manage the juror management process under the supervision and control of the Chief Judge. The term "Chief Judge" shall mean the Chief Judge of this District, or any supervising judge appointed by the Chief Judge.

(a) *Approved Management Methods.* The Court finds that electronic data processing methods can be advantageously used for managing this Plan. Therefore, a properly programmed electronic data processing system or a combination system employing both manual and electronic machine methods, may, at the Clerk's option after consultation with the Chief Judge, be used for all randomized drawings and to perform other clerical and record-keeping jury functions.

In the event of an emergency, computer malfunction, or any overt or obvious deviation from this Plan caused by automation, the Clerk, with the approval of the Chief Judge, shall manually, or by alternative electronic methods, proceed from the last step correctly implemented.

Section 1.06 Delegation of the Clerk's Management Responsibilities. In accordance with 28 U.S.C. §§ 1863(b)(1) and 1869(a), the Clerk of Court may delegate responsibility for the day-to-day operation of the jury management process to any authorized deputy clerk, or to any non-court person or agency authorized pursuant to Section 1.10 below.

Section 1.07 Jury Management Divisions. (*See* 28 U.S.C. § 1869(e) and Local Rule 120) To facilitate juror management activities, the Clerk is directed to align the Eastern District of California's counties into the following jury management divisions:

(a) *Sacramento Division.* consisting of the counties of Siskiyou, Modoc, Trinity, Shasta, Lassen, Tehama, Plumas, Glenn, Butte, Colusa, Sutter, Yuba, Sierra, Nevada, Yolo, Placer, El Dorado, Solano, Sacramento, Amador, Alpine, San Joaquin, and Mono.

(b) *Fresno Division.* Consisting of the counties of Merced, Mariposa, Madera, Fresno, Inyo, Kings, Tulare, Kern, Calaveras, Stanislaus, and Tuolumne.

Jurors will be selected for service from a single division or from a combination of divisions as the Chief Judge may from time to time direct. The provisions of this Plan apply to both divisions in the District, unless specifically indicated to the contrary.

Section 1.08 Emptying and Refilling the Master Jury Wheels. The Clerk of Court shall create and maintain a master jury wheel for each of the divisions within the District. In accordance with 28 U.S.C. § 1863(b)(4), the Clerk is directed to empty and refill the master jury wheels by October 1st each year, with a total number as may be deemed sufficient for a period of one (1) year. The Chief Judge may grant additional time to empty and refill the master jury wheels as needed.

Section 1.09 Emptying and Refilling the Qualified Jury Wheels. When the master wheels are emptied, the existing qualified wheels will continue to be used until the Clerk determines that an adequate number of persons from the new master wheels have been qualified. At that time, the old qualified wheels will be emptied and new qualified wheels created. Jurors from previous qualified jury wheels may serve at the same time with jurors selected from later qualified jury wheels.

Section 1.10 Use of Non–Court Personnel. The Clerk may use the services of non-court personnel to assist in the juror management process. For purposes of this plan, the phrase "*non-court personnel*" may include, but is not limited to:

(a) County or State of California officials, and their employees or agents, who are responsible for custody and maintenance of the source lists identified in Section 2.01 of this Plan.

(b) Owners, employees, operators and/or agents of computer or data processing centers, barcoding facilities, mail handling centers, document reproduction facilities, and optical scanning facilities, whose services are requested or employed by the Clerk to support the juror management process.

(c) Other non-court administrative or clerical persons whose services are requested or employed by the Clerk to select, process, and/or mail the various documents and records involved in the juror management process.

Section 1.11 Method and Manner for the Random Selection of Jurors. The randomized selection procedures set forth in this Plan ensure that the names chosen will represent all segments of the source file from which drawn, that the mathematical odds of any single name being picked are substantially equal, and that the possibility of human discretion or choice affecting the selection of any individual's name is eliminated.

(a) *Purely Randomized Process.* At the Clerk's option, and after consultation with the Chief Judge, the selection of names from the complete source list databases in electronic media for the master jury wheels may be accomplished by a purely randomized process through a properly programmed electronic data processing system. Similarly, at the option of the Clerk and after consultation with the Chief Judge, a properly programmed electronic data processing system for pure randomized selection may be used to select names from the master wheel to determine qualification for jury service, from the qualified wheel for summoning persons to serve as grand or petit jurors, from the pool of jurors to serve as a panel, and from the panel of jurors to serve as a jury. Such random selections of names from the source lists for inclusion in the master wheels by data computer personnel must ensure that each county within the jury division is substantially proportionally represented in the master jury wheel in accordance with 28 U.S.C. § 1863(b)(3). The purely randomized selection procedure may be used for all drawings. (*See* Section 2.03 herein for the procedures to ensure proper proportional county representation in the divisional master jury wheels.)

(1) The method and manner of purely randomized selection shall be as follows:

(i) Determining a "Quotient". The Clerk shall make the systematic randomized selection by taking the total number of names available for selection and dividing that number by the number of names needed for the master wheel. The number obtained will be the "quotient."

(ii) Determining a "Starting Number". After determining the "quotient," the Clerk shall establish a "starting number." This number will be the first name to be selected. The "starting number" will be manually drawn by lot beginning with the number one and ending with the same number as the "quotient." As an example of how both the "starting number" and the "quotient" are used, if we suppose the "quotient" to be "100" and the "starting number" to be "12," the first name chosen would be the 12th name on the list, the second name would be the 112th, etc., and continued in the same manner to the end of the list.

CHAPTER TWO. SOURCE LISTS, INITIAL RANDOM SELECTION, AND THE MASTER JURY WHEEL

Section 2.01 Source Lists (*See* 28 U.S.C. §§ 1861 and 1863(b)(2) and (3)).

The Court finds that California county voter registration lists and the State of California Department of Motor Vehicles records represent a fair cross section of the citizens residing within the communities in the Eastern District of California.

Section 2.02 Size of the Master Jury Wheels (*See* 28 U.S.C. § 1863(b)(4)). The names of all persons randomly selected from the voter registration records of the counties in each division and the names of all persons randomly selected from the State of California, Department of Motor Vehicle Records, will be equal in number and shall be placed in the master jury wheel for that division.

These two lists shall be merged and duplicate records purged. The Court takes notice that when two or more source lists are used, one person's name may appear more than once. The Clerk will, either manually or through automated systems, eliminate as reasonably as possible such duplications before any selection procedures begin.

(b) Pursuant to 28 U.S.C. § 1863 (b)(4) of the Act, the minimum number of names to be placed in the master jury wheels shall be at least one-half of one percent of the total number of names on all county voter registration records.

(c) The Chief Judge may order additional names to be placed in the master jury wheels from time to time as necessary.

Section 2.03 Substantial Proportional Representation and the Master Jury Wheels. In accordance with 28 U.S.C. § 1863(b)(3), the Clerk shall determine the number of records needed in the master wheel. The number of names drawn from each county shall be substantially in the same proportion to the total number drawn from all counties within the division.

Section 2.04 Filling the Master Jury Wheels. After first determining the total number of names needed for the master wheel and then the proportionate share of names to be drawn a combination of the voter registration records and the State of California Department of Motor Vehicle records, the Clerk shall proceed, either manually or through a combination of manual and computer methods, to make the initial selection of names from the record of each county.

CHAPTER THREE. DRAWING NAMES FROM THE MASTER JURY WHEEL, JUROR QUALIFICATION, AND THE QUALIFIED JURY WHEEL

Section 3.01 Drawing Names from the Master Jury Wheel. A general notice shall be posted in the Clerk's Office and on the Court's website that explains the process by which names are randomly and periodically drawn from the wheel.

The Clerk, either all at once or at periodic intervals, shall draw at random from the master jury wheels the names of as many persons as may be required to maintain an adequate number of names in the qualified jury wheels. The number of names to be drawn shall be determined by the Clerk based upon anticipated juror needs by the Court plus a margin of extra names sufficient to compensate for the estimated number that will turn out to be unavailable or ineligible.

At the option of the Clerk and after consultation with the court, a properly programmed electronic data processing system for pure randomized selection may be used to select names from the master wheel to determine qualification for jury service, and from the qualified wheel for summoning persons to serve as grand or petit jurors. Such random selections of names from the source list for inclusion in the master wheel by data computer personnel must insure that each county within the jury division is substantially proportionally represented in the master jury wheel in accordance with 28 U.S.C. § 1863 (b)(3). The selections of names from the source list, the master wheel, and the qualified wheel must also insure that the mathematical odds of any single name being picked are substantially equal.

Section 3.02 Juror Qualification Questionnaires. The juror qualification form prescribed by the Administrative Office of the United States Courts and approved by the Judicial Conference of the United States shall be used.

The Clerk will mail a juror qualification questionnaire notice to every person randomly selected pursuant to Section 3.01 of this plan (28 U.S.C. § 1864(a)). The notice will direct the juror to complete a juror qualification questionnaire through the Court's internet website, within ten (10) days. If a juror does not complete the juror qualification questionnaire online, a paper copy of the questionnaire may be mailed with instructions to complete and return the questionnaire to the Clerk by mail within ten days of receipt.

Section 3.03 Failure to Submit a Juror Qualification Questionnaire. If a person fails to submit a completed juror qualification questionnaire, the Clerk may note the failure in the juror's record. Upon Order of the Court, the Clerk thereafter may pursue such matter in accordance with the provisions of 28 U.S.C. § 1864(a) of the Act. No juror fees or costs for this appearance shall be paid, unless otherwise ordered by the Court.

Section 3.04 Determining Juror Qualification Status. The Chief Judge or designated judge, on their own initiative, or upon recommendation of the Clerk, shall determine solely on the basis of information provided on the juror qualification form and other competent evidence, whether a person is unqualified for, or exempt, or to be excused from jury service. The Clerk shall, by manual or computer means, enter this determination in the space provided on the juror qualification form. (28 U.S.C. § 1865(a)). The Clerk shall enter such determination on the juror qualification form or juror records in the database in the master jury wheel.

(a) *Disqualification from Jury Service.* In accordance with 28 U.S.C. § 1865(b), any person shall be deemed qualified to serve on grand and petit juries in this District unless such person:

(1) Is not a citizen of the United States, eighteen (18) years of age who has resided within the judicial district for one year;

(2) Is unable to read, write and understand the English language with a degree of proficiency sufficient to fill out satisfactorily the juror qualification form;

(3) Is unable to speak the English language;

(4) Is incapable, by reason of mental or physical infirmity, to render satisfactory jury service; or

(5) Has a charge pending against him for the commission of, or has been convicted in a State of Federal Court of record of, a crime punishable by imprisonment for more than one year and his civil rights have not been restored.

(b) *Exemption from Jury Service.* In accordance with 28 U.S.C. § 1863(b)(6), the following persons are barred from jury service on the grounds that they are exempt:

(1) Members in active service in the Armed Forces of the United States;

(2) Members of the fire or police departments of any state, district, territory, possession, or subdivision thereof; and

(3) Public officers in the executive, legislative, or judicial branches of the Government of the United States, or any state, district, territory, possession or subdivision thereof, who are actively engaged in the performance of their official duties. A "public officer" shall mean a person who is elected to public office or who is directly appointed by a person elected to public office.

(c) *Excuses From Jury Service on Individual Request.*

(1) Permanent Excuse. In accordance with 28 U.S.C. § 1863(b)(5)(A) and (B), the Court finds that jury service by members of the following occupational classes or groups of persons would entail undue hardship or extreme inconvenience to the members thereof, and the excuse of such members would not be inconsistent with §§ 1861 and 1862 of 28 U.S.C., and shall be granted upon individual written request to those:

(i) Over seventy (70) years of age;

(ii) persons who have, within the past two years, served as a federal grand or petit juror;

(iii) Volunteer safety personnel, specifically individuals serving a public agency in an official capacity, without compensation, as firefighters or members of a rescue squad or ambulance crew.

(2) Temporary Excuse. In addition to the members of groups and occupational classes subject to excuse from jury service on individual request, any person summoned for jury service may, upon written request, be excused by the Court, or by the Clerk of the Court, upon a showing of undue hardship or extreme inconvenience, for such period as the Court deems necessary, at the conclusion of which such person shall be notified again for jury service within a reasonable time or as the Court may direct. The name of such person shall be reinserted into the qualified jury wheel of the Court.

(i) Undue hardship or extreme inconvenience: as a basis for excuse from immediate jury service under this section shall mean great distance, either in miles or travel time, from the place of holding court, grave illness in the family or any other emergency which outweighs in immediacy and urgency the obligation to serve as a juror when summoned, or any other factor which the Court determines to constitute an undue hardship or to create an extreme inconvenience to the juror; and in addition, in situations where it is anticipated that a trial or grand jury proceeding may require more than thirty (30) days of service, the court may consider, as a further basis for temporary excuse, severe economic hardship to an employer which would result from the absence of a key employee during the period of such service.

Section 3.05   Qualified Jury Wheels. The Clerk shall maintain separate qualified jury wheels or devices similar in purpose and function for each division, and shall place in the wheels the names of all persons drawn from the master wheels and not disqualified, exempt or excused pursuant to this

Plan. The Clerk shall insure at all times an adequate number of names are maintained in each wheel. The Clerk may maintain these wheels by using an automated system.

CHAPTER FOUR.   SELECTION OF GRAND AND PETIT JURORS

Section 4.01   Selection and Impanelment of Grand and Petit Jurors (*See* 28 U.S.C. § 1866(a)). From time to time, the clerk shall draw at random from the qualified jury wheel such number of names of persons as may be required for assignment to grand and petit jury panels. The clerk shall post a general notice for public review in the clerk's office and on the court's website explaining the process by which names are periodically and randomly drawn.

Section 4.02   Summoning Grand and/or Petit Jurors (*See* 28 U.S.C. § 1866(b)). Upon Court Order, the Clerk shall randomly select, by manual or computer means, from the designated qualified jury wheel the designated number of persons to be summoned for a specific date. Names of persons summoned and appearing for service may be considered as a petit jury pool, from which separate trial panels will be randomly selected by lot. Pooling of jurors, staggered trial starts and multiple voir dire may be used in the assignment of jurors to petit jury panels. The Clerk shall prepare for the Court and counsel a separate list of names of persons assigned to each petit jury panel. Jurors shall complete and return their summons information sheets either by regular mail or through the Court's internet site.

The names of trial jurors may be released to the parties, the public, or the press at the conclusion of a trial (civil or criminal) only upon leave of the court. All requests for release of juror names must be made in writing to the presiding trial judge.

Section 4.03   Unanticipated Shortage of Jurors (*See* 28 U.S.C. § 1866(f)). When there is an unanticipated shortage of available petit jurors drawn from the qualified jury wheels, the Chief Judge or designated judge may require the United States Marshal to summon a sufficient number of additional petit jurors. These jurors will be selected at random, in a manner ordered by the Court, consistent with 28 U.S.C. § 1862.

Section 4.04   Petit Jury Term. In any two-year period, no person shall be required to:

(a) serve or attend court for prospective service as a petit juror for a total of more than thirty (30) days, except when necessary to complete service in a particular case, or

(b) serve as both a grand and petit juror.

A petit juror required to attend more than ten days in hearing one case may be paid, in the discretion of the trial judge, an additional fee, not exceeding the limit set forth by statute, for each day in excess of ten days on which the juror is required to hear such case.

A petit juror required to attend more than ten days of actual service may be paid, in the discretion of the judge, the appropriate fees at the end of the first ten days and at the end of every ten days of service thereafter.

The judge may order certification of additional attendance fees to be made effective commencing on the first day of extended service, without reference to the date of such certification.

Petit jurors appearing in the United States District Court for the Eastern District of California may, upon completion of their service, be released from further jury service obligations for a period of not less than two years. The Court reserves the right to modify the provisions of this petit jury policy when the interests of justice so require.

Section 4.05   Disclosure of Petit Juror Information.

(a) *To Attorneys and Parties.* When the Clerk has assigned a venire panel to a particular trial, the list of names so assigned shall be furnished to the attorneys for the parties and any parties appearing *pro se* in said trial at the beginning of jury selection, unless otherwise ordered by the trial judge. Notwithstanding this general policy, any trial judge may order the Clerk to keep jurors names confidential in any case where the interests of justice so require.

(b) *To the Public and the Media.* The names and information relating to any prospective or sitting petit jurors shall not be disclosed to the public or media outside open court, except upon order of the Court. Applications for disclosure of petit juror names or information to the media or public must be made by motion (with a memorandum of authorities) to the presiding trial judge. The presiding trial judge may order the Clerk to keep the jurors' names confidential in any case where the interests of justice so require.

Section 4.06   Grand Jury Impanelment (*See* 28 U.S.C. § 1863(b)(8)). From time to time as grand juries are required, the Court shall order the random drawing from each division's qualified wheel the names of persons as may be required for assignment to the grand jury panels. The total number of grand jurors to be summoned shall be based on a pro-rata share of the total number of persons on the voter registration record of each division as compared to the total number of persons on the voter registration records of all divisions. Special grand juries shall be selected in the same manner as regular grand juries.

(a) *Divisional Grand Juries.* If a grand jury is to be impaneled for service in a division only, the Clerk shall draw at random from the qualified wheel of that division such number of prospective grand jurors as the Chief Judge may direct.

Section 4.07   Term of Regular Grand Jury. Each grand jury shall serve until discharged by the Chief Judge, but no regular grand jury shall serve more than 18 months unless the Court extends the service of the grand jury upon a determination that such extension is in the public interest, in accordance with Rule 6(g) of the Federal Rules of Criminal Procedure.

Section 4.08   Term of Special Grand Jury. Each Special Grand Jury as defined in 18 U.S.C. § 3331, shall serve for a term of 18 months unless an order for its discharge or an extension of its term is entered by the Court in accordance with Sections 3331 or 3333 of 18 U.S.C.

Section 4.09   Alternate Grand Jurors. The Court may direct that alternate grand jurors be selected at the same time a grand jury is selected. Alternate grand jurors, in the order in which they were selected, may thereafter be impaneled to replace excused grand jurors. Alternate grand jurors shall be drawn in the same manner and shall have the same qualifications as the regular grand jurors, and if impaneled, shall be subject to the same challenges, shall take the same oath, and shall have the same authority as the regular grand jurors.

Section 4.10   Disclosure of Grand Juror Information (*See* 28 U.S.C. § 1863(b)(7)). Except as authorized by written order of the court, the names and information relating to any summoned or serving grand juror or grand jury panel will be confidential and not disclosed to any litigant or member of the public. Applications for disclosure of grand juror information must be made by motion (with a memorandum of authorities) to the Chief Judge and must show exceptional and compelling circumstances why disclosure should be allowed.

CHAPTER FIVE.   EXCLUSION OR EXCUSE FROM JURY SERVICE

Section 5.01   Exclusion or Excuse From Jury Service (28 U.S.C. § 1866(c)). Except as provided elsewhere in this Plan, no person or class of persons shall be disqualified, excluded, excused, or exempted from service as jurors; provided, however, that any person summoned for jury service may be:

(a) Excluded by the court on the grounds that such person may be unable to render impartial jury service or that his service as a juror would be likely to disrupt the proceedings;

(b) Excluded upon peremptory challenge as provided by law;

(c) Excluded pursuant to the procedure specified by law upon a challenge by any party for good cause shown;

(d) Excluded upon determination of the court, after hearing in open court, that service as a juror would be likely to threaten the secrecy of the proceedings, or otherwise adversely affect the integrity of jury deliberations, and that exclusion of such person will not be inconsistent with the policy stated in 28 U.S.C. §§ 1861 and 1862.

Section 5.02   Jury Service Limit. In any two (2) year period, no person shall be required to:

(a) serve or attend court for prospective service as a petit juror for a total of more than thirty (30) days, except when necessary to complete service in a particular case, or

(b) serve on more than one grand jury, or

(c) serve as both a grand and petit juror.

Section 5.03   Permanent Exclusion or Excuse from Jury Service. Whenever a person is permanently excluded or excused from jury service under this Chapter, the Clerk shall note the same on the questionnaire, or in the qualified jury wheel database.

CHAPTER SIX.   DISCLOSURE AND RETENTION OF JURY SELECTION RECORDS

Section 6.01   Release of Jury Plan Information. The clerk is authorized to provide a copy of this Juror Management Plan to any person requesting information about the juror management process, and may post the Plan to the court's public website. All other requests for information about the juror management process must be submitted in writing (with a memorandum of authorities) to the Clerk of Court, who will confer with the Chief Judge prior to releasing any information.

Section 6.02   Release of Juror Records (*See* 28 U.S.C. § 1867(f)). The contents of records and papers used in the juror management process will not be disclosed, except upon written order of the court. Applications for disclosure of juror management records must be made by motion (with a memorandum of authorities) to the Chief Judge and must show exceptional and compelling circumstances why disclosure should be allowed.

Section 6.03   Retention of Juror Records (*See* 28 U.S.C. § 1868). The clerk will keep all records and papers relating to the juror management process for four years following the emptying and refilling of the master jury wheels and the completion of service of all jurors selected from those master jury wheels, or for such longer periods of time as the Court may require. Such records may then be destroyed, providing the means used ensures the privacy of their contents.

Section 6.04   Request to Inspect Jury Wheel Records (*See* 28 U.S.C. § 1868). Applications to inspect juror management records to determine the validity of the selection of any jury must be made by motion (with a memorandum of authorities) to the Chief Judge, and must show exceptional and compelling circumstances why disclosure should be allowed.

[Adopted January 25, 2016, approved by the Judicial Council for the Ninth Circuit February 19, 2016, and made effective February 25, 2016.]

CRIMINAL JUSTICE ACT PLAN
(GENERAL ORDER NO. 582)
Statement of Policy

The objective of the Criminal Justice Act Plan for the Eastern District of California (CJA Plan) is to attain the constitutional ideal of equality before the law for all persons. This CJA Plan shall be administered so those accused of a crime, or otherwise eligible for services, are not deprived of their right to counsel due to any lack of financial resources. The CJA Plan shall be administered so all eligible persons receive timely appointed counsel. The CJA Plan must be administered so appointed counsel's services meet the legal profession's best practices, are cost-effective, and protect the defense function's independence in order that the rights of individual defendants are protected and enforced. This CJA Plan satisfies requirements of the United States Constitution, amend. VI, the *Criminal Justice Act* (CJA) (18 U.S.C. § 3006A), the *USA Patriot Improvement and Reauthorization Act of 2005* (18 U.S.C. § 3599*), Judicial Council of the Ninth Circuit—Criminal Justice Act Policies and Procedures*, dated October 20, 2016 and the *Guide to Judiciary Policy* (*Guide*), Volume 7A, in a way best meeting the Eastern District of California's needs.

I. AUTHORITY

Under the CJA (18 U.S.C. § 3006A) and the *Guide*, Volume 7A, the Judges of the United States District Court for the Eastern District of California (the Court) adopt this CJA Plan, as approved by the Ninth Circuit, to furnish representation in the Eastern District of California's federal court for any person financially unable to obtain representation required or entitled to by law.

II. COMPLIANCE

The Court, its Clerk, the Office of the Federal Defender for the Eastern District of California (FD–CAE), and private attorneys appointed under the CJA must comply with this CJA Plan, any General Orders issued by this District's District Judges pertaining to this CJA Plan, 18 U.S.C. § 3006A, and the *Guide*, Volume 7A as approved by the Judicial Conference of the United States or its Defender Services Committee.

The Court will post on the Court's website a current copy of the CJA Plan and any related General Orders. The FD–CAE's CJA Panel Administrator will provide new CJA counsel, upon that attorney's designation as a CJA counsel or upon their first appointment to the Panel, a current copy of this CJA Plan and any related General Orders thereon. The Panel Administrator shall also maintain a current copy of the CJA Plan, General Orders relating to the CJA Plan, and the *Guide* for CJA Panel member use.

III. DEFINITIONS

A. "Representation" includes counsel and investigative, expert, and any other necessary services.

B. "Appointed Attorney" is an attorney designated to represent a financially eligible person under the CJA and this CJA Plan. Such attorneys include private attorneys and FD attorneys.

C. "CJA Administrator" is a person(s) from the FD–CAE, designated by the Federal Defender, to administer the CJA Panel.

IV. ELIGIBILITY FOR CJA REPRESENTATION

A. Subject Matter Eligibility.
1. *Mandatory.* Representation shall be provided for any financially eligible person who:
   a. is charged with a felony or with a Class A misdemeanor;
   b. is a juvenile alleged to have committed an act of juvenile delinquency as defined in 18 U.S.C. § 5031;

c. is charged with a violation of probation, or faces a change of a term or condition of probation (unless the modification sought is favorable to the probationer, the government has not objected to the proposed change, and the probationer has waived their right to counsel);

d. is under arrest, when such representation is required by law;

e. is entitled to appointment of counsel in parole proceedings;

f. is charged with a violation of supervised release or faces modification, reduction, or enlargement of a condition, or extension or revocation of a term of supervised release;

g. is subject to a mental condition hearing under 18 U.S.C. § 4241 et seq;

h. is in custody as a material witness;

i. is seeking to set aside or vacate a death sentence under 28 U.S.C. § 2254 or § 2255;

j. is entitled to appointment of counsel in verification of consent proceedings in connection with a transfer of an offender to or from the United States for the execution of a penal sentence under 18 U.S.C. § 4109;

k. is entitled to appointment of counsel under the Sixth Amendment to the United States Constitution; or

l. faces loss of liberty in a case and federal law requires the appointment of counsel.

2. *Discretionary.* Whenever a District Judge or Magistrate Judge determines the interests of justice so require, representation may be provided for any financially eligible person who:

a. is charged with a petty offense (class B or C misdemeanor or infraction) for which a sentence of confinement is authorized;

b. is seeking relief under 28 U.S.C. §§ 2241, 2254, or 2255 other than to set aside or vacate a death sentence;

c. is charged with civil or criminal contempt and faces loss of liberty;

d. has been called as a witness before a grand jury, a court, the Congress, or a federal agency or commission which has the power to compel testimony, and there is reason to believe, either prior to or during such testimony, that the witness could be subject to a criminal prosecution, a civil or criminal contempt proceeding, or face loss of liberty;

e. had been advised by the United States Attorney or a law enforcement officer of the likelihood that federal criminal charges may be filed or that they are the target of a grand jury investigation;

f. is proposed by the United States Attorney for processing under a pretrial diversion program; or

g. is held for international extradition under 18 US.C. § 3181 et al.

3. *Ancillary Matters.* Whenever a District Judge or Magistrate Judge determines the interests of justice so require, representation may be provided for financially eligible persons in ancillary matters appropriate to the criminal proceedings, pursuant to 18 U.S.C. § 3006A(c). The following is a non-exhaustive list of reasons the Court might consider representation is reasonably necessary:

a. to protect a constitutional right;

b. to contribute in some significant way to the defense of the principal criminal charge;

c. to aid in preparation for the trial or disposition of the principal criminal charge;

d. to enforce the terms of a plea agreement in the principal criminal charge;

e. to preserve the claim of the CJA client to an interest in real or personal property subject to civil forfeiture proceeding under 18 U.S.C. § 983, 19 U.S.C. § 1602, 21 U.S.C. § 881, or similar statutes, which property, if recovered by the client, may be considered for reimbursement under 18 U.S.C. § 3006A(f); or

f. effectuate the return of real or personal property belonging to the CJA client, which may be subject to a motion for return of property under Fed.R.Crim.P. 41(g), which property, if recovered by the client, may be considered for reimbursement under 18 U.S.C. § 3006A(f).

B. Financial Eligibility.

1. *Presentation of the Accused for Financial Eligibility Determination.*

a. Duties of Law Enforcement. Upon arrest, and where the defendant has not retained or waived counsel, federal law enforcement officials must promptly notify, telephonically or electronically, the FD–CAE of an individual's arrest in connection with a federal criminal charge.

Law enforcement agency employees should not participate in completing the financial affidavit or seek information concerning financial eligibility from a person arrested or requesting counsel appointment.

b. Duties of the United States Attorney's Office

i. Upon an Indictment's return or unsealing of a criminal information's filing, and where the defendant has not retained or waived counsel, the United States Attorney or their designee will promptly notify, telephonically or electronically, the FD–CAE.

ii. Upon issuing a 'target letter,' and where the individual has not retained or waived counsel, the United States Attorney's Office (USAO) should promptly notify, telephonically or electronically, the FD–CAE. If the USAO knows of an actual or potential conflict between the target and the FD–CAE, the USAO should promptly notify the CJA Panel Administrator or the Federal Defender. The USAO should also let the CJA Panel Administrator know if any CJA Panel lawyers have a conflict in representing the individual.

iii. USAO employees should not participate in completing the financial affidavit from a person requesting counsel appointment.

c. Duties of the Pretrial Services Office

i. The Judicial Conference recognizes the importance of counsel's advice for persons subject to Bail Reform Act proceedings, 18 U.S.C. § 3141 et seq., before being interviewed by a pretrial services or probation officer. Accordingly, the FD–CAE shall be given a reasonable period of time within which to contact a person subject to 18 U.S.C. § 3142 proceedings. During this reasonable period of time, the pretrial services office shall not contact that person. Thereafter, the pretrial services officer will not conduct the pretrial service interview (PSI) of a financially eligible defendant without counsel present unless that defendant waives their right to counsel or otherwise knowingly consents to a PSI without counsel.

ii. When the Court has appointed counsel or designated the FD–CAE for appointment before the initial appearance, the pretrial services officer will provide counsel notice either telephonically or electronically, and will provide a reasonable opportunity for counsel to attend the defendant's PSI before the initial pretrial release or detention hearing.

iii. Pretrial Services Office employees should not participate in completing the financial affidavit or seek information concerning financial eligibility from a person requesting counsel appointment. This should not be construed as prohibiting the usual information gathering regarding the detention hearing.

d. Duties of the Office of the Federal Defender

i. In cases where the FD–CAE may be appointed, the FD–CAE will immediately investigate and determine whether an actual or potential conflict exists. If such conflict exists, FD–CAE will promptly notify the CJA Panel Administrator to facilitate CJA Panel counsel appointment.

ii. When a person indicates they are financially unable to retain counsel, whenever practicable, the FD–CAE will:

(a) discuss with the person their right to appointed counsel,

(b) assist their completing a financial affidavit (Form CJA 23), if counsel appointment seems likely, and

(c) arrange to have their matter promptly presented before a Magistrate Judge or District Judge to determine financial eligibility and counsel appointment.

2. *Factual Determination of Financial Eligibility.*

a. In every case where 18 U.S.C. § 3006A(a) and related statutes authorize counsel appointment, the Court must advise the person they have a right to be represented by counsel throughout the case and, if so desired, the court will appoint counsel to represent the person when they are financially unable to obtain counsel.

b. The completed financial eligibility affidavit (Form CJA 23) should reflect relevant information bearing on the person's financial eligibility for appointed counsel.

c.   Determining eligibility for representation under the CJA is a judicial function performed by the Court after making appropriate inquiries concerning the person's financial eligibility. Other court employees, the CJA Panel Administrator or the FD–CAE may be designated to obtain or verify facts relevant to the financial eligibility determination.

d.   In determining whether a person is "financially unable to obtain counsel," one should consider the cost of providing the person and their dependents with life's necessities, the cost of securing pretrial release, asset encumbrance, and the likely cost to retain counsel.

e.   The initial eligibility determination must be made without considering a person's family's financial ability to retain counsel unless their family indicates a willingness and ability to do so promptly.

f.   Any doubts about a person's eligibility should be resolved in the person's favor. Erroneous eligibility determinations may be corrected at a later time.

g.   If, at any time after the counsel appointment, a judge finds a person provided representation is financially able to retain private counsel or make partial payments towards the appointed representation, the judge may either terminate the counsel appointment or direct the defendant to contribute by paying the Court as provided in 18 U.S.C. § 3006A(f).

h.   If, at any stage of their proceedings, a judge finds a person can no longer financially pay retained counsel, the Court may appoint counsel in accord with this CJA Plan's procedures.

V.   TIMELY APPOINTMENT OF COUNSEL

A.   Eligible persons must receive appointed counsel as soon as feasible. This means as soon as possible after they are taken into custody, when they appear before a judicial officer, when they are formally charged or notified of the charges if formal charges are sealed, or when a judicial officer otherwise determines appointed counsel is appropriate under the CJA or this CJA Plan, whichever occurs earliest.

B.   Counsel appointment may be made retroactive to include representation provided prior to the judicial officer's formal appointment.

VI.   PROVIDING REPRESENTATION SERVICES

A.   Office of the Federal Defender and Private Counsel.   This CJA Plan provides for representation by the FD–CAE, for appointment and compensation of private counsel from a CJA Panel list approved by the Court and maintained by the CJA Panel Administrator, and, in limited circumstances, other private attorneys, in cases authorized under the CJA and related statutes.

B.   Panel Administration.   Administration of the CJA Panel in the Eastern District of California is hereby delegated and assigned to the FD–CAE.

C.   Case Apportionment.   Whenever possible, CJA Panel attorneys should be appointed in a substantial proportion of the cases where the Court determines a person is financially eligible for representation under the CJA and this CJA Plan. "Substantial" in this context means at least twenty-five percent (25%) of the annual CJA appointments.

D.   Number of Counsel.   More than one attorney may be appointed in any case to represent one person when the Court determines the representation or case is extremely complex or difficult.

E.   Capital Cases.   The guidelines and procedures for capital case representation services where the defendant (i) is charged with a crime that may be punished by death, or (ii) is seeking to vacate or set aside a death sentence in 28 U.S.C. §§ 2254 or 2255 proceedings, are set forth in this CJA Plan's section XIV.

VII.   OFFICE OF THE FEDERAL DEFENDER

A.   Establishment.   The FD–CAE was established in this district pursuant to the CJA and is responsible for appointed defense services throughout this District. The FD–CAE shall maintain full-time staffed offices in Sacramento and Fresno, and a seasonally/part-time staffed office in Yosemite National Park.

B. Supervision. The Federal Defender is responsible for supervising and managing the FD–CAE. Accordingly, the Federal Defender will be appointed to all cases assigned to the organization for subsequent assignment to staff attorneys at the Federal Defender's discretion. The Federal Defender will continually monitor office staff workloads to ensure high quality representation for all clients.

C. Standards and Professional Conduct. The FD–CAE shall provide high quality representation consistent with the legal profession's best practices, commensurate with services rendered by privately retained counsel. The FD–CAE must conform to the highest standards of professional conduct, including, but not limited to,

1. California laws and rules for lawyers practicing in California to include the California Rules of Professional Conduct and the California Business and Professions Code, §§ 6000 *et seq.*,

2. the American Bar Association's *Model Rules of Professional Conduct*, and *Defense Function* Criminal Justice Section standards, and

3. the *Guide*, Volume 2, Part A, Chapter 4, *Code of Conduct for Federal Public Defender Employees*.

D. CJA Panel Management and Training. The Federal Defender shall designate CJA Panel Administrators for Sacramento and for Fresno and shall be responsible for their supervision. The CJA Panel Administrator shall be responsible for the systematic distribution of cases to and management of the CJA Panel subject to provisions of the CJA, the *Guide* and this CJA Plan's provisions. The Federal Defender, in coordination with the CJA Panel Administrators and the CJA Panel Attorney District Representative(s), shall assess the Panel attorneys' training needs and will provide them training opportunities and other educational resources.

VIII.   CJA PANEL COMMITTEE

A.   Establishing a CJA Panel Committee.

1. *CJA Panel Committee Composition.* CJA Panel Committees in Fresno and Sacramento (CJA Committee) were established after consulting with the Federal Defender and the District Judges for the Fresno and Sacramento divisions. A Separate CJA Attorney Panel has been established and is administered by the Magistrate Judge in Redding. Each CJA Committee shall consist of:

- two experienced CJA Panel members,
- two experienced criminal law practitioners who are not CJA Panel members -the CJA Committee is encouraged to include in one of these positions a county public defender from an office within the respective divisions,
- an experienced attorney from the FD–CAE, and
- the CJA Panel Attorney District Representative and the CJA Panel Attorney District Representative elect.

The Federal Defender or their designee shall serve as the permanent CJA Committee chairperson. The CJA Panel Administrator shall serve as the permanent CJA Committee secretary.

2. *Term.* CJA Committee members shall serve terms of three years and may be extended for unlimited additional terms. Vacancies will be filled by remaining CJA Committee members' recommendation with the Chief District Judge's approval. The Federal Defender, CJA Panel Administrator, and CJA Panel Representative are members for as long as they hold those titles.

3. *Meetings.* The CJA Committee shall meet at least twice a year and at any other time the Chief District Judge requests the CJA Committee meet and consider an issue.

4. *Quorum and Decision Making.* CJA Committee decisions shall be by majority vote. The secretary is not a voting member of the CJA Committee. A quorum of four voting committee members shall be necessary to conduct business.

B.   CJA Committee Duties.

1. *Reviewing Panel Membership.* At least once a year, the CJA Committee shall examine applicant qualifications for CJA Panel membership and recommend the Chief Judge approve those attorneys deemed qualified and reject the applications from those attorneys not recommended for the CJA Panel. The CJA Committee shall recommend whether applicants should be on the A, B or C

general panel list, on the post-conviction panel list (for direct appeals and noncapital habeas appeals), or both. Please see definition of panel A, B and C on page 11, IX.C.3.

The CJA Committee shall consider whether applicants attended the free training sessions the FD–CAE regularly provides for the CJA Panel. For CJA Panel reappointments, the CJA Committee will consider how many appointments the member accepted or declined in the past year. The CJA Committee may also solicit input from the legal community concerning the quality of representation applicants provided.

The CJA Committee shall strive to create and maintain a diverse CJA Panel of the highest caliber federal criminal defense practitioners from our community. All qualified attorneys shall be encouraged to participate in furnishing CJA case representation without regard to race, color, religion, veteran status, sex, sexual orientation, gender identification or expression, age, national origin or disabling or medical condition.

2. *Annual Report.* Annually, in the first quarter of each year, the CJA Committee shall review the CJA Panel operation and administration for the preceding year. The CJA Committee Chairperson shall report its findings and recommendations to the Chief Judge. This report should include the current CJA Panel size and whether it should grow or not, efforts made to recruit qualified and diverse CJA Panel attorneys, and any recurring issues or difficulties CJA Panel members or their CJA clients encountered. The CJA Committee shall consult with the CJA Panel Administrator and the CJA Panel Representative in preparing this report.

3. *Removal from the Panel.* The CJA Committee shall follow the procedures set forth in Section IX of this CJA Plan and recommend to the Chief District Judge removing any CJA Panel member who:

    a. fails to satisfactorily fulfill their CJA Panel membership requirements during their service term, including failing to provide high quality representation to their CJA clients, or

    b. has engaged in other conduct such that their continued CJA Panel service is inappropriate.

4. *Mentoring.* The CJA Committee shall appoint CJA Panel members to serve as mentors to new, less experienced members of the CJA Panel. CJA Panel member mentor arrangements are voluntary.

IX. CJA PANEL MEMBERSHIP

The CJA Panel attorneys must provide high quality representation consistent with the legal profession's best practices and commensurate with those services rendered by privately retained counsel. CJA Panel attorneys are also expected to conform to the highest professional conduct standards, including, but not limited to:

    i. California laws and rules for lawyers practicing in California to include the California Rules of Professional Conduct and the California Business and Professions Code, §§ 6000 *et seq.*, and

    ii. the American Bar Association's *Model Rules of Professional Conduct*, and *Defense Function* Criminal Justice Section standards.

A. Approving CJA Panel Members. The existing, previously established CJA Panel of attorneys eligible and willing to accept CJA court appointments is hereby recognized. For future CJA Panel appointments, the CJA Committee through its Chairperson will recommend attorney CJA Panel membership to the Chief District Judge for their approval.

B. Panel Size. The CJA Panel size will be determined by the CJA Committee based on CJA Panel member caseloads and activity and by case filings, subject to the Chief District Judge's review. The CJA Panel must be large enough so its members can accept approximately 25% of all counsel appointments in the District, yet small enough so CJA Panel members will each receive an adequate number of appointments to maintain their federal criminal defense work proficiency.

C. CJA Panel Qualifications for Membership.

1. *Applications.* Application forms for CJA Panel membership are available online from the FD–CAE website. They may also be obtained directly from the CJA Panel Administrators.

2. *Eligibility.* New applicants practicing at least three years with federal criminal law experience will receive membership preference. CJA Panel applicants must:

a. be members in good standing of the California State Bar, the Eastern District of California bar, and the 9th Circuit Court of Appeals;

b. for the general panel, applicants must maintain a primary, satellite or shared office in this district—this requirement does not apply to post-conviction panel applicants; and

c. possess strong litigation and writing skills, and demonstrate proficiency with the Federal Rules of Evidence, the Federal Rules of Criminal Procedures, the Federal Rules of Appellate Procedure, federal sentencing procedures, the Bail Reform Act, and this District's Local Rules.

3. *Panel Appointment Types.* CJA Panel memberships are divided into two categories.

a. One category is the post-conviction panel, which is further divided into attorneys for direct appeals, habeas representations, and habeas appeals.

b. The second category is the general panel appointed on all other matters. The general panel is further subdivided into the:

1. "A List" made up of the most experienced panel members eligible for appointment in all cases, including the most complex and difficult cases;

2. "B List" for CJA Panel members eligible for all other case appointments types; and

3. "C list" consisting of less experienced CJA Panel members eligible for misdemeanor appointments, witnesses, and relatively simple felony case appointments.

Capital case appointment procedures are contained in section XIV of this CJA Plan.

CJA members may be appointed to accept more than one category of representations.

4. *Panel Terms.* Attorneys shall serve as a CJA Panel member for three years unless otherwise designated by the CJA Committee and approved by the Chief District Judge. CJA Panel General Panel C List attorneys shall serve an initial one-year term. Attorneys are eligible for unlimited additional terms. The CJA Panel Administrator will notify CJA Panel members, before their term expires, of the need to apply for CJA Panel reappointment. Panel members who do not reapply when their term expires will be dropped from the CJA Panel. Voluntary CJA Panel resignations, before term expiration, should be in writing directed to the CJA Panel Administrator or the Federal Defender.

5. *CJA Panel Membership Appointment.* After considering the CJA Committee recommendations, the Chief District Judge will determine whether to approve CJA Panel membership appointments or reappointments. The Chief District Judge will send the written decision back to the CJA Committee. The Federal Defender will notify all the applicants of the outcome.

6. *Training.* CJA Panel members are expected to attend mandatory training sessions offered by the FD–CAE.

7. *Removal From the CJA Panel.*

a. Mandatory Removal. Any CJA Panel member suspended or disbarred from the practice of law by any state court before whom such member is admitted, or who is suspended or disbarred from the Eastern District of California will be immediately removed from the CJA Panel.

b. Automatic Disciplinary Review. The CJA Committee will meet and conduct an automatic disciplinary review of any CJA Panel member against whom any state bar has issued a sanction or reprimand, or any CJA Panel member sanctioned or found in contempt by any federal or state court judge. Panel members must promptly self-report such events to the CJA Panel Administrator or the CJA Committee Chairperson.

c. Discretionary Disciplinary Review. A complaint against a CJA Panel member may be initiated by the CJA Committee, any federal judge of the district, another panel member, a defendant, or an FD–CAE lawyer. A complaint need not follow any particular form, but it must be in writing, not anonymous, and state the alleged deficiency with specificity. Complaints should be directed to the CJA Committee which will determine whether a full disciplinary review is necessary.

d. Disciplinary Review Procedures.

i. Reviewing Body. The CJA Committee may conduct the review before the full committee or may designate a subcommittee for this purpose.

ii. Notice. If the CJA Committee conducts a disciplinary review, it will notify the CJA Panel member of the specific allegations under review.

iii. Response. A CJA Panel member under review may respond to the allegations in writing and may request to appear before the CJA Committee.

iv. Protective Action. Prior to deciding the matter, the CJA Committee may recommend the CJA Panel member's suspension or removal from any pending appointed case or from the CJA Panel, and may take any other protective action, acting in the best interest of the client or the CJA Plan's administration, pending the outcome of this review. The Federal Defender, or their designee, may take any temporary protective action, acting in the best interests of the appointed clients of the panel member or the CJA Plan's administration, pending the outcome of a review by the Committee as a whole.

v. Review and Recommendation. After investigation and review, the CJA Committee may recommend closing the matter with no further action, or may recommend appropriate remedial action which might include:

- removing the attorney from the panel,
- limiting the attorney's participation to particular categories of cases,
- directing the attorney to complete specific training before receiving further panel appointments,
- assigning the attorney an experienced panel attorney as a mentor,
- directing the attorney to attend counseling for substance abuse issues, or
- any other appropriate remedial action.

vi. Final Disposition by the Court. The CJA Committee will forward its recommendation to the Chief District Judge for consideration and final approval.

vii. Confidentiality. Unless otherwise directed in the final disposition, information concerning the complaint, the disciplinary review, and the disposition will be kept confidential by the CJA Committee to the extent possible.

None of these procedures creates a property interest in being on or remaining on the CJA Panel.

X. CJA PANEL APPOINTMENTS

A. Appointment List. The CJA Panel Administrator will maintain a current list of all CJA Panel attorneys with current office addresses, email addresses, and telephone numbers. This list will also indicate the CJA Panel lawyer's eligible representation categories.

B. Appointment Procedure. CJA Panel member case appointments will ordinarily be made on a rotational basis. In a complex or otherwise difficult case, or in a case that would benefit from particular talents (such as a foreign language or expertise in a certain subject area), the CJA Panel Administrator may appoint counsel outside of the normal rotation. The CJA Panel Administrator might also vary from the rotation because CJA Panel members indicate, for whatever reason, they are unable to accept new cases for a period of time, to get counsel appointed expeditiously when the situation warrants, or when CJA Panel counsel has a large number of continuing representations still pending.

C. Appointing Attorneys Not on the CJA Panel. When a judge of this District finds special circumstances to exist, an attorney not on this District's CJA Panel may be appointed to represent a defendant on an ad hoc basis, provided the attorney has the experience level and knowledge that otherwise would qualify the attorney for CJA Panel membership. Reasons for such an appointment may include cost and time efficiencies, for example, if an attorney has previous experience with the particular defendant from a prior, concurrent or related civil or administrative representation. The Court must report such appointments to the CJA Panel Administrator. An attorney appointed under this provision is expected to adhere to the same rules and procedures as a CJA Panel attorney. An attorney appointed under this provision will be compensated at the same rate and subject to the same rules as a CJA Panel attorney.

D. Appointing CJA Panel Counsel Previously Retained. It may happen that CJA Panel counsel who was retained by a person requests to be appointed on a criminal case or investigation in this District. When that occurs, the judicial officer must consult with the CJA Panel Administrator or the Federal Defender. In determining whether or not to grant this request, the judicial officer should consider how long the attorney has been working with the now-financially eligible person, the nature of their fee agreement, and whether the attorney previously made such a request.

XI. CJA PANEL MEMBER DUTIES

A. Standards and Professional Conduct.

1. CJA Panel members must provide high quality representation consistent with the legal profession's best practices and commensurate with those services rendered by privately retained counsel.

2. Attorneys appointed under the CJA must conform to the highest standards of professional conduct, including, but not limited to:

    a. California laws and rules for lawyers practicing in California to include the California Rules of Professional Conduct and the California Business and Professions Code, §§ 6000 *et seq.*, and

    b. the American Bar Association's *Model Rules of Professional Conduct*, and *Defense Function* Criminal Justice Section standards.

3. Once counsel is appointed under the CJA, counsel will continue the representation until:

- the matter, including the appellate process is complete,
- substitute counsel has been appointed and counsel has been relieved,
- an order is entered allowing the client to proceed pro se, or
- the appointment is otherwise terminated by court order.

4. In complex non-capital representations likely to become extraordinary in terms of cost, the case may be referred to the Ninth Circuit Case Managing Attorney (CMA) by any stakeholder (Judge, appointed attorney, CJA Administrator, etc.) for case budgeting. Case budgeting is optional if the representation is expected to, or does, exceed $50,000. Any such representation which is expected to exceed $100,000 must be referred to the CMA by the appointed attorney for case budgeting. All capital cases must be budgeted. See section XIV for more capital case information.

5. CJA Panel members must consult with the Ninth Circuit Case Managing Attorney or with the National Litigation Support Team before contracting for discovery related services (such as scanning or OCR-ing documents) exceeding $10,000.

6. CJA Panel members must submit their final billing within 90 days after the Court files judgment or terminates the representation. Submissions after 90 days must be accompanied by a statement justifying the delay and may result in reductions or nonpayment.

7. If, at any time after appointment, CJA Panel counsel has reason to believe a client is financially able to retain or make partial payments for counsel, and CJA Panel counsel's information source is not protected as a privileged communication, CJA Panel counsel will advise the court.

8. In no circumstance may appointed CJA counsel require, request, or accept any payment, promise of payment, or any other valuable consideration for representation, unless, for some extraordinary reason, such payment is approved by Court order.

9. CJA Panel members must immediately notify the Federal Defender or the CJA Panel Administrator, in writing, if they are disbarred, suspended, sanctioned, or reprimanded by the Bar of any State. CJA Panel members must also notify the Federal Defender or the CJA Panel Administrator, in writing, within 30 days, if they are sanctioned or found in contempt by any state or federal court judge.

B. Training and Continuing Legal Education.

1. CJA Panel attorneys are expected to remain current with developments in federal criminal defense law, practice, and procedure.

2. CJA Panel attorneys are expected to attend trainings sponsored by the FD–CAE on a regular basis.

3. CJA Panel attorneys must know and comply with procedures related to eVoucher and procuring investigative, expert and other services necessary for efficient and effective representation.

C.   Facilities and Technology Requirements.

1.   CJA Panel attorneys must have and maintain facilities, resources, and technological capability to effectively and efficiently manage assigned cases.

2.   CJA Panel attorneys must comply with electronic filing and eVoucher requirements.

3.   Please see the Federal Defender's website for the current minimum technology requirements for CJA Panel attorneys.

XII.   CJA PANEL ATTORNEY COMPENSATION

A.   Policy.   Providing fair compensation to appointed counsel is a critical component of the administration of justice.   CJA Panel attorneys must be compensated for time expended in court and time reasonably expended out of court, and reimbursed for expenses reasonably incurred.

B.   Payment Procedures.

1.   Compensation claims must be submitted on the appropriate CJA form through the eVoucher system.

2.   The CJA Panel Administrator will review the claim for mathematical and technical accuracy and for conformity with the *Guide*, Volume 7A and, if correct, will forward the claim for consideration and action by the presiding judge.

3.   Absent extraordinary circumstances, the court should act on CJA compensation claims within 30 days of submission.   Vouchers should not be delayed or reduced to diminish Defender Services program costs as a response to adverse financial or budgetary circumstances.

4.   A presiding judge may, in their sound discretion, approve interim vouchers on a case-by-case basis.

5.   *Voucher Review.*   Any judge in this district may at any time informally request a voucher review from the CJA Panel Administrator or the Federal Defender or their designee.   If this informal review process does not resolve the judge's concerns and the judge, for reasons other than mathematical errors, intends to authorize payment for less than the compensation amount CJA Panel counsel claimed, then the judge or their chambers will notify CJA Panel counsel of the potential voucher reduction and give counsel an opportunity to provide additional information or documentation relevant to the voucher and the concerns raised by the judge before cuts to the voucher are made.

XIII.   INVESTIGATIVE, EXPERT AND OTHER SERVICES
PROCURED BY PANEL COUNSEL

A.   Authorization.   Counsel for a person financially unable to obtain investigative, expert, or other services necessary for an adequate defense may request such services in an *ex parte* application to the court as provided in 18 U.S.C. § 3006A(e)(1), regardless of whether counsel is appointed under the CJA.   Upon a finding that the services are necessary and the person is financially unable to obtain them, the Court must authorize counsel to obtain the services.

B.   Requests for Funds.   Requests to authorize funds for investigative, expert, and other services must be submitted in an *ex parte* application to the Court using the eVoucher system and must not be disclosed except with the consent of the person represented or as required by law or the policies set forth in the *Guide*, Volume 7A.

C.   Service Provider Rates.   Counsel must comply with rates and rules contained within the *Guide*, Volume 7A; General Order No. 575 (regarding limits on services provided without pre-authorization);   the *Judicial Council of the Ninth Circuit Criminal Justice Act Policies and Procedures* adopted on October 20, 2016, Appendix 2;   the *CJA Policy and Review Committee Recommendations* as approved by the Chief Judge of the Eastern District of California on February 1, 2017 (regarding paralegals and investigators); and the *Memorandum Request to Deviate from the new CJA Policies and Procedures Regarding Interpreter Service Providers in the Eastern District of California* as approved by the Judicial Council of the Ninth Circuit on April, 7, 2017.   Copies of these policies will be provided to new panel members, are available on the FD–CAE's website, and can be electronically provided, upon request, by the CJA Panel Administrator.

D.   Associate Attorneys.   It is the Eastern District of California's policy to encourage using associate attorneys, consistent with the *Guide*, to assist with representations upon the presiding judge's prior approval. The purpose of this policy is to reduce costs and to enlarge the pool of potential CJA Panel applicants. Associate attorneys should not, however, be used to make substantive court appearances or to advise clients. The encouraged use of associate attorneys is for tasks such as substantive research and writing under the supervision of the appointed attorney who is ultimately responsible for all work-product.

E. **Engagement Letters.** Eastern District of California CJA Panel attorneys are required to use an engagement letter when hiring service providers. A sample letter can be found in the *Judicial Council of the Ninth Circuit Criminal Justice Act Policies and Procedures* adopted on October 20, 2016, Appendix 3, page 34.

F. **Services Obtained by Person Represented by Retained.** Pursuant to 18 U.S.C. § 3006A(e), upon an ex parte application, the Court may authorize a person represented by retained counsel to obtain investigative, expert, or other services. The Court shall assess the defendant's financial eligibility by requiring submission of a financial eligibility affidavit (Form CJA 23) and may also request a copy of the legal services contract or other documentation deemed informative to the application. If the request is granted in full or in part, retained counsel shall make funding requests and submit vouchers for payment through eVoucher. Retained counsel shall use engagement letters for service providers funded in this manner (see XIII.E., above) and inform third parties of the proper billing practices for submission of vouchers. All funding requests and vouchers made pursuant to this provision are subject to the same reasonableness review as any CJA request or voucher.

XIV. APPOINTMENT OF COUNSEL AND CASE MANAGEMENT IN CJA CAPITAL CASES

A. **Applicable Legal Authority**. Appointing and compensating counsel in capital cases, and authorizing use and payment of persons providing investigative, expert, and other services, are governed by 18 U.S.C. §§ 3005, 3006A, and 3599; the *Guide*, Vol. 7A, Ch. 6; Eastern District of California Local Rule 191; and, in Fresno, the *Guide to Case Management and Budgeting in Capital Habeas Cases Eastern District of California, Fresno Division*.

B. **General Applicability and Appointment of Counsel Requirements.**

1. Unless otherwise specified, the provisions set forth in this section apply to all capital proceedings in the federal courts, whether those matters originated in a district court (federal capital trials) or in a state court (habeas proceedings under 28 U.S.C. § 2254). Such matters include those in which the death penalty may be or is being sought by the prosecution, motions for a new trial, direct appeal, applications for a writ of certiorari to the Supreme Court of the United States, all post-conviction proceedings under 28 U.S.C. §§ 2254 or 2255 seeking to vacate or set aside a death sentence, applications for stays of execution, competency proceedings, proceedings for executive or other clemency, and other appropriate motions and proceedings.

2. Any person charged with a crime punishable by death who is or becomes financially unable to retain representation is entitled to appointed counsel assistance throughout every stage of available judicial proceedings, including pretrial proceedings, trial, sentencing, motions for new trial, appeals, applications for writ of certiorari to the Supreme Court of the United States, and all available post-conviction processes, together with applications for stays of execution and other appropriate motions and procedures, competency proceedings, and proceedings for executive or other clemency as may be available to the defendant. *See* 18 U.S.C. § 3599(e).

3. Qualified counsel must be appointed in capital cases at the earliest possible opportunity.

4. Given the complex and demanding nature of capital cases, where appropriate, the court will utilize the expert services available through the Administrative Office of the United States Courts (AO); Defender Services Death Penalty Resource Counsel projects ("Resource Counsel projects") which include: (1) Federal Death Penalty Resource Counsel and Capital Resource Counsel Projects (for federal capital trials), (2) Federal Capital Appellate Resource Counsel Project, (3) Federal Capital Habeas § 2255 Project; and (4) National and Regional Habeas Assistance and Training Counsel Projects (§ 2254). These counsel are death penalty experts who may be relied upon by the court for assistance in selecting and appointing counsel, case budgeting, and legal, practical, and other matters arising in federal capital cases.

5. The Federal Defender or their designee should promptly notify and consult with the appropriate Resource Counsel projects about potential and actual federal capital trial, appellate, and habeas corpus cases, and consider their recommendations for appointing counsel.

6. The presiding judge may appoint an attorney furnished by a state or local public defender organization, legal aid agency, or other private, non-profit organization to represent a person charged with a capital crime or seeking federal death penalty habeas corpus relief provided the attorney is fully qualified. Such appointments may be in place of, or in addition to, appointing a federal defender organization, a CJA Panel attorney, or an attorney appointed *pro hac vice*. *See* 18 U.S.C. § 3006A(a)(3).

7. All attorneys appointed in federal capital cases must be well qualified, by virtue of their training, commitment, and distinguished prior capital defense experience at the relevant stage of the proceeding, to serve as counsel in this highly specialized and demanding litigation.

8. All attorneys appointed in federal capital cases must have sufficient time and resources to devote to the representation, taking into account their current caseloads and the extraordinary demands of federal capital cases.

9. All attorneys appointed in federal capital cases should comply with the American Bar Association's *2003 Guidelines for the Appointment and Performance of Defense Counsel in Death Penalty Cases* (Guidelines 1.1 and 10.2 et seq.), and their 2008 *Supplementary Guidelines for the Mitigation Function of Defense Teams in Death Penalty Cases.*

10. All attorneys appointed in federal capital cases should consult regularly with their appropriate Resource Counsel projects.

11. Questions about the appointment and compensation of counsel and the authorization and payment of investigative, expert, and other service providers in federal capital cases should be directed to the AO Defender Services Office, Legal and Policy Division Duty Attorney at 202–502–3030 or via email at ods_lpb@ao.uscourts.gov.

C. Appointing Trial Counsel in Federal Death–Eligible Cases.

1. *General Requirements.*

a. Appointing qualified capital trial counsel must occur no later than when a defendant is charged with a federal criminal offense where the death penalty is possible. *See* 18 U.S.C. § 3005.

b. To protect the rights of an individual who, although uncharged, is the subject of a federal death-eligible case investigation, the Court may appoint capital-qualified counsel upon request, consistent with Sections C.1, 2, and 3 of these provisions.

c. At the outset of every capital case, the court must appoint two attorneys, at least one of whom meets the qualifications for "learned counsel" as described below. If necessary for adequate representation, more than two attorneys may be appointed to represent a defendant in a capital case. *See* 18 U.S.C. § 3005.

d. When appointing counsel, the judge must consider the recommendation of the Federal Defender or their designee, who will consult with Federal Death Penalty Resource Counsel to recommend qualified counsel. *See* 18 U.S.C. § 3005.

e. To effectuate 18 U.S.C. § 3005's requirement that the Federal Defender's recommendation be provided to the court, the judge should ensure the Federal Defender has been notified of the need to appoint capital-qualified counsel.

f. Relying on a list for capital counsel appointment is not recommended because trial counsel selection should account for the particular case's and defendant's needs, and be based on individualized recommendations from the Federal Defender or their designee in conjunction with the Federal Death Penalty Resource Counsel and Capital Resource Counsel projects.

g. Out-of-district counsel, including Federal Defender Organization staff, who possess the requisite expertise may be considered for capital trial appointment to achieve high quality representation together with cost and other efficiencies.

h. In evaluating proposed trial counsel's qualifications, the Court should consider counsel's commitment to defending capital cases, their current caseload including other capital cases, and their willingness to effectively represent the client's interests.

2. *Learned Counsel Qualifications.*

a. Learned counsel must either be a member of this district's bar or be eligible for admission *pro hac vice* based on their qualifications. Counsel appointment from outside the jurisdiction is common in federal capital cases to achieve cost and other efficiencies together with high quality representation.

b. Learned counsel must meet the minimum experience standards set forth in 18 U.S.C. §§ 3005 and 3599.

c. Learned counsel should have distinguished prior experience in the trial, appeal, or post-conviction review of federal death penalty cases, or distinguished prior experience in state death penalty trials, appeals, or post-conviction review that, in combination with co-counsel, will assure high quality representation.

d. "Distinguished prior experience" contemplates excellence, not simply prior experience. Counsel with distinguished prior experience should be appointed, even if meeting this standard requires appointing counsel outside the district where the matter arises.

e. Learned counsel's suitability should be assessed considering the case's particular demands, the litigation stage, and the defendant.

f. Learned counsel must be willing and able to adjust other caseload demands to accommodate the extraordinary time required by the capital representation.

g. Learned counsel should satisfy the qualification standards endorsed by bar associations and other legal organizations regarding the quality of capital case representation.

3. *Second and Additional Counsel Qualifications.*

a. Second and additional counsel may, but are not required to, satisfy the learned counsel qualifications, as set forth above.

b. Second and additional counsel must be well qualified, by virtue of their distinguished prior criminal defense experience, training and commitment, to serve as counsel in this highly specialized and demanding litigation.

c. Second and additional counsel must be willing and able to adjust other caseload demands to accommodate the extraordinary time capital representation requires.

d. Second and additional counsel suitability should be assessed considering the individual case's demands, the litigation stage, and the defendant.

D. Direct Appeal Counsel in Federal Death Penalty Cases Appointment and Qualifications.

1. When appointing capital appellate counsel, the judge must consider the recommendation of the Federal Defender or their designee, who will consult with Federal Capital Appellate Resource Counsel to recommend qualified counsel.

2. Counsel appointed to represent a death-sentenced federal appellant should include at least one attorney who did not represent the appellant at trial.

3. Each trial counsel who withdraws should be replaced with similarly qualified counsel to represent the death-sentenced defendant on appeal.

4. Out-of-district counsel, including Federal Defender Organization staff, who possess the requisite expertise may be considered for capital appeal appointments to achieve high quality representation together with cost and other efficiencies.

5. Capital appellate counsel, between them, should have distinguished prior experience in federal criminal appeals and capital appeals.

6. At least one of the attorneys appointed as capital appellate counsel must have the requisite background, knowledge, and experience required by 18 U.S.C.§ 3599(c) or (d).

7. In evaluating proposed capital appellate counsel's qualifications, the Court should consider the qualification standards endorsed by bar associations and other legal organizations regarding the quality of capital case legal representation.

8. In evaluating proposed capital appellate counsel's qualifications, the Court should consider their commitment to defending capital cases, their current caseload including other capital cases, and their willingness to effectively represent the client's interests.

E. Post–Conviction Counsel in Federal Death Penalty Cases (28 U.S.C. § 2255) Appointment and Qualifications.

1. A financially eligible person seeking to vacate or set aside a death sentence in proceedings under 28 U.S.C. § 2255 is entitled to appointment of fully qualified counsel. *See* 18 U.S.C. § 3599(a)(2).

414

2.   Due to the complex, demanding, and protracted nature of death penalty proceedings, the Court should consider appointing at least two attorneys.

3.   Considering the accelerated timeline applicable to capital § 2255 proceedings, prompt counsel appointment is essential. Wherever possible, appointment should occur before the United States Supreme Court denies certiorari on direct appeal.

4.   When appointing counsel in a capital § 2255 matter, the Court should consider the recommendation of the Federal Defender or their designee, who will consult with the Federal Capital Habeas § 2255 Project.

5.   Out-of-district counsel, including Federal Defender Organization staff, who possess the requisite expertise may be considered for capital § 2255 case appointments to achieve high quality representation together with cost and other efficiencies.

6.   Counsel in § 2255 cases should have distinguished prior experience in federal post-conviction proceedings and capital post-conviction proceedings.

7.   When possible, post-conviction counsel should have distinguished prior experience in capital § 2255 representations.

8.   In evaluating proposed post-conviction counsel's qualifications, the Court should consider the qualification standards endorsed by bar associations and other legal organizations regarding the quality of capital case legal representation.

9.   In evaluating proposed post-conviction § 2255 counsel's qualification, the Court should consider their commitment to defending capital cases, their current caseload including other capital cases, and their willingness to effectively represent the client's interests.

F.   Counsel in Federal Capital Habeas Corpus Proceedings (28 U.S.C. § 2254 and Local Rule 191) Appointment and Qualifications.

1.   A financially eligible person seeking to vacate or set aside a death sentence under 28 U.S.C. § 2254 proceedings is entitled to appointment of qualified counsel. *See* 18 U.S.C. § 3599(a)(2).

2.   Due to the complex, demanding, and protracted nature of death penalty proceedings, the Court should consider appointing at least two attorneys.

3.   Pursuant to Eastern District of California Local Rule 191, the Eastern District Selection Board (Board), as approved by the Chief District Judge, will be the appointing authority for § 2254 matters. The Board shall be comprised of the Federal Defender or their designee, the Executive Director of the California Appellate Project, the Executive Director of the Habeas Corpus Resource Center, the State Public Defender, and a member of the California State Bar.

4.   Out-of-district counsel, including Federal Defender Organization staff, who possess the requisite expertise may be considered for capital § 2254 case appointment to achieve cost and other efficiencies together with high quality representation.

5.   For federal counsel to avail themselves of the full statute of limitations period to prepare a petition, the Court should appoint counsel and provide appropriate litigation resources at the earliest possible time permissible by law.

6.   Unless precluded by a conflict of interest, or replaced by similarly qualified counsel upon motion by the attorney or by the defendant, capital § 2254 counsel must represent the defendant throughout every subsequent stage of available judicial proceedings and all available post-conviction processes, together with applications for stays of execution and other appropriate motions and procedures, and must also represent the defendant in such competency proceedings and proceedings for executive or other clemency as may be available to the defendant. *See* 18 U.S.C. § 3599(e).

7.   Capital § 2254 case counsel should have distinguished prior experience in federal post-conviction proceedings and capital post-conviction proceedings.

8.   When possible, capital § 2254 counsel should have distinguished prior experience in capital § 2254 representations.

9.   In evaluating proposed capital § 2254 counsel's qualifications, the Court should consider the qualification standards endorsed by bar associations and other legal organizations regarding the quality of capital case legal representation.

10.   In evaluating proposed capital § 2254 counsel's qualifications, the Court should consider proposed counsel's commitment to defending capital cases, their current caseload including other capital cases, and their willingness to represent effectively the client's interests.

XV.   EFFECTIVE DATE

This Plan will become effective when approved by the Judicial Council of the Ninth Circuit.

[Dated: June 6, 1996, approved by the Judicial Conference of the Ninth Circuit effective June 21, 1996, and filed June 26, 1996. Amended effective June 19, 1998; August 31, 1999; July 27, 2017.]

SELECTED GENERAL ORDERS
GENERAL ORDER 92. PLAN FOR PROMPT DISPOSITION OF CRIMINAL CASES PURSUANT TO SPEEDY TRIAL ACT OF 1974

[**Publisher's Note:** *See also* General Order 479, *post.*]

(As Amended by General Order No. 231)

SECTION I: INTRODUCTORY MATERIAL

A. and B. [Omitted].

C. Copies of the Plan shall be made available for public inspection at the Office of the Clerk, United States District Court for the Eastern District of California at Sacramento, California, and Fresno, California. A copy of Section II shall be made available to practicing members of the Bar.

SECTION II: STATEMENT OF TIME LIMITS ADOPTED BY THE COURT AND PROCEDURES FOR IMPLEMENTING THEM

Pursuant to the requirements of Rule 50(b) of the Federal Rules of Criminal Procedure, the Speedy Trial Act of 1974 (18 U.S.C. §§ 3161–3174), and the Federal Juvenile Delinquency Act (18 U.S.C. §§ 5036, 5037), the judges of the United States District Court for the Eastern District of California have adopted the time limits and procedures set forth below as sections 1 through 13 of Section II of this Plan, in order to minimize undue delay and to further the prompt disposition of criminal cases and certain juvenile proceedings:

1. Applicability.

(a) *Offenses.* The time limits set forth herein are applicable to all criminal offenses triable in this Court, including cases triable by United States magistrates, except for petty offenses as defined in 18 U.S.C. § 1(3). Except as specifically provided, they are not applicable to proceedings under the Federal Juvenile Delinquency Act. [See 18 U.S.C. § 3172.]

(b) *Persons.* The time limits are applicable to persons accused who have not been indicted or informed against as well as those who have, and the word "defendant" includes such persons unless the context indicates otherwise.

(c) *Definitions.* A "judicial officer" is either a judge or a magistrate. The term "Court" includes any United States judge or magistrate assigned to the Eastern District of California. "Excludable time" means any period of delay set forth in 18 U.S.C. § 3161(h).

2. Priorities in Scheduling Criminal Cases. Preference shall be given to criminal proceedings as far as practicable, in accordance with Rule 50(a) of the Federal Rules of Criminal Procedure. The trial of defendants in custody solely because they are awaiting trial and of high-risk defendants as defined in subsection 5 should be given preference over other criminal cases. [See 18 U.S.C. § 3164(a).]

3. Time Within Which an Indictment or Information Must Be Filed.

(a) *Time Limits.* If an individual is arrested or served with a summons and the complaint charges an offense to be prosecuted in this district, any indictment or information subsequently filed in connection with such charge shall be filed within 30 days of arrest or service. [See 18 U.S.C. § 3161(b).]

(b) *Measurement of Time Periods.* If a person has not been arrested or served with a summons on a Federal charge, an arrest will be deemed to have been made at such time as the person (i) is held in custody solely for the purpose of responding to a Federal charge; (ii) is delivered to the custody of a Federal official in connection with a Federal charge; or (iii) appears before a judicial officer in connection with a Federal charge.

(c) *Related Procedures.*

(1) At the time of the earliest appearance before a judicial officer of a person who has been arrested for an offense not charged in an indictment or information, the judicial officer shall establish for the record the date on which the arrest took place.

(2) In the absence of a showing to the contrary, a summons shall be considered to have been served on the date of service shown on the return thereof.

4. Time Within Which Trial Must Commence.

(a) *Time Limits*. The trial of a defendant shall commence not later than 70 days after the last to occur of the following dates:

(1) The date on which an indictment or information is filed in this district;

(2) The date on which a sealed indictment or information is unsealed; or

(3) The date of the defendant's first appearance before a judicial officer of this district. [See 18 U.S.C. § 3161(c)(1).]

(b) *Retrial; Trial After Reinstatement of an Indictment or Information*. The retrial of a defendant shall commence within 70 days from the date the order occasioning the retrial becomes final, as shall the trial of a defendant upon an indictment or information dismissed by a trial court and reinstated following an appeal. If the retrial or trial follows an appeal or collateral attack, the court may extend the period if unavailability of witnesses or other factors resulting from passage of time make trial within 70 days impractical. The extended period shall not exceed 180 days. [See 18 U.S.C. §§ 3161(d)(2); 3161(e).]

(c) *Withdrawal of Plea*. If a defendant enters a plea of guilty or nolo contendere to any or all charges in an indictment or information and is subsequently permitted to withdraw the plea, the time limit shall be determined for all counts as if the indictment or information were filed on the day the order permitting withdrawal of the plea became final. [See 18 U.S.C. § 3161(1).]

(d) *Superseding Charges*. If, after an indictment or information has been filed, a complaint, indictment, or information is filed which charges the defendant with the same offense or with an offense required to be joined with that offense, the time limit applicable to the subsequent charge shall be determined as follows:

(1) If the original indictment or information was dismissed on motion of the defendant before the filing of the subsequent charge, the time limit shall be determined without regard to the existence of the original charge. [See 18 U.S.C. § 3161(d).]

(2) If the original indictment or information is pending at the time the subsequent charge is filed, the trial shall commence within the time limit for commencement of trial on the original indictment or information. [See 18 U.S.C. § 3161(h)(6).]

(3) If the original indictment or information was dismissed on motion of the United States Attorney before the filing of the subsequent charge, the trial shall commence within the time limit for commencement of trial on the original indictment or information, but the period during which the defendant was not under charges shall be excluded from the computations. Such period is the period between the dismissal of the original indictment or information and the date the time would have commenced to run on the subsequent charge had there been no previous charge. [See 18 U.S.C. § 3161(h)(6).]

(4) If the subsequent charge is contained in a complaint, the time within which an indictment or information must be obtained on the charge shall be determined without regard to the existence of the original indictment or information.

(e) *Measurement of Time Periods*. For the purposes of this section:

(1) If a defendant signs a written consent to be tried before a magistrate and no indictment or information charging the offense has been filed, the time limit shall run from the date of such consent.

(2) In the event of a transfer to this district under Rule 20 of the Federal Rules of Criminal Procedure, the indictment or information shall be deemed filed in this district when the papers in the proceeding or certified copies thereof are received by the clerk.

(3) A trial in a jury case shall be deemed to commence at the beginning of voir dire.

(4) A trial in a non-jury case shall be deemed to commence on the day the case is called, provided that some step in the trial procedure immediately follows.

(f) *Related Procedures*.

(1) At the time of the defendant's earliest appearance before a judicial officer of this district, the office shall take appropriate steps to assure that the defendant is represented by counsel and shall

appoint counsel where appropriate under the Criminal Justice Act and Rule 44 of the Federal Rules of Criminal Procedure.

(2) The Court shall have sole responsibility for setting cases for trial after consultation with counsel. At the time of arraignment or as soon thereafter as is practicable, each case shall be set for trial on a date certain. [See 18 U.S.C. § 3161(a).]

(3) Individual calendars shall be managed so that absent unusual circumstances every criminal case set for trial is reached within five (5) court days of the date originally set. A conflict in schedules of Assistant United States Attorneys shall not be ground for a continuance or a delay in the setting of a trial date except under circumstances approved by the Court and called to the Court's attention at the earliest practicable time. It is the duty of the United States Attorney to be familiar with the scheduling procedures of each judicial officer and to assign or reassign cases in such manner that the government will be ready for trial on the date set pursuant to subparagraph (2) above.

(4) The Chief Judge of the District shall have the ultimate responsibility for determining whether certain cases need to be reassigned in order to comply with the time requirements of this Plan.

(5) In the event that a complaint, indictment, or information is filed against a defendant charged in a pending indictment or information or in an indictment or information dismissed on motion of the United States Attorney, the trial on the new charge shall commence within the time limit specified above in paragraph (d) of this subsection, unless the Court makes a finding on the record that the new charge is not for the same offense charged in the original indictment or information or an offense required to be joined therewith.

(6) At the time of the filing of a complaint, indictment, or information such as described in subparagraph (5) above, the United States Attorney shall give written notice to the Court of that circumstance and of the government's position with respect to the computation of the time limits set forth in this Plan.

(7) All pretrial hearings shall be conducted as soon after the arraignment as is possible consistently with the priorities of other matters on the Court's criminal docket.

(8) The date first set for trial pursuant to subparagraph (2) of this paragraph shall not thereafter be changed to a date more than five days later, or to a date which does not comply with the limits set by this Plan for the time within which trial must commence, without the Court having made a determination on the record as provided in section 6 of this Plan as to whether excludable time has accrued or is accruing in the case, or whether a continuance is justified under 18 U.S.C. § 3161(h)(8). If the Court determines that no excludable time has accrued, it shall so rule on the record; if the Court determines that excludable time has accrued, or is accruing, it shall state on the record the amount of excludable time which has been found to have accrued.

(i) Any new trial date set pursuant to this subparagraph shall be within the limits set by this Plan for the time within which trial must commence, as adjusted to reflect any excludable time determined by the Court to have accrued or which will accrue by virtue of the granting of a continuance under 18 U.S.C. § 3161(h)(8).

(ii) If excludable time is accruing at the time of the Court's granting of a continuance, and the date the accrual of excludable time will cease cannot then be determined, the Court shall grant an indefinite continuance and it shall be the duty of the United States Attorney to move for a trial date to be set as soon as the accrual of excludable time appears to have ceased. At the time a trial date is then set, the Court shall make a determination on the record as to the amount of excludable time which has theretofore accrued.

5. Defendants in Custody and High–Risk Defendants.*

(a) *Time Limits.* Notwithstanding any longer time periods that may be permitted under sections 3 and 4, the following time limits will also be applicable to defendants in custody and high-risk defendants as herein defined:

(1) The trial of a defendant held in custody solely for the purpose of trial on a Federal charge shall commence within 90 days following the beginning of continuous custody.

(2) The trial of a high-risk defendant shall commence within 90 days of the designation as high-risk. [See 18 U.S.C. § 3164(b).]

(b) *Definition of "High–Risk Defendant."* A high-risk defendant is one reasonably designated by the United States Attorney as posing a danger to himself or any other person or to the community.

(c) *Measurement of Time Periods.* For the purposes of this section:

(1) A defendant is deemed to be in detention awaiting trial when he is arrested on a Federal charge or otherwise held for the purpose of responding to a Federal charge. Detention is deemed to be solely because the defendant is awaiting trial unless the person exercising custodial authority has an independent basis (not including a detainer) for continuing to hold the defendant.

(2) If a case is transferred pursuant to Rule 20 of the Federal Rules of Criminal Procedure and the defendant subsequently rejects disposition under Rule 20 or the court declines to accept the plea, a new period of continuous detention awaiting trial will begin at that time.

(3) A trial shall be deemed to commence as provided in sections 4(e)(3) and 4(e)(4).

(d) *Related Procedures.*

(1) If a defendant is being held in custody solely for the purpose of awaiting trial, the United States Attorney shall advise the court at the earliest practicable time of the date of the beginning of such custody.

(2) The United States Attorney shall advise the court at the earliest practicable time (usually at the hearing with respect to bail) if the defendant is considered by him to be high risk.

(3) If the court finds that the filing of a "high-risk" designation as a public record may result in prejudice to the defendant, it may order the designation sealed for such period as is necessary to protect the defendant's right to a fair trial, but not beyond the time that the court's judgment in the case becomes final. During the time the designation is under seal, it shall be made known to the defendant and his counsel but shall not be made known to other persons without the permission of the court.

6. Computation of Excludable Time.

(a) *Applicability.* In computing any time limit under sections 3, 4, or 5 herein, the periods of delay set forth in 18 U.S.C. § 3161(h) shall be excluded. Such periods of delay shall not be excluded in computing the minimum period before commencement of trial under section 7.

(b) *Procedures for Determination of Excludable Time.*

(1) Determinations concerning excludable time shall be made on the record by the Court. Counsel shall have five days from the date of the order in which to object to such a determination of the amount of excludable time. It is the duty of all counsel appearing in this Court to assist the Court in accurately determining and classifying the accrual of excludable time.

(2) The Court may grant a continuance under 18 U.S.C. § 3161(h)(8) for either a specific period of time or a period to be determined by reference to an event (such as recovery from illness) not within the control of the government. If the continuance is to a date not certain, the Court shall require one or both parties to inform the Court promptly when and if the circumstances that justify the continuance no longer exist. In addition, the Court shall require one or both parties to file periodic reports bearing on the continued existence of such circumstances. The Court shall determine the frequency of such reports in the light of the facts of the particular case.

(3) When a defendant is released on bond in another district for the purpose of returning to this district, said defendant shall appear on the date set by the Court in this district. At the time of such appearance, the Court shall note the dates of arrest, indictment, removal order, and any other significant event, and a determination as to the amount of excludable time shall be made forthwith, providing, however, that before a determination of excludable time is made the defendant shall have had the opportunity to consult with counsel and counsel shall have been given the opportunity to be heard on the matter.

(i) If the defendant appears without counsel, counsel shall be appointed, where appropriate. The case shall be set over to a date certain for a preliminary hearing if the defendant has not previously been indicted or had a preliminary hearing therein. If the defendant has previously been indicted or had a preliminary hearing therein, the case shall be set over to a date certain for arraignment.

(ii) If the defendant appears with counsel, the defendant shall be arraigned at that time if the defendant has previously been indicted or had a preliminary hearing therein. If the defendant has not previously been indicted or had a preliminary hearing therein, the case shall be set over to a date certain for a preliminary hearing.

(4) In any removal of a defendant under Rule 40 of the Federal Rules of Criminal Procedure, from this district to another, the Court before signing the warrant of removal shall make a determination on the record of the amount of excludable time accrued from the time of arrest to the time of the signing of the warrant of removal.

(5) When a defendant is returned to this district in custody, said defendant shall be brought immediately before a judicial officer. The dates of arrest, indictment, removal order and any other significant event shall be noted by the officer, and a determination as to the amount of excludable time shall be made forthwith, providing however, that before a determination of excludable time is made the defendant shall have had the opportunity to consult with counsel and counsel shall have been given the opportunity to be heard on the matter.

(i) If the defendant appears without counsel, counsel shall be appointed, where appropriate. The case shall be set over to a date certain for a preliminary hearing if the defendant has not previously been indicted or had a preliminary hearing therein, the case shall be set over to a date certain for arraignment.

(ii) If the defendant appears with counsel, the defendant shall be arraigned at that time if the defendant has previously been indicted or had a preliminary hearing therein. If the defendant has not previously been indicted or had a preliminary hearing therein, the case shall be set over to a date certain for a preliminary hearing.

(c) *Pre-Indictment Procedures.*

(1) In the event that the United States Attorney anticipates that an indictment or information will not be filed within the time limit set forth in section 3 hereof, the United States Attorney may file a written motion with the Court for a determination of excludable time or for a continuance under 18 U.S.C. § 3161(h)(8). The Court shall not grant such a motion until counsel for the defendant, whenever practicable, has been given the opportunity to be heard on the matter.

(2) The motion of the United States Attorney shall state (i) the period of time proposed for exclusion, and (ii) the basis of the proposed exclusion. If the motion is for a continuance under 18 U.S.C. § 3161(h)(8), it shall also state whether or not the defendant is being held in custody on the basis of the complaint. In appropriate circumstances, the motion may include a request that some or all of the supporting material be considered ex parte and in camera.

(3) The Court may grant a continuance under 18 U.S.C. § 3161(h)(8) for either a specific period of time or a period to be determined by reference to an event (such as recovery from illness) not within the control of the government. If the continuance is to a date not certain, the Court shall require one or both parties to inform the Court promptly when and if the circumstances that justify the continuance no longer exist. In addition, the Court shall require one or both parties to file periodic reports bearing on the continued existence of such circumstances. The Court shall determine the frequency of such reports in the light of the facts of the particular case.

(d) *Records of Excludable Time.*

(1) The clerk of the Court shall enter on the docket information with respect to any periods of excludable time as to each defendant which have been determined on the record by the Court. The clerk of the Court shall also enter on the docket any other information of record pertaining to excludable time.

(2) Any and all documents and records prepared or maintained by the clerk relating to excludable time shall be for information purposes only and shall not constitute evidence that such excludable time has occurred where in fact no determination has been made by a judicial officer in the manner prescribed by paragraph (b) of this section.

7. Minimum Period for Defense Preparation. Unless the defendant consents in writing to the contrary, the trial shall not commence earlier than 30 days from the date on which the indictment or information is filed or, if later, from the date on which counsel first enters an appearance or on which the defendant expressly waives counsel and elects to proceed pro se. For the purposes of this section the acceptance of a plea of guilty or nolo contendere does not constitute the commencement of trial. In circumstances in which the 70-day time limit for commencing trial on a charge in an indictment or information is determined by reference to an earlier indictment or information pursuant to section 4(d), the 30-day minimum period shall also be determined by reference to the earlier indictment or information. When prosecution is resumed on an original indictment or information following a mistrial, appeal, or withdrawal of a guilty plea, a new 30-day minimum period will not begin to run. The court will in all cases schedule trials so as to permit defense counsel adequate preparation time in the light of all the circumstances. See 18 U.S.C. § 3161(c)(2); § 3162(2).

8. Time Within Which Defendant Should Be Sentenced.

(a) *Time Limit.* A defendant shall ordinarily be sentenced within 75 days of conviction or the entering of a plea of guilty or nolo contendere.

(b) *Related Procedures.* If the defendant and defendant's counsel consent thereto, a presentence investigation may be commenced prior to a plea of guilty or nolo contendere or a conviction.

9. Juvenile Proceedings.

(a) *Time Within Which Trial Must Commence.* An alleged delinquent who is in detention pending trial shall be brought to trial within 30 days of the date on which such detention was begun, as provided in 18 U.S.C. § 5036.

(b) *Time of Dispositional Hearing.* If a juvenile is adjudicated delinquent, a separate dispositional hearing shall be held no later than 20 court days after trial, unless the Court has ordered further study of the juvenile in accordance with 18 U.S.C. § 5037(c).

10. Sanctions.

(a) *Dismissal.* The failure of the government or the Court to comply with the requirements of Title I of the Speedy Trial Act of 1974, 18 U.S.C. § 3161 et seq., may entitle the defendant involved to dismissal of the charges against said defendant. Nothing in this plan shall be construed to require that a case be dismissed in circumstances in which dismissal is not required by statute or the Interstate Agreement on Detainers. In particular, it should be noted that the time period for sentencing set in section 8 herein is a statement of this district's voluntarily assumed goal, and is not required or enforced by the Speedy Trial Act of 1974.

(b) *High–Risk Defendants.* A high-risk defendant whose trial has not commenced within the time limit set forth in 18 U.S.C. § 3164(b) shall, if the failure to commence trial was through no fault of the attorney for the government, have his release conditions automatically reviewed. A high-risk defendant who is found by the court to have intentionally delayed the trial of his case shall be subject to an order of the court modifying his nonfinancial conditions of release under Chapter 207 of Title 18, U.S.C., to ensure that he shall appear at trial as required. [See 18 U.S.C. § 3164(c).]

(c) *Discipline of Attorneys.* In a case in which counsel for the government or any defendant (i) knowingly allows the case to be set for trial without disclosing the fact that a necessary witness would be unavailable for trial, (ii) knowingly files a frivolous motion solely for the purpose of delay; (iii) makes a statement for the purpose of obtaining a continuance with knowledge that the statement is false and is material to the granting of the continuance, or (iv) otherwise willfully fails to proceed to trial without justification consistent with 18 U.S.C. § 3161 and this Plan, the Court may punish such counsel as provided in 18 U.S.C. §§ 3162(b) and (c).

(d) *Alleged Juvenile Delinquents.* An alleged delinquent in detention pending trial whose trial has not commenced within the time limit set forth in 18 U.S.C. § 5036 is entitled pursuant to that section to dismissal of the information against such person unless the United States Attorney shows that the delay was consented to or caused by the juvenile and the juvenile's counsel, or is in the interest of justice in the particular case.

11. Persons Serving Terms of Imprisonment.

If the United States Attorney knows that a person charged with an offense in this district is serving a term of imprisonment in any penal institution, the United States Attorney shall promptly seek to obtain the presence of the prisoner for trial, or cause a detainer to be filed, in accordance with the provisions of 18 U.S.C. § 3161(j).

12. Monitoring Compliance With Time Limits.

(a) As part of its continuing study of the administration of criminal justice in this district, the district's Speedy Trial Planning Group shall pay special attention to those cases in which there is a failure to comply with time limits set forth herein. From time to time, the Group may make appropriate recommendations to prevent repetition of failures.

(b) In addition to maintaining such statistical data as is required to be maintained by the Administrative Office of the United States Courts and by this Plan, including paragraph (c) of this section, the clerk will from time to time report to the other members of the Speedy Trial Planning Group the circumstances of each case in which there has been a determination by a judicial officer of a failure to comply with any time limit set forth herein, and of each case in which it appears to the clerk from facts of record that such a failure has occurred although no judicial determination of non-compliance has been made. Said report shall include any order or opinion which sets forth such a determination of non-compliance by a judicial officer, together with any order or opinion imposing a sanction for non-compliance.

(c) The clerk shall be prepared to provide promptly upon request of the Circuit Executive sufficient information on the status of all criminal cases in this district to permit the Circuit Executive to ascertain this district's degree of compliance with this Plan and the Speedy Trial Act of 1974.

13. Effective Dates.

(a) The amendments to the Speedy Trial Act made by Public Law 96–43 became effective August 2, 1979. To the extent that this revision of the district's plan does more than merely reflect the amendments, the revised plan shall take effect upon approval of the reviewing panel designated in accordance with 18 U.S.C. § 3165(c). However, the dismissal sanction and the sanctions against attorneys authorized by 18 U.S.C. § 3162 and reflected in sections 10(a) and (c) of this plan shall apply only to defendants whose cases are commenced by arrest or summons on or after July 1, 1980, and to indictments and informations filed on or after that date.

(b) If a defendant was arrested or served with a summons before July 1, 1979, the time within which an information or indictment must be filed shall be determined under the plan that was in effect at the time of such arrest or service.

(c) If a defendant was arraigned before August 2, 1979, the time within which the trial must commence shall be determined under the plan that was in effect at the time of such arraignment.

(d) If a defendant was in custody on August 2, 1979, solely because he was awaiting trial, the 90-day period under section 5 shall be computed from that date.

SECTIONS III TO VIII. [OMITTED]

[Dated: May 20, 1988.]

* If a defendant's presence has been obtained through the filing of a detainer with state authorities, the Interstate Agreement on Detainers, 18 U.S.C., Appendix, may require that trial commence before the deadline established by the Speedy Trial Act. See *U.S. v. Mauro,* 436 U.S. 340, 356–57 n. 24, 98 S.Ct. 1834, 1845 n. 24 (1978).

GENERAL ORDER 182. ORDER REFERRING BANKRUPTCY CASES AND PROCEEDINGS TO BANKRUPTCY JUDGES AND AUTHORIZING BANKRUPTCY APPEALS TO BE DECIDED BY THE NINTH CIRCUIT BANKRUPTCY APPELLATE PANEL[1]

PART I: REFERRAL OF BANKRUPTCY CASES AND PROCEEDINGS

The following provisions of the General Order of July 27, 1984 shall remain in full force and effect:

1.01 Cases and Proceedings Under Title 11, United States Code. This court hereby refers to the bankruptcy judges of this district all cases under Title 11, and all proceedings arising under Title 11 or arising in or related to cases under Title 11.

1.02 Cases and Proceedings Under the Bankruptcy Act of 1898. The bankruptcy judges of this district shall hear and determine cases and proceedings arising under the Bankruptcy Act of 1898, as amended, pursuant to sec. 403(a) of the Bankruptcy Reform Act of 1978.

PART II: BANKRUPTCY APPEALS

2.01 Bankruptcy Appellate Panel.

(a) Pursuant to 28 U.S.C. § 158(b)(2), this court hereby authorizes a bankruptcy appellate panel to hear and determine appeals from judgments, orders, and decrees entered by bankruptcy judges from this district, subject to the limitations set forth in subparagraphs (b)–(d).

(b) The bankruptcy appellate panel may hear and determine only those appeals in which all parties to the appeal consent thereto pursuant to paragraph 2.02 of this order.

(c) The bankruptcy appellate panel may hear and determine appeals from final judgments, orders, and decrees entered by bankruptcy judges and, with leave of the bankruptcy appellate panel, appeals from interlocutory orders and decrees entered by bankruptcy judges.

(d) The bankruptcy appellate panel may hear and determine appeals from judgments, orders, and decrees entered by bankruptcy judges after July 10, 1984, and appeals transferred to this court from the previous Ninth Circuit bankruptcy appellate panel by sec. 115(b) of the Bankruptcy Amendments and Federal Judgeship Act of 1984, P.L. 98–353. The bankruptcy appellate panel may not hear and determine appeals from judgments, orders, and decrees entered by bankruptcy judges between December 25, 1982, and July 10, 1984, under the Emergency Bankruptcy Rule of this district.

2.02   Form and Time of Consent.

(a) The consent of a party to allow an appeal to be heard and determined by the bankruptcy appellate panel shall be deemed to have been given unless written objection thereto is timely made in accordance with Paragraph 2 of the Amended Order Establishing and Continuing the Bankruptcy Appellate Panel of the Ninth Circuit, a copy of which is attached to this order and incorporated herein by reference.[2]

2.03   Rules Governing Bankruptcy Appeals.

(a) Practice in such bankruptcy appeals as may come before this district court shall be governed by Part VIII of the Rules of Bankruptcy Procedure, and shall be handled by the Clerk in accordance with the attached procedures regarding the processing of bankruptcy appeals.

(b) Notwithstanding subparagraph (a), the time for filing appellant's, appellee's, and reply briefs for consideration by the district court shall be 40 days, 30 days, and 14 days, respectively, in lieu of the time limits specified in Rule 8009(a) of the Rules of Bankruptcy Procedure, provided, however, that the district court or the bankruptcy appellate panel may shorten these time limits in appropriate cases.

[**Publisher's Note:** In General Order 182–A, effective October 1, 1995, the Court amended General Order 182 by adding paragraph 3.01, which is reproduced below.]

3.01   Each bankruptcy judge of the Eastern District of California is specially designated to conduct jury trials in core and non-core bankruptcy proceedings in cases commenced on or after October 22, 1994, upon the written consent of all parties to the action.

(a)   If the parties consent to a jury trial before a bankruptcy judge, they are deemed to have also consented to:

(i)   the application of all statutes of the United States or the Federal Rules of Civil Procedure that govern district court jury trials until such time Federal Rules are modified to cover jury trials in the bankruptcy court.

(ii)   the entry of a final order by the bankruptcy judge in a non-core proceeding.

(b)   Jury trials in bankruptcy court shall be subject to the jury plan in effect for the Eastern District.

PART III: EFFECTIVE DATE

This order shall become effective immediately and supersede all previous orders of this court regarding bankruptcy cases, proceedings, and appeals provided, however, that all prior actions of the bankruptcy appellate panel not inconsistent herewith are not affected by this order.

[Dated: December 6, 1996.]

[1] [**Publisher's Note:** On October 22, 1987, the Court entered General Order 223, providing as follows:

"GOOD CAUSE APPEARING, all the provisions of General Order Number 182 are hereby reenacted and shall remain in full force and effect, and shall specifically include the referral to the Bankruptcy Court for filing and all other purposes, Removal Applications as provided in Bankruptcy Rule 9027."]

[2] [**Publisher's Note:** For the Amended Order Establishing and Continuing the Bankruptcy Appellate Panel of the Ninth Circuit, please refer to the *California Rules of Court—Federal Bankruptcy Courts* pamphlet.]

ATTACHMENTS A AND B.   [OMITTED]

[Publisher's Note: Attachments A and B of the Procedures Regarding the Processing of Bankruptcy Appeals to the District Court are directed solely to the Clerk of the Court and have been omitted.]

ATTACHMENT C.   OPENING LETTER

UNITED STATES DISTRICT COURT
EASTERN DISTRICT OF CALIFORNIA

In re:

_____
             Debtor

_____
             Appellant,

             v.

_____
             Appellee.

_____

) District Court Case Number
) CV. _____
)
) Bankruptcy Court Case Number
) NO. _____
)
) Adversary Proceeding Number
) NO. _____
)
) Bankruptcy Appellate Panel Number
) NO. _____
)
)
)   OPENING LETTER
)
)

YOU ARE HEREBY NOTIFIED that your appeal from the bankruptcy court has been received in the district court and assigned the above district court case number. All pleadings filed in the district court should be in the form of an original plus two copies.

After a Notice of Appeal has been filed, the parties' next step in prosecuting this appeal is compliance with F.R.B.P. 8006 and 8007. These rules require the appellant to file within ten (10) days a designation of record, statement of issues on appeal and a notice regarding the ordering of transcripts *with the bankruptcy court*. Under these rules, the appellee may also file a supplemental designation of record and order transcripts. The party ordering transcripts must make satisfactory arrangements for payment of their costs. If transcripts are not to be ordered, appellant is required to file with the bankruptcy court a notice stating none are required.

Parties should note that the designation of record under F.R.B.P. 8006 is a necessary procedural step in prosecuting an appeal and the parties may not later include in their excerpts of record documents which have not been designated. The record and bankruptcy file will remain with the clerk of the bankruptcy court and the district court will review only those items in the record which counsel reproduces and includes in the excerpts of record filed at the time of the briefs, although under some circumstances the district court may call up the formal record.

It is the parties' responsibility to monitor the appeal to ensure transcripts are timely filed and the record is completed in a timely manner. Under F.R.B.P. 8007(a), the court reporter is required to file transcripts within thirty (30) days of receipt of the parties request, unless an extension has been granted.

After the record is complete, *the clerk of the bankruptcy court* will send a Certificate of Record (COR) to the clerk of the district court. Upon receipt of the COR, the district court will issue the briefing schedule. The briefing schedule will contain time deadlines and instructions regarding filing of briefs with the district court. Parties should be aware the time periods set forth in the briefing schedule are relatively short and the district court may require a showing of good cause for any extensions of time.

Once briefing is complete, the appeal will be set for oral argument before the presiding district court judge.

JACK L. WAGNER, CLERK
UNITED STATES DISTRICT COURT

Dated: _____

By: _____
      Deputy Clerk

    cc: All Counsel
           Courtroom Deputy
           Clerk, Bankruptcy Court
           Clerk, Bankruptcy Appellate Panel
           Hon. _____, Bankruptcy Judge

Adopted, Dec. 6, 1996.

ATTACHMENT D. BRIEFING SCHEDULE

UNITED STATES DISTRICT COURT
EASTERN DISTRICT OF CALIFORNIA

In re:

_____
Debtor

_____
Appellant,

v.

_____
Appellee.

) District Court Case Number
) CV. _____
)
) Bankruptcy Court Case Number
) NO. _____
)
) Adversary Proceeding Number
) NO. _____
)
) Bankruptcy Appellate Panel Number
) NO. _____
)
)
)   BRIEFING SCHEDULE
)

YOU ARE HEREBY NOTIFIED the clerk of the bankruptcy court has issued the Certificate of Record, certifying that the record on appeal is complete. This certificate was received and docketed by the district court on _____.

Pursuant to Federal Rule of Bankruptcy Procedure 8009, the *appellant's opening brief and excerpts of record* are due, filed in the district court, within *fifteen (15) days*, of the above date.

The *appellee's opening brief* is due, filed in the district court, within *fifteen (15) days* after service of appellant's brief.

The appellant may file a reply brief with the district court, within *ten (10) days* after service of appellee's brief.

Once all briefs have been submitted, the appellant is to notify the court in writing, within *ten (10) days* after service of appellant's reply brief, that the appeal is ready for oral argument.

All briefs and supporting documents filed with the district court should contain the following information and are required to be in the following format:

Briefs. The content of the briefs must comply with the requirements of: Bankruptcy Appellate Panel Rules 4 and 5; Federal Rules of Bankruptcy Procedure 8009 and 8010; and Federal Rules of Appellate Procedure 32(a). The length of opening briefs of appellant and appellee shall not exceed thirty (30) pages. The appellant's reply brief, if any, shall not exceed twenty (20) pages.

NOTE ON FORM AND NUMBER OF BRIEFS: The district court needs only the original plus one copy of all documents. Also, these documents shall not have a cover, rather they should comply with Local Rule 130 (i.e., 8½" by 11" white pleading paper, bound in the upper left corner and two hole punched.)

Excerpts of Record. The bankruptcy court record, including transcripts, is not forwarded to the district court unless requested by the district court. The parties are expected to include copies of all relevant parts of the record in their excerpts. In particular appellant's brief shall include at least: the complaint and answer(s) or other equivalent operative pleadings: the pretrial order, if any; the judgment or order from which the appeal is taken; other orders sought to be reviewed, if any; any supporting opinion, findings of fact or conclusions of law filed or delivered orally by the trial court (citations, if opinion is published); the motion and response upon which the court rendered judgment, if any; and the trial court docket sheet. Copies of any portion of a transcript referred to in a brief must be included in the excerpts.

Index. Each party should prepare an index to accompany the excerpts of record. The pages of the excerpts of record should be sequentially numbered and each document should be indicated with a tab. The index should refer to the record by tab and page number.

Notice Appeal Ready for Oral Argument. Counsel for appellant shall submit to the assigned district court judge's courtroom deputy, a notice that all documents are complete and the appeal may be calendared for argument. Appellant is required to submit an original and one (1) copy of this document within ten (10) days after service of the appellant's reply brief.

JACK L. WAGNER, CLERK
UNITED STATES DISTRICT COURT

Dated: _____

By: _____
    Deputy Clerk

cc: All Counsel
        Courtroom Deputy
        Clerk, Bankruptcy Court
        Hon. _____, Bankruptcy Judge

Adopted, Dec. 6, 1996.

GENERAL ORDER 188. PROCEDURES FOR ESTABLISHMENT OF A BRADSHAW PANEL IN SACRAMENTO

Pursuant to *Bradshaw v. Zoological Society of San Diego* (C.A.Cal.1981) 662 F.2d 1301, the following procedure for the appointment of counsel in Title VII [Title 42 U.S.C. Section 2000e–5(f)(1)] cases is hereby adopted by the court.

1.   The court's memorandum and procedure entitled, "Appointment of Counsel in Title VII Cases," shall be duplicated and provided to all plaintiffs eligible for court appointed counsel. (Example attached as Exhibit A hereto.*)

2.   The court shall establish and maintain with the Clerk a panel of attorneys for appointment in Title VII cases. This order shall be publicized in a manner calculated to insure the widest possible geographical representation of attorneys in the Eastern District. Counsel shall be compensated, as described below, for reasonable costs expended.

Unless subsequent experience dictates otherwise, the panel shall be open to those members of the bar of this court willing to serve. Counsel shall be appointed on a rotating basis with due regard, however, for the proximity of counsel's office to the residence of the client and the court in which the action is pending.

3.   Regulating cost expenditures and reimbursements, at least at the outset, shall be handled on a case by case basis with each expenditure pre-approved. A simple form shall be submitted ex parte for approval by the district court. This form will set out the nature of the contemplated expenditure, the reason for it, the anticipated amount and a summary of previous costs. A recommended form titled, "Request for Authority to Incur Costs (Appointed Counsel) and Request for Payment" is attached as Exhibit B.* In the event that costs become excessive, the judge may either disapprove a contemplated expenditure, schedule a discovery or status conference or take such other action as is deemed appropriate.

4.   Due to the responsibilities placed upon counsel in civil matters, e.g., Rule 11 of the Federal Rules of Civil Procedure, it is important that appointed counsel have a procedure to facilitate withdrawal when necessary. It is deemed advisable that this procedure allow for a withdrawal motion to be heard in camera by a judicial officer other than the trial judge so as to minimize prejudice to the plaintiff. Accordingly, rather than the procedure provided by Local Rule 182(b),** when counsel appointed by the court pursuant to this rule desires to withdraw, upon the filing of the motion, it shall be referred to another district judge or to a magistrate. The motion shall then be heard ex parte and in camera.

5.   It shall be the responsibility of counsel for plaintiff to reimburse the Clerk of the Court for all costs advanced pursuant to this procedure immediately upon settlement or other successful resolution of the case. Such reimbursement shall be made prior to any disbursement to counsel, plaintiff or any other person.

[Dated: January 14, 1986.]

  * [**Publisher's Note:** Exhibits A and B are available upon request from the Clerk's Office.]

 ** [**Publisher's Note:** See Local Rule 182(d), *ante*.]

GENERAL ORDER 255. RATE FOR COMPENSATION OF COUNSEL APPOINTED UNDER 21 U.S.C. § 848(q)

The court having considered the recommendations made by the Judicial Conference of the United States,

IT IS HEREBY ORDERED that, under 21 U.S.C. § 848(q)(10), the presumptive rate for compensation of counsel appointed pursuant to 21 U.S.C. § 848(q) and Local Rule 191(d) shall be One Hundred Ten Dollars ($110) per hour.

[Dated: December 20, 1989.]

GENERAL ORDER 345. CONSENT TO JURISDICTION
BY U.S. MAGISTRATE JUDGE

It appearing that the civil and criminal case dockets of the U.S. District Judges of this Court sitting in Fresno are extremely overcrowded; and it further appearing that such overcrowding is causing unnecessary delay in the disposition of civil cases, including cases brought by or on behalf of prisoner litigants and appeals of Social Security Disability Determinations. GOOD CAUSE APPEARING, the Judges of the Eastern District of California hereby adopt this General Order concerning the assignment of cases to U.S. Magistrate Judges.

Pursuant to this General Order all civil cases filed in or transferred to the Fresno court which are: 1) brought under 42 U.S.C. §§ 405(g), 1383(c)(3) and 1395ff seeking judicial review [of] a final decision of the Commissioner of Social Security; or 2) brought by or [on behalf of] a person in custody who is seeking habeas corpus relief (28 U.S.C. § 2241 et seq.), except cases involving the death penalty, or any relief authorized by 42 U.S.C. § 1981 et seq., shall be randomly assigned to a U.S. Magistrate Judge and no District Judge shall be assigned.

Following the assignment of a U.S. Magistrate Judge, forms of consent pursuant to 28 U.S.C. § 636(c), for each party, shall be stamped with a case number and served by the clerk on the plaintiff or petitioner and all parties who have appeared, the remaining forms shall be served at the same time and in the same manner as summons and complaint. Each party shall be required to notify the clerk of court in writing whether or not they consent to the jurisdiction of the U.S. Magistrate Judge for all purposes pursuant to 28 U.S.C. § 636(c), using the forms supplied by the clerk. Each party must file the completed form indicating whether they consent to the jurisdiction of the Magistrate Judge with the court, not later than 20 days after entry of appearance.

If all parties consent, the case will remain with the assigned magistrate judge, pursuant to 28 U.S.C. § 636(c).

If any party chooses not to consent, the case will be randomly assigned to a U.S. District Court Judge. The case will remain with the previously assigned U.S. Magistrate Judge who will manage the progress of the action and rule on all non-dispositive motions pursuant to 28 U.S.C. § 636(b)(1)(A) and all dispositive motions by findings and recommendations pursuant to 28 U.S.C. § 636(b)(1)(B) in accordance with Local Rule 72–304(c)(15) and (17).

[Dated: October 17, 1997.]

GENERAL ORDER 348. JUDICIAL ADVISORY COMMITTEE
OF THE EASTERN DISTRICT OF CALIFORNIA

By order of the U.S. District Court for the Eastern District of California (hereinafter the "District"), a Judicial Advisory Committee (hereinafter the "Committee") is hereby formed to provide advice and assistance to the court in its ongoing efforts to improve the administration of justice. The purpose, composition, and term of the Committee is as follows:

A. Purpose. In light of the expiration of the Civil Justice Reform Act of 1990 on December 1, 1997, the principal purpose of the Committee is to continue the work of the Civil Justice Reform Act Advisory Group by providing advice and assistance to the court on ways to ensure the prompt and efficient resolution of civil litigation. The Committee will also be a forum for the exchange of information on criminal justice issues and reforms. Among other things, the Committee shall regularly review the Local Rules of the District and submit proposals to the court for changes or additions to the Local Rules.

B. Composition. The Committee shall be composed of the following members:

1. The Chief Judge of the District;

2. The Chief Bankruptcy Judge of the District;

3. The Chief Magistrate Judge of the District;

4. The Co-chairs of the District's Lawyer Representatives Committee to the Ninth Circuit Judicial Conference;

5. The U.S. Attorney for the District or his/her designee;

6. The Federal Public Defender for the District or his/her designee;

7. The President of the Sacramento Chapter of the Federal Bar Association or his/her designee;

8. The President of the San Joaquin Valley Chapter of the Federal Bar Association or his/her designee;

9. The Chair of the Sacramento Valley Bankruptcy Forum or his/her designee;

10. The Chair of the Central California Bankruptcy Forum or his/her designee;

11. The California Attorney General or his/her designee;

12. The Co–Chairs of the District Conference Planning Committee;

13. Three or more at-large members appointed for three year staggered terms by the Chief Judge of the District;

14. A representative from the United States District Court, Eastern District of California Historical Society; and

15. A representative of the Federal Courts Committee of the State Bar of California, Litigation Section.

16. The Chair of the Local Rules Committee of the District;

17. The Clerk of Court of the District, or his/her Designee; and

18. The ADR and Pro Bono Director of the District.

All members of the Committee shall be judicial officers and employees of the District or attorneys in good standing with the California State Bar who reside in the Eastern District of California and who regularly appear before the judges of the District.

C. Chairperson and Vice Chairperson. A Chairperson and Vice Chairperson of the Committee shall be selected annually by the Chief Judge of the District in advance of each annual cycle of the Committee.

D. Sub–Committees. The Committee shall have one standing sub-committee called the "Local Rules Committee" and such ad hoc sub-committees as the Committee or the Chief Judge of the District may establish from time-to-time. Membership in the sub-committees is not limited to members of the Committee, but may include anyone who is selected by the Chief Judge of the District to serve on a sub-committee.

E. Term. The Committee shall exist until disbanded by order of the court and shall operate on an annual basis beginning on January 1 of each year.

[Dated: February 27, 2017.]

GENERAL ORDER 372. RELATION OF CRIMINAL CASES AND PETITIONER* FOR PROBATION ACTION OR VIOLATIONS OF SUPERVISED RELEASE

Good cause appearing, IT IS HEREBY ORDERED as follows:

Where a Notice of Related Cases is filed suggesting that a petition for probation action and/or violation of the terms of supervised release should be related to a new indictment, and the basis of the probation petition or alleged supervised release violation is the conduct underlying the new indictment, the two cases shall be related and the judge assigned to the new criminal case shall also be assigned the earlier case, unless the original sentencing judge desires to retain the first case, in which circumstance both cases shall be assigned to the original sentencing judge.

This Order supersedes General Order No. 275.

[Dated: October 12, 1999.]

* [**Publisher's Note:** So in original. Probably should be "Petition".]

GENERAL ORDER 479.   IN RE: PLAN FOR PROMPT DISPOSITION OF CRIMINAL CASES PURSUANT TO SPEEDY TRIAL ACT OF 1974

Under General Order No. 92, the court adopted its Plan for Prompt Disposition of Criminal Cases pursuant to the requirements of the Federal Rules of Criminal Procedure, the Speedy Trial Act of 1974, and the Federal Juvenile Delinquency Act.

Section 6 of the Plan sets forth the Computation of Excludable Time. Subsection 6(b)(1) requires that "Determinations concerning excludable time shall be made on the record by the Court" and Subsection 6 requires that "The clerk of the Court shall enter on the docket information with respect to any periods of excludable time as to each defendant which have been determined on the record by the Court."

In order to facilitate the recording of excludable time on the record and in docket entries, the court has developed Excludable Delay Codes with arabic numerals corresponding to specific statutory provisions of 18 U.S.C. § 3161(h) to be used at the discretion of each judge. Individual judges have found that the use of the codes helps to expedite court proceedings and the entry of docket information.

From time to time, it becomes necessary to update the Excludable Delay Codes to correspond to amendments to 18 U.S.C. § 3161(h). Therefore, the court adopts the attached updated Excludable Delay Codes as modified on August 24, 2009. Individual judges may utilize the codes at their discretion.

[Dated: October 15, 2009.]

EXCLUDABLE DELAY CODES

Modified on 8/24/09

18:3161	CODE	EXCLUDABLE DELAY CODES
(h)(1)(A)	A	Exam or hearing for mental or physical incapacity (18 U.S.C. § 4244)
(h)(1)(A)	B	NARA Exam (28 U.S.C. § 2902)
(h)(1)(B)	C	State or Federal trials or other charges pending
(h)(1)(C)	D	Interlocutory Appeals
(h)(1)(D)	E	Pretrial Motions (from filing to hearing or other prompt disp.)
(h)(1)(E)	F	Transfers from other districts
(h)(1)(F)	G	Proceedings under advisement not to exceed 30 days
	H	Miscellaneous proceedings: parole or probation revocation, deportation or extradition
(h)(2)	5	Deferral of prosecution under 28 U.S.C. § 2902
(h)(1)(F)	6	Transportation from another district or to/from examination or hospitalization in ten days or less
(h)(1)(G)	7	Consideration by court of proposed plea agreement
(h)(2)	I	Prosecution deferred by mutual agreement
(h)(3)(A)(B)	M	Unavailability of defendant or essential witness

18:3161	CODE	EXCLUDABLE DELAY CODES
(h)(4)	N	Period of mental or physical incompetence of defendant to stand trial
(h)(4)	O	Period of NARA Commitment or treatment
(h)(5)	P	Superseding indictment and/or new charges
(h)(6)	R	Defendant awaiting trial of co-defendant when no severance granted
(h)(7)(A)(B)	T	Continuance granted per (h)(7)—use "T" alone if more than one of the reasons below are given in support of continuance
(h)(7)(B)(i)	T1	1) Failure to continue would stop further proceedings or result in miscarriage of justice
(h)(7)(B)(ii)	T2	2) Case unusual or complex
(h)(7)(B)(iii)	T3	3) Indictment following arrest cannot be filed in 30 days
(h)(7)(B)(iv)	T4	4) Continuance granted in order to obtain or substitute counsel; give reasonable time to prepare
(i)	U	Time up to withdrawal of guilty plea
(b)	W	Grand jury indictment time extended 30 days

GENERAL ORDER 515. IN RE: RECUSAL WHEN FORMER JUDGE APPEARS AS COUNSEL

The District Judges of the Eastern District of California have met and have decided the issue of recusal of its judges when a former Eastern District judge (either district or magistrate) appears as counsel. The Court will follow the guidelines provided by the United States Federal Courts Committee on Codes of Conduct, Advisory Opinion No. 70, which in part states: "The Committee recommends that courts announce a policy that for a fixed period after the retirement or resignation of a colleague, judges recuse themselves in any case in which the former colleague appears as counsel." This general recusal will last for a one year period from the date that the former judge left the Court.

[Dated: December 7, 2011.]

GENERAL ORDER 539. IN RE: ADOPTION OF AMENDED PLAN FOR THE ADMINISTRATION OF THE NON–APPROPRIATED FUND

CHAPTER ONE. General Matters

Section 1.01 Purpose: The United States District Court has adopted this Attorney Admissions Fund Plan (the Plan) for the Eastern District of California. The purpose of the Plan is to provide guidance for receipting, depositing, disbursing, and accounting for monies maintained in the Court's Non–Appropriated Fund (the Fund). This Plan supersedes the plans adopted in General Orders 154, 259 and 377.

Section 1.02 Sources of Revenue:

(a) *Excess Attorney Admissions Fees*: Pursuant to Local Rule 180, attorneys applying for admission to this Court will be required to pay a prescribed fee, in excess of the basic fee set by the

Judicial Conference of the United States. This excess amount will be collected, deposited, and maintained by the Fund custodian as part of the Fund.

(b) *Pro Hac Vice Fees*: Pursuant to Local Rule 180, attorneys applying for Pro Hac Vice admission to this Court will be required to pay a prescribed fee. This amount will be collected, deposited, and maintained by the Fund custodian as part of the Fund.

(c) *Other Sources of Income*: The only other source of income for the Fund is any interest income accrued on the Attorney Admission fees.

Section 1.03 Constraints on the Use of Attorney Admission Fund Monies: The following guidelines and principles apply to the administration of the Fund:

(a) *Receipt and Deposit of Monies*: The Clerk of Court will receipt, deposit, and account for monies according to fiscal and accounting principles established in the most current version of the Attorney Admission Fund Guidelines (the Guidelines) adopted by the Judicial Conference of the United States (see Vol. 13, Chap. 12 of the Guide to Judiciary Policies, hereinafter referred to as the Guide).

(b) *Limitations on Deposits*:

(1) The Clerk of Court shall deposit all monies of the Fund only in federally insured banks or savings institutions. Whenever practical and feasible, all substantial sums should be deposited in interest-bearing accounts, government securities, or money market funds invested in government obligations, at the direction of the Court or the Judicial Advisory Committee (JAC).

(2) The Court shall avoid an unreasonable accumulation of attorney admission fees.

(c) *Separation of Fund Receipts From Other Judiciary Accounts*: Attorney admission funds shall be segregated from all other monies held in the custody of the Court.

(d) *Authorized Expenditures*: Expenditures from the Fund are to be used for the benefit of the bench and bar in the administration of justice. After considering the recommendations of the JAC or other judges, the Chief District Judge must enter an order authorizing all expenditures, except as provided in Section 2.02 "Pro Bono Expenses."

(e) *Limitations on Expenditures*:

(1) The Fund shall not be used to pay for goods or services for which appropriated funds may be legally used, even if the appropriated funds are exhausted or otherwise not available. Use of the Fund for any purpose for which appropriated funds may be legally used constitutes an impermissible augmentation of appropriations.

(a) Exception for Library Books and Periodicals: Notwithstanding the rule against augmentation, the Fund may be used to purchase books, periodicals and other resource materials for court libraries.

(b) Exception for Overtime Utilities and Courtroom Security Officer (CSO) Overtime Pay for Unofficial Court Functions: Notwithstanding the rule against augmentation, the Fund may be used to pay for overtime utilities and CSO overtime pay for unofficial court functions as noted in Section 2.01.

(2) The Fund shall not be used to supplement the salary of any court officer or employee, or other government official, or to provide a personal benefit to any judge or court employee, or his or her family member. A limited exception exists for the receipt of a de minimis personal benefit incidental to a proper expenditure from the Fund, e.g., meals, refreshments or hospitality items provided under section 2.01 of the Guide.

(3) The Fund shall not be used to pay for official or personal travel by a judge or court employee or by his or her family member. A limited exception exists that allows the Fund to be used to pay for local transportation of a judge or court employee to attend bench/bar events.

(4) The Fund shall not be used to pay for the printing of local rules.

(5) The Fund shall not be used to provide continuing legal education for any judge or employee of the Court.

CHAPTER TWO. Authorized Uses of the Fund

Section 2.01 Authorized Expenditures: The District Court and Bankruptcy Court shall use the Fund only for purposes that inure to the benefit of the members of the bench and the bar in the administration of justice. Subject to the provisions of Section 1.03, examples of proper common uses of the Fund include but are not limited to the following activities:

(a) *Attorney Admissions Proceedings*: Including expenses of admission committees and admission ceremonies.

(b) *Attorney Discipline Proceedings*: Including but not limited to expenses of investigating counsel for disciplinary enforcement, stenographers, meeting room rentals, postage, travel expenses and witness fees in disciplinary proceedings.

(c) *Attorney Lounge Facilities*: Including expenses to furnish, equip, and operate attorney lounge facilities, e.g., furniture; photocopiers and fax machines; beverage supplies or services; microwave, refrigerator, and other appliances; and television, telephone, and Internet service.

(d) *Auditing Fees*: Fees for services rendered by outside auditors or accountants in auditing the Fund.

(e) *Cash Donations*: In consultation with and following procedures established by the JAC, educational grants may be made to law-related educational or charitable organizations, such as a bar association, historical society, or law school, for purposes that advance the administration of justice.

(f) *Circuit Judicial Conference Expenses*: Expenses of circuit judicial conferences, to the extent permitted by the policy of the Judicial Conference of the United States.

(g) *Court Ceremonies*: Including expenses relating to judicial investitures, retirements, memorial or historical occasions, or other appropriate judicial or court-related proceedings advised and recommended by the JAC, but only for expenses for which appropriated funds may not be used.

(h) *District–Wide Bench/Bar Meetings*: Including expenses of meetings such as the Court's annual bench/bar meeting, the Court's district meeting at the circuit conference and other similar meetings, where various members of the bar are asked to assist in planning the meeting(s) and are invited to attend to discuss topics that are relevant and timely to both the Court and the members of the bar.

(i) *Educational Outreach*: Including expenses to promote and assist area high schools participating in the events, e.g., expenses related to transporting students to and from the Court for the Court's annual Open Doors to Federal Courts programs and similar events.

(j) *Historical Works*: Including expenses relating to the collection, restoration, preservation, and/or display of pictures, judicial portraits and photographs, oral histories, artwork, and other artifacts of historical significance.

(k) *Hospitality Items*: Hospitality items (e.g., food, beverages, and mementos) for which appropriated funds may not be used.

(*l*) *Lawyer Advisory Committee Meetings*: For expenses not payable out of appropriated funds, relating to matters that deal with the administration of justice.

(m) *Overtime Utilities and Court Security Officer (CSO) Overtime Pay for Unofficial Court Functions*: For overtime utility expenses and CSO overtime pay incurred for unofficial events and functions that benefit the bench and the bar in the administration of justice as determined by the Chief Judge. Such unofficial court functions include, but are not limited to:

(1) Receptions and other social events involving members of the Court and sponsored by a bar association.

(2) Bench and bar association-type meetings.

(3) Other events of legal-related groups, organizations, or entities using courthouse space (e.g., law school and high school moot-court competitions/trial advocacy competitions, CJA panel continuing education programs).

(4) Routine meetings of Inns of Court.

To expend funds under this provision, the Chief Judge of the District will make a determination that a particular court function (or series of related functions) is an unofficial court function that benefits the bench and the bar in and administration of justice prior to authorizing the disbursement of funds. In the Chief Judge's discretion, a determination may be made on recurring court functions as a group, rather than on an expenditure-by-expenditure basis. As to recurring court functions, the Chief Judge's determination shall be effective until the Chief Judge modifies the determination, or until appointment of a new Chief Judge.

(n) *Reimbursement to Jurors*: Reimbursement to jurors for lost or damaged personal property incident to their jury service, when compensation is not available from the United States under a statute such as the Federal Tort Claims Act.

(o) *Reimbursement for Lawyer Representatives Attending Ninth Circuit Judicial Conferences*: Upon request to the Chief District Judge, lawyer representatives may be reimbursed for the costs of their lodging and coach class airfare or mileage incurred to attend the Ninth Circuit Judicial Conference.

(p) *Surety Bonds*: Surety bonds for the custodian of the Fund and designated deputy clerks, to cover only the monies in the Fund.

(q) *Other Authorized Purpose*: Any other purpose for which appropriated funds may not legally be used that will benefit the bench and the bar in the administration of justice and that receives the approval of the JAC.

Section 2.02 Pro Bono Expenses: Upon appointment as pro bono counsel on behalf of indigent pro se civil litigants, an attorney acting as appointed pro bono counsel for indigent pro se civil litigants may petition the Court for reimbursement from the Fund of certain expenses incurred. Such reimbursement shall be governed exclusively by the provisions of General Order 510, adopted September 29, 2011.

CHAPTER THREE. Judicial Advisory Committee

Section 3.01 Role of the Court's Judicial Advisory Committee: The Court's Judicial Advisory Committee (the JAC), shall advise the District and Bankruptcy Courts on matters of policy in the administration of the Fund and make recommendations to the District and Bankruptcy Courts on proposed expenditures.

Section 3.02 Appointment Authority: With the consent of the Court, the Chief Judge will appoint members of the JAC and shall designate one member to act as Chair. Pursuant to General Order 414, amending General Orders 348 and 390, the JAC shall consist of:

(a) the Chief District Judge;

(b) the Chief Bankruptcy Judge;

(c) the Chief Magistrate Judge;

(d) the Co-chairs of the District's Lawyer Representatives Committee to the Ninth Circuit Judicial Conference;

(e) the U.S. Attorney for the District or his/her designee;

(f) the Federal Public Defender for the District or his/her designee;

(g) the President of the Sacramento Chapter of the Federal Bar Association or his/her designee;

(h) the President of the San Joaquin Valley Chapter of the Federal Bar Association or his/her designee;

(i) the Chair of the Sacramento Valley Bankruptcy Forum or his/her designee;

(j) the Chair of the Central California Bankruptcy Forum or his/her designee;

(k) the California Attorney General or his/her designee;

(*l*) the Co–Chairs of the District Conference Planning Committee;

(m) Three or More At–Large Members Appointed for Three Year Staggered Terms by the Chief Judge of the District;

(n) a Representative from the United States District Court, Eastern District of California Historical Society;

(o) a Representative of the Federal Courts Committee of the State Bar of California;

(p) the Chair of the Local Rules Committee of the District;

(q) the Clerk of Court of the District, or his/her Designee; and

(r) the ADR and Pro Bono Program Director.

Section 3.03 Terms of Office for Committee Members: Terms of office for members of the JAC will be established in the appointment order of the Chief Judge.

Section 3.04 Duties of the JAC: The JAC will advise the Court and the custodian on the administration of the Fund.

Section 3.05 Compensation for JAC Members: Members of the committee will serve without compensation.

CHAPTER FOUR. Court Responsibilities

Section 4.01 Fund Custodian and Responsibilities: The Clerk of the Court serves as the Fund custodian and is responsible for receiving, safeguarding, depositing, investing, disbursing, and accounting for all monies in the Fund according to any pertinent laws. The Fund custodian shall invest funds in excess of immediate needs in appropriate interest-bearing accounts at the direction of the Court or the JAC.

Section 4.02 Delegation of Fund Accounting Responsibilities: The Clerk of Court may delegate fund accounting and reporting responsibilities to any authorized deputy clerk.

Section 4.03 Surety Bonds Authorized: The Clerk of Court may recommend, and the JAC may authorize payment for surety bonds for the Fund custodian, and any authorized deputy clerk up to the amount of monies held by the Fund.

Section 4.04 Fund Accounting Procedures: The Fund custodian shall establish appropriate accounting and internal control procedures to administer the Fund and shall maintain records of all receipts, disbursements, and other significant activities relating to the Fund.

Section 4.05 Periodic Reporting Requirements:

(a) *Reports*: The Fund custodian will provide the Chief Judge with monthly balance statements and activity reports. The Fund custodian will provide the JAC with quarterly balance statements and activity reports.

(b) *Annual Report*: By December 1st of each year, the Fund custodian will prepare an annual report for the Chief Judge and the JAC, detailing the Fund activity for the previous fiscal year (covering the 12–month period from October 1–September 30).

(c) *Content of Reports*: The above reports must include:

(1) beginning balance of assets;

(2) revenue during reporting period (collections and investments);

(3) disbursements during reporting period;

(4) ending balance of assets (bank balances and undeposited collections);

(5) obligations, accounts payable or known future expenditures; and

(6) available balance.

(d) *Certification of Reports*: The Clerk of Court, as the Fund custodian, shall certify that the statements and reports accurately present the financial condition of the Fund.

Section 4.06 Final Accounting Upon Change of Fund Custodian:

(a) *Final Audit*: Before the departure of a Fund custodian, the Chief Judge may order that an exit audit be conducted to verify the financial status and condition of the Fund. Upon completion, the outgoing Fund custodian will verify the exit audit and statement attesting to the assets, liabilities, obligations, and financial condition of the Fund at the time of transfer to a new Fund custodian.

(b) *Acceptance of Custodial Responsibility*: Upon receipt of the exit audit and financial statement, and after verifying the financial condition of the Fund, the successor Fund custodian will file in the records of the Fund, a letter accepting custodial responsibility for all monies and accounts associated with the Fund.

Section 4.07 Audits and Inspections:

(a) *Regular Audits*: The Fund is subject to audit by the Administrative Office of the United States Courts and shall be included in the Court's annual internal audits.

(b) *Additional Audits*: If the JAC determines that additional audits are necessary, or appropriate, the Chief Judge may request an audit and use monies in the Fund to contract for services with an outside auditor or other disinterested person.

(c) *Written Results of Audits*: The Fund custodian shall provide written audit reports to the Chief Judge and the JAC. Reports may be made available, upon written request, to any attorney admitted pursuant to Local Rule 180.

Section 4.08 Dissolution of the Fund: The Chief Judge, with the consent of the Court, may dissolve the Fund whenever it is deemed necessary to do so. All outstanding obligations of the Fund shall be paid prior to dissolution, including any expenses resulting from a required terminal audit or inspection. Upon dissolution, monies remaining in the Fund shall be disposed of pursuant to court order in a manner that is consistent with the original purposes of the Fund.

[Dated: November 8, 2013.]

GENERAL ORDER 558. IN RE: ADOPTION OF AMENDED PLAN GOVERNING REIMBURSEMENT OF APPOINTED PRO BONO COUNSEL

This General Order supersedes General Order 510 in its entirety. Additionally, this General Order supersedes General Orders 154, 230, 259 and 377 to the extent they address reimbursement of pro bono counsel for indigent civil litigants.

The United States District Court for the Eastern District of California hereby adopts the following plan governing reimbursement of pro bono counsel appointed in indigent pro se civil cases. An attorney acting as appointed pro bono counsel for indigent pro se civil litigants may petition the Court for reimbursement from the Court's Non Appropriated Fund (Fund) of certain expenses incurred. Such reimbursement shall be governed exclusively by the provisions of this General Order.

Section 1. General Provisions.

A. All requests for reimbursement from the Fund shall be filed with and approved by the judge before whom a case is proceeding.

B. Except for good cause shown, requests for reimbursement may only be submitted during the pendency of the case in question or up to thirty (30) days following the entry of final judgment in the case.

C. When an attorney appointed as pro bono counsel for a pro se civil litigant is permitted to withdraw from representing the party in the case and the attorney wishes to seek payment of incurred expenses which may be reimbursable under this order, said attorney shall file a request for reimbursement within thirty (30) days of the entry of the order allowing the withdrawal. Except for good cause shown, the Court shall not allow reimbursement of expenses where the request was filed more than thirty (30) days after the entry of the order of withdrawal.

Section 2. Procedures for Requesting and Approving Reimbursement.

A. *Approval of certain expenses before they have been incurred.* Counsel seeking reimbursement of any single out-of-pocket expense costing $501 or more, and subject to Section 2(C), shall submit to the judge before whom a case is proceeding the form entitled "Request for Authority to Incur Costs" (available on the Court's website) prior to incurring any such expense. Except for good cause shown, the judge before whom a case is proceeding will only authorize such requests for reimbursement before such expenses have been incurred by pro bono counsel.

  1) After judicially-approved expenses have been incurred, counsel seeking reimbursement shall submit to the judge before whom a case is proceeding the form entitled "Request for Payment of Pro Bono Expenses" (available on the Court's website). The Court shall consider reimbursing counsel upon receipt of this properly completed and submitted form, upon review of whether the claimed expenses conform to those previously approved.

B. *Approval of certain expenses after they have been incurred.* Subject to the exceptions in Sections 2(C), 4(A)(3) and 4(A)(5)(ii) below, counsel requesting reimbursement of any out-of-pocket expense costing $500 or less shall submit to the judge before whom a case is proceeding the form entitled "Request for Payment of Pro Bono Expenses" (available on the Court's website) within the timeframe stated in Section 1 above.

  1) The judge before whom a case is proceeding may authorize reimbursement for these costs for good cause, even if the "Request for Payment of Pro Bono Expenses" form is submitted by pro bono counsel without previously submitting the "Request for Authority to Incur Costs" form and obtaining prior approval to incur the expenses from the judge before whom the case is proceeding as described in Section 2(A).

C. *Category–based exceptions.* Counsel reimbursed $501 or more under Section 2(B) for multiple expenses from the same general category (e.g., travel expenses) shall request advance approval and reimbursement for all subsequent expenses from that category incurred for that particular case in accordance with the procedures outlined in Section 2(A).

D. *Documentation requirements.* Counsel seeking reimbursement under this section must support all claimed expenses by attaching invoices, receipts or similar documentation to the submitted "Request for Payment of Pro Bono Expenses" form. Canceled checks do not constitute an acceptable form of documentation for this purpose.

Section 3.   Procedures for Reimbursing the Fund.

A. If at any time it appears that the indigent litigant is able to afford private counsel or otherwise elects to be represented by other counsel or to proceed in propria persona, the Court's appointment of pro bono counsel shall terminate on the motion of the Court or of the appointed attorney. The attorney and the litigant may then agree upon a fee arrangement for continued representation. The litigant is required to notify the judge before whom a case is proceeding of any change in his or her financial condition that may affect his or her ability to afford private counsel. If court appointment is thus terminated because of a change in the litigant's financial condition that resulted in the litigant being able to afford private counsel, the Court may require the litigant to repay to the Court any sums originally received as reimbursement for costs under this General Order.

B. In the event of settlement or other successful resolution of the case which results in a monetary award to the indigent litigant equal to or exceeding the reimbursed costs under this section, the indigent litigant through counsel shall reimburse the Fund for such out-of-pocket expenses allowed and reimbursed under this section. Counsel shall reimburse the Fund within thirty (30) days of settlement or judgment. Counsel shall ensure that such reimbursement occurs prior to any disbursement of judgment or settlement funds to counsel, plaintiff or any other person.

Section 4.   Costs and Expenses Eligible for Reimbursement.

A. Subject to the preceding sections and approval of the judge before whom a case is proceeding, the following costs and expenses are eligible for reimbursement from the Fund:

1) Costs of photocopies, photographs, and telephone toll calls: Counsel may request reimbursement for expenses incurred for photocopying, photographs used in furtherance of a client's case, toll calls, and other similar expenses not including overhead charges. Counsel may only request reimbursement for costs incurred outside of counsel's office space and necessary to the preparation of a client's case.

2) Certain deposition and transcript costs: In accordance with the provisions of Section 5(A)(5) below and California Business and Professions Code Section 8030.2, the costs of transcripts or depositions must be borne initially by the State of California's Transcript Reimbursement Fund (TRF). Counsel may request reimbursement from the Fund for such transcript or deposition costs that exceed the maximum allowed from the TRF. The Court's Pro Bono Program Director is available to assist pro bono counsel with the process of requesting reimbursement through the TRF.

3) Expert and non-expert witness costs: Counsel may request reimbursement for costs of retaining expert and non-expert witnesses whose services are necessary in preparing their client's case. Except for good cause shown, all such services require prior approval of the judge before whom a case is proceeding before they may be purchased, regardless of their cost.

4) Costs for service of papers: Counsel may request reimbursement of fees for service of papers that are not otherwise avoided, waived or recoverable.

5) Costs of travel: Attorneys may request reimbursement of costs and expenses incurred for travel related to a client's case, subject to the following:

i. Travel by privately owned automobile may be claimed at the rate currently authorized for federal judiciary employees who use a private automobile to conduct official business, plus parking fees, tolls and similar expenses. Applicable mileage rates may be found at www.gsa.gov.

ii. Travel other than by privately owned automobile requires prior approval by the Court. Travel information may be obtained from the Pro Bono Program Director.

iii. Costs of lodging and meals and incidentals (M&IE) shall not exceed the per diem rates authorized by the U.S. General Services Administration (GSA). When expenses of lodging are expected to exceed the GSA maximum lodging rate for the location, the Court may preauthorize the attorney reimbursement for the actual cost of lodging plus the applicable GSA locality M&IE allowance, provided that the total does not exceed 150 percent of the applicable GSA locality per diem rate. GSA rates may be found at www.gsa.gov.

6) Other costs and expenses: Counsel may request reimbursement for expenses other than those described in this section. Such reimbursement requests must comply with the requirements of previous sections, and request forms submitted to the judge before whom a case is proceeding shall include a detailed description of the expenses incurred.

Section 5. Costs and Expenses Not Eligible for Reimbursement.

A. Except for good cause shown and subject to the preceding sections, the following costs and expenses are not eligible for reimbursement from the Fund:

1) Attorneys' fees: Attorneys' fees may not be reimbursed from the Fund.

2) Printing of briefs: Costs incurred printing briefs, regardless of the printing method used, may not be reimbursed from the Fund.

3) Proceedings covered by the Criminal Justice Act (CJA): Costs incurred in proceedings where expenses are reimbursable under the CJA (18 U.S.C. § 3006A) may not be reimbursed from the Fund. Such expenses shall be reimbursed in accordance with CJA guidelines only.

4) Computer assisted legal research: Costs incurred conducting computer assisted legal research may not be reimbursed from the Fund.

5) Certain deposition and transcript costs: In accordance with the provisions of Section 4(A)(2) above and California Business and Professions Code Section 8030.2, initial costs incurred producing transcripts or depositions may not be reimbursed from the Fund and must be borne by the TRF. The Pro Bono Program Director is available to assist pro bono counsel with the reimbursement process through the TRF.

6) General office overhead and related expenses: Costs incurred for general office operations, including personnel costs, rent, telephone services, secretarial assistance, office photocopying equipment and any other general overhead expenses may not be reimbursed from the Fund.

7) Statutorily recovered fees: Expenses that may be statutorily recovered may not be reimbursed from the Fund.

8) Costs or fees taxed against the party: Costs or fees taxed against the indigent litigant or his or her pro bono counsel may not be reimbursed from the Fund.

[Dated: March 18, 2015.]

INDEX TO
UNITED STATES DISTRICT COURT
FOR THE EASTERN DISTRICT OF CALIFORNIA

UNITED STATES DISTRICT COURT
FOR THE NORTHERN DISTRICT OF CALIFORNIA

Including Amendments Received Through
December 1, 2021

CIVIL LOCAL RULES

RULE 1. TITLE; SCOPE; DEFINITIONS

RULE 1–1. TITLE

These are the Local Rules of Practice in Civil Proceedings before the United States District Court for the Northern District of California. They should be cited as "Civil L.R. ___."

[Effective September 1, 1995.]

RULE 1–2. SCOPE, PURPOSE AND CONSTRUCTION

(a) Scope. These local rules are promulgated pursuant to 28 U.S.C. § 2071 and Fed. R. Civ. P. 83. They apply to civil actions filed in this Court. The Court also has promulgated separate local rules in the following subject areas:

(1) Admiralty and Maritime;

(2) Alternative Dispute Resolution;

(3) Bankruptcy;

(4) Criminal Proceedings;

(5) Habeas Corpus Petitions; and

(6) Patent.

(b) Supplement to Federal Rules. These local rules supplement the applicable Federal Rules. They shall be construed so as to be consistent with the Federal Rules and to promote the just, efficient, speedy, and economical determination of every action and proceeding.

(c) Temporary Suspension of Local Rules. Any of these Local Rules may be temporarily suspended for good cause by General Order or by Order of the Chief Judge.

[Effective September 1, 1995. Amended effective July 1, 1997; December 1, 2000; December 1, 2021.]

RULE 1–3. EFFECTIVE DATE

These rules take effect on November 1, 2021. They govern civil cases filed on or after that date. For actions pending on November 1, 2021, if fewer than ten days remain to perform an act otherwise governed by these rules, the provisions of the local rules that were in effect on October 31, 2021, shall apply to that act.

[Effective September 1, 1995. Amended effective July 1, 1997; December 1, 2000; January 1, 2005; January 1, 2006; December 1, 2009; December 1, 2021.]

RULE 1–4. SANCTIONS AND PENALTIES FOR NONCOMPLIANCE

Failure by counsel or a party to comply with any duly promulgated local rule or any Federal Rule may be a ground for imposition of any authorized sanction.

[Effective September 1, 1995. Amended effective December 1, 2000.]

RULE 1–5. DEFINITIONS

(a) Clerk. "Clerk" refers to the Clerk or a Deputy Clerk of the Court.

(b) Court. Except where the context otherwise requires, the word "Court" refers to the United States District Court for the Northern District of California and to a Judge acting on behalf of that Court with respect to a matter within the Court's jurisdiction.

(c) Day. For computation of time under these local rules, "day" shall have the meaning given in Fed. R. Civ. P. 6(a).

(d) Ex Parte. "Without other party." Ex parte means contact with the Court without the advance knowledge or contemporaneous participation of all other parties.

(e) File. "File" means delivery to and acceptance by the Clerk of a document, including an electronic document, which is approved for filing and which will be included in the official files of the Court and noted in the docket of the case.

(f) Fed. R. Civ. P. "Fed. R. Civ. P." means the Federal Rules of Civil Procedure.

(g) Fed. R. Crim. P. "Fed. R. Crim. P." means the Federal Rules of Criminal Procedure.

(h) Fed. R. App. P. "Fed. R. App. P." means the Federal Rules of Appellate Procedure.

(i) Federal Rule. "Federal Rule" means any applicable Federal Rule.

(j) General Orders. "General Orders" are made by the Chief Judge or by the Court relating to Court administration. When the Court deems it appropriate, a General Order also may be used to promulgate modifications of these local rules. Such General Orders shall remain in effect until the rules are properly amended.

(k) General Duty Judge. The "General Duty Judge" is the Judge designated by the Chief Judge to act for the Court in matters for which there is no assigned Judge, or when the assigned Judge is unavailable. The name of the Judge serving as General Duty Judge shall be made available by the office of the Clerk.

(l) Judge. Unless the context otherwise indicates, the term "Judge," or "assigned Judge" refers to any United States District Judge, any United States Bankruptcy Judge, or to any full-time or part-time United States Magistrate Judge.

(m) Lodge. When a statute, rule, or order permits a document to be submitted to the Court but does not permit the document to be "filed" (e.g., proposed trial exhibits or deposition transcripts), the document may be "lodged" with the Clerk's office. The Clerk will stamp the document "Received" and promptly deliver it to the Chambers of the Judge for whom the document is intended.

(n) Meet and Confer. "Meet and confer" or "confer" means to communicate directly and to discuss in good faith the issue(s) required under the particular Rule or order. Unless these Local Rules otherwise provide or a Judge otherwise orders, such communication may take place by telephone. The mere sending of a written, electronic, or voice-mail communication, however, does not satisfy a requirement to "meet and confer" or to "confer." Rather, this requirement can be satisfied only through direct dialogue and discussion—either in a face to face meeting or in a telephone conversation.

Commentary

See Fed. R. Civ. P. 26(f).

(o) Standing Orders of Individual Judges. "Standing Orders" are orders by a Judge governing the conduct of a class or category of actions or proceedings assigned to that Judge. It is the policy of the Court to provide notice of any applicable Standing Orders to parties before they are subject to sanctions for violating such orders. Nothing in these local rules precludes a Judge from issuing Standing Orders to govern matters not covered by these local rules or by the Federal Rules.

(p) Unavailability. This Court is in continuous session. To the extent reasonably feasible, each active Judge of this Court will be available at his or her assigned courthouse during the normal hours the Clerk has established pursuant to Civil L.R. 77–1. A Judge who will be absent from the District for one court day or more shall post a notice to that effect on the official calendar of the Court. If a Judge is unavailable, any motion or matter requesting immediate judicial determination shall be referred to the General Duty Judge. If the General Duty Judge is unavailable, the Clerk shall assign the matter to any available Judge of this Court.

[Effective September 1, 1995. Amended effective July 1, 1997; December 1, 2000; October 1, 2002; July 2, 2012; January 1, 2018; December 1, 2021.]

RULE 3.   COMMENCEMENT AND ASSIGNMENT OF ACTION

RULE 3–1.   REGULAR SESSION

The Court shall be in continuous session in the following locations: San Francisco Division, Oakland Division, San Jose Division, and Eureka Division. From time to time sessions may be held at other locations within the district as the Court may order.

[Effective September 1, 1995. Amended effective July 1, 1997; July 2, 2012.]

RULE 3–2.   COMMENCEMENT AND ASSIGNMENT OF ACTION

(a) Civil Cover Sheet. Every complaint, petition, or other paper initiating a civil action (except for pro se prisoner complaints and petitions) must be filed with a completed civil cover sheet on a form approved by the Court.

Cross Reference

See Civil L.R. 3–6(b) *"Jury Demand; Marking of Civil Cover Sheet Insufficient;"* Civil L.R. 3–7(a) *"Civil Cover Sheet Requirement in Private Securities Actions"*

(b) Commencement of Action. An action may be commenced within the meaning of Fed. R. Civ. P. 3 at any office of the Clerk for this district. In cases that permit or require manual filing, once an action is commenced, subsequent manual filings may be made in any division within the district, except that manual filings in matters assigned to the San Francisco, San Jose, or Oakland divisions may not be filed in the Eureka–McKinleyville division.

(c) Assignment to a Division. The Clerk shall assign civil actions and proceedings pursuant to the Court's Assignment Plan (General Order No. 44). For those case categories which are not district-wide, the Clerk shall assign the case to the court division serving the county in which the action arises. A civil action arises in the county where a substantial part of the events or omissions giving rise to the claim occurred, or where a substantial part of the property that is the subject of the action is situated.

(d) San Francisco and Oakland. Except as provided in Civil L.R. 3–2(c), all civil actions that arise in the counties of Alameda, Contra Costa, Marin, Napa, San Francisco, San Mateo or Sonoma shall be assigned to the San Francisco Division or the Oakland Division.

(e) San Jose. Except as provided in Civil L.R. 3–2(c), all civil actions that arise in the counties of Santa Clara, Santa Cruz, San Benito or Monterey shall be assigned to the San Jose Division.

(f) Eureka. Except as provided in Civil L.R. 3–2(c), all civil actions that arise in the counties of Del Norte, Humboldt, Lake, and Mendocino, except for cases not assigned to the

Magistrate Judges pursuant to the Court's Assignment Plan, shall be assigned to the Eureka Division.

Cross Reference

See General Order No. 44, Assignment Plan.

(g) Assignment of Action to the Eureka Division. All cases assigned to the Eureka Division shall be assigned to the full-time Magistrate Judge presiding in that division. Such assignments are subject to the provisions of Civil L.R. 73 and require the consent of the parties. Any case for which all parties do not consent will be reassigned to a District Judge in the San Francisco, Oakland, or San Jose division.

(h) Transfer of Actions and Proceedings. Whenever a Judge finds, upon the Judge's own motion or the motion of any party, that (1) a civil action has not been assigned to the proper division within this district in accordance with this rule, or (2) that the convenience of the parties and witnesses and the interests of justice will be served by transferring the action to a different division within the district, the Judge may order such transfer, subject to the provisions of the Court's Assignment Plan.

[Effective September 1, 1995. Amended effective July 1, 1997; December 1, 2000; October 1, 2002; March 17, 2009; December 1, 2009; July 2, 2012; May 11, 2017; January 1, 2018; December 1, 2021.]

RULE 3–3. ASSIGNMENT OF ACTION TO A JUDGE

(a) Assignment. Immediately upon the filing of any civil action and its assignment to a division of the Court pursuant to Civil L.R. 3–2, the Clerk shall assign it to a Judge pursuant to the Assignment Plan of the Court (General Order No. 44). The Clerk may not make or change any assignment, except as provided in these local rules or in the Assignment Plan .

(b) Multiple Filings. Any single action filed in more than one division of this Court shall be transferred pursuant to Civil L.R. 3–2(h).

(c) Refiled Action. If any civil action or claim of a civil action is dismissed and subsequently refiled, the refiling party must file a Motion to Consider Whether Cases Should be Related pursuant to Civil L.R. 3–12. Upon a determination by a Judge that an action or claim pending before him or her is covered by this Local Rule, that Judge may transfer the refiled action to the Judge originally assigned to the action which had been dismissed. Any party who files an action in multiple divisions or dismisses an action and subsequently refiles it for the purpose of obtaining an assignment in contravention of Civil L.R. 3–3(b) shall be subject to appropriate sanctions.

[Effective September 1, 1995. Amended effective July 1, 1997; December 1, 2000; January 1, 2006; May 1, 2018; December 1, 2021.]

RULE 3–4. PAPERS PRESENTED FOR FILING

(a) First Page Requirements. The first page of each paper presented for filing must set forth:

(1) The name, address, telephone number, email address, and state bar number of counsel (or, if pro se, the name, address, telephone number, and email address of the party)

presenting the paper for filing. This information must appear in the upper left hand corner and must indicate the party represented by name as well as that party's status in the litigation (i.e., plaintiff, defendant, etc.). In multiparty actions or proceedings, reference may be made to the signature page for the complete list of parties represented;

Cross Reference

See Civil L.R. 3–9 *"Parties"*; Civil L. R. 3–11 *"Failure to Notify of Address Change;"* and Civil L.R. 11–3(e) *"Appearances and Service on Local Co–Counsel.*

(2) If not proceeding pro se and if proceeding *pro hac vice* in conformity with Civil L.R. 11–3, following the information required in Civil L.R. 3–4(a)(1), the name, address, telephone and state bar number of the member of the bar of the Court who maintains an office within the State of California; and

(3) Commencing on the eighth line of the page (except where additional space is required for counsel identification) there must appear:

(A) The title of this Court, including the appropriate division or location;

(B) The title of the action;

(C) The case number of the action followed by the initials of the assigned District Judge or Magistrate Judge and, if applicable, the initials of the Magistrate Judge to whom the action is referred for discovery or other pretrial activity;

(D) A title describing the paper; and

(E) Any other matter required by Civil L.R. 3.

(4) Any complaint or Notice of Removal of Action seeking review of federal agency determinations in immigration cases, Privacy Act cases, or Administrative Procedure Act cases must include, under the title of the document, whichever of the following is applicable: "Immigration Case," "Privacy Act Case," or "Administrative Procedure Act Case."

(5) *Presentation of Class Action.* If any complaint, counterclaim or cross-claim is sought to be maintained as a class action, it must bear the legend "Class Action" on its first page below the title describing the paper as a complaint, counterclaim or cross-claim.

(b) Caption for Consolidated Cases. When filing papers in cases consolidated pursuant to Fed. R. Civ. P. 42, the caption of each paper must denote the lead case number above all consolidated case numbers. Duplicate originals, however, are not required for associated cases.

(c) General Requirements.

(1) *Paper.* Papers presented for manual filing must be on 8-1/2 inch by 11 inch white paper with numbered lines, and must be flat, unfolded (unless necessary for the presentation of exhibits), without back or cover, and firmly bound.

(2) *Written Text.* Text must appear on one side only and must be double-spaced with no more than 28 lines per page, except for the identification of counsel, title of the case, footnotes, and quotations. Unless a Judge's standing order or other instruction from the court requires otherwise, text, including footnotes and quotations, must be:

(A) in a standard, proportionally spaced font (e.g., Times New Roman or Century Schoolbook);

(B) in 12 point type or larger; and

(C) spaced no more than 10 characters per horizontal inch.

(3) *Identification of Paper.* Except for exhibits, each paper filed with the Court must bear a footer on the lower margin of each page stating the title of the paper (e.g., "Complaint," "Defendant's Motion for Summary Judgment," etc.) or some clear and concise abbreviation. Once the Court assigns a case number to the action, that case number must be included in the footer.

Commentary

When a case is first filed, the footer on each page of the complaint need only bear the title of the paper (e.g., "Complaint"), but after assignment of a case number on filing, that number must be included in footers on any subsequently prepared papers (e.g., "Defendant's Motion for Summary Judgment—21–cv–12345–ABC.")

(d) Citation to Authorities. Unless otherwise directed by the assigned Judge, citation to authorities in any paper must include:

(1) In any citation to an Act of Congress, a parallel citation to the United States Code by title, section and date;

(2) In any citation to U.S. regulations, a citation to the Code of Federal Regulations by title and section, and the date of promulgation of the regulation;

(3) In any citation to a U.S. Supreme Court Case, a citation to United States Reports, Lawyers' Edition, or Supreme Court Reporter. If the case is not yet available in any of those formats but is available on electronic databases, citation must indicate the database, year, and any screen or page numbers, if assigned;

(4) In any citation to other federal courts, unless an alternate reporting service is widely available, a citation to the Federal Reporter, Federal Supplement, or Federal Rules Decisions must be used. If the case is not yet available in those formats but is available on electronic databases, citation must indicate the database, year, and any screen or page numbers, if assigned; and

(5) In any citation to a state court, citations must include either the official reports or any official regional reporting service (e.g., West Publishing). If the case is not yet available in those formats but is available on electronic databases, citation must indicate the database, year, and any screen or page numbers, if assigned.

(e) Prohibition of Citation to Uncertified Opinion or Order. Any order or opinion that is designated: "NOT FOR CITATION," pursuant to Civil L.R. 7–14 or pursuant to a similar rule of any other issuing court, may not be cited to this Court, either in written submissions or oral argument, except when relevant under the doctrines of law of the case, res judicata, or collateral estoppel.

See Civil L.R. 7–14 *"Designation 'Not For Citation'."* See also Ninth Circuit Court of Appeals Rule 36–3.

[Effective September 1, 1995. Amended effective July 1, 1997; December 1, 2000; January 1, 2005; July 2, 2012; December 1, 2021.]

RULE 3–5. JURISDICTIONAL STATEMENT

(a) Jurisdiction. Each complaint, petition, counterclaim, and cross-claim must include a separate paragraph entitled "Jurisdiction." The paragraph will identify the statutory or other basis for federal jurisdiction and the facts supporting such jurisdiction.

(b) Divisional Assignment. Each complaint or petition must include a paragraph entitled "Divisional Assignment." The paragraph must identify any basis for assignment to a particular location or division of the Court pursuant to Civil L.R. 3–2(c).

[Effective September 1, 1995. Amended effective July 1, 1997; December 1, 2000; December 1, 2021.]

RULE 3–6. JURY DEMAND

(a) Included in Pleading. A party may demand a jury trial as provided in Fed. R. Civ. P. 38(b). When a demand for jury trial is included in a pleading, the demand must be set forth at the end of the pleading. When the demand is made by a party who is represented by counsel, the pleading must be signed by the attorney for the party making the demand. In the caption of such pleading, immediately following the title of the pleading, the following must appear: "DEMAND FOR JURY TRIAL."

(b) Marking of Civil Cover Sheet Insufficient.. Marking the civil cover sheet to indicate a demand for jury trial is not a sufficient demand to comply with this Local Rule.

Commentary

See *Wall v. Nat'l R.R. Passenger Corp.*, 718 F.2d 906, 909 (9th Cir. 1983) (holding that "checking the jury demand box on the civil cover sheet is insufficient to meet the requirements of rule 38(b)").

[Effective September 1, 1995. Amended effective December 1, 2000; December 1, 2021.]

RULE 3–7. FILING AND CERTIFICATION IN PRIVATE SECURITIES ACTIONS

(a) Civil Cover Sheet Notation Requirement. If a complaint or other pleading contains a claim governed by the Private Securities Litigation Reform Act of 1995, Pub. L. No. 104–67, 109 Stat. 737 (1995), the following must be so noted in Block VI of the civil cover sheet: "Private Securities Litigation Reform Act."

See Civil L.R. 23–1 *"Private Securities Actions."*

(b) Certification by Filing Party Seeking to Serve as Lead Plaintiff. Any person or group of persons filing a complaint and seeking to serve as lead plaintiff in a civil action containing a claim governed by the Private Securities Litigation Reform Act of 1995, Pub. L. No. 104–67, 109 Stat. 737

(1995), must serve and file with the initial pleading a certificate under penalty of perjury which contains the following averments:

(1) The party has reviewed the complaint and authorized its filing;

(2) The party did not engage in transactions in the securities which are the subject of the action at the direction of plaintiff's counsel or in order to participate in this or any other litigation under the securities laws of the United States;

(3) The party is willing to serve as a representative party on behalf of a class, including providing testimony at deposition and trial, if necessary;

(4) The party has made no transactions during the class period in the debt or equity securities that are the subject of the action except those set forth in the certificate (as used herein, "equity security" shall have the same meaning as that term has for purposes of section 16(a) of the Securities Exchange Act of 1934, 15 U.S.C. § 78p(a));

(5) The party has not, within the three years preceding the date of the certification, sought to serve or served as a representative party on behalf of a class in an action involving alleged violations of the federal securities laws, except as set forth in the certificate; and

(6) The party will not accept any payment for serving as representative on behalf of a class beyond the party's pro rata share of any recovery, unless ordered or approved by the Court pursuant to section 27(a)(4) of the Securities Act, 15 U.S.C. § 77z–1(a)(4), or section 21D(a)(4) of the Securities Exchange Act, 15 U.S.C. § 78u–4(a)(4).

(c) Certification by Nonfiling Party Seeking to Serve as Lead Plaintiff. Any party seeking to serve as lead plaintiff, but who does not also file a complaint, need not file the certification required in Civil L.R. 3–7(b), but must at the time of initial appearance state that the party has reviewed a complaint filed in the action and either:

(1) Adopts its allegations or, if not,

(2) Specifies the allegations the party intends to assert.

(d) Certification by Lawyers Seeking to Serve as Class Counsel. Each lawyer seeking to serve as class counsel in any civil action containing a cause of action governed by the Private Securities Litigation Reform Act of 1995, Pub. L. No. 104–67, 109 Stat. 737 (1995), must serve and file a certificate under penalty of perjury which either:

(1) Affirms that the lawyer does not directly own or otherwise have a beneficial interest in securities that are the subject of the action; or

(2) Sets forth with specificity the extent of any such ownership or interest and explains why that ownership or interest does not constitute a conflict of interest sufficient to disqualify the attorney from representing the class.

Cross Reference

See also Civil L.R. 23 *"Class Actions."*

[Effective September 1, 1995. Amended effective July 1, 1997; December 1, 2000.]

RULE 3–8. CLAIM OF UNCONSTITUTIONALITY

(a) Federal Statute. In any action in which the constitutionality of an Act of Congress is questioned and neither the United States nor any officer, agency or employee thereof is a party, counsel raising the question must file a notice of such claim with the assigned Judge (or, if no assignment has been made, the Chief Judge) and serve a copy of such notice on the United States Attorney for this district. The notice must identify the statute and describe the basis for the claim that it is unconstitutional. The party must file the notice with a certificate of service pursuant to Civil L.R. 5–5.

(b) State Statute. In any action in which the constitutionality of a state statute is questioned and neither the state nor an agency, officer or employee of the state is a party, counsel raising the question must file notice of such claim with the assigned Judge (or, if no assignment has been made, the Chief Judge) and serve a copy of such notice on the State Attorney General. The notice must identify the statute and describe the basis for the claim that it is unconstitutional. The party must file the notice with a certificate of service pursuant to Civil L.R. 5–5.

Cross Reference

See 28 U.S.C. § 2403.

[Effective September 1, 1995. Amended effective December 1, 2000; October 1, 2002; July 2, 2012.]

RULE 3–9. PARTIES

(a) Natural Person Appearing Pro Se. Any party representing him or herself without an attorney must appear personally and may not delegate that duty to any other person who is not a member of the bar of this Court. A person representing him or herself without an attorney is bound by the Federal Rules, as well as by all applicable local rules. Sanctions (including default or dismissal) may be imposed for failure to comply with local rules.

Cross Reference

See Civil L.R. 11–1 *"The Bar of This Court."*

(b) Corporation or Other Entity. A corporation, unincorporated association, partnership or other such entity may appear only through a member of the bar of this Court.

Cross Reference

See Civil L.R. 11–1 *"The Bar of This Court."*

(c) Government or Governmental Agency. When these rules require an act be done personally by the party, and the party is a government or a governmental agency, the act must be done by a representative of the government or governmental agency who is knowledgeable about the facts of the case and the position of the government, and who has, to the greatest extent feasible, authority to do the required act.

Cross Reference

See Civil L.R. 11–2 *"Attorneys for the United States."* See also ADR L.R. 5–10(a)(2) and 6–9(a)(2).

[Effective September 1, 1995. Amended effective December 1, 2000.]

RULE 3–10. EX PARTE MOTION TO PROCEED IN FORMA PAUPERIS

(a) Motion to Proceed In Forma Pauperis. At the commencement of an action, any person wishing the Court to authorize prosecution or defense of the action without payment of fees or security, pursuant to 28 U.S.C. § 1915, must submit, with the proposed complaint, an Ex Parte Motion to Proceed In Forma Pauperis, pursuant to Civil L.R. 7–11. The Clerk shall file the complaint, assign a case number, and assign a presiding Judge.

(b) Content of Motion. The motion must contain:

(1) A request to proceed *in forma pauperis*;

(2) An affidavit or declaration under penalty of perjury providing the information required by Title 28 U.S.C. § 1915, on a form available at the Office of the Clerk and on the Court's website, or an equivalent form; and

(3) A proposed order.

(c) Determination of the Motion. The Judge may grant the motion, grant the motion (subject to partial payment of fees, costs or security), or deny the motion. If the motion is granted in part or denied, the order will state that the action is dismissed unless any outstanding fees, costs, or security is paid within the time set in the order.

Commentary

If, during the pendency of an action, any person wishes to prosecute or defend an action *in forma pauperis*, the person must file an Administrative Motion to Proceed *In Forma Pauperis* pursuant to Civil L.R. 7–11.

[Effective September 1, 1995. Amended effective July 1, 1997; December 1, 2000; January 1, 2005; August 10, 2010; September 8, 2011; September 15, 2015; December 1, 2021.]

RULE 3–11. FAILURE TO NOTIFY OF ADDRESS CHANGE

(a) Duty to Notify. An attorney or a party proceeding pro se whose address changes while an action is pending must promptly file with the Court and serve upon all opposing parties a Notice of Change of Address specifying the new address.

(b) Dismissal Due to Failure. The Court may, without prejudice, dismiss a complaint or strike an answer when:

(1) Mail directed to the attorney or pro se party by the Court has been returned to the Court as not deliverable; and

(2) The Court fails to receive within 60 days of this return a written communication from the attorney or pro se party indicating a current address.

[Effective September 1, 1995. Amended effective December 1, 2000.]

RULE 3–12. RELATED CASES

(a) Definition of Related Cases. An action is related to another when:

(1) The actions concern substantially the same parties, property, transaction or event; and

(2) It appears likely that there will be an unduly burdensome duplication of labor and expense or conflicting results if the cases are conducted before different Judges.

(b) Administrative Motion to Consider Whether Cases Should Be Related. Whenever a party knows or learns that an action, filed in or removed to this district is (or the party believes that the action may be) related to an action which is or was pending in this District as defined in Civil L.R. 3–12(a), the party must promptly file in the lowest-numbered case an Administrative Motion to Consider Whether Cases Should be Related, pursuant to Civil L.R. 7–11. In addition to complying with Civil L.R. 7–11, a copy of the motion, together with proof of service pursuant to Civil L.R. 5–5, must be served on all known parties to each apparently related action. A courtesy copy of the motion must be lodged with the assigned Judge in each apparently related case under Civil L.R. 5–1(e)(7).

(c) Sua Sponte Judicial Referral for Purpose of Determining Relationship. Whenever a Judge believes that a case pending before that Judge is related to another case, the Judge may refer the case to the Judge assigned to the lowest-numbered case with a request that the Judge assigned to the lowest-numbered case consider whether the cases are related. The referring Judge shall file and send a copy of the referral to all parties to all affected cases. The parties must file any response in opposition to or support of relating the cases pursuant to Civil L.R. 3–12(e). Alternatively, a Judge may order the parties to file a motion pursuant to Civil L.R. 3–12(b).

(d) Content of Motion. An Administrative Motion to Consider Whether Cases Should be Related must contain:

(1) The title and case number of each apparently related case;

(2) A brief statement of the relationship of the actions according to the criteria set forth in Civil L.R. 3–12(a).

(e) Response to Motion. Any opposition to or support of a Motion to Consider Whether Cases Should be Related must be filed in the lowest-numbered case pursuant to Civil L.R. 7–11. The opposition or statement of support must specifically address the issues in Civil L.R. 3–12(a) and (d) and be served on all parties and lodged with the Chambers of all Judges identified in the motion. If the motion identifies more than two potentially related cases, and a party contends that not all of the cases are related, the party must address whether any of the cases are related to one another.

(f) Order Granting or Denying Relationship. Upon a motion by a party or a referral by another Judge, after the time for filing support or opposition to the Motion to Consider Whether Cases Should Be Related has passed, the Judge in this District who is assigned to the lowest-numbered case will decide if the cases are or are not related and will notify the Clerk, who, in turn, will notify the parties.

(1) Due to the need for parties and affected Judges to have a speedy determination of the motion or referral, the Judge assigned to the lowest-numbered case shall act on the motion or referral within 14 days after the date a response is due. If the Judge assigned to the lowest-numbered case is not available for that period, the Clerk or counsel may bring the motion or referral to the General Duty Judge.

(2) If the Judge assigned to the lowest-numbered case decides that the cases are not related, no change in case assignment will be made. In cases where there are more than two potentially related cases, the Clerk shall submit the order to the Judges assigned to the other cases in order of filing with a form of order to decide within 14 days if the cases are or are not related. If no Judge relates any of the remaining cases, no change in case assignment will be made.

(3) If any Judge decides that any of the cases are related, pursuant to the Assignment Plan, the Clerk shall reassign all related higher-numbered cases to that Judge and shall notify the parties and the affected Judges accordingly.

(g) Effect of Order on Case Schedule. The case management conference in any reassigned case will be rescheduled by the newly assigned Judge. The parties shall adjust the dates for the conference, disclosures and report required by Fed. R. Civ. P. 16 and 26 accordingly. Unless the assigned Judge otherwise orders, upon reassignment, any deadlines set by the ADR Local Rules remain in effect and any dates for hearing noticed motions are automatically vacated and must be renoticed by the moving party before the newly assigned Judge. For cases ordered related after the initial case management conference, unless the assigned Judge otherwise orders, any deadlines established in the case management order shall continue to govern, except for the trial date, which will be rescheduled by the assigned Judge.

[Effective September 1, 1995. Amended effective July 1, 1997; December 1, 2000; January 1, 2006; December 1, 2009; July 2, 2012; November 1, 2014; September 15, 2015.]

RULE 3–13. NOTICE OF PENDENCY OF OTHER ACTION OR PROCEEDING

(a) Notice. Whenever a party knows or learns that an action filed or removed to this district involves all or a material part of the same subject matter and all or substantially all of the same parties as another action which is pending in any other federal or state court, the party must promptly file with the Court in the action pending before this Court and serve all opposing parties in the action pending before this Court with a Notice of Pendency of Other Action or Proceeding.

(b) Content of Notice. A Notice of Pendency of Other Action or Proceeding must contain:

(1) A description of the other action;

(2) The title and location of the court in which the other action or proceeding is pending; and

(3) A brief statement of:

(A) The relationship of the other action to the action or proceeding pending in this district; and

(B) If the other action is pending in another U.S. District Court, whether transfer should be effected pursuant to 28 U.S.C. § 1407 (Multi District Litigation Procedures) or whether other coordination might avoid conflicts, conserve resources and promote an efficient determination of the action; or

(C) If the other action is pending before any state court, whether proceedings should be coordinated to avoid con-

flicts, conserve resources and promote an efficient determination of the action.

(c) Procedure After Filing. No later than 14 days after service of a Notice of Pendency of Other Action, any party may file with the Court a statement supporting or opposing the notice. Such statement will specifically address the issues in Civil L.R. 3–13(b).

(d) Order. After the time for filing support or opposition to the Notice of Pendency of Other Actions or Proceedings has passed, the Judge assigned to the case pending in this district may make appropriate orders.

[Effective September 1, 1995. Amended effective July 1, 1997; December 1, 2000; December 1, 2009.]

RULE 3–14. DISQUALIFICATION OF ASSIGNED JUDGE

Whenever an affidavit of bias or prejudice directed at a Judge of this Court is filed pursuant to 28 U.S.C. § 144, and the Judge has determined not to recuse him or herself and found that the affidavit is neither legally insufficient nor interposed for delay, the Judge shall refer the request for disqualification to the Clerk for random assignment to another Judge.

Commentary

Recusal under 28 U.S.C. § 455 is normally undertaken by a Judge sua sponte. However, counsel may bring the issue to a Judge's attention by formal motion or raise it informally at a Case Management Conference or by a letter to the Judge, with a copy to the other parties in the case. This rule does not preclude a Judge from referring matters arising under 28 U.S.C. § 455 to the Clerk so that another Judge can determine disqualification. See also Civil L.R. 3–15.

[Former Rule 3–15 effective September 1, 1995. Amended effective July 1, 1997. Renumbered and amended effective December 1, 2000. Amended effective January 1, 2005. Renumbered and amended effective February 3, 2014.]

RULE 3–15. DISCLOSURE OF NON-PARTY INTERESTED ENTITIES OR PERSONS

(a) Certification. Upon making a first appearance in any proceeding in this Court, each party must file with the Clerk a "Certification of Interested Entities or Persons" pursuant to this Rule. The Rule does not apply to any governmental entity or its agencies.

(1) The Certification must disclose any persons, associations of persons, firms, partnerships, corporations (including parent corporations), or other entities other than the parties themselves known by the party to have either: (i) a financial interest of any kind in the subject matter in controversy or in a party to the proceeding; or (ii) any other kind of interest that could be substantially affected by the outcome of the proceeding.

(2) If a party has no disclosure to make pursuant to subparagraph (a)(1), that party must make a certification stating that no such interest is known other than that of the named parties to the action. A party has a continuing duty to supplement its

certification if an entity becomes interested within the meaning of section (1) during the pendency of the proceeding.

(3) For purposes of this Rule, the terms "proceeding" and "financial interest" shall have the meaning assigned by 28 U.S.C. § 455 (d)(1), (3) and (4), respectively.

(b) Form of Certification. The Certification of Interested Entities or Persons must take the following form, as is appropriate to the proceeding:

(1) If there is an interest to be certified: "Pursuant to Civil L.R. 3–15, the undersigned certifies that the following listed persons, associations of persons, firms, partnerships, corporations (including parent corporations) or other entities (i) have a financial interest in the subject matter in controversy or in a party to the proceeding, or (ii) have a non-financial interest in that subject matter or in a party that could be substantially affected by the outcome of this proceeding: (List names and identify their connection and interest). Signature, Attorney of Record."

(2) If there is no interest to be certified: "Pursuant to Civil L.R. 3–15, the undersigned certifies that as of this date, other than the named parties, there is no such interest to report. Signature, Attorney of Record."

(3) Certification, pursuant to this subsection, must be filed as a separate document.

[Former Rule 3–6 effective December 1, 2000. Amended effective October 1, 2002; March 1, 2007. Renumbered and amended effective February 3, 2014. Amended effective January 17, 2017.]

RULE 4. PROCESS: ISSUANCE AND SERVICE

RULE 4–1. LIMITATION ON SERVICE BY MARSHAL

Except for service on behalf of the United States or as required by Fed. R. Civ. P. 4(c)(2), or unless the Court orders otherwise for good cause shown, service of summons in a civil action shall not be made by the United States Marshal.

Commentary

28 U.S.C. § 566(c) provides that the United States Marshal shall execute writs, process and orders issued under the authority of the United States.

[Effective September 1, 1995. Amended effective July 1, 1997; December 1, 2000.]

RULE 4–2. SERVICE OF SUPPLEMENTARY MATERIAL

Along with the complaint and the summons or request for waiver of service, a party subject to Civil L.R. 16–2(a), (b), or (c), must serve the following Supplementary Material:

(a) A copy of the Order Setting Initial Case Management Conference and ADR deadlines issued pursuant to Civil L.R. 16–2(a), (b) or (c);

(b) Any pertinent Standing Orders of the assigned Judge;

(c) A copy of the assigned Judge's order and instructions for the preparation of a Case Management Statement or, if none, the Court's form found at cand.uscourts.gov, pursuant to Civil L.R. 16–10; and

(d) Except in cases assigned at the time of filing to a Magistrate Judge, a copy of the form allowing a party to consent to assignment of the case to a Magistrate Judge.

Commentary

The Clerk will provide the filing party with a copy of the Order Setting Initial Case Management Conference and ADR Deadlines, the form for Consent to Assignment of the Case to a Magistrate Judge, the form for preparation of the Case Management Statement, and any pertinent Standing Orders. The party must make copies of the schedules and forms for service. The Court's ADR processes and procedures are described in the handbook entitled "Dispute Resolution Procedures in the Northern District of California" available on the Court's ADR webpage, cand.uscourts.gov/adr. Limited printed copies of the ADR handbook are available from the Clerk's Office for parties in cases not subject to the Court's Electronic Case Filing (ECF) program under Civil L.R. 5–1(b).

[Effective September 1, 1995. Renumbered and amended effective December 1, 2000. Amended effective January 1, 2006; July 2, 2012; September 15, 2015; December 1, 2021.]

RULE 5. SERVICE AND FILING OF PLEADINGS AND OTHER PAPERS

RULE 5–1. ELECTRONIC CASE FILING

(a) Electronic Filing, Signing, or Verification. Pursuant to Fed. R. Civ. P. 5(d)(3), papers may be filed, signed, or verified by electronic means.

(b) Cases and Parties Subject to Electronic Filing. All cases, except where exempted by court order, are designated for participation in the Court's Electronic Case Filing ("ECF") system. Documents in sealed cases must be filed according to procedures established by the Clerk's Office and published on the Court's website. Sealed documents within unsealed cases shall be filed electronically, in compliance with Civil L.R. 79–5. Pro se parties must file case-initiating documents manually in each new action brought in the court. After manually filing case-initiating documents, pro se parties may file subsequent documents in the same case manually, or may register for ECF and file subsequent documents in the same case electronically. Parties represented by counsel in a case involving a pro se party must file documents electronically and serve them manually on the pro se party, unless the pro se party is a registered ECF user.

Commentary

Procedures and instructions for using the Court's ECF system consistent with these policies may be found on the Court's ECF webpage at cand.uscourts.gov/cases–e–filing/cm–ecf/. In addition to providing access to filing and retrieval of documents, the ECF webpage also contains instructions, a user manual, tutorials, an extensive listing of Frequently Asked Questions ("FAQs"), and information regarding changes in the ECF system, among other items. The initial point of contact for anyone having trouble filing a document on the ECF system is the email address or toll-free number posted on the Court's ECF webpage.

(c) Registration, Appearance and Access.

(1) *Attorney's Obligation to Register.* Each attorney of record is obligated to become an ECF user and obtain a user ID and password for access to the system upon filing a case in this district or before e-filing a document in an existing case in this district. Registration shall be on a form prescribed by the Clerk, which can be found on the ECF webpage at cand. uscourts.gov/cases–e–filing/cm–ecf/.

(2) *Notice of Appearance.*

(A) A Notice of Appearance must be e-filed whenever counsel joins a case.

(B) If counsel from the same firm replace one another as the representative of a client, a Notice of Substitution of Counsel must be e-filed.

(C) If a particular counsel ceases to be involved with a case when the party is still represented by other counsel, a Notice of Change in Counsel must be e-filed.

(D) The withdrawal of a party's sole remaining counsel is governed by Civil L.R. 11–5 and requires an order of the Court.

(E) The replacement of one firm by another as counsel for a party is governed by Civil L.R. 11–5 and requires an order of the Court.

(3) *Obligation to Keep Account Information Current.* An ECF user ID and password is the equivalent of a permanent, individual electronic signature for a registered attorney. Registered attorneys are required to keep their contact information current and may update their email address online via the ECF webpage.

(4) *Authorizing Use of User ID and Password by Others.* An ECF user may authorize another person to electronically file a document using the user ID and password of the ECF user. Nevertheless, the ECF user retains full responsibility for any document so filed.

(5) *Access.*

(A) Filing. Only the attorney-of-record as described in section (c)(1), a person authorized by the attorney-of-record as described in section (c)(4), or a pro se party who has registered for ECF as described in section (b) may electronically file documents.

(B) Retrieval. Any person may review at the Clerk's Office all filings, electronic or paper, that have not been sealed by the Court. Any ECF user also may access the ECF system and retrieve electronically filed documents that are not sealed, with the following exception:

(i) Exception. Only counsel for a party, or a pro se party who is an ECF user, may access the ECF system and retrieve any electronically filed document in a Social Security appeal or certain immigration cases pursuant to

Fed. R. Civ. P. 5.2(c). Any other ECF user may access and retrieve electronically only the docket for the case and any orders entered by the Court. Any person may have access to the full record at the Clerk's Office.

Commentary

Anyone who is a PACER user (even if not an ECF user) may retrieve publicly available documents in any case electronically filed in this district or nationwide.

(d) Filing and Service of Pleadings.

(1) *Filing Initiating Documents.* Except for manual filings by a pro se party who is filing case-initiating documents or is not a registered e-filer, all civil complaints and other case initiating documents in civil cases must be filed electronically.

(2) *Service and Answer.* After a defendant or third-party defendant has been served, defendant's counsel shall register to become an ECF user following the procedures outlined on the ECF webpage, and shall file the responsive pleading electronically. If the defendant or third-party defendant is pro se and is not a registered ECF user, the responsive pleading must be filed and served manually.

Cross Reference

See Civil L.R. 5–1(i) for rules governing the filing of documents with signatures other than those of the e-filer.

(3) *Completion of Filing.* Electronic transmission of a document in compliance with court procedures shall, upon receipt by the Clerk of the entire document and the sending of a Notice of Electronic Filing ("NEF") by the ECF system, constitute filing of the document for all purposes and shall constitute entry of that document on the docket maintained by the Clerk pursuant to Fed. R. Civ. P. 58 and 79, and Fed. R. Crim. P. 49 and 55.

(4) *Deadlines.* All electronic filings of documents must be completed as described in Civil L.R. 5–1(e)(3) prior to midnight in order to be considered timely filed that day.

(5) *Technical Failure.* The Clerk shall deem the ECF system to be subject to a technical failure on a given day if the system is unable to accept filings continuously or intermittently over the course of any period of time greater than one hour after 12:00 noon that day. Filings due on the day of a technical failure which were not filed solely due to such technical failure shall be due the next court day. Such delayed filings shall be accompanied by a declaration or affidavit attesting to the filer's failed attempts to file electronically at least two times after 12:00 noon separated by at least one hour on each day of delay due to such technical failure.

(6) *Docket.* The record of filings and entries created by the ECF system for each case shall constitute the docket for that case.

Commentary

In addition to receiving email notifications of filing activity, parties are encouraged to check the docket in their case on the ECF system at regular intervals.

(7) *Chambers Copies.* No chambers copy or "courtesy copy" of an electronically-filed document shall be submitted to the Court, unless required by a standing order of the assigned Judge or requested by the assigned Judge in a particular case.

(e) Manual Filing. Some types of documents shall only be filed manually and not electronically unless specifically authorized by the Court. A list of such documents may be found on the ECF webpage. Such documents shall be manually filed with the Clerk and served upon the parties in accordance with the applicable Federal Rules of Civil Procedure, Federal Rules of Criminal Procedure, and Local Rules for filing and service of paper documents. Parties manually filing a document shall file electronically a Manual Filing Notification.

(f) Proposed Orders. Proposed orders submitted by an ECF user in an ECF case shall be filed in PDF format, and attached to the applicable motion or other document. In addition, proposed orders shall be submitted in a standard word processing format (such as Microsoft Word) to the specific address on the Court's website for emailing proposed orders to the assigned Judge. Proposed orders must conform to the requirements of the assigned Judge's standing orders.

(g) Service of Electronically Filed Documents.

(1) *Generally.* Upon the filing of a document by a party, the ECF system will send to the registered attorneys for all parties in the case a Notice of Electronic Filing, which constitutes service on the receiving party. Exceptions to this are electronically filed civil complaints and other case-initiating documents, which must be served manually.

Cross Reference

See Civil L.R. 7–3 for rules for calculating due dates for opposition and reply briefs.

(2) *Service on Parties Who Have Not Registered as ECF Users.* When service of a document, other than a complaint or third-party complaint, is required to be made upon a person who is not a registered ECF user in that case, a paper copy of the document shall be served on the person (as otherwise required or permitted by the Federal Rules of Civil Procedure, Federal Rules of Criminal Procedure, and Local Rules). Service of these documents may alternatively be made by electronic means (e.g., email) if the recipient consented in writing to such service.

(3) *Service of the Court's Orders.* Orders filed by the Court in non-sealed cases will be served only via the emailed Notice of Electronic Filing. No manual service will be made by the Court except on a pro se party who is not an ECF user in a particular case.

(h) Signatures.

(1) *Generally.* A document electronically filed with the Court shall be deemed to be signed by the person ("Signatory") when the document identifies the person as a Signatory and the filing complies with either subsection (2) or (3). Any filing in accordance with any of these methods shall bind the Signatory as if the document was physically signed and filed, and shall function as the Signatory's signature whether for purposes of Rule 11 of the Federal Rules of Civil Procedure, to attest to the truthfulness of an affidavit or declaration, or for any other purpose.

(2) *ECF Users.* In the case of a Signatory who is an ECF user, such document shall be deemed signed, regardless of the existence of a physical signature on the document, provided that such document is filed using the user ID and password of the Signatory.

(3) *Others.* In the case of a Signatory who is not an ECF user, or who is an ECF user but whose user ID and password are not utilized in the electronic filing of the document (as in the case of documents requiring multiple signatures), the filer of the document shall attest that each of the other Signatories have concurred in the filing of the document, which shall serve in lieu of their signatures on the document. The filer's attestation may be incorporated into the document itself, or take the form of a declaration attached to the document. The filer shall maintain records to support this concurrence for subsequent production for the Court, if so ordered, or for inspection upon request by a party, until one year after the final resolution of the action (including appeal, if any). The filer may attach a scanned image of the signature page of the document being electronically filed in lieu of maintaining the paper record for subsequent production if required.

(4) *Criminal Cases.* Notwithstanding the provisions of section 5–1(e)(3), in a criminal case, any document signed by a criminal defendant and any document containing multiple signatures shall be scanned in its entirety to ensure that all signatures are visible. Certain documents that may be used by various agencies shall also be scanned in their entirety; a list of such documents may be found on the ECF webpage.

(i) Sanctions for Non–Compliance. Failure of counsel to timely register or otherwise comply with ECF filing requirements may result in sanctions as the Court deems appropriate.

[Effective September 1, 1995. Amended effective July 1, 1997. Renumbered and amended effective December 1, 2000. Amended effective January 1, 2005; March 17, 2009; July 2, 2012; July 15, 2013; February 3, 2014; May 1, 2018; December 1, 2021.]

RULE 5–2. MANUAL FILING [WITHDRAWN]

RULE 5–3. FACSIMILE FILINGS

(a) Method of Filing. A party may have an agent file with the Court a facsimile copy of an original document that must be manually filed. For purposes of this rule, any facsimile filing agency shall be regarded as an agent of the filing party, not an agent of the Court. Also for purposes of this rule, the image of the original manual signature appearing on a facsimile copy filed pursuant to this rule shall constitute an original signature for all Court purposes.

(b) Procedures. Facsimile copies may be filed as follows:

(1) The facsimile copy is <u>not</u> transmitted directly to the Clerk by electronic or telephonic means;

(2) The facsimile copy complies with the requirements of Civil L.R. 3–4; and

(3) The facsimile copy is accompanied by a certificate of service.

(c) Disposition of the Original Document. The following procedures shall govern disposition of the original document whenever a facsimile copy is filed pursuant to Civil L.R. 5–3(b):

(1) The original signed document shall not be substituted into the Court's records, except upon Court order;

(2) Any party filing a facsimile copy of a document must maintain the original transmitted document and the transmission record of that document until the conclusion of the case, including any applicable appeal period. A transmission record for purposes of this rule is a paper printed by the facsimile machine upon which the original document was transmitted. The record must state the telephone number of the receiving machine, the number of pages sent, the transmission time and an indication that no error in transmission occurred.

(3) Upon request by a party or the Court, the filing party must provide for review the original transmitted document from which a facsimile copy was produced.

[Effective December 1, 2000. Amended effective December 1, 2009; July 2, 2012; December 1, 2021.]

RULE 5–4. DROP BOX FILINGS

(a) **Documents Which May Be Filed.** Most documents that are required or permitted to be manually filed may be deposited in a Clerk's Office drop box, subject to the following:

(1) Any papers in support of or in opposition to a matter scheduled for hearing within 7 days of filing may not be filed through use of a drop box;

(2) Initial pleadings or other case-initiating documents that are required or permitted to be manually filed may be deposited for filing in a drop box at any courthouse of the district — and any applicable filing fee must be included, with payment only in the form of a check;

(3) Except for documents covered by (a)(1) above, after regular hours of the Clerk's Office, a document required or permitted to be manually filed may be filed by deposit in the Clerk's Office drop box at the courthouse in which the Chambers of the assigned Judge are located.

(b) **Drop Box Locations and Availability.** The Court will maintain drop boxes at each division of the Clerk's Office. The Clerk will regulate the hours during which materials may be filed through use of a drop box.

Commentary

Questions regarding current availability and use of the drop box should be directed to the Clerk. The Clerk has set the following general schedule for location and availability of drop boxes:

Drop Box Location	Availability	Restrictions
Clerk's Office Entrance 16th Floor 450 Golden Gate Avenue San Francisco	Before 9:00 a.m. & After 4:00 p.m.	Federal Building closed to public after 6:00 p.m. and before 6:00 a.m. on weekdays, and all weekends and federal holidays.
Courthouse Lobby 1st Floor 1301 Clay Street Oakland	Before 9:00 a.m. & After 4:00 p.m.	Federal Building closed to public after 5:00 p.m. and before 7:00 a.m., and on weekends and federal holidays.
Clerk's Office Entrance 2nd Floor 280 South 1st Street San Jose	Before 9:00 a.m. & After 4:00 p.m.	Federal Building closed to public after 5:00 p.m. and before 7:30 a.m., and on weekends and federal holidays.

(c) **Filing Date of Drop Box Documents.** Before a document is deposited in a drop box for filing, the back side of the last page of the document must be stamped "Received" using the device available at the drop box.

(1) The document will be marked by the Clerk as "Filed" on the same date indicated by the "Received" stamp, except when the "Received" date is a weekend or Court holiday, in which case it will be marked as "Filed" on the first day following the weekend or Court holiday.

(2) Where the back side of the last page of the document has not been stamped "Received" with the device available at the drop box, the Clerk will mark the document as "Filed" on the day the Clerk emptied the drop box of the document.

Commentary

Questions regarding availability and use of the drop box should be directed to the Clerk. The Clerk's Office policy is to empty and lock the drop box at the beginning of each day when the Clerk's Office opens. When the Clerk's Office closes, the drop box is reopened so that it may be used again for filing.

[Effective December 1, 2000. Amended effective July 2, 2012; February 3, 2014; December 1, 2021.]

RULE 5–5. CERTIFICATE OF SERVICE

(a) **Form.** Whenever any pleading or other paper presented for filing is required (or permitted by any rule or other provision of law) to be served upon any party or person, unless it is served by ECF, it must bear or have attached to it:

(1) An acknowledgment of service by the person served; or

(2) Certificate of service stating the date, place, and manner of service, and the name, street address, or electronic address of each person served, certified by the person who made service, pursuant to 28 U.S.C. § 1746.

(b) **Sanction for Failure to Provide Certificate.** Failure to provide an acknowledgment or certificate of service shall not be a ground for the Clerk to refuse to file a paper or pleading. However, any such document may be disregarded by the Judge if an adverse party timely objects on the ground of lack of service.

Cross Reference

See Fed. R. Civ. P. 4(d).

Commentary

Pursuant to Civil L.R. 5–1, except for civil complaints and other case-initiating documents in civil cases, parties are not required to include a certificate or acknowledgment of service upon registered ECF users when a document is filed electronically. Notification to those parties will be provided by the Court's electronic filing system.

[Effective September 1, 1995. Renumbered and amended effective December 1, 2000. Amended effective June 2, 2011; September 8, 2011; July 2, 2012; July 15, 2013; December 1, 2021.]

RULE 6. TIME

RULE 6–1. ENLARGING OR SHORTENING TIME

(a) When Stipulation Permissible Without Court Order. Parties may stipulate in writing, without a Court order, to extend the time within which to answer or otherwise respond to the complaint, or to enlarge or shorten the time in matters not required to be filed or lodged with the Court, provided the change will not alter the date of any event or any deadline already fixed by Court order. Such stipulations shall be promptly filed pursuant to Civil L.R. 5.

(b) When Court Order Necessary to Change Time. A Court order is required for any enlargement or shortening of time that alters an event or deadline already fixed by Court order or that involves papers required to be filed or lodged with the Court (other than an initial response to the complaint). A request for a Court order enlarging or shortening time may be made by written stipulation pursuant to Civil L.R. 6–2 or motion pursuant to Civil L.R. 6–3. Any stipulated request or motion which affects a hearing or proceeding on the Court's calendar must be filed no later than 14 days before the scheduled event.

[Effective December 1, 2000. Amended effective December 1, 2009.]

RULE 6–2. STIPULATED REQUEST FOR ORDER CHANGING TIME

(a) Form and Content. The parties may file a stipulation, conforming to Civil L.R. 7–12, requesting an order changing time that would affect the date of an event or deadline already fixed by Court order, or that would accelerate or extend time frames set in the Local Rules or in the Federal Rules. The stipulated request must be accompanied by a declaration that:

(1) Sets forth with particularity, the reasons for the requested enlargement or shortening of time;

(2) Discloses all previous time modifications in the case, whether by stipulation or Court order; and

(3) Describes the effect the requested time modification would have on the schedule for the case.

(b) Action by the Court. After receiving a stipulated request under this Rule, the Judge may grant, deny or modify the requested time change.

[Effective December 1, 2000. Amended effective January 1, 2005.]

RULE 6–3. MOTION TO CHANGE TIME

(a) Form and Content. A motion to enlarge or shorten time may be no more than 5 pages in length and must be accompanied by a proposed order and by a declaration that:

(1) Sets forth with particularity, the reasons for the requested enlargement or shortening of time;

(2) Describes the efforts the party has made to obtain a stipulation to the time change;

(3) Identifies the substantial harm or prejudice that would occur if the Court did not change the time; and

(4) If the motion is to shorten time for the Court to hear a motion:

(i) Describes the moving party's compliance with Civil L.R. 37–1(a), where applicable, and

(ii) Describes the nature of the underlying dispute that would be addressed in the motion and briefly summarizes the position each party had taken.

(5) Discloses all previous time modifications in the case, whether by stipulation or Court order;

(6) Describes the effect the requested time modification would have on the schedule for the case.

(b) Opposition to Motion to Change Time. Unless otherwise ordered, a party who opposes a motion to enlarge or shorten time must file an opposition not to exceed 5 pages, accompanied by a declaration setting forth the basis for opposition, no later than 4 days after receiving the motion.

(c) Delivery of Manually Filed Documents to Other Parties. A party manually filing an administrative motion to enlarge or shorten time must deliver a copy of the motion, proposed order and supporting declaration to all other parties on the day the motion is filed. The objecting party must deliver a copy of its opposition to all parties on the day the opposition is filed.

(d) Action by the Court. After receiving a motion to enlarge or shorten time and any opposition, the Judge may grant, deny, modify the requested time change or schedule the matter for additional briefing or a hearing.

[Effective December 1, 2000. Amended effective December 1, 2009; July 2, 2012.]

RULE 7. MOTION PRACTICE

RULE 7–1. MOTIONS

(a) Types of Motions. Any written request to the Court for an order must be presented by one of the following means:

(1) A duly noticed motion pursuant to Civil L.R. 7–2;

(2) A motion to enlarge or shorten time pursuant to Civil L.R. 6–1;

(3) When authorized, an ex parte motion pursuant to Civil L.R. 7–10;

(4) When applicable, a motion for administrative relief pursuant to Civil L.R. 7–11;

(5) A stipulation of the affected parties pursuant to Civil L.R. 7–12; or

(6) A motion regarding an Order or Recommendation of a Magistrate Judge pursuant to Civil L.R. 72–2 or 72–3.

(b) To Whom Motions Made. Motions must be directed to the Judge to whom the action is assigned, except as that Judge may otherwise order. In the Judge's discretion, or upon request by counsel and with the Judge's approval, a motion may be determined without oral argument or by telephone conference call.

(c) Unassigned Case or Judge Unavailable. A motion may be presented to the General Duty Judge or, if unavailable, to the Chief Judge or Acting Chief Judge when:

(1) The assigned Judge is unavailable as defined in Civil L.R. 1–5(p) and an emergency requires prompt action; or

(2) An order is necessary before an action can be filed.

[Effective September 1, 1995. Amended effective July 1, 1997; December 1, 2000; January 1, 2005; April 20, 2010; December 1, 2021.]

RULE 7–2. NOTICE AND SUPPORTING PAPERS

(a) Time. Except as otherwise ordered or permitted by the assigned Judge or these Local Rules, and except for motions made during the course of a trial or hearing, all motions must be filed, served and noticed in writing on the motion calendar of the assigned Judge for hearing not less than 35 days after filing of the motion. Fed. R. Civ. P. 6(d), which extends deadlines that are tied to service (as opposed to filing), does not apply and thus does not extend this deadline.

(b) Form. In one filed document not exceeding 25 pages in length, a motion must contain:

(1) On the first page in the space opposite the caption and below the case number, the noticed hearing date and time;

(2) In the first paragraph, notice of the motion including date and time of hearing;

(3) In the second paragraph, a concise statement of what relief or Court action the movant seeks; and

(4) In the succeeding paragraphs, the points and authorities in support of the motion —in compliance with Civil L.R. 7–4(a).

(c) Proposed Order. Unless excused by the Judge who will hear the motion, each motion must be accompanied by a proposed order.

(d) Affidavits or Declarations. Each motion must be accompanied by affidavits or declarations pursuant to Civil L.R. 7–5.

Commentary

The time periods set forth in Civil L.R. 7–2 and 7–3 regarding notice, response, and reply to motions are minimum time periods. For complex motions, parties are encouraged to stipulate to or seek a Court order establishing a longer notice period with correspondingly longer periods for response or reply. See Civil L.R. 1–4 and 1–5.

[Effective September 1, 1995. Amended effective December 1, 2000; July 2, 2012; February 3, 2014; December 1, 2021.]

RULE 7–3. OPPOSITION; REPLY; SUPPLEMENTARY MATERIAL

(a) Opposition. Any opposition to a motion may include a proposed order, affidavits, or declarations, as well as a brief or memorandum under Civil L.R. 7–4. Any evidentiary and procedural objections to the motion must be contained within the brief or memorandum. Pursuant to Civil L.R. 7–4(b), such brief or memorandum may not exceed 25 pages of text. The opposition must be filed and served not more than 14 days after the motion was filed. Fed. R. Civ. P. 6(d), which extends deadlines that are tied to service (as opposed to filing), does not apply and thus does not extend this deadline.

(b) Statement of Nonopposition. If the party against whom the motion is directed does not oppose the motion, that party must file with the Court a Statement of Nonopposition within the time for filing and serving any opposition.

(c) Reply. Any reply to an opposition may include affidavits or declarations, as well as a supplemental brief or memorandum under Civil L.R. 7–4. Any evidentiary and procedural objections to the opposition must be contained within the reply brief or memorandum. Pursuant to Civil L.R. 7–4(b), the reply brief or memorandum may not exceed 15 pages of text. The reply to an opposition must be filed and served not more than 7 days after the opposition was due. Fed. R. Civ. P. 6(d), which extends deadlines that are tied to service (as opposed to filing), does not apply and thus does not extend this deadline.

(d) Supplementary Material. Once a reply is filed, no additional memoranda, papers or letters may be filed without prior Court approval, except as follows:

(1) *Objection to Reply Evidence.* If new evidence has been submitted in the reply, the opposing party may file and serve an Objection to Reply Evidence, which may not exceed 5 pages of text, stating its objections to the new evidence, which may not include further argument on the motion. The Objection to Reply Evidence must be filed and served not more than 7 days after the reply was filed. Fed. R. Civ. P. 6(d), which extends

deadlines that are tied to service (as opposed to filing), does not apply and thus does not extend this deadline.

(2) Before the noticed hearing date, counsel may bring to the Court's attention a relevant judicial opinion published after the date the opposition or reply was filed by filing and serving a Statement of Recent Decision. Such Statement shall contain a citation to and provide a copy of the new opinion without argument.

[Effective September 1, 1995. Amended effective July 1, 1997; December 1, 2000; September 14, 2010; June 2, 2011; September 8, 2011; July 2, 2012; December 19, 2016; December 1, 2021.]

RULE 7–4. BRIEF OR MEMORANDUM OF POINTS AND AUTHORITIES

(a) **Content.** In addition to complying with the applicable provisions of Civil L.R. 3–4, a brief or memorandum of points and authorities filed in support, opposition or reply to a motion must contain:

(1) On the first page in the space opposite the caption and below the case number, the noticed hearing date and time;

(2) If in excess of 10 pages, a table of contents and a table of authorities;

(3) A statement of the issues to be decided;

(4) A succinct statement of the relevant facts; and

(5) Argument by the party, citing pertinent authorities.

(b) **Length.** Unless the Court expressly orders otherwise pursuant to a party's request made prior to the due date, briefs or memoranda filed with opposition papers may not exceed 25 pages of text and the reply brief or memorandum may not exceed 15 pages of text.

Cross Reference

See Civil L.R. 7–11 regarding request to exceed page limitations.

Commentary

Although Civil L.R. 7–4(b) limits briefs to 25 pages of text, counsel should not consider this a minimum as well as a maximum limit. Briefs with less than 25 pages of text may be excessive in length for the nature of the issues addressed.

[Effective September 1, 1995. Amended effective July 1, 1997; December 1, 2000; August 10, 2010; September 8, 2011.]

RULE 7–5. AFFIDAVIT OR DECLARATION

(a) **Affidavit or Declaration Required.** Factual contentions made in support of or in opposition to any motion must be supported by an affidavit or declaration and by appropriate references to the record. Extracts from depositions, interrogatory answers, requests for admission and other evidentiary matters must be appropriately authenticated by an affidavit or declaration.

(b) **Form.** An affidavit or declaration may contain only facts, must conform as much as possible to the requirements of Fed. R. Civ. P. 56(e), and must avoid conclusions and argument. Any statement made upon information or belief must

specify the basis therefor. An affidavit or declaration not in compliance with this rule may be stricken in whole or in part.

[Effective September 1, 1995. Amended effective December 1, 2000; December 1, 2021.]

RULE 7–6. ORAL TESTIMONY CONCERNING MOTION

No oral testimony will be received in connection with any motion, unless otherwise ordered by the assigned Judge.

[Effective September 1, 1995.]

RULE 7–7. CONTINUANCE OF HEARING OR WITHDRAWAL OF MOTION

(a) **Before Opposition Is Filed.** Except for cases where the Court has issued a Temporary Restraining Order, a party who has filed a motion may file a notice continuing the originally noticed hearing date for that motion to a later date if:

(1) No opposition has been filed; and

(2) The notice of continuance is filed prior to the date on which the opposition is due pursuant to Civil L.R. 7–3(a).

(b) **After Opposition Is Filed.** After an opposition to a motion has been filed, the noticed hearing date may be continued to a subsequent date as follows:

(1) When parties affected by the motion have not previously stipulated to continue the hearing date, unless the hearing date has been reserved with or specially set by the Judge, the parties affected by the motion may stipulate in writing pursuant to Civil L.R. 6–1(a) to continue the hearing date; or

(2) Upon order of the assigned Judge.

(c) **Keeping Track of Hearing Dates.** Counsel are responsible for knowing hearing dates on motions.

(d) **Effect on Time for Filing Opposition or Reply.** Unless otherwise ordered by the Court, the continuance of the hearing of a motion does not extend the time for filing and serving the opposing papers or reply papers.

(e) **Withdrawal.** Within the time for filing and serving a reply, the moving party may file and serve a notice of withdrawal of the motion. Upon the filing of a timely withdrawal, the motion will be taken off-calendar. Otherwise, the Court may proceed to decide the motion.

[Effective September 1, 1995. Amended effective July 1, 1997; December 1, 2000; June 2, 2011; July 2, 2012; December 1, 2021.]

RULE 7–8. MOTIONS FOR SANCTIONS— FORM AND TIMING

Any motion for sanctions, regardless of the sources of authority invoked, must comply with the following:

(a) The motion must be separately filed and the date for hearing must be set in conformance with Civil L.R. 7–2;

(b) The form of the motion must comply with Civil L.R. 7–2;

(c) The motion must comply with any applicable Fed. R. Civ. P. and must be made as soon as practicable after the filing party learns of the circumstances that it alleges make the motion appropriate; and

(d) Unless otherwise ordered by the Court, no motion for sanctions may be served and filed more than 14 days after entry of judgment by the District Court.

[Effective September 1, 1995. Amended effective July 1, 1997; December 1, 2000.]

RULE 7–9. MOTION FOR RECONSIDERATION

(a) **Leave of Court Requirement.** Before the entry of a judgment adjudicating all of the claims and the rights and liabilities of all the parties in a case, any party may make a motion before a Judge requesting that the Judge grant the party leave to file a motion for reconsideration of any interlocutory order on any ground set forth in Civil L.R. 7–9(b). No party may notice a motion for reconsideration without first obtaining leave of Court to file the motion.

Cross Reference

See Fed. R. Civ. P. 54(b) regarding discretion of Court to reconsider its orders prior to entry of final judgment.

Commentary

This local rule does not apply to motions for reconsideration of a Magistrate Judge's order pursuant to 28 U.S.C. § 636(b)(1)(A). See Civil L.R. 72.

(b) **Form and Content of Motion for Leave.** A motion for leave to file a motion for reconsideration must be made in accordance with the requirements of Civil L.R. 7–9. The moving party must specifically show reasonable diligence in bringing the motion and one of the following:

(1) That at the time of the motion for leave, a material difference in fact or law exists from that which was presented to the Court before entry of the interlocutory order for which reconsideration is sought. The party also must show that in the exercise of reasonable diligence the party applying for reconsideration did not know such fact or law at the time of the interlocutory order; or

(2) The emergence of new material facts or a change of law occurring after the time of such order; or

(3) A manifest failure by the Court to consider material facts or dispositive legal arguments which were presented to the Court before such interlocutory order.

(c) **Prohibition Against Repetition of Argument.** No motion for leave to file a motion for reconsideration may repeat any oral or written argument made by the applying party in support of or in opposition to the interlocutory order which the party now seeks to have reconsidered. Any party who violates this restriction shall be subject to appropriate sanctions.

(d) **Determination of Motion.** Unless otherwise ordered by the assigned Judge, no response need be filed and no hearing will be held concerning a motion for leave to file a motion to reconsider. If the Judge decides to order the filing of additional papers or that the matter warrants a hearing, the Judge will fix an appropriate schedule.

[Effective September 1, 1995. Amended effective July 1, 1997; December 1, 2000; February 3, 2014; December 1, 2021.]

RULE 7–10. EX PARTE MOTIONS

Unless otherwise ordered by the assigned Judge, a party may file an ex parte motion, that is, a motion filed without notice to opposing party, only if a statute, Federal Rule, local rule, or Standing Order authorizes ex parte filing. The motion must include a citation to the statute, rule, or order which permits the use of an ex parte motion to obtain the relief sought.

Cross Reference

See, e.g., Civil L.R. 65–1 *"Temporary Restraining Orders."*

[Effective September 1, 1995. Amended effective July 1, 1997. Renumbered and amended effective December 1, 2000. Amended effective October 1, 2002; January 1, 2005; December 1, 2021.]

RULE 7–11. MOTION FOR ADMINISTRATIVE RELIEF

The Court recognizes that during the course of case proceedings a party may require a Court order with respect to miscellaneous administrative matters, not otherwise governed by a federal statute, Federal Rule, local rule, or standing order of the assigned Judge. These motions would include matters such as motions to exceed otherwise applicable page limitations or motions to file documents under seal, for example.

(a) **Form and Content of Motions.** A motion for an order concerning a miscellaneous administrative matter may not exceed 5 pages (not counting declarations and exhibits), must set forth specifically the action requested and the reasons supporting the motion, and must be accompanied by a proposed order and by either a stipulation under Civil L.R. 7–12 or by a declaration that explains why a stipulation could not be obtained. If the motion is manually filed, the moving party must deliver the motion and all attachments to all other parties on the same day that the motion is filed.

(b) **Opposition to or Support for Motion for Administrative Relief.** Any opposition to or support for a Motion for Administrative Relief may not exceed 5 pages (not counting declarations and exhibits), must set forth succinctly the reasons in opposition or support, must be accompanied by a proposed order, and must be filed no later than 4 days after the motion has been filed. The opposition or support and all attachments thereto, if manually filed, must be delivered to all other parties the same day it is manually filed.

(c) **Action by the Court.** Unless otherwise ordered, a Motion for Administrative Relief is deemed submitted for immediate determination without hearing on the day after the opposition is due.

[Effective September 1, 1995. Amended effective July 1, 1997. Renumbered and amended effective December 1, 2000. Amended effective October 1, 2002. Renumbered and amended effective January 1, 2005. Amended effective January 1, 2006; December 1, 2009; July 2, 2012; December 1, 2021.]

RULE 7–12. STIPULATIONS

Every stipulation requesting judicial action must be in writing signed by all affected parties or their counsel. A proposed form of order may be submitted with the stipulation and may consist of an endorsement on the stipulation of the words, "PURSUANT TO STIPULATION, IT IS SO ORDERED," with spaces designated for the date and the signature of the Judge.

[Effective September 1, 1995. Renumbered effective December 1, 2000. Renumbered effective January 1, 2005.]

RULE 7–13. NOTICE REGARDING SUBMITTED MATTERS

Whenever any motion or other matter has been under submission for more than 120 days, a party, individually or jointly with another party, may file with the Court a notice that the matter remains under submission, or may ask the Northern District of California Ombudsperson to provide such notice to the Court. If judicial action is not taken, subsequent notices may be filed at the expiration of each 120–day period thereafter until a ruling is made.

This rule does not preclude a party from filing an earlier notice if it is warranted by the nature of the matter under submission (e.g., motion for extraordinary relief).

[Effective July 1, 1997. Renumbered and amended effective December 1, 2000. Renumbered effective January 1, 2005. Amended effective July 2, 2012; November 1, 2014; December 1, 2021.]

RULE 7–14. DESIGNATION NOT FOR CITATION

It is within the sole discretion of the issuing Judge to determine whether an order or opinion issued by that Judge shall not be citable. Any order or opinion which the issuing Judge determines shall not be citable shall bear in the caption before the title of the Court "NOT FOR CITATION."

Cross Reference

See Civil L.R. 3–4(e) "Prohibition of Citation to Uncertified Opinion or Order."

[Effective December 1, 2000. Amended effective October 1, 2002. Renumbered effective January 1, 2005.]

RULE 10. FORM OF PAPERS

RULE 10–1. AMENDED PLEADINGS

Any party filing or moving to file an amended pleading must reproduce the entire proposed pleading and may not incorporate any part of a prior pleading by reference.

[Effective September 1, 1995. Amended effective December 1, 2000.]

RULE 11. ATTORNEYS

RULE 11–1. THE BAR OF THIS COURT

(a) Members of the Bar. Except as provided in Civil L.R. 11–2, 11–3, and 11–9, and Fed. R. Civ. P. 45(f), an attorney must be a member of the bar of this Court to practice in this Court and in the Bankruptcy Court of this District.

(b) Eligibility for Membership. To be eligible for admission to and continuing membership in the bar of this Court, an attorney must be an active member in good standing of the State Bar of California. For any attorney admitted to the bar of this court before September 1, 1995 based on membership in the bar of a jurisdiction other than California, continuing membership in the bar of that jurisdiction is an acceptable alternative basis for eligibility.

(c) Procedure for Admission. Each applicant for admission must present to the Clerk a sworn petition for admission in the form prescribed by the Court. Prior to admission to the bar of this Court, an attorney must certify:

(1) Knowledge of the contents of the Federal Rules of Civil and Criminal Procedure and Evidence, the Rules of the United States Court of Appeals for the Ninth Circuit, and the Local Rules of this Court;

(2) Familiarity with the Alternative Dispute Resolution Programs of this Court;

(3) Understanding and commitment to abide by the Standards of Professional Conduct of this Court set forth in Civil L.R. 11–4; and

(4) Familiarity with the Guidelines for Professional Conduct in the Northern District of California.

(d) Admission Fees. Each attorney admitted to practice before this Court under this Local Rule must pay to the Clerk the fee fixed by the Judicial Conference of the United States, together with an assessment in an amount to be set by the Court. The assessment will be placed in the Court Non–Appropriated Fund for library, educational, and other appropriate uses.

(e) Admission. The Clerk or a Judge may admit an applicant to the bar of the Court after the applicant signs the prescribed oath and pays the prescribed fees, and after the Clerk verifies the applicant's qualifications.

(f) Certificate of Good Standing. A member of the bar of this Court who is in good standing may obtain a Certificate of Good Standing by presenting a written request to the Clerk and paying the prescribed fee.

(g) Reciprocal Administrative Change in Attorney Status. Upon notice from the State Bar of California (or the bar of another jurisdiction that is the basis for membership in the bar of this Court) that an attorney is deceased, has been placed on "voluntary inactive" status, or has resigned for reasons not relating to discipline, the Clerk will note "deceased," "resigned," or "voluntary inactive," as appropriate, on the attorney's admission record. An attorney on "voluntary inactive" status will remain inactive on the roll of this Court until such time as the State Bar or the attorney has notified the Court that the attorney has been restored to "active" status. An attorney who has resigned and wishes to be readmitted must petition the Court for admission in accordance with subparagraphs (c) and (d) of this Rule.

(1) The following procedure will apply to actions taken in response to information provided by the State Bar of California (or by another jurisdiction that is the basis for membership in the bar of this Court) of a suspension for (a) a period of less than 30 days for any reason or (b) a change in an attorney's status that is temporary in nature and may be reversed solely by the attorney's execution of one or more administrative actions. Upon receipt of notification from the State Bar that an attorney has been suspended for any of the following, the Clerk will note the suspension on the attorney's admission record:

(A) Noncompliance with Rule 9.22 child and family support;

(B) Failure to pass PRE;

(C) Failure to pay bar dues;

(D) Failure to submit documentation of compliance with continuing education requirements.

While suspended, an attorney is not eligible to practice in this Court or in the Bankruptcy Court of this District. In the event that an attorney files papers or otherwise practices law in this Court or in the Bankruptcy Court while an administrative notation of suspension is pending on the attorney's admission record, the Clerk will verify the attorney's disciplinary status with the State Bar (or other jurisdiction, if applicable). If the attorney is not then active and in good standing, the Chief District Judge will issue to the attorney an order to show cause in accordance with Civil L.R. 11–7(b)(1).

Upon receipt by the Court of notification from the State Bar that the attorney's active status has been restored, the reinstatement will be noted on the attorney's admission record.

(2) In response to information provided by the State Bar of California (or other jurisdiction that is the basis for membership in the bar of this Court) that an attorney has been placed on disciplinary probation but is still allowed to practice, the Clerk will note the status change on the attorney's admission record. An attorney with that status must, in addition to providing the notice to the Clerk required by Civil L.R. 11–7(a)(1), report to the Clerk all significant developments related to the probationary status. Upon receipt by the Court of notification from the State Bar that the attorney's good standing has been restored, the change will be noted on the attorney's admission record.

[Effective September 1, 1995. Amended effective July 1, 1997; December 1, 2000; January 1, 2005; July 2, 2012; February 3, 2014; November 1, 2014; December 1, 2021.]

RULE 11–2. COUNSEL FOR THE UNITED STATES

An attorney employed or retained by the United States government or any of its agencies may, without satisfying the membership requirements of LR 11–1, practice in this Court in all actions or proceedings within the scope of his or her employment or retention by the United States.

[Effective December 1, 2000. Amended effective July 2, 2012; December 1, 2021.]

RULE 11–3. PRO HAC VICE

(a) **Application.** An attorney who is not a member of the bar of this Court may apply to appear pro hac vice in a particular action in this district by submitting to the Clerk, together with the written application, a true and correct copy of a certificate of good standing or other similar official document issued by the appropriate authority governing attorney admissions for the relevant bar. Said certificate or other document must be dated no more than one year prior to the date of application for admission. The applicant must also submit an oath certifying the following:

(1) That he or she is an active member in good standing of the bar of a United States Court or of the highest court of another State or the District of Columbia, specifying such bar;

(2) That he or she agrees to abide by the Standards of Professional Conduct set forth in Civil L.R. 11–4, and to become familiar with the Local Rules and Alternative Dispute Resolution Programs of this Court and, where applicable, with the Bankruptcy Local Rules;

(3) That an attorney, identified by name and office address, who is a member of the bar of this Court in good standing and who maintains an office within the State of California, is designated as co-counsel.

(4) The number of times the applicant has been granted pro hac vice admission by the Court in the 12 months preceding the application.

(b) **Time of Application.** An attorney seeking to appear pro hac vice must submit the application and admission fee at the time of the filing of a complaint or the attorney's first appearance in the case. A failure to meet this deadline may result in denial of the application.

(c) **Disqualification from Pro Hac Vice Appearance.** Unless authorized by an Act of Congress or by an order of the assigned Judge, an applicant is not eligible for permission to practice pro hac vice if the applicant:

(1) Resides in the State of California; or

(2) Is regularly engaged in the practice of law in the State of California.

This disqualification shall not be applicable if the pro hac vice applicant (i) has been a resident of California for less than one year; (ii) has registered with, and completed all required applications for admission to, the State Bar of California; and (iii) has officially registered to take or is awaiting results from the California State Bar exam.

(d) **Approval.** The Clerk shall present the application to the assigned Judge for approval. The assigned Judge shall have discretion to accept or reject the application, or excuse the admission fee.

(e) Admission Fee. At the time the application is submitted, an attorney requesting to practice under Civil L.R. 11–3 must pay to the Clerk the Pro Hac Vice admission fee set by the Court's fee schedule, available at cand.uscourts.gov/court–fees. The Clerk will not present an application to the assigned Judge unless the filing fee has been paid or a request to waive the filing fee has been submitted. The fee will be placed in the Court's Non–Appropriated Fund for library, educational, and other appropriate uses. If the assigned Judge rejects the application, the fee will be refunded at the attorney's request.

(f) Appearances and Service on Local Co–Counsel. All papers filed by the attorney must indicate appearance pro hac vice. Service of papers on and communications with local co-counsel designated pursuant to Civil L.R. 11–3(a)(3) shall constitute notice to the party.

[Effective December 1, 2000. Amended effective January 1, 2006; July 2, 2012; December 1, 2021.]

RULE 11–4. STANDARDS OF PROFESSIONAL CONDUCT

(a) Duties and Responsibilities. Every member of the bar of this Court and any attorney permitted to practice in this Court under Civil L.R. 11 must:

(1) Be familiar and comply with the standards of professional conduct required of members of the State Bar of California;

(2) Comply with the Local Rules of this Court;

(3) Maintain respect due to courts of justice and judicial officers;

(4) Practice with the honesty, care, and decorum required for the fair and efficient administration of justice;

(5) Discharge all obligations to client(s) and the Court; and

(6) Assist those in need of counsel when requested by the Court.

Commentary

The California Standards of Professional Conduct are contained in the State Bar Act, the Rules of Professional Conduct of the State Bar of California, and decisions of any court applicable thereto.

(b) Prohibition Against Bias. The practice of law before this Court must be free from prejudice and bias. Treatment free of bias must be accorded all other attorneys, litigants, judicial officers, jurors, and support personnel. Any violation of this policy should be brought to the attention of the Clerk or any Judge for action under Civ. L.R. 11–6.

(c) Prohibition against Ex Parte Communication. Except as otherwise provided by law or these Local Rules or otherwise ordered by the Court, an attorney or party to an action must refrain from contacting the assigned Judge or the Judge's law clerks or otherwise communicating with a Judge or the Judge's staff regarding a pending matter, without prior notice to opposing counsel.

Commentary

This rule is not intended to prohibit communications with Court staff regarding scheduling or general case management.

[Effective September 1, 1995. Amended effective December 1, 2000; July 2, 2012; November 1, 2014; September 15, 2015; December 1, 2021.]

RULE 11–5. WITHDRAWAL FROM CASE

(a) Order Permitting Withdrawal. Counsel may not withdraw from an action until relieved by order of the Court after written notice has been provided, reasonably in advance, to the client and to all other parties who have appeared in the case.

(b) Conditional Withdrawal. When withdrawal by an attorney from an action is not accompanied by simultaneous appearance of substitute counsel or agreement of the party to appear pro se, leave to withdraw may be subject to the condition that papers may continue to be served on counsel for forwarding purposes, unless and until the client appears by other counsel or pro se. When this condition is imposed, counsel must notify the party of this condition. Any filed consent by the party to counsel's withdrawal under these circumstances must include acknowledgment of this condition.

[Effective September 1, 1995. Amended effective December 1, 2000; July 2, 2012; December 1, 2021.]

RULE 11–6. DISCIPLINE

(a) General. In the event that a Judge has cause to believe that an attorney (as defined in subsection (b) below) has engaged in unprofessional conduct, the Judge may, in addition to any action authorized by applicable law, do either or both of the following:

(1) Refer the matter to the Court's Standing Committee on Professional Conduct; or

(2) Refer the matter to the Chief District Judge. If the alleged unprofessional conduct arises in the Bankruptcy Court, the Judge shall first refer the matter to the Chief Bankruptcy Judge, who may in turn refer it to the Chief District Judge.

(b) "Attorney" Defined. For purposes of Civil L.R. 11–6, the term "attorney" refers to any attorney who is or has been admitted to practice in any State, or admitted to membership in the bar of this Court, or admitted to practice in this Court pro hac vice pursuant to Civil L.R. 11–3. The term "attorney" may include law corporations and partnerships, when the alleged conduct occurs in the course and scope of employment by the corporation or partnership.

(c) Standing Committee on Professional Conduct. The Court will appoint, as special counsel for disciplinary proceedings pending before the Court, a Standing Committee on Professional Conduct consisting of a minimum of 7 and a maximum of 11 members, depending on the number of disciplinary matters referred to or active before the committee, and the Chief District Judge will designate one of the members to serve as Chair. All members of the Standing Committee must be members in good standing of the bar who practice regularly in this court. Members shall serve staggered 4–year terms in 2 approximately equal groups, such that the members of one group are replaced or reappointed every 2 years. The

Standing Committee may organize itself and conduct its affairs by subcommittees of one or more members as it deems advisable. All final actions of the Standing Committee require a majority vote. The Standing Committee will submit a confidential report of its activities annually to the Clerk, the Chief District Judge, the Clerk of the Bankruptcy Court and Chief Bankruptcy Judge and the Professional Conduct Liaison Judge.

(d) Professional Conduct Liaison Judge. The Chief District Judge shall appoint a District Judge to oversee the administration of this Local Rule and to serve as liaison to the Standing Committee. The Chief District Judge may delegate some or all of the powers of the Chief District Judge under this rule to the Professional Conduct Liaison Judge.

(e) Matters Referred to the Standing Committee. Any Judge may enter an order of referral to the Standing Committee on Professional Conduct to initiate an investigation into a charge or information that a member of the bar of this Court, an attorney appearing pro hac vice, or an attorney employed or retained by the United States (see Civil L.R. 11–2) has engaged in unprofessional conduct in the practice of law before this Court. The Alternative Dispute Resolution Magistrate Judge may enter an order of referral based upon information provided by, and at the request of, the Alternative Dispute Resolution Department. An order of referral to the Standing Committee on Professional Conduct may be made on the public docket of an active case or may be directed to the Clerk confidentially without a case number, with a copy of the referral order served by U.S. Mail or by electronic mail on the subject attorney. Upon receipt of an order of referral, the Clerk will open a new miscellaneous case under seal, file the original order of referral and any accompanying exhibits thereto, and transmit a copy to the chair of the Standing Committee. Unless otherwise directed by the Court, the Standing Committee shall investigate the alleged or suspected unprofessional conduct in accordance with the following procedures:

(1) Investigations shall be conducted formally or informally as the Standing Committee deems appropriate to the circumstances of the case. Investigations shall be confidential unless the Professional Conduct Liaison Judge, upon application by the Standing Committee or the attorney who is subject to the investigation, determines that there is a compelling reason to make the matter public.

(2) At the written request of the Standing Committee, the Chief District Judge may direct the issuance of subpoenas and subpoenas duces tecum.

(3) At the conclusion of its investigation, the Standing Committee may, if it deems appropriate, finally resolve any referred matter informally or by consent; if the attorney who was the subject of the investigation has admitted unprofessional conduct, however, the Standing Committee should obtain a written consent specifying a remedial plan. The Standing Committee shall prepare a final report summarizing its proceedings, its findings, any informal or stipulated resolution and its recommendation, if any, to the Court. If the Standing Committee's determination is to file a petition for formal discipline, it shall so state in the final report. The final report shall be marked "CONFIDENTIAL: ATTORNEY DISCI-PLINE MATTER" and shall include a proposed order directing the Clerk to close the file. The Standing Committee shall direct the original final report to the Chief District Judge and a copy to the referring Judge. Upon filing the final report and closing the file, the Clerk shall serve the final report on the attorney under investigation.

(4) If a majority of the members determine that public reprimand, suspension, disbarment, monetary sanctions or other formal discipline is warranted, and the respondent attorney does not consent, the Standing Committee shall institute a disciplinary proceeding by filing with the Clerk a sealed petition that specifies the alleged misconduct. Upon the filing of the petition, the Clerk shall assign a new civil case number to the matter and shall randomly assign it to a District Judge other than the referring Judge or the Professional Conduct Liaison Judge in the same manner as any other sealed civil action or proceeding. Unless otherwise directed by the assigned Judge, the proceeding shall then be presented by one or more members of the Standing Committee. For a matter arising in the Bankruptcy Court of this District, the assigned Judge may, sua sponte or upon motion by the respondent attorney, refer the matter to the Clerk of the Bankruptcy Court for assignment to a Bankruptcy Judge, other than the referring Judge, for hearing and a report and recommendation.

(5) After a civil case is assigned under subsection (4) above, the assigned judge shall issue an order to show cause setting a date for hearing, addressed to the respondent attorney, requiring the attorney to appear and show cause why he or she should not be disciplined as stated in the Judge's order. The order shall direct that a copy thereof, together with a copy of the petition, be served on the respondent in a manner permitted by Fed. R. Civ. P. 5(b) not less than 35 days in advance of the date specified for hearing. Any response must be filed no more than 14 days later. In the event the matter cannot be resolved solely based on the petition, response, and hearing thereon, the Judge may order such additional proceedings as the circumstances warrant. Written findings of fact and an order based thereon shall be filed by the Judge when dismissing the proceeding or when imposing discipline. Documents presented for manual filing in the case shall be marked "CONFIDENTIAL: ATTORNEY DISCIPLINE MATTER." The entire case shall be maintained under seal and court proceedings shall be closed to the public unless, upon written motion from either the Standing Committee or the respondent attorney, the Judge determines that the interests of justice would be best be served by opening all or part of the proceedings to the public. The Judge's final order, if imposing discipline, together with portions of the file deemed by the Judge to be appropriate for public disclosure, will be unsealed and made accessible to the public on the Court's website and any other means ordered by the Judge and will be disseminated to the Judges of the Northern District of California by the Clerk 7 days after the final order is filed, absent an extension by the Court. An order imposing discipline under this Rule may be appealed to the Court of Appeals.

(6) Records other than court files, such as the confidential reports of the Standing Committee, shall be maintained as directed by the Chief District Judge.

(7) After an order imposing discipline is filed, the Standing Committee may provide the Clerk with a list of other courts before which the Standing Committee knows the respondent attorney to have been admitted to practice. The list shall be compiled from information obtained in the course of the Standing Committee's work on the case, and shall not require a separate investigation. The Clerk shall give prompt notice of the order of discipline to the disciplinary body of each such court.

(f) Costs. Out-of-pocket expenses necessarily incurred by the Standing Committee in carrying out its responsibilities under these rules, if presented for reimbursement within 90 days of the conclusion of the proceeding, will be paid by the Court.

[Effective December 1, 2000. Amended effective July 2, 2012; November 1, 2014; December 1, 2021.]

RULE 11–7. RECIPROCAL DISCIPLINE AND DISCIPLINE FOLLOWING FELONY CONVICTION

(a) Required Notice of Change in Status. Any attorney admitted to practice in this Court or any attorney appearing pro hac vice who is convicted of a felony, suspended, disbarred or placed on disciplinary probation by any court, or who resigns from the bar of any court with an investigation into allegations of unprofessional conduct pending, must give notice to the Clerk and the Clerk of the Bankruptcy Court in writing within 14 days of such event.

(b) Order to Show Cause. Unless referred to the Standing Committee on Professional Conduct, matters subject to reciprocal discipline on the grounds listed in paragraph (a) above shall be handled as follows:

(1) Whenever a member of the bar of this Court or any attorney appearing pro hac vice who is convicted of a felony, disbarred, suspended for reasons other than those noted in Civil L.R. 11–1(g) or who resigns from the bar of any court with an investigation into allegations of unprofessional conduct pending, the Chief District Judge will enter an order suspending that member on an interim basis from practice before this Court and affording the member an opportunity to show cause, within 28 days, why a suspension or disbarment order should not be entered. If the attorney files a response stating that imposition of an order of suspension or disbarment from this Court is not contested, or if the attorney does not respond to the Order to Show Cause within the time specified, then the Court shall enter an order of suspension or disbarment.

(2) An attorney who wishes to contest reciprocal discipline must file with the Court a timely response to the order to show cause. The Chief District Judge may then act on the matter, order it randomly assigned to another Judge or refer it to the Standing Committee on Professional Conduct for report and recommendation. The response to the Order to Show Cause must set forth facts establishing one or more of the following: (a) the procedure in the other jurisdiction was so lacking in notice or opportunity to be heard as to constitute a deprivation of due process; (b) there was such an infirmity of proof establishing the misconduct as to give rise to a clear conviction that the Court should not accept as final the other

jurisdiction's conclusion(s) on that subject; (c) imposition of like discipline would result in a grave injustice; or (d) other substantial reasons exist so as to justify not accepting the other jurisdiction's conclusion(s). In addition, together with the response to the Order to Show Cause, the attorney must lodge with the Court a certified copy of the entire record from the other jurisdiction or bear the burden of persuading the Court that less than the entire record will suffice. This procedure may not be used to relitigate a felony conviction.

(3) An attorney disbarred, suspended or placed on disciplinary probation under the reciprocal discipline provisions of this rule may seek reinstatement upon completion of the period of suspension, disbarment or disciplinary probation by filing a petition for admission with the Clerk as provided in Civil L.R. 11–1(c) and paying the admission fee in accordance with 11–1(d). An attorney disbarred by reason of a felony conviction may not petition for reinstatement until at least one year after entry of the disbarment order.

Cross Reference

See Fed. R. Civ. P. 11(c), 16(f), 37.

[Effective December 1, 2000. Amended effective December 1, 2009; July 2, 2012.]

RULE 11–8. SANCTIONS FOR UNAUTHORIZED PRACTICE

A person who exercises, or pretends to be entitled to exercise, any of the privileges of membership in the bar of this Court, when that person is not entitled to exercise such privileges, may be referred to the Standing Committee in addition to any action authorized by applicable law.

[Effective September 1, 1995. Amended effective July 1, 1997; December 1, 2000; July 2, 2012.]

RULE 11–9. STUDENT PRACTICE

(a) Permission to Appear. With the approval of the assigned Judge, a certified law student who complies with these Local Rules and acts under the supervision of a member of the bar of this Court may engage in the permitted activities set forth in this Local Rule.

(b) Permitted Activities. With respect to a matter pending before this Court, a certified law student may:

(1) Negotiate for and on behalf of the client or appear at Alternative Dispute Resolution (ADR) proceedings, provided that the activity is conducted under the general supervision of a supervising attorney;

(2) Appear on behalf of a client in the trial of a misdemeanor or petty offense, provided the appearance is under the general supervision of a supervising attorney who is immediately available to attend the proceeding if the Judge decides to require the presence of the supervising attorney and, if the client is a criminal defendant, the client has filed a consent with the Court; and

(3) Appear on behalf of a client in any other proceeding or public trial, provided the appearance is under the direct and

immediate supervision of a supervising attorney, who is present during the proceedings.

(c) Requirements for Eligibility. To be eligible to engage in the permitted activities, a law student must submit to the Clerk:

(1) An application for certification on a form established for that purpose by the Court. The Clerk is authorized to issue a certificate of eligibility;

(2) A copy of a Notice of Student Certification or Recertification from the State Bar of California, or a certificate from the registrar or dean of a law school accredited by the American Bar Association or the State Bar of California that the law student has completed at least one-third of the graduation requirements and is continuing study at the law school, (or, if a recent graduate of the law school, that the applicant has registered to take or is awaiting results of the California State Bar Examination). The certification may be withdrawn at any time by the registrar or dean by providing notice to that effect to the Court; and

(3) Certification from a member of the bar of this Court that he or she will serve as a supervising attorney for the law student. The certification may be withdrawn at any time by a supervising attorney by providing notice to that effect to the Court.

(d) Requirements of Supervising Attorney. A supervising attorney must:

(1) Be admitted or otherwise permitted to practice before this Court;

(2) Sign all documents to be filed by the student with the Court;

(3) Assume professional responsibility for the student's work in matters before the Court; and

(4) Assist and counsel the student in the preparation of the student's work in matters before the Court.

(e) Termination of Privilege. The privilege of a law student to appear before this Court under this rule may be terminated by the Court at any time in the discretion of the Court, without the necessity to show cause.

[Effective September 1, 1995. Renumbered and amended effective December 1, 2000. Amended effective July 2, 2012.]

RULE 16. CASE MANAGEMENT AND PRETRIAL CONFERENCES

RULE 16–1. DEFINITIONS

"Scheduling," "discovery," or "status" conferences under Fed. R. Civ. P. 16 and 26 shall be designated as "case management conferences" in this Court. All statements, proposed orders, or other documents prepared in connection with such conferences must be referred to as such.

[Effective September 1, 1995. Amended effective March 25, 1997; December 1, 2000; February 21, 2003.]

RULE 16–2. ORDER SETTING INITIAL CASE MANAGEMENT CONFERENCE

(a) Issuance and Service of Order. Once an action is initiated in this Court, the Clerk shall issue an Order Setting Initial Case Management Conference and ADR Deadlines. The Order shall set the following dates, among others: (1) the date for the Initial Case Management Conference on the assigned Judge's calendar; and (2) the deadline for filing the ADR Certification required by Civil L.R. 16–8(b). The plaintiff must serve on each defendant a copy of the Order, along with the supplementary materials specified by Civil L.R. 4–2. This Order shall not be issued in categories of cases that are excluded under the Federal Rules of Civil Procedure, these Local Rules, or an order of this Court.

(b) Case Management Schedule in Removed Cases. When a case is removed from a state court to this Court, upon the filing of the notice of removal the Court shall issue to the removing party an Order Setting Initial Case Management Conference, as described in subsection (a), above. The removing party must serve the other parties in the case with a copy of the Order and the supplementary materials specified in Civil L.R. 4–2. Unless ordered otherwise by the Court, the filing of a motion for remand does not relieve the parties of any obligations under this rule.

(c) Case Management Schedule in Transferred Cases. When a civil action is transferred to this district, the Court shall issue to the plaintiff an Order Setting Initial Case Management Conference, as described in subsection (a), above. The plaintiff must serve the other parties in the case with a copy of the Order and the pertinent supplementary materials specified in Civil L.R. 4–2.

(d) Relief from Case Management Schedule. By serving and filing a motion with the assigned Judge pursuant to Civil L.R. 7, a party, including a party added later in the case, may seek relief from an obligation imposed by Fed. R. Civ. P. 16 or 26 or the Order Setting Initial Case Management Conference. The motion must:

(1) Describe the circumstances which support the request;

(2) Affirm that counsel for the moving party has conferred with all other counsel in an effort to reach agreement about the matter and, for each other party, report whether that party supports or opposes the request for relief;

(3) Be accompanied by a proposed revised case management schedule; and

(4) If applicable, indicate any changes required in the ADR process or schedule in the case.

(e) Limitation on Stipulations. Any stipulation that would vary the date of a Case Management Conference shall have no effect unless approved by the assigned Judge before the date set for the conference. Any stipulation must comply with Civil L.R. 7–12.

[Effective September 1, 1995. Amended effective July 1, 1997; December 1, 2000; February 21, 2003; January 1, 2005; January 1, 2006; May 1, 2018; December 1, 2021.]

RULE 16–3. LEAD TRIAL COUNSEL REQUIRED TO CONFER

Unless otherwise ordered, the conferring and planning that is mandated by Fed. R. Civ. P. 26(f) and by ADR Local Rule 3–5 must be done by lead trial counsel for each party.

[Effective September 1, 1995. Renumbered and amended effective December 1, 2000.]

RULE 16–4. PROCEDURE IN BANKRUPTCY APPEALS

Appeals from the United States Bankruptcy Court to the United States District Court are governed by the Federal Rules of Bankruptcy Procedure and the Bankruptcy Local Rules of this district.

Cross Reference

See Fed. R. Bankr. P. 8001 through 8020 and B.L.R. 8001–1 through 8011–1.

[Effective December 1, 2000. Amended effective January 1, 2005; May 1, 2008.]

RULE 16–5. PROCEDURE IN ACTIONS FOR REVIEW ON AN ADMINISTRATIVE RECORD

In actions for District Court review on an administrative record, the defendant must serve and file an answer, together with a certified copy of the transcript of the administrative record, within 90 days of receipt of service of the summons and complaint. Within 28 days of receipt of defendant's answer, plaintiff must file a motion for summary judgment pursuant to Civil L.R. 7–2 and Fed. R. Civ. P. 56. Defendant must serve and file any opposition or counter-motion within 28 days of service of plaintiff's motion. Plaintiff may serve and file a reply within 14 days after service of defendant's opposition or counter-motion. Unless the Court orders otherwise, upon the conclusion of this briefing schedule, the matter will be deemed submitted for decision by the District Court without oral argument.

[Effective December 1, 2000. Amended effective December 1, 2009.]

RULE 16–6. PROCEDURE IN U.S. DEBT COLLECTION CASES

These cases shall proceed as follows:

(a) Identification. The first page of the complaint must identify the action by using the words "Debt Collection Case;"

(b) Assignment. Upon filing the complaint, the matter will be assigned to a Magistrate Judge for all pre-trial proceedings; and

(c) Collection Proceedings. If the United States files an application under the Federal Debt Collection Procedures Act, either pre-judgment or post-judgment, such matter will be assigned to a Magistrate Judge.

[Effective December 1, 2000.]

RULE 16–7. PROCEDURE IN OTHER EXEMPT CASES

Unless otherwise provided in these local rules, in categories of cases that are exempted by Fed. R. Civ. P. 26(a)(1)(B) from the initial disclosure requirements of Fed. R. Civ. P. 26(a)(1), promptly after the commencement of the action the assigned judge will schedule a Case Management Conference or issue a case management order without such conference. Discovery shall proceed in such cases only at the time, and to the extent, authorized by the Judge in the case management order.

[Effective December 1, 2000.]

RULE 16–8. ALTERNATIVE DISPUTE RESOLUTION (ADR) IN THE NORTHERN DISTRICT

(a) District Policy Regarding ADR. It is the policy of this Court to assist parties involved in civil litigation to resolve their disputes in a just, timely and cost-effective manner. The Court has created and makes available its own Alternative Dispute Resolution (ADR) programs for which it has promulgated local rules. The Court also encourages civil litigants to consider use of ADR programs operated by private entities. At any time after an action has been filed, the Court on its own initiative or at the request of one or more parties may refer the case to one of the Court's ADR programs.

Cross Reference

See ADR L.R. 1–2 *"Purpose and Scope;"* ADR L.R. 2–3 *"Referral to ADR Program."* The Court's ADR processes and procedures are described on the Court's ADR webpage: cand.uscourts.gov/adr.

(b) ADR Certification. In cases assigned to the ADR Multi–Option Program, no later than the date specified in the Order Setting Initial Case Management Conference and ADR Deadlines (presumptively 21 days before the date set for the initial case management conference), counsel and client must sign, serve and file an ADR Certification. The certification must be made on a form established for this purpose by the Court and in conformity with the instructions approved by the Court. Separate Certifications may be filed by each party. If the client is a government or governmental agency, the certificate must be signed by a person who meets the requirements of Civil L.R. 3–9(c). If the date of the initial case management conference is changed, unless otherwise ordered the ADR Certification deadline adjusts accordingly.

Counsel and client must certify that both have:

(1) Read the document entitled *"Alternative Dispute Resolution Procedures Handbook"* on the ADR webpage, found at cand.uscourts.gov/adr;

(2) Discussed with each other the available dispute resolution options provided by the Court and private entities; and

(3) Considered whether their case might benefit from any of the available dispute resolution options.

Counsel must further certify that they have discussed selection of an ADR process and an appropriate deadline for an ADR session with counsel for the other parties to the case and shall indicate whether they intend to stipulate to an ADR process and deadline or prefer to discuss ADR selection with the assigned Judge at the case management conference.

Cross Reference

See ADR L.R. 3–5.

Commentary

Certification forms and the document entitled *Alternative Dispute Resolution Procedures Handbook* are available on the Court's ADR webpage at cand.uscourts.gov/adr. The Clerk's Office will print copies upon request for pro se parties.

(c) Stipulation to ADR Process. If the parties agree to participate in an ADR process and they wish the Court to make an ADR referral in advance of the case management conference, they may file a Stipulation and Proposed Order selecting an ADR process.

(d) Selection at Case Management Conference.

(1) *Consideration of ADR Processes.* Counsel must include in their joint case management statement a report on the status of ADR, specifying which ADR process option they have selected and a proposed deadline by which the parties will conduct the ADR session or, if they do not agree, setting forth which option and timing each party prefers. Unless the assigned Judge already has approved a stipulation to an ADR process, counsel must be prepared to discuss all of the subjects about which they were required to meet and confer under ADR L.R. 3–5(a). If the ADR legal staff holds an ADR Phone Conference in advance of the initial case management conference, they ordinarily will make a recommendation to the assigned Judge.

(2) *Selection by Stipulation or Order.* If the parties agree to a particular ADR process at the case management conference and the assigned Judge approves, the Judge will issue an order referring the case to that process. Alternatively, even if the parties do not agree, the Judge may issue an order referring the case to Early Neutral Evaluation (ENE), Mediation, or a Settlement Conference.

(3) *Deferred Referral or Exemption.* If, considering the views of the parties, the Judge at the case management conference concludes that the case is not ripe for an ADR referral or that no ADR process is likely to deliver benefits to the parties sufficient to justify the resources devoted to it, the Judge may defer making an ADR referral or may exempt the case from participating in any ADR process.

(e) ADR Phone Conference. An ADR Phone Conference conducted by a member of the ADR legal staff may be set to assist the parties or the assigned Judge in selecting or customizing an ADR process, in aid of the administration of a case that has been referred to an ADR process, or as otherwise directed by the Court. An ADR Phone Conference may be set at the request of the parties on the form established for that purpose by the Court, by referral from the assigned Judge, or at the initiative of the ADR legal staff.

Cross Reference

See ADR L.R. 3–5 "Selecting an ADR Process" and ADR L.R. 3–5(d) "Selection Through ADR Phone Conference."

Commentary

Forms for "ADR Certification," "Stipulation to an ADR Process" and "Request for ADR Telephone Conference" are available on the Court's ADR webpage at cand.uscourts.gov/adr. The Clerk's Office will print copies upon request for pro se parties for a nominal fee.

[Effective December 1, 2000. Amended effective February 21, 2003; January 1, 2006; September 8, 2011; July 2, 2012; September 15, 2015; May 1, 2018; December 1, 2021.]

RULE 16–9. CASE MANAGEMENT STATEMENT AND PROPOSED ORDER

(a) Joint or Separate Case Management Statement. Unless otherwise ordered, no later than the date specified in Fed. R. Civ. P. 26(f), counsel must file a Joint Case Management Statement addressing all of the topics set forth in the Standing Order for All Judges of the Northern District of California—Contents of Joint Case Management Statement, which can be found on the Court's website located at cand.uscourts.gov/forms. If one or more of the parties is not represented by counsel, the parties may file separate case management statements. If a party is unable, despite reasonable efforts, to obtain the cooperation of another party in the preparation of a joint statement, the complying party may file a separate case management statement, accompanied by a declaration describing the conduct of the uncooperative party which prevented the preparation of a joint statement. Separate statements must also address all of the topics set forth in the Standing Order referenced above.

(b) Case Management Statement in Class Action. Any party seeking to maintain a case as a class action must include in the Case Management Statement required by Civil L.R. 16–9(a) the following additional information:

(1) The specific paragraphs of Fed. R. Civ. P. 23 under which the action is maintainable as a class action;

(2) A description of the class or classes in whose behalf the action is brought;

(3) Facts showing that the party is entitled to maintain the action under Fed. R. Civ. P. 23(a) and (b); and

(4) A proposed date for the Court to consider whether the case can be maintained as a class action.

[Former Rule 16–7 effective September 1, 1995. Renumbered as Rule 16–13 and amended, effective July 1, 1997. Renumbered and amended effective December 1, 2000. Amended effective January 1, 2006; March 1, 2007; December 1, 2021.]

RULE 16–10. CASE MANAGEMENT CONFERENCE

(a) Initial Case Management Conference. Unless otherwise ordered, no later than the date specified in the Order Setting Initial Case Management Conference, the Court will conduct an initial Case Management Conference. Subject to 28 U.S.C. § 636, the assigned District Judge may designate a Magistrate Judge to conduct the initial Case Management Conference and other pretrial proceedings in the case. Unless excused by the Judge, lead trial counsel for each party must attend the initial Case Management Conference. Requests to participate in the conference remotely (e.g., telephonic or videoconference) must be filed and served at least 7 days before the conference or in accordance with the Standing Orders of the assigned Judge.

(b) Case Management Orders. After a Case Management Conference, the Judge will enter a Case Management Order or sign the Joint Case Management Statement and Proposed Order submitted by the parties. This order will comply with Fed. R. Civ. P. 16(b) and will identify the principal issues in the case, establish deadlines for joining parties and amending pleadings, identify and set the date for filing any motions that should be considered early in the pretrial period, establish a disclosure and discovery plan, set appropriate limits on discovery, and refer the case to ADR unless such a referral would be inappropriate. In addition, in the initial Case Management Order or in any subsequent case management order, the Court may establish deadlines for:

(1) Commencement and completion of any ADR proceedings;

(2) Disclosure of proposed expert or other opinion witnesses pursuant to Fed. R. Civ. P. 26(a)(2), as well as supplementation of such disclosures;

(3) Conclusion of pretrial discovery and disclosure;

(4) Hearing pretrial motions;

(5) Counsel to meet and confer to prepare joint final pretrial conference statement and proposed order and coordinated submission of trial exhibits and other material;

(6) Filing joint final pretrial conference statement and proposed order;

(7) Lodging exhibits and other trial material, including copies of all exhibits to be offered and all schedules, summaries, diagrams and charts to be used at the trial other than for impeachment or rebuttal. Each proposed exhibit must be premarked for identification. Upon request, a party must make the original or the underlying documents of any exhibit available for inspection and copying;

(8) Serving and filing briefs on all significant disputed issues of law, including procedural and evidentiary issues;

(9) In jury cases, serving and filing requested voir dire questions, jury instructions, and forms of verdict; or in court cases, serving and filing proposed findings of fact and conclusions of law;

(10) Serving and filing statements designating excerpts from depositions (specifying the witness and page and line references), from interrogatory answers and from responses to requests for admission to be offered at the trial other than for impeachment or rebuttal;

(11) A date by which parties objecting to receipt into evidence of any proposed testimony or exhibit must advise and confer with the opposing party with respect to resolving such objection;

(12) A final pretrial conference and any necessary Court hearing to consider unresolved objections to proposed testimony or exhibits;

(13) A trial date and schedule;

(14) Determination of whether the case will be maintained as a class action; and

(15) Any other activities appropriate in the management of the case, including use of procedures set forth in the Manual for Complex Litigation.

(c) Subsequent Case Management Conferences. Pursuant to Fed. R. Civ. P. 16, the assigned Judge or Magistrate Judge may, sua sponte or in response to a stipulated request or motion, schedule subsequent case management conferences during the pendency of an action. Each party must be represented at such subsequent case management conferences by counsel having authority with respect to matters under consideration.

(d) Subsequent Case Management Statements. Unless otherwise ordered, no fewer than 7 days before any subsequent case management conference, the parties must file a Joint Case Management Statement, reporting progress or changes since the last statement was filed and making proposals for the remainder of the case development process. Such statements must report the parties' views about whether using some form of ADR would be appropriate.

[Former Rule 16–8 effective September 1, 1995. Renumbered as Rule 16–14 and amended, effective July 1, 1997. Renumbered and amended effective December 1, 2000. Amended effective October 1, 2002; December 1, 2009; July 2, 2012; September 15, 2015; December 1, 2021.]

RULE 23.   CLASS ACTIONS

RULE 23–1.   PRIVATE SECURITIES ACTIONS

(a) Filing and Serving Required Notices. Not later than 21 days after filing the complaint in any action governed by the Private Securities Litigation Reform Act of 1995, Pub. L. No. 104–67, 109 Stat. 737 (1995), the party filing that complaint and seeking to serve as lead plaintiff must serve and file a copy of any notice required by the Act.

Cross Reference

See Civil L.R. 3–7 *"Civil Cover Sheet and Certification in Private Securities Actions."*

(b) Motion to Serve as Lead Plaintiff. Not later than 60 days after publication of the notices referred to in Civil L.R. 23–1(a), any party seeking to serve as lead plaintiff must serve and file a motion to do so. The motion must set forth whether the party claims entitlement to the presumption set forth in section 27(a)(3)(B)(iii)(I) of the Securities Act or section 21D(a)(3)(B)(iii)(I) of the Securities Exchange Act or that the presumption is rebutted and the reasons therefor.

Commentary

A *"Model Stipulation and Proposed Consolidation Order for Securities Fraud Class Actions"* is available from the Clerk in civil actions containing a claim governed by the Private Securities Litigation Reform Act of 1995, Pub. L. No. 104–67, 109 Stat. 737 (1995), and is part of the materials provided to the filing party for service on all parties in the action pursuant to Civil L.R. 4–2. See also the Court's "Forms" page at: cand.uscourts.gov/forms.

[Repealed and adopted effective July 1, 1997. Amended effective December 1, 2000; December 1, 2009; July 2, 2012; September 15, 2015; December 1, 2021.]

RULE 26. GENERAL PROVISIONS GOVERNING DISCOVERY

RULE 26–1. CUSTODIAN OF DISCOVERY DOCUMENTS

The party propounding interrogatories, requests for production of documents, or requests for admission must retain the original of the discovery request and the original response. That party shall be the custodian of these materials. Fed. R. Civ. P. 30(f) identifies the custodian of the original transcript or recording of a deposition.

Commentary

Counsel should consider stipulating to sharing computer-readable copies of discovery requests, such as interrogatories and requests for production of documents, as well as responses to such requests, to save costs and to facilitate expeditious pretrial discovery.

[Effective September 1, 1995. Renumbered and amended effective December 1, 2000.]

RULE 30. DEPOSITIONS

RULE 30–1. REQUIRED CONSULTATION REGARDING SCHEDULING

For the convenience of witnesses, counsel and parties, before noticing a deposition of a party or witness affiliated with a party, the noticing party must confer about the scheduling of the deposition with opposing counsel or, if the party is pro se, the party. A party noticing a deposition of a witness who is not a party or affiliated with a party must also meet and confer about scheduling, but may do so after serving the nonparty witness with a subpoena.

[Effective September 1, 1995. Renumbered and amended effective December 1, 2000. Amended effective January 1, 2005.]

RULE 30–2. NUMBERING OF DEPOSITION PAGES AND EXHIBITS

(a) Sequential Numbering of Pages. The pages of the deposition of a single witness, even if taken at different times, must be numbered sequentially.

(b) Sequential Numbering of Exhibits. Documents identified as exhibits during the course of depositions and at trial must be numbered and organized as follows:

(1) At the outset of the case, counsel must meet and confer regarding the sequential numbering system that will be used for exhibits throughout the litigation, including trial.

(2) If the pages of an exhibit are not numbered internally and it is necessary to identify pages of an exhibit, then each page must receive a page number designation preceded by the exhibit number (e.g., Exhibit 100–2, 100–3, 100–4).

(3) To the extent practicable, any exhibit which is an exact duplicate of an exhibit previously numbered must bear the same exhibit number regardless of which party is using the exhibit. Any version of any exhibit which is not an exact duplicate must be marked and treated as a different exhibit, bearing a different exhibit number.

(4) In addition to exhibit numbers, documents may bear other numbers or letters used by the parties for internal control purposes.

[Effective September 1, 1995. Renumbered and amended effective December 1, 2000.]

RULE 33. INTERROGATORIES

RULE 33–1. FORM OF ANSWERS AND OBJECTIONS

Answers and objections to interrogatories must set forth each question in full before each answer or objection.
[Effective December 1, 2000.]

RULE 33–2. DEMANDS THAT A PARTY SET FORTH THE BASIS FOR A DENIAL OF A REQUESTED ADMISSION

A demand that a party set forth the basis for a denial of an admission requested under Fed. R. Civ. P. 36 will be treated as a separate discovery request (an interrogatory) and is allowable only to the extent that a party is entitled to propound additional interrogatories.

Cross Reference

To the same effect, see Civil L.R. 36–2.

Commentary

Under Fed. R. Civ. P. 36, a party is not required to set forth the basis for an unqualified denial.

[Effective December 1, 2000. Amended effective September 8, 2011.]

RULE 33–3. MOTIONS FOR LEAVE TO PROPOUND MORE INTERROGATORIES THAN PERMITTED BY FED. R. CIV. P. 33

A motion for leave to propound more interrogatories than permitted by Fed. R. Civ. P. 33 must be accompanied by a memorandum which sets forth each proposed additional interrogatory and explains in detail why it is necessary to propound the additional questions.

[Effective December 1, 2000.]

RULE 34. PRODUCTION OF DOCUMENTS AND THINGS

RULE 34–1. FORM OF RESPONSES TO REQUESTS FOR PRODUCTION

A response to a request for production or inspection made pursuant to Fed. R. Civ. P. 34(a) must set forth each request in full before each response or objection.

[Effective September 1, 1995. Amended effective December 1, 2000.]

RULE 36. REQUESTS FOR ADMISSION

RULE 36–1. FORM OF RESPONSES TO REQUESTS FOR ADMISSION

Responses to requests for admission must set forth each request in full before each response or objection.

[Effective September 1, 1995. Amended effective December 1, 2000.]

RULE 36–2. DEMANDS THAT A PARTY SET FORTH THE BASIS FOR A DENIAL OF A REQUESTED ADMISSION

A demand that a party set forth the basis for a denial of a requested admission will be treated as a separate discovery request (an interrogatory) and is allowable only to the extent that a party is entitled to propound additional interrogatories.

Cross Reference

To the same effect, see Civil L.R. 33–2.

Commentary

Under Fed. R. Civ. P. 36, a party is not required to set forth the basis for an unqualified denial.

[Effective December 1, 2000. Amended effective September 8, 2011.]

RULE 37. MOTIONS TO COMPEL DISCLOSURE OR DISCOVERY OR FOR SANCTIONS

RULE 37–1. PROCEDURES FOR RESOLVING DISPUTES

(a) Conference Between Counsel Required. The Court will not entertain a request or a motion to resolve a disclosure or discovery dispute unless, pursuant to Fed. R. Civ. P. 37, counsel have previously conferred for the purpose of attempting to resolve all disputed issues. If counsel for the moving party seeks to arrange such a conference and opposing counsel refuses or fails to confer, the Judge may impose an appropriate sanction, which may include an order requiring payment of all reasonable expenses, including attorney's fees, caused by the refusal or failure to confer.

(b) Requests for Intervention During a Discovery Event. If a dispute arises during a discovery event the parties must attempt to resolve the matter without judicial intervention by conferring in good faith. If good faith negotiations between the parties fail to resolve the matter, and if disposition of the dispute during the discovery event likely would result in substantial savings of expense or time, counsel or a party may contact the chambers of the assigned District Judge or Magistrate Judge to ask if the Judge is available to address the problem through a telephone conference during the discovery event.

[Effective September 1, 1995. Amended effective December 1, 2000.]

RULE 37–2. FORM OF MOTIONS TO COMPEL

In addition to complying with applicable provisions of Civil L.R. 7, a motion to compel further responses to discovery requests must set forth each request in full, followed immediately by the objections and/or responses thereto. For each such request, the moving papers must detail the basis for the party's contention that it is entitled to the requested discovery and must show how the proportionality and other requirements of Fed. R. Civ. P. 26(b)(2) are satisfied.

[Effective December 1, 2000.]

RULE 37–3. DISCOVERY CUT–OFF; DEADLINE TO FILE MOTIONS TO COMPEL

Unless otherwise ordered, as used in any order of this Court or in these Local Rules, a "discovery cut-off" is the date by which all responses to written discovery are due and by which all depositions must be concluded.

Where the Court has set a single discovery cut-off for both fact and expert discovery, no motions to compel discovery may be filed more than 7 days after the discovery cut-off.

Where the Court has set separate deadlines for fact and expert discovery, no motions to compel fact discovery may be filed more than 7 days after the fact discovery cut-off, and no motions to compel expert discovery may be filed more than 7 days after the expert discovery cut-off.

Discovery requests that call for responses or depositions after the applicable discovery cut-off are not enforceable, except by order of the Court for good cause shown.

Commentary

Counsel should initiate discovery requests and notice depositions sufficiently in advance of the cut-off date to comply with this local rule.

[Effective December 1, 2000. Formerly Rule 26–2, redesignated effective April 20, 2010. Amended effective December 1, 2021.]

RULE 40. TRIAL

RULE 40–1. CONTINUANCE OF TRIAL DATE; SANCTIONS FOR FAILURE TO PROCEED

No continuance of a scheduled trial date will be granted except by order of the Court issued in response to a motion made in accordance with the provisions of Civil L.R. 7. Failure of a party to proceed with the trial on the scheduled trial date may result in the assessment of jury costs and the imposition of appropriate sanctions, including dismissal or

RULE 54. COSTS

RULE 54–1. FILING OF BILL OF COSTS

(a) Time for Filing and Content. No later than 14 days after entry of judgment or order under which costs may be claimed, a prevailing party claiming taxable costs must serve and file a bill of costs. The bill must state separately and specifically each item of taxable costs claimed. It must be supported by an affidavit, pursuant to 28 U.S.C. § 1924, that the costs are correctly stated, were necessarily incurred, and are allowable by law. Appropriate documentation to support each item claimed must be attached to the bill of costs.

(b) Effect of Service. Service of bill of costs shall constitute notice pursuant to Fed. R. Civ. P. 54(d), of a request for taxation of costs by the Clerk.

(c) Waiver of Costs. Any party who fails to file a bill of costs within the time period provided by this rule will be deemed to have waived costs.

Commentary

The 14–day time period set by this rule is inapplicable where a statute authorizing costs establishes a different time deadline, (e.g., 28

RULE 37–4. MOTIONS FOR SANCTIONS UNDER FED. R. CIV. P. 37

When, in connection with a dispute about disclosure or discovery, a party moves for an award of attorney fees or other form of sanction under Fed. R. Civ. P. 37, the motion must:

(a) Comply with Civil L.R. 7–8 and Civil L.R. 7–2; and

(b) Be accompanied by competent declarations which:

(1) Set forth the facts and circumstances that support the motion;

(2) Describe in detail the efforts made by the moving party to secure compliance without intervention by the Court; and

(3) If attorney fees or other costs or expenses are requested, itemize with particularity the otherwise unnecessary expenses, including attorney fees, directly caused by the alleged violation or breach, and set forth an appropriate justification for any attorney-fee hourly rate claimed.

[Effective December 1, 2009.]

entry of default. Jury costs may be also assessed for failure to provide the Court with timely notice of a settlement.

Commentary

Counsel should consult any Standing Orders issued by the assigned Judge with respect to the conduct of trial. Such orders are available on the individual Judges' pages of the Court's website: cand.uscourts.gov/judges.

[Effective September 1, 1995. Amended effective December 1, 2000; July 2, 2012; November 1, 2014; December 1, 2021.]

U.S.C. § 2412(d)(1)(B) (setting 30 days from final judgment as time limit to file for fees under Equal Access to Justice Act)).

[Effective September 1, 1995. Amended effective December 1, 2000; January 1, 2005; July 2, 2012; December 1, 2021.]

RULE 54–2. OBJECTIONS TO BILL OF COSTS

(a) Time for Filing Objections. Within 14 days after service by any party of its bill of costs, the party against whom costs are claimed must serve and file any specific objections to any item of cost claimed in the bill, succinctly setting forth the grounds of each objection.

(b) Meet and Confer Requirement. Any objections filed under this Local Rule must contain a representation that counsel met and conferred in an effort to resolve disagreement about the taxable costs claimed in the bill, or that the objecting party made a good faith effort to arrange such a conference.

[Effective September 1, 1995. Amended effective January 1, 2005; December 1, 2009.]

RULE 54–3. STANDARDS FOR TAXING COSTS

(a) Fees for Filing and Service of Process.

(1) The Clerk's filing fee is allowable if paid by the claimant.

(2) Fees of the marshal as set forth in 28 U.S.C. § 1921 are allowable to the extent actually incurred. Fees for service of process by someone other than the marshal acting pursuant to Fed. R. Civ. P. 4(c) are allowable to the extent reasonably required and actually incurred.

(b) Reporters' Transcripts.

(1) The cost of transcripts necessarily obtained for an appeal is allowable.

(2) The cost of a transcript of a statement by a Judge from the bench which is to be reduced to a formal order prepared by counsel is allowable.

(3) The cost of other transcripts is not normally allowable unless, before it is incurred, it is approved by a Judge or stipulated to be recoverable by counsel.

(c) Depositions.

(1) The cost of an original and one copy of any deposition (including videotaped depositions) taken for any purpose in connection with the case is allowable.

(2) The expenses of counsel for attending depositions are not allowable.

(3) The cost of reproducing exhibits to depositions is allowable if the cost of the deposition is allowable.

(4) Notary fees incurred in connection with taking depositions are allowable.

(5) The attendance fee of a reporter when a witness fails to appear is allowable if the claimant made use of available process to compel the attendance of the witness.

(d) Reproduction and Exemplification.

(1) The cost of reproducing and certifying or exemplifying government records used for any purpose in the case is allowable.

(2) The cost of reproducing disclosure or formal discovery documents when used for any purpose in the case is allowable.

(3) The cost of reproducing copies of motions, pleadings, notices, and other routine case papers is not allowable.

(4) The cost of reproducing trial exhibits is allowable to the extent that a Judge requires copies to be provided.

(5) The cost of preparing charts, diagrams, videotapes, and other visual aids to be used as exhibits is allowable if such exhibits are reasonably necessary to assist the jury or the Court in understanding the issues at the trial.

(e) Witness Expenses. Per diem, subsistence, and mileage payments for witnesses are allowable to the extent reasonably necessary and provided for by 28 U.S.C. § 1821. No other witness expenses, including fees for expert witnesses, are allowable.

(f) Fees for Masters and Receivers. Fees to masters and receivers are allowable.

(g) Costs on Appeal. Other costs not provided for in these Rules but authorized under Fed. R. App. P. 39 are allowable.

(h) Costs of Bonds and Security. Premiums on undertaking bonds and costs of providing security required by law, by order of a Judge, or otherwise necessarily incurred are allowable.

[Effective September 1, 1995. Amended effective December 1, 2021.]

RULE 54–4. DETERMINATION OF TAXABLE COSTS

(a) Supplemental Documentation. The Clerk may require and consider further affidavits and documentation as necessary to determine allowable costs.

(b) Taxation of Costs. No sooner than 14 days after a bill of costs has been filed, the Clerk shall tax costs after considering any objections filed pursuant to Civil L.R. 54–2. Costs shall be taxed in conformity with 28 U.S.C. §§ 1920 and 1923, Civil L.R. 54–3, and all other applicable statutes and rules. On the bill of costs or in a separate notice, the Clerk shall indicate which, if any, of the claimed costs are allowed and against whom such costs are allowed. The Clerk shall serve copies of the notice taxing costs on all parties on the day in which costs are taxed.

[Effective September 1, 1995. Amended effective January 1, 2005; December 1, 2009; December 1, 2021.]

RULE 54–5. MOTION FOR ATTORNEY'S FEES

(a) Time for Filing Motion. Motions for awards of attorney's fees by the Court must be served and filed within 14 days of entry of judgment by the District Court, unless otherwise ordered by the Court after a stipulation to enlarge time under Civil L.R. 6–2 or a motion under Civil L.R. 6–3. Filing an appeal from the judgment does not extend the time for filing a motion. Counsel for the respective parties must meet and confer for the purpose of resolving all disputed issues relating to attorney's fees before making a motion for award of attorney's fees.

Commentary

Fed. R. Civ. P. 54(d)(2)(B) sets a time period of 14 days from the entry of judgment to file a motion for attorney's fees. Counsel who desire to seek an order extending the time to file such a motion, either by stipulation (See Civil L.R. 6–2) or by motion (See Civil L.R. 6–3), are advised to seek such an order as expeditiously as practicable.

(b) Form of Motion. Unless otherwise ordered, the motion for attorney fees must be supported by declarations or affidavits containing the following information:

(1) A statement that counsel have met and conferred for the purpose of attempting to resolve any disputes with respect to the motion or a statement that no conference was held, with certification that the applying attorney made a good faith effort to arrange such a conference, setting forth the reason the conference was not held; and

(2) A statement of the services rendered by each person for whose services fees are claimed, together with a summary of the time spent by each person, and a statement describing the manner in which time records were maintained. Depending on the circumstances, the Court may require production of an abstract of or the contemporary time records for inspection,

including *in camera* inspection, as the Judge deems appropriate; and

(3) A brief description of relevant qualifications and experience and a statement of the customary hourly charges of each

such person or of comparable prevailing hourly rates or other indication of value of the services.

[Effective September 1, 1995. Amended effective July 1, 1997; December 1, 2000; October 1, 2002. Renumbered effective January 1, 2005. Amended effective December 1, 2009; December 1, 2021.]

RULE 56. SUMMARY JUDGMENT

RULE 56–1. NOTICE OF MOTION

Motions for summary judgment or summary adjudication and opposition to such motions must be noticed as provided in Civil L.R. 7–2 and 7–3.

[Effective February 1, 2010.]

RULE 56–2. SEPARATE OR JOINT STATEMENT OF UNDISPUTED FACTS

(a) No Separate Statement Allowed Without Court Order. Unless required by the assigned Judge, no separate statement of undisputed facts or joint statement of undisputed facts shall be submitted.

(b) Procedure if Joint Statement Ordered. If the assigned Judge orders the submission of a joint statement of undisputed facts, the parties shall confer and submit, on or before a date set by the assigned Judge, a joint statement of undisputed facts. If the nonmoving party refuses to join in

the statement, the moving party will nevertheless be permitted to file the motion, accompanied by a separate declaration of counsel explaining why a joint statement was not filed. Whether or not sanctions should be imposed for failure to file a joint statement of undisputed facts is a matter within the discretion of the assigned Judge.

[Effective September 1, 1995. Amended effective December 1, 2000. Renumbered effective December 1, 2009. Renumbered effective February 1, 2010.]

RULE 56–3. ISSUES DEEMED ESTABLISHED

Statements contained in an order of the Court denying a motion for summary judgment or summary adjudication shall not constitute issues deemed established for purposes of the trial of the case, unless the Court so specifies.

[Effective September 1, 1995. Amended effective December 1, 2000. Renumbered effective December 1, 2009. Renumbered effective February 1, 2010.]

RULE 65. INJUNCTIONS

RULE 65–1. TEMPORARY RESTRAINING ORDERS

(a) Documentation Required. A motion for temporary restraining order must be accompanied by:

(1) A copy of the complaint;

(2) A separate memorandum of points and authorities in support of the motion;

(3) The proposed temporary restraining order and order to show cause;

(4) Other supporting documents that the party wishes the Court to consider; and

(5) A declaration by counsel certifying that notice has been provided to the opposing party, or explaining why such notice could not be provided.

(b) [Withdrawn].

(c) Form of Temporary Restraining Order. The moving party must include both a proposed temporary restraining order and a proposed order to show cause setting the time and date for a hearing on a motion for preliminary injunction,

which shall be scheduled pursuant to Fed. R. Civ. P. 65(b). Proposed orders submitted under this Rule must provide a place for the Judge to set a deadline by which the temporary restraining order and all supporting pleadings and papers must be served upon the adverse party.

(d) Notification to Clerk.

(1) The filing party should alert the Court to the filing of a motion for temporary restraining order by emailing or calling the courtroom deputy clerk for the judge assigned to the case.

(2) Motions filed after hours or on weekends must follow instructions provided in ECF.

[Effective September 1, 1995. Amended effective December 1, 2000; October 1, 2002; July 2, 2012; December 1, 2021.]

RULE 65–2. MOTION FOR PRELIMINARY INJUNCTION

Motions for preliminary injunctions unaccompanied by a temporary restraining order are governed by Civil L.R. 7–2.

[Effective September 1, 1995. Amended effective December 1, 2000.]

RULE 65.1. SECURITY

RULE 65.1–1. SECURITY

(a) When Required. Upon demand of any party, where authorized by law and for good cause shown, the Court may require any party to furnish security for costs which can be awarded against such party in an amount and on such terms as the Court deems appropriate.

(b) Qualifications of Surety. Every bond must have as surety either:

(1) A corporation authorized by the Secretary of the Treasury of the United States to act as surety on official bonds under 31 U.S.C. §§ 9301–9306;

(2) A corporation authorized to act as surety under the laws of the State of California;

(3) Two natural persons, who are residents of the Northern District of California, each of whom separately own real or personal property not exempt from execution within the district. (The total value of these two persons' property should be sufficient to justify the full amount of the suretyship); or

(4) A cash deposit of the required amount made with the Clerk and filed with a bond signed by the principals.

(c) Court Officer as Surety. No Clerk, marshal or other employee of the Court may be surety on any bond or other undertaking in this Court. No member of the bar of this Court appearing for a party in any pending action may be surety on any bond or other undertaking in that action. However, cash deposits on bonds may be made by members of the bar of this Court on certification that the funds are the property of a specified person who has signed as surety on the bond. Upon exoneration of the bond, such monies shall be returned to the owner and not to the attorney.

(d) Examination of Surety. Any party may apply for an order requiring any opposing party to show cause why it should not be required to furnish further or different security, or to require the justification of personal sureties.

[Effective September 1, 1995. Amended effective December 1, 2021.]

RULE 66. PREJUDGMENT REMEDIES

RULE 66–1. APPOINTMENT OF RECEIVER

(a) Time for Motion. A motion for the appointment of a receiver in a case may be made after the complaint has been filed and the summons issued.

(b) Temporary Receiver. A temporary receiver may be appointed with less notice than required by Civil L.R. 7–2 or, in accordance with the requirements and limitations of Fed. R. Civ. P. 65(b), without notice to the party sought to be subjected to a receivership or to creditors.

(c) Permanent Receiver. Concurrent with the appointment of a temporary receiver or upon motion noticed in accordance with the requirements of Civil L.R. 7–2, the Judge may, upon a proper showing, issue an order to show cause, requiring the parties and the creditors to show cause why a permanent receiver should not be appointed.

(d) Parties to Be Notified. Within 7 days of the issuance of the order to show cause, the defendant must provide to the temporary receiver or, if no temporary receiver has been appointed, to the plaintiff, a list of the defendant's creditors, and their addresses. Not less than 14 days before the hearing on the order to show cause, notice of the hearing must be mailed to the listed creditors by the temporary receiver, or, if none, by the plaintiff.

(e) Bond. The Court may require any appointed receiver to furnish a bond in such amount as the Court deems reasonable.

[Effective September 1, 1995. Amended effective December 1, 2009.]

RULE 66–2. EMPLOYMENT OF ATTORNEYS, ACCOUNTANTS OR INVESTIGATORS

The receiver may not employ an attorney, accountant or investigator without a Court order. The compensation of all such employees shall be fixed by the Court.

[Effective September 1, 1995. Amended effective December 1, 2000.]

RULE 66–3. MOTION FOR FEES

All motions for fees for services rendered in connection with a receivership must set forth in reasonable detail the nature of the services. The motion must include as an exhibit an itemized record of time spent and services rendered.

[Effective September 1, 1995. Amended effective December 1, 2000; December 1, 2021.]

RULE 66–4. DEPOSIT OF FUNDS

A receiver must deposit all funds received into the institution selected by the Court as its designated depository pursuant to 28 U.S.C. § 2041. The account title shall include the case name and number. At the end of each month, the receiver must deliver to the Clerk a statement of account, copies of canceled checks, and any other records of transactions.

[Effective September 1, 1995. Amended effective December 1, 2000; December 1, 2021.]

RULE 66–5. REPORTS

Within 30 days of appointment, a permanent receiver must serve and file with the Court a verified report and petition for instructions. The report and petition must contain a summary of the operations of the receiver, an inventory of the assets and their appraised value, a schedule of all receipts and disbursements, and a list of all creditors, their addresses and the amounts of their claims. The petition must contain the receiver's recommendation as to the continuance of the receivership and reasons therefor. At the hearing, the Judge will determine whether the receivership will be continued and, if so, will set a schedule for future reports of the receiver.

[Effective September 1, 1995. Amended effective December 1, 2000; December 1, 2021.]

RULE 66–6. NOTICE OF HEARINGS

The receiver must give all interested parties notice of the time and place of hearings of the following in accordance with Civil L.R. 7–2:

(a) Petitions for instructions;

(b) Petitions for the payment of dividends to creditors;

(c) Petitions for confirmation of sales of property;

(d) Reports of the receiver;

(e) Motions for fees of the receiver or of any attorney, accountant or investigator, the notice to state the services performed and the fee requested; and

(f) Motions for discharge of the receiver.

[Effective September 1, 1995.]

RULE 72. MAGISTRATE JUDGES; PRETRIAL ORDERS

RULE 72–1. POWERS OF MAGISTRATE JUDGE

Each Magistrate Judge appointed by the Court is authorized to exercise all powers and perform all duties conferred upon Magistrate Judges by 28 U.S.C. § 636, by the local rules of this Court and by any written order of a District Judge designating a Magistrate Judge to perform specific statutorily authorized duties in a particular action.

[Effective September 1, 1995.]

RULE 72–2. MOTION FOR RELIEF FROM NONDISPOSITIVE PRETRIAL ORDER OF MAGISTRATE JUDGE

(a) Form of Objection. Any objection filed pursuant to Fed. R. Civ. P. 72(a) and 28 U.S.C. § 636(b)(1)(A) must be made as a "Motion for Relief from Nondispositive Pretrial Order of Magistrate Judge."

. (b) Contents of Motion. Any motion filed pursuant to this rule may not exceed 5 pages (not including declarations and exhibits) and must include:

(1) A specific statement of the portions of the Magistrate Judge's findings, recommendation, or report to which an objection is made;

(2) A statement of the Court action requested;

(3) A statement of the reasons and authority supporting the motion; and

(4) A proposed order.

(c) Service of Motion. The moving party must deliver any manually filed motion and all attachments to all other parties on the same day that the motion is filed.

(d) Opportunity for Response; Ruling on Motion. Unless otherwise ordered by the assigned District Judge, no response need be filed and no hearing will be held concerning the motion. The District Judge may deny the motion by written order at any time, but may not grant it without first giving the opposing party an opportunity to respond. If no order denying the motion or setting a briefing schedule is made within 14 days of filing the motion, the motion shall be deemed denied. The Clerk shall notify parties when a motion has been deemed denied.

[Effective September 1, 1995. Amended effective December 1, 2000; December 1, 2009; April 20, 2010; July 2, 2012; December 1, 2021.]

RULE 72–3. MOTION FOR DE NOVO DETERMINATION OF DISPOSITIVE MATTER REFERRED TO MAGISTRATE JUDGE

(a) Form of Motion and Response. Any objection filed pursuant to Fed. R. Civ. P. 72(b) and 28 U.S.C. § 636(b)(1)(B) must be made as a "Motion for De Novo Determination of Dispositive Matter Referred to Magistrate Judge." The motion must be made pursuant to Civil L.R. 7–2 and must specifically identify the portions of the Magistrate Judge's findings, recommendation, or report to which objection is made and the reasons and authority supporting the motion.

(b) Associated Administrative Motions. At the time a party files a motion under Civil L.R. 72–3(a) or a response, the party may accompany it with a separately filed motion for "Administrative Motion to Augment the Record" or an "Administrative Motion for an Evidentiary Hearing." Any associated administrative motion must be made in accordance with Civil L.R. 7–11.

(c) Record Before District Judge. Except when the Court grants a motion under Civil L.R. 72–3(b), the Court's review and determination of a motion filed pursuant to Civil L.R. 72–3(a) shall be upon the record of the proceedings before the Magistrate Judge.

Commentary

Procedures governing review of a pretrial order by a Magistrate Judge on matters not dispositive of a claim or defense are governed by Fed. R. Civ. P. 72(a) and 28 U.S.C. § 636(b)(1)(A). Procedures governing consideration of a Magistrate Judge's findings, report and recommendations on pretrial matters dispositive of a claim or defense are governed by Fed. R. Civ. P. 72(b) and 28 U.S.C. § 636(b)(1)(B) & (C).

[Effective September 1, 1995. Amended effective December 1, 2000; April 20, 2010; December 1, 2021.]

RULE 73.   MAGISTRATE JUDGES; TRIAL BY CONSENT

RULE 73–1.   TIME FOR CONSENT TO MAGISTRATE JUDGE

(a) Cases Initially Assigned to a Magistrate Judge. In cases that are initially assigned to a Magistrate Judge, unless the Clerk or the Magistrate Judge has set a different deadline in an individual case:

(1) Parties must either file written consent to the jurisdiction of the Magistrate Judge, or request reassignment to a District Judge, by the deadline for filing the initial case management conference statement.

(2) If a motion that cannot be heard by the Magistrate Judge without the consent of the parties, pursuant to 28 U.S.C. § 636(c), is filed prior to the initial case management conference, the parties must either file written consent to the jurisdiction of the Magistrate Judge, or request reassignment to a District Judge, no later than 7 days after the motion is filed.

(b) Cases Initially Assigned to a District Judge. In cases that are assigned to a District Judge, the parties may consent at any time to the Court reassigning the case to a Magistrate Judge for all purposes, including entry of final judgment, pursuant to 28 U.S.C. § 636(c).

[Effective January 1, 2005. Amended effective December 1, 2009; November 1, 2014; May 1, 2018; December 1, 2021.]

RULE 77.   DISTRICT COURT AND CLERK

RULE 77–1.   LOCATIONS AND HOURS

(a) Locations.

(1) The Office of the Clerk for the San Francisco Division is located at the Philip Burton Federal Building and United States Courthouse, 450 Golden Gate Avenue, San Francisco, California 94102.

(2) The Office of the Clerk for the Oakland Division is located at the Ronald V. Dellums Federal Building and United States Courthouse, 1301 Clay Street, Oakland, California 94612.

(3) The Office of the Clerk for the San Jose Division is located at the Robert F. Peckham Federal Building and United States Courthouse, 280 South First Street, San Jose, California 95113.

(4) The Eureka–McKinleyville United States Courthouse is located at 3140 Boeing Avenue, McKinleyville, California 95519. There is no Office of the Clerk in the Eureka–McKinleyville Courthouse.

(b) Hours. The regular hours of the Offices of the Clerk are from 9:00 a.m. to 4:00 p.m. each day except Saturdays, Sundays, and Court holidays. For current front desk hours, see the Court's website at cand.uscourts.gov.

Commentary

See Civil L.R. 5–4 regarding after-hours drop box filing.

[Effective September 1, 1995. Amended effective July 1, 1997; December 1, 2000; July 2, 2012; September 15, 2015; December 1, 2021.]

RULE 77–2.   ORDERS GRANTABLE BY CLERK

The Clerk is authorized to sign and enter orders specifically allowed to be signed by the Clerk under the Federal Rules of Civil Procedure and these local rules. The Clerk may file such orders as effective on a previous date when appropriate and as permitted by law. In addition, the Clerk may sign and enter the following orders without further direction of a Judge:

(a) Orders specifically appointing persons to serve process in accordance with Fed. R. Civ. P. 4;

(b) Orders on consent noting satisfaction of a judgment, providing for the payment of money, withdrawing stipulations, annulling bonds, exonerating sureties, or setting aside a default;

(c) Orders of dismissal on consent, with or without prejudice, except in cases to which Fed. R. Civ. P. 23, 23.1, or 66 apply;

(d) Orders establishing a schedule for case management in accordance with Civil L.R. 16;

(e) Orders relating or reassigning cases on behalf of the Executive Committee; and

(f) Orders taxing costs pursuant to Civil L.R. 54–4.

Cross Reference

See ADR L.R. 4–11(d) "*Nonbinding Arbitration; Entry of Judgment on Award.*"

[Effective September 1, 1995. Amended effective December 1, 2000; December 1, 2021.]

RULE 77–3.   PHOTOGRAPHY AND PUBLIC BROADCASTING

Unless allowed by a District Judge or Magistrate Judge with respect to his or her own chambers or assigned courtroom for ceremonial purposes, or for participation in a pilot or other project authorized by the Judicial Council of the Ninth Circuit or the Judicial Conference of the United States, photography, public broadcasting, televising, audio-recording, or video-recording in the courtroom or its environs in connection with any judicial proceeding is prohibited. Electronic transmittal of courtroom proceedings and presentation of evidence within the confines of the courthouse is permitted if authorized by the presiding Judge. The term "environs" as used in this rule means all floors on which chambers, courtrooms, or Offices of the Clerk are located, with the exception of any space specifically designated as a Press Room. Nothing in this rule is intended to restrict the use of electronic means to receive or present evidence during Court proceedings.

[Effective September 1, 1995. Amended effective December 1, 2000; February 17, 2009; December 22, 2009; February 1, 2010; September 8, 2011; December 1, 2021.]

RULE 77–4. OFFICIAL NOTICES

The following media are designated by this Court as its official means of giving public notice of calendars, General Orders, employment opportunities, policies, proposed modifications of these local rules, or any matter requiring public notice. The Court may designate any one or a combination of these media for purposes of giving notice as it deems appropriate:

(a) Bulletin Board. A bulletin board for posting of official notices shall be located at the Office of the Clerk at each courthouse of this district.

(b) Website. The Court website located at cand.uscourts.gov is designated as the district's official website and may be used for the posting of official notices.

(c) Newspapers. The following newspapers are designated as official newspapers of the Court for the posting of official notices:

(1) The Recorder; or

(2) The Daily Journal; or

(3) The San Jose Post–Record, for matters pending in the San Jose Division, in addition to the newspapers listed in subparagraphs (1) and (2); or

(4) The Times Standard, for matters pending before a Judge sitting in Eureka.

[Effective September 1, 1995. Amended effective December 1, 2000; September 15, 2015; December 1, 2021.]

RULE 77–5. SECURITY OF THE COURT

The Court, or any Judge, may from time to time make such orders or impose such requirements as may be reasonably necessary to assure the security of the Court and of all persons in attendance.

[Effective September 1, 1995.]

RULE 77–6. WEAPONS IN THE COURTHOUSE AND COURTROOM

(a) Prohibition on Unauthorized Weapons. Only the United States Marshal, Deputy Marshals, and Court Security Officers are authorized to carry weapons within the confines of the courthouse, courtrooms, secured judicial corridors, and chambers of the Court. When the United States Marshal

deems it appropriate, upon notice to any affected Judge, the Marshal may authorize duly authorized law enforcement officers to carry weapons in the courthouse or courtroom.

(b) Use of Weapons as Evidence. In all cases in which a weapon is to be introduced as evidence, before bringing the weapon into a courtroom, the United States Marshal or Court Security Officer on duty must be notified. Before a weapon is brought into a courtroom, it must be inspected by the United States Marshal or Court Security Officer to ensure that it is inoperable and appropriately marked as evidence, and the assigned Judge shall be notified of such inspection.

[Effective September 1, 1995. Amended effective December 1, 2000; December 1, 2021.]

RULE 77–7. COURT LIBRARY

The Court maintains a law library primarily for the use of Judges and personnel of the Court. In addition, attorneys admitted to practice in this Court may use the library as needed for actions or proceedings pending in the Court. The library is operated in accordance with such rules and regulations as the Court may from time to time adopt.

[Effective September 1, 1995. Amended effective December 1, 2021.]

RULE 77–8. COMPLAINTS AGAINST JUDGES

Pursuant to 28 U.S.C. § 351(a), any person alleging that a Judge of this Court has engaged in conduct prejudicial to the effective and expeditious administration of the business of the Court, or alleging that a Judge is unable to discharge all of the duties of office by reason of mental or physical disability, may file with the Clerk of the Court for the United States Court of Appeals for the Ninth Circuit a written complaint containing a brief statement of the facts constituting such conduct. Upon request, the Clerk of this Court will provide to any person wishing to file such a complaint:

(a) A copy of the Rules for Judicial–Conduct and Judicial–Disability Proceedings promulgated by the Judicial Conference of the United States, and the Ninth Circuit Judicial Council's Local Rules for Misconduct Proceedings, both of which are available at: ca9.uscourts.gov/misconduct/judicial_misconduct.php;

(b) A copy of the Ninth Circuit Judicial Council's complaint form; and

(c) A pre-addressed envelope to the Clerk of Court for the Ninth Circuit Court of Appeals, marked "COMPLAINT OF MISCONDUCT" or "COMPLAINT OF DISABILITY." No judge's name may appear on the envelope.

[Effective September 1, 1995. Amended effective September 15, 2015; December 1, 2021.]

RULE 79. BOOKS AND RECORDS KEPT BY THE CLERK

RULE 79–1. TRANSCRIPT AND DESIGNATION OF RECORD ON APPEAL

If a party timely orders a transcript in accordance with the requirements of Fed. R. App. P. 10(b), but fails to make

satisfactory arrangements to pay the court reporter at or before the time of the order, the court reporter must promptly notify the Clerk of Court and the party. Within 14 days after receipt of such notice from the court reporter, the ordering the transcript must make satisfactory arrangements for payment. The reporters' transcript must be filed within 28 days of the date such arrangements have been made. If the party fails to make satisfactory arrangements for payment within 14 days, the Clerk of Court shall certify to the Court of Appeals for the Ninth Circuit that the party has failed to comply with Fed. R. App. P. 10(b)(4).

Cross Reference

See Ninth Circuit Rule 10–3 *"Ordering the Reporter's Transcript."*

[Effective September 1, 1995. Amended effective December 1, 2000; December 1, 2009; December 1, 2021.]

RULE 79–2. EXCLUSIONS FROM RECORD ON APPEAL

The Clerk will not include in the record on appeal the following items unless their inclusion is specifically requested in writing and supported by a brief statement of the reason therefor:

(a) Summonses and returns;

(b) Subpoenas and returns;

(c) Routine procedural motions and orders, such as motions for extensions of or shortening time; and

(d) Routine procedural notices.

[Effective September 1, 1995. Amended effective December 1, 2021.]

RULE 79–3. FILES; CUSTODY AND WITHDRAWAL

All files of the Court shall remain in the custody of the Clerk. The "original copy" of a document filed via ECF is the electronic file stored on ECF. Physical documents belonging to the files of the Court may be taken from the custody of the Clerk only in extraordinary circumstances, by special order of a Judge and with a proper receipt signed by the person obtaining the record or document.

[Effective September 1, 1995. Amended effective December 1, 2021.]

RULE 79–4. CUSTODY AND DISPOSITION OF EXHIBITS AND TRANSCRIPTS

(a) Custody of Exhibits During Trial or Evidentiary Hearing. Unless the Court directs otherwise, each exhibit admitted into evidence during a trial or other evidentiary proceeding shall be held in the custody of the Clerk.

(b) Removal of Exhibits Upon Conclusion of Proceeding. The Court will retain custody of admitted exhibits for 14 days after the conclusion of a proceeding (e.g., receipt of a jury verdict). During this 14 day period, exhibits will be available for public inspection. After this 14 day period expires, any exhibit placed in the custody of the Clerk pursuant to Civil L.R. 79–4(a) must be removed within 5 days by the party that submitted it into evidence. Unless otherwise permitted by the Court, the party that submitted an exhibit into evidence must maintain custody of that exhibit until:

(1) 14 days after expiration of the time for filing a notice of appeal, if no notice of appeal is filed in the proceeding by any party; or

(2) 14 days after a mandate issues from the Court of Appeals, if an appeal was taken by any party to the proceeding.

(c) Disposition of Unclaimed Exhibits. Unless otherwise directed by the Court, the Clerk may destroy or otherwise dispose of exhibits not reclaimed within 21 days after the time set for removal under this rule.

[Effective September 1, 1995. Amended effective December 1, 2009; September 15, 2015; December 1, 2021.]

RULE 79–5. FILING DOCUMENTS UNDER SEAL IN CIVIL CASES

(a) Right of Access. The public has a right of access to the Court's files. This local rule applies in all instances where a party seeks to conceal information from the public by filing a document, or portions of a document, under seal. A party must explore all reasonable alternatives to filing documents under seal, minimize the number of documents filed under seal, and avoid wherever possible sealing entire documents (as opposed to merely redacting the truly sensitive information in a document).

(b) Necessity of Filing a Motion to Seal. A party must file a motion to seal a document at the same time that the party submits the document. Filing a motion to seal permits the party to provisionally file the document under seal, pending the Court's ruling on the motion to seal. A party need not file a motion to seal if a federal statute or a prior court order in the same case expressly authorizes the party to file certain documents (or portions of documents) under seal.

(c) Contents of Motion to Seal. Reference to a stipulation or protective order that allows a party to designate certain documents as confidential is not sufficient to establish that a document, or portions thereof, are sealable. A motion to seal a party's own document (as opposed to a document designated as confidential by another party, as discussed in subsection (f)) must be filed as an Administrative Motion to File Under Seal in conformance with Civil L.R. 7–11. This requirement applies even if the motion is joined by the opposing party. The motion must include the following:

(1) a specific statement of the applicable legal standard and the reasons for keeping a document under seal, including an explanation of:

(i) the legitimate private or public interests that warrant sealing;

(ii) the injury that will result if sealing is denied; and

(iii) why a less restrictive alternative to sealing is not sufficient;

(2) evidentiary support from declarations where necessary; and

(3) a proposed order that is narrowly tailored to seal only the sealable material, and which lists in table format each document or portion thereof that is sought to be sealed.

(d) Procedure for Filing Declarations or Exhibits. Where the document to be sealed is a declaration or an exhibit to a document filed electronically, an otherwise blank page reading "EXHIBIT FILED UNDER SEAL" shall replace the exhibit in the document filed on the public docket, and the exhibit to be filed under seal shall be filed separately as an attachment to the Administrative Motion to File Under Seal.

(e) Procedure for Filing Pleadings and Briefs. Only in rare circumstances should a party seek to file portions of a pleading or brief under seal. For redacted pleadings and briefs, the following procedure applies:

(1) the party shall redact the confidential information from the pleading or brief filed on the public docket; and

(2) the party shall file the unredacted pleading or brief under seal, as an attachment to an Administrative Motion to File Under Seal. The unredacted version must include the phrase "FILED UNDER SEAL" prominently marked on the first page and must highlight the portions for which sealing is sought.

Motions to seal entire pleadings or briefs are strongly disfavored and will be granted only in extraordinary circumstances.

(f) Motion to Consider Whether Another Party's Material Should be Sealed. For any document a party ("Filing Party") seeks to seal because that document has been designated as confidential by another party or non-party (the "Designating Party"), the Filing Party must, instead of filing an Administrative Motion to File Under Seal, file an Administrative Motion to Consider Whether Another Party's Material Should Be Sealed.

(1) This motion must identify each document or portions thereof for which sealing is sought, but the Filing Party need not satisfy the showing required in subsection (c)(1) above.

(2) In the event the Designating Party is not an ECF user in the case, the Filing Party must serve the motion on the Designating Party the same day the motion is filed.

(3) Within 7 days of the motion's filing, the Designating Party must file a statement and/or declaration as described in subsection (c)(1). A failure to file a statement or declaration

may result in the unsealing of the provisionally sealed document without further notice to the Designating Party.

(4) If any party wishes to file a response, it must do so no later than 4 days after the Designating Party files its statement and/or declaration. Responses may not exceed 5 pages absent leave of the Court.

(5) In the event a single document contains various portions that more than one party bears the burden of showing is sealable, the filing party must file separate motions pursuant to 79–5(c) and 79–5(f) as appropriate. Each party must then satisfy its own burden with respect to that portion of the document that it seeks to seal.

(6) Additionally, overly broad requests to seal may result in the denial of the motion.

(g) Effect and Duration of Court's Ruling on Motion to Seal.

(1) When the Court grants a motion to seal or otherwise permits a document to remain under seal, the document will remain under seal until further order of the Court.

(2) When the Court denies a motion to seal, it will determine whether to consider the information sought for sealing and require its public filing, permit its withdrawal without considering the information, or order any other disposition it deems proper.

(3) Parties or non-parties may, at any time, file a motion requesting that the Court unseal a document. If a motion to unseal is filed more than 3 years after the case is closed, there will be a strong presumption that the document will be unsealed.

(h) Manual Filing of Sealed Documents. When a pro se party who is not an e-filer wishes to manually file a document under seal, the pro se party shall place the document and the Administrative Motion to File Under Seal in a sealed envelope, marked with the case caption and the phrase "FILED UNDER SEAL."

[Effective September 1, 1995. Amended effective July 1, 1997; December 1, 2000; January 1, 2005; December 1, 2009; October 1, 2013; December 1, 2021.]

RULE 83. AMENDMENT OF THE LOCAL RULES

RULE 83–1. METHOD OF AMENDMENT

The local rules of this Court may be modified or amended by a majority vote of the active Judges of the Court in accordance with the procedures set forth in this rule. New rules may be proposed or existing rules may be amended at the suggestion of any judge or member of the public, and will generally be vetted by the Local Rules Committee, which will make a recommendation to the Court before a vote is taken. Attorney Advisory Committees will be appointed to advise and assist the Court when called upon to do so by the Local Rules Committee.

[Former Rule 83–3 effective September 1, 1995. Amended effective December 1, 2000; February 3, 2014.]

RULE 83–2. PROCEDURE FOR PUBLIC COMMENT ON LOCAL RULES

(a) Public Submissions. Any person may submit written suggestions for amendments to the local rules at any time. Such suggestions shall be directed to the Chief Judge, who will refer the matter to the Local Rules Committee for consideration, unless the circumstances warrant putting the matter immediately before the full Court.

(b) Publication. Before becoming effective, any proposed substantive modification of the local rules shall be subject to public comment in accordance with Fed. R. Civ. P. 83 and posted on the Court's website. Proposed amendments for form, style, grammar, consistency, or any other non-substantive modifications, need not be submitted for public comment.

[Effective September 1, 1995. Renumbered and amended effective February 3, 2014. Amended effective December 1, 2021.]

ADMIRALTY AND MARITIME LOCAL RULES
RULE 1. TITLE AND SCOPE OF RULES

RULE 1–1. TITLE

These are the Local Rules of Practice in Admiralty and Maritime Claims before the United States District Court for the Northern District of California. They should be cited as "Admir. L.R. __."

[Effective September 1, 1995.]

RULE 1–2. SCOPE

These admiralty local rules apply only to civil proceedings that are governed by the Supplemental Rules for Certain Admiralty and Maritime Claims of the Federal Rules of Civil Procedure ("Fed. R. Civ. P. Supp."): maritime attachment and garnishment; actions in rem; possessory, petitory and partition actions; actions for exoneration from or limitation of liability; and, with respect to Fed. R. Civ. P. Supp. G, to statutory condemnation and forfeiture proceedings analogous to maritime actions in rem. The Federal Rules of Civil Procedure and the civil local rules of this court are also applicable in these proceedings, but to the extent that the civil local rules are inconsistent with these admiralty local rules, these admiralty local rules govern.

Cross Reference

See Fed. R. Civ. P. Supp. A, G.

Commentary

Fed. R. Civ. P. Supp. G, which governs statutory condemnation and forfeiture proceedings analogous to maritime actions in rem, took effect on December 1, 2006. See Admir. L.R. 12, infra. Prior to enactment of Fed. R. Civ. P. Supp. G, statutory condemnation and civil forfeitures procedures were interspersed amongst other Supplemental Admiralty Rules, particularly Fed. R. Civ. P. Supp. C. The effort to create Fed. R. Civ. P. Supp. G resulted from a desire to formulate a comprehensive rule governing civil forfeiture procedures, to consolidate those procedures in a single rule to the extent possible, and to avoid confusion with the admiralty and maritime procedures contained in Fed. R. Civ. P. Supp. A through F.

[Effective September 1, 1995. Amended effective January 1, 2005; August 2008.]

RULE 2. PLEADING IN ADMIRALTY AND MARITIME PROCEEDINGS

RULE 2–1. VERIFICATION OF PLEADINGS

Verification of every pleading, statement of right or interest, or other paper as required by Fed. R. Civ. P. Supp. B, C, D, and G shall be upon oath or solemn affirmation, or in the form provided by 28 U.S.C. § 1746, by a party or by an authorized officer of a corporate party. If no party or authorized corporate officer is present within the district, verification of a complaint may be made by an agent, attorney in fact, or attorney of record, who shall state the sources of the knowledge, information and belief contained in the complaint; declare that the document verified is true to the best of that knowledge, information, and belief; state why verification is not made by the party or an authorized corporate officer; and state that the affiant is authorized to so verify. A verification not made by a party or authorized corporate officer will be deemed to have been made by the party as if verified personally. If the verification was not made by a party or authorized corporate officer, any interested party may move, with or without requesting a stay, for the personal oath of a party or an authorized corporate officer, which shall be procured by commission or as otherwise ordered.

Cross Reference

See 28 U.S.C. § 1746.

[Effective September 1, 1995. Amended effective January 1, 2005; August, 2008.]

RULE 2–2. ITEMIZED DEMAND FOR JUDGMENT

The demand for judgment in every complaint filed under Fed. R. Civ. P. Supp. B or C, except a demand for a salvage award, shall allege the dollar amount of the debt or damages for which the action was commenced. The demand for judgment shall also allege the nature of other items of damage. The amount of the special bond posted under Fed. R. Civ. P. Supp. E(5)(a) may be based upon these allegations.

Cross Reference

See Fed. R. Civ. P. Supp. B, C, E(5)(a).

[Effective September 1, 1995.]

RULE 2–3. AFFIDAVIT THAT DEFENDANT IS NOT FOUND WITHIN THE DISTRICT

The affidavit required by Fed. R. Civ. P. Supp. B(1) to accompany the complaint seeking a money judgment shall describe the efforts made by and on behalf of plaintiff to find the defendant within the district.

Cross Reference

See Fed. R. Civ. P. Supp. B(1).

[Effective September 1, 1995. Amended effective August, 2008.]

RULE 2–4. USE OF STATE PROCEDURES

When the plaintiff invokes a state procedure in order to attach or garnish as permitted by the Federal Rules of Civil Procedure or Fed. R. Civ. P. Supp. B(1)(e), the process of attachment or garnishment shall identify the state law upon which the attachment or garnishment is based.

Cross Reference

See Fed. R. Civ. P. 64, Fed. R. Civ. P. Supp. B(1)(e).

[Effective August, 2008.]

RULE 3.   JUDICIAL AUTHORIZATION AND PROCESS

RULE 3–1.   REVIEW BY JUDGE

(a) **Authorization to Issue Process.** Before the clerk will issue a summons and process of arrest, attachment or garnishment to any party, including intervenors, under Fed. R. Civ. P. Supp. B and C, the pleadings, the affidavit required by Fed. R. Civ. P. Supp. B and accompanying supporting papers must be reviewed by a judge, as defined in Civil L.R. 1–5(*l*). If the judge finds the conditions set forth in Fed. R. Civ. P. Supp. B or C exist, the judge shall authorize the clerk to issue appropriate process. Supplemental process or alias process may thereafter be issued by the clerk upon application without further order of the court.

Cross Reference

See Fed. R. Civ. P. Supp. B, C.

(b) **Exigent Circumstances.** If the plaintiff or his attorney certifies by affidavit submitted to the clerk that exigent circumstances make review impracticable, the clerk shall issue a summons and warrant of arrest or process of attachment and garnishment.

Cross Reference

See Fed. R. Civ. P. Supp. B, C.

(c) **Personal Appearance.** Unless otherwise required by the judge, the review by the judge will not require the presence of the applicant or its attorney but shall be based upon the pleadings and other papers submitted on behalf of that party.

(d) **Order.** Upon approving the application for arrest, attachment or garnishment, the judge will issue an order to the clerk authorizing the clerk to issue an order for arrest, attachment or garnishment. The proposed form of order authorizing the arrest, attachment or garnishment, and the order of arrest, attachment or garnishment shall be submitted with the other documents for review.

(e) **Request for Review.** Except in case of exigent circumstances, application for review shall be made by filing a Notice of Request for Review in Accordance with Fed. R. Civ. P. Supp. B or C with the clerk and stating therein the process sought and any time requirements within which the request must be reviewed. The clerk shall contact the judge to whom the matter is assigned to arrange for the necessary review. It will be the duty of the applicant to ensure that the application has been reviewed, and upon approval, presented to the clerk for issuance of the appropriate order.

[Effective September 1, 1995. Amended effective August, 2008.]

RULE 3–2.   WHEN ASSIGNED JUDGE UNAVAILABLE

If the judge to whom a case under these admiralty local rules has been assigned is not available, as defined in Civil L.R. 1–5(n), any matter pertaining to arrest, attachment, garnishment, security or release may be presented to any other judge in the district without reassigning the case.

[Effective September 1, 1995.]

RULE 3–3.   RETURN DATE

In an action under Fed. R. Civ. P. Supp. D, a judge may order that the claim and answer be filed on a date earlier than 21 days after arrest. The order may also set a date for expedited hearing of the action.

[Effective September 1, 1995. Amended effective December 1, 2009.]

RULE 3–4.   PROCESS HELD IN ABEYANCE

If a party does not wish the process to be issued at the time of filing the action, the party shall request that issuance of process be held in abeyance. It will not be the responsibility of the clerk or the marshal to ensure that process is issued at a later date.

Cross Reference

See Fed. R. Civ. P. Supp. E(3)(b).

[Effective September 1, 1995. Amended effective August, 2008.]

RULE 4.   ATTACHMENT, GARNISHMENT AND ARREST OF PROPERTY

RULE 4–1.   ORDER TO SHOW CAUSE REGARDING INTANGIBLE PROPERTY

The summons issued pursuant to Fed. R. Civ. P. Supp. C(3) shall direct the person having control of intangible property to show cause, no later than 14 days after service, why the intangible property should not be delivered to the court to abide the judgment. Pursuant to ex parte motion made under Civil L.R. 7–11, for good cause shown, a judge may lengthen or shorten the time. Service of the summons has the effect of an arrest of the intangible property and brings it within the control of the court. The person who is served may deliver or pay over to the marshal the intangible property proceeded against to the extent sufficient to satisfy the plaintiff's claim. If such delivery or payment is made, the person served is excused from the duty to show cause. Claimants Persons * asserting a right of possession or any ownership interest in the property may show cause as provided in Fed. R. Civ. P. Supp. C(6) why the property should not be delivered to or retained by the court.

[Effective September 1, 1995. Amended effective August, 2008; December 1, 2009.]

* So in original.

Cross Reference

See Fed. R. Civ. P. Supp. C, Fed. R. Civ. P. 6(a).

RULE 4–2. NOTICE OF ACTION AND ARREST

(a) Publication. The public notice specified by Fed. R. Civ. P. Supp. C(4) shall be published once in a newspaper named in Civil L.R. 77–4, and plaintiff's attorney shall file a copy of the notice as it was published with the clerk. The notice shall contain:

(1) The court, title, and number of the action;

(2) The date of the arrest;

(3) The identity of the property arrested;

(4) The name, address, and telephone number of the attorney for plaintiff;

(5) A statement that any person who asserts a right of possession or any ownership interest in the property pursuant to Fed. R. Civ. P. Supp. C(6) must file a verified statement of right or interest within 14 days of the execution of process or within the period specified by court order;

(6) A statement that any person required to file a verified statement of right or interest must also file and serve an answer to the complaint within 21 days after filing the statement of interest or right, and that otherwise, default may be entered and condemnation ordered;

(7) A statement that applications for intervention under Fed. R. Civ. P. 24 by persons claiming maritime liens or other interests against the property shall be filed within the time fixed by the court; and

(8) The name, address, and telephone number of the marshal.

(b) Filing of Proof of Publication. No later than thirty 30 days after the date of publication, plaintiff shall cause to be filed with the clerk sworn proof of publication by or on behalf of the publisher of the newspaper in which notice was published, together with a copy of the publication or reproduction thereof.

Cross Reference

See Fed. R. Civ. P. Supp. C(3), Fed. R. Civ. P. 6(a).

[Effective September 1, 1995. Amended effective January 1, 2005; August, 2008; December 1, 2009.]

RULE 4–3. SERVICE BY MARSHAL— WHEN REQUIRED

Only a marshal shall arrest or attach a vessel or tangible property aboard a vessel. If other tangible or intangible property is the subject of the action, the clerk may deliver the warrant to a marshal, a person or organization contracted with by the United States, a person specially appointed by the court for that purpose, or, if the action is brought by the United States, any officer or employee of the United States.

Cross Reference

See Fed. R. Civ. P. Supp. B(1)(d)(i), C(3)(b).

[Effective September 1, 1995. Amended effective August 2008.]

RULE 4–4. INSTRUCTIONS TO THE MARSHAL

The party who requests a warrant of arrest or process of attachment or garnishment shall provide instructions to the marshal or the person authorized to serve the warrant pursuant to Admir. L.R. 4–3.

[Effective September 1, 1995.]

RULE 4–5. PROPERTY IN POSSESSION OF UNITED STATES OFFICER

When the property to be attached or arrested is in the custody of an employee or officer of the United States, the marshal will deliver a copy of the complaint and warrant of arrest or summons and process of attachment or garnishment to that officer or employee if present, and otherwise to the custodian of the property. The marshal will instruct the officer, employee or custodian to retain custody of the property until ordered to do otherwise by a judge.

[Effective September 1, 1995.]

RULE 4–6. SECURITY DEPOSIT FOR ARREST OR ATTACHMENT OF VESSELS

The first party who seeks arrest or attachment of a vessel or property aboard a vessel shall deposit with the marshal the sum estimated by the marshal to be sufficient to cover the expenses of the marshal including, but not limited to, dockage, keepers, maintenance and insurance for at least 14 days. The marshal is not required to execute process until the deposit is made. The party shall advance additional sums from time to time as requested to cover the marshal's estimated expenses until the property is released or disposed of as provided in Fed. R. Civ. P. Supp. E.

[Effective September 1, 1995. Amended effective August, 2008; December 1, 2009.]

RULE 4–7. UNDERTAKINGS IN LIEU OF ARREST

If, before or after commencement of suit, plaintiff accepts any written undertaking to respond on behalf of the vessel or other property sued in return for foregoing its arrest or stipulating to the release of such vessel or other property, the undertaking shall become a defendant in place of the vessel or other property sued and be deemed referred to under the name of the vessel or other property in any pleading, order or judgment in the action referred to in the undertaking. The preceding shall apply to any such undertaking, subject to its own terms and whether or not it complies with Civil L.R. 65.1–1 and has been approved by a judge or clerk.

Cross Reference

See Fed. R. Civ. P. Supp. E(5).

[Effective September 1, 1995. Amended effective August 2008.]

RULE 4–8. ADVERSARY HEARING

The adversary hearing following arrest or attachment or garnishment that is called for in Fed. R. Civ. P. Supp. E(4)(f) shall be conducted upon 3 court days written notice to plaintiff, unless otherwise ordered. This local rule shall have no application to suits for seamen's wages when process is issued upon a certification of sufficient cause filed pursuant to Title 46, U.S.C. §§ 603 and 604 or to action by the United States for forfeitures.

Cross Reference

See Fed. R. Civ. P. Supp. E(4)(f), Fed. R. Civ. P. 6(a).

[Effective September 1, 1995. Amended effective August 2008.]

RULE 5. DEFENSE; LIMITATION OF LIABILITY

RULE 5–1. DEPOSIT OF SECURITY FOR COSTS

The amount of security for costs under Fed. R. Civ. P. Supp. F(1) shall be $1,000 unless otherwise ordered, and may be combined with the security for value and interest.

[Effective September 1, 1995.]

RULE 5–2. ORDER OF PROOF AT TRIAL

Where the vessel interests seeking statutory limitation of liability have raised the statutory defense by way of answer or complaint, the plaintiff in the former or the damage claimant in the latter shall proceed with its proof first, as is normal at civil trials.

[Effective September 1, 1995.]

RULE 6. JUDGMENT, DEFAULT AND DEFAULT JUDGMENT

RULE 6–1. DEFAULT IN ACTION IN REM

(a) Notice Required. A party seeking a default judgment in an action in rem must show that due notice of the action and arrest of the property has been given:

(1) In actions subject to Fed. R. Civ. P. Supp. G:

i. Through execution of process in accordance with Fed. R. Civ. P. Supp. G(3); and

ii. In accordance with Fed. R. Civ. P. Supp. G(4).

(2) In actions not subject to Fed. R. Civ. P. Supp. G:

i. By publication as required in Fed. R. Civ. P. Supp. C(4);

ii. By service upon the master or other person having custody of the property; and

iii. By service under Fed. R. Civ. P. 5(b) upon every other person who has not appeared in the action and is known to have an interest in the property.

(b) Persons With Recorded Interests.

(1) In actions subject to Fed. R. Civ. P. Supp. G:

i. In accordance with Fed. R. Civ. P. Supp. G(4).

(2) In actions not subject to Fed. R. Civ. P. Supp. G:

i. If the defendant property is a vessel documented under the laws of the United States, plaintiff must attempt to notify all persons named in the United States Coast Guard Certificate of Ownership;

ii. If the defendant property is a vessel numbered as provided in the Federal Boat Safety Act, plaintiff must attempt to notify the persons named in the records of the issuing authority;

iii. If the defendant property is of such character that there exists a governmental registry of recorded property interests or security interests in the property, the plaintiff must attempt to notify all persons named in the records of each such registry.

(c) Failure to Give Notice. Failure to give notice as provided by this local rule shall be grounds for setting aside the default under applicable rules, but shall not affect title to property sold pursuant to order of sale or judgment.

[Effective September 1, 1995. Amended effective August, 2008.]

RULE 6–2. ENTRY OF DEFAULT AND DEFAULT JUDGMENT

After the time for filing an answer has expired, the plaintiff may apply for entry of default under Fed. R. Civ. P. 55(a). Judgment may be entered under Fed. R. Civ. P. 55(b) at any time after default has been entered. Default will be entered upon a showing that:

(a) In actions subject to Fed. R. Civ. P. Supp. G:

(1) Notice has been given as required by Admir. L.R. 6–1(a)(1) and (b)(1); (2) No one has filed timely and responsive pleadings pursuant to the requirements of Fed. R. Civ. P. Supp. G(5).

(b) In actions not subject to Fed. R. Civ. P. Supp. G:

(1) Notice has been given as required by Admir. L.R. 6–1(a)(2) and (b)(2);

(2) The time to answer has expired; and

(3) No one has filed a verified statement of right of possession or ownership interest in the property.

[Effective September 1, 1995. Amended effective January 1, 2005; August, 2008.]

RULE 6–3.   RATE OF PREJUDGMENT INTEREST ALLOWED

Unless a judge directs otherwise or as provided by statute, prejudgment interest shall be awarded at the rate authorized in 28 U.S.C. § 1961, providing for interest on judgments.

Cross Reference

See Fed. R. Civ. P. 55, Fed. R. Civ. P. Supp. C and G.

[Effective September 1, 1995.   Amended effective August, 2008.]

RULE 7.   SECURITY

RULE 7–1.   SECURITY FOR COSTS

In an action under the Supplemental Rules for Certain Admiralty and Maritime Claims of the Federal Rules of Civil Procedure, a party may move upon notice to all parties for an order to compel an adverse party to post security for costs with the clerk pursuant to Fed. R. Civ. P. Supp. E(2)(b). Unless otherwise ordered, the amount of security shall be $1,000. The party so ordered shall post the security within 7 days after the order is entered. A party who fails to post security when due may not participate further in the proceedings. A party may move for an order increasing the amount of security for costs.

Cross Reference

See Fed. R. Civ. P. Supp. E.

[Effective September 1, 1995.   Amended effective August, 2008; December 1, 2009.]

RULE 7–2.   APPRAISAL

An order for appraisal of property so that security may be given or altered will be entered by the clerk at the request of any interested party. If the parties do not agree in writing upon an appraiser, a judge will appoint the appraiser. The appraiser shall be sworn to the faithful and impartial discharge of the appraiser's duties before any federal or state officer authorized by law to administer oaths. The appraiser shall give one day's notice of the time and place of making the appraisal to counsel of record. The appraiser shall promptly file the appraisal with the clerk and serve it upon counsel of record. The appraiser's fee will be paid by the moving party, unless otherwise ordered or agreed. The appraiser's fee is a taxable cost of the action.

Cross Reference

See Fed. R. Civ. P. Supp. E(5), Fed. R. Civ. P. Supp. F(7).

[Effective September 1, 1995.   Amended effective August, 2008.]

RULE 8.   INTERVENTION

RULE 8–1.   INTERVENOR'S LIEN OR OTHER NON–POSSESSORY OR NON–OWNERSHIP CLAIM IN ADMIRALTY AND MARITIME CASES

(a) **Filing of Intervening Complaint.** When a vessel or other property has been arrested, attached or garnished in an action filed pursuant to Fed. R. Civ. P. Supp. B, C(6), or D, and the vessel or property is in the hands of the marshal or custodian substituted therefor,* anyone having a lien or other non-possessory or non-ownership based claim against the vessel or property is required to present said claim by filing an intervening complaint, and not by filing an original complaint, unless otherwise ordered by a judge. The clerk shall promptly deliver a conformed copy of the complaint in intervention and the intervener's warrant of arrest or process of attachment or garnishment to the marshal, who shall deliver the same to the vessel or custodian of the property. Interveners shall thereafter be subject to the rights and obligations of parties, and the vessel or property shall stand arrested, attached or garnished by the intervener. An intervener shall not be required to advance a security deposit to the marshal.

(b) **Sharing Marshal's Fees and Expenses.** An intervener shall owe a debt to the first plaintiff, enforceable on motion, consisting of the intervener's share of the marshal's fees and expenses in the proportion that the intervener's claim bears to the sum of all the claims. If a party plaintiff permits vacation of an arrest, attachment or garnishment, remaining plaintiffs share the responsibility to the marshal for fees and expenses in proportion to the remaining claims and for the duration of the marshal's custody because of each claim.

[Effective September 1, 1995.   Amended effective January 1, 2005; August, 2008.]

* So in original.

RULE 9.   CUSTODY SALE AND RELEASE OF PROPERTY

RULE 9–1.   CUSTODY OF PROPERTY

(a) **Safekeeping of Property.** When a vessel, cargo or other property is brought into the marshal's custody by arrest or attachment, the marshal shall arrange for adequate safekeeping, which may include the placing of keepers on or near the vessel. A substitute custodian in place of the marshal may be appointed by order of the court.

(b) **Insurance.** The marshal may procure insurance to protect the marshal, deputies, keepers and substitute custodians, from liabilities assumed in arresting and holding the vessel, cargo or other property, and in performing whatever services may be undertaken to protect the vessel, cargo or other property, and to maintain the court's custody. The party who applies for removal of the vessel, cargo or other property to another location, for designation of a substitute custodian, or for other relief that will require an additional premium, shall reimburse the marshal therefor. The premiums charged for the liability insurance are taxable as administrative costs while the vessel, cargo or other property is in custody of the court.

(c) Vessel Operations. Following arrest or attachment of a vessel, no cargo handling, repairs or movement may be made without an order of court. The applicant for such an order shall give notice to the marshal and to all parties of record. Upon proof of adequate insurance coverage of the applicant to indemnify the marshal for his or her liability, the court may direct the marshal to permit cargo handling, repairs, movement of the vessel or other operations. Before or after the marshal has taken custody of a vessel, cargo or other property, any party of record may move for an order to dispense with keepers or to remove or place the vessel, cargo or other property at a specified facility, to designate a substitute custodian, or for similar relief. Notice of the motion shall be given to the marshal and to all parties of record. The judge will require that adequate insurance on the property will be maintained by the successor to the marshal, before issuing the order to change arrangements.

(d) Claims by Suppliers for Payment of Charges. A person who furnishes supplies or services to a vessel, cargo or other property in custody of the court who has not been paid and claims the right to payment as an expense of administration shall file an invoice with the clerk in the form of a verified claim at any time before the vessel, cargo or other property is released or sold. The supplier must serve copies of the claim on the marshal, substitute custodian if one has been appointed, and all parties of record. The court may consider the claims individually or schedule a single hearing for all claims.

[Effective September 1, 1995.]

RULE 9–2. SALE OF PROPERTY IN ACTIONS NOT SUBJECT TO FED. R. CIV. P. SUPP.G

(a) Notice. Notice of sale of arrested or attached property shall be published in one or more newspapers to be specified in the order for sale. Unless otherwise ordered by a judge upon a showing of urgency or impracticality or unless otherwise provided by law, such notice shall be published for at least 6 consecutive publication days before the date of sale.

(b) Payment of Bid. Unless otherwise provided in the order, in all public auction sales by the marshal under orders of sale in admiralty and maritime claims, the marshal shall require of the last and highest bidder at the sale a minimum deposit in cash, certified check or cashier's check, of the full purchase price if it does not exceed $1,000, and otherwise $1,000 or ten percent of the bid, whichever is greater. The balance, if any, of the purchase price shall be paid in cash, certified check or cashier's check before confirmation of the sale or within 3 court days of the dismissal of any opposition which may have been filed. Notwithstanding the above, a

plaintiff or intervening plaintiff foreclosing a properly recorded preferred mortgage on, or other valid security interest in the vessel may bid, without payment of cash, certified check or cashier's check, up to the total amount of the secured indebtedness as established by affidavit filed and served by that party on all other parties no later than 14 days prior to the date of sale.

(c) Report and Confirmation. At the conclusion of the sale, the marshal shall forthwith file a written report to the court of the fact of sale, the price obtained and the name and address of the buyer. The clerk of the court shall endorse upon such report the time and date of its filing. If within 3 court days no written objection is filed, the sale shall stand confirmed as of course, without the necessity of any affirmative action thereon by the court and the clerk upon request shall so state to the marshal in writing; except that no sale shall stand confirmed until the buyer has complied fully with the terms of his purchase. If no opposition to the sale is filed, the expenses of keeping the property pending confirmation of sale shall be charged against the party bearing expenses before the sale (subject to taxation as costs), except that if confirmation is delayed by the purchaser's failure to pay any balance which is due on the price, the cost of keeping the property subsequent to the 3–day period hereinabove specified shall be borne by the purchaser.

(d) Penalty for Late Payment of Balance. A successful bidder who fails to pay the balance of the bid within the time allowed under these local rules or a different time specified by the court shall also pay the marshal the costs of keeping the property from the date payment of the balance was due to the date the bidder pays the balance and takes delivery of the property. Unless otherwise ordered by the court, the marshal shall refuse to release the property until this additional charge is paid.

(e) Penalty for Default in Payment of Balance. A successful bidder who fails to pay the balance of the bid within the time allowed is in default and the court may at any time thereafter order a sale to the second highest bidder or order a new sale as appropriate. Any sum deposited by the bidder in default shall be applied to pay any additional costs incurred by the marshal by reason of the default including costs incident to resale. The balance of the deposit, if any, shall be retained in the registry subject to further order of the court, and the court shall be given written notice of its existence whenever the registry deposits are reviewed.

(f) Opposition to Sale. A party filing an opposition to the sale, whether seeking the reception of a higher bid or a new public sale by the marshal, shall give prompt notice to all other parties and to the purchaser. Such party shall also prior to filing an opposition, secure the marshal's endorsement upon it acknowledging deposit with the marshal of the necessary expense of keeping the property for at least 7 days. Pending the court's determination of the opposition, such party shall also advance any further expense at such times and in such amounts as the marshal shall request, or as the court orders upon application of the marshal or the opposing party. Such expense may later be subject to taxation as costs. In the event of failure to make such advance, the opposition shall fail without necessity for affirmative action thereon by the court.

If the opposition fails, the expense of keeping the property during its pendency shall be borne by the party filing the opposition.

(g) Disposition of Deposits.

(1) *Objection Sustained.* If an objection is sustained, sums deposited by the successful bidder will be returned to the bidder forthwith. The sum deposited by the objector will be applied to pay the fees and expenses incurred by the marshal in keeping the property until it is resold, and any balance remaining shall be returned to the objector. The objector will be reimbursed for the expense of keeping the property from the proceeds of a subsequent sale.

(2) *Objection Overruled.* If the objection is overruled, the sum deposited by the objector will be applied to pay the expense of keeping the property from the day the objection was filed until the day the sale is confirmed, and any balance remaining will be returned to the objector forthwith.

Cross Reference

See Fed. R. Civ. P. Supp. E, Fed. R. Civ. P. 6(a).

[Effective September 1, 1995. Amended effective August, 2008; December 1, 2009.]

RULE 10.   DESERTING SEAMAN CASES

RULE 10–1.   SERVICE

Upon filing a verified petition for return of wages deposited in the registry of the court by a Coast Guard official to whom the duties of shipping commissioner have been delegated pursuant to the provisions of 46 U.S.C. § 11505, a copy of the petition shall be served forthwith on the United States Attorney and a copy mailed to the Attorney General of the United States, after which a sworn return of such service and mailing shall be filed.

[Effective September 1, 1995.]

RULE 10–2.   TIME TO PLEAD

The United States has 21 days after receipt of a copy of the petition by the United States Attorney in which to file its responsive pleading and claim.

[Effective September 1, 1995. Amended effective December 1, 2009.]

RULE 11.   DECEASED SEAMEN

RULE 11–1.   RECEIPT OF MONEY, PROPERTY OR WAGES

When the court receives the money, property or wages of a deceased seaman, pursuant to 46 U.S.C. §§ 10705–10707, the clerk of the court shall receive any cash or check and perform an inventory of the money, property or wages. The next of kin of the deceased seaman may claim the money, property or wages by filing with the clerk a Kinsman's Petition for Wages and Effects of Deceased Seaman.

[Effective September 1, 1995.]

RULE 11–2.   DISPOSITION OF UNCLAIMED MONEY, PROPERTY OR WAGES

If a claim for the money, property or wages of a deceased seaman has not been substantiated and allowed 6 years after receipt of the money, property or wages, or if, 6 years after its receipt it appears to the court that no claim will have to be satisfied, any property shall be sold; and the money, wages and proceeds from the sale shall be deposited by the clerk in the United States Treasury fund for unclaimed monies.

[Effective September 1, 1995.]

RULE 12.   FORFEITURE ACTIONS IN REM

RULE 12–1.   SCOPE

Civil forfeiture actions in rem arising from a federal statute shall proceed pursuant to Fed. R. Civ. P. Supp. G.

Cross Reference

See Fed. R. Civ. P. Supp. G.

[Effective August, 2008. Renumbered effective December 1, 2009.]

LOCAL RULES FOR ALTERNATIVE DISPUTE RESOLUTION

RULE 1. PURPOSE AND SCOPE OF RULES

RULE 1–1. TITLE

These are the Local Rules for Alternative Dispute Resolution in the United States District Court for the Northern District of California. They should be referred to as "ADR L.R. ____."

[Effective January 1, 2009.]

RULE 1–2. PURPOSE AND SCOPE

(a) **Purpose.** The Court recognizes that full, formal litigation of claims can impose large economic burdens on parties and can delay resolution of disputes for considerable periods. The Court also recognizes that sometimes an alternative dispute resolution procedure can improve the quality of justice by improving the parties' clarity of understanding of their case, their access to evidence, and their satisfaction with the process and result. The Court adopts these ADR Local Rules to make available to litigants a broad range of court-sponsored ADR processes to provide quicker, less expensive and potentially more satisfying alternatives to continuing litigation without impairing the quality of justice or the right to trial. The Court offers diverse ADR services to enable parties to use the ADR process that promises to deliver the greatest benefits to their particular case. In administering these Local Rules and the ADR program, the Court will take appropriate steps to assure that no referral to ADR results in imposing on any party an unfair or unreasonable economic burden.

Commentary

The Alternative Dispute Resolution Act of 1998, 28 U.S.C. §§ 651–58, requires each federal district court to authorize by local rule the use of at least one ADR process in all civil actions. In accordance with § 651(c), the Court has examined the effectiveness of its ADR programs and has adopted improvements consistent with the Act.

(b) **Scope.** These ADR Local Rules are effective May 1, 2018, and shall govern actions pending or commenced on or after that date. These rules supplement the Civil Local Rules of the Court and, except as otherwise indicated, apply to all civil actions filed in this Court. Cases subject to these ADR Local rules also remain subject to the other local rules of the Court.

(c) **Magistrate Judges Consent Cases.** In cases initially assigned to a Magistrate Judge, even prior to the filing of consents by all parties to jurisdiction by a Magistrate Judge under 28 U.S.C. § 636(c), the Magistrate Judge shall have the authority to refer cases to ADR programs and to grant relief from the requirements of these ADR local rules. Consents or declinations shall be filed in advance of any Mediation, ENE, or settlement conference proceeding under these rules.

[Effective January 1, 2009. Amended effective December 1, 2009; September 15, 2015; May 1, 2018.]

RULE 2. GENERAL PROVISIONS

RULE 2–1. ADR UNIT

(a) **Staff and Responsibilities.** The ADR Unit shall consist of a Director of ADR Programs and such attorneys, case administrators and support personnel as the Court may authorize. The ADR Director and legal staff shall be attorneys with expertise in ADR procedures. The ADR Unit shall be responsible for designing, implementing, administering and evaluating the Court's ADR Programs. These responsibilities extend to educating litigants, lawyers, Judges and Court staff about the ADR Program and rules. In addition, the ADR Unit shall be responsible for overseeing, screening and training neutrals to serve in the Court's ADR programs. The ADR Director and legal staff also serve as neutrals in selected cases.

(b) **ADR Website and Handbook.** The ADR Unit's website, located at cand.uscourts.gov/adr, contains information about the Court's ADR processes and their comparative benefits, answers to frequently asked questions, various forms approved by the Court and information about becoming a neutral in the Court's programs.

(c) **Contacting the ADR Unit.** The address, phone and fax numbers, and email address of the ADR Unit are:

U.S. District Court–ADR Unit
450 Golden Gate Avenue, 16th Floor
San Francisco, CA 94102
Telephone: (415) 522–2199
Fax: (415) 522–4112
General email: ADR@cand.uscourts.gov

Requests to be excused from appearing at an ADR session:
ADR_Attendance@cand.uscourts.gov
Reports of violations of the ADR Local Rules:
ADR_RulesViolations@cand.uscourts.gov

Commentary

The Court encourages litigants and counsel to consult the ADR website and to contact the ADR Unit to discuss the suitability of ADR options for their cases or for assistance in tailoring an ADR process to a specific case.

[Effective January 1, 2009. Amended effective July 2, 2012; September 15, 2015.]

RULE 2–2. ADR MAGISTRATE JUDGE

The Court shall designate one of its magistrate judges as the ADR Magistrate Judge. The ADR Magistrate Judge is responsible for overseeing the ADR Unit, consulting with the ADR Director and legal staff on matters of policy, program design and evaluation, education, training and administration. The ADR Magistrate Judge shall rule on all requests to be excused from appearing in person at ENE and Mediation sessions, and shall hear and determine all complaints alleging violations of these ADR local rules. If the ADR Magistrate Judge is unavailable or precluded from hearing and determining an attendance request or complaint alleging violations of these ADR local rules because of a conflict of interest or because he or she is also the case's assigned Judge, the matter shall be referred to the Chief Magistrate Judge. If the Chief Magistrate Judge is unavailable or precluded from hearing and determining the matter, it shall be referred to the General Duty Judge. If the General Duty Judge is unavailable or precluded from hearing and determining the matter, it shall be referred to the Chief Judge.

Cross Reference

See ADR L.R. 4–9, 5–10 and 6–10 for attendance. See ADR L.R. 2–4(c) for violations.

[Effective January 1, 2009. Amended effective September 15, 2015.]

RULE 2–3. REFERRAL TO ADR PROGRAM BY STIPULATION, MOTION OR ORDER

Subject to pertinent jurisdictional and resource constraints, a case may be referred to a Court ADR process by order of the assigned Judge following a stipulation by all parties, by motion of a party under Civil L.R. 7, or on the Judge's initiative. A stipulation and proposed order selecting an ADR process must (1) designate the specific ADR process the parties have selected, (2) specify the time frame within which the ADR process will be completed, and (3) set forth any other information the parties would like the Court to know. The parties may use the form provided by the Court.

Commentary

A form stipulation and proposed order is available on the ADR website: cand.uscourts.gov/adr. The Clerk's Office will print copies upon request for pro se parties.

Cross Reference

See ADR L.R. 3–4 for Court ADR Processes and ADR L.R. 5–2 and 6–2 for eligible cases.

[Effective January 1, 2009. Amended effective July 2, 2012.]

RULE 2–4. VIOLATION OF THE ADR LOCAL RULES

(a) **Informal Resolution.** Without prejudice to the use of more formal procedures set forth in sections (b) and (c) below, a complaint alleging that any person or party, including the neutral, has materially violated any of the ADR local rules other than ADR L.R. 7 (pertaining to judicially hosted settlement conferences) may be presented informally to the ADR Director, or to such legal staff as the Director may designate, who will attempt to resolve the matter to the satisfaction of all concerned.

(b) **Reporting Violation.**

(1) *Complaints Alleging Material Violations.* A formal complaint alleging that any person or party, including the neutral, has materially violated any of the ADR local rules other than ADR L.R. 7 (pertaining to judicially hosted settlement conferences) must be presented in writing directly to the ADR Magistrate Judge in care of the ADR Unit at the address listed in ADR L.R. 2–1(c), or emailed to ADR_Rules Violations@cand.uscourts.gov. Such a letter of complaint must be accompanied by a competent declaration. Copies of the letter of complaint and declaration must be sent contemporaneously to all other parties and the neutral (if a neutral has been appointed). The letter of complaint and declaration must be marked "Confidential–Not to be Filed" and must neither be filed nor disclosed to the assigned Judge.

(2) *Report by Neutral.* A neutral who perceives a material violation of these ADR local rules shall make a written report directly to the ADR Magistrate Judge in care of the ADR Unit at the address listed in ADR L.R. 2–1(c), or emailed to ADR_RulesViolations@cand.uscourts.gov and contemporaneously provide copies to all counsel. Such report must be marked "Confidential–Not to be Filed" and must neither be filed nor disclosed to the assigned Judge.

(c) **Proceeding in Response to Complaint or Report of Violation and Sanctions.** If, upon receiving an appropriately presented and supported complaint or report of a material violation of these ADR local rules, the ADR Magistrate Judge determines that the matter warrants further proceedings, the ADR Magistrate Judge may refer the matter to the ADR Director to explore the possibility of resolving the complaint informally in accordance with section (a) above. If no such referral is made, or if the matter is not resolved informally, the ADR Magistrate Judge shall take appropriate action. The ADR Magistrate Judge may issue an order to show cause why sanctions should not be imposed. The response to any such order to show cause, and any additional briefing on the matter, shall be marked "Confidential–Not to be Filed," must neither be filed nor disclosed to the assigned Judge, and must be presented in writing directly to the ADR Magistrate Judge in care of the ADR Unit at the address listed in ADR L.R. 2–1(c), or emailed to ADR_RulesViolations@cand.uscourts. gov, with copies sent contemporaneously to all other parties and the neutral (if a neutral has been appointed). Any such sanctions proceedings shall be conducted on the record but under seal. The ADR Magistrate Judge will afford all interested parties an opportunity to be heard before deciding whether to impose sanctions. Any objections to the ADR Magistrate Judge's order resolving the sanctions issue must be made by motion under Civil L.R. 7 before the General Duty Judge, unless the General Duty Judge is the assigned Judge or is otherwise precluded from hearing the matter, in which case the objections shall be made to the Chief Judge. Any such objection shall be marked "Confidential–Not to be Filed" and must be delivered directly to the appropriate Judge in care of the ADR Unit at the address listed in ADR L.R. 2–1(c), or emailed to ADR_RulesViolations@cand.uscourts.gov within 14 days of the filing of the ADR Magistrate Judge's order resolving the sanctions issue. Such objection shall not be filed or disclosed to the assigned Judge, and shall be served immediately on the ADR Magistrate Judge, all other counsel, the neutral and the ADR Unit.

Commentary

The Court encourages parties to use the informal resolution procedure set forth in ADR L.R. 2–4(a) prior to submitting a formal complaint. Under *Zambrano v. City of Tustin*, 885 F.2d 1473 (9th Cir. 1989), the district court may impose fee shifting sanctions for a violation of a local rule only on a finding of bad faith, willfulness, recklessness, or gross negligence.

[Effective January 1, 2009. Amended effective December 1, 2009; September 15, 2015; May 1, 2018.]

RULE 2–5. NEUTRALS

(a) Panel. The ADR Unit shall maintain a panel of neutrals serving in the Court's ADR programs. Neutrals will be selected from time to time by the Court from applications submitted by lawyers willing to serve or by other persons as set forth in section (b)(3) below. Neutrals will be appointed to renewable terms of 4 years. The legal staff of the ADR Unit may serve as neutrals.

(b) Qualifications and Training. Each lawyer serving as a neutral in a Court ADR program must be a member of the bar of this Court or a member of the faculty of an accredited law school and must successfully complete initial and periodic training as required by the Court. Additional minimum requirements for serving on the Court's panel of neutrals, which the Court may modify in individual circumstances for good cause, are as follows:

(1) *ENE Evaluators.* Evaluators must have been admitted to the practice of law for at least 15 years and have considerable experience with civil litigation in federal court. Evaluators must also have substantial expertise in the subject matter of the cases assigned to them and must have the temperament and training to listen well, facilitate communication across party lines and, if called upon, assist the parties with settlement negotiations.

(2) *Mediators.* Lawyer mediators must have been admitted to the practice of law for at least 7 years and must be knowledgeable about civil litigation in federal court. Mediators shall have strong Mediation process skills and the temperament and training to listen well, facilitate communication across party lines and assist the parties with settlement negotiations. Mediators who are not lawyers may also be selected to serve on the Court's panel of mediators if they have appropriate professional credentials in another discipline and are knowledgeable about civil litigation in federal court. A non-lawyer mediator may be appointed to a case only with the consent of the parties.

(c) Oath. Persons serving as neutrals in any of the Court's ADR programs must take the oath or affirmation prescribed in 28 U.S.C. § 453.

(d) Disqualification of Neutrals.

(1) *Applicable Standards.* No person may serve as a neutral in a case in a Court ADR program in violation of:

(A) the standards set forth in 28 U.S.C. § 455, or

(B) any applicable standard of professional responsibility or rule of professional conduct, or

(C) other guidelines adopted by the Court concerning disqualification of neutrals.

(2) *Mandatory Disqualification and Notice of Recusal.* A prospective neutral who discovers a circumstance requiring disqualification must immediately notify the parties and the ADR Unit in writing. The parties may not waive a basis for disqualification that is described in 28 U.S.C. Section 455 (b).

(3) *Disclosure and Waiver of Non–Mandatory Grounds for Disqualification.* If a prospective neutral discovers a circumstance that would not compel disqualification under an applicable standard of professional responsibility or rule of professional conduct or other guideline, or under § 455(b), but that might be covered by § 455(a), the neutral shall promptly disclose that circumstance to all counsel in writing, as well as the ADR Unit. A party who has an objection to the neutral based upon an allegation that the neutral has a conflict of interest must present this objection in writing to the ADR Unit and all counsel within 7 days of learning the source of the potential conflict or shall be deemed to have waived objection.

(4) *Objections Not Based on Disclosures by Neutral.* Within 7 days of learning the identity of a proposed neutral, a party who objects to service by that neutral must deliver to the ADR Unit and to all other counsel a writing that specifies the bases for the objection. The ADR Director shall determine whether the proposed neutral will serve or whether another neutral should be appointed. Appeal from such a determination must be made directly to the ADR Magistrate Judge within 7 days of the notice of the ADR Director's determination.

(e) Immunities. All persons serving as neutrals in any of the Court's ADR programs are performing quasi-judicial functions and are entitled to the immunities and protections that the law accords to persons serving in such capacity.

[Effective January 1, 2009. Amended effective December 1, 2009; September 15, 2015.]

RULE 2–6. EVALUATION OF ADR PROGRAMS

Congress has mandated that the Court's ADR programs be evaluated. Neutrals, counsel and clients must promptly respond to any inquiries or questionnaires from persons authorized by the Court to evaluate the programs. Responses to such inquiries will be used for research and monitoring purposes only and the sources of specific information will not be disclosed to the assigned Judge or in any report.

[Effective January 1, 2009.]

RULE 3. ADR MULTI–OPTION PROGRAM

RULE 3–1. PURPOSE

The ADR Multi–Option Program is designed to encourage litigants in a broad range of cases to use ADR and to provide parties with sophisticated assistance in identifying the ADR process that is best suited to their particular case.

[Effective January 1, 2009.]

RULE 3–2. DESCRIPTION

Most civil cases are assigned at filing to the ADR Multi–Option Program, in which the parties are presumptively required to participate in one non-binding ADR process offered by the Court (Early Neutral Evaluation, Mediation or a Settlement Conference with a Magistrate Judge). With the assigned Judge's permission, the parties may substitute an ADR process offered by a private provider. On or before the date set forth in the Order Setting Initial Case Management Conference and ADR Deadlines, counsel and client must sign, serve, and file the ADR Certification as set forth in ADR L.R. 3–5, and counsel must meet and confer in an effort to agree on an ADR process option. If, after meeting and conferring, the parties need specialized assistance to select or customize an ADR process, they may request a joint phone conference with the legal staff of the ADR Unit. Counsel must include in their joint case management statement a report on the status of ADR, specifying which ADR process option they have selected and a proposed deadline by which the parties will conduct the ADR session, or, if they do not agree, setting forth which option and timing each party prefers. Unless the assigned Judge already has approved a stipulation to an ADR process, the assigned Judge will discuss ADR options with counsel at the initial case management conference. With the benefit of input from the parties and, if provided, from the legal staff of the ADR Unit, the Judge will select one of the ADR processes offered by the Court, unless persuaded that the case is not ripe for an ADR referral or that no ADR process is likely to deliver benefits to the parties sufficient to justify the resources devoted to it.

Commentary

Counsel are encouraged to reach agreements about what information the parties need to exchange, formally or informally, in order to be ready to participate in ADR. Counsel should stipulate to an ADR process that will take place within the presumptive 90–day deadline set forth in ADR L.R. 3–7 if they agree that the parties will be ready to participate meaningfully in the selected ADR process in that time frame. Counsel should defer their selection of an ADR process to the case management conference if they disagree or have questions about the most appropriate ADR process or timing.

Cross Reference

See Case Management Conference provisions of Civil L.R. 16.

[Effective January 1, 2009. Amended effective September 15, 2015; May 1, 2018.]

RULE 3–3. ASSIGNMENT TO ADR MULTI–OPTION PROGRAM

(a) **Automatic Assignment.** In accordance with Civil L.R. 16–2, most civil cases are assigned to the ADR Multi–Option Program by the Clerk when the complaint or notice of removal is filed. Notice of such assignment will be given in the Order Setting Initial Case Management Conference and ADR Deadlines issued under Civil L.R. 16–2.

(b) **By Stipulation, Motion or Order.** Cases not assigned at filing may be assigned to the ADR Multi–Option Program, or to a specific ADR process, by order of the assigned Judge following a stipulation by all parties, on motion by a party under Civil L.R. 7, or on the Judge's initiative.

(c) **Relief From Automatic Referral.** Any party whose case has been referred automatically to the ADR Multi–Option Program may file with the assigned Judge a motion for relief from automatic referral under Civil L.R. 7.

[Effective January 1, 2009. Amended effective September 15, 2015.]

RULE 3–4. ADR OPTIONS

(a) **Court–Sponsored ADR Processes.** The Court-sponsored ADR options for cases assigned to the ADR Multi–Option Program include:

1. Early Neutral Evaluation (ENE);

2. Mediation; and

3. Settlement Conference with a Magistrate Judge.

A case may be referred to ENE, Mediation or a Settlement Conference only by order of the assigned Judge.

(b) **Private ADR.** A private ADR procedure may be substituted for a Court process if the parties so stipulate and the assigned Judge approves. Private ADR proceedings, however, are not subject to the provisions of the ADR Local Rules including attendance, confidentiality, enforcement and immunity.

[Effective January 1, 2009. Amended effective September 15, 2015; May 1, 2018.]

RULE 3–5. SELECTING AN ADR PROCESS

(a) **Meet and Confer to Select ADR Process.** In cases assigned to the ADR Multi–Option Program, as soon as feasible after filing or removal and no later than the deadline to meet and confer (presumptively 21 days before the date set for the initial case management conference), counsel must meet and confer to discuss the available ADR processes, to identify the process each believes will be most helpful to the parties' settlement efforts, to specify any formal or informal exchange of information needed before an ADR session, and to attempt to agree on an ADR process and a deadline for the ADR session. If the date of the initial case management conference is changed, unless otherwise ordered the meet and confer deadline adjusts accordingly.

(b) **ADR Certification.** In cases assigned to the ADR Multi–Option Program, no later than the date specified in the Order Setting Initial Case Management Conference and ADR Deadlines (presumptively 21 days before the date set for the initial case management conference), counsel and client must sign, serve, and file an ADR Certification. The certification must be filed on a form established for that purpose by the Court and in conformity with the instructions approved by the Court. Separate certifications may be filed by each party. If the client is a government or government agency, the certificate shall be signed by a person who meets the requirements of Civil L.R. 3–9(c). If the date of the initial case management conference is changed, unless otherwise ordered the ADR Certification deadline adjusts accordingly.

Counsel and client must certify that both have:

(1) Read the handbook entitled "Alternative Dispute Resolution Procedures Handbook" on the Court's ADR website (found at cand.uscourts.gov/adr);

(2) Discussed with each other the available dispute resolution options provided by the Court and private entities; and

(3) Considered whether their case might benefit from any of the available dispute resolution options.

Counsel must further certify that they have discussed selection of an ADR process and an appropriate deadline for an ADR session with counsel for the other parties to the case and must indicate whether they intend to stipulate to an ADR process and deadline or prefer to discuss ADR selection with the assigned Judge at the case management conference.

(c) Stipulation to ADR Process. If the parties agree to participate in an ADR process and they wish the Court to make an ADR referral in advance of the case management conference, they may file a Stipulation and Proposed Order selecting an ADR process.

(d) Selection at Case Management Conference.

(1) *Consideration of ADR Processes.* Counsel must include in their joint case management statement a report on the status of ADR, specifying which ADR process option they have selected and a proposed deadline by which the parties will conduct the ADR session or, if they do not agree, setting forth which option and timing each party prefers. Unless the assigned Judge already has approved a stipulation to an ADR process, counsel must be prepared to discuss all of the subjects about which they were required to meet and confer under ADR L.R. 3–5(a). If the ADR legal staff holds an ADR Phone Conference in advance of the initial case management conference, they ordinarily will make a recommendation to the assigned Judge.

(2) *Selection by Stipulation or Order.* If the parties agree to a particular ADR process at the case management conference and the assigned Judge approves, the Judge will issue an order referring the case to that process. Alternatively, even if the parties do not agree, the Judge may issue an order referring the case to ENE, Mediation, or a Settlement Conference.

(3) *Deferred Referral or Exemption.* If, considering the views of the parties, the Judge at the case management conference concludes that the case is not ripe for an ADR referral or that no ADR process is likely to deliver benefits to the parties sufficient to justify the resources devoted to it, the Judge may defer making an ADR referral or may exempt the case from participating in any ADR process.

[Effective January 1, 2009. Amended effective July 2, 2012; September 15, 2015; May 1, 2018.]

RULE 3–6. ADR PHONE CONFERENCE

An ADR Phone Conference conducted by a member of the ADR legal staff may be set to assist the parties or the assigned Judge in selecting or customizing an ADR process, in aid of the administration of a case that has been referred to an ADR process, or as otherwise directed by the Court. An ADR Phone Conference may be set at the request of the parties on the form established for that purpose by the Court, by referral from the assigned Judge, or at the initiative of the ADR legal staff. Unless otherwise specified in the order referring the matter for an ADR Phone Conference or the Notice Setting ADR Phone Conference, the following procedures shall apply:

(a) Participants. Counsel who will be primarily responsible for handling the trial of the matter must participate in the conference. Clients and their insurance carriers may participate as well. Counsel may request an in-person ADR conference at the Court in lieu of the phone conference by calling the ADR Unit.

(b) Participation in the Conference Call. For the convenience of the parties, the Court provides a dial-in conference line for all ADR phone conferences. Unless otherwise directed, counsel should reserve one half-hour for each such conference call.

(c) Preparation. Before the phone conference, counsel are expected to have complied with ADR L.R. 3–5(a) and (b).

(d) Request to Continue the ADR Phone Conference. Requests to continue the ADR Phone Conference must be directed to the ADR Unit at (415) 522–2199 or ADR@cand.uscourts.gov.

(e) Confidentiality. Absent express agreement to the contrary, ADR phone conferences are not confidential. ADR legal staff may report their impressions and make recommendations to the assigned Judge following the phone conference.

Commentary

Forms for ADR Certification, Stipulation to an ADR Process, and Request for ADR Phone Conference, and the handbook entitled "Alternative Dispute Resolution Procedures Handbook" are available on the Court's website: cand.uscourts.gov/adr. The Clerk's Office will print copies upon request for pro se parties.

[Effective May 1, 2018.]

RULE 3–7. TIMING OF ADR PROCESS IN THE ADR MULTI–OPTION PROGRAM

Unless otherwise ordered, the ADR session must be held within 90 days after the entry of an order referring the case to a specific ADR process.

Commentary

Parties are permitted to request a longer or shorter deadline on a case specific basis.

Cross Reference

See ADR L.R. 5–4 and 6–4.

[Former Rule 3–6 effective January 1, 2009. Amended effective September 15, 2015. Renumbered Rule 3–7 and amended, effective May 1, 2018.]

RULE 5.   EARLY NEUTRAL EVALUATION

RULE 5–1.   DESCRIPTION

In Early Neutral Evaluation (ENE) the parties and their counsel, in a confidential session, make compact presentations of their claims and defenses, including key evidence as developed at that juncture, and receive a non-binding evaluation by an experienced neutral lawyer with subject matter expertise. The Evaluator also helps identify areas of agreement, offers case-planning suggestions and, if requested by the parties, settlement assistance.

[Effective January 1, 2009.]

RULE 5–2.   ELIGIBLE CASES

Subject to the availability of administrative resources and of an Evaluator with subject matter expertise, appropriate civil cases may be referred to ENE by order of the assigned Judge following a stipulation by all parties, on motion by a party under Civil L.R. 7, or on the Judge's initiative.

[Effective January 1, 2009.]

RULE 5–3.   EVALUATORS

(a) Appointment. After entry of an order referring a case to ENE, the ADR Unit will appoint from the Court's panel an Evaluator who has expertise in the subject matter of the lawsuit, is available during the appropriate period and has no apparent conflict of interest. The Court will notify the parties of the appointment. The rules governing conflicts of interest and the procedure for objecting to an Evaluator are set forth in ADR L.R. 2–5(d). The procedures for party input into the selection process are posted on the ADR website at cand.uscourts.gov/adr.

(b) Compensation. ENE Evaluators shall volunteer up to two hours of preparation time and the first four hours in an ENE session. After four hours in an ENE session, the Evaluator may (1) continue to volunteer his or her time or (2) give the parties the option of either concluding the proceeding or paying the Evaluator. The ENE proceeding will continue only if all parties and the Evaluator agree. If all parties agree to continue, the Evaluator may then charge his or her hourly rate or such other rate that all parties agree to pay. If more substantial preparation by the Evaluator is desired, the parties may discuss appropriate alternative payment arrangements with the Evaluator. Alternative arrangements must be approved by the ADR Legal Staff. No party may offer or give the Evaluator any gift.

(c) Payment. All terms and conditions of payment must be clearly communicated to the parties. The parties may agree to pay the fee in other than equal portions. The parties must pay the Evaluator directly, or the Evaluator's law firm or employer, as directed by the Evaluator. On a questionnaire form provided by the Court, the Evaluator shall promptly report to the ADR Unit the amount of any payment received.

[Effective January 1, 2009. Amended effective September 15, 2015.]

RULE 5–4.   TIMING AND SCHEDULING THE ENE SESSION

(a) Scheduling by Evaluator. Promptly after being appointed to a case, the Evaluator must arrange for the pre-session phone conference under ADR L.R. 5–7 and, after consulting with all parties, must fix the date and place of the ENE session within the deadlines set by paragraph (c) below, or the order referring the case to ENE.

(b) Cooperating With the Evaluator. Counsel must respond promptly to and cooperate fully with the Evaluator with respect to scheduling the pre-session phone conference and the ENE session.

(c) Deadline for Conducting Session. Unless otherwise ordered, the ENE session must be held within 90 days after the entry of the order referring the case to ENE.

Commentary

If the parties believe that the deadline for conducting an ENE is not appropriate, they should promptly seek an extension of time in accordance with the procedures set forth in ADR L.R. 5–5.

[Effective January 1, 2009. Amended effective September 15, 2015.]

RULE 5–5.   REQUESTS TO EXTEND DEADLINE

(a) Motion Required. Requests for extension of the deadline for conducting an ENE session must be made by the parties no later than 14 days before the session is to be held and must be directed to the assigned Judge, in a motion or stipulation and proposed order under Civil L.R. 7, with a copy to the other parties, the Evaluator (if appointed) and the ADR Unit.

(b) Content of Motion. Such motion must:

(1) Detail the considerations that support the request;

(2) Indicate whether the other parties concur in or object to the request; and

(3) Be accompanied by a proposed order setting forth a new deadline by which the ENE session shall be held.

[Effective January 1, 2009. Amended effective December 1, 2009; September 15, 2015.]

RULE 5–6.   EX PARTE CONTACT PROHIBITED

Except with respect to scheduling matters, there shall be no ex parte communications between parties or counsel and the Evaluator, including private caucuses to discuss settlement, until after the Evaluator has committed his or her Evaluation to writing and all parties have agreed that ex parte communications with the evaluator may occur.

[Effective January 1, 2009.]

RULE 5–7.   PHONE CONFERENCE BEFORE ENE SESSION

The Evaluator shall schedule a brief joint phone conference before the ENE session with counsel who will attend the ENE session to discuss matters such as the scheduling of the ENE session, the procedures to be followed, compensation of the neutral, the nature of the case, the content of the written ENE statements, and which client representatives will attend. The Evaluator may schedule additional joint pre-session calls as appropriate.

Commentary

If more than one pre-session phone conference is conducted, all counsel do not necessarily need to participate in every call but the lead counsel who will attend the ENE session must participate in at least one pre-session phone conference. See ADR L.R. 5–10(b).

[Effective January 1, 2009. Amended effective September 15, 2015; May 1, 2018.]

RULE 5–8. WRITTEN ENE STATEMENTS

(a) Time for Submission. No later than 7 days before the first ENE session unless otherwise directed by the Evaluator, each party must submit directly to the Evaluator, and must serve on all other parties, a written ENE Statement.

(b) Prohibition Against Filing. The statements constitute confidential information as defined in ADR L.R. 5–12, must not be filed and the assigned Judge shall not have access to them.

(c) Content of Statement. The statements must be concise, may include any information that may be useful to the Evaluator, and must, unless otherwise directed by the Evaluator:

(1) Identify, by name and title or status:

(A) The person(s) with decision-making authority, who, in addition to counsel, will attend the ENE session as representative(s) of the party, and

(B) Persons connected with a party opponent (including an insurer representative) whose presence might substantially improve the utility of the ENE session or the prospects for settlement;

(2) Describe briefly the substance of the suit, addressing the party's views of the key liability issues and damages and discussing the key evidence;

(3) Address whether there are legal or factual issues whose early resolution would reduce significantly the scope of the dispute or contribute to settlement negotiations;

(4) Identify the discovery that is necessary to equip the parties for meaningful settlement negotiations; and

(5) Include copies of documents out of which the suit arose (e.g., contracts), or whose availability would materially advance the purposes of the Evaluation session, (e.g., medical reports or documents by which special damages might be determined).

[Effective January 1, 2009. Amended effective December 1, 2009; September 15, 2015.]

RULE 5–9. SPECIAL PROVISIONS FOR PATENT, COPYRIGHT, OR TRADEMARK CASES

Unless otherwise directed by the Evaluator, the following provisions apply to the written ENE statements submitted under ADR L.R. 5–8.

(a) Patent Cases. When a claim in a case alleges infringement of a utility patent, or when a party seeks a declaratory judgment that a utility patent is not infringed, is invalid, or is unenforceable, each party must attach to its written ENE statement a copy of each document the party has been required to generate (by the date the written ENE statements are due) under Patent L.R. 3–1, 3–3, or 3–5(a), or under any case-specific order modifying the requirements of these provisions of the Patent Local Rules. A party whose duty has arisen only under Patent L.R. 3–5(a) may satisfy the requirements hereby imposed by attaching to its written ENE statement a copy of documents it was required to generate under Patent L.R. 3–3.

(b) Copyright Cases. To the extent then known or readily available and feasible, a party who bases a claim on copyright must include as exhibits the copyright registration (or, if there is no relevant copyright registration yet, the relevant copyright application) and one or more demonstrative exemplars of the copying and infringement. Such party must also present whatever direct or indirect evidence it has of copying, and shall indicate whether it intends to elect statutory or actual damages. Each party in a copyright case who is accused of infringing shall set forth in its written statement the dollar volume of sales of and profits from the allegedly infringing works that it and any entities for which it is legally responsible have made.

(c) Trademark Cases. To the extent then known or readily available and feasible, a party who bases a claim on trademark or trade dress infringement, or on other unfair competition, must include as an exhibit its registration, if any, exemplars of both its use of its mark and use of the allegedly infringing mark, both including a description or representation of the goods or services on or in connection with which the marks are used, and any evidence it has of actual confusion. If "secondary meaning" is in issue, such a party must also describe the nature and extent of the advertising it has done with its mark and the volume of goods it has sold under its mark. Both parties must describe in their Evaluation statements how the consuming public is exposed to their respective marks and goods or services, including, if available, photographic or other demonstrative evidence. Each party in a trademark or unfair competition case who is accused of infringement must set forth the dollar volume of sales of and profits from goods or services bearing the allegedly infringing mark.

[Effective January 1, 2009. Amended effective September 15, 2015.]

RULE 5–10. ATTENDANCE AT SESSION

(a) Parties. All named parties and their counsel are required to attend the ENE session in person unless excused under paragraph (d) below. This requirement reflects the Court's view that the principal values of ENE include affording litigants opportunities to articulate directly to other parties and a neutral their positions and interests and to hear, first hand, both their opponent's version of the matters in dispute and a neutral assessment of the merits of the case and the relative strengths of each party's legal positions.

(1) *Corporation or Other Non–Governmental Entity.* A party other than a natural person (e.g., a corporation or an association) satisfies this attendance requirement if represented by a person (other than outside counsel) who has final authority to settle and who is knowledgeable about the facts of the case. If final authority to settle is vested only in a governing board, claims committee, or equivalent body and cannot be delegated to a representative, an entity must disclose (in writing or electronically) this fact to all other parties and the Evaluator at least 14 days before the ENE session will occur. This required disclosure must identify the board, committee, body, or persons in whom final settlement authority is vested. In this instance the party must send the person (in addition to counsel of record) who has, to the greatest extent feasible, authority to recommend a settlement, and who is knowledgeable about the facts of the case, the entity's position, and the procedures and policies under which the entity decides whether to accept proposed settlements.

(2) *Government Entity.* A unit or agency of government satisfies this attendance requirement if represented by a person (in addition to counsel of record) who has, to the greatest extent feasible, authority to settle, and who is knowledgeable about the facts of the case, the governmental unit's position, and the procedures and policies under which the governmental unit decides whether to accept proposed settlements. If the action is brought by the government on behalf of one or more individuals, at least one such individual also must attend.

(b) **Counsel.** Each party must be accompanied at the ENE session by the lawyer who will be primarily responsible for handling the trial of the matter.

(c) **Insurers.** Insurer representatives are required to attend in person unless excused under paragraph (d) below, if they have accepted coverage, or the duty to defend, even if subject to a reservation of rights.

(d) **Request to Be Excused.** A person who is required to attend an ENE session may be excused from attending in person only after a showing that personal attendance would impose an extraordinary or otherwise unjustifiable hardship. A person seeking to be excused must submit, no fewer than 14 days before the date set for the session, a letter to the ADR Magistrate Judge in care of the ADR Unit at the address listed in ADR L.R. 2–1(c), or emailed to ADR_Attendance@cand.uscourts.gov, simultaneously copying all counsel and the Evaluator. The letter must:

(1) Set forth all considerations that support the request;

(2) State realistically the amount in controversy in the case;

(3) Identify by name and title or status the individual(s) seeking to be excused;

(4) Identify by name and title or status all those persons who will attend;

(5) Identify by name and title or status the person(s) with decision-making authority, and

(6) Indicate whether the other party or parties and the Evaluator join in or object to the request.

The request may not be filed or disclosed to the assigned judge.

(e) **Opposing a Request to Be Excused or Seeking to Compel Attendance by an Appropriate Party Representative.**

(1) A party who opposes another party's request to be excused from attending in person an ENE session may submit to the ADR Magistrate Judge in care of the ADR Unit at the address listed in ADR L.R. 2–1(c), or emailed to ADR_Attendance@cand.uscourts.gov, within 4 days of receiving a copy of the request, a letter setting forth all grounds for the opposition. Such a letter must be served simultaneously on all parties and the Evaluator- and may not be filed or disclosed to the assigned judge.

(2) A party who alleges that another party will not be represented at an ENE session by an appropriate representative may submit to the ADR Magistrate Judge in care of the ADR Unit at the address listed in ADR L.R. 2–1(c), or emailed to ADR_Attendance@cand.uscourts.gov, as far in advance of the session as practicable, a letter setting forth the bases for this allegation, along with a proposed order. Within 4 days of receiving a copy of such a letter, the party so challenged may submit to the ADR Magistrate Judge a responsive letter. Such letters must be sent to the ADR Magistrate Judge in care of the ADR Unit at the address listed in ADR L.R. 2–1(c), or emailed to ADR_Attendance@cand.uscourts.gov and served simultaneously on all other parties and the Evaluator— and may not be filed or disclosed to the assigned judge.

(f) **Participation by Telephone.** Unless otherwise ordered, a person excused from appearing in person at an ENE session must participate by telephone for the duration of the session or until excused by the neutral.

Commentary

Ordinarily, a corporation or other entity, including a governmental entity or an insurer, satisfies the attendance requirement by sending a person or persons who can agree to a settlement without the necessity of gaining approval from anyone else. Exceptions to this general practice must be disclosed and addressed in advance of the session.

[Effective January 1, 2009. Amended effective December 1, 2009; September 15, 2015.]

RULE 5–11.   PROCEDURE AT ENE SESSION

(a) **Components of ENE Session.** The Evaluator shall:

(1) Permit each party (through counsel or otherwise), orally and through documents or other media, to present its claims or defenses and to describe the principal evidence on which they are based;

(2) Help the parties identify areas of agreement and, where feasible, enter stipulations;

(3) Assess the relative strengths and weaknesses of the parties' contentions and evidence, and explain carefully the reasoning that supports these assessments;

(4) Estimate, where feasible, the likelihood of liability and the dollar range of damages;

(5) Help the parties devise a plan for sharing the important information and/or conducting the key discovery that will equip them as expeditiously as possible to enter meaningful

settlement discussions or to position the case for disposition by other means;

(6) Help the parties assess litigation costs realistically;

(7) If the parties are interested, help them, through private caucusing or otherwise, explore the possibility of settling the case; and

(8) Determine whether some form of follow up to the session would contribute to the case development process or to settlement.

(b) Process Rules. The session shall be informal. Rules of evidence shall not apply. There shall be no formal examination or cross-examination of witnesses and no recording of the presentations or discussion shall be made.

(c) Evaluation and Settlement Discussions. If all parties agree, they may proceed to discuss settlement after the evaluation has been written but before it is presented. The evaluation must be presented orally on demand by any party. Copies of the written evaluation may be provided to the parties at the discretion of the Evaluator. The parties also may agree to discuss settlement after the evaluation has been presented.

[Effective January 1, 2009. Amended effective September 15, 2015.]

RULE 5–12.   CONFIDENTIALITY

(a) Confidential Treatment. Except as provided in subdivision (b) of this local rule, this Court, the Evaluator, all counsel and parties, and any other persons attending the ENE session shall treat as "confidential information" the contents of the written ENE Statements, anything that was said, any position taken, and any view of the merits of the case expressed by any participant in connection with any ENE session. "Confidential information" shall not be:

(1) Disclosed to anyone not involved in the litigation;

(2) Disclosed to the assigned Judge; or

(3) Used for any purpose, including impeachment, in any pending or future proceeding in this Court.

(b) Limited Exceptions to Confidentiality. This rule does not prohibit:

(1) Disclosures as may be stipulated by all parties and the Evaluator;

(2) Disclosure of the terms of a fully executed settlement agreement signed during or arising out of the ENE session;

(3) Disclosures made in a subsequent confidential ADR or settlement proceeding under these Rules;

(4) A report to or an inquiry by the ADR Magistrate Judge pursuant to ADR L.R. 2–4 regarding a possible violation of the ADR Local Rules;

(5) The Evaluator from discussing the ENE session with the Court's ADR staff, who must maintain the confidentiality of the ENE session;

(6) Any participant or the Evaluator from responding to an appropriate request for information duly made by persons authorized by the Court to monitor or evaluate the Court's ADR program in accordance with ADR L.R. 2–6; or

(7) Disclosures as are otherwise required by law.

(c) Confidentiality Agreement. The Evaluator may ask the parties and all persons attending the ENE session to sign a confidentiality agreement on a form provided by the Court.

Commentary

Ordinarily, anything that was said in connection with an ENE session is to be treated as confidential in the same manner and for the same reasons as with Mediation. Please see the legal authorities cited in the commentary to ADR Local Rule 6–12(c).

[Effective January 1, 2009. Amended effective September 15, 2015; May 1, 2018.]

RULE 5–13.   FOLLOW UP

(a) Discussion at Close of ENE. At the close of the ENE session, the Evaluator and the parties shall discuss whether it would be beneficial to schedule any follow up to the session.

(b) Follow Up the Evaluator May Order. The Evaluator may order these kinds of follow up without stipulation:

(1) Responses to settlement offers or demands;

(2) A focused phone conference;

(3) Exchanges of letters between counsel addressing specified legal or factual issues; or

(4) Written or telephonic reports to the Evaluator, e.g., describing how discovery or other events occurring after the ENE session have affected a party's analysis of the case or position with respect to settlement.

(c) Stipulation to Follow Up Session. With the consent of all parties, the Evaluator may schedule one or more follow up ENE sessions that may include additional evaluation, settlement discussions, or case development planning.

(d) Limitations on Authority of Evaluator. Evaluators have no authority to compel parties to conduct or respond to discovery or to file motions. Nor do Evaluators have authority to determine what the issues in any case are, to impose limits on parties' pretrial activities, or to impose sanctions.

[Effective January 1, 2009. Amended effective May 1, 2018.]

RULE 5–14.   CERTIFICATION OF SESSION

Within 14 days of the close of each ENE session, and on the form Certification of Session provided by the Court, the Evaluator must report to the ADR Unit: the date of the session, whether any follow up is scheduled, and whether the case settled in whole or in part. The ADR Unit will enter this information on the docket.

[Effective January 1, 2009. Amended effective December 1, 2009; September 15, 2015.]

RULE 6. MEDIATION

RULE 6–1. DESCRIPTION

Mediation is a flexible, non-binding, confidential process in which a neutral person (the mediator) facilitates settlement negotiations. The mediator improves communication across party lines, helps parties articulate their interests and understand those of their opponent, probes the strengths and weaknesses of each party's legal positions, identifies areas of agreement and helps generate options for a mutually agreeable resolution to the dispute. The mediator generally does not give an overall evaluation of the case. A hallmark of Mediation is its capacity to expand traditional settlement discussion and broaden resolution options, often by exploring litigant needs and interests that may be formally independent of the legal issues in controversy.

[Effective January 1, 2009.]

RULE 6–2. ELIGIBLE CASES

Subject to the availability of administrative resources and of a suitable mediator, appropriate civil cases may be referred to Mediation by order of the assigned Judge following a stipulation by all parties, on motion by a party under Civil L.R. 7, or on the Judge's initiative.

[Effective January 1, 2009.]

RULE 6–3. MEDIATORS

(a) **Appointment.** After entry of an order referring a case to Mediation, the ADR Unit will appoint from the Court's panel a mediator who is available during the appropriate period and has no apparent conflict of interest. The Court will notify the parties of the appointment. The rules governing conflicts of interest and the procedure for objecting to a mediator are set forth in ADR L.R. 2–5(d). The procedures for party input into the selection process are posted on the ADR website at www.cand.uscourts.gov/adr.

(b) **Standards of Conduct.** Mediators on the Court's panel agree to adhere to applicable standards of professional conduct as may be officially adopted by the Court.

(c) **Compensation.** Mediators shall volunteer up to two hours of preparation time and the first four hours in a Mediation. After four hours of Mediation, the mediator may (1) continue to volunteer his or her time or (2) give the parties the option of either concluding the proceeding or paying the mediator. The proceeding will continue only if all parties and the mediator agree. If all parties agree to continue, the mediator may then charge his or her hourly rate or such other rate that all parties agree to pay. If more substantial preparation by the mediator is desired, the parties may discuss appropriate alternative payment arrangements with the mediator. Alternative arrangements must be approved by the ADR Legal Staff. No party may offer or give the mediator any gift.

(d) **Payment.** All terms and conditions of payment must be clearly communicated to the parties. The parties may agree to pay the fee in other than equal portions. The parties must pay the mediator directly, or the mediator's law firm or employer, as directed by the mediator. On a form questionnaire provided by the Court, the mediator must promptly report to the ADR Unit the amount of any payment received.

[Effective January 1, 2009. Amended effective September 15, 2015.]

RULE 6–4. TIMING AND SCHEDULING THE MEDIATION

(a) **Scheduling by Mediator.** Promptly after being appointed to a case, the mediator must arrange for the pre-Mediation conference under ADR L.R. 6–6 and, after consulting with all parties, must fix the date and place of the Mediation within the deadlines set by paragraph (c) below, or the order referring the case to Mediation.

(b) **Cooperating With the Mediator.** Counsel must respond promptly to and cooperate fully with the mediator with respect to scheduling the pre-session phone conference and the Mediation session.

(c) **Deadline for Conducting Mediation.** Unless otherwise ordered, the Mediation must be held within 90 days after the entry of the order referring the case to Mediation.

[Effective January 1, 2009. Amended effective September 15, 2015.]

RULE 6–5. REQUEST TO EXTEND THE DEADLINE

(a) **Motion Required.** Requests for extension of the deadline for conducting a Mediation must be made no later than 14 days before the session is to be held and must be directed to the assigned Judge, in a motion or stipulation and proposed order under Civil L.R. 7, with a copy to the other parties, the mediator (if appointed) and the ADR Unit.

(b) **Content of Motion.** Such motion must:

(1) Detail the considerations that support the request;

(2) Indicate whether the other parties concur in or object to the request; and

(3) Be accompanied by a proposed order setting forth a new deadline by which the Mediation shall be held.

[Effective January 1, 2009. Amended effective December 1, 2009.]

RULE 6–6. PHONE CONFERENCE BEFORE MEDIATION

The mediator must schedule a brief joint phone conference before the Mediation session with counsel who will attend the Mediation session to discuss matters such as the scheduling of the Mediation, the procedures to be followed, compensation of the neutral, the nature of the case, the content of the written Mediation statements, and which client representatives will attend. The mediator may schedule additional pre-session calls either jointly or separately as appropriate.

Commentary

If more than one pre-session phone conference is conducted, all counsel do not necessarily need to participate in every call but the lead counsel who will attend the Mediation session must participate in at least one pre-session phone conference. *See* ADR L.R. 6–10(b).

[Effective January 1, 2009. Amended effective September 15, 2015; May 1, 2018.]

RULE 6–7. WRITTEN MEDIATION STATEMENTS

(a) Time for Submission. No later than 7 days before the first Mediation session, unless otherwise directed by the mediator, each party must submit directly to the mediator, and must serve on all other parties, a written Mediation Statement.

(b) Prohibition Against Filing. The statements constitute confidential information as defined in ADR L.R. 6–12, must not be filed and the assigned Judge shall not have access to them.

(c) Content of Statement. The statements must be concise, may include any information that may be useful to the mediator, and must, unless otherwise directed by the mediator:

(1) Identify, by name and title or status:

(A) The person(s) with decision-making authority, who, in addition to counsel, will attend the Mediation as representative(s) of the party, and

(B) Persons connected with a party opponent (including an insurer representative) whose presence might substantially improve the utility of the Mediation or the prospects for settlement;

(2) Describe briefly the substance of the suit, addressing the party's views of the key liability issues and damages and discussing the key evidence;

(3) Identify the discovery or motions that promise to contribute most to equipping the parties for meaningful settlement negotiations;

(4) Except to the extent prohibited by applicable laws of privilege or by these local rules, describe the history and current status of any settlement negotiations;

(5) Provide additional information about any needs, interests or other considerations not described elsewhere in the statement that might be pertinent to settlement; and

(6) Include copies of documents likely to make the Mediation more productive or to materially advance settlement prospects.

Commentary

Ordinarily, parties should be able to include in their Mediation statements a description of the history and status of any settlement negotiations. An exception may exist for negotiations held during a prior Mediation or ENE session, if all parties do not agree to the disclosure of these negotiations. *See* ADR L.R. 5–12 and 6–12. Such prohibitions are distinct from rules prohibiting the admission into evidence of settlement offers and demands which ordinarily would not prevent inclusion of the settlement history in a Mediation statement. *See, e.g.*, Fed. R. Evid. 408.

[Effective January 1, 2009. Amended effective December 1, 2009; September 15, 2015.]

RULE 6–8. SPECIAL PROVISIONS FOR PATENT, COPYRIGHT, OR TRADEMARK CASES

Unless otherwise directed by the mediator, the following provisions apply to the written Mediation statements submitted under ADR L.R. 6–7.

(a) Patent Cases. When a claim in a case alleges infringement of a utility patent, or when a party seeks a declaratory judgment that a utility patent is not infringed, is invalid, or is unenforceable, each party must attach to its written Mediation statement a copy of each document the party has been required to generate (by the date the written Mediation statements are due) under Patent L.R. 3–1, 3–3, or 3–5(a), or under any case-specific order modifying the requirements of these provisions of the Patent Local Rules. A party whose duty has arisen only under Patent L.R. 3–5(a) may satisfy the requirements hereby imposed by attaching to its written Mediation statement a copy of documents it was required to generate under Patent L.R. 3–3.

(b) Copyright Cases. To the extent then known or readily available and feasible, a party who bases a claim on copyright must include as exhibits the copyright registration (or, if there is no relevant copyright registration yet, the relevant copyright application) and one or more demonstrative exemplars of the copying and infringement. Such party must also present whatever direct or indirect evidence it has of copying, and shall indicate whether it intends to elect statutory or actual damages. Each party in a copyright case who is accused of infringing shall set forth in its written statement the dollar volume of sales of and profits from the allegedly infringing works that it and any entities for which it is legally responsible have made.

(c) Trademark Cases. To the extent then known or readily available and feasible, a party who bases a claim on trademark or trade dress infringement, or on other unfair competition, must include as an exhibit its registration, if any, exemplars of both its use of its mark and use of the allegedly infringing mark, both including a description or representation of the goods or services on or in connection with which the marks are used, and any evidence it has of actual confusion. If "secondary meaning" is in issue, such a party must also describe the nature and extent of the advertising it has done with its mark and the volume of goods it has sold under its mark. Both parties must describe in their Mediation statements how the consuming public is exposed to their respective marks and goods or services, including, if available, photographic or other demonstrative evidence. Each party in a trademark or unfair competition case who is accused of infringement must set forth the dollar volume of sales of and profits from goods or services bearing the allegedly infringing mark.

[Effective January 1, 2009. Amended effective September 15, 2015.]

RULE 6–9. CONTACT WITH MEDIATOR BEFORE THE MEDIATION

Before the Mediation, the mediator may ask each party to submit only to the mediator an additional confidential written statement or may discuss the case in confidence with a lawyer (and a party representative as appropriate) by telephone. Confidential Mediation statements may address such matters as the party's views about his/her own interests, the interests of the other side, analysis of the best and worst alternatives to a negotiated settlement, the strengths and weaknesses of the legal case, and an estimated budget to litigate the case. The mediator must not disclose any party's confidential communication without permission.

[Effective January 1, 2009. Amended effective September 15, 2015.]

RULE 6–10. ATTENDANCE AT SESSION

(a) **Parties.** All named parties and their counsel are required to attend the Mediation in person unless excused under paragraph (d) below. This requirement reflects the Court's view that the principal values of Mediation include affording litigants opportunities to articulate directly to the other parties and a neutral their positions and interests and to hear, first hand, their opponent's version of the matters in dispute. Mediation also enables parties to search directly with their opponents for mutually agreeable solutions.

(1) *Corporation or Other Non–Governmental Entity.* A party other than a natural person (e.g., a corporation or an association) satisfies this attendance requirement if represented by a person (other than outside counsel) who has final authority to settle and who is knowledgeable about the facts of the case. If final authority to settle is vested only in a governing board, claims committee, or equivalent body and cannot be delegated to a representative, an entity must disclose (in writing or electronically) this fact to all other parties and the mediator at least 14 days before the Mediation session will occur. This required disclosure must identify the board, body, or persons in whom final settlement authority is vested. In this instance the party must send the person (in addition to counsel of record) who has, to the greatest extent feasible, authority to recommend a settlement, and who is knowledgeable about the facts of the case, the entity's position, and the procedures and policies under which the entity decides whether to accept proposed settlements.

(2) *Government Entity.* A unit or agency of government satisfies this attendance requirement if represented by a person (in addition to counsel of record) who has, to the greatest extent feasible, authority to settle, and who is knowledgeable about the facts of the case, the governmental unit's position, and the procedures and policies under which the governmental unit decides whether to accept proposed settlements. If the action is brought by the government on behalf of one or more individuals, at least one such individual also must attend.

(b) **Counsel.** Each party must be accompanied at the Mediation by the lawyer who will be primarily responsible for handling the trial of the matter.

(c) **Insurers.** Insurer representatives are required to attend in person unless excused under paragraph (d) below, if they have accepted coverage, or the duty to defend, even if subject to a reservation of rights.

(d) **Request to Be Excused.** A person who is required to attend a Mediation may be excused from attending in person only after a showing that personal attendance would impose an extraordinary or otherwise unjustifiable hardship. A person seeking to be excused must submit, no fewer than 14 days before the date set for the Mediation, a letter to the ADR Magistrate Judge in care of the ADR Unit at the address listed in ADR L.R. 2–1(c), or emailed to ADR_Attendance@cand.uscourts.gov, simultaneously copying all counsel and the mediator. The letter must:

(1) Set forth all considerations that support the request;

(2) State realistically the amount in controversy in the case;

(3) Identify by name and title or status the individual(s) seeking to be excused;

(4) Identify by name and title or status all those persons who will attend;

(5) Identify by name and title or status the person(s) with decision-making authority, and

(6) Indicate whether the other party or parties and the mediator join in or object to the request.

The request may not be filed or disclosed to the assigned judge.

(e) **Opposing a Request to be Excused or Seeking to Compel Attendance by an Appropriate Party Representative.**

(1) A party who opposes another party's request to be excused from attending in person a Mediation session may submit to the ADR Magistrate Judge in care of the ADR Unit at the address listed in ADR L.R. 2–1(c), or emailed to ADR_Attendance@cand.uscourts.gov, within 4 days of receiving a copy of the request, a letter setting forth all grounds for the opposition. Such a letter must be served simultaneously on all other parties and the mediator—and may not be filed or disclosed to the assigned judge.

(2) A party who alleges that another party will not be represented at a Mediation session by an appropriate representative may submit to the ADR Magistrate Judge, as far in advance of the session as practicable, a letter setting forth the bases for this allegation. Within 4 days of receiving a copy of such a letter, the party so challenged may submit to the ADR Magistrate Judge a responsive letter. Such letters must be sent to the ADR Magistrate Judge in care of the ADR Unit at the address listed in ADR L.R. 2–1(c), or emailed to ADR_Attendance@cand.uscourts.gov and served simultaneously on all other parties and the mediator—and may not be filed or disclosed to the assigned judge.

(f) **Participation by Telephone.** Unless otherwise ordered, a person excused from appearing in person at a Mediation must participate by telephone for the duration of the session or until excused by the neutral.

Commentary

Ordinarily, a corporation or other entity, including a governmental entity or an insurer, satisfies the attendance requirement by sending a person or persons who can agree to a settlement without the necessity of gaining approval from anyone else. Exceptions to this general practice must be disclosed and addressed in advance of the session.

[Effective January 1, 2009. Amended effective December 1, 2009; September 15, 2015.]

RULE 6–11. PROCEDURE AT MEDIATION

(a) **Procedure.** The Mediation shall be informal. Mediators shall have discretion to structure the Mediation so as to maximize the benefits of the process.

(b) **Separate Caucuses.** The mediator may hold separate, private caucuses with each side or each lawyer or, if the parties agree, with the clients only. The mediator may not disclose communications made during such a caucus to another party or counsel without the consent of the party who made the communication.

[Effective January 1, 2009.]

RULE 6–12. CONFIDENTIALITY

(a) **Confidential Treatment.** Except as provided in subdivision (b) of this local rule, this Court, the mediator, all counsel and parties, and any other persons attending the Mediation shall treat as "confidential information" the contents of the written Mediation Statements, anything that was said, any position taken, and any view of the merits of the case expressed by any participant in connection with any Mediation. "Confidential information" shall not be:

(1) Disclosed to anyone not involved in the litigation;

(2) Disclosed to the assigned Judge or

(3) Used for any purpose, including impeachment, in any pending or future proceeding in this Court.

(b) **Limited Exceptions to Confidentiality.** This rule does not prohibit:

(1) Disclosures as may be stipulated by all parties and the mediator;

(2) Disclosure of the terms of a fully executed settlement agreement signed during or arising out of the Mediation;

(3) Disclosures made in a subsequent confidential ADR or settlement proceeding;

(4) A report to or an inquiry by the ADR Magistrate Judge pursuant to ADR L.R. 2–4 regarding a possible violation of the ADR Local Rules;

(5) The mediator from discussing the Mediation with the Court's ADR staff, who must maintain the confidentiality of the Mediation;

(6) Any participant or the mediator from responding to an appropriate request for information duly made by persons authorized by the Court to monitor or evaluate the Court's ADR program in accordance with ADR L.R. 2–6;

(7) Disclosures as are otherwise required by law.

(c) **Confidentiality Agreement.** The mediator may ask the parties and all persons attending the Mediation to sign a confidentiality agreement on a form provided by the Court.

Commentary

Ordinarily, anything that was said in connection with a Mediation is confidential. *See, e.g.,* Fed. R. Evid. 408; *Folb v. Motion Picture Industry Pension & Health Plans,* 16 F. Supp. 2d 1164 (C.D. Cal. 1998); Cal. Evid. Code §§ 703.5 and 1115–28; *Simmons v. Ghaderi,* 44 Cal.4th 570 (2008); *Rojas v. Superior Court,* 33 Cal. 4th 407 (2004); *Foxgate Homeowner's Assn. v. Bramalea California, Inc.,* 26 Cal.4th 1 (2001). The law may provide some limited circumstances in which the need for disclosure outweighs the importance of protecting the confidentiality of a Mediation. *E.g.,* threats of death or substantial bodily injury (*see* Or. Rev. Stat. § 36.220(6)); use of Mediation to commit a felony (*see* Colo. Rev. Stat. § 13–22–307); right to effective cross examination in a quasi-criminal proceeding (*see Rinaker v. Superior Court,* 62 Cal.App.4th 155 (3d Dist. 1998); lawyer duty to report misconduct (*see In re Waller,* 573 A.2d 780 (D.C. App. 1990); need to prevent manifest injustice (*see* Ohio Rev. Code § 2317.023(c)(4); *see also* Uniform Mediation Act, § 6 (2001). Accordingly, after application of legal tests which are appropriately sensitive to the policies supporting the confidentiality of Mediation proceedings, the Court may consider whether the interest in Mediation confidentiality outweighs the asserted need for disclosure. *See* amended opinion in *Olam v. Congress Mortgage Co.,* 68 F. Supp. 2d 1110 (N.D. Cal. 1999). Nothing in this commentary is intended to imply that, absent truly exigent circumstances, confidential matters may be disclosed without prior approval by the Court.

[Effective January 1, 2009. Amended effective September 15, 2015; May 1, 2018.]

RULE 6–13. FOLLOW UP

At the close of the Mediation session, the mediator and the parties shall jointly determine whether it would be appropriate to schedule some type of follow up. Such follow up could include, but need not be limited to, written or telephonic reports that the parties might make to one another or to the mediator, exchange of specified kinds of information, or another Mediation session.

[Effective January 1, 2009.]

RULE 6–14. CERTIFICATION OF SESSION

Within 14 days of the close of each Mediation session and on the form Certification of Session provided by the Court, the mediator must report to the ADR Unit: the date the session was held, whether the case settled in whole or in part, and whether any follow up is scheduled. The ADR Unit will enter this information on the docket.

[Effective January 1, 2009. Amended effective December 1, 2009; September 15, 2015.]

RULE 7. SETTLEMENT CONFERENCES

RULE 7–1. DESCRIPTION

In a settlement conference, a judicial officer, usually a Magistrate Judge, facilitates the parties' efforts to negotiate a settlement. Some settlement Judges use Mediation techniques in the settlement conference to improve communication among the parties, probe barriers to settlement, and assist in formulating resolutions. A settlement Judge might articulate views about the merits of the case or the relative strengths and weaknesses of the parties' legal positions.

[Effective January 1, 2009.]

RULE 7–2. REFERRAL TO A SETTLEMENT CONFERENCE

Cases are referred to a settlement conference by order of the assigned Judge following a written stipulation by all parties, on motion by a party under Civil L.R. 7, or the Judge's initiative. A settlement conference generally will be conducted by a Magistrate Judge, but in some limited circumstances may be conducted by a District Judge. Upon written stipulation of all parties, the assigned Judge, in the exercise of his or her discretion, may conduct a settlement conference.

(a) Timing. A party may request a settlement conference at any time after the action has been commenced.

(b) Referral to a Settlement Judge. The parties may stipulate to a preference for one or more particular Magistrate Judges or District Judges. The Court will attempt to honor the preference, subject to intra-division needs and the availability of the Magistrate Judges and District Judges.

[Effective January 1, 2009. Amended effective September 15, 2015; May 1, 2018.]

RULE 7–3. DIRECTIVES FROM THE SETTLEMENT JUDGE

Within any constraints fixed by the referring Judge, the settlement Judge shall notify the parties of the time and date of the settlement conference. The settlement Judge also shall notify the parties of his or her requirements for pre-conference submissions and for attendance at the settlement conference. The settlement Judge may order parties to attend. Unless the settlement Judge otherwise specifies, "attendance" at a settlement conference is governed by the following:

(a) Corporation or Other Non–Governmental Entity. A party other than a natural person (e.g., a corporation or an association) satisfies this attendance requirement if represented by a person (other than outside counsel) who has final authority to settle and who is knowledgeable about the facts of the case. If final authority to settle is vested only in a governing board, claims committee, or equivalent body and cannot be delegated to a representative, an entity must disclose (in writing or electronically) this fact to all other parties and the settlement judge at least 14 days before the settlement conference will occur. This required disclosure must identify the board, body, or persons in whom final settlement authority is vested. In this instance the party must send the person (in addition to counsel of record) who has, to the greatest extent feasible, authority to recommend a settlement, and who is knowledgeable about the facts of the case, the entity's position, and the procedures and policies under which the entity decides whether to accept proposed settlements.

(b) Government Entity. A unit or agency of government satisfies this attendance requirement if represented by a person (in addition to counsel of record) who has, to the greatest extent feasible, authority to settle, and who is knowledgeable about the facts of the case, the governmental unit's position, and the procedures and policies under which the governmental unit decides whether to accept proposed settlements. If the action is brought by the government on behalf of one or more individuals, at least one such individual also must attend.

(c) Insurers. Unless excused by the settlement Judge, insurer representatives are required to attend in person if they have accepted coverage, or the duty to defend, even if subject to a reservation of rights.

Commentary

Ordinarily, a corporation or other entity, including a governmental entity or an insurer, satisfies the attendance requirement by sending a person or persons who can agree to a settlement without the necessity of gaining approval from anyone else. Exceptions to this general practice must be disclosed and addressed in advance of the settlement conference.

[Effective January 1, 2009. Former ADR L.R. 7–4 renumbered and amended effective September 15, 2015.]

RULE 7–4. SETTLEMENT CONFERENCE CONFIDENTIALITY

(a) Confidential Treatment. Except as provided by a case-specific order entered in advance of the settlement conference or in subdivision (b) of this local rule, this Court, the settlement Judge, all counsel and parties, and any other persons attending the settlement conference shall treat as "confidential information" the contents of any written settlement conference statements, anything that was said, any position taken, and any view of the merits of the case expressed by any participant in connection with any settlement conference. "Confidential information" shall not be:

(1) Disclosed to anyone not involved in the litigation;

(2) Disclosed to the assigned Judge; or

(3) Used for any purpose, including impeachment, in any pending or future proceeding in this Court.

(b) Limited Exceptions to Confidentiality. This rule does not prohibit:

(1) Disclosures as may be stipulated by all parties;

(2) Disclosure of the terms of a fully executed or binding settlement agreement on the record arising out of the Settlement Conference;

(3) Disclosures made in a subsequent confidential ADR or settlement proceeding;

(4) The settlement Judge from discussing the settlement conference with the Court's ADR staff, who must maintain the confidentiality of the settlement conference;

(5) Any participant or the settlement Judge from responding to an appropriate request for information duly made by persons authorized by the Court to monitor or evaluate the Court's ADR program in accordance with ADR L.R. 2–6;

(6) Disclosures as are necessary to preserve the Court's capacity to enforce lawful orders or to discipline contumacious conduct; or

(7) Disclosures as otherwise required by law.

Commentary

It is the established practice in this district that a settlement Judge does not, formally or informally, disclose to the assigned Judge the substance of any settlement discussions. See Commentary for ADR L.R. 6–12.

[Effective January 1, 2009. Amended effective December 1, 2009. Former ADR L.R. 7–5 renumbered and amended effective September 15, 2015; May 1, 2018.]

RULE 8.　OTHER ADR PROCESSES

RULE 8–1.　OTHER COURT ADR PROCESSES

(a) Non–Binding Arbitration. Non–binding arbitration is an adjudicative process in which an arbitrator or a panel of three arbitrators issues a non-binding judgment ("award" or "decision") on the merits after an expedited, adversarial hearing. Either party may reject the non-binding award or decision and request a trial *de novo*. Non–binding arbitration occurs earlier in the life of a case than a trial and is less formal and less expensive. Because testimony is taken under oath and is subject to cross-examination, arbitration can be especially useful in cases that turn on credibility of witnesses. Arbitrators do not facilitate settlement discussions. Parties considering a non-binding arbitration are encouraged to contact the ADR Unit for assistance in structuring a non-binding arbitration tailored to their case.

(b) Non–Binding Summary Bench or Jury Trial. A summary bench or jury trial is a flexible, non-binding process designed to promote settlement in complex, trial-ready cases headed for protracted trials. The process provides litigants and their counsel with an advisory verdict after a short hearing in which the evidence may be presented in condensed form, usually by counsel and sometimes through witnesses. This procedure, as ordinarily structured, provides the litigants an opportunity to ask questions and hear the reactions of the Judge or jury. The Judge's or jury's nonbinding verdict and reactions to the legal and factual arguments are used as bases for subsequent settlement negotiations. Parties considering a non-binding summary trial are encouraged to contact the ADR Unit for assistance in structuring a summary trial tailored to their case.

(c) Special Masters. Under Fed. R.Civ. P. 53, the Court may appoint special masters to serve a wide variety of functions, including, but not limited to: discovery manager, fact finder or host of settlement negotiations. The Court may refer a case to a special master on its own initiative, on the request of a party, or upon stipulation of the parties. The precise roles and responsibilities of the special master shall be defined in the case specific order of reference. Generally the parties pay the special master's fees.

[Effective January 1, 2009. Amended effective September 15, 2015; May 1, 2018.]

RULE 8–2.　PRIVATE ADR

There are numerous private sector providers of ADR services including arbitration, Mediation, fact-finding, neutral evaluation and private judging. Private providers may be lawyers, law professors, retired Judges or other professionals with expertise in dispute resolution techniques. Virtually all private sector providers charge fees for their services. The Court does not ordinarily refer cases to private providers except on the stipulation of the parties. The assigned Judge will take appropriate steps to assure that a referral to private ADR does not result in an imposition on any party of an unfair or unreasonable economic burden.

Commentary

Private ADR proceedings are not subject to the provisions of the ADR Local Rules including attendance, confidentiality, enforcement, and immunity. See ADR L.R. 3–4(b).

[Effective January 1, 2009. Amended effective September 15, 2015.]

HABEAS CORPUS LOCAL RULES
RULE 2254. HABEAS CORPUS LOCAL RULES

RULE 2254-1. TITLE

These are the Local Rules of Practice which govern petitions for writs of habeas corpus filed in the United States District Court for the Northern District of California pursuant to 28 U.S.C. § 2254. They should be cited as "Habeas L.R. ___." These rules are effective December 1, 2009 and shall govern habeas corpus actions pending or commenced on or after that date.

These rules are intended to supplement the "Rules Governing Section 2254 Cases in the United States District Courts." The Civil Local Rules of this Court are also applicable in these proceedings, except to the extent that they are inconsistent with these Habeas Corpus Local Rules. The application of these rules to a particular petition may be modified by the Judge to whom the petition is assigned.

[Effective September 1, 1995. Amended effective May 1, 2000; January 1, 2005; December 1, 2009.]

I. HABEAS CORPUS PETITIONS IN NON-CAPITAL CASES

RULE 2254-2. SCOPE

Habeas L.R. 2254-2 to 2254-10 shall apply to a petition for a writ of habeas corpus pursuant to 28 U.S.C. § 2254 in a noncapital case, that is a petition attacking something other than a judgment imposing a penalty of death.

[Effective September 1, 1995. Amended effective May 1, 2000.]

RULE 2254-3. FILING PETITION

(a) **Venue.** The following noncapital petitions for writs of habeas corpus shall be filed in this District:

(1) Petitions challenging the lawfulness of a conviction or sentence for which the petitioner was convicted and sentenced in the following counties: Alameda, Contra Costa, Del Norte, Humboldt, Lake, Marin, Mendocino, Monterey, Napa, San Benito, San Francisco, San Mateo, Santa Clara, Santa Cruz and Sonoma; or

(2) Petitions challenging the manner in which the sentence is being executed, such as loss of good time credits, where the petitioner is confined in an institution located in a county listed in Habeas L.R. 2254-3(a)(1) at the time the petition is filed.

(b) **Transfer of Venue.** If a petition is filed in this District which does not conform to Habeas L.R. 2254-3(a), venue shall be transferred to:

(1) The district of conviction or sentencing if the petition is challenging the conviction or sentence; or

(2) The district of confinement if the petition is challenging the manner in which the sentence is being executed.

(c) **Place for Filing.** Noncapital petitions as to which venue lies in this District shall be filed in San Francisco.

(d) **Form and Content.** Noncapital petitions shall be filed on a form supplied by the Clerk, and shall be filled in by printing or typewriting. In the alternative, the petition may be in a typewritten, word-processed or other legible written form which contains all of the information required by the Court's form.

(e) **Pro Se Petitions.** Noncapital petitions filed by persons who are appearing pro se shall be on a form established for that purpose by the Court and shall be completed in conformity with the instructions approved by the Court. Copies of the forms, instructions and pertinent provisions of these Habeas Corpus Local Rules shall be supplied to pro se petitioners by the Clerk upon request or upon the filing of papers which appear to be a request by a person appearing pro se for relief which should be presented by a petition for habeas corpus pursuant to 28 U.S.C. § 2254.

(f) **Requests to Proceed In Forma Pauperis.** Persons seeking leave to proceed in forma pauperis must complete the application established for that purpose by the Court. Copies of the application form, instructions and pertinent provisions of the local rules shall be supplied to in forma pauperis applicants by the Clerk upon request or upon the filing of papers which appear to be a request by a person to proceed in forma pauperis. The Clerk shall refer a completed application to the assigned Judge for determination.

(g) **Number of Copies.** An original and one copy of the petition shall be filed by a petitioner represented by counsel. A pro se petitioner need only file the original.

[Effective September 1, 1995. Amended effective May 1, 2000.]

RULE 2254-4. ASSIGNMENT TO JUDGES

(a) **Assignment to District Judge.** The assignment of noncapital habeas corpus petitions to a Judge shall be made in accordance with the provisions of the Assignment Plan of the Court.

(b) **Assignment to Magistrate Judge.** Pursuant to 28 U.S.C. § 636(b)(1)(B), a Magistrate Judge may be designated by the Court to perform all duties under these rules.

[Effective September 1, 1995. Amended effective May 1, 2000.]

RULE 2254-5. DISCOVERY

No discovery pursuant to Fed. R. Civ. P. 26-37 shall be conducted with respect to a petition for writ of habeas corpus in noncapital cases without leave of the Court.

[Effective September 1, 1995. Renumbered and amended effective May 1, 2000.]

RULE 2254-6. BRIEFING SCHEDULE

(a) **Schedule.** Unless the Judge summarily dismisses the petition under Rule 4 of the Rules Governing § 2254 Cases, the schedule and procedure set forth in this Rule shall apply, subject to modification by the assigned Judge. Requests for enlargement of any time period in this rule shall comply with the applicable Civil Local Rules for enlargement of time.

Cross Reference

See Civil L.R. 6 "Time."

(b) Answer to Petition. After the Court orders a response to the petition, within 60 days of service of a noncapital petition, the respondent shall serve and file:

(1) An answer to the petition with accompanying points and authorities;

(2) The matters defined in Rule 5 of the Rules Governing § 2254 Cases;

(3) Portions of the trial and appellate record that are relevant to a determination of the issues presented by the petition which have not been previously filed; and

(4) Certificate of service, pursuant to Civil L.R. 5–5.

(c) Traverse. Within 30 days after the respondent has filed the answer, the petitioner may serve and file a traverse.

[Effective September 1, 1995. Amended effective May 1, 2000; January 1, 2005; July 2, 2012.]

RULE 2254–7. EVIDENTIARY HEARING

(a) Request for Evidentiary Hearing. A request for an evidentiary hearing by either party shall be made within 14 days from the filing of the traverse, or within 14 days from the expiration of the time for filing the traverse. The request shall include a specification of which factual issues require a hearing and a summary of what evidence the party proposes to offer. An opposition to the request for an evidentiary hearing shall be made within 14 days from the filing of the request. Any reply shall be filed within 7 days from the filing of the opposition. The Court will then give due consideration to whether an evidentiary hearing will be held.

(b) Transcript of Evidentiary Hearing. If an evidentiary hearing is held and any party orders a transcript, the transcript will be prepared and immediately provided to the petitioner and to the respondent for use in such briefing and argument as the Court may order. Upon the preparation of the transcript, the Court may establish a reasonable schedule for further briefing and argument of the issues considered at the hearing.

[Effective September 1, 1995. Renumbered and amended effective May 1, 2000. Amended effective December 1, 2009.]

RULE 2254–8. ORAL ARGUMENT

(a) Request for Oral Argument. A request for an oral argument by either party shall be made within 14 days from the filing of the traverse, or within 14 days from the expiration of the time for filing the traverse or, if an evidentiary hearing is granted, within 14 days after a decision of the Court with respect to the subject matter of the evidentiary hearing. The request shall include a specification of the issues to be addressed at the argument.

(b) Notice of Hearing. Upon request of a party, the Court, in its discretion, may set the matter down for oral argument. Within 30 days after an evidentiary hearing or within 30 days after the Court has denied a request for an evidentiary hearing, the assigned Judge shall notify the parties whether the Court will hear oral argument and the date of the hearing or whether the matter shall be submitted for decision without oral argument.

[Effective September 1, 1995. Renumbered effective May 1, 2000. Amended effective December 1, 2009.]

RULE 2254–9. RULINGS

The Court's rulings shall be in the form of a written opinion which will be filed. The Clerk shall serve the parties with a copy of the ruling pursuant to Fed. R. Civ. P. 77(d).

[Effective September 1, 1995. Renumbered and amended effective May 1, 2000.]

II. HABEAS CORPUS PETITIONS IN CAPITAL CASES

RULE 2254–20. APPLICABILITY

Habeas L.R. 2254–20 et seq. shall govern the procedures for a first petition for a writ of habeas corpus filed in this District under chapter 153 of Title 28 of the U.S. Code in which the petitioner seeks relief from a judgment imposing a penalty of death. A subsequent filing may be deemed a first petition under this Rule if the original filing was not dismissed on the merits.

[Effective May 1, 2000.]

RULE 2254–21. NOTICES FROM CALIFORNIA ATTORNEY GENERAL

The California Attorney General shall send to the Clerk the following reports:

(a) Monthly Report. Monthly, the Attorney General shall send a list of all scheduled executions in California and a list of death penalty cases emanating from state trial courts in the Northern District that have been affirmed on appeal by the California Supreme Court, or that have been orally argued before the California Supreme Court and are awaiting decision.

(b) Quarterly Report. The Attorney General shall send to the Clerk quarterly a list of all death penalty cases in California that have been affirmed on appeal.

[Effective May 1, 2000.]

RULE 2254–22. VENUE

(a) Policy Statement. Subject to the provisions of 28 U.S.C. § 2241(d), it is the policy of this Court that a petition for writ of habeas corpus in a capital case should be heard in the district in which the petitioner was convicted, rather than in the district of the petitioner's present confinement.

(b) Venue in the District. A capital habeas corpus proceeding is properly commenced in this District if the petitioner challenges the lawfulness of a conviction and death sentence imposed in the following counties: Alameda, Contra Costa, Del Norte, Humboldt, Lake, Marin, Mendocino, Monterey, Napa, San Benito, San Francisco, San Mateo, Santa Clara, Santa Cruz and Sonoma.

(c) Transfer of Venue. If a proceeding is commenced in this District which does not conform to Habeas L.R. 2254-22(a) and (b) the Clerk shall immediately advise the Clerk of the Court of the district of conviction and shall present the matter to the General Duty Judge for an order transferring the matter to the district of conviction. The Clerk shall also prepare a proposed temporary stay order pursuant to Habeas L.R. 2254-24(b).

[Effective May 1, 2000.]

RULE 2254-23. COMMENCEMENT OF PROCEEDINGS

(a) Place of Filing. The first paper or pleading with respect to relief from a judgment imposing a penalty of death for which venue lies in this district shall be filed in the Office of the Clerk at the San Francisco Courthouse. All subsequent papers or pleadings shall be filed in the Office of the Clerk at the courthouse where the assigned Judge maintains his or her chambers.

(b) First Paper or Pleading. The first paper or pleading may be either an application for appointment of counsel or a petition for writ of habeas corpus. The Clerk will have available forms for the application for appointment of counsel. A sample form is available at cand.uscourts.gov. In addition to other matters appropriate to the nature of the first paper or pleading filed pursuant to Habeas L.R. 2254-23(b), the first paper or pleading shall:

(1) Identify by case number any applications for relief with respect to the same matter which the petitioner has filed in any federal court; and

(2) Set forth any scheduled execution date.

(c) Service on the Respondent. An attorney representing a party filing a first paper or pleading in a capital habeas corpus proceeding shall serve a copy of the paper or pleading on the California Attorney General. When a first paper or pleading is filed by a person who is not represented by an attorney, the Clerk shall promptly serve the Attorney General with a copy of that paper or pleading.

(d) Filing Fee. Concurrently with the filing of the initial pleading, or if the filing is made on an emergency basis, then as soon thereafter as reasonably practicable, the petitioner either shall pay the $5 statutory filing fee or shall submit a completed in forma pauperis application. Civil L.R. 3-10 shall govern proceedings with respect to the application.

(e) Assignment to a Judge. After commencement of a proceeding involving a request for a writ of habeas corpus in which it appears that venue is proper in this District, the Clerk shall assign or reassign the matter to a Judge in accordance with the Assignment Plan of the Court.

[Effective May 1, 2000. Amended effective July 2, 2012.]

RULE 2254-24. STAYS OF EXECUTION

(a) Stay Pending Final Disposition. Upon the filing of a first paper or pleading by a petitioner who was convicted and sentenced to death in this District, unless the pleading is patently frivolous, the Judge will order a stay of execution pending final disposition of the proceedings in this Court.

(b) Temporary Stay for Transfer of Venue. When a first paper or pleading is filed by a petitioner who was convicted and sentenced to death in another district, the Clerk shall include a proposed order staying execution with the order presented to a Judge pursuant Habeas L.R. 2254-22(c). The signed stay of execution shall remain in effect until the transferee court acts on it.

(c) Stay Pending Appeal. If the Court dismisses or denies the petition and issues a certificate of probable cause for appeal or a certificate of appealability, the Court will grant a stay of execution which shall remain in effect until the United States Court of Appeals for the Ninth Circuit acts upon the appeal or the order of stay.

(d) Notice of Stay. Upon the granting of any stay of execution, the Clerk will immediately notify the Warden of San Quentin Prison and the Attorney General. The Attorney General shall ensure that the Clerk has a twenty-four hour telephone number to the Warden.

[Effective May 1, 2000.]

RULE 2254-25. COUNSEL

(a) In General. Each petitioner in a proceeding for a writ of habeas corpus in a capital case shall be represented by counsel unless the petitioner has clearly elected to proceed pro se and the assigned Judge is satisfied, after a hearing, that the petitioner's election is intelligent and voluntary.

(b) Appointment and Compensation. Unless the petitioner is represented by retained counsel or has been permitted to proceed pro se, the Court shall appoint counsel at the earliest appropriate time if it finds that the requirement of 21 U.S.C. § 848(q)(4)(B), that the defendant is financially unable to obtain adequate representation, has been satisfied. The assigned Judge, in his or her discretion, will determine whether more than one attorney is necessary for adequate representation of the petitioner. Appointment and compensation of counsel shall be governed by § 6.01(A)(2) of Volume VII of the Guide to Judiciary Policies and Procedures, Appointment of Counsel in Criminal Cases, and by 21 U.S.C. § 848(q)(6), (7) & (10)(A). The presumptive rate for compensation of lead counsel or co-lead counsel shall be $125.00 per hour. The presumptive rate for compensation of second counsel shall be $100.00 per hour.

(c) Selection Board. A selection board appointed by the Chief Judge of the District will certify a panel of attorneys qualified for appointment in capital habeas cases. The selection board will consist of a representative of the Federal Public Defender for the Northern District, a representative of the California Appellate Project (CAP), a representative of the Habeas Corpus Resource Center (HCRC), a representative of the State Public Defender, and a representative of the private bar. The selection board may suggest one or more counsel for appointment. The Court also may request suggestions from the selection board for one or more counsel.

[Effective May 1, 2000.]

RULE 2254–26. CASE MANAGEMENT AND BUDGETING

After a capital habeas corpus proceeding has been assigned to a Judge and counsel has been appointed, the assigned Judge shall conduct an initial case management conference to discuss anticipated proceedings in the case. In all cases where attorneys' fees and investigative and expert expenses are reimbursed pursuant to 21 U.S.C. §§ 848(q)(4)–(10), the petitioner's counsel will be required to prepare phased budgets for submission to the Court. Following the initial case management conference, the assigned Judge may schedule additional case management conferences in advance of each of the budgeting phases. The assigned judge also may schedule one or more ex parte conferences with the petitioner's counsel to implement the budgeting process.

[Effective May 1, 2000.]

RULE 2254–27. LODGING OF THE RECORD

(a) **Material to Be Lodged.** As soon as practicable, but in any event within 21 days from the date of the initial case management conference, the respondent shall lodge with the Court the following:

(1) Transcripts of the state trial court proceedings;

(2) The appellant's and respondent's briefs on direct appeal to the California Supreme Court, and the opinion or orders of that Court;

(3) The petitioner's and the respondent's pleadings in any state court habeas corpus proceedings, and all opinions, orders and transcripts of such proceedings;

(4) Copies of all pleadings, opinions and orders in any previous federal habeas corpus proceeding filed by the petitioner, or on the petitioner's behalf, which arose from the same conviction;

(5) An index of all materials described in items (1) through (4) above. The respondent shall mark and number the materials so that they can be uniformly cited. The respondent shall serve the index upon counsel for the petitioner;

(6) If any item identified in paragraphs (1) through (4) above does not become available until a later date, the respondent shall provide a supplemental lodging and index within 21 days of its availability.

(b) **Missing Documents.** If counsel for the petitioner claims that the respondent has not complied with the requirements of paragraph (a) above, or if counsel for the petitioner does not have copies of all the documents the respondent has lodged with the Court, counsel for the petitioner shall notify the Court in writing as soon as practicable, with a copy to the respondent. The respondent will provide copies of the missing documents to the Court and to the petitioner's counsel, as appropriate.

[Effective May 1, 2000. Amended effective December 1, 2009.]

RULE 2254–28. FINALIZED PETITION

(a) **Form.** The term "finalized petition" shall refer to the petition filed by retained or appointed counsel, or by a petitioner who has expressly waived counsel and elected to proceed pro se under Habeas L.R. 2254–25(a). The finalized petition shall comply with the requirements of 28 U.S.C. § 2242 and the Rules Governing Section 2254 Cases in the United States District Courts, Rule 2(c). The finalized petition shall be filed on a form supplied by the Clerk, and shall be filled in by printing or typewriting. In the alternative, the finalized petition may be in a typewritten, word-processed or other legible written form which contains all of the information required by the Court's form.

(b) **Contents.** All assertions of historical or procedural fact shall be accompanied by citations to the state trial record or other record of proceedings and shall appear in a style comporting with the designations employed in the index of materials prepared in accordance with Habeas L.R. 2254–27(a)(5). The finalized petition shall:

(1) State whether the petitioner has previously sought relief arising out of the same matter from this Court or any other federal court, together with the ruling and reasons of such court;

(2) Include a table of contents which sets forth the headings and subheadings in the petition;

(3) Set forth each factual allegation or group of related allegations in a separately numbered or lettered paragraph;

(4) Identify where in the record each claim was exhausted; and

(5) Set forth any scheduled execution date.

(c) **Filing and Service.** Counsel for the petitioner shall file an original and two copies of the finalized petition and shall serve a copy of the petition on counsel for the respondent. A pro se petitioner need only file the original. The Clerk shall serve a copy of a finalized pro se petition on the Attorney General.

[Effective May 1, 2000.]

RULE 2254–29. SCHEDULE OF PROCEEDINGS FOR CONSIDERING THE FINALIZED PETITION

(a) **Presumptive Schedule.** Unless the Judge summarily dismisses the petition under Rule 4 of the Rules Governing § 2254 Cases, the following schedule and procedure shall apply, subject to modification by the assigned Judge. Requests for enlargement of any time period in this Rule shall comply with the Civil L.R. 7–8.

(b) **Meet and Confer Regarding Exhaustion.** If the respondent contends that any claims in the petition are unexhausted and declines to waive exhaustion, counsel for the respondent shall make a good faith effort to confer with counsel for the petitioner regarding the exhausted status of each such claim. Unless relieved by written order of the Court upon good cause shown, counsel for the petitioner shall confer with counsel for the respondent within 14 days after service of a letter from the respondent requesting such a conference. The letter shall identify each claim that respondent contends is unexhausted, specify the basis for asserting that the claim is unexhausted and provide any legal authority that the respondent contends is dispositive of the exhausted status of that claim.

(c) Motion Regarding Exhaustion. If, after the conference held pursuant to Habeas L.R. 2254–29(b), the parties continue to dispute the exhausted status of one or more claims, then no later than forty-five (45) days after service of the petition, the respondent shall file a motion asking the Court to determine the status of the claim(s). In connection with any motion relating to exhaustion disputes, the parties shall file a joint statement identifying:

(1) The claims the parties agree are exhausted;

(2) The claims the parties agree are not exhausted; and

(3) The claims as to which the parties disagree on exhaustion.

(d) Answer and Request for Case Management Conference. Within forty-five (45) days from the service of the finalized petition, or, if the respondent has filed a motion pursuant to Habeas L.R. 2254–29(c), then within such time as the Court may order, the respondent shall file an answer to the petition and may file accompanying points and authorities. The answer shall conform to Rule 5 of the Rules Governing § 2254 Cases. Concurrently with the filing of the answer, the respondent shall file a request that a case management conference be held within forty-five (45) days.

(e) Meet and Confer Regarding Case Management Conference Statement. No later than fourteen (14) days prior to the date set by the Court for a case management conference, counsel for the petitioner and the respondent shall meet and confer to prepare a joint statement setting forth the parties' positions regarding:

(1) The status of any claims the respondent identifies as procedurally defaulted, and the appropriate procedure for addressing those claims;

(2) The scheduling of motions for any evidentiary hearings; and

(3) The scheduling of any other pleadings or proceedings necessary for resolving the petition, including motions for summary judgment.

(f) Filing of Joint Statement. No later than seven (7) days prior to the case management conference, counsel for the petitioner and the respondent shall file the joint statement for the Case Management Conference.

(g) Case Management Conference. At the Case Management Conference, the Court shall set a schedule for: (1) resolving any issues of procedural default; (2) motions for evidentiary hearings; and (3) any other pleadings or proceedings necessary for resolving the petition, including motions for summary judgment.

(h) Discovery. No discovery pursuant to Fed. R. Civ. P. 26–37 shall be had without leave of the Court. Any permitted discovery shall comply with the Federal Rules of Civil Procedure and the Local Rules of this Court.

(i) Request for Evidentiary Hearing. A request for an evidentiary hearing shall include:

(1) A specification of which issues require a hearing;

(2) A discussion of the legal basis for holding a hearing on each issue; and

(3) A summary of the evidence the party proposes to offer.

(j) Evidentiary Hearing. The Court will determine whether an evidentiary hearing will be held. If an evidentiary hearing is held and any party orders a transcript, the transcript will be prepared and immediately provided to the petitioner and to the respondent for use in such briefing and argument as the Court may order.

(k) Oral Argument. If no evidentiary hearing is held, the Court will determine whether to set the matter for oral argument.

[Effective May 1, 2000. Amended effective December 1, 2009.]

RULE 2254–30. NOTIFICATION OF RULINGS

The Clerk will immediately notify the warden of San Quentin Prison and the Attorney General whenever relief is granted on a petition. The Clerk will immediately notify the Clerk of the United States Court of Appeals for the Ninth Circuit by telephone of (i) the issuance of a final order denying or dismissing a petition without a certificate of probable cause or appealability, or (ii) the denial of a stay of execution.

[Effective May 1, 2000.]

RULE 2254–31. TRANSMISSION OF RECORD

(a) When Petition Denied and Certificate of Appealability Denied. When the petitioner files a notice of appeal from an order denying habeas relief, and the District Court has denied a certificate of probable cause or appealability and denied a stay of execution, the Clerk will transmit to the Court of Appeals immediately:

(1) A copy of the notice of appeal;

(2) A copy of the order(s) denying the certificate and stay;

(3) A copy of the docket sheet; and

(4) The entire record of proceedings in the District Court, including any lodged state court records.

(b) When Petition Denied and Certificate of Appealability Granted. When the petitioner files a notice of appeal from an order denying habeas relief, and the District Court has granted a certificate of probable cause or appealability and granted a stay of execution, the Clerk shall retain the record of proceedings until requested by the Court of Appeals to transmit it. The Clerk will transmit to the Court of Appeals immediately:

(1) A copy of the notice of appeal;

(2) A copy of the order(s) granting the certificate and stay; and

(3) A copy of the docket sheet.

(c) When Petition Granted. When the respondent files a notice of appeal from an order granting habeas relief, the Clerk shall retain the record of proceedings until requested by

the Court of Appeals to transmit it. The Clerk shall transmit to the Court of Appeals immediately:

(1) A copy of the notice of appeal; and

(2) A copy of the docket sheet.

[Effective May 1, 2000.]

CRIMINAL LOCAL RULES

I. SCOPE, PURPOSE AND CONSTRUCTION

RULE 1–1. TITLE

These are the Local Rules of Practice in Criminal proceedings before the United States District Court for the Northern District of California. They should be cited as "Crim. L.R. ___."

[Effective September 1, 1996.]

RULE 2–1. PURPOSE AND CONSTRUCTION

These Rules are promulgated pursuant to 28 U.S.C. § 2071 and Fed. R. Crim. P. 57. They supplement the Federal Rules of Criminal Procedure and shall be construed so as to be consistent with those Rules. The provisions of the Civil Local Rules of the Court shall apply to criminal actions and proceedings, except where they may be inconsistent with these criminal local rules, the Federal Rules of Criminal Procedure or provisions of law specifically applicable to criminal cases.

Cross Reference

See Civil L.R. 1–5(i) "General Orders" and Civil L.R. 1–5(m) "Standing Orders of Individual Judges."

[Effective September 1, 1996. Amended effective May 1, 2000.]

RULE 2–2. DEFINITIONS

Unless the context requires otherwise, the definitions contained in Civil L.R. 1–5 apply to these local rules.

(a) Fed. R. Evid. "Fed. R. Evid." means the Federal Rules of Evidence.

(b) Probation Officer. "Probation Officer" refers to a United States Probation Officer appointed by the United States District Court.

[Effective September 1, 1996.]

RULE 2–3. CERTIFICATE OF SERVICE

(a) Party Certificate of Service. Whenever these local rules or other provision of law requires any pleading or paper which is presented for filing in a criminal case to be served upon any party or person, it shall bear on it or have attached to it a certificate of service in a form which complies with Civil L.R. 5–5(a).

(b) Clerk's Certificate of Service. Unless the Judge or these local rules require otherwise, any written order of the Court in a criminal case shall bear on it or have attached to it a certificate of service by the Clerk.

[Effective September 1, 1996. Amended effective May 1, 2000; July 2, 2012.]

RULE 2–4. LODGING COPY FOR CHAMBERS

Unless the Court orders otherwise, an extra copy of any document filed in a criminal case shall be marked "Chambers Copy," and shall be provided to the Clerk's Office pursuant to Civil L.R. 5–2(b) and 5–1(e)(7).

[Effective September 1, 1996. Amended effective July 2, 2012.]

II. PRELIMINARY PROCEEDINGS

RULE 5–1. CRIMINAL CASE PROCEEDINGS BEFORE ASSIGNMENT TO A DISTRICT JUDGE

(a) Calendar for Proceedings in Criminal Cases Before Assignment. Each courthouse of this District shall maintain a criminal calendar to hear any matter in a criminal case which has been assigned to that courthouse and which arises before the case is assigned to a District Judge.

Cross Reference

See Crim. L.R. 18–1(a), (b) or (c).

(b) Proceedings Before Magistrate Judge Prior to Assignment. At each courthouse a Magistrate Judge shall be designated to hear and decide matters arising before the case has been assigned to a District Judge in criminal cases which have been assigned to that courthouse. The designated Magistrate Judge is empowered to hear and decide any matter on that calendar unless a federal statute or federal rule requires that the matter be decided by a District Judge.

(c) Initial Appearance After Arrest. Whenever a person is arrested in this District for a federal offense, the person shall be brought without unnecessary delay before a Magistrate Judge. The Magistrate Judge before whom the person is brought shall preside over the initial appearance in accordance with Fed. R. Crim. P. 5. All subsequent proceedings shall be conducted at the courthouse where the case has been assigned pursuant to Crim. L.R. 7–1.

(d) Proceedings Before a District Judge Prior to Assignment. When a matter arises in a criminal case before the case has been assigned to a District Judge which a federal statute or federal rule requires be presented to or decided by a District Judge, it shall be presented to the General Duty Judge.

Cross Reference

See Civil L.R. 1–5(j) *"General Duty Judge."*

[Effective September 1, 1996. Amended effective January 1, 2005; January 1, 2018.]

III. INDICTMENT AND INFORMATION

RULE 6–1. IMPANELMENT OF GRAND JURY

The General Duty Judge is empowered to impanel one or more grand juries as the public interest requires. Upon a determination by a General Duty Judge to impanel a grand jury for a particular courthouse, he or she shall summon a sufficient number of legally qualified residents of the counties served by that courthouse pursuant to Civil L.R. 3–2 to satisfy the requirements of Fed. R. Crim. P. 6(a).

[Effective September 1, 1996. Amended effective January 1, 2018.]

RULE 6–2. GRAND JURY ADMINISTRATION

(a) **Motions Pertaining to Composition or Term of Impaneled Grand Jury.** A request by the government or a grand juror for an order pertaining to service on or the term of an impaneled grand jury shall be made by *ex parte* motion or request to the Judge who impaneled the grand jury. If that Judge is unavailable within the meaning of Civil L.R. 1–5(n), the motion or request shall be made to the General Duty Judge. Such motions or requests may pertain to matters such as:

(1) A request by a member of a grand jury or by the government that a grand juror be excused;

(2) A request by the government to appoint an alternate grand juror;

(3) A motion to extend the term of a grand jury.

(b) **Motions Regarding Grand Jury Process or Proceedings.** Any government motion regarding those parts of the grand jury's process or proceedings or in aid of its process or proceedings which must be conducted in secret pursuant to Fed. R. Crim. P. 6, may be made under seal by ex parte motion to the General Duty Judge. Unless otherwise ordered by the General Duty Judge pursuant to ex parte request, any such motion filed by a private party shall be accompanied by proof of service of the motion upon the office of the United States Attorney for this District.

[Effective September 1, 1996. Amended effective May 1, 2000; January 1, 2018.]

RULE 7–1. ASSIGNMENT OF CRIMINAL CASE

(a) **Designation in Caption of Pleading.** In the caption of each complaint, indictment or information immediately following the identification of the pleading, the government shall identify the courthouse to which the action should be assigned pursuant to Crim. L.R. 18–1. After a complaint, indictment or information has been filed in this District and assigned to the appropriate courthouse pursuant to Crim. L.R. 18–1, the Clerk shall assign it to a District Judge pursuant to the Assignment Plan of the Court. The case shall also be assigned to the designated criminal calendar Magistrate Judge at that courthouse.

(b) **Proceedings Before Magistrate Judge After Assignment.** After a case has been assigned to a District Judge pursuant to Crim. L.R. 7–1(a), the criminal calendar Magistrate Judge may conduct the following proceedings as deemed appropriate:

(1) Appoint counsel;

(2) Appoint an interpreter;

(3) Conduct an arraignment and schedule an appearance before the assigned District Judge;

(4) Accept or enter a plea of not guilty;

(5) Conduct a probation or supervised release preliminary revocation hearing;

(6) Hear and determine motions or matters regarding release or detention;

(7) Set a schedule for disclosure of information pursuant to Fed. R. Crim. P. 16;

(8) In a case transferred to this District under Fed. R. Crim. P. 20, order a presentence report and schedule a date for arraignment, plea and sentencing consistent with the time necessary to effect the transfer;

(9) Order a presentence report where a defendant who is represented by counsel has agreed to plead guilty;

(10) In cases pending before the Magistrate Judge, declare forfeiture of bail and conduct proceedings pursuant to Fed. R. Crim. P. 46(e);

(11) After issuance of an order of forfeiture, enforcement, remission or exoneration by a District Judge pursuant to Fed. R. Crim. P. 46(e), conduct further proceedings pertaining to the bond as may be referred by the District Judge;

(12) Conduct proceedings under Fed. R. Crim. P. 40;

(13) Conduct proceedings for extradition;

(14) Conduct such other proceedings which may be performed by a Magistrate Judge as ordered by the assigned District Judge.

[Effective September 1, 1996. Amended effective December 1, 2009.]

RULE 8–1. NOTICE OF RELATED CASE IN A CRIMINAL ACTION

(a) **Notice Requirement.** Whenever a party to a criminal action pending in this District knows or learns that the action is related to a civil or criminal action, which is or was pending in this District, that party shall promptly file a "Notice of Related Case in a Criminal Action" with the Judge assigned to the earliest filed action, shall lodge a copy of the notice with the chambers of each Judge assigned to each related case and shall serve all known parties with a copy of the notice.

Commentary

A Judge's involvement in any pre-indictment miscellaneous proceeding (e.g., issuance of search warrant) is not a basis for assignment of any resulting criminal action to that Judge as a related case.

(b) Definition of Related Case for Criminal Action. Any pending criminal action is related to another civil or criminal action when:

(1) Both actions concern one or more of the same defendants and the same alleged events, occurrences, transactions or property; or

(2) Both actions appear likely to entail substantial duplication of labor if heard by different Judges or might create conflicts and unnecessary expenses if conducted before different Judges.

(c) Content of Notice. A Notice of Related Case in a Criminal Action shall contain:

(1) The title and case number of each related case;

(2) A description of each related case;

(3) A brief statement of the relationship of each action according to the criteria set forth in Crim. L.R. 8–1(b);

(4) A statement by the party with respect to whether assignment to a single Judge is or is not likely to conserve judicial resources and promote an efficient determination of the action.

(d) Response to Notice. No later than 7 days after service of a Notice of Related Case in a Criminal Action, any party may serve and file a statement to support or oppose the notice. Such statement shall specifically address the issues in Crim. L.R. 8–1(b) and (c).

(e) Related Case Order. After the time for filing support or opposition to the notice has passed, the Judge assigned to the earliest-filed case shall issue an order that indicates whether the later-filed case is related or not, and if the case is related, whether the later-filed case is to be reassigned to that Judge. After the Judge issues the related case order, the Clerk shall reassign the case if ordered to do so and shall serve a copy of the order upon the parties and the assigned Judge in the later-filed case.

[Effective September 1, 1996. Amended effective October 1, 2002; January 1, 2003; December 1, 2009; February 3, 2014.]

IV. PREPARATION FOR DISPOSITION BY TRIAL OR SETTLEMENT

RULE 11–1. VOLUNTARY SETTLEMENT CONFERENCE

(a) Joint Request for Referral. At any time prior to the final pretrial conference, the attorney for the government and the attorney for a defendant, acting jointly, may request that the assigned Judge refer the case to another Judge or Magistrate Judge to conduct a settlement conference. In a multiple defendant case, all defendants need not join in the request in order for the assigned Judge to refer for settlement conference the case pending against a requesting defendant.

(b) Order of Referral. Upon a request made pursuant to Crim. L.R. 11–1(a), the assigned Judge may, in his or her discretion, refer the case to another Judge or Magistrate Judge available to conduct the settlement conference. In conjunction with the referral, the assigned Judge may order the pretrial services officer of the Court to provide a report of any prior criminal proceedings involving the defendant to the parties and the settlement Judge.

(c) Conduct of Settlement Conference. The role of the settlement Judge is to assist the parties in exploring a voluntary settlement in a criminal case. The settlement Judge shall schedule a conference taking into consideration the trial schedule in the case. The attorney for the government and the principal attorney for the defendant shall attend the conference. The defendant need not be present at the conference, but shall be present at the courthouse for consultation with defense counsel, unless the defendant's presence is excused by the settlement judge. At least 7 days before the settlement conference, the Deputy Clerk for the settlement Judge shall notify the marshal to bring a defendant who is in custody to the courthouse to be available for consultation with his or her defense counsel. The settlement conference shall not be reported, unless the parties and the settlement judge agree that it should be on the record. Neither the settlement Judge, nor the parties nor their attorneys shall communicate any of the substance of the settlement discussions to the assigned Judge or to any other person. No statement made by any participant in the settlement conference shall be admissible at the trial of any defendant in the case. If a resolution of the case is reached which involves a change in the plea, the settlement Judge shall not take the plea.

(d) Withdrawal of Request for Referral. Participation in a settlement conference is voluntary. Any party may unilaterally withdraw its request for a settlement conference at any time.

[Effective September 1, 1996. Amended effective May 1, 2000; April 19, 2005; December 1, 2009.]

RULE 12–1. PRETRIAL MOTIONS

Unless good cause is shown, all defenses, objections or requests pursuant to Fed. R. Crim. P. 12, which are capable of determination without the trial of the general issue, must be raised by pretrial motion and noticed for hearing on or before the deadline set by the assigned Judge or Magistrate Judge for hearing all pretrial motions. Motions shall be noticed in accordance with Crim. L.R. 47–1.

[Effective September 1, 1996.]

RULE 12.4–1 DISCLOSURE OF NONGOVERNMENTAL CORPORATE PARTY

(a) Certification. The disclosure statement required pursuant to Fed. R. Crim. P. 12.4(a)(1) must be entitled "Certification of Nongovernmental Corporate Party." If a party has no disclosure to make pursuant to this rule, that party must make a certification stating that no such interest is known.

(b) Form of Certification. The certification required by subpart (a) of this rule must take the following form, as is appropriate to the proceeding:

(1) If there is any interest to be certified: "Pursuant to Fed. R. Crim. P. 12.4(a)(1) and Crim. L.R. 12.4–1(a), the undersigned certifies that the following parent or publicly held corporation owns 10 per cent or more of the stock of (name of party), a non-governmental corporate party to this action: (List name of parent or publicly held corporation). Signature, Attorney of Record."

(2) If there is no interest to be certified: "Pursuant to Fed. R. Crim. P. 12.4(a)(1) and Crim. L.R. 12.4–1(a), the undersigned certifies that as of this date, other than the named parties, there is no parent or publicly held corporation which owns 10 per cent or more of the stock of (name of party), a non-governmental corporate party to this action. Signature, Attorney of Record."

(3) Certification, pursuant to subpart (a) of this rule, must be filed as a separate and distinct document.

(4) Any supplemental filing required pursuant to Fed. R. Crim. P. 12.4(b) must be entitled "Supplemental Certification of Nongovernmental Corporate Party" and must comply with the form requirements of subpart (b)(1) of this rule.

(5) When an action is assigned to a district judge pursuant to Crim. L.R. 7–1(a) or is reassigned to another judge pursuant to Crim. L.R. 8–1 or General Order No. 44—Assignment Plan, each party must lodge with the Clerk a chambers copy for the newly assigned judge of any previously filed certification required by this rule.

[Effective January 1, 2005.]

RULE 12.4–2 DISCLOSURE OF ORGANIZATIONAL VICTIM

(a) Certification. The government's disclosure statement required pursuant to Fed. R. Crim. P. 12.4(a)(2) must be entitled "Certification of Organizational Victim."

(b) Form of Certification. The certification required by subpart (a) of this rule must take the following form:

(1) "Pursuant to Fed. R. Crim. P. 12.4(a)(2) and Crim. L.R. 12.4–2(a), the undersigned certifies that the following organization is a victim of the alleged criminal activity charged herein: (name of victim). The parent or publicly held corporation owning 10 per cent or more of the stock of (name of victim) is: (List name of parent or publicly held corporation, if obtainable. If unobtainable, state "Not obtainable."). Signature, Attorney of Record."

(2) Certification, pursuant to subpart (a) of this rule, must be filed as a separate document.

(3) Any supplemental filing required pursuant to Fed. R. Crim. P. 12.4(b) must be entitled "Supplemental Certification of Organizational Victim" and must comply with the form requirements of subpart (b)(1) of this rule.

(4) When an action is assigned to a district judge pursuant to Crim. L.R. 7–1(a) or is reassigned to another judge pursu-

ant to Crim. L.R. 8–1 or General Order No. 44—Assignment Plan, each party must lodge with the Clerk a chambers copy for the newly assigned judge of any previously filed certification required by this rule.

[Effective January 1, 2005.]

RULE 16–1. PROCEDURES FOR DISCLOSURE AND DISCOVERY IN CRIMINAL ACTIONS

(a) Meeting of Counsel. Within 14 days after a defendant's plea of not guilty, the attorney for the government and the defendant's attorney shall confer with respect to a schedule for disclosure of the information as required by Fed. R. Crim. P. 16 or any other applicable rule, statute or case authority. The date for holding the conference can be extended to a day within 21 days after entry of plea upon stipulation of the parties. Any further stipulated delay requires the agreement of the assigned Judge pursuant to Civil L.R. 7–12.

(b) Order Setting Date for Disclosure. In the absence of a stipulation by the parties, a schedule for disclosure of information as required by Fed. R. Crim. P. 16 or any other applicable rule, statute or case authority may be set sua sponte by the assigned Judge or Magistrate Judge. If a party has conferred with opposing counsel as required by Crim. L.R. 16–1(a), the party may make a motion pursuant to Crim. L.R. 47–1 and 47–2 to impose a schedule for such disclosure.

(c) Supplemental Disclosure. In addition to the information required by Fed. R. Crim. P. 16, in order to expedite the trial of the case, in accordance with a schedule established by the parties at the conference held pursuant to Crim. L.R. 16–1(a) or by the assigned Judge pursuant to Crim. L.R. 16–1(b), the government shall disclose the following:

(1) *Electronic Surveillance.* A statement of the existence or non-existence of any evidence obtained as a result of electronic surveillance;

(2) *Informers.* A statement of the government's intent to use as a witness an informant, i.e., a person who has or will receive some benefit from assisting the government;

(3) *Evidence of Other Crimes, Wrongs or Acts.* A summary of any evidence of other crimes, wrongs or acts which the government intends to offer under Fed. R. Evid. 404(b), and which is supported by documentary evidence or witness statements in sufficient detail that the Court may rule on the admissibility of the proffered evidence; and

(4) *Co-conspirator's Statements.* A summary of any statement the government intends to offer under Fed. R. Evid. 801(d)(2)(E) in sufficient detail that the Court may rule on the admissibility of the statement.

[Effective September 1, 1996. Amended effective December 1, 2009.]

RULE 16–2. MOTION TO COMPEL DISCOVERY

(a) Content of Motion. A motion to compel disclosure or discovery shall be accompanied by a declaration by counsel which shall set forth:

(1) The date of the conference held pursuant to Crim. L.R. 16–1(a);

(2) The name of the attorney for the government and defense counsel present at the conference;

(3) The matters which were agreed upon; and

(4) The matters which are in dispute and which require the determination of the Court.

[Effective September 1, 1996. Amended effective May 1, 2000.]

RULE 17–1. SUBPOENA TO TESTIFY IN A CRIMINAL CASE; FORMS

A party seeking to compel the appearance of a witness to testify at a criminal proceeding pursuant to Rule 17(a) or (b) of the Federal Rules of Criminal Procedure, or a party seeking to compel the appearance of a witness to testify and bring documents to a criminal proceeding pursuant to Rule 17(c), must utilize form CAND 89A, "SUBPOENA TO TESTIFY IN A CRIMINAL CASE." Forms are available at the Court's website: cand.uscourts.gov.

[Effective February 1, 2006; January 1, 2018.]

RULE 17–2. SUBPOENA TO PRODUCE DOCUMENTS OR OBJECTS IN ADVANCE OF TRIAL OR HEARING

(a) Order Required. No subpoena in a criminal case may require the production of books, papers, documents or other objects in advance of the trial, hearing or proceeding at which these items are to be offered in evidence, unless the Court has entered an order pursuant to Rule 17(c) of the Federal Rules of Criminal Procedure.

(1) An order permitting issuance of a Rule 17(c) subpoena may be obtained by filing either a noticed motion pursuant to Crim. L.R. 47–2 or, for good cause, an ex parte motion without advance notice to the opposing party. An ex parte motion and order thereon may be filed under seal for good cause. A party requesting a subpoena must support its request by a declaration specifying the facts supporting the issuance of the subpoena along with a proposed order.

Cross Reference

This rule relieves the party filing an ex parte motion from providing advance notice of the motion to the opposing party as required by Crim. L.R. 47–3. However, subsection (e) below requires notice to the opposing party of a subpoena seeking personnel or complaint records from a law enforcement agency.

(2) The Court will determine whether the material sought should be produced. In issuing an order granting the motion, the Court may place limits on the scope of the requested production.

(b) Return of Subpoena. Any Rule 17(c) subpoena must be returnable to the Court and the items sought therein must be delivered to the Court at the place, date and time indicated. The subpoena may advise, however, that no appearance is necessary if the items are produced in advance of the date specified, either to the Court, in an envelope delivered to the Clerk's Office, or directly to the issuing attorney whose name and address appears at the bottom of the subpoena.

(c) Protection for the Recipient. Any Rule 17(c) subpoena must advise the subpoenaed party that if compliance would be unreasonable or oppressive, it may file a motion to quash or modify the subpoena, for an in camera review of the documents, or for an order to permit production only pursuant to a protective order. Motions filed under this subsection must comply with Crim. L.R. 47–2.

(d) Time for Production. No Rule 17(c) subpoena may require the production of documents or objects in fewer than 14 days from the date the subpoena is served, absent good cause, which must be demonstrated in the motion seeking the order for issuance of the subpoena. If the items sought are voluminous, more than 14 days should be permitted to avoid unnecessary motions to quash or modify.

(e) Production of Personnel or Complaint Records From Law Enforcement Agency. In addition to complying with the preceding subsections, if the Rule 17(c) subpoena is directed to a law enforcement agency and seeks the production of personnel or complaint records, the party requesting the subpoena must provide notice of the subpoena to the opposing party in the manner described in subsection (1) below.

(1) A party serving a Rule 17(c) subpoena on a law enforcement agency seeking the production, in advance of trial or hearing, of personnel or complaint records of an officer currently or formerly employed by that agency must serve the opposing party with a copy of the subpoena on the same date that the subpoena is served on the agency.

(2) The term "law enforcement agency" means all police or sheriff's departments, including citizen review boards, and including, but not limited to, state or local transit, public housing or park agencies; agencies with the authority to investigate violations of state, county or municipal law; prison, jail or corrections agencies; and parole and probation agencies.

(f) Forms. A party seeking to compel only the production of books, papers, documents or other objects pursuant to Rule 17(c), in advance of the trial, hearing or proceeding at which these items are to be offered in evidence, must utilize form CAND 89B, "SUBPOENA TO PRODUCE DOCUMENTS OR OBJECTS IN A CRIMINAL CASE." Forms are available at the Court's website: cand.uscourts.gov.

[Effective February 1, 2006. Amended effective December 1, 2009; January 1, 2018.]

RULE 17.1–1 PRETRIAL CONFERENCE

(a) Time for Pretrial Conference. On request of any party or on the Judge's own motion, the assigned Judge may hold one or more pretrial conferences in any criminal action or proceeding.

(b) Pretrial Conference Statement. Unless otherwise ordered, not less than 7 days prior to the pretrial conference, the parties shall file a pretrial conference statement addressing the matters set forth below, if pertinent to the case:

(1) Disclosure and contemplated use of statements or reports of witnesses under the Jencks Act, 18 U.S.C. § 3500, or Fed. R. Crim. P. 26.2;

(2) Disclosure and contemplated use of grand jury testimony of witnesses intended to be called at the trial;

(3) Disclosure of exculpatory or other evidence favorable to the defendant on the issue of guilt or punishment;

(4) Stipulation of facts which may be deemed proved at the trial without further proof by either party and limitation of witnesses;

(5) Appointment by the Court of interpreters under Fed. R. Crim. P. 28;

(6) Dismissal of counts and elimination from the case of certain issues, e.g., insanity, alibi and statute of limitations;

(7) Joinder pursuant to Fed. R. Crim. P. 13 or the severance of trial as to any co-defendant;

(8) Identification of informers, use of lineup or other identification evidence and evidence of prior convictions of defendant or any witness, etc.;

(9) Pretrial exchange of lists of witnesses intended to be called in person or by deposition to testify at trial, except those who may be called only for impeachment or rebuttal;

(10) Pretrial exchange of documents, exhibits, summaries, schedules, models or diagrams intended to be offered or used at trial, except materials that may be used only for impeachment or rebuttal;

(11) Pretrial resolution of objections to exhibits or testimony to be offered at trial;

(12) Preparation of trial briefs on controverted points of law likely to arise at trial;

(13) Scheduling of the trial and of witnesses;

(14) Request to submit questionnaire for prospective jurors pursuant to Crim. L.R. 24–1, voir dire questions, exercise of peremptory and cause challenges and jury instructions;

(15) Any other matter which may tend to promote a fair and expeditious trial.

[Effective September 1, 1996. Amended effective October 1, 2002; December 1, 2009.]

V. VENUE

RULE 18–1. INTRADISTRICT ASSIGNMENT OF CRIMINAL ACTIONS

(a) Assignment to San Francisco. Unless otherwise ordered, the Clerk shall assign all criminal actions and proceedings involving offenses allegedly committed in the counties of Del Norte, Humboldt, Lake, Marin, Mendocino, Napa, San Francisco, San Mateo or Sonoma to a Judge assigned to the San Francisco Courthouse.

(b) Assignment to Oakland. Unless otherwise ordered, the Clerk shall assign all criminal actions and proceedings involving offenses allegedly committed in the counties of Alameda and Contra Costa to a Judge assigned to the Oakland Courthouse.

(c) Assignment to San Jose. Unless otherwise ordered, the Clerk shall assign all criminal actions and proceedings involving offenses allegedly committed in the counties of Santa Clara, Santa Cruz, San Benito or Monterey to a Judge assigned to the San Jose Courthouse.

(d) Extradition. The Clerk shall assign any extradition proceeding to the courthouse which, pursuant to Crim. L.R. 18–1, serves the county in which the defendant is a resident, or if not a resident, the county in which the defendant is physically present at the time the defendant is apprehended.

[Adopted effective September 1, 1996. Amended, effective May 1, 2000.]

RULE 18–2. INTRADISTRICT TRANSFER

Upon a Judge's own motion or the motion of any party, unless the case was specially assigned pursuant to the Assignment Plan, a Judge may order the Clerk to transfer a criminal case to a different courthouse if it appears that the case was not properly assigned under Crim. L.R. 18–1(a), (b), (c) or (d) or that a transfer would be in the interest of justice based upon the convenience of the defendant and the witnesses and the prompt administration of justice.

Cross Reference

See 18 U.S.C. § 3236 (trial of homicide shall be in county in which the offense occurred).

[Adopted effective September 1, 1996.]

RULE 20–1. ASSIGNMENT, PLEA OR SENTENCING UNDER RULE 20

Any criminal case transferred to this District pursuant to Fed. R. Crim. P. 20 shall be commenced in the courthouse which, pursuant to Crim. L.R. 18–1(a), (b), or (c), serves the county in which the defendant is a resident, or if not a resident, the county in which the defendant is physically present at the time the defendant is apprehended.

[Adopted effective September 1, 1996.]

VI. TRIAL

RULE 24–1. PROCEDURE FOR EXERCISE OF PEREMPTORY CHALLENGES

Peremptory challenges to which each party may be entitled under Fed. R. Crim. P. 24(b) shall be exercised in the manner directed by the assigned Judge. Generally, the government may exercise the first challenge, the defense may exercise the second challenge, the next by the government, the next two by the defense, and alternating in this fashion until the government exercises its sixth challenge and the defense its tenth.

[Adopted effective September 1, 1996. Renumbered effective December 1, 2009.]

RULE 24–2. PASSING A PEREMPTORY CHALLENGE

If a party passes a peremptory challenge and if the opposing party also passes, the jury shall be deemed selected. However, if a party passes a peremptory challenge and the opposing party exercises a challenge, the party who previously passed may exercise any unused challenge.

[Adopted effective September 1, 1996. Renumbered effective December 1, 2009. Amended effective January 14, 2013.]

VII. JUDGMENT

RULE 32–1. SCHEDULING OF THE SENTENCING HEARING

(a) Setting the Date for Sentencing. Unless referral is waived or delayed pursuant to Crim. L.R. 32–1(b) or (c), at the time of a finding of guilt or entry of a plea of guilty, the defendant shall be referred to the Probation Officer for this Court for investigation and preparation of a presentence report. Unless it determines otherwise, the Court shall set the defendant's sentencing hearing:

(1) no earlier than 75 days after the referral date, for an in-custody defendant; or

(2) no earlier than 95 days after the referral date, for an out-of-custody defendant.

Commentary

This local rule is designed to allow sufficient time for investigation and preparation of a presentence report and the identification and narrowing of issues requiring judicial resolution before sentencing. Pursuant to Fed. R. Crim. P. 32(a), at the time of a finding of guilt or entry of a plea of guilty for good cause shown, counsel may request the Court to adjust requirements set out by the various sections of Crim. L.R. 32 (e.g., shortening or lengthening the time between judgment and sentencing or modify the requirements regarding materials to be filed prior to sentencing.).

Offenses to which the sentencing guidelines are not applicable (offenses prior to November 1, 1987) shall also comply with the time limits established by this rule.

Cross Reference

See Crim. L.R. 32–3(a) (Duty of defense counsel and defendant to report to probation office on the day of referral).

(b) Immediate or Expedited Sentencing. If the defendant waives his or her right to a presentence report and the Court finds that it is able to exercise its sentencing authority meaningfully without a presentence report, the Court may immediately sentence the defendant or set a sentencing hearing on an expedited schedule.

(c) Delayed Referral and Sentencing. For good cause shown, the Court may delay referral of the case to the Probation Officer. Upon referral, unless otherwise ordered, the time periods set forth in Crim. L.R. 32–1(a) shall apply.

(d) Notification to Probation Officer. On the day a defendant is referred to the Probation Officer, the Clerk shall transmit to the Probation Officer written notice of referral and of the date set for sentencing of the defendant.

[Adopted effective September 1, 1996.]

RULE 32–2. RESCHEDULING THE DATE FOR SENTENCING

(a) Stipulation or Motion. At any time prior to filing the final presentence report, the parties may file a stipulation or a party may make a motion to change a date for the sentencing hearing in a case. The stipulation or motion shall be served upon the opposing party and the Probation Officer. The stipulation or motion shall contain:

(1) Good cause for the change;

(2) Certification that the moving party has conferred with opposing counsel and the Probation Officer and that those parties will be available on the changed date if the motion is granted;

(3) Certification that the moving party has conferred with the Courtroom Deputy Clerk for the assigned Judge and that the changed date is available on the calendar of the assigned Judge; and

(4) A proposed order.

(b) Response or Opposition to Motion to Reschedule. Any response or opposition to a motion to reschedule the date for a sentencing hearing shall conform with the requirements of Crim. L.R. 47–3(c).

(c) Continuance by the Probation Officer. In the event there is a delay in obtaining information necessary for completing the presentence report, the Probation Officer may make a motion pursuant to Civil L.R. 7–11 that the date for sentencing be changed. The motion shall include:

(1) Certification that the Probation Officer has conferred with counsel for the parties and the courtroom Deputy Clerk with respect to the new date; that the date is available for the parties and the hearing calendar of the assigned Judge or whether there is any objection to the change by a party; and

(2) A proposed order.

(d) Effect of Rescheduling of Sentencing on Deadlines. Unless otherwise stated, if the Judge grants a motion to change the date for sentencing, unless otherwise ordered, the deadlines set in Crim. L.R. 32–3, 32–4 and 32–5 shall automatically adjust and be calculated from the new sentencing date.

[Adopted effective September 1, 1996. Amended, effective May 1, 2000; January 1, 2005.]

RULE 32–3. INITIATION OF THE PRESENTENCE INVESTIGATION

(a) Duty to Assist Probation Office Scheduling. On the day the defendant is referred to the Probation Officer, the defendant's counsel (and, if the defendant is out of custody, the defendant as well) shall immediately report to the Probation Officer for the purpose of assisting in the presentence investigation.

Cross Reference

Fed. R. Crim. P. 32(b)(2) (Right of defense counsel to notice and opportunity to attend interview).

(b) Sentencing Information in Government's Possession. Within 7 days after receiving a written request from the Probation Officer for information (e.g., indictment, plea agreement, investigative report, etc.), the attorney for the government shall respond to the request and may supply other relevant information. The attorney for the government shall serve a copy of the material on defense counsel, except material already in the possession of defense counsel.

(c) Deadline for Submission of Material Regarding Sentence. Any material a party wishes the Probation Officer to consider for purposes of the proposed presentence report shall be submitted to the Probation Officer at least 45 days before the date set for sentencing. The party shall serve a copy of the material on opposing counsel, except for material already in the possession of opposing counsel.

[Adopted effective September 1, 1996.]

RULE 32–4. PROPOSED PRESENTENCE REPORT

(a) Distribution of Proposed Presentence Report. Pursuant to Fed. R. Crim. P. 32(b)(6)[1] at least 35 days before the date set for sentencing, the Probation Officer shall furnish to defense counsel (or a pro se defendant) and to the attorney for the government, a proposed presentence report.

(b) Parties' Response to Proposed Presentence Report. Within 14 days after the proposed presentence report has been furnished pursuant to Fed. R. Crim. P. 32(b)(6),[2] a party shall deliver to the Probation Officer and to opposing counsel a written response to the proposed presentence report which shall comply with Crim. L.R. 32–4(c).

(c) Content of Response to Proposed Presentence Report.

(1) *Statement of No Opposition.* If a party does not object to factual statements or computations of offense level under the guidelines of the United States Sentencing Commission, the party shall notify the Probation Officer in writing that the party has no objections under Fed. R. Crim. P. 32(b)(6).[3]

(2) *Statement of Opposition.* If Crim. L.R. 32–4(c)(1) does not apply, the written response required by Crim. L.R. 32–4(b) shall identify and address any objections to factual statements or guideline computations in the proposed report. The response shall not be filed with the sentencing Judge. Such objections must:

(A) Set out each objection to the proposed presentence report, including each material factual statement disputed and how that party's version of the facts differs from those stated in the proposed presentence report, as well as citation to material facts omitted from the proposed presentence report;

(B) Specifically cite the evidentiary support for that party's version of the material facts; and

(C) State any variation the party contends should be made from the guideline computation recommended in the proposed presentence report.

Commentary

This rule is intended to implement the informal process of identifying and narrowing issues that will ultimately require judicial resolution. Parties should be aware that the objections not raised to the Probation Officer may not be considered by the Court absent a showing of good cause. See Fed. R. Crim. P. 32–5(b)(6)(D).[4]

(d) Presentence Conference With Probation Officer. If the response of a party contains objections, the party shall attend any meeting called by the Probation Officer pursuant to Fed. R. Crim. P. 32(b)(6)(B).[5] If the presence of a party or parties is not feasible, the Probation Officer may conduct the conference telephonically.

Commentary

This rule does not mandate that a presentence conference occur. If the Probation Officer feels that one is not needed, the Probation Officer need not call such a conference. However, if the Probation Officer does call such a conference, attorneys *must* attend and participate.

Participants in the presentence conference process should consider disseminating documents by electronic means (e.g., by fax transmission) in order to speed dissemination of the proposed presentence report. Crim. L.R. 32–3 presumes that the U.S. Probation Offices in the Northern District of California will establish regulations and procedures for the expeditious disclosure of the proposed presentence report to the defendant, defense counsel and the attorney for the government.

(e) Conference With In–Custody Defendant. If requested by the probation office and to the extent its available resources permit, the U.S. Marshal shall bring an in-custody defendant to a courthouse on a date scheduled for an initial or subsequent interview with the Probation Officer pursuant to Fed. R. Crim. P. 32 or for disclosure of the presentence report to the defendant pursuant to Crim. L.R. 32–4 and 32–5.

Commentary

This rule is designed to aid efforts by the Probation Officer to expedite meetings with defense counsel and the defendant and to reduce the cost of presentence interviews. It is contemplated that the Marshal would utilize any excess capacity to transport or hold a defendant in order to facilitate an interview.

[Adopted effective September 1, 1996. Amended effective December 1, 2009.]

[1] [**Publisher's Note:** So in original. Probably should read "Fed. R. Crim. P. 32(e)(2)".]

[2] [**Publisher's Note:** So in original. Probably should read "Fed. R. Crim. P. 32(e)(2)".]

[3] [**Publisher's Note:** So in original. Probably should read "Fed. R. Crim. P. 32(f)".]

4 [**Publisher's Note:** So in original. Probably should read "Fed. R. Crim. P. 32(f)(1)".]

5 [**Publisher's Note:** So in original. Probably should read "Fed. R. Crim. P. 32(f)(2)".]

RULE 32–5. FINAL PRESENTENCE REPORT

(a) **Final Presentence Report and Attachments.** At least 14 days before the date set for sentencing, the Probation Officer shall disclose a copy of the final presentence report and recommendations to defense counsel (or a pro se defendant), attorney for the government and lodge a copy with the sentencing Judge. The final presentence report shall be accompanied by a separate enclosure containing any of the following documents:

(1) Plea agreement;

(2) Character reference letters;

(3) Victim-witness letters;

(4) Certification by the Probation Officer that the proposed and final presentence reports were disclosed to defense counsel (or pro se defendant) and the dates of those disclosures; and

(5) Any other matter for consideration by the Court which pertains to sentencing.

Commentary

The final presentence report shall include or contain an addendum setting forth objections that remain unresolved following the process set out in Crim. L.R. 32–4.

While this rule requires attachments to the final presentence report be in a separate enclosure, the Probation Officer may attach the materials to the copy of the final report which is furnished to the attorney for the government and attorney for the defendant, rather than in a separate enclosure. The Probation Officer does not need to supply a party with material which originated with that party.

(b) **Sentencing Memorandum.** The parties may submit a sentencing memorandum addressing sentencing issues as set forth below and must submit a sentencing memorandum if a departure or evidentiary hearing is requested. Any sentencing memorandum shall be filed no later than 7 days prior to the date set for sentencing. If the sentencing memorandum requests a departure, the title of the memorandum shall state "Motion for Departure;" and if the sentencing memorandum requests an evidentiary hearing, the title of the memorandum shall state "Request for Evidentiary Hearing." The sentencing memorandum shall contain the following:

(1) *Unresolved Objections Identified in the Final Presentence Report.* The sentencing memorandum need not reassert objections any party has made that are identified in the final presentence report as unresolved objections; however, a party's sentencing memorandum may elaborate on objections identified in the final presentence report and shall indicate whether or not the party requests an evidentiary hearing to resolve any objection.

(2) *Departures.* Any party requesting a departure that has not been identified in the final presentence report must file a sentencing memorandum that states the sentence requested, the grounds for the departure, and the legal authority for the departure.

(3) *Other Matters.* The sentencing memorandum may include any other matter that a party believes should be considered in connection with sentencing.

Commentary

With the prior approval of the Court, the sentencing memorandum may be filed under seal.

(c) **Response to Sentencing Memorandum.** A response, if any, to the opposing party's memorandum may be filed no later than 3 days prior to the date set for sentencing. If a party requests an evidentiary hearing to resolve any issue raised in the reply or the opposing party's sentencing memorandum, the title of the reply shall state "Request for Evidentiary Hearing."

Commentary

If the sentencing memorandum is filed under seal, the reply to the sentencing memorandum must be filed under seal.

(d) **Evidentiary Hearing.** If the sentencing memorandum or reply requests an evidentiary hearing, in addition to so stating in the title of the document, the pleading shall set forth:

(1) The factual issues to be resolved at the evidentiary hearing; and

(2) The names of the witnesses to be called and a description of their proposed testimony.

(e) **Judicial Notice of Evidentiary Hearing or Unsolicited Departure.** If the sentencing Judge is considering departing for a reason not identified in the final presentence report or requested by a party or if the sentencing Judge decides to conduct an evidentiary hearing, the Judge shall notify the parties and the Probation Officer and may schedule a conference with the parties and the Probation Officer to decide any issues relating to the departure or evidentiary hearing. If the Court issues no notice of an evidentiary hearing, no evidentiary hearing will be held on the date set for sentencing.

Commentary

This local rule outlines the procedure for formal litigation relating to sentencing that follows the informal proceedings set out in Crim. L.R. 32–1 through 32–4. This rule anticipates that litigants will have undertaken in good faith to resolve objections informally with opposing counsel and the Probation Officer and thereby identified and narrowed the issues requiring judicial resolution. It seeks to avoid duplication of efforts by relieving litigants from reasserting in memoranda those objections of which the Court will be apprised by the final presentence report, but it requires objections to be raised in the informal process of Crim. L.R. 32–4 by imposing a requirement that good cause be shown before such an objection not previously made can be considered.

[Adopted effective September 1, 1996. Amended effective December 1, 2009; July 2, 2012.]

RULE 32–6. SENTENCING PROCEEDINGS

(a) **Form of Judgment.** After imposition of sentence, without unnecessary delay, the Court shall enter judgment on the form entitled "Judgment in a Criminal Case" adopted by the Administrative Office of the United States Courts.

(b) Statement of Reasons. The Court provides a statement of reasons pursuant to 18 U.S.C. § 3553(c)(1) when:

(1) The Court completes and attaches the form entitled "Statement of Reasons" to the form of judgment entered pursuant to Crim. L.R. 32–6(a); or

(2) The sentencing Judge states in open court the reason for imposing a sentence and orders the court reporter or recorder to prepare immediately a transcript of the proceedings, which the Clerk shall attach to the judgment form required by Crim. L.R. 32–6(a). The court reporter or recorder shall deliver a copy of the transcript to the Probation Officer.

(3) Disclosure of Statements of Reasons. A statement of reasons is a confidential record of the Court. Except as otherwise authorized by statute, federal rule or regulation or unless expressly authorized by order of the Court, such records shall be disclosed only to the Court, court personnel, the defendant, defense counsel and the attorney for the government.

(c) Record of Finding Regarding Accuracy of Presentence Report. When the sentencing Judge makes a finding with respect to the accuracy of the presentence report pursuant to Fed. R. Crim. P. 32(c)(1), the Judge shall be deemed to have provided a record of the finding if he or she:

(1) Includes the finding in the statement of reasons pursuant to Crim. L.R. 32–6(b)(1) or (2); or

(2) Orders the Probation Officer to incorporate the finding in an addendum to the final presentence report, a copy of which shall be provided to the Court and the parties at least 5 days before the final presentence report is submitted to the Bureau of Prisons.

[Former Rule 32–7 effective September 1, 1996. Renumbered as Rule 32–6, effective July 1, 1997. Renumbered as Rule 32–7, effective May 1, 2000. Amended effective October 1, 2002. Renumbered and amended effective January 1, 2005. Amended effective December 1, 2009; November 9, 2020.]

RULE 32–7. CONFIDENTIAL CHARACTER OF PRESENTENCE REPORT

(a) Disclosure of Presentence Reports and Related Records. A presentence report, probation, supervised release report, violation report and related documents to be offered in a sentencing or violation hearing are confidential records of the Court. Except as otherwise required by Fed. R. Crim. P. 26.2, authorized by statute, federal rule or regulation or unless expressly authorized by order of the Court, such records shall be disclosed only to the Court, court personnel, the defendant, defense counsel and the attorney for the government in connection with sentencing, violation hearings, appeal or collateral review.

(b) Request for Disclosure Under Circumstances Not Covered by Statute. Anyone seeking an order authorizing disclosure of a presentence report which is not authorized by statute, federal rule or regulation shall file a motion pursuant to Crim. L.R. 47–1 with the sentencing Judge or, if no longer sitting, with the General Duty Judge Such motion shall state with particularity the reason disclosure is sought and to whom the report will be provided. No disclosure shall be made

under this Crim. L.R. 32–7(b) except upon an order issued by this Court. The motion shall be served upon the defendant, last defense counsel of record, the attorney for the government and the Probation Officer of record.

Commentary

Other than as allowed by any regulations of the Probation Office for disclosure (e.g., for disclosure to U.S. Marshal in the case of an absconding defendant or to other U.S. Probation Offices for purposes of supervision or other sentencings of the defendant; therapists with whom the defendant is engaged as a result of a court ordered study or condition of supervision; or U.S. Sentencing Commission pursuant to 28 U.S.C. § 994(w), a presentence report should not be disclosed.

[Former Rule 32–8 effective September 1, 1996. Renumbered as Rule 32–7, effective July 1, 1997. Renumbered as Rule 32–8, effective May 1, 2000. Renumbered and amended effective January 1, 2005. Amended effective January 1, 2018.]

RULE 32.1–1. REVOCATION OF PROBATION OR SUPERVISED RELEASE

(a) Petition for Revocation. The following procedures shall be followed with respect to any petition by a Probation Officer for revocation of probation or supervised release:

(1) The petition shall be filed and noticed for hearing before the sentencing Judge or sentencing Magistrate Judge. If the sentencing judicial officer is unavailable, the petition shall be presented to the Criminal Calendar Magistrate Judge for the courthouse where the probationer or releasee was originally sentenced or to the General Duty Judge;

(2) The petition shall be accompanied by a summons and proposed order that the probationer or releasee appear and show cause why probation or supervised release should not be revoked. Alternatively, the petition may request that the Court issue an arrest warrant. If a warrant is sought, the probation office shall recommend bail in a specified amount or that the probationer or releasee be held without release on bail; and

(3) Unless otherwise ordered, the Probation Officer shall serve a copy of the petition and order on the probationer or releasee, last known counsel of record and the attorney for the government.

(b) Preliminary Revocation Hearing. A preliminary hearing to determine whether or not there is probable cause to believe that a violation has occurred may be conducted by a criminal calendar Magistrate Judge. If the Magistrate Judge finds the existence of probable cause, the Magistrate Judge shall set the matter for a revocation hearing before the assigned Judge or sentencing Magistrate Judge.

(c) Appearance by Attorney for the Government. An attorney for the government may appear on behalf of the government at any proceeding to revoke probation or supervised release.

(d) Order Regarding Disposition of Petition. The disposition of a petition for violation of probation or supervised release and the facts upon which it is based shall be set forth on the form adopted by the Administrative Office of the United States Courts for that purpose.

(e) Presentence Report and Recommendation for Revocation of Probation or Supervised Release. A Probation Officer may initiate a revocation proceeding by the Submission of a Form 12 to the Court that placed the defendant on probation or supervised release. If the Court decides that a hearing is appropriate, it shall notify the parties and the Probation Officer. The Probation Officer shall have no further contact with the Court with respect to the Form 12 prior to the hearing on the violation.

If, after a hearing, the defendant is found to have violated the terms of probation or supervised release, the Probation Officer shall prepare a dispositional report and recommendation. At least 7 days before the date set for sentencing after the Court has revoked a term of probation or supervised release, the Probation Officer shall disclose a copy of a dispositional report and recommendation to defense counsel (or to a *pro se* defendant) and to the attorney for the government, and shall lodge a copy with the sentencing Judge.

[Adopted effective September 1, 1996. Amended effective May 1, 2000; January 1, 2018.]

VIII. [RESERVED]

IX. SUPPLEMENTARY AND SPECIAL PROCEEDINGS

RULE 40–1. ASSIGNMENT OF RULE 40 CASES

For purposes of assignment of proceedings under Fed. R. Crim. P. 40, the "nearest available federal Magistrate Judge" shall be deemed to be a Magistrate Judge sitting at the courthouse which serves the county in which the defendant is a resident, or, if not a resident, the county in which the defendant is physically present at the time the defendant is apprehended.

[Adopted effective September 1, 1996.]

RULE 41–1. ASSIGNMENT OF RULE 41 MOTION OR PROCEEDINGS

When no criminal case has been filed, proceedings under Fed. R. Crim. P. 41 shall be assigned as a miscellaneous matter to the General Duty Judge. When a criminal case is pending or has been completed, proceedings under Fed. R. Crim. P. 41 shall bear the original case number and shall be assigned to the District Judge assigned to the pending or completed criminal case.

[Adopted effective September 1, 1996. Amended effective January 1, 2018.]

X. GENERAL PROVISIONS

RULE 44–1. RIGHT TO AND APPOINTMENT OF COUNSEL

(a) Retained Counsel. If a defendant appears without counsel in a criminal proceeding, the Court may grant a reasonable continuance if the defendant expresses a desire to retain counsel.

(b) Appointed Counsel. If a defendant requests appointment of counsel by the Court, the Court shall appoint counsel in accordance with the plan of the Court adopted pursuant to the Criminal Justice Act of 1964.

(c) Proceeding Pro Se. A defendant may elect to proceed without counsel, provided the defendant waives the right to counsel in a manner approved by the Judge or Magistrate Judge. However, if requested by the pro se defendant, the Court may designate counsel to advise the pro se defendant.

[Adopted effective September 1, 1996.]

RULE 44–2. APPEARANCE AND WITHDRAWAL OF COUNSEL

(a) Appearance of Counsel. Whether retained or appointed, an attorney appearing for a defendant in a criminal case shall promptly inform the Court by either a written or oral representation on the record that he or she is making a general appearance on behalf of the defendant.

(b) Withdrawal of Counsel. An attorney who wishes to withdraw must file a motion to withdraw, showing good cause for allowing the attorney to withdraw. Failure of the defendant to pay agreed compensation may not necessarily be deemed good cause. Notice of the motion shall be given to the defendant and all parties to the case. The attorney continues to represent the party until entry of a court order granting leave to withdraw.

(c) Duration of Representation.

(1) *District Court Proceedings.* Unless such leave is granted pursuant to Crim. L.R. 44–2(b), the attorney shall continue to represent the defendant until the case is dismissed, or the defendant is acquitted or, if convicted, until the expiration of the time for making post-trial motions and for filing notice and appeal pursuant to Fed. R. App. P. 4(b).

(2) *On Appeal.* If an appeal is filed, the attorney shall continue to serve until leave to withdraw is granted by the Court having jurisdiction of the case or until other counsel has been appointed by that court as provided in 18 U.S.C. § 3006A and in other applicable provisions of law.

[Adopted effective September 1, 1996. Amended effective May 1, 2000.]

RULE 44-3. PRO SE DEFENDANT
IN CRIMINAL CASE

(a) Manner of Giving Notice to Pro Se Defendant. If a defendant appears pro se, a party shall be deemed to comply with any requirement of these local rules for giving notice to defense counsel if such notice is personally served upon a defendant who is in custody or if such notice is mailed to the last known address of a defendant who is out of custody.

(b) Actions Required by Pro Se Defendant. Any act these local rules require to be done by defense counsel shall be performed by the defendant, if appearing pro se.

[Adopted effective September 1, 1996.]

RULE 46-1. MOTIONS TO RELEASE
OR DETAIN

Subject to the provisions of 18 U.S.C. §§ 3141-3145, 3148-3149, Magistrate Judges shall hear and determine all motions to release or detain except as otherwise ordered by the Court.

[Adopted effective September 1, 1996.]

RULE 46-2. POSTING SECURITY

When the release of a defendant is conditioned upon the deposit of cash (i.e., currency, check or money order) with the Court, such deposit shall be made with the cashier of the office of the Clerk of this Court during the regular business hours set forth in Civil L.R. 77-1(b). When the release of a defendant is conditioned upon the deposit of other security (e.g., deed of trust) with the Court, such deposit shall be made with the Magistrate Judge who set the bail or with a person designated by the Magistrate Judge in accordance with the "Guidelines in Posting Real Property as Bail in Lieu of Cash/Surety Bond; Surrendering Passport(s)," or as modified by the Court. A copy of the guideline is available from the office of the Clerk.

[Adopted effective September 1, 1996.]

RULE 47-1. MOTION IN CRIMINAL CASE

(a) Types of Motions. Any request to the Court for an order in a criminal case must be presented by:

(1) Noticed motion pursuant to Crim. L.R. 47-2;

(2) For good cause shown, ex parte motion pursuant to Crim. L.R. 47-3; or

(3) Stipulation of the affected parties pursuant to Crim. L.R. 47-4;

(b) To Whom Made. Unless otherwise ordered by the assigned Judge, all motions in criminal cases shall be noticed in writing on the criminal motions calendar of the assigned Judge.

[Adopted effective September 1, 1996. Amended effective July 1, 1997; May 1, 2000.]

RULE 47-2. NOTICED MOTION
IN A CRIMINAL CASE

(a) Time. Except as the assigned Judge directs or these criminal local rules require, all motions in criminal cases shall be filed, served and noticed in writing for hearing not less than 14 days after service of the motion or, if the Judge specially sets a date for hearing, not less than 14 days before the date specially set. This rule does not apply to motions during the course of trial or hearing.

(b) Format. Except as otherwise specifically provided, the format of motions shall comply with the requirements of Civil L.R. 7-2(b) and (c). Motions presenting issues of fact shall be supported by affidavits or declarations which shall comply with the requirements of Civil L.R. 7-5.

(c) Time Under the Speedy Trial Act. When filing any motion or papers concerning any matter to which an exclusion under 18 U.S.C. § 3161 may apply, the government shall indicate in a concluding paragraph entitled "Speedy Trial Act Implications," the number of days remaining before trial must commence as of the date the motion or paper is filed. If the defendant has any objection to the government's calculation, the objection and the defendant's calculation shall be stated in any response to the motion or papers.

(d) Opposition or Reply. Any opposition to a noticed motion shall be served and filed not more than 7 days after the motion is filed. Any reply shall be served and filed not more than 4 days after the opposition is due. Any opposition or reply shall comply with Civil L.R. 7-3(b), (c) and (d); 7-4 and 7-5, with respect to format and length unless otherwise ordered.

[Adopted effective September 1, 1996. Amended effective October 1, 2002; January 1, 2003; December 1, 2009; March 12, 2012.]

RULE 47-3. EX PARTE MOTION
IN A CRIMINAL CASE

(a) Form and Content of Ex Parte Motion. An ex parte motion shall contain:

(1) In one filed document not exceeding 5 pages in length, the motion, a memorandum of points and authorities which shall contain a citation to the rule or order which permits use of an ex parte motion to obtain the relief sought;

(2) Affidavits or declarations setting forth specific facts which support granting the requested relief without notice or with limited notice to the opposing party;

(3) A proposed form of order.

Cross Reference

See e.g., Crim. L.R. 6-2 [ex parte motion re grand jury].

[Adopted effective September 1, 1996. Amended effective May 1, 2000; July 2, 2012.]

RULE 47-4. STIPULATION

A stipulation requesting judicial action shall be in writing signed by all affected parties or their counsel. A proposed form of order may be submitted with the stipulation and may consist of an endorsement on the stipulation of the words, "PURSUANT TO STIPULATION, IT IS SO ORDERED," with spaces designated for the date and signature of the Judge.

Cross Reference

See e.g., Crim. L.R. 11–1(a) [stipulation to voluntary settlement conference] and Crim. L.R. 32–2(a) and (c) [stipulation to change date of sentencing].

[Adopted effective September 1, 1996. Renumbered effective May 1, 2000.]

RULE 55–1. CUSTODY AND DISPOSITION OF EXHIBITS

Excepting contraband, firearms and other sensitive items, or unless the Judge hearing the matter otherwise orders, the procedures set forth in Civil L.R. 79–4(a) and (b) shall govern the custody and disposition of exhibits in criminal proceedings before the Court, except, without further order of a court, a party to a criminal case may take possession of the evidence that party offered upon the declaration of a mistrial.

[Adopted effective September 1, 1996. Amended effective May 1, 2000; October 10, 2013.]

RULE 56–1. FILING DOCUMENTS UNDER SEAL IN CRIMINAL CASES

(a) Electronic Filing of Sealed Documents in Criminal Cases Not Permitted. An administrative motion to file documents under seal, and the documents in support thereof, must be manually filed if the sealing of the motion itself is desired, otherwise the administrative motion must be e-filed. Until further notice, the electronic filing ("e-filing") of the documents sought to be sealed in criminal cases is not permitted. Under seal filings in criminal cases must be submitted manually, in hard copy form. Following the Court's ruling on a motion to seal, any publicly-filed documents shall be e-filed.

(b) Specific Court Order Required. Except as provided in Crim. L.R. 56–1(c)(1), no document may be filed under seal (i.e., closed to inspection by the public) except pursuant to a court order that authorizes the sealing of the particular document, or portions thereof. A sealing order may issue only upon a request that establishes that a document is sealable because, for example, the safety of persons or a legitimate law enforcement objective would be compromised by the public disclosure of the contents of the document. The request must be narrowly tailored to seek sealing only of sealable material, and must conform with Crim. L.R. 56–1(c).

Commentary

As a public forum, the Court has a policy of providing to the public full access to documents filed with the Court. The Court recognizes that, in some cases, the Court must consider information that, if made available to the public, would compromise the safety of persons (e.g., cooperating defendants) and/or thwart legitimate law enforcement objectives (e.g., the arrest of a defendant who poses a substantial risk of evading capture). This rule governs requests in criminal cases to file under seal documents or things, whether pleadings, memoranda, declarations, documentary evidence or other evidence. This rule is designed to ensure that the assigned Judge receives in chambers a confidential copy of the unredacted and complete document, annotated to identify which portions are sealable, that a separate unredacted and sealed copy is maintained for appellate review, and that, where appropriate, a redacted copy is filed and available for public review with the minimum redactions necessary to protect sealable information.

(c) Request to File Document, or Portions Thereof, Under Seal. A party seeking to file a document, or portions thereof, under seal ("the Submitting Party") must:

(1) File and serve (unless the motion is filed ex parte) an Administrative Motion to File Under Seal, in conformance with Civil L.R. 7–11. The administrative motion, and any attachments thereto, may be filed under seal before a sealing order is obtained. Any documents filed under seal must be contained in a sealed envelope or other suitable container with a cover sheet affixed to the envelope or container, setting forth the information required by Civil L.R. 3–4(a) and prominently displaying the notation "DOCUMENTS SUBMITTED UNDER SEAL."

(2) The administrative motion must be accompanied by the following attachments:

(A) A **declaration** establishing that the document sought to be filed under seal, or portions thereof, are sealable.

(B) A **proposed order** that is narrowly tailored to seal only the sealable material, and which lists in table format each document or portion thereof that is sought to be sealed.

(C) A **redacted version** of the document that is sought to be filed under seal. The redacted version shall prominently display the notation " REDACTED VERSION OF DOCUMENT(S) SOUGHT TO BE SEALED." A redacted version need not be filed if the submitting party is seeking to file the entire document under seal.

(D) An **unredacted version** of the document sought to be filed under seal. The unredacted version must indicate, by highlighting or other clear method, the portions of the document that have been omitted from the redacted version, and prominently display the notation "UNREDACTED VERSION OF DOCUMENT(S) SOUGHT TO BE SEALED."

(3) Provide a courtesy copy of the administrative motion, declaration, proposed order, and both the redacted and unredacted versions of all documents sought to be sealed, in accordance with Civil L.R. 5–1(e)(7).

The courtesy copy of unredacted declarations and exhibits should be presented in the same form as if no sealing order was being sought; in other words, if a party is seeking to file under seal one or more exhibits to a declaration, or portions thereof, the courtesy copy should include the declaration with all of the exhibits attached, including the exhibits, or portions thereof, sought to be filed under seal, with the portions to be sealed highlighted or clearly noted as subject to a sealing motion.

The courtesy copy should be an exact copy of what was filed. The courtesy copy must be contained in a sealed envelope or other suitable container with a cover sheet affixed to the envelope or container, setting forth the information required by Civil L.R. 3–4(a) and prominently displaying the notation

"COURTESY [or CHAMBERS] COPY—DOCUMENTS SUBMITTED UNDER SEAL."

The courtesy copies of sealed documents will be disposed of in accordance with the assigned judge's discretion. Ordinarily these copies will be recycled, not shredded, unless special arrangements are made.

(d) Effect of Court's Ruling on Administrative Motion to File Under Seal. Upon the Court's ruling on the Administrative Motion to File Under Seal, further action by the Submitting Party may be required.

(1) If the Administrative Motion to File Under Seal is granted in its entirety then the document filed under seal will remain under seal and the public will have access only to the redacted version, if any, accompanying the motion.

(2) If the Administrative Motion to File Under Seal is denied in its entirety, the document sought to be sealed will not be considered by the Court unless the Submitting Party files an unredacted version of the document within 7 days after the motion is denied.

(3) If the Administrative Motion to File Under Seal is denied or granted in part, the document sought to be sealed will not be considered by the Court unless the Submitting Party files a redacted version of the document which comports with the Court's order within 7 days after the motion is denied.

(e) Effect of Seal. Unless otherwise ordered by the Court, any document filed under seal shall be kept from public inspection, including inspection by attorneys and parties to the action. Nothing in this rule is intended to affect the normal records disposition policy of the United States Courts.

[Adopted effective September 1, 1996. Amended effective May 1, 2000; October 1, 2013.]

RULE 58–1. DESIGNATION OF MAGISTRATE JUDGES TO TRY MISDEMEANORS AND OTHER PETTY OFFENSES

Subject to the limitation of 18 U.S.C. § 3401, Magistrate Judges are specially designated to try persons accused of and sentence persons convicted of misdemeanors committed within this District. In addition, Magistrate Judges may dispose of misdemeanors which are transferred to this District under Fed. R. Crim. P. 20. A Magistrate Judge may direct the Probation Officer to conduct a presentence investigation of any person convicted of a misdemeanor and to render a report to the Magistrate Judge prior to the imposition of sentence.

[Adopted effective September 1, 1996.]

RULE 58–2. APPEAL FROM CONVICTION BY MAGISTRATE JUDGE

(a) Assignment to District Judge. When an appeal from a judgment of conviction or sentence by a Magistrate Judge to a District Judge is made pursuant to Fed. R. Crim. P. 58(g)(2), the Clerk shall assign the appeal to a District Judge in the same manner as an indictment or felony information would be assigned.

(b) Record. If a transcript is desired by a party, the party shall order the transcript from the Court reporter in accordance with the procedure prescribed by Fed. R. App. P. 10(b). If the proceedings were recorded by audio tape, the audio tape shall constitute the record of the proceedings. Upon request, the Clerk shall duplicate and provide a copy of the audio tape to the requesting party at the rate provided for in 28 U.S.C. § 1914. No transcript shall be made of an audio tape unless ordered by the assigned District Judge pursuant to motion by the requesting party. The record shall be deemed complete 14 days after the notice of appeal is filed if no transcript is ordered or upon filing of the transcript or upon lodging the audio tape with the assigned District Judge.

(c) Hearing. After the record is complete, the Clerk for the assigned District Judge shall notify the parties of the time set for hearing the appeal. The hearing shall be not more than 90 days after the date of the notice.

(d) Time for Filing and Serving Briefs. The appellant shall serve and file an opening brief not later than 35 days before the date set for the hearing pursuant to Crim. L.R. 58–2(c). The appellee shall serve and file a responsive brief not later than 21 days before the hearing date. The appellant may serve and file a reply not later than 14 days before the hearing date.

(e) Length. Unless the Court expressly orders otherwise pursuant to ex parte request made prior to the due date, the opening and responsive briefs shall not exceed 25 pages and the reply shall not exceed 10 pages.

[Adopted effective September 1, 1996. Amended effective May 1, 2000; December 1, 2009.]

RULE 58–3. VIOLATION NOTICES

Pursuant to Rule 58(d)(1), Federal Rules of Criminal Procedure, the prosecution of petty offenses initiated by citation or violation notice shall be terminated upon receipt by the Clerk of the District Court of the amount, if any, of the fixed sum indicated as a fine on the face of the citation or violation notice. Such sums may be revised from time to time by General Order of the Court.

[Adopted effective September 1, 1996.]

RULE 59–1. EFFECTIVE DATE

These rules are effective December 1, 2009 and shall govern all criminal proceedings commenced on or after that date. Unless otherwise ordered by the Assigned Judge, these rules shall also be applicable to any case commenced prior to December 1, 2009, except when fewer than 10 days remain before a party must perform an act regulated by these local rules, in which case the former procedure for performing that act shall apply.

[Adopted effective September 1, 1996. Amended effective May 1, 2000; January 1, 2005; February 1, 2006; December 1, 2009.]

PATENT LOCAL RULES

1. SCOPE OF RULES

RULE 1–1. TITLE

These are the Local Rules of Practice for Patent Cases before the United States District Court for the Northern District of California. They should be cited as "Patent L.R. —."

[Effective December 1, 2000.]

RULE 1–2. SCOPE AND CONSTRUCTION

These rules apply to all civil actions filed in or transferred to this Court which allege infringement of a utility patent in a complaint, counterclaim, cross-claim or third party claim, or which seek a declaratory judgment that a utility patent is not infringed, is invalid or is unenforceable. The Civil Local Rules of this Court shall also apply to such actions, except to the extent that they are inconsistent with these Patent Local Rules. If the filings or actions in a case do not trigger the application of these Patent Local Rules under the terms set forth herein, the parties shall, as soon as such circumstances become known, meet and confer for the purpose of agreeing on the application of these Patent Local Rules to the case and promptly report the results of the meet and confer to the Court.

[Effective December 1, 2000. Amended effective March 1, 2008.]

RULE 1–3. MODIFICATION OF THESE RULES

The Court may modify the obligations or deadlines set forth in these Patent Local Rules based on the circumstances of any particular case, including, without limitation, the simplicity or complexity of the case as shown by the patents, claims, products, or parties involved. Such modifications shall, in most cases, be made at the initial case management conference, but may be made at other times upon a showing of good cause. In advance of submission of any request for a modification, the parties shall meet and confer for purposes of reaching an agreement, if possible, upon any modification.

[Adopted effective March 1, 2008.]

RULE 1–4. EFFECTIVE DATE

These Patent Local Rules take effect on December 1, 2009. They govern patent cases filed on or after that date. For actions pending prior to December 1, 2009, the provisions of the Patent Local Rules that were in effect on November 30, 2009, shall apply, except that the time periods for actions pending before December 1, 2009 shall be those set forth in and computed as in the Federal Rules of Civil Procedure and the Patent Local Rules that took effect on December 1, 2009.

[Effective December 1, 2000. Renumbered and amended effective March 1, 2008. Amended effective December 1, 2009.]

2. GENERAL PROVISIONS

RULE 2–1. GOVERNING PROCEDURE

(a) Notice of Pendency of Other Action Involving Same Patent.

(1) When actions concerning the same patent are filed within two years of each other by the same plaintiff, they will be deemed related.

(2) Whenever a party knows or learns that actions concerning the same patent have been filed within two years of each other by the same plaintiff, the party must promptly file in each such case A Notice of Pendency of Other Action Involving Same Patent.

(3) Pursuant to the Assignment Plan, the Clerk will reassign the related higher-numbered cases to the Judge assigned to the lowest-numbered case and will file the appropriate notification on the docket of each reassigned case.

(4) If the Judge determines that the reassignment is not in compliance with subsection (1), the Judge may refer the matter to the Executive Committee for resolution.

(5) Even if a case is not deemed related to a pending case pursuant to this rule, a party may still seek a related case determination pursuant to Civil L.R. 3–12.

(6) If the lowest-numbered case is assigned to a magistrate judge to whom the parties have consented to preside over the action, the magistrate judge will retain that case even if consent is not entered in higher-numbered cases deemed related pursuant to subsection (1).

(b) Initial Case Management Conference. When the parties confer pursuant to Fed. R. Civ. P. 26(f), in addition to the matters covered by Fed. R. Civ. P. 26, the parties shall discuss and address in the Case Management Statement filed pursuant to Fed. R. Civ. P. 26(f) and Civil L.R. 16–9, the following topics:

(1) Proposed modification of the obligations or deadlines set forth in these Patent Local Rules to ensure that they are suitable for the circumstances of the particular case (see Patent L.R. 1–3);

(2) The scope and timing of any claim construction discovery (including disclosure of and discovery from any expert witness permitted by the court) and damages discovery;

(3) The format of the Claim Construction Hearing, including whether the Court will hear live testimony, the order of presentation, and the estimated length of the hearing; and

(4) How the parties intend to educate the court on the technology at issue.

(5) The parties shall provide the court with a non-binding, good-faith estimate of the damages range expected for the

case along with an explanation for the estimates. If either party is unable to provide such information, that party shall explain why it cannot and what specific information is needed before it can do so. Such party shall also state the time by which it should be in a position to provide that estimate and explanation.

[Effective December 1, 2000. Amended effective March 1, 2008; November 1, 2014; January 17, 2017.]

RULE 2–2. CONFIDENTIALITY

Discovery cannot be withheld on the basis of confidentiality absent Court order. The Protective Order authorized by the Northern District of California shall govern discovery unless the Court enters a different protective order. The approved Protective Order can be found on the Court's website.

[Effective December 1, 2000. Amended effective March 1, 2008.]

RULE 2–3. CERTIFICATION OF DISCLOSURES

All statements, disclosures, or charts filed or served in accordance with these Patent Local Rules shall be dated and signed by counsel of record. Counsel's signature shall constitute a certification that to the best of his or her knowledge, information, and belief, formed after an inquiry that is reasonable under the circumstances, the information contained in the statement, disclosure, or chart is complete and correct at the time it is made.

[Effective December 1, 2000. Amended effective March 1, 2008.]

RULE 2–4. ADMISSIBILITY OF DISCLOSURES

Statements, disclosures, or charts governed by these Patent Local Rules are admissible to the extent permitted by the Federal Rules of Evidence or Procedure. However, the statements and disclosures provided for in Patent L.R. 4–1 and 4–2 are not admissible for any purpose other than in connection with motions seeking an extension or modification of the time periods within which actions contemplated by these Patent Local Rules shall be taken.

[Effective December 1, 2000. Amended effective March 1, 2008.]

RULE 2–5. RELATIONSHIP TO FEDERAL RULES OF CIVIL PROCEDURE

Except as provided in this paragraph or as otherwise ordered, it shall not be a ground for objecting to an opposing party's discovery request (e.g., interrogatory, document request, request for admission, deposition question) or declining to provide information otherwise required to be disclosed pursuant to Fed. R. Civ. P. 26(a)(1) that the discovery request or disclosure requirement is premature in light of, or otherwise conflicts with, these Patent Local Rules, absent other legitimate objection. A party may object, however, to responding to the following categories of discovery requests (or decline to provide information in its initial disclosures under Fed. R. Civ. P. 26(a)(1)) on the ground that they are premature in light of the timetable provided in the Patent Local Rules:

(a) Requests seeking to elicit a party's claim construction or damages positions;

(b) Requests seeking to elicit from the patent claimant a comparison of the asserted claims and the accused apparatus, product, device, process, method, act, or other instrumentality;

(c) Requests seeking to elicit from an accused infringer a comparison of the asserted claims and the prior art; and

(d) Requests seeking to elicit from an accused infringer the identification of any advice of counsel, and related documents.

Where a party properly objects to a discovery request (or declines to provide information in its initial disclosures under Fed. R. Civ. P. 26(a)(1)) as set forth above, that party shall provide the requested information on the date on which it is required to be provided to an opposing party under these Patent Local Rules or as set by the Court, unless there exists another legitimate ground for objection.

[Effective December 1, 2000. Amended effective March 1, 2008; January 17, 2017.]

3. PATENT DISCLOSURES

RULE 3–1. DISCLOSURE OF ASSERTED CLAIMS AND INFRINGEMENT CONTENTIONS

Not later than 14 days after the Initial Case Management Conference, a party claiming patent infringement shall serve on all parties a "Disclosure of Asserted Claims and Infringement Contentions." Separately for each opposing party, the "Disclosure of Asserted Claims and Infringement Contentions" shall contain the following information:

(a) Each claim of each patent in suit that is allegedly infringed by each opposing party, including for each claim the applicable statutory subsections of 35 U.S.C. § 271 asserted;

(b) Separately for each asserted claim, each accused apparatus, product, device, process, method, act, or other instrumentality ("Accused Instrumentality") of each opposing party of which the party is aware. This identification shall be as specific as possible. Each product, device, and apparatus shall be identified by name or model number, if known. Each method or process shall be identified by name, if known, or by any product, device, or apparatus which, when used, allegedly results in the practice of the claimed method or process;

(c) A chart identifying specifically where and how each limitation of each asserted claim is found within each Accused Instrumentality, including for each limitation that such party contends is governed by 35 U.S.C. § 112(6), the identity of the structure(s), act(s), or material(s) in the Accused Instrumentality that performs the claimed function.

(d) For each claim which is alleged to have been indirectly infringed, an identification of any direct infringement and a description of the acts of the alleged indirect infringer that contribute to or are inducing that direct infringement. Insofar as alleged direct infringement is based on joint acts of multiple parties, the role of each such party in the direct infringement must be described.

(e) Whether each limitation of each asserted claim is alleged to be literally present or present under the doctrine of equivalents in the Accused Instrumentality;

(f) For any patent that claims priority to an earlier application, the priority date to which each asserted claim allegedly is entitled; and

(g) If a party claiming patent infringement wishes to preserve the right to rely, for any purpose, on the assertion that its own or its licensee's apparatus, product, device, process, method, act, or other instrumentality practices the claimed invention, the party shall identify, separately for each asserted claim, each such apparatus, product, device, process, method, act, or other instrumentality that incorporates or reflects that particular claim.

(h) Identify the timing of the point of first infringement, the start of claimed damages, and the end of claimed damages; and

(i) If a party claiming patent infringement alleges willful infringement, the basis for such allegation.

[Effective December 1, 2000. Amended effective March 1, 2008; December 1, 2009; January 17, 2017.]

RULE 3–2. DOCUMENT PRODUCTION ACCOMPANYING DISCLOSURE

With the "Disclosure of Asserted Claims and Infringement Contentions," the party claiming patent infringement shall produce to each opposing party or make available for inspection and copying:

(a) Documents (e.g., contracts, purchase orders, invoices, advertisements, marketing materials, offer letters, beta site testing agreements), and third party or joint development agreements) sufficient to evidence each discussion with, disclosure to, or other manner of providing to a third party, or sale of or offer to sell, or any public use of, the claimed invention prior to the date of application for the patent in suit. A party's production of a document as required herein shall not constitute an admission that such document evidences or is prior art under 35 U.S.C. § 102;

(b) All documents evidencing the conception, reduction to practice, design, and development of each claimed invention, which were created on or before the date of application for the patent in suit or the priority date identified pursuant to Patent L.R. 3–1(f), whichever is earlier;

(c) A copy of the file history for each patent in suit;

(d) All documents evidencing ownership of the patent rights by the party asserting patent infringement;

(e) If a party identifies instrumentalities pursuant to Patent L.R. 3–1(g), documents sufficient to show the operation of any aspects or elements of such instrumentalities the patent claimant relies upon as embodying any asserted claims;

(f) All agreements, including licenses, transferring an interest in any patent-in-suit;

(g) All agreements that the party asserting infringement contends are comparable to a license that would result from a hypothetical reasonable royalty negotiation;

(h) All agreements that otherwise may be used to support the party asserting infringement's damages case;

(i) If a party identifies instrumentalities pursuant to Patent L.R. 3–1(g), documents sufficient to show marking of such embodying accused instrumentalities and if it wants to preserve the right to recover lost profits based on such products, sales, revenues, costs and profits of such embodying accused instrumentalities; and

(j) All documents comprising or reflecting a F/RAND commitment or agreement with respect to the asserted patent(s).

The producing party shall separately identify by production number which documents correspond to each category.

[Effective December 1, 2000. Amended effective March 1, 2008; January 17, 2017.]

RULE 3–3. INVALIDITY CONTENTIONS

Not later than 45 days after service upon it of the "Disclosure of Asserted Claims and Infringement Contentions," each party opposing a claim of patent infringement, shall serve on all parties its "Invalidity Contentions" which shall contain the following information:

(a) The identity of each item of prior art that allegedly anticipates each asserted claim or renders it obvious. Each prior art patent shall be identified by its number, country of origin, and date of issue. Each prior art publication shall be identified by its title, date of publication, and where feasible, author and publisher. Each alleged sale or public use shall be identified by specifying the item offered for sale or publicly used or known, the date the offer or use took place or the information became known, and the identity of the person or entity which made the use or which made and received the offer, or the person or entity which made the information known or to whom it was made known. For pre-AIA claims, prior art under 35 U.S.C. § 102(f) shall be identified by providing the name of the person(s) from whom and the circumstances under which the invention or any part of it was derived. For pre-AIA claims, prior art under 35 U.S.C. § 102(g) shall be identified by providing the identities of the person(s) or entities involved in and the circumstances surrounding the making of the invention before the patent applicant(s);

(b) Whether each item of prior art anticipates each asserted claim or renders it obvious. If obviousness is alleged, an explanation of why the prior art renders the asserted claim obvious, including an identification of any combinations of prior art showing obviousness;

(c) A chart identifying specifically where and how in each alleged item of prior art each limitation of each asserted claim is found, including for each limitation that such party contends is governed by 35 U.S.C. § 112(6), the identity of the structure(s), act(s), or material(s) in each item of prior art that performs the claimed function; and

(d) Any grounds of invalidity based on 35 U.S.C. § 101, indefiniteness under 35 U.S.C. § 112(2) or enablement or written description under 35 U.S.C. § 112(1) of any of the asserted claims.

[Effective December 1, 2000. Amended effective March 1, 2008; January 17, 2017.]

RULE 3–4. DOCUMENT PRODUCTION ACCOMPANYING INVALIDITY CONTENTIONS

With the "Invalidity Contentions," the party opposing a claim of patent infringement shall produce or make available for inspection and copying:

(a) Source code, specifications, schematics, flow charts, artwork, formulas, or other documentation sufficient to show the operation of any aspects or elements of an Accused Instrumentality identified by the patent claimant in its Patent L.R. 3–1(c) chart;

(b) A copy or sample of the prior art identified pursuant to Patent L.R. 3–3(a) which does not appear in the file history of the patent(s) at issue. To the extent any such item is not in English, an English translation of the portion(s) relied upon shall be produced;

(c) All agreements that the party opposing infringement contends are comparable to a license that would result from a hypothetical reasonable royalty negotiation;

(d) Documents sufficient to show the sales, revenue, cost, and profits for accused instrumentalities identified pursuant to Patent L.R. 3–1(b) for any period of alleged infringement; and

(e) All agreements that may be used to support the party denying infringement's damages case.

The producing party shall separately identify by production number which documents correspond to each category.

[Effective December 1, 2000. Amended effective March 1, 2008; January 17, 2017.]

RULE 3–5. DISCLOSURE REQUIREMENT IN PATENT CASES FOR DECLARATORY JUDGMENT OF INVALIDITY

(a) Invalidity Contentions If No Claim of Infringement. In all cases in which a party files a complaint or other pleading seeking a declaratory judgment that a patent is invalid Patent L.R. 3–1 and 3–2 shall not apply unless and until a claim for patent infringement is made by a party. If the defendant does not assert a claim for patent infringement in its answer to the complaint, no later than 14 days after the defendant serves its answer, or 14 days after the Initial Case Management Conference, whichever is later, the party seeking a declaratory judgment of invalidity shall serve upon each opposing party its Invalidity Contentions that conform to Patent L.R. 3–3 and produce or make available for inspection and copying the documents described in Patent L.R. 3–4.

(b) Inapplicability of Rule. This Patent L.R. 3–5 shall not apply to cases in which a request for a declaratory judgment

that a patent is invalid is filed in response to a complaint for infringement of the same patent.

[Effective December 1, 2000. Amended effective March 1, 2008; December 1, 2009.]

RULE 3–6. AMENDMENT TO CONTENTIONS

Amendment of the Infringement Contentions or the Invalidity Contentions may be made only by order of the Court upon a timely showing of good cause. Non-exhaustive examples of circumstances that may, absent undue prejudice to the non-moving party, support a finding of good cause include: (a) A claim construction by the Court different from that proposed by the party seeking amendment; (b) Recent discovery of material, prior art despite earlier diligent search; and (c) Recent discovery of nonpublic information about the Accused Instrumentality which was not discovered, despite diligent efforts, before the service of the Infringement Contentions. The duty to supplement discovery responses does not excuse the need to obtain leave of court to amend contentions.

[Effective December 1, 2000. Amended effective March 1, 2008.]

RULE 3–7. ADVICE OF COUNSEL

Not later than 30 days after service by the Court of its Claim Construction Ruling, each party relying upon advice of counsel as part of a patent-related claim or defense for any reason shall:

(a) Produce or make available for inspection and copying any written advice and documents related thereto for which the attorney-client and work product protection have been waived;

(b) Provide a written summary of any oral advice and produce or make available for inspection and copying that summary and documents related thereto for which the attorney-client and work product protection have been waived; and

(c) Serve a privilege log identifying any other documents, except those authored by counsel acting solely as trial counsel, relating to the subject matter of the advice which the party is withholding on the grounds of attorney-client privilege or work product protection.

A party who does not comply with the requirements of this Patent L.R. 3–7 shall not be permitted to rely on advice of counsel for any purpose absent a stipulation of all parties or by order of the Court.

[Effective December 1, 2000. Renumbered and amended effective March 1, 2008. Amended effective January 17, 2017.]

RULE 3–8. DAMAGES CONTENTIONS

Not later than 50 days after service of the Invalidity Contentions, each party asserting infringement shall:

(a) Identify each of the category(-ies) of damages it is seeking for the asserted infringement, as well as its theories of recovery, factual support for those theories, and computations of damages within each category, including:

1. lost profits;
2. price erosion;
3. convoyed or collateral sales;
4. reasonable royalty; and

5. any other form of damages.

(b) To the extent a party contends it is unable to provide a fulsome response to the disclosures required by this rule, it shall identify the information it requires.

[Effective January 17, 2017.]

RULE 3–9. RESPONSIVE DAMAGES CONTENTIONS

Not later than 30 days after service of the Damages Contentions served pursuant to Patent L.R. 3–8, each party denying

infringement shall identify specifically how and why it disagrees with those contentions. This should include the party's affirmative position on each issue. To the extent a party contends it is unable to provide a fulsome response to the disclosures required by this rule, it shall identify the information it requires.

[Effective January 17, 2017.]

4. CLAIM CONSTRUCTION PROCEEDINGS

RULE 4–1. EXCHANGE OF PROPOSED TERMS FOR CONSTRUCTION

(a) Not later than 14 days after service of the "Invalidity Contentions" pursuant to Patent L.R. 3–3, not later than 42 days after service upon it of the "Disclosure of Asserted Claims and Infringement Contentions" in those actions where validity is not at issue (and Patent L.R. 3–3 does not apply), or, in all cases in which a party files a complaint or other pleading seeking a declaratory judgment not based on validity, not later than 14 days after the defendant serves an answer that does not assert a claim for patent infringement (and Patent L.R. 3–1 does not apply), each party shall serve on each other party a list of claim terms which that party contends should be construed by the Court, and identify any claim term which that party contends should be governed by 35 U.S.C. § 112(6).

(b) The parties shall thereafter meet and confer for the purposes of limiting the terms in dispute by narrowing or resolving differences and facilitating the ultimate preparation of a Joint Claim Construction and Prehearing Statement. The parties shall also jointly identify the 10 terms likely to be most significant to resolving the parties' dispute, including those terms for which construction may be case or claim dispositive.

[Effective December 1, 2000. Amended effective March 1, 2008; December 1, 2009.]

RULE 4–2. EXCHANGE OF PRELIMINARY CLAIM CONSTRUCTIONS AND EXTRINSIC EVIDENCE

(a) Not later than 21 days after the exchange of the lists pursuant to Patent L.R. 4–1, the parties shall simultaneously exchange proposed constructions of each term identified by either party for claim construction. Each such "Preliminary Claim Construction" shall also, for each term which any party contends is governed by 35 U.S.C. § 112(6), identify the structure(s), act(s), or material(s) corresponding to that term's function.

(b) At the same time the parties exchange their respective "Preliminary Claim Constructions," each party shall also identify all references from the specification or prosecution history that support its proposed construction and designate any supporting extrinsic evidence including, without limitation, dictionary definitions, citations to learned treatises and prior art,

and testimony of percipient and expert witnesses. Extrinsic evidence shall be identified by production number or by producing a copy if not previously produced. With respect to any supporting witness, percipient or expert, the identifying party shall also provide a description of the substance of that witness' proposed testimony that includes a listing of any opinions to be rendered in connection with claim construction.

(c) The parties shall thereafter meet and confer for the purposes of narrowing the issues and finalizing preparation of a Joint Claim Construction and Prehearing Statement.

[Effective December 1, 2000. Amended effective March 1, 2008; December 1, 2009.]

RULE 4–3. JOINT CLAIM CONSTRUCTION AND PREHEARING STATEMENT AND EXPERT REPORTS

Not later than 60 days after service of the "Invalidity Contentions," the parties shall complete and file a Joint Claim Construction and Prehearing Statement, which shall contain the following information:

(a) The construction of those terms on which the parties agree;

(b) Each party's proposed construction of each disputed term, together with an identification of all references from the specification or prosecution history that support that construction, and an identification of any extrinsic evidence known to the party on which it intends to rely either to support its proposed construction or to oppose any other party's proposed construction, including, but not limited to, as permitted by law, dictionary definitions, citations to learned treatises and prior art, and testimony of percipient and expert witnesses;

(c) An identification of the terms whose construction will be most significant to the resolution of the case up to a maximum of 10. The parties shall also identify any term among the 10 whose construction will be case or claim dispositive. If the parties cannot agree on the 10 most significant terms, the parties shall identify the ones which they do agree are most significant and then they may evenly divide the remainder with each party identifying what it believes are the remaining most significant terms. However, the total terms identified by all parties as most significant cannot exceed 10. For example, in a case involving two parties, if the parties agree upon the identification of five terms as most significant, each may only identify two additional terms as most significant; if the parties agree upon eight such terms, each party may only identify only one additional term as most significant.

(d) The anticipated length of time necessary for the Claim Construction Hearing;

(e) Whether any party proposes to call one or more witnesses at the Claim Construction Hearing, and the identity of each such witness.

(f) An identification of any factual findings requested from the Court related to claim construction.

Unless the parties agree otherwise, not later than 60 days after service of the "Invalidity Contentions," any party that intends to rely on any witness who will give expert testimony to support that party's proposed constructions shall serve the other party or parties with a claim construction expert report for that witness. Such reports shall comply with the disclosure requirements of Fed. R. Civ. P. 26(A)(2)(B).

[Effective December 1, 2000. Amended effective March 1, 2008; January 17, 2017; November 4, 2020.]

RULE 4–4. COMPLETION OF CLAIM CONSTRUCTION DISCOVERY

Not later than 30 days after service and filing of the Joint Claim Construction and Prehearing Statement, the parties shall complete all discovery relating to claim construction, including any depositions with respect to claim construction of any witnesses, including experts, identified in the Preliminary Claim Construction statement (Patent L.R. 4–2) or Joint Claim Construction and Prehearing Statement (Patent L.R. 4–3).

[Effective December 1, 2000. Amended effective March 1, 2008.]

RULE 4–5. CLAIM CONSTRUCTION BRIEFS

(a) Not later than 45 days after serving and filing the Joint Claim Construction and Prehearing Statement, the party claiming patent infringement, or the party asserting invalidity if there is no infringement issue present in the case, shall serve and file an opening brief and any evidence supporting its claim construction.

(b) Not later than 14 days after service upon it of an opening brief, each opposing party shall serve and file its responsive brief and supporting evidence.

(c) Not later than 7 days after service upon it of a responsive brief, the party claiming patent infringement, or the party asserting invalidity if there is no infringement issue present in the case, shall serve and file any reply brief and any evidence directly rebutting the supporting evidence contained in an opposing party's response.

[Effective December 1, 2000. Amended effective March 1, 2008.]

RULE 4–6. CLAIM CONSTRUCTION HEARING

Subject to the convenience of the Court's calendar, two weeks following submission of the reply brief specified in Patent L.R. 4–5(c), the Court shall conduct a Claim Construction Hearing, to the extent the parties or the Court believe a hearing is necessary for construction of the claims at issue.

[Effective December 1, 2000. Amended effective March 1, 2008.]

RULE 4–7. GOOD FAITH PARTICIPATION

A failure to make a good faith effort to narrow the instances of disputed terms or otherwise participate in the meet and confer process of any of the provisions of section 4 may expose counsel to sanctions, including under 28 U.S.C. § 1927.

[Effective March 1, 2008.]

SELECTED FORMS
MODEL PROTECTIVE ORDER FOR NON–COMPLEX CRIMINAL CASES

BRIAN J. STRETCH (CABN 163973)
Acting United States Attorney

DAVID R. CALLAWAY (CABN 121782)
Chief, Criminal Division

[AUSA Name] (CABN   )
Assistant United States Attorney

   [Address line 1]
[Address line 2]
Telephone:
FAX:
Email:

Attorneys for United States of America

UNITED STATES DISTRICT COURT
NORTHERN DISTRICT OF CALIFORNIA
DIVISION

UNITED STATES OF AMERICA,	Case No. CR
Plaintiff,	STIPULATION AND PROTECTIVE ORDER [PROPOSED] [1]
v.	
[Defendant Name(s)],	
Defendant.	

With the agreement of the parties, the Court enters the following Protective Order:

Defendant is charged with [insert offenses]. Upon receipt of a discovery request, the United States will produce documents and other materials pertaining to the defendant[s] and the charged offense[s] to defense counsel. The discovery to be provided includes documents or other materials falling into one or more of the following categories (collectively, "Protected Information"):

1. Personal Identifying Information of any individual (other than his or her name), including without limitation any person's date of birth, social security number, residence or business address, telephone numbers, email addresses, driver's license number, professional license number, family members names, or criminal histories ("Personal Identifying Information");

2. Financial information of any individual or business, including without limitation bank account numbers, credit or debit card numbers, account passwords, contact information, and taxpayer identification numbers ("Financial Information"); and

3. Medical records or other patient information of any individual covered by the Health Insurance Portability and Accountability Act of 1996 (HIPPA) ("Medical Information").

To ensure that Protected Information is not subject to unauthorized disclosure or misuse,

IT IS HEREBY ORDERED that defense counsel of record, their investigators, assistants, and employees (collectively, "the defense team") may review with the defendant all discovery material produced by the government, but shall not provide a defendant with copies of, or permit defendant to make copies of, or have unsupervised access to, any discovery material produced by the government

---

[1] This sample Protective Order ("Order") is not intended to cover every situation (*e.g.*, trade secrets or cases in which exposure of protected material could endanger a victim or witness), nor does it cover disclosure of Confidential Source information. Those situations, among others, may require more robust protections than are contained in this sample Order. The Court and the parties should tailor any proposed protective order to suit the needs of a particular case. This Order is also not intended to affect the obligations of either party or the timing of when discoverable materials must be produced. Those obligations are governed by Rule 16 of the Federal Rules of Criminal Procedure, Rule 16–1 of the Northern District of California Criminal Local Rules, and 18 U.S.C. § 3500 and Rule 26.2 of the Federal Rules of Criminal Procedure (the Jencks Act).

that contains Protected Information, unless the Personal Identifying Information, Financial Information, and/or Medical Information has first been **entirely redacted** from the discovery materials. The government and defense counsel are ordered to work together to ensure that these materials are protected, but that defendant has as much access to the materials as can be provided consistent with this Court's order. Discovery material that clearly pertains to a specific defendant and does not contain Protected Information regarding any other person (*e.g.*, defendant's own bank records, telephone records, and business records) may be provided to that defendant unredacted.

Defense counsel may also provide unredacted copies of Protected Information to any experts retained to assist with the preparation of the defense in the captioned case. The defendant, all members of the defense team, and any experts who receive discovery under this Order shall be provided a copy of this Order along with those materials and shall initial and date the order reflecting their agreement to be bound by it.

The materials provided pursuant to this protective order may only be used for the specific purpose of preparing or presenting a defense in this matter: [insert if such use is contemplated and agreed to by the parties] *and related ancillary proceedings, e.g., immigrations proceedings, S.E.C. civil proceedings, Social Security administrative proceedings*] unless specifically authorized by the Court.

This Order shall also apply to any copies made of any materials covered by this Order.

IT IS FURTHER ORDERED that neither a defendant nor any member of the defense team shall provide any discovery material produced by the government—whether or not the material constitutes or contains Protected Information within the meaning of this Order—to any third party (*i.e.*, any person who is not a member of the defense team) or make any public disclosure of the same, other than in a court filing, without the government's express written permission or further order of this Court. If a party files a pleading that references or contains or attaches Protected Information subject to this Order, that filing must be under seal.[2]

IT IS FURTHER ORDERED that defense counsel shall return materials subject to this Protective Order (including any copies) to the United States within 14 days after whichever event occurs last in time: dismissal of all charges against the defendant; defendant's acquittal; defendant's sentencing; or the conclusion of any direct appeal. After the United States receives documents and materials subject to this Order, it shall maintain those documents and materials until the period for filing a motion under 28 U.S.C. § 2255 has expired. After the statutory period for filing a motion under 28 U.S.C. § 2255 has expired, the United States is free to destroy documents and materials subject to this Order. If defendant is represented by counsel and files a motion pursuant to 28 U.S.C. § 2255, the United States will provide counsel with the documents and materials subject to this Protective Order under the terms of this Order. Defendant's attorney in any motion under 28 U.S.C. § 2255 shall return the documents and materials subject to this Protective Order within 14 days after the district court's ruling on the motion or 14 days after the conclusion of any direct appeal of the district court's order denying the motion, whichever is later. This stipulation is without prejudice to either party applying to the Court to modify the terms of any protective order. This Court shall retain jurisdiction to modify this Order upon motion of either party even after the conclusion of district court proceedings in this case.

         IT IS SO STIPULATED.   BRIAN J. STRETCH
                                             United States Attorney

Dated: _____
                                  [INSERT NAME]
                                  Assistant United States Attorney

                                  _____
                                  [INSERT NAME]
                                  Counsel for Defendant

IT IS SO ORDERED.

Dated: _____
                                  [INSERT NAME]
                                  United States District Judge

[Effective April 2018.]

2 This Order authorizes such filings under seal and the parties are not required to seek additional authorization from the Court to do so.

STIPULATED PROTECTIVE ORDER FOR STANDARD LITIGATION

UNITED STATES DISTRICT COURT
NORTHERN DISTRICT OF CALIFORNIA

Case No.

Plaintiff,

v.

STIPULATED PROTECTIVE
ORDER FOR STANDARD
LITIGATION

Defendant.

1. PURPOSES AND LIMITATIONS

Disclosure and discovery activity in this action are likely to involve production of confidential, proprietary, or private information for which special protection from public disclosure and from use for any purpose other than prosecuting this litigation may be warranted. Accordingly, the parties hereby stipulate to and petition the court to enter the following Stipulated Protective Order. The parties acknowledge that this Order does not confer blanket protections on all disclosures or responses to discovery and that the protection it affords from public disclosure and use extends only to the limited information or items that are entitled to confidential treatment under the applicable legal principles. The parties further acknowledge, as set forth in Section 12.3, below, that this Stipulated Protective Order does not entitle them to file confidential information under seal; Civil Local Rule 79-5 sets forth the procedures that must be followed and the standards that will be applied when a party seeks permission from the court to file material under seal.

2. DEFINITIONS

2.1 <u>Challenging Party</u>: a Party or Non–Party that challenges the designation of information or items under this Order.

2.2 <u>"CONFIDENTIAL" Information or Items</u>: information (regardless of how it is generated, stored or maintained) or tangible things that qualify for protection under Federal Rule of Civil Procedure 26(c).

2.3 <u>Counsel (without qualifier)</u>: Outside Counsel of Record and House Counsel (as well as their support staff).

2.4 <u>Designating Party</u>: a Party or Non–Party that designates information or items that it produces in disclosures or in responses to discovery as "CONFIDENTIAL."

2.5 <u>Disclosure or Discovery Material</u>: all items or information, regardless of the medium or manner in which it is generated, stored, or maintained (including, among other things, testimony, transcripts, and tangible things), that are produced or generated in disclosures or responses to discovery in this matter.

2.6 <u>Expert</u>: a person with specialized knowledge or experience in a matter pertinent to the litigation who has been retained by a Party or its counsel to serve as an expert witness or as a consultant in this action.

2.7 <u>House Counsel</u>: attorneys who are employees of a party to this action. House Counsel does not include Outside Counsel of Record or any other outside counsel.

2.8 <u>Non–Party</u>: any natural person, partnership, corporation, association, or other legal entity not named as a Party to this action.

2.9 <u>Outside Counsel of Record</u>: attorneys who are not employees of a party to this action but are retained to represent or advise a party to this action and have appeared in this action on behalf of that party or are affiliated with a law firm which has appeared on behalf of that party.

2.10 <u>Party</u>: any party to this action, including all of its officers, directors, employees, consultants, retained experts, and Outside Counsel of Record (and their support staffs).

2.11 <u>Producing Party</u>: a Party or Non–Party that produces Disclosure or Discovery Material in this action.

2.12 <u>Professional Vendors</u>: persons or entities that provide litigation support services (e.g., photocopying, videotaping, translating, preparing exhibits or demonstrations, and organizing, storing, or retrieving data in any form or medium) and their employees and subcontractors.

2.13 <u>Protected Material</u>: any Disclosure or Discovery Material that is designated as "CONFIDEN-TIAL."

2.14 <u>Receiving Party</u>: a Party that receives Disclosure or Discovery Material from a Producing Party.

3. SCOPE

The protections conferred by this Stipulation and Order cover not only Protected Material (as defined above), but also (1) any information copied or extracted from Protected Material; (2) all copies, excerpts, summaries, or compilations of Protected Material; and (3) any testimony, conversations, or presentations by Parties or their Counsel that might reveal Protected Material. However, the protections conferred by this Stipulation and Order do not cover the following information: (a) any information that is in the public domain at the time of disclosure to a Receiving Party or becomes part of the public domain after its disclosure to a Receiving Party as a result of publication not involving a violation of this Order, including becoming part of the public record through trial or otherwise; and (b) any information known to the Receiving Party prior to the disclosure or obtained by the Receiving Party after the disclosure from a source who obtained the information lawfully and under no obligation of confidentiality to the Designating Party. Any use of Protected Material at trial shall be governed by a separate agreement or order.

4. DURATION

Even after final disposition of this litigation, the confidentiality obligations imposed by this Order shall remain in effect until a Designating Party agrees otherwise in writing or a court order otherwise directs. Final disposition shall be deemed to be the later of (1) dismissal of all claims and defenses in this action, with or without prejudice; and (2) final judgment herein after the completion and exhaustion of all appeals, rehearings, remands, trials, or reviews of this action, including the time limits for filing any motions or applications for extension of time pursuant to applicable law.

5. DESIGNATING PROTECTED MATERIAL

5.1 <u>Exercise of Restraint and Care in Designating Material for Protection</u>. Each Party or Non–Party that designates information or items for protection under this Order must take care to limit any such designation to specific material that qualifies under the appropriate standards. The Designating Party must designate for protection only those parts of material, documents, items, or oral or written communications that qualify—so that other portions of the material, documents, items, or communications for which protection is not warranted are not swept unjustifiably within the ambit of this Order.

Mass, indiscriminate, or routinized designations are prohibited. Designations that are shown to be clearly unjustified or that have been made for an improper purpose (e.g., to unnecessarily encumber or retard the case development process or to impose unnecessary expenses and burdens on other parties) expose the Designating Party to sanctions.

If it comes to a Designating Party's attention that information or items that it designated for protection do not qualify for protection, that Designating Party must promptly notify all other Parties that it is withdrawing the mistaken designation.

5.2 <u>Manner and Timing of Designations</u>. Except as otherwise provided in this Order (see, e.g., second paragraph of section 5.2(a) below), or as otherwise stipulated or ordered, Disclosure or Discovery Material that qualifies for protection under this Order must be clearly so designated before the material is disclosed or produced.

Designation in conformity with this Order requires:

(a) for information in documentary form (e.g., paper or electronic documents, but excluding transcripts of depositions or other pretrial or trial proceedings), that the Producing Party affix the legend "CONFIDENTIAL" to each page that contains protected material. If only a portion or portions of the material on a page qualifies for protection, the Producing Party also must clearly identify the protected portion(s) (e.g., by making appropriate markings in the margins).

A Party or Non–Party that makes original documents or materials available for inspection need not designate them for protection until after the inspecting Party has indicated which material it would like copied and produced. During the inspection and before the designation, all of the material made available for inspection shall be deemed "CONFIDENTIAL." After the inspecting Party has identified the documents it wants copied and produced, the Producing Party must determine which documents, or portions thereof, qualify for protection under this Order. Then, before producing the specified documents, the Producing Party must affix the "CONFIDENTIAL" legend to each page that contains Protected Material. If only a portion or portions of the material on a page qualifies for protection, the Producing Party also must clearly identify the protected portion(s) (e.g., by making appropriate markings in the margins).

(b) for testimony given in deposition or in other pretrial or trial proceedings, that the Designating Party identify on the record, before the close of the deposition, hearing, or other proceeding, all protected testimony.

(c) for information produced in some form other than documentary and for any other tangible items, that the Producing Party affix in a prominent place on the exterior of the container or containers in which the information or item is stored the legend "CONFIDENTIAL." If only a portion or portions of the information or item warrant protection, the Producing Party, to the extent practicable, shall identify the protected portion(s).

5.3 Inadvertent Failures to Designate. If timely corrected, an inadvertent failure to designate qualified information or items does not, standing alone, waive the Designating Party's right to secure protection under this Order for such material. Upon timely correction of a designation, the Receiving Party must make reasonable efforts to assure that the material is treated in accordance with the provisions of this Order.

6. CHALLENGING CONFIDENTIALITY DESIGNATIONS

6.1 Timing of Challenges. Any Party or Non–Party may challenge a designation of confidentiality at any time. Unless a prompt challenge to a Designating Party's confidentiality designation is necessary to avoid foreseeable, substantial unfairness, unnecessary economic burdens, or a significant disruption or delay of the litigation, a Party does not waive its right to challenge a confidentiality designation by electing not to mount a challenge promptly after the original designation is disclosed.

6.2 Meet and Confer. The Challenging Party shall initiate the dispute resolution process by providing written notice of each designation it is challenging and describing the basis for each challenge. To avoid ambiguity as to whether a challenge has been made, the written notice must recite that the challenge to confidentiality is being made in accordance with this specific paragraph of the Protective Order. The parties shall attempt to resolve each challenge in good faith and must begin the process by conferring directly (in voice to voice dialogue; other forms of communication are not sufficient) within 14 days of the date of service of notice. In conferring, the Challenging Party must explain the basis for its belief that the confidentiality designation was not proper and must give the Designating Party an opportunity to review the designated material, to reconsider the circumstances, and, if no change in designation is offered, to explain the basis for the chosen designation. A Challenging Party may proceed to the next stage of the challenge process only if it has engaged in this meet and confer process first or establishes that the Designating Party is unwilling to participate in the meet and confer process in a timely manner.

6.3 Judicial Intervention. If the Parties cannot resolve a challenge without court intervention, the Designating Party shall file and serve a motion to retain confidentiality under Civil Local Rule 7 (and in compliance with Civil Local Rule 79–5, if applicable) within 21 days of the initial notice of challenge or within 14 days of the parties agreeing that the meet and confer process will not resolve their dispute, whichever is earlier. Each such motion must be accompanied by a competent declaration affirming that the movant has complied with the meet and confer requirements imposed in the preceding paragraph. Failure by the Designating Party to make such a motion including the required declaration within 21 days (or 14 days, if applicable) shall automatically waive the confidentiality designation for each challenged designation. In addition, the Challenging Party may file a motion challenging a confidentiality designation at any time if there is good cause for doing so, including a challenge to the designation of a deposition transcript or any portions thereof. Any motion brought pursuant to this provision must be accompanied by a competent declaration affirming that the movant has complied with the meet and confer requirements imposed by the preceding paragraph.

The burden of persuasion in any such challenge proceeding shall be on the Designating Party. Frivolous challenges, and those made for an improper purpose (e.g., to harass or impose unnecessary expenses and burdens on other parties) may expose the Challenging Party to sanctions. Unless the Designating Party has waived the confidentiality designation by failing to file a motion to retain confidentiality as described above, all parties shall continue to afford the material in question the level of protection to which it is entitled under the Producing Party's designation until the court rules on the challenge.

7. ACCESS TO AND USE OF PROTECTED MATERIAL

7.1 <u>Basic Principles</u>. A Receiving Party may use Protected Material that is disclosed or produced by another Party or by a Non–Party in connection with this case only for prosecuting, defending, or attempting to settle this litigation. Such Protected Material may be disclosed only to the categories of persons and under the conditions described in this Order. When the litigation has been terminated, a Receiving Party must comply with the provisions of section 13 below (FINAL DISPOSITION).

Protected Material must be stored and maintained by a Receiving Party at a location and in a secure manner that ensures that access is limited to the persons authorized under this Order.

7.2 <u>Disclosure of "CONFIDENTIAL" Information or Items</u>. Unless otherwise ordered by the court or permitted in writing by the Designating Party, a Receiving Party may disclose any information or item designated "CONFIDENTIAL" only to:

(a) the Receiving Party's Outside Counsel of Record in this action, as well as employees of said Outside Counsel of Record to whom it is reasonably necessary to disclose the information for this litigation and who have signed the "Acknowledgment and Agreement to Be Bound" that is attached hereto as Exhibit A;

(b) the officers, directors, and employees (including House Counsel) of the Receiving Party to whom disclosure is reasonably necessary for this litigation and who have signed the "Acknowledgment and Agreement to Be Bound" (Exhibit A);

(c) Experts (as defined in this Order) of the Receiving Party to whom disclosure is reasonably necessary for this litigation and who have signed the "Acknowledgment and Agreement to Be Bound" (Exhibit A);

(d) the court and its personnel;

(e) court reporters and their staff, professional jury or trial consultants, mock jurors, and Professional Vendors to whom disclosure is reasonably necessary for this litigation and who have signed the "Acknowledgment and Agreement to Be Bound" (Exhibit A);

(f) during their depositions, witnesses in the action to whom disclosure is reasonably necessary and who have signed the "Acknowledgment and Agreement to Be Bound" (Exhibit A), unless otherwise agreed by the Designating Party or ordered by the court. Pages of transcribed deposition testimony or exhibits to depositions that reveal Protected Material must be separately bound by the court reporter and may not be disclosed to anyone except as permitted under this Stipulated Protective Order.

(g) the author or recipient of a document containing the information or a custodian or other person who otherwise possessed or knew the information.

8. PROTECTED MATERIAL SUBPOENAED OR ORDERED PRODUCED IN OTHER LITIGATION

If a Party is served with a subpoena or a court order issued in other litigation that compels disclosure of any information or items designated in this action as "CONFIDENTIAL", that Party must:

(a) promptly notify in writing the Designating Party. Such notification shall include a copy of the subpoena or court order;

(b) promptly notify in writing the party who caused the subpoena or order to issue in the other litigation that some or all of the material covered by the subpoena or order is subject to this Protective Order. Such notification shall include a copy of this Stipulated Protective Order; and

(c) cooperate with respect to all reasonable procedures sought to be pursued by the Designating Party whose Protected Material may be affected.

If the Designating Party timely seeks a protective order, the Party served with the subpoena or court order shall not produce any information designated in this action as "CONFIDENTIAL" before a determination by the court from which the subpoena or order issued, unless the Party has obtained the Designating Party's permission. The Designating Party shall bear the burden and expense of seeking protection in that court of its confidential material—and nothing in these provisions should be construed as authorizing or encouraging a Receiving Party in this action to disobey a lawful directive from another court.

9. A NON–PARTY'S PROTECTED MATERIAL SOUGHT TO BE PRODUCED IN THIS LITIGATION

(a) The terms of this Order are applicable to information produced by a Non–Party in this action and designated as "CONFIDENTIAL". Such information produced by Non–Parties in connection with this litigation is protected by the remedies and relief provided by this Order. Nothing in these provisions should be construed as prohibiting a Non–Party from seeking additional protections.

(b) In the event that a Party is required, by a valid discovery request, to produce a Non–Party's confidential information in its possession, and the Party is subject to an agreement with the Non–Party not to produce the Non–Party's confidential information, then the Party shall:

(1) promptly notify in writing the Requesting Party and the Non–Party that some or all of the information requested is subject to a confidentiality agreement with a Non–Party;

(2) promptly provide the Non–Party with a copy of the Stipulated Protective Order in this litigation, the relevant discovery request(s), and a reasonably specific description of the information requested; and

(3) make the information requested available for inspection by the Non–Party.

(c) If the Non–Party fails to object or seek a protective order from this court within 14 days of receiving the notice and accompanying information, the Receiving Party may produce the Non–Party's confidential information responsive to the discovery request. If the Non–Party timely seeks a protective order, the Receiving Party shall not produce any information in its possession or control that is subject to the confidentiality agreement with the Non–Party before a determination by the court. Absent a court order to the contrary, the Non–Party shall bear the burden and expense of seeking protection in this court of its Protected Material.

10. UNAUTHORIZED DISCLOSURE OF PROTECTED MATERIAL

If a Receiving Party learns that, by inadvertence or otherwise, it has disclosed Protected Material to any person or in any circumstance not authorized under this Stipulated Protective Order, the Receiving Party must immediately (a) notify in writing the Designating Party of the unauthorized disclosures, (b) use its best efforts to retrieve all unauthorized copies of the Protected Material, (c) inform the person or persons to whom unauthorized disclosures were made of all the terms of this Order, and (d) request such person or persons to execute the "Acknowledgment and Agreement to Be Bound" that is attached hereto as Exhibit A.

11. INADVERTENT PRODUCTION OF PRIVILEGED OR OTHERWISE PROTECTED MATERIAL

When a Producing Party gives notice to Receiving Parties that certain inadvertently produced material is subject to a claim of privilege or other protection, the obligations of the Receiving Parties are those set forth in Federal Rule of Civil Procedure 26(b)(5)(B). This provision is not intended to modify whatever procedure may be established in an e-discovery order that provides for production without prior privilege review. Pursuant to Federal Rule of Evidence 502(d) and (e), insofar as the parties reach an agreement on the effect of disclosure of a communication or information covered by the attorney-client privilege or work product protection, the parties may incorporate their agreement in the stipulated protective order submitted to the court.

12. MISCELLANEOUS

12.1 Right to Further Relief. Nothing in this Order abridges the right of any person to seek its modification by the court in the future.

12.2 Right to Assert Other Objections. By stipulating to the entry of this Protective Order no Party waives any right it otherwise would have to object to disclosing or producing any information or item on any ground not addressed in this Stipulated Protective Order. Similarly, no Party waives any right to object on any ground to use in evidence of any of the material covered by this Protective Order.

12.3 <u>Filing Protected Material</u>. Without written permission from the Designating Party or a court order secured after appropriate notice to all interested persons, a Party may not file in the public record in this action any Protected Material. A Party that seeks to file under seal any Protected Material must comply with Civil Local Rule 79–5. Protected Material may only be filed under seal pursuant to a court order authorizing the sealing of the specific Protected Material at issue. Pursuant to Civil Local Rule 79–5, a sealing order will issue only upon a request establishing that the Protected Material at issue is privileged, protectable as a trade secret, or otherwise entitled to protection under the law. If a Receiving Party's request to file Protected Material under seal pursuant to Civil Local Rule 79–5(d) is denied by the court, then the Receiving Party may file the information in the public record pursuant to Civil Local Rule 79–5(e) unless otherwise instructed by the court.

13. FINAL DISPOSITION

Within 60 days after the final disposition of this action, as defined in paragraph 4, each Receiving Party must return all Protected Material to the Producing Party or destroy such material. As used in this subdivision, "all Protected Material" includes all copies, abstracts, compilations, summaries, and any other format reproducing or capturing any of the Protected Material. Whether the Protected Material is returned or destroyed, the Receiving Party must submit a written certification to the Producing Party (and, if not the same person or entity, to the Designating Party) by the 60 day deadline that (1) identifies (by category, where appropriate) all the Protected Material that was returned or destroyed and (2) affirms that the Receiving Party has not retained any copies, abstracts, compilations, summaries or any other format reproducing or capturing any of the Protected Material. Notwithstanding this provision, Counsel are entitled to retain an archival copy of all pleadings, motion papers, trial, deposition, and hearing transcripts, legal memoranda, correspondence, deposition and trial exhibits, expert reports, attorney work product, and consultant and expert work product, even if such materials contain Protected Material. Any such archival copies that contain or constitute Protected Material remain subject to this Protective Order as set forth in Section 4 (DURATION).

IT IS SO STIPULATED, THROUGH COUNSEL OF RECORD.

DATED: _____   _____

                                 Attorneys for Plaintiff

DATED: _____   _____

                                 Attorneys for Defendant

PURSUANT TO STIPULATION, IT IS SO ORDERED.
DATED: _____   _____

                                 United States District/Magistrate
                                 Judge

EXHIBIT A

ACKNOWLEDGMENT AND AGREEMENT TO BE BOUND

I, _____ [print or type full name], of _____ [print or type full address], declare under penalty of perjury that I have read in its entirety and understand the Stipulated Protective Order that was issued by the United States District Court for the Northern District of California on [date] in the case of _____ [**insert formal name of the case and the number and initials assigned to it by the court**]. I agree to comply with and to be bound by all the terms of this Stipulated Protective Order and I understand and acknowledge that failure to so comply could expose me to sanctions and punishment in the nature of contempt. I solemnly promise that I will not disclose in any manner any information or item that is subject to this Stipulated Protective Order to any person or entity except in strict compliance with the provisions of this Order.

I further agree to submit to the jurisdiction of the United States District Court for the Northern District of California for the purpose of enforcing the terms of this Stipulated Protective Order, even if such enforcement proceedings occur after termination of this action.

I hereby appoint _____ [print or type full name] of _____ [print or type full address and telephone number] as my California agent for service of process in connection with this action or any proceedings related to enforcement of this Stipulated Protective Order.

Date: _____

City and State where sworn and signed: _____

Printed name: _____

Signature: _____

STIPULATED PROTECTIVE ORDER FOR LITIGATION INVOLVING PATENTS, HIGHLY SENSITIVE CONFIDENTIAL INFORMATION AND/OR TRADE SECRETS

UNITED STATES DISTRICT COURT
NORTHERN DISTRICT OF CALIFORNIA

Case No. C

Plaintiff,	STIPULATED PROTECTIVE ORDER FOR LITIGATION INVOLVING PATENTS, HIGHLY SENSITIVE CONFIDENTIAL INFORMATION AND/OR TRADE SECRETS
v.	
Defendant.	

1. PURPOSES AND LIMITATIONS

Disclosure and discovery activity in this action are likely to involve production of confidential, proprietary, or private information for which special protection from public disclosure and from use for any purpose other than prosecuting this litigation may be warranted. Accordingly, the parties hereby stipulate to and petition the court to enter the following Stipulated Protective Order. The parties acknowledge that this Order does not confer blanket protections on all disclosures or responses to discovery and that the protection it affords from public disclosure and use extends only to the limited information or items that are entitled to confidential treatment under the applicable legal principles. The parties further acknowledge, as set forth in Section 14.4, below, that this Stipulated Protective Order does not entitle them to file confidential information under seal; Civil Local Rule 79–5 sets forth the procedures that must be followed and the standards that will be applied when a party seeks permission from the court to file material under seal.

2. DEFINITIONS

2.1 Challenging Party: a Party or Non–Party that challenges the designation of information or items under this Order.

2.2 "CONFIDENTIAL" Information or Items: information (regardless of how it is generated, stored or maintained) or tangible things that qualify for protection under Federal Rule of Civil Procedure 26(c).

2.3 Counsel (without qualifier): Outside Counsel of Record and House Counsel (as well as their support staff).

[2.4 Optional: Designated House Counsel: House Counsel who seek access to "HIGHLY CONFIDENTIAL—ATTORNEYS' EYES ONLY" information in this matter.]

2.5 Designating Party: a Party or Non–Party that designates information or items that it produces in disclosures or in responses to discovery as "CONFIDENTIAL" or "HIGHLY CONFI-DENTIAL—ATTORNEYS' EYES ONLY" [Optional: or "HIGHLY CONFIDENTIAL—SOURCE CODE"].

2.6 Disclosure or Discovery Material: all items or information, regardless of the medium or manner in which it is generated, stored, or maintained (including, among other things, testimony, transcripts, and tangible things), that are produced or generated in disclosures or responses to discovery in this matter.

2.7 Expert: a person with specialized knowledge or experience in a matter pertinent to the litigation who (1) has been retained by a Party or its counsel to serve as an expert witness or as a consultant in this action, (2) is not a past or current employee of a Party or of a Party's competitor, and (3) at the time of retention, is not anticipated to become an employee of a Party or of a Party's competitor.

2.8 "HIGHLY CONFIDENTIAL—ATTORNEYS' EYES ONLY" Information or Items: ex-tremely sensitive "Confidential Information or Items," disclosure of which to another Party or Non–Party would create a substantial risk of serious harm that could not be avoided by less restrictive means.

[2.9 Optional: "HIGHLY CONFIDENTIAL—SOURCE CODE" Information or Items: ex-tremely sensitive "Confidential Information or Items" representing computer code and associated comments and revision histories, formulas, engineering specifications, or schematics that define or otherwise describe in detail the algorithms or structure of software or hardware designs, disclosure of which to another Party or Non–Party would create a substantial risk of serious harm that could not be avoided by less restrictive means.]

2.10 House Counsel: attorneys who are employees of a party to this action. House Counsel does not include Outside Counsel of Record or any other outside counsel.

2.11 Non–Party: any natural person, partnership, corporation, association, or other legal entity not named as a Party to this action.

2.12 Outside Counsel of Record: attorneys who are not employees of a party to this action but are retained to represent or advise a party to this action and have appeared in this action on behalf of that party or are affiliated with a law firm which has appeared on behalf of that party.

2.13 Party: any party to this action, including all of its officers, directors, employees, consultants, retained experts, and Outside Counsel of Record (and their support staffs).

2.14 Producing Party: a Party or Non–Party that produces Disclosure or Discovery Material in this action.

2.15 Professional Vendors: persons or entities that provide litigation support services (e.g., photocopying, videotaping, translating, preparing exhibits or demonstrations, and organizing, storing, or retrieving data in any form or medium) and their employees and subcontractors.

2.16 Protected Material: any Disclosure or Discovery Material that is designated as "CONFI-DENTIAL," or as "HIGHLY CONFIDENTIAL—ATTORNEYS' EYES ONLY." [Optional: or as "HIGHLY CONFIDENTIAL—SOURCE CODE."]

2.17 Receiving Party: a Party that receives Disclosure or Discovery Material from a Producing Party.

3. SCOPE

The protections conferred by this Stipulation and Order cover not only Protected Material (as defined above), but also (1) any information copied or extracted from Protected Material; (2) all copies, excerpts, summaries, or compilations of Protected Material; and (3) any testimony, conversa-tions, or presentations by Parties or their Counsel that might reveal Protected Material. However, the protections conferred by this Stipulation and Order do not cover the following information: (a) any information that is in the public domain at the time of disclosure to a Receiving Party or becomes part of the public domain after its disclosure to a Receiving Party as a result of publication not involving a violation of this Order, including becoming part of the public record through trial or otherwise; and (b) any information known to the Receiving Party prior to the disclosure or obtained by the Receiving Party after the disclosure from a source who obtained the information lawfully and under no obligation of confidentiality to the Designating Party. Any use of Protected Material at trial shall be governed by a separate agreement or order.

4. DURATION

Even after final disposition of this litigation, the confidentiality obligations imposed by this Order shall remain in effect until a Designating Party agrees otherwise in writing or a court order otherwise directs. Final disposition shall be deemed to be the later of (1) dismissal of all claims and defenses in this action, with or without prejudice; and (2) final judgment herein after the completion and exhaustion of all appeals, rehearings, remands, trials, or reviews of this action, including the time limits for filing any motions or applications for extension of time pursuant to applicable law.

5. DESIGNATING PROTECTED MATERIAL

5.1 Exercise of Restraint and Care in Designating Material for Protection. Each Party or Non–Party that designates information or items for protection under this Order must take care to limit any such designation to specific material that qualifies under the appropriate standards. To the extent it is practical to do so, the Designating Party must designate for protection only those parts of material, documents, items, or oral or written communications that qualify—so that other portions of the material, documents, items, or communications for which protection is not warranted are not swept unjustifiably within the ambit of this Order.

Mass, indiscriminate, or routinized designations are prohibited. Designations that are shown to be clearly unjustified or that have been made for an improper purpose (e.g., to unnecessarily encumber or retard the case development process or to impose unnecessary expenses and burdens on other parties) expose the Designating Party to sanctions.

If it comes to a Designating Party's attention that information or items that it designated for protection do not qualify for protection at all or do not qualify for the level of protection initially asserted, that Designating Party must promptly notify all other parties that it is withdrawing the mistaken designation.

5.2 Manner and Timing of Designations. Except as otherwise provided in this Order (see, e.g., second paragraph of section 5.2(a) below), or as otherwise stipulated or ordered, Disclosure or Discovery

Material that qualifies for protection under this Order must be clearly so designated before the material is disclosed or produced.

Designation in conformity with this Order requires:

(a) for information in documentary form (e.g., paper or electronic documents, but excluding transcripts of depositions or other pretrial or trial proceedings), that the Producing Party affix the legend "CONFIDENTIAL" or "HIGHLY CONFIDENTIAL—ATTORNEYS' EYES ONLY" [Optional: or "HIGHLY CONFIDENTIAL—SOURCE CODE"] to each page that contains protected material. If only a portion or portions of the material on a page qualifies for protection, the Producing Party also must clearly identify the protected portion(s) (e.g., by making appropriate markings in the margins) and must specify, for each portion, the level of protection being asserted.

A Party or Non–Party that makes original documents or materials available for inspection need not designate them for protection until after the inspecting Party has indicated which material it would like copied and produced. During the inspection and before the designation, all of the material made available for inspection shall be deemed "HIGHLY CONFIDENTIAL—ATTORNEYS' EYES ONLY." After the inspecting Party has identified the documents it wants copied and produced, the Producing Party must determine which documents, or portions thereof, qualify for protection under this Order. Then, before producing the specified documents, the Producing Party must affix the appropriate legend ("CONFIDENTIAL" or "HIGHLY CONFIDENTIAL—ATTORNEYS' EYES ONLY" [Optional: or "HIGHLY CONFIDENTIAL—SOURCE CODE]) to each page that contains Protected Material. If only a portion or portions of the material on a page qualifies for protection, the Producing Party also must clearly identify the protected portion(s) (e.g., by making appropriate markings in the margins) and must specify, for each portion, the level of protection being asserted.

(b) for testimony given in deposition or in other pretrial or trial proceedings, that the Designating Party identify on the record, before the close of the deposition, hearing, or other proceeding, all protected testimony and specify the level of protection being asserted. When it is impractical to identify separately each portion of testimony that is entitled to protection and it appears that substantial portions of the testimony may qualify for protection, the Designating Party may invoke on the record (before the deposition, hearing, or other proceeding is concluded) a right to have up to 21 days to identify the specific portions of the testimony as to which protection is sought and to specify the level of protection being asserted. Only those portions of the testimony that are appropriately designated for protection within the 21 days shall be covered by the provisions of this Stipulated Protective Order. Alternatively, a Designating Party may specify, at the deposition or up to 21 days afterwards if that period is properly invoked, that the entire transcript shall be treated as "CONFIDENTIAL" or "HIGHLY CONFIDENTIAL—ATTORNEYS' EYES ONLY."

Parties shall give the other parties notice if they reasonably expect a deposition, hearing or other proceeding to include Protected Material so that the other parties can ensure that only authorized individuals who have signed the "Acknowledgment and Agreement to Be Bound" (Exhibit A) are present at those proceedings. The use of a document as an exhibit at a deposition shall not in any way affect its designation as "CONFIDENTIAL" or "HIGHLY CONFIDENTIAL—ATTORNEYS' EYES ONLY."

Transcripts containing Protected Material shall have an obvious legend on the title page that the transcript contains Protected Material, and the title page shall be followed by a list of all pages (including line numbers as appropriate) that have been designated as Protected Material and the level of protection being asserted by the Designating Party. The Designating Party shall inform the court reporter of these requirements. Any transcript that is prepared before the expiration of a 21–day period for designation shall be treated during that period as if it had been designated "HIGHLY CONFIDENTIAL—ATTORNEYS' EYES ONLY" in its entirety unless otherwise agreed. After the expiration of that period, the transcript shall be treated only as actually designated.

(c) for information produced in some form other than documentary and for any other tangible items, that the Producing Party affix in a prominent place on the exterior of the container or containers in which the information or item is stored the legend "CONFIDENTIAL" or "HIGHLY CONFIDENTIAL—ATTORNEYS' EYES ONLY" [*Optional*: or "HIGHLY CONFIDENTIAL— SOURCE CODE"]. If only a portion or portions of the information or item warrant protection, the Producing Party, to the extent practicable, shall identify the protected portion(s) and specify the level of protection being asserted.

5.3 Inadvertent Failures to Designate. If timely corrected, an inadvertent failure to designate qualified information or items does not, standing alone, waive the Designating Party's right to secure protection under this Order for such material. Upon timely correction of a designation, the Receiving Party must make reasonable efforts to assure that the material is treated in accordance with the provisions of this Order.

6. CHALLENGING CONFIDENTIALITY DESIGNATIONS

6.1 Timing of Challenges. Any Party or Non–Party may challenge a designation of confidentiality at any time. Unless a prompt challenge to a Designating Party's confidentiality designation is necessary to avoid foreseeable, substantial unfairness, unnecessary economic burdens, or a significant disruption or delay of the litigation, a Party does not waive its right to challenge a confidentiality designation by electing not to mount a challenge promptly after the original designation is disclosed.

6.2 Meet and Confer. The Challenging Party shall initiate the dispute resolution process by providing written notice of each designation it is challenging and describing the basis for each challenge. To avoid ambiguity as to whether a challenge has been made, the written notice must recite that the challenge to confidentiality is being made in accordance with this specific paragraph of the Protective Order. The parties shall attempt to resolve each challenge in good faith and must begin the process by conferring directly (in voice to voice dialogue; other forms of communication are not sufficient) within 14 days of the date of service of notice. In conferring, the Challenging Party must explain the basis for its belief that the confidentiality designation was not proper and must give the Designating Party an opportunity to review the designated material, to reconsider the circumstances, and, if no change in designation is offered, to explain the basis for the chosen designation. A Challenging Party may proceed to the next stage of the challenge process only if it has engaged in this meet and confer process first or establishes that the Designating Party is unwilling to participate in the meet and confer process in a timely manner.

6.3   Judicial Intervention.   If the Parties cannot resolve a challenge without court intervention, the Designating Party shall file and serve a motion to retain confidentiality under Civil Local Rule 7 (and in compliance with Civil Local Rule 79–5, if applicable) within 21 days of the initial notice of challenge or within 14 days of the parties agreeing that the meet and confer process will not resolve their dispute, whichever is earlier.[1]   Each such motion must be accompanied by a competent declaration affirming that the movant has complied with the meet and confer requirements imposed in the preceding paragraph.   Failure by the Designating Party to make such a motion including the required declaration within 21 days (or 14 days, if applicable) shall automatically waive the confidentiality designation for each challenged designation.   In addition, the Challenging Party may file a motion challenging a confidentiality designation at any time if there is good cause for doing so, including a challenge to the designation of a deposition transcript or any portions thereof.   Any motion brought pursuant to this provision must be accompanied by a competent declaration affirming that the movant has complied with the meet and confer requirements imposed by the preceding paragraph.

The burden of persuasion in any such challenge proceeding shall be on the Designating Party. Frivolous challenges and those made for an improper purpose (e.g., to harass or impose unnecessary expenses and burdens on other parties) may expose the Challenging Party to sanctions.   Unless the Designating Party has waived the confidentiality designation by failing to file a motion to retain confidentiality as described above, all parties shall continue to afford the material in question the level of protection to which it is entitled under the Producing Party's designation until the court rules on the challenge.

7.   ACCESS TO AND USE OF PROTECTED MATERIAL

7.1   Basic Principles.   A Receiving Party may use Protected Material that is disclosed or produced by another Party or by a Non–Party in connection with this case only for prosecuting, defending, or attempting to settle this litigation.   Such Protected Material may be disclosed only to the categories of persons and under the conditions described in this Order.   When the litigation has been terminated, a Receiving Party must comply with the provisions of section 15 below (FINAL DISPOSITION).

Protected Material must be stored and maintained by a Receiving Party at a location and in a secure manner[2] that ensures that access is limited to the persons authorized under this Order.

7.2   Disclosure of "CONFIDENTIAL" Information or Items.   Unless otherwise ordered by the court or permitted in writing by the Designating Party, a Receiving Party may disclose any information or item designated "CONFIDENTIAL" only to:

(a) the Receiving Party's Outside Counsel of Record in this action, as well as employees of said Outside Counsel of Record to whom it is reasonably necessary to disclose the information for this litigation and who have signed the "Acknowledgment and Agreement to Be Bound" that is attached hereto as Exhibit A;

(b) the officers, directors, and employees (including House Counsel) of the Receiving Party to whom disclosure is reasonably necessary for this litigation and who have signed the "Acknowledgment and Agreement to Be Bound" (Exhibit A);

(c) Experts (as defined in this Order) of the Receiving Party to whom disclosure is reasonably necessary for this litigation and who have signed the "Acknowledgment and Agreement to Be Bound" (Exhibit A);

(d) the court and its personnel;

(e) court reporters and their staff, professional jury or trial consultants, and Professional Vendors to whom disclosure is reasonably necessary for this litigation and who have signed the "Acknowledgment and Agreement to Be Bound" (Exhibit A);

(f) during their depositions, witnesses in the action to whom disclosure is reasonably necessary and who have signed the "Acknowledgment and Agreement to Be Bound" (Exhibit A), unless otherwise agreed by the Designating Party or ordered by the court.   Pages of transcribed deposition testimony or exhibits to depositions that reveal Protected Material must be separately bound by the court reporter and may not be disclosed to anyone except as permitted under this Stipulated Protective Order.

(g) the author or recipient of a document containing the information or a custodian or other person who otherwise possessed or knew the information.

7.3   Disclosure of "HIGHLY CONFIDENTIAL—ATTORNEYS' EYES ONLY" [*Optional*: and "HIGHLY CONFIDENTIAL—SOURCE CODE"] Information or Items.   Unless otherwise ordered by the court or permitted in writing by the Designating Party, a Receiving Party may disclose any information or item designated "HIGHLY CONFIDENTIAL—ATTORNEYS' EYES ONLY" [*Optional*: or "HIGHLY CONFIDENTIAL—SOURCE CODE"] only to:

(a) the Receiving Party's Outside Counsel of Record in this action, as well as employees of said Outside Counsel of Record to whom it is reasonably necessary to disclose the information for this litigation and who have signed the "Acknowledgment and Agreement to Be Bound" that is attached hereto as Exhibit A;

[(b) *Optional as deemed appropriate in case-specific circumstances:* Designated House Counsel of the Receiving Party[3] (1) who has no involvement in competitive decision-making, (2) to whom disclosure is reasonably necessary for this litigation, (3) who has signed the "Acknowledgment and Agreement to Be Bound" (Exhibit A), and (4) as to whom the procedures set forth in paragraph 7.4(a)(1), below, have been followed];[4]

(c) Experts of the Receiving Party (1) to whom disclosure is reasonably necessary for this litigation, (2) who have signed the "Acknowledgment and Agreement to Be Bound" (Exhibit A), and (3) as to whom the procedures set forth in paragraph 7.4(a)(2), below, have been followed];

(d) the court and its personnel;

(e) court reporters and their staff, professional jury or trial consultants,[5] and Professional Vendors to whom disclosure is reasonably necessary for this litigation and who have signed the "Acknowledgment and Agreement to Be Bound" (Exhibit A); and

(f) the author or recipient of a document containing the information or a custodian or other person who otherwise possessed or knew the information.

7.4   Procedures for Approving or Objecting to Disclosure of "HIGHLY CONFIDENTIAL—ATTORNEYS' EYES ONLY" [*Optional*: or "HIGHLY CONFIDENTIAL—SOURCE CODE"] Information or Items to Designated House Counsel[6] or Experts.[7]

(a)(1) Unless otherwise ordered by the court or agreed to in writing by the Designating Party, a Party that seeks to disclose to Designated House Counsel any information or item that has been designated "HIGHLY CONFIDENTIAL—ATTORNEYS' EYES ONLY" pursuant to paragraph 7.3(b) first must make a written request to the Designating Party that (1) sets forth the full name of the Designated House Counsel and the city and state of his or her residence, and (2) describes the Designated House Counsel's current and reasonably foreseeable future primary job duties and responsibilities in sufficient detail to determine if House Counsel is involved, or may become involved, in any competitive decision-making.[8]

(a)(2) Unless otherwise ordered by the court or agreed to in writing by the Designating Party, a Party that seeks to disclose to an Expert (as defined in this Order) any information or item that has been designated "HIGHLY CONFIDENTIAL—ATTORNEYS' EYES ONLY" [*Optional*: or "HIGHLY CONFIDENTIAL—SOURCE CODE"] pursuant to paragraph 7.3(c) first must make a written request to the Designating Party that (1) identifies the general categories of "HIGHLY CONFIDENTIAL—ATTORNEYS' EYES ONLY" [*Optional*: or "HIGHLY CONFIDENTIAL—SOURCE CODE"] information that the Receiving Party seeks permission to disclose to the Expert, (2) sets forth the full name of the Expert and the city and state of his or her primary residence, (3) attaches a copy of the Expert's current resume, (4) identifies the Expert's current employer(s), (5) identifies each person or entity from whom the Expert has received compensation or funding for work in his or her areas of expertise or to whom the expert has provided professional services, including in connection with a litigation, at any time during the preceding five years,[9] and (6) identifies (by name and number of the case, filing date, and location of court) any litigation in connection with which the Expert has offered expert testimony, including through a declaration, report, or testimony at a deposition or trial, during the preceding five years.[10]

(b) A Party that makes a request and provides the information specified in the preceding respective paragraphs may disclose the subject Protected Material to the identified Designated House Counsel or Expert unless, within 14 days of delivering the request, the Party receives a written objection from the Designating Party. Any such objection must set forth in detail the grounds on which it is based.

(c) A Party that receives a timely written objection must meet and confer with the Designating Party (through direct voice to voice dialogue) to try to resolve the matter by agreement within seven days of the written objection. If no agreement is reached, the Party seeking to make the disclosure to Designated House Counsel or the Expert may file a motion as provided in Civil Local Rule 7 (and in compliance with Civil Local Rule 79–5, if applicable) seeking permission from the court to do so. Any such motion must describe the circumstances with specificity, set forth in detail the reasons why the disclosure to Designated House Counsel or the Expert is reasonably necessary, assess the risk of harm that the disclosure would entail, and suggest any additional means that could be used to reduce that risk. In addition, any such motion must be accompanied by a competent declaration describing the parties' efforts to resolve the matter by agreement (i.e., the extent and the content of the meet and confer discussions) and setting forth the reasons advanced by the Designating Party for its refusal to approve the disclosure.

In any such proceeding, the Party opposing disclosure to Designated House Counsel or the Expert shall bear the burden of proving that the risk of harm that the disclosure would entail (under the safeguards proposed) outweighs the Receiving Party's need to disclose the Protected Material to its Designated House Counsel or Expert.

8. PROSECUTION BAR [*Optional*]

Absent written consent from the Producing Party, any individual who receives access to "HIGHLY CONFIDENTIAL—ATTORNEYS' EYES ONLY" [*Optional*: or "HIGHLY CONFIDENTIAL—SOURCE CODE"] information shall not be involved in the prosecution of patents or patent applications relating to [insert subject matter of the invention and of highly confidential technical information to be produced], including without limitation the patents asserted in this action and any patent or application claiming priority to or otherwise related to the patents asserted in this action, before any foreign or domestic agency, including the United States Patent and Trademark Office ("the Patent Office").[11] For purposes of this paragraph, "prosecution" includes directly or indirectly drafting, amending, advising, or otherwise affecting the scope or maintenance of patent claims.[12] To avoid any doubt, "prosecution" as used in this paragraph does not include representing a party challenging a patent before a domestic or foreign agency (including, but not limited to, a reissue protest, ex parte reexamination or *inter partes* reexamination). This Prosecution Bar shall begin when access to "HIGHLY CONFIDENTIAL—ATTORNEYS' EYES ONLY" [*Optional*: or "HIGHLY CONFIDENTIAL—SOURCE CODE"] information is first received by the affected individual and shall end two (2) years after final termination of this action.[13]

9. SOURCE CODE [*Optional*]

(a) To the extent production of source code becomes necessary in this case, a Producing Party may designate source code as "HIGHLY CONFIDENTIAL—SOURCE CODE" if it comprises or includes confidential, proprietary or trade secret source code.

(b) Protected Material designated as "HIGHLY CONFIDENTIAL—SOURCE CODE" shall be subject to all of the protections afforded to "HIGHLY CONFIDENTIAL—ATTORNEYS' EYES ONLY" information [*Optional*: including the Prosecution Bar set forth in Paragraph 8], and may be disclosed only to the individuals to whom "HIGHLY CONFIDENTIAL—ATTORNEYS' EYES ONLY" information may be disclosed, as set forth in Paragraphs 7.3 and 7.4, with the exception of Designated House Counsel.[14]

(c) Any source code produced in discovery shall be made available for inspection, in a format allowing it to be reasonably reviewed and searched, during normal business hours or at other mutually agreeable times, at an office of the Producing Party's counsel or another mutually agreed upon location.[15] The source code shall be made available for inspection on a secured computer in a secured room without Internet access or network access to other computers, and the Receiving Party shall not copy, remove, or otherwise transfer any portion of the source code onto any recordable media or recordable device. The Producing Party may visually monitor the activities of the Receiving Party's representatives during any source code review, but only to ensure that there is no unauthorized recording, copying, or transmission of the source code.[16]

(d) The Receiving Party may request paper copies of limited portions of source code that are reasonably necessary for the preparation of court filings, pleadings, expert reports, or other papers, or for deposition or trial, but shall not request paper copies for the purposes of reviewing the source code other than electronically as set forth in paragraph (c) in the first instance. The Producing Party shall provide all such source code in paper form including bates numbers and the label "HIGHLY CONFIDENTIAL—SOURCE CODE." The Producing Party may challenge the amount of source code requested in hard copy form pursuant to the dispute resolution procedure and timeframes set forth in Paragraph 6 whereby the Producing Party is the "Challenging Party" and the Receiving Party is the "Designating Party" for purposes of dispute resolution.

(e) The Receiving Party shall maintain a record of any individual who has inspected any portion of the source code in electronic or paper form. The Receiving Party shall maintain all paper copies of any printed portions of the source code in a secured, locked area. The Receiving Party shall not create any electronic or other images of the paper copies and shall not convert any of the information contained in the paper copies into any electronic format. The Receiving Party shall only make additional paper copies if such additional copies are (1) necessary to prepare court filings, pleadings, or other papers (including a testifying expert's expert report), (2) necessary for deposition, or (3) otherwise necessary for the preparation of its case. Any paper copies used during a deposition shall be retrieved by the Producing Party at the end of each day and must not be given to or left with a court reporter or any other unauthorized individual.[17]

10. PROTECTED MATERIAL SUBPOENAED OR ORDERED PRODUCED IN OTHER LITIGATION

If a Party is served with a subpoena or a court order issued in other litigation that compels disclosure of any information or items designated in this action as "CONFIDENTIAL" or "HIGHLY CONFIDENTIAL—ATTORNEYS' EYES ONLY" [*Optional*: or "HIGHLY CONFIDENTIAL—SOURCE CODE"] that Party must:

(a) promptly notify in writing the Designating Party. Such notification shall include a copy of the subpoena or court order;

(b) promptly notify in writing the party who caused the subpoena or order to issue in the other litigation that some or all of the material covered by the subpoena or order is subject to this Protective Order. Such notification shall include a copy of this Stipulated Protective Order; and

(c) cooperate with respect to all reasonable procedures sought to be pursued by the Designating Party whose Protected Material may be affected.[18]

If the Designating Party timely seeks a protective order, the Party served with the subpoena or court order shall not produce any information designated in this action as "CONFIDENTIAL" or "HIGHLY CONFIDENTIAL—ATTORNEYS' EYES ONLY" [*Optional*: or "HIGHLY CONFIDENTIAL—SOURCE CODE"] before a determination by the court from which the subpoena or order issued, unless the Party has obtained the Designating Party's permission. The Designating Party shall bear the burden and expense of seeking protection in that court of its confidential material—and nothing in these provisions should be construed as authorizing or encouraging a Receiving Party in this action to disobey a lawful directive from another court.

11. A NON–PARTY'S PROTECTED MATERIAL SOUGHT TO BE PRODUCED IN THIS LITIGATION

(a) The terms of this Order are applicable to information produced by a Non–Party in this action and designated as "CONFIDENTIAL" or "HIGHLY CONFIDENTIAL—ATTORNEYS' EYES ONLY" [*Optional*: or "HIGHLY CONFIDENTIAL—SOURCE CODE"]. Such information produced by Non–Parties in connection with this litigation is protected by the remedies and relief provided by this Order. Nothing in these provisions should be construed as prohibiting a Non–Party from seeking additional protections.

(b) In the event that a Party is required, by a valid discovery request, to produce a Non–Party's confidential information in its possession, and the Party is subject to an agreement with the Non–Party not to produce the Non–Party's confidential information, then the Party shall:

1. promptly notify in writing the Requesting Party and the Non–Party that some or all of the information requested is subject to a confidentiality agreement with a Non–Party;

2. promptly provide the Non–Party with a copy of the Stipulated Protective Order in this litigation, the relevant discovery request(s), and a reasonably specific description of the information requested; and

3. make the information requested available for inspection by the Non–Party.

(c) If the Non–Party fails to object or seek a protective order from this court within 14 days of receiving the notice and accompanying information, the Receiving Party may produce the Non–Party's confidential information responsive to the discovery request. If the Non–Party timely seeks a protective order, the Receiving Party shall not produce any information in its possession or control that is subject to the confidentiality agreement with the Non–Party before a determination by the court.[19] Absent a court order to the contrary, the Non–Party shall bear the burden and expense of seeking protection in this court of its Protected Material.

12. UNAUTHORIZED DISCLOSURE OF PROTECTED MATERIAL

If a Receiving Party learns that, by inadvertence or otherwise, it has disclosed Protected Material to any person or in any circumstance not authorized under this Stipulated Protective Order, the Receiving Party must immediately (a) notify in writing the Designating Party of the unauthorized disclosures, (b) use its best efforts to retrieve all unauthorized copies of the Protected Material, (c) inform the person or persons to whom unauthorized disclosures were made of all the terms of this Order, and (d) request such person or persons to execute the "Acknowledgment and Agreement to Be Bound" that is attached hereto as Exhibit A.

13. INADVERTENT PRODUCTION OF PRIVILEGED OR OTHERWISE PROTECTED MATERIAL

When a Producing Party gives notice to Receiving Parties that certain inadvertently produced material is subject to a claim of privilege or other protection, the obligations of the Receiving Parties are those set forth in Federal Rule of Civil Procedure 26(b)(5)(B).[20] This provision is not intended to modify whatever procedure may be established in an e-discovery order that provides for production without prior privilege review. Pursuant to Federal Rule of Evidence 502(d) and (e), insofar as the parties reach an agreement on the effect of disclosure of a communication or information covered by the attorney-client privilege or work product protection, the parties may incorporate their agreement in the stipulated protective order submitted to the court.

14. MISCELLANEOUS

14.1 Right to Further Relief. Nothing in this Order abridges the right of any person to seek its modification by the court in the future.

14.2 Right to Assert Other Objections. By stipulating to the entry of this Protective Order no Party waives any right it otherwise would have to object to disclosing or producing any information or item on any ground not addressed in this Stipulated Protective Order. Similarly, no Party waives any right to object on any ground to use in evidence of any of the material covered by this Protective Order.

[14.3 *Optional:* Export Control. Disclosure of Protected Material shall be subject to all applicable laws and regulations relating to the export of technical data contained in such Protected Material, including the release of such technical data to foreign persons or nationals in the United States or elsewhere. The Producing Party shall be responsible for identifying any such controlled technical data, and the Receiving Party shall take measures necessary to ensure compliance.]

14.4 Filing Protected Material. Without written permission from the Designating Party or a court order secured after appropriate notice to all interested persons, a Party may not file in the public record in this action any Protected Material. A Party that seeks to file under seal any Protected Material must comply with Civil Local Rule 79–5. Protected Material may only be filed under seal pursuant to a court order authorizing the sealing of the specific Protected Material at issue. Pursuant to Civil Local Rule 79–5, a sealing order will issue only upon a request establishing that the Protected Material at issue is privileged, protectable as a trade secret, or otherwise entitled to protection under the law. If a Receiving Party's request to file Protected Material under seal pursuant to Civil Local Rule 79–5(e) is denied by the court, then the Receiving Party may file the Protected Material in the public record pursuant to Civil Local Rule 79–5(e)(2) unless otherwise instructed by the court.

15. FINAL DISPOSITION

Within 60 days after the final disposition of this action, as defined in paragraph 4, each Receiving Party must return all Protected Material to the Producing Party or destroy such material. As used in this subdivision, "all Protected Material" includes all copies, abstracts, compilations, summaries, and any other format reproducing or capturing any of the Protected Material. Whether the Protected Material is returned or destroyed, the Receiving Party must submit a written certification to the Producing Party (and, if not the same person or entity, to the Designating Party) by the 60–day deadline that (1) identifies (by category, where appropriate) all the Protected Material that was returned or destroyed and (2) affirms that the Receiving Party has not retained any copies, abstracts, compilations, summaries or any other format reproducing or capturing any of the Protected Material. Notwithstanding this provision, Counsel are entitled to retain an archival copy of all pleadings, motion papers, trial, deposition, and hearing transcripts, legal memoranda, correspondence, deposition and trial exhibits, expert reports, attorney work product, and consultant and expert work product, even if such materials contain Protected Material. Any such archival copies that contain or constitute Protected Material remain subject to this Protective Order as set forth in Section 4 (DURATION).

IT IS SO STIPULATED, THROUGH COUNSEL OF RECORD.

DATED: _____   _____
                                    Attorneys for Plaintiff

DATED: _____   _____
                                    Attorneys for Plaintiff

PURSUANT TO STIPULATION, IT IS SO ORDERED.

DATED: _____   _____
                                    [Name of Judge]
                                    United States District/Magistrate Judge

1 Alternative: It may be appropriate in certain circumstances for the parties to agree to shift the burden to move on the Challenging Party after a certain number of challenges are made to avoid an abuse of the process. The burden of persuasion would remain on the Designating Party.

2 It may be appropriate under certain circumstances to require the Receiving Party to store any electronic Protected Material in password-protected form.

3 It may be appropriate under certain circumstances to limit the number of Designated House Counsel who may access "HIGHLY CONFIDENTIAL—ATTORNEYS' EYES ONLY" information under this provision.

4 This Order contemplates that Designated House Counsel shall not have access to any information or items designated "HIGHLY CONFIDENTIAL—SOURCE CODE." It may also be appropriate under certain circumstances to limit how Designated House Counsel may access "HIGHLY CONFIDENTIAL—ATTORNEYS' EYES ONLY" information. For example, Designated House Counsel may be limited to viewing "HIGHLY CONFIDENTIAL—ATTORNEYS' EYES ONLY" information only if it is filed with the court under seal, or in the presence of Outside Counsel of Record at their offices.

5 Alternative: The parties may wish to allow disclosure of information not only to professional jury or trial consultants, but also to mock jurors, to further trial preparation. In that situation, the parties may wish to draft a simplified, precisely tailored Undertaking for mock jurors to sign.

6 Alternative: The parties may exchange names of a certain number of Designated House Counsel instead of following this procedure.

7 Alternative: "CONFIDENTIAL" or "HIGHLY CONFIDENTIAL—ATTORNEYS' EYES ONLY" information or items may be disclosed to an Expert without disclosure of the identity of the Expert as long as the Expert is not a current officer, director, or employee of a competitor of a Party or anticipated to become one.

8 It may be appropriate in certain circumstances to require any Designated House Counsel who receives "HIGHLY CONFIDENTIAL—ATTORNEYS' EYES ONLY" information pursuant to this Order to disclose any relevant changes in job duties or responsibilities prior to final disposition of the litigation to allow the Designating Party to evaluate any later-arising competitive decision-making responsibilities.

9 If the Expert believes any of this information is subject to a confidentiality obligation to a third-party, then the Expert should provide whatever information the Expert believes can be disclosed without violating any confidentiality agreements, and the Party seeking to disclose to the Expert shall be available to meet and confer with the Designating Party regarding any such engagement.

10 It may be appropriate in certain circumstances to restrict the Expert from undertaking certain limited work prior to the termination of the litigation that could foreseeably result in an improper use of the Designating Party's "HIGHLY CONFIDENTIAL—ATTORNEYS' EYES ONLY" information.

11 It may be appropriate under certain circumstances to require Outside and House Counsel who receive access to "HIGHLY CONFIDENTIAL—ATTORNEYS' EYES ONLY" information to implement an "Ethical Wall."

12 Prosecution includes, for example, original prosecution, reissue and reexamination proceedings.

13 Alternative: It may be appropriate for the Prosecution Bar to apply only to individuals who receive access to another party's "HIGHLY CONFIDENTIAL—ATTORNEYS' EYES ONLY" technical or source code information pursuant to this Order, such as under circumstances where one or more parties is not expected to produce "HIGHLY CONFIDENTIAL—ATTORNEYS' EYES ONLY" information that is technical in nature or "HIGHLY CONFIDENTIAL—SOURCE CODE" information,

14 It may be appropriate under certain circumstances to allow House Counsel access to derivative materials including "HIGHLY CONFIDENTIAL—SOURCE CODE" information, such as exhibits to motions or expert reports,

15 Alternative: Any source code produced in discovery shall be made available for inspection in a format through which it could be reasonably reviewed and searched during normal business hours or other mutually agreeable times at a location that is reasonably convenient for the Receiving Party and any experts to whom the source code may be disclosed. This alternative may be appropriate if the Producing Party and/or its counsel are located in a different jurisdiction than counsel and/or experts for the Receiving Party.

16   It may be appropriate under certain circumstances to require the Receiving Party to keep a paper log indicating the names of any individuals inspecting the source code and dates and times of inspection, and the names of any individuals to whom paper copies of portions of source code are provided.

17   The nature of the source code at issue in a particular case may warrant additional protections or restrictions, For example, it may be appropriate under certain circumstances to require the Receiving Party to provide notice to the Producing Party before including "HIGHLY CONFIDENTIAL—SOURCE CODE" information in a court filing, pleading, or expert report.

18   The purpose of imposing these duties is to alert the interested parties to the existence of this Protective Order and to afford the Designating Party in this case an opportunity to try to protect its confidentiality interests in the court from which the subpoena or order issued.

19   The purpose of this provision is to alert the interested parties to the existence of confidentiality rights of a Non–Party and to afford the Non–Party an opportunity to protect its confidentiality interests in this court.

20   *Alternative*: The parties may agree that the recipient of an inadvertent production may not "sequester" or in any way use the document(s) pending resolution of a challenge to the claim of privilege or other protection to the extent it would be otherwise allowed by Federal Rule of Civil Procedure 26(b)(5)(B) as amended in 2006. This could include a restriction against "presenting" the document(s) to the court to challenge the privilege claim as may otherwise be allowed under Rule 26(b)(5)(B) subject to ethical obligations.

An alternate provision could state: "If information is produced in discovery that is subject to a claim of privilege or of protection as trial-preparation material, the party making the claim may notify any party that received the information of the claim and the basis for it. After being notified, a party must promptly return or destroy the specified information and any copies it has and may not sequester, use or disclose the information until the claim is resolved. This includes a restriction against presenting the information to the court for a determination of the claim."

EXHIBIT A

ACKNOWLEDGMENT AND AGREEMENT TO BE BOUND

I, _____ [print or type full name], of _____ [print or type full address], declare under penalty of perjury that I have read in its entirety and understand the Stipulated Protective Order that was issued by the United States District Court for the Northern District of California on [date] in the case of _____ **[insert formal name of the case and the number and initials assigned to it by the court]**. I agree to comply with and to be bound by all the terms of this Stipulated Protective Order and I understand and acknowledge that failure to so comply could expose me to sanctions and punishment in the nature of contempt. I solemnly promise that I will not disclose in any manner any information or item that is subject to this Stipulated Protective Order to any person or entity except in strict compliance with the provisions of this Order.

I further agree to submit to the jurisdiction of the United States District Court for the Northern District of California for the purpose of enforcing the terms of this Stipulated Protective Order, even if such enforcement proceedings occur after termination of this action.

I hereby appoint _____ [print or type full name] of _____ [print or type full address and telephone number] as my California agent for service of process in connection with this action or any proceedings related to enforcement of this Stipulated Protective Order.

Date: _____

City and State where sworn and signed: _____

Printed name: _____
                        [printed name]

Signature: _____
                [signature]

[Amended effective August 20, 2014.]

PATENT LOCAL RULE 2–2 INTERIM MODEL PROTECTIVE ORDER

UNITED STATES DISTRICT COURT
NORTHERN DISTRICT OF CALIFORNIA

Case No. C

Plaintiff,

v.

Defendant.

PATENT LOCAL RULE 2–2 INTERIM
MODEL PROTECTIVE ORDER

1. <u>PURPOSES AND LIMITATIONS</u>

Disclosure and discovery activity in this action are likely to involve production of confidential, proprietary, or private information for which special protection from public disclosure and from use for any purpose other than prosecuting this litigation may be warranted. This Order does not confer blanket protections on all disclosures or responses to discovery and the protection it affords from public disclosure and use extends only to the limited information or items that are entitled to confidential treatment under the applicable legal principles. As set forth in Section 14.4 below, this Protective Order does not entitle the Parties to file confidential information under seal; Civil Local Rule 79–5 sets forth the procedures that must be followed and the standards that will be applied when a party seeks permission from the court to file material under seal.

2. <u>DEFINITIONS</u>

2.1 <u>Challenging Party</u>: a Party or Non–Party that challenges the designation of information or items under this Order.

2.2 <u>"CONFIDENTIAL" Information or Items</u>: information (regardless of how it is generated, stored or maintained) or tangible things that qualify for protection under Federal Rule of Civil Procedure 26(c).

2.3 <u>Counsel (without qualifier)</u>: Outside Counsel of Record and House Counsel (as well as their support staff).

2.4 <u>Designated House Counsel</u>: House Counsel who seek access to "HIGHLY CONFIDENTIAL—ATTORNEYS' EYES ONLY" information in this matter.

2.5 <u>Designating Party</u>: a Party or Non–Party that designates information or items that it produces in disclosures or in responses to discovery as "CONFIDENTIAL," "HIGHLY CONFIDENTIAL—ATTORNEYS' EYES ONLY," or "HIGHLY CONFIDENTIAL—SOURCE CODE."

2.6 <u>Disclosure or Discovery Material</u>: all items or information, regardless of the medium or manner in which it is generated, stored, or maintained (including, among other things, testimony, transcripts, and tangible things), that are produced or generated in disclosures or responses to discovery in this matter.

2.7 <u>Expert</u>: a person with specialized knowledge or experience in a matter pertinent to the litigation who (1) has been retained by a Party or its counsel to serve as an expert witness or as a consultant in this action, (2) is not a past or current employee of a Party or of a Party's competitor, and (3) at the time of retention, is not anticipated to become an employee of a Party or of a Party's competitor.

2.8 <u>"HIGHLY CONFIDENTIAL—ATTORNEYS' EYES ONLY" Information or Items</u>: extremely sensitive "Confidential Information or Items," disclosure of which to another Party or Non–Party would create a substantial risk of serious harm that could not be avoided by less restrictive means.

2.9 <u>"HIGHLY CONFIDENTIAL—SOURCE CODE" Information or Items</u>: extremely sensitive "Confidential Information or Items" representing computer code and associated comments and revision histories, formulas, engineering specifications, or schematics that define or otherwise describe in detail the algorithms or structure of software or hardware designs, disclosure of which to another Party or Non–Party would create a substantial risk of serious harm that could not be avoided by less restrictive means.

2.10   House Counsel: attorneys who are employees of a party to this action.   House Counsel does not include Outside Counsel of Record or any other outside counsel.

2.11   Non–Party: any natural person, partnership, corporation, association, or other legal entity not named as a Party to this action.

2.12   Outside Counsel of Record: attorneys who are not employees of a party to this action but are retained to represent or advise a party to this action and have appeared in this action on behalf of that party or are affiliated with a law firm which has appeared on behalf of that party.

2.13   Party: any party to this action, including all of its officers, directors, employees, consultants, retained experts, and Outside Counsel of Record (and their support staffs).

2.14   Producing Party: a Party or Non–Party that produces Disclosure or Discovery Material in this action.

2.15   Professional Vendors: persons or entities that provide litigation support services (e.g., photocopying, videotaping, translating, preparing exhibits or demonstrations, and organizing, storing, or retrieving data in any form or medium) and their employees and subcontractors.

2.16   Protected Material: any Disclosure or Discovery Material that is designated as "CONFIDENTIAL," "HIGHLY CONFIDENTIAL—ATTORNEYS' EYES ONLY," or "HIGHLY CONFIDENTIAL—SOURCE CODE."

2.17   Receiving Party: a Party that receives Disclosure or Discovery Material from a Producing Party.

3.   SCOPE

The protections conferred by this Order cover not only Protected Material (as defined above), but also (1) any information copied or extracted from Protected Material; (2) all copies, excerpts, summaries, or compilations of Protected Material; and (3) any testimony, conversations, or presentations by Parties or their Counsel that might reveal Protected Material.   However, the protections conferred by this Order do not cover the following information: (a) any information that is in the public domain at the time of disclosure to a Receiving Party or becomes part of the public domain after its disclosure to a Receiving Party as a result of publication not involving a violation of this Order, including becoming part of the public record through trial or otherwise;   and (b) any information known to the Receiving Party prior to the disclosure or obtained by the Receiving Party after the disclosure from a source who obtained the information lawfully and under no obligation of confidentiality to the Designating Party.   Any use of Protected Material at trial shall be governed by a separate agreement or order.

4.   DURATION

Even after final disposition of this litigation, the confidentiality obligations imposed by this Order shall remain in effect until a Designating Party agrees otherwise in writing or a court order otherwise directs.   Final disposition shall be deemed to be the later of (1) dismissal of all claims and defenses in this action, with or without prejudice;   and (2) final judgment herein after the completion and exhaustion of all appeals, rehearings, remands, trials, or reviews of this action, including the time limits for filing any motions or applications for extension of time pursuant to applicable law.

5.   DESIGNATING PROTECTED MATERIAL

5.1   Exercise of Restraint and Care in Designating Material for Protection.   Each Party or Non–Party that designates information or items for protection under this Order must take care to limit any such designation to specific material that qualifies under the appropriate standards.   To the extent it is practical to do so, the Designating Party must designate for protection only those parts of material, documents, items, or oral or written communications that qualify—so that other portions of the material, documents, items, or communications for which protection is not warranted are not swept unjustifiably within the ambit of this Order.

Mass, indiscriminate, or routinized designations are prohibited.   Designations that are shown to be clearly unjustified or that have been made for an improper purpose (e.g., to unnecessarily encumber or retard the case development process or to impose unnecessary expenses and burdens on other parties) expose the Designating Party to sanctions.

If it comes to a Designating Party's attention that information or items that it designated for protection do not qualify for protection at all or do not qualify for the level of protection initially asserted, that Designating Party must promptly notify all other Parties that it is withdrawing the mistaken designation.

5.2 <u>Manner and Timing of Designations</u>. Except as otherwise provided in this Order (see, e.g., second paragraph of section 5.2(a) below), or as otherwise stipulated or ordered, Disclosure or Discovery Material that qualifies for protection under this Order must be clearly so designated before the material is disclosed or produced.

Designation in conformity with this Order requires:

(a) <u>for information in documentary form</u> (e.g., paper or electronic documents, but excluding transcripts of depositions or other pretrial or trial proceedings), that the Producing Party affix the legend "CONFIDENTIAL," "HIGHLY CONFIDENTIAL—ATTORNEYS' EYES ONLY," or "HIGHLY CONFIDENTIAL—SOURCE CODE" to each page that contains protected material. If only a portion or portions of the material on a page qualifies for protection, the Producing Party also must clearly identify the protected portion(s) (e.g., by making appropriate markings in the margins) and must specify, for each portion, the level of protection being asserted.

A Party or Non–Party that makes original documents or materials available for inspection need not designate them for protection until after the inspecting Party has indicated which material it would like copied and produced. During the inspection and before the designation, all of the material made available for inspection shall be deemed "HIGHLY CONFIDENTIAL—ATTORNEYS' EYES ONLY." After the inspecting Party has identified the documents it wants copied and produced, the Producing Party must determine which documents, or portions thereof, qualify for protection under this Order. Then, before producing the specified documents, the Producing Party must affix the appropriate legend ("CONFIDENTIAL," "HIGHLY CONFIDENTIAL—ATTORNEYS' EYES ONLY," or "HIGHLY CONFIDENTIAL—SOURCE CODE") to each page that contains Protected Material. If only a portion or portions of the material on a page qualifies for protection, the Producing Party also must clearly identify the protected portion(s) (e.g., by making appropriate markings in the margins) and must specify, for each portion, the level of protection being asserted.

(b) <u>for testimony given in deposition or in other pretrial or trial proceedings</u>, that the Designating Party identify on the record, before the close of the deposition, hearing, or other proceeding, all protected testimony and specify the level of protection being asserted. When it is impractical to identify separately each portion of testimony that is entitled to protection and it appears that substantial portions of the testimony may qualify for protection, the Designating Party may invoke on the record (before the deposition, hearing, or other proceeding is concluded) a right to have up to 21 days to identify the specific portions of the testimony as to which protection is sought and to specify the level of protection being asserted. Only those portions of the testimony that are appropriately designated for protection within the 21 days shall be covered by the provisions of this Protective Order. Alternatively, a Designating Party may specify, at the deposition or up to 21 days afterwards if that period is properly invoked, that the entire transcript shall be treated as "CONFIDENTIAL" or "HIGHLY CONFIDENTIAL—ATTORNEYS' EYES ONLY."

Parties shall give the other parties notice if they reasonably expect a deposition, hearing, or other proceeding to include Protected Material so that the other parties can ensure that only authorized individuals who have signed the "Acknowledgment and Agreement to Be Bound" (Exhibit A) are present at those proceedings. The use of a document as an exhibit at a deposition shall not in any way affect its designation as "CONFIDENTIAL" or "HIGHLY CONFIDENTIAL—ATTORNEYS' EYES ONLY."

Transcripts containing Protected Material shall have an obvious legend on the title page that the transcript contains Protected Material, and the title page shall be followed by a list of all pages (including line numbers as appropriate) that have been designated as Protected Material and the level of protection being asserted by the Designating Party. The Designating Party shall inform the court reporter of these requirements. Any transcript that is prepared before the expiration of a 21–day period for designation shall be treated during that period as if it had been designated "HIGHLY CONFIDENTIAL—ATTORNEYS' EYES ONLY" in its entirety unless otherwise agreed. After the expiration of that period, the transcript shall be treated only as actually designated.

(c) <u>for information produced in some form other than documentary and for any other tangible items</u>, that the Producing Party affix in a prominent place on the exterior of the container or containers in which the information or item is stored the legend "CONFIDENTIAL," "HIGHLY CONFIDENTIAL—ATTORNEYS' EYES ONLY," or "HIGHLY CONFIDENTIAL—SOURCE CODE." If only a portion or portions of the information or item warrant protection, the Producing Party, to the extent practicable, shall identify the protected portion(s) and specify the level of protection being asserted.

5.3   Inadvertent Failures to Designate.   If timely corrected, an inadvertent failure to designate qualified information or items does not, standing alone, waive the Designating Party's right to secure protection under this Order for such material.   Upon timely correction of a designation, the Receiving Party must make reasonable efforts to assure that the material is treated in accordance with the provisions of this Order.

6.   CHALLENGING CONFIDENTIALITY DESIGNATIONS

6.1   Timing of Challenges.   Any Party or Non–Party may challenge a designation of confidentiality at any time.   Unless a prompt challenge to a Designating Party's confidentiality designation is necessary to avoid foreseeable, substantial unfairness, unnecessary economic burdens, or a significant disruption or delay of the litigation, a Party does not waive its right to challenge a confidentiality designation by electing not to mount a challenge promptly after the original designation is disclosed.

6.2   Meet and Confer.   The Challenging Party shall initiate the dispute resolution process by providing written notice of each designation it is challenging and describing the basis for each challenge.   To avoid ambiguity as to whether a challenge has been made, the written notice must recite that the challenge to confidentiality is being made in accordance with this specific paragraph of the Protective Order.   The parties shall attempt to resolve each challenge in good faith and must begin the process by conferring directly (in voice to voice dialogue; other forms of communication are not sufficient) within 14 days of the date of service of notice.   In conferring, the Challenging Party must explain the basis for its belief that the confidentiality designation was not proper and must give the Designating Party an opportunity to review the designated material, to reconsider the circumstances, and, if no change in designation is offered, to explain the basis for the chosen designation.   A Challenging Party may proceed to the next stage of the challenge process only if it has engaged in this meet and confer process first or establishes that the Designating Party is unwilling to participate in the meet and confer process in a timely manner.

6.3   Judicial Intervention.   If the Parties cannot resolve a challenge without court intervention, the Designating Party shall file and serve a motion to retain confidentiality under Civil Local Rule 7 (and in compliance with Civil Local Rule 79–5, if applicable) within 21 days of the initial notice of challenge or within 14 days of the parties agreeing that the meet and confer process will not resolve their dispute, whichever is earlier.   Each such motion must be accompanied by a competent declaration affirming that the movant has complied with the meet and confer requirements imposed in the preceding paragraph.   Failure by the Designating Party to make such a motion including the required declaration within 21 days (or 14 days, if applicable) shall automatically waive the confidentiality designation for each challenged designation.   In addition, the Challenging Party may file a motion challenging a confidentiality designation at any time if there is good cause for doing so, including a challenge to the designation of a deposition transcript or any portions thereof.   Any motion brought pursuant to this provision must be accompanied by a competent declaration affirming that the movant has complied with the meet and confer requirements imposed by the preceding paragraph.

The burden of persuasion in any such challenge proceeding shall be on the Designating Party.   Frivolous challenges and those made for an improper purpose (e.g., to harass or impose unnecessary expenses and burdens on other parties) may expose the Challenging Party to sanctions.   Unless the Designating Party has waived the confidentiality designation by failing to file a motion to retain confidentiality as described above, all parties shall continue to afford the material in question the level of protection to which it is entitled under the Producing Party's designation until the court rules on the challenge.

7.   ACCESS TO AND USE OF PROTECTED MATERIAL

7.1   Basic Principles.   A Receiving Party may use Protected Material that is disclosed or produced by another Party or by a Non–Party in connection with this case only for prosecuting, defending, or attempting to settle this litigation.   Such Protected Material may be disclosed only to the categories of persons and under the conditions described in this Order.   When the litigation has been terminated, a Receiving Party must comply with the provisions of section 15 below (FINAL DISPOSITION).

Protected Material must be stored and maintained by a Receiving Party at a location and in a secure manner that ensures that access is limited to the persons authorized under this Order.

7.2   Disclosure of "CONFIDENTIAL" Information or Items.   Unless otherwise ordered by the court or permitted in writing by the Designating Party, a Receiving Party may disclose any information or item designated "CONFIDENTIAL" only to:

(a) the Receiving Party's Outside Counsel of Record in this action, as well as employees of said Outside Counsel of Record to whom it is reasonably necessary to disclose the information for this litigation and who have signed the "Acknowledgment and Agreement to Be Bound" that is attached hereto as Exhibit A;

(b) the officers, directors, and employees (including House Counsel) of the Receiving Party to whom disclosure is reasonably necessary for this litigation and who have signed the "Acknowledgment and Agreement to Be Bound" (Exhibit A);

(c) Experts (as defined in this Order) of the Receiving Party to whom disclosure is reasonably necessary for this litigation and who have signed the "Acknowledgment and Agreement to Be Bound" (Exhibit A);

(d) the court and its personnel;

(e) court reporters and their staff, professional jury or trial consultants, and Professional Vendors to whom disclosure is reasonably necessary for this litigation and who have signed the "Acknowledgment and Agreement to Be Bound" (Exhibit A);

(f) during their depositions, witnesses in the action to whom disclosure is reasonably necessary and who have signed the "Acknowledgment and Agreement to Be Bound" (Exhibit A), unless otherwise agreed by the Designating Party or ordered by the court. Pages of transcribed deposition testimony or exhibits to depositions that reveal Protected Material must be separately bound by the court reporter and may not be disclosed to anyone except as permitted under this Protective Order.

(g) the author or recipient of a document containing the information or a custodian or other person who otherwise possessed or knew the information.

7.3 Disclosure of "HIGHLY CONFIDENTIAL—ATTORNEYS' EYES ONLY" and "HIGHLY CONFIDENTIAL—SOURCE CODE" Information or Items. Unless otherwise ordered by the court or permitted in writing by the Designating Party, a Receiving Party may disclose any information or item designated "HIGHLY CONFIDENTIAL—ATTORNEYS' EYES ONLY" or "HIGHLY CONFIDENTIAL—SOURCE CODE" only to:

(a) the Receiving Party's Outside Counsel of Record in this action, as well as employees of said Outside Counsel of Record to whom it is reasonably necessary to disclose the information for this litigation and who have signed the "Acknowledgment and Agreement to Be Bound" that is attached hereto as Exhibit A;

(b) Designated House Counsel of the Receiving Party (1) who has no involvement in competitive decision-making, (2) to whom disclosure is reasonably necessary for this litigation, (3) who has signed the "Acknowledgment and Agreement to Be Bound" (Exhibit A), and (4) as to whom the procedures set forth in paragraph 7.4(a)(1), below, have been followed;[1]

(c) Experts of the Receiving Party (1) to whom disclosure is reasonably necessary for this litigation, (2) who have signed the "Acknowledgment and Agreement to Be Bound" (Exhibit A), and (3) as to whom the procedures set forth in paragraph 7.4(a)(2), below, have been followed;

(d) the court and its personnel;

(e) court reporters and their staff, professional jury or trial consultants, and Professional Vendors to whom disclosure is reasonably necessary for this litigation and who have signed the "Acknowledgment and Agreement to Be Bound" (Exhibit A); and

(f) the author or recipient of a document containing the information or a custodian or other person who otherwise possessed or knew the information.

7.4 Procedures for Approving or Objecting to Disclosure of "HIGHLY CONFIDENTIAL— ATTORNEYS' EYES ONLY" or "HIGHLY CONFIDENTIAL—SOURCE CODE" Information or Items to Designated House Counsel or Experts.

(a)(1) Unless otherwise ordered by the court or agreed to in writing by the Designating Party, a Party that seeks to disclose to Designated House Counsel any information or item that has been designated "HIGHLY CONFIDENTIAL—ATTORNEYS' EYES ONLY" pursuant to paragraph 7.3(b) first must make a written request to the Designating Party that (1) sets forth the full name of the Designated House Counsel and the city and state of his or her residence and (2) describes the Designated House Counsel's current and reasonably foreseeable future primary job duties and responsibilities in sufficient detail to determine if House Counsel is involved, or may become involved, in any competitive decision-making.

(a)(2) Unless otherwise ordered by the court or agreed to in writing by the Designating Party, a Party that seeks to disclose to an Expert (as defined in this Order) any information or item that has been designated "HIGHLY CONFIDENTIAL—ATTORNEYS' EYES ONLY" or "HIGHLY CONFIDENTIAL—SOURCE CODE" pursuant to paragraph 7.3(c) first must make a written request to the Designating Party that (1) identifies the general categories of "HIGHLY CONFIDENTIAL—ATTORNEYS' EYES ONLY" or "HIGHLY CONFIDENTIAL—SOURCE CODE" information that the Receiving Party seeks permission to disclose to the Expert, (2) sets forth the full name of the Expert and the city and state of his or her primary residence, (3) attaches a copy of the Expert's current resume, (4) identifies the Expert's current employer(s), (5) identifies each person or entity from whom the Expert has received compensation or funding for work in his or her areas of expertise or to whom the expert has provided professional services, including in connection with a litigation, at any time during the preceding five years,[2] and (6) identifies (by name and number of the case, filing date, and location of court) any litigation in connection with which the Expert has offered expert testimony, including through a declaration, report, or testimony at a deposition or trial, during the preceding five years.

(b) A Party that makes a request and provides the information specified in the preceding respective paragraphs may disclose the subject Protected Material to the identified Designated House Counsel or Expert unless, within 14 days of delivering the request, the Party receives a written objection from the Designating Party. Any such objection must set forth in detail the grounds on which it is based.

(c) A Party that receives a timely written objection must meet and confer with the Designating Party (through direct voice to voice dialogue) to try to resolve the matter by agreement within seven days of the written objection. If no agreement is reached, the Party seeking to make the disclosure to Designated House Counsel or the Expert may file a motion as provided in Civil Local Rule 7 (and in compliance with Civil Local Rule 79–5, if applicable) seeking permission from the court to do so. Any such motion must describe the circumstances with specificity, set forth in detail the reasons why disclosure to Designated House Counsel or the Expert is reasonably necessary, assess the risk of harm that the disclosure would entail, and suggest any additional means that could be used to reduce that risk. In addition, any such motion must be accompanied by a competent declaration describing the parties' efforts to resolve the matter by agreement (i.e., the extent and the content of the meet and confer discussions) and setting forth the reasons advanced by the Designating Party for its refusal to approve the disclosure.

In any such proceeding, the Party opposing disclosure to Designated House Counsel or the Expert shall bear the burden of proving that the risk of harm that the disclosure would entail (under the safeguards proposed) outweighs the Receiving Party's need to disclose the Protected Material to its Designated House Counsel or Expert.

8. PROSECUTION BAR

Absent written consent from the Producing Party, any individual who receives access to "HIGHLY CONFIDENTIAL—ATTORNEYS' EYES ONLY" or "HIGHLY CONFIDENTIAL—SOURCE CODE" information shall not be involved in the prosecution of patents or patent applications relating to the subject matter of this action, including without limitation the patents asserted in this action and any patent or application claiming priority to or otherwise related to the patents asserted in this action, before any foreign or domestic agency, including the United States Patent and Trademark Office ("the Patent Office"). For purposes of this paragraph, "prosecution" includes directly or indirectly drafting, amending, advising, or otherwise affecting the scope or maintenance of patent claims.[3] To avoid any doubt, "prosecution" as used in this paragraph does not include representing a party challenging a patent before a domestic or foreign agency (including, but not limited to, a reissue protest, ex parte reexamination or inter partes reexamination). This Prosecution Bar shall begin when access to "HIGHLY CONFIDENTIAL—ATTORNEYS' EYES ONLY" or "HIGHLY CONFIDENTIAL—SOURCE CODE" information is first received by the affected individual and shall end two (2) years after final termination of this action.

9. SOURCE CODE

(a) To the extent production of source code becomes necessary in this case, a Producing Party may designate source code as "HIGHLY CONFIDENTIAL—SOURCE CODE" if it comprises or includes confidential, proprietary or trade secret source code.

(b) Protected Material designated as "HIGHLY CONFIDENTIAL—SOURCE CODE" shall be subject to all of the protections afforded to "HIGHLY CONFIDENTIAL—ATTORNEYS' EYES ONLY" information, including the Prosecution Bar set forth in Paragraph 8, and may be disclosed only to the individuals to whom "HIGHLY CONFIDENTIAL—ATTORNEYS' EYES ONLY" information may be disclosed, as set forth in Paragraphs 7.3 and 7.4, with the exception of Designated House Counsel.

(c) Any source code produced in discovery shall be made available for inspection, in a format allowing it to be reasonably reviewed and searched, during normal business hours or at other mutually agreeable times, at an office of the Producing Party's counsel or another mutually agreed upon location. The source code shall be made available for inspection on a secured computer in a secured room without Internet access or network access to other computers, and the Receiving Party shall not copy, remove, or otherwise transfer any portion of the source code onto any recordable media or recordable device. The Producing Party may visually monitor the activities of the Receiving Party's representatives during any source code review, but only to ensure that there is no unauthorized recording, copying, or transmission of the source code.

(d) The Receiving Party may request paper copies of limited portions of source code that are reasonably necessary for the preparation of court filings, pleadings, expert reports, or other papers, or for deposition or trial, but shall not request paper copies for the purpose of reviewing the source code other than electronically as set forth in paragraph (c) in the first instance. The Producing Party shall provide all such source code in paper form, including bates numbers and the label "HIGHLY CONFIDENTIAL—SOURCE CODE." The Producing Party may challenge the amount of source code requested in hard copy form pursuant to the dispute resolution procedure and timeframes set forth in Paragraph 6 whereby the Producing Party is the "Challenging Party" and the Receiving Party is the "Designating Party" for purposes of dispute resolution.

(e) The Receiving Party shall maintain a record of any individual who has inspected any portion of the source code in electronic or paper form. The Receiving Party shall maintain all paper copies of any printed portions of the source code in a secured, locked area. The Receiving Party shall not create any electronic or other images of the paper copies and shall not convert any of the information contained in the paper copies into any electronic format. The Receiving Party shall only make additional paper copies if such additional copies are (1) necessary to prepare court filings, pleadings, or other papers (including a testifying expert's expert report), (2) necessary for deposition, or (3) otherwise necessary for the preparation of its case. Any paper copies used during a deposition shall be retrieved by the Producing Party at the end of each day and must not be given to or left with a court reporter or any other unauthorized individual.

10. PROTECTED MATERIAL SUBPOENAED OR ORDERED PRODUCED IN OTHER LITIGATION

If a Party is served with a subpoena or a court order issued in other litigation that compels disclosure of any information or items designated in this action as "CONFIDENTIAL," "HIGHLY CONFIDENTIAL—ATTORNEYS' EYES ONLY," or "HIGHLY CONFIDENTIAL—SOURCE CODE," that Party must:

(a) promptly notify in writing the Designating Party. Such notification shall include a copy of the subpoena or court order;

(b) promptly notify in writing the party who caused the subpoena or order to issue in the other litigation that some or all of the material covered by the subpoena or order is subject to this Protective Order. Such notification shall include a copy of this Protective Order; and

(c) cooperate with respect to all reasonable procedures sought to be pursued by the Designating Party whose Protected Material may be affected.[4]

If the Designating Party timely seeks a protective order, the Party served with the subpoena or court order shall not produce any information designated in this action as "CONFIDENTIAL," "HIGHLY CONFIDENTIAL—ATTORNEYS' EYES ONLY." or "HIGHLY CONFIDENTIAL—SOURCE CODE" before a determination by the court from which the subpoena or order issued, unless the Party has obtained the Designating Party's permission. The Designating Party shall bear the burden and expense of seeking protection in that court of its confidential material—and nothing in these provisions should be construed as authorizing or encouraging a Receiving Party in this action to disobey a lawful directive from another court.

11. A NON–PARTY'S PROTECTED MATERIAL SOUGHT TO BE PRODUCED IN THIS LITIGATION

(a) The terms of this Order are applicable to information produced by a Non–Party in this action and designated as "CONFIDENTIAL," "HIGHLY CONFIDENTIAL—ATTORNEYS' EYES

ONLY," or "HIGHLY CONFIDENTIAL—SOURCE CODE." Such information produced by Non–Parties in connection with this litigation is protected by the remedies and relief provided by this Order. Nothing in these provisions should be construed as prohibiting a Non–Party from seeking additional protections.

(b) In the event that a Party is required, by a valid discovery request, to produce a Non–Party's confidential information in its possession, and the Party is subject to an agreement with the Non–Party not to produce the Non–Party's confidential information, then the Party shall:

    1. promptly notify in writing the Requesting Party and the Non–Party that some or all of the information requested is subject to a confidentiality agreement with a Non–Party;

    2. promptly provide the Non–Party with a copy of the Protective Order in this litigation, the relevant discovery request(s), and a reasonably specific description of the information requested; and

    3. make the information requested available for inspection by the Non–Party.

(c) If the Non–Party fails to object or seek a protective order from this court within 14 days of receiving the notice and accompanying information, the Receiving Party may produce the Non–Party's confidential information responsive to the discovery request. If the Non–Party timely seeks a protective order, the Receiving Party shall not produce any information in its possession or control that is subject to the confidentiality agreement with the Non–Party before a determination by the court.[5] Absent a court order to the contrary, the Non–Party shall bear the burden and expense of seeking protection in this court of its Protected Material.

12. UNAUTHORIZED DISCLOSURE OF PROTECTED MATERIAL

If a Receiving Party learns that, by inadvertence or otherwise, it has disclosed Protected Material to any person or in any circumstance not authorized under this Protective Order, the Receiving Party must immediately (a) notify in writing the Designating Party of the unauthorized disclosures, (b) use its best efforts to retrieve all unauthorized copies of the Protected Material, (c) inform the person or persons to whom unauthorized disclosures were made of all the terms of this Order, and (d) request such person or persons to execute the "Acknowledgment and Agreement to Be Bound" that is attached hereto as Exhibit A.

13. INADVERTENT PRODUCTION OF PRIVILEGED OR OTHERWISE PROTECTED MATERIAL

When a Producing Party gives notice to Receiving Parties that certain inadvertently produced material is subject to a claim of privilege or other protection, the obligations of the Receiving Parties are those set forth in Federal Rule of Civil Procedure 26(b)(5)(B). This provision is not intended to modify whatever procedure may be established in an e-discovery order that provides for production without prior privilege review. Pursuant to Federal Rule of Evidence 502(d) and (e), insofar as the parties reach an agreement on the effect of disclosure of a communication or information covered by the attorney-client privilege or work product protection, the parties may incorporate their agreement in a stipulated protective order submitted to the court.

14. MISCELLANEOUS

14.1 _Right to Further Relief._ Nothing in this Order abridges the right of any person to seek its modification by the court in the future.

14.2 _Right to Assert Other Objections._ No Party waives any right it otherwise would have to object to disclosing or producing any information or item on any ground not addressed in this Protective Order. Similarly, no Party waives any right to object on any ground to use in evidence of any of the material covered by this Protective Order.

14.3 _Export Control._ Disclosure of Protected Material shall be subject to all applicable laws and regulations relating to the export of technical data contained in such Protected Material, including the release of such technical data to foreign persons or nationals in the United States or elsewhere. The Producing Party shall be responsible for identifying any such controlled technical data, and the Receiving Party shall take measures necessary to ensure compliance.

14.4 _Filing Protected Material._ Without written permission from the Designating Party or a court order secured after appropriate notice to all interested persons, a Party may not file in the public record in this action any Protected Material. A Party that seeks to file under seal any Protected Material must comply with Civil Local Rule 79–5. Protected Material may only be filed under seal pursuant to a court order authorizing the sealing of the specific Protected Material at issue. Pursuant to Civil Local Rule 79–5, a sealing order will issue only upon a request establishing that the Protected Material at issue is privileged, protectable as a trade secret, or otherwise entitled to protection under the law. If a Receiving Party's request to file Protected Material under seal pursuant to Civil Local Rule 79–5(e) is denied by the court, then the Receiving Party may file the Protected Material in the public record pursuant to Civil Local Rule 79–5(e)(2) unless otherwise instructed by the court.

15. FINAL DISPOSITION

Within 60 days after the final disposition of this action, as defined in paragraph 4, each Receiving Party must return all Protected Material to the Producing Party or destroy such material. As used in this subdivision, "all Protected Material" includes all copies, abstracts, compilations, summaries, and any other format reproducing or capturing any of the Protected Material. Whether the Protected Material is returned or destroyed, the Receiving Party must submit a written certification to the Producing Party (and, if not the same person or entity, to the Designating Party) by the 60 day deadline that (1) identifies (by category, where appropriate) all the Protected Material that was returned or destroyed and (2) affirms that the Receiving Party has not retained any copies, abstracts, compilations, summaries or any other format reproducing or capturing any of the Protected Material. Notwithstanding this provision, Counsel are entitled to retain an archival copy of all pleadings, motion papers, trial, deposition, and hearing transcripts, legal memoranda, correspondence, deposition and trial exhibits, expert reports, attorney work product, and consultant and expert work product, even if such materials contain Protected Material. Any such archival copies that contain or constitute Protected Material remain subject to this Protective Order as set forth in Section 4 (DURATION).

IT IS SO ORDERED.

DATED: _____   _____

[Name of Judge]
United States District/Magistrate Judge

[1] This Order contemplates that Designated House Counsel shall not have access to any information or items designated "HIGHLY CONFIDENTIAL—SOURCE CODE."

[2] If the Expert believes any of this information is subject to a confidentiality obligation to a third-party, then the Expert should provide whatever information the Expert believes can be disclosed without violating any confidentiality agreements, and the Party seeking to disclose to the Expert shall be available to meet and confer with the Designating Party regarding any such engagement.

[3] Prosecution includes, for example, original prosecution, reissue and reexamination proceedings.

[4] The purpose of imposing these duties is to alert the interested parties to the existence of this Protective Order and to afford the Designating Party in this case an opportunity to try to protect its confidentiality interests in the court from which the subpoena or order issued.

[5] The purpose of this provision is to alert the interested parties to the existence of confidentiality rights of a Non–Party and to afford the Non–Party an opportunity to protect its confidentiality interests in this court.

EXHIBIT A

ACKNOWLEDGMENT AND AGREEMENT TO BE BOUND

I, _____ [print or type full name], of _____ [print or type full address], declare under penalty of perjury that I have read in its entirety and understand the Protective Order that was issued by the United States District Court for the Northern District of California on _____ [date] in the case of _____ **[insert formal name of the case and the number and initials assigned to it by the court]**. I agree to comply with and to be bound by all the terms of this Protective Order, and I understand and acknowledge that failure to so comply could expose me to sanctions and punishment in the nature of contempt. I solemnly promise that I will not disclose in any manner any information or item that is subject to this Protective Order to any person or entity except in strict compliance with the provisions of this Order.

I further agree to submit to the jurisdiction of the United States District Court for the Northern District of California for the purpose of enforcing the terms of this Protective Order, even if such enforcement proceedings occur after termination of this action.

I hereby appoint _____ [print or type full name] of _____ [print or type full address and telephone number] as my California agent for service of process in connection with this action or any proceedings related to enforcement of this Protective Order.

Date: _____

City and State where sworn and signed: _____

Printed name: _____
               [printed name]

Signature: _____
          [signature]

[Amended effective August 20, 2014.]

JOINT CASE MANAGEMENT STATEMENT & [PROPOSED] ORDER

UNITED STATES DISTRICT COURT
NORTHERN DISTRICT OF CALIFORNIA

)
)   Case Number: C 18–xxxx
)
)   **JOINT CASE MANAGEMENT**
Plaintiff(s),   )   **STATEMENT & [PROPOSED] ORDER**
)
)
vs.   )
)
)
Defendant(s).   )
)
)
_____)

The parties to the above-entitled action jointly submit this JOINT CASE MANAGEMENT STATEMENT & PROPOSED ORDER pursuant to the *Standing Order for All Judges of the Northern District of California* and Civil Local Rule 16–9.

    1. Jurisdiction & Service. *The basis for the court's subject matter jurisdiction over plaintiff's claims and defendant's counterclaims, whether any issues exist regarding persona jurisdiction or venue, whether any parties remain to be served, and, if any parties remain to be served, a proposed deadline for service.*

    2. Facts. *A brief chronology of the facts and a statement of the principal factual issues in dispute.*

    3. Legal Issues. *A brief statement, without extended legal argument, of the disputed points of law, including reference to specific statutes and decisions.*

    4. Motions. *All prior and pending motions, their current status, and any anticipated motions.*

    5. Amendment of Pleadings. *The extent to which parties, claims, or defenses are expected to be added or dismissed and a proposed deadline for amending the pleadings.*

    6. Evidence Preservation. *A brief report certifying that the parties have reviewed the Guidelines Relating to the Discovery of Electronically Stored Information ("ESI Guidelines"), and confirming that the parties have met and conferred pursuant to Fed. R. Civ. P. 26(f) regarding reasonable and proportionate steps taken to preserve evidence relevant to the issues reasonably evident in this action. See ESI Guidelines 2.01 and 2.02, and Checklist for ESI Meet and Confer.*

    7. Disclosures. *Whether there has been full and timely compliance with the initial disclosure requirements of Fed. R. Civ. P. 26 and a description of the disclosures made. For ADA and employment cases, see General Order Nos. 56 and 71.*

    8. Discovery. *Discovery taken to date, if any, the scope of anticipated discovery, any proposed limitations or modifications of the discovery rules, a brief report on whether the parties have considered entering into a stipulated e-discovery order, a proposed discovery plan pursuant to Fed. R. Civ. P. 26(f), and any identified discovery disputes.*

    9. Class Actions. *If a class action, a proposal for how and when the class will be certified.*

    10. Related Cases. *Any related cases or proceedings pending before another judge of this court, or before another court or administrative body.*

    11. Relief. *All relief sought through complaint or counterclaim, including the amount of any damages sought and a description of the bases on which damages are calculated. In addition, any party from whom damages are sought must describe the bases on which it contends damages should be calculated if liability is established.*

    12. Settlement and ADR. *Prospects for settlement, ADR efforts to date, and a specific ADR plan for the case, including which ADR process option the parties have selected and a proposed* *deadline, or if the parties do not agree, each party's preferred option and timing, in compliance with ADR L.R. 3–5. In addition, the parties should include a description of key discovery or motions necessary to position the parties to negotiate a resolution.*

    13. Consent to Magistrate Judge For All Purposes. *Whether **all** parties will consent to have a magistrate judge conduct all further proceedings including trial and entry of judgment.* _____ YES _____ NO

    14. Other References. *Whether the case is suitable for reference to binding arbitration, a special master, or the Judicial Panel on Multidistrict Litigation.*

    15. Narrowing of Issues. *Issues that can be narrowed by agreement or by motion, suggestions to expedite the presentation of evidence at trial (e.g., through summaries or stipulated facts), and any request to bifurcate issues, claims, or defenses.*

    16. Expedited Trial Procedure. *Whether this is the type of case that can be handled under the Expedited Trial Procedure of General Order 64, Attachment A. If all parties agree, they shall instead of this Statement, file an executed Agreement for Expedited Trial and a Joint Expedited Case Management Statement, in accordance with General Order No. 64, Attachments B and D.*

    17. Scheduling. *Proposed dates for completion of initial ADR session, designation of experts, discovery cutoff, hearing of dispositive motions, pretrial conference and trial.*

    18. Trial. *Whether the case will be tried to a jury or to the court and the expected length of the trial.*

    19. Disclosure of Non-party Interested Entities or Persons. *Whether each party has filed the "Certification of Interested Entities or Persons" required by Civil Local Rule 3–15. In addition, each party must restate in the case management statement the contents of its certification by identifying any persons, firms, partnerships, corporations (including parent corporations) or other entities known by the party to have either: (i) a financial interest in the subject matter in controversy or in a party to the proceeding; or (ii) any other kind of interest that could be substantially affected by the outcome of the proceeding.*

    20. Professional Conduct. *Whether all attorneys of record for the parties have reviewed the Guidelines for Professional Conduct for the Northern District of California.*

    21. Other. *Such other matters as may facilitate the just, speedy and inexpensive disposition of this matter.*

Dated: _____

                             Counsel for plaintiff

Dated: _____

                             Counsel for defendant

CASE MANAGEMENT ORDER

    The above JOINT CASE MANAGEMENT STATEMENT & PROPOSED ORDER is approved as the Case Management Order for this case and all parties shall comply with its provisions. [In addition, the Court makes the further orders stated below:]

    IT IS SO ORDERED.

Dated: _____

              UNITED STATES DISTRICT/MAGISTRATE JUDGE

[Effective September 1, 1995. Amended effective March 1, 2000. Abrogated effective March 1, 2007. Amended effective January 26, 2012; November, 2012; May, 2013; August, 2014; May 2018.]

STIPULATION AND [PROPOSED] ORDER SELECTING ADR PROCESS

UNITED STATES DISTRICT COURT
NORTHERN DISTRICT OF CALIFORNIA

	CASE No C
Plaintiff(s)	
v.	STIPULATION AND [PROPOSED] ORDER SELECTING ADR PROCESS
Defendant(s)	

Counsel report that they have met and conferred regarding ADR and have reached the following stipulation pursuant to Civil L.R. 16-8 and ADR L.R. 3-5. The parties agree to participate in the following ADR process:

- ☐ **Early Neutral Evaluation (ENE)** (ADR L.R. 5)

- ☐ **Mediation** (ADR L.R. 6)

- ☐ **Early Settlement Conference with a Magistrate Judge** (ADR L.R. 7)

- ☐ **Private ADR** (*specify process and provider*)

The parties agree to hold the ADR session by:

- ☐ the presumptive deadline *(90 days from the date of the order referring the case to ADR)*

- ☐ other requested deadline:

Date: _____

_____
Attorney for Plaintiff

Date: _____

_____
Attorney for Defendant

☐ IT IS SO ORDERED.
☐ IT IS SO ORDERED WITH THE FOLLOWING MODIFICATIONS:

DATE: _____   _____
                        U.S. DISTRICT/MAGISTRATE JUDGE

Important! E-file this form in ECF using the appropriate event among these choices: "Stipulation & Proposed Order Selecting Mediation" or "Stipulation & Proposed Order Selecting ENE" or "Stipulation & Proposed Order Selecting Early Settlement Conference with a Magistrate Judge" or "Stipulation & Proposed Order Selecting Private ADR."

Form ADR-Stip rev. 1-15-2019

[Effective May 1, 2000. Amended effective December, 2011. November, 2016; January, 2017; May 1, 2018; January 15, 2019.]

REQUEST FOR ADR PHONE CONFERENCE
UNITED STATES DISTRICT COURT
NORTHERN DISTRICT OF CALIFORNIA

Plaintiff(s)	Case No. C
v.	REQUEST FOR ADR PHONE CONFERENCE
Defendant(s)	

Counsel hereby request an ADR Phone Conference with a member of the legal staff of the ADR Program.

Date of Case Management Conference: _____.

The following counsel will participate in the ADR phone conference:

Attorney Name & Party Representing	Phone & Email Address

ADR Local Rule 3-6(a) requires that lead trial counsel participate in the ADR Phone Conference. The ADR Unit (adr@cand.uscourts.gov) will notify you of the date and time of your phone conference.

Date: Signed: _____
                                          Attorney for Plaintiff

Date: Signed: _____
                                          Attorney for Defendant

Important! *E-file this form in ECF using event name: "Request for ADR Phone Conference."*

Form ADR-TC rev. 5-1-2018

[Effective May 1, 2000. Amended effective December, 2005; November, 2016; May 1, 2018.]

ELECTRONICALLY STORED INFORMATION
GUIDELINES FOR THE DISCOVERY OF ELECTRONICALLY STORED INFORMATION

GENERAL GUIDELINES

Guideline 1.01 (Purpose). Discoverable information today is mainly electronic. The discovery of electronically stored information (ESI) provides many benefits such as the ability to search, organize, and target the ESI using the text and associated data. At the same time, the Court is aware that the discovery of ESI is a potential source of cost, burden, and delay.

These Guidelines should guide the parties as they engage in electronic discovery. The purpose of these Guidelines is to encourage reasonable electronic discovery with the goal of limiting the cost, burden and time spent, while ensuring that information subject to discovery is preserved and produced to allow for fair adjudication of the merits. At all times, the discovery of ESI should be handled by the parties consistently with Fed. R. Civ. P. 1 to "secure the just, speedy, and inexpensive determination of every action and proceeding."

These Guidelines also promote, when ripe, the early resolution of disputes regarding the discovery of ESI without Court intervention.

Guideline 1.02 (Cooperation). The Court expects cooperation on issues relating to the preservation, collection, search, review, and production of ESI. The Court notes that an attorney's zealous representation of a client is not compromised by conducting discovery in a cooperative manner. Cooperation in reasonably limiting ESI discovery requests on the one hand, and in reasonably responding to ESI discovery requests on the other hand, tends to reduce litigation costs and delay. The Court emphasizes the particular importance of cooperative exchanges of information at the earliest possible stage of discovery, including during the parties' Fed. R. Civ. P. 26(f) conference.

Guideline 1.03 (Discovery Proportionality). The proportionality standard set forth in Fed. R. Civ. P. 26(b)(1) should be applied to the discovery plan and its elements, including the preservation, collection, search, review, and production of ESI. To assure reasonableness and proportionality in discovery, parties should consider factors that include the importance of the issues at stake in the action, the amount in controversy, the parties' relative access to relevant information, the parties' resources, the importance of the discovery in resolving the issues, and whether the burden or expense of the proposed discovery outweighs its likely benefit. To further the application of the proportionality standard, discovery requests for production of ESI and related responses should be reasonably targeted, clear, and as specific as practicable.

ESI DISCOVERY GUIDELINES

Guideline 2.01 (Preservation).

a) At the outset of a case, or sooner if feasible, counsel for the parties should discuss preservation. Such discussions should continue to occur periodically as the case and issues evolve.

b) In determining what ESI to preserve, parties should apply the proportionality standard referenced in Guideline 1.03. The parties should strive to define a scope of preservation that is proportionate and reasonable and not disproportionately broad, expensive, or burdensome.

c) Parties are not required to use preservation letters to notify an opposing party of the preservation obligation, but if a party does so, the Court discourages the use of overbroad preservation letters. Instead, if a party prepares a preservation letter, the letter should provide as much detail as possible, such as the names of parties, a description of claims, potential witnesses, the relevant time period, sources of ESI the party knows or believes are likely to contain relevant information, and any other information that might assist the responding party in determining what information to preserve.

d) If there is a dispute concerning the scope of a party's preservation efforts, the parties or their counsel should meet and confer and fully discuss the reasonableness and proportionality of the preservation. If the parties are unable to resolve a preservation issue, then the issue should be raised promptly with the Court.

e) The parties should discuss what ESI from sources that are not reasonably accessible will be preserved, but not searched, reviewed, or produced. As well as discussing ESI sources that are not reasonably accessible, the parties should consider identifying data from sources that (1) the parties believe could contain relevant information but (2) determine, under the proportionality factors, should not be preserved.

Guideline 2.02 (Rule 26(f) Meet and Confer). At the required Rule 26(f) meet and confer conference, when a case involves electronic discovery, the topics that the parties should consider discussing include: 1) preservation; 2) systems that contain discoverable ESI; 3) search and production; 4) phasing of discovery; 5) protective orders; and 6) opportunities to reduce costs and increase efficiency. In order to be meaningful, the meet and confer should be as sufficiently detailed on these topics as is appropriate in light of the specific claims and defenses at issue in the case. Some or all of the following details may be useful to discuss, especially in cases where the discovery of ESI is likely to be a significant cost or burden:

a) The sources, scope and type of ESI that has been and will be preserved —considering the needs of the case and other proportionality factors— including date ranges, identity and number of potential custodians, and other details that help clarify the scope of preservation;

b) Any difficulties related to preservation;

c) Search and production of ESI, such as any planned methods to identify discoverable ESI and filter out ESI that is not subject to discovery, or whether ESI stored in a database can be produced by querying the database and producing discoverable information in a report or an exportable electronic file;

d) The phasing of discovery so that discovery occurs first from sources most likely to contain relevant and discoverable information and is postponed or avoided from sources less likely to contain relevant and discoverable information;

e) The potential need for a protective order and any procedures to which the parties might agree for handling inadvertent production of privileged information and other privilege waiver issues pursuant to Fed. R. Evid. 502(d) or (e), including a Rule 502(d) Order;

f) Opportunities to reduce costs and increase efficiency and speed, such as by conferring about the methods and technology used for searching ESI to help identify the relevant information and sampling methods to validate the search for relevant information, using agreements for truncated or limited privilege logs, or by sharing expenses like those related to litigation document repositories.

The Court encourages the parties to address any agreements or disagreements related to the above matters in the joint case management statement required by Civil Local Rule 16–9.

Guideline 2.03 (Cooperation and Informal Discovery Regarding ESI). The Court strongly encourages an informal discussion about the discovery of ESI (rather than deposition) at the earliest reasonable stage of the discovery process. Counsel, or others knowledgeable about the parties' electronic systems, including how potentially relevant data is stored and retrieved, should be involved or made available as necessary. Such a discussion will help the parties be more efficient in framing and responding to ESI discovery issues, reduce costs, and assist the parties and the Court in the event of a dispute involving ESI issues.

Guideline 2.04 (Disputes Regarding ESI Issues). Disputes regarding ESI that counsel for the parties are unable to resolve shall be presented to the Court at the earliest possible opportunity, such as at the initial Case Management Conference. If the Court determines that any counsel or party in a case has failed to cooperate and participate in good faith in the meet and confer process, the Court may require additional meet and confer discussions, if appropriate.

Guideline 2.05 (E–Discovery Liaison(s)). In most cases, the meet and confer process will be aided by participation of e-discovery liaisons as defined in this Guideline. If a dispute arises that involves the technical aspects of e-discovery, each party shall designate an e-discovery liaison who will be knowledgeable about and responsible for discussing their respective ESI. An e-discovery liaison will be, or have access to those who are, knowledgeable about the location, nature, accessibility, format, collection, searching, and production of ESI in the matter. Regardless of whether the e-discovery liaison is an attorney (in- house or outside counsel), an employee of the party, or a third party consultant, the e-discovery liaison should:

a) Be prepared to participate in e-discovery dispute resolution to limit the need for Court intervention;

b) Be knowledgeable about the party's e-discovery efforts;

c) Be familiar with, or gain knowledge about, the party's electronic systems and capabilities in order to explain those systems and answer related questions; and

d) Be familiar with, or gain knowledge about, the technical aspects of e-discovery in the matter, including electronic document storage, organization, and format issues, and relevant information retrieval technology, including search methodology.

EDUCATION GUIDELINES

Guideline 3.01 (Judicial Expectations of Counsel). It is expected that counsel for the parties, including all counsel who have appeared, as well as all others responsible for making representations to the Court or opposing counsel (whether or not they make an appearance), will be familiar with the following in each litigation matter:

a) The electronic discovery provisions of the Federal Rules of Civil Procedure, including Rules 26, 33, 34, 37, and 45, and Federal Rule of Evidence 502;

b) The Advisory Committee Report on the 2015 Amendments to the Federal Rules of Civil Procedure, available at www.uscourts.gov/rules-policies/archives/committee-reports/advisory-committee-rules-civil-procedure-may-2014; and

c) These Guidelines and this Court's *Checklist for Rule 26(f) Meet and Confer Regarding ESI and Stipulated E–Discovery Order for Standard Litigation.*

[Effective November 26, 2012. Amended effective December 1, 2015.]

CHECKLIST FOR RULE 26(f) MEET AND CONFER REGARDING ELECTRONICALLY STORED INFORMATION

In cases where the discovery of electronically stored information ("ESI") is likely to be a significant cost or burden, the Court encourages the parties to engage in on-going meet and confer discussions and use the following Checklist to guide those discussions. These discussions should be framed in the context of the specific claims and defenses involved. The usefulness of particular topics on the checklist, and the timing of discussion about these topics, may depend on the nature and complexity of the matter.

I. Preservation.

☐ The ranges of creation or receipt dates for any ESI to be preserved.

☐ The description of data from sources that are not reasonably accessible and that will not be reviewed for responsiveness or produced, but that will be preserved pursuant to Federal Rule of Civil Procedure 26(b)(2)(B).

☐ The description of data from sources that (a) the party believes could contain relevant information but (b) has determined, under the proportionality factors, is not discoverable and should not be preserved.

☐ Whether or not to continue any interdiction of any document destruction program, such as ongoing erasures of e-mails, voicemails, and other electronically-recorded material.

☐ The names and/or general job titles or descriptions of custodians for whom ESI will be preserved (e.g., "HR head," "scientist," "marketing manager," etc.).

☐ The number of custodians for whom ESI will be preserved.

☐ The list of systems, if any, that contain ESI not associated with individual custodians and that will be preserved, such as enterprise databases.

☐ Any disputes related to scope or manner of preservation.

II. Liaison.

☐ The identity of each party's e-discovery liaison.

III.   Informal Discovery About Location and Types of Systems.

☐ Identification of systems from which discovery will be prioritized (e.g., email, finance, HR systems).

☐ Description of systems in which potentially discoverable information is stored.

☐ Location of systems in which potentially discoverable information is stored.

☐ How potentially discoverable information is stored.

☐ How discoverable information can be collected from systems and media in which it is stored.

IV.   Proportionality and Costs.

☐ The amount and nature of the claims being made by either party.

☐ The nature and scope of burdens associated with the proposed preservation and discovery of ESI.

☐ The likely benefit of the proposed discovery.

☐ Costs that the parties will share to reduce overall discovery expenses, such as the use of a common electronic discovery vendor or a shared document repository, or other cost-saving measures.

☐ Limits on the scope of preservation or other cost-saving measures.

☐ Whether there is relevant ESI that will not be preserved pursuant to Fed. R. Civ. P. 26(b)(1), requiring discovery to be proportionate to the needs of the case.

V.   Search.

☐ The search method(s), including specific words or phrases or other methodology, that will be used to identify discoverable ESI and filter out ESI that is not subject to discovery.

☐ The quality control method(s) the producing party will use to evaluate whether a production is missing relevant ESI or contains substantial amounts of irrelevant ESI.

VI.   Phasing.

☐ Whether it is appropriate to conduct discovery of ESI in phases.

☐ Sources of ESI most likely to contain discoverable information and that will be included in the first phases of Fed. R. Civ. P. 34 document discovery.

☐ Sources of ESI less likely to contain discoverable information from which discovery will be postponed or avoided.

☐ Custodians (by name or role) most likely to have discoverable information and whose ESI

☐ will be included in the first phases of document discovery.

☐ Custodians (by name or role) less likely to have discoverable information and from whom discovery of ESI will be postponed or avoided.

☐ The time period during which discoverable information was most likely to have been created or received.

VII.   Production.

☐ The formats in which structured ESI (database, collaboration sites, etc.) will be produced.

☐ The formats in which unstructured ESI (email, presentations, word processing, etc.) will be produced.

☐ The extent, if any, to which metadata will be produced and the fields of metadata to be produced.

☐ The production format(s) that ensure(s) that any inherent searchablility of ESI is not degraded when produced.

VIII. Privilege.

☐ How any production of privileged or work product protected information will be handled.

☐ Whether the parties can agree upon alternative ways to identify documents withheld on the grounds of privilege or work product to reduce the burdens of such identification.

☐ Whether the parties will enter into a Fed. R. Evid. 502(d) Stipulation and Order that addresses inadvertent or agreed production.

[Amended effective December 1, 2015.]

RECOMMENDATIONS FOR ESI DISCOVERY IN FEDERAL CRIMINAL CASES

Introduction to Recommendations for
ESI Discovery in Federal Criminal Cases

Today, most information is created and stored electronically. The advent of electronically stored information (ESI) presents an opportunity for greater efficiency and cost savings for the entire criminal justice system, which is especially important for the representation of indigent defendants. To realize those benefits and to avoid undue cost, disruption and delay, criminal practitioners must educate themselves and employ best practices for managing ESI discovery.

The Joint Electronic Technology Working Group (JETWG) was created to address best practices for the efficient and cost-effective management of post-indictment ESI discovery between the Government and defendants charged in federal criminal cases. JETWG was established in 1998 by the Director of the Administrative Office of the U.S. Courts (AOUSC) and the Attorney General of the United States. It consists of representatives of the Administrative Office of U.S. Courts' (AOUSC) Office of Defender Services (ODS), the Department of Justice (DOJ), Federal Defender Organizations (FDO), private attorneys who accept Criminal Justice Act (CJA) appointments, and liaisons from the United States Judiciary and other AOUSC offices.

JETWG has prepared recommendations for managing ESI discovery in federal criminal cases, which are contained in the following three documents:

1. Recommendations for ESI Discovery in Federal Criminal Cases. The Recommendations provide the general framework for managing ESI, including planning, production, transmission, dispute resolution, and security.

2. Strategies and Commentary on ESI Discovery in Federal Criminal Cases. The Strategies provide technical and more particularized guidance for implementing the recommendations, including definitions of terms. The Strategies will evolve in light of changing technology and experience.

3. ESI Discovery Checklist. A one-page Checklist for addressing ESI production issues.

The Recommendations, Strategies, and Checklist are intended for cases where the volume and/or nature of the ESI produced as discovery significantly increases the complexity of the case. They are not intended for all cases. The Recommendations, Strategies, and Checklist build upon the following basic principles:

Principle 1: Lawyers have a responsibility to have an adequate understanding of electronic discovery. (See #4 of the Recommendations.)

Principle 2: In the process of planning, producing, and resolving disputes about ESI discovery, the parties should include individuals with sufficient technical knowledge and experience regarding ESI. (See #4 of the Recommendations.)

Principle 3: At the outset of a case, the parties should meet and confer about the nature, volume, and mechanics of producing ESI discovery. Where the ESI discovery is particularly complex or produced on a rolling basis, an on-going dialogue may be helpful. (See #5 of the Recommendations and Strategies.)

Principle 4: The parties should discuss what formats of production are possible and appropriate, and what formats can be generated. Any format selected for producing discovery should maintain the ESI's integrity, allow for reasonable usability, reasonably limit costs, and, if possible, conform to industry standards for the format. (See #6 of the Recommendations and Strategies.)

Principle 5: When producing ESI discovery, a party should not be required to take on substantial additional processing or format conversion costs and burdens beyond what the party has already done or would do for its own case preparation or discovery production. (See #6 of the Recommendations and Strategies.)

Principle 6: Following the meet and confer, the parties should notify the court of ESI discovery production issues or problems that they reasonably anticipate will significantly affect the handling of the case. (See #5(s) of the Strategies.)

Principle 7: The parties should discuss ESI discovery transmission methods and media that promote efficiency, security, and reduced costs. The producing party should provide a general description and maintain a record of what was transmitted. (See #7 of the Recommendations and Strategies.)

Principle 8: In multi-defendant cases, the defendants should authorize one or more counsel to act as the discovery coordinator(s) or seek appointment of a Coordinating Discovery Attorney. (See #8 of the Recommendations and Strategies.)

Principle 9: The parties should make good faith efforts to discuss and resolve disputes over ESI discovery, involving those with the requisite technical knowledge when necessary, and they should consult with a supervisor, or obtain supervisory authorization, before seeking judicial resolution of an ESI discovery dispute or alleging misconduct, abuse, or neglect concerning the production of ESI. (See #9 of the Recommendations.)

Principle 10: All parties should limit dissemination of ESI discovery to members of their litigation team who need and are approved for access, and they should also take reasonable and appropriate measures to secure ESI discovery against unauthorized access or disclosure. (See #10 of the Recommendations.)

The Recommendations, Strategies, and Checklist set forth a collaborative approach to ESI discovery involving mutual and interdependent responsibilities. The goal is to benefit all parties by making ESI discovery more efficient, secure, and less costly.

Recommendations for ESI Discovery Production in Federal Criminal Cases

1. **Purpose.** These Recommendations are intended to promote the efficient and cost-effective post-indictment production of electronically stored information (ESI) in discovery[1] between the Government and defendants charged in federal criminal cases, and to reduce unnecessary conflict and litigation over ESI discovery by encouraging the parties to communicate about ESI discovery issues, by creating a predictable framework for ESI discovery, and by establishing methods for resolving ESI discovery disputes without the need for court intervention.

ESI discovery production involves the balancing of several goals:

a) the parties must comply with their legal discovery obligations;

b) the volume of ESI in many cases may make it impossible for counsel to personally review every potentially discoverable item, and, as a consequence, the parties increasingly will employ software tools for discovery review, so ESI discovery should be done in a manner to facilitate electronic search, retrieval, sorting, and management of discovery information;

c) the parties should look for ways to avoid unnecessary duplication of time and expense for both parties in the handling and use of ESI;

d) subject to subparagraph (e), below, the producing party should produce its ESI discovery materials in industry standard formats;

e) the producing party is not obligated to undertake additional processing desired by the receiving party that is not part of the producing party's own case preparation or discovery production[2]; and

f) the parties must protect their work product, privileged, and other protected information.

The following Recommendations are a general framework for informed discussions between the parties about ESI discovery issues. The efficient and cost-effective production of ESI discovery materials is enhanced when the parties communicate early and regularly about any ESI discovery issues in their case, and when they give the court notice of ESI discovery issues that will significantly affect the handling of the case.

2. Scope: Cases Involving Significant ESI. No single approach to ESI discovery is suited to all cases. These Recommendations are intended for cases where the volume and/or nature of the ESI produced as discovery significantly increases the complexity of the case.[3] In simple or routine cases, the parties should provide discovery in the manner they deem most efficient in accordance with the Federal Rules of Criminal Procedure, local rules, and custom and practice within their district.

Due to the evolving role of ESI in criminal cases, these Recommendations and the parties' practices will change with technology and experience. As managing ESI discovery becomes more routine, it is anticipated that the parties will develop standard processes for ESI discovery that become the accepted norm.

3. Limitations. These Recommendations and the accompanying Strategies do not alter the parties' discovery obligations or protections under the U.S. Constitution, the Federal Rules of Criminal Procedure, the Jencks Act, or other federal statutes, case law, or local rules. They may not serve as a basis for allegations of misconduct or claims for relief and they do not create any rights or privileges for any party.

4. Technical Knowledge and Experience. For complex ESI productions, each party should involve individuals with sufficient technical knowledge and experience to understand, communicate about, and plan for the orderly exchange of ESI discovery. Lawyers have a responsibility to have an adequate understanding of electronic discovery.

5. Planning for ESI Discovery Production—The Meet and Confer Process. At the outset of a case involving substantial or complex ESI discovery, the parties should meet and confer about the nature, volume, and mechanics of producing ESI discovery. The parties should determine how to ensure that any "meet and confer" process does not run afoul of speedy trial deadlines. Where the ESI discovery is particularly complex or produced on a rolling basis, an on-going dialogue during the discovery phase may be helpful. In cases where it is authorized, providing ESI discovery to an incarcerated defendant presents challenges that should be discussed early. Also, cases involving classified information will not fit within the Recommendations and Strategies due to the unique legal procedures applicable to those cases. ESI that is contraband (*e.g.*, child pornography) requires special discovery procedures. The Strategies and Checklist provide detailed recommendations on planning for ESI discovery.

6. Production of ESI Discovery. Production of ESI discovery involves varied considerations depending upon the ESI's source, nature, and format. Unlike certain civil cases, in criminal cases the parties generally are not the original custodian or source of the ESI they produce in discovery. The ESI gathered by the parties during their investigations may be affected or limited by many factors, including the original custodian's or source's information technology systems, data management practices, and resources; the party's understanding of the case at the time of collection; and other factors. Likewise, the electronic formats used by the parties for producing ESI discovery may be affected or limited by several factors, including the source of the ESI; the format(s) in which the ESI was originally obtained; and the party's legal discovery obligations, which may vary with the nature of the material. The Strategies and Checklist provide detailed recommendations on production of ESI discovery.

General recommendations for the production of ESI discovery are:

a. The parties should discuss what formats of production are possible and appropriate, and what formats can be generated. Any format selected for producing discovery should, if possible, conform to industry standards for the format.[4]

b. ESI received from third parties should be produced in the format(s) it was received or in a reasonably usable format(s). ESI from the government's or defendant's business records should be produced in the format(s) in which it was maintained or in a reasonably usable format(s).

c. Discoverable ESI generated by the government or defense during the course of their investigations (*e.g.*, investigative reports, witness interviews, demonstrative exhibits, etc.) may be handled differently than in 6(a) and (b) above because the parties' legal discovery obligations and practices vary according to the nature of the material, the applicable law, evolving legal standards, the parties' policies, and the parties' evolving technological capabilities.

d. When producing ESI discovery, a party should not be required to take on substantial additional processing or format conversion costs and burdens beyond what the party has already done or would do for its own case preparation or discovery production. For example, the producing party need not convert ESI from one format to another or undertake additional processing of ESI beyond what is required to satisfy its legal disclosure obligations. If the receiving party desires ESI in a condition different from what the producing party intends to produce, the parties should discuss what is reasonable in terms of expense and mechanics, who will bear the burden of any additional cost or work, and how to protect the producing party's work product or privileged information. Nonetheless, with the understanding that in certain instances the results of processing ESI may constitute work product not subject to discovery, these recommendations operate on the general principle that where a producing party elects to engage in processing of ESI, the results of that processing should, unless they constitute work product, be produced in discovery along with the underlying ESI so as to save the receiving party the expense of replicating the work.

7. **Transmitting ESI Discovery.** The parties should discuss transmission methods and media that promote efficiency, security, and reduce costs. In conjunction with ESI transmission, the producing party should provide a general description and maintain a record of what was transmitted. Any media should be clearly labeled. The Strategies and Checklist contain detailed recommendations on transmission of ESI discovery, including the potential use of email to transmit ESI.

8. **Coordinating Discovery Attorney.** In cases involving multiple defendants, the defendants should authorize one or more counsel to act as the discovery coordinator(s) or seek the appointment of a Coordinating Discovery Attorney[5] and authorize that person to accept, on behalf of all defense counsel, the ESI discovery produced by the government. Generally, the format of production should be the same for all defendants, but the parties should be sensitive to different needs and interests in multiple defendant cases.

9. **Informal Resolution of ESI Discovery Matters.**

a. Before filing any motion addressing an ESI discovery issue, the moving party should confer with opposing counsel in a good-faith effort to resolve the dispute. If resolution of the dispute requires technical knowledge, the parties should involve individuals with sufficient knowledge to understand the technical issues, clearly communicate the problem(s) leading to the dispute, and either implement a proposed resolution or explain why a proposed resolution will not solve the dispute.

b. The Discovery Coordinator within each U.S. Attorney's Office should be consulted in cases presenting substantial issues or disputes.

c. To avoid unnecessary litigation, prosecutors and Federal Defender Offices[6] should institute procedures that require line prosecutors and defenders (1) to consult with a supervisory attorney before filing a motion seeking judicial resolution of an ESI discovery dispute, and (2) to obtain authorization from a supervisory attorney before suggesting in a pleading that opposing counsel has engaged in any misconduct, abuse, or neglect concerning production of ESI.

d. Any motion addressing a discovery dispute concerning ESI production should include a statement of counsel for the moving party relating that after consultation with the attorney for the opposing party the parties have been unable to resolve the dispute without court action.

10. **Security: Protecting Sensitive ESI Discovery From Unauthorized Access or Disclosure.** Criminal case discovery entails certain responsibilities for all parties in the careful handling of a variety of sensitive information, for example, grand jury material, the defendant's records, witness identifying information, information about informants, information subject to court protective orders, confidential personal or business information, and privileged information. With ESI discovery, those responsibilities are increased because ESI is easily reproduced and disseminated, and unauthorized access or disclosure could, in certain circumstances, endanger witness safety; adversely affect national security or homeland security; leak information to adverse parties in civil suits; compromise privacy, trade secrets, or classified, tax return, or proprietary information; or prejudice the fair administration of justice. The parties' willingness to produce early, accessible, and usable ESI discovery will be enhanced by safeguards that protect sensitive information from unauthorized access or disclosure.

All parties should limit dissemination of ESI discovery to members of their litigation team who need and are approved for access. They should also take reasonable and appropriate measures to secure ESI discovery against unauthorized access or disclosure.

During the initial meet and confer and before ESI discovery is produced, the parties should discuss whether there is confidential, private or sensitive information in any ESI discovery they will be providing. If such information will be disclosed, then the parties should discuss how the recipients will prevent unauthorized access to, or disclosure of, that ESI discovery, and, absent agreement on appropriate security, the producing party should seek a protective order from the court addressing management of the particular ESI at issue. The producing party has the burden to raise the issue anew if it has concerns about any ESI discovery it will provide in subsequent productions. The parties may choose to have standing agreements so that their practices for managing ESI discovery are not discussed in each case. The Strategies contains additional guidance in sections 5(f), 5(p), and 7(e).

[1] The Recommendations and Strategies are intended to apply only to disclosure of ESI under Federal Rules of Criminal Procedure 16 and 26.2, *Brady*, *Giglio*, and the Jencks Act, and they do not apply to, nor do they create any rights, privileges, or benefits during, the gathering of ESI as part of the parties' criminal or civil investigations. The legal principles, standards, and practices applicable to the discovery phase of criminal cases serve different purposes than those applicable to criminal and civil investigations.

[2] One example of the producing party undertaking additional processing for its discovery production is a load file that enables the receiving party to load discovery materials into its software.

[3] Courts and litigants will continue to seek ways to identify cases deserving special consideration. While the facts and circumstances of cases will vary, some factors may include: (1) a large volume of ESI; (2) unique ESI issues, including native file formats, voluminous third-party records, non-standard and proprietary software formats; and/or (3) multiple defendant cases accompanied by a significant volume of ESI.

[4] An example of "format of production" might be TIFF images, OCR text files, and load files created for a specific software application. Another "format of production" would be native file production, which would accommodate files with unique issues, such as spreadsheets with formulas and databases. ESI in a particular case might warrant more than one format of production depending upon the nature of the ESI.

[5] Coordinating Discovery Attorneys (CDA) are AOUSC contracted attorneys who have technological knowledge and experience, resources, and staff to effectively manage complex ESI in multiple defendant cases. The CDAs may be appointed by the court to provide in-depth and significant hands-on assistance to CJA panel attorneys and FDO staff in selected multiple-defendant cases that require technology and document management assistance. They can serve as a primary point of contact for the U.S. Attorneys Office to discuss ESI production issues for all defendants, resulting in lower overall case costs for the parties. If a panel attorney or FDO is interested in utilizing the services of the CDA, they should contact the National Litigation Support Administrator or Assistant National Litigation Support Administrator for the Office of Defender Services at 510–637–3500.

[6] For private attorneys appointed under the Criminal Justice Act (CJA), this subsection (c) is not applicable.

Strategies and Commentary
on ESI Discovery in Federal Criminal Cases

1. **Purpose.** This commentary contains strategies for implementing the ESI discovery Recommendations and specific technical guidance. Over time it will be modified in light of experience and changing technology. Definitions of common ESI terms are provided in paragraph 11, below.

2. **Scope of ESI Gathered.** In order to promote efficiency and avoid unnecessary costs, when gathering ESI the parties should take into consideration the nature, volume, and mechanics of managing ESI.

3. **Limitations.** Nothing contained herein creates any rights or privileges for any party.

4. **Technical Knowledge and Experience.** No additional commentary.

5. **Planning for ESI Discovery Production—The Meet and Confer Process.** To promote efficient ESI discovery, the parties may find it useful to discuss the following:

a. *ESI Discovery Produced.* The parties should discuss the ESI being produced according to the following general categories:

    i. Investigative materials (investigative reports, surveillance records, criminal histories, etc.)

    ii. Witness statements (interview reports, transcripts of prior testimony, Jencks statements, etc.)

    iii. Documentation of tangible objects (*e.g.*, records of seized items or forensic samples, search warrant returns, etc.)

    iv. Third parties' ESI digital devices (computers, phones, hard drives, thumb drives, CDs, DVDs, cloud computing, etc., including forensic images)

    v. Photographs and video/audio recordings (crime scene photos; photos of contraband, guns, money; surveillance recordings; surreptitious monitoring recordings; etc.)

vi. Third party records and materials (including those seized, subpoenaed, and voluntarily disclosed)

vii. Title III wire tap information (audio recordings, transcripts, line sheets, call reports, court documents, etc.)

viii. Court records (affidavits, applications, and related documentation for search and arrest warrants, etc.)

ix. Tests and examinations

x. Experts (reports and related information)

xi. Immunity agreements, plea agreements, and similar materials

xii. Discovery materials with special production considerations (such as child pornography; trade secrets; tax return information; etc.)

xiii. Related matters (state or local investigative materials, parallel proceedings materials, etc.)

xiv. Discovery materials available for inspection but not produced digitally

xv. Other information

b. *Table of Contents.* If the producing party has not created a table of contents prior to commencing ESI discovery production, it should consider creating one describing the general categories of information available as ESI discovery. In complex discovery cases, a table of contents to the available discovery materials can help expedite the opposing party's review of discovery, promote early settlement, and avoid discovery disputes, unnecessary expense, and undue delay.[1] Because no single table of contents is appropriate for every case, the producing party may devise a table of contents that is suited to the materials it provides in discovery, its resources, and other considerations.[2]

c. *Forms of Production.* The producing party should consider how discoverable materials were provided to it or maintained by the source (*e.g.*, paper or electronic), whether it has converted any materials to a digital format that can be used by the opposing party without disclosing the producing party's work product, and how those factors may affect the production of discovery materials in electronic formats. For particularized guidance *see* paragraph 6, below. The parties should be flexible in their application of the concept of "maintained by the source." The goals are to retain the ESI's integrity, to allow for reasonable usability, and to reasonably limit costs.[3]

d. *Proprietary or Legacy Data.* Special consideration should be given to data stored in proprietary or legacy systems, for example, video surveillance recordings in an uncommon format, proprietary databases, or software that is no longer supported by the vendor. The parties should discuss whether a suitable generic output format or report is available. If a generic output is not available, the parties should discuss the specific requirements necessary to access the data in its original format.

e. *Attorney–Client, Work Product, and Protected Information Issues.*[4] The parties should discuss whether there is privileged, work product, or other protected information in third-party ESI or their own discoverable ESI and proposed methods and procedures for segregating such information and resolving any disputes.[5]

f. *Confidential and Personal Information.* The parties should identify and discuss the types of confidential or personal information present in the ESI discovery, appropriate security for that information, and the need for any protective orders or redactions. *See also,* section 5(p) below.

g. *Incarcerated Defendant.* If the defendant is incarcerated and the court or correctional institution has authorized discovery access in the custodial setting, the parties should consider what institutional requirements or limitations may affect the defendant's access to ESI discovery, such as limitations on hardware or software use.[6]

h. *ESI Discovery Volume.* To assist in estimating the receiving party's discovery costs and to the extent that the producing party knows the volume of discovery materials it intends to produce immediately or in the future, the producing party may provide such information if such disclosure would not compromise the producing party's interests. Examples of volume include the number of pages of electronic images of paper-based discovery, the volume (*e.g.*, gigabytes) of ESI, the number and aggregate length of any audio or video recordings, and the number and volume of digital devices. Disclosures concerning expected volume are not intended to be so detailed as to require a party to disclose what they intend to produce as discovery before they have a legal obligation to produce the particular discovery material (*e.g.*, Jencks material). Similarly, the parties' estimates are not binding and may not serve as the basis for allegations of misconduct or claims for relief.

i. *Naming Conventions and Logistics.* The parties should, from the outset of a case, employ naming conventions that would make the production of discovery more efficient. For example, in a Title III wire tap case generally it is preferable that the naming conventions for the audio files, the monitoring logs, and the call transcripts be consistent so that it is easy to cross-reference the audio calls with the corresponding monitoring logs and transcripts. If at the outset of discovery production a naming convention has not yet been established, the parties should discuss a naming convention before the discovery is produced. The parties should discuss logistics and the sharing of costs or tasks that will enhance ESI production.

j. *Paper Materials.* For options and particularized guidance on paper materials *see* paragraphs 6(a) and(e), below.

k. *Any Software and Hardware Limitations.* As technology continues to evolve, the parties may have software and hardware constraints on how they can review ESI. Any limitations should be addressed during the meet and confer.

l. *ESI From Seized or Searched Third–Party ESI Digital Devices.* When a party produces ESI from a seized or searched third-party digital device (*e.g.*, computer, cell phone, hard drive, thumb drive, CD, DVD, cloud computing, or file share), the producing party should identify the digital device that held the ESI, and, to the extent that the producing party already knows, provide some indication of the device's probable owner or custodian and the location where the device was seized or searched. Where the producing party only has limited authority to search the digital device (*e.g.*, limits set by a search warrant's terms), the parties should discuss the need for protective orders or other mechanisms to regulate the receiving party's access to or inspection of the device.

m. *Inspection of Hard Drives and/or Forensic (Mirror) Images.* Any forensic examination of a hard drive, whether it is an examination of a hard drive itself or an examination of a forensic image of a hard drive, requires specialized software and expertise. A simple copy of the forensic image may not be sufficient to access the information stored, as specialized software may be needed. The parties should consider how to manage inspection of a hard drive and/or production of a forensic image of a hard drive and what software and expertise will be needed to access the information.

n. *Metadata in Third Party ESI.* If a producing party has already extracted metadata from third party ESI, the parties should discuss whether the producing party should produce the extracted metadata together with an industry-standard load file, or, alternatively, produce the files as received by the producing party from the third party.[7] Neither party need undertake additional processing beyond its own case preparation, and both parties are entitled to protect their work product and privileged or other protected information. Because the term "metadata" can encompass different categories of information, the parties should clearly describe what categories of metadata are being discussed, what the producing party has agreed to produce, and any known problems or gaps in the metadata received from third parties.

o. *A Reasonable Schedule for Producing and Reviewing ESI.* Because ESI involves complex technical issues, two stages should be addressed. First, the producing party should transmit its ESI in sufficient time to permit reasonable management and review. Second, the receiving party should be pro-active about testing the accessibility of the ESI production when it is received. Thus, a schedule should include a date for the receiving party to notify the producing party of any production issues or problems that are impeding use of the ESI discovery.

p. *ESI Security.* During the first meet and confer, the parties should discuss ESI discovery security and, if necessary, the need for protective orders to prevent unauthorized access to or disclosure of ESI discovery that any party intends to share with team members via the internet or similar system, including:

i. what discovery material will be produced that is confidential, private, or sensitive, including, but not limited to, grand jury material, witness identifying information, information about informants, a defendant's or co-defendant's personal or business information, information subject to court protective orders, confidential personal or business information, or privileged information;

ii. whether encryption or other security measures during transmission of ESI discovery are warranted;[8]

iii. what steps will be taken to ensure that only authorized persons have access to the electronically stored or disseminated discovery materials;

iv. what steps will be taken to ensure the security of any website or other electronic repository against unauthorized access;

v. what steps will be taken at the conclusion of the case to remove discovery materials from the a website or similar repository; and

vi. what steps will be taken at the conclusion of the case to remove or return ESI discovery materials from the recipient's information system(s), or to securely archive them to prevent unauthorized access.

Note: Because all parties want to ensure that ESI discovery is secure, the Department of Justice, Federal Defender Offices, and CJA counsel are compiling an evolving list of security concerns and recommended best practices for appropriately securing discovery. Prosecutors and defense counsel with security concerns should direct inquiries to their respective ESI liaisons[9] who, in turn, will work with their counterparts to develop best practice guidance.

q. *Other Issues.* The parties should address other issues they can anticipate, such as protective orders, "claw-back" agreements[10] between the government and criminal defendant(s), or any issues related to the preservation or collection of ESI discovery.

r. *Memorializing Agreements.* The parties should memorialize any agreements reached to help forestall later disputes.

s. *Notice to Court.*

i. Preparing for the meet and confer: A defendant who anticipates the need for technical assistance to conduct the meet and confer should give the court adequate advance notice if it will be filing an ex parte funds request for technical assistance.

ii. Following the meet and confer: The parties should notify the court of ESI discovery production issues or problems that they anticipate will significantly affect when ESI discovery will be produced to the receiving party, when the receiving party will complete its accessibility assessment of the ESI discovery received,[11] whether the receiving party will need to make a request for supplemental funds to manage ESI discovery, or the scheduling of pretrial motions or trial.

6. Production of ESI Discovery.

a. *Paper Materials.* Materials received in paper form may be produced in that form,[12] made available for inspection, or, if they have already been converted to digital format, produced as electronic files that can be viewed and searched. Methods are described below in paragraph 6(b).

b. *Electronic Production of Paper Documents.* Three possible methodologies:

i. Single–Page TIFFs. Production in TIFF and OCR format consists of the following three elements:

(1) Paper documents are scanned to a picture or image that produces one file per page. Documents should be unitized. Each electronic image should be stamped with a unique page label or Bates number.

(2) Text from that original document is generated by OCR and stored in separate text files without formatting in a generic format using the same file naming convention and organization as image file.

(3) Load files that tie together the images and text.

ii. Multi–Page TIFFS. Production in TIFF and OCR format consists of the following two elements:

(1) Paper documents are scanned to a picture or image that produces one file per document. Each file may have multiple pages. Each page of the electronic image should be stamped with a unique page label or Bates number.

(2) Text from that original document is generated by OCR and stored in separate text files without formatting in a generic format using the same file naming convention and organization as the image file.

iii. PDF. Production in multi-page, searchable PDF format consists of the following one element:

(1) Paper documents scanned to a PDF file with text generated by OCR included in the same file. This produces one file per document. Documents should be unitized. Each page of the PDF should be stamped with a unique Bates number.

iv. . Note re: color documents. Paper documents should not be scanned in color unless the color content of an individual document is particularly significant to the case.[13]

c. *ESI Production.* Three possible methodologies:

i. Native Files as Received. Production in a native file format without any processing consists of a copy of ESI files in the same condition as they were received.

ii. ESI Converted to Electronic Image. Production of ESI in a TIFF or PDF and extracted text format consists of the following four elements:

(1) Electronic documents converted from their native format into a picture / image. The electronic image files should be computer generated, as opposed to printed and then imaged. Each electronic image should be stamped with a unique Bates number.

(2) Text from that original document is extracted or pulled out and stored without formatting in a generic format.

(3) Metadata (*i.e.*, information about that electronic document), depending upon the type of file converted and the tools or methodology used, that has been extracted and stored in an industry standard format. The metadata must include information about structural relationships between documents, *e.g.*, parent-child relationships.

(4) Load files that tie together the images, text, and metadata.

iii. Native Files With Metadata. Production of ESI in a processed native file format consists of the following four elements:

(1) The native files.

(2) Text from that original document is extracted or pulled out and stored without formatting in a generic format.

(3) Metadata (*i.e.*, information about that electronic document), depending upon the type of file converted and the tools or methodology used, that has been extracted and stored in an industry standard format. The metadata must include information about structural relationships between documents, *e.g.*, parent-child relationships.

(4) Load files that tie together the native file, text, and metadata.

d. *Forensic Images of Digital Media.* Forensic images of digital media should be produced in an industry-standard forensic format, accompanied by notice of the format used.

e. *Printing ESI to Paper.* The producing party should not print ESI (including TIFF images or PDF files) to paper as a substitute for production of the ESI unless agreed to by the parties.

f. *Preservation of ESI Materials Received From Third Parties.* A party receiving potentially discoverable ESI from a third party should, to the extent practicable, retain a copy of the ESI as it was originally produced in case it is subsequently needed to perform quality control or verification of what was produced.

g. *Production of ESI From Third Parties.* ESI from third parties may have been received in a variety of formats, for example, in its original format (native, such as Excel or Word), as an image (TIFF or PDF), as an image with searchable text (TIFF or PDF with OCR text), or as a combination of any of these. The third party's format can affect or limit the available options for production as well as what associated information (metadata) might be available. ESI received from third parties should be produced in the format(s) it was received or in a reasonably usable format(s). ESI received from a party's own business records should be produced in the format(s) in which it was maintained or in a reasonably usable form(s). The parties should explore what formats of production[14] are possible and appropriate, and discuss what formats can be generated. Any format selected for producing discovery should, if possible and appropriate, conform to industry standards for the format.

h. *ESI Generated by the Government or Defense.* Paragraphs 6(f) and 6(g) do not apply to discoverable materials generated by the government or defense during the course of their investigations (*e.g.*, demonstrative exhibits, investigative reports and witness interviews—*see* subparagraph i, below, etc.) because the parties' legal discovery obligations and practices vary according to the nature of the material, the applicable law, evolving legal standards, and the parties' evolving technological capabilities. Thus, such materials may be produced differently from third party ESI. However, to the extent practicable, this material should be produced in a searchable and reasonably usable format. Parties should consult with their investigators in advance of preparing discovery to ascertain the investigators' ESI capabilities and limitations.

i. *Investigative Reports and Witness Interviews.* Investigative reports and witness interviews may be produced in paper form if they were received in paper form or if the final version is in paper form. Alternatively, they may be produced as electronic images (TIFF images or PDF files), particularly when needed to accommodate any necessary redactions. Absent particular issues such as redactions or substantial costs or burdens of additional processing, electronic versions of investigative reports and witness interviews should be produced in a searchable text format (such as ASCII text, OCR text, or plain text (.txt)) in order to avoid the expense of reprocessing the files. To the extent possible, the electronic image files of investigative reports and witness interviews should be computer-generated (as opposed to printed to paper and then imaged) in order to produce a higher-quality searchable text which will enable the files to be more easily searched and cost-effectively utilized.[15]

j. *Redactions.* ESI and/or images produced should identify the extent of redacted material and its location within the document.

k. *Photographs and Video and Audio Recordings.* A party producing photographs or video or audio recordings that either were originally created using digital devices or have previously been digitized should disclose the digital copies of the images or recordings if they are in the producing party's possession, custody or control. When technically feasible and cost-efficient, photographs and video and audio recordings that are not already in a digital format should be digitized into an industry standard format if and when they are duplicated. The producing party is not required to convert materials obtained in analog format to digital format for discovery.

l. *Test Runs.* Before producing ESI discovery a party should consider providing samples of the production format for a test run, and once a format is agreed upon, produce all ESI discovery in that format.

m. *Access to Originals.* If the producing party has converted paper materials to digital files, converted materials with color content to black and white images, or processed audio, video, or other materials for investigation or discovery, it should provide reasonable access to the originals for inspection and/or reprocessing.

7. Transmitting ESI Discovery.

a. ESI discovery should be transmitted on electronic media of sufficient size to hold the entire production, for example, a CD, DVD, or thumb drive.[16] If the size of the production warrants a large capacity hard drive, then the producing party may require the receiving party to bear the cost of the hard drive and to satisfy requirements for the hard drive that are necessary to protect the producing party's IT system from viruses or other harm.

b. The media should be clearly labeled with the case name and number, the producing party, a unique identifier for the media, and a production date.

c. A cover letter should accompany each transmission of ESI discovery providing basic information including the number of media, the unique identifiers of the media, a brief description of the contents including a table of contents if created, any applicable bates ranges or other unique production identifiers, and any necessary passwords to access the content. Passwords should not be in the cover letter accompanying the data, but in a separate communication.

d. The producing party should retain a write-protected copy of all transmitted ESI as a preserved record to resolve any subsequent disputes.

e. *Email Transmission.* When considering transmission of ESI discovery by email, the parties' obligation varies according to the sensitivity of the material, the risk of harm from unauthorized disclosure, and the relative security of email versus alternative transmission. The parties should consider three categories of security:

i. Not Appropriate for Email Transmission: Certain categories of ESI discovery are never appropriate for email transmission, including, but not limited to, certain grand jury materials; materials affecting witness safety; materials containing classified, national security, homeland security, tax return, or trade secret information; or similar items.

ii. Encrypted Email Transmission: Certain categories of ESI discovery warrant encryption or other secure transmission due to their sensitive nature. The parties should discuss and identify those categories in their case. This would ordinarily include, but not be limited to, information about informants, confidential business or personal information, and information subject to court protective orders.

    iii. Unencrypted Email Transmission: Other categories of ESI discovery not addressed above may be appropriate for email transmission, but the parties always need to be mindful of their ethical obligations.[17]

8. Coordinating Discovery Attorney. Coordinating Discovery Attorneys (CDA) are AOUSC contracted attorneys who have technological knowledge and experience, resources, and staff to effectively manage complex ESI in multiple defendant cases. The CDAs may be appointed by the court to provide additional in-depth and significant hands-on assistance to CJA panel attorneys and FDO staff in selected multiple-defendant cases that require technology and document management assistance. They can serve as a primary point of contact for the US Attorneys Office to discuss ESI production issues for all defendants, resulting in lower overall case costs for the parties. If you have any questions regarding the services of a CDA, please contact either Sean Broderick (National Litigation Support Administrator) or Kelly Scribner (Assistant National Litigation Support Administrator) at 510–637–3500, or by email: sean_broderick@fd.org, kelly_scribner@fd.org.

9. Informal Resolution of ESI Discovery Matters. No additional commentary.

10. Security: Protecting Sensitive ESI Discovery From Unauthorized Access or Disclosure. See sections 5(f)—Confidential and personal information, 5(p)—ESI security, and 7(e)—Email Transmission of the Strategies for additional guidance.

11. Definitions. To clearly communicate about ESI, it is important that the parties use ESI terms in the same way. Below are common ESI terms used when discussing ESI discovery:

    a. *Cloud Computing.* With cloud computing, the user accesses a remote computer hosted by a cloud service provider over the Internet or an intranet to access software programs or create, save, or retrieve data, for example, to send messages or create documents, spreadsheets, or databases. Examples of cloud computing include Gmail, Hotmail, Yahoo! Mail, Facebook, and on-line banking.

    b. *Coordinating Discovery Attorney (CDA).* An AOUSC contracted attorney who has technological knowledge and experience, resources, and staff to effectively manage complex ESI in multiple-defendant cases, and who may be appointed by a court in selected multiple-defendant cases to assist CJA panel attorneys and/or FDO staff with discovery management.

    c. *Document Unitization.* Document unitization is the process of determining where a document begins (its first page) and ends (its last page), with the goal of accurately describing what was a "unit" as it was received by the party or was kept in the ordinary course of business by the document's custodian. A "unit" includes attachments, for example, an email with an attached spreadsheet. Physical unitization utilizes actual objects such as staples, paper clips and folders to determine pages that belong together as documents. Logical unitization is the process of human review of each individual page in an image collection using logical cues to determine pages that belong together as documents. Such cues can be consecutive page numbering, report titles, similar headers and footers, and other logical cues.

    d. *ESI (Electronically Stored Information).* Any information created, stored, or utilized with digital technology. Examples include, but are not limited to, word-processing files, e-mail and text messages (including attachments); voicemail; information accessed via the Internet, including social networking sites; information stored on cell phones; information stored on computers, computer systems, thumb drives, flash drives, CDs, tapes, and other digital media.

    e. *Extracted Text.* The text of a native file extracted during ESI processing of the native file, most commonly when native files are converted to TIFF format. Extracted text is more accurate than text created by the OCR processing of document images that were created by scanning and will therefore provide higher quality search results.

    f. *Forensic Image (Mirror Image) of a Hard Drive or Other Storage Device.* A process that preserves the entire contents of a hard drive or other storage device by creating a bit-by-bit copy of the original data without altering the original media. A forensic examination or analysis of an imaged hard drive requires specialized software and expertise to both create and read the image. User created files, such as email and other electronic documents, can be extracted, and a more complete analysis of the hard drive can be performed to find deleted files and/or access information. A forensic or mirror image is not a physical duplicate of the original drive or device; instead it is a file or set of files that contains all of the data bits from the source device. Thus a forensic or mirror image cannot simply be opened and viewed as if you were looking at the original device. Indeed, forensic or mirror images of multiple hard drives or other storage devices can be stored on a single recipient hard drive of sufficient capacity.

g. *Image of a Document or Document Image.* An electronic "picture" of how the document would look if printed. Images can be stored in various file formats, the most common of which are TIFF and PDF. Document images, such as TIFF and PDF, can be created directly from native files, or created by scanning hard copy.

h. *Load File.* A cross reference file used to import images or data into databases. A data load file may contain Bates numbers, metadata, path to native files, coded data, and extracted or OCR text. An image load file may contain document boundary, image type and path information. Load files must be obtained and provided in software-specific formats to ensure they can be used by the receiving party.

i. *Metadata.* Data that describes characteristics of ESI, for example, the author, date created, and date last accessed of a word processing document. Metadata is generally not reproduced in full form when a document is printed to paper or electronic image. Metadata can describe how, when and by whom ESI was created, accessed, modified, formatted, or collected. Metadata can be supplied by applications, users or the file system, and it can be altered intentionally or inadvertently. Certain metadata can be extracted when native files are processed for litigation. Metadata is found in different places and in different forms. Some metadata, such as file dates and sizes, can easily be accessed by users; other metadata can be hidden or embedded and unavailable to computer users who are not technically adept. Note that some metadata may be lost or changed when an electronic copy of a file is made using ordinary file copy methods.

j. *Native File.* A file as it was created in its native software, for example a Word, Excel, or PowerPoint file, or an email in Outlook or Lotus Notes.

k. *OCR (Optical Character Recognition).* A process that converts a picture of text into searchable text. The quality of the created text can vary greatly depending on the quality of the original document, the quality of the scanned image, the accuracy of the recognition software and the quality control process of the provider. Generally speaking, OCR does not handle handwritten text or text in graphics well. OCR conversion rates can range from 50 to 98% accuracy depending on the underlying document. A full page of text is estimated to contain 2,000 characters, so OCR software with even 90% accuracy would create a page of text with approximately 200 errors.

l. *Parent—Child Relationships.* Related documents are described as having a parent/child relationship, for example, where the email is the parent and an attached spreadsheet is the child.

m. *PDF.* "Portable Document Format." A file format created by Adobe that allows a range of options, including electronic transmission, viewing, and searching.

n. *TIFF.* "Tagged Image File Format." An industry-standard file format for storing scanned and other digital black-and-white, grey-scale, and full-color images.

[1] *See, e.g.*, U.S. v. Skilling, 554 F.3d 529, 577 (5th Cir. 2009) (no *Brady* violation where government disclosed several hundred million page database with searchable files and produced set of hot documents and indices).

[2] A table of contents is intended to be a general, high-level guide to the categories of ESI discovery. Because a table of contents may not be detailed, complete, or free of errors, the parties still have the responsibility to review the ESI discovery produced. With ESI, particular content usually can be located using available electronic search tools. There are many ways to construct a general table of contents. For example, a table of contents could be a folder structure as set forth above in paragraph 2(a)(i–xv), where like items are placed into folders.

[3] For example, when the producing party processes ESI to apply Bates numbers, load it into litigation software, create TIFF images, etc., the ESI is slightly modified and no longer in its original state. Similarly, some modification of the ESI may be necessary and proper in order to allow the parties to protect privileged information, and the processing and production of ESI in certain formats may result in the loss or alteration of some metadata that is not significant in the circumstances of the particular case.

[4] Attorney-client and work product (see, e.g., F.R.Crim.P. 16(a)(2) and (b)(2)) issues arising from the parties' own case preparation are beyond the scope of these Recommendations, and they need not be part of the meet and confer discussion.

[5] If third party records are subject to an agreement or court order involving a selective waiver of attorney-client or work product privileges (*see* F.R.E. 502), then the parties should discuss how to handle those materials.

[6] Because pretrial detainees often are held in local jails (for space, protective custody, cost, or other reasons) that have varying resources and security needs, there are no uniform practices or rules for pretrial detainees' access to

ESI discovery. Resolution of the issues associated with such access is beyond the scope of the Recommendations and Strategies.

[7] The producing party is, of course, limited to what it received from the third party. The third party's processing of the information can affect or limit what metadata is available.

[8] The parties should consult their litigation support personnel concerning encryption or other security options.

[9] Federal Defender Organizations and CJA panel attorneys should contact Sean Broderick (National Litigation Support Administrator) or Kelly Scribner (Assistant National Litigation Support Administrator) at 510–637–3500, or by email: sean_broderick@fd.org, kelly_scribner@fd.org. Prosecutors should contact Andrew Goldsmith (National Criminal Discovery Coordinator) at Andrew.Goldsmith@usdoj.gov or John Haried (Assistant National Criminal Discovery Coordinator) at John.Haried@usdoj.gov.

[10] A "claw back" agreement outlines procedures to be followed to protect against waiver of privilege or work product protection due to inadvertent production of documents or data.

[11] *See* paragraph 5(*o*) of the Strategies, above.

[12] The decision whether to scan paper documents requires striking a balance between resources (including personnel and cost) and efficiency. The parties should make that determination on a case-by-case basis.

[13] Color scanning substantially slows the scanning process and creates huge electronic files which consume storage space, making the storage and transmission of information difficult. An original signature, handwritten marginalia in blue or red ink, and colored text highlights are examples of color content that may be particularly significant to the case.

[14] An example of "format of production" might be TIFF images, OCR text files, and load files created for a specific software application. Another "format of production" would be native file production, which would accommodate files with unique issues, such as spreadsheets with formulas and databases.

[15] For guidance on making computer generated version of investigative reports and witness interview reports, see the description of production of TIFF, PDF, and extracted text format in paragraphs 6(b)(ii)(1) and (ii).

[16] Rolling productions may, of course, use multiple media. The producing party should avoid using multiple media when a single media will facilitate the receiving party's use of the material.

[17] Illustrative of the security issues in the attorney-client context are ABA Op. 11–459 (Duty to Protect the Confidentiality of E–Mail Communications with One's Client) and ABA Op. 99–413 (Protecting the Confidentiality of Unencrypted E–Mail).

ESI Discovery Production Checklist

☐ Is this a case where the volume or nature of ESI significantly increases the case's complexity?
☐ Does this case involve classified information?
☐ Does this case involve trade secrets, or national security or homeland security information?
☐ Do the parties have appropriate technical advisors to assist?
☐ Have the parties met and conferred about ESI issues?
☐ Have the parties addressed the format of ESI being produced? Categories may include:
    ☐ Investigative reports and materials
    ☐ Witness statements
    ☐ Tangible objects
    ☐ Third party ESI digital devices (computers, phones, etc.)
    ☐ Photos, video and audio recordings
    ☐ Third party records
    ☐ Title III wire tap information
    ☐ Court records
    ☐ Tests and examinations
    ☐ Experts
    ☐ Immunity and plea agreements
    ☐ Discovery materials with special production considerations
    ☐ Related matters

☐ Discovery materials available for inspection but not produced digitally

☐ Other information

☐ Have the parties addressed ESI issues involving:

    ☐ Table of contents?

    ☐ Production of paper records as either paper or ESI?

    ☐ Proprietary or legacy data?

    ☐ Attorney-client, work product, or other privilege issues?

    ☐ Sensitive confidential, personal, grand jury, classified, tax return, trade secret, or similar information?

    ☐ Whether email transmission is inappropriate for any categories of ESI discovery?

    ☐ Incarcerated defendant's access to discovery materials?

    ☐ ESI discovery volume for receiving party's planning purposes?

    ☐ Parties' software or hardware limitations?

    ☐ Production of ESI from 3rd party digital devices?

    ☐ Forensic images of ESI digital devices?

    ☐ Metadata in 3rd party ESI?

    ☐ Redactions?

    ☐ Reasonable schedule for producing party?

    ☐ Reasonable schedule for receiving party to give notice of issues?

    ☐ Appropriate security measures during transmission of ESI discovery, *e.g.*, encryption?

    ☐ Adequate security measures to protect sensitive ESI against unauthorized access or disclosure?

    ☐ Need for protective orders, clawback agreements, or similar orders or agreements?

    ☐ Collaboration on sharing costs or tasks?

    ☐ Need for receiving party's access to original ESI?

    ☐ Preserving a record of discovery produced?

☐ Have the parties memorialized their agreements and disagreements?

☐ Do the parties have a system for resolving disputes informally?

☐ Is there a need for a designated discovery coordinator for multiple defendants?

☐ Do the parties have a plan for managing/returning ESI at the conclusion of the case?

SUGGESTED PRACTICES REGARDING DISCOVERY IN COMPLEX CASES

Based on meetings with representatives from the Court, the United States Attorney's Office, and the CJA Committee for the Northern District of California, the following is a protocol of suggested practices regarding discovery in wiretap and other complex, document-intensive cases. This document is not intended to expand the parties' discovery obligations under Federal Rule of Criminal Procedure 16, the Jencks Act, or other federal statutes or rules. Paragraphs 1 through 8 of the suggested practices correspond to paragraphs 1 through 8 of the "Second Agreement Regarding Discovery in Complex Cases."

1. Pertinent Call Tapes.

a. The parties are encouraged to use digital media for audio files because digital files may be easier to review and less expensive to reproduce for a multi-defendant case.

b. Generally, it is preferable that the naming conventions for the audio files, the monitoring logs, and the transcripts be consistent so that it is easy to cross-reference the audio calls with the corresponding monitoring logs and transcripts. If at the outset of a case, a naming convention has not yet been established, the prosecution and defense should meet and confer regarding a naming convention before the files are produced.

2. Pleading Documents. Pleading documents should be Bates-stamped in chronological order using the Bates sequence used for disclosure of other discovery in the case. The parties are encouraged to consider printing all Title III pleadings (including affidavits) into Adobe .pdf format and disclosing the .pdf format simultaneously with the hard copies.

3. Non–Pertinent Calls.

a. As with pertinent calls, the parties are encouraged to use digital media for audio files because digital files may be easier to review and less expensive to reproduce for a multi-defendant case.

b. As with pertinent calls, generally it is preferable that the naming conventions of audio files, monitoring logs, and transcripts be consistent. If at the outset of a case, a naming convention has not established, the parties should meet and refer regarding a naming convention.

4. Investigative Reports.

a. The parties should meet and confer at the outset of a case as to whether both parties want to convert investigative reports into an electronic .pdf format with an OCR (optical character recognition) overlay.

b. If both parties want the investigative reports in electronic format, then the parties should meet and confer about whether they can divide the costs for this process between the parties.

5. Pen Register Data. The United States Attorney's Office will ask the investigative agencies to ask the telephone companies to provide pen register data in electronic format so that it can be disclosed in this format.

6. Monitoring Logs.

a. In wiretap cases, the AUSA will ask federal agencies to use an electronic format for monitoring logs and monitoring data.

b. The AUSA is encouraged to disclose the data in ASCII tab or comma-delimited format. To the extent that fields or information are excluded from this digital information, the AUSA will notify the defense that data was omitted.

7. Translations and Transcriptions.

a. If possible, the parties should provide electronic version of transcripts or translations in Wordperfect or Rich Text Format (RTF), and also in ASCII format.

b. As discussed above, generally it is preferable that the naming conventions for the audio files, the monitoring logs, and the transcripts be consistent so that it is easy to cross-reference the audio calls with the corresponding monitoring logs and transcripts. If at the outset of a case, a naming convention has not yet been established, the prosecution and defense should meet and confer regarding a naming convention for the translations and transcripts that corresponds to the titles of audio and monitoring files.

8. Consensual and Surveillance Tapes and Videos. The parties are encouraged to use digital media for tapes and videos because digital files may be easier to review and less expensive to reproduce for a multi-defendant case.

9. Indices. On a case-by-case basis, the parties are encouraged to discuss the joint production of indices that will be mutually beneficial to both parties, and will result in cost-savings to both parties.

10. Disclosure of Hard Copies of Discovery.

a. In situations where discovery is available initially only as a hard copy (as opposed to electronically), the parties should provide a complete Bates-numbered hard copy set to the discovery coordinator or to the discovery/copying vendor.

b. As with the production of investigative reports, and in situations where discovery is available initially only as a hard copy, the parties should meet and confer as to whether both parties want to convert the discovery to an electronic .pdf format with an OCR (optical character recognition) overlay.

c. If both parties want the discovery in electronic format, then the parties should meet and confer at the outset of the case about whether they can divide the costs for this process between the parties.

d. A recommended procedure for the conversion is as follows. The hard copy of the discovery should be scanned into a high-quality .pdf format (using Adobe .pdf software) with an optical character recognition (OCR) overlay. The vendor should be asked to simultaneously produce a set of .tif (image) files. (This can usually be done at no additional cost.)

11. Computer/Digital Discovery. Discovery in computer cases will be dealt with on a case-by-case basis. The parties should meet and confer at the outset of the case about what should be provided in discovery. The defense will be responsible for purchasing and providing a blank hard drive or blank medium upon which a copy can be made of the computer media that will be disclosed.

12. Complex Case Discovery Orders. Copies of stipulated discovery orders in complex cases will be provided to the Northern District CJA Supervising Attorney. The parties are encouraged to review these orders at the outset of new complex cases in order to expedite arriving at new agreements and to expedite the disclosure of discovery.

SELECTED GENERAL ORDERS
GENERAL ORDER NO. 2. CRIMINAL JUSTICE ACT PLAN
I. AUTHORITY

The judges of the United States District Court for the Northern District of California adopt this Plan, as approved by the Ninth Circuit, for furnishing representation in federal court for any person financially unable to obtain adequate representation as required by the Criminal Justice Act (CJA) of 1964, as amended, 18 U.S.C. § 3006A, and the Guidelines for Administering the CJA and Related Statutes, Volume 7A, Guide to Judiciary Policy (CJA Guidelines).

II. STATEMENT OF POLICY

A. Objectives. The objectives of this Plan are to attain the goal of equal justice under the law by providing all eligible persons with timely appointed counsel services that are consistent with the best practices of the legal profession, to ensure that services are cost-effective without compromising the quality of representation, to promote the independence of the defense function so that the rights of individual defendants are safeguarded and enforced, and to particularize the requirements of the CJA, the USA Patriot Improvement and Reauthorization Act of 2005 (recodified at 18 U.S.C. § 3599), CJA Guidelines, Ninth Circuit CJA Policies and Procedures, and Local Rules of the Northern District of California in a way that meets the needs of this district.

This Plan must be administered so that those accused of a crime, or otherwise eligible for services under the CJA, will not be deprived of the right to counsel, or any element of representation necessary to an effective defense, due to lack of financial resources.

B. Representational Services. This Plan provides for representational services by the Federal Public Defender for the Northern District of California and for the appointment and compensation of private attorneys from an approved panel list ("CJA Panel") and other private attorneys in limited circumstances, in cases authorized under the CJA and related statutes.

C. Panel Administration. Administration of the CJA Panel, as set forth in this Plan, is hereby delegated and assigned to the Court.

D. Compliance. The Court, its clerk, the Federal Public Defender, private attorneys appointed under the CJA, federal law enforcement officers, the United States Attorney's Office, and the Pretrial Services Office must comply with the CJA Guidelines, approved by the Judicial Conference or its Committee on Defender Services, the Ninth Circuit's CJA Policies and Procedures, and with this Plan. The Court will ensure that a current copy of the CJA Plan is made available on the Court's website and provided to counsel upon the attorney's designation as a member of the CJA Panel.

III. DEFINITIONS

A. "Appointed Attorney" is an attorney designated to represent a financially eligible person under the CJA and this Plan. Such attorneys include private attorneys, the Federal Public Defender, and its staff attorneys.

B. "CJA Panel Administrator" is a person employed by the Federal Public Defender to perform tasks related to the administration of the CJA Panel including case assignments.

C. "CJA Supervising Attorney" is an attorney employed by the Court who oversees the CJA Department, budgeting and funding of cases, including coordinating CJA attorneys in multi-defendant cases, and voucher review.

D. "Panel Attorney District Representative" (PADR) is a member of the district's CJA Panel who is selected by the Federal Public Defender, with approval from the Chief District Judge, to serve as a representative of the district's CJA Panel for the Defender Services CJA PADR program and local CJA committees.

E. "Representation" includes counsel, service providers (such as paralegals, investigators, or experts), litigation support vendors, and expenses.

IV. ELIGIBILITY FOR CJA REPRESENTATION

A. Subject–Matter Eligibility.

1. *Mandatory.* Representation must be provided for any financially eligible person who:

    a. is charged with a felony or with a Class A misdemeanor;

    b. is a juvenile alleged to have committed an act of juvenile delinquency as defined in 18 U.S.C. § 5031;

    c. is charged with a violation of probation, or faces a change of a term or condition of probation (unless the modification sought is favorable to the probationer and the government has not objected to the proposed change);

    d. is under arrest, when appointed representation is required by law;

    e. is entitled to appointed counsel in parole proceedings;

    f. is charged with a violation of supervised release or faces modification, reduction, or enlargement of a condition, or extension or revocation of a term of supervised release;

    g. is subject to a mental condition hearing under 18 U.S.C. chapter 313;

    h. is in custody as a material witness;

    i. is seeking to set aside or vacate a death sentence or when an evidentiary hearing is warranted in a non-capital proceeding under 28 U.S.C. § 2254 or § 2255;

    j. is entitled to appointment of counsel in verification of consent proceedings in connection with a transfer of an offender to or from the United States for the execution of a penal sentence under 18 U.S.C. § 4109;

    k. is entitled to appointment of counsel under the Sixth Amendment to the Constitution; or

    l. faces loss of liberty in a case, and federal law requires the appointment of counsel.

2. *Discretionary.* Whenever a district judge or magistrate judge determines that the interests of justice so require, representation may be provided for any financially eligible person who:

    a. is charged with a petty offense (Class B or C misdemeanor, or an infraction) for which a sentence to confinement is authorized;

    b. is seeking relief under 28 U.S.C. §§ 2241, 2254, or 2255 other than to set aside or vacate a death sentence, unless an evidentiary hearing is warranted (see above IV(A)(1)(i));

    c. is charged with civil or criminal contempt and faces loss of liberty;

    d. has been called as a witness before a grand jury, a court, the Congress, or a federal agency or commission which has the power to compel testimony, and there is reason to believe, either prior to or during testimony, that the witness could be subject to a criminal prosecution, a civil or criminal contempt proceeding, or face loss of liberty;

    e. has been advised by the United States attorney or a law enforcement officer that they are the target of a grand jury investigation;

    f. is proposed by the United States attorney for processing under a pretrial diversion program; or

    g. is held for international extradition under 18 U.S.C. chapter 209.

3. *Ancillary Matters.* The Court has the discretion to appoint counsel for financially eligible persons in ancillary matters appropriate to the criminal proceedings under 18 U.S.C. § 3006A(c). In determining whether representation in an ancillary matter is appropriate to the criminal proceedings, the Court should consider whether such representation is reasonably necessary to:

    a. protect a constitutional right;

    b. contribute in some significant way to the defense of the principal criminal charge;

    c. aid in preparation for the trial or disposition of the principal criminal charge;

    d. enforce the terms of a plea agreement in the principal criminal charge;

e. preserve the claim of the CJA client to an interest in real or personal property subject to civil forfeiture proceeding under 18 U.S.C. § 983, 19 U.S.C. § 1602, 21 U.S.C. § 881, or similar statutes, which property, if recovered by the client, may be considered for reimbursement under 18. U.S.C. § 3006A(f); or

f. effectuate the return of real or personal property belonging to the CJA client, which may be subject to a motion for return of property under Fed. R. Crim. P. 41(g), which property, if recovered by the client, may be considered for reimbursement under 18 U.S.C. § 3006A(f).

B. Financial Eligibility.

1. *Presentation of Accused for Financial Eligibility Determination.*

a. Duties of Federal Law Enforcement Officers

1) For the purpose of ensuring that eligible persons have access to counsel as soon as practicable, federal law enforcement officials must promptly notify, telephonically or electronically, the appropriate court personnel and the Federal Public Defender of an arrest, unless the person has retained counsel.

2) Employees of law enforcement agencies may not participate in the completion of the financial affidavit or seek to obtain information concerning financial eligibility from a person requesting the appointment of counsel.

b. Duties of United States Attorney's Office

1) Upon the return or unsealing of an indictment, the filing of a criminal complaint or information, and where the defendant has not retained counsel, the United States Attorney's Office will promptly notify, telephonically or electronically, appropriate court personnel and the Federal Public Defender.

2) Upon issuance of a target letter, and where the individual has not retained counsel, the United States Attorney's Office must promptly notify, telephonically or electronically, the appropriate court personnel and the Federal Public Defender, unless the United States Attorney's Office is aware of an actual or potential conflict with the target and the Federal Public Defender, in which case they must promptly notify the CJA Panel Administrator.

3) Employees of the United States Attorney's Office may not participate in the completion of the financial affidavit or seek to obtain information concerning financial eligibility from a person requesting the appointment of counsel.

c. Duties of the Federal Public Defender

1) In cases in which the Federal Public Defender may be appointed, the office will immediately investigate and determine whether an actual or potential conflict exists and, if so, must promptly notify the CJA Panel Administrator to facilitate the timely appointment of other counsel.

2) Whenever practicable, the Federal Public Defender will discuss with the person the right to appointed counsel and arrange to have the matter promptly presented before a judicial officer of this Court to determine financial eligibility and counsel appointment.

d. Duties of Pretrial Services Office

1) When counsel has been appointed, the pretrial services officer will provide counsel opportunity to attend any interview of the defendant by the pretrial services officer prior to the initial pretrial release or detention hearing.

2) The pretrial services officer will not conduct the pretrial services interview of a financially eligible defendant until counsel has been appointed and given an opportunity to attend the interview.

2. *Eligibility Determination.* In every case where 18 U.S.C. § 3006A(a) and related statutes authorize appointment of counsel, the Court must advise the person that he or she has a right to be represented by counsel throughout the case and that, if so desired, the Court will appoint counsel to represent the person if he or she is financially unable to obtain counsel.

The completed financial eligibility affidavit (Form CJA 23) should reflect relevant information bearing on the person's financial eligibility for appointed counsel.

Determining eligibility for representation under the CJA is a judicial function performed by the Court after making appropriate inquiries concerning the person's financial eligibility. Other employees of the Court or the Federal Public Defender may be designated to obtain or verify the facts relevant to the financial eligibility determination if the Defender Organization is not available.

3. *Standards.* In determining whether a person is "financially unable to obtain counsel," the Court should consider the cost of providing the person and the person's dependents with life's necessities, the cost of securing pretrial release, asset encumbrance, and the likely cost to retain counsel.

The initial eligibility determination must be made without regard to the financial ability of the person's family to retain counsel unless the person's family indicates a willingness and ability to do so promptly.

Any doubts about a person's eligibility should be resolved in the person's favor; erroneous determinations of eligibility may be corrected later.

If at any time after appointment appointed counsel has reason to believe that a person is financially able to retain private counsel or make partial payment for the appointed representation, and disclosure would not conflict with counsel's ethical duties, counsel will advise the Court.

If at any time after the appointment of counsel a judge finds that a person provided representation is financially able to retain private counsel or make partial payment for the appointed representation, the judge may terminate the counsel appointment or direct the defendant to pay available funds as provided in 18 U.S.C. § 3006A(f).

If at any stage of the proceedings a judge finds that a person is no longer financially able to pay retained counsel, counsel will be appointed in accordance with the general provisions set forth in this Plan.

If at any stage of the proceedings a judge finds that a pro se or privately represented person is not financially able to pay other representation costs, including investigative, expert, or other services, funding may be authorized for those costs in accordance with the general provisions set forth in this Plan.

V. TIMELY APPOINTMENT OF COUNSEL

A. Eligible persons must receive appointed counsel as soon as feasible. This means as soon as possible after receiving a target letter, after being taken into custody, upon appearing before a judicial officer, when formally charged, when notified of charges if formal charges are sealed, or when a judicial officer otherwise determines appointed counsel is appropriate under the CJA or this Plan, whichever occurs earliest.

B. Financially eligible persons will be provided appointed counsel prior to being interviewed by a pretrial services officer. The Federal Public Defender will maintain a schedule of "on call" or "duty day" attorneys, who are employees of the Federal Public Defender, to advise persons who are in custody, or who otherwise may be entitled to counsel under the CJA, during the pretrial services interview process.

C. Appointment of counsel may be made retroactive to include representation provided prior to appointment.

VI. FEDERAL PUBLIC DEFENDER OF THE NORTHERN DISTRICT OF CALIFORNIA

A. **Establishment.** The Federal Public Defender of the Northern District of California is established in this district under the CJA and is responsible for rendering defense services on appointment throughout this district.

B. **Staff Supervision and Case Workload.** The Federal Public Defender is responsible for supervising and managing the defender organization. Accordingly, the Federal Public Defender will be appointed in all cases assigned to that organization for subsequent assignment to staff attorneys at the Federal Public Defender's discretion. The Federal Public Defender will continually monitor staff workloads to ensure high-quality representation for all clients.

C. **Standards and Professional Conduct.** The Federal Public Defender must provide high-quality representation consistent with the best practices of the legal profession. The Federal Public Defender must conform to the highest standards of professional conduct, including but not limited to the American Bar Association's Model Rules of Professional Conduct, Code of Conduct for Federal Public Defender Employees and other standards for professional conduct adopted by the Court.

D. Private Practice of Law. Neither the Federal Public Defender nor any defender employee may engage in the private practice of law except as authorized by the Federal Public Defender Code of Conduct.

E. Panel Attorney Training. In coordination with the PADR, CJA Supervising Attorney, and the CJA Administration Committee, the Federal Public Defender will assess the training needs of the CJA Panel and provide regularly scheduled training opportunities and other educational resources that include updates regarding substantive law, sharing best practices in federal criminal defense, and presentations on courtroom and office technology.

VII.   CJA ADMINISTRATION COMMITTEE

A. Establishment. The CJA Administration Committee has been established by the Court in consultation with the Federal Public Defender to assist the Court in administering the Act and will promulgate regulations necessary to implement this Plan including the selection, oversight, and management of CJA Panel members. The CJA Administration Committee Chair may establish subcommittees both standing and ad hoc, that include non-members that have the necessary expertise and qualifications to address specific CJA related issues such as recruiting panel members, training, mentoring, reviewing complaints, and reviewing voucher reductions.

B. Composition. At a minimum, the CJA Administration Committee must consist of:

1.   the Chair, appointed by the Chief Judge;

2.   three District Judges with one from each of the San Francisco, Oakland, and San Jose divisions;

3.   two Magistrate Judges;

4.   the Federal Public Defender or delegate, who will be a permanent member of the CJA Administration Committee;

5.   the district's current PADR or delegate, who will be a permanent member of the CJA Administration Committee;

6.   the district's CJA Supervising Attorney, who will be a permanent member of the CJA Administration Committee;

7.   three experienced criminal defense attorneys with prior panel experience; and

8.   the Clerk or designee thereof who will act as administrative coordinator.

C. Terms. Court members of the CJA Administration Committee who are judicial officers serve at the pleasure of the Chief Judge. Except for the Federal Public Defender, PADR, CJA Supervisory Attorney, and ex officio administrator, members will serve for three years and may be extended for one additional three-year term. Terms will be staggered to ensure continuity on the CJA Administration Committee and rotation of members. Vacancies will be filled upon recommendation of the Chair, with input from the Federal Public Defender, PADR, and the CJA Supervising Attorney, and upon approval by the Chief District Judge.

D. Diversity. The CJA Administration Committee will ensure the creation of a diverse panel.

E. Meeting Requirement. The CJA Administration Committee will meet at least once a year and at any time the Court or a committee member asks the committee to consider an issue.

F. Training. The CJA Administration Committee will assist the Federal Public Defender in devising and presenting training programs for the CJA Panel.

G. Quorum. Six members shall constitute a quorum.

H. Annual Report. Annually, the CJA Administration Committee shall review panel operation and administration for the preceding year and provide a report to the Chief District Judge describing efforts to recruit qualified and diverse panel members, any proposed changes to panel size, any recurring issues or difficulties panel attorneys or their clients encounter, and any other operating difficulties, along with recommendations for appropriate changes.

I. CJA Panel Membership. There shall be four panel selection subcommittees to select members for the San Francisco/Oakland, San Jose, Appellate, and Eureka Panels. The Chairs of each committee shall be selected by the Chair of the CJA Administration Committee in consultation with the Chief Judge.

J. Recruitment. The CJA Panel Selection Committees will strive to create and maintain a diverse CJA Panel of the highest caliber federal criminal defense practitioners. In conjunction with a mentoring program, the Committee will devise a recruitment strategy that identifies and trains a diverse set of viable panel applicants.

K. Panel Selection Committees.

1. *San Francisco/Oakland and San Jose Panel Selection Subcommittees.* The Chair of the CJA Administration Committee shall select a District Judge member of each panel selection subcommittee, who shall select the Magistrate Judge and attorney members of his or her panel selection subcommittee, subject to approval by the Chair of the CJA Administration Committee. The trial panel selection subcommittees shall consist of at least one District Judge, one Magistrate Judge, two experienced criminal attorneys with prior panel experience, the Federal Public Defender and/or a designee, the CJA Supervising Attorney, and the current CJA Panel Attorney District Representative. With the exception of the Federal Public Defender, members of each panel selection subcommittee shall have their chambers or principal place of business in the geographic area served by that subcommittee.

2. *Appellate Panel Selection Subcommittee.* The Chair of the CJA Administration Committee shall select a District Judge member of the Appeals Selection Subcommittee, who shall select the Magistrate Judge and attorney members of his or her panel selection subcommittee, subject to approval by the Chair of the CJA Administration Committee. The Appellate Selection Subcommittee shall consist of at least one District Judge, one Magistrate Judge, two experienced criminal attorneys with prior panel and appellate experience and the Federal Public Defender and/or a designee.

3. *Eureka Panel Selection Subcommittee.* This subcommittee shall consist of the resident Magistrate Judge in conjunction with the Chair of the CJA Administration Committee and the Federal Defender or a designee.

4. *Meetings.* The panel selection subcommittees shall annually review attorney applications and recommend attorneys for appointment to the panel.

5. *Terms.* Each non-judicial member of the Panel Selection Subcommittees, except ex officio members, shall serve a three-year term and may be reappointed by the Chair of the CJA Administration Committee for one successive term.

6. *Process of Selecting Panel Attorneys.* The four panel selection subcommittees shall select panel attorneys based on their proven experience and competence in the field of criminal defense, proof that they meet the minimum requirement as set forth in this Plan, and their willingness to serve indigent defendants. The panel selection subcommittees will present their appointment recommendations to the Chair of the CJA Administration Committee, who will present them to a quorum of the CJA Administration Committee for approval, after which the Chair of the CJA Administration Committee will present the list of the recommended panel attorneys to the Chief Judge for final approval.

7. *Additional Panel Selection Subcommittee Responsibilities.* At least annually, the panel selection subcommittees shall (a) review the operation and administration of their panels over the preceding year and make recommendations to the CJA Administration Committee regarding the selection, recommendation and appointment process, and panel management, and (b) determine the continued availability and willingness of each panel member to accept appointments.

VIII. CJA PANEL MEMBERSHIP

A. Establishment. The existing, previously established panels of attorneys who are eligible and willing to be appointed to provide representation under the CJA are hereby recognized. The Court will approve additional attorneys for membership on the CJA Panel after receiving recommendations from the CJA Administration Committee. Nothing in this Plan creates a property interest in being or remaining on the CJA Panel.

B. Size. The CJA Panel size will be determined by the CJA Administration Committee, subject to the Court's review, based on panel member caseloads and activity. The CJA Panel must be large enough to provide a sufficient number of experienced attorneys to handle the CJA caseload, yet small enough so panel members will each receive an adequate number of appointments to maintain their federal criminal defense work proficiency, enabling them to provide high quality representation consistent with the best practices of the legal profession.

C. Qualifications and Membership.

1. *Equal Opportunity.* All qualified attorneys are encouraged to apply for CJA Panel membership.

2. *Application.* Application forms for CJA Panel membership are available from the Federal Public Defender during the annual application time period.

3. *Eligibility.*

    a. General Qualifications: CJA Panel applicants must have the following general qualifications:

    1) be members in good standing of the State Bar of California, federal bar of this district, and the Ninth Circuit Court of Appeals;

    2) except for capital habeas panel members, maintain a primary, satellite, or shared office in the specific court Division of the District for the applicable panel at the time the attorney submits an application for the panel membership and during the entire term of membership;

    3) possess strong litigation and writing skills;

    4) demonstrate proficiency with the Bail Reform Act, Recommendations for Electronically Stored Information Discovery Production in Federal Criminal Cases (ESI Protocol), Federal Rules of Evidence, Federal Rules of Criminal Procedure, Federal Rules of Appellate Procedure, United States Sentencing Guidelines, federal sentencing procedures, and this District's Local Rules;

    5) have the training and ability to manage and effectively utilize electronic case presentation equipment and software in the courtroom and manage electronic discovery;

    6) have significant experience representing persons charged with serious criminal offenses and demonstrate a commitment to the defense of people who lack the financial means to hire an attorney.

Attorneys who do not possess the experience set forth above but believe they have equivalent other experience, or who have completed a mentoring program, are encouraged to apply and set forth in writing the details of that experience for the committee's consideration.

    b. CJA Trial Panels. Trial Panel memberships are divided into two specialized panels.

    1) "Tier One" made up of the most experienced panel members eligible for appointment in all cases, including the most complex and difficult cases;

    2) "Tier Two" members are eligible for appointment in the following types of cases:

      (a) 18 U.S.C. § 922(g) cases;

      (b) 21 U.S.C. § 841 cases that do not involve mandatory minimum sentences alleged in the initial indictment, conspiracy allegations, wiretaps, or weapons; and

      (c) Other less serious cases identified as appropriate by the Federal Public Defender or the defender's legal staff.

    c. Minimum Relevant Professional Experience. All panel members must be of good standing in the State Bar of California and have their primary place of business in the Northern District of California.

    1) Trial Panel Membership Tier One: At a minimum, counsel must have five years of continuous private federal criminal practice, or seven years of criminal practice in state or federal court, or three years of experience as an Assistant United States Attorney or Assistant Federal Public Defender; and five federal or state felony jury trials. Two of the required trials may be replaced with equivalent experience such as unusually complex matters which are settled short of trial, criminal appeals which require unusual knowledge or effort, or substantial civil jury trials.

    2) Any applicant who has not tried two federal felony jury trials must audit two cases from start to finish pursuant to the mentor program established under the Plan. Successful completion of the mentor program will satisfy the requirements necessary to serve on a trial panel, but it does not guarantee admission. This audit shall include watching at least one federal felony jury trial.

3) Trial Panel Membership Tier Two: At a minimum, counsel must have five years of continuous criminal practice and three felony jury trials in either state or federal court. Tier Two panel members have the ability to apply for the Tier One panel after two years.

4) Appellate Panel Membership: Ten federal or state felony appeals or combination thereof. Five of the required appeals may be replaced with equivalent experience such as criminal trials, habeas corpus proceedings, or complex criminal matters settled short of trial.

5) Members of the San Francisco/Oakland Trial Panels must be willing to take cases in either venue.

6) Such additional qualifications as may be established by the CJA Administration Committee.

D. Term Limits for Panel Attorneys. Each panel member will serve for a three-year term. A panel member's term will continue until the conclusion of any active representation under this Plan, but no new appointments will be offered. Subject to the provisions of this Plan, members of the panels shall serve at the pleasure of the Court.

E. Re–Appointment and Re–Application.

1.   In considering the re-appointment of CJA Panel members, the CJA Panel Committee may:

a.   solicit input from the legal community and the Court concerning the quality of representation provided by attorneys seeking reappointment;

b.   request a personal interview with the CJA Panel member; and

c.   consider the number of cases the CJA Panel member accepted and declined during the review period, the member's participation in training opportunities, whether the member continues to meet this Plan's technology and facilities requirements, whether the member has been the subject of any complaints, and whether the member continues to meet the prerequisites and obligations of CJA panel members or applicants as set forth in this Plan.

2.   The CJA Panel Administrator will notify CJA Panel members, within 3 months prior to the expiration of their current term, of the need to apply for reappointment to the CJA Panel and will set forth the procedures and deadlines for reapplying.

F. Leaves of Absence. A panel member may take a leave of absence not to exceed three months without being required to resign from the panel, which can be initiated by the panel member sending a letter to the CJA Supervising Attorney. The leave of absence will not extend the panel attorney's term. The CJA Administration Committee may permit longer leave periods if justified.

IX. CJA PANEL MEMBER DUTIES

A. Standards and Professional Conduct.

1.   CJA panel members must provide high quality representation consistent with the legal profession's best practices. CJA Panel attorneys will be guided in their practice by the Federal Adaptation of the National Legal Aid and Defender Association Performance Guidelines for Criminal Defense Representations and the ABA's Criminal Justice Standards for the Defense Function.

2.   Attorneys appointed under the CJA must conform to the highest standard of professional conduct, including but not limited to the American Bar Association's Model Rules of Professional Conduct and all other standards for professional conduct adopted by the Court.

3.   CJA Panel members must immediately notify the Federal Public Defender, in writing, if they are disbarred, suspended, sanctioned, or reprimanded by any licensing authority, grievance commit- tee, or administrative body. CJA Panel members must also notify the Federal Public Defender in writing, within 30 days, if they are sanctioned or found in contempt by any state or federal court judge.

B. Training and Continuing Legal Education.

1.   CJA Panel attorneys are expected to remain current with developments in federal criminal defense law, practice, and procedure, including electronic discovery techniques.

2.   CJA panel members are encouraged to annually attend CLE or federal criminal practice training, hosted by the Office of the Federal Public Defender, the Defender Services Office, or by the Court. Participation in federal criminal practice trainings will be considered during the panel application process.

3. The effective defense of indigent federal criminal defendants requires counsel to remain current with developments in case law, forensics, ethics, and other related fields.

C. Facilities and Technology Requirements.

1. CJA panel attorneys must have the facilities, resources, and technological capability to effectively and efficiently manage assigned cases, including the availability of office space to meet with clients and the technological resources to receive, review, organize, and otherwise manage electronic discovery and records.

2. CJA panel attorneys must know and comply with the requirements of electronic filing and eVoucher, including how to submit requests for investigative, expert, and other services.

3. CJA panel attorneys shall maintain competence with technology including using email, word processing, spreadsheets, keyword searching tools, and application to open ZIP files, and creating searchable PDF documents.

X. MENTOR PROGRAM.

The Federal Public Defender shall administer this program. If requested by the Federal Public Defender, the trial panel member is encouraged to serve as a mentor to a non-panel attorney ("mentee") who has not tried two federal criminal jury trials. The mentor shall provide an opportunity for the mentee to audit all aspects of a federal criminal case, including client conferences, strategy determination, motion and trial preparation, and court appearances, and the mentee shall be part of the defense team for the purposes of creating duties of loyalty and confidentiality owed to the client. To complete the requirements of the program, mentees need to audit two federal criminal cases from start to finish including at least one jury trial and two of each of the following: arraignment, detention hearing, motion hearing, and sentencing.

XI. COUNSEL APPOINTMENT IN NON–CAPITAL CASES

A. Apportionment of Cases. CJA Panel attorneys will be appointed in a sufficient number of cases per year so that attorneys remain proficient in criminal defense work.

B. Number of Counsel. More than one attorney may be appointed in any case determined by the Court to be unusual or complex or to otherwise involve exceptional circumstances. Separate from the formal appointment of counsel, particularly in cases involving trials or evidentiary hearings, the Court welcomes and will consider seriously requests by appointed counsel to associate junior counsel. Panel members should propose associate counsel who they are willing to mentor and train specifically as future panel members and are encouraged to identify associate lawyers, especially those from diverse backgrounds and those with fewer years of experience as federal lawyers.

C. Appointment List. The CJA Panel Administrator will maintain a current list of all CJA Panel attorneys, with current office addresses, email addresses, and telephone numbers, as well as a statement of qualifications and experience.

D. Appointment Procedure. The Federal Public Defender is responsible for overseeing the appointment of cases to panel attorneys. The Federal Public Defender will maintain a record of panel attorney appointments and data reflecting the proportion of appointments among the CJA Panel and the Federal Public Defender. If the Federal Public Defender cannot accept an appointment, the CJA Panel Administrator shall refer a panel attorney for the Court's appointment.

1. Appointment of cases to CJA panel members will ordinarily be made on a strict rotational basis. Exceptions are allowed only when the representation calls for a specialization or demand.

2. Under special circumstances, the Court may appoint an attorney who is not a member of the District's CJA Panel. Such special circumstances may include cases in which the Court determines that the appointment of an attorney is in the interests of justice, judicial economy, or continuity of representation, or for any other compelling reason. Other circumstances may include large multi-defendant cases for which there is an insufficient number of CJA Panel attorneys in the District. It is not anticipated that special circumstances will arise often, and the procedures set forth in the Plan are presumed to be sufficient in the vast majority of cases in which counsel are to be appointed. Appointments made under this section will be reported to the CJA Administration Panel Committee.

E. Continuing Representation.

1. Once counsel is appointed under the CJA, counsel will continue the representation until:

    a. the matter is closed, including conclusion of any appellate or certiorari proceedings;

    b. substitute counsel has filed a notice of appearance;

    c. an order is entered allowing the client to proceed pro se; or

    d. the appointment is otherwise terminated by Court order.

2. If trial counsel prefers to withdraw in favor of new counsel on appeal, trial counsel will first file the notice of appeal in the district court to preserve the client's right to appeal and then move to withdraw in the Court of Appeals, asking for appointment of substitute counsel.

XII.   REMOVAL FROM THE PANEL

A. Mandatory Removal. Any attorney whose right to practice in this District or the State of California has been suspended or revoked shall be automatically removed from the panel.

B. Discretionary Removal. For good cause shown, the CJA Administration Committee may remove an attorney from the panel for engaging in unethical behavior, improper billing, or misconduct or for failing to represent his or her client in a vigorous, competent, professional, or ethical way.

C. Removal Procedure.

1. *Filing a Complaint.* Any person who believes that a panel member's conduct should be investigated may file a complaint addressed to the Chair of the CJA Administration Committee and delivered to the CJA Unit in a sealed envelope marked "confidential." A complaint should be made as soon as possible after the event arises so that fair consideration of the facts is possible; a complaint is subject to dismissal when the passage of time has rendered adequate investigation impracticable. A complaint must meet the following requirements:

    a. The complaint may be in letter format, not to exceed five typewritten or legible handwritten pages, and it must contain a thorough statement of what occurred, the time and place of the occurrence(s), and any other information that would assist investigation, such as the presence of witnesses and their names and contact information.

    b. Supporting documentation should be attached.

    c. The complaint must be signed, and the complainant's address and daytime phone provided. Anonymous complaints are disfavored; it is within the discretion of the CJA Administrative Committee to decide whether an anonymous complaint merits further investigation.

2. *Investigating a Complaint.* Within 21 days of receipt of the complaint, the Chair of the CJA Administration Committee shall determine whether the complaint should be investigated and forward this recommendation to the other committee members. If the other members agree with the Chair's determination, the Chair shall provide a copy of the complaint to the panel member who is the subject of the complaint and request that the panel member, within 14 days, submit a written response by letter addressed to the Chair. The CJA Administration Committee may undertake any investigation necessary to resolve the matter or may appoint a subcommittee to do so. The investigation may include interviewing the complainant, the panel attorney and witnesses. The CJA Administration Committee will provide the results of this investigation to the panel attorney and provide that attorney with an opportunity to respond.

3. *Investigating a Complaint Involving Allegations of Criminal Activity.* If the complaint alleges criminal activity, the CJA Administration Committee is not required to notify the panel attorney of the complaint if disclosure could jeopardize the investigation.

4. *Bases for Automatic Dismissal of the Complaint.* Within 21 days of receipt of the complaint, the Chair of the CJA Administration Committee shall automatically dismiss the complaint without further action if:

    a. It alleges activities that can no longer be adequately investigated because of the passage of time;

    b. It lacks sufficient detail; or

    c. The allegations are clearly frivolous or untrue.

When a complaint is dismissed for any of these reasons, the subject panel member shall receive a copy of the complaint with a written statement of dismissal from the Chair of the CJA Administration Committee.

5. *Final Determination by CJA Administration Committee.* Within 90 days of receipt of a complaint, the CJA Administration Committee will dismiss a complaint if the allegations are found to be untrue or, if true, insufficiently serious to warrant removal from the panel. The CJA Administration Committee may impose other sanctions short of removal, such as censure, a term of probation, or any other sanction it deems appropriate under the circumstances. If the CJA Administration Committee finds the allegations to be true and warranting removal, the Chair will notify the panel member of his/her removal from the panel. A notice of removal should occur no more than 90 days from the date the complainant filed the complaint, although the Chair of the CJA Administration Committee may extend this deadline for good cause.

6. *Reapplication to the Panel Following Removal.* Any member who is removed from the panel, whether for mandatory or discretionary reasons, may reapply for panel membership after waiting one year from the date of removal.

7. *Miscellany.* The original complaint and all papers, records and reports will be kept in confidential files by the Clerk of the Court.

The Chair of the CJA Administration Committee may extend a deadline for good cause shown.

The entire complaint process shall remain confidential until the Chair of the Administration Committee

    a. formally dismisses the complaint, or

    b. formally removes the attorney from the panel.

These procedures are not meant to preclude remedies available through malpractice or negligence suits arising from the provision of representational services.

If the CJA Administration Committee finds the allegations to be true and warranting removal from the panel, the Chair may, after consultation with the Chief Judge, refer the matter to the Court's Standing Committee on Professional Conduct.

XIII. SPECIAL PROVISIONS FOR CAPITAL CASES

A. Capital Cases. For purposes of this plan, "capital cases" are those involving the death penalty and include: (1) prosecutions under any provision of federal law carrying a potential penalty of death; (2) direct appeals from cases wherein the death penalty was imposed by a federal court; (3) postconviction proceedings in which an individual sentenced to death by a federal court is seeking to set aside or vacate the conviction or sentence under 28 U.S.C. § 2255; and (4) habeas corpus proceedings in which an individual sentenced to death by a state court is seeking to set aside or vacate the conviction or sentence under 28 U.S.C. § 2254.

B. Applicable Legal Authority. The appointment and compensation of counsel in capital cases and the authorization and payment of persons providing investigative, expert, and other services are governed by 18 U.S.C. §§ 3005, 3006A, and 3599; CJA Guidelines, Ch. 6; and General Order 50.

C. Counsel Qualifications.

1. In addition to the requirements for Panel membership set out in Section VIII of this Plan, counsel appointed in capital cases to represent financially-eligible persons will meet the statutory requirements set out in 18 U.S.C. §§ 3005 and 3599(b)–(d) as expanded upon below, as well as any applicable circuit rules.

2. All attorneys appointed in capital cases must (1) be well qualified as demonstrated by their training, commitment to the defense of capital cases, and distinguished prior criminal defense experience at the relevant stage of the proceeding; (2) have sufficient time and resources to devote to the representation, considering their current caseload and the extraordinary demands of a capital case; (3) meet all applicable guidelines adopted by the American Bar Association concerning representation of persons in death penalty cases; and (4) consult regularly with the appropriate Death Penalty Resource Counsel project available through the Defender Services division of the Administrative Office of the United States Courts.

3. In trial-level capital cases requiring the appointment of "learned counsel," such counsel must meet the minimum standards in 18 U.S.C. §§ 3005 and 3599(b) or (d). Learned counsel should have distinguished prior experience in the trial, appeal, or postconviction review of federal or state death-penalty cases that, in combination with co-counsel, will assure high-quality representation. "Distinguished prior experience" contemplates excellence, not simply prior experience.

4. In direct appeals and post-conviction proceedings under 18 U.S.C. §§ 2254 or 2255, appointed counsel must meet the minimum standards required by 18 U.S.C. § 3599(c) or (d) and should have distinguished prior experience in federal criminal appeals, capital appeals, federal post-conviction proceedings, or capital post-conviction proceedings.

5. Out-of-district counsel, including Defender Organization staff, who possess the requisite expertise may be considered for appointment in capital cases to achieve high-quality representation.

6. An attorney furnished by a state or local public defender organization or legal aid agency or other private, non-profit organization to represent a person charged with a capital crime or seeking federal capital habeas corpus relief may be appointed if the attorney is fully qualified. This appointment may be in place of, or in addition to, the appointment of a federal defender organization or a CJA panel attorney or an attorney appointed pro hac vice. (See 18 U.S.C. § 3006A(a)(3).)

D. Appointment of Counsel.

1. *Pre–Trial.* No later than when a defendant receives a target letter alleging the commission of a capital offense or is charged with a federal criminal offense where the statute authorizes the death penalty, the Court must appoint two attorneys, at least one of whom meets the qualifications for "learned counsel." If necessary, for adequate representation, more than two attorneys may be appointed. Consistent with Section V.A of this Plan, the Court may appoint capitally qualified counsel for an individual that, although uncharged, is the subject of an investigation in a federal death-eligible case. When appointing counsel, the judge must consider the recommendation of the Federal Public Defender who will consult with Death Penalty Resource Counsel to recommend qualified counsel.

2. *Direct Appeals.* Counsel representing a death-sentenced federal appellant should include at least one attorney who did not represent the appellant at trial. Each trial counsel who withdraws should be replaced with similarly qualified counsel to represent the defendant on appeal. When appointing counsel, the Court must consider the recommendation of the Federal Public Defender who will consult with Federal Capital Appellate Resource Counsel to recommend qualified counsel.

3. *Post–Conviction Proceedings.* In any post-conviction proceeding under 18 U.S.C. §§ 2255 or 2254, the Court must appoint at least one qualified attorney and may consider appointing at least two given the complex, demanding, and protracted nature of death penalty proceedings. When appointing counsel, the Court should consider the recommendation of the Federal Public Defender, who will consult with the appropriate Resource Counsel project to recommend qualified counsel. For § 2255 proceedings, appointment should take place, if possible, prior to denial of certiorari on direct appeal by the United States Supreme Court. For § 2254 proceedings, appointment should take place at the earliest time permissible by law to permit federal counsel to avail themselves of the full statute-of-limitations period to prepare a petition.

E. Case Budgeting and Resources. All capital cases, unless staffed only by the Federal Public Defender's office, must be budgeted. As early as practicable after appointment, counsel or the Court should refer the case to the CJA Supervisory Attorney. Questions about the appointment and compensation of counsel and the authorization and payment of investigative, expert, and other service providers in capital cases also may be directed to the appropriate Death Penalty Resource Counsel project or the AO Defender Services Office, Legal and Policy Division Duty Attorney at 202–502–3030.

XV. EFFECTIVE DATE

This plan shall take effect when approved by the Judges of the Northern District of California and the Judicial Council of the Ninth Circuit.

[Dated: January 22, 2020.]

GENERAL ORDER NO. 6.   PLAN FOR THE RANDOM
SELECTION OF GRAND AND PETIT JURORS

This Jury Plan is adopted by the United States District Court for the Northern District of California, in accordance with the provisions of the Jury Selection and Service Act of 1968 (Public Law 90–274) ("Jury Act"), as amended and codified in 28 U.S.C. § 1861–1878.

I. DEFINITIONS

The phrase "Jury Selection Process" in this Plan means all activities associated with the master jury wheels and relating to the random selection, qualification, summoning, and service of grand and petit jurors.

The word "Clerk" in this Plan means the Clerk of this court and any and all of his or her deputies.

The phrase "Chief Judge" in this Plan means the Chief Judge of this court, the acting Chief Judge, or such other judge as the Chief Judge may designate.

II. DIVISIONS

Pursuant to 28 U.S.C. § 1869(e), the Northern District of California is hereby divided into jury divisions for jury selection purposes as follows:

- San Francisco–Oakland jury division, consisting of the counties of Alameda, Contra Costa, Marin, Napa, San Francisco, San Mateo, and Sonoma.

- San Jose jury division, consisting of the counties of Monterey, San Benito, Santa Clara, and Santa Cruz.

- Eureka jury division, consisting of the counties of Del Norte, Humboldt, Lake, and Mendocino.

A separate divisional master jury wheel will be maintained for each division. This Plan applies to each of the divisional master jury wheels. Jurors will be selected for service from a single jury division for petit juries, unless the Chief Judge directs otherwise. Jurors may be selected for service from a combination of divisions for grand juries.

III. POLICY

All litigants in this court entitled to trial by jury have the right to grand and petit jurors selected at random from a fair cross section of the community in the district or jury division wherein the court convenes. All citizens have the opportunity to be considered for service on grand and petit juries and have an obligation to serve as jurors when summoned for that purpose.

No citizen qualified for service will be excluded from service as a grand or petit juror on account of race, color, religion, sex, national origin, economic status, disability, age, sexual orientation or gender identity.

No employer shall discharge, threaten to discharge, intimidate, or coerce any permanent employee over such employee's jury service, or the attendance or scheduled attendance in connection with such jury service. Any employer who acts in violation of this section shall be subject to penalties specified by 28 U.S.C. § 1875.

IV. MANAGEMENT AND SUPERVISION OF JURY SELECTION PROCESS

In accordance with 28 U.S.C. § 1863(b)(1) and 1869(a), the Clerk is authorized to manage the Jury Selection Process under the supervision and control of the Chief Judge. The Clerk may delegate responsibility for the day-to-day operation of the Jury Selection Process to any authorized deputy clerk, or to any authorized non-court personnel, which may include:

- County or state officials, and their employees or agents, who are responsible for custody and maintenance of the source lists identified in Section V of this Plan.

- Owners, employees, operators and/or agents of computer or data processing centers, bar-coding facilities, mail handling centers, document reproduction facilities, and optical scanning facilities, and similar facilities whose services are requested or employed by the Clerk to support the Jury Selection Process.

- Other non-court administrative or clerical persons whose services are requested or employed by the Clerk to select, process, and/or mail the various documents and records involved in the Jury Selection Process.

V. USE OF MULTIPLE–SOURCE LIST.

To foster the policy and protect the rights secured by 28 U.S.C. §§ 1861 and 1862, driver's license and state ID information will be used to supplement voter record information for the creation of master jury wheels. The court finds this "multiple-source list" represents a fair cross section of the citizens residing in the district. Additional sources may be added in the future if feasible.

VI. RANDOM SELECTION

The Clerk will use randomized selection procedures to ensure that the names chosen will represent all segments of the source lists from which the names are drawn, that the mathematical odds of any single name being picked are substantially equal, and that the possibility of human discretion or choice affecting the selection of any individual's name is eliminated.

A properly-programmed electronic data processing system may be used for all randomized drawings, including:

- selecting names from the complete multiple-source list proportionate to the number of registered voters in each county to create the master jury wheels;
- selecting names from a master jury wheel for the purpose of determining qualification for jury service;
- selecting from a pool of persons qualified for service to serve as grand or petit jurors;
- selecting from a pool of jurors to serve as a panel; and
- selecting from a panel of jurors to serve as a jury.

The electronic data processing system may also be used to perform clerical and recordkeeping jury functions.

In the event of an emergency, computer malfunction, or any overt or obvious deviation from this Plan caused by automation, the Clerk will manage these functions manually.

VII. MASTER JURY WHEELS

The Clerk shall maintain a master jury wheel for each of the jury divisions within the district. The names of all persons randomly selected from the multiple-source list from the counties in a jury division shall be placed in the master jury wheel for that jury division. The minimum number of names to be placed initially in these master jury wheels shall be as follows:

- San Francisco–Oakland jury division — 30,000
- San Jose jury division — 10,000
- Eureka jury division — 7,000

The foregoing minimum number of names represents well in excess of one-half of one percent of the total number of registered voters for each jury division and is in substantial compliance with the mandate of the Jury Act.

In accordance with 28 U.S.C. § 1863(b)(4), the master jury wheel of each jury division will be emptied and refilled by August 31 of each year. If additional time is needed to empty and refill the master jury wheels, permission must be obtained from the Chief Judge of the Ninth Circuit.

Jurors qualified from a previous jury wheel may serve at the same time as jurors qualified from a newly-filled jury wheel.

VIII. DRAWING OF NAMES FROM THE MASTER JURY WHEELS

From time to time, the Clerk will draw at random from the master jury wheel of each jury division the names of as many persons as may be required for jury service in each jury division. The Clerk will mail to every person whose name is thus drawn a juror summons and qualification notice accompanied by instructions to complete the questionnaire via the court's website within ten days. The qualification notice will explain that a paper copy of the questionnaire can be mailed upon request.

In any case in which it appears that there is a substantive omission, ambiguity, or error in a juror qualification questionnaire, the Clerk will inform that person that additions or corrections must be made within five days.

If a person fails to complete a juror qualification questionnaire, the Clerk may issue a summons directing the person to appear in the Clerk's Office to complete the qualification questionnaire. No juror fees or costs for this appearance will be paid, unless otherwise ordered by the court pursuant to 28 U.S.C. § 1864(a). The court may impose penalties authorized by 28 U.S.C § 1864(b) for failure to appear as directed.

IX. DETERMINATION OF STATUS OF SUMMONED INDIVIDUALS

Except as provided herein and in 28 U.S.C. § 1866(c), no person or class of persons may be disqualified, excluded, excused or exempted from service as jurors. The Clerk, under supervision of the court, will determine solely on the basis of information provided on the juror qualification form and other competent evidence whether a person is unqualified for, exempt from, or otherwise eligible to be excused from jury service. The Clerk will record each such determination in the electronic data processing system or on the juror qualification questionnaire.

X. QUALIFICATION

The Clerk must deem any person qualified to serve on grand and petit juries in this court unless such person:

- Is not a citizen of the United States who is eighteen years old and who has resided for a period of one year within the judicial district;

- Is unable to read, write, and understand the English language with a degree of proficiency sufficient to fill out satisfactorily the juror qualification form;

- Is unable to speak the English language;

- Is incapable, by reason of mental or physical infirmity, of rendering satisfactory jury service; or

- Has a charge pending against him or her for the commission of, or has been convicted in a state or federal court of record of, a crime punishable by imprisonment for more than one year and his or her civil rights have not been restored.

XI. EXEMPTION

The court hereby finds that exemption of the following groups of persons or occupational classes is in the public interest and would not be inconsistent with the Jury Act; accordingly, members who are employed full-time in the following groups are exempt from jury service:

- Members in active service in the armed forces of the United States;

- Members of the fire or police departments of any state, district, territory, possession, or subdivision thereof; and

- Public officers in the executive, legislative, or judicial branches of the government of the United States, or any state, district or territory or possession, or subdivision thereof, who are actively engaged in the performance of official duties. Public officer means a person who is either elected to public office or who is directly appointed by a person or persons elected to public office.

XII. EXCUSES ON INDIVIDUAL REQUEST

The court finds that jury service by the groups of persons or occupational classes listed below would entail undue hardship or extreme inconvenience to the members thereof and excuse of the members thereof would not be inconsistent with 28 U.S.C. §§ 1861 and 1862. The Clerk will excuse, upon individual request, members of the following groups:

- Persons over 75 years of age;

- Persons who within the last year have served on one or more petit or grand juries in any state court, or who have reported in person to the courthouse in response to a jury summons;

- Persons who serve without compensation as firefighters or members of a rescue squad or ambulance crew for a public agency.

The court, or the Clerk as authorized by the court, may excuse a person summoned for jury service upon a showing of undue hardship or extreme inconvenience if required to serve.

Upon request, the Clerk may defer for up to six months the service of a person summoned.

In any one-year period, no person may be required to (1) serve or attend court more than once or be on standby for prospective service as a petit juror for a total of more than two weeks, except when necessary to complete service in a particular case, or (2) serve on more than one grand jury, or (3) serve as both a grand and petit juror.

XIII. PETIT JURY PANELS

The Clerk will draw at random from the pool of qualified prospective jurors the number of persons anticipated to be necessary for assignment to petit jury panels. Unless otherwise ordered by the Chief Judge, the term of service of prospective petit jurors will be two weeks. During the two-week period, prospective petit jurors will be required to report to the courthouse no more than once unless the jury-selection process in the case to which they are assigned is continuing. Prospective jurors who report for jury selection but are not selected as jurors for any trial will have satisfied their jury service obligation upon completion of voir dire, empanelment of the final jury, or discharge by the judge. Prospective jurors who are selected as trial jurors will have satisfied their jury service obligation upon completion of the trial.

A petit juror serving more than 10 days on one case will be paid an additional $10 per day over the regular attendance fee for each day over 10 days served. 28 U.S.C. § 1871(b)(2).

XIV. GRAND JURY PANELS

At least one grand jury will be impaneled serving the entire district, and will serve its term of service at San Francisco. To impanel district-wide grand juries, the Clerk will draw at random from a pool of qualified persons of each jury division for the grand jury panel such number of prospective grand jurors in the same ratio that the number of registered voters in each jury division bears to the total number of registered voters in the district.

The court may order additional grand juries to serve in other places as the court may designate and at such times as the court may order. For a grand jury to be impaneled for service in one jury division only, the Clerk will draw at random from a pool of qualified persons of that jury division for the grand jury panel such number of prospective grand jurors as necessary.

Each grand jury must serve until discharged by the Chief Judge, but no regular, criminal grand jury will serve more than 18 months unless the court extends the service of the grand jury for a period of six months or less, upon a determination that such extension is in the public interest. Each special grand jury, as defined in 18 U.S.C. § 3331, will serve for a term of 18 months unless an order for its discharge or an extension of its term is entered by the court in accordance with 18 U.S.C. § 3331 or § 3333.

Alternate jurors may be designated at the time a grand jury is selected, and may thereafter be impaneled to replace excused jurors in the order in which they were designated. Alternate jurors are subject to the same challenges, and, if impaneled, will take the same oath and will have the same functions and powers as the regular grand jurors.

The impanelment of every regular or special grand jury will not be conducted in open court or within public view.

A grand juror attending more than 45 days of actual service will be paid an additional $10 per day over the regular attendance fee for each day over 45 days. 28 U.S.C. § 1871(b)(3).

XV. CHALLENGES TO THE SELECTION PROCEDURES

Any challenge to this Plan or the court's compliance with the provisions of this Plan or compliance with the provisions of the Jury Act must be made within the times and in the manner provided in 28 U.S.C. § 1867.

XVI. DISCLOSURE OF JURY RECORDS

The contents of records or papers used by the Clerk in connection with the Jury Selection Process will not be disclosed, except upon written order of the court. Applications for disclosure of records related to the Jury Selection Process must be made by motion to the trial judge and must set forth why disclosure should be allowed.

When the Clerk has assigned a venire panel to a particular trial, the list of names so assigned may be furnished to the attorneys for the parties and any parties appearing *pro se* in said trial on the day jury selection begins, unless otherwise ordered by the trial judge.

The names of prospective and sitting petit jurors will be disclosed to the public or media outside open court only upon order of the court. A request for such disclosure must be made to the trial judge pursuant to Civil Local Rule 7–11.

Except as authorized by written order of the court, the names and information relating to any summoned or serving grand juror or grand jury panel will be kept confidential and not disclosed to any litigant or member of the public. Applications for disclosure of grand juror information must be made by motion to the trial judge and must set forth why disclosure should be allowed. A motion for the names of grand jurors that is not related to a particular trial may be made by filing a miscellaneous action with the Clerk.

XVII. MAINTENANCE OF RECORDS

In accordance with 28 U.S.C. § 1868, the Clerk will keep all records and papers relating to the Jury Selection Process for four years following the emptying and refilling of the master jury wheels and the completion of service of all jurors selected from those master jury wheels, or for such longer periods of time as the court may require. Such records may then be destroyed, providing the means used ensures the privacy of their contents.

XVIII. MODIFICATIONS AND EFFECTIVE DATE

Modifications to this Plan may be made from time to time by this court upon approval of the Ninth Circuit Reviewing Panel of the Judicial Council, and must be made when so directed by the Reviewing Panel.

The effective date of this Plan will be established by a separate order of this court after this Plan has been approved by the reviewing panel of the Ninth Circuit.

The prior Jury Plan will be superseded as of the effective date of this revised Plan.

A copy of the revised Plan, as approved by the reviewing panel, will be provided to the Administrative Office of the United States Courts and the Attorney General of the United States.

[Dated: September 23, 2021.]

GENERAL ORDER NO. 14.   PLAN FOR PROMPT
DISPOSITION OF CRIMINAL CASES

Section I.   Introductory Material.

A.   The Plan for Prompt Disposition of Criminal Cases for the Northern District of California is set forth in Section II of this report. The Plan has been approved and adopted by the Court upon the recommendation of the Planning Group.

B.   The Planning Group for the Northern District of California consists of the following individuals:

Chief Judge Robert F. Peckham, Chairman

Judge Alfonso J. Zirpoli

Judge William H. Orrick

Judge William W. Schwarzer

Chief Magistrate Richard S. Goldsmith

G. William Hunter, United States Attorney

James F. Hewitt, Federal Public Defender

Glen E. Robinson, United States Marshal

Michael E. Sterrett, Attorney-in-Charge, Organized Crime & Racketeering Section, Dept. of Justice

Jerrold M. Ladar, Private Attorney

Weyman I. Lundquist, Private Attorney

William L. Whittaker, Clerk of Court

Harry W. Schloetter, Chief Probation Officer

Jay L. Schaefer, Reporter

C.   Copies of the Plan and this report will be available for public inspection at the Office of the Clerk of the United States District Court in San Francisco and in San Jose. Copies of the Plan (Section II) will be distributed upon request to members of the Bar who practice before the District Court.

Section II.   Plan for Achieving Prompt Disposition of Criminal Cases.   Pursuant to the requirements of Rule 50(b) of the Federal Rules of Criminal Procedure, the Speedy Trial Act of 1974

(18 U.S.C., Chapter 208), the Speedy Trial Act Amendments of 1979 (Pub.L. No. 96–43, 93 Stat. 327), and the Federal Juvenile Delinquency Act (18 U.S.C., §§ 5036, 5037), the Judges of the United States District Court for the Northern District of California have adopted the following time limits and procedures to minimize undue delay and to further the prompt disposition of criminal cases and certain juvenile proceedings:

1. *Applicability.*

(a) Offenses. The time limits set forth herein are applicable to all criminal offenses triable in this court, including cases triable by United States Magistrates, except for petty offenses as defined in 18 U.S.C. § 1(3). Except as specifically provided, they are not applicable to proceedings under the Federal Juvenile Delinquency Act. [§ 3172]

(b) Persons. The time limits are applicable to persons accused who have not been indicted or informed against as well as those who have, and the word "defendant" includes such persons unless the context indicates otherwise.

2. *Priorities in Scheduling Criminal Cases.* Preference shall be given to criminal proceedings as far as practicable as required by Rule 50(a) of the Federal Rules of Criminal Procedure. The trial of defendants in custody solely because they are awaiting trial and of high-risk defendants as defined in Section 5 should be given preference over other criminal cases. [§ 3164(a)]

3. *Time Within Which an Indictment or Information Must Be Filed.*

(a) Time Limits. If an individual is arrested or served with a summons and the Complaint charges an Offense to be prosecuted in this district, any Indictment or Information subsequently filed in connection with such charge shall be filed within thirty (30) days of arrest or service. [§ 3161(b)]

(b) Grand Jury Not in Session. If the defendant is charged with a felony to be prosecuted in this district, and no grand jury in the district has been in session during the 30–day period prescribed in subsection (a), such period shall be extended an additional 30 days. [§ 3161(b)]

(c) Measurement of Time Periods.

(1) Arrest. If a person has not been arrested or served with a summons on a Federal charge, an arrest will be deemed to have been made at such time as the person: (i) is held in custody solely for the purpose of responding to a Federal charge; (ii) is delivered to the custody of a Federal official in connection with a Federal charge; or (iii) appears before a judicial officer in connection with a Federal charge.

(2) Summons. In the absence of a showing to the contrary, a summons shall be considered to have been served on the date of service shown on the return thereof.

(3) Superseding Charges. See section 4(d), infra.

4. *Time Within Which Trial Must Commence.*

(a) Time Limits. The trial of a defendant shall commence not later than 70 days after the last to occur of the following dates:

(1) The date on which an indictment or information is filed in this district;

(2) The date on which a sealed indictment or information is unsealed; or

(3) The date of the defendant's first appearance before a judicial officer of this district. [§ 3161(c)(1)]

(b) Retrial; Trial After Reinstatement of an Indictment or Information. The retrial of a defendant shall commence within 70 days from the date the order occasioning the retrial becomes final, as shall the trial of a defendant upon an indictment or information dismissed by a trial court and reinstated following an appeal. If the retrial or trial follows an appeal or collateral attack, the court may extend the period if unavailability of witnesses or other factors resulting from passage of time make trial within 70 days impractical. The extended period shall not exceed 180 days. [§ 3161(d)(2), (e)]

(c) Withdrawal of Plea. If a defendant enters a plea of guilty or nolo contendere to any or all charges in an indictment or information and is subsequently permitted to withdraw the plea, the time limit shall be determined for all counts as if the indictment or information were filed on the day the order permitting withdrawal of the plea became final. [§ 3161(i)]

(d) Superseding Charges.

(1) Indictment or Information Superseded. If, after an indictment or information has been filed, an indictment or information is filed which charges the defendant with the same offense or with an offense required to be joined with that offense, the time limit applicable to the subsequent charge will be determined as follows:

(i) If the original indictment or information was dismissed on motion of the defendant before the filing of the subsequent charge, the time limit to trial (under section 4(a), above) shall be determined without regard to the existence of the original charge. [§ 3161(d)(1)]

(ii) If the original indictment or information is pending at the time the subsequent charge is filed, the trial shall commence within the time limit for commencement of trial on the original indictment or information. [§ 3161(h)(6)]

(iii) If the original indictment or information was dismissed on motion of the United States Attorney before the filing of the subsequent charge, the trial shall commence within the time limit for commencement of trial on the original indictment or information, but the period during which the defendant was not under charges shall be excluded from the computations. Such period is the period between dismissal of the original indictment or information and the date the time would have commenced to run on the subsequent charge (under section 4(a), above) had there been no previous charge.

(2) Complaint Superseded. If any charge contained in a complaint filed against a defendant is dismissed or otherwise dropped, and thereafter a complaint, indictment or information is filed which charges the defendant with the same offense or an offense based on the same conduct or arising from the same criminal episode, the time limits set forth in sections 3 and 4 of this plan, which are applicable to such subsequent charge, shall be determined without regard to the existence of the original charge. [§ 3161(d)(1)]

(3) Subsequent Charge in Complaint. If any charge contained in a complaint, information or indictment filed against a defendant is dismissed or otherwise dropped, and thereafter a complaint is filed which charges the defendant with the same offense or an offense based on the same conduct or arising out of the same criminal episode, the time limit within which an indictment or information must be obtained shall be determined without regard to the existence of the original complaint, information or indictment. [§ 3161(d)(1)]

(4) Same Offense Charged. Under (d)(1)(ii) and (iii), above, unless the court finds that the subsequent charge is not for the same offense charged in the original indictment or information, or not for an offense required to be joined therewith, the trial on the subsequent charge shall commence within the time limit for commencement of trial on the original indictment or information.

(e) Measurement of Time Periods. For the purposes of this section:

(1) If a defendant signs a written consent to be tried before a magistrate and no indictment or information charging the offense has been filed, the time limit shall run from the date of such consent.

(2) In the event of a transfer to this district under Rule 20 of the Federal Rules of Criminal Procedure, the indictment or information shall be deemed filed in this district when the papers in the proceeding or certified copies thereof are received by the clerk.

(3) A trial in a jury case shall be deemed to commence at the beginning of voir dire.

(4) A trial in a non-jury case shall be deemed to commence on the day the case is called, provided that some step in the trial procedure immediately follows.

(f) Related Procedures.

(1) Earliest Appearance. At the time of the defendant's earliest appearance before a judicial officer of this district, the officer will take appropriate steps to assure that the defendant is represented by counsel and shall appoint counsel where appropriate under the Criminal Justice Act and Rule 44 of the Federal Rules of Criminal Procedure.

(2) Setting Trial Date. The court shall have sole responsibility for setting cases for trial after consultation with counsel. At the time of arraignment or as soon thereafter as is practicable, each case will be set for trial on a weekly or other short-term calendar. [§ 3161(a)]

(3) Pre-trial Motions. Except as otherwise ordered by the court, all motions shall be filed within ten (10) days from the date of arraignment.

(4) Pre-trial Hearings. All pre-trial hearings shall be conducted as soon after the arraignment as possible, consistent with the priorities of other matters on the court's criminal docket.

(5) Trial Date. Individual calendars shall be managed so that it will be reasonably anticipated that every criminal case set for trial will be reached during the week of original setting. All counsel shall advise the court at the time of trial setting or as soon as practicable thereafter, of conflicts with the trial date. A conflict in schedules of Assistant United States Attorneys or defense counsel will not be a ground for a continuance or delayed setting unless the court determines that such a continuance of the trial date is in the ends of justice under section 3161(h)(8). (See Section 5(c), infra.)

(6) Notice by Government. At the time of the filing of a complaint, indictment, or information, including a superseding complaint, indictment or information, the United States Attorney shall give written notice to the court of that circumstance and of the government's position with respect to the computation of time limits, as required by section 6(b)(3).

5. *Defendants in Custody and High–Risk Defendants.*

(a) Time Limits. Notwithstanding any longer time periods that may be permitted under sections 3 and 4, the following time limits will also be applicable to defendants in custody and high-risk defendants as herein defined:

(1) The trial of a defendant held in custody solely for the purpose of trial on a federal charge shall commence within 90 days following the beginning of continuous custody.

(2) The trial of a high-risk defendant shall commence within 90 days of the designation as high-risk. [§ 3161(b)]

(b) Definition and Notice.

(1) If a defendant is being held in custody solely for the purpose of awaiting trial, the United States Attorney shall so advise the court and the clerk at the time custody commences or as soon as possible thereafter.

(2) A high-risk defendant is one designated by the United States Attorney as posing a danger to himself or any other person or to the community. The United States Attorney shall notify the court and the clerk of such designation at the time the designation is made.

(3) If the court finds that the filing of a "high-risk" designation as a public record may result in prejudice to the defendant, it may order the designation sealed for such period as is necessary to protect the defendant's right to a fair trial, but not beyond the time that the court's judgment in the case becomes final. During the time the designation is under seal, it shall be made known to the defendant and defense counsel but shall not be made known to other persons without the permission of the court.

(c) Measurement of Time Periods. For the purposes of this section:

(1) A defendant is deemed to be in detention awaiting trial when he or she is arrested on a federal charge or otherwise held for the purpose of responding to a federal charge. Detention is deemed to be solely because the defendant is awaiting trial unless the person exercising custodial authority has an independent basis (not including a detainer) for continuing to hold the defendant.

(2) If a case is transferred pursuant to Rule 20 of the Federal Rules of Criminal Procedure and the defendant subsequently rejects disposition under Rule 20 or the court declines to accept the plea, a new period of continuous detention awaiting trial will begin at that time.

(3) A trial shall be deemed to commence as provided in sections 4(e)(3) and (4), above.

6. *Exclusion of Time From Computations.*

(a) Applicability. In computing any time limit under Sections 3, 4, or 5, the periods of delay set forth in 18 U.S.C. § 3161(h) shall be excluded. Such periods of delay shall not be excluded in computing the minimum period for commencement of trial under Section 7, infra.

(b) Determination and Recordation of Excludable Time.

(1) Court. Determinations concerning excludable time shall normally be made on the record by the court or the magistrate.

(2) Counsel.

(i) Counsel shall have five (5) days from the date of the court's determination of excludable time in which to object to the determination. Counsel shall have the responsibility for examining the clerk's records of excludable time for completeness and accuracy.

(ii) All motions, opposition to motions, and other papers filed and orders presented to the court for signing in any criminal proceeding shall state which, if any, of the exclusions under § 3161 are applicable and how much time should be excluded, as provided in Local Rule 340–2.

(iii) The attorney for the Government and the attorney for the defendant may at any time enter into stipulations with respect to the accuracy of the docket entries recording excludable time. To the extent that the amount of time stipulated by the parties does not exceed the amount recorded on the docket for any excludable period of delay, the stipulation shall be conclusive as between the parties unless it has no basis in fact or law. It shall similarly be conclusive as to a co-defendant for the limited purpose of determining, under 18 U.S.C. § 3161(h)(7), whether time has run against the defendant entering into the stipulation. To the extent that the amount of time stipulated exceeds the amount recorded on the docket, the stipulation shall have no effect unless approved by the Court.

(3) United States Attorney. The United States Attorney shall calculate and record excludable time with respect to proceedings prior to the filing of an indictment or information. Excludable time calculations shall be reported to the court and to the clerk at the time the information or indictment is filed or as soon as possible thereafter.

(4) Clerk. The Clerk of the Court shall enter on the docket information with respect to the excludable periods of time which have been determined for each defendant.

(5) Documents and records prepared or maintained by the Clerk or the United States Attorney relating to excludable time are for informational purposes only and shall not constitute evidence that such excludable time has occurred in fact in the absence of a judicial determination or stipulation.

(c) Continuances.

(1) Request for Continuance. In the event that either party seeks a continuance under § 3161(h)(8), counsel for that party shall file a written motion stating:

(i) the period of time proposed for exclusion;

(ii) the basis of the proposed exclusion; and

(iii) whether or not the defendant is being held in custody. In appropriate circumstances, the motion may include a request that some or all of the supporting material be considered ex parte and in camera.

(2) Order Granting Continuance. If it is determined that a continuance is justified, the Court shall set forth its findings in the record, either orally or in writing. If the continuance is granted under 18 U.S.C. § 3161(h)(8), the Court shall also set forth its reason for finding that the ends of justice served by granting the continuance outweigh the best interests of the public and the defendant in a speedy trial. If the continuance is to a date not certain, the Court shall require one or both parties to inform the Court promptly when and if the circumstances that justify the continuance no longer exist. In addition, the Court shall require one or both parties to file periodic reports bearing on the continued existence of such circumstances. The Court shall determine the frequency of such reports in the light of the facts of the particular case.

(3) Pre–Indictment Continuance.

(i) In the event that the United States Attorney anticipates that an Indictment or Information will not be filed within the time limit set forth in Section 3, the Government may file a written motion with the Court for a determination of excludable time. In the event that the Government seeks a continuance under 18 U.S.C. § 3161(h)(8), the United States Attorney shall file a written motion with the Court requesting such a continuance and shall provide the Court with the record of excludable time maintained pursuant to section 6(b)(3), above.

(4) Post–Indictment Continuance.

(i) In the event that the Court continues a trial beyond the time limits set forth in section 4 or 5 of this plan, the Court shall determine whether the limit may be recomputed by excluding time pursuant to 18 U.S.C. § 3161(h).

7. *Minimum Period for Defense Preparation.* Unless the defendant consents in writing to the contrary, the trial shall not commence earlier than 30 days from the date on which the indictment or information is filed or, if later, from the date on which the defendant first appears through counsel or on which the defendant expressly waives counsel and elects to proceed pro se.

(a) In circumstances in which the 70-day time limit for commencing trial on a charge in an indictment or information is determined by reference to an earlier indictment or information pursuant to section 4(d), above, the 30-day minimum period shall also be determined by reference to the earlier indictment or information.

(b) When prosecution is resumed on an original indictment or information following a mistrial, appeal, or withdrawal of a guilty plea, a new 30–day minimum period will not begin to run.

(c) A change of counsel or of pro se status shall not restart the 30–day minimum period. The Court will in all cases schedule trials so as to permit counsel adequate preparation time in light of all the circumstances. [§ 3161(c)(2)]

8. *Time Within Which Defendant Should Be Sentenced.*

(a) Time Limit. A defendant shall ordinarily be sentenced within 45 days of the date of the conviction or plea of guilty or nolo contendere.

(b) Presentence Report. If the defendant and defense counsel consent on the record, a presentence investigation may be commenced prior to a plea of guilty or nolo contendere or a conviction.

9. *Juvenile Proceedings.*

(a) Time Within Which Trial Must Commence. An alleged delinquent who is in detention pending trial shall be brought to trial within 30 days of the date on which such detention was begun, as provided in 18 U.S.C. § 5036.

(b) Time of Dispositional Hearing. If a juvenile is an adjudicated delinquent, a separate dispositional hearing shall be held no later than 20 court days after trial, unless the court has ordered further study of the juvenile in accordance with 18 U.S.C. § 5037(c).

10. *Sanctions.*

(a) Dismissal Not Required. Failure to comply with the requirements of Title I of the Speedy Trial Act may entitle the defendant to dismissal of the charges. Nothing in this plan shall be construed to require that a case be dismissed or a defendant released from custody in circumstances in which dismissal or release would not be required by 18 U.S.C. § 3162 or § 3164.[1] The Court retains the power to dismiss a case for unnecessary delay pursuant to Rule 48(b) of the Federal Rules of Criminal Procedure.

[1] Dismissal may also be required in some cases under the Interstate Agreement on Detainers, 18 U.S.C., Appendix.

(b) High–Risk Defendants. A high-risk defendant whose trial has not commenced within the time limit set forth in 18 U.S.C. § 3164(b) shall, if the failure to commence trial was through no fault of the attorney for the government, have the release conditions automatically reviewed. A high-risk defendant who is found by the court to have delayed intentionally the trial of his or her case shall be subject to an order of the court modifying the nonfinancial conditions of release under Chapter 207 of Title 18, U.S.C., to ensure that the defendant shall appear at trial as required. [§ 3164(c)]

(c) Discipline of Attorneys. In a case in which counsel: (1) knowingly allows the case to be set for trial without disclosing the fact that a necessary witness would be unavailable for trial, (2) files a motion solely for the purpose of delay knowing it is frivolous and without merit, (3) makes a statement for the purpose of obtaining a continuance knowing it to be false and which is material to granting of the continuance, or (4) otherwise willfully fails to proceed to trial without justification consistent with 18 U.S.C. § 3161, the Court may punish such counsel as provided in 18 U.S.C. § 3162(b) and (c). The sanctions which may be imposed on such attorney include: (i) reducing up to 25% the compensation of an attorney appointed under the Criminal Justice Act; (ii) fining retained counsel up to 25% of their fee; (iii) fining the attorney for the Government up to $250; (iv) prohibiting the attorney for the Government from practicing before that Court for not more than 90 days; or (v) filing a report with the appropriate disciplinary committee.

(d) Alleged Juvenile Delinquents. An alleged delinquent in custody whose trial has not commenced within the time limit set forth in 18 U.S.C. § 5036 shall be entitled to dismissal of the case pursuant to that section unless the Attorney General shows that the delay was consented to or caused by the juvenile or the juvenile's counsel, or would be in the interest of justice in the particular case.

11. *Persons Serving Terms of Imprisonment.* If the United States Attorney knows that a person charged with an offense is serving a term of imprisonment in any penal institution, the United States Attorney shall promptly seek to obtain the presence of the prisoner for trial, or cause a detainer to be filed, in accordance with the provisions of 18 U.S.C. § 3161(j).

12. *Additional Responsibilities.*

(a) Magistrate or District Judge.

(1) At the time the defendant first appears in court with counsel, the court shall establish for the record the date of arrest or summons, indictment or filing of information or complaint, and the date of other significant Speedy Trial Act events. The court shall also establish the date of the first appearance through counsel for the purposes of section 7 of this plan and determine excludable time pursuant to section 6, above.

(2) If the court orders the defendant or the case removed or transferred under the Federal Rules of Criminal Procedure, the court shall determine the amount of excludable time through the day the order for removal or transfer is signed.

(b) Marshal. The Marshal shall report to the clerk as soon as possible:

(1) The names and reasons for detention of all persons taken into custody;

(2) The change of status of any person in custody; and

(3) The arrest of a defendant out of the district on a warrant issued by this court.

(c) District Planning Group. As part of its continuing study of the administration of criminal justice in this district, the District Planning Group will pay special attention to those cases in which there is a failure to comply with the time limits set forth herein. From time to time, the Group may make appropriate recommendations to the court.

(d) Responsibilities of Clerk. In addition to maintaining statistical data as required by the Administrative Office of the United States Courts, the Clerk will from time to time report to the other members of the Planning Group concerning failures to comply with any time limit set forth herein. The Clerk will provide the Circuit Council with any information it requests on the status of criminal cases in this district.

13. *Effective Date.*

(a) This plan shall take effect upon approval of the reviewing panel designated in accordance with 18 U.S.C. § 3165(c). This plan supersedes those previously in effect. However, the dismissal sanction and the sanctions against attorneys authorized by 18 U.S.C. § 3162 and reflected in sections 10(a) and (c) of this plan shall apply only to defendants whose cases are commenced by arrest or summons on or after July 1, 1980, and to indictments and informations filed on or after that date.

(b) If a defendant was arrested or served with a summons before July 1, 1979, the time within which an information or indictment must be filed shall be determined under the plan that was in effect at the time of such arrest or service.

(c) If a defendant was arraigned before August 2, 1979, the time within which the trial must commence shall be determined under the plan that was in effect at the time of such arraignment.

(d) The provisions of 18 U.S.C. § 3164, reflected in section 5 of this plan, became effective on August 2, 1979, the date the Speedy Trial Act amendments were signed.

Section III.   Summary of Experience Under the Act Within the District.

A. *Progress Toward Meeting the Permanent Time Limits.* The court has made substantial progress towards meeting the time limits. As experience with the act increases, more findings of excludable time are being made, thus increasing the rate of compliance. With the expanded exclusion for motions (§ 3161(h)(1)(F)) and the increasing use of § 3161(h)(8), there should be full compliance by July 1, 1980.

B. *Problems Encountered.* A lack of awareness and understanding of the Speedy Trial Act has been the major obstacle to compliance. The anticipation of sanctions on July 1, 1980, and increasing experience with the act are facilitating compliance efforts.

C. *Incidence of, and Reasons for, Requests or Allowances of Extensions of Time Beyond the District's Standards.* The reasons for extensions beyond the time limit to trial are described in Table 2 of Section VIII (Statistics).[1] The longer extensions were granted under § 3161(h)(8), frequently because of the unavailability of counsel, the complexity of the case, or the number of defendants.

[1] For Statistical Tables, contact the Clerk of Court's office.

D. *Reasons Why Exclusions Were Inadequate to Accommodate Reasonable Periods of Delay.* The exclusions, as amended, would have been adequate, had they been recorded, to bring all criminal cases into compliance.

E. *The Effect on Criminal Justice Administration of Prevailing Time Limits.* A reduction in the number of criminal filings and a change in the nature and complexity of cases commenced since the act was implemented make the effects of the Speedy Trial Act difficult to isolate. From the year ending June 30, 1976 through the year ending in 1979, the median time (actual days) from filing to disposition of criminal cases has increased from 3.2 to 4.4 months, while the percentage of defendants not in compliance with the 30 and 60–day time limits (actual days minus excludable time) has decreased.

The act focuses greater attention on criminal cases, causes more cases to be reassigned, and causes more court activity, including determination of excludable time; whether cases will terminate more quickly (in terms of total elapsed days, not "net" time countable under the act), however, remains an open question.

F. *Effect of Compliance With the Time Limits on the Civil Calendar.* The Speedy Trial Act has not yet had an effect on the civil calendar. Since the act became effective, there has been a 10% increase in the annual civil filings but the median time from filing to disposition has decreased from 9 to 8 months. However, with several lengthy criminal trials scheduled and three judgeships presently vacant, there could soon be a serious interruption in the scheduling of civil trials.

G. *Frequency of Use of Sanctions Under 18 U.S.C. § 3164.* (Release from custody or modification of release conditions.) No sanctions have been imposed under § 3164.

Section IV. Procedures and Innovations That Have Been Adopted by the District Court to Expedite the Disposition of Criminal Cases.

1. The district regularly convenes an expanded planning group that includes, in addition to the members required by statute, three district judges, the Special Agent–in–Charge of the Organized Crime Strike Force, and the Chief Assistants of United States Attorney and Marshal. The group addresses a variety of problems including some beyond immediate scope of the Speedy Trial Act.

2. The Court has adopted the following local rule (340–2): "All motions and other papers filed in any criminal action or proceeding shall show on the first page beneath the file number which, if any, of the exclusions under 18 U.S.C. § 3161 may be applicable to the action sought or opposed by the motion or other paper, and the resulting excludable time."

3. Additional responsibilities of the Court, Magistrates, United States Attorney and Marshal are described in section II.

4. A weekly COURTRAN print-out (Appendix) enables the court and Clerk's Office to monitor criminal cases closely.

SPEEDY TRIAL SUMMARY REPORT
(Defendants awaiting Trial, Rule 20
defendants awaiting arraignment,
defendants in U.S. CUSTODY awaiting trial
and explanation of pending excludable intervals)

as of —/—/—

JUDGE NAME	DOCKET	MAXIMUM TRIAL DATE	MINIMUM TRIAL DATE	PENDING EXCLUD-ABLE TIME TO BE ADDED	DAYS CURRENTLY IN U.S. CUSTODY
SAMPLE, VICTOR LUIZ	CR479–1	03/17/79	02/02/79	43 *	0

****

* PENDING EXCLUDABLE INTERVALS

DOCKET NO.	TYPE EXCL. STARTED	START DATE	REASON STARTED	EXP. DATE (if applicable)
CR479–1	T,M	1/15/79	Ends of Justice outweigh need for speedy trial and Unavailability of essential witness	

*** No Defendants in U.S. CUSTODY awaiting trial***
*** No Rule 20 Defendants awaiting arraignment***
1 DEFENDANT in this report

Section V. Statement of Additional Resources to Achieve Compliance With the Act. With the filling of all judgeships and the maintenance of the present staffing levels of the Clerk, United States Attorney, Marshal, and Probation Office, no additional resources will be needed to comply with the Speedy Trial Act.

Section VI. Recommendations for Changes in Rules. Rule 20 of the Federal Rules of Criminal Procedure should be amended to allow the defendant to waive venue in the district in which a complaint is pending and consent to be charged in the arresting district. At the present time, the defendant can waive indictment and trial under Rules 7, 11, and 20(b). Permitting the waiver of venue would further expedite Rule 20 proceedings.

Section VII. Incidence and Length of, Reasons for, and Remedies for Detention Prior to Trial. The judges in this district have uniformly applied the standards of the Bail Reform Act. Statistics concerning the number of defendants detained and the length of detention are reported in the tables in Section VIII (Statistics).[1]

[1] For Statistical Tables, contact the Clerk of Court's office.

[Dated: April 7, 1980.]

GENERAL ORDER NO. 19. PLAN FOR THE ADMINISTRATION AND OPERATION OF THE COURT NON–APPROPRIATED FUND

I. Introduction

In conformity with the "Guidelines for Non–Appropriated Funds Maintained by the Courts of the United States" issued by the Director of the Administrative Office of the United States Courts on October 7, 1981, the Court adopts this Plan to establish standards and procedures for the administration and operation of non-appropriated funds held and collected by the Court for the benefit of the bench and the bar.

II. Sources of Funds

The funds to be administered in accordance with this Plan include:

A. All funds on deposit with the Clerk under the designation "Library Fund" on the date of adoption of this Plan.

B. All funds received by the Clerk pursuant to Civil LR 11–1(d) and 11–3(d).

C. All income derived from the sources described in IIA and B, above.

These funds collectively are referred to herein as "non-appropriated funds" or "the Fund."

III. Fund Custodian

The Clerk of the Court is hereby appointed custodian of the Fund. The Clerk shall:

A. Receive, safeguard, deposit, disburse and account for all funds, as prescribed in this Plan and in pertinent laws;

B.   Establish an accounting system approved by the court;

C.   Ensure that a financial statement and operating report is prepared quarterly, sign it and distribute a copy to each judge of the court, thereby certifying that the statement and report accurately presents the financial condition of the fund;

D.   Ensure that a budget is prepared and regularly maintained, based on spending and commitment decisions;

E.   Invest funds in federally insured interest bearing accounts, government securities or money market funds invested in government obligations;

F.   Perform such other functions as the court may direct.

IV. Purpose and Uses of the Fund

The Fund is to be used for the benefit of the bench and the bar in the administration of justice, in accordance with The Guide to Judiciary Policy, Vol. 13 § 1220. Its uses may include, but are not limited to:

A.   Providing for the court library useful books, treatises, periodicals, research aids, equipment, facilities and services not available through the Administrative Office of the United States Courts;

B.   Collection and preservation of records of historical value to the court;

C.   Development of the history of the court;

D.   Enhancing the level of advocacy in the court;

E.   Covering costs of attorney admission proceedings (including expenses of admissions, committees, and admissions ceremonies);

F.   Covering the costs of attorney discipline proceedings (including expenses of investigating counsel for disciplinary enforcement, travel expenses and witness fees in disciplinary proceedings);

G.   Covering costs of the annual Northern District Judicial Conference and costs associated with the court's participation in the annual Ninth Circuit Judicial Conference, including, but not limited to: site fees; public service awards; lodging and meals for speakers and presenters; subsidized lodging; meals and participation fees for government and public interest attorneys; and signage and printed and digital conference materials;

H.   Providing adequate facilities for attorneys practicing in the court;

I.   Covering costs of special projects or acquisitions to further the administration of justice within the district including, without limitation, providing assistance to litigants without counsel and disseminating information about court proceedings.

V. Administration of the Fund

The Fund shall be administered by a Court Non–Appropriated Fund Committee appointed by the Chief Judge, consisting of the Chief Judge, ex officio, a chairperson and four other judicial officers, at least one of whom shall be from the San Jose division, and one of whom shall be from the Oakland Division. This Committee shall be responsible for overseeing the Clerk in his custodial responsibilities, reviewing and approving the quarterly accountings rendered by the Clerk, and making recommendations to the Court on proposed expenditures from the Fund.

The chairperson (or, in the chairperson's absence, the Chief Judge) shall have the authority to approve individual disbursements not exceeding $5,000. The Committee, or a majority thereof, shall have the authority to approve individual disbursements not exceeding $25,000. All expenditures in excess of $25,000 may be authorized only by a majority of a quorum of active judges.

Any judge, staff member or member of the bar of this court may recommend to the Committee uses for non-appropriated funds.

When non-appropriated funds are administered by a grantee (such as, for example, the court's Lawyer Representatives in connection with the annual Northern District Judicial Conference), the grantee must submit to the Non–Appropriated Fund Committee an accounting of the expenses paid for with non-appropriated funds and shall provide such supporting documentation as the court requests. Such accounting should be submitted as soon as practicable after the non-appropriated funds at issue are spent. Unless otherwise provided in the grant, every grantee with custody of non-appropriated funds for a period greater than ninety (90) days shall submit a quarterly accounting of the funds and a status report on the project or program for which the non-appropriated funds were granted.

From time to time, if the Chief Judge determines that the Court or the Non–Appropriated fund Committee would benefit from advice from members of the bar with respect to particular matters of policy or administration of the Fund, the Chief Judge may appoint a Non–Appropriated Fund Advisory Committee. The Advisory Committee shall be composed of five members of the bar. One member shall be the president of the Federal Bar Association for the Northern District of California. The Chief Judge shall designate the terms of the members of the Advisory Committee and the particular matter for which the Advisory Committee's advice is sought.

VI. Audit

The financial records, disbursements, receipts and earning statements shall be audited by the Audit Division of the Administrative Office of the United States Courts as a part of their periodic reviews of the business of the court; and the Clerk as part of the court's annual internal audit. The Court Non–Appropriated Fund Committee may direct that an audit be performed by an outside auditor at any time. The cost of such audit, if any, shall be paid out of the Fund.

[Dated: May 18, 2011.]

GENERAL ORDER NO. 24. ORDER REFERRING BANKRUPTCY CASES AND PROCEEDINGS TO BANKRUPTCY JUDGES AND AUTHORIZING BANKRUPTCY APPEALS TO BE DECIDED BY THE NINTH CIRCUIT BANKRUPTCY APPELLATE PANEL

PART I: REFERRAL OF BANKRUPTCY CASES AND PROCEEDINGS

1.01   Cases and Proceedings Under Title 11, United States Code.

(a) This court hereby refers to the bankruptcy judges of this district all cases under title 11, and all proceedings arising under title 11 or arising in or related to cases under title 11.

(b) If a bankruptcy judge or district judge determines that entry of a final order or judgment by a bankruptcy judge would not be consistent with Article III of the United States Constitution in a particular proceeding referred under this order and determined to be a core matter, the bankruptcy judge shall, unless otherwise ordered by the district court, hear the proceeding and submit proposed findings of fact and conclusions of law to the district court made in compliance with Fed. R. Civ. P. 52(a)(1) in the form of findings and conclusions stated on the record or in an opinion or memorandum of decision.

(c) The district court may treat any order of the bankruptcy court as proposed findings of fact and conclusions of law in the event the district court concludes that the bankruptcy judge could not have entered a final order or judgment consistent with Article III of the United States Constitution.

1.02   Cases and Proceedings Under the Bankruptcy Act of 1898.   The bankruptcy judges of this district shall hear and determine cases and proceedings arising under the Bankruptcy Act of 1898, as amended, pursuant to sec. 403(a) of the Bankruptcy Reform Act of 1978.

PART II: BANKRUPTCY APPEALS

2.01   Bankruptcy Appellate Panel.

(a) Pursuant to 28 U.S.C. § 158(b)(2), this court hereby authorizes a bankruptcy appellate panel to hear and determine appeals from judgments, orders, and decrees entered by bankruptcy judges from this district, subject to the limitations set forth in subparagraphs (b)–(d).

(b) The bankruptcy appellate panel may hear and determine only those appeals in which all parties to the appeal consent thereto pursuant to paragraph 2.02 of this order.

(c) The bankruptcy appellate panel may hear and determine appeals from final judgments, orders, and decrees entered by bankruptcy judges and, with leave of the bankruptcy appellate panel, appeals from interlocutory orders and decrees entered by bankruptcy judges.

(d) The bankruptcy appellate panel may hear and determine appeals from judgments, orders, and decrees entered by bankruptcy judges after July 10, 1984, and appeals transferred to this court from the previous Ninth Circuit bankruptcy appellate panel by sec. 115(b) of The Bankruptcy Amendments and Federal Judgeship Act of 1984, P.L. 98–353. The bankruptcy appellate panel may not hear and determine appeals from judgments, orders, and decrees entered by bankruptcy judges between December 25, 1982, and July 10, 1984, under the Emergency Bankruptcy Rule of this district.

2.02 Form and Time of Consent. The consent of a party to allow an appeal to be heard and determined by the bankruptcy appellate panel shall be deemed to have been given unless written objection thereto is timely made in accordance with Paragraph 2 of the Amended Order Establishing and Continuing the Bankruptcy Appellate Panel of the Ninth Circuit, a copy of which is attached to this order and incorporated herein by reference.

2.03 Rules Governing Bankruptcy Appeals. Practice in such bankruptcy appeals as may come before this district court shall be governed by Part VIII of the Rules of Bankruptcy Procedure, except as provided in this order or in rules subsequently adopted by this district court.

PART III: EFFECTIVE DATE

This order shall become effective immediately and supersede all previous orders of this court regarding bankruptcy cases, proceedings, and appeals provided, however, that all prior actions of the bankruptcy appellate panel not inconsistent herewith are not affected by this order.

**UNITED STATES BANKRUPTCY APPELLATE PANEL
OF THE NINTH CIRCUIT**

**AMENDED ORDER CONTINUING
THE BANKRUPTCY APPELLATE PANEL
OF THE NINTH CIRCUIT**

**JUDICIAL COUNCIL OF THE NINTH CIRCUIT
AMENDED ORDER CONTINUING
THE BANKRUPTCY APPELLATE PANEL OF THE NINTH CIRCUIT**

1. **Continuing the Bankruptcy Appellate Panel Service.**

(a) Pursuant to 28 U.S.C. § 158(b)(1) as amended by the Bankruptcy Reform Act of 1994, the judicial council hereby reaffirms and continues a bankruptcy appellate panel service which shall provide panels to hear and determine appeals from judgments, orders and decrees entered by bankruptcy judges from districts within the Ninth Circuit.

(b) Panels of the bankruptcy appellate panel service may hear and determine appeals originating from districts that have authorized such appeals to be decided by the bankruptcy appellate panel service pursuant to 28 U.S.C. § 158(b)(6).

(c) All appeals originating from those districts shall be referred to bankruptcy appellate panels unless a party elects to have the appeal heard by the district court in the time and manner and form set forth in 28 U.S.C. § 158(c)(1) and in paragraph 3 below.

(d) Bankruptcy appellate panels may hear and determine appeals from final judgments, orders and decrees entered by bankruptcy judges and, with leave of bankruptcy appellate panels, appeals from interlocutory orders and decrees entered by bankruptcy judges.

(e) Bankruptcy appellate panels may hear and determine appeals from final judgments, orders, and decrees entered after the district court from which the appeal originates has issued an order referring bankruptcy cases and proceedings to bankruptcy judges pursuant to 28 U.S.C. § 157(a).

2. **Immediate Reference to Bankruptcy Appellate Panels.** Upon filing of the notice of appeal, all appeals are immediately referred to the bankruptcy appellate panel service.

3. **Election to District Court—Separate Written Statement Required.** A party desiring to transfer the hearing of an appeal from the bankruptcy appellate panel service to the district court pursuant to 28 U.S.C. § 158(c)(1) shall timely file a separate written statement of election expressly stating that the party elects to have the appeal transferred from the bankruptcy appellate panel service to the district court.

(a) *Appellant.* If the appellant wishes to make such an election, appellant must file a separate written statement of election with the clerk of the bankruptcy court at the time of filing the notice of appeal. Appellant shall submit the same number of copies of the statement of election as copies of the notice of appeal. See Bankruptcy Rule 8001(a). When such an election is made, the clerk of the bankruptcy court shall forthwith transfer the case to the district court. The clerk of the bankruptcy court shall give notice to all parties and the clerk of the bankruptcy appellate panels of the transfer at the same time and in the same manner as set forth for serving notice of the appeal in Bankruptcy Rule 8004.

(b) *All Other Parties.* In all appeals where appellant does not file an election, the clerk of the bankruptcy court shall forthwith transmit a copy of the notice of appeal to the clerk of the bankruptcy appellate panels. If any other party wishes to have the appeal heard by the district court, that party must, within thirty (30) days after service of the notice of appeal, file with the clerk of the bankruptcy appellate panels a written statement of election to transfer the appeal to the district court. Upon receipt of a timely statement of election filed under this section, the clerk of the bankruptcy appellate panels shall forthwith transfer the appeal to the appropriate district court and shall give notice of the transfer to the parties and the clerk of the bankruptcy court. Any question as to the timeliness of an election shall be referred by the clerk of the bankruptcy appellate panels to a bankruptcy appellate panel motions panel for determination.

4. Motions During Election Period. All motions relating to an appeal shall be filed with the bankruptcy appellate panel service unless the case has been transferred to a district court. The bankruptcy appellate panels may not dismiss or render a final disposition of an appeal within thirty (30) days from the date of service of the notice of appeal, but may otherwise fully consider and dispose of all motions.

5. Panels. Each appeal shall be heard and determined by a panel of three judges from among those appointed pursuant to paragraph 6, provided however that a bankruptcy judge shall not participate in an appeal originating in a district for which the judge is appointed or designated under 28 U.S.C. § 152. In addition, the panel may hear and determine appeals en banc under rules promulgated by and approved as provided in section 8 of this order.

6. Membership of Bankruptcy Appellate Panels. The bankruptcy appellate panel shall consist of seven members serving seven-year terms (subject to reappointment to one additional three-year term). The judicial council shall periodically examine the caseload of the bankruptcy appellate panel service to assess whether the number of bankruptcy judges serving should change. Appointment of regular and pro tem bankruptcy judges to service on the bankruptcy appellate panel shall be governed by regulations promulgated by the Judicial Council.

(a) When a three-judge panel cannot be formed from the judges designated under subparagraph (a) to hear a case because judges have recused themselves, are disqualified from hearing the case because it arises from their district, or are otherwise unable to participate, the Chief Judge of the Ninth Circuit may designate one or more other bankruptcy judge(s) from the circuit to hear the case.

(b) In order to provide assistance with the caseload or calendar relief, to constitute an en banc panel, or otherwise to assist the judges serving, or to afford other bankruptcy judges with the opportunity to serve on the bankruptcy appellate panels, the Chief Judge of the Ninth Circuit may designate from time to time one or more other bankruptcy judge(s) from the circuit to participate in one or more panel sittings.

7. Chief Judge. The members of the bankruptcy appellate panel service by majority vote shall select one of their number to serve as chief judge.

8. Rules of Procedure.

(a) Practice before the bankruptcy appellate panels shall be governed by Part VIII of the Federal Rules of Bankruptcy Procedure, except as provided in this order or by rule of the bankruptcy appellate panel service adopted under subparagraph (b).

(b) The bankruptcy appellate panel service may establish rules governing practice and procedure before bankruptcy appellate panels not inconsistent with the Federal Rules of Bankruptcy Procedure. Such rules shall be submitted to, and approved by, the Judicial Council of the Ninth Circuit.

9. Places of Holding Court. Bankruptcy appellate panels may conduct hearings at such times and places within the Ninth Circuit as it determines to be appropriate.

10. Clerk and Other Employees.

(a) *Clerk's Office.* The members of the bankruptcy appellate panel service shall select and hire the clerk of the bankruptcy appellate panel. The clerk of the bankruptcy appellate panel may select and hire staff attorneys and other necessary staff. The chief judge shall have appointment authority for the clerk, staff attorneys and other necessary staff. The members of the bankruptcy appellate panel shall determine the location of the principal office of the clerk.

(b) *Law Clerks.* Each judge on the bankruptcy appellate panel service shall have appointment authority to hire an additional law clerk.

11. Effective Date. This Order shall be effective as to all appeals originating in those bankruptcy cases that are filed after the effective date of this Order. For all appeals originating in those bankruptcy cases that were filed before October 22, 1994, the Judicial Council's prior Amended Order, as revised October 15, 1992, shall apply. This Order, insofar as just and practicable, shall apply to all appeals originating in those bankruptcy cases that were filed after the effective date of the Bankruptcy Reform Act of 1994, October 22, 1994, but before the date of this Order.

[Dated: February 22, 2016.]

GENERAL ORDER NO. 31. DEPOSIT AND INVESTMENT OF REGISTRY FUNDS

The Court's registry funds consist of monies deposited with the court for cash bail, appeal and other bonds, temporary restraining orders and preliminary injunctions, interpleader funds, restitution, and other monies ordered to be deposited into the court in a pending or closed case.

The Court's registry funds are pooled with registry funds from other courts and invested, via the Court Registry Investment System ("CRIS"), in short-term nonmarketable Government Account Series ("GAS") securities managed under the Federal Investments Program of the United States Department of the Treasury's Bureau of the Fiscal Service. These short-term GAS securities, each maturing within 100 days or less, are laddered within the Liquidity Fund to ensure that sufficient funds are available to meet the disbursement needs of participating courts. The Administrative Office of the U.S. Courts ("AO") manages CRIS.

The AO has established a Minors' Fund within CRIS to invest post-adjudication deposits held on behalf of minors until their age of majority, which is often longer than 100 days. The Minors' Fund provides liquidity but is comprised of a laddered portfolio of one-year securities maturing each month. Thus, the fund improves the match between investment holdings and the length of time each minor's funds remain invested, thereby capitalizing on higher-yielding securities. Accordingly, all funds held in the CRIS Liquidity Fund on behalf of minors were transferred to the Minors' Fund in March 2014.

The AO has also established a Disputed Ownership Fund ("DOF") pool within CRIS for courts to invest interpleader deposits filed under 28 U.S.C. § 1335 and eliminate the need for the appointment of a DOF administrator in each case to undertake the tax administration responsibilities needed to comply with the IRS reporting requirements for interpleader funds. This centralized approach for the tax administration of DOFs will be cost-effective to litigants and reduce risks related to managing the DOFs individually. A court order to deposit funds into the DOF is required for interpleader cases filed under 28 U.S.C. § 1335.

I. Receipt of Funds

A. No money shall be sent to the Court or its officers for deposit in CRIS without a court order signed by the presiding judge in the case or proceeding.

B. Unless provided for elsewhere in this Order, all monies, including cash bail, appeal and other bonds, temporary restraining orders and preliminary injunctions, and interpleader funds ordered to be paid to the Court or received by its officers in any case pending or closed, shall be deposited in the Court's registry fund through CRIS with the Treasurer of the United States in the name and to the credit of this Court, pursuant to 28 U.S.C. § 2041.

C. The party making the deposit or transferring funds to CRIS shall serve the order authorizing the deposit or transfer on the Clerk of Court.

D. Restitution monies shall be deposited in the court's registry only by court order and shall be held there until the court orders them distributed, together with interest earned, to the recipients named in the order.

II. Investment of Registry Funds

A. When, by order of the Court, funds on deposit with the Court are to be placed in some form of interest-bearing account or invested in a court-approved, interest-bearing instrument in accordance with Rule 67 of the Federal Rules of Civil Procedure, CRIS, administered by the AO under 28 U.S.C. § 2045, shall be the only investment mechanism authorized.

B. Interpleader funds deposited under 28 U.S.C. § 1335 meet the IRS definition of a DOF, a taxable entity that requires tax administration. Interpleader funds shall be deposited in the DOF established within the CRIS and administered by the AO, which shall be responsible for meeting all DOF tax administration requirements. A court order granting motion for interpleader deposits under 28 U.S.C. § 1335 must be accompanied with the deposit in order for the funds to be deposited into the DOF.

C. The Director of the AO is designated as custodian for all CRIS funds. The Director or the Director's designee shall perform the duties of custodian. Funds held in the CRIS remain subject to the control and jurisdiction of the Court.

D. Money from each case deposited in CRIS, with the exception of funds held on behalf of minors and interpleader funds, shall be held in the Liquidity Fund.

E. Post–adjudication deposits held on behalf of minors until their age of majority will be deposited into the Minors' Fund. Estimated withdrawal dates are required for the funds to be deposited into the Minors' Fund.

F. An account for each case will be established in CRIS bearing the name of the case that gave rise to the investment in the fund. Income generated from fund investments will be distributed to each case based on the ratio each account's principal and earnings has to the aggregate principal and income total in either the Liquidity or Minors' Fund after the CRIS fee has been applied. Reports showing the interest earned and the principal amounts contributed in each case are available from the FedInvest/CMS application to litigants and/or their counsel.

G. For each interpleader case, an account will be established in the CRIS DOF, titled in the name of the case giving rise to the deposit invested in the fund. Income generated from fund investments will be distributed to each case after the DOF fee has been applied and tax withholdings have been deducted from the fund. Reports showing the interest earned and the principal amounts contributed in each case will be available through the FedInvest/CMS application for each court participating in the CRIS and made available to litigants and/or their counsel. On appointment of an administrator authorized to incur expenses on behalf of the DOF in a case, the case DOF funds should be transferred to another investment account as directed by court order.

III. Fees and Taxes

A. The Director of the AO, as custodian, is authorized and directed by this Order to deduct the CRIS fee of an annualized 10 basis points on assets on deposit for all CRIS funds, excluding the case funds held in the DOF, for the management of investments in the CRIS. According to the Court's Miscellaneous Fee Schedule, the CRIS fee is assessed from interest earnings to the pool before a pro rata distribution of earnings is made to court cases.

B. The Director of the AO, as custodian, is authorized and directed by this Order to deduct the DOF fee of an annualized 20 basis points on assets on deposit in the DOF for management of investments and tax administration. According to the Court's Miscellaneous Fee Schedule, the DOF fee is assessed from interest earnings to the pool before a pro rata distribution of earnings is made to court cases. The custodian is further authorized and directed by this Order to withhold and pay federal taxes due on behalf of the DOF.

[Dated: October 15, 2019.]

GENERAL ORDER NO. 32. MODIFICATION OF PROBATION SUPERVISED RELEASE CONDITIONS FOR PLACEMENT IN A COMMUNITY TREATMENT CENTER

In 1990, this General Order was enacted, authorizing the Probation Office of this Court to place a probationer or supervised releasee (hereinafter, the "probationer") arrested for alleged violations of probation or supervised release in a community treatment center (also known as a halfway house) for a term not to exceed five court days or until further order of the Court. The stated reason for the enactment of this General Order was that "the probation officer finds it difficult to arrange placement through the Bureau of Prisons, who [sic] is given the responsibility for payment of all Public Law placements."

Federal Rule of Criminal Procedure 32.1(a) provides that "[a] person held in custody for violating probation or supervised release must be taken without unnecessary delay before a magistrate judge" for, among other things, a determination whether to release or detain the probationer pending further proceedings pursuant to 18 U.S.C. § 3143. The magistrate judge sometimes orders the probationer "released" to a community treatment center.

An Administrative Office of the United States Courts memorandum dated May 1, 1991 ("Probation Revocation Issues") governs the funding procedures for "residential placement" of a probationer pending probation revocation proceedings, specifying two distinct scenarios:

(a) "If the judicial officer modifies the probation order to include residential placement as a condition of supervision and sets a limit not to exceed 120 days, the Bureau of Prisons provides funding"; and

(b) "If the judicial officer orders the pretrial release of an alleged probation violator pending a violation hearing . . . funding . . . will be provided by the [P]retrial [S]ervices [O]ffice for a period not to exceed 30 days."

Under the second scenario—funding provided by the Pretrial Services Office—the Probation Office retains responsibility under the May 1, 1991 memorandum for supervision of the probationer.

The large number of revocation proceedings in which release to a community treatment center is ordered by the criminal duty magistrate judge in accordance with the above-cited authorities has created a growing budgetary burden for the Pretrial Services Office. In order to address this concern, the Court now orders the following additional procedure to apply in all cases in which a magistrate judge orders a probationer released to a community treatment center pending a violation hearing:

No later than three days after release of the probationer to a community treatment facility pending a violation hearing, the Probation Office will deliver to the chambers of the sentencing judge (or, in the absence of the sentencing judge, the general duty judge), a request, accompanied by a proposed order, to modify the probation order to include residential placement as a condition of supervision for no more than 120 days. Upon entry of the sentencing judge or duty judge's order thus modifying the probation order, the Probation Office will promptly notify the Pretrial Services Office and the Bureau of Prisons that responsibility for funding the probationer's residential placement has been transferred to the Bureau of Prisons.

[Dated: September 19, 2012.]

GENERAL ORDER NO. 40. PROHIBITION OF BIAS

Prologue. The Court is committed to ensuring that all forms of bias and prejudice are eliminated from the practice of law in our district. Accordingly, the Court enacts the following General Order and shall amend its local rules to implement the policy set forth herein. It should be noted that the General Order is intended to govern the conduct of attorneys and litigants since existing law already places a duty of fair treatment on judges and court employees. While the enforcement procedures set forth in paragraphs (2) through (6) apply only to attorneys, paragraph (1) calls upon all participants involved in court business to treat all individuals with respect and courtesy.

Duties and Procedures.

(1) The practice of law before the United States District Court for the Northern District of California must be free from prejudice and bias in any form. Treatment free of bias must be accorded all other attorneys, litigants, judicial officers, courtroom jurors or support personnel. The duty to exercise non-biased behavior includes the responsibility to avoid comment or behavior manifesting prejudice or bias toward another. This duty is owed by all attorneys, judges, judicial officers and court personnel in connection with cases pending before the district court.

(2) The purpose of the facilitation process set forth herein shall be principally to promote understanding and education through voluntary peer review of biased behavior. To implement the policy set forth in paragraph (1), the Court shall appoint a committee of attorneys practicing in the Northern District to constitute the Advisory Committee on Professional Conduct ("the Committee"). The roster of the Committee shall remain on file with the Clerk of the Court. It shall be the responsibility of the Committee, serving at the discretion of the Court as an advisory adjunct, to hear complaints of biased behavior and to provide a forum for the voluntary resolution of conflicts of this nature.

(3) Upon being directly notified of an alleged violation of paragraph (1) or upon referral from the Court, the chair of the Committee shall, after consultation with the complaining party, appoint a member of the Committee or other appropriate, neutral facilitator who shall provide the parties a copy of this rule, and then attempt to facilitate a resolution of the matter. When deemed necessary in a particular case by the Committee, the chair of the Committee may appoint a facilitator who is not on the roster. Participation by the parties shall be voluntary, but the Court, by this rule, encourages participation. All matters that are the subject of facilitation, including the names of the parties, shall remain absolutely confidential.

(4) Attorneys are encouraged to resolve alleged violations of paragraph (1) informally, without resort to the processes set forth herein. If attempts at informal resolution fail or would be inappropriate, an alleged violation of paragraph (1) may be raised through: a) referral to the Committee; or b) formal presentation to the Court. When the matter has been presented to the Court, the Court has discretion to send the matter to the Committee for facilitation. However, nothing in this rule shall affect the Court's inherent power to use its processes to ensure that the practice of law before the Court is free from bias. Where a Judge or Magistrate Judge is alleged to have engaged in biased behavior, enforcement of paragraph (1) shall be made with reference to Title 28 U.S.C. § 372(c) and to the Rules of the Judicial Council of the Ninth Circuit Governing Complaints of Judicial Misconduct or Disability.

(5) All communications by the parties and witnesses pursuant to an investigation under this rule shall be deemed confidential. Unless required by law, the Committee shall not retain written records of the facilitation processes. However, the Committee may collect data on types of alleged violations or underlying anecdotes that might be useful in educational programs, provided that the identities of participants shall not be disclosed.

(6) Notwithstanding the foregoing, any violation of paragraph (1) committed in the presence of the Court should be addressed promptly by the Court. Any violation, whether or not committed in the presence of the Court (such as misconduct in the presence of witnesses or jurors), that affects the integrity of the judicial process should be promptly raised with the Court.

[Dated: January 10, 1995.]

GENERAL ORDER NO. 42. LIMITATIONS ON REFERRALS OF MATTERS TO MAGISTRATE JUDGES

It is the policy of the court to promote the efficient utilization of magistrate judges and to avoid the unnecessary duplication of judicial action. Good cause appearing,

IT IS HEREBY ORDERED that the following matters shall not be referred to a magistrate judge:

1. Civil pretrial matters that are dispositive of a claim or defense and require a de novo review by a district judge under Rule 72(b), F.R.Civ.P. unless: (a) the parties consent to final disposition of the matter by a magistrate judge pursuant to Rule 73, F.R.Civ.P.; or (b) the matter requires an evidentiary hearing which can be conducted by a magistrate judge without being repeated before a district judge. Case dispositive matters include motions for summary judgment, for judgment on the pleadings, for injunctive relief, to dismiss for failure to state a claim upon which relief can be granted, to dismiss or permit maintenance of a class action, and to involuntarily dismiss an action. See 28 U.S.C. § 636(b)(1)(A);

2. Prisoner petitions and habeas corpus cases unless: (a) the parties consent to final disposition of the matter by a magistrate judge pursuant to Rule 73, F.R.Civ.P.; or (b) the matter is not a capital habeas case and requires an evidentiary hearing which can be conducted by a magistrate judge without being repeated before a district judge;

3. Case dispositive matters in criminal felony cases including motions to dismiss an indictment or information made by a defendant or to suppress evidence;

4. Acceptance of guilty pleas of a defendant in a criminal felony case pursuant to Rule 11, F.R.Crim.P. unless there are exceptional circumstances that warrant referral; and

5. Claim Construction hearings and determinations in patent infringement cases pursuant to Patent Local Rule 4–6, unless the parties consent to disposition by a magistrate judge pursuant to Rule 73, F.R.Civ.P.

Exceptions to this Order in individual cases or in emergency circumstances may be granted by the Executive Committee.

[Dated: January 16, 2001.]

GENERAL ORDER NO. 43. PROCEDURES—EXECUTION SCHEDULED WITHIN SEVEN DAYS

I. PURPOSE

The purpose of this General Order is to ensure prompt, orderly processing of death penalty-related cases and requests for stays filed when an execution is imminent. To this end, it allocates and centralizes responsibility for making the initial decisions required for proper filing and assignment of these cases. It also provides that these decisions shall conform to existing local rules, general orders and the Assignment Plan, except as specifically otherwise noted in this order.

II. PROCEDURES

A. Application. The procedures set forth in this General Order shall be in effect during the seven days preceding a scheduled execution of any California state inmate under sentence of death. While they are in effect, the procedures apply to filings by or on behalf of that inmate.

B. Duties of the Clerk of Court.

1. The Clerk shall at all times maintain a record of all filings in this Court by California inmates sentenced to death that seek *habeas corpus* or civil rights relief from the execution of the sentence of death, showing the name of the petitioner, the date of each filing and the Judge to whom the cases are assigned.

2. When an execution is scheduled, the Clerk shall determine whether the condemned inmate has previously filed an action that seeks *habeas corpus* or civil rights relief from the execution of the sentence of death in this or any other district court in California. If so, the Clerk shall assist the San Francisco General Duty Judge ("the General Duty Judge") in making arrangements so that the Judge assigned the prior case will be immediately available to decide any emergency stay requests based on any new filing that may be assigned or transferred to that Judge pursuant to this General Order.

3. The San Francisco Office of the Clerk of Court shall remain open for telephone and filing access, on an emergency basis, after the close of normal business hours on the last court day before a scheduled execution, until notice is received that: the execution has gone forward; or, the execution is stayed and all applications to vacate the stay have been denied; or, the execution warrant has expired.

4. During the time described in B.3. above, the Clerk shall designate a person or persons to receive the filings on an emergency basis and make the required telephone calls, and a person or persons to serve as messenger to deliver papers to and from the General Duty Judge, the assigned Judge, and the Court of Appeals. The Clerk shall maintain 24-hour telephone and facsimile numbers for: the Judge assigned to any previous action that seeks *habeas corpus* or civil rights relief from the execution of the sentence of death filed by the inmate whose execution is scheduled, the Office of the Clerk and Motions Panel of the Ninth Circuit Court of Appeals, the Warden of San Quentin Prison and the United States Supreme Court staff attorney responsible for coordinating emergency applications in capital cases.

5. Immediately upon receipt of papers presented for filing that request a stay of execution the Clerk shall deliver the papers to the General Duty Judge, and shall notify the Judge assigned to that inmate's previous related filings, if any.

6. If the General Duty Judge is unavailable within one hour after the Clerk attempts to contact him or her, or not available immediately if the execution is scheduled within the hour, the Clerk shall contact the Chief Judge immediately for designation of a Duty Judge. If the Chief Judge is not available, the Clerk shall call each active judge of the court in order of seniority, and then each senior judge, until an available Judge is located. That Judge will act as General Duty Judge for the purposes of this order.

C. Duties of the General Duty Judge.

1. During the seven days preceding a scheduled execution, the General Duty Judge shall be immediately available during normal business hours. After the close of normal business hours on the last court day before a scheduled execution, the General Duty Judge shall be in the Bay Area and immediately available by telephone until notice is received that: the execution has gone forward; or, the execution is stayed and all applications to vacate the stay have been denied; or, the execution warrant has expired. The Clerk shall provide a cellular telephone and facsimile machine, if needed, to the General Duty Judge.

2. The General Duty Judge shall act as the decision-maker in applying the rules and procedures of the court. Before the inmate's papers requesting a stay of execution are filed, the General Duty Judge shall decide, among other things, whether the inmate has previously filed in this court an action that seeks *habeas corpus* or civil rights relief from the execution of the sentence of death, and whether the inmate has previously sought *habeas* relief in another district court. The General Duty Judge shall then instruct the Clerk how the case shall be assigned, in accordance with subsection C.3. below.

3. Local court rules and the Assignment Plan shall apply to the assignment of all cases where an emergency stay of execution is requested, except as set forth in this order.

a. If the inmate has previously filed in this court an action that seeks *habeas corpus* relief from the conviction and sentence of death, the new filing shall be assigned to the Judge assigned to the prior petition. If the inmate has not previously filed in this court a *habeas corpus* petition seeking relief from the conviction and sentence of death but has previously filed an action that seeks civil rights relief from the execution of the sentence of death, the case shall be assigned to the Judge assigned to the prior civil rights proceeding.

b. If the inmate has previously sought habeas corpus relief from the conviction and sentence of death in another district court, the General Duty Judge shall transfer any new *habeas* filing seeking such relief to that district court. The Clerk shall assign any such case a miscellaneous case number and immediately transmit a copy of the transfer order by facsimile to the other district.

c. If the case is not assigned or transferred pursuant to C.3.a. or b. above, or if the Judge of this Court who had the prior case or petition is no longer sitting or has taken senior status and elected not to hear death-penalty-related cases, the Clerk shall assign the case randomly either from the Capital *Habeas Corpus* category if it falls within that category or from the Prisoner Petitions case category. Consistent with the Court's Assignment Plan, cases assigned pursuant to this subparagraph may not be assigned to a newly-appointed judge until after that judge has received his or her first capital *habeas corpus* assignment.

d. If an inmate files a Notice of Related Case seeking to relate the newly filed case to another case not filed by that inmate, the procedures of Local Rule 3–12(e) shall be followed, except that the Notice of Related Case shall be submitted immediately to the Judge assigned to the earliest filed case, without waiting for support or opposition. If the Clerk cannot contact that Judge to obtain an immediate ruling on the related case request within one hour of the filing of the Notice of Related Case, or immediately if the execution is scheduled within the hour, the request to relate the cases shall be deemed denied without prejudice.

e. Notwithstanding the above, the General Duty Judge shall have the power to assign any patently frivolous execution-related filing by or on behalf of the prisoner to himself or herself as a miscellaneous filing, and to dismiss such filing summarily as provided by law.

4. The Clerk shall attempt to reach the Judge to whom the case should be assigned pursuant to C.3.a., c. or d. above. If the Clerk cannot contact that Judge within one hour of the filing of the request for the stay of execution, or immediately if the execution is scheduled within the hour, the General Duty Judge shall decide the request for the stay.

5. The regularly assigned General Duty Judge and Chief Judge may transfer the duties of the General Duty Judge to another Judge of the Court.

[Dated: July 18, 2000.]

GENERAL ORDER NO. 44. ASSIGNMENT PLAN

A. Purpose. This plan is adopted pursuant to 28 U.S.C. § 137 and Civil Local Rule 3–3(a). The purpose of the plan is to:

1. Provide an equitable system for a proportional division of the caseload among the district and magistrate judges of the court;

2. Ensure that cases are randomly and blindly assigned, except as otherwise provided herein to promote efficient case management;

3. Provide for necessary adjustments to caseload assignments; and

4. Provide a basis for monitoring the operation of the case assignment system.

B. Administration. The Executive Committee shall have the power to make and review all orders of assignment and reassignment consistent with this plan. As provided in Civil L.R. 77–2(e), the Clerk, when directed by the committee or as specifically provided for in this plan, may sign orders on behalf of the Executive Committee.

C. Case Numbers. Each case commenced in or transferred to the court pursuant to Civil L.R. 3–2 shall be assigned a case number by the Clerk upon filing. A separate sequence of case numbers shall be maintained for criminal and civil cases. Case numbers shall conform to the format approved by the Administrative Office of the United States Courts.

D. Assignment of Cases.

1. Unless otherwise required by the Executive Committee, cases shall be assigned by the Clerk to the judges holding chambers in the courthouse or courthouses serving the county in which the action arises.

2. Cases shall be assigned blindly and at random by the Clerk by means of an automated system approved by the judges of the court. Such system will be designed to accomplish the following:

   a. Proportionate, random and blind assignment of cases;

   b. Except as set forth in paragraphs (D)(4) through (D)(7), an approximately equal distribution among the active judges of the court of newly filed civil and criminal cases within each of the case categories established by the court

   c. A high level of security so as to reasonably avoid prediction of the results of any case assignment;

   d. A system of credits and debits to adjust for reassignments of cases among and between judges;

   e. A record of all assignments and reassignments made.

3. Notwithstanding any other provision of the Assignment Plan, the Clerk shall maintain a district-wide system of assignment for prisoner petitions (including death penalty habeas corpus), bankruptcy, intellectual property rights, Social Security, federal tax suits, antitrust and securities class actions. Venue for cases in these categories shall be proper in any courthouse in this District. These cases shall not be reassigned on the basis of intra-district venue.

4. Notwithstanding any other provision of the Assignment Plan, the Clerk shall assign cases transferred to this District pursuant to Federal Rule of Criminal Procedure 20 in the following manner. Assignment of Rule 20 cases shall be made prior to execution of a consent to transfer in the manner set forth in Criminal L.R. 20–1. Any subsequent Rule 20 proceeding involving the same defendant and arising out of the same or superseding charges shall be deemed to be a related case and shall be assigned to the originally assigned judge.

5. Notwithstanding any other provision of the Assignment Plan, the Clerk shall assign any non-capital habeas petition filed by a prisoner to the same judge who was assigned any previous petitions filed by or on behalf of that prisoner.

6. Notwithstanding any other provision of the Assignment Plan, the Clerk shall assign any non-habeas civil complaint filed by a prisoner within five (5) years after the filing of the first civil complaint by that party to the same judge to whom the first such complaint was assigned. After five (5) years, the next new civil complaint filed by that prisoner shall be assigned to a different judge, in accordance with paragraph (D)(2) above, who shall then be assigned that prisoner's civil filings for the next five (5) years. Thereafter, a different judge shall be assigned for each subsequent five-year period.

7. Notwithstanding any other provision of the assignment plan, the Clerk shall assign a bankruptcy matter to the same judge who was assigned any previously filed bankruptcy matter arising from the same case in the United States Bankruptcy Court.

E.   Assignment of Cases to Magistrate Judges.

1.   The full-time magistrate judges of this District shall be included in the civil case assignment system in the same manner as active district judges, except for capital habeas corpus petitions, securities class actions, and bankruptcy appeals or bankruptcy withdrawal of reference cases. With respect to such assignments, the following shall apply:

a.   In cases assigned at filing to a magistrate judge, the magistrate judge shall conduct all proceedings including a jury or bench trial and shall order the entry of a final judgment upon the written consent of all parties in the case in accordance with 28 U.S.C. § 636(c) and Fed. R. Civ. P. 73.

b.   In all cases assigned at filing to a magistrate judge the Clerk shall provide all parties with a copy of the forms adopted by the court for "Notice of Assignment of Case To A United States Magistrate Judge for Trial." The form shall indicate that upon written consent of the parties the magistrate judges of this District have been designated to conduct any and all proceedings in a civil case, including a jury or nonjury trial and order the entry of a final judgment. Prior to the magistrate judge taking any dispositive action in the case, the Clerk shall obtain from the parties written consent to the jurisdiction of the magistrate judge in accordance with 28 U.S.C. § 636(c) and Fed. R. Civ. P. 73.

c.   If a party declines to consent to a United States magistrate judge, the Clerk shall reassign the case to a district judge on a random basis or in accordance with paragraphs (D)(5) and (D)(6), if applicable.

2.   Upon filing, the following will be assigned to a magistrate judge for all pretrial proceedings. When the case is ready for trial, upon consent of the parties, it will be retained by the magistrate judge for trial. If all parties do not so consent, the Clerk will randomly assign the case to a district judge in the division where the case is pending.

a.   All actions filed by the United States to recover on a claim for a debt;

b.   Pre-judgment or post-judgment applications by the United States under the Federal Debt Collection Procedures Act.

3.   Upon filing, unless exempted by Local Rule, order of a judge of this court, or other provision of this general order, all civil miscellaneous matters will be randomly assigned in the first instance to a magistrate judge who will either resolve the matter or, if necessary, prepare a report and recommendation and request assignment of the matter to the district judge who was the general duty judge on the date the miscellaneous matter was filed. Any objections to the magistrate judge's order or report and recommendation will be resolved by that district judge. See Fed. R. Civ. P. 72. Matters from the Eureka division shall be reassigned, as necessary, to the general duty judge.

4.   For cases reassigned to a magistrate judge subsequent to initial case assignment (e.g. at a case management conference), the parties may consent to the assignment of a magistrate judge sitting in any division.

[Dated: January 1, 2018.]

GENERAL ORDER NO. 47.   EXECUTIVE COMMITTEE

A.   Introduction. This General Order establishes an Executive Committee as a Standing Committee of the Court. As the established policy of this Court is that all policy decisions are made by the Court as a whole, meetings of the Executive Committee shall not be a substitute for the regular monthly meetings of the Court, and any judge may have an item placed on the agenda for discussion at a regular monthly meeting.

B.   Membership. The Executive Committee of the Court shall be a Standing Committee of the United States District Court for the Northern District of California. The Executive Committee shall consist of five voting members and two *ex officio* members as follows:

1.   The Chief Judge, who will serve as Chair of the Executive Committee;

2.   The Judge designated as successor Chief Judge pursuant to 28 U.S.C. § 136(e);

3.   A Judge sitting in the San Francisco Courthouse, based upon active judge seniority;

4.   A Judge sitting in the Oakland Courthouse, based on active judge seniority; and

5.   A Judge sitting in the San Jose Courthouse based on active judge seniority.

6. An invitation shall be extended to the immediate Past Chief Judge of the Court and to the Chief Magistrate Judge to serve *ex officio* without vote.

C. Term. Each member (except *ex officio*) shall serve for a period of three years. Members may serve no more than one consecutive three-year term. If any of the three judges selected on the basis of seniority is unable to serve out his or her term, the judge sitting in that courthouse who is next in seniority among the active judges shall become a member. If a judge assumes an unexpired term vacated by another judge, the assuming judge shall serve for three years starting on the day following the last day of service of the judge who did not complete his or her service.

D. Meetings. Executive Committee meetings shall be called as the Chief Judge deems appropriate or at the request of any member of the Committee. Three voting members of the Committee shall constitute a quorum.

E. Authority, Duties and Responsibilities. The Executive Committee shall have the following authority, duties and responsibilities:

1. To act for the Court between regular monthly meetings of the Court on matters needing attention before the next regular monthly meeting;

2. To act as the Budget Committee;

3. To act as the Assignment Committee; and

4. To assist the Chief Judge in such matters as the Chief or the Court may request.

F. Review. Any action taken by the Executive Committee shall be placed on the agenda of the next regular monthly meeting for review by the Court.

[Dated: February 21, 2012.]

GENERAL ORDER NO. 50. CRIMINAL JUSTICE ACT PROCEDURES FOR ATTORNEY COMPENSATION AND FUNDING FOR NEEDED SERVICES

I. VOUCHER SUBMISSIONS AND APPROVAL

A. Introduction. The following policies and procedures are applicable to representations for attorneys appointed under the Criminal Justice Act, 18 U.S.C. § 3006A (referred to herein as the "CJA"), death-eligible and capital habeas representations for attorneys appointed under 18 U.S.C. § 3005 or § 3599(a), and payment for investigative, expert and other services.

Claims and payments shall be made in accordance with the provisions as set forth herein, Volume 7 of the Guide to Judiciary Policy, the CJA Plan of the United States District Court for the Northern District of California (General Order 2, referred to herein as the "Plan"), the fiscal policies of the Administrative Office of the United States Courts, the policies of the Ninth Circuit Judicial Council, the CJA Policy Manual for the Northern District of California, and any other guidelines that may be implemented by the CJA Administration Committee.

Questions about this general order should be directed to the Court's CJA Unit (cja@cand.uscourts. gov).

B. Court Compensation Policies.

1. Providing fair compensation to appointed counsel is a critical component of the administration of justice. CJA panel attorneys must be compensated for time expended in court and time reasonably expended out of court and reimbursed for expenses reasonably incurred. In determining the reasonableness of out-of-court time, the court must consider three factors:

a. whether the work was performed;

b. whether the work performed was a reasonable means of achieving the client's aims in the litigation; and

c. whether the time spent to accomplish that work was reasonable.

2. Voucher reductions will be limited to mathematical errors; instances in which work billed was not compensable, undertaken, or completed; and instances in which the hours billed clearly exceed what was reasonably required to complete the task.

3. Vouchers and funding requests for service providers and other litigation costs will not be delayed or reduced to lessen Defender Services program costs in response to adverse financial circumstances.

4. Absent extraordinary circumstances, the Court will act on compensation claims within 30 days of submission.

5. Payment vouchers and amounts paid to counsel or service providers will not be disclosed except as required by law or CJA Guidelines.

C. Claim Submission.

1. Claims for compensation must be submitted on the appropriate CJA form through the Court's eVoucher system. Information regarding eVoucher is available at cand.uscourts.gov/cja/evoucher. The following forms are only available through eVoucher:

> **CJA–20**—Attorney voucher in a criminal case or other representations including grand jury witness and supervised release violations
>
> **CJA–21**—Expert and service provider voucher in a criminal case or other representations including grand jury witness and supervised release violations
>
> **CJA–26**—Statement for a Compensation Claim in Excess of the Statutory Case Compensation Maximum
>
> **CJA–30**—Attorney voucher in a capital (death-eligible) case or capital habeas representation.[1]
>
> **CJA–31**—Expert and service provider voucher in a capital (death-eligible) case or capital habeas representation.

All other forms referred to in this General Order can be found at cand.uscourts.gov/cja/forms.

2. Claims for compensation will be submitted no later than 60 days after final disposition of the case, unless good cause is shown.

D. Delegated Authority for Claim Approval. This Court has delegated to the CJA Supervising Attorney the authority to approve vouchers and authorize payment as follows:

1. Vouchers for attorney services;

2. Vouchers for interpreters, investigators, and paralegals requesting payment for less than $2,500 or that are within pre-authorized funding limits in all felony, misdemeanor, non-capital habeas, and other criminal proceedings;

3. Vouchers for all other service providers requesting payment under $800 or that are within funding limits pre-authorized by the assigned Judge in felony, misdemeanor, non-capital habeas, and other criminal proceedings;

4. Vouchers for attorneys and service providers in capital habeas cases in which the expenditures were previously authorized in a budget that was approved by the assigned Judge; and

5. Vouchers for transcript services, interpreter services, and routine travel.

The Court retains ultimate review and approval authority.

E. Interim Vouchers. Prior to the completion of the case, any attorney providing representation under the CJA may submit interim vouchers for payment of fees and reimbursement of allowable expenses

Interim vouchers should be submitted every 60 days unless the voucher amount is less than $1,400.

F. Final Vouchers.

1. For completed cases and cases in which the services of the CJA attorney have been terminated for any reason, vouchers must be submitted no later than 60 days after the attorney ceases representation without regard to the amount of the claim or the date of any previously submitted interim voucher.

2. Attorneys must provide good cause to justify payment of any voucher submitted more than 60 days after representation is completed.

G. Statutory Maximums. When compensation exceeds, or is expected to exceed, the statutory maximums permitted under 18 U.S.C. § 3006A(d)(3), the attorney must submit a CJA–26 through eVoucher showing why payment in excess of the statutory maximum is necessary to provide fair compensation to the attorney.

H. Case Budgeting.

1. *Budget Forms:* Budgets should be submitted every 6 months and must be submitted through the eVoucher system as attachments to a CJA–26 or BUDGETAUTH. All budget forms are available at cand.uscourts.gov/cja/forms.

2. Budgets are required in the following cases:

a. Complex Cases: Any case in which the case maximum is expected to exceed 300 hours is considered a complex case. The attorney is required to complete and submit a Confidential Ex Parte Application for CJA Funds in a Complex Case.

b. Capital Cases: Any case where the defendant is "death-eligible" is considered a capital case. The Lead Attorney is required to complete and submit a Capital Case Funding Authorization.

c. Capital Habeas Cases: Lead Attorney is required to submit a budget at each phase of the representation. Lead counsel is required to complete and submit a:

1. Capital Habeas Funding Application; and

2. Capital Habeas Confidential Case Evaluation.

I. Details Required in Attorney Vouchers. Without violating the Canons of Ethics or disclosing attorney work product, attorneys must include sufficient detail to permit meaningful review. If a voucher contains insufficient detail for auditing purposes, it will be returned to the attorney to resubmit with sufficient detail. To provide sufficient detail, an attorney must:

1. Delineate discrete services. Separate, unrelated services may not be "bundled" in one entry.

2. Describe witness interviews with sufficient information to distinguish between individuals, e.g. "Witness 1" or "W1" or "witness A.K.".

3. Identify the participants in telephone conversation or conferences and general topics discussed.

4. Specify topics researched and the pleadings filed as a result of the research by ECF docket number.

5. List the type of documents, number of pages reviewed, and Bates numbers when review exceeds one hour. (e.g. FBI 302s, 77 pages SC300–377).

J. Voucher Review Procedure. The CJA Department will perform an initial review for accuracy and compensability under the CJA Guidelines and Ninth Circuit CJA Policies and Procedures. In determining whether services provided by counsel are compensable, the guidelines for ancillary appointment of counsel in Section IV.A.3 of General Order 2, the Criminal Justice Act Plan, may be considered. After this review, vouchers will be forwarded for consideration and action by the presiding judge or his or her designee, who will review claims for overall reasonableness.

K. Voucher Reductions and Independent Review Procedures.

1. *Reductions* Claims for compensation under the CJA will not be reduced without affording counsel notice and an opportunity to be heard.

a. When contemplating a voucher reduction, the CJA Department will notify CJA counsel of any proposed reduction and offer counsel the opportunity to justify the submission.

b. If counsel indicates that the reduction is not contested, or if no response is received within ten days, the CJA Department will process the reduced voucher.

c. If counsel responds and provides information justifying the claimed time or expense, the voucher will be approved as submitted.

2. *Independent Review Procedures.*

a. Judicial Approval: The CJA Supervising Attorney must obtain the approval of the assigned Judge for a proposed voucher reduction greater than $375.

b. Fee Review Committee: A voucher reduction in excess of $375 may be reviewed by the Fee Review Committee (FRC) at the request of either the assigned Judge or the attorney. The attorney must submit the request for review in writing to the CJA Supervising Attorney. The assigned Judge will give significant weight to the FRC's recommendation in making a final determination. Information regarding the Fee Review Committee can be found at cand.uscourts.gov/cja/feereview.

L. No Receipt of Other Payment. Appointed counsel may not require, request, or accept any payment or promise of payment or any other valuable consideration for representation under the CJA, unless such payment is approved by order of the Court.

II. Investigative, Expert, and Other Services; Litigation Expenses

Counsel for a person financially unable to obtain investigative, expert, or other services necessary for an adequate defense may request CJA funding in an *ex parte* application to the Court as provided in 18 U.S.C. § 3006A(e)(1), regardless of whether counsel is appointed under the CJA. Upon finding that the services are necessary, and that the person is financially unable to obtain them, the presiding judge or designee must authorize the funding.

Cost Considerations. CJA counsel are expected to use lower-cost service providers such as investigators or paralegals to undertake tasks not requiring attorney expertise. In multi-defendant cases with multiple CJA attorneys, counsel must make all reasonable efforts to coordinate with each other to reduce costs, including coordinating and sharing discovery and utilizing shared investigators and other services to the extent possible.

Attorneys are responsible for obtaining qualified experts and service providers and for conducting careful review of experts' and service providers' bills to assure that the charges are accurate and reasonable and that they contain sufficient detail.

Delegation. This Court has delegated to the CJA Supervising Attorney the authority to approve requests for associates, paralegals, interpreters, and investigators.

A. Requests for Services.

1. *Applications.* To request funds for investigative, expert, and other services, an attorney must submit a Funding Request by email to the CJA Unit (cja@cand.uscourts.gov). The Funding Request must provide sufficient detail to demonstrate that the service is reasonably necessary, the hourly rate charged by the provider, and that the estimated number of hours needed to complete the work is reasonable. The request must not be disclosed except with the consent of the person represented or as required by law or CJA Guidelines.

2. *Obtaining Services Without Prior Request.* Attorneys may obtain investigative, expert or other services without prior authorization if necessary for adequate representation under the following circumstances:

    a. Interpreters, investigators, and paralegals: the total cost of services for each such provider may not exceed $2,500 plus the cost of expenses reasonably incurred.

    b. All other service providers: the total cost of services per case may not exceed $800 plus the costs of expenses reasonably incurred.

B. Nunc Pro Tunc Requests.
If an attorney obtains services without seeking prior approval or the service provider exceeds the specific terms of the funding authorization, as soon as possible the attorney must submit a Funding Request justifying the services, a request for *nunc pro tunc* authorization to the date services were first rendered, and a thorough explanation of why prior authorization could not have reasonably been obtained. *Nunc pro tunc* requests to compensate service providers will be considered and authorized only upon a showing of good cause, such as when a service not previously contemplated required immediate action. If the assigned Judge denies the request in whole or in part, the Court will not be liable for refusal to pay for services rendered without prior approval or in excess of authorized funds.

C. Payment to Experts and Service Providers.
A separate voucher must be created in eVoucher for each expert or service provider.

1. Paralegals, investigators, and mitigation specialists have access to eVoucher and are required to enter their time directly into the system.

2. All other experts and service providers must submit their invoices to the attorney.

3. Invoices should contain adequate detail of the services performed and include supporting documentation.

4. Each invoice for expert and service provider services must be accompanied by a Certificate of Service ("COS") verifying services invoiced.

5. The attorney is responsible for attaching the invoice, any documentation, and the COS on behalf of the expert or service provider to the voucher.

6. The attorney is responsible for reviewing and submitting the voucher on behalf of all service providers.

7. Interpreters must use the CJA Interpreter Invoice.

   D. Compliance. Counsel must comply with Judicial Conference policies set forth in CJA Guidelines, Ch. 3.

III. CJA DOCUMENTATION

   A. Confidentiality. All CJA documents are filed in the confidential CJA financial files maintained by the Clerk's Office. Documents maintained in the CJA financial files shall not be disclosed to the public except as provided by statute, by the Guide to Judiciary Policy, or by order of the Court. Accordingly, it is not necessary for the attorney to request sealing of CJA documents.

   B. Standardized Forms. Where the Administrative Office of the United States Courts provides standard forms, such forms shall be used in connection with all actions taken under the Plan and the provisions set forth herein.

[Dated: January 22, 2020.]

   1 Once a case is designated as capital, even if de-authorized, the attorney will use the CJA–30/CJA–31 throughout the representation.

GENERAL ORDER NO. 51. LOCAL RULES OF THE BANKRUPTCY COURT

   Pursuant to Fed.R.Bankr.P. 9029(a), the bankruptcy judges of this district, acting through a majority of their number, are hereby authorized to make and amend local rules governing practice and procedure in all cases and proceedings arising under the district court's bankruptcy jurisdiction, provided that the bankruptcy judges shall provide the chief judge of the district court with advance notice of the proposed adoption of any such rule or amendment sufficient to permit circulation, review, and comment by the judges of the district court, and provided further that the district court shall retain full authority to order that any proposed rule or amendment not take effect and to abrogate any such rule or amendment after it takes effect.

[Dated: January 16, 2001.]

GENERAL ORDER NO. 52. COLLATERAL FORFEITURE SCHEDULE

   Pursuant to Federal Rule of Criminal Procedure 58(d)(1) and Criminal Local Rule 58–3, IT IS ORDERED that effective January 1, 2010, the attached schedule* is adopted as the list of offenses for which collateral may be posted in the amounts fixed, by persons charged with those offenses who prefer to post and forfeit bail in lieu of appearing to answer a citation. It is further ORDERED that the attached schedule supersedes all previous schedules. The Clerk is ORDERED to disseminate a copy of this order and the revised schedule to each federal law enforcement agency within the District.

[Dated: December 22, 2009.]

   * For the most current Collateral Forfeiture Schedule, please contact the Clerk's Office.

GENERAL ORDER NO. 55. BOND EXONERATION AND
THE POSTING AND RETURN OF PROPERTY
I. Purpose

   The purpose of this General Order is to ensure that property is correctly posted as security for a bond in a criminal case and is returned in conformance with the law promptly after entry of final judgment.

II. Guidelines for Posting Real Property to Secure a Person's Release From Custody

   A. Introduction. The following are guidelines for posting real property to support a pretrial release bond in the United States District Court for the Northern District of California. When the court sets a bond to secure a person's pretrial release and orders the bond secured by real property, certain documents will be required to prove the value and ownership of the property and to secure the court's interest. The documents are typically prepared by the defense, presented to the government for approval and then lodged with the court. These guidelines are intended to assist parties to generate accurate and reliable documentation without undue delay, expense or burden.

B. Required Documents. The court requires accurate information concerning the value of and title to any property posted as security for a bond. For each piece of real property posted, documents must be provided to show (1) that the property has enough equity to support its portion of the bond amount, and (2) that the person(s) posting the property is/are the true and only owner(s). There will be no deviation from the requirements set forth below regarding (1) the Obligation, (2) the Deed of Trust, or (3) the Reconveyance (see B.3, 4 & 5 below.)

1. *Valuation Documents.* Documents that show the current fair market value of property are to be used in this process. Appraisals conducted by licensed appraisers are recognized as the most effective means of capturing the fair market value of property. Other methods, such as property profiles or comparative market analyses, may be considered when particular circumstances diminish valuation concerns or when otherwise appropriate.

2. *Title Documents.* Documents prepared by a title insurance company or a title research company that show (a) the current legal owners, and (b) encumbrances, liens and/or mortgages on the property must be submitted. Such documents usually include a preliminary title report and/or litigation report. Other documents may be considered when warranted by particular circumstances, such as the posting of multiple properties.

3. *Obligation.* This document guarantees that the owner(s) of the property understand(s) that the property is being posted as security for the defendant's release from custody. Defendants and sureties must be advised that if the defendant fails to appear and abide by all other conditions imposed by the court, the property is subject to forfeiture by the United States. The obligation must be signed by each person who holds title to the property. The form is attached hereto as *Form CAND GO–55–A.*

4. *Deed of Trust and Assignment of Rents.* This document conveys the interest in the property to the court. The document must be signed by all parties who hold title to the property. The document must also conform to the legal requirements of a document conveying interest in real property. Both the "beneficiary" and "trustee" for the property must be "Susan Y. Soong, Clerk of the Court." The deed of trust must have the case name, case number and the amount of the bond on its face. A sample form is attached as *Form CAND GO–55–B.* The deed of trust must be recorded with the County Recorder in the county where the property lies. The deed of trust should not be recorded until the entire bond package has been approved.

5. *Reconveyance.* A fully prepared reconveyance deed must be lodged with the court at the time the property bond is posted. A sample form is attached as *Form CAND GO–55–C.* The sample reconveyance document may not satisfy the requirements of states other than California. The preparer of the reconveyance document is responsible for verifying the requirements of any other state in which property lies and providing the proper documents to the Clerk.

The Clerk's Office will automatically use the lodged reconveyance document to reconvey the Clerk's interest in the property upon exoneration of the bond. If changed circumstances make this reconveyance document obsolete, the submitting party must submit a new reconveyance document to the Clerk's Office along with clear instructions to use it in place of the one previously submitted.

The Clerk's Office will not alter or amend the reconveyance document submitted at the time the bond package is lodged and does not warrant its accuracy or assume liability for the reconveyance document or its recording. The submitting party is solely responsible for its accuracy and recording.

C. Review Process. A flexible, case-by case approach to the valuation of property may result in the parties agreeing on different combinations of the valuation and title documents outlined below. The documents listed in II.B must be given to the prosecutor assigned to the case for review and approval before being submitted to the court. The parties should make good faith efforts to resolve informally any issues and/or disagreements regarding the sufficiency of documents before bringing such matters before the court. The court will not be involved in the valuation or approval of a bond package unless there is a dispute between the parties and only after good faith efforts have failed to resolve it.

D. Lodging the Bond Package With the Court. When all the above documents have been prepared and approved by the parties or by the court and the deed of trust has been recorded, the documents must be lodged with the Clerk of the Court.

The Clerk's Office will only lodge recorded deeds of trust. A conformed or certified copy from the recording office of the recorded deed of trust will suffice to show proof of recording. The Clerk's Office will issue a receipt in exchange for the lodged documents.

III. Procedure for Exoneration of Bond and Reconveyance of Property

A. Unless otherwise requested by one of the parties, upon final judgment in any criminal matter in which a bond has been posted, the court on its own motion will either (1) exonerate the bond at the time of sentencing, or (2) order the bond exonerated upon the self-surrender of the defendant to the Bureau of Prisons for service of the defendant's sentence. Unless otherwise provided by the court, an order of dismissal or judgment of acquittal exonerates the bond without further action by the court and any cash bond plus interest is to be returned to the owner identified on the *Affidavit of Owner of Cash Security (Form CAND GO–55–D)*.

B. Upon exoneration of the bond, the Clerk of the Court will reconvey the property by executing the reconveyance document lodged with the court by the posting party, and sending the executed reconveyance document to the address for the posting party which appears on the reconveyance document. The posting party is responsible for recording the reconveyance document with the respective county recorder.

C. Subject to the provisions of 28 USC § 2044, if cash or cash equivalents are posted, the owner(s) of the cash or cash equivalents, *i.e.*, the defendant or a surety or sureties, must proceed in the manner described in the attached *Procedures For Bond Posting & Exoneration*, and complete the *Affidavit of Owner of Cash Security (Form CAND GO–55–D)*. If more than $10,000 in cash and/or cash equivalents is posted for a defendant charged with an offense involving a controlled substance, racketeering, or money laundering, then *Receipt of Cash Bail of More than $10,000 in a Specified Criminal Case (Form CAND GO–55–E)* and Parts I and II of *IRS Form 8300 (which may be downloaded from irs.gov)* must also be completed.

D. All travel documents surrendered at the time of the posting of the bond shall be submitted to Pretrial Services. All other personal and real property related to the posting of the bond shall be submitted to the Clerk of the Court.

1. Bond Exoneration—Return of Travel Documents or Personal Property. Except as hereinafter provided, travel documents surrendered to Pretrial Services, and other personal property of the defendant submitted to the Clerk of the Court at the time of the posting of the bond, will be sent to the defendant or defendant's attorney upon execution of the order exonerating bond, execution of an order of dismissal, or entry of a judgment of acquittal. If, however, a travel document is known to have been issued in a false name, it will be sent to the appropriate passport agency (unless the document is being held for evidentiary purposes in another proceeding).

2. Documents or Property Unable to Be Returned. If the defendant's attorney is no longer representing the defendant and there is no known address for the defendant or attorney, the travel document or personal property will be held by Pretrial Services or the Clerk of the Court, respectively, until such time as the defendant requests its release. After 5 years, the travel document will be sent to the appropriate passport agency. An expired travel document will be sent to the appropriate passport agency irrespective of the outcome of the criminal case. If the defendant is convicted, all travel documents will be sent to the appropriate passport agency.

E. If the bond is exonerated for any reason other than entry of final judgment, the defendant's attorney must submit a proposed order of exoneration.

F. If any judge of this court orders the forfeiture of a bond, then cash or cash equivalents or property, real or otherwise, posted for the purpose of securing the bond will be forfeited up to the amount of the bond and any interest earned on the cash or cash equivalents will be disbursed pursuant to the court order forfeiting bond.

UNITED STATES DISTRICT COURT NORTHERN DISTRICT OF CALIFORNIA

OFFICE OF THE CLERK

PROCEDURES FOR BOND POSTING & EXONERATION

When a defendant is permitted to post bail in the form of cash and/or cash equivalents (currency, personal check, cashier's check or money order), the posting and exoneration of bail will be in accordance with the following procedures. These procedures relate to General Order 55.

POSTING OF CASH & CASH EQUIVALENTS GENERALLY

Each person delivering cash and/or cash equivalents must complete the *Affidavit of Owner of Cash Security* (*Form CAND GO–55–D*) providing, under penalty of perjury, his or her name, address, Social Security Number (SSN), Taxpayer Identification Number (TIN), Individual Taxpayer Identification Number (ITIN) or Employer Identification Number (EIN) and the amount of cash owned by that person posted as bail. In the event of cash being posted by more than one person, the cashier will issue a separate receipt to each owner of the cash based on the information provided on the *Affidavit of Owner of Cash Security*.

Cash bail bonds that are posted with the court are invested in the Court Registry Investment System (CRIS) pursuant to General Order 31. Upon exoneration of bail, an order of dismissal or judgment of acquittal, the Clerk's Office will refund cash and/or cash equivalents and the interest earned on those funds only if a SSN, TIN, ITIN or EIN has been provided. A completed *Affidavit of Owner of Cash Security* (*Form CAND GO–55–D*) must accompany the bail, whether it is remitted in person, by mail or express delivery, or in some other fashion.

POSTING OF CASH IN AMOUNT GREATER THAN $10,000 (CERTAIN OFFENSES)

If more than $10,000 in cash is posted as bail for any individual charged with a specified criminal offense involving a controlled substance, racketeering, or money laundering, the person who posts the bail with the court and the person on whose behalf the bond is posted must complete, in addition to the *Affidavit of Owner of Cash Security* (*Form CAND GO–55–D*), the *Receipt of Cash Bail of More than $10,000 in a Specified Criminal Case* (*Form CAND GO–55–E*) and *Parts I and II of IRS Form 8300* (irs.gov).

"Cash" for purposes of this section includes United States and foreign currency or a cashier's check, money order, bank draft or traveler's check having a face amount of $10,000 or less; it does not include any personal check, regardless of the amount.

A combination of forms of cash each less than $10,000 but exceeding $10,000 when added together (e.g. $6,000 in currency together with a $7,000 cashier's check) triggers the requirements set forth in this section.

Monetary instruments with a face amount of more than $10,000 are not treated as cash. The IRS 8300 form is not required to be filed by the Clerk of Court since the bank or financial institution that issues the instrument must file the necessary information with the IRS.

If multiple payments are made in cash to satisfy bail and the initial payment does not exceed $10,000, the initial payment and subsequent payments must be aggregated, the payment that causes the aggregate amount to exceed $10,000 in cash triggers the requirements set forth in this section.

REFUNDING OF CASH & CASH EQUIVALENTS AFTER BOND EXONERATION, DISMISSAL OR ACQUITTAL

Upon the exoneration of bail, an order of dismissal or judgment of acquittal, the Clerk's Office will return the bail and any interest earned thereon to: (a) the name(s) and address(s) provided on the *Affidavit of Owner of Cash Security*; or (b) the name and address contained in any applicable court order identifying the owner of the bail. It is the obligation of the person or persons to whom, under the above provisions, the exonerated bail will be returned to notify the financial unit of the Clerk's Office, in writing, of any address changes.

TRANSFER OF BAIL FROM ANOTHER DISTRICT

In any case in which bail received in another district court has been transferred to this district court, it is the responsibility of defense counsel to obtain a court order identifying the owner of the money, and to have the owner complete the *Affidavit of Owner of Cash Security* (*Form CAND GO–55–D*).

UNITED STATES DISTRICT COURT

NORTHERN DISTRICT OF CALIFORNIA

OFFICE OF THE CLERK

OBLIGATION

We, the undersigned, represent and/or agree that:

1. We are the owners of the property pledged in the attached Deed of Trust;

2. In consideration for the release of defendant _____
    on bond in the matter of the United States v. _____,
    Case No. CR_____, we pledge the amount of $ _____ to be secured
    by the above-mentioned Deed of Trust executed in favor of the United States District
    Court, Northern District of California.

3. In the event bail is eventually exonerated in said matter, said beneficiary of the Deed of
    Trust is authorized and requested to execute and acknowledge the Reconveyance
    document also attached hereto;

4. In the event bail is eventually forfeited for failure to comply with the terms of the bail
    order, said beneficiary is authorized to request the trustee under the Deed of Trust to
    proceed with foreclosure under the terms of the Deed of Trust and to submit this
    document together with the order forfeiting bail and the Deed of Trust as conclusive
    evidence of default.

_____   _____
Signature   Date

_____   _____
Signature   Date

Form CAND GO-55-A (rev. 3/2015)

ATTORNEY OF RECORD

WHEN RECORDED MAIL TO:
Susan Y. Soong, Clerk of the US District
Court for the Northern District of California
450 Golden Gate Avenue, 16th Floor
San Francisco, CA 94102

THIS SPACE FOR RECORDER'S USE

SHORT FORM DEED OF TRUST AND ASSIGNMENT OF RENTS SECURING A PERSONAL SURETY BOND TO THE UNITED STATES DISTRICT COURT

THIS DEED OF TRUST, made this _____ day of _____, 20___ between _____

herein called TRUSTOR, whose address is: _____ and Susan Y. Soong, Clerk, United States District Court for the Northern District of California, herein called both TRUSTEE and BENEFICIARY

WITNESSETH: That Trustor IRREVOCABLY GRANTS, TRANSFERS AND ASSIGNS TO TRUSTEE IN TRUST, WITH POWER OF SALE, that property in _____ County, California, described as: *(ATTACH PROPERTY DESCRIPTION ON SEPARATE PAGE)* TOGETHER WITH the rents, issues and profits thereof, SUBJECT, HOWEVER, to the right, power and authority given to and conferred upon Beneficiary by paragraph (10) of the provisions incorporated herein by reference to collect and apply such rents, issues and profits.

For the purpose of securing performance of each agreement of Trustor incorporated by reference or contained herein under the bond(s) posted on behalf of defendant(s) _____ in Case No. CR _____ which includes an obligation by said Trustor's surety (ies) in the amount of $ _____ secured by _____.

TO PROTECT THE SECURITY OF THIS DEED OF TRUST, TRUSTOR AGREES: By the execution and delivery of this Deed of Trust and the note or the Personal Surety Bond secured hereby, that provisions (1) to (14), inclusive, (which provisions, identical in all counties, are printed on the reverse hereof) of the fictitious deed of trust recorded in the book and at the page of Official Records in the office of the County Recorder of the County where said property is located, noted below with the County name, viz:

COUNTY	BOOK	PAGE	COUNTY	BOOK	PAGE	COUNTY	BOOK	PAGE	COUNTY	BOOK	PAGE
Alameda	435477	12 140	Kings	122	578	Placer	1998	591	Sierra	79	652
Alpine	50	344 372	Lake	942	153	Plumas	291	119	Siskiyou	824	414
Amador	555	343	Lassen	354	756	Riverside	1975	10181	Solano	1978	55321
Butte	290	464	Los Angeles	78 730503	—	Sacramento	78 37 07	114	Sonoma	3421	862
Calaveras	415	244	Madera	406	233	San Benito	432	10	Stanislaus	3074	305
Colusa	401	325	Marin	3400	70	San Bernardino	6490	1393	Sutter	520	678
Contra Costa	3914	236	Mariposa	165	384	San Diego	1975	76 28521	Tehama	765	109
Del Norte	219	441	Mendocino	1 to	523	San Francisco	C851	703	Trinity	152	632
El Dorado	1649	92	Merced	2130	925	San Joaquin	7420	187	Tulare	3645	778
Fresno	7089	711	Modoc	255	590	San Luis Obispo	2064	293	Tuolumne	539	129
Glenn	65	343	Mono	246	573	San Mateo	7759	2037	Ventura	5158	219
Humboldt	1606	559	Monterey	357	711	Santa Barbara	78 30910	—	Yolo	1310	148
Imperial	1415	1241	Napa	1063	386	Santa Clara	5757	19	Yuba	671	093
Inyo	252	93	Nevada	465	297	Santa Cruz	2933	275			
Kern	5128	521	Orange	2749	725	Shasta	1530	350			

are hereby adopted and incorporated herein and made a part hereof as though fully set forth herein at length; that Trustor will observe and perform said provisions; and that the references to property, obligations, and parties in said provisions shall be construed to refer to the property, obligations, and parties set forth in the Deed of Trust. Trustor requests that a copy of any Notice of Default and of any Notice of Sale hereunder be mailed to him at his address hereinbefore set forth.

A NOTARY PUBLIC OR OTHER OFFICER COMPLETING THIS CERTIFICATE VERIFIES ONLY THE IDENTITY OF THE INDIVIDUAL WHO SIGNED THE DOCUMENT TO WHICH THIS CERTIFICATE IS ATTACHED, AND NOT THE TRUTHFULNESS, ACCURACY, OR VALIDITY OF THAT DOCUMENT.

STATE OF CALIFORNIA
COUNTY OF _____ } ss

SIGNATURE OF TRUSTOR

Sign: _____
Print Name: _____
Sign: _____
Print Name: _____

On _____, 20___, before me, _____, Notary Public, personally appeared _____

who proved to me on the basis of satisfactory evidence to be the person(s) whose name(s) is/are subscribed to the within instrument and acknowledged to me that he/she/they executed the same in his/her/their authorized capacity(ies), and that by his/her/their signature(s) on the instrument the person(s), or the entity upon behalf of which the person(s) acted, executed the instrument. I certify under PENALTY OF PERJURY under the laws of the State of California that the foregoing paragraph is true and correct.

WITNESS my hand and official seal.

_____
SIGNATURE OF NOTARY PUBLIC   [SEAL]
Form CAND GO-55-B (rev. 10/2015)

DO NOT RECORD THIS PAGE

To Protect the Security of This Deed of Trust, Trustor Agrees:

(1) To keep said property in good condition and repair, not to remove or demolish any building thereon, to complete or restore promptly and in good and workmanlike manner any building which may be constructed, damaged or destroyed thereon and to pay when due all claims for labor performed and materials furnished therefor, to comply with all laws affecting said property or requiring any alterations or improvements to be made thereon, not to commit or permit waste thereof, not to commit, suffer or permit any act upon said property in violations of law, to cultivate, irrigate, fertilize, fumigate, prune and do all other acts which from the character or use of said property may be reasonably necessary, the specific enumerations herein not excluding the general.

2) To provide, maintain and deliver to Beneficiary fire insurance satisfactory to and with loss payable to Beneficiary. The amount collected under any fire or other insurance policy may be applied by Beneficiary upon indebtedness secured hereby and in such order as Beneficiary may determine, or, at option of Beneficiary, the entire amount so collected or any part thereof may be released to Trustor. Such application or release shall not cure or waive any default or notice of default hereunder or invalidate any act done pursuant to such notice.

(3) To appear in and defend any action or proceeding purporting to affect the security hereof or the rights or powers of Beneficiary or Trustee, and to pay all costs and expenses including cost of evidence of title and attorney's fees in a reasonable sum, in any such action or proceeding in which Beneficiary or Trustee may appear and in any suit brought by Beneficiary to foreclose this Deed.

(4) To pay at least ten days before delinquency all taxes and assessments affecting said property, including assessments on appurtenant water stock, when due, all encumbrances, charges and liens, with interest, on said property or any part thereof, which appear to be prior or superior hereto, all costs, fees and expenses of this Trust. Should Trustor fail to make any payment or to do any act as herein provided, then Beneficiary or Trustee, but without obligation so to do and without notice to or demand upon Trustor and without releasing Trustor from any obligation hereof, may make or do the same in such manner and to such extent as either may deem necessary to protect the security hereof. Beneficiary or Trustee being authorized to enter upon said property for such purposes, appear in and defend any action or proceeding purporting to affect the security hereof or the rights or powers of Beneficiary or Trustee, pay, purchase, contest or compromise any encumbrance, charge or lien which in the judgment of either appears to be prior or superior hereto, and in exercising any such powers, pay necessary expenses, employ counsel and pay his reasonable fees.

(5) To pay immediately and without demand all sums so expended by Beneficiary or Trustee, with interest from date of expenditure at the amount allowed by law in effect at the date hereof, and to pay for any statement provided for by law in effect at the date hereof regarding the obligation secured hereby any amount demanded by the Beneficiary not to exceed the maximum allowed by law at the time when said statement is demanded.

(6) That any award of damages in connection with any condemnation for public use of or injury to said property or any part thereof is hereby assigned and shall be paid to Beneficiary, who may apply or release such moneys received by him in the same manner and with the same effect as above provided for disposition of proceeds of fire or other insurance.

(7) That by accepting payment of any sum secured hereby after its due date, Beneficiary does not waive his rights either to require prompt payment when due of all other sums so secured or to declare default for failure so to pay.

(8) That at any time or from time to time, without liability therefor and without notice, upon written request of Beneficiary and presentation of this Deed and said note for endorsement, and without affecting the personal liability of any person for payment of the indebtedness secured hereby, Trustee may reconvey any part of said property, consent to the making of any map or plot thereof; join in granting any easement thereon or join in any extension agreement or any agreement subordinating the lien or charge hereof.

(9) That upon written request of Beneficiary state that all sums secured hereby have been paid, and upon surrender of this Deed and said note to Trustee for cancellation and retention and upon payment of its fees, Trustee shall reconvey, without warranty, the property then held hereunder. The recitals in such reconveyance of any matters or facts shall be conclusive proof of the truthfulness thereof. The grantee in such reconveyance may be described as "The person or persons legally entitled thereto." Five years after issuance of such full reconveyance, Trustee may destroy said note and this Deed (unless directed in such request to retain them).

(10) That as additional security, Trustor hereby gives to and confers upon Beneficiary the right, power and authority, during the continuance of these Trusts, to collect the rents, issues and profits of said property, reserving unto Trustor the right, prior to any default by Trustor in payment of any indebtedness secured hereby or in performance of any agreement hereunder, to collect the rents, issues and profits of said property, reserving unto Trustor the right, prior to any default by Trustor in payment of any indebtedness secured hereby or in performance of any agreement hereunder, to collect and retain such rents, issues and profits as they become due and payable. Upon any such default, Beneficiary may at any time without notice, either in person, by agent or by a receiver to be appointed by a court, and without regard to the adequacy of any security for the indebtedness hereby secured, enter upon and take possession of said property or any part thereof, in his own name sue for or otherwise collect such rents, issues and profits, including those past due and unpaid, and apply the same, less costs and expenses of operation and collection, including reasonable attorney's fees upon any indebtedness secured hereby, and in such order as Beneficiary may determine. The entering upon and taking possession of said property, the collection of such rents, issues and profits and the application thereof as aforesaid, shall not cure or waive any default or notice of default hereunder or invalidate any act done pursuant to such notice.

(11) That upon default by Trustor in payment of any indebtedness secured hereby or in performance of any agreement hereunder, Beneficiary may declare all sums secured hereby immediately due and payable by delivery to Trustee of written declaration of default and demand for sale and of written notice of default and of election to cause to be sold said property, which notice Trustee shall cause to be filed for record. Beneficiary also shall deposit with Trustee this Deed, said note and all documents evidencing expenditures secured hereby. After the lapse of such time as may then be required by law following the recordation of said notice of default, and notice of sale having been given as then required by law, Trustee, without demand on Trustor, shall sell said property at the time and place fixed by it in said notice of sale, either as a whole or in separate parcels, and in such order as it may determine, at public auction to the highest bidder for cash in lawful money of the United States, payable at time of sale. Trustee may postpone sale of all or any portion of said property by public announcement at such time and place of sale, and from time to time thereafter may postpone such sale by public announcement at the time fixed by the preceding postponement. Trustee shall deliver to such purchaser its deed conveying the property so sold, but without any covenant or warranty, express or implied. The recitals in such deed of any matters or facts shall be conclusive proof of the truthfulness thereof. Any person, including Trustor, Trustee or Beneficiary as herein defined, may purchase at such sale. After deducting all costs, fees and expenses of Trustee and of this Trust, including cost of evidence of title in connection with sale, Trustee shall apply the proceeds of sale to payment of all sums expended under the terms hereof not then repaid, with accrued interest at the amount allowed by law in effect at the date hereof, all other sums then secured hereby, and the remainder, if any, to the person or persons legally entitled thereto.

(12) Beneficiary, or any successor in ownership of any indebtedness secured hereby, may from time to time, by instrument in writing, substitute a successor or successors to any Trustee named herein or acting hereunder, which instrument, executed by the Beneficiary and duly acknowledged and recorded in the office of the recorder of the county or counties where said property is situated, shall be conclusive proof of proper substitution of such successor Trustee or Trustees, who shall, without conveyance from the Trustee predecessor, succeed to all its title, estate, rights, powers and duties. Said instrument must contain the name of the original Trustor, Trustee and Beneficiary hereunder, the book and page where this Deed is recorded and the name and address of the new Trustee.

(13) That this Deed applies to, inures to the benefit of and binds all parties hereto, their heirs, legatees, devisees, administrators, executors, successors and assigns. The term Beneficiary shall mean the owner and holder, including pledgees, of the note secured hereby, whether or not named as Beneficiary herein in this Deed, whenever the context so requires, the masculine gender includes the feminine and/or neuter, and the singular number includes the plural.

(14) That Trustee accepts this Trust when this Deed, duly executed and acknowledged, is made a public record as provided by law. Trustee is not obligated to notify any party hereto of pending sale under any other Deed of Trust or of any action or proceeding in which Trustor, Beneficiary or Trustee shall be a party unless brought by Trustee.

WHEN RECORDED MAIL TO:

THIS SPACE FOR RECORDER'S USE

FULL RECONVEYANCE

Susan Y. Soong, Clerk, United States District Court for the Northern District of California as Trustee and Beneficiary under that certain Deed of Trust dated the _____ day of _____, 20___, executed by _____ as Trustor(s) and recorded on the _____ day of _____, 20___ as instrument number _____ in Book _____ at Page _____ of Official Records, in the Office of the Recorder of _____ County, California, having been requested in writing by the holder of the obligations secured by said Deed of Trust to reconvey the estate granted to Trustee under said Deed of Trust, DOES HEREBY RECONVEY to the person or persons legally entitled thereto, without warranty, all the estate, title & interest acquired by Trustee under said Deed of Trust.

Dated: _____   _____

Susan Y. Soong,
Clerk of Court, United States District Court

A NOTARY PUBLIC OR OTHER OFFICER COMPLETING THIS CERTIFICATE
VERIFIES ONLY THE IDENTITY OF THE INDIVIDUAL WHO SIGNED THE
DOCUMENT TO WHICH THIS CERTIFICATE IS ATTACHED, AND NOT THE
TRUTHFULNESS, ACCURACY, OR VALIDITY OF THAT DOCUMENT.

STATE OF CALIFORNIA

COUNTY OF SAN FRANCISCO   ss

On _____, before me, _____, Notary Public, personally appeared _____, who proved to me on the basis of satisfactory evidence to be the person(s) whose name(s) is/are subscribed to the within instrument and acknowledged to me that he/she/they executed the same in his/her/their authorized capacity(ies), and that by his/her/their signature(s) on the instrument the person(s), or the entity upon behalf of which the person(s) acted, executed the instrument.

I certify under PENALTY OF PERJURY under the laws of the State of California that the foregoing paragraph is true and correct.

WITNESS my hand and official seal.

_____
SIGNATURE OF NOTARY PUBLIC   [SEAL]

Form CAND GO-55-C (rev. 10/2015)

643

UNITED STATES DISTRICT COURT
NORTHERN DISTRICT OF CALIFORNIA

OFFICE OF THE CLERK

AFFIDAVIT OF OWNER OF CASH SECURITY
(CASH & CASH EQUIVALENTS)

Case Name: United States v. _____

Case Number: CR_____

By my signature below, on the date signed, I, the owner of the cash or cash equivalents listed below, hereby certify under penalty of perjury that:

1. The below amount of cash or cash equivalents appearing next to my signature and deposited as security on the foregoing bond is owned by me and is to be returned to me with interest earned based on the ratio of the cash or cash equivalents deposited at the below address upon exoneration of this bond,

2. The SSN/TIN/ITIN/EIN shown below is my correct taxpayer identification number,

3. I am not subject to backup withholding because (a) I am exempt from backup withholding, or (b) I have not been notified by the Internal Revenue Service (IRS) that I am subject to backup withholding as a result of a failure to report all interest or dividends, or (c) the IRS has notified me that I am no longer subject to backup withholding, and

4. I am a U.S. Citizen or other U.S. person defined by the IRS for federal tax purposes as (a) an individual who is a U.S. citizen or U.S. resident alien, (b) a partnership, corporation, company, or association created or organized in the United States or under the law of the United States, (c) an estate (other than a foreign estate) or (d) a domestic trust (as defined in Regulations section 301.7701-7).

5. I am exempt from Foreign Account Tax Compliance (FATCA) reporting.

Name: _____

Address: _____

SSN/TIN/ITIN/EIN (required for disbursement upon exoneration): _____

Telephone Numbers:
Home: _____   Work: _____   Mobile: _____

Amount of Cash & Cash Equivalents provided as bail:

    Currency: $ _____

    Personal check: $ _____

    Cashier's check: $ _____

    Money order: $ _____

    Other: $ _____

I declare under penalty of perjury that the information provided on this form is true and correct.

_____   _____
             Signature   Date

Form CAND GO-55-D (rev. 10/2019)

UNITED STATES DISTRICT COURT

NORTHERN DISTRICT OF CALIFORNIA

OFFICE OF THE CLERK

RECEIPT OF CASH BAIL OF MORE THAN $10,000
IN A SPECIFIED CRIMINAL CASE

REPORTING REQUIREMENT

The Clerk of Court must file IRS Form 8300 with the Internal Revenue Service if more than $10,000 in cash is received as bail for any individual(s) charged with certain criminal offenses involving a controlled substance, racketeering, or money laundering no later than the 15th day after the date the cash bail is received, with a copy to the U.S. Attorney in both the jurisdiction of the defendant's residence and the jurisdiction in which the offense occurred. A copy of the IRS Form 8300 is provided to each person posting bail whose name is on the IRS Form 8300 by January 31st of the year following the year in which the cash is received.

If multiple payments are made and the initial payment does not exceed $10,000, the initial payment and subsequent payments must be aggregated and the information return must be filed by the 15th day after receipt of the payment that causes the aggregate amount to exceed $10,000. Payments made to satisfy separate bail requirements are not required to be aggregated.

INSTRUCTIONS

Please complete all fields below and Parts I and II on IRS Form 8300 (irs.gov) — Report of Cash Payments Over $10,000 Received in a Trade or Business. Please type or hand-write legibly; this information will be forwarded to the Internal Revenue Service.

Case Name: United States v. _____   **Case Number**: _____

Date Cash Bail Posted: _____   **Amount**: _____

Specified Criminal Offense:

- ☐ A Federal criminal offense involving a controlled substance;
- ☐ Racketeering (as defined in Section 1951, 1952 or 1955 of Title 18 of the United States Code);
- ☐ Money laundering (as defined in Section 1956 or 1957 of Title 18 of the United States Code).

Under penalty of perjury, I declare that to the best of my knowledge and belief the information I have furnished above and on the attached IRS Form 8300 is true, correct, and complete.

_____   _____
            Signature of Owner of Cash   Date

Form CAND GO-55-E (rev. 10/2019)

[Dated: October 15, 2019.]

GENERAL ORDER NO. 56.   AMERICANS WITH
DISABILITIES ACT ACCESS LITIGATION

In any action which asserts denial of a right of access protected by Titles II or III of the Americans with Disabilities Act, 42 U.S.C. §§ 12131–89, pursuant to Federal Rule of Civil Procedure 16, the Court ORDERS that the following shall apply:

1. Service. Pursuant to Federal Rule of Civil Procedure 4(m), plaintiff shall promptly complete service on all defendants. A plaintiff who is unable to complete service on all defendants within 60 days may, prior to the expiration of that period, file a Motion for Administrative Relief pursuant to Civil Local Rule 7–11 requesting an extension of the schedule required by this Order.

2. Responsive Pleading. Within the time allowed for responsive pleading under Federal Rule of Civil Procedure 12, a defendant may either (a) answer or (b) file a motion under Rule 12(b). Filing a motion under Rule 12(b) does not automatically relieve the parties of the requirements of this Order.

3. Stay of Proceedings and Relief from Requirements of this Order. All discovery, motion practice (except for motions under Rule 12(b) and motions to appear pro hac vice), and other proceedings are STAYED unless the assigned judge orders otherwise. Requests to lift the stay to conduct specific discovery, to file any other motion, to be relieved of any of the requirements of this Order, or to enforce any of the requirements of this Order may be made by stipulation and proposed order under Civil Local Rule 7–12 or by filing a Motion for Administrative Relief under Civil Local Rule 7–11.

4. Initial Disclosures and Production of Documents.

a) Initial disclosures required by Federal Rule of Civil Procedure 26(a)(1) shall be completed no later than 7 days prior to the joint site inspection required by Paragraph 7. Examples of what the initial disclosures must contain include:

- Each party shall disclose all information in that party's possession or control that may be used to support its claims or defenses regarding the accessibility of the premises, transportation service, examination, course, program, service, activity, website, mobile software application, or other technology.

- Defendant shall disclose all information in defendant's possession or control regarding the construction or alteration history of the subject premises if defendant intends to dispute liability on that basis.

- In a Title II action, defendant shall disclose all information in defendant's possession or control regarding programmatic compliance, a transition plan, or a self-evaluation plan if defendant intends to dispute liability on that basis.

- If plaintiff claims damages, plaintiff shall set forth the damages computation required by Rule 26(a)(1)(A)(iii) but need not include attorneys' fees and costs.

- Plaintiff shall disclose the day, month, and year of all dates on which plaintiff claims to have sought access to the premises, transportation service, examination, course, program, service, activity, website, mobile software application, or other technology and shall disclose any documentary evidence regarding the alleged access efforts and barriers plaintiff encountered.

- If a defendant claims the injunctive relief sought is not readily achievable, that defendant shall disclose all information in its possession or control supporting that defense, including information pertaining to the factors stated in 42 U.S.C. § 12181(9) and to any alternative methods that are used to provide access.

These examples are illustrative of the type of information initial disclosures must contain and do not restrict any obligation imposed by Federal Rule of Civil Procedure 26(a).

b) Notwithstanding the stay imposed by Paragraph 3, upon request, a party promptly shall provide to the requesting party any documents identified in the initial disclosures.

5. Settlement Discussions.

a) The parties are encouraged to discuss settlement at their earliest opportunity. In those discussions, plaintiff is not required to make a monetary demand until the parties agree on the resolution of claims for injunctive relief and all other material terms, conditioned only on resolution of claims for damages, attorneys' fees, and costs. Once they come to such an agreement in principle, plaintiff promptly shall make a demand for settlement of the case in its entirety. The demand shall specify separately the amount sought as damages, the amount sought as attorneys' fees, and the amount sought as costs. Plaintiff shall not require execution of a written agreement as a precondition to making a monetary demand. If a monetary demand would facilitate discussions, plaintiff is not precluded by this Order from discussing claims for injunctive and monetary relief at the same time. Nothing in this Order is intended to preclude or to determine the effect of an offer of judgment under Federal Rule of Civil Procedure 68.

b) Whenever plaintiff makes a monetary demand, defendant may request and plaintiff then promptly shall provide an itemization of costs, an overall summary of the major categories of work performed, the total number of hours each time keeper spent on each category of work, and each time keeper's billing rate. If plaintiff prefers, plaintiff may instead provide complete, detailed time records (redacted, if necessary, for attorney-client privilege and work product).

6. Experts. This Order does not require any party to engage an expert, including a Certified Access Specialist (CASp). In simpler cases it may be possible for parties to reach agreement regarding corrective actions without engaging experts, or without the preparation of written expert reports. If the parties believe that a case would benefit from expert assistance, the Court encourages them to jointly engage an expert. Before scheduling the joint site inspection and the settlement meeting required in Paragraphs 7 and 8 of this Order, counsel shall confer regarding the possibility of retaining a joint expert and shall disclose whether they intend to have a separate expert or consultant in attendance. If written expert reports are prepared, they shall be exchanged.

7. Joint Site Inspection.

a) No later than 60 days after service of the complaint, counsel and any unrepresented parties (accompanied by their experts or consultants and the parties themselves, if the parties so elect or if required in order to comply with Section (c) below) shall meet in person at the subject premises to conduct a joint site inspection. If the parties agree that plaintiff alleges only violations unrelated to a physical location (such as programmatic or policy violations), or if the parties already have reached an agreement resolving claims for injunctive relief and all other material terms, conditioned only on resolution of claims for damages, attorneys' fees, and costs, the parties may proceed directly to the required settlement meeting described in Paragraph 8 of this Order, in which case the settlement meeting shall be scheduled within 60 days after service of the Complaint.

b) The parties shall inspect together the portions or aspects of the subject premises, transportation service, examination, course, program, service, activity, website, mobile software application, or other technology that are claimed to violate the Americans with Disabilities Act. Plaintiff shall specify all claimed access violations and, to the extent possible at the site, the corrective actions or policy changes requested of defendant. With respect to each claimed violation, defendant shall specify, to the extent possible at the site, whether defendant is willing to undertake the requested corrective actions or has an alternate proposal. If defendant claims any proposed corrective action is not readily achievable or otherwise is not required by law, defendant shall specify the factual basis for this claim.

c) Each party shall be represented at the joint site inspection by a person with knowledge about the facts of the case and the authority to settle the injunctive relief claims. If a plaintiff asserts claims based on the accessibility of a website or mobile software application, a defendant also shall be represented at the joint site inspection by person(s) with the best possible technical knowledge regarding the website or mobile software application at issue.

8. Settlement Meeting.

a) The joint site inspection shall be followed by an in-person settlement meeting. The settlement meeting may occur at the same time and location as the joint site inspection or may be scheduled separately, but not later than 35 days after the joint site inspection.

b) Participation in the settlement meeting cannot be satisfied by telephone, video conference, or exchanging letters, emails, or texts. The parties themselves and their counsel must be personally present. Governmental entities, corporations, and non-governmental entities must be represented by a person (in addition to counsel of record) who has, to the greatest extent feasible, authority to settle and who is knowledgeable about the facts of the case.

c) Plaintiff shall be prepared at the outset of the settlement meeting to provide defendant with the demand for settlement described in Paragraph 5(a) of this Order.

d) If a party believes that it would be unsafe or otherwise inappropriate for a required individual to appear in person at the settlement meeting, that party may seek relief from the requirement of personal attendance in the manner set forth in Paragraph 3 of this Order.

9. **Mediation.** Within 42 days from the joint site inspection or settlement meeting, whichever occurs first, the parties shall file either the form Notice of Settlement of ADA Access Case or the form Notice of Need for Mediation and Certification of Counsel, both available on the Court's website. Unless settled, the matter will then be referred automatically to mediation for a session to be scheduled as soon as feasible, and in no event later than 90 days from the date the Notice of Need for Mediation and Certification of Counsel is filed, unless otherwise ordered by the assigned judge. The mediator shall preside over settlement negotiations that address all issues presented by the matter, including requests for injunctive relief, damages, and attorneys' fees. The mediator and the parties shall address the issues in the manner and order set forth in Paragraph 5 of this Order. Should a settlement be reached, counsel shall ensure that the parties make a written record of the essential terms of the settlement sufficient to permit any party to move to enforce the settlement should it not be consummated according to its terms. Should any settlement be conditioned upon future conduct such as remediation, upon submission of an appropriate order of dismissal that includes retention of jurisdiction to enforce the settlement the assigned judge will retain jurisdiction to enforce the settlement.

10. **Request for Case Management Conference.** If the case does not resolve within 7 days of the mediator's filing of a Certification of ADR Session reporting that the mediation process is concluded and that the case did not settle in its entirety, plaintiff shall file the form Notice Requesting Case Management Conference, available on the Court's website.

[Dated: January 1, 2020.]

GENERAL ORDER NO. 58. REGULATING POSSESSION AND USE OF ELECTRONIC DEVICES IN THE COURTHOUSE

The purposes of this General Order are to promote security for all persons who enter federal courthouses (meaning the portions of federal buildings occupied by the District Court and any other facility in which a District Court judicial proceeding is held), to protect the integrity of judicial proceedings, to facilitate legitimate use of electronic devices for communication or for the storage, retrieval, or presentation of information, and to comply with the mandates of the Federal Rules of Criminal Procedure and the policies of the Judicial Conference of the United States.

I. "As used in this General Order, the phrase "electronic device" embraces all equipment, including cameras, that can be used for:

A. Wireless communication; or

B. Receiving, creating, capturing, storing, retrieving, sending, or broadcasting any signals or any text, sound, or images; or

C. Accessing the Internet or any other network or off-site system or equipment for communicating or for storing or retrieving information.

II. Federal Rule of Criminal Procedure 53 prohibits "the taking of photographs in the courtroom during judicial proceedings or the broadcasting of judicial proceedings from the courtroom."

III. Policy of the Judicial Conference of the United States prohibits, in both civil and criminal cases in all district courts, broadcasting, televising, recording, or photographing courtroom proceedings for the purpose of public dissemination, subject to strictly-defined exceptions such as the Cameras in Courts pilot which concluded July 18, 2015.

IV. This District has adopted the following specific rules in furtherance of the national policies cited above:

A. Court security personnel will screen all electronic devices before permitting them to be brought into the courthouse. The purpose of this screening is to make sure that the items do not contain weapons, dangerous devices or materials, or contraband. Court security personnel may bar from the courthouse, or from portions of a building in which judicial proceedings are held, any item that appears to pose a threat to security or safety.

B. Photography and video and audio recording are prohibited in the common areas of the courthouse (i.e. the corridors and other areas outside the courtrooms) as well as in the courtrooms.

Photographing or recording any court proceeding from a location outside the courthouse in conjunction with an appearance made by telephone or videoconference is also prohibited. Exceptions to these prohibitions may be authorized only by express written permission of the Chief Judge.

C. Subject to the screening described in paragraph IV.A and to other provisions of this General Order, electronic devices may be brought into the courthouse and may be used in a non-disruptive manner in the common areas of the courthouse for purposes other than photography and video and audio recording.

D. Absent a more restrictive order (i.e., a specific judge's standing order or an order entered in a specific case), only the text functions of electronic devices (such as typing documents, emailing, text messaging and tweeting) may be used in a non-disruptive manner in courtrooms while proceedings are in session. Users of electronic devices may connect to the Internet and transmit communications. Electronic devices must be silenced and only keyboards that can be operated quietly will be allowed. Any judge may order, in a standing order or in a specific case or proceeding, restrictions on the use of electronic devices, up to and including prohibiting all use of electronic devices in the courtroom.

E. Jurors may not use electronic devices in courtrooms during judicial proceedings or in jury rooms during, or in connection with, deliberations. Grand jurors may not use electronic devices during, or in connection with, any proceedings before, or deliberations by, the grand jury.

In response to a violation of any provision of this General Order, or of any court order addressing matters covered by this General Order, court security personnel may order immediate compliance, direct the offender to leave the courtroom or the building, temporarily confiscate the device(s) used in violation of these rules, and/or report the violation to the presiding judge, the Chief Judge, the Clerk of Court and/or the United States Attorney.

[Dated: September 15, 2015.]

GENERAL ORDER NO. 59. ELECTRONIC AVAILABILITY
OF TRANSCRIPTS OF COURT PROCEEDINGS

Pursuant to the requirements of the E–Government Act of 2002 and in accordance with the policy adopted by the Judicial Conference of the United States (the "Conference") in September 2007, transcripts of proceedings before United States District Judges and Magistrate Judges in the Northern District of California that are filed with the Court shall also be filed in electronic format. The Court will follow Conference policy as to when such transcripts will be electronically available to the public as delineated below. The Court will also follow the requirements of the E–Government Act relating to the redaction of personal identification information from transcripts before they are made electronically available to the general public as further delineated below. That policy, as delineated below, establishes a procedure for counsel to request the redaction from the transcript of specific personal data identifiers before the transcript is made electronically available to the general public. The personal identifiers that must be redacted are as follows: social security numbers; financial account numbers; names of minor children; dates of birth; and, home addresses of individuals.

1. Any transcript of a proceeding filed on or after May 15, 2008 shall be electronically filed through the Court's Case Management/Electronic Case Files (CM/ECF) system. Any transcript of a sealed proceeding shall be filed in accordance with whatever procedure is in effect for the filing of sealed documents at the time of filing.

2. For the first 90 days after the transcript is electronically filed, access to the transcript in CM/ECF will be restricted to (a) court staff; (b) public terminal users; (c) attorneys of record or parties who have purchased the transcript from the court reporter or transcriber; and (d) other persons as directed by the court.

3. The Clerk shall provide to all parties electronic notice of the filing and of the redaction requirements. Redaction is limited to the following personal identifiers which must be redacted: (a) Social Security numbers; (b) financial account numbers; (c) names of minor children; (d) dates of birth; and, (e) home addresses of individuals. Within five business days of the filing of an official transcript, a party must file electronically a Notice of Intent to Request Redaction for any transcript in need of such redaction on the court-approved form, which shall be available on the forms page of the Court's Internet site: http://www.cand.uscourts.gov. The Clerk shall provide the court reporter

with a copy of the filed form. If no such notice is filed, the Court will assume no redaction of personal identifiers from the transcript is necessary.

4. If a party files a Notice of Intent to Request Redaction, within 21 calendar days from the filing of the transcript with the Clerk, or longer if ordered by the Court, the party must submit directly to the court reporter a statement indicating where the personal identifiers appear in the transcript by page and line and how they are to be redacted. The format of redactions shall comply with Civil Local Rule 3–17. For example, if a party wanted to redact the Social Security number 123–45–6789 appearing on page 12, line 9 of the transcript, the statement would read: "Redact the Social Security number on page 12, line 9 to read xxx–xx–6789." A party is only responsible for reviewing and indicating the redactions in the testimony of the witnesses it called and its own statements (e.g., opening statements and closing arguments). Only the personal identifiers listed above may be redacted by the court reporter on a party's request. Within 31 calendar days of the original transcript filing date, the court reporter or transcriber shall perform the redactions and electronically file a redacted version of the transcript. If a party wants other information redacted from the transcript, that party must move the Court for further redaction by noticed motion served on all parties and the court reporter. The transcript will not be electronically available to the general public until the Court has ruled on any such motion. Counsel appointed pursuant to the Criminal Justice Act may claim compensation, at the applicable rate, for the time spent reviewing the transcript and preparing the request for redaction, as well as for costs associated with obtaining a copy of the transcript.

5. If a transcript is redacted by the court reporter pursuant to this General Order, the following certification shall be used: "I certify that the foregoing is a correct transcript from the record of the proceedings in the above-entitled matter, as amended by the redaction of certain personal identifiers at the request of the parties [and by the Court]."

6. To minimize the need for redaction of a transcript, counsel are admonished to minimize their use of unnecessary personal identifiers at any proceeding at which a record is being taken.

7. Nothing in this order or Conference policy is intended to create a private right of action against a court reporter for any failure to redact the required information or for any errors associated with such redaction. This order and Conference policy do not affect in any way the obligation of the court reporter to file promptly with the Clerk of Court the court reporter's original records of a proceeding or the inclusion of a filed transcript with the records of the court pursuant to Title 28 USC § 753, nor do they affect the obligation of the Clerk to make the official transcript included in the court file available for copying by the public without further compensation to the court reporter.

[Dated: April 25, 2008.]

GENERAL ORDER NO. 61. IMMIGRATION MANDAMUS CASES

In any civil action seeking a writ of mandamus regarding immigration benefits, filed pursuant to the mandamus statute, 28 U.S.C. § 1361, and/or the Administrative Procedure Act, 5 U.S.C. §§ 701 et seq., the court **ORDERS**, pursuant to Federal Rule of Civil Procedure 16, that the following shall apply:

1. Plaintiff shall identify each such action as an "IMMIGRATION MANDAMUS CASE" in the case caption on the first page of the complaint.

2. The clerk's office shall file in each such action a procedural order which specifies that (a) the defendant shall serve and file an answer within 60 days of receipt of service of the summons and complaint; (b) subject to sub-paragraph (c), the plaintiff may file a motion for summary judgment at any time permitted by the Federal Rules of Civil Procedure and this court's local rules, in which event defendant may respond as permitted by the Federal Rules of Civil Procedure and this court's local rules; (c) if the plaintiff has not filed a motion for summary judgment within 90 days of filing the complaint, the defendant shall be the party who shall first file a motion for summary judgment, and the defendant must serve and file that motion within 120 days of service of the complaint; (d) unless a motion pursuant to Federal Rule of Civil Procedure 56(f) is filed, the plaintiff shall serve and file any opposition and/or counter-motion within 30 days of service of defendant's motion; (e) defendant may serve and file a reply and/or opposition within 14 days of service of plaintiff's opposition or counter-motion; and (f) if plaintiff filed a counter-motion, plaintiff may serve and file a reply within 14 days of service of defendant's opposition.

3. For scheduling purposes, motions shall be noticed in accordance with Civil Local Rule 7–2. If a party wishes to have the court decide the matter on the briefs and without oral argument, a party may make that request pursuant to Civil Local Rule 7–1(b).

4. Unless the court orders otherwise, no case management conference will be held, and no ADR process is required.

5. Any party who wishes to have a case management conference, pursuant to Civil Local Rule 16–10, may request that the court set a case management conference, consistent with the time frame set forth in Civil Local Rule 16–2. The rules set forth under Federal Rule of Civil Procedure 26 and Civil Local Rules 16–9 and 16–10 shall apply.

6. The court on its own motion or on the joint request of the parties may waive any requirement of this order.

[Dated: May 19, 2011.]

GENERAL ORDER NO. 64.   EXPEDITED TRIAL PROCEDURE

An Expedited Trial offers an abbreviated, efficient and cost effective litigation and trial process. The Northern District of California adopts the following Expedited Trial Procedure as a General Order of the Court:

Attachment A—Procedure for Expedited Trials

Attachment B—(Form) Agreement for Expedited Trial and Request for Approval

Attachment C—(Form) Standing Order for All Judges of the Northern District of California—Contents of Joint Case Management Statement

Attachment D—(Form) Standing Order for All Judges of the Northern District of California—Joint Expedited Case Management Statement

[Dated: June 21, 2011.]

ATTACHMENT A. PROCEDURE FOR EXPEDITED TRIALS

1. **Expedited Trial Procedure.** The court encourages parties to agree to an expedited trial. The Expedited Trial Procedure is meant to offer an abbreviated, efficient and cost-effective litigation and trial alternative. Subject to the approval of the assigned judge, the following procedures shall govern. "Expedited Trial" means a consensual, binding trial before a jury or before a judge with limited discovery and limited rights to appeal.

2. **Effective Date.** The parties shall file a written agreement, using the court form titled "Agreement for Expedited Trial and Request for Approval." Neither the agreement nor its existence shall be disclosed to the jury. The time schedule for expedited procedures and trial shall begin on the date the agreement is approved by the court.

3. **Termination of Agreement.** The agreement may be terminated by the court upon a showing that one or more parties have not participated in good faith with the provisions of this General Order or that previously undisclosed facts have been discovered that make it inappropriate to proceed pursuant to the agreement.

4. **Applicable Rules.** The provisions of the Expedited Trial Agreement, as approved by the court, shall supersede and govern over any inconsistencies or conflicts that arise between it and the Federal Rules of Civil Procedure or the Local Rules of this Court. Otherwise, all Federal Rules of Civil Procedure, Rules of Evidence, and Local Rules of this Court shall apply.

5. **Initial Disclosures.** If initial disclosures have not been exchanged, or if they are not yet due, the disclosures required by Rule 26(a)(1)(A) shall be exchanged within seven (7) days after the agreement is approved by the court.

6. **Expedited Trial Conference.** Immediately upon the filing of the agreement, plaintiff shall contact the courtroom deputy for the assigned judge and request an initial expedited trial conference. The conference shall occur no later than thirty (30) days after the filing of the agreement. Upon request of any party, the court shall permit counsel to appear by telephone. A Joint Expedited Trial Statement shall be filed seven (7) days before the conference addressing all of the topics set forth in the Standing Order for All Judges of the Northern District of California—Joint Expedited Case Management Statement, found on the Court's website: www.cand.uscourts.gov.

A case management order shall be issued following the conference. Unless otherwise ordered by the court, the order shall require the parties to exchange the documents described in Rule 26(a)(3) of the Federal Rules of Civil Procedure no later than fifteen (15) days before the pretrial conference and shall require the parties to complete all discovery no later than ninety 90 days after the expedited trial conference. All Rule 12 and pleading issues shall be resolved by the court at the expedited trial conference, except as provided in section 10 of this General Order. The court may determine the extent, if any, that previous case management orders on matters subject to the expedited rules shall supersede or be combined with any previous orders.

7. **Pretrial Conference.** The pretrial conference shall be held no later than one hundred fifty (150) days after the agreement is approved by the court.

8. **Discovery.** Unless otherwise ordered by the court or by agreement of the parties, discovery shall be limited to ten (10) interrogatories per side, ten (10) document requests, ten (10) requests for admission, and fifteen (15) hours of depositions, per side. The parties may agree or the court may order, that the time for response to written discovery be shortened. Deposition time limits are inclusive of fact witnesses and expert witnesses.

9. **Expert Witnesses.** No party shall call more than one expert witness to testify, unless permitted by the court or by agreement of the parties.

10. **Pretrial Motions.** No pretrial motion shall be filed without leave of court, which shall be sought by a letter not to exceed one page. If leave is granted, the motion shall be in letter form, filed with the clerk, unless otherwise ordered. The response to the motion shall be by letter filed with the clerk not later than seven calendar days after receipt of the motion.

Unless otherwise permitted, no letter shall exceed three pages. A letter reply, not to exceed one page may be filed within three days after receipt of opposition. The court may decide the motion without a hearing. If the court finds that a hearing is necessary, it may establish a briefing schedule and order further briefing. Pendency of a dispositive motion shall not stay any other proceedings.

11. Trial Date. Unless otherwise ordered, trial shall be held no later than six months after the agreement is approved by the court.

12. Trial. Jury trial will be before six jurors and may proceed before a five-person jury if a juror is unable to serve through conclusion of trial and deliberations. The court shall conduct all voir dire and shall determine time limits for opening statements and closing argument. Each side shall have three hours to present evidence, not including time for opening statement and time for closing argument. There shall be no findings of fact or conclusions of law in non-jury trials. In multi-party trials, plaintiffs shall divide the three hours among themselves, and defendants shall divide the three hours among themselves. If the parties cannot agree to a division of trial time, the judge shall order a division.

13. Post–Trial Motions.

(a) Post-trial motions shall be limited to determination of costs and attorney's fees, correcting a judgment for clerical error, conforming the verdict to the agreement, enforcement of judgment and motions for a new trial.

(b) Within ten (10) court days after notice of entry of a jury verdict, a party may file with the clerk and serve on each adverse party a notice of intention to move for a new trial on any of the grounds specified in section 13(c) of these procedures. The notice shall be deemed to be a motion for a new trial.

(c) Grounds for motions for a new trial shall be limited to: (1) judicial misconduct that materially affected the substantial rights of a party; (2) misconduct of the jury; (3) corruption, fraud, or other undue means employed in the proceedings of the court or jury.

14. Judgment. Judgment shall be entered within 30 days after a bench trial, except as ordered by the court for good cause.

15. Appeal. Before filing an appeal, a party shall make a motion for a new trial pursuant to paragraph 13 of these procedures. If the motion for a new trial is denied, the party may appeal the judgment and seek a new trial only on grounds specified in subsection 13(c). All other grounds for appeal shall be waived and are not permitted, unless the parties agree otherwise.

ATTACHMENT B. AGREEMENT FOR EXPEDITED
TRIAL AND REQUEST FOR APPROVAL

UNITED STATES DISTRICT COURT
NORTHERN DISTRICT OF CALIFORNIA

	)	Case Number: C 11–xxxx
	)	
	)	
	)	**AGREEMENT FOR EXPEDITED TRIAL**
	)	**AND REQUEST FOR APPROVAL**
Plaintiff(s),	)	
	)	
vs.	)	
	)	
	)	
	)	
	)	
	)	
	)	
Defendant(s).	)	
	)	
	)	

The parties agree that all litigation in the above captioned matter shall be governed by General Order No. 64, Procedure for Expedited Trials of the United States District Court for the Northern District of California ("the Expedited Trial Procedure"). This Agreement, when approved by the court, shall be binding on the parties and on the court, subject to the Termination of Agreement provision set forth in paragraph 3 of Attachment A to General Order No. 64.

In addition to the terms set forth in General Order No. 64, the parties elect and agree to the following:

☐ 1. That regardless of the ultimate decision of the jury or the court, plaintiff will receive no less than $ ___ in damages from defendant(s), and defendant will pay no more than $ ___ in damages to plaintiff. (The floor/ceiling amounts may be kept under seal by filing this document in accordance with Local Rule 79–5.)

☐ 2. That plaintiff will receive no less than $ ___ in attorney fees and defendant will pay no more than $ ___ in attorney fees. The judge shall determine attorney fees within the range agreed by the parties. (The floor/ceiling amounts may be kept under seal by filing this document in accordance with Local Rule 79–5.)

☐ 3. That the judge may order equitable relief consistent with and within the options agreed to by the parties, *e.g.*, injunctive relief, promises to implement policies or practices, etc.

☐ 4. That the following trade-offs to reduce the scope of the litigation and the trial be adopted (*e.g.*, to forego pretrial motions, such as motions to dismiss, motions for summary judgments, etc., in exchange for limitations on damages, including waiver of punitive damages): _____.

☐ 5. That the following limitations on Pre–Trial Conference obligations to the extent permitted by the court be adopted: _____.

☐ 6. That the number of peremptory challenges will be reduced to _____ per side.

☐ 7. That limits on evidentiary matters (*e.g.*, allow hearsay, limit objections in deposition to form and reserving all others) will be altered as follows: _____

☐ 8. Other: _____

The parties agree that any and all rights to appeal from the judgment are waived by all parties, except as provided in section 15 of Attachment A to General Order No. 64.

Dated: _____
                                                    Counsel for plaintiff

Dated: _____
                                                    Counsel for defendant

IT IS ORDERED that the forgoing Agreement is approved. The parties shall request an Initial Expedited Trial Proceeding and file a Joint Expedited Trial Statement.

Dated: _____
                                        UNITED STATES DISTRICT JUDGE

ATTACHMENT C. STANDING ORDER FOR ALL JUDGES OF THE NORTHERN DISTRICT OF CALIFORNIA—CONTENTS OF JOINT CASE MANAGEMENT STATEMENT

All judges of the Northern District of California require identical information in Joint Case Management Statements filed pursuant to Civil Local Rule 16–9. The parties must include the following information in their statement which, except in unusually complex cases, should not exceed ten pages:

1. Jurisdiction and Service: The basis for the court's subject matter jurisdiction over plaintiff's claims and defendant's counterclaims, whether any issues exist regarding personal jurisdiction or venue, whether any parties remain to be served, and, if any parties remain to be served, a proposed deadline for service.

2. Facts: A brief chronology of the facts and a statement of the principal factual issues in dispute.

3. Legal Issues: A brief statement, without extended legal argument, of the disputed points of law, including reference to specific statutes and decisions.

4. Motions: All prior and pending motions, their current status, and any anticipated motions.

5. Amendment of Pleadings: The extent to which parties, claims, or defenses are expected to be added or dismissed and a proposed deadline for amending the pleadings.

6. Evidence Preservation: A brief report certifying that the parties have reviewed the Guidelines Relating to the Discovery of Electronically Stored Information ("ESI Guidelines"), and confirming that the parties have met and conferred pursuant to Fed. R. Civ. P. 26(f) regarding reasonable and proportionate steps taken to preserve evidence relevant to the issues reasonably evident in this action. *See ESI Guidelines 2.01 and 2.02, and Checklist for ESI Meet and Confer.*

7. Disclosures: Whether there has been full and timely compliance with the initial disclosure requirements of Fed. R. Civ. P. 26, and a description of the disclosures made.

8. Discovery: Discovery taken to date, if any, the scope of anticipated discovery, any proposed limitations or modifications of the discovery rules, a brief report on whether the parties have considered entering into a stipulated e-discovery order, a proposed discovery plan pursuant to Fed. R. Civ. P. 26(f), and any identified discovery disputes.

9. Class Actions: If a class action, a proposal for how and when the class will be certified.

10. Related Cases: Any related cases or proceedings pending before another judge of this court, or before another court or administrative body.

11. Relief: All relief sought through complaint or counterclaim, including the amount of any damages sought and a description of the bases on which damages are calculated. In addition, any party from whom damages are sought must describe the bases on which it contends damages should be calculated if liability is established.

12. Settlement and ADR: Prospects for settlement, ADR efforts to date, and a specific ADR plan for the case, including compliance with ADR L.R. 3–5 and a description of key discovery or motions necessary to position the parties to negotiate a resolution.

13. Consent to Magistrate Judge for All Purposes: Whether **all** parties will consent to have a magistrate judge conduct all further proceedings including trial and entry of judgment. ___ Yes ___ No

14. Other References: Whether the case is suitable for reference to binding arbitration, a special master, or the Judicial Panel on Multidistrict Litigation.

15. Narrowing of Issues: Issues that can be narrowed by agreement or by motion, suggestions to expedite the presentation of evidence at trial (e.g., through summaries or stipulated facts), and any request to bifurcate issues, claims, or defenses.

16. Expedited Trial Procedure: Whether this is the type of case that can be handled under the Expedited Trial Procedure of General Order No. 64 Attachment A. If all parties agree, they shall instead of this Statement, file an executed Agreement for Expedited Trial and a Joint Expedited Case Management Statement, in accordance with General Order No. 64 Attachments B and D.

17. Scheduling: Proposed dates for designation of experts, discovery cutoff, hearing of dispositive motions, pretrial conference and trial.

18.   Trial: Whether the case will be tried to a jury or to the court and the expected length of the trial.

19.   Disclosure of Non-party Interested Entities or Persons: Whether each party has filed the "Certification of Interested Entities or Persons" required by Civil Local Rule 3–15. In addition, each party must restate in the case management statement the contents of its certification by identifying any persons, firms, partnerships, corporations (including parent corporations) or other entities known by the party to have either: (i) a financial interest in the subject matter in controversy or in a party to the proceeding; or (ii) any other kind of interest that could be substantially affected by the outcome of the proceeding.

20.   Professional Conduct: Whether all attorneys of record for the parties have reviewed the Guidelines for Professional Conduct for the Northern District of California.

21.   Such other matters as may facilitate the just, speedy and inexpensive disposition of this matter.

[Effective July 1, 2011. Amended effective November 27, 2012; August 24, 2015.]

ATTACHMENT D. STANDING ORDER FOR ALL JUDGES OF THE NORTHERN DISTRICT OF CALIFORNIA—CONTENTS OF JOINT EXPEDITED CASE MANAGEMENT STATEMENT

Commencing July 1, 2011, all judges of the Northern District of California will require the following information in Joint Expedited Case Management Statements filed pursuant to General Order No. 64, which should not exceed five pages:

1. <u>Expedited Trial Approval</u>: Date Expedited Trial Agreement approved by the Court.

2. <u>Motions</u>: All prior and pending motions, their current status, and any anticipated motions.

3. <u>Disclosures</u>: Whether there has been full and timely compliance with the initial disclosure requirements of Fed. R. Civ. P. 26 and General Order No. 64 Attachment A, ¶ 5.

4. <u>Discovery</u>: Discovery taken to date, if any, the scope of anticipated discovery, any proposed limitations or modifications of the discovery rules, and a proposed discovery plan pursuant to Fed. R. Civ. P. 26(f) and General Order No. 64, Attachment A, ¶ 8.

5. <u>Settlement and ADR</u>: Whether the parties wish a settlement conference before a magistrate judge or some other form of ADR.

6. <u>Consent to Magistrate Judge For All Purposes</u>: Whether all parties will consent to have a magistrate judge conduct all further proceedings including trial and entry of judgment.

7. <u>Narrowing of Issues</u>: Issues that can be narrowed by agreement or by motion, suggestions to expedite the presentation of evidence at trial (e.g., through summaries or stipulated facts), and any request to bifurcate issues, claims, or defenses.

8. <u>Scheduling</u>: Proposed dates for designation of experts, discovery cutoff, hearing of motions permitted by General Order No. 64, Attachment A, ¶ 10, pretrial conference, and trial.

9. <u>Trial</u>: Whether the case will be tried to a jury or to the court.

10. Such other matters as may facilitate the just, speedy and inexpensive disposition of this matter.

GENERAL ORDER NO. 65.   CAMERAS IN THE COURTROOM PILOT PROJECT

Rule 53 of the Federal Rules of Criminal Procedure and policies of the Judicial Conference of the United States ("JCUS") prohibit, in both civil and criminal proceedings in federal district courts, the taking of photographs in courtrooms during judicial proceedings and the broadcasting of judicial proceedings from courtrooms.   To evaluate the effect of cameras in courtrooms, the JCUS, in consultation with the Federal Judicial Center, undertook a pilot project to allow, subject to tightly-drawn parameters, the recording of proceedings in selected district courts beginning July 18, 2011 (the "pilot project").

The United States District Court for the Northern District of California was one of the fourteen participating district courts in the pilot project.   The national pilot project concluded on July 18, 2015, but this district has been authorized by the JCUS and the Ninth Circuit Judicial Council to continue to record proceedings and to post them on uscourts.gov.   The program will continue to be governed by: the national "Pilot Guidelines" available at cand.uscourts.gov/cameras/guidelines; the procedures to implement the pilot project adopted by this Court and published at cand.uscourts.gov/cameras; and this General Order.

Cameras in the Courtroom

Revised September 15, 2016

The Northern District of California has been participating since October 3, 2011, in the Cameras in the Courtroom Pilot Project created by the Judicial Conference of the United States.   The Court's General Order 65 adopts the Pilot Project Guidelines issued by the Judicial Conference's Court Administration and Case Management Committee.   The national pilot project officially concluded on July 18, 2015, but this District, along with the Western District of Washington and the District of Guam, has been authorized to continue making the Pilot Project available.

Pursuant to the Court's procedures set out below, civil hearings and bench and jury trials may be recorded by local court personnel and published to a web page where they will be available for viewing or download by Darties, counsel and the general public.

Procedures

1.   Hearings and trials in any civil case assigned to a judge participating in the Pilot Project are eligible for video recording, upon request and with the consent of the parties and the presiding judge.

a.   The judges currently participating in the Pilot Project are Judges Alsup, Breyer, Chen, Chesney, Chhabria, Davila, Donato, Freeman, Gonzalez Rogers, Illston, Koh, Orrick, Tigar, White and Wilken.

b.   A Notice of Eligibility for Video Recording will be disseminated with the Order Setting Initial Case Management Conference and ADR Deadlines in every case assigned to the judges participating in the Pilot Project.

c.   When a hearing or trial is noticed or scheduled in a civil case before a participating judge, the judge, any party to the case, or the media may submit a Request for Video Recording through the Court's website.   The presiding judge's Courtroom Deputy and the Court's Information Technology Department will receive notification if a request is submitted.   Requests for video recording must be submitted at least 21 calendar days before the hearing date.

d.   If a Request for Video Recording is submitted, a Notice of Request for Video Recording will be filed on the case docket.

e.   Consent to recording will be presumed unless a party submits an Objection to Video Recording (.pdf)[1] through the Court's website within 7 calendar days of the date the Notice of Request for Video Recording is filed.   Do not e-file an Objection to Video Recording (.pdf)[1]; it will not become part of the public record in the case.

f.   When completing an Objection to Video Recording (.pdf)[1], a party may object to the recording of all or a portion of the proceeding or of only a certain witness or witnesses.

g.   The presiding judge's Courtroom Deputy will file a Notice Regarding Video Recording on the case docket, which will inform the parties, the requester and the public whether the proceeding, or a portion of it, will be recorded.

659

2. After a proceeding is video recorded, it will be made available to the public on the U.S. Courts Cameras in Courts web page (USCourts.gov)[2]. Videos will be made available as soon as possible, but the Court cannot provide exact dates or guarantee quality.

3. The presiding judge always maintains the discretion not to record any or all of a proceeding or not to publish any or all of a proceeding that has been recorded. Logistical issues such as availability of equipment and staff may also prevent recording.

Questions regarding the Northern District's participation in the Pilot Project should be directed to cameras@cand.uscourts.gov. Additional information about the Pilot Project can be found at the U.S. Courts Cameras in Courts web page (USCourts.gov)[2].

UNITED STATES DISTRICT COURT
NORTHERN DISTRICT OF CALIFORNIA

OBJECTION/RESPONSE TO REQUEST FOR VIDEO RECORDING

THIS FORM IS NOT TO BE FILED IN THE PUBLIC RECORD.

This form responds to the Request for Video Recording pending in this case.

Consent to recording is presumed unless this form is submitted no more than 7 days after the date of the Request for Video Recording.

View all rules and procedures at: cand.uscourts.gov/cameras.

INSTRUCTIONS:
1. Complete required fields.
2. Lock and Save form using the button at the bottom of the page.
3. Email this form to cameras@cand.uscourts.gov. Do not e-file!

Today's Date: _____   Date of Request: _____

Your Name: _____   Phone: _____

Email: _____   Case No: _____

Case Name: _____

Party you represent: _____

PLEASE SELECT ONE OF THE FOLLOWING:

☐ I **consent** to the Request for Video Recording, except as to the following witnesses, issues or types of evidence. (Please specify and explain.)

☐ I **consent** to the video recording request, subject to the following reservation or comment. (Please specify and explain.)

I **object** to the video recording of any part of this hearing. (Please state why you do not consent.)

CAND-01VR *Rev. Mar 2018*   [Lock and Save Form]   [Clear/Reset Form]

[Amended effective July 19, 2016.]

1 https://cand.uscourts.gov/wp-content/uploads/2018/11/CAND-Objection-to-Video-Recording-2018.pdf.   Publisher's Note: The form is also reproduced *infra*.

2 http://www.uscourts.gov/about-federal-courts/cameras-courts

GENERAL ORDER NO. 66. PROCEDURE FOR POST–JUDGMENT REVIEW OF SENTENCES IN CRACK COCAINE CASES PURSUANT TO UNITED STATES SENTENCING COMMISSION'S AMENDMENT TO POLICY STATEMENT § 1B1.10

On June 30, 2011, the United States Sentencing Commission ("USSG") promulgated an amendment to Policy Statement § 1B1.10 authorizing retroactive changes to sentences imposed for certain crack cocaine convictions. Absent contrary Congressional action, the amendment will go into effect on November 1, 2011. There are a number of defendants sentenced in the Northern District of California who, due to this amendment, may be eligible under 18 U.S.C. § 3582(c)(2) to seek reductions in sentences imposed on them for crack cocaine offenses. To recognize the potential for resolution of the matter by stipulation and to expedite appointment of counsel, disclosure of information relevant to sentencing and to conserve judicial resources, this General Order sets forth the procedures that shall apply to any defendant who contends that, pursuant to the June 30, 2011 amendment to USSG § 1B1.10, ("Applicable Case"), he or she is eligible for a change in sentence.

1. Upon the filing of a proposed stipulation, motion, application or request for a change in sentence in an Applicable Case, the Clerk of Court shall docket the matter under the case number of the underlying case and assign it to the Judge who presided over the underlying case for disposition pursuant to Criminal Local Rule 47–1 (Motion in Criminal Case) or 47–3 (Ex Parte Motion in Criminal Case) or 47–4 (Stipulation), respectively. If the originally assigned Judge is unavailable, the case shall be reassigned pursuant to General Order 44.D.

2. Unless the assigned Judge orders otherwise, the Federal Public Defender's Office is reappointed to represent any defendant in an Applicable Case whom it originally represented with respect to the underlying offense.

3. Unless the assigned Judge orders otherwise, the CJA panel attorney is reappointed to represent the defendant in an Applicable Case, whom he or she originally represented in the underlying case. If the original CJA panel attorney is unavailable or is otherwise unable to accept or declines the appointment, a new CJA panel attorney shall be appointed according to the regular procedures of our District for the appointment of a CJA panel attorney.

4. If a proposed stipulation, motion or application is filed by a defendant pro se, the Clerk of Court shall notify the Federal Public Defender's Office and the United States Attorney's Office of the filing.

5. No new financial affidavit will be required for a defendant in an Applicable Case who was previously represented by the Federal Public Defender's Office or by a CJA panel attorney.

6. In accordance with Criminal Local Rule 44–2(a), counsel may inform the Court of his or her appearance on behalf of the defendant by filing a notice of appearance electronically. No separate court appearance for identification of counsel is required.

7. Criminal Local Rule 32–7(b) governs the disclosure of presentence reports. Upon notice to it by the defense attorney or by counsel for the government that a defendant might be eligible for a change of sentence, without further order of the Court, the Probation Office is authorized to disclose the original presentence report and statement of reasons and any related documents to: (1) the Federal Public Defender's Office and other counsel for the defendant who is appointed pursuant to this General Order or who is subsequently appointed or retained; and (2) the United States Attorney's Office.

[Dated: October 11, 2011.]

GENERAL ORDER NO. 67. PROCEDURES FOR ASSIGNMENT OF PATENT CASES

A. **Purpose.** This Court, having been selected to participate in the Patent Pilot Project pursuant to Pub. L. No. 111–349, adopts the following procedures for the assignment of patent or plant variety protection cases which allege that a patent has been infringed or seek a declaratory judgment that a patent is not infringed, is invalid, or is unenforceable, and have been filed or transferred to this Court on or after January 1, 2012.

B. Procedures.

1. Patent Pilot Judges are active and senior District Judges who have volunteered, or who in the future volunteer, to receive assignments of patent cases under the Patent Pilot Project. District Judges may volunteer to be Patent Pilot Judges at any time. The list of current Patent Pilot Judges will be maintained by the Clerk of Court and posted on the Court's website. *See* http://cand.uscourts. gov/patentpilot.

2. Patent Magistrate Judges are Magistrate Judges with a particular interest in presiding over patent cases. A Magistrate Judge may be designated as a Patent Magistrate Judge if he or she so requests, but will preside over only patent cases in which the parties have consented to a Magistrate Judge for all purposes. See 28 U.S.C. § 636(c). A Patent Magistrate Judge will not be counted as a Patent Pilot Judge for the purposes of meeting any of the requirements for the district to become or retain its status as a Patent Pilot Project district. However, the Court will strive to increase the number of patent cases assigned to Patent Magistrate Judges consistent with 28 U.S.C. § 636(c). Magistrate Judges may request to be designated as Patent Magistrate Judges at any time. The list of Patent Magistrate Judges will be maintained by the Clerk of Court and posted on the Court's website. *See* http://cand.uscourts.gov/patentpilot.

3. All newly filed patent cases will be initially assigned pursuant to General Order No. 44 and Civil Local Rules 3–2 and 3–3. However, each non–Patent Pilot Judge will be allowed to decline up to three (3) patent cases in one 12–month period.

4. When a non–Patent Pilot Judge declines a case, it will be randomly assigned to a Patent Pilot Judge.

5. The Patent Pilot Judge who receives the declined case will then have removed from his or her caseload the number of newly filed non-prisoner cases which have a total weight, using the weights prescribed by the Administrative Office of the Courts, roughly equal to, but not less than, the weight of the declined patent case assignment. Those removed cases will then be reassigned to the judge who declined the patent case assignment. If a judge relates a declined case away from the Patent Pilot Judge who has already given up an equivalent of newly filed non-prisoner cases, that Patent Pilot Judge will have a new ballot added to the patent wheel.

6. As reflected in General Order No. 44 and Civil Local Rules 3–2 and 3–3, it is the policy and practice of this Court to maintain an equitable system for a proportionate division of civil cases among the District Judges and Magistrate Judges. For the limited purpose of the Court's participation in the Patent Pilot Project, the venue-based assignment of civil cases will be suspended for the purpose of re-balancing the caseloads of judges who exercise the option to decline patent cases and the Patent Pilot Judges who receive those declined cases, as detailed above.

7. This General Order does not prohibit reassignment of patent cases necessitated by recusals or orders relating cases pursuant to Civil Local Rule 3–12 or Patent Local Rule 2–1.

8. The Patent Pilot Project will be reviewed annually and each time a District Judge volunteers as, or discontinues serving as, a Patent Pilot Judge. Revisions to these procedures will be made as necessary.

[Dated: February 17, 2015.]

GENERAL ORDER NO. 68. POLICY ON COURT REFUNDS OF FEE OVERPAYMENTS

The Judicial Conference of the United States has a long-standing policy that generally prohibits the refunding of fees, subject to the following narrow exceptions: duplicate payments or other erroneous overpayments of fees, special assessments, fines or restitution may be refunded. The court hereby delegates its authority to the Clerk of Court to administer refunds in such limited circumstances. Records of all fee refunds shall be maintained for a minimum of seven years.

I. The following refund procedures apply to fees not paid electronically via Pay.gov:

A. If a party discovers an overpayment, the party may request a refund by writing to the Clerk of Court. The letter should explain the circumstances leading to the request and specify the amount of the requested refund.

B. Upon receipt of a request for a refund or, in the event that court staff discover an overpayment, a Clerk's Office supervisor will review the information and, if appropriate, approve the refund.

C. If approved by a supervisor, the request or court-initiated overpayment information will be transmitted to the Financial Administrator for review and data entry, and thereafter to the Chief Deputy of Administration for final processing of the refund. If for any reason the request is denied, the requesting party shall be promptly notified of the reason for the denial.

II. The following procedures apply to fees paid electronically via Pay.gov:

A. The Clerk of Court may refund only duplicate payments in which the payor has inadvertently paid the filing fee more than once in the same case, resulting in two or more identical credit card charges and erroneous payments in which the payor has inadvertently made a fee payment when no fee was due.

B. To request a refund after making a duplicate or erroneous overpayment, the payor should, complete an Application for Refund form, which is available under the Forms section of the court's website. The Application for Refund should then be submitted to the Clerk of Court via the court's CM/ECF system by selecting "Application for Refund" from the CM/ECF events menu.

C. Upon receipt of the Application for Refund, the Financial Administrator may approve or deny an application for refund.

D. The approval or denial of the application for refund will be entered on the case docket.

E. If the Financial Administrator denies an application for refund, the payor may make written request to the Clerk of Court to review the basis for the denial, if the Clerk of Court upholds the denial, the payor may, within ten business days of the Clerk's denial, file a motion making a request that the assigned judge or the Chief Judge if it is not case specific review the denial.

F. All authorized refunds shall be processed through the electronic credit card system, Pay.gov. If the payor's credit card is no longer valid, the Clerk of Court may cause a check to be issued through the United States Treasury. In no event shall the Clerk of Court make a cash refund.

G. In the event that an attorney or law firm repeatedly requests refunds for mistakes made when paying filing fees online, the Clerk of Court may request that the Chief Judge issue an order to show cause why additional requests for refunds by that attorney or law firm should not be denied. The order to show cause will be filed under a miscellaneous case.

[Dated: November 11, 2011.]

GENERAL ORDER NO. 69. PROCESS FOR SUBPOENAING & USING PERSONNEL OR COMPLAINT RECORDS OF STATE LAW ENFORCEMENT OFFICERS TESTIFYING IN FEDERAL COURT

I. PURPOSE

The purpose of this general order is to provide a streamlined process for subpoenaing and reviewing personnel and complaint records (hereafter, "records") of state law enforcement officers who have been or will be subpoenaed to testify in a federal criminal proceeding. It does not eliminate or limit any of the requirements of Northern District of California Criminal Local Rules (cited herein as "Crim. L.R.") 17-2 and 47-2, including the ability of the subpoenaed party to move to quash or modify the subpoena or to request an in camera review of the records.

II. PROCESS FOR OBTAINING AND USING RECORDS

A. Introduction. This General Order was generated by representatives from the Court, the United States Attorney's Office, the Federal Public Defender and the Court's Criminal Justice Act (CJA) Administration and Criminal Practice Committees. It contains a process for subpoenaing, obtaining, reviewing, and using personnel and complaint records and reflects the agreements of the Federal Public Defender and the United States Attorney to facilitate that process.

The General Order streamlines the request for production, production, and use of the records in four ways:

First, it establishes a process for production of records pursuant to a model protective order that provides for the return of all subpoenaed records at the end of the case, and it requires the defendant to move *in limine* in advance of a hearing or trial to introduce any records that the defendant believes are admissible. A sample form model protective order is attached as *Exhibit A*.

Second, the Federal Public Defender will provide training to all Assistant Federal Public Defenders and CJA panel lawyers on the General Order and the drafting of narrowly-framed Rule 17(c) subpoenas that comply with the requirements of Crim. L.R. 17–2.

Third, the General Order and the model protective order will be attached to the Rule 17(c) subpoenas requesting records.

Fourth, the United States Attorney's office will provide training to all Assistant United States Attorneys and will explain the expedited process to local law enforcement agencies that may receive Rule 17(c) subpoenas for personnel records.

The General Order is intended to minimize the need for judicial review of subpoena requests and documents produced pursuant to subpoena requests. It also should decrease the number of motions to quash because it offers local law enforcement agencies the protection of an automatic protective order, a mechanism for return of records, and an assurance that the Court will rule on the admissibility of any records in advance of a hearing or trial.

B. Form and Content of Subpoena. Any subpoena for personnel and complaint records of a state law enforcement officer who has been or will be called to testify in a federal criminal proceeding shall comply with the form and content requirements of Crim. L.R. 17–2. Specifically, the defendant shall submit to the Court an appropriate request for a Rule 17(c) subpoena directed to the custodian of records, setting forth the records requested, and specifying any particular records that the defendant believes are subject to disclosure based upon the facts of the case. Notice of this request for a Rule 17(c) subpoena must be given to the Government at the time the request is made. The defendant shall use the subpoena form entitled "Subpoena to Produce State Law Enforcement Personnel or Complaint Records in a Criminal Case" (attached as *Exhibit B* to this General Order), which advises the subpoenaed party that if compliance would be unreasonable or oppressive, it may move to quash or modify the subpoena or seek an in camera review of the records and which states that any records obtained pursuant to this subpoena will be subject to the model protective order restricting the release and use of the records sought. *See* Crim. L.R. 17–2(c). The model protective order and this General Order shall be attached to the subpoena.

C. Timing of Subpoena Requests.

1. *Motion Hearings.* If the records sought relate to officers who are expected to testify at an evidentiary hearing regarding a pre-trial motion, the request for a subpoena must be filed no later than the filing date of the defendant's motion. The return date for the subpoena shall be 14 days from service of the subpoena (unless the Court finds good cause for an earlier date under Crim. L.R. 17–2(d)). Should the subpoenaed party decide to file a motion to quash, it shall be filed on or before the return date and noticed for a hearing on the Court's next available criminal calendar but no fewer than 14 days later. *See* Crim. L.R. 47–2. The defendant shall be served with a copy of the motion to quash and shall file an opposition to the motion to quash 7 days after the motion to quash is filed. An optional reply is due 4 days after the opposition is filed.

If the Court rules on the defendant's motion without an evidentiary hearing, the serving party shall notify the subpoenaed party that it does not have to produce the requested documents and that any pending motion to quash is moot.

If the Court denies a motion to quash after ordering an evidentiary hearing, the Court shall allow the defendant sufficient time to review the records and make an appropriate in limine motion under seal seeking the admission of the records prior to the evidentiary hearing. The Court shall allow the Government sufficient time to file an opposition to the in limine motion. The Court shall decide any motions in limine on the date of the evidentiary hearing (unless the Court sets a different date).

If the defendant intends to subpoena personnel and complaint records in anticipation of an evidentiary hearing on a pretrial motion, Crim. L.R. 47–2's 14–day period to notice criminal motions will mean that the subpoenaed party may return records or file a motion to quash on or shortly after the initial motion hearing. The Court and the parties should consider these timing issues when setting a briefing and hearing schedule.

2. *Trial.* If the records sought relate to trial testimony, the request for a subpoena shall be filed no later than 40 days before the date set for the pretrial conference. Any subpoena shall be issued

and served no later than 35 days before the pretrial conference. The return date for the subpoena shall be 14 days from service of the subpoena (unless the Court finds good cause for an earlier date under Crim. L.R. 17–2(d)). Should the subpoenaed party decide to file a motion to quash, it shall be filed on or before the return date and noticed for a hearing on the Court's next available criminal calendar but not fewer than 14 days later (as required by Crim. L.R. 47–2). The defendant shall be served with a copy of the motion to quash and shall file an opposition to the motion to quash 7 days after the motion is filed. An optional reply is due 4 days after the opposition is filed.

Assuming service of a subpoena 35 days before the pretrial conference, the process allows a motion to quash to be noticed and heard 7 days before the pretrial conference. Should the motion to quash be denied, the Court shall allow the defendant sufficient time to review the records and make an appropriate in limine motion seeking the admission of relevant records prior to trial. The Court shall allow the Government sufficient time to file an opposition to any in limine motion.

D. Use of Subpoenaed Records. If no motion to quash is filed, or should the motion to quash be denied, the subpoenaed records shall be delivered to the Court (or to the requesting party if the subpoenaed party elects that procedure under Crim. L.R. 17–2(b)) in accordance with the schedule established above. If returned to the Court, the Court shall deliver the records to counsel for the defendant and the Government subject to the model protective order, which restricts the release of the records absent an order from the Court and which requires the return of the records at the conclusion of the case. If returned to the requesting party, the requesting party shall deliver a copy of the records to the opposing party subject to the same protective order.

If, after a review of the records, the defendant believes that material contained in those records is admissible either at an evidentiary hearing or at trial, the defendant shall make an appropriate in limine motion seeking admission of the records at issue in accordance with the schedule outlined below. The motion shall be made under seal in order to comply with the protective order regarding the public disclosure of the records.

If the Court agrees that the material is admissible, it shall grant the in limine motion, and the material will be admitted as ordered by the Court.

E. Timing of Motions *In Limine*.

1. *Motion Hearings.* If no motion to quash is filed, the defendant's motion in limine seeking admission of the subpoenaed records shall be filed no later than 14 days before the evidentiary hearing. The Government shall file any opposition no later than 7 days after the motion is filed. An optional reply is due 4 days after the opposition is filed. The Court will decide the motion in limine at the evidentiary hearing (unless the Court sets a different date).

2. *Trial.* If no motion to quash is filed, the defendant shall file an in limine motion seeking admission of the subpoenaed records no fewer than 14 days before the pretrial conference. The Government shall file any opposition 7 days after the motion is filed. An optional reply is due 4 days after the opposition is filed. The Court will decide the motion *in limine* at the pretrial conference (unless the Court sets a different date).

[Dated: June 19, 2012.]

EXHIBIT A TO GENERAL ORDER 69
See Forms Library for interactive version

UNITED STATES DISTRICT COURT
NORTHERN DISTRICT OF CALIFORNIA

UNITED STATES OF AMERICA,	)
	) Case Number: CR —————
Plaintiff,	)
	) PROTECTIVE ORDER RE: SUBPOENAED
	) PERSONNEL OR COMPLAINT RECORDS
vs.	) RECEIVED FROM LAW ENFORCEMENT
	)
———————————	) AGENCY UNDER FED. R. CRIM. P. 17(c) &
	) N.D. CAL. CRIM. L. R. 17–2(e)
Defendant(s).	)
	)
———————————————	)

Law enforcement personnel and/or complaint records (hereafter, "records") were subpoenaed from state or local agencies and returned to:

☐ the Court   ☐ the requesting party

and are hereby delivered to:

☐ both parties.
☐ the requesting party, who must produce a copy to the Government or make the records available for inspection and duplication.
☐ the Government by the requesting party, either by a copy of the records or, if no copy is attached, by this notice that the records are available for inspection and duplication.

Use of the records in this case shall be governed by General Order No. 69: *Process for Subpoenaing and Using Personnel and Complaint Records of State Law Enforcement Officers Testifying in Federal Court.* The parties may not use the records in any court proceeding or otherwise disclose any portion of the records or their contents without a court order. At the conclusion of the case, including the final disposition of an appeal of any conviction, the parties shall return the records to the court or the producing agency.

☐ The producing party asks that the assigned district judge file this protective order in the public record.

☐ The producing party sent the records directly to the requesting party, who now submits this order to the assigned district judge for filing in the public record.

IT IS SO ORDERED.

Dated: ———————————   ——————————————————
                              UNITED STATES DISTRICT JUDGE

EXHIBIT B TO GENERAL ORDER 69
Visit Forms Library for interactive version

UNITED STATES OF AMERICA,	SUBPOENA TO PRODUCE
	STATE LAW ENFORCEMENT
Plaintiff,	PERSONNEL OR COMPLAINT RECORDS
v.	IN A CRIMINAL CASE
	Case No.:
Defendant(s).	

TO:

YOU ARE COMMANDED to produce at the place, date, and time specified the personnel or complaint records indicated below. You shall produce the records pursuant to General Order 69 and pursuant to the attached protective order. If compliance would be unreasonable or oppressive, you may file a motion within 14 days of receipt of this subpoena requesting the court to quash or modify the subpoena or to review the documents in camera.

INDEX TO
UNITED STATES DISTRICT COURT
FOR THE NORTHERN DISTRICT OF CALIFORNIA

677

UNITED STATES DISTRICT COURT
FOR THE CENTRAL DISTRICT OF CALIFORNIA

Including Amendments Received Through
December 1, 2021

CHAPTER I. LOCAL CIVIL RULES, INTEGRATED WITH TITLES OF FEDERAL RULES OF CIVIL PROCEDURE

I. SCOPE OF RULES; FORM OF ACTION

F.R.CIV.P. 1. SCOPE AND PURPOSE

L.R. 1–1. APPLICABILITY

These Local Rules apply to all civil actions and proceedings in the United States District Court for the Central District of California.

[Effective October 1, 2001.]

L.R. 1–2. GENERAL ORDERS

The Clerk shall maintain a file of General Orders of the Court which shall be available for inspection by the public during regular office hours.

[Effective October 1, 2001.]

L.R. 1–3. APPLICABILITY OF RULES TO PERSONS APPEARING WITHOUT ATTORNEYS

Persons appearing pro se are bound by these rules, and any reference in these rules to "attorney" or "counsel" applies to parties pro se unless the context requires otherwise.

[Effective October 1, 2001.]

L.R. 1–4. DEFINITIONS

Unless the context requires otherwise, as used in these Local Rules:

(a) "Court" includes the judge or magistrate judge to whom a civil or criminal action, proceeding, case or matter has been assigned;

(b) "Declaration" includes any declaration under penalty of perjury executed in conformance with 28 U.S.C. § 1746, and any properly executed affidavit;

(c) "Defendant" means any party against whom a claim for relief is made or against whom an indictment or information is pending in a criminal case;

(d) "F.R.App.P." means the Federal Rules of Appellate Procedure;

(e) "F.R.Civ.P." means the Federal Rules of Civil Procedure;

(f) "F.R.Crim.P." means the Federal Rules of Criminal Procedure;

(g) "F.R.Evid." means the Federal Rules of Evidence;

(h) "Judge" refers to a United States District Judge or other judicial officer acting in any matter assigned to a United States District Judge;

(i) "Person" includes natural person, corporation, partnership or other association of individuals;

(j) "Plaintiff" means any party claiming affirmative relief by complaint, counterclaim or cross-claim;

Wherever applicable, each gender includes the other gender and the singular includes the plural.

[Effective October 1, 2001.]

F.R.CIV.P. 2. ONE FORM OF ACTION

II. COMMENCING AN ACTION; SERVICE OF PROCESS, PLEADINGS, MOTIONS, AND ORDERS

F.R.CIV.P. 3. COMMENCING AN ACTION

L.R. 3–1. CIVIL COVER SHEET AND OTHER FORMS REQUIRED AT THE TIME OF FILING A NEW ACTION

All civil actions presented to the Clerk for filing must be accompanied by a Civil Cover Sheet (Form CV–071) completed and signed by the attorney or party presenting the matter. In all cases where jurisdiction is invoked in whole or in part under 28 U.S.C. § 1338 (regarding patents, plant variety protection, copyrights and trademarks), the attorney or party presenting the matter must also provide at the time of filing the required notice to the Patent and Trademark Office in patent, plant variety protection and trademark matters (Form AO–120) and the required notice to the Copyright Office in copyright matters (Form AO–121). Copies of the Civil Cover Sheet and other forms are available from the Court's website, www.cacd.uscourts.gov.

[Effective October 1, 2001. Amended effective December 1, 2014.]

L.R. 3–2. FILING OF INITIATING DOCUMENTS

Unless exempted from electronic filing pursuant to L.R. 5–4.2, case-initiating documents, such as complaints and notices of removal, and all concurrently filed documents must be prepared in the English language and must be filed electronically using the Court's CM/ECF System, in accordance with the applicable Federal Rules of Civil Procedure and the Local Rules of this Court.

[Effective January 1, 2008. Amended effective June 1, 2012; December 1, 2013; December 1, 2014.]

F.R.CIV.P. 4. SUMMONS

L.R. 4–1. SUMMONS—PRESENTATION FOR ISSUANCE

The summons must be prepared using an approved form of summons, available from the Court's website, www.cacd.uscourts.gov. Unless exempted from electronic filing pursuant to L.R. 5–4.2, the summons must be presented electronically for issuance by the Clerk, using the Court's CM/ECF System.

[Effective October 1, 2001. Amended effective December 1, 2014.]

L.R. 4–2. SUMMONS—SERVICE OF PROCESS— UNITED STATES MARSHAL—CIVIL CASES

Except as otherwise provided by order of the Court, or when required by the treaties or statutes of the United States, process shall not be presented to the United States Marshal for service.

[Effective October 1, 2001.]

L.R. 4–3. SUMMONS—SERVICE OF PROCESS— UNITED STATES GOVERNMENT

Civil process on behalf of the United States government or an officer or agency thereof shall be made by the United States Marshal upon request by the government.

[Effective October 1, 2001.]

L.R. 4–4. SUMMONS—SERVICE OF PROCESS— HABEAS CORPUS PROCEEDINGS

In all cases where a petitioner has filed a habeas corpus petition under 28 U.S.C. § 2241 or § 2254, which challenges the judgment of a state court or the decision of a state agency, the procedures for service of the petitions and related orders will be pursuant to the agreement between the Attorney General of California and the Court set forth in Appendix B to these Local Rules. In all cases where a petitioner has filed a habeas corpus petition under 28 U.S.C. § 2241 or a motion under 28 U.S.C. § 2255, which challenges the judgment of a federal court or a decision of a federal agency, the procedures for service of the petitions, motions, and related orders will be pursuant to the agreement between the United States Attorneys' Office and the Court set forth in Appendix C to these Local Rules.

[Effective December 1, 2012. Amended effective June 1, 2013.]

L.R. 4–5. SUMMONS—SERVICE OF PROCESS DIRECTED TO FOREIGN COUNTRIES OR TO PERSONS OR ENTITIES WITHIN THEM

Any party requesting that the Clerk of Court mail a summons, complaint, or other documents under F.R.Civ.P. 4(f)(2)(C)(ii) or comparable statute or rule must file such request in the docket of the case in which service is sought. The request must identify the federal rule, statute, or other authority that authorizes the Clerk to effect service by mail and must include a declaration demonstrating that the filer has determined that service by mail is not prohibited by the law of the foreign country. The request must be electronically filed unless the filer is exempt under L.R. 5–4.2(a). An additional copy of the request must be brought or mailed to the Clerk's Office together with copies of the documents to be served, in a form proper for service under the applicable rule or statute, with a postage-paid envelope addressed to the person or entity upon whom service is sought, return receipt requested. After mailing the documents, the Clerk must file proof of mailing in the docket of the case; if the signed receipt is returned by the postal service to the Clerk's Office, the Clerk must file the returned receipt in the docket of the case as well. The mailing of documents by the Clerk under this rule does not constitute a judicial determination that service by mail is authorized, appropriate, or effective.

[Effective December 1, 2021.]

F.R.CIV.P. 4.1. SERVING OTHER PROCESS

F.R.CIV.P. 5. SERVING AND FILING PLEADINGS AND OTHER PAPERS

L.R. 5–1. LODGING DOCUMENTS

"Lodge" means to deliver to the Clerk a document which is tendered to the Court but is not approved for filing, such as depositions, exhibits, or a proposed form of order. Unless excluded from electronic filing pursuant to L.R. 5–4.2, all lodged documents shall be submitted electronically, in the same manner as documents that are electronically filed. Parties electronically lodging proposed orders or other proposed documents that require a judge's signature must comply with L.R. 5–4.4.

[Effective October 1, 2001. Amended effective January 1, 2010; June 1, 2012.]

L.R. 5–2. FILING IN FORMA PAUPERIS

An action to be filed in forma pauperis shall be accompanied by a motion, with supporting declaration. The declaration shall set forth information sufficient to establish that the movant will be unable to pay the fees and costs or give security therefor. The Clerk shall supply forms which may be used for an application to proceed in forma pauperis.

[Effective October 1, 2001. Amended effective December 1, 2003.]

L.R. 5–3. SERVING DOCUMENTS

Unless service is governed by F.R.Civ.P. 4, documents must be served as follows:

L.R. 5–3.1. Service of Documents Not Filed Electronically.

L.R. 5–3.1.1. *Service.* Documents presented to the Clerk for filing or lodging in paper format pursuant to L.R. 5–4.2 must be served in accordance with F.R.Civ.P. 5. All documents served under this L.R. 5–3.1.1 must be accompanied by a proof of service in the form required by L.R. 5–3.1.2.

L.R. 5–3.1.2. *Proof of Service.* Proof of service for documents served pursuant to L.R. 5–3.1.1 must be made by declaration of the person accomplishing the service. If the proof of service declaration is attached to the original document, it must be attached as the last page(s) of the document. The proof of service declaration must include the following information:

    (a) The day and manner of service;

    (b) Each person and/or entity served;

    (c) The title of each document served; and

    (d) The method of service employed (e.g., personal, mail, substituted, etc.).

L.R. 5–3.2. Service of Documents Filed Electronically.

L.R. 5–3.2.1. *Service.* Upon the electronic filing of a document, a "Notice of Electronic Filing" ("NEF") will be automatically generated by the CM/ECF System and sent by email to: (1) all attorneys who have appeared in the case in this Court and (2) all *pro se* parties who have been granted leave to file documents electronically in the case pursuant to L.R. 5–4.1.1 or who have appeared in the case and are registered to receive service through the CM/ECF System pursuant to L.R. 5–3.2.2. Unless service is governed by F.R.Civ.P. 4 or L.R. 79–5.3, service with this electronic NEF will constitute service pursuant to the Federal Rules of Civil and Criminal Procedure, and the NEF itself will constitute proof of service for individuals so served.

Individuals who have not appeared in the case in this Court or who are not registered for the CM/ECF System must be served in accordance with F.R.Civ.P. 5, and proof of service on such individuals must be made by declaration in the form required by L.R. 5–3.1.2.

L.R. 5–3.2.2. *Electronic Service for Pro Se Litigants.* A non-incarcerated pro se litigant who has not been granted leave to file documents electronically in a particular case pursuant to L.R. 5–4.1.1 may nevertheless register to receive electronic service of documents through the Court's CM/ECF System.

L.R. 5–3.2.3. *Consent to Electronic Service [Abrogated].*

[Effective October 1, 2001. Amended effective January 1, 2008; February 7, 2008; January 1, 2010; June 1, 2012; June 1, 2013; December 1, 2014; December 1, 2015; December 1, 2018.]

L.R. 5–4. FILING DOCUMENTS

L.R. 5–4.1 Electronic Filing in Civil Cases. Except as provided in L.R. 5–4.2, all documents filed in civil cases must be filed electronically using the Court's CM/ECF System. Sending a document by email does not constitute an electronic filing. To file documents using the CM/ECF System, an attorney must obtain an individual account login and password from the federal judiciary's national Public Access to Court Electronic Records ("PACER") system (www.pacer.gov) and

link this account to the Court's CM/ECF System. After the attorney's PACER account has been linked to the Court's CM/ECF System, the attorney must use the PACER-issued login and password to file documents through the Court's CM/ECF System.

L.R. 5–4.1.1 *Pro Se Litigants.* After entering an appearance in a civil case, any non-incarcerated pro se litigant may seek leave of Court to use the CM/ECF System to file documents electronically in that particular case. Leave to file electronically must be sought by motion, which must demonstrate that the pro se litigant has access to the equipment and software necessary to prepare documents for filing in PDF format and to connect to the Court's CM/ECF System.

If granted leave to file electronically, the pro se litigant must register to use the Court's CM/ECF System within five days of being served with the order granting leave. Registration must be initiated online through the Court's website and will require the litigant to have an active PACER account. After the registration process has been completed, the litigant will be able to file documents electronically only in the case in which leave to do so was granted. Leave to file electronically must be separately sought and granted, and the registration process separately completed, in each case in which the pro se litigant wishes to file electronically.

L.R. 5–4.1.2 *Authorization of Electronic Filing.* The Clerk will accept documents filed, signed, or verified by electronic means in compliance with these Local Rules. Any such document constitutes a written document for the purposes of applying these Local Rules and the Federal Rules of Civil Procedure.

L.R. 5–4.1.3 *Applicability of Other Rules.* Except as otherwise ordered in accordance with applicable statutes and rules, all Federal Rules of Civil Procedure and Local Rules shall continue to apply to cases that are subject to electronic filing.

L.R. 5–4.1.4 *Definitions.*

    (1) "CM/ECF System" refers to the automated Case Management/Electronic Case Filing system implemented by the Court. The CM/ECF System is available at https://ecf.cacd.uscourts.gov or at such other web address as may be specified by the Clerk on the Court's website.

    (2) "CM/ECF Website" refers to the CM/ECF Website operated by this Court to provide information regarding the CM/ECF System, including procedures and instructions for using the system. The CM/ECF Website is available at www.cacd.uscourts.gov/cmecf or at such other web address as may be specified by the Clerk on the Court's website.

    (3) "Notice of CM/ECF Unavailability" refers to a Public Notice from the Clerk regarding scheduled maintenance that will make the CM/ECF System unavailable. Such Notices are placed on the CM/ECF Website. In the event of an unscheduled system outage not preceded by a Notice of CM/ECF Unavailability, refer to L.R. 5–4.6.2.

    (4) The "Notice of Electronic Filing" ("NEF") generated pursuant to L.R. 5–3.2 for each electronically filed document will include the time of filing, the name of the parties and attorney(s) filing the document, the type of document, the text of the docket entry, the name of parties and/or attor-

ney(s) receiving the NEF, a hyperlink to the filed document that allows recipients to retrieve the document automatically, and the names of any attorneys or parties who have appeared in the case but who are not registered to receive service through the CM/ECF System.

(5) "PDF" refers to Portable Document Format, a specific computer file format that is the only format in which a document may be electronically filed.

L.R. 5–4.2 Exceptions to Electronic Filing in Civil Cases. Documents exempted from electronic filing pursuant to one of the subsections listed below shall be presented to the Clerk for filing or lodging in paper format, and shall comply with the requirements of L.R. 11 and all other applicable Local and Federal Rules.

(a) *Exemptions for Particular Filers.* The following filers are exempt from the requirement to file documents electronically:

(1) Pro Se Litigants. Unless otherwise ordered by the Court (*see* L.R. 5–4.1.1), pro se litigants shall continue to present all documents to the Clerk for filing in paper format. Documents received by the Clerk from pro se litigants under this rule will be scanned by the Clerk into the CM/ECF System. Once scanned, the original documents will be destroyed.

(2) Other Exceptional Cases Involving Unregistered Filers. For good cause shown, the Court may grant an exemption from the obligation to file electronically to an attorney who is not registered to file documents through the CM/ECF System. Any such exemption will not exceed one calendar year, but may be renewed upon good cause shown. If an attorney granted such an exemption thereafter registers to file documents through the CM/ECF System, that registration will abrogate any exemption granted under this rule. Documents received by the Clerk from an attorney granted an exemption pursuant this rule will be scanned by the Clerk into the CM/ECF System. Once scanned, the original documents will be destroyed.

(b) *Documents Excluded from Electronic Filing.* The following documents are excluded from the electronic filing requirement of L.R. 5–4.1:

(1) Nonpaper Exhibits. Nonpaper physical exhibits may not be filed at any time or in any format. Such exhibits must either be lodged with the Clerk under L.R. 11–5.1 (if submitted as an exhibit to a document) or submitted under L.R. 79–3 or 79–4 at the time of a trial or hearing.

(2) Oversized Paper Exhibits. Any exhibit on a sheet of paper that is too large or irregularly shaped to be scanned into PDF format may not be filed. It must either be lodged with the Clerk in paper format under L.R. 11–5.4 (if submitted as an exhibit to a document) or submitted under L.R. 79–3 or 79–4 at the time of a trial or hearing.

(3) Under–Seal and Other Documents Excluded from the Public Case File. Documents filed under seal or otherwise excluded from the public case file (such as documents filed pursuant to L.R. 5.2–2.2) shall be filed electronically if required by L.R. 79–5. Otherwise, such documents shall be filed in paper form, in accordance with the Federal Rules of Civil and Criminal Procedure and the Local Rules of this Court.

(4) Other Exceptions. For good cause shown, the Court may permit a particular document or exhibit to be filed or lodged in paper format, rather than electronically. If permission to file or lodge a document or exhibit in paper format is obtained, the document or exhibit shall be filed or lodged in compliance with L.R. 11–4. Unless the filer is exempted from electronic filing pursuant to L.R. 5–4.2(a), the filer shall first file electronically a Notice of Manual Filing or Lodging describing the document or exhibit being filed or lodged in paper format, and present a copy of the Notice of Manual Filing or Lodging, together with its NEF (see L.R. 5–3.2.1), with the document to be filed or lodged.

L.R. 5–4.3 Format of Electronically Filed Documents. In addition to the specific requirements for electronically filed documents set forth below, all documents subject to electronic filing shall comply with the general format requirements of L.Rs. 11–3, 11–5, 11–6, 11–7, and 11–8.

L.R. 5–4.3.1 *Technical Requirements (File Format and Size Limitations).* Documents filed electronically must be submitted in PDF. Except as provided elsewhere in this L.R. 5–4, the document filed with the Court must be created using word-processing software, then published to PDF from the original word-processing file (to permit the electronic version of the document to be searched). PDF IMAGES CREATED BY SCANNING PAPER DOCUMENTS ARE PROHIBITED, except that exhibits submitted as attachments to a document and records in bankruptcy appeals, habeas corpus proceedings, and administrative review cases such as Social Security appeals, ERISA, and IDEA cases may be scanned and attached, in text-searchable PDF form, if the filer does not possess a word-processing-file version of the attachment. Individual PDF files shall not exceed 35 MB in size, and shall contain no more than one document or portion of one document per file. PDF files that exceed 35 MB must be divided into subvolumes.

Where scanned signature pages are authorized under L.R. 5–4.3.4(a), only the signature pages may be scanned; the remainder of the document must be generated by publishing to PDF from the original word-processing file.

L.R. 5–4.3.2 *Redaction.* It is the responsibility of the filer to ensure full compliance with the redaction requirements of Federal Rule of Civil Procedure 5.2 and L.R. 5.2–1.

L.R. 5–4.3.3 *Hyperlinks.* Electronically filed documents may contain the following types of hyperlinks:

(1) Hyperlinks to other portions of the same document;

(2) Hyperlinks to other documents filed within the CM/ECF system; and

(3) Hyperlinks to a location on the Internet that contains a source document for a citation.

Hyperlinks may not be used to link to sealed or restricted documents. Hyperlinks to cited authority may not replace standard citation format. Complete citations must be included in the text of the filed document. Neither a hyperlink, nor any site to which it refers, shall be considered part of the record, but are simply mechanisms for accessing material cited in a filed document.

The court accepts no responsibility for, and does not endorse, any product, organization, or content at any hyperlinked site, or at any site to which that site may be linked. The court accepts no responsibility for the availability or functionality of any hyperlink. Court staff cannot assist counsel or parties in preparing hyperlinked documents, and should not be contacted for any such purpose.

L.R. 5–4.3.4 *Signatures.*

(a) Signatures on Electronically Filed Documents. An electronically filed document must be signed using one of the following methods:

(1) Documents Requiring the Signature of a Single Registered CM/ECF Filer. In the case of a document in which there is only one signatory, who is a registered CM/ECF filer, the document must be filed using that signatory's PACER login and password, which will function as the signatory's signature. Electronically filed documents must also include a signature block as provided in L.R. 11–1, and the signature must be represented on the signature line with either an "/s/" or a digitized personalized signature.

(2) Documents Requiring the Signatures of Multiple Registered CM/ECF Filers. In the case of a single document (such as a stipulation) in which there are multiple signatories, all of whom are registered CM/ECF filers, the document must be filed using the PACER login and password of one of those signatories and must include signature blocks for each required signatory, with the signatures indicated on each signature line using one of the following methods:

(i) the signatures of all signatories may be indicated on the document with an "/s/," and the filer must attest on the signature page of the document that all other signatories listed, and on whose behalf the filing is submitted, concur in the filing's content and have authorized the filing; or

(ii) the signatures of all signatories may be indicated using digitized personalized signatures.

(3) Documents Requiring Signatures Other Than Those of CM/ECF Filers. In the case of documents requiring signatures other than those of registered CM/ECF filers (such as declarations), the filer must scan the hand-signed signature page(s) of the document in PDF format and electronically file the document as required by L.R. 5–4.3.1.

(b) Maintenance of Original Hand-Signed Documents. For any electronically filed document containing a scanned copy of a hand-signed page, the filer must maintain the original, signed document. The original must be available for subsequent production to the assigned judge, whether ordered upon request by a party or the judge's own motion, until one year after final resolution of the action (including the appeal, if any).

(c) Effect of Signatures on Electronically Filed Documents. Any filing under this L.R. 5–4.3.4 will bind the signatories as if the document were physically signed and filed, whether for purposes of Rule 11 of the Federal Rules of Civil Procedure, to attest to the truthfulness of an affidavit or declaration, or for any other purpose.

(d) Responsibility for Use of Login and Password. A person registered to file documents through the CM/ECF System may authorize another to file a document using his or her PACER login and password if the document is filed on behalf of a party represented by the person registered to file. The person registered will be responsible for any document so filed. If at any time a registered CM/ECF filer believes that the security of his or her password has been compromised, he or she must immediately notify the PACER Service Center.

(e) Prohibition Against Filing on Behalf of Party Not Represented by the Registered CM/ECF Filer. Unless otherwise ordered by the Court, a registered CM/ECF filer's PACER login and password may not be used to file a document on behalf of a party not represented by that registered CM/ECF filer.

L.R. 5–4.4 Submission of Proposed Orders, Judgments, or Other Proposed Documents That Require a Judge's Signature.

L.R. 5–4.4.1 *Electronic Lodging of Proposed Orders.* Parties submitting proposed orders or other proposed documents that require a judge's signature must comply with both this L.R. 5–4.4.1 and L.R. 5–4.4.2, unless exempted from electronic filing pursuant to L.R. 5–4.2. When a proposed order or other proposed document accompanies an electronic filing, the proposed order or other proposed document shall be in PDF format and included, as an attachment, with the main electronically filed document (e.g., stipulations, applications, motions). Proposed orders or other proposed documents (such as a proposed judgment or proposed findings of fact) that are not lodged with a main document shall be electronically lodged as an attachment to a Notice of Lodging; if the proposed document is being submitted in response to a court order, the filer shall link the Notice of Lodging to that court order.

L.R. 5–4.4.2 *Submission of Word–Processing Versions of Proposed Orders.* After a document requiring a judge's signature has been lodged under L.R. 5–4.4.1, a WordPerfect or Microsoft Word copy of the proposed document, along with a PDF copy of the electronically filed main document, must be emailed to the assigned judge's generic chambers email address, either by using the "Proposed Orders" link within the CM/ECF System or by sending a separate email with the subject line in the following format: Court's divisional office, year, case type, case number, document control number assigned to the main document at the time of filing, judge's initials, and filer (party) type and name (e.g., for Los Angeles: LA08CV00123–6–ABC–Defendant and Counter Plaintiff Corp. A; for Santa Ana: SA08CV00124–8–DEF–Defendant and Counter Plaintiff Corp. B; for Riverside: ED08CV00125–10–GHI–Defendant and Counter Plaintiff Corp. C).

L.R. 5–4.5 Mandatory Chambers Copies. A "mandatory chambers copy" is an exact duplicate of an electronically filed document submitted in paper format directly to the assigned judge. Unless otherwise ordered by the assigned judge, one mandatory chambers copy of every electronically filed document must be delivered to the chambers of the assigned judge, or other designated location, no later than 12:00 noon on the following business day. Mandatory chambers copies must comply with L.R. 11–3, *et seq.* (i.e., blue-backing, font size, page-numbering, tabbing of exhibits, etc.), unless otherwise directed by the assigned judge. Mandatory chambers copies must be prominently labeled MANDATORY CHAMBERS COPY on the face page. Mandatory chambers copies must be printed from CM/ECF, and must include: (1) the CM/ECF–generated header (consisting of the case number, document control number, date of filing, page number, etc.) at the top of each page; and (2) the NEF (see L.R. 5–3.2.1) as the last page of the document. The Court's CM/ECF Website contains additional instructions by judges for delivery of mandatory chambers copies, including each judge's designated delivery location, and any differences in the required number of copies or delivery deadline.

L.R. 5–4.6 Deadlines.

L.R. 5–4.6.1 *Timeliness.* Unless otherwise provided by order of the assigned judge, all electronic transmissions of documents must be completed prior to midnight Pacific Standard Time or Pacific Daylight Time, whichever is in effect at the time, in order to be considered timely filed on that day.

L.R. ·5–4.6.2 *Technical Failures.* If a registered CM/ECF filer needs to file a document electronically, but is unable to do so, the filer must immediately contact the CM/ECF Help Desk by e-mail or telephone as posted on the CM/ECF Website, unless a "Notice of CM/ECF Unavailability" covering that time period has been posted on the Court's CM/ECF Website. If no Notice of CM/ECF Unavailability has been posted, the filer shall attempt to file the document electronically at least two times, separated by at least one hour. If, after at least two attempts, the filer cannot electronically file the document, the document will be accepted for filing by the Clerk in paper format that same day, if time permits. If a filer has complied with this section, and the delay of being unable to file a document electronically causes the document to be untimely, the filing shall be accompanied by a declaration or affidavit setting forth the facts of the filer's failed attempts to file electronically, together with an appropriate application for leave to file the document. Nothing in this Local Rule authorizes the Court to extend a deadline that, by statute or rule, may not be extended.

A history of technical failures lasting longer than one hour will be posted on the CM/ECF Website.

L.R. 5–4.7 Effectiveness of Electronic Filings.

L.R. 5–4.7.1 *Entry of Documents.* Except as otherwise provided in this L.R. 5–4, the acceptance by the Clerk of a document electronically filed shall constitute entry of that pleading or other document on the docket maintained by the Clerk under Federal Rules of Civil Procedure 58, 77, and 79.

L.R. 5–4.7.2 *Certification of Electronic Documents.* Pursuant to Federal Rules of Civil Procedure 44(a)(1) and 44(c), the method of electronic certification described herein is deemed proof of an official court record maintained by the Clerk of Court. The NEF (see L.R. 5–3.2.1) contains the date of electronic distribution and identification of the United States

District Court for the Central District of California as the sender. An encrypted verification code appears in the electronic document stamp section of the NEF. The electronic document stamp shall be used for the purpose of confirming the authenticity of the transmission and associated document(s) with the Clerk of Court, as necessary. When a document has been electronically filed in the CM/ECF System, the official record is the electronic recording of the document kept in the custody of the Clerk of Court. The NEF provides certification that the associated document(s).is a true and correct copy of the original filed with the Court.

L.R. 5–4.7.3 *Court Orders.* Any order or other Court-issued document filed electronically without the original signature of a judge or clerk has the same force and effect as if the judge or clerk had signed a paper copy of the order.

L.R. 5–4.8 Maintenance of Personal Contact Information.

L.R. 5–4.8.1 *Obligation to Maintain Personal Contact Information.* Attorneys and pro se parties registered to file or receive service of documents through the CM/ECF System are required to maintain and update their personal contact account information through PACER, including name, law firm or other affiliation, business address, telephone number, facsimile number, and email address. Attorneys and pro se parties with pending cases must also separately file and serve notice of the change in contact information as required by L.R. 83–2.4.

L.R. 5–4.8.2 *Obligation to Maintain Electronic Post Office Box.* Every attorney and pro se party registered to file or receive service of documents through the CM/ECF System will be responsible for maintaining an "electronic post office box," or storage area in the attorney's or party's computer system, that is adequate to handle all documents that will be sent electronically; for making certain that the e-mail service provider used does not limit the size of attachments; and for ensuring that the Court's NEF transmissions (see L.R. 5–3.2.1) are not blocked.

[Effective August 22, 2002. Amended effective February 7, 2008; January 1, 2010; June 1, 2012; June 1, 2013. Technical revisions effective December 1, 2013. Amended effective June 1, 2014; December 1, 2014; June 1, 2015; December 1, 2015; December 1, 2019; June 1, 2020; December 1, 2020.]

F.R.CIV.P. 5.1. CONSTITUTIONAL CHALLENGE TO A STATUTE—NOTICE, CERTIFICATION, AND INTERVENTION

F.R.CIV.P. 5.2. PRIVACY PROTECTION FOR FILINGS MADE WITH THE COURT

L.R. 5.2–1. REDACTION

It is the responsibility of the filer to ensure full compliance with the redaction requirements of Federal Rule of Civil Procedure 5.2. In addition, the filer shall redact passport numbers and driver license numbers in their entirety, and shall ensure that any document that contains a home address (except any proof of service filed as required by Federal Rule of Civil Procedure 4(*l*)) shall include only the city and state. This restriction on including passport numbers, driver license numbers, and full home addresses shall not apply to a filing exempted by Federal Rule of Civil Procedure 5.2(b); to an under-seal filing as set forth in Federal Rule of Civil Procedure 5.2(d), (f), or (g); or where the redaction requirement with respect to that information has been waived as provided in Federal Rule of Civil Procedure 5.2(h).

Parties shall carefully examine the documents, exhibits, or attachments to be filed with the Court in order to protect any sensitive and private information. The responsibility for redacting or placing under seal protected personal data identifiers rests solely with counsel and the parties. The Clerk will not review any pleadings or documents for compliance.

Counsel and the parties are cautioned that failure to redact or place under seal protected personal data identifiers may subject them to the disciplinary power of the Court. If a redacted version of the document is filed, counsel shall maintain possession of the unredacted document pending further order of the Court or resolution of the action (including the appeal, if any) and shall, at the request of opposing counsel or parties, provide a copy of the complete document.

[Effective June 1, 2012. Amended effective December 1, 2013; June 1, 2018.]

L.R. 5.2–2. EXCEPTIONS

L.R. 5.2–2.1 Remote Access Limitations. Cases subject to the limitations on remote access to electronic files set forth in F.R.Civ.P. 5.2(c) are exempted from the redaction requirements of F.R.Civ.P. 5.2(a) and of L.R. 5.2–1.

L.R. 5.2–2.2 Documents to Be Excluded From the Public Case File. The documents listed below are not to be included in the public case file, and are therefore excluded from the redaction requirements of F.R.Civ.P. 5.2 and L.R. 5.2–1:

(1) Unexecuted summonses or warrants, supporting applications, and affidavits;

(2) Pretrial bail reports;

(3) Presentence investigation reports;

(4) Statements of reasons in the judgment of conviction;

(5) Juvenile records;

(6) Documents containing identifying information about jurors or potential jurors;

(7) Financial affidavits filed in seeking representation pursuant to the Criminal Justice Act;

(8) Ex parte requests for authorization of investigative, expert, or other services pursuant to the Criminal Justice Act; and

(9) Sealed documents.

[Effective June 1, 2012. Amended effective December 1, 2013.]

F.R.CIV.P. 6. COMPUTING AND EXTENDING TIME; TIME FOR MOTION PAPERS

L.R. 6–1. NOTICE AND SERVICE OF MOTION

Unless otherwise provided by rule or order of the Court, no oral motions will be recognized and every motion shall be presented by written notice of motion. The notice of motion shall be filed with the Clerk not later than twenty-eight (28) days before the date set for hearing, and shall be served on each of the parties electronically or, if excepted from electronic filing, either by deposit in the mail or by personal service. If mailed, the notice of motion shall be served not later than thirty-one (31) days before the Motion Day designated in the notice. If served personally, or electronically, the notice of motion shall be served not later than twenty-eight (28) days before the Motion Day designated in the notice. The Court may order a shorter time. Unless otherwise ordered by the Court, the Clerk shall place each motion on the Motion Day calendar for the date designated in the written notice of motion.

[Effective October 1, 2001. Amended effective January 1, 2010; December 1, 2013.]

III. PLEADINGS AND MOTIONS

F.R.CIV.P. 7. PLEADINGS ALLOWED; FORM OF MOTIONS AND OTHER PAPERS

L.R. 7–1. STIPULATIONS

Stipulations will be recognized as binding only when made in open court, on the record at a deposition, or when filed in the proceeding. Written stipulations affecting the progress of the case shall be filed with the Court, be accompanied by a separate order as provided in L.R. 52–4.1, and will not be effective until approved by the judge, except as authorized by statute or the F.R.Civ.P.

[Effective October 1, 2001. Amended effective January 1, 2010.]

L.R. 7–2. APPLICABILITY

The provisions of this rule shall apply to motions, applications, petitions, orders to show cause, and all other proceedings except a trial on the merits (all such being included within the term "motion" as used herein) unless otherwise ordered by the Court or provided by statute, the F.R.Civ.P., or the Local Rules.

[Effective October 1, 2001.]

L.R. 7–3. CONFERENCE OF COUNSEL PRIOR TO FILING OF MOTIONS

In all cases not listed as exempt in L.R. 16–12, and except in connection with discovery motions (which are governed by L.R. 37–1 through 37–4) and applications for temporary restraining orders or preliminary injunctions, counsel contemplating the filing of any motion shall first contact opposing counsel to discuss thoroughly, *preferably in person*, the substance of the contemplated motion and any potential resolution. The conference shall take place at least seven (7) days prior to the filing of the motion. If the parties are unable to reach a resolution which eliminates the necessity for a hearing, counsel for the moving party shall include in the notice of motion a statement to the following effect:

"This motion is made following the conference of counsel pursuant to L.R. 7–3 which took place on (date)."

[Effective October 1, 2001. Amended effective December 1, 2003; January 1, 2010; June 1, 2013.]

L.R. 7–4. MOTIONS

The Court may decline to consider a motion unless it meets the requirements of L.R. 7–3 through 7–8. On the first page of the notice of motion and every other document filed in connection with any motion, there shall be included, under the title of the document, the date and time of the motion hearing, and the name of the judicial officer before whom the motion has been noticed. The notice of motion shall contain a concise statement of the relief or Court action the movant seeks.

[Effective October 1, 2001. Amended effective December 1, 2003; June 1, 2012; June 1, 2018.]

L.R. 7–5. MOVING PAPERS

There shall be served and filed with the notice of motion:

(a) A brief but complete memorandum in support thereof and the points and authorities upon which the moving party will rely; and

(b) The evidence upon which the moving party will rely in support of the motion.

[Effective October 1, 2001. Amended, effective December 1, 2009.]

L.R. 7–6. EVIDENCE ON MOTIONS

Factual contentions involved in any motion and opposition to motions shall be presented, heard, and determined upon declarations and other written evidence (including documents, photographs, deposition excerpts, etc.) alone, except that the Court may, in its discretion, require or allow oral examination of any declarant or any other witness.

[Effective October 1, 2001.]

L.R. 7–7. FORM AND CONTENT OF DECLARATIONS

Declarations shall contain only factual, evidentiary matter and shall conform as far as possible to the requirements of F.R.Civ.P. 56(c)(4).

[Effective October 1, 2001. Amended effective December 1, 2010.]

L.R. 7–8. PRESENCE OF DECLARANTS— CIVIL CASES

On motions for and orders to show cause re preliminary injunctions, motions to be relieved from default and other motions where an issue of fact is to be determined (*e.g.*, civil contempt, but excluding motions contesting venue and personal jurisdiction), not later than fourteen (14) days prior to the hearing, a party desiring to cross-examine any declarant who is not beyond the subpoena power of the Court and who is reasonably available to the party offering the declaration may serve by hand (or facsimile or by electronic filing) and file a notice of request to cross-examine such declarant. If the party offering the declaration disputes that the declarant is within the subpoena power of the Court and reasonably available to the offering party, such party shall serve and file an objection to the notice of request to cross-examine not later than eleven (11) days prior to the hearing. The offering party shall be under no obligation to produce the declarant unless the Court has granted the request to cross-examine by written order not later than three (3) days prior to the hearing. No declaration of a declarant with respect to whom such a request has been granted shall be considered unless such declarant is personally present and available at the hearing for such cross-examination as the Court may permit. The Court may, in the alternative, order that the cross-examination be done by deposition taken on two (2) days' notice with the transcript being lodged five (5) days prior to the hearing. The Court may impose sanctions pursuant to these Local Rules against any party or counsel who requests the presence of any declarant without a good-faith intention to cross-examine the declarant.

[Effective October 1, 2001. Amended effective December 1, 2003; January 1, 2008; January 1, 2010.]

L.R. 7–9. OPPOSING PAPERS

Each opposing party shall, not later than ten (10) days after service of the motion in the instance of a new trial motion and not later than twenty-one (21) days before the date designated for the hearing of the motion in all other instances, serve upon all other parties and file with the Clerk either (a) the evidence upon which the opposing party will rely in opposition to the motion and a brief but complete memorandum which shall contain a statement of all the reasons in opposition thereto and the points and authorities upon which the opposing party will rely, or (b) a written statement that that party will not oppose the motion. Evidence presented in all opposing papers shall comply with the requirements of L.R. 7–6, 7–7 and 7–8.

[Effective October 1, 2001. Amended effective December 1, 2003; January 1, 2010.]

L.R. 7–10. REPLY PAPERS

A moving party may, not later than fourteen (14) days before the date designated for the hearing of the motion, serve and file a reply memorandum, and declarations or other rebuttal evidence. Absent prior written order of the Court, the opposing party shall not file a response to the reply.

[Effective October 1, 2001. Amended effective December 1, 2003; January 1, 2010.]

L.R. 7–11. CONTINUANCE OF HEARING DATE

Unless the order for continuance shall specify otherwise, the entry of an order continuing the hearing of a motion automatically extends the time for filing and serving opposing papers and reply papers to twenty-one (21) days and fourteen (14) days, respectively, preceding the new hearing date. A stipulation to continue shall provide the date the opposition and reply papers are due to be filed with the Court.

[Effective October 1, 2001. Amended effective January 1, 2010.]

L.R. 7–12. FAILURE TO FILE REQUIRED DOCUMENTS

The Court may decline to consider any memorandum or other document not filed within the deadline set by order or local rule. The failure to file any required document, or the failure to file it within the deadline, may be deemed consent to the granting or denial of the motion, with the exception that a motion pursuant to F.R.Civ.P. 56 may not be granted solely based on the failure to file an opposition.

[Effective October 1, 2001. Amended effective December 1, 2003; June 1, 2012; June 1, 2014.]

L.R. 7–13. SANCTIONS FOR LATE FILING

A party filing any document in support of, or in opposition to, any motion noticed for hearing as above provided after the time for filing the same shall have expired, also shall be subject to the sanctions of L.R. 83–7 and the F.R.Civ.P.

[Effective October 1, 2001.]

L.R. 7–14. APPEARANCES AT HEARING

Counsel for the moving party and the opposing party shall be present on the hearing date and shall have such familiarity with the case as to permit informed discussion and argument of the motion. Failure of any counsel to appear, unless excused by the Court in advance pursuant to L.R. 7–15 or otherwise, may be deemed consent to a ruling upon the motion adverse to that counsel's position.

[Effective October 1, 2001.]

L.R. 7–15. ORAL ARGUMENT—WAIVER

Counsel may, with the consent of the Court, waive oral argument. Counsel who have agreed to waive oral argument shall advise the court clerk of such agreement by no later than noon on the fifth day preceding the hearing date. The court clerk shall advise the parties by no later than noon on the court day preceding the hearing date as to whether the Court has consented to the waiver of oral argument. The Court may dispense with oral argument on any motion except where an oral hearing is required by statute, the F.R.Civ.P. or these Local Rules.

[Effective October 1, 2001. Amended effective January 1, 2010.]

L.R. 7–16. ADVANCE NOTICE OF WITHDRAWAL OR NON–OPPOSITION

Any moving party who intends to withdraw a motion before the hearing date, and any opposing party who no longer intends to oppose a motion, must file and serve a notice of withdrawal of the motion or opposition immediately, preferably no later than 7 days before the hearing.

[Effective October 1, 2001. Amended effective December 1, 2010; June 1, 2020.]

L.R. 7–17. RESUBMISSION OF MOTIONS PREVIOUSLY ACTED UPON

If any motion, application or petition has been made to any judge of this Court and has been denied in whole or in part or has been granted conditionally or on terms, any subsequent motion for the same relief in whole or in part, whether upon the same or any allegedly different state of facts, shall be presented to the same judge whenever possible. If presented to a different judge, it shall be the duty of the moving party to file and serve a declaration setting forth the material facts and circumstances as to each prior motion, including the date and judge involved in the prior motion, the ruling, decision, or order made, and the new or different facts or circumstances claimed to warrant relief and why such facts or circumstances were not shown to the judge who ruled on the motion. Any failure to comply with the foregoing requirements shall be the basis for setting aside any order made on such subsequent motion, either sua sponte or on motion or application, and the offending party or attorney may be subject to the sanctions provided by L.R. 83–7.

[Effective October 1, 2001.]

L.R. 7–18. MOTION FOR RECONSIDERATION

A motion for reconsideration of an Order on any motion or application may be made only on the grounds of (a) a material difference in fact or law from that presented to the Court that, in the exercise of reasonable diligence, could not have been known to the party moving for reconsideration at the time the Order was entered, or (b) the emergence of new material facts or a change of law occurring after the Order was entered, or (c) a manifest showing of a failure to consider material facts presented to the Court before the Order was entered. No motion for reconsideration may in any manner repeat any oral or written argument made in support of, or in opposition to, the original motion. Absent good cause shown, any motion for reconsideration must be filed no later than 14 days after entry of the Order that is the subject of the motion or application.

[Effective October 1, 2001. Amended effective December 1, 2020.]

L.R. 7–19. EX PARTE APPLICATION

An application for an ex parte order shall be accompanied by a memorandum containing, if known, the name, address, telephone number and e-mail address of counsel for the opposing party, the reasons for the seeking of an ex parte order, and points and authorities in support thereof. An applicant also shall lodge the proposed ex parte order.

L.R. 7–19.1. Notice of Application. It shall be the duty of the attorney so applying (a) to make reasonable, good faith efforts orally to advise counsel for all other parties, if known, of the date and substance of the proposed ex parte application and (b) to advise the Court in writing and under oath of efforts to contact other counsel and whether any other counsel, after such advice, opposes the application.

L.R. 7–19.2. Waiver of Notice. If the judge to whom the application is made finds that the interest of justice requires that the ex parte application be heard without notice (which in the instance of a TRO means that the requisite showing under F.R.Civ.P. 65(b) has been made), the judge may waive the notice requirement of L.R. 7–19.1.

[Effective October 1, 2001. Amended effective January 1, 2010; December 1, 2010.]

L.R. 7–20. ORDERS ON MOTIONS AND APPLICATIONS

A separate proposed order shall be lodged with any motion or application requiring an order of the Court, pursuant to L.R. 52–4.1. Unless exempted from electronic filing pursuant to L.R. 5–4.2, each proposed order shall comply with L.R. 5–4.4.

[Effective October 1, 2001. Amended effective June 1, 2012.]

F.R.CIV.P. 7.1 DISCLOSURE STATEMENT

L.R. 7.1–1 NOTICE OF INTERESTED PARTIES

To enable the Court to evaluate possible disqualification or recusal, counsel for all non-governmental parties must file with their first appearance a Notice of Interested Parties, which must list all persons, associations of persons, firms, partnerships, and corporations (including parent corporations, clearly identified as such) that may have a pecuniary interest in the outcome of the case, including any insurance carrier that may be liable in whole or in part (directly or indirectly) for a judgment in the action or for the cost of defense. A corporate party may include in the Notice filed under this L.R. 7.1–1 any disclosures required under F.R.Civ.P. 7.1; if this information is included in the corporation's Notice of Interested Parties, the corporation is not required to file a separate Disclosure Statement under F.R.Civ.P. 7.1.

If the Notice of Interested Parties is filed with the Clerk in paper format under L.R. 5–4.2, an original and two copies must be filed. If the Notice of Interested Parties is filed electronically, Mandatory Chambers Copies must be delivered to the assigned district and magistrate judges. Counsel must promptly file an amended Notice if any material change occurs in the status of interested parties, as through merger or acquisition or a change in the carrier that may be liable for any part of a judgment.

The Notice must include the following certification:

"The undersigned, counsel of record for _____, certifies that the following listed party (or parties) may have a pecuniary interest in the outcome of this case. These representations are made to enable the Court to evaluate possible disqualification or recusal.

(Here list the names of all such parties and identify their connection and interest.)

Signature, Attorney of Record for:"

[Effective December 1, 2003. Amended effective December 1, 2005; January 1, 2008; December 1, 2012; June 1, 2019.]

F.R.CIV.P. 8. GENERAL RULES OF PLEADING

L.R. 8–1. JURISDICTION—ALLEGATIONS

The statutory or other basis for the exercise of jurisdiction by this Court shall be plainly stated in the first paragraph of any document invoking this Court's jurisdiction.

[Effective October 1, 2001.]

L.R. 8–2. THREE–JUDGE COURT— IDENTIFICATION IN PLEADING

If a party contends that the matter filed requires hearing by a court composed of three judges, the words "Three–Judge Court" shall be typed immediately below the docket number.

[Effective October 1, 2001.]

L.R. 8–3. RESPONSE TO INITIAL COMPLAINT

A stipulation extending the time to respond to the initial complaint shall be filed with the Clerk. If the stipulation, together with any prior stipulations, does not extend the time for more than a cumulative total of thirty (30) days from the date the response initially would have been due, the stipulation need not be approved by the judge. Any such stipulation must have as its title "Stipulation to Extend Time to Respond to Initial Complaint By Not More than 30 days (L.R. 8–3)". Directly beneath the title, the parties shall state when the Complaint was served, when a response currently is due, and when it will be due following the filing of the stipulation. For example:

```
John Smith        )  CV 08–20000–ABC (RZx)
                  )  Stipulation to Extend
                  )  Time to Respond to Initial
   v.             )  Complaint By Not More
                  )  Than 30 Days (L.R. 8–3)
                  )
                  )
James Jones       )  Complaint served:
                  )  September 15, 2008
                  )  Current response date:
                  )  October 6, 2008
                  )  New response date:
                  )  November 5, 2008
```

This rule shall not apply to answers, replies or other responses to cross-claims, counterclaims, third-party complaints or any amended or supplemental pleadings.

[Effective October 1, 2001. Amended effective February 16, 2009.]

F.R.CIV.P. 9.   PLEADING SPECIAL MATTERS

F.R.CIV.P. 10.   FORM OF PLEADINGS

F.R.CIV.P. 11.   SIGNING PLEADINGS, MOTIONS, AND OTHER PAPERS; REPRESENTATIONS TO THE COURT; SANCTIONS

L.R. 11–1.   SIGNATURE OF COUNSEL

All documents, except declarations, shall be signed by the attorney for the party or the party appearing pro se. The name of the person signing the document shall be clearly typed below the signature line.

[Effective October 1, 2001.]

L.R. 11–2.   FACSIMILE DOCUMENTS

Documents may not be transmitted by facsimile directly to the Clerk's office for filing. However, copies of facsimile documents shall be accepted for filing, provided that they are legible. The original of any faxed document, including the original signature of the attorney, party or declarant, shall be maintained by the filing party until the conclusion of the case, including any applicable appeal period, subject to being produced upon order of the Court.

[Effective October 1, 2001.]

L.R. 11–3.   DOCUMENTS PRESENTED TO THE COURT—FORM AND FORMAT

L.R. 11–3.1   Legibility. All pleadings, motions, affidavits, declarations, briefs, points and authorities, and other documents, including all exhibits thereto (hereinafter collectively referred to as "documents"), presented for filing or lodging with the Clerk shall be typewritten or printed, or prepared by a photocopying or other duplicating process that will produce clear and permanent copies equally legible to printing, in black or dark blue ink.

L.R. 11–3.1.1. *Font.* Either a proportionally spaced or a monospaced font may be used. A proportionally spaced font must be standard (e.g., non-condensed) 14–point or larger, or as the Court may otherwise order. A monospaced font may not contain more than 10–1/2 characters per inch.

L.R. 11–3.2   Paper. All documents shall be formatted for 8½ × 11 inch paper, and shall be numbered on the left margin with not more than 28 lines per page. The lines on each page shall be double-spaced and numbered consecutively with line 1 beginning at least one inch below the top edge of the paper. All documents presented to the Clerk for filing or lodging in paper format, and all mandatory chambers copies, shall be submitted on opaque, unglazed, white paper (including recycled paper) not less than 13–pound weight; only one side of the paper shall be used.

L.R. 11–3.3   Pagination. All documents shall be numbered consecutively at the bottom of each page.

L.R. 11–3.4   Original; Copies. The original of a document shall be labeled as the original and shall consist entirely of the original pages, except as otherwise allowed by these rules. All copies, including mandatory chambers copies if required by the assigned judge's orders or written procedures, are to be clearly identified as such.

L.R. 11–3.5   Pre–Punching of Documents. All documents presented for filing or lodging with the Clerk in paper format, and all mandatory chambers copies, if required by the assigned judge's orders or written procedures, shall be pre-punched with two (2) normal-size holes (approximately 1/4″ diameter), centered 2–3/4 inches apart, 1/2 to 5/8 inches from the top edge of the document. All pages shall be firmly bound at the top.

L.R. 11–3.6   Spacing. The typing or printing on the document shall be double spaced, including citations and quotations.

L.R. 11–3.6.1 *Footnotes—Exception.* Footnotes may be single spaced.

L.R. 11–3.6.2 *Real Property Description—Exception.* The description of real property may be single spaced.

L.R. 11–3.6.3 *Corporate Surety Bonds—Exception.* Printed forms of corporate surety bonds and undertakings may be single spaced and have unnumbered lines if they comply generally with the space requirements of this rule.

L.R. 11–3.7   Quotations. Quotations from cited cases or other authorities more than one sentence in length shall be clearly indented not less than 5 spaces nor more than 20 spaces.

L.R. 11–3.8   Title Page. On the first page of all documents:

(a) The name, California bar number, office address (or residence address if no office is maintained), the telephone and facsimile numbers, and the e-mail address of the attorney or a party appearing pro se presenting the document shall be placed commencing with line 1 at the left margin. The e-mail address shall be placed immediately beneath the name of the attorney. Immediately beneath, the party on whose behalf the document is presented shall be identified. All this information shall be single spaced. When a document is presented, the information set forth in this paragraph shall be supplied for each attorney or party appearing pro se who joins in the presentation of that document.

(b) The space between lines 1 and 7 to the right of the center of the page shall be left blank for use by the Clerk.

(c) The title of the Court shall be centered on or below line 8.

(d) The names of the parties shall be placed below the title of the Court and to the left of center, and single spaced. If the parties are too numerous, the names may be continued on the second or successive pages in the same space. In all documents, after the initial pleadings, the names of the first-named party only on each side shall appear.

(e) The docket number of the case shall be placed to the right of the center of the page and immediately opposite the names of the parties on the first page. Immediately below the docket number shall appear a concise description of the nature of the document (e.g., notice of motion, memorandum in support or opposition). Immediately below the description shall appear the time and date of the hearing on the matter to which the document is addressed.

(f) The title of a complaint or petition shall state the nature of the action or proceeding.

L.R. 11–3.9 Citations.

L.R. 11–3.9.1 *Acts of Congress.* All citations to Acts of Congress shall include a parallel citation to the United States Code by title and section.

L.R. 11–3.9.2 *Regulations.* All citations to regulations shall include a citation to the Code of Federal Regulations by title and section, and the date of promulgation of the regulation.

L.R. 11–3.9.3. *Cases.* Citation to a U.S. Supreme Court case must be to the United States Reports, Lawyers' Edition, or Supreme Court Reporter if available. Citation to a case from any other federal court must be to the Federal Reporter, Federal Supplement, or Federal Rules Decisions if available. Citation to a state court case must be to the official state reporter or any regional reporter published by West Publishing Company if available. If a case is not available in the foregoing sources, but is available on an electronic database (e.g., LEXIS or Westlaw), citation to the case must include the case name, the database identifier, the court, the date of decision, any code or number used by the database to identify the case, and any screen or page numbers assigned.

L.R. 11–3.10 Translations Required. Claim–Initiating Documents, as defined in L.R. 3–2, must be presented for filing in the English language. All other documents must be presented in English unless:

(a) an English translation is concurrently provided; or (b) the Court orders otherwise upon a showing of good cause.

[Effective October 1, 2001. Amended effective February 1, 2005; December 1, 2005; January 1, 2008; April 1, 2009; January 1, 2010; June 1, 2012; December 1, 2012; December 1, 2013; June 1, 2014.]

L.R. 11–4. COPIES

L.R. 11–4.1. In General.

L.R. 11–4.1.1. *Electronically Filed Documents.* Mandatory chambers copies of all electronically filed documents must be provided in accordance with L.R. 5–4.5. Unless otherwise ordered by the judge, all mandatory chambers copies must include the Notice of Electronic Filing (NEF) as the last page of the document, and must be blue-backed. The backing must extend no more than one inch below the bound pages, and the short title of the document must be typed on its lower right-hand corner.

L.R. 11–4.1.2. *Non–Electronically Filed Documents.* [DELETED].

L.R. 11–4.2. Three–Judge Court. If the matter is one that is to be heard by a three-judge court, mandatory chambers copies of all electronically filed documents shall be provided to each assigned judge in accordance with L.R. 5–4.5. For documents exempted from electronic filing pursuant to 5–4.2 and filed with the Clerk in paper format, three clear, conformed, and legible copies of the original shall be provided to the Clerk (one for the use of each of the assigned judges).

L.R. 11–4.3. Carbon Copies. [DELETED].

L.R. 11–4.4. Conformed Copy. Copies shall be conformed to the original but need not be executed. Conformed copies shall be identical to the original in content, pagination, additions, deletions and interlineations.

L.R. 11–4.5. Request for Conformed Copy. If the party presenting a document for filing in paper format requests the Clerk to return a conformed copy by United States mail, an extra copy shall be submitted by the party for that purpose accompanied by a postage-paid, self-addressed envelope.

[Effective October 1, 2001. Amended effective January 1, 2010; June 1, 2012; December 1, 2012; June 1, 2014; December 1, 2019.]

L.R. 11–5. EXHIBITS TO DOCUMENTS

L.R. 11–5.1 Nonpaper Physical Exhibits to Documents. Nonpaper physical exhibits may not be attached to any document. A nonpaper physical exhibit submitted as an exhibit to a document must be placed in a secure container (labeled with the case name and number, the docket number of the document to which it relates, and the name, address, telephone number, and email address of the submitting party) and lodged with a separately filed Notice of Lodging, which must include a description of the exhibit. Unless the filer is exempt from electronic filing under L.R. 5–4.2(a), the Notice of Lodging must be filed electronically before lodging the exhibit, and the Notice of Lodging, together with its NEF (see L.R. 5–3.2.1), must be presented with the exhibit to be lodged. Counsel of record for the submitting party must maintain copies of all exhibits submitted under this rule for the time required in L.R. 79–3. No originals may be submitted under this rule unless it is impossible to make a copy in any format. If it is not possible to make a copy in any format, the submitting party must clearly state that fact in the Notice of Lodging and must label the exhibit as the "ORIGINAL." Unless the Notice of Lodging requests that an exhibit be returned to counsel, all exhibits submitted under this rule, including originals, will be destroyed. Exhibits submitted under this rule do not become part of the Court's case file, are not considered Court records, and are not available for public viewing while under submission to the Court without a Court order. No contraband or valuable, sensitive, or dangerous exhibits may be submitted under this rule; such exhibits may be submitted only at the time of a trial or hearing as permitted under L.R. 79–4.

L.R. 11–5.2 Paper Exhibits to Documents—Attachment and Numbering. Unless compliance is impracticable, paper exhibits must be filed as attachments to the document to which they relate and must be numbered at the bottom of each page consecutively to the principal document. Exhibits filed electronically must comply with this rule unless precluded by L.R. 5–4.3.1.

L.R. 11–5.3 Exhibit Numbers on Paper Exhibits to Documents. The exhibit number must be placed immediately above or below the page number on each page of the exhibit. Exhibits must be tabbed in sequential order.

L.R. 11–5.4 Size of Paper Exhibits to Documents. Whenever possible, exhibits must be formatted for 8½ × 11 inch paper and filed under L.R. 11–5.2. Exhibits that are too large to scan must be folded in such a manner as not to exceed an 8½ × 11 inch sheet and lodged with the Clerk in paper format. Unless otherwise exempt from electronic filing under L.R. 5–4.2(a), the party presenting exhibits to the Clerk for lodging in paper format must first electronically file a Notice of Lodging setting forth why the exhibits cannot be filed electronically. The Notice of Lodging, together with its NEF (see L. R. 5–3.2.1), must be presented with the exhibits to be lodged. Counsel of record for the submitting party must maintain copies of all exhibits submitted under this rule for the time required in L.R. 79–3. No originals may be submitted under this rule unless it is impossible to make a copy in any format. If it is not possible to make a copy in any format, the submitting party must clearly state that fact in the Notice of Lodging and must label the exhibit as the "ORIGINAL." Unless the Notice of Lodging Requests that an exhibit be returned to counsel, all exhibits submitted under this rule, including originals, will be destroyed. Exhibits submitted under this rule do not become part of the Court's case file, are not considered Court records, and are not available for public viewing while under submission to the Court without a Court order.

L.R. 11–5.5 Small Paper Exhibits to Documents. An exhibit smaller than 8½ × 11 inches must be attached to an 8½ × 11 inch sheet, scanned, and electronically filed unless exempt under L.R. 5–4.2.

[Effective October 1, 2001. Amended effective January 1, 2010; June 1, 2012. Technical revisions effective December 1, 2013. Amended effective December 1, 2020.]

L.R. 11–6. POINTS AND AUTHORITIES—TRIAL BRIEFS—LENGTH

No memorandum of points and authorities, pre-trial brief, trial brief, or post-trial brief shall exceed 25 pages in length, excluding indices and exhibits, unless permitted by order of the judge.

[Effective October 1, 2001.]

L.R. 11–7. APPENDICES

Appendices shall not include any matters which properly belong in the body of the memorandum of points and authorities or pre-trial or post-trial brief.

[Effective October 1, 2001.]

L.R. 11–8. TABLE OF CONTENTS AND TABLE OF AUTHORITIES

Any memorandum of points and authorities or any brief exceeding ten (10) pages in length, excluding exhibits, shall be accompanied by an indexed table of contents setting forth the headings or subheadings contained in the body thereof, and by an indexed table of the cases, statutes, rules, and other authorities cited.

[Effective October 1, 2001.]

L.R. 11–9. SANCTIONS

The presentation to the Court of frivolous motions or opposition to motions (or the failure to comply fully with this rule) subjects the offender at the discretion of the Court to the sanctions of L.R. 83–7.

[Effective October 1, 2001.]

F.R.CIV.P. 12. DEFENSES AND OBJECTIONS: WHEN AND HOW PRESENTED; MOTION FOR JUDGMENT ON THE PLEADINGS; CONSOLIDATING MOTIONS; WAIVING DEFENSES; PRETRIAL HEARING

F.R.CIV.P. 13. COUNTERCLAIM AND CROSSCLAIM

F.R.CIV.P. 14. THIRD–PARTY PRACTICE

F.R.CIV.P. 15. AMENDED AND SUPPLEMENTAL PLEADINGS

L.R. 15–1. SEPARATE DOCUMENT

Any proposed amended pleading must be filed as an attachment to the related motion or stipulation. In addition, unless exempted from electronic filing by L.R. 5–4.2(a)(1), a party who obtains leave of Court to file an amended pleading must promptly thereafter file the pleading approved by the Court as a separate document in the Court's CM/ECF System.

[Effective October 1, 2001. Amended effective January 1, 2010; December 1, 2014.]

L.R. 15–2. COMPLETE DOCUMENT

Every amended pleading filed as a matter of right or allowed by order of the Court shall be complete including exhibits. The amended pleading shall not refer to the prior, superseded pleading.

[Effective October 1, 2001.]

L.R. 15–3. DATE OF SERVICE

An amended pleading allowed by order of the Court shall be deemed served upon the parties who have previously appeared on the date the motion to amend is granted or the stipulation therefor is approved. Service of amended pleadings on a party who has not previously appeared shall be made as provided in L.R. 4.

[Effective October 1, 2001. Technical revisions effective December 1, 2013.]

L.R. 15–4. MANNER OF FILING [DELETED EFFECTIVE DECEMBER 1, 2014]

F.R.CIV.P. 16. PRETRIAL CONFERENCES; SCHEDULING; MANAGEMENT

L.R. 16–1. APPLICABILITY

All civil actions or proceedings (including Admiralty) shall be pre-tried pursuant to F.R.Civ.P. 16 unless exempted by this rule or expressly waived in whole or in part by order of the Court.

[Effective October 1, 2001.]

L.R. 16–2. MEETING OF COUNSEL BEFORE FINAL PRETRIAL CONFERENCE

At least forty (40) days before the date set for the Final Pretrial Conference, lead trial counsel for the parties shall meet in person and shall accomplish the following:

L.R. 16–2.1. Subject Matter Jurisdiction. The parties shall assure themselves that this Court has jurisdiction of the subject matter. If any party questions the existence of subject matter jurisdiction, that party shall raise the issue by motion to be heard prior to the Final Pretrial Conference.

L.R. 16–2.2. Stipulation to Facts. The parties shall make every effort to stipulate to facts upon which the parties know or have reason to know there can be no dispute. A stipulation to the existence of a fact does not, unless expressly stated, stipulate to its admissibility in evidence.

L.R. 16–2.3. Disclosure of Exhibits. The parties shall disclose all exhibits to be used at trial other than those contemplated to be used solely for impeachment, as set forth in F.R.Civ.P. 26(a)(3)(A)(iii). The disclosures of exhibits shall be filed with the Court as provided in L.R. 16–6. Exhibits shall be marked in accordance with the procedures set forth in L.R. 26–3.

L.R. 16–2.4. Disclosure of Witnesses. The parties shall disclose the information required by F.R.Civ.P. 26(a)(3)(A)(i) and (ii) as to witnesses (including expert witnesses) to be called at trial other than those contemplated to be used solely for impeachment. The information shall be filed with the Court as provided in L.R. 16–5.

L.R. 16–2.5. Expert Witnesses. The parties shall discuss the status of expert witness designations, expert witnesses, and any issues concerning experts to be raised at the Final Pretrial Conference.

L.R. 16–2.6. Evidentiary Matters. The parties shall attempt to resolve any objections to the admission of testimony, documents, or other evidence.

L.R. 16–2.7. Depositions. Each party intending to present any evidence by way of deposition testimony shall:

(a) Identify on the original transcript the testimony the party intends to offer by bracketing the questions and answers in the margins. The opposing party shall likewise countermark any testimony that it plans to offer. The parties shall agree between themselves on a separate color to be used by each party which shall be consistently used by that party for all depositions offered in the case.

(b) Identify any objections to the proffered evidence in the margins of the deposition by briefly stating the ground for the objection.

(c) At the time of lodging under L.R. 32–1, also serve and file an index of the portions of the deposition offered, stating the pages and lines offered, objections, and the grounds for the objections.

L.R. 16–2.8. Contentions of Law and Fact. Each party shall disclose to every other party which of the party's pleaded claims and defenses the party plans to pursue, together with the party's contentions regarding the applicable facts and law.

L.R. 16–2.9. Settlement. The parties shall exhaust all possibilities of settlement.

[Effective October 1, 2001. Amended effective December 1, 2003; December 1, 2006; June 1, 2009.]

L.R. 16–3. DISCLOSURE OF GRAPHIC AND ILLUSTRATIVE MATERIAL

If not already disclosed as a part of the exhibits in accordance with L.R. 16–2.3, the parties shall disclose copies of all graphic or illustrative material to be shown the trier of fact as illustrating the testimony of a witness at least eleven (11) days before trial. Graphic or illustrative material not so disclosed may not be used at trial except by order of the Court on a finding of good cause for the failure to disclose.

[Effective December 1, 2006.]

L.R. 16–4. MEMORANDUM OF CONTENTIONS OF FACT AND LAW

Not later than twenty-one (21) days before the Final Pretrial Conference, each party shall serve and file a Memorandum of Contentions of Fact and Law. The Memorandum shall include the following parts:

L.R. 16–4.1 Claims and Defenses. The Memorandum shall contain:

(a) A summary statement of the claims Plaintiff has pleaded and plans to pursue. For example:

Claim 1: Defendant A breached his contract with Plaintiff;

Claim 2: Defendant A violated the Americans with Disabilities Act, 42 U.S.C. § 12101 et seq.

(b) *The Elements Required to Establish Plaintiff's Claims.* The elements shall be listed separately for each claim, as found in standard jury instructions or case law. For example:

Elements Required to Establish
Plaintiff's Claim for Violation
of the Americans with Disabilities Act

1. Plaintiff has a disability within the meaning of the Americans with Disabilities Act;

2. Plaintiff was a qualified individual; and

3. Plaintiff's disability was a motivating factor in the decision not to hire Plaintiff.

See Ninth Circuit Manual of Model Civil Jury Instructions § 12.1C (2007).

(c) In Plaintiff's Memorandum, a brief description of the key evidence in support of each of the claims. In Defendant's Memorandum, a brief description of the key evidence in opposition to each of the claims. The evidence should be listed separately for each claim.

(d) A summary statement of the counterclaims and affirmative defenses Defendant has pleaded and plans to pursue. For example:

Counterclaim 1: Plaintiff conspired with Third Party Defendant C to violate the Sherman Antitrust Act, 15 U.S.C. § 1;

Counterclaim 2: Plaintiff breached his fiduciary duty to Defendant.

First Affirmative Defense: Plaintiff's claim for breach of contract is barred by the four-year statute of limitations found in Cal. Civ. Proc. Code § 337.

Second Affirmative Defense: Under the doctrine of res judicata, Plaintiff's Complaint is barred by the final judgment entered in *Plaintiff v. Smith*, Los Angeles Superior Court Case No. 123456 (Judgment entered February 10, 1998).

Third Affirmative Defense: Defendant's decision not to hire Plaintiff was justified by business necessity.

(e) The elements required to establish Defendant's counterclaims and affirmative defenses. The elements shall be listed separately for each claim, as found, for example, in standard jury instructions or case law. For example:

Elements Required to Establish
Defendant's Affirmative Defense
of Business Necessity

1. The criterion by which the hiring decision was made was uniformly applied;

2. The criterion by which the hiring decision was made is job-related;

3. The criterion by which the hiring decision was made is consistent with business necessity;

4. The criterion cannot be met by a person with Plaintiff's disability, even with a reasonable accommodation.

See Ninth Circuit Manual of Model Civil Jury Instructions § 12.11 (2007).

(f) In Defendant's Memorandum, a brief description of the key evidence relied on in support of each counterclaim and affirmative defense. In Plaintiff's Memorandum, a brief description of the key evidence relied on in opposition to each counterclaim and affirmative defense. The evidence should be listed separately for each element of each counterclaim and affirmative defense.

(g) Similar statements for all third parties.

(h) Identification of any anticipated evidentiary issues, together with the party's position on those issues; and

(i) Identification of any issues of law, such as the proper interpretation of a governing statute, which are germane to the case, together with the party's position on those issues.

L.R. 16–4.2 [Abrogated].

L.R. 16–4.3 Bifurcation of Issues. The Memorandum shall contain any request for bifurcation of issues and an explanation for the request.

L.R. 16–4.4 Jury Trial. The Memorandum shall state whether any issues are triable to a jury as a matter of right and, if so, whether a timely demand for jury has been made, or whether the matter will be tried to the Court (F.R.Civ.P. 38, L.R. 38). If less than all issues are triable to a jury, the issues triable to a jury and to the Court shall be listed separately, with appropriate citation of authorities.

L.R. 16–4.5 Attorneys' Fees. If a party claims that attorneys' fees are recoverable, the Memorandum shall discuss the factual and legal basis of such claim.

L.R. 16–4.6 Abandonment of Issues. The Memorandum shall identify any pleaded claims or affirmative defenses which have been abandoned.

[Effective October 1, 2001. Renumbered and amended effective December 1, 2006. Technical revisions effective December 1, 2013.]

L.R. 16–5. WITNESS LIST

Each party shall serve and file under separate cover, at the same time as the Memorandum of Contentions of Fact and Law, a witness list containing the information required by F.R.Civ.P. 26(a)(3)(A). An asterisk shall be placed next to the names of those witnesses whom the party may call only if the need arises. Any objections to the use under F.R.Civ.P. 32 of a deposition designated under F.R.Civ.P. 26(a)(3)(A) shall be stated in the Final Pretrial Conference Order.

[Effective October 1, 2001. Renumbered and amended effective December 1, 2006. Amended effective January 1, 2010.]

L.R. 16–6. EXHIBITS

L.R. 16–6.1. Joint Exhibit List. Not later than twenty-one (21) days before the Final Pretrial Conference, all parties shall file a joint list of exhibits containing the information required by F.R.Civ.P. 26(a)(3)(A)(iii). The exhibits shall be listed in numerical order. When an exhibit has been numbered at a deposition, the same number shall be used for that exhibit at trial. If an exhibit has not been marked at a deposition, it shall be given the appropriate number in accordance with the requirements of L.R. 26–3. It is recognized that not all exhibits marked at depositions may be offered at trial so that there may be gaps in the numerical sequence on the exhibit list. An asterisk shall be placed next to the exhibits which a party may offer only if the need arises.

The exhibit list shall be substantially in the form indicated by the following example:

Case Title: _____ Case No. _____

No. of Exhibit	Description	Date Identified	Date Admitted
3	1/30/80 letter from Doe to Roe		
105	$500 check dated 2/3/82 drawn on Roe payable to Doe		
1002*	Handwritten notes dated 1/16/80		

* [An asterisk shall be placed next to the exhibits which a party may offer if the need arises.]

L.R. 16–6.2. Enlarged Copies of Exhibits. At trial, an enlarged copy of an exhibit may be used with the original exhibit. The enlarged copy shall be given the same number as the original exhibit, with a subdesignation (e.g., Exh. 24A) and shall be returned to counsel by the Clerk at the conclusion of the trial.

L.R. 16–6.3. Objections to Exhibits. The list of objections required by F.R.Civ.P. 26(a)(3)(B) shall be included in the proposed Final Pretrial Conference Order. The grounds for all objections shall be stated separately as to each exhibit.

L.R. 16–6.4. Marking of Exhibits for Trial. Counsel shall prepare official exhibit tags to be placed on all exhibits for trial. These exhibit tags may be obtained from the Clerk.

[Effective October 1, 2001. Renumbered and amended effective December 1, 2006. Amended effective June 1, 2009; January 1, 2010.]

L.R. 16–7. FINAL PRETRIAL CONFERENCE ORDER

A Final Pretrial Conference Order shall be prepared by plaintiff's counsel and signed by all counsel. It is the duty of all counsel to cooperate with plaintiff's counsel in the preparation and submission of the Final Pretrial Conference Order as required by this rule. Failure of counsel to comply shall subject counsel to the sanctions provided by L.R. 83–7 and 28 U.S.C. § 1927.

L.R. 16–7.1. Lodging. Plaintiff shall lodge the Final Pretrial Conference Order with the Clerk eleven (11) days before the date set for the Final Pretrial Conference.

L.R. 16–7.2. Form. The Final Pretrial Conference Order shall be substantially in the form shown in Pretrial Form No. 1 set forth in Appendix A to these Local Rules.

[Effective October 1, 2001. Renumbered and amended effective December 1, 2006.]

L.R. 16–8. FINAL PRETRIAL CONFERENCE

Each party appearing at the Final Pretrial Conference shall be represented by the attorney (or the party, if appearing *pro se*) who is then contemplated to have charge of the conduct of the trial on behalf of such party. At the Final Pretrial Conference the Court will consider:

L.R. 16–8.1. Unserved Parties. Any party not theretofore dismissed who is unserved at the time of the Final Pretrial Conference will be dismissed from the action without prejudice.

L.R. 16–8.2. Other Matters. Any matter arising from the Memorandums of Contentions of Fact and Law, Witness or Joint Exhibit Lists, Proposed Final Pretrial Conference Order, or other matter which needs to be addressed.

L.R. 16–8.3. Setting of Trial Date. The Court expects that at the Final Pretrial Conference the parties will then be ready to proceed to trial. If not previously set, the trial date shall be set at the earliest date permitted by the Court's calendar.

[Effective October 1, 2001. Renumbered and amended effective December 1, 2006.]

L.R. 16–9. CONTINUANCES

No continuance of the Final Pretrial Conference shall be granted merely on the stipulation of the parties. If the Court is satisfied that counsel are preparing the case diligently and that additional time is required to comply with this rule, the Final Pretrial Conference may be continued upon submission of a timely stipulation signed by all counsel setting forth the reasons for the requested continuance. The stipulation also shall describe what has been accomplished in preparing the case for the Final Pretrial Conference. No continuance of the Final Pretrial Conference will be granted unless the stipulation has been lodged before the date upon which the Final Pretrial Conference Order must be lodged with the Court. Counsel shall inform the Clerk immediately by telephone or other expeditious means when a stipulation is to be submitted for continuance of the Final Pretrial Conference.

A motion for continuance of the Final Pretrial Conference may be noticed upon five (5) days' notice to be heard not later than the last Motion Day before the date for which the Final Pretrial Conference has been set.

[Effective October 1, 2001. Renumbered and amended effective December 1, 2006.]

L.R. 16–10. TRIAL BRIEF

Unless the Court otherwise orders, at least seven (7) days before trial is scheduled to commence, each party may serve and file a trial brief which may:

(a) Update the Memorandum of Contentions of Fact and Law by citing newly decided cases;

(b) Brief such issues as directed by the Court; and

(c) Reply to the Memorandum of Contentions of Fact and Law of any other party.

[Effective October 1, 2001. Renumbered and amended effective December 1, 2006.]

L.R. 16–11. WAIVER OF PRETRIAL

In their report to the Court pursuant to F.R.Civ.P. 26(f), the parties may suggest to the Court that the matter should not be subject to the pretrial procedures in L.R. 16–2 through 16–10, and may request a waiver of those procedures. The report shall explain why counsel request the waiver.

L.R. 16–11.1. Procedure on Waiver. If the Court agrees that the case should not be subject to L.R. 16–2 through 16–10, the Court shall so indicate in its scheduling order entered under F.R.Civ.P. 16(b).

L.R. 16–11.2. Preparation for Trial. When the Court has granted a waiver of L.R. 16–2 through 16–10, the lead trial attorneys for the parties shall meet thirty (30) days before the date set for commencement of the trial and each party shall file not less than fourteen (14) days before the date set for commencement of the trial:

(a) A succinct statement of the factual and legal issues;

(b) Unless otherwise ordered by the Court, in non-jury cases, the direct testimony of all witnesses reasonably available to the party, in declaration or narrative form, who shall be subject to cross examination at trial by the opposing party as provided in L.R. 43–1;

(c) A witness list;

(d) An exhibit list;

(e) Depositions to be used at trial marked as required by L.R. 16–2.7; and

(f) A trial brief which provides the theory of the case and statutory or precedential support for the theory together with any unusual evidentiary or legal questions which may be anticipated at trial.

L.R. 16–11.3. Guideline for Granting Waiver. Unless otherwise ordered by the Court, waiver of L.R. 16–2 through 16–10 shall apply only to cases that are realistically estimated to consume no more than two (2) trial days.

[Effective October 1, 2001. Renumbered and amended effective December 1, 2006.]

L.R. 16–12. EXEMPTIONS

In the following categories of cases, the Court need not issue a scheduling order or hold a Final Pretrial Conference under F.R.Civ.P. 16:

(a) Petitions filed under 28 U.S.C. §§ 2241 et seq., or their functional equivalents;

(b) Actions for judicial review of a decision by the Commissioner of Social Security under 42 U.S.C. § 405(g);

(c) Any case in which the plaintiff is appearing pro se, is in custody, and is not an attorney;

(d) Any case removed to this Court from the small claims division of a state court;

(e) Appeals from the bankruptcy court;

(f) Extradition cases;

(g) Actions to enforce or quash an administrative summons or subpoena; and

(h) Actions by the United States to collect on a student loan guaranteed by the United States.

[Effective October 1, 2001. Renumbered and amended effective December 1, 2006. Amended effective January 1, 2010.]

L.R. 16–13. REPRESENTATION AT CONFERENCES

Each party appearing at any Scheduling or Pretrial Conference held under F.R.Civ.P. 16 shall be represented by the attorney (or the party if appearing pro se) who is then contemplated to have charge of the conduct of the trial on behalf of such party.

[Effective October 1, 2001. Renumbered and amended effective December 1, 2006.]

L.R. 16–14. MODIFICATION OF SCHEDULING ORDERS AND PRETRIAL ORDERS

Any application to modify an order entered pursuant to F.R.Civ.P. 16 shall be made to the judicial officer who entered the order.

[Effective October 1, 2001. Renumbered effective December 1, 2006.]

L.R. 16–15. POLICY RE SETTLEMENT & ADR

It is the policy of the Court to encourage disposition of civil litigation by settlement when such is in the best interest of the parties. The Court favors any reasonable means to accomplish this goal. Nothing in this rule shall be construed to the contrary. The parties are urged first to discuss and to attempt to reach settlement among themselves without resort to these procedures. It is also the policy of the Court that unless an Alternative Dispute Resolution (ADR) Procedure is selected by the parties, the judge assigned to preside over the civil case (the trial judge) may participate in facilitating settlement.

L.R. 16–15.1. Proceedings Mandatory. Unless exempted by the trial judge, the parties in each civil case shall participate in one of the ADR Procedures set forth in this rule or as otherwise approved by the trial judge.

L.R. 16–15.2. Time for Proceedings. Except as otherwise ordered by the Court, a Request: ADR Procedure Selection, signed by counsel for both sides, shall be filed with the parties' F.R.Civ.P. 26(f) report. Unless otherwise ordered, no later than forty-five (45) days before the Final Pretrial Conference, the parties shall participate in the ADR process approved by the Court.

L.R. 16–15.3. Court–Ordered Proceedings. If the parties do not file a timely Request: ADR Procedure Selection, the trial judge may order the parties to participate in any of the ADR Procedures set forth in this rule.

L.R. 16–15.4. Suggested ADR Procedures.

ADR PROCEDURE NO. 1—The parties shall appear before the district judge or magistrate judge assigned to the case for such settlement proceedings as the judge may conduct or direct.

ADR PROCEDURE NO. 2—The parties shall appear before a neutral selected from the Court's Mediation Panel.

ADR PROCEDURE NO. 3—The parties shall participate in a private dispute resolution proceeding.

L.R. 16–15.5. Requirements for ADR Procedures. With the exception of subsection (a) which applies only to settlement proceedings before a district judge or magistrate judge, the following requirements shall apply to all ADR Procedures unless otherwise ordered by the settlement judge or the neutral:

(a) *Statement of Case.* The parties shall submit in writing to the settlement judge, in camera (but not file), a confidential settlement statement (not to exceed five (5) pages) setting forth the party's statement of the case and the party's settlement position, including the last offer or demand made by that party and a separate statement of the offer or demand the party is prepared to make at the settlement conference. This confidential settlement statement shall be delivered to the settlement judge at least five (5) days before the date of the conference.

(b) *Appearance by Party.* Each party shall appear at the settlement proceeding in person or by a representative with final authority to settle the case, which in the case of lawsuits brought by or against the United States or any of its agencies as a party, shall involve the attendance of an attorney charged with responsibility for the conduct of the case and who has final settlement authority as provided by his or her superiors. A corporation or other non-governmental entity satisfies this attendance requirement if represented by a person who has final settlement authority and who is knowledgeable about the facts of the case. Representatives of insurers with decision-making authority are required to attend settlement proceedings, unless personal attendance is excused by the settlement officer. At the discretion of the settlement officer, and only with the settlement officer's express authorization, parties residing outside the District may have a representative with final settlement authority available by telephone during the entire proceeding, in lieu of personal appearance.

(c) *Appearance by Lead Trial Attorney.* Each party shall be represented at the settlement proceeding by the attorney who is expected to try the case, unless excused by the settlement officer.

(d) *Preparation by Party.* Each party shall have made a thorough analysis of the case prior to the settlement proceeding and shall be fully prepared to discuss all economic and non-economic factors relevant to a full and final settlement of the case.

L.R. 16–15.6. Optional Requirements for ADR Procedures. In settlement proceedings before a district judge or magistrate judge, any of the following procedures may be required:

(a) An opening statement by each counsel.

(b) With the agreement of the parties, a "summary" or "mini-trial," tried either to the settlement officer or to a mock jury.

(c) Presentation of the testimony, summary of testimony or report of expert witnesses.

(d) A closing argument by each counsel.

(e) Any combination of the foregoing.

L.R. 16–15.7. Report of Settlement. If a settlement is reached, counsel shall (a) immediately report the settlement to the trial judge's courtroom deputy clerk; and (b) timely memorialize the terms of the settlement.

L.R. 16–15.8. Confidentiality. This rule applies only to ADR Procedure No. 2, mediations conducted by the Court's Mediation Panel.

(a) *Confidential Treatment.* Except as provided in subsection (b) of this local rule, this Court, the mediator, all counsel and parties, and any other persons attending the mediation shall treat as "confidential information" the contents of the written mediation statements, any documents prepared for the purpose of, in the course of, or pursuant to the mediation, anything that happened or was said relating to the subject matter of the case in mediation, any position taken, and any view of the merits of the case expressed by any participant in connection with any mediation. "Confidential information" shall not be:

(1) disclosed to anyone not involved in the litigation;

(2) disclosed to the assigned judges; or

(3) used for any purpose, including impeachment, in any pending or future proceeding in this Court or any other forum.

(b) *Limited Exceptions to Confidentiality.* This rule does not prohibit:

(1) disclosures as may be stipulated by all parties and the mediator;

(2) disclosures as may be stipulated by all parties, without the consent of the mediator, for use in a subsequent confidential ADR or settlement proceeding;

(3) a report to or an inquiry by the ADR Judge regarding a possible violation of policies and procedures governing the ADR program;

(4) the mediator from discussing the mediation process with the Court's ADR staff, who shall maintain the confidentiality of the process;

(5) any participant or the mediator from responding to an appropriate request for information duly made by persons authorized by the Court to monitor or evaluate the Court's ADR program;

(6) disclosures as are required by General Order, related ADR forms, and as otherwise required by law; or

(7) in an action or proceeding to enforce a settlement, the admission of a written settlement agreement or a settlement placed on the record, reached as a result of mediation.

(c) *Confidentiality Agreement.* The mediator may ask the parties and all persons attending the mediation to sign a confidentiality agreement on a form provided by the Court and available on the court website. The confidentiality provisions of this section apply regardless of whether a confidentiality agreement is signed.

(d) *Scope.* Nothing in this rule is intended to limit any applicable privilege or rule of evidence designed to protect mediation confidentiality, and any such broader protection shall control if applicable.

L.R. 16–15.9. Rule Non–Exclusive. Nothing in this rule shall preclude or replace any settlement practice used by any district judge or magistrate judge of the Court. The provisions of this rule are not exclusive and nothing in this rule shall preclude any district judge or magistrate judge of the Court from dispensing with any provision of this rule as to any case or category of cases, as the judge, in his or her discretion, determines to be appropriate.

[Effective October 1, 2001. Amended effective September 1, 2004. Renumbered and amended effective December 1, 2006. Amended effective January 1, 2010; December 1, 2011.]

IV. PARTIES

F.R.CIV.P. 17. PLAINTIFF AND DEFENDANT; CAPACITY; PUBLIC OFFICERS

L.R. 17–1. MINORS OR INCOMPETENTS

L.R. 17–1.1. Minors or Incompetents—Appointment of Guardian Ad Litem. When the appointment of a guardian ad litem is required by F.R.Civ.P. 17(c)(2), a relative or friend of the minor or incompetent person, the minor if age 14 or over, or other suitable person must file a Petition for the Appointment of a Guardian Ad Litem at the time of the minor's or incompetent person's first appearance.

L.R. 17–1.2 Minors or Incompetents—Settlement of Claim of Minor or Incompetent. No claim in any action involving a minor or incompetent person shall be settled, compromised, or dismissed without leave of the Court embodied in an order, judgment, or decree.

L.R. 17–1.3 Minors or Incompetents—Settlement of Claim Procedure. Insofar as practicable, hearings on petitions to settle, compromise, or dismiss a claim in an action involving a minor or incompetent person shall conform to Cal. Civ. Proc. Code § 372 and California Rule of Court 3.1384.

L.R. 17–1.4 Minors or Incompetents—Attorney's Fees. In all actions involving the claim of a minor or incompetent person, whether resolved by settlement or judgment after trial, the Court shall fix the amount of attorney's fees.

L.R. 17–1.5 Minors or Incompetents—Judgment or Settlement Funds. All monies or property recovered on behalf of a minor or incompetent person, either by settlement or judgment, shall be paid into the registry of the Court unless otherwise ordered by the Court. All monies received by the Clerk representing a settlement or judgment on behalf of a minor or incompetent person shall be deposited by the Clerk in accordance with L.R. 67–1 and 67–2.

L.R. 17–1.6 Minors or Incompetents—Disbursement of Funds. All monies or property deposited with the Clerk pursuant to L.R. 17–1.5 shall be disbursed by the Clerk only in accordance with an order of the Court.

L.R. 17–1.6.1 *Conformance to State Law.* Unless otherwise ordered by the Court, disbursement of funds of California residents or foreign nationals under this L.R. 17–1.6 shall be made by the Clerk in accordance with the provisions of California Probate Code §§ 3600 et seq. If the minor, incompetent person, guardian, custodian, or parent is a resident of a state of the United States other than California, the funds or property shall be disbursed pursuant to restrictions of the state of residence similar to the provisions of California Probate Code §§ 3600 et seq.

L.R. 17–1.7 Minors or Incompetents—Letters of Guardianship or Custody—Bond. Before any funds or property are ordered distributed to any guardian or custodian, the following documents shall be filed with this Court:

(a) A certified copy of letters of guardianship or an order of appointment as custodian of the estate of an incompetent; and

(b) A certificate by a state court certifying that a surety bond has been filed by the guardian or custodian in a sum at least equal to the amount of money or value of property to be distributed.

L.R. 17–1.7.1 *Corporate Guardian.* If letters of guardianship or an order of appointment as custodian of the estate of an incompetent person have been issued to a corporate guardian authorized by state law to so act, no certificate showing filing of a bond shall be necessary.

[Effective October 1, 2001. Amended effective December 1, 2005; January 1, 2010; June 1, 2012. Former Rule 83–5 renumbered effective December 1, 2014.]

F.R.CIV.P. 18. JOINDER OF CLAIMS

F.R.CIV.P. 19. REQUIRED JOINDER OF PARTIES

L.R. 19–1. FICTITIOUSLY NAMED PARTIES

No complaint or petition shall be filed that includes more than ten (10) Doe or fictitiously named parties.

[Effective October 1, 2001.]

L.R. 19–2. MISJOINDER

No complaint or petition alleging violation of copyright, patent or trademark shall contain causes of action of different owners claiming violation of different copyrights, patents or trademarks, unless the complaint or petition is accompanied by a declaration of counsel setting forth grounds showing that the interests of justice will be advanced, and a multiplicity of actions avoided, by such joinder.

[Effective October 1, 2001.]

F.R.CIV.P. 20. PERMISSIVE JOINDER OF PARTIES

F.R.CIV.P. 21. MISJOINDER AND NONJOINDER OF PARTIES

F.R.CIV.P. 22. INTERPLEADER

F.R.CIV.P. 23. CLASS ACTIONS

L.R. 23–1. CAPTION

The title of any pleading purporting to commence a class action shall include the legend: "(Title of Pleading) Class Action."

[Effective October 1, 2001.]

L.R. 23–2. CLASS ALLEGATIONS

Any pleading purporting to commence a class action shall contain a separate section entitled "Class Action Allegations."

The information required in L.R. 23–2.1 and 23–2.2 shall be set forth in that section.

L.R. 23–2.1. Statutory Reference. The section shall contain a reference to the portion or portions of F.R.Civ.P. 23 under which it is contended that the suit is properly maintainable as a class action.

L.R. 23–2.2. Class Action Requisites. The section shall contain appropriate allegations thought to justify the action's proceeding as a class action, including, but not limited to:

(a) The definition of the proposed class;

(b) The size (or approximate size) of the proposed class;

(c) The adequacy of representation by the representative(s) of the class;

(d) The commonality of the questions of law and fact;

(e) The typicality of the claims or defenses of the representative(s) of the class;

(f) If proceeding under F.R.Civ.P. 23(b)(3), allegations to support the findings required by that subdivision; and

(g) The nature of notice to the proposed class required and/or contemplated.

[Effective October 1, 2001.]

L.R. 23–3. CERTIFICATION

At the earliest possible time after service of a pleading purporting to commence a class action other than an action subject to the Private Securities Litigation Reform Act of 1995, P.L. 104–67, 15 U.S.C. § 77z–1 et seq., but no later than any deadline set by the assigned judge, the proponent of the class must file a motion for certification that the action is maintainable as a class action.

[Effective October 1, 2001. Technical revisions effective December 1, 2013. Amended effective December 1, 2019.]

F.R.CIV.P. 23.1. DERIVATIVE ACTIONS

F.R.CIV.P. 23.2. ACTIONS RELATING TO UNINCORPORATED ASSOCIATIONS

F.R.CIV.P. 24. INTERVENTION

F.R.CIV.P. 25. SUBSTITUTION OF PARTIES

V. DISCLOSURES AND DISCOVERY

F.R.CIV.P. 26. DUTY TO DISCLOSE; GENERAL PROVISIONS GOVERNING DISCOVERY

L.R. 26–1. CONFERENCE OF PARTIES; REPORT

At the conference of parties held pursuant to F.R.Civ.P. 26(f), the parties shall discuss the following matters in addition to those noted in F.R.Civ.P. 26(f):

(a) Complex Cases. The complexity of the case, and whether all or part of the procedures of the Manual For Complex Litigation (current edition) should be utilized. Counsel may propose to the Court modifications of the procedures in the Manual to facilitate the management of a particular action.

(b) Motion Schedule. The dispositive or partially dispositive motions which are likely to be made, and a cutoff date by which all such motions shall be made.

(c) ADR. Selection of one of the three ADR Procedures specified in L.R. 16–15.4 as best suited to the circumstances of the case, and when the ADR session should occur. For cases in the Court–Directed ADR Program, counsel are directed to furnish and discuss with their clients the Notice to Parties of Court–Directed ADR Program in preparation for this conference. A settlement conference with a magistrate judge is generally not available for such cases.

(d) Trial Estimate. A preliminary estimate of the time required for trial.

(e) Additional Parties. The likelihood of appearance of additional parties.

(f) Expert Witnesses. The proposed timing of disclosures under F.R.Civ.P. 26(a)(2).

In their written report required by F.R.Civ.P. 26(f), the parties shall include their views and proposals, including any areas of disagreement, on the matters listed in this local rule. The Court will consider this report in making a referral to ADR.

[Effective October 1, 2001. Amended effective December 1, 2011.]

L.R. 26–2. DISCOVERY DOCUMENTS—FILING

When a discovery request or response is required for use in a proceeding, only that part of the document which is in issue shall be filed. All such discovery documents shall be held by the attorney pending use for the period specified in L.R. 79–3 for the retention of exhibits, unless otherwise ordered by the Court. Discovery documents lodged with the Court for a motion or a trial which are not used in said motion or trial shall be returned by the clerk to the party lodging the document at the conclusion of the motion or trial.

[Effective October 1, 2001.]

L.R. 26–3. EXHIBITS IN DISCOVERY

L.R. 26–3.1. Numbering of Exhibits. Documents introduced in discovery shall be numbered sequentially. Only one exhibit number shall be assigned to any given document. Exhibits shall be numbered without regard to the identity of the party introducing the exhibits.

If possible, each new exhibit shall be given the next available number. If it is not possible to do so (as, for example, when multiple depositions are conducted on the same day), then the parties shall break the sequence and use higher numbers to avoid duplication.

L.R. 26–3.2. Duplicate Exhibits. Any exhibit which is an exact duplicate of an exhibit previously numbered shall bear the same exhibit number regardless of which party is using the exhibit. Any version of any exhibit which is not an exact duplicate shall be marked and treated as a different exhibit bearing a different exhibit number.

L.R. 26–3.3. Inadvertent Numbering of a Duplicate Exhibit. If, through inadvertence, the same exhibit has been marked with different exhibit numbers, the parties shall assign the lowest such exhibit number to the exhibit and conform all deposition transcripts and exhibits to reflect the lowest number. The superseded number shall not be reused by the parties.

Example: If the same exhibit has been marked as 52 in the deposition of A and 125 in the depositions of B, C and/or D, the exhibit marked 125 shall be renumbered 52 and the depositions of B, C and D shall be conformed to the renumbered exhibit. Thereafter, number 125 shall not be used.

L.R. 26–3.4. Designation of Exhibit Sub–Parts. If it is necessary to identify sub-parts of a document that has been marked as an exhibit, then such sub-parts shall be designated by the number of the exhibit followed by a number designation.

Example: If a three-page contract is marked as Exhibit No. 12, the pages of the contract may be marked as Exhibits 12–1, 12–2, and 12–3; the entire document shall be referred to as Exhibit 12.

L.R. 26–3.5. Exhibits—Internal Control Numbering. In addition to exhibit numbers, documents may bear other numbers or letters used by the parties for internal control purposes.

[Effective October 1, 2001. Amended effective December 1, 2003.]

F.R.CIV.P. 27. DEPOSITIONS TO PERPETUATE TESTIMONY

F.R.CIV.P. 28. PERSONS BEFORE WHOM DEPOSITIONS MAY BE TAKEN

F.R.CIV.P. 29. STIPULATIONS ABOUT DISCOVERY PROCEDURE

F.R.CIV.P. 30. DEPOSITIONS BY ORAL EXAMINATION

F.R.CIV.P. 31. DEPOSITIONS BY WRITTEN QUESTIONS

F.R.CIV.P. 32. USING DEPOSITIONS IN COURT PROCEEDINGS

L.R. 32–1. USE AT TRIAL OR AN EVIDENTIARY HEARING

Deposition transcripts to be used at trial or an evidentiary hearing shall be marked as provided in L.R. 16–2.7. The original deposition shall be lodged with the Clerk on or before the first day of a trial or at least ten (10) days before an evidentiary hearing unless required to be filed earlier under L.R. 16–11.2. In addition, all original depositions not so lodged shall be brought to court by the attorney in custody of the same for any trial. Any party may by notice require an original deposition to be lodged for a trial or an evidentiary hearing. At a trial or an evidentiary hearing, the Court may order a lodged deposition to be filed or received in evidence, or may direct a party to prepare extracts from a deposition to be filed or received in evidence. The requirement for marking depositions shall not apply to depositions intended to be used at trial solely for impeachment.

[Effective October 1, 2001. Amended effective December 1, 2006; December 1, 2013.]

L.R. 32–2. ORIGINAL OF TRANSCRIPT

The original transcript of a deposition shall, unless otherwise stipulated to on the record at the deposition, after signing and correction, or waiver of the same, as provided in F.R.Civ.P. 30(e), be sent to the attorney noticing the deposition. The said attorney shall maintain control of the original deposition until final disposition of the case or until called upon to lodge the original deposition with the Court pursuant to L.R. 32–1. A copy of a deposition signed and certified as required in F.R.Civ.P. 30(e) and (f) may be used in lieu of an original.

[Effective October 1, 2001. Amended effective December 1, 2003.]

F.R.CIV.P. 33. INTERROGATORIES TO PARTIES

L.R. 33–1. NUMBERING

Interrogatories shall be numbered sequentially without repeating the numbers used on any prior set of interrogatories propounded by that party.

[Effective October 1, 2001.]

L.R. 33–2. ANSWERS AND OBJECTIONS

The party answering or objecting to interrogatories shall quote each interrogatory in full immediately preceding the statement of any answer or objection thereto.

[Effective October 1, 2001.]

L.R. 33–3. ORIGINAL

The original of the interrogatories served on the opposing party shall be held by the attorney propounding the interrogatories pending use or further order of the Court.

[Effective October 1, 2001.]

F.R.CIV.P. 34. PRODUCING DOCUMENTS, ELECTRONICALLY STORED INFORMATION, AND TANGIBLE THINGS, OR ENTERING ONTO LAND, FOR INSPECTION AND OTHER PURPOSES

L.R. 34–1. NUMBERING

Requests for production shall be numbered sequentially without repeating the numbers used on any prior set of requests for production propounded by that party.

[Effective October 1, 2001.]

L.R. 34–2. RESPONSES AND OBJECTIONS

The party responding or objecting to requests for production shall quote each request for production in full immediately preceding the statement of any response or objection thereto.
[Effective October 1, 2001.]

L.R. 34–3. ORIGINAL

The original of the requests for production of documents or to inspect tangible things served on the opposing party shall be held by the attorney propounding the requests pending use or further order of the Court.
[Effective October 1, 2001.]

F.R.CIV.P. 35. PHYSICAL AND MENTAL EXAMINATIONS

F.R.CIV.P. 36. REQUESTS FOR ADMISSION

L.R. 36–1. NUMBERING

Requests for admissions shall be numbered sequentially without repeating the numbers used on any prior set of requests propounded by that party.
[Effective October 1, 2001.]

L.R. 36–2. ANSWERS AND OBJECTIONS

The party answering or objecting to requests for admission shall quote each request in full immediately preceding the statement of any answer or objection thereto.
[Effective October 1, 2001.]

L.R. 36–3. ORIGINAL

The original of the requests for admission served on the opposing party shall be held by the attorney propounding the requests pending use or further order of the Court.
[Effective October 1, 2001.]

F.R.CIV.P. 37. FAILURE TO MAKE DISCLOSURES OR TO COOPERATE IN DISCOVERY; SANCTIONS

L.R. 37–1. PRE–FILING CONFERENCE OF COUNSEL

Before filing any motion relating to discovery under F.Rs.Civ.P. 26–37, counsel for the parties must confer in a good-faith effort to eliminate the necessity for hearing the motion or to eliminate as many of the disputes as possible. It is the responsibility of counsel for the moving party to arrange for this conference. If both counsel are located in the same county, the conference must take place in person at the office of the moving party's counsel unless the parties agree to meet someplace else. If both counsel are not located in the same county, the conference may take place telephonically. Unless relieved by written order of the Court upon good cause shown, counsel for the opposing party must confer with counsel for the moving party within ten days after the moving party

serves a letter requesting such conference. The moving party's letter must identify each issue and/or discovery request in dispute, state briefly as to each such issue/request the moving party's position (and provide any legal authority the moving party believes is dispositive of the dispute as to that issue/request), and specify the terms of the discovery order to be sought.
[Effective October 1, 2001. Amended effective December 1, 2003; January 1, 2010; December 1, 2019.]

L.R. 37–2. MOVING PAPERS

If counsel are unable to settle their differences, they must formulate a written stipulation unless otherwise ordered by the Court. The stipulation must be filed and served with the notice of motion.

L.R. 37–2.1 Form of Joint Stipulation. The stipulation must be set forth in one document signed by both counsel. The stipulation must contain all issues in dispute and, as to each such issue, the contentions and points and authorities of each party. The stipulation may not refer the Court to any other documents. For example, if the sufficiency of an answer to an interrogatory is at issue, the stipulation must contain, verbatim, both the interrogatory and the allegedly insufficient answer, followed by each party's contentions as to that particular interrogatory, separately stated. If the allegations made in a prior filing are relevant, a copy of that prior filing should be attached as an exhibit. Exhibits to the stipulation may include declarations prepared in conformity with L.R. 7–7. The specification of the issues in dispute, and the parties' contentions and points and authorities as to such issues, may be preceded by an introductory statement from each party, provided that no party's introductory statement may exceed three pages in length. When a party states its contentions on a particular issue, such party must also state how it proposed to resolve the dispute over that issue at the conference of counsel.

Although the stipulation should present the disputed issues as concisely as the subject matter permits, the page limitation established by L.R. 11–6 does not apply to stipulations regarding discovery disputes. Any stipulation exceeding ten pages in length, excluding exhibits, must be accompanied by an indexed table of contents setting forth the headings or subheadings contained in the body thereof but need not be accompanied by a table of authorities.

The title page of the stipulation must state the date and time of the motion hearing, the discovery cutoff date, the pretrial-conference date, and the trial date. In addition, a copy of the order establishing the initial case schedule, as well as any amendments, must be attached to the stipulation or to a declaration filed in support of the motion.

L.R. 37–2.2 Preparation of Joint Stipulation. Following the conference of counsel, counsel for the moving party must personally deliver, e-mail, or fax to counsel for the opposing party the moving party's portion of the stipulation, together with all declarations and exhibits to be offered in support of the moving party's position. Unless the parties agree otherwise, within seven days of receipt of the moving party's material, counsel for the opposing party must personally deliver, e-mail, or fax to counsel for the moving party the opposing party's portion of the stipulation, together with all declarations and exhibits to be offered in support of the opposing party's position. After the opposing party's material is added to the stipulation by the moving party's counsel, the stipulation must be provided to opposing counsel, who must sign it (electronically or otherwise) and return it to counsel for the moving party no later than the end of the next business day, so that it can be filed with the notice of motion.

L.R. 37–2.3 Supplemental Memorandum. After the Joint Stipulation is filed, each party may file a supplemental memorandum of law not later than fourteen days before the hearing date. Unless otherwise ordered by the Court, a supplemental memorandum may not exceed five pages in length. No other separate memorandum of points and authorities may be filed by either party in connection with the motion.

L.R. 37–2.4 Failure to File Joint Stipulation. The Court will not consider any discovery motion in the absence of a joint stipulation or a declaration from counsel for the moving party establishing that opposing counsel (a) failed to confer in a timely manner under L.R. 37–1; (b) failed to provide the opposing party's portion of the joint stipulation in a timely manner under L.R. 37–2.2; or (c) refused to sign and return

the joint stipulation after the opposing party's portion was added. If such declaration accompanies the motion, then L.Rs. 6–1, 7–9 and 7–10 apply.

[Effective October 1, 2001. Amended effective December 1, 2003; April 1, 2008; January 1, 2010; June 1, 2012; December 1, 2015; December 1, 2019; December 1, 2021.]

L.R. 37–3. HEARING ON MOTION

The motion must be noticed to be heard on a regular Motion Day for the appropriate judge at least twenty-one days after the filing of the motion. Unless the Court in its discretion otherwise allows, no discovery motions may be filed or heard on an ex parte basis absent a showing of irreparable injury or prejudice not attributable to the lack of diligence of the moving party.

[Effective October 1, 2001. Amended effective December 1, 2019.]

L.R. 37–4. COOPERATION OF COUNSEL—SANCTIONS

The failure of any counsel to comply with or cooperate in the foregoing procedures may result in the imposition of sanctions.

[Effective October 1, 2001.]

VI. TRIALS

F.R.CIV.P. 38. RIGHT TO A JURY TRIAL; DEMAND

L.R. 38–1. JURY TRIAL DEMAND— INCLUDED IN PLEADING

If the demand for jury trial is included in a pleading, it shall be set forth at the end thereof and be signed by the attorney for the party making the demand. The caption of such a pleading shall also contain the following: "DEMAND FOR JURY TRIAL."

[Effective October 1, 2001.]

L.R. 38–2. JURY TRIAL DEMAND—REMOVED CASES WHERE JURY TRIAL NOT DE-MANDED PRIOR TO REMOVAL

In all such cases removed to this Court which are not at issue at the time of removal, the demand for jury trial must be filed within 14 days after service of the last responsive pleading addressed to an issue triable by right by a jury. If the matter already is at issue at the time of removal, the demand must be filed within 14 days after the filing of the notice of removal if the demand is made by the removing party, and within 14 days after service of filing of the notice of removal if the demand is made by a party other than the removing party.

[Effective October 1, 2001. Amended effective June 1, 2020.]

L.R. 38–3. JURY TRIAL DEMAND—MARKING CIVIL COVER SHEET INSUFFICIENT

Marking the Civil Cover Sheet shall not be deemed a sufficient demand to comply with F.R.Civ.P. 38(b) or L.R. 38–1 and 38–2.

[Effective October 1, 2001.]

L.R. 38–4. EXCEPTIONS

The provisions of L.R. 38–3 shall not prevent the use of printed forms provided by the Clerk or by the Administrative Office of the United States Courts.

[Effective October 1, 2001.]

F.R.CIV.P. 39. TRIAL BY JURY OR BY THE COURT

F.R.CIV.P. 40. SCHEDULING CASES FOR TRIAL

L.R. 40–1. CONTINUANCES

Any application for continuance of any trial or similar proceeding shall be served and filed at least five (5) days before the day set for the trial or proceeding. The application shall set forth in detail the reasons therefor.

L.R. 40–1.1. Notice of Application for Continuance. Counsel shall notify the court clerk immediately when a stipulation for the continuance of a hearing, pre-trial conference, trial or other proceeding is to be submitted for approval of the Court.

L.R. 40–1.2. Application for Continuance—Approval of the Court. No continuance (whether stipulated to by counsel or not) shall be effective unless approved in writing or announced in open court by the judge.

[Effective October 1, 2001.]

L.R. 40–2. NOTICE OF SETTLEMENT

Counsel shall inform the court clerk immediately by telephone or other expeditious means when a case set for trial or other proceeding has been settled.

[Effective October 1, 2001.]

L.R. 40–3. LATE NOTIFICATION

In any civil case, failure to comply with the provisions of L.R. 40–1 or 40–2 may subject counsel or the parties to the following sanctions:

(a) Payment of costs and attorneys' fees of an opposing party;

(b) Payment of reasonable charges reflecting the costs of compensating jurors for their unnecessary appearance; and

(c) Such other sanctions as may seem proper to the Court under the circumstances.

Notwithstanding compliance with L.R. 40–2, if counsel fails to inform the court clerk of settlement by 4 p.m. on the last business day prior to trial, the Court may assess counsel or the parties reasonable charges reflecting the costs of compensating jurors for their unnecessary appearance.

[Effective October 1, 2001. Amended effective June 1, 2014.]

F.R.CIV.P. 41. DISMISSAL OF ACTIONS

L.R. 41–1. DISMISSAL—UNREASONABLE DELAY

Civil suits which have been pending for an unreasonable period of time without any action having been taken therein may, after notice, be dismissed for want of prosecution.

[Effective October 1, 2001.]

L.R. 41–2. DISMISSAL—EFFECT

Unless the Court provides otherwise, any dismissal pursuant to L.R. 41–1 shall be without prejudice.

[Effective October 1, 2001.]

L.R. 41–3. REINSTATEMENT—SANCTIONS

If any action dismissed pursuant to L.R. 41–1 is reinstated, the Court may impose such sanctions as it deems just and reasonable.

[Effective October 1, 2001.]

L.R. 41–4. REFILING OF DISMISSED ACTION

If any action dismissed pursuant to L.R. 41–1 is refiled as a new action, the party filing the later action shall comply with the requirements of L.R. 83–1.2.2.

[Effective October 1, 2001.]

L.R. 41–5. DISMISSAL—FAILURE TO APPEAR

If a party, without notice to the Court, fails to appear at the noticed call of any action or proceeding, the matter is subject to dismissal for want of prosecution.

[Effective October 1, 2001.]

L.R. 41–6. DISMISSAL—FAILURE OF PRO SE PLAINTIFF TO KEEP COURT APPRISED OF CURRENT ADDRESS

A party proceeding *pro se* must keep the Court and all other parties informed of the party's current address as well as any telephone number and email address. If a Court order or other mail served on a *pro se* plaintiff at his address of record is returned by the Postal Service as undeliverable and the *pro se* party has not filed a notice of change of address within 14 days of the service date of the order or other Court document, the Court may dismiss the action with or without prejudice for failure to prosecute.

[Effective October 1, 2001. Amended effective December 1, 2003; January 1, 2010; December 1, 2020.]

F.R.CIV.P. 42. CONSOLIDATION; SEPARATE TRIALS

F.R.CIV.P. 43. TAKING TESTIMONY

L.R. 43–1. NON–JURY TRIAL—NARRATIVE STATEMENTS

In any matter tried to the Court, the judge may order that the direct testimony of a witness be presented by written narrative statement subject to the witness' cross-examination at the trial. Such written, direct testimony shall be adopted by the witness orally in open court, unless such requirement is waived.

[Effective October 1, 2001.]

F.R.CIV.P. 44. PROVING AN OFFICIAL RECORD

F.R.CIV.P. 44.1. DETERMINING FOREIGN LAW

F.R.CIV.P. 45. SUBPOENA

L.R. 45–1. MOTIONS RELATING TO DISCOVERY SUBPOENAS

Except with respect to motions transferred to this district pursuant to F.R.Civ.P. 45(f), L.R. 37 applies to all motions relating to discovery subpoenas served on (a) parties and (b) non-parties represented by counsel.

[Effective October 1, 2001. Amended effective June 1, 2014.]

F.R.CIV.P. 46. OBJECTING TO A RULING OR ORDER

F.R.CIV.P. 47. SELECTING JURORS

F.R.CIV.P. 48. NUMBER OF JURORS; VERDICT; POLLING

F.R.CIV.P. 49. SPECIAL VERDICT; GENERAL VERDICT AND QUESTIONS

L.R. 49–1. REQUEST FOR SPECIAL VERDICT OR INTERROGATORIES

Any request for a special verdict or a general verdict accompanied by answers to interrogatories shall be filed and served at least seven (7) days before trial is scheduled to commence.

[Effective October 1, 2001. Amended effective January 1, 2010.]

L.R. 49–2. FORM—PRESENTATION BY COUNSEL

Special verdicts or interrogatories shall not bear any identification of the party presenting the form. Identification shall be made only on a separate page appended to the front of the special verdict or interrogatory form.

[Effective October 1, 2001.]

F.R.CIV.P. 50. JUDGMENT AS A MATTER OF LAW IN A JURY TRIAL; RELATED MOTION FOR A NEW TRIAL; CONDITIONAL RULING

F.R.CIV.P. 51. INSTRUCTIONS TO THE JURY; OBJECTIONS; PRESERVING A CLAIM OF ERROR

L.R. 51–1. REQUESTS FOR INSTRUCTIONS

Proposed instructions shall be in writing and shall be filed and served at least seven (7) days before trial is scheduled to begin unless a different filing date is ordered by the Court. The parties jointly shall submit a single set of instructions as to which they agree. In addition, each party shall submit separately those proposed instructions as to which all parties do not agree.

[Effective October 1, 2001. Amended effective December 1, 2003; January 1, 2010.]

L.R. 51–2. FORM OF REQUESTS

Each requested instruction shall:

(a) Be set forth in full on a separate page;

(b) Embrace only one subject or principle of law; and

(c) Not repeat the principle of law contained in any other request.

[Effective October 1, 2001.]

L.R. 51–3. IDENTITY OF REQUESTING PARTY

The identity of the party requesting the instructions shall be set forth on a cover page only and shall not be disclosed on the proposed instructions.

[Effective October 1, 2001.]

L.R. 51–4. CITATION OF AUTHORITY

The authority for or source of each proposed instruction shall be set forth on a separate page or document and shall not be disclosed on the proposed instruction.

[Effective October 1, 2001.]

L.R. 51–5. OBJECTIONS

Objections shall be filed and served on or before the first day of trial unless the Court permits oral objections.

L.R. 51–5.1. Separate Objections. Written objections shall be numbered and shall specify distinctly the objectionable matter in the proposed instruction. Each objection shall be accompanied by citation of authority. Where applicable, the objecting party shall submit an alternative instruction covering the subject or principle of law.

[Effective October 1, 2001.]

F.R.CIV.P. 52. FINDINGS AND CONCLUSIONS BY THE COURT; JUDGMENT ON PARTIAL FINDINGS

L.R. 52–1. NON–JURY TRIAL—FINDINGS OF FACT AND CONCLUSIONS OF LAW

In any matter tried to the Court without a jury requiring findings of fact and conclusions of law, counsel for each party shall lodge and serve proposed findings of fact and conclusions of law at least seven (7) days before trial.

[Effective October 1, 2001. Amended effective December 1, 2003; January 1, 2010.]

L.R. 52–2. OTHER FINDINGS OF FACT AND CONCLUSIONS OF LAW

In all other cases where findings of fact and conclusions of law are required under F.R.Civ.P. 41, 52, and 65, the attorney directed to do so by the Court shall lodge and serve proposed findings of fact within seven (7) days of the decision.

[Effective October 1, 2001. Amended effective January 1, 2010.]

L.R. 52–3. FORMAT

Proposed findings of fact shall:

(a) Be in separately numbered paragraphs;

(b) Be in chronological order; and

(c) Not make reference to allegations contained in pleadings.

Conclusions of law shall follow the findings of fact and:

(a) Shall be in separately numbered paragraphs, and

(b) May include brief citations of appropriate authority.

[Effective October 1, 2001.]

L.R. 52–4.   ORDERS

Each order shall be prepared by the attorney directed to do so by the Court. The order shall comply with the requirements of L.R. 58–10. Within five (5) days of the ruling, the attorney preparing the order shall serve it on all parties and lodge it with the Clerk.

L.R. 52–4.1.   Separate Order. A separate proposed order shall be submitted with any stipulation, application, motion, or request of the parties requiring an order of the court. If the proposed order is the result of a stipulation, the pertinent elements requested in the stipulation shall be set forth in the order. Unless the filer is exempted from electronic filing pursuant to L.R. 5–4.2(a), the proposed order shall be submitted as provided in L.R. 5–4.4.

[Effective October 1, 2001. Amended effective January 1, 2010; June 1, 2012.]

L.R. 52–5.   SIGNING OF ORDERS
FOR ABSENT JUDGES

Except as otherwise provided by F.R.Civ.P. 63, application for any order in a civil action (including cases on appeal) shall be made to the judge to whom the case is assigned. If the judge to whom the action is assigned is not available and there is an emergency necessitating an order, the judge's court clerk shall be consulted to determine whether a judge of this Court has been designated to handle matters in the absence of the assigned judge. If a designation has been made, the application shall be presented to the designated judge. If no designation has been made by the assigned judge, then the matter shall be presented to the Chief Judge, or in the Chief Judge's absence, to any other available judge. If no emergency exists, the application will be held by the assigned judge's court clerk until the assigned judge is available.

[Effective October 1, 2001. Amended effective December 1, 2003.]

L.R. 52–6.   SERVICE OF DOCUMENT

The attorney whose duty it is to prepare any document required by L.R. 52–1, 52–2, or 52–4 shall serve a copy on opposing counsel on the same day that the document is lodged with the Court. Alternatively, the attorney preparing the document may present it to opposing counsel for approval as to form before the document is lodged.

[Effective October 1, 2001. Amended effective June 1, 2012.]

L.R. 52–7.   SEPARATE OBJECTION

Opposing counsel may, within seven (7) days after service of a copy of a document prepared pursuant to L.R. 52–1, 52–2, or 52–4, file and serve objections to the form of the document and the grounds thereof. The failure to file timely objections shall be deemed a waiver of any defects in the form of the document.

[Effective October 1, 2001. Amended effective January 1, 2010; June 1, 2012.]

L.R. 52–8.   ENDORSEMENT OF COUNSEL

Unless the Court otherwise directs, no document governed by L.R. 52–1, 52–2, or 52–4 will be signed by the judge unless either opposing counsel shall have endorsed thereon an approval as to form, or the time for objection has expired. If it finds the ends of justice so requires, the Court may conduct a hearing on the proper form of the document, or it may sign the document as prepared or as modified.

[Effective October 1, 2001. Amended effective June 1, 2012.]

L.R. 52–9.   ORDER UPON STIPULATION
[DELETED]

F.R.CIV.P. 53.   MASTERS

L.R. 53–1.   APPOINTMENT

Appointment of a master pursuant to F.R.Civ.P. 53 shall be made by written order of the Court.

[Effective October 1, 2001.]

L.R. 53–2.   FEES AND EXPENSES

A master's fees and expenses, when approved by the Court, shall be paid as the Court orders. Those amounts are recoverable as costs under L.R. 54–3. 9.

[Effective October 1, 2001. Technical revisions effective December 1, 2013.]

VII.   JUDGMENT

F.R.CIV.P. 54.   JUDGMENT; COSTS

L.R. 54–1.   DETERMINATION
OF PREVAILING PARTY

The "prevailing party" entitled to costs under F.R.Civ.P. 54(d) is the party in whose favor judgment is entered, unless otherwise determined by the Court. When a case is dismissed or otherwise terminated voluntarily, the Court may, upon request, determine the prevailing party.

[Effective October 1, 2001. Amended effective December 1, 2012; December 1, 2018.]

L.R. 54–2. APPLICATION TO TAX COSTS UNDER F.R.CIV.P. 54(d); BILL OF COSTS

To request that any allowable costs be taxed, a prevailing party entitled to costs under F.R.Civ.P. 54(d)(1) must file an Application to the Clerk to Tax Costs as required by L.R. 54–2.1. Parties applying for or objecting to an Application to the Clerk to Tax Costs under F.R.Civ.P. 54(d) must familiarize themselves with the Court's Bill of Costs Handbook, available on the Court's website at www.cacd.uscourts.gov.

L.R. 54–2.1. Filing and Form of Application to the Clerk to Tax Costs. Within 14 days after the entry of judgment or order under which costs may be claimed, a prevailing party claiming taxable costs must file and serve, in accordance with L.Rs. 5–3 and 5–4.1, a completed Form CV–59 "Application to the Clerk to Tax Costs," including a detailed bill of costs. The bill must state separately and specifically each item of taxable costs claimed. Sufficient documentation to support the amount and taxability of each item, such as an invoice, receipt, or other record of the expenditure, must be attached to the Form CV–59 when filed. If a court order or stipulation is required by these rules to support a particular item of costs, the order or stipulation must also be attached to the Form CV–59. Failure to include an item in a timely filed Application to the Clerk to Tax Costs or to attach sufficient documentation to support an item will constitute grounds for not taxing that item. Failure to file an Application to the Clerk to Tax Costs within the time provided by this rule will be grounds for denial.

L.R. 54–2.2. Objections. Within 14 days after service of an Application to the Clerk to Tax Costs under L.R. 54–2.1, any party against whom costs are claimed may file and serve written objections to any cost claimed in the application. The grounds for each objection must be specifically stated. In the absence of a timely objection, any allowable item may be taxed as requested in the application. Any objections filed under this rule must contain a representation that counsel met and conferred in an effort to resolve disagreement about the taxable costs claimed in the bill, or that the objecting party made a good faith effort to arrange such a conference.

L.R. 54–2.3. Response to Objections. Within 3 days after service of an objection under L.R. 54–2.2, the party applying for costs may file and serve a written response to the objection.

L.R. 54–2.4. Clerk's Determination—Finality. No hearing on the application will be held unless the Clerk notifies the parties otherwise. After considering any objections to the proposed bill of costs and any responses thereto, the Clerk will electronically file the bill of costs annotated to identify all taxed costs. The Clerk's determination shall be final unless modified by the Court upon review under L.R. 54–2.5. The Clerk has no discretion to tax any item not identified as taxable in this L.R. 54 and its subparts.

L.R. 54–2.5. Review of Clerk's Determination. A party may seek review of the Clerk's taxation of costs by filing and serving a motion to retax costs within seven (7) days of the Clerk's decision. That review will be limited to the record made before the Clerk and encompass only those items specifically identified in the motion.

[Effective October 1, 2001. Amended effective December 1, 2012; June 1, 2013; December 1, 2014; December 1, 2018.]

L.R. 54–3. ITEMS TAXABLE AS COSTS

L.R. 54–3.1. Clerk's Fees. Fees listed in the Judicial Conference Schedule of Fees District Court Miscellaneous Fee Schedule, issued in accordance with 28 U.S.C. § 1914, that are actually paid to the Clerk in connection with a case are taxable. Pro hac vice fees and other fees not included in the District Court Miscellaneous Fee Schedule are not taxable.

L.R. 54–3.2. Fees for Service of Process. Reasonable fees for service of process under F.R.Civ.P. 4 (whether served by the United States Marshal or other persons authorized by F.R.Civ.P. 4) and reasonable fees for service of subpoenas under F.R.Civ.P. 45 are taxable, including reasonable fees for research, surveillance, wait time, and parking incurred in connection with service.

L.R. 54–3.3. United States Marshal's Fees. Fees and commissions paid to the United States Marshal under 28 U.S.C. § 1921 are taxable.

L.R. 54–3.4. Transcripts of Court Proceedings. Except as allowed by L.R. 54–4, the cost of a transcript of any court proceeding is not taxable unless, before the cost is incurred, it is approved by the Court or stipulated by counsel in writing to be recoverable. Unless the order or stipulation otherwise specifies, the taxable cost of such a transcript will be limited to the cost of the original and one copy of the transcript prepared after the proceeding for ordinary, non-expedited delivery and billed at the rates set by the Judicial Conference of the United States.

L.R. 54–3.5. Depositions. Costs incurred in connection with oral depositions are taxable only to the extent set forth below:

(a) *Transcripts:* The reasonable cost of preparing the original transcription of the oral portion of a deposition for ordinary, non-expedited delivery after the deposition is taxable if the transcript is used for any purpose in connection with the case. Any additional charges paid to expedite the preparation of the transcription, and any charges for "real time" views of the transcription during the deposition, are not taxable unless the judge so orders or counsel stipulate in writing before the costs are incurred. The reasonable cost of one additional copy of the transcript, in any form (including a rough draft), is taxable. The reasonable cost of one copy of the transcript is also taxable when purchased by a party that did not purchase the original. The transcript rates set by the Judicial Conference of the United States will generally be considered reasonable. For transcripts billed at higher rates to be taxable, an explanation of why higher rates were reasonable under the circumstances must be provided. In addition, reasonable fees for the following are taxable:

1. binding,
2. Bates stamping,
3. non–expedited shipping and handling,

4. ASCII disks,

5. production and code compliance charges,

6. electronic transmission charges for non-expedited electronic delivery of a transcript,

7. miniscripts, and

8. witness handling charges.

The cost of videotaping or recording depositions is not taxable unless recording the deposition by video or audio means was ordered by the Court before the taking of the deposition. Failure to provide itemized invoices breaking out the per-page cost of transcripts from other costs, such as expediting, binding, or shipping fees, will be sufficient grounds for not taxing the cost.

(b) *Reporters and Other Persons Required to Take, Report, or Transcribe a Deposition:* The reasonable fees of a stenographic reporter and, if necessary to take the deposition, a notary and an interpreter, are taxable for time attending a deposition and for time appearing at a properly noticed deposition when a deponent fails to appear. Reasonable travel and subsistence expenses of reporters, notaries, and interpreters are also taxable. Fees for video and audio technicians are not taxable unless recording the deposition by video or audio means was ordered by the Court before the taking of the deposition. Attorneys' fees and expenses incurred while taking or defending the deposition are not taxable.

(c) *Exhibits:* The cost of copying or reproducing exhibits used at the deposition and made a part of the deposition transcript is taxable.

L.R. 54–3.6. Witness Fees. Statutory witness fees, including attendance, mileage or other travel expenses, a per diem subsistence allowance, and any other fees or expenses provided in 28 U.S.C. § 1821, are taxable when paid to a witness (including an officer or employee of a corporation or other entity if not a party in his or her own capacity and a party if subpoenaed by an opposing party):

(a) Who actually attends any court proceeding scheduled in connection with the case or before any person authorized to take the witness's deposition, or

(b) With a subpoena directing the witness's appearance.

Taxable attendance and subsistence fees include fees paid for time reasonably spent in travel. No other witness expenses, including fees for expert witnesses, are allowable.

L.R. 54–3.7. Interpreter's Fees. Reasonable fees, expenses, and costs paid to interpreters for interpretation or oral translation services provided at any court proceeding or deposition in the case are taxable, including the salaries, fees, expenses, and costs of special interpretation services provided under 28 U.S.C. § 1828. Document translation costs are not taxable.

L.R. 54–3.8. Docket Fees. Docket fees are taxable as provided by 28 U.S.C. § 1923 if actually incurred.

L.R. 54–3.9. Court–Appointed Experts, Masters, Commissioners, and Receivers. The reasonable fees and expenses of court-appointed experts, masters, commissioners, and receivers are taxable.

L.R. 54–3.10. Certification, Exemplification and Reproduction of Documents. Reasonable document preparation costs are taxable, including:

(a) The cost of copies of documents necessarily filed and served, including the cost of copying and delivering Mandatory Chambers Copies required by the Court;

(b) The cost of copies of documents or other materials admitted into evidence when the original is not available or the copy is substituted for the original at the request of an opposing party;

(c) Fees for an official certification of proof respecting the nonexistence of a document or record;

(d) Patent Office charges for the patent file wrappers and prior art patents necessary to the prosecution or defense of a proceeding involving a patent;

(e) Notary fees incurred in notarizing a document when the cost of the document is taxable;

(f) Fees for certification or exemplification of any document or record necessarily obtained for use in the case; and

(g) The cost of physically replicating or reproducing material necessarily obtained for use in the case (including copies obtained to be produced in discovery) in any format in which such material is required to be produced and with any required characteristics (such as metadata or manipulability) intact. To claim costs incurred in producing material in a required format, the agreement or order imposing the relevant requirements must be attached.

Any party seeking taxation of costs under this local rule must provide a consolidated itemization of copying costs, setting forth with specificity, particularity, and clarity the distinct tasks and services performed. Only costs associated with copying documents or reproducing other material for actual use in the case are allowed. Costs incurred for the convenience of counsel or as prefatory steps in the discovery process before copying documents for actual production are not recoverable.

L.R. 54–3.11. Premiums on Undertakings and Bonds. Premiums paid on undertakings, bonds, security stipulations, or substitutes therefor, where required by law or Court order, or where necessary to enable a party to secure a right granted in the proceeding, are taxable.

L.R. 54–3.12. Other Costs. Upon order of the Court, the reasonable cost of the physical preparation and duplication of the following items may be taxed:

(a) Summaries, computations, polls, surveys, statistical comparisons, maps, charts, diagrams, and other visual aids reasonably necessary to assist the jury or the Court in understanding the issues at the trial;

(b) Photographs, if admitted in evidence or attached to documents necessarily filed and served upon the opposing party; and

(c) The cost of models.

The intellectual effort involved in the production of these materials may not be taxed.

L.R. 54–3.13. State Court Costs. Costs incurred in state court before removal that are recoverable under state statutes shall be recoverable by the prevailing party in this Court.

[Effective October 1, 2001. Amended effective December 1, 2003; January 1, 2008; December 1, 2012; December 1, 2018.]

L.R. 54–4. ITEMS TAXABLE AS COSTS ON APPEAL

An application to tax costs on appeal that are taxable in the District Court under F.R.App.P. 39(e) shall be filed in the District Court no later than twenty-eight (28) days after the date the mandate or judgment is issued by the Court of Appeals.

[Effective October 1, 2001. Amended effective December 1, 2003; January 1, 2008; January 1, 2010; December 1, 2012; December 1, 2018.]

L.R. 54–5. ITEMS TAXABLE AS COSTS ON A BANKRUPTCY APPEAL TO THE DISTRICT COURT

A Notice of Application to the Clerk to Tax Costs and Proposed Bill of Costs on a bankruptcy appeal decided in the District Court is to be filed within fourteen (14) days of the entered date of the order deciding that bankruptcy appeal. Taxable costs for bankruptcy appeals decided by the District Court shall be as provided for in Rule 8014 of the Federal Rules of Bankruptcy Procedure. To recover the costs of printing or otherwise reproducing briefs or excerpts of the record, a statement by counsel that the cost is no higher than is generally charged for such reproduction in the local area and that no more copies were reproduced than were actually necessary shall be required. No Clerk's fees not actually paid shall be recoverable.

[Effective October 1, 2001. Amended effective December 1, 2003; December 1, 2012; December 1, 2018.]

L.R. 54–6. WRIT OF EXECUTION FOR ATTORNEY'S FEES AND COSTS

The Clerk shall, upon request, issue a writ of execution to recover attorney's fees awarded by the Court following a judgment and any separate award of costs by the Clerk:

(a) Upon presentation of a certified copy of the final judgment and separate Bill of Costs and, if appropriate, a certified copy of the order awarding attorney's fees; or

(b) Upon presentation of a mandate of the Court of Appeals to recover costs taxed by the appellate court.

[Former Rule L.R. 54–9 renumbered and amended December 1, 2018.]

L.R. 54–7. FILING DATE FOR REQUESTS FOR ATTORNEYS' FEES

Any motion or application for attorneys' fees shall be served and filed within fourteen (14) days after the entry of judgment or other final order, unless otherwise ordered by the Court.

Such motions and their disposition shall be governed by L.R. 7–3, *et seq.*

[Former Rule L.R. 54–10 renumbered and amended December 1, 2018.]

L.R. 54–8. FILING DATE FOR MOTIONS TO AWARD COSTS NOT GOVERNED BY F.R.CIV.P. 54(d)

Any motion for an award of costs not governed by F.R.Civ.P. 54(d), such as a motion for a discretionary award of costs under 28 U.S.C. § 1919, shall be served and filed within fourteen (14) days after the entry of judgment or other final order, unless otherwise ordered by the Court. Such motions and their disposition shall be governed by L.R. 7–3, *et seq.*

[Former Rule L.R. 54–11 renumbered and amended December 1, 2018.]

F.R.CIV.P. 55. DEFAULT; DEFAULT JUDGMENT

L.R. 55–1. DEFAULT JUDGMENTS

When application is made to the Court for a default judgment, the application shall be accompanied by a declaration in compliance with F.R.Civ.P. 55(b)(1) and/or (2) and include the following:

(a) When and against what party the default was entered;

(b) The identification of the pleading to which default was entered;

(c) Whether the defaulting party is an infant or incompetent person, and if so, whether that person is represented by a general guardian, committee, conservator or other representative;

(d) That the Servicemembers Civil Relief Act (50 U.S.C. App. § 521) does not apply; and

(e) That notice has been served on the defaulting party, if required by F.R.Civ.P. 55(b)(2).

[Effective October 1, 2001. Amended effective June 2, 2008.]

L.R. 55–2. DEFAULT JUDGMENT— UNLIQUIDATED DAMAGES

If the amount claimed in a judgment by default is unliquidated, the applicant may submit evidence of the amount of damages by declarations. Notice must be given to the defaulting party of the amount requested. The party against whom judgment is sought may submit declarations in opposition.

[Effective October 1, 2001.]

L.R. 55–3. DEFAULT JUDGMENT—SCHEDULE OF ATTORNEYS' FEES

When a promissory note, contract or applicable statute provides for the recovery of reasonable attorneys' fees, those fees shall be calculated according to the following schedule:

Amount of Judgment	Attorneys' Fees Awards
$0.01–$1,000	30% with a minimum of $250.00
$1,000.01–$10,000	$300 plus 10% of the amount over $1,000
$10,000.01–$50,000	$1200 plus 6% of the amount over $10,000
$50,000.01–$100,000	$3600 plus 4% of the amount over $50,000
Over $100,000	$5600 plus 2% of the amount over $100,000

This schedule shall be applied to the amount of the judgment exclusive of costs. An attorney claiming a fee in excess of this schedule may file a written request at the time of entry of the default judgment to have the attorney's fee fixed by the Court. The Court shall hear the request and render judgment for such fee as the Court may deem reasonable.

[Effective October 1, 2001. Amended effective December 1, 2003.]

F.R.CIV.P. 56.   SUMMARY JUDGMENT

L.R. 56–1.   DOCUMENTS REQUIRED FROM MOVING PARTY

A party filing a notice of motion for summary judgment or partial summary judgment shall lodge a proposed "Statement of Uncontroverted Facts and Conclusions of Law." Such proposed statement shall set forth the material facts as to which the moving party contends there is no genuine dispute. A party seeking summary judgment shall lodge a proposed Judgment; a party seeking partial summary judgment shall lodge a proposed Order.

[Effective October 1, 2001. Amended effective December 1, 2010; June 1, 2012.]

L.R. 56–2.   STATEMENT OF GENUINE DISPUTES OF MATERIAL FACT BY OPPOSING PARTY

Any party who opposes the motion shall serve and file with the opposing papers a separate document containing a concise "Statement of Genuine Disputes" setting forth all material facts as to which it is contended there exists a genuine dispute necessary to be litigated.

[Effective October 1, 2001. Amended effective December 1, 2003; December 1, 2010.]

L.R. 56–3.   DETERMINATION OF MOTION

In determining any motion for summary judgment or partial summary judgment, the Court may assume that the material facts as claimed and adequately supported by the moving party are admitted to exist without controversy except to the extent that such material facts are (a) included in the "Statement of Genuine Disputes" and (b) controverted by declaration or other written evidence filed in opposition to the motion.

[Effective October 1, 2001. Amended effective December 1, 2010; June 1, 2011.]

L.R. 56–4.   MOTIONS UNDER F.R.CIV.P. 56(d) [ABROGATED EFFECTIVE DECEMBER 1, 2010]

F.R.CIV.P. 57.   DECLARATORY JUDGMENT

F.R.CIV.P. 58.   ENTERING JUDGMENT

L.R. 58–1.   ENTRY OF JUDGMENTS AND ORDERS

The entry of judgments and orders by the Clerk through notation in the appropriate civil docket pursuant to F.R.Civ.P. 58 and 79 shall be made at the earliest practicable time.

[Effective October 1, 2001.]

L.R. 58–2.   ENTRY OF JUDGMENTS—COSTS

Entry of judgment shall not be delayed pending taxation of costs to be included therein pursuant to L.R. 54.

[Effective October 1, 2001. Amended effective January 1, 2010.]

L.R. 58–3.   ENTRY OF JUDGMENTS AND ORDERS—CLERK'S ORDERS AND JUDGMENTS

Orders and judgments signed by the Clerk pursuant to F.R.Civ.P. 55(a) and 77(c) and L.R. 58–1 shall be noted in the civil docket. That notation shall constitute entry of the judgment or order as provided by F.R.Civ.P. 58 and 79 (a).

[Effective October 1, 2001.]

L.R. 58–4.   ENTRY OF JUDGMENTS AND ORDERS—SETTLEMENT OF ORDERS OR JUDGMENTS

Entry of judgments or orders shall not be made by the Clerk until the Court has settled the form of judgment or order as provided in L.R. 52–8.

[Effective October 1, 2001.]

L.R. 58–5.   JUDGMENT BY CLERK

Judgments may be entered by the Clerk without further direction from the judge in the following instances:

(a) Judgments on the verdict of a jury as provided in F.R.Civ.P. 58 unless the judge directs otherwise;

(b) Judgments by default as set forth in F.R.Civ.P. 55(b)(1), provided that no judgment shall be entered without a declaration that any natural person against whom it is sought is not an infant, incompetent person, or exempted under the Servicemembers Civil Relief Act, 1940; and

(c) Judgments on offers of judgment as set forth in F.R.Civ.P. 68. The Clerk may require the party obtaining a judgment or order to prepare and present same.

[Effective October 1, 2001. Amended effective January 1, 2010.]

L.R. 58–6.   ENTRY OF JUDGMENT— MEMORANDUM OF DECISION, OPINION, MINUTE ORDER

Notation in the civil docket of entry of a memorandum of decision, an opinion of the Court, or a minute order of the Clerk shall not constitute entry of judgment pursuant to F.R.Civ.P. 58 and 79(a) unless specifically ordered by the judge.

[Effective October 1, 2001.]

L.R. 58–7.   ENTRY OF JUDGMENT— SETTLEMENT OF INTEREST

If interest is accruing or will accrue on any judgment, decree or order, the party preparing the proposed form of judgment, decree or order shall indicate by memorandum attached thereto the applicable interest rate as computed under 28 U.S.C. § 1961(a) or 26 U.S.C. § 6621 and the amount of interest to be added for each day the document remains unsigned.

[Effective October 1, 2001.]

L.R. 58-8. ENTRY OF JUDGMENT— AWARD—TAX CASES

In tax cases involving overpayments or deficiencies, and in such other cases as it deems appropriate, the Court may withhold entry of judgment to permit the parties to submit, either separately or jointly by stipulation, the computation of the amount of money to be awarded in accordance with the Court's determination of the issues.

[Effective October 1, 2001.]

L.R. 58-9. JUDGMENT, ORDER, DECREE— UNITED STATES A PARTY—DUTY OF CLERK

When a judgment, order or decree is entered by the Court directing any officer of the United States to perform any act, unless such officer is present in Court when the order is made, the Clerk shall forthwith transmit a copy of the judgment, order or decree to the officer ordered to perform the act.

[Effective October 1, 2001.]

L.R. 58-10. SIGNATURE LINE FOR SIGNATURE OF JUDGE

At least two lines of the text of any order or judgment shall appear on the page that has the line provided for the signature of the judge. Next to the signature line shall be the word "Dated:" with a blank left for the judge to write in the date. At least two lines above the signature line shall be left blank for the judge's signature.

[Effective October 1, 2001.]

L.R. 58-11. DEFAULT JUDGMENT— SEPARATE DOCUMENT

A proposed default judgment shall be submitted as a separate document in compliance with F.R.Civ.P. 58.

[Effective October 1, 2001.]

F.R.CIV.P. 59. NEW TRIAL; ALTERING OR AMENDING A JUDGMENT

L.R. 59-1. NEW TRIAL—PROCEDURE

L.R. 59-1.1. Specification of Ground—Error of Law. If the ground for the motion is an error of law occurring at the trial, the error shall be specifically stated.

L.R. 59-1.2. Specification of Ground—Insufficiency of Evidence. If the ground for the motion is the insufficiency of the evidence, the motion shall specify with particularity the respects in which the evidence is claimed to be insufficient.

L.R. 59-1.3. Specification of Ground—Newly Discovered Evidence. If the ground for the motion is newly discovered evidence, the motion shall be supported by a declaration by the party, or the agent of the party having personal knowledge of the facts, showing:

(a) When the evidence was first discovered;

(b) Why it could not with reasonable diligence have been produced at trial;

(c) What attempts were made to discover and present the evidence at trial;

(d) If the evidence is oral testimony, the nature of the testimony and the willingness of the witness to so testify; and

(e) If the evidence is documentary, the documents or duly authenticated copies thereof, or satisfactory evidence of their contents where the documents are not then available.

L.R. 59-1.4. New Trial—Hearing. The motion shall be considered upon:

(a) The pleadings and documents on file;

(b) The minutes of the court clerk;

(c) The reporter's notes or transcript; and

(d) Declarations, if the ground is other than error of law or insufficiency of the evidence and the facts or circumstances relied on do not otherwise appear in the file.

L.R. 59-1.5. New Trial—Declarations—Time for Filing. Declarations in support of a motion for a new trial shall be filed concurrently with the motion unless the Court fixes a different time.

L.R. 59-1.6. New Trial—Calendaring of Motion. The motion for a new trial shall be noticed and heard (if required by the Court) as provided in L.R. 7-3 et seq.

[Effective October 1, 2001. Amended effective June 1, 2012.]

F.R.CIV.P. 60. RELIEF FROM A JUDGMENT OR ORDER

F.R.CIV.P. 61. HARMLESS ERROR

F.R.CIV.P. 62. STAY OF PROCEEDINGS TO ENFORCE A JUDGMENT

F.R.CIV.P. 62.1. INDICATIVE RULING ON A MOTION FOR RELIEF THAT IS BARRED BY A PENDING APPEAL

F.R.CIV.P. 63. JUDGE'S INABILITY TO PROCEED

VIII. PROVISIONAL AND FINAL REMEDIES

F.R.CIV.P. 64. SEIZING A PERSON OR PROPERTY

L.R. 64–1. ISSUANCE OF WRIT

All writs or other process issued for the seizure of persons or property pursuant to F.R.Civ.P. 64 shall be issued, attested, signed and sealed as required for writs issued out of this Court.

[Effective October 1, 2001. Amended effective December 1, 2003.]

L.R. 64–2. WRITS OR OTHER PROCESS OF SEIZURE—CIVIL CASES—EXECUTION AND RETURN

Any writ or other process for seizure in a civil action shall only be directed to, executed and returned by the United States Marshal or by a state or local law enforcement officer authorized by state law or a private person specially appointed by the Court for that purpose. Unless otherwise relieved by the Court, an attorney for the seizing party must be available to the seizing officer at the time of the seizure.

[Effective October 1, 2001.]

L.R. 64–3. PROCESS REQUIRING ENTRY UPON PREMISES

An order of Court requiring entry upon private premises without notice shall only be executed by the United States Marshal, a state or local law enforcement officer, or a private person specially appointed by the Court for that purpose. If process is to be executed by a private person, the private person shall be accompanied by a United States Marshal or a state or local law enforcement officer, who shall be present upon the premises during the execution of the order.

[Effective October 1, 2001.]

L.R. 64–4. APPLICATIONS CONCERNING PROVISIONAL REMEDIES

Applications concerning provisional remedies other than injunctive relief shall be made to a magistrate judge of this Court, unless otherwise ordered.

[Effective October 1, 2001. Amended effective December 1, 2003.]

F.R.CIV.P. 65. INJUNCTIONS AND RESTRAINING ORDERS

L.R. 65–1. TEMPORARY RESTRAINING ORDERS AND PRELIMINARY INJUNCTIONS

A party seeking a temporary restraining order ("TRO") must submit an application, a proposed TRO, a declaration setting forth the facts and certification required by F.R.Civ.P. 65(b)(1)(A) and (B), and a proposed order to show cause why a preliminary injunction should not issue. If the TRO is denied, the Court may set the hearing on the order to show cause without regard to the twenty-eight (28) days notice of motion requirement of L.R. 6–1.

When a TRO is not sought, an application for a preliminary injunction must be made not by order to show cause but by notice of motion filed and served as required by L.R. 6–1. Proof of service of a motion for preliminary injunction must demonstrate that all adverse parties have been notified as required by F.R.Civ.P. 65(a)(1).

[Effective October 1, 2001. Amended effective December 1, 2003; textual correction entered by the Court on or about January 28, 2010; December 1, 2021.]

L.R. 65–2. APPROVAL OF BONDS, UNDERTAKINGS AND STIPULATIONS OF SECURITY

The Clerk is authorized to approve on behalf of the Court all bonds, undertakings and stipulations of security given in the form and amount prescribed by statute, order of the Court or stipulation of counsel, which comply with the requirements of L.R. 65–3, and contain a certificate by an attorney pursuant to L.R. 65–5, except where the approval of a judge is specifically required by law.

[Effective October 1, 2001.]

L.R. 65–3. BONDS OR UNDERTAKINGS— SURETIES—QUALIFICATIONS

No bond or undertaking requiring third-party sureties will be approved unless it bears the names and addresses of third-party sureties and is accompanied by a declaration by the surety stating that:

(a) The surety is a resident of the State of California;

(b) The surety who intends to deed real property as security owns the real property within the State of California;

(c) The security posted by the surety is worth the amount specified in the bond or undertaking, over and above just debts and liabilities; and

(d) The property, real or personal, which is to be conveyed as security, is not exempt from execution and prejudgment attachment.

If specifically approved by the Court, real property in any other state of the United States may be part of the surety's undertaking.

[Effective October 1, 2001.]

L.R. 65–4. BONDS OR UNDERTAKINGS— CORPORATE SURETY

Before any corporate surety bond or undertaking is accepted by the Clerk, the corporate surety must have on file with the Clerk a duly authenticated copy of a power of attorney appointing the agent executing the bond or undertaking. The appointment shall be in a form to permit recording in the State of California.

[Effective October 1, 2001.]

L.R. 65–5. BONDS OR UNDERTAKINGS—CERTIFICATE BY ATTORNEY

A bond or undertaking presented to the Clerk for acceptance must be accompanied by a certificate by the attorney for the presenting party in substantially the following form:

This bond (or undertaking) has been examined pursuant to L.R. 65–3 and is recommended for approval. It (is) (is not) required by law to be approved by a judge.

Date	Attorney

[Effective October 1, 2001.]

L.R. 65–6. CERTIFICATE BY ATTORNEY—MEANING

A certificate by an attorney made pursuant to L.R. 65–5 certifies to the Court that:

(a) The attorney has carefully examined the bond or undertaking;

(b) The attorney knows the content of the bond or undertaking;

(c) The attorney knows the purpose for which the bond or undertaking is executed;

(d) In the attorney's opinion, the bond or undertaking is in due form;

(e) The attorney believes the declarations of qualification by the surety are true; and

(f) The attorney has determined whether the bond or undertaking is required by law to be approved by a judge.

[Effective October 1, 2001.]

L.R. 65–7. BONDS OR UNDERTAKINGS—APPROVAL OF JUDGE

If a bond or undertaking is required by law to be approved by a judge, it shall be presented to the judge with the attorney's certificate required by L.R. 65–5 before it is filed by the Clerk.

[Effective October 1, 2001.]

L.R. 65–8. BONDS OR UNDERTAKINGS—SUMMARY ADJUDICATION OF OBLIGATION AND EXECUTION—PROCEEDING

An indemnitee or party in interest seeking a judgment on a bond or undertaking shall proceed by Motion for Summary Adjudication of Obligation and Execution. Service of the motion on personal sureties shall be made pursuant to F.R.Civ.

P.5(b). Service shall be made on a corporate surety as provided in 31 U.S.C. § 9306.

[Effective October 1, 2001.]

L.R. 65–9. BONDS OR UNDERTAKINGS—SURETY—JUDGES AND ATTORNEYS

No bankruptcy judge, magistrate judge, or district judge, and no attorney appearing in the case, will be accepted as surety upon any bond or undertaking in any action or proceeding in this Court.

[Effective October 1, 2001. Amended effective January 1, 2010.]

L.R. 65–10. BONDS OR UNDERTAKINGS—CASH DEPOSIT

In any civil proceeding, a cashier's check may be deposited with the Clerk in lieu of any bond or undertaking requiring a personal or corporate surety. Such deposit shall be subject to all of the provisions of the F.R.Civ.P. applicable to bonds and undertakings.

[Effective October 1, 2001. Amended effective April 1, 2008.]

F.R.CIV.P. 65.1 PROCEEDINGS AGAINST A SURETY

F.R.CIV.P. 66. RECEIVERS

L.R. 66–1. TEMPORARY RECEIVER

Upon good cause shown by verified pleadings or declaration, the Court may in its discretion appoint a temporary receiver without notice to creditors.

[Effective October 1, 2001.]

L.R. 66–2. TEMPORARY RECEIVER—TERM OF APPOINTMENT

A temporary receiver shall not be appointed for a period longer than the next Motion Day following the expiration of twenty (20) days after the date of appointment.

[Effective October 1, 2001.]

L.R. 66–3. PERMANENT RECEIVER—ORDER TO SHOW CAUSE

Concurrently with appointment of a temporary receiver, the Court shall issue an order to show cause requiring the parties and the creditors of the defendant to show cause why a permanent receiver should not be appointed.

[Effective October 1, 2001.]

L.R. 66–4. PERMANENT RECEIVER—NOTICE

A copy of the Court's order to show cause why a permanent receiver should not be appointed shall be served on the defendant, any other parties to the action, and all known creditors of the defendant by the person requesting appointment of a receiver.

L.R. 66–4.1. Notice—Change of Form. The Court may in its discretion, prescribe a different form of notice, other persons upon whom the notice shall be served, and the time for and manner of service.

[Effective October 1, 2001.]

L.R. 66–5. SCHEDULE OF CREDITORS

A schedule of names, addresses and amounts of claims of all known creditors of the defendant shall be filed by the temporary receiver within five (5) days after appointment of a permanent receiver. If no temporary receiver has been appointed, the defendant shall file that schedule within the same time.

L.R. 66–5.1 Known Creditors—Defined. Known creditors shall mean those creditors who are listed as such in the records or books of account of the person or entity for which a receiver is appointed.

[Effective October 1, 2001.]

L.R. 66–6. PERMANENT RECEIVERS— REPORTS

L.R. 66–6.1. Report Required. Within six months of appointment, and semi-annually thereafter, the receiver shall serve and file with the Court a report showing:

(a) The receipts and expenditures of the receivership; and

(b) All acts and transactions performed in the receivership.

[Effective October 1, 2001.]

L.R. 66–7. PERMANENT RECEIVERS— NOTICE OF HEARING

The receiver shall give notice by mail to all parties to the action and to all known creditors of the defendant of the time and place for hearing of:

(a) Petitions for the payment of dividends to creditors;

(b) Petitions for the confirmation of sales of real property and personal property;

(c) Reports of the receiver;

(d) Applications for instructions concerning administration of the estate;

(e) Applications for discharge of the receiver; and

(f) Applications for fees and expenses of the receiver, the attorney for the receiver and any other person appointed to aid the receiver.

The provisions of L.R. 6–1 shall apply to such notice.

[Effective October 1, 2001.]

L.R. 66–8. PERMANENT AND TEMPORARY RECEIVERS—ADMINISTRATION OF ESTATE

Except as otherwise ordered by the Court, a receiver shall administer the estate as nearly as possible in accordance with the practice in the administration of estates in bankruptcy.

L.R. 66–8.1. Permanent Receivers—Attorney—Records. A receiver, the attorney for the receiver, and such other persons appointed by the Court or employed by the receiver to aid the receivership, shall keep an itemized record of time spent and services rendered.

L.R. 66–8.2. Failure to Maintain Itemized Record. Failure to maintain the itemized records required by L.R. 66–8.1 may be grounds for denying reimbursement or compensation.

[Effective October 1, 2001.]

F.R.CIV.P. 67. DEPOSIT INTO COURT

L.R. 67–1. ORDER OF DEPOSIT— SERVICE ON THE CLERK

For purposes of F.R.Civ.P. 67, service on the Clerk of Court of an order for deposit to an interest-bearing account means personal service on the Clerk, Chief Deputy Clerk, Finance Director or Fiscal Operations Officer.

[Effective October 1, 2001. Amended effective December 1, 2003.]

L.R. 67–2. REGISTRY FEE ON FUNDS DEPOSITED

Whenever money is deposited into Court and is deposited by the Clerk into an interest-bearing account, by order of the Court or otherwise, the Clerk is authorized and directed by this rule to deduct from the income earned on the investment a registry fee not to exceed the amount prescribed by the Judicial Conference of the United States.

[Effective October 1, 2001.]

L.R. 67–3. FINANCIAL INSTITUTION FEE ON FUNDS DEPOSITED

Whenever money is deposited into Court and is deposited by the Clerk into an interest-bearing account, there may be transaction or service fees charged by the financial institution where the money is deposited. Where there are not sufficient funds in the interest accrued to cover transaction or service fees, transaction or service fees may be deducted from the principal amount deposited into the account.

[Effective December 1, 2010.]

F.R.CIV.P. 68. OFFER OF JUDGMENT

F.R.CIV.P. 69. EXECUTION

L.R. 69–1. WRITS AND EXAMINATIONS

A motion concerning execution of a judgment shall be made to the assigned District Judge, unless the motion relates to the scheduling and conducting of judgment debtor and third party examinations pursuant to Cal. Code Civ. Proc. §§ 708.110 et seq. or other post-judgment discovery, in which case the motion shall be made to the assigned Magistrate Judge.

[Effective December 1, 2003.]

F.R.CIV.P. 70. ENFORCING A JUDGMENT FOR A SPECIFIC ACT

F.R.CIV.P. 71. ENFORCING RELIEF FOR OR AGAINST A NONPARTY

IX. SPECIAL PROCEEDINGS

F.R.CIV.P. 71.1. CONDEMNING REAL OR PERSONAL PROPERTY

F.R.CIV.P. 72. MAGISTRATE JUDGES: PRETRIAL ORDER

L.R. 72–1. DUTIES AND FUNCTIONS OF MAGISTRATE JUDGES

United States Magistrate Judges of this Court are authorized to perform all of the duties and functions prescribed and authorized by 28 U.S.C. § 636, or any other statutes or Federal Rules of Procedure which authorize Magistrate Judges to perform judicial duties or functions, as set forth in General Order No. 05–07, or any successor General Order. Magistrate Judges shall have the inherent power of judicial officers to implement and enforce their own orders and to regulate proceedings before them, to the extent permitted by law.

[Effective October 1, 2001. Amended and renumbered effective December 1, 2003. Amended effective June 1, 2012.]

L.R. 72–2. NONDISPOSITIVE RULINGS ON PRETRIAL MATTERS

L.R. 72–2.1. Motions for Review of Nondispositive Rulings. Any party objecting under F.R.Civ.P. 72(a) to a Magistrate Judge's ruling on a pretrial matter not dispositive of a claim or defense must file a motion for review by the assigned District Judge, designating the specific portions of the ruling objected to and stating the grounds for the objection. Such motion shall be filed within fourteen (14) days of an oral ruling which the Magistrate Judge indicates will not be followed by a written ruling, or within fourteen (14) days of service of a written ruling.

L.R. 72–2.2. Effectiveness of Magistrate Judge's Ruling Pending Review. Regardless of whether a motion for review has been filed, the Magistrate Judge's ruling remains in effect unless the ruling is stayed or modified by the Magistrate Judge or the District Judge.

[Effective October 1, 2001. Renumbered and amended effective December 1, 2003. Amended effective January 1, 2010.]

L.R. 72–3. DISPOSITIVE MOTIONS AND PRISONER PETITIONS

L.R. 72–3.1. Duties of Magistrate Judge. Upon the assignment of a case covered by F.R.Civ.P. 72, the Magistrate Judge shall conduct all necessary proceedings. Pursuant to Rule 10 of the Rules Governing Section 2254 Cases in the United States District Courts, the duties imposed upon a Judge of the District Court may be performed by a full-time Magistrate Judge (except in death penalty cases).

L.R. 72–3.2. Summary Dismissal of Habeas Corpus Petition. The Magistrate Judge promptly shall examine a petition for writ of habeas corpus, and if it plainly appears from the face of the petition and any exhibits annexed to it that the petitioner is not entitled to relief, the Magistrate Judge may prepare a proposed order for summary dismissal and submit it and a proposed judgment to the District Judge.

L.R. 72–3.3. Report by Magistrate Judge. In habeas cases that are not summarily dismissed, and in all other matters covered by F.R.Civ.P. 72(b) that the Magistrate Judge determines can be resolved without trial, the Magistrate Judge shall file a report which may contain proposed findings of fact, conclusions of law and recommendations for disposition. If the Magistrate Judge concludes that a trial by a District Judge is required, the Magistrate Judge shall so report to the District Judge.

L.R. 72–3.4. Objections to Report Where Party in Custody. If a party is in custody at the time of the filing of the Magistrate Judge's report, the time for filing objections allowed under F.R.Civ.P. 72(b) shall be twenty (20) days or such further time as the Magistrate Judge may order.

L.R. 72–3.5. Determination of Objections by District Judge. If no objections are filed within the time allowed, the Magistrate Judge shall submit the matter to the District Judge on the basis of the original report. If objections are timely filed, the Magistrate Judge may issue a revised or supplemental report or submit the matter to the District Judge on the basis of the original report.

L.R. 72–3.6. Filing of Transcript. If an evidentiary hearing was conducted by the Magistrate Judge, the party objecting shall obtain and file a certified transcript of the hearing or pertinent part thereof. Upon application, the Magistrate Judge may extend the time to file the transcript.

[Effective October 1, 2001. Renumbered and amended effective December 1, 2003.]

L.R. 72–4. POST–JUDGMENT MATTERS

Following entry of judgment, all motions or other matters not covered by L.R. 69–1 shall be considered and determined by the District Judge.

[Effective October 1, 2001. Renumbered and amended effective December 1, 2003.]

L.R. 72–5.   MOTION TO DISQUALIFY MAGISTRATE JUDGE

A motion to disqualify a Magistrate Judge pursuant to 28 U.S.C. §§ 144 or 455 shall be made to the assigned District Judge. If such a motion is filed in a case to which no District Judge has been assigned, the motion shall be assigned to a District Judge for decision. A copy of the motion shall be submitted to the assigned Magistrate Judge, who shall not proceed with the matter until the motion has been determined. If the District Judge denies the motion, the case shall proceed as originally assigned. If the District Judge grants the motion, the case shall be returned to the Clerk for reassignment.

[Effective October 1, 2001. Renumbered and amended effective December 1, 2003. Amended effective December 1, 2012.]

F.R.CIV.P. 73.   MAGISTRATE JUDGES: TRIAL BY CONSENT; APPEAL

L.R. 73–1.   AUTHORIZATION

Any full-time Magistrate Judge may exercise the authority provided by Title 28, U.S.C. § 636(c), and may conduct any or all proceedings, including a jury or non-jury trial, in a civil case.

[Effective October 1, 2001. Amended and renumbered effective December 1, 2003.]

L.R. 73–2.   DIRECT ASSIGNMENT OF CASES TO MAGISTRATE JUDGE

L.R. 73–2.1.   Notice. When a case is assigned initially only to a magistrate judge, the Clerk shall provide a Notice and Consent Form to the initiating party advising the parties that they may consent to have the assigned magistrate judge conduct all further proceedings in the case, including the entry of final judgment. The Notice shall advise the parties that they may consent to proceed only before the assigned magistrate judge. The initiating party must serve the Notice and Consent Form on each party at the time of service of the summons and complaint or other initial pleading.

L.R. 73–2.2.   Proof of Service. In any case in which only a magistrate judge is initially assigned, plaintiff must file a proof of service within 10 days of service of the summons and complaint.

L.R. 73–2.3.   Execution of Statement of Consent. If the parties agree to the exercise of jurisdiction by the magistrate judge, all counsel and any party appearing pro se shall jointly or separately execute and file a statement of consent setting forth such election.

L.R. 73–2.4.   Filing of Statement of Consent. If all parties execute and file a statement of consent, the magistrate judge will preside over the case for all purposes, including trial and entry of final judgment as provided by 28 U.S.C. § 636(c) and Federal Rule of Civil Procedure 73(b). Appeal from a final judgment entered at a magistrate judge's direction may be taken to the court of appeals as would any other appeal from a district-court judgment.

L.R. 73–2.4.1. *Cases Originally Filed in District Court.* Except as provided in L.R. 73–2.4.1.1, a case originally filed in District Court and initially assigned only to a magistrate judge shall be randomly reassigned to a district judge if any defendant has not filed a statement of consent within 42 days after service of the summons and complaint upon that defendant, if the plaintiff has not filed a statement of consent within 42 days after service upon the first-served defendant, if any party applies for a temporary restraining order, or if any party makes a motion that the magistrate judge concludes cannot be decided by the magistrate judge and must be addressed before the period for consent expires.

L.R. 73–2.4.1.1. Exception for United States, its Agencies, Officers and Employees. If the United States, an agency of the United States, or an officer or employee of the United States is a defendant, a case originally filed in District Court and initially assigned only to a magistrate judge shall be randomly reassigned to a district judge if the government defendant has not filed a statement of consent within 60 days after service of the summons and complaint upon that defendant, if any party applies for a temporary restraining order, or if any party makes a motion that the magistrate judge concludes cannot be decided by the magistrate judge and must be addressed before the period for consent expires.

L.R. 73–2.4.2. *Cases Removed From State Court.* A case initially assigned only to a magistrate judge following removal under 28 U.S.C. § 1441 et seq. shall be randomly reassigned to a district judge if, within 14 days after the notice of removal is filed, plaintiff(s) and all defendants upon whom service has been effected have not filed a statement of consent, if any party applies for a temporary restraining order, or if any party makes a motion that the magistrate judge concludes cannot be decided by the magistrate judge and must be addressed before the period for consent expires.

L.R. 73–2.5.   Party Added After Election to Proceed Before Magistrate Judge. If a party is added to the case after all previous parties have elected to proceed before a magistrate judge, the newly-added party may file a statement of consent within 42 days after the order allowing intervention, or after service of the summons and appropriate pleading. If the newly-added party does not file a statement of consent within this period, the case shall be randomly reassigned to a district judge for further proceedings.

L.R. 73–2.6.   Discovery Assignment. For any case which is originally assigned only to a magistrate judge and then later reassigned to a district judge, a magistrate judge shall be randomly assigned to hear all referred discovery matters.

[Effective January 2, 2009. Amended effective February 16, 2009; January 1, 2010; June 1, 2011.]

L.R. 73–3.   CONSENT IN CASES ASSIGNED FOR REPORT AND RECOMMENDATION

In any case assigned to a district judge and referred to a magistrate judge, pursuant to 28 U.S.C. § 636(b), for a report and recommendation, the parties may, at any time prior to the entry of judgment, consent that the assigned magistrate judge may handle the case for all purposes. Upon the filing of the appropriate consent forms, the Clerk will reassign the case solely to the magistrate judge.

[Effective October 1, 2001. Amended and renumbered effective December 1, 2003. Repealed effective January 2, 2009. Amended effective February 16, 2009.]

X. DISTRICT COURTS AND CLERKS; CONDUCTING BUSINESS; ISSUING ORDERS

F.R.CIV.P. 77. CONDUCTING BUSINESS; CLERK'S AUTHORITY; NOTICE OF AN ORDER OR JUDGMENT

L.R. 77–1. PROCEDURES FOR EMERGENCY MATTERS

When court action is required prior to the next business day, relief should be sought by filing, during normal business hours, a written application for a temporary restraining order ("TRO") pursuant to F.R.Civ.P. 65 and L.R. 65–1, unless otherwise provided by federal statute, federal or local rule, or court order. After filing an application for a TRO, the filer must immediately notify the courtroom deputy for the assigned judge by telephone. If it is anticipated that an application for a TRO will be filed outside normal business hours, the filer must notify the courtroom deputy for the assigned judge in advance, during normal business hours. If an application for a TRO is or will be filed before a judge is assigned to the case, the filer should contact the Civil Intake Department in the Clerk's Office for the division in which the case is pending: Western Division (213) 894–3535, Eastern Division (951) 328–4470, or Southern Division (714) 338–4786. Failure to notify the court as directed may delay judicial action. In highly unusual circumstances, a filer may not be able to anticipate before the close of business that relief will need to be sought prior to the next business day in a new civil case not already assigned to a judge. If a new civil case is opened and an application for a TRO or similar document is filed after 4:30 p.m., and court attention is needed prior to the next business day, the filer should call the Court at (213) 894–0028 and follow the Emergency Filing Procedures set forth on the Court's website at www.cacd.uscourts.gov/court–procedures/filing–procedures/emergency–filing–procedures. Requests for emergency relief directed to this number should be exceedingly rare.

[Effective December 1, 2003. Amended effective December 1, 2015; December 1, 2017; June 1, 2020.]

F.R.CIV.P. 78. HEARING MOTIONS; SUBMISSION ON BRIEFS

L.R. 78–1. MOTION DAYS

Each Monday, commencing at 10:00 a.m., shall be "Motion Day" on which motions will be heard unless set for another day or hour by order of the Court. If Monday is a national holiday, any motion noticed for that day shall be considered noticed for the next succeeding motion calendar of the judge

F.R.CIV.P. 74. [ABROGATED]

F.R.CIV.P. 75. [ABROGATED]

F.R.CIV.P. 76. [ABROGATED]

before whom the motion is calendared without special order or further notice.

[Effective October 1, 2001.]

F.R.CIV.P. 79. RECORDS KEPT BY THE CLERK

L.R. 79–1. CLERK'S OFFICE—REMOVAL OF RECORDS AND FILES

No records or objects belonging in the files of the Court may be taken from the office or custody of the Clerk except upon written order of the Court.

[Effective October 1, 2001.]

L.R. 79–2. RECEIPT FOR REMOVAL

Any person removing records pursuant to L.R. 79–1 shall give the Clerk a descriptive receipt using the form prescribed by the Clerk.

L.R. 79–2.1. Clerk's Office—Removal of Records and Files—Court Officers. The provisions of L.R. 79–1 shall not apply to a judge, master, examiner employed by the United States, United States Magistrate Judge, a judge's law clerk, court reporter, or court clerk requiring records or objects in the exercise of official duty. Any court officer removing records or objects shall provide the Clerk with a receipt as required in L.R. 79–2.

[Effective October 1, 2001.]

L.R. 79–3. RETENTION AND DISPOSITION OF EXHIBITS

This rule governs all models, diagrams, CDs, DVDs, audio or video recordings in any format, documents, and exhibits in any other form submitted at the time of a trial or hearing, except those subject to L.R. 79–4. Exhibits submitted under this rule will be retained by the Court until the completion of the trial or hearing or as otherwise directed by the Court, at which time they will be returned to counsel for the submitting party. Counsel notified that exhibits are ready to be returned under this rule must immediately arrange to pick up those exhibits. Exhibits not reclaimed by counsel within 30 days of this notification may be destroyed. After exhibits are returned to counsel under this rule, counsel must maintain custody of those exhibits until the earliest of expiration of the time for appeal when no appeal is taken, entry of stipulation waiving or abandoning the right to appeal, final disposition of the appeal, or Court order allowing destruction of the exhibits.

[Effective October 1, 2001. Amended effective December 1, 2020.]

L.R. 79–4. CONTRABAND AND VALUABLE, SENSITIVE, AND DANGEROUS EXHIBITS

No contraband or valuable, sensitive, or dangerous exhibits (including but not limited to narcotics, firearms, ammunition, explosives, pornographic materials, poisonous or dangerous chemicals, intoxicating liquors, jewelry, money or articles of high monetary value, counterfeit money, fine art, and items of historical significance) submitted at the time of a trial or hearing will be retained by the Court even during the pendency of the trial or hearing unless specifically authorized by the Court. Such exhibits must remain at all times in the custody of either counsel for the submitting party or the case agent for any relevant law-enforcement agency. They must maintain custody of all contraband and all valuable, sensitive, and dangerous exhibits until the earliest of expiration of the time for appeal when no appeal is taken, entry of stipulation waiving or abandoning the right to appeal, final disposition of the appeal, or Court order allowing destruction of the exhibits.

[Effective October 1, 2001. Amended effective December 1, 2020.]

L.R. 79–5. CONFIDENTIAL COURT RECORDS—UNDER SEAL

L.R. 79–5.1. Definition. A case or document that is "under seal" or "sealed" is one that is closed to inspection by the public. A person seeking to have a case or document sealed must follow the procedures set forth below. Parties should be familiar with the difference between *in camera* review (*see* L.R. 79–6) and under seal filings.

L.R. 79–5.2. Procedures. Unless otherwise indicated in this L.R. 79–5.2, no case or document may be filed under seal without first obtaining approval by the Court.

All documents to be filed under seal and all Applications for Leave to File Under Seal must be filed electronically using the Court's CM/ECF System, unless otherwise indicated in this rule or exempted from electronic filing pursuant to L.R. 5–4.2. Before electronically filing any under-seal documents or any Applications for Leave to File Under Seal, filers must familiarize themselves with the Court's Guide to Electronically Filing Under–Seal Documents in Civil Cases, available on the Court's website at www.cacd.uscourts.gov. Failure to comply with the instructions in this Guide may result in the disclosure of confidential information.

Where this rule directs that documents must be presented for filing in paper format, the original and the judge's copy of all such documents must be submitted for filing in separate sealed envelopes, with a copy of the title page attached to the front of each envelope, and must be accompanied by a PDF version of the documents on a CD, unless otherwise ordered by the judge.

L.R. 79–5.2.1. *Under-Seal Civil Cases.*

(a) Case–Initiating Documents.

(i) If Filing Under Seal Is Already Expressly Authorized. If a statute, rule, regulation, or prior court order expressly provides that a case is to be filed under seal, the complaint (or other initiating document) and all concurrently filed documents must be presented to the Clerk for filing in paper format, in accordance with the applicable Federal Rules of Civil Procedure and the Local Rules of this Court. The caption must clearly indicate the authority for filing the case under seal by including, immediately under the title of the document: "FILED UNDER SEAL PURSUANT TO _____." If filing under seal is authorized by a court order, a copy of the order must be provided with the case-initiating document.

(ii) All Other Circumstances. In the absence of prior express authorization to file a case under seal, the filer must present to the Clerk for filing in paper format: (1) the case-initiating document(s); (2) an Application for Leave to File Case Under Seal; (3) a declaration establishing good cause or demonstrating compelling reasons why the strong presumption of public access in civil cases should be overcome; and (4) a proposed order. While the Application is pending, the Clerk must seal the case and all associated documents. If the Application is denied, the Clerk must, unless otherwise ordered by the Court, immediately unseal the case and all documents filed therein, and may do so without first notifying the filing party.

(b) Subsequent Documents. All documents filed in sealed cases must be presented to the Clerk for filing in paper format. All such documents will be accepted as filed under seal, without the need for a separate Application for Leave to File Under Seal.

L.R. 79–5.2.2. *Under-Seal Documents in Non-Sealed Civil Cases.* In a non-sealed civil case, no document may be filed under seal without prior approval by the Court. A person seeking to file documents under seal must follow the procedures set forth below in subsection (a), unless someone else has designated these documents as confidential pursuant to a protective order, in which event those involved must follow the procedures set forth in subsection (b). Once the Court has granted leave to file under seal, documents to be filed under seal must be filed in accordance with subsection (c).

(a) Documents Not Designated by Another as Confidential Pursuant to a Protective Order. A person seeking leave of Court to file some or all of a document under seal (the "Filing Party") must file an Application for Leave to File Under Seal ("Application"). When possible, the Filing Party should file the Application in time to receive a determination before filing the motion or other paper that the proposed sealed document is intended to support. The Application will be open to public inspection. It must, however, describe the nature of the information that the Filing Party asserts should be closed to public inspection, and must be accompanied by:

(i) A declaration (1) establishing good cause or demonstrating compelling reasons why the strong presumption of public access in civil cases should be overcome, with citations to the applicable legal standard, and (2) informing the Court whether anyone opposes the Application. That the information may have been designated confidential pursuant to a protective order is not sufficient justification for filing under seal; a person seeking to file such documents under seal must comply with L.R. 79–5.2.2(b).

(ii) A proposed order, narrowly tailored to seal only the sealable material, and listing in table form each document or portion thereof to be filed under seal.

(iii) A redacted version of any document(s) of which only a portion is proposed to be filed under seal, conspicuously labeled "REDACTED VERSION OF DOCUMENT PROPOSED TO BE FILED UNDER SEAL."

(iv) An unredacted version of the document(s) proposed to be filed under seal, conspicuously labeled "UNREDACTED VERSION OF DOCUMENT PROPOSED TO BE FILED UNDER SEAL," with any proposed redactions highlighted.

The declaration and the unredacted version of any document proposed for sealing will be closed to public inspection, but the redacted versions of those documents, the proposed order, and the docket entry text will be publicly viewable.

The Filing Party must provide a mandatory chambers copy of the Application and all associated documents as required by L.R. 5–4.5. The declaration and unredacted versions of documents for which sealing is sought must be provided in sealed envelopes, with a copy of the title page attached to the front of each envelope. The proposed order must be emailed to chambers as required by L.R. 5–4.4.2.

If the Application is granted, the Filing Party must thereafter file the sealed document pursuant to L.R. 79–5.2.2(c). The Clerk will not convert the PROPOSED sealed document submitted with the Application into a new filing.

If the Application is denied in its entirety, the document(s) proposed to be filed under seal will not be considered by the Court in connection with any pending motion, unless the Filing Party files an unredacted version of the document(s) within 3 days after the Application is denied.

If the Application is denied in part, the document(s) proposed to be filed under seal will not be considered by the Court in connection with any pending motion unless the Filing Party files a revised redacted version of the document(s) that comports with the Court's order within 3 days after the Application is denied.

(b) Documents Designated by Another as Confidential Pursuant to a Protective Order. At least 3 days before seeking to file under seal a document containing information previously designated as confidential by another pursuant to a protective order, the Filing Party must confer with the person that designated the material confidential (the "Designating Party") in an attempt to eliminate or minimize the need for filing under seal by means of redaction. If the document cannot be suitably redacted by agreement, the Filing Party may file an Application pursuant to subsection (a), but the supporting declaration must identify the material previously designated as confidential, as well as the Designating Party, and must describe in detail the efforts made to resolve the issue. The declaration must be served on the Designating Party on the same day it is filed, and

proof of this service must be filed with the declaration. Subsequently:

(i) Within 4 days of the filing of the Application, the Designating Party must file a declaration establishing that all or part of the designated material is sealable, by showing good cause or demonstrating compelling reasons why the strong presumption of public access in civil cases should be overcome, with citations to the applicable legal standard. If the Designating Party maintains that only part of the designated material is sealable, the Designating Party must file with its declaration a copy of the relevant material with proposed redactions highlighted. The declaration and, if applicable, the document highlighting proposed redactions will be closed to public inspection. Failure to file a declaration or other required document may be deemed sufficient grounds for denying the Application.

(ii) If the Application is denied, the Filing Party may file the document in the public case file (i.e., unsealed) no earlier than 4 days, and no later than 10 days, after the Application is denied, unless the Court orders otherwise.

(c) After Leave of Court Has Been Granted. Once the Court has granted leave to file a document under seal, the Filing Party must thereafter file the document with whatever motion or other document the under-seal filing is intended to support. The Clerk will not convert the PROPOSED sealed document submitted with the Application into a new filing. The caption of the under-seal document must clearly indicate the authority for filing the document under seal by including, immediately under the title of the document: "FILED UNDER SEAL PURSUANT TO ORDER OF THE COURT DATED _____"; if filed electronically, the under-seal document must also be linked, during the filing process, to the order authorizing its filing. Any document filed pursuant to this L.R. 79–5.2.2(c) that misstates the basis for filing under seal may be subject to public disclosure, and may subject the filer to sanctions.

L.R. 79–5.3. Service of Documents Filed Under Seal. Filing a document under seal does not exempt the filer from the service requirements imposed by federal statutes, rules, or regulations, or by the Local Rules of this Court. Because documents filed under seal (even those filed electronically) are visible on CM/ECF or PACER only to Court personnel and the person who filed the document, a person electronically filing a document under seal may not rely on the Court's CM/ECF System to effect service as provided in L.R. 5–3.2.1. Service of such documents must be made in accordance with F.R.Civ.P. 5. At the time of filing, the documents must be accompanied either by a Proof of Service in the form required by L.R. 5–3.1.2 or by a declaration explaining why service is not required.

[Effective October 1, 2001. Amended effective November 25, 2002; December 1, 2003. L.R. 79–5.4 effective July 1, 2005. Amended effective January 1, 2008; February 7, 2008; April 1, 2008; December 1, 2011; June 1, 2012. Technical revisions effective December 1, 2013. Amended effective December 1, 2015.]

L.R. 79–6. CONFIDENTIAL COURT RECORDS— IN CAMERA REVIEW

L.R. 79–6.1. In Camera Review. A document accepted by the Court for review *in camera* will not, while under review, be made part of the Court's official case file, or be made available for inspection by the public or any party, and need not be served on any party when presented to the Court for review.

L.R. 79–6.2. Prior Court Approval Required. No document may be presented for review *in camera* without prior approval of the Court. A person seeking *in camera* review of a document must describe its general nature and establish why it should be reviewed *in camera*, citing the applicable legal standard.

L.R. 79–6.3. After Review. After reviewing a document *in camera*, the Court may order it to be filed publicly or under seal, with or without service, or otherwise disclosed to other parties. Unless the Court orders it to be filed, or unless otherwise ordered by the Court, a document reviewed *in camera* must afterward be retained by the counsel or party that presented it until final disposition of an appeal, entry of a stipulation waiving or abandoning the right to appeal, expiration of the time for appeal (where no appeal is taken), or order of the Court, whichever occurs first.

[Effective December 1, 2015.]

L.R. 79–7. CONFIDENTIAL COURT RECORDS—DISCLOSURE

L.R. 79–7.1. Non–Disclosure of Confidential Court Records. Except upon written order of the Court, or as otherwise provided in this L.R. 79–7.1, the Clerk shall not disclose to the public, including attorneys and parties appearing in the case, a document that has been filed under seal or, for a case that has been sealed, the docket of that case. A document filed under seal in a civil case pending on or after the effective date of this L.R. 79–7.1 will, upon request, be open to inspection by the public and the parties to the case without further action by the Court 10 years from the date the case is closed. However, the party that filed the document in question or a party that designated the document as confidential pursuant to a protective order may, upon showing good cause prior to that date, seek an order to extend non-disclosure to a specific date beyond the 10 years provided by this rule. Nothing in this rule is intended to affect the normal records disposition policy or schedule of the United States Courts.

L.R. 79–7.2. Procedure for Disclosure of Confidential Court Records. An application for disclosure of cases or documents filed under seal must be made to the Court in writing and must be filed by the person seeking disclosure. The application shall set forth with particularity the need for specific information in such records. The procedures of L.R. 7–3 *et seq.* shall govern the hearing of any such application. A nonparty seeking access to a sealed document may intervene in a case for the purpose of filing an application for disclosure of the document.

[Effective December 1, 2015.]

F.R.CIV.P. 80. STENOGRAPHIC TRANSCRIPT AS EVIDENCE

XI. GENERAL PROVISIONS

F.R.CIV.P. 81. APPLICABILITY OF THE RULES IN GENERAL; REMOVED ACTIONS

F.R.CIV.P. 82. JURISDICTION AND VENUE UNAFFECTED

F.R.CIV.P. 83. RULES BY DISTRICT COURTS; JUDGE'S DIRECTIVES

L.R. 83–1. ASSIGNMENT OF CASES—NOTICE OF RELATED CASES IN CENTRAL DISTRICT, OTHER ACTIONS, OR PETITIONS TO MULTI-DISTRICT PANEL

L.R. 83–1.1 Assignment of Cases. All actions shall be assigned when commenced to individual judges and magistrate judges of this Court in the manner provided by General Order.

L.R. 83–1.2 Refiling of Actions.

L.R. 83–1.2.1. *Improper Refiling of Actions.* It is not permissible to dismiss and thereafter refile an action for the purpose of obtaining a different judge.

L.R. 83–1.2.2. *Duty on Refiling of Actions.* Whenever an action is dismissed by a party or by the Court before judgment and thereafter the same or essentially the same claims, involving the same or essentially the same parties, are alleged in another action, the later-filed action shall be assigned to the judge to whom the first-filed action was assigned. It shall be the duty of every attorney in any such later-filed action to bring those facts to the attention of the Court in the Civil Cover Sheet and by the filing of a Notice of Related Case(s) pursuant to L.R. 83–1.3.

L.R. 83–1.3 Notice of Related Cases

L.R. 83–1.3.1. *Notice of Related Civil Cases.* It shall be the responsibility of the parties to promptly file a Notice of Related Cases whenever two or more civil cases filed in this District:

(a) arise from the same or a closely related transaction, happening or event;

(b) call for determination of the same or substantially related or similar questions of law and fact, or;

(c) for other reasons would entail substantial duplication of labor if heard by different judges.

That cases may involve the same patent, trademark, or copyright does not, by itself, constitute a circumstance contemplated by (a), (b), or (c).

The Notice of Related Cases must include a brief factual statement that explains how the cases in question are related under the foregoing factors. All facts that appear relevant to such a determination must be set forth.

The Notice must be filed at the time any case (including a notice of removal or bankruptcy appeal) appearing to relate to another is filed, or as soon thereafter as it reasonably should appear that the case relates to another. The Notice must be served on all parties who have appeared in the case and concurrently with service of the complaint.

L.R. 83–1.3.2. *Notice of Related Civil Forfeiture and Criminal Cases.* It shall be the responsibility of the parties to promptly file a Notice of Related Cases whenever a civil forfeiture case and a criminal case:

(a) arise from the same or a closely related transaction, happening, or event;

(b) call for determination of the same or substantially related or similar questions of law and fact; or

(c) involve one or more defendants from the criminal case in common, and would entail substantial duplication of labor if heard by different judges.

The Notice must include a brief factual statement that explains how the cases in question are related under the foregoing factors.

The Notice must be filed at the time a civil forfeiture case appearing to relate to a criminal case is filed, or as soon thereafter as it appears such cases are related. The Notice must be served on all parties who have appeared in the case and concurrently with service of the complaint.

L.R. 83–1.3.3. *Opposition.* Within five days of receiving service of a Notice of Related Cases, or within five days of first appearing in the case, any party to the case may file and serve a short statement setting forth reasons that the case does not qualify as a related case under these rules.

L.R. 83–1.3.4. *Continuing Duty.* It shall be the continuing duty of the attorney in any case to file a Notice of Related Cases as required by these rules.

L.R. 83–1.4 Notice of Pendency of Other Actions or Proceedings.

L.R. 83–1.4.1. *Notice.* Whenever a civil action filed in or removed to this Court involves all or a material part of the subject matter of an action then pending before the United States Court of Appeals, Bankruptcy Appellate Panel, Bankruptcy Court or any other federal or state court or administrative agency, the attorney shall file a "Notice of Pendency of Other Actions or Proceedings" with the original complaint or petition filed in this Court. The duty imposed by L.R. 83–1.4 continues throughout the time an action is before this Court.

L.R. 83–1.4.2. *Notice—Contents.* The Notice of Pendency of Other Actions or Proceedings shall contain:

(a) A description sufficient to identify all other actions or proceedings;

(b) The title of the court or administrative body in which the other actions or proceedings are pending;

(c) The names of the parties or participants in such other actions or proceedings;

(d) The names, addresses and telephone numbers of the attorneys in such other actions or proceedings; and

(e) A brief factual statement setting forth the basis for the attorney's belief that the action involves all or a material part of the subject matter of such other actions or proceedings.

L.R. 83–1.4.3. *Notice of Petition to the Judicial Panel on Multidistrict Litigation—Duty of Counsel.* The attorney shall comply with L.R. 83–1.4 promptly upon learning that an action or proceeding filed in this Court is the subject of or is related to an action which is before the Judicial Panel on Multidistrict Litigation, or which has been transferred by it pursuant to 28 U.S.C. § 1407.

[Effective October 1, 2001. Amended effective December 1, 2003; July 1, 2005; March 1, 2008; December 1, 2014.]

L.R. 83–2. ATTORNEYS; PARTIES WITHOUT ATTORNEYS

L.R. 83–2.1 Attorneys.

L.R. 83–2.1.1 *Appearance Before the Court.*

L.R. 83–2.1.1.1 Who May Appear. Except as provided in L.R. 83–2.1.3, 83–2.1.4, 83–2.1.5, and 83–4.5, L.Bankr.R. 8, J.P.M.L. R. 2.1(c), and F.R.Civ.P. 45(f), an appearance before the Court on behalf of another person, an organization, or a class may be made only by members of the Bar of this Court, as defined in L.R. 83–2.1.2.

L.R. 83–2.1.1.2 Effect of Appearance. Any attorney who appears for any purpose submits to the discipline of this Court in all respects pertaining to the conduct of the litigation.

L.R. 83–2.1.1.3 Form of Appearance—Professional Corporations and Unincorporated Law Firms. No appearance may be made and no pleadings or other documents may be signed in the name of any professional law corporation or unincorporated law firm (both hereinafter referred to as "law firm") except by an attorney admitted to the Bar of or permitted to practice before this Court. A law firm may appear in the following form of designation or its equivalent:

John Smith
A Member of Smith and Jones, P.C.
Attorneys for Plaintiff

L.R. 83–2.1.2 *The Bar of This Court.*

L.R. 83–2.1.2.1 In General. Admission to and continuing membership in the Bar of this Court are limited to persons of good moral character who are active members in good standing of the State Bar of California. If an attorney admitted to the Bar of this Court ceases to meet these criteria, the attorney will be subject to the disciplinary rules of the Court, infra.

L.R. 83–2.1.2.2 Admission to the Bar of this Court. Each applicant for admission to the Bar of this Court must complete an Application for Admission to the Bar of the Central District of California (Form G–60) and submit it to the Court electronically through the Court's website, together with the admission fee prescribed by the Judicial Conference of the United States and such other fees as may from time to time be required by General Order of this Court. The completed Application for Admission to the Bar of the Central District of California must include certification that the applicant is familiar with the Court's Local Civil and Criminal Rules and with the Federal Rules of Civil Procedure, Criminal Procedure, and Evidence.

L.R. 83–2.1.2.3 Continuing Membership in the Bar of this Court. Each attorney admitted to the Bar of this Court must, in order to remain a member of the Bar of this Court, pay the annual renewal fee imposed by General Order of the Court.

L.R. 83–2.1.3 *Pro Hac Vice Practice.*

L.R. 83–2.1.3.1 Who May Apply for Permission to Practice Pro Hac Vice. An attorney who is not a member of the State Bar of California may apply for permission to appear pro hac vice in a particular case in this Court if the attorney:

(a) is a member in good standing of, and eligible to practice before, the bar of any United States Court, or of the highest court of any State, Territory, or Insular Possession of the United States;

(b) is of good moral character;

(c) has been retained to appear before this Court; and

(d) is not disqualified under L.R. 83–2.1.3.2.

L.R. 83–2.1.3.2 Disqualification from Pro Hac Vice Appearance. Unless authorized by the Constitution of the United States or Acts of Congress, an applicant is not eligible for permission to practice *pro hac vice* if the applicant:

(a) resides in California;

(b) is regularly employed in California; or

(c) is regularly engaged in business, professional, or other similar activities in California.

L.R. 83–2.1.3.3 How to Apply for Permission to Appear Pro Hac Vice.

(a) Each applicant for permission to appear *pro hac vice* must complete an Application of Non–Resident Attorney to Appear in a Specific Case (Form G–64, available on the Court's website), which must include:

(1) certification that the applicant is familiar with the Court's Local Civil and Criminal Rules and with the Federal Rules of Civil Procedure, Criminal Procedure, and Evidence;

(2) identification of Local Counsel as required by L.R. 83–2.1.3.4; and

(3) a list of all *pro hac vice* applications made to this Court in the previous three years.

(b) The completed Application of Non–Resident Attorney to Appear in a Specific Case must be electronically filed by the identified Local Counsel in each case in which the applicant seeks to appear, together with the following:

(1) a separate proposed Order;

(2) the *pro hac vice* fee set by General Order of the Court (unless the applicant is employed by the United States or any of its departments or agencies, in which case no fee is required); and

(3) a Certificate of Good Standing from each state bar in which the applicant is a member, issued no more than 30 days before filing the Application of Non–Resident Attorney to Appear in a Specific Case.

(c) Approval of the applicant's *pro hac vice* application will be at the discretion of the assigned judge in each case in which an application is submitted.

By practicing in this Court, the registered *pro hac vice* attorney submits to the disciplinary authority of the Central District of California.

L.R. 83–2.1.3.4 Designation of Local Counsel. Every attorney seeking to appear pro hac vice must designate as Local Counsel an attorney with whom the Court and opposing counsel may readily communicate regarding the conduct of the case and upon whom documents may be served. An attorney may be designated as Local Counsel only if he or she: (1) is a member of the Bar of this Court and (2) maintains an office within the District for the practice of law, in which the attorney is physically present on a regular basis to conduct business.

L.R. 83–2.1.3.5 Designation of Co–Counsel. A judge to whom a case is assigned may, in the exercise of discretion, require the designation of an attorney who is a member of the Bar of this Court and who maintains an office within the District as co-counsel with authority to act as attorney of record for all purposes.

L.R. 83–2.1.4 *Attorneys for the United States, or Its Departments or Agencies.*

L.R. 83–2.1.4.1 Attorney for the United States or its Departments or Agencies. (a) Any person who is eligible for admission to the Bar of this Court under L.R. 83–2.1.2 and who is employed by the United States or any of its departments or agencies may practice in this Court in all actions or proceedings within the scope of his or her employment by the United States without being admitted to the Bar of this Court and without paying any associated admission fee. To register for permission to practice under this L.R. 83–2.1.4.1(a), the federal government attorney must comply with the other requirements of L.R. 83–2.1.2, including completion of an Application for Admission to the Bar of the Central District of California (Form G–60), which must be submitted to the Court electronically through the Court's website.

(b) Any person who is not eligible for admission under L.R. 83–2.1.2 or 83–2.1.3, who is employed within this state and is a member in good standing of, and eligible to practice before, the bar of any United States Court, the District of Columbia Court of Appeals, or the highest court of any State, Territory or Insular Possession of the United States, and is of good moral character, may be granted leave of court to practice in this Court in any matter for which such person is employed or retained by the United States, or its departments or agencies. The application for such permission must include a certification filed with the Clerk showing that the applicant has applied to take the next succeeding Bar Examination for admission to the State Bar of California for which that applicant is eligible. No later than one year after submitting the foregoing application, the applicant must submit to this Court proof of admission to the State Bar of California. Failure to do so will result in revocation of permission to practice in this Court.

L.R. 83–2.1.4.2 Special Assistant United States Attorneys. Notwithstanding L.R. 83–2.1.4.1, any United States Armed Forces attorney who has been appointed a Special Assistant United States Attorney under 28 U.S.C. sections 515 and 543 may handle misdemeanor matters before this Court.

Attorneys employed by the United States Department of Justice specially appointed by the United States Attorney General to conduct any kind of legal proceeding, civil or criminal, under 28 U.S.C. § 515(a), may appear without filing an Application of Nonresident Attorney to Appear in a Specific Case.

L.R. 83–2.1.5 *Registered Legal Services Attorney.* A registered legal services attorney authorized to appear in the state courts of California under California Rules of Court, Rule 9.45, may apply for permission to appear in a case before this Court under the conditions set forth in that rule. Such an applicant must complete an Application of Registered Legal Services Attorney to Practice Before the Court (Form CV–99, available on the Court's website), which must include:

(a) certification that the applicant is a registered legal services attorney authorized to practice law in the state courts of California pursuant to California Rules of Court, Rule 9.45 (or a successor rule);

(b) certification that the applicant is familiar with the Court's Local Civil and Criminal Rules and with the Federal Rules of Civil Procedure, Criminal Procedure, and Evidence; and

(c) identification of a supervising attorney who is a member in good standing of the Bar of this Court, and who must appear with the registered legal services attorney as one of the attorneys of record.

The completed Application of Registered Legal Services Attorney to Practice Before the Court must be electronically filed by the supervising attorney in each case in which the applicant seeks to appear, together with a separate proposed Order. Approval of the application will be at the discretion of the assigned judge in each case in which an application is submitted.

By practicing in this Court, the registered legal services attorney submits to the disciplinary authority of the Central District of California.

L.R. 83–2.2 Parties Without Attorneys.

L.R. 83–2.2.1 *Individuals.* Any person representing himself or herself in a case without an attorney must appear *pro se* for such purpose. That representation may not be delegated to any other person — even a spouse, relative, or co-party in the case. A non-attorney guardian for a minor or incompetent person must be represented by counsel.

L.R. 83–2.2.2 *Organizations.* Only individuals may represent themselves *pro se.* No organization or entity of any other kind (including corporations, limited liability corporations, partnerships, limited liability partnerships, unincorporated associations, trusts) may appear in any action or proceeding unless represented by an attorney permitted to practice before this Court under L.R. 83–2.1.

L.R. 83–2.2.3 *Compliance With Federal Rules.* Any person appearing *pro se* is required to comply with these Local Rules, and with the F.R.Civ.P., F.R.Crim.P., F.R.Evid. and F.R.App.P.

L.R. 83–2.2.4 *Sanctions.* Failure to comply with the rules enumerated in L.R. 83–2.2.3 may be grounds for dismissal or judgment by default.

L.R. 83–2.3 Withdrawal and Substitution of Attorneys.

L.R. 83–2.3.1 *Appearance by Attorney.* Whenever a party has appeared by an attorney, the party may not thereafter appear or act pro se, except upon order made by the Court after notice to such attorney and to any other parties who have appeared in the action.

L.R. 83–2.3.2 *Motion for Withdrawal.* An attorney may not withdraw as counsel except by leave of court. A motion for leave to withdraw must be made upon written notice given reasonably in advance to the client and to all other parties who have appeared in the action. The motion for leave to withdraw must be supported by good cause. Failure of the client to pay agreed compensation is not necessarily sufficient to establish good cause.

L.R. 83–2.3.3 *Individuals.* When an attorney of record for any reason ceases to act for a party, such party must appear pro se or appoint another attorney by a written substitution of attorney signed by the party and the attorneys.

L.R. 83–2.3.4 *Organizations.* An attorney requesting leave to withdraw from representation of an organization of any kind (including corporations, limited liability corporations, partnerships, limited liability partnerships, unincorporated associations, trusts) must give written notice to the organization of the consequences of its inability to appear pro se.

L.R. 83–2.3.5 *Delays by Substitution of Attorneys.* Unless good cause is shown and the ends of justice require, no substitution or relief of attorney will be approved that will cause delay in prosecution of the case to completion.

L.R. 83–2.4 Notification of Change of Name, Address, Firm Association, Telephone Number, Facsimile Number or E–Mail Address. An attorney who is a member of the bar of this Court or who has been authorized to appear in a case in this Court, and any party who has appeared pro se in a case pending before the Court, and who changes his or her name, office address (or residence address, if no office is maintained), law firm association (if any), telephone number, facsimile number, or e-mail address must, within five (5) days of the change, notify the Clerk of Court in writing. If any actions are currently pending, the attorney or party must file and serve a copy of the notice upon all parties.

L.R. 83–2.5 Communications With the Judge. Attorneys or parties to any action or proceeding shall refrain from writing letters to the judge, sending e-mail messages to the judge, making telephone calls to chambers, or otherwise communicating with a judge in a pending matter unless opposing counsel is present. All matters must be called to a judge's attention by appropriate application or motion filed in compliance with these Local Rules.

[Effective October 1, 2001. Amended effective December 1, 2003; February 1, 2005; April 1, 2008; April 1, 2009; January 1, 2010; December 1, 2010; June 1, 2012; June 1, 2013; December 1, 2013; June 1, 2014; December 1, 2019; June 1, 2020; December 1, 2020.]

L.R. 83–3. ATTORNEY DISCIPLINARY RULES OF THE COURT

L.R. 83–3.1 Discipline. Nothing contained in these Rules shall be construed to deny the Court its inherent power to maintain control over the proceedings conducted before it or to deny the Court those powers derived from statute, rule or procedure, or other rules of court. When alleged attorney misconduct is brought to the attention of the Court, whether by a Judge of the Court, any lawyer admitted to practice before the Court, any officer or employee of the Court, or otherwise, the Court may, in its discretion, dispose of the matter through the use of its inherent, statutory, or other powers; refer the matter to an appropriate state bar agency for investigation and disposition; refer the matter to the Standing Committee on Discipline; or take any other action the Court deems appropriate. These procedures are not mutually exclusive.

L.R. 83–3.1.1 *The Standing Committee on Discipline.* At all times the Court will maintain a Standing Committee on Discipline (hereinafter "Committee"). The Committee shall consist of 13 attorneys who are members of the Bar of the Court. However, in the event of any vacancy or vacancies, the Committee may continue to perform any of the functions herein authorized so long as there are nine members in office.

Committee members shall be appointed by the Chief Judge with the concurrence of the Executive Committee. The Chief Judge shall designate one member to serve as the chair. A Committee member shall serve for a term of one to three years but may continue in office, upon order of the Chief Judge, beyond said three-year term until the completion of any disciplinary proceeding (which includes the initial investigation to presentation of disciplinary recommendations to the Court) in which the member is participating. Each committee member's term shall commence on January 1 of the year specified in the appointment, and appointments shall be staggered so that each year the terms of four members, not including the Chair, shall end. Should any Committee member not complete a three-year term, that member's replacement shall complete the length of term remaining. The Chair of the Committee shall serve a term of three years as Chair, regardless of previous time served as a Committee member.

The Chair of the Committee shall organize the Committee into four sections of three members each. Each section shall consist of one member who has one year remaining on his term, one member who has two years remaining on his term, and one member who has three years remaining on his term. The Chair of the Committee may assign any matter before the Committee to one of the sections for initial investigation and further proceedings described in these rules. Except for the

requirement of seven affirmative votes for the imposition of discipline as specified in Rule 83–3.1.5, the Committee may perform or decide any matter arising under these rules by a majority vote. For any Committee meeting, a quorum of seven is required.

The Clerk of the Court shall be advised of, and keep a current list of, all matters referred to the Committee and each section, to assist the Court, the Committee, and the affected attorney or complaining person, in recording the status of each matter.

L.R. 83–3.1.2 *Standards of Professional Conduct—Basis for Disciplinary Action.* In order to maintain the effective administration of justice and the integrity of the Court, each attorney shall be familiar with and comply with the standards of professional conduct required of members of the State Bar of California and contained in the State Bar Act, the Rules of Professional Conduct of the State Bar of California, and the decisions of any court applicable thereto. These statutes, rules and decisions are hereby adopted as the standards of professional conduct, and any breach or violation thereof may be the basis for the imposition of discipline. The Model Rules of Professional Conduct of the American Bar Association may be considered as guidance.

L.R. 83–3.1.3 *Possible Disciplinary Penalties.* An order imposing discipline under this Rule may consist of any of the following:

(a) disbarment,

(b) suspension not to exceed three years,

(c) public or private reproval,

(d) monetary penalties (which may include an order to pay the costs of the proceedings), and/or

(e) acceptance of resignation.

In lieu of any of the foregoing disciplinary steps, the Court's Standing Committee on Discipline may issue an admonition as defined by California State Bar Rules, to wit, where the offense is not serious, or not intentional, or involved mitigating circumstances, or no significant harm resulted.

Any suspension, reproval, or acceptance of resignation may be subject to specified conditions, which may include but are not limited to continuing legal education requirements, counseling, and/or supervision of practice and periods of probation.

Any disbarment, suspension, or acceptance of resignation from this Court will result in termination of the attorney's ability to file documents electronically through the Court's CM/ECF System. E-filing privileges will be restored upon application of the practitioner showing proof of an order of reinstatement.

L.R. 83–3.1.4 *Who May Originate Complaints—Initial and Further Investigation—Hearing and Opportunity for Attorney Involved to Appear and Present Evidence.* A complaint that an attorney has violated any of the standards of conduct specified in Rule 83–3.1.2, may come to the Committee from any District, Bankruptcy or Magistrate Judge of the Court or from any other person. The complaint shall be in writing addressed to the Committee in care of the Clerk of Court. Within 10 days of receipt, the Clerk shall serve a copy of the complaint on the Chair of the Committee, the attorney affected and the Clerk of the Bankruptcy Court.

Within 10 days of receipt of any such complaint, the Committee chair shall assign the matter of possible disciplinary action based on the complaint to one of the sections of the Committee for initial investigation and possible disciplinary proceedings. Any attorney of the assigned section who cannot participate shall so notify the Chair within 10 days of assignment so that a replacement can be assigned.

Within 60 days of receipt, the section to which such a complaint is referred shall conduct and complete an initial investigation. If the section determines that the complaint should not be the subject of further disciplinary action, and the Committee concurs in that determination, the matter will thereupon be closed. Notice of closing shall be promptly sent to the complainant, the attorney affected and the Chief Judge. If the Committee determines that the complaint should be further investigated as being one that may result in disciplinary action, the section shall thereupon within 60 days conduct and complete such further investigation and inquiries as it deems necessary. The section, in so doing, may take the testimony of witnesses and may seek from the Chief Judge, or his or her designee, any subpoena necessary for its investigation and the Clerk shall promptly issue any such requested subpoena. The affected attorney may also apply to the Chief Judge, or his or her designee, for any necessary subpoenas.

All final disciplinary actions will be distributed to the judicial officers of the Court. Final disciplinary action, including the name of the attorney, will be posted on the Court's website when it consists of (a) disbarment; (b) suspension; (c) public reproval; or (d) resignation with charges pending. It may be ordered posted if the disciplinary action consists of monetary penalties.

Other final disciplinary actions may be posted, without the name of the attorney, to promote understanding of the level of practice expected in this district.

The deadlines in this paragraph may be extended by the Committee Chair for a period of up to six months, for good cause at the request of the section or the affected attorney. The deadlines may be extended for a longer time in consultation with the Chief Judge.

L.R. 83–3.1.4.1 Appointment of Prosecutor. At the request of the investigating section, concurred in by the Chair of the Committee, the Chief Judge may appoint a member of the Bar of the Court who is not a Committee member to (1) supervise and conduct such further investigation as may be appropriate; (2) prosecute the matter at any hearing conducted by the section or the Committee or any other proceeding the Court may require before entering an order of discipline; and (3) defend any order of discipline on appeal.

By order of the Chief Judge, with the concurrence of the Executive Committee, the prosecutor shall be compensated for services out of the Attorneys' Admission Fund.

L.R. 83–3.1.4.2 Duties of the Chief Judge. If the Chief Judge is recused or otherwise is unavailable to perform the duties as outlined in this rule, the duties shall be referred to the next available district judge in regular active service who is senior in commission of all the active judges.

L.R. 83–3.1.4.3 Indemnification of Prosecutor, Section, and Committee. Any expenses incurred in the prosecution of a disciplinary proceeding and any award of court costs against the Section, the Committee or the prosecutor shall likewise be paid out of the Attorneys' Admission Fund.

L.R. 83–3.1.5 Right of Attorney Involved to a Hearing and to Present Evidence. Before recommending the imposition of any discipline, the investigating Section shall provide to the attorney involved a statement of the charges and a description of the discipline which the Section is considering recommending. The Section, upon request of the attorney involved, shall conduct a hearing on the charges, which hearing shall be recorded electronically or by a court reporter. The attorney involved shall have the right to be represented by counsel and to be personally heard under oath at said hearing. The attorney involved may also present sworn testimony of relevant witnesses and may submit briefing and evidentiary exhibits at said hearing. Following the said hearing, the section shall formulate its findings of fact and conclusions of law in writing together with a statement of the discipline, if any, which it recommends. Where the imposition of discipline is recommended, the Section shall, within 30 days of the hearing or of the completion of the investigation, transmit to the Committee, along with its recommendation, copies of its proposed findings of fact and conclusions of law, the exhibits which it received in evidence and the record of testimony which was presented to it. The Committee shall thereafter promptly adopt, modify or reject the section's recommended action. The Committee may, but need not, hear any further statement by the attorney affected or his or her counsel, or receive any further evidence or briefing. If the Committee determines to recommend the imposition of discipline, it must do so at a meeting, which may be held telephonically, with at least seven members voting in favor of the recommendation.

L.R. 83–3.1.6 Confidentiality of Proceedings. The record in a disciplinary proceeding shall not be public (unless otherwise ordered by the Court) but shall become public if and when a final order imposing discipline is entered. If the final order imposing discipline consists of private reproval, the record shall only be made public upon an order of the Court.

L.R. 83–3.1.7 Presentation of Disciplinary Recommendations to the Court. When the Committee has determined that discipline should not be imposed, the matter will thereupon be closed. Notice of the closing shall be promptly sent to the complainant, the attorney affected, the Chief Judge, and the Clerk of the Court.

When the Committee has determined that discipline should be imposed, it shall promptly transmit to the Chief Judge and the Clerk of the Court its recommendation (in court document format) and the complete record, including the section's proposed findings of fact and conclusions of law, and shall request an order of the Court imposing the recommended discipline. A copy of the Committee's recommendation shall also be sent to the attorney affected and his or her counsel.

Within 15 days of the Chief Judge receiving a Committee recommendation, the matter of whether the Court should impose discipline shall be assigned to three judges of the

Court selected at random in the same manner as civil cases are distributed, but not to include any judge who originated the complaint. The judges to whom the matter is assigned are not required to conduct any further hearing, to hear the attorney involved or his or her counsel, or to receive any further evidence or briefing before determining to issue an appropriate order. The assigned judges shall adopt, modify or reject the Committee's recommendation for the imposition of discipline. The decision of said judges shall be final. If the judges assigned determine to impose discipline, they shall sign and file an appropriate order imposing it.

Appeals from such orders shall be in accordance with the F.R.A.P.

L.R. 83–3.1.8 *Application For Reinstatement.* Any attorney who has been suspended or disbarred under the Local Rules may make an application for reinstatement. The application for reinstatement shall be by written motion filed in paper format addressed to the Committee. The Committee shall consider the application and make a recommendation to the Chief Judge. The Chief Judge may, with the concurrence of the Executive Committee, adopt, modify or reject the recommendation of the Committee concerning the application. Before making its recommendation, the Committee is not required to hear the attorney affected or his or her counsel and is not required to hear any testimony or receive any other evidence or briefing. Nor shall the Chief Judge or the Executive Committee be required to do so before deciding on the application.

L.R. 83–3.2 Enforcement of Attorney Discipline.

L.R. 83–3.2.1 *Disbarment or Suspension by Other Courts or Conviction of a Crime.* Upon receipt of reliable information that a member of the Bar of this Court or any attorney appearing pro hac vice (1) has been suspended or disbarred from the practice of law by the order of any United States Court, or by the Bar, Supreme Court, or other governing authority of any State, territory or possession, or the District of Columbia, or (2) has resigned from the Bar of any United States Court or of any State, territory or possession, or the District of Columbia while an investigation or proceedings for suspension or disbarment was pending, or (3) has been convicted of a crime, other than in this Court, the elements or underlying facts of which may affect the attorney's fitness to practice law, this Court shall issue an Order to Show Cause why an order of suspension or disbarment should not be imposed by this Court.

Upon the filing of a judgment or conviction demonstrating that any attorney admitted to practice before this Court has been convicted in this Court of any serious crime as herein defined, the Chief Judge or his or her designee shall enter an order immediately suspending that attorney, whether the conviction resulted from a plea of guilty, nolo contendere, verdict after trial, or otherwise, and regardless of the pendency of any appeal. The suspension so ordered shall remain in effect until final disposition of the disciplinary proceedings to be commenced upon such conviction. A copy of such order shall be immediately served upon the attorney. Upon good cause shown, the Chief Judge or his or her designee may set aside such order when it appears in the interest of justice to do so.

The term "serious crime" shall include any felony and any lesser crime a necessary element of which, as determined by the statutory or common law definition of such crime in the jurisdiction in which it was entered, involves false swearing, misrepresentation, fraud, deceit, bribery, extortion, misappropriation, theft, or the use of dishonesty, or an attempt, conspiracy, or solicitation of another to commit a "serious crime."

If the attorney files a response stating that imposition of an order of suspension or disbarment from this Court is not contested, or if the attorney does not respond to the Order to Show Cause within the time specified, then the Court shall issue an order of suspension or disbarment. The order shall be filed by the Chief Judge or his or her designee.

L.R. 83–3.2.2 *Alternatives.* As an alternative to suspension or disbarment, the Committee may consider, and the Court may accept, the attorney's resignation, if the attorney both:

(a) Files a written response setting forth his or her status for the practice of law in all other jurisdictions where the attorney was or is admitted; and

(b) Tenders his or her resignation from the Bar of this Court.

A resignation with charges pending is not effective until accepted by the Court. An attorney will be on inactive status while the Court considers whether to accept the resignation. The acceptance of a resignation may be subject to additional conditions including but not limited to those under L.R. 83–3.1.3 and referral to, or resignation from, the Bar of another jurisdiction.

L.R. 83–3.2.3 *Contested Matters.* If the attorney files a written response to the Order to Show Cause within the time specified stating that the entry of an order of suspension or disbarment is contested, then the Chief Judge or other district judge who may be assigned shall determine whether an order of suspension or disbarment or other appropriate order shall be entered. Where an attorney has been suspended or disbarred by another Bar, or has resigned from another Bar while disciplinary proceedings were pending, the attorney in the response to the Order to Show Cause, must set forth facts establishing one or more of the following: (a) the procedure in the other jurisdiction was so lacking in notice or opportunity to be heard as to constitute a deprivation of due process; (b) there was such an infirmity of proof establishing the misconduct as to give rise to a clear conviction that the Court should not accept as final the other jurisdiction's conclusion(s) on that subject; (c) imposition of like discipline would result in a grave injustice; or (d)other substantial reasons exist so as to justify not accepting the other jurisdiction's conclusion(s). In addition, at the time the response is filed, the attorney must produce a certified copy of the entire record from the other jurisdiction or bear the burden of persuading the Court that less than the entire record will suffice.

L.R. 83–3.2.4 *Reinstatement.* Unless stated otherwise by order of the Court, an attorney who has been suspended or disbarred from the Bar of this Court because of his resignation, suspension or disbarment from the Bar of another court will be reinstated upon proof of reinstatement as an active member in good standing in such other Bar.

L.R. 83–3.2.5 *Discipline by Agencies.* Information that a member of the Bar of this Court has been suspended or disbarred from practice by the order of any federal or state administrative agency, shall be treated as a complaint which can be the basis of disciplinary action by this Court. The matter shall be referred to the Committee for investigation, hearing and recommendation as provided hereinabove in the case of other complaints. All parties in interest are advised of the United States Bankruptcy Court for the Central District of California's Fourth Amended General Order No. 96–05 or any successor General Order governing attorney discipline proceedings in the Bankruptcy Court.

L.R. 83–3.2.6 *Notice of Disciplinary Action to State Bar and Other Courts.* The Clerk shall give prompt notice of any conviction of any attorney admitted to this bar of a serious crime as herein defined or imposing discipline under this Rule 83–3 to the Circuit Court of Appeals, to the Bankruptcy Court, to the California State Bar, and to the Bar or disciplinary body of those courts to which the attorney involved has been admitted to practice and of which the Clerk is aware.

L.R. 83–3.2.7 *Powers of an Individual Judge to Deal With Contempt or Other Misconduct Not Affected.* Disciplinary proceedings under Rule 83–3 shall not affect, or be affected by, any proceedings for criminal contempt under the U.S. Criminal Code, nor shall anything contained in this Rule 83–3 be construed to deny any judge of this Court said judge's inherent power to maintain control over the proceedings conducted before said judge, nor to deny the judge those powers derived from any statute or rule of court. Misconduct of any attorney in the presence of a court or in any manner in respect to any matter pending in a court may be dealt with directly by the judge in charge of the matter or at said judge's option, referred to the Committee, or both.

L.R. 83–3.3 Practice Prohibited While on Inactive Status. Any attorney previously admitted to the Bar of this Court who no longer is enrolled as an active member of the Bar, Supreme Court, or other governing authority of any State, territory or possession, or the District of Columbia, shall not practice before this Court. Upon receipt of reliable information that such attorney is practicing before the Bar of this Court, this Court shall issue an Order to Show Cause why the attorney should not be disbarred from this Court, and shall proceed with the Order to Show Cause in the manner set forth in L.R. 83–3.2.1.

L.R. 83–3.4 Obligation to Notify Court of Felony Conviction or Change of Status. Any attorney admitted to the Bar of this Court or admitted *pro hac vice* shall promptly notify the Clerk of this Court of (1) the attorney's conviction of any felony, or (2) the imposition of discipline in any other jurisdiction, or (3) the attorney's resignation from the Bar while disciplinary investigation or proceedings were pending in any other jurisdiction.

[Effective October 1, 2001. Amended effective December 1, 2003; July 1, 2005; January 1, 2010; June 1, 2012. Technical revisions effective December 1, 2013. Amended effective June 1, 2020.]

L.R. 83–4. STUDENT PRACTICE

L.R. 83–4.1 Consent. An eligible law student acting under the supervision of a member of the bar of this Court may appear on behalf of any client, including federal, state, or local government bodies, if the client has filed a written consent with the Court. Additional written consent must be given if one eligible student is replaced by another.

L.R. 83–4.2 Requirements. An eligible student must:

(a) be enrolled and in good standing in a law school accredited by the American Bar Association or the State Bar of California;

(b) have completed one-half of the legal studies required for graduation;

(c) have completed a course in evidence. For civil cases, an eligible law student must have also completed a course in civil procedure. For criminal cases, an eligible law student must have completed courses in criminal law and criminal procedure. An eligible law student must also have knowledge of and be familiar with the Federal Rules of Civil and Criminal Procedure as well as the Federal Rules of Evidence, the Rules of Professional Conduct of the State Bar of California and applicable statutory rules, and rules of this Court;

(d) be certified by the dean of a law school as being adequately trained to fulfill all responsibilities as a legal intern to the Court in compliance with L.R. 83–4.2(a) and (b);

(e) not accept compensation for his or her legal services directly or indirectly from a client; and

(f) file with the Clerk of the Court all documents required to comply with this rule.

L.R. 83–4.3 Supervising Attorney. The supervising attorney must:

(a) have such substantial litigation experience to satisfy the Court of his or her ability to supervise the student;

(b) be registered for the Court's CM/ECF System;

(c) file with the Clerk of the Court to whom each case has been assigned a "Request to Undertake the Supervision of an Eligible Law Student." The undertaking, if approved by the Court, may be withdrawn by the supervising attorney by filing a written notice with the Clerk of the Court and by giving notice of such withdrawal to the affected student;

(d) appear with the student in any oral presentations before this Court;

(e) sign all documents filed with this Court;

(f) assume personal professional responsibility for the student's work in matters before this Court;

(g) assist and counsel the student in the preparation of the student's work in matters before this Court; and

(h) be responsible to supplement oral or written work of the student as necessary to assure proper representation of the client. All written work will be filed over the signature of the supervising attorney. Written work may also be signed by the eligible law student who participated in such written work. The student, in signing the written work, must indicate his or her status as an eligible law student.

L.R. 83–4.4 Law School Dean's Certification. The dean's certification of the student:

(a) must be filed with the Clerk of the Court and must remain in effect for a period of three years or until withdrawn;

(b) must state that he or she knows of no reason which would render the law student ineligible under this rule;

(c) may be withdrawn for good cause by the dean with notice to the Court and to the student. Certification may only be withdrawn by the dean for good cause. Such cause must be stated in the notice filed with the Court.

L.R. 83–4.5 Student Appearance. Upon fulfilling the requirements of this rule, the student may appear and make oral presentations before this Court when accompanied by the supervising attorney.

L.R. 83–5 [Reserved]

[Effective October 1, 2001. Amended effective June 1, 2013; June 1, 2020.]

L.R. 83–5.   [RESERVED]

[Renumbered as L.R. 17–1 and amended effective December 1, 2014.]

L.R. 83–6.   POSSESSION AND USE OF ELECTRONIC DEVICES

Any person entering any courthouse, as defined below, will be subject to this L.R. 83–6 and all its subparts.

L.R.   83–6.1 Definitions.

L.R. 83–6.1.1 *Electronic Devices.* As used in this L.R. 83–6, the phrase "electronic device" means all equipment, including computers, cameras, cellular telephones, tablets, smart watches, and similar devices, that can be used for:

(a) Wireless communication;

(b) Receiving, creating, capturing, storing, retrieving, sending, or broadcasting any signals or any text, sound, or images; or

(c) Accessing the internet or any other network or off-site system or equipment for communicating or for storing or retrieving information.

L.R. 83–6.1.2 *Courthouse.* As used in this L.R. 83–6, the term "courthouse" means those portions of federal buildings occupied by the United States District Court for the Central District of California and any other facility within the Central District in which a District Court judicial proceeding is held.

L.R. 83–6.1.3 *Permissible Uses [AMENDED AND RENUMBERED TO L.R. 83–6.3].*

L.R. 83–6.1.4 *Prohibited Uses [AMENDED AND RENUMBERED TO L.R. 83–6.4].*

L.R. 83–6.1.5 *Restricted Areas [AMENDED AND RENUMBERED TO L.R. 83–6.5].*

L.R. 83–6.2 Possession. Subject to the conditions set forth in this L.R. 83–6, possession of electronic devices is permitted in all courthouses; however, court security personnel will screen electronic devices before permitting them to be brought into a courthouse and may bar from any courthouse any item that appears to pose a threat to security or safety.

L.R.   83–6.2.1 *[DELETED].*

L.R.   83–6.2.2 *[DELETED].*

L.R.   83–6.2.3 *[DELETED].*

L.R. 83–6.3 Permissible Uses of Electronic Devices. Except as provided in L.R. 83–6.5, electronic devices may be used in all Central District courthouses in a non-disruptive manner for purposes other than taking photographs, making audio or video recordings, or broadcasting, televising, transmitting or live streaming audio or video.

L.R.   83–6.3.1 *Official Recordings [AMENDED AND RENUMBERED TO L.R. 83–6.8.1].*

L.R.   83–6.3.2 *Video Testimony [AMENDED AND RENUMBERED TO L.R. 83–6.8.2].*

L.R.   83–6.3.3 *Ceremonial Functions [AMENDED AND RENUMBERED TO L.R. 83–6.8.3].*

L.R.   83–6.3.4 *Press Conferences [AMENDED AND RENUMBERED TO L.R. 83–6.8.4].*

L.R.   83–6.3.5 *Dictating Equipment [AMENDED AND RENUMBERED TO L.R. 83–6.8.5].*

L.R. 83–6.4 Prohibited Uses. Except as otherwise provided in this L.R. 83–6 or as expressly approved in advance by the court in writing, electronic devices must not be used in any public area of a courthouse to take photographs, make audio or video recordings, or broadcast, televise, transmit or live stream any audio or video. Use of electronic devices in areas of a courthouse occupied by other federal agencies will be subject to such regulations as those agencies may impose.

L.R.   83–6.4.1 *Violations of Rule [AMENDED AND RENUMBERED TO L.R. 83–6.9.1].*

L.R.   83–6.4.2 *Contempt [AMENDED AND RENUMBERED TO L.R. 83–6.9.2].*

L.R. 83–6.5 Restricted Areas. Except as approved in advance by the court, all electronic devices must be turned off completely in the following areas at the designated times: (1) all courtrooms at all times; (2) any other room in which court proceedings are being held, while those proceedings are in progress; (3) any designated jury room, during jury deliberations; and (4) any area where relevant restrictions are posted.

L.R. 83–6.6 Use of Electronic Devices From Remote Locations. Photographing or recording any part of any court proceeding from a location outside the courthouse is prohibited, including in conjunction with an appearance made by telephone or videoconference.

L.R. 83–6.7 Use of Electronic Devices by Jurors. Jurors may not use electronic devices for any purpose during judicial proceedings or in jury rooms during, or in connection with, deliberations. Grand jurors may not use electronic devices for any purpose during, or in connection with, any proceedings before, or deliberations by, the grand jury.

L.R.   83–6.8 Exceptions.

L.R. 83–6.8.1 *Official Recordings.* Nothing in this L.R. 83–6 shall prohibit recordings made by official court reporters, recorders, or judges in the performance of their official duties. No use may be made of an official recording of a court proceeding without an express, written order of the court.

L.R. 83–6.8.2 *Video Testimony.* Nothing in this L.R. 83–6 shall prohibit the recording of depositions for trial purposes, or the preparation and perpetuation of testimony, taken by or under the direction of a judge of this court or a duly designated visiting judge.

L.R. 83–6.8.3 *Ceremonial and Educational Functions.* Nothing in this L.R. 83–6 shall prohibit the taking or making of photographs or audio or video recordings at ceremonial functions (including naturalization ceremonies, investiture ceremonies, memorial services, etc.) or educational functions (moot court, training, meetings, etc.) if specifically authorized by the Chief Judge or the judge presiding at such an event and subject to any limitations set by that judge. Any judge authorizing the use of electronic devices at such an event will notify the U.S. Marshals Service in advance of the event that use of such devices is authorized.

L.R. 83–6.8.4 *Press Conferences.* Nothing in this L.R. 83–6 shall prohibit the use of any equipment or devices at press conferences or public announcements made by the U.S. Attorney, the Federal Public Defender, or the District Court Executive, who will provide the United States Marshals Service advance written notification of such press conferences or public announcements. A Court Security Officer will escort communications media personnel and their equipment to and from the site of such press conference or public announcement.

L.R. 83–6.8.5 *Dictation.* Nothing in this L.R. 83–6 shall prohibit attorneys admitted to practice before this court or bona fide members of the print or electronic media (that is, newspaper, magazine, radio, online, or television) from using electronic devices to take dictation by making audio recordings in the following areas: the attorney's lounge, a press room, a witness room, or the Clerk's Office.

L.R. 83–6.9 Enforcement.

L.R. 83–6.9.1 *Violations of Rule.* In response to a violation of this L.R. 83–6 or of any court order addressing matters covered by this rule, court security personnel may order immediate compliance, direct the offender to leave the courtroom or the building, temporarily confiscate the device(s) used in violation of this rule, report the violation to the presiding judge, the Chief Judge, the Clerk of Court, or the United States Attorney, or take any other action allowed by law.

L.R. 83–6.9.2 *Contempt.* A violation of L.R. 83–6 may constitute contempt of court.

[Effective October 1, 2001. Amended effective December 1, 2003; November 16, 2006; December 1, 2012; December 1, 2016; June 1, 2020.]

L.R. 83–7. SANCTIONS—VIOLATION OF RULE

The violation of or failure to conform to any of these Local Rules may subject the offending party or counsel to:

(a) monetary sanctions, if the Court finds that the conduct was willful, grossly negligent, or reckless;

(b) the imposition of costs and attorneys' fees to opposing counsel, if the Court finds that the conduct rises to the level of bad faith and/or a willful disobedience of a court order; and/or

(c) for any of the conduct specified in (a) and (b) above, such other sanctions as the Court may deem appropriate under the circumstances.

[Effective October 1, 2001.]

L.R. 83–8. VEXATIOUS LITIGANTS

L.R. 83–8.1 Policy. It is the policy of the Court to discourage vexatious litigation and to provide persons who are subjected to vexatious litigation with security against the costs of defending against such litigation and appropriate orders to control such litigation. It is the intent of this rule to augment the inherent power of the Court to control vexatious litigation and nothing in this rule shall be construed to limit the Court's inherent power in that regard.

L.R. 83–8.2 Orders for Security and Control. On its own motion or on motion of a party, after opportunity to be heard, the Court may, at any time, order a party to give security in such amount as the Court determines to be appropriate to secure the payment of any costs, sanctions or other amounts which may be awarded against a vexatious litigant, and may make such other orders as are appropriate to control the conduct of a vexatious litigant. Such orders may include, without limitation, a directive to the Clerk not to accept further filings from the litigant without payment of normal filing fees and/or without written authorization from a judge of the Court or a Magistrate Judge, issued upon such showing of the evidence supporting the claim as the judge may require.

L.R. 83–8.3 Findings. Any order issued under L.R. 83–8.2 shall be based on a finding that the litigant to whom the order is issued has abused the Court's process and is likely to continue such abuse, unless protective measures are taken.

L.R. 83–8.4 Reference to State Statute. Although nothing in this rule shall be construed to require that such a procedure be followed, the Court may, at its discretion, proceed by reference to the Vexatious Litigants statute of the State of California, Cal. Code Civ. Proc. §§ 391–391.8.

[Effective October 1, 2001. Technical revisions effective December 1, 2013.]

L.R. 83–9. TIME LIMITS FOR DECISIONS BY COURT

L.R. 83–9.1. Time Limit Established. The Court shall render and file its decision on motions and non-jury trials within 120 days after the matter is submitted for decision.

L.R. 83–9.1.1. *"Submitted" Defined.*

(a) A motion shall be deemed submitted for decision (i) on the date the Court announces on the record in open court, at the conclusion of the hearing thereon, that the matter is submitted for decision; or (ii) on the date the last memorandum or other document is permitted to be filed. If no oral argument is conducted on the motion, a motion shall be deemed submitted for decision as of the date the last memorandum or other pleading is permitted to be filed.

(b) A non-jury trial shall be deemed submitted for decision (i) on the date the Court announces on the record in open court, at the conclusion of the trial, that the matter is submitted for decision; or (ii) on the date the last memorandum or other document is permitted to be filed.

L.R. 83–9.2. Duty of Counsel. If the Court does not render and file its decision on a submitted matter within 120 days of submission, all counsel shall, within 130 days after the matter is submitted for decision, file with the Court a joint request that such decision be made without further delay. A copy of such request shall be sent to the Chief Judge.

L.R. 83–9.3. Duty of Court to Respond. Unless the Court makes its decision within 30 days after the filing of a joint request, it shall, within the same time period, advise the parties in writing of the date by which the decision will be made. A copy of such written advice shall be filed in the case and sent to the Chief Judge.

L.R. 83–9.4. Follow–Up Duty of Counsel. In the event the Court fails timely to make its decision or to advise the parties of an intended decision date, as required by L.R. 83–9.3, counsel shall then file a joint request with the Chief Judge to establish an intended decision date. A copy of such request shall be filed in the case.

L.R. 83–9.5. Date of Intended Decision. Upon receipt of a request under L.R. 83–9.4, the Chief Judge shall, after consultation with the judge to whom the matter is assigned, establish a firm intended decision date by which the Court's decision shall be made. Such setting of a final intended decision date shall be in writing, shall be filed in the case, and shall be served on the parties.

[Effective October 1, 2001. Amended effective June 1, 2012; December 1, 2012.]

L.R. 83–10. APPEALS—DESIGNATION OF REPORTER'S TRANSCRIPT

The designation of a reporter's transcript on appeal shall specify each hearing date or dates ordered from the court reporter. That designation shall be made on the appropriate form, which is available from the Clerk.

[Effective October 1, 2001.]

L.R. 83–11 THROUGH 83–15 [RESERVED]

L.R. 83–16. HABEAS CORPUS PETITIONS AND MOTIONS UNDER 28 U.S.C. SECTION 2255

L.R. 83–16.1. Court Forms. A petition for a writ of habeas corpus or a motion filed pursuant to 28 U.S.C. § 2255 shall be submitted on the forms approved and supplied by the Court.

L.R. 83–16.2. Verification—Other Than by Person in Custody. If the petition or motion is verified by a person other than the individual in custody, the person verifying the document shall set forth the reason why it has not been verified by the person in custody. The person verifying the document shall allege only facts personally known to that person. If facts are alleged upon information and belief, the source of the information and belief shall be stated.

L.R. 83–16.3. Habeas Corpus—Exclusion, Deportation and Removal Cases. A next friend petition for a writ of habeas corpus in exclusion, deportation and removal cases must allege that the petitioner has been authorized by the applicant for admission or respondent in the proceedings to file the petition. If the petition is filed by a relative who is the father, mother, husband, wife, brother, sister, uncle or aunt of the applicant for admission in the proceedings, that fact shall be alleged and authorization to file the petition need not be shown.

[Effective October 1, 2001.]

L.R. 83–17. SPECIAL REQUIREMENTS FOR HABEAS CORPUS PETITIONS INVOLVING THE DEATH PENALTY

L.R. 83–17.1. Applicability. This rule shall govern the procedures for a first federal habeas proceeding under Chapter 153 of Title 28 of the United States Code in which a petitioner seeks relief from a judgment imposing the penalty of death. The application of this rule may be modified by the judge to whom the case is assigned. These rules shall supplement the Rules Governing Section 2254 Cases in the United States District Courts.

L.R. 83–17.2. Timely Notice of Execution Dates From California Attorney General. Whenever an execution date is set for a petitioner who was convicted and sentenced in a county within the jurisdiction of the Central District of California, the California Attorney General shall notify the Court of the date of the scheduled execution by preparing and filing Form CV–138, Notice of Setting of Date For Execution of Sentence on Judgment of Death, within seven (7) days of the state court's setting of the execution date. The Attorney General shall ensure that the notice is filed under the same case number as the original petition for writ of habeas corpus filed in this Court.

L.R. 83–17.3. Initial Filings and Petitions.

(a) A prisoner under a judgment of death may file a petition for writ of habeas corpus or a request for appointment of counsel. Such filings shall be made in the Western Division (Los Angeles) of the Central District. Upon such filing, the case shall be randomly assigned to a district judge through the district-wide Death Penalty Assignment Wheel. After filing and assignment, the matter shall be immediately referred to the Capital Case Committee for the appointment of counsel.

(b) Petitions shall be submitted on a form supplied by the Clerk of Court, filled in by printing or typewriting, or as a legible typewritten document which contains all of the information required by that form. All petitions or requests for appointment of counsel: (i) shall state whether the petitioner has previously sought habeas relief arising out of the same matter from this court or any other federal court, together with a copy of the ruling; and (ii) shall clearly identify in the caption any scheduled execution date. Any petition exceeding ten (10) pages in length, excluding exhibits, shall be accompanied by an indexed table of contents setting forth the headings or subheadings contained in the body thereof.

(c) A pro se petitioner need only file the original of the petition. If the petitioner is represented by counsel, counsel for the petitioner shall file the petition in accordance with L.R. 5–4. No filing fee is required.

(d) If the petitioner is not represented by counsel, the Clerk of Court shall immediately serve the California Attorney General's Office by mail, e-mail or fax when an initial filing is received by the Court.

(e) When a petition or request for appointment of counsel is filed by a petitioner who was convicted outside of this district, the Clerk of the Court shall immediately advise the Clerk of the Court of the district in which the petitioner was convicted, and prepare a stay and transfer order for signature of a district court judge.

L.R. 83–17.4. Appointment of Counsel.

(a) *Initial Appointment of Counsel.* Upon receipt of the habeas corpus petition or the initial request for appointment of counsel, unless the petition is patently frivolous, or the request for appointment of counsel is clearly premature, the Federal Public Defender's Office ("FPDO") will be appointed. If the FPDO has already been assigned the maximum number of cases, as determined by the Defender Services Committee of the United States Judicial Conference, and the FPDO has not agreed to an excess appointment, or otherwise has a conflict or cannot accept the appointment, lead and second counsel must be selected and appointed from a panel of attorneys, qualified for appointment in capital habeas corpus cases. In exceptional circumstances, the Court may appoint an attorney who is not a member of the panel.

(b) *Subsequent Appointment of Second Counsel.* If second counsel is not appointed at the time lead counsel is appointed, and lead counsel recommends that second counsel be appointed, lead counsel must apply to the assigned judge for appointment of a second counsel.

(c) *Substitution of First or Second Counsel.* If the assigned judge, in his or her discretion, determines that the substitution of counsel is necessary, section (a) applies.

L.R. 83–17.5. Transfer of Venue.

(a) Subject to the provisions of 28 U.S.C. § 2241(d), it is the policy of this Court that a petition should be heard in the district in which petitioner was convicted, rather than in the district of petitioner's present confinement.

(b) If an order for transfer of venue is made on a first petition for habeas corpus, the Court shall order a stay of execution which shall continue until such time as the transferee court acts upon the petition or the order of stay.

L.R. 83–17.6. Stays of Execution.

(a) *Stay Pending Final Disposition.* Upon the filing of a habeas corpus petition, unless the petition is patently frivolous or clearly premature, the Court may issue a stay of execution pending final disposition of the petition in the district court.

(b) *Stay for the Request for Appointment of Counsel.* Upon the filing of a request for appointment of counsel, unless the request is patently frivolous or clearly premature, the Court

must issue a temporary stay of execution. The stay must terminate not later than 90 days after counsel is appointed or the request for appointment of counsel is withdrawn or denied.

(c) *Stay Pending Appeal.* If the petition is denied and a certificate of appealability is issued, the Court may grant a stay of execution which will continue in effect until the Court of Appeals acts upon the appeal or the order of stay.

(d) *Notice of Stay.* Upon the granting of any stay of execution, the Clerk of the Court must immediately notify the Custodian of the prisoner and the California Attorney General. The California Attorney General must assure that the Clerk of the Court has a twenty-four (24) hour telephone number to the Custodian.

L.R. 83–17.7. Procedures for Considering the Petition.

Unless the Court summarily dismisses the petition under Rule 4 of the Rules Governing Section 2254 Cases in the United States District Courts, the following schedule and procedures shall apply subject to modification by the Court. Requests for enlargement of any time period in this rule shall comply with the applicable Local Rules of the Court.

(a) Respondent shall as soon as practicable, but in any event on or before thirty (30) days from the date of service of the petition, electronically lodge the following with the Court in accordance with L.R. 5–1 and 5–4.3.1:

(i) Transcripts of the state trial court proceedings.

(ii) Appellant's and respondent's briefs on direct appeal to the California Supreme Court, and the opinion or orders of that court.

(iii) Petitioner's and respondent's briefs in any state court habeas corpus proceedings, and all opinions, orders and transcripts of such proceedings.

(iv) An index of all materials described in paragraphs (a)(i) through (a)(iii) above. Such materials are to be marked and numbered so that they can be uniformly cited.

(v) If any items identified in paragraphs (a)(i)through (a)(iv) are not available, respondent shall state when, if at all, such missing material can be filed.

(b) If counsel for petitioner claims that respondent has not complied with the requirements of paragraph (a), or if counsel for petitioner does not have copies of all the documents lodged with the Court by respondent, counsel for petitioner shall promptly file written notice thereof. Respondent shall supply copies of the missing documents forthwith, and file notice of compliance.

(c) (i) In the interest of expediting habeas death penalty cases, it is the policy of the Court to entertain unexhausted claims if the respondent expressly waives the exhaustion issue. However, if the respondent declines to waive the exhaustion issue with respect to any or all claims in the petition, prior to filing a motion, counsel for respondent must make a good faith effort to confer with counsel for petitioner regarding the exhausted status of each such claim. Unless relieved by written order of the Court upon good cause shown, counsel for petitioner must confer with counsel for respondent within seven (7) days after service of a letter requesting such conference. The respondent's letter must identify each claim that respondent contends is unexhausted, specify the basis for asserting that the claim is unexhausted, and provide any legal authority that respondent contends is dispositive of the exhausted status of that claim.

(ii) If, after the meeting, the parties continue to dispute the exhausted status of one or more claims, the respondent must file an appropriate motion no later than twenty-eight (28) days after service of the petition. In connection with any motion relating to exhaustion disputes, the parties must file a joint statement indicating (1) which claims the parties agree have been fairly presented to the state supreme court, (2) which claims the parties agree have not been fairly presented to the state supreme court, and (3) on which claims the parties disagree whether the claim has been fairly presented to the state supreme court. For each claim whose exhaustion status is in dispute, the petitioner must cite the specific pages of the state court record that petitioner contends fairly presented the claim to the state supreme court.

(d) If respondent does not intend to challenge the exhausted status of any claim in the petition, or is willing to expressly waive exhaustion as to all such claims, respondent must file an answer within twenty-eight (28) days from the date of service of the petition. Respondent must include in the answer the matters defined in Rule 5 of the Rules Governing Section 2254 Cases in the United States District Courts and must attach any other relevant documents not already lodged or filed. An answer that exceeds ten (10) pages in length, excluding exhibits, must be accompanied by an indexed table of contents setting forth the headings or subheadings contained in the body thereof.

(e) Unless otherwise ordered by the Court, within twenty-eight (28) days after respondent has filed the answer, petitioner may file a reply to the respondent's answer.

(f) No discovery shall be had without leave of the Court. A request for discovery shall be presented to the Court by way of a joint stipulation in substantially the same format as required by L.R. 37–2.1. The joint stipulation shall identify the discovery requested, a statement explaining the need for the requested discovery, and opposing counsel's position regarding the need for the requested discovery.

(g) Any request for an evidentiary hearing by either party must be made within twenty-eight (28) days from the filing of the reply to the respondent's answer, or within twenty-eight (28) days from the expiration of the time for filing the reply. The request must include a specification of the factual issues and the legal reasoning that require a hearing and a summary of the evidence of each claim the movant proposes to offer at the hearing. Any opposition must be filed within twenty-one (21) days after the request for an evidentiary hearing was filed. A reply to the opposition must be filed within fourteen (14) days after the opposition was filed.

L.R. 83–17.8. Evidentiary Hearing. If an evidentiary hearing is held, the proceedings must be recorded and a transcript of the proceedings must be prepared. The parties must agree to an equitable division of the cost and which party will order the transcript. In the absence of agreement, the parties may apply to the Court for an order allocating the cost.

L.R. 83–17.9. Budgeting Capital Habeas Cases.

(a) Budgeting Required. In all cases where attorneys' fees and investigative and expert fees and expenses are reimbursed pursuant to 18 U.S.C. § 3599, petitioner's counsel is required to prepare and submit to the Court a budget for each phase of the proceedings. The Court may schedule one or more ex parte conferences with petitioner's counsel to implement the budgeting process.

(b) Filing of Budget Related Documents. Once the Court orders that a proper showing of the need for confidentiality of budget related documents has been made, the petitioner may file future budget related documents under seal without further approval by the Court. The title page for budget related documents, filed after the Court has so ordered, must contain the following language: "To Be Filed Under Seal Pursuant to Local Rule 79–5.1."

L.R. 83–17.10. Rulings. The Clerk of Court must immediately notify the Custodian of the prisoner and the California Attorney General whenever relief is granted on a petition.

The Clerk of the Court must immediately notify the Clerk of the United States Court of Appeals for the Ninth Circuit by telephone of:

(a) the issuance of a final order denying or dismissing a petition without a certificate of appealability, or

(b) the denial of a stay of execution.

When a notice of appeal is filed, and if the certificate of appealability was denied in full, the Clerk of the Court must immediately transmit the record to the Court of Appeals. In all other instances the record must only be transmitted upon a request from the Court of Appeals.

After the issuance of the mandate of a reviewing court that results in the denial with prejudice of all habeas relief, and if the Court so orders, the respondent must lodge a complete copy of the state court record and all other items identified in L.R. 83–17.7 by the date set by the Court.

[Effective October 1, 2001. Amended effective December 1, 2003; March 22, 2006; January 1, 2010; November 1, 2010; June 1, 2015; December 1, 2016.]

F.R.CIV.P. 84. FORMS

F.R.CIV.P. 85. TITLE

L.R. 85–1. SHORT TITLE

These rules may be cited as the Local Rules.

[Effective October 1, 2001.]

F.R.CIV.P. 86. EFFECTIVE DATES

LOCAL CIVIL APPENDICES
APPENDIX A.   PRETRIAL FORM NO. 1
UNITED STATES DISTRICT COURT
CENTRAL DISTRICT OF CALIFORNIA

(TITLE OF CASE)   ) CASE NO. _____

)

) FINAL PRETRIAL

) CONFERENCE ORDER

)

)

_____)

Following pretrial proceedings, pursuant to F.R.Civ.P. 16 and L.R. 16, IT IS ORDERED:

1.   The parties are: [list]

Each of these parties has been served and has appeared.   All other parties named in the pleadings and not identified in the preceding paragraph are now dismissed.

The pleadings which raise the issues are: [list]

2.   Federal jurisdiction and venue are invoked upon the grounds: [Give a concise statement of facts necessary to confer federal jurisdiction and venue.   State whether the facts requisite to federal jurisdiction are denied or admitted.]

3.   The trial is estimated to take ____ trial days.   [Where counsel cannot agree set forth each side's estimate.]

4.   The trial is to be a jury (non-jury) trial.

[If a jury trial add: At least seven (7) days prior to the trial date the parties shall file and serve by e-mail, fax, or personal delivery: (a) proposed jury instructions as required by L.R. 51–1 and (b) any special questions requested to be asked on voir dire.]

[If a non-jury trial add: At least seven (7) days prior to the trial date the parties shall lodge and serve by e-mail, fax, or personal delivery the findings of fact and conclusions of law the party expects the Court to make upon proof at the time of trial as required by L.R. 52–1.]

5.   The following facts are admitted and require no proof: [list admitted facts]

6.   The following facts, though stipulated, shall be without prejudice to any evidentiary objection: [list facts not to be contested though not admitted]

7.   [This section of the Final Pretrial Conference Order is intended to finalize, in advance of trial, the claims and defenses to be presented at trial.   In accordance with F.R.Civ.P. 16(c), parties will be precluded from presenting claims or defenses not set forth in this order, in the manner required by this order, unless the order is modified to prevent manifest injustice.   Only claims or defenses contained in the complaint and answer and any court authorized amendment or supplement may be included in this Final Pretrial Conference Order.   If a party chooses to abandon a claim or defense previously alleged, it may do so by not including it in this order, and the failure to include any pleaded claim or defense will be deemed to effect such a waiver.   The following format must be employed:]

Plaintiff(s):

(a) Plaintiff plans to pursue the following claims against the following defendants:

[Here list claims in summary fashion, for example:

   Claim 1: Defendant A breached his contract with Plaintiff;

   Claim 2: Defendant A violated the Americans with Disabilities Act, 42 U.S.C. § 12101 et seq.]

(b) The elements required to establish Plaintiff's claims are: [List the elements separately for each claim, as found in standard jury instructions or case law.   The parties should strive to agree on the elements.   If the parties cannot agree on an element, then each party may state its version of the elements.]

(c) In brief, the key evidence Plaintiff relies on for each of the claims is: [List separately for each element of each claim.]

Defendant(s):

(a) Defendant plans to pursue the following counterclaims and affirmative defenses: [Insofar as defenses are concerned, Defendant should identify only *affirmative* defenses, which are those matters on which the Defendant bears the burden of proof. They are matters which would defeat Plaintiff's claim even if Plaintiff established the elements of the claim. Examples of such affirmative defenses—which must have been pleaded in Defendant's Answer—appear in F.R.Civ.P. 8(c). Insofar as counterclaims are concerned, Defendant should follow the same format as Plaintiff in listing claims.]

(b) The elements required to establish Defendant's counterclaims and affirmative defenses are: [List the elements separately for each counterclaim or affirmative defense as found in standard jury instructions or case law. The parties should strive to agree on the elements. If the parties cannot agree on an element, then each party may state its version of the elements.]

(c) In brief, the key evidence Defendant relies on for each counterclaim and affirmative defense is: [List separately for each element of each counterclaim or defense.]

Third Party Plaintiffs and Defendants:

[Claims and defenses in third-party cases should be analyzed and set forth in the same way as those of plaintiffs and defendants. Separate proposed pretrial conference orders will not be accepted.]

8.   In view of the admitted facts and the elements required to establish the claims, counterclaims and affirmative defenses, the following issues remain to be tried: [list ultimate issues, not evidentiary issues]

9.   All discovery is complete.

10.   All disclosures under F.R.Civ.P. 26(a)(3) have been made.

The joint exhibit list of the parties has been filed under separate cover as required by L.R. 16–6.1. Unless all parties agree that an exhibit shall be withdrawn, all exhibits will be admitted without objection at trial, except those exhibits listed below:

Plaintiff objects to Exhibit Nos. _____

Defendant objects to Exhibit Nos. _____

The objections and grounds therefor are: [list exhibit and grounds for objections separately as to each exhibit]

11.   Witness lists of the parties have been filed with the Court.

Only the witnesses identified in the lists will be permitted to testify (other than solely for impeachment).

Each party intending to present evidence by way of deposition testimony has marked such depositions in accordance with L.R. 16–2.7. For this purpose, the following depositions shall be lodged with the Clerk as required by L.R. 32–1: [list]

[if appropriate:] Plaintiff (Defendant) objects to the presentation of testimony by deposition of the following witnesses:

12.   The following law and motion matters and motions in limine, and no others, are pending or contemplated: [state "none" or list]

13.   Bifurcation of the following issues for trial is ordered. [State "none" or identify those issues to be tried during the first stage of the trial and those to be tried later.]

14.   The foregoing admissions having been made by the parties, and the parties having specified the foregoing issues remaining to be litigated, this Final Pretrial Conference Order shall supersede the pleadings and govern the course of the trial of this cause, unless modified to prevent manifest injustice.

Dated: _____, 20____.

_____
                                        UNITED STATES DISTRICT JUDGE

Approved as to form and content.

_____

Attorney for Plaintiff

_____

Attorney for Defendant

_____

Attorney for (indicate party represented)

[Effective April 1, 1998.   Amended effective December 1, 2006; January 1, 2010; June 1, 2012.]

APPENDIX B.   AGREEMENT ON ACCEPTANCE OF SERVICE

To facilitate and assure timely service of process and to provide adequate time to answer habeas corpus petitions under 28 U.S.C. § 2241 or § 2254, the Clerk of Court of the United States District Court for the Central District of California and the Offices of the Attorney General of the State of California for Los Angeles and San Diego agree to the following procedures. This agreement addresses cases in which the United States District Judge or Magistrate Judge determines that service documents are to issue in all cases where petitioners have filed a habeas corpus petitions under 28 U.S.C. § 2241 or 28 U.S.C. § 2254.

1.   General Provisions

A. At case opening, the case manager will add an appropriate entity which specifies the Attorney General as a "Notice Only Party" to the court's Case Management and Electronic Case Filing System (CM/ECF). The Attorney General's Office will thereby receive electronic notice of all case filings and activity, including the case initiating documents, to any e-mail accounts specified by that office in their "Notice Only" designation. If the Attorney General ultimately enters an appearance on behalf of one or more defendants in the case, the "Notice Only Party" will be terminated and the attorney/(s) who enters his/her appearance will be designated as the counsel to whom notice is sent.

B. These procedures shall take effect for any case filed after June 1, 2013, and remain in effect until terminated by the Attorney General or the Clerk.

2.   Habeas Corpus Petitions

Pursuant to the Rules 4 and 5 Governing § 2254 Cases and 28 U.S.C. § 2243, following preliminary review by the Court, the respondent is only required to answer or otherwise respond to the petition if ordered to do so by the court. In its order the Court will fix the time by which response must be made. The Attorney General agrees that entry of the order to respond on the docket by the clerk complies with the requirement of service of the petition on the respondent, the Attorney General, or other appropriate officer and will accept service of the same.

[Amended effective December 1, 2012; June 1, 2013.]

APPENDIX C. AGREEMENT ON ACCEPTANCE OF SERVICE

To facilitate and assure timely service of process and to provide adequate time to answer habeas corpus petitions under 28 U.S.C. § 2241 and 28 U.S.C. § 2255, the Clerk of Court of the United States District Court for the Central District of California and the United States Attorney's Office of the Central District of California agree to the following procedures. This agreement addresses cases in which the United States District Judge or Magistrate Judge determines that service documents are to issue in all cases where petitioners have filed habeas corpus petitions under 28 U.S.C. § 2241 and motions under 28 U.S.C. § 2255.

1. General Provisions

A. At case opening, the case manager will add an appropriate entity which specifies the U.S. Attorney's Office as a "Notice Only Party" to the court's Case Management and Electronic Case Filing System (CM/ECF). The U.S. Attorney's Office will thereby receive electronic notice of all case filings and activity, including the case initiating documents, to any e-mail accounts specified by that office in their "Notice Only" designation. If the U.S. Attorney's Office ultimately enters an appearance on behalf of one or more defendants in the case, the "Notice Only Party" will be terminated and the attorney/(s) who enters his/her appearance will be designated as the counsel to whom notice is sent.

B. These procedures shall take effect for any case filed after June 1, 2013, and remain in effect until terminated by the U.S. Attorney's Office or the Clerk.

2. Habeas Corpus Petitions

Pursuant to the Rules 4 and 5 Governing § 2254 Cases and 28 U.S.C. § 2243, following preliminary review by the Court, the respondent is only required to answer or otherwise respond to the petition if ordered to do so by the court. In its order the Court will fix the time by which response must be made. The U.S. Attorney's Office agrees that entry of the order to respond on the docket by the clerk complies with the requirement of service of the petition on the respondent, the U.S. Attorney's Office, or other appropriate officer and will accept service of the same.

[Effective June 1, 2013.]

CHAPTER II.   RULES FOR ADMIRALTY AND MARITIME CLAIMS AND ASSET FORFEITURE ACTIONS

The reference in parentheses following the local rule number is the corresponding Rule or Supplemental Rule of the Federal Rules of Civil Procedure.

RULE A.   (RA–A)—SCOPE AND DEFINITIONS

A.1.   (RA–A.1.) Scope.   These local rules may be referred to as "local admiralty rules." They apply only to civil actions that are governed by Supplemental Rule A of the Supplemental Rules for Admiralty or Maritime Claims and Asset Forfeiture Actions (Supplemental Rule or Rules). All other local rules are applicable in these cases, but to the extent that another local rule is inconsistent with the applicable local admiralty rules, the local admiralty rules shall govern.

A.2.   (RA–A.2.) Officers of the Court.   As used in the local admiralty rules, "Judicial Officer" means a United States District Judge or a United States Magistrate Judge, "Clerk of the Court" means the Clerk of the District Court and includes deputy clerks of court; and "Marshal" means the United States Marshal and includes deputy marshals.

A.3.   (83, RA–A.1.) Citation.   The local admiralty rules may be cited by the letters "LAR" and the capital letter and numbers in parentheses that appear at the beginning of each section. The capital letter is intended to associate the local admiralty rule with the Supplemental Rule that bears the same capital letter.

[Effective April 1, 1998. Amended effective December 1, 2010.]

RULE B.   (RB–B)—ATTACHMENT AND GARNISHMENT

B.1.   (83, RB–B.1.) Identification of State Law Invoked.   When the plaintiff invokes a state procedure in order to attach or garnish as permitted by the Rules or the Supplemental Rules, the process of attachment or garnishment shall identify the state law upon which the attachment or garnishment is based.

B.2.   (RB–B.1.) Affidavit that Defendant is Not Found Within the District.   The affidavit required by Supplemental Rule B(1) to accompany the complaint shall list the efforts made by and on behalf of plaintiff to find and serve the defendant within the district. The phrase "not found within the district" in Supplemental Rule B(1) means that, in an in personam action, the defendant cannot be served with the summons and complaint as provided in F.R.Civ.P. 4(e)(2) or 4(h)(1).

[Effective April 1, 1998. Amended effective January 1, 2010; December 1, 2010.]

RULE C.   (RC–C)—ACTIONS IN REM: SPECIAL PROVISIONS

C.1 (RC–C.1) Undertakings in Lieu of Arrest.   If, before or after commencement of suit, plaintiff accepts any written undertaking to respond on behalf of the vessel or other property sued in return for foregoing the arrest or stipulating to the release of such vessel or other property, the undertaking shall become a defendant in place of the vessel or other property sued and be deemed referenced as the name of the vessel or other property in any pleading, order or judgment in the action referenced in the undertaking. The preceding shall apply to any such undertaking, subject to its own terms and whether or not it complies with Rule 65–2 *et seq.* of Chapter I of these Rules, or has been approved by a Judge or Clerk.

C.2 (RC–C.2) Intangible Property.   The summons issued pursuant to Supplemental Rule C(3)(c) shall direct the person having control of intangible property to show cause no later than fourteen (14) days after service why the intangible property should not be delivered to the Court to abide the judgment. A judicial officer for good cause shown may lengthen or shorten the time. Service of the summons has the effect of an arrest of the intangible property and brings it within the control of the Court. Service of the summons to show cause requires a garnishee wishing to retain possession of the property to establish grounds for doing so, including specification of the measures taken to segregate and safeguard the intangible property arrested. The person who is served may deliver or pay over to the Marshal the intangible property proceeded against to the extent sufficient to satisfy the plaintiff's claim. If such delivery or payment is made, the person served is excused from the duty to show cause. A person who asserts a right of possession or ownership of the property may show cause as provided in Supplemental Rule C(6)(a) why the property should not be delivered to the Court.

C.3 (RC–C.3) Notice of Action and Arrest.

(a) *Publication.*   The notice required by Supplemental Rule C(4) shall be published once and plaintiff's attorney shall file a copy of the notice as it was published with the Clerk. The notice shall contain:

(i) The Court, title, and number of the action;

(ii) The date of the arrest;

(iii) The identity of the property arrested;

(iv) The name, address and telephone number of the attorney for plaintiff;

(v) A statement that the claim of a person who is entitled to possession or who claims an interest pursuant to Supplemental Rule C(6)(a) must be filed with the Clerk and served on the attorney for plaintiff within fourteen (14) days after publication;

(vi) A statement that an answer to the complaint must be filed and served within thirty (30) days after publication, and that otherwise, default may be entered and condemnation ordered;

(vii) A statement that applications for intervention under Federal Rule 24 by persons claiming maritime liens or other interests shall be filed within the time fixed by the Court; and,

(viii) The name, address and telephone number of the Marshal.

(b) *Filing of Proof of Publication.* Plaintiff shall cause to be filed with the Clerk not later than thirty (30) days after the date of publication sworn proof of publication by or on behalf of the publisher of the newspaper in which notice was published, together with a copy of the publication or reproduction thereof.

C.4 (RC–C.4) Default in Action In Rem.

(a) *Notice Required.* A party seeking a default judgment in an action in rem must show that due notice of the action and arrest of the property has been given:

(1) by publication as required in Local Admiralty Rule C.3;

(2) by service upon the master or other person having custody of the property; and

(3) by first-class mail to every other person who has not appeared in the action and is known to have an interest in the property.

(b) *Persons with Recorded Interest.*

(1) If the defendant property is a vessel documented under the laws of the United States, plaintiff must attempt to notify by first-class mail all persons named in the United States Coast Guard certificate of ownership.

(2) If the defendant property is a vessel numbered as provided in the Federal Boat Safety Act, plaintiff must attempt to notify by first-class mail the persons named in the records of the issuing authority.

(3) If the defendant property is of such character that there exists a governmental registry of recorded property interests or security interests in the property, the plaintiff must attempt to notify by first-class mail all persons named in the records of each such registry.

(c) *Failure to Give Notice.* Failure to give notice as provided by this Rule shall be grounds for setting aside the default under applicable rules but shall not affect title to property sold pursuant to order of sale or judgment.

C.5 (RC–C.5) Entry of Default and Default Judgment.
After the time for filing an answer has expired, the plaintiff may apply for entry of default under F.R.Civ.P. 55(a). Default will be entered upon showing that:

(a) Notice has been given as required by Local Admiralty Rule C.4(a); and

(b) Notice has been attempted as required by Local Admiralty Rule C.4(b), where appropriate; and

(c) The time for answer has expired; and

(d) No one has appeared to claim the property. Judgment may be entered under F.R.Civ.P. 55(b) at any time after default has been entered.

C.6 (RC–C.3) Application for Order Authorizing Issuance of Warrant for Arrest of Vessel or Other Property.
Any application for an order authorizing issuance of a warrant for the arrest of a vessel or other property under the Supplemental Rules for Admiralty and Maritime Claims must include, if known, the name, address, telephone number, and email address of both the owner of the vessel or other property at issue and the owner's counsel.

[Effective April 1, 1998. Amended effective October 1, 2001; December 1, 2010; December 1, 2018.]

RULE D. (RD–D)—POSSESSORY, PETITORY AND PARTITION ACTIONS

D.1. (RD–D.1.) Return Date. In an action under Supplemental Rule D, a judicial officer may order that the claim and answer be filed on a date earlier than twenty-one (21) days after arrest. The order may also set a date for expedited hearing of the action.

[Effective April 1, 1998. Amended effective December 1, 2010.]

RULE E. (RE–E)—ACTIONS IN REM AND QUASI IN REM: GENERAL PROVISIONS

E.1 (RE–E.1) Itemized Demand for Judgment. The demand for judgment in every complaint filed under Supplemental Rule B or C except a demand for a salvage award shall allege the dollar amount of the debt or damages for which the action was commenced. The demand for judgment shall also allege the nature of other items of damage. The amount of the special bond posted under Supplemental Rule E(5)(a) may be based upon these allegations.

E.2 (83, RE–E.1) Itemized Demand for Salvage Award. In an action for a salvage reward, the complaint shall allege the dollar value of the vessel, cargo, freight, and other property salved, and the dollar amount of the reward claimed.

E.3 (RE–E.2) Verification and Pleadings. Every complaint in Supplemental Rule B, C and D actions shall be verified upon oath or solemn affirmation, or in the form provided by 28 U.S.C. § 1746, by a party or by an authorized officer of a corporate party. If no party or authorized corporate officer is present within the district, verification of a complaint may be made by an agent, attorney in fact, or attorney of record, who shall state the sources of the knowledge, information and belief contained in the complaint; declare that the document verified is true to the best of that knowledge, information, and belief; state why verification is not made by the party or an authorized corporate officer; and state that the affiant is authorized so to verify. A verification not made by a party or authorized corporate officer will be deemed to have been made by the party as if verified personally. If the verification was not made by a party or authorized corporate officer, any interested party may move, with or without requesting a stay, for the personal oath of a party or an authorized corporate officer, which shall be procured by commission or as otherwise ordered.

E.4 (83–RE.3) Review by Judicial Officer.

(a) *Authorization to Issue Process.* Before the Clerk will issue a summons and process of arrest, attachment or garnishment to any party, including intervenors, under Supplemental Rules B and C, the pleadings, the affidavit required by Rule B, and accompanying supporting documents must be reviewed by a judicial officer. If the judicial officer finds the conditions set forth in Rules B or C appear to exist, as appropriate, the judicial officer shall authorize the Clerk to issue process. Supplemental process or alias process may thereafter be issued by the Clerk upon application without further order of the Court.

(b) *Exigent Circumstances.* If the plaintiff or plaintiff's attorney certifies by affidavit or declaration pursuant to 28 U.S.C. § 1746 submitted to the Clerk that exigent circumstances make review impracticable and sets forth in detail the facts that establish the exigent circumstances, the Clerk shall issue a summons and warrant of arrest or process of attachment and garnishment.

(c) *Personal Appearance.* Unless otherwise required by the judicial officer, the review by the judicial officer will not require the presence of the applicant or the applicant's attorney but shall be based upon the pleadings and other documents submitted on behalf of that party.

(d) *Order.* Upon approving the application for arrest, attachment or garnishment, the judicial officer will issue an order to the Clerk authorizing the Clerk to issue an order for arrest, attachment, or garnishment. The proposed form of order authorizing the arrest, attachment, or garnishment, and the order for arrest, attachment, or garnishment shall be submitted with the other documents for review.

(e) *Request for Review.* Except in case of exigent circumstances, application for review shall be made by filing a Notice of Request for Review In Accordance With Supplemental Rule B or C with the Clerk and stating therein the process sought and any time requirements within which the request must be reviewed. The Clerk shall contact the judicial officer to whom the matter is assigned (or if that officer is not available, another judicial officer) to arrange for the necessary review. It will be the duty of the applicant to ensure that the application has been reviewed and, upon approval, presented to the Clerk for issuance of the appropriate order.

E.5 (83–E.3) Process Held in Abeyance. If a party does not wish the process to be issued at the time of filing the action, the party shall request that issuance of process be held in abeyance. It will not be the responsibility of the Clerk or the Marshal to ensure that process is issued at a later date.

E.6 (83–C.3) Service by Marshal Required. Only a Marshal shall serve a warrant of arrest or process of maritime attachment or garnishment on a vessel, cargo or other tangible property. Upon completion of service, the Marshal shall file proof thereof in the appropriate form.

E.7 (83) Instructions to the Marshal. The party who requests a warrant of arrest or process of attachment or garnishment shall provide instructions to the Marshal.

E.8 (83) Property in Possession of United States Officer. When the property to be attached or arrested is in the custody of an employee or officer of the United States, the Marshal will deliver a copy of the complaint and warrant of arrest or summons and process of attachment or garnishment to that officer or employee, if present, and otherwise to the custodian of the property. The Marshal will instruct the officer or employee or custodian to retain custody of the property until ordered to do otherwise by a judicial officer.

E.9 (83–E.2) Security for Costs. In an action under the Supplemental Rules, a party may move upon notice to all parties for an order to compel an adverse party to post security for costs with the Clerk pursuant to Supplemental Rule E(2)(b). Unless otherwise ordered, the amount of security shall be $500.00. The party so ordered shall post the security within seven (7) days after the order is entered. A party who fails to post security when due may not participate further in the proceedings. A party may move for an order increasing the amount of security for costs.

E.10 (83–E.4) Adversary Hearing. Upon application of any interested party, the adversary hearing following arrest or attachment or garnishment under Supplemental Rule E(4)(f) shall be conducted promptly by a judicial officer. The Court may order such notice as it deems appropriate.

E.11 (83) Appraisal. An order for appraisal of property so that security may be given or altered will be entered by the Clerk at the request of any interested party. If the parties do not agree in writing upon an appraiser, a judicial officer will appoint the appraiser. The appraiser shall be sworn to the faithful and impartial discharge of the appraiser's duties before any federal or state officer authorized by law to administer oaths. The appraiser shall give twenty-four (24) hours notice of the time and place of making the appraisal to counsel of record. The appraiser shall promptly file the appraisal with the Clerk and serve it upon counsel of record. The appraiser's fee will be paid by the moving party, unless otherwise ordered or agreed but it is a taxable cost of the action.

E.12 (83) Security Deposit for Arrest or Attachment of Vessels. The first party who seeks arrest or attachment of a vessel or property aboard a vessel shall deposit with the Marshal the sum estimated by the Marshal to be sufficient to cover the expenses of the Marshal including, but not limited to, dockage, keepers, maintenance, and insurance for at least fourteen (14) days. The Marshal is not required to execute process until the deposit is made. The party shall advance additional sums from time to time as directed by the Marshal to cover the Marshal's estimated expenses until the property is released or disposed of as provided in Supplemental Rule E. A party who fails to advance such additional sums may not participate further in the proceedings except by order of the Court. The Marshal may, upon notice to all parties, petition the Court for an order to release the vessel if additional sums are not advanced within seven (7) days after the request, or seek such other appropriate relief as the Court deems proper.

E.13 (83) Intervenor's Claims.

(a) *Presentation of Claim.* When a vessel or other property has been arrested, attached, or garnished, and is in the hands of the Marshal or substitute custodian, anyone having a claim against the vessel or property is required to present the claim by filing an intervening complaint and obtaining a warrant of arrest or process of maritime attachment and garnishment, and not by filing an original complaint, unless otherwise ordered by a judicial officer. The intervening party shall file a Notice of Request for Review pursuant to Local Admiralty Rule E.4(e). Upon obtaining judicial approval for issuance of process, the intervening party shall forthwith deliver a conformed copy of the complaint in intervention and the intervenor's warrant of arrest or process of attachment or garnishment to the Marshal, who shall deliver the same to the vessel or custodian of the property. Intervenors shall thereafter be subject to the rights and obligations of parties, and the vessel or property shall stand arrested, attached, or garnished by the intervenor. An intervenor shall not be required to advance a security deposit to the Marshal.

(b) *Sharing Marshal's Fees and Expenses.* An intervenor shall owe a debt to the first plaintiff, enforceable on motion, consisting of the intervenor's share of the Marshal's fees and expenses in the proportion that the intervenor's claim bears to the sum of all the claims. If a party plaintiff permits vacation of an arrest, attachment or garnishment, remaining plaintiffs share the responsibility to the Marshal for fees and expenses in proportion to the remaining claims and for the duration of the Marshal's custody because of each claim.

E.14 (83) Custody of Property.

(a) *Safekeeping of Property.* When a vessel, cargo or other property is brought into the Marshal's custody by arrest or attachment, the Marshal shall arrange for adequate safekeeping, which may include the placing of keepers on or near the vessel. A substitute custodian in place of the Marshal may be appointed by order of the Court. The custodian shall have liability of not less than $10,000.00. Notice of the application to appoint a substitute custodian must be given to all parties and the Marshal. The application must show the name of the proposed substitute custodian, the location of the vessel during the period of custody, and the proposed insurance coverage.

(b) *Insurance.* The Marshal may procure insurance to protect the Marshal, his deputies, keepers, and substitute custodians, from liabilities assumed in arresting and holding the vessel, cargo, or other property, and in performing whatever services may be undertaken to protect the vessel, cargo, or other property and to maintain the Court's custody. The party applying for removal of the vessel, cargo or other property to another location, for designation of a substitute custodian, or for other relief that will require an additional premium, shall reimburse the Marshal therefor. The premiums charged for the liability insurance are taxable as administrative costs while the vessel, cargo, or other property is in the custody of the Court.

(c) *Vessel Operations.* Following arrest or attachment of a vessel, no cargo handling, repairs, or movement may be made without an order of Court. The applicant for such an order shall give notice to the Marshal and to all parties of record. Upon proof of adequate insurance coverage of the applicant to indemnify any liability of the Marshal, the Court may direct the Marshal to permit cargo handling, repairs, movement of the vessel, or other operations. Before or after the Marshal has taken custody of a vessel, cargo or other property, any party of record may move for an order to dispense with keepers or to remove or place the vessel, cargo, or other property at a specified facility, to designate a substitute custodian, or for similar relief. Notice of the motion shall be given

to the Marshal and to all parties of record. The judicial officer will require that adequate insurance on the property will be maintained by the successor to the Marshal, before issuing the order to change arrangements.

(d) *Claims by Suppliers for Payment of Charges.* A person who furnishes supplies or services to a vessel, cargo, or other property in custody of the Court who has not been paid and claims the right to payment as an expense of administration shall file an invoice with the Clerk in the form of a verified claim at any time before the vessel, cargo, or other property is released or sold. The supplier must serve copies of the claim on the Marshal, substitute custodian if one has been appointed, and all parties of record. The Court may consider the claims individually or may schedule a single hearing for all claims.

E.15 (83—E.9) Sale of Property.

(a) *Notice.* Notice of sales of arrested or attached property shall be published in one or more newspapers to be specified in the order for sale. Unless otherwise ordered by a judge upon a showing of urgency or impracticality or unless otherwise provided by law, such notice shall be published for at least seven (7) days before the date of sale.

(b) *Payment of Bid.* Unless otherwise provided in the order, in all public auction sales by the Marshal under orders of sale in admiralty and maritime claims, the Marshal shall require of the last and highest bidder at the sale a minimum deposit in cash, certified check or cashier's check, of the full purchase price if it does not exceed $500 and otherwise $500 or ten percent (10%) of the bid, whichever is greater. The balance, if any, of the purchase price shall be paid in cash, certified check or cashier's check before confirmation of the sale or within seven (7) days of the dismissal of any opposition which may have been filed, exclusive of Saturdays, Sundays and legal holidays. Notwithstanding the above, a plaintiff or intervening plaintiff foreclosing a properly recorded and endorsed preferred mortgage on, or other valid security interest in the vessel may bid, without payment of cash, certified check or cashier's check, up to the total amount of the secured indebtedness as established by affidavit filed and served by that party on all other parties not later than fourteen (14) days prior to the date of sale.

(c) *Report and Confirmation.* At the conclusion of the sale, the Marshal shall forthwith file a written report to the Court setting forth the notice given; the fact of sale; the date of the sale; the names, addresses, and bid amounts of the bidders; the price obtained; and any other pertinent information. The Clerk of the Court shall endorse upon such report the time and date of its filing. If within seven (7) days, no written objection is filed, the sale shall stand confirmed as of course, without the necessity of any affirmative action thereon by the Court and the Clerk upon request shall so state to the Marshal in writing; except that no sale shall stand confirmed until the buyer has complied fully with the terms of his purchase. If no opposition to the sale is filed, the expenses of keeping the property pending confirmation of sale shall be charged against the party bearing expenses before the sale (subject to taxation as costs), except that if confirmation is delayed by the purchaser's failure to pay any balance which is due on the price, the cost of keeping the property subsequent to the seven (7) day period hereinabove specified shall be borne by the purchaser.

(d) *Penalty for Late Payment of Balance.* A successful bidder who fails to pay the balance of the bid within the time allowed under these rules or a different time specified by the Court shall also pay the Marshal the costs of keeping the property up to the date the bidder pays the balance and takes delivery of the property. Unless otherwise ordered by the Court, the Marshal shall refuse to release the property until this additional charge is paid.

(e) *Penalty for Default in Payment of Balance.* A successful bidder who fails to pay the balance of the bid within the time allowed is in default and the Court may at any time thereafter order a sale to the second highest bidder or order a new sale as appropriate. Any sum deposited by the bidder in default shall be applied to pay any additional costs incurred by the Marshal by reason of the default, including costs incident to resale. The balance of the deposit, if any, shall be retained in the registry subject to further order of the Court, and the Court shall be given written notice of its existence whenever the registry deposits are reviewed.

(f) *Opposition to Sale.* A party filing an opposition to the sale, whether seeking the reception of a higher bid or a new public sale by the Marshal, shall give prompt notice to all other parties and to the purchaser. Such party shall also, prior to filing an opposition, secure the Marshal's endorsement upon it acknowledging deposit with the Marshal of the necessary expense of keeping the property for at least seven (7) days. Pending the Court's determination of the opposition, such party shall also advance any further expense at such times and in such amounts as the Marshal shall request, or as the Court orders upon application of the Marshal or the opposing party. Such expense may later be subject to taxation as costs. In the event of failure to make such advance, the opposition shall fail without necessity for affirmative action thereon by the Court. If the opposition fails, the expense of keeping the property during the pendency of the opposition shall be borne by the party filing the opposition.

(g) *Disposition of Deposits.*

(i) Objection Sustained. If an objection is sustained, sums deposited by the successful bidder will be returned to the bidder forthwith. The sum deposited by the objector will be applied to pay the fees and expenses incurred by the Marshal in keeping the property until it is resold, and any balance remaining shall be returned to the objector. The objector will be reimbursed for the expense of keeping the property from the proceeds of a subsequent sale.

(ii) Objection Overruled. If the objection is overruled, the sum deposited by the objector will be applied to pay the expense of keeping the property from the day the objection was filed until the day the sale is confirmed, and any balance remaining will be returned to the objector forthwith.

[Effective April 1, 1998. Amended effective October 1, 2001; January 1, 2010; December 1, 2010; June 1, 2012; December 1, 2018.]

RULE F. (RF–F)—LIMITATION OF LIABILITY

F.1. (83–F.1.) Security for Costs. The amount of security for costs under Supplemental Rule F(1) shall be $1,000 unless otherwise ordered and it may be combined with the security for value and interest.

F.2. (83) Order of Proof at Trial. Where the vessel interests seeking statutory limitation of liability have raised the statutory defense by way of answer or complaint, the plaintiff in the former or the damage claimant in the latter shall proceed with its proof first, as is normal at civil trials.

[Effective April 1, 1998. Amended effective December 1, 2010.]

RULE G. (83, RG–G)—MISCELLANEOUS

G.1 (83) Deserting Seamen Cases.

(a) *Service.* Upon filing a verified petition for return of wages deposited in the registry of the Court pursuant to the provisions of 46 U.S.C. § 11505, a copy of the petition shall be served forthwith on the United States Attorney and a copy mailed to the Attorney General of the United States, after which a sworn return of such service and mailing shall be filed.

(b) *Time to Plead.* The United States has twenty-one (21) days after receipt of a copy of the petition by the United States Attorney in which to file its responsive pleading and claim.

G.2 (83) Rate of Prejudgment Interest Allowed. Unless a judge directs otherwise or as provided by statute, prejudgment interest shall be awarded at the rate authorized in 28 U.S.C. § 1961, providing for interest on judgments.

G.3 (83) Assignment of Actions. If the judge to whom a case under the Local Admiralty Rules has been assigned is not readily available, any matter pertaining to arrest, attachment, garnishment, security or release may be presented to any other judicial officer in the district without reassigning the case.

[Effective April 1, 1998. Amended effective December 1, 2010; December 1, 2012.]

CHAPTER III. LOCAL CRIMINAL RULES
I. APPLICABILITY

F.R.CRIM.P. 1.   SCOPE; DEFINITIONS

F.R.CRIM.P. 2.   INTERPRETATION

II. PRELIMINARY PROCEEDINGS

F.R.CRIM.P. 3.   THE COMPLAINT

F.R.CRIM.P. 4.   ARREST WARRANT OR SUMMONS ON A COMPLAINT

F.R.CRIM.P. 4.1.   COMPLAINT, WARRANT, OR SUMMONS BY TELEPHONE OR OTHER RELIABLE ELECTRONIC MEANS

F.R.CRIM.P. 5.   INITIAL APPEARANCE

L.Cr.R. 5-1.   REQUEST TO RECALL WARRANT OF REMOVAL

The United States Attorney must immediately notify the Court whenever a charging district drops all charges against a defendant who has been ordered transferred to that district under F.R.Crim.P. 5(c)(3) but the transfer has not taken place. The United States Attorney should do so by filing a Request to Recall Warrant of Removal in the case in which the transfer was ordered and notifying the magistrate judge on duty when the Request is filed.

[Effective December 1, 2019.]

F.R.CRIM.P. 5.1.   PRELIMINARY HEARING

III. THE GRAND JURY, THE INDICTMENT, AND THE INFORMATION

F.R.CRIM.P. 6.   THE GRAND JURY

F.R.CRIM.P. 7.   THE INDICTMENT AND THE INFORMATION

L.Cr.R. 7-1.   INDICTMENT OR INFORMATION—COPIES

The United States Attorney shall deliver to the Clerk sufficient copies of the indictment or information so that a copy may be delivered to each defendant and the judge or magistrate judge assigned to the case.

L.Cr.R. 7-2.   SUPERSEDING INDICTMENT OR INFORMATION

A superseding indictment or information shall be filed promptly with the Clerk in paper format and assigned the same number as the original indictment or information, followed by the letter (A) for the first superseding indictment or information, (B) for the second, etc.

L.Cr.R. 7-3.   NOTICE OF COMPLEX CASE

If a criminal case includes eight or more defendants in the indictment or if the presentation of evidence (including cross-examination) in the government's case-in-chief will exceed twelve trial days, the case is considered "complex." In such cases, the government must file with the Court, at the time the indictment is filed, a Notice of Complex Case that indicates the grounds for considering the case complex. Likewise, upon the filing of a superseding indictment in a case not previously identified as complex, the government must file a Notice of Complex Case if the case now qualifies as such.

[Effective December 1, 2014.]

L.Cr.R. 7-4.   NOTICE OF RELATED CRIMINAL CASES

It shall be the responsibility of the parties to promptly file a Notice of Related Cases whenever a criminal case previously filed and one or more informations or indictments later filed:

(a) arise out of the same conspiracy, common scheme, transaction, series of transactions or events; or

(b) involve one or more defendants in common, and would entail substantial duplication of labor in pretrial, trial or sentencing proceedings if heard by different judges.

The Notice must be filed and served in each later-filed case, must identify the previously filed case(s), and must set forth the reasons why counsel believes the cases are related. Whenever practicable, the United States Attorney shall file the Notice with the indictment or information and serve it on defense counsel promptly after defense counsel's identity has been ascertained.

[Amended effective July 1, 2005. Former Rule 50-3 renumbered effective December 1, 2014.]

L.Cr.R. 7–5. NOTICE OF RELATED SUPERVISED–RELEASE CASE

It shall be the responsibility of the government to promptly file a Notice of Related Supervised–Release Case whenever a criminal case charges a violation of 8 U.S.C. § 1326 against a defendant who is serving a term of supervised release in this district for a previous violation of 8 U.S.C. §§ 1325 or 1326. Whenever practicable, the United States Attorney shall file the Notice with the charging document and serve it on defense counsel promptly after defense counsel's identity has been ascertained.

[Effective December 1, 2014.]

L.Cr.R. 7–6. NOTICE OF CASE RELATED TO PRE–INDICTMENT DEATH–ELIGIBLE MATTER

Every ex parte application for the appointment of counsel to represent the target of a federal investigation relating to potential charges that might be considered punishable by death ("Pre–Indictment Death–Eligible Matter") is assigned to a district judge immediately, without waiting for an indictment to be filed. When the indictment or other charging document is eventually filed, therefore, the government must, if aware of a previously filed Pre–Indictment Death–Eligible Matter related to any of the crimes charged, concurrently file a Notice of Case Related to Pre–Indictment Death–Eligible Matter identifying the previously assigned matter.

[Effective June 1, 2019.]

F.R.CRIM.P. 8. JOINDER OF OFFENSES OR DEFENDANTS

F.R.CRIM.P. 9. ARREST WARRANT OR SUMMONS ON AN INDICTMENT OR INFORMATION

L.Cr.R. 9–1. RETURN OF SERVICE

The officer who executes the warrant or serves the summons shall make prompt return thereof and shall include in such return the fact of service of the information or indictment and the time and place of service.

IV. ARRAIGNMENT AND PREPARATION FOR TRIAL

F.R.CRIM.P. 10. ARRAIGNMENT

L.Cr.R. 10–1. SERVICE OF COPY OF INDICTMENT OR INFORMATION

A copy of the indictment or information shall be served upon the defendant with the summons or upon execution of a warrant for arrest.

L.CR.R. 10–2. DUTY OF DEFENDANT [ABROGATED EFFECTIVE DECEMBER 1, 2015]

F.R.CRIM.P. 11. PLEAS

F.R.CRIM.P. 12. PLEADINGS AND PRETRIAL MOTIONS

L.Cr.R. 12–1. MOTION TO SUPPRESS

The following procedures govern a motion to suppress:

L.Cr.R. 12–1.1 Declaration in Support. A motion to suppress shall be supported by a declaration on behalf of the defendant, setting forth all facts then known upon which it is contended the motion should be granted. The declaration shall contain only such facts as would be admissible in evidence and shall show affirmatively that the declarant is competent to testify to the matters stated therein.

L.Cr.R. 12–1.2 Response of Government. Unless otherwise ordered by the Court, the government shall file a response and any declarations in opposition to the motion not later than seven (7) days after service of the motion.

L.Cr.R. 12–1.3 Availability of Declarants. Any declarant in connection with a motion to suppress shall be made available for cross-examination at the hearing of the motion, unless no party desires to cross-examine the declarant. If a party does not desire to cross-examine a declarant, that party shall file and serve a notice to that effect no later than one week before the hearing.

F.R.CRIM.P. 12.1. NOTICE OF AN ALIBI DEFENSE

F.R.CRIM.P. 12.2. NOTICE OF AN INSANITY DEFENSE; MENTAL EXAMINATION

F.R.CRIM.P. 12.3. NOTICE OF A PUBLIC–AUTHORITY DEFENSE

F.R.CRIM.P. 12.4. DISCLOSURE STATEMENT

F.R.CRIM.P. 13. JOINT TRIAL OF SEPARATE CASES

F.R.CRIM.P. 14. RELIEF FROM PREJUDICIAL JOINDER

F.R.CRIM.P. 15. DEPOSITIONS

F.R.CRIM.P. 16. DISCOVERY AND INSPECTION

F.R.CRIM.P. 17. SUBPOENA

L.Cr.R. 17–1. SUBPOENA—ISSUANCE UNDER RULE 17(b)—WITNESS WITHIN THE DISTRICT

Defense counsel shall apply to the Clerk for a witness subpoena under F.R.Crim.P.17(b), when the witness will be served within this District. The Clerk may issue such a subpoena in blank. No subpoena so issued may be served outside of this District. By filling in a subpoena issued in blank, defense counsel represents that counsel believes the defendant is unable to pay the witness fees and that the presence of the witness is necessary to an adequate defense.

L.Cr.R. 17–2. SUBPOENA—ISSUANCE UNDER RULE 17(b)—WITNESS OUTSIDE THE DISTRICT

When a witness will be served outside this District, defense counsel shall apply for issuance of a subpoena under F.R.Crim.P. 17(b) to the judge or magistrate judge to whom the case is assigned, and defense counsel shall represent that the defendant is unable to pay for the witness fees and that

the presence of the witness is necessary to an adequate defense.

L.Cr.R. 17–3. SUBPOENA—FEES— PRIVATE SERVICE

No fee will be allowed for the private service of any subpoena issued by or at the request of defense counsel, except when such private service has been expressly authorized by written order of Court.

L.Cr.R. 17–4. SUBPOENA—CONFIDENTIALITY

If a subpoena is issued pursuant to an application under seal, the issuance or service of the subpoena shall not be disclosed to anyone, except as necessary to the Marshal's service, or upon order of the Court.

F.R.CRIM.P. 17.1. PRETRIAL CONFERENCE

V. VENUE

F.R.CRIM.P. 18. PLACE OF PROSECUTION AND TRIAL
F.R.CRIM.P. 19. (RESERVED)
F.R.CRIM.P. 20. TRANSFER FOR PLEA AND SENTENCE

F.R.CRIM.P. 21. TRANSFER FOR TRIAL
F.R.CRIM.P. 22. (TRANSFERRED)

VI. TRIAL

F.R.CRIM.P. 23. JURY OR NONJURY TRIAL
F.R.CRIM.P. 24. TRIAL JURORS

L.Cr.R. 24–1. NONDISCLOSURE OF JURORS' IDENTITY

Neither the Clerk nor any other person having access to the names or addresses of jurors or venire persons in connection with their official duties shall disclose the name or address of any juror or any person summoned for jury duty, except in connection with the summoning or notification of jurors, as certified in vouchers for payment of attendance fees and allowances, where required to do so by applicable law, or upon order of the Court.

F.R.CRIM.P. 25. JUDGE'S DISABILITY
F.R.CRIM.P. 26. TAKING TESTIMONY
F.R.CRIM.P. 26.1. FOREIGN LAW DETERMINATION

F.R.CRIM.P. 26.2. PRODUCING A WITNESS'S STATEMENT
F.R.CRIM.P. 26.3. MISTRIAL
F.R.CRIM.P. 27. PROVING AN OFFICIAL RECORD
F.R.CRIM.P. 28. INTERPRETERS
F.R.CRIM.P. 29. MOTION FOR A JUDGMENT OF ACQUITTAL
F.R.CRIM.P. 29.1. CLOSING ARGUMENT
F.R.CRIM.P. 30. JURY INSTRUCTIONS
F.R.CRIM.P. 31. JURY VERDICT

VII. POST–CONVICTION PROCEDURES

F.R.CRIM.P. 32.   SENTENCING AND JUDGMENT

L.Cr.R. 32–1.   SUPERVISED RELEASE AND PROBATION—GENERAL CONDITIONS

All persons placed on supervised release or probation as the result of a judgment of conviction in this Court will be subject to such general conditions of supervised release or probation as may from time to time be promulgated by General Order.

[Amended effective December 1, 2020.]

L.Cr.R. 32–2.   SUPERVISED RELEASE AND PROBATION—GENERAL CONDITIONS— DUTY OF PROBATION OFFICER

The Probation Officer must advise each person receiving a supervised release or probationary sentence of the general conditions of supervised release or probation.

[Amended effective December 1, 2020.]

L.Cr.R. 32–3.   PRESENTENCE INVESTIGATION ("PSI") REPORT

L.Cr.R. 32–3.1 Minimum Custody Cases. The Probation Officer must make a tentative determination of the Guideline sentencing range as soon as practicable after the case is referred for preparation of the PSI Report. If the probable sentencing range for the offense(s) or conviction is unlikely to exceed 4—10 months of imprisonment and the defendant is detained, the Probation Officer must:

(a) Give priority to the expedited preparation of the PSI Report.

(b) Promptly inform the Court of such determination and of the completion date of the expedited PSI Report so that the Court can determine whether the sentencing date should be advanced.

L.Cr.R. 32–3.2 Presentence Investigation Reports. The Probation & Pretrial Services Office will disclose the PSI Report to counsel electronically, either by email or through the Court's CM/ECF System. Counsel must observe strictly the requirements of F.R.Crim.P. 32(f) regarding objections to presentence reports.

L.Cr.R. 32–3.3 [Abrogated].

L.Cr.R. 32–3.4 Defense Counsel to Provide Defendant with Copy of PSI Report. Promptly after the receipt of the PSI Report, defense counsel must provide the PSI Report to the defendant for review and must arrange for an interpreter, if necessary, to assist in the defendant's review of the report.

L.Cr.R. 32–3.5 Supervised Release and Probation Records. Presentence investigations and reports, supervised release and probation supervision records, and related reports of studies and recommendations are confidential records of this Court. If filed under seal in the Court's case file, such records may be requested only as provided in L.R. 79–7.2. Records that have not been docketed in the case or filed in the Court's case file may be requested only as provided in the subpoena regulations of the United States Courts. The determining officer under those regulations is the Chief United States Probation & Pretrial Services Officer, who will consult with the Chief United States District Judge and the presiding judge in the case regarding the proper response.

[Technical revisions effective December 1, 2013. Amended effective December 1, 2020.]

F.R.CRIM.P. 32.1.   REVOKING OR MODIFYING PROBATION OR SUPERVISED RELEASE

L.Cr.R. 32.1–1.   SUPERVISED RELEASE AND PROBATION—ARREST OF VIOLATOR— DUTY OF MARSHAL

After taking into custody any person charged with a violation of supervised release or probation, the Marshal must immediately give written notice to the United States Attorney, the Probation Officer, and the Clerk of the date of such arrest and the place of confinement of the alleged probation violator.

[Amended effective December 1, 2020.]

L.Cr.R. 32.1–2.   SUPERVISED RELEASE AND PROBATION VIOLATION—NOTICE TO ATTORNEY FOR DEFENDANT

The Clerk must promptly inform any attorney of record for an alleged supervised release or probation violator of the arrest of the violator and the place of confinement. If no attorney of record appears or the attorney of record cannot be found, the notice must be given to the Federal Public Defender.

[Amended effective December 1, 2020.]

F.R.CRIM.P. 32.2.   CRIMINAL FORFEITURE

F.R.CRIM.P. 33.   NEW TRIAL

F.R.CRIM.P. 34.   ARRESTING JUDGMENT

F.R.CRIM.P. 35.   CORRECTING OR REDUCING A SENTENCE

F.R.CRIM.P. 36.   CLERICAL ERROR

F.R.CRIM.P. 37.   INDICATIVE RULING ON A MOTION FOR RELIEF THAT IS BARRED BY A PENDING APPEAL

F.R.CRIM.P. 38.   STAYING A SENTENCE OR A DISABILITY

F.R.CRIM.P. 39.   (RESERVED)

VIII. SUPPLEMENTARY AND SPECIAL PROCEEDINGS

F.R.CRIM.P. 40. ARREST FOR FAILING TO APPEAR IN ANOTHER DISTRICT OR FOR VIOLATING CONDITIONS OF RELEASE SET IN ANOTHER DISTRICT

F.R.CRIM.P. 41. SEARCH AND SEIZURE

F.R.CRIM.P. 42. CRIMINAL CONTEMPT

IX. GENERAL PROVISIONS

F.R.CRIM.P. 43. DEFENDANT'S PRESENCE

F.R.CRIM.P. 44. RIGHT TO AND APPOINTMENT OF COUNSEL

L.Cr.R. 44–1 WITHDRAWAL OF COUNSEL

An attorney, whether appointed or retained, may not withdraw as counsel except by leave of court. A motion for leave to withdraw must be made upon written notice given reasonably in advance to the client and to all other parties who have appeared in the action. The motion for leave to withdraw must be supported by good cause. Failure of the client to pay agreed compensation is not necessarily sufficient to establish good cause.

[Effective June 1, 2014.]

F.R.CRIM.P. 45. COMPUTING AND EXTENDING TIME

F.R.CRIM.P. 46. RELEASE FROM CUSTODY; SUPERVISING DETENTION

L.Cr.R. 46–1. AUTHORITY OF MAGISTRATE JUDGES

Except as set forth in these rules, any Magistrate Judge has the authority to fix or modify bail, approve or disapprove sureties and bonds, and conduct detention hearings and issue release and detention orders, as provided by 18 U.S.C. § 3142, including with respect to bail or detention recommended or set in another district in a case arising in this or another district.

L.Cr.R. 46–1.1 Death Penalty Case. A Magistrate Judge shall not fix bail or act upon any motion related to bail in any case in which the complaint, information or indictment charges an offense for which the death penalty may be imposed, except upon specific authorization from the Criminal Duty Judge.

L.Cr.R. 46–1.2 Bail Previously Fixed by District Judge. [Abrogated effective June 1, 2013.]

L.Cr.R. 46–1.3 Detention Hearing Held After Arraignment. If a defendant arrested on an indictment makes his first appearance before a Magistrate Judge prior to the arraignment, and a detention hearing pursuant to 18 U.S.C. § 3142(f) is continued beyond the time the case is assigned to a District Judge, the Magistrate Judge shall retain the case for determination of the detention or release of the defendant, unless otherwise ordered by the assigned District Judge.

L.Cr.R. 46–1.4 Review by Criminal Duty Judge—Hearing Only If Ordered. No defendant aggrieved by any order of the Magistrate Judge fixing or modifying bail shall have the right to a hearing before the Criminal Duty Judge on such matter and no such hearing shall be calendared before such Judge unless the Criminal Duty Judge has so ordered.

L.Cr.R. 46–2. MODIFICATION OF CONDITIONS OF BAIL

Twenty-four hours after bail has been set, a defendant unable to meet the conditions of bail may apply for review and modification of the conditions of bail. For good cause, the United States Attorney or the United States Probation & Pretrial Services Office also may apply to the Court for modification of the conditions of bail.

[Amended effective December 1, 2020.]

L.Cr.R. 46–2.1. WRITTEN CONSENT OF SURETY AND THIRD–PARTY CUSTODIAN

Any request for modification of conditions of bail, whether made by motion or by stipulation, must include the written consent of each surety and any third-party custodian to the proposed modification.

[Effective December 1, 2005. Amended effective December 1, 2016.]

L.Cr.R. 46–3. METHODS OF BAIL

The Court may admit a defendant to bail in any one or more of the following methods:

- Personal recognizance bond
- Appearance bond without surety
- Appearance bond with cash deposit
- Appearance bond with surety (not justified)
- Appearance bond with surety (justified)
- Cash or other collateral appearance bond
- Corporate surety bond.

Any person admitted to bail shall execute, as principal, a bond for appearance at the time and place designated for appearance before any Magistrate Judge or District Judge of this Court. All bonds except corporate surety bonds shall be on a form approved by the Court and obtained from the Clerk.

L.Cr.R. 46–3.1 Appearance Bond—Surety's Affidavit Where No Justification Required. If the Court requires that a bond be backed by a surety without justification, the surety, by affidavit or declaration under penalty of perjury, shall state:

(a) The surety resides within the Central District of California or, if approved by the Court, that the surety resides elsewhere;

(b) The surety agrees to be bound by the bond and by the provisions of L.Cr.R. 46–6;

(c) The surety will notify the Court and counsel of any change of address.

L.Cr.R. 46–3.2 Appearance Bond—Affidavit by Owner of Cash Security. If the Court requires that a bond be backed by a cash deposit, the depositor, by affidavit or declaration under penalty of perjury, shall state where he resides, and also that:

(a) The depositor is the owner of the cash;

(b) The owner agrees to be bound by the bond and by the provisions of L.Cr.R. 46–6;

(c) The owner will notify the Court and counsel of any change of address.

L.Cr.R. 46–3.3 Appearance Bond—Surety's Affidavit Where Justification Required. If the Court requires that a bond be backed by a surety with justification, the surety, by affidavit or declaration under penalty of perjury, shall state:

(a) The surety resides within the Central District of California or, if approved by the Court, that the surety resides elsewhere;

(b) The surety agrees to be bound by the bond and by the provisions of L.Cr.R. 46–6;

(c) The surety will notify the Court and counsel of any change of address;

(d) The surety owns real property within the State of California or in any other state, if the Court permits property in another state to be used as security;

(e) The property pledged is worth the amount specified in the bond, in excess of the just debts and liabilities of the surety pertaining to the property;

(f) The property is not otherwise exempt from execution;

(g) The following information as to the property pledged, with supporting documentation:

(1) A legal description of the property, together with street address;

(2) The exact form in which title to property is held;

(3) The name and address of each titleholder;

(4) The interest of each titleholder;

(5) The present fair market value of the property;

(6) The encumbrances or liens upon the property and the name and address of each holder of an encumbrance or lien;

(7) The value of the equity after deducting all encumbrances and liens;

(8) The number of bonds or undertakings for bail entered into by defendant that are discharged.

L.Cr.R. 46–3.3.1 *Documentation—Deed of Trust.* A surety must execute a deed of trust naming the Clerk as beneficiary.

L.Cr.R. 46–3.4 Review of Surety and Documentation by United States Attorney. Any affidavit of surety and any documentation required by this Rule must be presented to the Office of the United States Attorney. Within six (6) office working hours, an attorney employed by that office shall report to the Court approval or disapproval of the documentation presented. If disapproved, the United States Attorney shall specify the reason for disapproval.

L.Cr.R. 46–3.4.1 *Disapproval or Failure to Respond by United States Attorney—Hearing.* At the request of an aggrieved party, the Court, upon two (2) hours notice to the United States Attorney, shall hold a hearing on the reasons for disapproval or the failure of the United States Attorney to respond.

L.Cr.R. 46–4. APPEARANCE BONDS UNDER $10,000

Unless a District Judge or a Magistrate Judge specifically requires to the contrary, appearance bonds of $10,000 or less shall be approved if (1) the signature of the surety is executed on the affidavit of surety attached to the bond, and (2) the affidavit of surety sets forth the real or personal property intended for justification, if any, and lists all encumbrances or liens against the property, alleging that the surety is worth the face amount specified in excess of liabilities.

L.Cr.R. 46–5. CORPORATE SURETY—BOND

A corporate surety bond shall be executed by the defendant and authorized attorney-in-fact and shall be substantially in the form and content as approved forms of bonds available in the office of the Clerk. No corporate surety bond shall be accepted or approved by the Court unless the surety meets the conditions of Local Civil Rule 65–4.

L.Cr.R. 46–5.1 Corporate Surety—Statement Upon Filing. A corporate surety shall file a statement setting forth the existence or non-existence of an indemnitor or indemnitors. If an indemnitor is obtained, the corporate surety shall certify in writing that all the responsibilities of indemnity have been explained to the indemnitor and that the indemnitor has acknowledged understanding of those obligations. Among the matters explained shall be:

● If a condition of the bond is breached, the bond must be forfeited;

● The Court is not required to set aside a forfeiture; and

● The indemnitor faces liability for forfeiture, court costs, attorney's fees, and other matters related to the indemnity.

If an alternate method of posting bond is provided, the corporate surety also shall certify it has advised the indemnitor that such an alternative is available and that the indemnitor desires to proceed with a corporate surety, knowing of the alternate method of posting bond.

L.Cr.R. 46–5.2 Corporate Surety—Failure to Comply. If the corporate surety fails to comply with any of the provisions of Local Criminal Rule 46–5.1, the surety shall not be permitted to proceed upon any indemnity and shall be required to return to the indemnitor any security posted, whether the Court orders forfeiture or not.

L.Cr.R. 46–6. BOND—SUMMARY ADJUDICATION OF OBLIGATION

A bond or undertaking presented for filing shall contain consent of the principal and surety that, in case of default or contumacy on the part of the principal or surety, the Court, upon ten (10) days notice, may render a judgment summarily in accordance with the obligation undertaken and issue a writ of execution upon such judgment. An indemnitee or party in interest seeking a judgment on a bond or undertaking shall proceed by Motion for Summary Adjudication of Obligation and Execution. Service may be made on a corporate surety as provided in 31 U.S.C. § 9306.

L.Cr.R. 46–7. BOND—EXONERATION

Upon completion of the obligations of the defendant, the Court shall order the bond exonerated and the Clerk shall return any monies deposited with the Court to the person or persons making such deposit. No assignment of any monies deposited with the Court shall be recognized, unless filed with the Clerk within ten (10) days of the making thereof. If a deed of trust has been recorded, the Clerk shall deliver a Full Reconveyance upon exoneration.

L.Cr.R. 46–8. COURT OFFICERS AS SURETY

The provisions of Local Civil Rule 65–9 shall apply to all bonds and undertakings in criminal actions.

F.R.CRIM.P. 47. MOTIONS AND SUPPORTING AFFIDAVITS

F.R.CRIM.P. 48. DISMISSAL

F.R.CRIM.P. 49. SERVING AND FILING PAPERS

L.Cr.R. 49–1. SERVING AND FILING DOCUMENTS

L.Cr.R. 49–1.1 Mandatory Electronic Filing in Criminal Cases. Except as provided in L.Cr.R. 49–1.2, all documents filed in criminal cases must be filed electronically using the Court's CM/ECF System. Sending a document by email does not constitute an electronic filing. To file documents using the CM/ECF System, an attorney must obtain an individual account login and password from the federal judiciary's national Public Access to Court Electronic Records ("PACER") system (www.pacer.gov) and link this account to the Court's CM/ECF System. After the attorney's PACER account has been linked to the Court's CM/ECF System, the attorney must use the PACER–issued login and password to file documents through the Court's CM/ECF System.

L.Cr.R. 49–1.1.1 *Authorization of Electronic Filing.* The Clerk will accept documents filed, signed, or verified by electronic means in compliance with these Local Rules. Any such document constitutes a written document for the purposes of applying these Local Rules and the Federal Rules of Criminal Procedure.

L.Cr.R. 49–1.1.2 *Applicability of Other Rules.* Except as otherwise ordered in accordance with applicable statutes and rules, all Federal Rules of Criminal Procedure and Local Criminal Rules shall continue to apply to criminal cases that are subject to electronic filing.

L.Cr.R. 49–1.1.3 *Definitions.* The definitions set forth in Local Rule 5–4.1.3 shall apply to this Local Criminal Rule 49–1 and to any cross-reference to Local Rule 5–4 contained in this Local Rule.

L.Cr.R. 49–1.2 Exceptions to Electronic Filing in Criminal Cases. Documents exempted from electronic filing pursuant to one of the subsections listed below shall be presented to the Clerk for filing or lodging in paper format, and shall comply with the requirements of L.R. 11 and all other applicable Local and Federal Rules.

(a) *Exemptions for Particular Filers.* The following filers are exempt from the requirement to file documents electronically:

(1) Pro Se Litigants. Unless otherwise ordered by the Court, pro se litigants shall continue to present all documents to the Clerk for filing in paper format. Documents received by the Clerk from pro se litigants under this rule will be scanned by the Clerk into the CM/ECF System. Once scanned, the original paper documents will be destroyed.

(2) Other Exceptional Cases Involving Unregistered Filers. For good cause shown, the Court may grant an exemption from the obligation to file electronically to a filer who is not registered with the Court's CM/ECF. Any such exemption shall not exceed one calendar year, but may be renewed upon good cause shown. If any filer granted such an exemption thereafter registers for the Court's CM/ECF System, that registration shall abrogate any exemption granted under this rule. Documents received by the Clerk under this rule will be scanned by the Clerk into the CM/ECF System. Once scanned, the original paper documents will be destroyed.

(b) *Documents Excluded from Electronic Filing.* The following documents are excluded from the electronic filing requirement of Local Criminal Rule 49–1.1:

(1) Nonpaper and Oversized Paper Exhibits. Nonpaper physical exhibits may not be filed at any time in any format. Such exhibits must either be lodged with the Clerk under L.R. 11–5.1 (if submitted as an exhibit to a document) or submitted under L.R. 79–3 or 79–4 at the time of a trial or

hearing. Any exhibit on a sheet of paper too large or irregularly shaped to be scanned into PDF format may not be filed. It must either be lodged with the Clerk in paper format under L.R. 11–5.4 (if submitted as an exhibit to a document) or submitted under L.R. 79–3 or 79–4 at the time of a trial or hearing.

(2) Criminal Case–Initiating Documents. Complaints, indictments, informations, and other case-initiating documents in criminal cases ("Criminal Case–Initiating Documents") shall be filed with the Clerk in paper format rather than electronically, in accordance with the applicable Federal Rules of Criminal Procedure and the Local Criminal Rules of this Court. All Criminal Case–Initiating Documents shall be submitted to the division of the Court to which the case is assigned. All Criminal Case–Initiating Documents shall also be submitted in electronic form (PDF format only) by close of business the following business day. Submission of these documents must be made by e-mail to the criminal intake e-mail box for the division to which the case is assigned. The intake e-mail box address for each division is indicated on the Court's CM/ECF Website. Attorneys who fail to timely e-mail PDF copies of these documents shall be subject to such sanctions as may be imposed by the Court.

(3) Under–Seal and In–Camera Documents, and Other Documents Excluded from the Public Case File. Applications and proposed orders to seal or file in camera, along with the document for which protection is sought, and any documents for which under-seal or in-camera filing is authorized by statute, rule, or prior court order must be presented for filing in paper form. Unless the documents are subject to L.Cr.R. 49–1.2(b)(4), or the Court orders otherwise, the original and the judge's copy of the documents must be submitted for filing in separate sealed envelopes, with a copy of the title page attached to the front of each envelope, and must be accompanied by a PDF version of the documents on a CD.

Other documents excluded from the public case file pursuant to L.Cr.R. 49.1–2 shall not be filed electronically, but shall be filed, if appropriate, as otherwise provided in the Local Rules of this Court, and in accordance with the Federal Rules of Civil and Criminal Procedure.

(4) Criminal Duty Matters. The following documents filed in criminal duty matters, before a case is assigned to a district judge, shall be filed with the Clerk in paper form rather than electronically:

(a) Applications for Pen Registers, Search Warrants, Seizure Warrants, Arrest Warrants, Wire Taps, Cell Site Information, Tracking Services, and other such documents;

(b) Bond–Related Documents; and

(c) Under–Seal and In–Camera Documents.

All such documents shall also be submitted in electronic form (PDF format only) by close of business the following business day. Submission of these documents must be made by e-mail to the criminal intake e-mail box for the division to which the case is assigned. The intake e-mail box address for each division is indicated on the Court's CM/ECF Website. Attorneys who fail to timely e-mail PDF

copies of these documents shall be subject to such sanctions as may be imposed by the Court.

(5) Other Exceptions. For good cause shown, the Court may permit a particular document or exhibit to be filed or lodged in paper format, rather than electronically. If permission to file or lodge a document or exhibit in paper format is obtained, the document or exhibit shall be filed or lodged in compliance with L.R. 11–4. Unless the filer is exempted from electronic filing pursuant to Local Criminal Rule 49–1.2(a), the filer shall first file electronically a Notice of Manual Filing or Lodging describing the document or exhibit being filed or lodged in paper format, and present a copy of the Notice of Manual Filing or Lodging, together with its NEF (see L.R. 5–3.2.1), with the document to be filed or lodged.

L.Cr.R. 49–1.3 General Applicability of Civil Electronic Filing Rules; Exceptions and Supplemental Rules for Criminal Cases.

L.Cr.R. 49–1.3.1 *General Applicability of Civil Electronic Filing Rules.* Except as provided in Local Criminal Rule 49–1.3.2, any electronically filed document shall comply with the provisions of Local Civil Rule 5–4.3, 5–4.4, 5–4.5, and 5–4.6. Attorneys registered to file documents through the CM/ECF System must comply with Local Civil Rule 5–4.8.

L.Cr.R. 49–1.3.2 *Special Rules for Criminal Cases.*

(a) Redaction. It is the responsibility of the filer to ensure full compliance with the redaction requirements of Federal Rule of Criminal Procedure 49.1 and L.Cr.R. 49.1–1.

(b) Service. Where service is required by the Federal Rules of Criminal Procedure, service shall be in accordance with Local Civil Rule 5–3.

(c) Proposed Orders. An electronically lodged proposed order shall comply with the requirements of Local Civil Rule 5–4.4, except that, for criminal cases, the subject line of the e-mail transmitting the word-processing version of the proposed order required by Local Civil Rule 5–4.4.2 shall include the defendant's last name and initial of first name as the filer (e.g., for Los Angeles: LA08CR00123–6–ABC–Doe J; for Santa Ana: SA08CR00124–8–DEF–Smith A; for Riverside: ED08CR00125–10–GHI–Jones B).

[Effective December 1, 2011. Amended effective June 1, 2012; December 1, 2013; June 1, 2014; December 1, 2015; June 1, 2020; December 1, 2020.]

F.R.CRIM.P. 49.1. PRIVACY PROTECTION FOR FILINGS MADE WITH THE COURT

L.Cr.R. 49.1–1. REDACTION

It is the responsibility of the filer to ensure full compliance with the redaction requirements of Federal Rule of Criminal Procedure 49.1. In addition, the filer shall redact passport numbers and driver license numbers in their entirety, and shall ensure that any document that contains a home address shall include only the city and state. This restriction on including passport numbers, driver license numbers, and full home addresses shall not apply to a filing exempted by Federal Rule of Criminal Procedure 49.1(b); to an under-seal filing as set forth in Federal Rule of Criminal Procedure 49.1(d), (f), or (g); or where the protection of Federal Rule of Criminal Procedure 49.1(h) has been waived with respect to that information.

Parties shall carefully examine the documents, exhibits, or attachments to be filed with the Court in order to protect any sensitive and private information. The responsibility for redacting or placing under seal protected personal data identifiers rests solely with counsel and the parties. The Clerk will not review any pleadings or documents for compliance.

Counsel and the parties are cautioned that failure to redact or place under seal protected personal data identifiers may subject them to the full disciplinary power of the Court. If a redacted version of the document is filed, counsel shall maintain possession of the unredacted document pending further order of the Court or resolution of the action (including the appeal, if any) and shall, at the request of opposing counsel or parties, provide a copy of the complete document.

[Effective June 1, 2012. Amended effective December 1, 2013.]

L.Cr.R. 49.1–2. EXCEPTIONS

The documents listed below are not to be included in the public case file, and are therefore excluded from the redaction requirements of F.R.Crim.P. 49.1 and L.Cr.R. 49.1–1:

(1) Unexecuted summonses or warrants, supporting applications, and affidavits;

(2) Pretrial bail reports;

(3) Presentence investigation reports;

(4) Statements of reasons in the judgment of conviction;

(5) Juvenile records;

(6) Documents containing identifying information about jurors or potential jurors;

(7) Financial affidavits filed in seeking representation pursuant to the Criminal Justice Act;

(8) Ex parte requests for authorization of investigative, expert, or other services pursuant to the Criminal Justice Act; and

(9) Sealed documents.

[Effective June 1, 2012. Technical revisions effective December 1, 2013.]

F.R.CRIM.P. 50. PROMPT DISPOSITION

L.Cr.R. 50–1. ASSIGNMENT OF CASES

Criminal cases shall be assigned to the individual calendars of the District Judges or Magistrate Judges (if the case is triable by a Magistrate Judge) as shall be provided by General Order.

L.Cr.R. 50–2. SIGNING OF ORDERS FOR ABSENT JUDGES

Any motion or request in an action or proceeding (including cases on appeal) shall be made to the judge to whom the case is assigned. If the assigned judge is not available and an emergency necessitates an order, the Clerk shall be consulted to determine whether a judge of this Court has been designated to handle matters in the absence of the assigned judge. If a designation has been made, the application shall be presented to the designated judge. If no designation has been made, then the matter shall be presented to the Criminal Duty judge or, in his or her absence, to any other available judge. If no emergency exists, the application will be held by the Clerk until the assigned judge is available.

F.R.CRIM.P. 51. PRESERVING CLAIMED ERROR

F.R.CRIM.P. 52. HARMLESS AND PLAIN ERROR

F.R.CRIM.P. 53. COURTROOM PHOTOGRAPHING AND BROADCASTING PROHIBITED

F.R.CRIM.P. 54. (TRANSFERRED)

F.R.CRIM.P. 55. RECORDS

F.R.CRIM.P. 56. WHEN COURT IS OPEN

F.R.CRIM.P. 57. DISTRICT COURT RULES

L.Cr.R. 57–1. APPLICABILITY OF LOCAL CIVIL RULES

When applicable directly or by analogy, the Local Rules of the Central District of California shall govern the conduct of criminal proceedings before the District Court, unless otherwise specified.

L.Cr.R. 57–2. DUTIES AND FUNCTIONS OF MAGISTRATE JUDGES

United States Magistrate Judges of this Court are authorized to perform all of the duties and functions prescribed and authorized by 28 U.S.C. § 636, or any other statutes or Federal Rules of Procedure which authorize Magistrate Judges to perform judicial duties or functions, as set forth in General Order No. 05–07, or any successor General Order. Magistrate Judges shall have the inherent power of judicial officers to implement and enforce their own orders and to regulate proceedings before them, to the extent permitted by law.

[Amended effective June 1, 2012.]

L.Cr.R. 57–3. SETTLEMENT OF COMPLEX CASES

L.Cr.R. 57–3.1 Policy. It is the Court's policy to facilitate the parties' efforts to dispose of complex criminal cases without trial. It is also the Court's policy that the judge assigned to preside over a complex criminal case (the trial judge) may ask if parties desire a settlement conference but shall not participate in facilitating settlement. Participation in settlement conferences under this rule shall be completely voluntary.

L.Cr.R. 57–3.2 Definition. A "complex" criminal case is defined in L.Cr.R. 7–3.

L.Cr.R. 57–3.3 Request for Conference. A settlement conference can be requested only by the attorney for the government and the attorney for the defendant acting jointly. (This rule does not require that all defendants in a multi-defendant case join in the request.)

L.Cr.R. 57–3.3.1 *Time of Request.* A settlement conference may be requested at any time up to the settlement conference cut-off date established by the trial judge. If no cut-off date is established, a settlement conference request may be made at any time up to twenty-one (21) days before the date scheduled for the commencement of trial, unless a later request is permitted by the trial judge.

L.Cr.R. 57–3.3.2 *Form of Request.* The request for a settlement conference shall be in writing and shall be signed by both the attorney for the government and the attorney for the defendant, and the defendant personally. It shall list the dates on which counsel are available for the conference and shall be filed in the case.

L.Cr.R. 57–3.3.3 *Response to Request.* Upon a timely request for a settlement conference, the trial judge may, at his or her discretion, refer the matter for assignment to a settlement judge.

L.Cr.R. 57–3.3.4 *Withdrawal of Request.* A request for a settlement conference may be withdrawn unilaterally by any requesting party at any time. A withdrawal shall be in writing, shall be signed by the attorney and shall be filed in the case.

L.Cr.R. 57–3.4 Settlement Judge. The role of the settlement judge shall be limited to facilitating a voluntary settlement between parties in criminal cases. The settlement judge shall not preside over any aspect of the case other than facilitation of a voluntary settlement according to this Rule. All matters related to the case other than settlement shall be handled by the trial judge.

L.Cr.R. 57–3.5 Conduct of Conference.

L.Cr.R. 57–3.5.1 *Availability of Defendant.* The defendant shall not be present during settlement discussions, unless otherwise ordered by the settlement judge. However, the defendant shall be available (a) in the courtroom of the settlement judge, if the defendant is not in custody or (b) in the Marshal's lock-up, if the defendant is under pretrial detention, unless the defendant's availability is waived by the settlement judge.

L.Cr.R. 57–3.5.2 *Criminal History.* If so requested by either counsel at least 10 days before the settlement conference, the Probation Officer, without order of the Court, must provide a summary of the defendant's criminal history to both counsel within 7 days of the request.

L.Cr.R. 57–3.5.3 *Non–recordation.* The settlement conference shall not be reported.

L.Cr.R. 57–3.5.4 *Written Agreement.* If a settlement is agreed to by both counsel and approved by the defendant, the plea agreement shall be reduced to writing and executed by the parties within three (3) court days from the settlement conference.

L.Cr.R. 57–3.6 Restrictions on Participants.

L.Cr.R. 57–3.6.1 *Settlement Judge.* The settlement judge shall not take a guilty plea from and shall not sentence any defendant in the case. The settlement judge shall not communicate any of the substance of the settlement discussions to the trial judge.

L.Cr.R. 57–3.6.2 *Statements Inadmissible at Trial.* No statement made by any participant at the settlement conference shall be admissible at the trial of any defendant in the case.

L.Cr.R. 57–3.6.3 *Counsel.* Neither counsel shall disclose the substance of the settlement discussions or the comments and recommendations of the settlement judge to the trial judge, except as expressly provided for by the terms of the written plea agreement.

L.Cr.R. 57–3.7 Discretion of Trial Judge Unaffected. Nothing in this rule shall be construed to limit in any way the discretion of the trial judge under F.R.Crim.P. 11(c).

[Amended effective April 1, 2008; June 1, 2012; December 1, 2014; December 1, 2020.]

F.R.CRIM.P. 58. PETTY OFFENSES AND OTHER MISDEMEANORS

L.Cr.R. 58–1. AUTHORITY OF MAGISTRATE JUDGE OVER CASES CHARGING MISDEMEANOR AND OTHER PETTY OFFENSES

United States Magistrate Judges of this Court are authorized to conduct proceedings in any case charging a misdemeanor or infraction as provided in 18 U.S.C. § 3401, and order a presentence report in any such case pending before a Magistrate Judge.

F.R.CRIM.P. 59. MATTERS BEFORE A MAGISTRATE JUDGE

F.R.CRIM.P. 60. VICTIM'S RIGHTS

F.R.CRIM.P. 61. TITLE

L.Cr.R. 61–1. SHORT TITLE

These rules may be cited as the "Local Criminal Rules."

[Renumbered and amended effective June 1, 2009.]

CHAPTER IV. LOCAL RULES GOVERNING BANKRUPTCY APPEALS, CASES, AND PROCEEDINGS

I. APPEALS

RULE 1 (8001). SCOPE OF RULES[1]

This Chapter of the Local Rules governs bankruptcy appeals, motions to withdraw the reference, and other bankruptcy related matters that are presented to the District Court. An extensively revised and reorganized version of the national appellate bankruptcy rules, which appear in Part VIII of the Federal Rules of Bankruptcy Procedure, Rule 8001 *et seq.*, became effective on December 1, 2014. This Chapter of the Local Rules was thereafter revised to conform to those national appellate bankruptcy rules. Attorneys and litigants are advised to consult the Local Bankruptcy Rules of the United States Bankruptcy Court for the Central District of California, Rule 8000–1 *et seq.*, and the Federal Rules of Bankruptcy Procedure, Rule 8001 *et seq.*, as well as the official Advisory Committee Notes appended to each individual rule.

Unless the Federal Rules of Bankruptcy Procedure or these Local Rules state otherwise, the Federal Rules of Appellate Procedure, the Federal Rules of Civil Procedure, the Federal Rules of Evidence, and the Ninth Circuit Rules shall apply.

[Effective April 1, 1998. Amended effective December 1, 2011; December 1, 2015.]

[1] Citations to these rules should be in the following format: C.D. Cal. L. Bankr. R. ____."

RULE 2. NOTICE OF APPEAL

2.1 (8012) Certification of Interested Parties and Notice of Related Cases. Certification as to interested parties and notice of related cases, as prescribed in Local Civil Rules 7.1–1 and 83–1.3, shall be filed by the appellant with the notice of appeal.

2.2 (8002) Premature Notice of Appeal. If the appellant files a notice of appeal before the entry of the judgment or order being appealed, then the appellant shall forward to the clerk of the district court a copy of the judgment or order being appealed immediately upon entry of that judgment or order.

[Effective April 1, 1998. Amended effective October 1, 2001; December 1, 2011; December 1, 2015.]

RULE 3 (8006–3). THE RECORD ON APPEAL [ABROGATED EFFECTIVE DECEMBER 1, 2015]

[ABROGATED (Rule 3 addressed The Record on Appeal, which is now covered by Fed. R. Bankr. P. 8010 & 8018.)]

[Effective April 1, 1998. Amended effective December 1, 2011; Abrogated effective December 1, 2015.]

RULE 4. BRIEFS

4.1 (8018(b)) Briefs in Cases Involving Multiple Appellants or Appellees. In cases involving more than one appellant or appellee, including cases consolidated for purposes of the appeal, all parties are encouraged to join in a single brief to the greatest extent practicable.

4.2 (8018(a)) Extensions of Time for Filing Briefs. A motion for an extension of time for filing a brief shall be filed in the district court within the time limits prescribed by Fed. R. Bankr. P. 8018 and shall be accompanied by a proof of service of the motion reflecting service on the other interested parties. The motion and accompanying declaration shall state the date the brief is due, how many previous extensions have been granted, when the brief was first due, and whether any previous requests for extension of time have been denied. The motion and declaration must also state the reason(s) why such an extension is necessary, the amount of additional time requested, and the position of the opponent(s) as to the proposed extension or why the moving party has been unable to obtain a statement of the opponent's position.

[Effective April 1, 1998. Amended effective December 1, 2011; December 1, 2013; December 1, 2015.]

RULE 5. MOTIONS

5.1 (8026(b)) Emergency Motion; Appendix. Any emergency motion shall include an appendix that provides the following information:

5.1.1 (8026(b)) *Conformed Copy of Notice of Appeal.* A conformed copy of the notice of appeal;

5.1.2 (8026(b)) *Conformed Copy of Judgment, Order or Decree.* A conformed copy of the judgment, order, or decree from which the appeal is taken;

5.1.3 (8026(b)) *Stay Pending Appeal.* If the emergency motion seeks a stay pending appeal, a copy of the bankruptcy court's order denying the movant a stay pending appeal or an affidavit by the movant stating that a stay had been denied;

5.2 (8026(b)) Withdrawal of the Election to the District Court. Motions to withdraw the election for the bankruptcy appeal to be heard by the district court and to refer the matter to the Bankruptcy Appellate Panel shall be filed in the district court in accordance with Local Civil Rule 7.

[Effective April 1, 1998. Amended effective December 1, 2011; December 1, 2015.]

RULE 6 (8014–6). COSTS ON APPEAL [ABROGATED EFFECTIVE DECEMBER 1, 2015]

[ABROGATED (Rule 6 addressed Costs on Appeal, which is now covered by Fed. R. Bankr. P. 8021.)]

[Effective April 1, 1998. Amended effective October 1, 2001; December 1, 2011; Abrogated effective December 1, 2015.]

RULE 7 (8001–7). VOLUNTARY DISMISSALS OF APPEALS [ABROGATED EFFECTIVE DECEMBER 1, 2015]

[ABROGATED (Rule 7 addressed Voluntary Dismissals of Appeals, which is now covered by Fed. R. Bankr. P. 8023.)]

[Effective April 1, 1998. Amended effective December 1, 2011; Abrogated effective December 1, 2015.]

RULE 8 (8026(B)). PRO HAC VICE APPEARANCES

Attorneys who have been granted permission to appear pro hac vice in a particular case or in a particular proceeding in a case by the bankruptcy court in accordance with Bankruptcy Court Local Rule 2090–1(b) may proceed pro hac vice in that same bankruptcy case or proceeding if it is subsequently filed in or referred to the district court.

[Effective April 1, 1998. Amended effective March 1, 2000; December 1, 2011; December 1, 2012; December 1, 2015.]

II. MOTIONS TO WITHDRAW THE REFERENCE

RULE 9 (5011). MOTIONS TO WITHDRAW THE REFERENCE

A motion to withdraw the reference of a case or proceeding pending in the bankruptcy court shall be filed, with proof of service of the motion reflecting service on the other interested parties, with the clerk of the district court. Such a motion shall be made in accordance with F.R.B.P. 5011. Certification as to interested parties and notice of related cases, as prescribed in Local Civil Rules 7.1–1 and 83–1.3, shall be filed by the moving party with the motion to withdraw. A conformed copy of the motion to withdraw shall be delivered by the moving party to the bankruptcy judge presiding over the case or proceeding.

Opposition and reply papers to the motion to withdraw shall be filed in the district court in accordance with Local Civil Rule 7. Opposition papers shall include a certification as to interested parties and notice of related cases as prescribed in Local Civil Rules 7.1–1 and 83–1.3.

[Effective April 1, 1998. Amended effective October 1, 2001. Amended effective December 1, 2011; December 1, 2015.]

PLAN OF THE UNITED STATES DISTRICT COURT, CENTRAL DISTRICT OF CALIFORNIA FOR THE RANDOM SELECTION OF GRAND AND PETIT JURORS [GENERAL ORDER 19-07]

Pursuant to the Jury Selection and Service Act of 1968, as amended, 28 U.S.C. § 1861 *et seq.* ("Act"), the following amended Jury Selection Plan ("Plan") is hereby adopted by the United States District Court for the Central District of California ("Court"), subject to approval by the Ninth Circuit Judicial Council and to such rules and regulations as may be adopted from time to time by the Judicial Conference of the United States.

1. **Applicability of Plan.** This Plan applies to the Central District of California ("District"), including all three of its divisions: (1) the Western Division, which includes the counties of Los Angeles, San Luis Obispo, Santa Barbara, and Ventura; (2) the Southern Division, which includes the county of Orange; and (3) the Eastern Division, which includes the counties of Riverside and San Bernardino. 28 U.S.C. § 84(c). These three statutory divisions shall constitute the divisions contemplated by the Act, as provided in 28 U.S.C. § 1869(e)(1).

2. **Declaration of Policy.** It is the policy of the Court that all litigants in this Court entitled to trial by jury shall have the right to grand and petit juries selected at random from a fair cross section of the community in the division wherein the Court convenes.

It is further the policy of the Court that all citizens shall have the opportunity to be considered for service on grand and petit juries of the Court and shall have an obligation to serve as jurors when summoned for that purpose. No citizen shall be excluded from service as a grand or petit juror on the basis of race, color, religion, gender, sexual orientation, national origin, or economic status.

3. **Management and Supervision of Jury Selection Process.** The Clerk of the Court, any authorized deputy clerk, or any other person designated to assist the clerk (collectively "Clerk"), shall manage the jury selection process under the supervision and control of the chief judge of the Court, a judge acting pursuant to 28 U.S.C. § 136(e), or such other judge of the district court as the chief judge may designate ("Chief Judge"). The Clerk is authorized to use non–Court personnel to assist in the performance of functions under this Plan. Non–Court personnel shall be given detailed instructions regarding any work they are asked to perform, and shall be required to certify that all work performed has been completed pursuant to those instructions. The instructions provided, and the certifications returned upon completion, will be considered "Juror Selection Records," and will be retained and made available to the public pursuant to Section 12 of this Plan.

4. **Sources of Prospective Jurors' Names.** The names of prospective jurors shall be drawn from the names of registered voters, licensed drivers, and holders of California Identification Cards (issued by the California Department of Motor Vehicles) who reside within one of the seven counties in the District. The Clerk shall obtain the names of all registered voters residing in the District by requesting voter registration lists, as defined in 28 U.S.C. § 1869(c) ("Voter Lists"), either from the Office of the California Secretary of State or from the Registrar of Voters or equivalent office in each of the seven counties in the District. The Clerk shall obtain the names of all licensed drivers and holders of California Identification Cards residing within the District by requesting from the California Department of Motor Vehicles ("DMV") information regarding individuals who hold a California driver's license or identification card and who reside in one of the seven counties in the District ("DMV Records").

The Clerk shall obtain updated Voter Lists and DMV Records (collectively, "Source Data") for the District every year, in advance of the annual emptying and refilling of the Master Jury Wheels described in Section 5, below. The Clerk shall obtain the Source Data by requesting, in writing, that each agency provide a list of the required names, together with addresses and any other information necessary to achieve the goals of the Act. The Clerk shall also require that each agency, when providing the list, provide a declaration certifying that the requested information was forwarded to the Court in accordance with the Clerk's written request. The Source Data, the Clerk's written requests for the Source Data, and the declarations from each agency providing Source Data will be considered "Juror Selection Records," and will be retained and made available to the public pursuant to Section 12 of this Plan.

5. **Creation and Maintenance of Master Jury Wheels.** Having obtained the Source Data for each county in the District, the Clerk shall use that information to establish and maintain one "Master Jury Wheel," in electronic form, for each of the three divisions within the District. First,

using a properly programmed electronic data processing system, the Source Data for each county shall be merged into a single list, and duplicate records of the same person and the records of persons under the age of 18 years eliminated. The resulting list will be referred to as the county's "Merged Source List."

Next, in accordance with 28 U.S.C. § 1863(b)(3), the Clerk shall randomly select names from the Merged Source List for each county in the District, using a purely randomized process through a properly programmed electronic data processing system designed to ensure that the mathematical odds of any single name being picked from a Merged Source List are substantially equal. The selected names shall be placed in the Master Jury Wheel for the division in which the county is located, in such numbers as to ensure that each county is substantially proportionally represented in that division's Master Jury Wheel.

For purposes of determining proportional representation in the Master Jury Wheel, the number of registered voters in each county shall be compared to the total number of registered voters in the division, and a percentage calculated; the number of names drawn from a county's Merged Source List for inclusion in the division's Master Jury Wheel shall be in an amount equal to the same percentage of that division's Master Jury Wheel. For example, if, in a division with two counties, County A has 20% of the registered voters for the division, and County B has 80% of the registered voters, then 20% of the names in the division's Master Jury Wheel should be drawn from County A's Merged Source List, and 80% of the names in the division's Master Jury Wheel should be drawn from County B's Merged Source List.

The minimum number of names to be placed in each Master Jury Wheel shall be at least one-half of 1% of the total number of persons on the Merged Source Lists for the counties in that division. The Court finds that placing names selected from the Merged Source Lists for the counties in a division using a purely randomized process into the Master Jury Wheel for that division in such amounts, with each county in the division substantially proportionally represented, will result in a Master Jury Wheel for each division that includes a fair cross section of the persons residing in that division.

Each Master Jury Wheel shall be emptied and refilled annually prior to January 1. If necessary to assure an adequate supply of qualified jurors, the Chief Judge may order that any Master Jury Wheel be supplemented from time to time with additional names selected from the Merged Source Lists on a random basis, in substantially proportional amounts from each county in the relevant division. Jurors selected from previous Master Jury Wheels may serve at the same time as jurors selected from later Master Jury Wheels.

The Merged Source Lists, the list of names placed in the Master Jury Wheels, and any Orders of the Chief Judge directing that a Master Jury Wheel be supplemented with additional names shall be considered "Juror Selection Records," and will be retained and made available to the public pursuant to Section 12 of this Plan.

6. Random Selection of Names From the Master Jury Wheels: One–Step Summoning and Qualification of Prospective Jurors. Pursuant to 28 U.S.C. § 1878, the Court adopts a one-step process to summon and qualify prospective petit and grand jurors. The Clerk shall use this one-step approach in lieu of the two separate procedures (a qualification process, followed by a separately issued summons) otherwise provided for by the Act.

Accordingly, throughout the term of the Master Jury Wheels, the Clerk shall regularly select names at random from the Master Jury Wheel for each division as required for assignment to grand and petit juries in that division, in such numbers as are estimated to meet the Court's projected needs. Names of prospective jurors shall be selected from the Master Jury Wheels using a purely randomized process through a properly programmed electronic data processing system designed to ensure that the mathematical odds of any single name being picked from a Master Jury Wheel are substantially equal. Once a name has been selected from a Master Jury Wheel, that name shall not be eligible to be drawn again until after the Master Jury Wheel has been emptied and re-filled. The Clerk shall post a copy of this General Order in all Jury Assembly Rooms and on the Court's website to explain the process by which names are randomly and periodically drawn from the Master Jury Wheels.

Every person whose name is so drawn shall be mailed a summons for jury service ("Summons"). Pursuant to 28 U.S.C. § 1864(a), each person summoned for jury service shall be instructed to complete and return a juror qualification form ("Questionnaire") within ten days. Questionnaires may be completed and submitted online through the Court's website, or completed and returned to the Clerk by mail, e-mail, or fax. The Questionnaire shall be in a form prescribed by the

Administrative Office of the United States Courts and approved by the Judicial Conference of the United States. Any person who mails Summonses to prospective jurors shall make the affidavit of service required by 28 U.S.C. § 1866(b).

Each Questionnaire submitted by a prospective juror shall be reviewed upon receipt to determine: (1) whether the Questionnaire has been completed; and (2) whether, based on the information provided in or with the Questionnaire, the prospective juror should be disqualified from jury service (see Section 9 of this Plan), exempted from jury service (see Section 10 of this Plan), or excused from jury service for some period of time (see Section 11 of this Plan). A prospective juror may ask to be temporarily excused from jury service by requesting a postponement of jury service to a later date; prospective jurors whose service is postponed will be re-summoned in advance of the new reporting date.

A person shall be deemed qualified and available to serve as summoned unless postponed, disqualified, exempted, or excused by the Court, or by the Clerk, acting under supervision of the Court. For any juror postponed, disqualified, exempted, or excused on the basis of information provided in or with the Questionnaire, the Clerk shall note this determination in the records of the Court, and make the results regarding each potential juror available to that juror in advance of the juror's Summons date.

The Clerk shall record the names of prospective jurors who fail to return the Questionnaire. If any Questionnaires are returned as undeliverable, the Clerk shall note that fact. Prospective jurors who fail to return the Questionnaire or who submit Questionnaires requiring further investigation may be summoned for a personal interview before the Clerk should other means of communication fail to elicit a satisfactory response. Except for extraordinary cause shown, such appearance shall be without attendance fees or travel allowance.

Each Summons shall include the date on which the prospective juror's two-week on-call period begins. All prospective jurors must call in as directed in the Summons, and report if directed to do so. Prospective jurors not directed to report on the first call-in date must continue to call in as directed throughout the on-call period.

Each week, the Clerk shall determine the number of prospective jurors estimated to be necessary to meet the Court's projected needs for petit jurors, and direct that number of prospective jurors to report for service. Prospective jurors will be directed to report in the order in which their names were randomly drawn from the Master Jury Wheel prior to the mailing of the Summons.

The Clerk shall maintain a record of the following: the names of persons sent a Summons; whether the Summons was returned as undeliverable; whether each prospective juror submitted or returned a Questionnaire; whether each Questionnaire submitted was completed; whether any Questionnaires were returned to prospective jurors for additional information; whether each prospective juror was postponed, disqualified, exempted, or excused; whether each prospective juror was directed to report during the on-call period; and whether each prospective juror reported as directed. This record, and the following documents, will be considered Juror Selection Records: the affidavits of service completed pursuant to 28 U.S.C. § 1866(b); any Summons returned as undeliverable, with its original envelope; and all submitted or returned Questionnaires. All Juror Selection Records will be retained and made available to the public pursuant to Section 12 of this Plan.

7. Selection of Petit Jurors. Prospective jurors summoned for petit jury service and not postponed, disqualified, exempted, or excused in advance of the call-in date shall report as directed to the appropriate divisional Jury Assembly Room. The Clerk shall record the names of any prospective jurors who fail to appear as directed.

Prospective jurors who report as directed may raise at that time additional grounds for postponement, disqualification, exemption, or excuse. All prospective jurors who report as directed will be deemed qualified and available to serve as summoned unless determined not to be for one of these reasons (as defined in Sections 9–11 of this Plan), by the Clerk, acting under supervision of the Court, or by a district or magistrate judge of the Court. Prospective jurors who report as directed, and who are not postponed, disqualified, exempted, or excused shall be considered "Present and Available" for jury service. The Clerk shall maintain records, which will be considered Juror Selection Records, noting whether each person directed to appear on a particular day is Present and Available to serve as directed, and if not, why: non-deliverable Summons, failure to respond to the Summons, postponement, disqualification, exemption, or excuse. Any orders to show cause issued to persons who fail to respond to a Summons will also be considered Juror Selection Records. All Juror Selection Records will be retained and made available to the public pursuant to Section 12 of this Plan.

When those persons who are Present and Available to begin petit jury service on a particular day are gathered in the Jury Assembly Room, the Clerk shall administer to them the appropriate oath. The Clerk shall then draw from such persons the number required for immediate assignment to petit jury panels, using a purely randomized process through a properly programmed electronic data processing system designed to ensure that the mathematical odds of any single name being picked from among all prospective jurors then present are substantially equal. Jurors selected for petit jury panels shall then be sent to the appropriate courtroom.

Pursuant to 28 U.S.C. § 1863(b)(7), the list of juror names for a particular petit jury panel may be released to the parties and the public at any time with the approval of the judge presiding at trial, or by the Chief Judge if the judge presiding at trial is unavailable. The names of such jurors and associated juror information may be kept confidential in any case where the interests of justice so require. Unless the Court orders that the list be kept confidential, the petit jury panel list shall also be considered a Juror Selection Record, to be maintained and disclosed pursuant to Section 12 of this Plan.

The judge (whether a district, magistrate, or bankruptcy judge) presiding over the trial for which the petit jury panel is called ("Presiding Judge") may excuse jurors upon a showing of undue hardship or extreme inconvenience, for such period as the Presiding Judge deems necessary. The Presiding Judge may also find that a juror is exempt from, or not qualified for, jury service. Jurors postponed by the Presiding Judge to a future date shall be re-summoned in advance of that date. Jurors excused but not postponed to a future date, and jurors found to be exempt or disqualified, shall be released from jury service.

The Presiding Judge may exclude a juror:

(a) on the ground that such person may be unable to render impartial jury service or that his service as a juror would be likely to disrupt the proceedings;

(b) upon peremptory challenge as provided by law;

(c) pursuant to the procedure specified by law upon a challenge by any party for good cause shown; or

(d) upon determination by the court that his service as a juror would be likely to threaten the secrecy of the proceedings, or otherwise adversely affect the integrity of jury deliberations.

Any person excluded from a particular jury under (a), (b), or (c) shall be eligible to sit on another jury if the basis for the initial exclusion would not be relevant to the juror's ability to serve on a different jury. The Presiding Judge may therefore direct that jurors excluded from a jury under (a), (b), or (c) return to the Jury Assembly Room for possible random selection to another petit jury panel. No person shall be excluded under (d) unless the Presiding Judge, in open court, determines that such is warranted and that exclusion of the person will not be inconsistent with 28 U.S.C. §§ 1861–1862. The number of persons excluded under (d) shall not exceed 1% of the number of persons who return executed Questionnaires during the year between two consecutive fillings of the Master Jury Wheel. The names of persons excluded under (d), together with detailed explanations for the exclusions, shall be forwarded immediately to the Ninth Circuit Judicial Council. Jurors excluded under this paragraph and not directed by the presiding judge to return to the Jury Assembly Room for possible random selection to another petit jury panel shall be released from jury service.

The Clerk shall maintain a record of whether each juror selected for a petit jury panel was excused, disqualified, exempted, excluded, or selected to serve as a juror or alternate juror. This record, as well as any findings made in excluding jurors under subsection (d), above, will be considered Juror Selection Records.

At the end of each day, all prospective jurors who were present and available to serve that day who have not been assigned to a petit jury panel shall be dismissed, and shall be deemed to have completed jury service. Prospective jurors summoned for jury service and not postponed, disqualified, exempted, or excused, and who have not been assigned to a petit jury panel by the end of the on-call period or initial appearance, will be deemed to have completed jury service. The Clerk will maintain records, which will be considered Juror Selection Records, of all prospective jurors who are deemed to have completed service pursuant to this paragraph. All Juror Selection Records will be retained and made available to the public pursuant to Section 12 of this Plan.

8. **Selection of Grand Jurors.** Prospective jurors summoned for grand jury service and who are not, in advance of the call-in date, postponed, disqualified, exempted, excused, or directed to report

instead for potential service as a petit juror shall report as directed to the location where grand jury impanelment is to be held. The Clerk shall record the names of any prospective jurors who fail to report as directed.

Prospective jurors who report as directed may raise at that time additional grounds for postponement, disqualification, exemption, or excuse. All prospective jurors who report as directed will be deemed qualified and available to serve as summoned unless determined to be otherwise for one of these reasons (as defined in Sections 9–11 of this Plan), by the Clerk, acting under supervision of the Court, or by a district or magistrate judge of the Court.

Prospective jurors who report as directed, and who are not then postponed, disqualified, exempted, or excused shall be considered "Present and Available" for jury service. For each person directed to appear on a particular day, the Clerk shall record whether the person is Present and Available to serve as directed, and if not, shall record the reason why: non-deliverable Summons, failure to respond to the Summons, postponement, disqualification, exemption, or excuse.

When those persons who are Present and Available to begin grand jury service on a particular day are gathered, the Clerk shall then draw from such persons the number required for immediate assignment to a grand jury, using a purely randomized process through a properly programmed electronic data processing system designed to ensure that the mathematical odds of any single name being picked from among all prospective jurors then present are substantially equal. The Clerk shall administer the appropriate oath to those chosen for grand jury service, and the Chief Judge shall give them necessary instructions.

The names of grand jurors chosen and sworn shall not be disclosed except on order of the Court. At the end of each day, all prospective jurors who were Present and Available to serve that day who have not been assigned to a grand jury panel shall be dismissed, and shall be deemed to have completed jury service.

9. **Qualifications for Jury Service.** In accordance with the provisions of 28 U.S.C. § 1865(b), any person whose name is drawn from a Master Source List shall be deemed qualified to serve on grand or petit juries in this Court unless it is determined that the person:

a. is not a citizen of the United States who has reached the age of 18 years and has resided for a period of one year within the District;

b. is unable to read, write, and understand the English language with a degree of proficiency sufficient to fill out satisfactorily the juror qualification form;

c. is unable to speak the English language;

d. is incapable, by reason of mental or physical infirmity, to render satisfactory jury service; or

e. has a charge pending against him or her for the commission of, or has been convicted in a state or federal court of record of, a crime punishable by imprisonment for more than one year and his or her civil rights have not been restored.

Persons summoned for jury duty who are determined to be disqualified from jury service shall be released from jury service.

10. **Exemptions from Jury Service.** The following persons, when employed on a full-time basis, are barred from jury service on the ground that they are exempt:

a. members in active service in the Armed Forces of the United States (including only the Army, Navy, Air Force, Marine Corps, and Coast Guard);

b. members of the professional fire or police departments of any State, the District of Columbia, any territory or possession of the United States, or any subdivision of a State, the District of Columbia, or such territory or possession; and

c. public officers (i.e., persons either elected to public office or directly appointed by a person elected to public office) in the executive, legislative, or judicial branches of the Government of the United States, or of any State, the District of Columbia, any territory or possession of the United States, or any subdivision of a State, the District of Columbia, or such territory or possession, who are actively engaged in the performance of official duties.

Persons summoned for jury duty who are determined to be exempt from jury service shall be released from jury service.

11. Individual Requests for Postponement or Excuse.

(a) *Postponement.* Persons summoned for jury duty may request that service be postponed to a future date. If a request for postponement is granted, a juror will be re-summoned in advance of the requested date.

(b) *Groups Whose Members May Request Excuse.* Persons summoned for jury duty may request that service be excused on the following grounds:

(i) Volunteer Safety Personnel. Upon individual request, individuals serving a public agency in an official capacity, without compensation, as firefighters or members of a rescue squad or ambulance crew, shall be excused from jury service.

(ii) Prior Jury Service. The Court finds that jury service by persons who have recently been selected and seated as a grand or petit juror or an alternate juror in either a United States District Court or a state trial court would entail undue hardship or extreme inconvenience to them and that excusing such persons would not be inconsistent with the Act. For purposes of this section, "recent jury service" includes the following: (1) service on a grand jury within the prior two years; (2) service on a petit jury within the prior year; or (3) service on one or more petit juries within the prior two years for an amount of time that, when combined with the prospective service, will exceed 30 days. Accordingly, persons who provide proof of recent jury service shall be excused from jury service upon individual request.

(iii) Care Givers. The Court finds that jury service by a person who has the obligation to care for children, the elderly, or other dependents, when the obligation of such care prevents the person from engaging in full-time employment outside the home, would entail undue hardship or extreme inconvenience to that person, and that excusing such a person would not be inconsistent with the Act. Accordingly, such persons shall be excused from jury service upon individual request.

(iv) Permanent Excuse. The Court finds that any person who provides documentation from a state or federal court showing that he or she has received a permanent excuse from serving as a juror should be excused from jury service in this Court.

(c) *Individual Showing of Undue Hardship or Extreme Inconvenience.* A prospective juror may make an individual request to be excused from jury service on the grounds that the following would create undue harm or extreme inconvenience:

(i) great distance, either in miles or travel time, from the place of holding court;

(ii) grave illness of the prospective juror or a family member for whom the prospective juror must care that prevents the juror from serving now or in the foreseeable future;

(iii) any other emergency which outweighs in immediacy and urgency the obligation to serve as a juror when summoned;

(iv) business, employment, or financial hardship to the juror;

(v) any other factor that the court determines to constitute an undue hardship or to create an extreme inconvenience to the juror;

(vi) in situations where it is anticipated that a trial or grand jury proceeding may require more than thirty days of service, severe economic hardship to an employer which would result from the absence of a key employee during the period of such service.

Persons summoned for jury duty who are excused from jury service but not postponed to a future date certain shall be released from jury service.

12. Juror Statistics and Records.
A Report on Operation of the Jury Selection Plan ("Form AO–12") shall be completed each time a Master Jury Wheel is refilled and any time there is a change in this Plan. All completed AO–12s will be considered "Juror Selection Records."

All records identified in this Plan as "Juror Selection Records" and that are created during the life of a Master Jury Wheel shall be retained by the Clerk until four years after the later of the following two events (the "Release Date"): (1) the date that that Master Jury Wheel is emptied and refilled; or (2) the date the last of the jurors selected to serve on a jury during the life of that Wheel completes his or her service. Prior to the Release Date, Juror Selection Records shall not be disclosed, except as necessary in the preparation or presentation of a motion under 28 U.S.C. § 1867(a), (b), or (c); a party preparing such a motion, or any party in a case in which such a motion has been filed, may inspect, reproduce, and copy Juror Selection Records regarding the Master Jury Wheel from which either the grand or petit jury in the case was selected, at all reasonable times, and at the party's expense, during the preparation or pendency of such a motion. During the four years after the Release Date, all Juror Selection Records shall be available for public inspection for the purpose of determining the validity of the selection of any jury; these records will not be available for reproduction or copying without an order of the Court. Except as otherwise provided in this Plan, the contents of records or papers not identified in this Plan as Juror Selection Records shall be disclosed only upon an order of the Court. Parties seeking the disclosure of anything not identified as Juror Selection Records must apply to the Court for an order of disclosure; if such an application is made, it shall be referred to the Chief Judge.

13. Sanctions for Late Settlement in Civil Cases. In any civil case in which a settlement is reached and the Court is notified of settlement later than the close of business on the last business day before jurors are scheduled to appear for jury selection, the Court may assess reasonable charges reflecting the costs to the government of compensating said jurors for their unnecessary appearance. Said charges may be assessed against one or more of the parties, or against one or more counsel, as the Court deems proper, and the amount collected shall be deposited by the Clerk into the Treasury of the United States.

14. Effective Date and Review of Plan. This Plan shall become effective upon filing by the Clerk of this Court after approval by the Judicial Council of the Ninth Circuit. Copies of the approved Plan will be sent to the Administrative Office of the United States Courts and the United States Attorney General. This Plan will be reviewed annually by the Chief Deputy of Operations to ensure that it complies with all legislation and Judicial Conference rules and regulations, encompasses the most effective procedures, and reflects the policy preferences of the court.

[Filed October 25, 2013. Approved by the Ninth Circuit Judicial Council October 23, 2013. Amended effective July 15, 2019.]

SPEEDY TRIAL ACT PLAN [GENERAL ORDER 11–14]

1. **Authority.** Pursuant to the requirements of the Speedy Trial Act (18 U.S.C. § 3161 et seq.), the Federal Juvenile Delinquency Act (18 U.S.C. § 5031 et seq.), and the Bail Reform Act of 1984 (18 U.S.C. §§ 3141–3156), the judges of the United States District Court for the Central District of California have adopted the following plan setting forth time limits and procedures to minimize undue delay and to further the prompt disposition of criminal cases and certain juvenile proceedings. This plan took effect upon approval of the Judicial Council of the Ninth Circuit on July 9, 2009. Minor, non-substantive changes to the plan were adopted by the Court on October 28, 2011. This plan supersedes General Order No. 11–05, filed June 17, 2011.

2. **Applicability.**

a. *Offense.* The time limits set forth herein are applicable to any criminal offense which is in violation of any Act of Congress and is triable by any court established by Act of Congress (other than a Class B or C misdemeanor or infraction, or an offense triable by court-martial, military commission, provost court, or other military tribunal).

b. *Judge.* The terms "judge," "judicial officer" or "court" mean, unless otherwise indicated, any United States district or magistrate judge.

c. *Persons.* The time limits are applicable to persons accused who have not been indicted or informed against as well as those who have, and the word "defendant" includes such persons unless the context indicates otherwise.

3. **Priorities in Scheduling Criminal Cases.** Preference shall be given to criminal proceedings as far as practicable as required by Rule 50 of the Federal Rules of Criminal Procedure. The trial or other disposition of cases involving a detained person who is being held in detention solely because he is awaiting trial, and a released person who is awaiting trial and has been designated by the attorney for the Government as being of high risk, shall be accorded priority. (18 U.S.C. § 3164(a).)

4. **Time Within Which an Indictment or Information Must Be Filed.**

a. *Time Limits.* If an individual is arrested or served with a summons and the complaint charges an offense to be prosecuted in this district, any indictment or information subsequently filed in connection with such charge shall be filed within 30 days of the arrest or service. (18 U.S.C. § 3161(b).)

b. *Measurement of Time Periods.* If a person has not been arrested or served with a summons on a federal charge, an arrest will be deemed to have been made at the earliest of such times as the person:

    i.   is held in custody solely for the purpose of responding to a federal charge;

    ii.   is delivered to the custody of a federal official in connection with a federal charge; or

    iii.   appears before a judicial officer in connection with a federal charge.

c. *Related Procedures.*

    i.   At the time of the earliest appearance before a judicial officer of a person who has been arrested for an offense not charged in an indictment or information, the prosecuting agency shall inform the judicial officer of the date on which the arrest took place for the record.

    ii.   In the absence of a showing to the contrary, a summons shall be considered to have been served on the date of service shown on the return thereof. A summons served by mail shall be considered to have been served on the date shown on the receipt thereof.

5. **Time Within Which Trial Must Commence.**

a. *Time Limits.*

    i.   Unless the defendant consents in writing to the contrary, the trial shall not commence earlier than 30 days from the date on which the defendant first appears before a judicial officer of this district either through counsel or on which the defendant expressly waives counsel and elects to proceed pro se. (18 U.S.C. § 3161(c)(2).)

    ii.   In any case in which a plea of not guilty is entered, the trial of a defendant charged in an information or indictment with commission of an offense shall commence within 70 days from the filing date (and making public) of the information or indictment, or from the date the defendant has appeared before a judicial officer of the court in which such charge is pending, whichever date last occurs. If a defendant consents in writing to be tried before a magistrate judge on a complaint, the trial shall commence within 70 days from the date of such consent. (18 U.S.C. § 3161(c)(1).)

iii. The trial of any detained person who is being held in detention solely because he is awaiting trial or of a released person who is awaiting trial and has been designated by the attorney for the Government as being of high risk shall commence not later than 90 days following the beginning of such continuous detention or designation of high risk by the attorney for the Government. The periods of delay enumerated in 18 U.S.C. § 3161(h) are excluded in computing the time limitation specified in this paragraph. (18 U.S.C. § 3164(a) and (b).)

b. *Superseding Charges.* If, after an indictment or information has been filed, a complaint, indictment, or information is filed which charges the defendant with the same offense or with an offense required to be joined with that offense, the time limit applicable to the subsequent charge shall be determined as follows.

i. If the original indictment or information was dismissed on motion of the defendant before the filing of the subsequent charge, the time limit shall be determined without regard to the existence of the original charge. (18 U.S.C. § 3161(d)(1).) A dismissal of the indictment on order of the judge with the consent of the defendant shall be considered dismissed on motion of the defendant.

ii. If the original indictment or information was dismissed on motion of the United States Attorney and thereafter a charge is filed against the defendant for the same offense, or any offense required to be joined with that offense, the trial shall commence within the time limit for commencement of trial on the original indictment or information, but any period of delay from the date the charge was dismissed to the date the time limit would commence to run as to the subsequent charge shall be excluded from the computations. (18 U.S.C. § 3161(h)(5).)

iii. If the original indictment or information is pending at the time the subsequent charge is filed, the trial shall commence within the time limit for commencement of the trial on the original indictment or information. (18 U.S.C. § 3161(h)(5).)

c. *Withdrawal of Plea.* If a defendant enters a plea of guilty or nolo contendere to any or all charges in an indictment or information and subsequently is permitted to withdraw the plea, the time limit shall be determined for all counts as if the indictment or information were filed on the day the order permitting withdrawal of plea became final. (18 U.S.C. § 3161(f).)

d. *Retrial and Trial on Charges Reinstated.* If a defendant is to be tried upon an indictment or information dismissed by the trial court and reinstated following an appeal, or if the defendant is to be tried again following a declaration by the trial judge of a mistrial or following an order of such judge for a new trial, the trial shall commence 70 days from the date the order occasioning the trial or retrial becomes final. If the defendant is to be tried again following an appeal or collateral attack, the trial shall commence within 70 days from the date the action occasioning the retrial becomes final, except that the court retrying may extend the period for retrial not to exceed 180 days from the date the action occasioning the retrial becomes final if unavailability of witnesses or other factors resulting from the passage of time shall make trial within 70 days impractical. The periods of delay enumerated in 18 U.S.C. § 3161(h) are excluded in computing the time limitations specified in this section. (18 U.S.C. §§ 3161(d)(2) and 3161(e).)

e. *Measurement of Time Periods.* For purposes of this section:

i. If a defendant signs a written consent to be tried before a magistrate on a complaint and no indictment or information charging the offense has been filed, the time limit for trial shall run from the date of such consent.

ii. In the event of a transfer to this district under Rule 20 of the Federal Rules of Criminal Procedure, the indictment or information shall be deemed filed in this district when the papers in the proceeding or certified copies thereof are received by the clerk of the court.

iii. A trial in a jury case shall be deemed to commence at the beginning of voir dire.

iv. A trial in a non-jury case shall be deemed to commence on the day the case is called, provided that some substantial step in the trial procedure immediately follows.

f. *Related Procedures.*

i. The court shall provide defendants with counsel as soon as feasible after they are taken into custody, when they appear before a district or magistrate judge, when they are formally charged or notified of charges if formal charges are sealed, or when a district or magistrate judge otherwise considers appointment of counsel appropriate under the Criminal Justice Act, whichever occurs earliest. (Criminal Justice Act; Rule 44 of the Federal Rules of Criminal Procedure; Criminal Justice Act Plan for the Central District of California.)

ii. The court shall have sole responsibility for setting cases for trial after consultation with the counsel for the defendant and the attorney for the Government. At the arraignment or as soon thereafter as is practicable, each case shall be set for trial. (18 U.S.C. § 3161(a).)

iii. A conflict in schedules of the Assistant United States Attorney or defense counsel shall not be grounds for a continuance or delay in the setting of a trial date except under circumstances approved by the court and called to the court's attention at the earliest practicable time.

iv. At or promptly after the time of the filing of a complaint, indictment, or information such as described in above subparagraph 5(b)(ii) or (iii), the United States Attorney shall inform the court of that circumstance and his or her position with respect to the computation of the time limits.

v. Pre-trial hearings deemed necessary to assist counsel in the preparation or disposition of their case shall be conducted as soon after the arraignment as possible, consistent with the priorities of other matters on the court's criminal docket.

6. Defendants in Custody.

a. *Time Limits.* Notwithstanding any longer time periods that may be permitted under paragraphs 4 and 5 above, the trial of a defendant held in custody solely for the purpose of trial on a federal charge shall commence within 90 days following the beginning of continuous custody.

b. *Measurement of Time Periods.* For the purposes of this section:

i. A defendant is deemed to be in detention awaiting trial when he is arrested on a federal charge or otherwise held for the purpose of responding to a federal charge. Detention is deemed to be solely because the defendant is awaiting trial unless the person exercising custodial authority has an independent basis (not including detainer) for continuing to hold the defendant.

ii. If a case is transferred pursuant to Rule 20 of the Federal Rules of Criminal Procedure and the defendant subsequently rejects disposition under Rule 20 or the court declines to accept the plea, a new period of continuous detention awaiting trial will begin at that time.

iii. A trial shall be deemed to commence as provided in subparagraphs 5(e)(iii) and (iv).

7. Minimum Time for Defense Preparation.
Unless the defendant consents in writing to the contrary, the trial shall not commence earlier than 30 days from the date on which the defendant first appears before a judicial officer of this district either through counsel or on which the defendant expressly waives counsel and elects to proceed pro se. In circumstances in which the 70–day time limit for commencing trial on a charge in an indictment or information is determined by reference to an earlier indictment or information pursuant to subparagraph 5(b), the 30–day minimum period shall also be determined by reference to the earlier indictment or information.

When prosecution is resumed on an original indictment or information following a mistrial, appeal or withdrawal of a guilty plea, a new 30–day minimum period will not begin to run. The court will in all cases schedule trials so as to permit defense counsel adequate preparation time in the light of all the circumstances. (18 U.S.C. § 3161(c)(2).)

8. Exclusion of Time From Computations.

a. *Applicability.* In computing any time limit under above paragraphs 4, 5, and 6, the periods of delay set forth in 18 U.S.C. § 3161(h) shall be excluded. Such periods of delay shall not be excluded in computing the minimum period for commencement of trial under paragraph 7 above.

b. *Basis for Excludable Time.* At the time it orders time excluded from the computation of any time limit under 18 U.S.C. § 3161, the court shall set forth on the record, in writing or orally, the basis for the finding of excludable time.

c. *Stipulations.*

i. The attorney for the Government and the attorney for the defendant may at any time enter into stipulations with respect to excludable time.

ii. To the extent that the amount of time stipulated exceeds the amount listed in the case record, the stipulation shall have no effect unless approved by the court.

d. *Pre–Indictment Procedures.*

i. In the event that the United States Attorney anticipates that an indictment or information will not be filed within the time limit set forth in paragraph 4 herein, the United States Attorney shall file a written motion with the court for a determination of excludable time. In the event that the United States Attorney seeks a continuance under 18 U.S.C. § 3161(h)(7), the United States Attorney shall file a written motion with the court requesting such a continuance.

ii.   The motion of the United States Attorney shall state:

(1) the period of time proposed for exclusion;

(2) the basis of the proposed exclusion; and

(3) if the motion is for a continuance under 18 U.S.C. § 3161(h)(7), it shall also state whether the defendant is being held in custody on the basis of the complaint.

In appropriate circumstances, the motion may include a request that some or all of the supporting material be considered ex parte and *in camera*.

iii.   The court will grant an extension of time within which an indictment or information must be filed under 18 U.S.C. § 3161(h)(7) only for a specific period of time.

e.   *Post–Indictment Procedures.*

i.   In the event the court extends the time for a trial beyond the time limit set forth in paragraphs 5, 6, and 7, the court shall determine whether the limit may be recomputed by excluding time pursuant to 18 U.S.C. § 3161(h). If it is determined that an extension is justified, the court shall state for the record, either orally or in writing, the fact or facts on which the determination is made. Any ex parte determination that time is excludable shall be subject to a motion to vacate the determination made within five days of the entry of the decision on the docket. No action following the determination that time is excludable will be deemed final until the time for such motion to vacate has passed. In the absence of a need for an extension of time, the court will not ordinarily rule on the excludability of any period of time.

9.   Time Within Which Defendant Should Be Sentenced.

a.   *Time Limit.* A defendant shall ordinarily be sentenced within 120 days of conviction. In particular, it should be noted that the time period for sentencing set forth herein is a statement of this district's voluntarily assumed goal, and is not required nor enforced by the Speedy Trial Act.

b.   *Related Procedures.* For good cause, the court may order a presentence investigation commenced prior to a conviction.

10.   Juvenile Proceedings.

a.   *Definitions.* "Juvenile" is a person who has not attained his 18th birthday, or for the purpose of proceedings and disposition for an alleged act of juvenile delinquency, a person who has not attained his 21st birthday, and "juvenile delinquency" is the violation of a law of the United States committed by a person prior to his 18th birthday which would have been a crime if committed by an adult or a violation by such a person of 18 U.S.C. § 922(x). (18 U.S.C. § 5031.)

b.   *Time Within Which Trial Must Commence.* An alleged delinquent who is in detention pending trial shall be brought to trial within 30 days of the date on which such detention was begun. (18 U.S.C. § 5036.)

c.   *Time of Dispositional Hearing.* If a juvenile is adjudicated delinquent, a separate dispositional hearing shall be held no later than 20 days after trial, unless the court has ordered further study of the juvenile in accordance with 18 U.S.C. § 5037(e). (18 U.S.C. § 5037(a).)

11.   Sanctions.

a.   *Dismissal.* Failure to comply with the requirements of the Speedy Trial Act, 18 U.S.C. § 3161 et seq., may entitle the defendant to dismissal of the charges against him. Nothing in this plan shall be construed to require that a case be dismissed in circumstances in which dismissal would not be by 18 U.S.C. § 3161 et seq. or the Interstate Agreement on Detainers.

b.   *Alleged Juvenile Delinquents.* If an alleged delinquent in detention pending trial is not brought to trial within 30 days from the date upon which such detention was begun, the information shall be dismissed on motion of the alleged delinquent or at the direction of the court, unless the United States Attorney shows that additional delay was caused by the juvenile or his counsel, or consented to by the juvenile and his counsel, or would be in the interest of justice in the particular case. (18 U.S.C. § 5036.)

c.   *Discipline of Attorneys.* The court may punish counsel as provided in 18 U.S.C. §§ 3162(b) and (c) in any case in which counsel for the defendant or the attorney for the Government:

    i. Knowingly allows the case to be set for trial without disclosing the fact that a necessary witness would be unavailable for trial;

    ii. Files a motion solely for the purpose of delay which he knows is totally frivolous and without merit;

    iii. Makes a statement for the purpose of obtaining a continuance which he knows to be false and which is material to the granting of a continuance; or

    iv. Otherwise willfully fails to proceed to trial without justification consistent with 18 U.S.C. § 3161. (18 U.S.C. § 3162.)

12. Persons Serving Terms of Imprisonment. If the United States Attorney knows that a person charged with an offense is serving a term of imprisonment in any penal institution, the United States Attorney shall promptly undertake to obtain the presence of the prisoner for trial, or cause a detainer to be filed, in accordance with the provisions of 18 U.S.C. § 3161(j).

[Effective July 9, 2009. Amended effective October 28, 2011.]

SELECTED GENERAL ORDERS

GENERAL ORDER NO. 03–01. IN THE MATTER OF FINANCIAL DISCLOSURE DURING PRESENTENCE INVESTIGATION

WHEREAS a defendant's disclosure of financial information during the presentence investigation would increase the probability of the defendant providing the type of information necessary to adequately analyze his or her financial condition and ability to pay financial sanctions, and

WHEREAS a defendant's cooperation is essential in obtaining such financial information,

IT IS HEREBY ORDERED that the following documents shall be provided by the defendant to the Probation Officer within 14 calendar days from the date of the guilty plea or verdict, unless another deadline is set by the Probation Officer:

1. An affidavit fully describing (a) the financial resources of the defendant, including a complete listing of all assets owned or controlled by the defendant and any transfers or sales of assets since the defendant's arrest; (b) the financial needs and earning ability of the defendant, the defendant's spouse (or significant other), and the defendant's dependents living at home; and (c) such other information that the Court requires. [18 U.S.C. § 3664(d)(3)];

2. All supporting financial documents requested by the Probation Officer, including but not limited to bills, pay stubs, credit card statements, and bank account statements;

3. A signed release authorizing credit report inquiries;

4. Copies of filed federal and state income tax returns for the last five years or a signed release authorizing their disclosure.

[Dated: March 11, 2003.]

GENERAL ORDER NO. 05–07. IN THE MATTER OF ASSIGNMENT OF DUTIES TO MAGISTRATE JUDGES

(SUPERSEDES GENERAL ORDERS 104, 104–A, 104–B, 104–C, 104–D, 104–E, 104–F and 194, 194–A, 194–B, 194–C, 194–D, 194–E, 194–F, 194–G, 194–H, 194–I, 97–3 and 01–13)

This General Order shall amend and supersede General Orders numbered 104 through 104–F, General Orders numbered 194 through 194–I, General Order 97–3 and General Order 01–13. All references to this general order and any subsequent amendments may be referenced as General Order 194.

IT IS HEREBY ORDERED that, unless restricted by General Order of this Court, United States Magistrate Judges of this Court are authorized to perform all of the duties and functions prescribed and authorized by 28 U.S.C. § 636, or any other statutes or Federal Rules of Procedure which authorize Magistrate Judges to perform judicial duties or functions.

Magistrate Judges shall have the inherent power of judicial officers to implement and enforce their own orders and regulate proceedings before them, to the extent permitted by law.

IT IS FURTHER ORDERED that the following civil and criminal matters shall be referred to the full-time Magistrate Judges:

Civil Matters:

1. Social Security disability cases (including post-judgment applications for attorney's fees);

2. Federal habeas corpus petitions;

3. Pro se § 1983 and *Bivens* cases for pretrial purposes (except for cases where a federal judicial officer is named as a defendant);

4. State habeas corpus petitions (except for death penalty cases);

5. Applications for letters rogatory and requests for international assistance;

6. Applications for provisional remedies other than injunctive relief, including writs of attachment sought pursuant to Cal.Civ.Proc. Code § 481.010, *et seq.*;

7. Judgment debtor and third party examinations pursuant to Cal.Civ.Proc. Code § 708.110, *et seq.* and other post-judgment discovery as provided by Fed.R.Civ.P. 69(a);

8. Discovery-related matters upon referral by the District Judge to whom the case is assigned;

9. Applications for warrants of arrest pursuant to Admiralty Rule C(3) and release from arrest pursuant to Admiralty Rule E(4)(f);

10. Any and all proceedings in a civil case (including jury and non-jury trials, and the entry of final judgment) upon the consent of the parties in accordance with the Local Rules;

11. Guardian ad litem applications;

12. Proceedings relating to naturalization matters;

13. Attorney admissions;

14. Jury excusals and grand jury empanelments;

15. Extradition proceedings pursuant to 18 U.S.C. § 3181, *et seq.*;

16. Settlement conferences in cases to which the Magistrate Judge is assigned, upon referral by the District Judge;

17. Upon referral by the District Judge to whom the case is assigned, and except as limited by General Order of this Court, any additional duty related to civil cases not inconsistent with the Constitution or laws of the United States.

Criminal Matters:

1. Process complaints and issue appropriate summonses or arrest warrants, and dismiss complaints upon the request of the United States Attorney;

2. Issue and accept returns of search and seizure warrants;

3. Review applications for and issue orders relating to the installation of a pen register, trap and trace, transponder or other surveillance device;

4. Conduct initial appearance proceedings and appoint counsel when necessary;

5. Conduct preliminary examinations;

6. Set bail for material witnesses;

7. Conduct removal hearings and issue warrants of removal;

8. Accept waivers of indictment;

9. Conduct extradition proceedings;

10. Conduct proceedings in cases charging misdemeanors and infractions as provided in 18 U.S.C. § 3401, and order a presentence investigation report in any such case pending before such Magistrate Judge;

11. Conduct post-indictment arraignment proceedings and appoint counsel when necessary;

12. In accordance with the instructions of the District Judge to whom the case is assigned, accept not guilty pleas and set the case for trial and/or further proceedings before the District Judge;

13. Accept a plea of guilty and impose sentence in a case involving an information or indictment charging a misdemeanor offense originating in another district, which has been transferred to this district, if the defendant consents to proceed before a Magistrate Judge;

14. Receive the Grand Jury reports, order that any indictments returned be filed, issue warrants and appropriate summonses, and set conditions for release on an indictment or information;

15. Review and issue orders relating to applications for the sealing of indictments, affidavits for search warrants and complaints and warrants, and other applications for sealing documents related to cases prior to the assignment of the case to a District Judge;

16. Issue subpoenas, writs of habeas corpus ad prosequendum or ad testificandum, or other orders necessary to obtain the presence of parties, witnesses, or evidence needed for the arraignment calendar or other court proceedings;

17. Exonerate or forfeit bonds, set aside forfeitures, and reinstate bail in proceedings pending before the Magistrate Judges;

18. Administer the Central Violations Bureau and recommend amendments to the bail schedule;

19. Fix or modify bail and conduct detention hearings and issue release and detention orders, as provided by 18 U.S.C. § 3142(f), (h) and (i);

20. Approve personal and corporate surety bonds and bonds requiring personal sureties;

21. Conduct *Nebbia* hearings;

22. In proceedings pending before the Magistrate Judge, appoint a psychiatrist, when appropriate, under 18 U.S.C. § 4241 and conduct the competency hearing;

23. In proceedings pending before the Magistrate Judge, issue bench warrants for the failure of defendants or witnesses to appear.

IT IS FURTHER ORDERED that the following matters shall be referred to the part-time Magistrate Judges:

1. Process complaints and issue appropriate summonses or arrest warrants;

2. Issue search and seizure warrants;

3. Conduct initial appearance proceedings, and set any required preliminary examination before a full-time Magistrate Judge;

4. Administer oaths and affirmations, issue orders pursuant to 18 U.S.C. § 3142 concerning release or detention of persons pending trial;

5. Conduct proceedings in cases charging misdemeanors and infractions as provided in 18 U.S.C. § 3401, and order a presentence investigation report in any such case pending before such Magistrate Judge.

6. Perform such other duties of the full-time Magistrate Judges as may be assigned by the Chief District Judge, or the Chief District Judge's designee.

IT IS FURTHER ORDERED that, except in cases pending before the particular Magistrate Judge for all purposes, the following civil and criminal matters shall not be referred to the Magistrate Judges:

Civil:

1. Applications or motions for attorney's fees and costs except in Social Security disability cases referred to the Magistrate Judges.

2. Capital habeas corpus petitions;

3. Motions under 28 U.S.C. § 2255, petitions for writs of habeas corpus or other writ petitions directed to a conviction and/or sentence sustained in this Court;

4. Applications or motions seeking contempt except as provided in 28 U.S.C. § 636(e) or any successor statute;

5. Applications or motions seeking entry of default judgment;

6. Applications or motions seeking injunctive or mandamus relief, including temporary restraining orders;

7. Post-judgment applications or motions, except proceedings relating to the scheduling and conducting of judgment debtor and third party examinations pursuant to Cal. Civ. Proc. Code §§ 708.110, *et seq.* and other post-judgment discovery as provided by Fed.R.Civ.P. 69(a);

8. Potentially dispositive motions listed in 28 U.S.C. § 636(b)(1)(A), except in social security disability cases, non-capital state or federal habeas corpus petitions, and pro se § 1983 and *Bivens* cases;

9. Pretrial matters not relating to discovery; and

10. Jury selection, jury returns, and all other jury tasks (except grand and petit jury excusals).

Criminal Matters:

1. Criminal discovery;

2. Pretrial conferences and related matters; and

3. Jury selection, return of jury verdicts, and all other petit jury tasks.

IT IS FURTHER ORDERED that civil cases filed and assigned to Magistrate Judges shall be subject to the following:

1. When a case is filed that is referable to a Magistrate Judge for a report and recommendation, the Magistrate Judge shall be randomly drawn from a district-wide Report and Recommendation Assignment Wheel, subject to the special assignment rules hereinafter specified.

If a pro se civil rights plaintiff secures counsel or all the civil rights claims are dismissed without leave to amend, then the reference under this General Order shall be vacated automatically by the Clerk of the Court, and the case shall be returned to the assigned District Judge with the assigned Magistrate Judge redesignated as the discovery Magistrate Judge. If a civil rights case is not referred to a Magistrate Judge under this General Order at the time it is filed, but the case is later determined to be referable or later becomes referable based on subsequent developments, then the case may be referred at the discretion of the assigned District Judge to a Magistrate Judge randomly drawn from the district-wide Report and Recommendation Assignment Wheel.

2. Once a case is randomly assigned to a Magistrate Judge for a report and recommendation, all subsequent habeas corpus cases, pro se civil rights and *Bivens* cases, and Social Security cases filed by that same party shall be directly assigned to the most recently assigned Magistrate Judge. The Magistrate Judge shall receive one credit in the Report and Recommendation Assignment Wheel for each case directly assigned. This rule shall not apply when either the original case or the subsequent case has multiple plaintiffs or petitioners. Rather, in those instances, the subsequent case shall be randomly assigned to a Magistrate Judge in accordance with this General Order.

3. Once a case is randomly assigned to a Magistrate Judge for a report and recommendation, if the reference thereafter is vacated by the District Judge, the same Magistrate Judge shall be directly assigned to the case for discovery. No card adjustments shall be made in the Assignment Wheels.

4. If a District Judge vacates a reference to a Magistrate Judge for discovery and instead refers the matter to a Magistrate Judge for a report and recommendation, the case shall be randomly assigned to a new Magistrate Judge for the report and recommendation if no discovery matters were heard by the discovery Magistrate Judge. If such assignment is made, the discovery Magistrate Judge shall receive a debit in the Discovery Assignment Wheel.

If any discovery matters were heard by the discovery Magistrate Judge, the case shall be directly assigned to the same Magistrate Judge for the report and recommendation. If such transfer is made, the Magistrate Judge shall receive a credit in the Report and Recommendation Assignment Wheel and a debit in the Discovery Assignment Wheel.

5. If a case filed by a pro se litigant is assigned to a Magistrate Judge for discovery, and the same pro se litigant subsequently files a case which is to be assigned to a Magistrate Judge for a report and recommendation, the report and recommendation case shall be directly assigned to the discovery Magistrate Judge only if any discovery matters were heard by that Magistrate Judge. If such assignment is made, the Magistrate Judge shall receive a credit in the Report and Recommendation Wheel.

If no discovery matters were heard, a new Magistrate Judge shall be randomly assigned the report and recommendation case.

6. If it is determined upon the filing of a new report and recommendation case that the same pro se litigant has a discovery case and a report and recommendation case pending before different Magistrate Judges, the new report and recommendation case shall be directly assigned to the Magistrate Judge who was randomly assigned to the most recent report and recommendation case.

The pending discovery case shall be directly assigned to the Magistrate Judge assigned to the most recent report and recommendation case if no discovery matters have been heard. If such transfer is made, the Discovery Assignment Wheel shall be respectively debited and credited for the transferor and transferee Magistrate Judge.

7. The Magistrate Judge randomly assigned a discovery case shall be directly assigned all subsequent discovery cases accepted by the originally assigned District Judge as related cases. Case credit for these direct assignments shall be limited to ten (10) unless otherwise ordered by the Chief Magistrate Judge.

IT IS FURTHER ORDERED that the Magistrate Judge to whom any particular action or proceeding is assigned and referred for a report and recommendation may transfer the case by order of the transferor and transferee Magistrate Judges. If such a transfer is made, it shall be respectively debited and credited in the Report and Recommendation Assignment Wheel.

[Dated: November 3, 2005. Amended effective February 28, 2006.]

GENERAL ORDER NO. 11–10.   IN THE MATTER OF ALTERNATIVE DISPUTE RESOLUTION (ADR) PROGRAM [SUPERSEDES GENERAL ORDERS NO. 04–01 AND NO. 07–01]

1. Scope and Purpose.

1.1. *Scope.* This General Order ("Order") governs the elective and presumptive referral of certain actions to the Alternative Dispute Resolution (ADR) Program for mediation with a neutral from the Mediation Panel (previously known as the Attorney Settlement Officer Panel) appointed by the Court. The Order shall be effective on December 1, 2011 and applies to actions which fall within the scope of this Order, regardless of when the actions commenced.

1.2. *Purpose.* The Court finds that the number of criminal and civil cases in this District, together with the adoption of Congressional requirements for the priority scheduling of criminal trials and the shortage of Judges in this District, have placed significant pressures on litigants, counsel, and the Court. The purpose of the ADR Program is to alleviate some of these pressures and to encourage the fair, speedy, and economical resolution of controversies by referring suitable cases to an impartial neutral who is experienced in one or more designated areas of law and in the process of alternative dispute resolution.

2. Administration.

2.1. *ADR Judge.* A district judge shall be appointed by the Chief Judge to serve as Chair of the ADR Committee. That judge will also serve as the ADR Judge of this Court. The ADR Judge shall serve as the primary liaison between the Court and ADR Program staff, consulting with staff on matters of policy, program design and evaluation, education, training and administration.

2.2. *Appointment of the ADR Program Director.* The ADR Program shall be coordinated by an ADR Program Director at the direction of the Clerk of Court.

2.3. *Duties of the ADR Program Director.* The duties of the ADR Program Director shall be established by the Court, and shall include the following:

(a) Maintain, on the Court website, the current list of panel members available to act as mediators;

(b) Report to the Court on the status and effectiveness of the ADR Program, and maintain records, including disposition and success rates, for this purpose;

(c) Serve as a neutral in selected cases;

(d) Perform any additional duties as the Court may direct which are necessary for the efficient administration of the ADR Program.

2.4. *Duties of the Bar.* The Central District's Lawyer Representatives' Mediation Panel Selection Committee will assist the Court with the ADR Program in the following ways:

(a) Recruit suitable candidates for the Mediation Panel;

(b) Review candidate applications for the Mediation Panel and provide advice to the Court in connection with the selection and appointment of panel members; and

(c) Perform such additional duties as the Court may direct which are necessary for the efficient administration of the ADR Program.

3. Mediator Qualifications and Selection.

3.1. *Qualifications.* A person may serve as a member of the Mediation Panel if:

(a) the person has been a United States Appellate, District, Magistrate or Bankruptcy Judge, or a California Judicial Officer; or

(b) the person is currently a member in good standing of the Bar of the United States District Court, Central District of California, with at least 10 years legal practice experience, substantial experience with or knowledge of civil litigation in federal court, and significant expertise in one or more of the following areas:

(1) Admiralty

(2) Americans with Disabilities Act

(3) Antitrust

(4) Bankruptcy

(5) Business/Commercial Litigation

(6) Civil Rights

(7) Class Actions

(8) Consumer Credit

(9) Copyright/Trademark

(10) Employment/Discrimination/Wrongful Termination

(11) Environmental

(12) ERISA

(13) Foreclosure

(14) Insurance Coverage/Bad Faith

(15) Labor

(16) Patent

(17) Personal Injury

(18) Products Liability

(19) Real Estate/Construction

(20) Securities

(21) Tax

The Court may modify these and other minimum requirements in individual circumstances for good cause. The Court shall only make such modification upon a determination that the applicant has demonstrated satisfactory evidence of sufficient education, training, skills and/or experience.

3.2. *Training Requirements.* In order to qualify for appointment to the Mediation Panel, an applicant shall successfully complete a court-conducted training course in mediation or provide proof that he or she has successfully completed a court-approved training course in mediation. In order to qualify for subsequent reappointments to the Mediation Panel, an applicant shall agree to periodically participate in court-conducted or court-approved refresher or advanced training. The Court may, in its discretion, waive the training requirements upon application by the individual.

3.3. *Application for Appointment to Mediation Panel.* An application for appointment to the Mediation Panel may be obtained from the ADR Program Director or downloaded from the Court's website, www.cacd.uscourts.gov. The application shall be submitted to the ADR Program Director.

3.4. *Appointment of Mediators to Panel.* Mediators shall be appointed to the Mediation Panel by the Court. A panel member may ask the ADR Program Director at any time to have his or her name removed from the panel roster. The Court may, in its sole discretion, remove any person from the Mediation Panel who violates this Order, *see* Section 11, or is unable to commit sufficient time to, or otherwise meet the requirements of, panel membership.

3.5. *Term of Appointment.* Appointment to the Mediation Panel shall be for a term of two years. The term may be renewed at the discretion of the Court upon the consent and re-application of the panel member. Panel members who do not reapply for appointment at the expiration of the two-year term will be removed from the panel roster.

3.6. *Oath Required.* Every mediator appointed to the Mediation Panel shall take the oath or affirmation prescribed in 28 U.S.C. § 453.

3.7. *Minimum Case Requirement.* Panel members are expected to mediate a minimum of two cases per appointment term. At least one case per term shall be a case that has been assigned by the Court. Panel members who do not meet the minimum case requirement will not be reappointed at the end of their term unless they contact the ADR Program Director and establish good cause for reappointment.

3.8. *Compensation.*

(a) Volunteer time. Panel members shall volunteer their preparation time and the first three hours of a mediation session. After three hours of a mediation session, the panel member may (1) give the parties the option of concluding the mediation; (2) continue the mediation and volunteer his or her time; or (3) continue the mediation on such terms and rates as the panel member and all parties agree. The mediation session will continue beyond three hours only if all parties and the panel member agree.

(b) Payment. If the mediation session continues beyond three hours, the terms and conditions of payment must be clearly communicated in writing to the parties. The parties may agree to pay the fee in other than equal portions. The parties must pay the mediator directly, or the mediator's law firm or employer, as directed by the mediator. On a form survey provided by the Court (in the form attached as "Exhibit I", *see* section 8.8 below), the mediator must promptly report to the ADR Program the amount of payment received.

3.9. *Limits on Role of Mediator.* The panel member has no authority to render a decision or to dictate a settlement.

3.10. *Immunities.* Panel members are performing quasi-judicial functions and are entitled to the immunities and protections that the law accords to persons serving in such capacity.

3.11. *Disqualification of Mediators.*

(a) Applicable Standards. No person may serve as a neutral in a case in the Court's ADR Program in violation of:

(1) the standards set forth in 28 U.S.C. § 455; or

(2) any applicable standard of professional responsibility or rule of professional conduct; or

(3) other guidelines adopted by the Court concerning disqualification of neutrals.

(b) Mandatory Disqualification and Notice of Recusal. A prospective neutral who discovers a circumstance requiring disqualification must immediately notify the parties and the ADR Program Director in writing. The parties may not waive a basis for disqualification that is described in 28 U.S.C. § 455(b).

(c) Disclosure and Waiver of Non–Mandatory Grounds for Disqualification. If a prospective neutral discovers a circumstance that would not compel disqualification under an applicable standard of professional responsibility or rule of professional conduct or other guideline, or under 28 U.S.C. § 455(b), but that might be covered by 28 U.S.C. § 455(a) (impartiality might reasonably be questioned), the neutral shall promptly disclose that circumstance in writing to all parties and the ADR Program Director. A party who has an objection to the neutral based upon an allegation that the neutral has a conflict of interest must present this objection in writing to the ADR Program Director within 10 calendar days of learning the source of the potential conflict or shall be deemed to have waived objection.

(d) Objections Not Based on Disclosure By Neutral. Within 7 days of learning the identity of a proposed neutral, a party who objects to service by that neutral must deliver to the ADR Program Director and to all other counsel a writing that specifies the bases for the objection. The ADR Program Director shall determine whether the proposed neutral will serve or whether another neutral should be appointed.

3.12. *Related Cases/Multiple Cases With Common Party.* A panel member may conduct a mediation for a group of related cases or a group of cases with one common party if (1) all parties to all cases agree, in writing, (2) all parties to all cases agree, in writing, to compensation terms and rates of the mediator, subject to the limitations of section 3.8 above, and (3) the panel member discloses to all parties the number of cases in which the panel member has previously conducted mediations involving any of the parties participating in the current proceeding.

3.13. *Members of Mediation Panel.* All attorneys who are serving on the Court's Attorney Settlement Officer Panel as of the date this Order becomes effective shall automatically be appointed as members of the Mediation Panel after they have taken the oath or affirmation prescribed in 28 U.S.C. § 453.

4. ADR Program General Provisions.

4.1. *Referral to the Court's Mediation Panel.* Cases may be referred to the ADR Program for mediation with a neutral from the Mediation Panel in one of two ways: 1) through the Court–Directed ADR Program, as described in section 5 below; and 2) under Civil L.R. 16–15, as described in section 6 below.

4.2. *Description: Mediation.* Mediation is a flexible, non-binding, confidential process in which a neutral person (the mediator) facilitates settlement negotiations. The mediator improves communication across party lines, helps parties articulate their interests and understand those of their opponent, probes the strengths and weaknesses of each party's legal positions, identifies areas of agreement and helps generate options for a mutually agreeable resolution to the dispute. A hallmark of mediation is its capacity to expand traditional settlement discussion and broaden resolution options, often by exploring litigant needs and interests that may be formally independent of the legal issues in controversy.

4.3. *Status of Discovery, Motions and Trial During the ADR Process.* Any case referred to the ADR Program continues to be subject to management by the judge to whom it is assigned. Selection of a case for ADR has no effect on the normal progress of the case toward trial. Referral of a case to ADR is not grounds for avoiding or postponing any deadline or obligation imposed by the case management order, unless so ordered by the Court.

4.4. *Cases Assigned to a Magistrate Judge Pursuant to 28 U.S.C. § 636(c) and the Local Civil Rules.* The provisions of this Order are applicable to those cases that are assigned to a magistrate judge pursuant to 28 U.S.C. § 636(c) and the Civil Local Rules if the magistrate judge determines that the case would benefit from participation in the ADR Program.

4.5. *Case Types Exempted.* The following case types shall not be referred to the Mediation Panel:

(a) habeas corpus and extraordinary writs;

(b) immigration and naturalization;

(c) prisoner civil rights;

(d) social security;

(e) petitions to enforce IRS summonses.

4.6. *Cases Involving a Self–Represented Party.* The Court, in its discretion, may order a case involving a self-represented party to the Mediation Panel. In such cases, within seven (7) days of the Order/Referral to ADR, the party proceeding without a lawyer and the opposing counsel must arrange for a phone conference with the ADR Program Director to discuss ADR options.

5. Referral of Cases to the Court–Directed ADR Program.

5.1. *Court–Directed ADR Program.* With the exception of those case types exempted in section 4.5 above and cases involving a party who is not represented by counsel (*see* section 4.6), all civil cases which are assigned to judges participating in the Court–Directed ADR Program are presumptively referred to the Mediation Panel or a private dispute resolution process. The participating judges are listed on the court website, www.cacd.uscourts.gov, ADR section, under "List of District Judges Participating in the ADR Program." In all such cases, a "Notice to Parties of Court–Directed ADR Program" in the form attached as "Exhibit C" will be provided to counsel at the time of the filing of the complaint or notice of removal for service on all parties. Counsel are required to furnish and discuss with their clients the "Notice to Parties: Court Policy on Settlement and Use of Alternative Dispute Resolution" (the "ADR Notice to Parties") and the ADR options available to them before the conference described in section 5.2 below.

5.2. *The Parties' Duty to Consider ADR, Confer and Report.* Unless otherwise ordered, at the conference of the parties held pursuant to Fed. R. Civ. P. 26(f) and Civil L.R. 26–1, counsel shall meet and confer about whether their case is best suited to a mediation with a neutral selected from the Mediation Panel or a private mediation, and when the mediation should occur. *See* Civil L.R. 26–1(c). The parties shall include their shared or separate views regarding the appropriate ADR procedure and proposed date of the session in the written report required by Fed. R. Civ. P. 26(f) and Civil L.R. 26–1.

5.3. *Order/Referral to ADR.* After considering the parties' written report required by Fed. R. Civ. P. 26(f) and Civil L.R. 26–1, the assigned judge will file an Order/Referral to ADR, in the form attached as "Exhibit B."

5.4. *Discretionary Referral.* For cases that do not meet the criteria of section 5.1 of this Order but which the assigned judge determines would benefit from participation in this Program, the assigned judge may file an "Order/Referral to ADR," in the form attached hereto as "Exhibit B."

5.5. *Cases Transferred to a Judge Participating in the Court–Directed ADR Program.* For cases that are transferred to a judge participating in the Court–Directed ADR Program, a "Notice to Parties of Court–Directed ADR Program" in the form attached as "Exhibit C" will be provided to counsel at the time of the transfer by the courtroom deputy clerk for the judge receiving the case.

5.6. *Cases Transferred From a Judge Participating in the Court–Directed ADR Program to a Judge Not Participating in the Court–Directed ADR Program.* The provisions of this section are applicable to those cases that are transferred to a judge who is not participating in the Court–Directed ADR Program but who determines that the case would benefit from and should remain in the Court–Directed ADR Program. If the judge who is not participating in the Court–Directed ADR Program determines that the transferred case would not benefit from mediation with a neutral selected from the Mediation Panel or private mediation, then an order vacating the referral in the form attached hereto as "Exhibit D" will be prepared and filed by the courtroom deputy clerk for the judge receiving the case.

5.7. *Change in Ordered ADR Procedure.* If all parties wish to request a change from the ordered ADR Procedure—from the Mediation Panel to private mediation or from private mediation to the Mediation Panel—the parties shall file a Request: ADR Procedure Selection (Exhibit A). In such instances, counsel shall also notify the ADR Program Director of this change.

6. Referral of Cases to ADR Program Pursuant to Civil Local Rule 16–15.2.

6.1. *Cases Referred Pursuant to the Court–Directed ADR Program Excepted.* Nothing in this section shall apply to cases referred to the ADR Program pursuant to the Court–Directed ADR Program. Rules for the Court–Directed ADR Program are found in section five of this Order.

6.2. *The Parties' Duty to Consider ADR, Confer and Report.* Unless otherwise ordered, at the conference of the parties held pursuant to Fed. R. Civ. P. 26(f) and Civil L.R. 26–1, counsel shall meet and confer about which of the three ADR procedures specified in Civil L.R. 16–15.4 (a settlement proceeding before the assigned district judge or magistrate judge, the Mediation Panel or private mediation) is best suited to the case and when the ADR session should occur. *See* Civil L.R. 26–1(c). The parties shall include their shared or separate views regarding the appropriate ADR procedure and proposed date of the session in the written report required by Fed. R. Civ. P. 26(f) and Civil L.R. 26–1. This report must be accompanied by a Request: ADR Procedure Selection, in the form attached as "Exhibit A." *See* Civil L.R. 16–15.2.

6.3. *Order/Referral to ADR.* After considering the parties' written report and Request: ADR Procedure Selection, the assigned judge will file an Order/Referral to ADR, in the form attached as "Exhibit B."

6.4. *Referral to or Change in ADR at Any Time After Issuance of Initial Case Management or Scheduling Order.* At any time after issuance of the initial case management or scheduling order and before entry of final judgment, if all parties agree that referral to a particular ADR procedure is appropriate, or wish to request a change to the ordered ADR procedure, the parties shall file a Request: ADR Procedure Selection (Exhibit A).

7. Selection and Assignment of Mediator.

7.1. *Selection of Mediator.*

(a) By Stipulation. The parties may stipulate to a mediator from the Mediator Panel list maintained by the ADR Program Director and made available on the Court's website. Upon obtaining the consent of the selected mediator, the parties shall file a Stipulation Regarding Selection of Mediator, in the form attached hereto as "Exhibit E." If the parties have not filed a Stipulation Regarding Selection of Mediator within twenty-one (21) days from the Order/Referral to ADR, the ADR Program Director will assign a mediator.

(b) By Assignment. If the parties are unable to stipulate to a mediator, they may ask that the ADR Program Director assign a mediator from the Panel list. Such request for assignment shall be made by filing a Stipulation Regarding Selection of Mediator, in the form attached hereto as "Exhibit E."

7.2. *Notice of Assignment of Mediator.* A "Notice of Assignment of Mediator" in the form attached hereto as "Exhibit F" shall be filed by the ADR Program in every case in which a mediator from the Mediation Panel is selected by the parties or assigned by the ADR Program Director. The ADR Program will provide the panel member with a copy of the Notice of Assignment, a copy of the current docket sheet and copies of any documents from the case file identified by the panel member as being necessary for his or her preparation for the mediation.

8. Procedures for Scheduling and Conducting the Mediation.

8.1. *Mediator's Initial Communication With Counsel.* Within thirty (30) days of the Notice of Assignment of Mediator, the panel member must communicate with counsel to schedule the mediation session. The communication may take the form of a brief joint telephone conference with counsel, as described below, or in writing, at the mediator's discretion. A joint telephone conference with counsel would likely include a discussion of the following matters:

(a) fixing a mutually convenient date, time and place for the mediation;

(b) the procedures to be followed during the mediation;

(c) who shall attend the session on behalf of each party;

(d) what material or exhibits shall be provided to the mediator prior to the mediation or brought by the parties to the mediation;

(e) any issues or matters that the mediator would like the parties to address in their written mediation statements;

(f) page limitations for mediation statements;

(g) whether the parties are likely to want to continue beyond the three pro bono hours offered by the panel member and, if so, the terms and rates of the panel member (see section 3.8 above); and

(h) any other matters that might enhance the quality of the mediation.

8.2. *Notice: Date and Location of Mediation.* Within thirty-five (35) days of the Notice of Assignment of Mediator, the mediator shall advise the ADR Program of the scheduled date of the mediation by filing a Notice of Mediation Date, in the form attached as "Exhibit G," or by other communication. The mediator shall strive to schedule the mediation for the earliest possible date after the parties have had reasonable time to evaluate their case, thus minimizing the expense of the litigation. The mediation must be completed within the time-frame ordered by the assigned judge or, if no completion date has been ordered, no later than forty-five (45) days before the Final Pretrial Conference. *See* Civil L.R. 16–15.2. Counsel may seek a continuance of the ADR deadline from the assigned judge for good cause. The Court shall provide suitable space for the mediation if a request is made to the ADR Program Director. If, for any reason, the mediator is unable, within thirty-five (35) days of the Notice of Assignment, to set a mediation date, the mediator shall notify the ADR Program Director that a mediation could not be scheduled.

8.3. *Continuances and Rescheduling.* No continuance or rescheduling of the mediation shall be granted except upon agreement of the mediator. The ADR Program Director shall be notified of any continuance or rescheduling of the mediation. Any continuance of the mediation beyond the completion date ordered by the judge or imposed by local rule must be approved by the assigned judge.

8.4. *Mediation Statements.*

(a) Content and Timing. At the request of the mediator, each party shall submit directly to the mediator a confidential mediation statement no later than seven (7) calendar days before the session. The mediation statement shall outline the underlying facts of the dispute, the key legal issues in the case, possible areas of agreement and options for settlement, and the settlement history of the dispute, if any. The mediation statement shall also identify, by name, and title or status:

(1) the person(s) with decision-making authority who, in addition to counsel, will attend the mediation on behalf of the party; and

(2) person(s) connected with either party (including insurer representatives) whose presence at the mediation might substantially improve the productivity of the mediation or the prospects for settlement.

(b) *Confidential Nature of Statement.* Mediation statements shall be subject to the protection afforded by the confidentiality provisions contained in section 9 below. Mediation statements must not be filed and the assigned judge shall not have access to them. The mediator may, with the consent of the parties, request that counsel serve the statements on other parties to the lawsuit.

8.5. *Appearance by Party Representative.* Each party shall appear at the mediation in person or by a representative with final authority to settle the case, which in the case of lawsuits brought against the United States or any of its agencies as a party, shall involve the attendance of an attorney charged with responsibility for the conduct of the case and who has final settlement authority as provided by his or her superiors. A corporation or other non-governmental entity satisfies this attendance requirement if represented by a person who has final settlement authority and who is knowledgeable about the facts of the case. Representatives of insurers with decision-making authority are required to attend mediation sessions, unless personal attendance is excused by the mediator. At the discretion of mediator, and only with the mediator's express authorization, parties residing outside the Central District may have a representative with final settlement authority available by telephone during the entire proceeding, in lieu of personal appearance. *See* Civil L.R. 16–15.5(b).

8.6. *Attendance of Trial Attorney.* Each party shall be represented at the mediation by the attorney who is expected to try the case, unless excused for good cause by the mediator, in accordance with Civil L.R. 16–15.5(c).

8.7. *Participant Surveys.* At the time of the mediation, the mediator shall distribute to each litigant and attorney an "ADR Program Participant Survey" in the form attached hereto as Exhibit J, to be returned directly to the ADR Program. The Participant Surveys are not to be filed with the Court.

8.8. *Attendance Sheet and 'Survey for Mediators and Report of Payment."* The mediator shall collect contact information from each mediation participant on the Mediation Attendance Record in the form attached hereto as "Exhibit H." The mediator shall submit the completed form directly to the ADR Program, with the "Survey for Mediators and Report of Payment," in the form attached hereto as "Exhibit I." The Mediation Attendance Record and Mediator Survey are not to be filed with the court. The ADR Program will use the Attendance Record to follow up with those participants of the mediation session who have not yet returned an "ADR Program Participant Survey," in the form attached hereto as "Exhibit J."

8.9. *Report to the Court.* Within five days after the conclusion of the mediation session, the mediator shall electronically file with the Court a "Mediation Report" in the form attached hereto as "Exhibit K," advising the Court as to whether the parties appeared at the mediation as required by Civil L.R. 16–15.5(b) and whether or not the case settled. Regardless of the outcome of the mediation session, the mediator will not provide the judge with any details of the substance of the mediation session. With the filing of the Mediation Report, the parties are advised that they must notify the trial judge's courtroom deputy clerk of the fact of settlement and promptly file documents regarding the final disposition of the case. *See* Civil L.R. 16–15.7.

If no mediation was held, the mediator shall electronically file with the Court a Mediation Report, indicating that a mediation did not take place. If the case did not settle at the mediation session but is later settled with the assistance of the mediator, the mediator shall file a subsequent Mediation Report.

9. Confidentiality.

9.1. *Confidential Treatment.* Except as provided in section 9.2 below, this Court, the mediator, all counsel and parties, and any other persons attending the mediation shall treat as "confidential information" the contents of the written mediation statements, any documents prepared for the purpose of, in the course of, or pursuant to the mediation, anything that happened or was said relating to the subject matter of the case in mediation, any position taken, and any view of the merits of the case expressed by any participant in connection with any mediation. "Confidential information" shall not be:

(a) disclosed to anyone not involved in the litigation;

(b) disclosed to the assigned judges; or

(c) used for any purpose, including impeachment, in any pending or future proceeding in this court or any other forum.

9.2. *Limited Exceptions to Confidentiality.* This rule does not prohibit:

(a) disclosures as may be stipulated by all parties and the mediator;

(b) disclosures as may be stipulated by all parties, without the consent of the mediator, for use in a subsequent confidential ADR or settlement proceeding;

(c) a report to or an inquiry by the ADR Judge pursuant to sections 10 and 11 below, regarding a possible violation of policies and procedures governing the ADR Program;

(d) the mediator from discussing the mediation process with the ADR Program staff, who shall maintain the confidentiality of the process;

(e) any participant or the mediator from responding to an appropriate request for information duly made by persons authorized by the Court to monitor or evaluate the Court's ADR program;

(f) disclosures as are required by this Order, related ADR forms, and as otherwise required by law; or

(g) in an action or proceeding to enforce a settlement, the admission of a written settlement agreement or a settlement placed on the record, reached as a result of mediation.

9.3. *Confidentiality Agreement.* The mediator may ask the parties and all persons attending the mediation to sign a confidentiality agreement on a form provided by the Court and attached as "Exhibit L." The confidentiality provisions of this section apply regardless of whether a confidentiality agreement is signed.

9.4. *Scope.* Nothing in this rule is intended to limit any applicable privilege or rule of evidence designed to protect mediation confidentiality, and any such broader protection shall control if applicable. *See* Civil L.R. 16–15.8.

10. Violations of This Order by Counsel or a Party.

10.1. *Informal Resolution.* Without prejudice to the use of more formal procedures set forth in sections 10.2 and 10.3 below, a complaint alleging that any person or party has materially violated this Order may be presented informally to the ADR Program Director, who will attempt to resolve the matter to the satisfaction of all concerned.

10.2. *Reporting Violation.* A formal complaint alleging that any person or party has materially violated this Order must be presented in writing (not electronically) to the ADR Program Director, who will refer the matter to the ADR Judge. The letter of complaint must be accompanied by a competent declaration. Copies of the letter and declaration must be sent contemporaneously to all other parties. If the assigned judge is the ADR Judge, the ADR Program Director will refer the letter of complaint and declaration to the Vice Chair of the ADR Committee or the Vice Chair's designee. The declaration must be marked "Confidential–Not to be Filed" and must neither be filed nor disclosed to the assigned judge.

10.3. *Proceeding in Response to Complaint or Report of Violation and Sanctions.* If, upon receiving an appropriately presented and supported complaint or report of a material violation of this Order, the ADR Judge determines that the matter warrants further proceedings, the ADR Judge may refer the matter to the ADR Program Director to explore the possibility of resolving the complaint informally in accordance with section 10.1 above. If no such referral is made, or if the matter is not resolved informally, the ADR Judge for this matter shall take appropriate action. The ADR Judge may issue an order to show cause why sanctions should not be imposed. Any such sanctions proceedings shall be conducted on the record but under seal. The ADR Judge will afford all interested parties an opportunity to be heard before deciding whether to impose sanctions.

11. Violation of This Order by a Panel Member.

11.1. *General Provision.* This rule is intended to promote the fair and timely resolution of complaints related to a mediator's performance in discharging his or her duties as a panel member. This section shall not limit the Court's authority to, in its sole discretion, determine who may be included on or removed from the panel or to take any other action not specifically contemplated by this section, in order to ensure that the quality of services provided by the Court Mediation Panel is commensurate with the Court's expectations and consistent with the Court's role in the administration of justice.

11.2. *Confidentiality of Complaint Proceedings.* No information or record concerning the receipt, investigation or resolution of any complaint made under this section may be open to the public. The Court shall maintain sufficient information about each complaint and its disposition to identify any history or patterns of complaints submitted under this section.

11.3. *Informal Complaints.* Informal complaints regarding a panel member's performance shall be brought to the attention of the ADR Program Director, who will conduct a preliminary review to determine whether the complaint can be informally resolved or merits a formal investigation.

11.4. *Formal Complaint Set Forth in Writing.* Any complaint regarding a panel member's performance that cannot be resolved informally shall be submitted in writing to the ADR Program Director. The complaint is not to be filed nor presented to the assigned judge. The complaint shall describe with particularity the matter, conduct and circumstances triggering the complaint. The ADR Program Director shall send the complainant a written acknowledgment that the complaint has been received.

11.5. *Proceedings in Response to Formal Complaint.* The ADR Committee shall promptly review the complaint to determine whether the matter warrants further investigation. If the ADR Committee determines that further investigation is warranted, the ADR Judge shall conduct an investigation, or appoint a subcommittee of ADR Committee members to conduct an investigation, and present a report of the investigation to the full committee. As part of such investigation, the panel member shall be afforded an opportunity to respond to the complaint. Upon conclusion of the investigation and receipt of the report, the ADR Committee shall make a final determination as to what, if any, action shall be taken.

11.6. *Notice of Final Action in Response to Formal Complaint.* The Court shall notify the complainant and the panel member, in writing, of the final disposition of the complaint.

12. Effective Date. This General Order shall become effective on December 1, 2011.

[Filed: August 15, 2011.]

EXHIBIT A. ADR PROCEDURE SELECTION

Name, Address and Telephone Number
of Attorney(s):

_____

UNITED STATES DISTRICT COURT
CENTRAL DISTRICT OF CALIFORNIA
_____
CASE NUMBER

Plaintiff(s)

v.   _____

REQUEST:
ADR PROCEDURE SELECTION

Defendant(s).
_____

Pursuant to Civil L.R.16–15, the parties request that the Court approve the following ADR procedure:

☐ **ADR PROCEDURE NO. 1**—The parties shall appear before the ☐ district judge *or* ☐ magistrate judge assigned to the case for such settlement proceedings as the judge may conduct or direct.

☐ **ADR PROCEDURE NO. 2**—The parties shall appear before a neutral selected from the Court's Mediation Panel for mediation.

☐ **ADR PROCEDURE NO. 3**—The parties shall participate in a private dispute resolution proceeding.

Dated: _____   _____

                               Attorney for Plaintiff _____

Dated: _____   _____

                               Attorney for Plaintiff _____

Dated: _____   _____

                               Attorney for Defendant _____

Dated: _____   _____

                               Attorney for Defendant _____

NOTE: If additional signatures are required, attach an additional page to this request.

[Effective January, 2012.]

EXHIBIT B.   ORDER/REFERRAL TO ADR

Name & Address:

_____

UNITED STATES DISTRICT COURT
CENTRAL DISTRICT OF CALIFORNIA
CASE NUMBER
_____

Plaintiff(s)

v.   _____

ORDER/REFERRAL TO ADR

Defendant(s).

_____

The Court, having considered the parties' Request: ADR Procedure Selection, the Notice to Parties of Court–Directed ADR Program, or the report submitted by the parties pursuant to Fed. R. Civ. P. 26(f) and Civil L.R. 26–1, hereby:

ORDERS this case referred to:

☐ **ADR PROCEDURE NO. 1:** (☐ district judge *or* ☐ magistrate judge assigned to the case for such settlement proceedings as the judge may conduct or direct).

☐ **ADR PROCEDURE NO. 2:** This case is referred to the ADR Program. Within twenty-one (21) days, plaintiff shall obtain the consent of a neutral listed on the Court's Mediation Panel who will conduct the mediation, and file form ADR–2, Stipulation Regarding Selection of Panel Mediator. If the parties have not selected and obtained the consent of a Panel Mediator within twenty-one (21) days, the ADR Program (213–894–2993) will assign one. Forms and a list of the Panel Mediators are available on the Court website, www.cacd. uscourts.gov. Absent extraordinary circumstances, parties cannot request a continuance within three (3) business days of a scheduled mediation.

☐ **ADR PROCEDURE NO. 3:** (Private mediation).

The ADR proceeding is to be completed no later than: _____

The Court further sets a status conference for: _____

For ADR Procedure Nos. 1 and 3, counsel are responsible for contacting the judge or private mediator at the appropriate time to arrange for further proceedings.

[Effective January, 2012.]

EXHIBIT C.   NOTICE TO PARTIES OF COURT–DIRECTED ADR PROGRAM

UNITED STATES DISTRICT COURT
CENTRAL DISTRICT OF CALIFORNIA

CASE NUMBER

PLAINTIFF(S)

v.

NOTICE TO PARTIES OF
COURT–DIRECTED ADR PROGRAM

DEFENDANT(S)

NOTICE TO PARTIES:

It is the policy of this Court to encourage settlement of civil litigation when such is in the best interest of the parties. The Court favors any reasonable means, including alternative dispute resolution (ADR), to accomplish this goal. *See* Civil L.R. 16–15. Unless exempted by the trial judge, parties in all civil cases must participate in an ADR process before trial. *See* Civil L.R. 16–15.1.

The district judge to whom the above-referenced case has been assigned is participating in an ADR Program that presumptively directs this case to either the Court Mediation Panel or to private mediation. *See* General Order No. 11–10, § 5. For more information about the Mediation Panel, visit the Court website, www.cacd.uscourts.gov, under "ADR."

Pursuant to Civil L.R. 26–1(c), counsel are directed to furnish and discuss with their clients the attached ADR Notice To Parties *before* the conference of the parties mandated by Fed.R.Civ.P. 26(f). Based upon the consultation with their clients and discussion with opposing counsel, counsel must indicate the following in their Joint 26(f) Report: 1) whether the case is best suited for mediation with a neutral from the Court Mediation Panel or private mediation; and 2) when the mediation should occur. *See* Civil L.R. 26–1(c).

At the initial scheduling conference, counsel should be fully prepared to discuss their preference for referral to the Court Mediation Panel or to private mediation and when the mediation should occur. The Court will enter an Order/Referral to ADR at or around the time of the scheduling conference.

Clerk, U.S. District Court

By _____

_____
Date   Deputy Clerk

UNITED STATES DISTRICT COURT
CENTRAL DISTRICT OF CALIFORNIA

NOTICE TO PARTIES: COURT POLICY ON SETTLEMENT
AND USE OF ALTERNATIVE DISPUTE RESOLUTION (ADR)

Counsel are required to furnish and discuss this Notice with their clients.

Despite the efforts of the courts to achieve a fair, timely and just outcome in all cases, litigation has become an often lengthy and expensive process. For this reason, it is this Court's policy to encourage parties to attempt to settle their disputes, whenever possible, through alternative dispute resolution (ADR).

ADR can reduce both the time it takes to resolve a case and the costs of litigation, which can be substantial. ADR options include mediation, arbitration (binding or non-binding), neutral evaluation (NE), conciliation, mini-trial and fact-finding. ADR can be either Court-directed or privately conducted.

The Court's ADR Program offers mediation through a panel of qualified and impartial attorneys who will encourage the fair, speedy and economic resolution of civil actions. Panel Mediators each have at least ten years of legal experience and are appointed by the Court. They volunteer their preparation time and the first three hours of a mediation session. This is a cost-effective way for parties to explore potential avenues of resolution.

This Court requires that counsel discuss with their clients the ADR options available and instructs them to come prepared to discuss the parties' choice of ADR option (settlement conference before a magistrate judge; Court Mediation Panel; private mediation) at the initial scheduling conference. Counsel are also required to indicate the client's choice of ADR option in advance of that conference. *See* Civil L.R. 26–1(c) and Fed.R.Civ.P. 26(f).

Clients and their counsel should carefully consider the anticipated expense of litigation, the uncertainties as to outcome, the time it will take to get to trial, the time an appeal will take if a decision is appealed, the burdens on a client's time, and the costs and expenses of litigation in relation to the amounts or stakes involved.

With more than 14,700 civil cases filed in the District in 2013, less than 1 percent actually went to trial. Most cases are settled between the parties; voluntarily dismissed; resolved through Court-directed or other forms of ADR; or dismissed by the Court as lacking in merit or for other reasons provided by law.

For more information about the Court's ADR Program, the Mediation Panel, and the profiles of mediators, visit the Court website, www.cacd.uscourts.gov, under "ADR."

[Effective January, 2012. Amended effective July, 2012; May 13, 2013; September, 2014.]

**EXHIBIT D.   NOTICE TO PARTIES OF COURT–DIRECTED
ADR PROGRAM—VACATING REFERRAL**

UNITED STATES DISTRICT COURT
CENTRAL DISTRICT OF CALIFORNIA

CASE NUMBER

Plaintiff(s)

v.

NOTICE TO PARTIES OF COURT–DIRECTED
ADR PROGRAM—VACATING REFERRAL

Defendant(s).

TO: ALL PARTIES OF RECORD

Reference of the above-captioned case to the Court–Directed ADR Program, General Order No. 11–10, § 5, is vacated. All further ADR procedures in this action shall be pursuant to General Order No. 11–10, § 6, and Civil L.R. 16–15.

Clerk, U.S. District Court

Dated: _____   By: _____
                                     Deputy Clerk

[Effective January, 2012.]

EXHIBIT E. STIPULATION REGARDING SELECTION OF PANEL MEDIATOR

Name, Address and Telephone Number of
Attorney(s):

_____

**UNITED STATES DISTRICT COURT
CENTRAL DISTRICT OF CALIFORNIA**
CASE NUMBER

_____

Plaintiff(s)

v.   _____

**STIPULATION REGARDING
SELECTION OF PANEL MEDIATOR**

Defendant(s).   _____

CHECK ONLY ONE BOX:

☐   The parties stipulate that _____ may serve as the
Panel Mediator in the above-captioned case. Plaintiff has obtained the Panel
Mediator's consent to conduct the mediation.

☐   The parties request that the ADR Program staff assign to the above-
captioned case a Panel Mediator with expertise in the following area of law:
_____

Dated: _____   _____
                                Attorney for Plaintiff _____

Dated: _____   _____
                                Attorney for Plaintiff _____

Dated: _____   _____
                                Attorney for Defendant _____

Dated: _____   _____
                                Attorney for Defendant _____

Attorney for Plaintiff to electronically file original document.

[Effective January, 2012.]

EXHIBIT F. NOTICE OF ASSIGNMENT OF PANEL MEDIATOR

UNITED STATES DISTRICT COURT
CENTRAL DISTRICT OF CALIFORNIA

CASE NUMBER

Plaintiff(s)

v.

_____

NOTICE OF ASSIGNMENT
OF PANEL MEDIATOR

Defendant(s).   _____

_____ is assigned to serve as the Panel Mediator in the above captioned case. This assignment is made because:

☐ The parties have stipulated to appointment of the Panel Mediator.

☐ The ADR Program staff has assigned the Panel Mediator.

The mediation in this case is to be completed no later than:

☐ _____, as ordered by the assigned judge.

☐ forty-five days prior to the final pretrial conference, consistent with Civil L.R. 16–15.2.

Counsel shall familiarize themselves with the requirements of General Order No. 11–10 which governs the ADR Program. Within thirty (30) days of this Notice, the Mediator will communicate with counsel to set the date of the mediation within the time requirements set forth above. *See* General Order No. 11–10, § 8.1.

Counsel are reminded that the written mediation statements which may be required by the Mediator (*see* General Order No. 11–10, § 8.4) shall NOT be filed with the Court. Counsel are further reminded that each party shall appear at the mediation in person or by a representative with final authority to settle the case. *See* General Order No. 11–10, § 8.5.

Clerk, U.S. District Court

Dated: _____   By: _____

ADR Program Director

ADR Program Office to electronically file original and cc: Mediator

[Effective January, 2012.]

EXHIBIT G.   NOTICE OF MEDIATION DATE

UNITED STATES DISTRICT COURT
CENTRAL DISTRICT OF CALIFORNIA

CASE NUMBER

Plaintiff(s)

v.

NOTICE OF
MEDIATION DATE

Defendant(s).

**YOU ARE HEREBY NOTIFIED THAT THE PANEL MEDIATOR HAS
SCHEDULED A MEDIATION IN THE ABOVE–CAPTIONED CASE**
for _____ at _____ ☐a.m. / ☐p.m.
LOCATION: _____
**The mediation session must be completed and an ADR–03 Report must be filed
on or before the Court-ordered completion date.**
Continuances are not favored and can only be granted by the Mediator up to the
Court-ordered completion date. Absent extraordinary circumstances, parties cannot
request a continuance within three (3) business days of a scheduled mediation.
Dated: _____   **Panel Mediator:** _____
                                        Address: _____
                                                             _____
                                                             _____
                                        Phone: _____

[Effective January, 2012.]

EXHIBIT H.   MEDIATION ATTENDANCE FORM

The Court deleted form ADR–18, *Mediation Attendance Form*, effective August 29, 2013.

[Effective January, 2012. Deleted effective August 29, 2013.]

EXHIBIT I.   ADR PROGRAM SURVEY FOR MEDIATORS AND REPORT OF PAYMENT

The Court deleted and replaced the form ADR–16, *Survey for Mediators and Report of Payment*, with an online system (Survey Monkey) to capture the responses to surveys from Panel Mediators. The survey is available on the ADR page of the Court website.

[Effective January, 2012. Abrogated effective August 29, 2013.]

EXHIBIT J.   ADR PROGRAM PARTICIPATION SURVEY

The Court deleted and replaced the form ADR–15, *ADR Program Participant Survey*, with an online system (Survey Monkey) to capture the responses to surveys from mediation participants. The survey is available on the ADR page of the Court website.

[Effective January, 2012. Abrogated effective August 29, 2013.]

EXHIBIT K.   MEDIATION REPORT

UNITED STATES DISTRICT COURT
CENTRAL DISTRICT OF CALIFORNIA

CASE NUMBER

Plaintiff(s)

v.
_____

MEDIATION REPORT

Defendant(s).
_____

Instructions: The mediator must file this Report within 5 days after the conclusion of a mediation session even if the negotiations continue. If the case later settles with the assistance of the mediator, the mediator must file a subsequent Report.

1. ☐ A mediation was held on (date): _____.

    ☐ A mediation did not take place because the case settled before the session occurred.

2. ☐ The individual parties and their respective trial counsel, designated corporate representatives, and/or representatives of the party's insurer:

    ☐ Appeared as required by Civil L.R. 16–15.5(b).

    ☐ Did not appear as required by Civil L.R. 16–15.5(b).

        ☐ Plaintiff or plaintiff's representative failed to appear.

        ☐ Defendant or defendant's representative failed to appear.

        ☐ Other:

3. ☐ Did the case settle?

    ☐ Yes, fully, on _____ (date).

    ☐ Yes, partially, and further facilitated discussions are expected. *(See No. 4 below.)*

    ☐ Yes, partially, and further facilitated discussions are **not** expected.

    ☐ No, and further facilitated discussions are expected. *(See No. 4 below.)*

    ☐ No, and further facilitated discussions are **not** expected.

4. ☐ If further facilitated discussions are expected, by what date will you check in with the parties? _____

Dated: _____   _____

                                           Signature of Mediator

                                     _____

                                           Name of Mediator (print)

The Mediator is to electronically file original document.

Instructions: The mediator must file this Report within 5 days after the conclusion of a mediation session even if the negotiations continue. If the case later settles with the assistance of the mediator, the mediator must file a subsequent Report.

1. ☐ A mediation was held on (date): _____.

    ☐ A mediation did not take place because the case settled before the session occurred.

2. ☐ The individual parties and their respective trial counsel, designated corporate representatives, and/or representatives of the party's insurer:

    ☐ Appeared as required by Civil L.R. 16–15.5(b).

    ☐ Did not appear as required by Civil L.R. 16–15.5(b).

        ☐ Plaintiff or plaintiff's representative failed to appear.

        ☐ Defendant or defendant's representative failed to appear.

        ☐ Other:

3. ☐ Did the case settle?

    ☐ Yes, fully, on _____ (date).

    ☐ Yes, partially, and further facilitated discussions are expected. *(See No. 4 below.)*

    ☐ Yes, partially, and further facilitated discussions are **not** expected.

    ☐ No, and further facilitated discussions are expected. *(See No. 4 below.)*

    ☐ No, and further facilitated discussions are **not** expected.

4. ☐ If further facilitated discussions are expected, by what date will you check in with the parties? _____.

        Dated: _____   _____

                                                Signature of Mediator

                                  _____

                                     Name of Mediator (print)

        The Mediator is to electronically file original document.

[Effective January, 2012; January, 2014.]

EXHIBIT L. MEDIATION CONFIDENTIALITY AGREEMENT

UNITED STATES DISTRICT COURT
CENTRAL DISTRICT OF CALIFORNIA
CASE NUMBER:

Plaintiff(s)
v.
_____

MEDIATION
CONFIDENTIALITY AGREEMENT

Defendant(s). _____

RETURN A COPY OF THIS AGREEMENT TO THE ADR PROGRAM OFFICE. DO NOT FILE WITH THE COURT.

Consistent with Central District of California Civil L.R. 16–15, General Order 11–10, related Federal Rules of Evidence and to the extent applicable, California Evidence Code Sections 703.5 and 1115–1128, the participants in mediation in the above-captioned case agree that:

1. No written or oral communication made by any party, attorney, mediator or other participant in a mediation in the above-named case may be used for any purpose in any pending or future proceeding unless all parties, including the mediator, so agree.

2. The parties agree that evidence admissible or subject to discovery or disclosure shall not be inadmissible or protected from disclosure solely by reason of its introduction or use in the mediation. Disclosure of information that otherwise is privileged shall not alter its privileged character.

3. The parties shall not subpoena the mediator or any documents submitted to or prepared by the mediator in connection with or during the mediation. The mediator shall not testify voluntarily on behalf of a party.

4. This agreement shall not preclude the reporting of information to the Central District of California ADR Program Office pursuant to General Order 11–10.

5. In an action or proceeding to enforce a settlement, this agreement shall not render inadmissable a written settlement agreement, or a settlement placed on the record, reached as a result of the mediation.

Dated: _____   _____

Print Name _____   Print Name _____

Signature _____   Signature _____

Email address _____   Email address _____

Describe Role in Mediation _____   Describe Role in Mediation _____

Print Name _____   Print Name _____

Signature	Signature
Email address	Email address
Describe Role in Mediation	Describe Role in Mediation
Print Name	Print Name
Signature	Signature
Email address	Email address
Describe Role in Mediation	Describe Role in Mediation
Print Name	Print Name
Signature	Signature
Email address	Email address
Describe Role in Mediation	Describe Role in Mediation
Print Name	Print Name
Signature	Signature
Email address	Email address
Describe Role in Mediation	Describe Role in Mediation

NOTE: If additional signatures are required, attach an additional page to this request.

[Amended effective August 29, 2013; January, 2014.]

GENERAL ORDER NO. 12–02. IN THE MATTER OF DIRECT ASSIGNMENT OF CIVIL CASES TO MAGISTRATE JUDGES

1. **IT IS ORDERED** that every full-time magistrate judge who has completed thirty-six months of service with the Court and maintains his or her regular caseload as determined by the Court shall

be included in the pool of judicial officers available for random selection as the assigned judge for all civil cases, except in those cases excluded below. A full-time magistrate judge without thirty-six months of service who maintains his or her caseload as determined by the Court may volunteer to be included in the pool of judicial officers available for random selection.

2. Except in the categories of cases described below, each eligible magistrate judge shall be randomly assigned two civil cases each month, and no district judge will be assigned to those cases, except as provided hereafter. A magistrate judge may volunteer to be assigned more than two cases each month.

3. **Cases Excluded.** The following categories of cases are excluded from direct assignment to magistrate judges: class actions, death penalty habeas corpus petitions, bankruptcy appeals or bankruptcy withdrawal of reference cases, cases referred to a magistrate judge for a Report and Recommendation under General Order 05–07 (as amended by General Order 06–01) or any successor General Order, and cases in which a request for a temporary restraining order or motion for preliminary injunction is presented when the action is initiated.

4. **Clerk's Notice and Consent Form.** When a case is randomly assigned to a magistrate judge, the Clerk shall provide a Notice and Consent Form to the plaintiff or removing party, who must serve the Notice and Consent Form on each party at the time of service of the summons and complaint or other initial pleading. The Notice shall instruct the parties, if they agree to a magistrate judge's exercise of jurisdiction over the case, to file a joint statement or separate statements of consent. A separate statement of consent must be filed by newly-added parties, setting forth such an election, in order for the magistrate judge to retain civil trial jurisdiction. The Notice shall advise the parties that they are free to withhold consent without adverse substantive consequences. The parties shall file the statement(s) of consent no later than the time provided in the Local Rules of this court.

5. **Magistrate Judge Serves as Judge for All Purposes.** The assigned magistrate judge initially shall be responsible for all case management and scheduling activities and shall decide all non-dispositive pretrial and discovery matters. If all parties consent in writing to the magistrate judge's exercise of civil trial jurisdiction, the case shall remain assigned to the magistrate judge for all purposes, including trial and entry of final judgment pursuant to 28 U.S.C. § 636(c) and Federal Rule of Civil Procedure 73. Appeal from a final judgment entered at a magistrate judge's direction may be taken to the court of appeals as would any other appeal from a district court judgment.

6. **Reassignment of Case.** A case initially assigned to a magistrate judge pursuant to this Order shall be randomly reassigned to a district judge if a party has not consented to the exercise of jurisdiction by the magistrate judge within the time required by the Local Rules. A magistrate judge shall be randomly assigned to the reassigned case as the discovery judge.

7. If, prior to the statement(s) of consent being filed, a party files a motion or application that the magistrate judge determines is a motion for review under L.R. 72–2.1, the motion shall be determined by the Chief District Judge or shall be randomly assigned to a district judge for determination.

8. If, prior to the statement(s) of consent being filed, a party files a motion or application that the magistrate judge concludes he or she lacks authority to rule upon, and, in the magistrate judge's view, the motion or application may require immediate judicial attention, the motion or application shall be determined by the Chief District Judge or shall be randomly assigned to a district judge for determination.

9. If, prior to the statement(s) of consent being filed, a magistrate judge has issued an order to show cause why the case should not be dismissed or remanded or why a default judgment should not be entered, and the time for response to the Order to Show Cause has expired, the determination of whether the case should be dismissed or remanded or a default should be entered shall be made by the Chief District Judge or the matter shall be randomly assigned to a district judge for resolution. If the district judge does not dismiss or remand the case or enter judgment by default, the case shall remain with the magistrate judge for further proceedings consistent with this General Order and the Local Rules.

10. This General Order shall be effective upon filing by the Clerk. The program governed by this General Order shall be reviewed two years after April 20, 2011.

[Dated: April 6, 2012.]

GENERAL ORDER NO. 13–05. IN THE MATTER OF REFERENCE OF CASES AND PROCEEDINGS TO THE BANKRUPTCY JUDGES OF THE CENTRAL DISTRICT OF CALIFORNIA, AND REFERENCE OF APPEALS TO THE BANKRUPTCY APPELLATE PANEL

(Supersedes General Order Nos. 266, 266–A, 269, and 96–04)

The following is hereby ORDERED:

(1) **Referral of Bankruptcy Cases and Proceedings.** Pursuant to 28 U.S.C. § 157(a), the Court hereby refers to the bankruptcy judges for the Central District of California all cases under Title 11 of the United States Code ("Title 11") and all proceedings arising under Title 11 or arising in or related to a case under Title 11.

(2) **Authority of Bankruptcy Judges.** The bankruptcy judges of the Central District of California may, upon consent of the parties, hear, determine, and enter final orders and judgments in any proceeding referred to the bankruptcy judges under this court's General Orders, regardless of whether that proceeding may be designated as "core" or "non-core" within the meaning of 28 U.S.C. § 157. Absent the parties' consent, the bankruptcy judges of the Central District of California may:

(a) hear, determine, and enter final orders and judgments in all cases under Title 11 and all core proceedings arising under Title 11, or arising in a case under Title 11, that may be heard and determined by a non-Article III tribunal; and

(b) in non-core proceedings, and in core proceedings that may not be determined by a non-Article III tribunal, hear proceedings and submit proposed findings of fact and conclusions of law to the district court; any final order or judgment in such a proceeding shall be entered by the district judge after considering the bankruptcy judge's proposed findings and conclusions and after reviewing de novo those matters to which any party has timely and specifically objected.

(3) **Jury Trials.** Pursuant to 28 U.S.C. § 157(e), the court hereby specially designates all bankruptcy judges of the Central District of California to conduct jury trials, with the express consent of all the parties, in all proceedings referred to the bankruptcy judges under this court's General Orders in which the right to a jury trial applies. Jury trials in bankruptcy court shall be subject to the jury plan in effect for the Central District. If the parties consent to a jury trial in a proceeding before a bankruptcy judge, they will be deemed to have consented to the entry of a final order by the bankruptcy judge in that proceeding.

(4) **Transferring Cases Back to District Court.** If the bankruptcy judge to whom a case is assigned determines that a specific case or proceeding should be heard in the district court, that bankruptcy judge may, on the judge's own motion, transfer the case or proceeding to the district court. The transfer order shall include a statement of legal authorization as to the basis for transfer to the district court.

(5) **Appeals.** Pursuant to 28 U.S.C. § 158(b)(2), the court hereby authorizes a bankruptcy appellate panel to hear and determine, upon the consent of all the parties: appeals from final judgments, orders, and decrees entered by bankruptcy judges from this district; and, with leave of the panel, appeals from interlocutory judgments, orders, and decrees entered by bankruptcy judges from this district. The appeals the bankruptcy appellate panel may hear under this paragraph include: appeals filed in the district court on or after July 10, 1984, the effective date of enactment of the Bankruptcy Amendments and Federal Judgeship Act of 1984 ("Act"); and appeals transferred from the bankruptcy appellate panel to the district court pursuant to section 115(b) of the Act.

(6) **Effective Date.** This General Order shall become effective upon filing by the Clerk of this Court.

[Dated: July 1, 2013.]

GENERAL ORDER NO. 13–09. IN THE MATTER OF PLAN FOR THE COMPOSITION, ADMINISTRATION, AND MANAGEMENT OF THE PANEL OF PRIVATE ATTORNEYS UNDER THE CRIMINAL JUSTICE ACT

(Supersedes General Order Nos. 98–06, 07–06, and 08–08)

The Criminal Justice Act of 1964, as amended (18 U.S.C. § 3006A) (the "CJA"), requires each United States district court to place in operation a plan for furnishing representation for any person financially unable to obtain adequate representation in certain circumstances. The Court has established such a plan (the "Criminal Justice Act Plan").

IT IS HEREBY ORDERED that the attached Plan for the Composition, Administration and Management of the Panel of Private Attorneys under the Criminal Justice Act is adopted by the Court.

This General Order shall be effective upon approval of the Criminal Justice Act Plan by the Judicial Council of the Ninth Circuit.

I. AUTHORITY

Pursuant to the Criminal Justice Act of 1964, as amended (18 U.S.C. § 3006A) (the "CJA"), and the *Guidelines for Administering the CJA and Related Statutes* ("*CJA Guidelines*"), Volume 7A of the *Guide to Judiciary Policy*, the judges of the United States District Court for the Central District of California adopt this amended Plan for furnishing representation in federal court in accordance with the CJA for any person financially unable to pay for adequate representation.

II. STATEMENT OF POLICY

A. Objectives.

1. The objective of this Plan is to attain equality before the law for all persons. Therefore, this Plan will be administered so that those accused of crimes, or otherwise eligible for services under the CJA, will not be deprived because they are financially unable to pay for an adequate defense.

2. The further objective of this Plan is to tailor the requirements of the CJA, the USA Patriot Improvement and Reauthorization Act of 2005 (recodified at 18 U.S.C. § 3599), and the *CJA Guidelines* in a way that meets the needs of this district.

B. Compliance.

1. The Office of the Federal Public Defender (to the extent applicable) and all private attorneys appointed under the CJA must comply with: (1) the CJA Guidelines approved by the Judicial Conference of the United States or its Committee on Defender Services; (2) this Plan; (3) the Central District of California CJA Trial Attorney Panel Manual (the "Panel Manual"); and (4) all applicable local rules, General Orders, and local policies and procedures.

2. The Clerk of Court will maintain and make available on the Court's website a current copy of this Plan, the Panel Manual, a current copy of the *CJA Guidelines* and the Court-adopted policies, guidelines, and procedures related to the CJA for the use of members of the CJA Panel, and will make known to such attorneys their availability.

III. DEFINITIONS

A. "Representation" includes counsel and investigative, expert, and other services.

B. "Appointed attorney" includes private attorneys, the Federal Public Defender, and staff attorneys of the Office of the Federal Public Defender.

IV. PROVISION OF REPRESENTATION

A. Circumstance.

1. *Mandatory.* Representation **shall** be provided for any financially eligible person who:

a. is charged with a felony or a Class A misdemeanor;

b. is a juvenile alleged to have committed an act of juvenile delinquency as defined in 18 U.S.C. § 5031;

c. is charged with a violation of probation;

d. is under arrest, when such representation is required by law;

e. is charged with a violation of supervised release or faces modification, reduction, or enlargement of a condition, or extension or revocation of a term of supervised release;

f. is subject to a mental condition hearing under chapter 313 of title 18, United States Code;

g. is in custody as a material witness;

h. is entitled to appointment of counsel under the sixth amendment to the Constitution;

i. faces loss of liberty in a case, and Federal law requires the appointment of counsel; or

j. is entitled to the appointment of counsel under 18 U.S.C. § 4109;

k. or otherwise provided by law.

2. *Discretionary.* Whenever the United States magistrate judge or the court determines that the interests of justice so require, representation may be provided for any financially eligible person who:

a. is charged with a Class B or C misdemeanor, or an infraction for which a sentence to confinement is authorized;

b. is seeking relief under 28 U.S.C. §§ 2241, 2254, or 2255;

c. is charged with civil or criminal contempt and faces loss of liberty;

d. has been called as a witness before a grand jury, a court, the Congress, or a federal agency or commission which has the power to compel testimony, and there is reason to believe, either prior to or during testimony, that the witness could be subject to a criminal prosecution, a civil or criminal contempt proceeding, or face loss of liberty;

e. is proposed by the United States attorney for processing under a pretrial diversion program; or

f. is held for international extradition under chapter 209 of title 18, United States Code.

3. *Ancillary Matters.* Representation may also be furnished for financially eligible persons in ancillary matters appropriate to the proceedings under subsection (c) of the CJA.

B. Timely Appointment of Counsel. Counsel shall be provided to eligible persons as soon as feasible after they are taken into custody, when they appear before a district judge or magistrate judge, when they are formally charged or notified of charges if formal charges are sealed, or when a district judge or magistrate judge otherwise considers appointment of counsel appropriate under the CJA, whichever occurs earliest.

C. Number and Qualifications of Counsel.

1. *Number.* More than one attorney may be appointed in any case determined by the Court to be extremely difficult. Such appointments of co-counsel or associate counsel should be rarely made and only in exceptional circumstances. Such appointments should be made only upon a showing of good cause and in furtherance of the interests of justice, the best interests of the client, and cost-savings to the Court.

In a capital case, the following applies:

a. Federal Capital Prosecutions. Pursuant to 18 U.S.C. § 3005, a person charged with a federal capital offense is entitled to the appointment of two attorneys, at least one of whom must be learned in the law applicable to capital cases. Pursuant to 18 U.S.C. § 3599(a)(1), if necessary for adequate representation, more than two attorneys may be appointed to represent a defendant in such a case.

b. Capital Habeas Corpus Proceedings. Pursuant to 18 U.S.C. § 3599(a)(2), a financially eligible person seeking to vacate or set aside a death sentence in proceedings under 28 U.S.C. §§ 2254 or 2255 is entitled to appointment of one or more qualified attorneys. Due to the complex, demanding, and protracted nature of death penalty proceedings, judicial officers should consider appointing at least two counsel.

2. *Qualifications.* Qualifications for appointed counsel shall be determined by the Court. In capital cases, the following also applies:

a. Appointment of Counsel Prior to Judgment. Pursuant to 18 U.S.C. § 3599(b), at least one of the attorneys appointed must have been admitted to practice in the court in which the case will be prosecuted for not less than five years, and must have had not less than three years experience in the actual trial of felony prosecutions in that court. Pursuant to 18 U.S.C. § 3005, at least one of the attorneys appointed must be knowledgeable in the law applicable to capital cases. Pursuant to

18 U.S.C. § 3005, in appointing counsel in capital prosecutions, the Court shall consider the recommendation of the Federal Public Defender.

b. **Appointment of Counsel After Judgment.** Pursuant to 18 U.S.C. § 3599(c), at least one of the attorneys appointed must have been admitted to practice in the court of appeals for not less than five years, and must have had not less than three years experience in the handling of appeals in felony cases in the court.

c. **Attorney Qualification Waiver.** Pursuant to 18 U.S.C. § 3599(d), the presiding judicial officer, for good cause, may appoint an attorney who may not qualify under 18 U.S.C. § 3599(b) or (c), but who has the background, knowledge, and experience necessary to represent the defendant properly in a capital case, giving due consideration to the seriousness of the possible penalty and the unique and complex nature of the litigation.

d. **Presumptive Qualification of the Office of the Federal Public Defender.** The Office of the Federal Public Defender is qualified for assignment of any capital case without further inquiry.

D. Eligibility for Representation.

1. *Fact Finding.* The determination of eligibility for representation under the CJA is a judicial function to be performed by a district judge or magistrate judge after making appropriate inquiries concerning the person's financial condition.

2. *Disclosure of Change in Eligibility.* If, at any time after appointment, counsel obtains information that a client is financially able to make payment, in whole or in part, for legal or other services in connection with his or her representation, and the source of the attorney's information is not protected as a privileged communication, counsel shall advise the Court.

V. OFFICE OF THE FEDERAL PUBLIC DEFENDER

A. Establishment.

1. The Office of the Federal Public Defender of the Central District of California, previously established in this district pursuant to the provisions of the CJA, is the federal public defender organization for this district.

2. The Office of the Federal Public Defender shall be responsible for providing legal services throughout the district.

B. Supervision of the Office of the Federal Public Defender. The Federal Public Defender shall be responsible for the supervision and management of the Office of the Federal Public Defender. Accordingly, the Federal Public Defender will be appointed in all cases assigned to that office for subsequent assignment to staff attorneys at the discretion of the Federal Public Defender.

VI. PRIVATE ATTORNEYS

A. Establishment of the CJA Trial Attorney Panel. This District maintains a panel of attorneys ("CJA Trial Attorney Panel") who are eligible and willing to be appointed to provide representation under the CJA.

1. *Appointment of Counsel.* Private attorneys from the CJA Trial Attorney Panel shall be appointed in the cases in which the Federal Public Defender has a conflict of interest or is otherwise unable to accept appointment.

2. *Appointment of Non–Panel Attorneys in Exceptional Circumstances.* In exceptional circumstances where good cause has been shown (such as the interest of justice, judicial economy, or continuity of representation), an attorney who is not a Deputy Federal Public Defender or a member of the CJA Trial Attorney Panel may be appointed to represent the financially eligible person. Non-panel attorneys are subject to all of the CJA Trial Attorney Panel duties and obligations. In order to preserve the integrity of the panel selection process, such appointments should be rare.

3. *Composition, Administration, and Management.* Details regarding the organization and management of the CJA Trial Attorney Panel are contained in the Court's CJA Trial Attorney Panel Manual, and may be amended as necessary.

4. *Continuing Legal Education and Training.* Panel members are required to complete eight hours of continuing legal education in the area of criminal law each year. The Office of Defender

Services and the Federal Public Defender's Office provide a wide variety of training programs that are available to panel members at no cost. Many of the training programs offered by the Office of Defender Services qualify for California's MCLE requirements. The Federal Public Defender for the Central District of California is an approved MCLE provider for the State Bar of California. In addition, panel members are required to attend one annual meeting of the entire CJA Trial Attorney Panel. This meeting addresses issues concerning the administration of the panel, and provides training for panel members. Additional professional conduct requirements and panel member qualifications are referenced in the Panel Manual.

5. *Removal.* Panel attorneys serve at the pleasure of the Court, as membership is a privilege, not a right. An attorney may be suspended or removed from the panel at any time at the discretion of the CJA Committee. The CJA Committee may also decide to do one or more of the following: renew an attorney for a term less than three years, place the attorney on probation, require training, or take any other action or impose any other conditions it deems appropriate. While the suspension or removal is considered final by the Court, an attorney may submit an application for panel membership, if he or she believes performance issues have been adequately addressed. An application may be submitted for a term beginning at least one full year after the suspension, removal, or non-renewal.

There is no right to review the CJA Committee's decisions concerning panel membership, including selection, non-renewal, and removal.

B. Establishment of Capital Habeas Attorney Panel. This District maintains a panel of attorneys qualified for appointment to represent petitioners in capital habeas corpus cases ("Capital Habeas Attorney Panel").

1. *Appointment of Counsel.* In cases in which appointment of counsel is mandatory under Part IV.A.1.i, supra, the Court shall appoint the Federal Public Defender as counsel of record where there is no conflict of interest, up to a fixed number of cases each year consistent with funding and staffing levels of the Office of the Federal Public Defender related to these types of cases. If the Office of the Federal Public Defender has already been assigned the maximum number of cases as determined by the Defender Services Committee of the United States Judicial Conference, and has not agreed to an excess appointment, or is otherwise prevented from accepting the appointment, the Court shall appoint counsel from the Capital Habeas Attorney Panel, pursuant to Local Rule 83–17 of the Local Rules for the United States District Court for the Central District of California, and General Order 10–08, or any successor local rule or general order.

2. *Composition, Administration, and Management.* Details regarding the establishment and administration of the Capital Habeas Attorney Panel are contained in General Order 10–08, or any successor local rule or general order, and the Court's CJA Trial Attorney Panel Manual, and may be amended as necessary.

C. Establishment of Appellate Attorney Panel. This District maintains a panel of attorneys qualified for appointment to represent petitioners in appellate cases ("Appellate Attorney Panel"). The appointment, composition, administration, and management of the appellate panel was delegated by the Ninth Circuit to the Office of the Federal Public Defender in 1996.

VII. DUTIES OF APPOINTED COUNSEL

A. Standards. The quality of representation to be rendered to a person represented by appointed counsel will be commensurate with the quality rendered if counsel were privately employed by the person. Counsel shall fulfill his or her professional responsibility as an officer of the Court, and the limited amount of compensation accruing in no respect diminishes such responsibility. Counsel who is unable to personally fulfill his or her obligation to a defendant for any reason should immediately so notify the assigned judge and the CJA Committee Chair in writing.

B. Professional Conduct. Attorneys appointed pursuant to the CJA must conform to the highest standards of professional conduct. Each attorney must be familiar with and comply with the standards of professional conduct required of members of the State Bar of California and contained in the State Bar Act, the Rules of Professional Conduct of the State Bar of California, and the decisions of any applicable court. These statutes, rules, and decisions are the standards of professional conduct. The Model Code of Professional Conduct of the American Bar Association may be considered for guidance.

C. No Receipt of Other Payment. Appointed counsel may not require, request, or accept any payment or promise of payment or any other valuable consideration from any source for representation or expenses under the appointment, unless such payment is approved by order of the Court.

D. Continuing Representation. The objective of this Plan is to maintain continuity of counsel wherever possible barring a conflict of interest. Once counsel is appointed under the CJA, counsel shall continue the representation through the earliest of the following: (1) exhaustion of all appeals and any review by certiorari (as governed by Ninth Circuit Rule 4-1 or any successor Rule or Plan addressing appointment and continuity of counsel); (2) substitution of counsel has been approved by the Court; or (3) entry of an order allowing the person represented to proceed pro se. Counsel desiring to be relieved from representation on appeal must comply with Ninth Circuit Rule 4-1, or any successor Rule or Plan.

Appointment as counsel also requires representation of the client in connection with issues concerning probation revocation, supervised release violations and remand following appeal, provided the client qualifies for representation under the CJA, and the trial attorney panel member remains on the panel, unless either of items (2) or (3) above has occurred, or unless otherwise specifically ordered by the Court.

VIII. RESOURCES

Answers to questions concerning appointment under the Act can generally be found in the applicable federal statutes: 18 U.S.C. § 3006A—Adequate Representation of Defendants, 18 U.S.C. § 3005—Counsel and Witnesses in Capital Cases, 18 U.S.C. § 3599—Counsel for Financially Unable Defendants, 18 U.S.C. § 983(b)—Civil Forfeiture Proceedings), the Guide to Judiciary Policy, Vol. 7, the CJA section of the Court's website (http://www.cacd.uscourts.gov/attorneys/cja), and this Court's CJA Trial Attorney Panel Manual. All other questions should be directed to the CJA Supervising Attorney.

IX. SUPERSESSION

This Plan supersedes all prior Criminal Justice Act Plans of this Court.

X. EFFECTIVE DATE

This Plan shall become effective when approved by the Judicial Council of the Ninth Circuit.

[Dated: July 30, 2013. Approved by the Judicial Council of the Ninth Circuit September 10, 2013. Filed: September 17, 2013.]

GENERAL ORDER NO. 20–04. IN THE MATTER OF ADOPTION OF STANDARD CONDITIONS OF PROBATION AND SUPERVISED RELEASE AND SENTENCING ORDERS AND CONDITIONS OF PROBATION AND SUPERVISED RELEASE PERTAINING TO FINANCIAL SANCTIONS [SUPERSEDES GENERAL ORDER NO. 18–10]

This General Order supersedes General Order No. 18–10. IT IS HEREBY ORDERED that the Judges of the Central District of California adopt: (1) the standard conditions of probation and supervised release set forth in Section I, below, to apply in every case in which probation or supervised release is imposed; (2) the sentencing orders set forth in Section II, below, to apply in every case in which a fine or restitution has been ordered; and (3) the conditions of probation and supervised release set forth in Section III, below, to apply in every case in which probation or supervised release is imposed in addition to the imposition of a fine or restitution. The presiding judge may impose any other conditions the judge deems advisable, consistent with existing or future law, in individual cases of supervision.

I. STANDARD CONDITIONS OF PROBATION AND SUPERVISED RELEASE

1) The defendant must not commit another federal, state, or local crime;

2) The defendant must report to the probation office in the federal judicial district of residence within 72 hours of imposition of a sentence of probation or release from imprisonment, unless otherwise directed by the probation officer;

3) The defendant must report to the probation office as instructed by the court or probation officer;

4) The defendant must not knowingly leave the judicial district without first receiving the permission of the court or probation officer;

5) The defendant must answer truthfully the inquiries of the probation officer, unless legitimately asserting his or her Fifth Amendment right against self-incrimination as to new criminal conduct;

6) The defendant must reside at a location approved by the probation officer and must notify the probation officer at least 10 days before any anticipated change or within 72 hours of an unanticipated change in residence or persons living in defendant's residence;

7) The defendant must permit the probation officer to contact him or her at any time at home or elsewhere and must permit confiscation of any contraband prohibited by law or the terms of supervision and observed in plain view by the probation officer;

8) The defendant must work at a lawful occupation unless excused by the probation officer for schooling, training, or other acceptable reasons and must notify the probation officer at least ten days before any change in employment or within 72 hours of an unanticipated change;

9) The defendant must not knowingly associate with any persons engaged in criminal activity and must not knowingly associate with any person convicted of a felony unless granted permission to do so by the probation officer. This condition will not apply to intimate family members, unless the court has completed an individualized review and has determined that the restriction is necessary for protection of the community or rehabilitation;

10) The defendant must refrain from excessive use of alcohol and must not purchase, possess, use, distribute, or administer any narcotic or other controlled substance, or any paraphernalia related to such substances, except as prescribed by a physician;

11) The defendant must notify the probation officer within 72 hours of being arrested or questioned by a law enforcement officer;

12) For felony cases, the defendant must not possess a firearm, ammunition, destructive device, or any other dangerous weapon;

13) The defendant must not act or enter into any agreement with a law enforcement agency to act as an informant or source without the permission of the court;

14) As directed by the probation officer, the defendant must notify specific persons and organizations of specific risks posed by the defendant to those persons and organizations and must permit the probation officer to confirm the defendant's compliance with such requirement and to make such notifications;

15) The defendant must follow the instructions of the probation officer to implement the orders of the court, afford adequate deterrence from criminal conduct, protect the public from further crimes of the defendant; and provide the defendant with needed educational or vocational training, medical care, or other correctional treatment in the most effective manner.

II. STATUTORY PROVISIONS PERTAINING TO PAYMENT AND COLLECTION OF FINANCIAL SANCTIONS

1) The defendant must pay interest on a fine or restitution of more than $2,500, unless the court waives interest or unless the fine or restitution is paid in full before the fifteenth (15th) day after the

date of the judgment under 18 U.S.C. § 3612(f)(1). Payments may be subject to penalties for default and delinquency under 18 U.S.C. § 3612(g). Interest and penalties pertaining to restitution, however, are not applicable for offenses completed before April 24, 1996. Assessments, restitution, fines, penalties, and costs must be paid by certified check or money order made payable to "Clerk, U.S. District Court." Each certified check or money order must include the case name and number. Payments must be delivered to:

> United States District Court, Central District of California
> Attn: Fiscal Department
> 255 East Temple Street, Room 1178
> Los Angeles, CA 90012

or such other address as the Court may in future direct.

2) If all or any portion of a fine or restitution ordered remains unpaid after the termination of supervision, the defendant must pay the balance as directed by the United States Attorney's Office. 18 U.S.C. § 3613.

3) The defendant must notify the United States Attorney within thirty (30) days of any change in the defendant's mailing address or residence address until all fines, restitution, costs, and special assessments are paid in full. 18 U.S.C. § 3612(b)(1)(F).

4) The defendant must notify the Court (through the Probation Office) and the United States Attorney of any material change in the defendant's economic circumstances that might affect the defendant's ability to pay a fine or restitution, as required by 18 U.S.C. § 3664(k). The Court may also accept such notification from the government or the victim, and may, on its own motion or that of a party or the victim, adjust the manner of payment of a fine or restitution under 18 U.S.C. § 3664(k). See also 18 U.S.C. § 3572(d)(3) and for probation 18 U.S.C. § 3563(a)(7).

5) Payments will be applied in the following order:

a. Special assessments under 18 U.S.C. § 3013;

b. Restitution, in this sequence (under 18 U.S.C. § 3664(i), all nonfederal victims must be paid before the United States is paid):

> Non-federal victims (individual and corporate),
> Providers of compensation to non-federal victims,
> The United States as victim;

c. Fine;

d. Community restitution, under 18 U.S.C. § 3663(c); and

e. Other penalties and costs.

III. CONDITIONS OF PROBATION AND SUPERVISED RELEASE PERTAINING TO FINANCIAL SANCTIONS

1) As directed by the Probation Officer, the defendant must provide to the Probation Officer: (1) a signed release authorizing credit report inquiries; (2) federal and state income tax returns or a signed release authorizing their disclosure and (3) an accurate financial statement, with supporting documentation as to all assets, income and expenses of the defendant. In addition, the defendant must not apply for any loan or open any line of credit without prior approval of the Probation Officer.

2) The defendant must maintain one personal checking account. All of defendant's income, "monetary gains," or other pecuniary proceeds must be deposited into this account, which must be used for payment of all personal expenses. Records of all other bank accounts, including any business accounts, must be disclosed to the Probation Officer upon request.

3) The defendant must not transfer, sell, give away, or otherwise convey any asset with a fair market value in excess of $500 without approval of the Probation Officer until all financial obligations imposed by the Court have been satisfied in full.

This General Order will be effective upon filing by the Clerk.

[Dated: April 8, 2020.]

GENERAL ORDER NO. 21–02. IN RE: FEDERAL RULE OF CRIMINAL PROCEDURE 5(f) AND THE DUE PROCESS PROTECTIONS ACT

Pursuant to Federal Rule of Criminal Procedure 5(f) and the Due Process Protections Act, Pub. L. No. 116–182, 134 Stat. 894 (Oct. 21, 2020), the United States District Court for the Central District of California issues the following order:

In all criminal proceedings, the prosecutor is ordered to comply with the disclosure obligations under *Brady v. Maryland*, 373 U.S. 83 (1963), and its progeny and is reminded of the possible consequences of not doing so, including exclusion of evidence, adverse jury instructions, dismissal of charges, contempt, referral to a disciplinary authority, and sanctions.

The judge presiding at the first scheduled court date when both prosecutor and defense counsel are present shall inform the prosecution and defense of the substance of this Order and an acknowledgment of compliance with this requirement shall be reflected in the docket in each case.

[Dated: March 8, 2021.]

GENERAL ORDER NO. 21–05. IN THE MATTER OF ATTORNEY ADMISSION, ANNUAL RENEWAL, AND PRO HAC VICE FEES [SUPERCEDES GENERAL ORDER NO. 20–07]

IT IS HEREBY ORDERED that each applicant for admission to the Bar of the Central District of California must pay to the Clerk the admission fee of $188, as prescribed by the Judicial Conference of the United States, plus an additional fee that the Clerk will place to the credit of the Attorney Admission Fund. The total fee for admission to the Bar of this Court is therefore as follows:

Lawyers Admitted to the California Bar—Fewer than 3 Years:	$281
Lawyers Admitted to the California Bar—3 or More Years:	$331

IT IS HEREBY FURTHER ORDERED that, unless exempted by this General Order, every attorney who has been a member of the Bar of the Central District of California for at least one year must pay an annual renewal fee of $25. This annual renewal fee will be due on September 1 of each year for all attorneys admitted to the Court's Bar before September 1 of the prior year. Attorneys who fail to pay the fee by September 30 will be subject to removal from the rolls of the Court's Bar. Attorneys removed from the rolls of the Bar under this General Order must, in order to practice before this Court, reapply for membership under Local Rule 83–2.1.2.2 and pay the full fee for admission set forth above.

IT IS HEREBY FURTHER ORDERED that each applicant for permission to appear *pro hac vice* in a case pending before this Court must pay to the Clerk a fee of $500 per case, all of which the Clerk will place to the credit of the Attorney Admission Fund.

[Dated: April 2, 2021.]

SELECTED CLERK'S NOTICES

NOTICE: ELECTRONIC AVAILABILITY OF TRANSCRIPTS

At its September 2007 session, the Judicial Conference approved a new policy regarding the availability of transcripts of court proceedings. Effective May 27, 2008, all ordered transcripts will be electronically filed by the court reporter into the CM/ECF system.

The transcript will be available to attorneys of record or parties and the general public for viewing only in the Clerk's Office Records Section public terminal for a period of 90 days after it is filed. During this 90–day period, a copy of the transcript may be obtained from the court reporter or transcriber, and an attorney who obtains the transcript from the court reporter or transcriber will be given remote electronic access to the transcript through the CM/ECF system. Within 5 business days from the date of filing of the transcript, parties may electronically file a Notice of Intent to Redact. A Request to Redact specifying page and line number of the required redaction(s) shall be filed within 21 days from the filing of the transcript. Responsibility for redacting rests solely with counsel and the parties. The Clerk will not review the transcripts for compliance. (Please refer to Local Rule 79–5.4) After the 90–day period has ended, the transcript will be available through PACER.

If a notice to redact is electronically filed and the request to redact is not filed within the prescribed time period, an Order to Show Cause will be set by the Court. More information on this topic is available at the CM/ECF website accessible from www.cacd.uscourts.gov.

[Adopted effective May 27, 2008.]

INDEX TO
UNITED STATES DISTRICT COURT
FOR THE CENTRAL DISTRICT OF CALIFORNIA

UNITED STATES DISTRICT COURT
FOR THE SOUTHERN DISTRICT OF CALIFORNIA

Including Amendments Received Through
December 1, 2021

PREAMBLE TO LOCAL RULES

The Local Rules of Practice for the United States District Court for the Southern District of California are contained herein. These rules are divided into two parts: civil and criminal. Civil rules may be cited as "CivLR___"; criminal rules may be cited as "CrimLR___."

Rules covering admiralty and habeas corpus proceedings may be found at the end of the civil rules, cited as A.1–E.1; and HC.1, HC.2, et seq.

[Effective August 18, 1997.]

CIVIL LOCAL RULES

CIVIL RULE 1.1   SCOPE AND AVAILABILITY OF LOCAL RULES

a. Title and Citation. These are the Local Civil Rules of Practice for the United States District Court for the Southern District of California. They may be cited as "CivLR ____."

b. Effective Date. These Rules become effective on January 30, 2016.

c. Scope of the Rules; Construction, Definitions. These rules supplement the Federal Rules of Civil Procedure, and they must be construed so as to be consistent with those rules and to promote the just, efficient and economical determination of every action and proceeding. The provisions of the Civil Rules must apply to all actions and proceedings, including criminal, bankruptcy and admiralty, and actions and proceedings before magistrate judges, except where they may be inconsistent with rules or provisions of law specifically applicable thereto.

d. In any case for the convenience of the parties in interest, or in the interest of justice, a judge may waive the applicability of these rules.

e. Definitions.

1. "Attorney" or "counsel" includes an attorney, proctor, advocate, solicitor, counsel, or counselor;

2. "Brief" includes briefs, memoranda, points and authorities and other written argument or compilation of authorities;

3. "Civil action" includes any action, case, proceeding or matter of a civil nature;

4. "Clerk" means the Clerk of the United States District Court for the Southern District of California and deputy clerks, unless the context otherwise requires;

5. "Court" includes the district judge or magistrate judge to whom a civil or criminal action, proceeding, case or matter has been assigned;

6. "Court Clerk" means a deputy clerk assigned to the courtroom of a judge or magistrate judge of this Court;

7. "Declaration" includes any declaration under penalty of perjury executed in conformance with 28 U.S.C. § 1746, and any properly executed affidavit;

8. "Defendant" means any party against whom a claim for relief is made or against whom an indictment or information is pending in a criminal case;

9. "Fed.R.App.P." means the Federal Rules of Appellate Procedure;

10. "Fed.R.Civ.P." means the Federal Rules of Civil Procedure;

11. "Fed.R.Crim.P." means the Federal Rules of Criminal Procedure;

12. "Fed.R.Evid." means the Federal Rules of Evidence;

13. "File" means the delivery to and acceptance by the Clerk or the court clerk of a document which will be noted in the civil or criminal docket;

14. "Judge" refers to any United States District Judge exercising jurisdiction with respect to a particular action or proceeding in said court or, to a part-time or full-time United States Magistrate Judge, to whom such action or proceeding has been assigned for purposes relevant to the context in which such reference occurs;

15. "Lodge" means to submit by email or otherwise any document(s) to the Clerk of Court (unless otherwise specified by these rules or by order of the Court);

16. "Motion" includes all motions, applications, petitions or other requests made for judicial action;

17. "Person" includes natural person, corporation, partnership or other association of individuals;

18. "Plaintiff" means any party claiming affirmative relief by complaint, counterclaim or cross-claim.

[Effective December 2, 1991. Renumbered effective August 18, 1997. Amended effective January 1, 2000; October 25, 2004; December 1, 2009; January 1, 2014.]

CIVIL RULE 1.2   AVAILABILITY OF LOCAL RULES

a. Availability. The Clerk must post updated copies of these rules on the Court website, www.casd.uscourts.gov. Changes to the Local Rules must be advertised in the Court's official newspaper for publication of notices; on the Court's website, and provide for a period of public comment prior to them taking effect. The Clerk must make copies of these rules available on request or upon payment of a nominal charge, which may be set by general order.

b. Notice After Adoption. Immediately upon the adoption of these rules or of any change in these rules, copies of the new and revised local rules must be provided to such publications and persons as the Chief Judge deems appropriate.

[Effective August 18, 1997. Amended, effective November 19, 2001; December 1, 2009.]

CIVIL RULE 2.1   PROFESSIONALISM

a. Code of Conduct. The following Code of Conduct establishes the principles of civility and professionalism that will govern the conduct of all participants in cases and proceedings pending in this Court. It is to be construed in the broadest sense and governs conduct relating to such cases and proceedings, whether occurring in the presence of the Court or occurring outside of the presence of the Court. This Code of Conduct is not intended to be a set of rules that lawyers can use to incite ancillary litigation on the question whether the standards have been observed, but the Court may take any appropriate measure to address violations, including, without limitation, as set forth in Civil L. Rule 2.2.

1. *Principles of Civility.* To borrow from others who have considered the importance of civility in our state and federal courts, we should all understand that the law preserves our freedom, and it is the courts that preserve our laws. Fair,

impartial and accessible courts are fundamental to the preservation of our democracy. We—judges, lawyers, court staff, parties—all have a responsibility in ensuring that we preserve the legacy of this institution by conducting ourselves according to the Golden Rule—to treat others as we ourselves would like to be treated.

In seeking justice through the courts, attorneys and parties subject themselves to an inherently adversarial system. Although adversarial, the experience does not have to, and should not, be antagonistic or hostile. Civility is paramount and not to be confused with weakness. Civility in action and words is fundamental to the effective and efficient functioning of our system of justice and public confidence in that system.

The Federal Rules and this court's Local and Chambers' Rules serve as safeguards to ensure that the principles of equity and fairness govern the procedural course of all litigation. At the same time, these resources, without more, may not sufficiently quell incivility amongst those who litigate in this court. The Court has therefore adopted the following Code of Conduct. No one is above the law and, equally important, no one is entitled to act in such a way that erodes the public's trust in the administration of justice, impartiality, and the search for the truth. Civility should not only be aspirational, but rather it should be inherent within us all. Nevertheless, this Code of Conduct serves as the Court's reminder that we owe it to ourselves, one another, and our justice system to act in accordance with the principles of fairness and equal treatment that underpin the law of our land.

This court is committed to ensuring that all who work within it and come before it treat each other with decency, dignity, and respect. As such, the Court expects that all who practice in this court will adhere to this Code of Conduct in all of their interactions within the courts of this judicial district, in order to nurture, rather than tarnish, the practice of law and to maintain the public's faith in the legitimacy of our judicial system. The Court acknowledges the substantial work of the San Diego County Bar Association in developing the Association's Attorney Civility and Practice Guidelines, which this court has adopted, in substantial part, in this Code of Conduct.

2. *Duties Owed to the Court.*

a) We expect lawyers to be courteous and respectful to the Court and all court and court-related personnel.

b) We expect lawyers arguing for an extension of existing law to clearly state that fact and why.

c) We expect lawyers appearing in court to dress neatly and appropriately and encourage their clients to do the same.

d) We expect lawyers to be on time and adhere to time constraints.

e) We expect lawyers to be prepared for all court appearances.

f) We expect lawyers to attempt to resolve disputes promptly, fairly and reasonably, with resort to the Court for judicial relief only if necessary.

g) We expect lawyers to discourage and refuse to accept a role in litigation that is meritless or designed primarily to harass or drain the financial resources of the opposing party.

h) We expect lawyers to honor and maintain the integrity of our justice system, including by not impugning the integrity of its proceedings, or its members.

3. *Duties Owed to Other Lawyers, Parties and Witnesses.*

a) We expect lawyers to address legal arguments with other lawyers professionally, and not personally.

b) We expect lawyers to treat adverse witnesses, litigants and opposing counsel with courtesy, fairness and respect.

c) We expect lawyers to conduct themselves in the discovery process as if a judicial officer were present.

d) We expect lawyers to not arbitrarily or unreasonable withhold consent to a reasonable request for cooperation or accommodation.

e) We expect lawyers to refrain from attributing to an opponent a position the opponent has not clearly taken.

f) We expect lawyers to be accurate in written communications intended to make a record.

g) We expect lawyers to refrain from proposing a stipulation in the presence of the Court or trier of fact unless the other parties have previously agreed to it.

h) We expect lawyers to refrain from interrupting an opponent's legal argument unless making an appropriate objection for a legitimate basis.

i) We expect lawyers in court to address opposing lawyers through the Court.

j) We expect lawyers to seek sanctions sparingly, and not to obtain a tactical advantage or for any other improper purpose.

k) We expect lawyers to refrain from seeking to disqualify opposing counsel for any improper purpose or for any reason not supported by fact or law.

l) We expect lawyers to encourage other lawyers to conform to the standards in this Code of Conduct.

m) We expect lawyers to conduct themselves so that they may conclude each case amicably with the opposing party.

[Effective March 18, 2020.]

CIVIL RULE 2.2   DISCIPLINE

a.   General. In the event any attorney engages in conduct which may warrant discipline or other sanctions, the Court or any judge may, in addition to initiating proceedings for contempt under Title 18 U.S.C. 401 and Rule 42, Fed. R. Crim.P., or imposing other appropriate sanctions, refer the matter to the disciplinary body of any court before which the attorney has been admitted to practice.

b.   Charge or Conviction of Felony.

1. Any attorney charged with or convicted of a felony must report the charge or conviction within fourteen (14) days to the Clerk of the Court.

2. An attorney on the Court's CJA panel or one appointed by the Court who is charged with a felony will not be assigned any further cases and will be relieved on cases on which the

attorney is appointed until further order of the Court. The attorney's cases will be reassigned as directed by the judge supervising those cases on which the attorney is relieved.

3. A non-court appointed attorney charged with a felony must show cause why they should not be removed from any pending civil or criminal case due to a conflict of interest. It will be the attorney's burden to demonstrate to each judge assigned a case on which the charged attorney wishes to appear that there is no conflict and the attorney can appropriately discharge their duties to the client.

4. Any attorney admitted to practice in this court who enters a plea of guilty to a felony, or is found guilty of a felony, must immediately be suspended from practice before this court. Upon the felony conviction becoming final, the attorney must be disbarred. The disbarred attorney may make a motion in this court within sixty days of disbarment for an order of modification of the disbarment order, as justice may require.

c. The Standing Committee on Discipline. The Court will appoint from time to time, by an order entered in its minutes, a "Standing Committee on Discipline" consisting of a least five members of the bar and will designate one of the members to serve as chairperson of the committee. The members of the committee will continue in office for a period of two years or until further order of the Court.

d. Discipline Following Disciplinary Proceedings in Other Courts. Upon receipt of information that an attorney admitted or permitted to practice in this court has been suspended or disbarred from practice before any court of competent jurisdiction, this court will issue an Order to Show Cause why an order of suspension or disbarment should not be imposed by this court.

If an attorney opposes the imposition of prospective discipline, in the response to the Order to Show Cause, the attorney must set forth facts establishing one or more of the following:

1. The procedure in the other jurisdiction was so lacking in notice or opportunity to be heard as to constitute a deprivation of due process;

2. There was such infirmity of proof establishing the misconduct as to give rise to a clear conviction that the Court should not accept as final the other jurisdiction's conclusion(s) on that subject;

3. Imposition of like discipline would result in a grave injustice; or

4. Other substantial reasons exist so as to justify not accepting the other jurisdiction's conclusion(s).

In addition, at the time the response is filed, the attorney must produce a certified copy of the entire record from the other jurisdiction or bear the burden of persuading the Court that less than the entire record will suffice.

If an attorney files a response stating the imposition of an order of suspension or disbarment from this court is not contested, or if the attorney does not respond to the Order to Show Cause within the time specified, then the Chief Judge will issue an order of suspension or disbarment.

If the attorney files a written response to the Order to Show Cause within the time specified stating that the entry of an order of suspension or disbarment is contested, then the Chief Judge will determine whether an order of suspension or disbarment should issue.

e. Original Disciplinary Investigations and Proceedings Initiated in This Court. The "Standing Committee on Discipline" will investigate any charge or information, referred by one of the judges, that any member of the bar of this court or that any attorney permitted to practice in the Court has been guilty of unprofessional conduct. At the request of the committee, the Chief Judge will direct the issuance of subpoenas and subpoenas duces tecum as may be required by the investigation.

In cases where a majority of the members deem it advisable, the committee will institute and prosecute a disciplinary proceeding by filing with the Clerk an appropriate petition on behalf of the committee addressed to the judges of this court. Upon the filing of the petition, the proceeding will be assigned to one of the judges in the same manner as any other civil action or proceeding.

The judge to whom the proceeding is assigned will issue an order to show cause why the respondent should not be disbarred, suspended or otherwise disciplined as prayed in the petition. The order to show cause will be served upon the respondent, not more than twenty-one (21) days from the date of the order. The order will further require that a copy of the order and a copy of the petition, be served in the respondent in a manner permitted by Fed.R.Civ.P 5(b) not less than fourteen (14) days in advance of the date specified for showing cause. Except as otherwise provided by local rule, the proceeding must be governed by the Fed.R.Civ.P. Written findings of fact and an order based thereon must be filed by the judge when dismissing the proceeding or when imposing discipline. Any investigation or proceeding in accordance with this local rule must not be public unless otherwise ordered by the Court or unless and until a disbarment, suspension or public reproval has been administered.

The Clerk will give prompt notice of any motion, petition or order made under Civil Local Rule 2.2. e to the United States Attorney and to the disciplinary body of the court(s) to which the attorney has been admitted to practice.

f. Contempt. Disciplinary matters, proceedings and investigations under Civil Local Rule 2.2 will not affect, or be affected by, any proceeding for contempt under Title 18 U.S.C. 401 or Fed.R.Crim.P 42.

[Former CivLR 83.5 effective August 18, 1997. Amended effective August 10, 1999; May 14, 2002; October 25, 2004; December 1, 2009; June 4, 2019. Renumbered as CivLR 2.2 and amended effective March 18, 2020.]

CIVIL RULE 3.1   DESIGNATION OF NATURE OF ACTION (CIVIL COVER SHEET)

For administrative purposes only, every complaint, petition or other paper initiating a civil action or proceeding must be accompanied by a completed civil cover sheet and must set forth immediately below the docket number one or more of the following categories most nearly descriptive of the subject matter of the action or proceeding:

  a. Admiralty—Maritime Claims (except Jones Act)

  b. Antitrust

  c. Contract

  d. Copyright/Trademark/Unfair Competition

  e. Patent

  f. Labor Relations

  g. Tax

  h. Tort/Personal Injury (including Jones Act)/Property Damage Fraud/Other (specify)

  i. Government Collection/Forfeiture/Penalty

  j. Civil Rights

  k. Land Condemnation

  l. Habeas Corpus

  m. Review of Administrative Action

  n. Federal Securities

  o. Miscellaneous (specify)

[Effective August 18, 1997. Amended, effective April 6, 1998; December 1, 2009.]

CIVIL RULE 3.2   ACTIONS IN FORMA PAUPERIS

a. Affidavit. All actions sought to be filed in forma pauperis, pursuant to 28 U.S.C. § 1915, must be accompanied by an affidavit that includes a statement of all assets which shows inability to pay initial fees or give security. This affidavit must consist of a declaration in support of request to proceed in forma pauperis. This declaration must contain the following:

1. A statement as to current employment including the amount of wages or salary per month and the name and address of the current employer.

2. A statement, if not currently employed, as to the date of last employment and the amount of wages or salary per month which was received.

3. A statement as to any money received within the past twelve months from any of the following sources:

  a) Business, profession, or self-employment;

  b) Rent payments, interest, or dividends;

  c) Pensions, annuities, or life insurance payments;

  d) Gifts or inheritances;

  e) Any other source.

The statement must include a description of each source of money and the amount of money received from each source during the past twelve months.

4. A statement as to any cash in possession and as to any money in a financial institution, including checking, savings, and any other accounts. The statement must include any money available to the declarant.

5. A statement as to any real estate, stocks, bonds, notes, automobiles, investments, or other valuable property (excluding ordinary household furnishings and clothing). The statement must describe the property and state its approximate value.

6. A statement as to all persons who depend upon the declarant for support. The statement must include the relationship of the dependents and the amount contributed toward their support.

7. A statement that, because of poverty, there is an inability to pay the initial costs of the proceeding or give security therefore, and the declarant's belief that the declarant is entitled to relief.

This declaration must be executed under penalty of perjury.

b. Prison Account Certification. In actions by incarcerated persons who seek to bring a civil action or appeal a judgment in forma pauperis, the affidavit requesting leave to proceed in forma pauperis must contain a certified copy of the trust fund account statement (or institutional equivalent) for the prisoner for the 6–month period immediately preceding the filing of the suit or notice of appeal, obtained from the appropriate official of each prison at which the prisoner is or was confined.

c. Partial Fee Assessment for Prisoners. In considering a prisoner's requests to proceed in forma pauperis, the Court must assess and, when funds exist, collect, as a partial payment of any court fees required by law, an initial partial filing fee of 20 percent of the greater of (1) the average monthly deposits to the prisoner's account; or (2) the average monthly balance in the prisoner's account for the 6–month period immediately preceding the filing of the complaint or notice of appeal. Thereafter, the prisoner is required to make monthly payments of 20 percent of the preceding month's income credited to the prisoner's account. The agency having custody of the prisoner must forward payments from the prisoner's account to the Clerk of the Court each time the amount in the account exceeds $10 until the filing fees are paid.

d. Partial Fee Assessment for Non–Prisoners. In considering a non-prisoner's request to proceed in forma pauperis, the Court may, in its discretion, impose a partial filing fee which is less than the full filing fee that is required by law, but which is commensurate with the applicant's ability to pay.

e. Partial Fee Waiver. In all actions sought to be filed in forma pauperis pursuant to 28 U.S.C. § 1915(a), and in which the person has insufficient assets or means by which to pay the full or assessed partial filing fee, the person may submit an application for waiver of the initial partial filing fee. In order to qualify for a waiver, the person must justify depletions of the previously adequate account or income history to show that the depletion was not a deliberate attempt to avoid payment of initial filing fees.

f. In Forma Pauperis Procedure. All persons must submit the request to proceed in forma pauperis, accompanied by the affidavit required by 28 U.S.C. § 1915(a)(1) and Civil Local Rule 3.2.a, at the time the suit or notice of appeal is submitted for filing. Incarcerated persons must also attach the 6–month prison account certification required by 28 U.S.C. § 1915(a)(2) and Civil Local Rule 3.2.b. Applications for partial fee waivers (if any) pursuant to 28 U.S.C. § 1915(b)(4) and Civil Local Rule 3.2.e. may also be submitted at the time the suit or notice of appeal is submitted for filing. NO PARTIAL FEE CHECKS WILL BE ACCEPTED UNTIL THE COURT REVIEWS THE AFFIDAVIT AND ACCOUNT INFORMATION SUBMITTED IN SUPPORT OF A PRISONER'S REQUEST TO PROCEED IN FORMA PAUPERIS AND ISSUES AN ORDER ASSESSING THE AMOUNT OF INITIAL FEE WHICH IS DUE. The Clerk of the Court is authorized to return any partial fee check submitted prior to the Court's partial fee assessment order.

g. Fee Collection Cap. In no event will the fee collected exceed the amount of fees permitted by statute for the commencement of a civil action or an appeal of a civil action or criminal judgment.

[Effective August 18, 1997. Amended, effective October 25, 2004; December 1, 2009.]

CIVIL RULE 4.1 SERVICE

a. Service of Process. Service of process, i.e., service of the summons and complaint, must be performed in accordance with Rule 4, Fed. R. Civ. P.

All complaints must be served within ninety (90) days. Any extension will be granted only upon good cause shown.

b. Failure to Serve. On the one hundredth (100th) day following the filing of the complaint, or on the fourteenth (14th) day following an extension of time to serve, if proof of service has not yet been filed, the Clerk will prepare an order to show cause with notice to plaintiff why the case should not be dismissed without prejudice and submit it to the assigned district judge for signature.

c. Instructions to Marshal. Where service of a summons and pleading is to be made by United States marshal upon a person or entity, the party at whose request the summons is issued is responsible for providing the United States marshal's office with appropriate instructions regarding the person upon whom service is to be made, in what capacity the service is to be made (official or individual), and at what address service is to be made. Failure to comply with these instructions may cause the marshal not to perform service.

d. Service of Pleadings Other Than Original Complaint. Service of an amended complaint, counterclaim, cross-claim, or third-party complaint, must be made upon each new party to the litigation, whether or not multiple parties are represented by a single attorney. Service of all other pleadings authorized to be served in accordance with Rule 5, Fed.R.Civ.P., must be complete when served upon the attorney for a party, if the party is represented by an attorney. Where an attorney represents multiple parties, service of one copy of a pleading, other than an amended complaint, an amended counterclaim, or an amended third-party complaint, will constitute service of all parties represented by that attorney, unless the Court otherwise orders.

The summons must be prepared by the attorney, or the party, if the party is proceeding pro se, upon forms supplied by the Clerk, and must be presented concurrently with the filing of a complaint or petition commencing the action.

[Effective August 18, 1997. Amended effective August 10, 1999; October 25, 2004; December 1, 2009; January 30, 2016.]

CIVIL RULE 4.5 FEE SCHEDULE

Fees will be charged for the following services in accordance with the Miscellaneous Fee Schedule approved by the Judicial Conference of the United States:

a. Filing of a civil case;

b. Filing a Habeas Corpus Petition;

c. Notice of Appeal;

d. Appeal to District Court from judgment and conviction in misdemeanor case;

e. Ninth Circuit docket fees when filing notice of appeal;

f. Filing or indexing any paper not in a case or proceeding, including registration of petitions to perpetuate testimony, filing power of attorney, letters rogatory or letters of request, filing of papers by trustees;

g. Search of the records;

h. Certification of any document or paper;

i. Exemplification of any document is twice the amount of the fee for certification;

j. Reproducing any record or paper, magnetic tape recording, or microfiche retrieval of a record from storage;

k. For a check paid into the Court which is returned for lack of funds;

l. For admission of attorneys to practice, including a certificate of admission, or for a duplicate certificate of admission;

m. For the handling of registry funds deposited with the Court;

n. For usage of electronic access to court data; and

o. For filing an action brought under Title III of the Cuban Liberty and Democratic Solidarity Act.

(A copy of the fee schedule can be obtained from the Court's website, or upon request to the Clerk of Court.)

[Effective August 18, 1997. Amended, effective January 16, 1998; August 10, 1999; December 1, 2009.]

CIVIL RULE 5.1 FORM; PAPER; LEGIBILITY; NATURE OF DOCUMENTS TO BE FILED

a. Legibility. Each document filed, including exhibits where practicable, must be in English, plainly written, or typed in double space on one side of the document, line numbered in the left margin with not more than 28 lines per page, and letter size. Documents filed in paper format must be flat and unfolded, without backing sheet, double spaced on one side of the paper or printed or prepared by means of a duplicating process on opaque, unglazed white paper. Quotations in excess of three lines must be indented and single spaced. Typewritten text must be no less than 10–point type in the Courier font or equivalent, spaced 10 characters per horizontal inch. Printed text, produced on a word processor or other computer, may be proportionally spaced allowing 28 lines on one side of the document, provided the type is no smaller than 14–point standard font (e.g. Times New Roman). The text of footnotes and quotations must also conform to these font requirements. Approved templates are available on the Court's website (www.casd.uscourts.gov) and may be amended by the Court over time as deemed appropriate.

b. Original; Copies. The original of a document must be labeled as the original. All copies are to be clearly identified as such. The case number must appear in the lower right corner of each page, although it is not required on the title page or on the complaint, petition or other document which opens the case. The typed number must be inserted in the following format: year, case type, four-digit case number with leading zeros if necessary (96cv0010). Case types are as follows: civil = cv, criminal = cr, magistrate judge = mj, miscellaneous = mc.

c. Interlineations. There must be no erasures or interlineations on a document unless they are noted by the Clerk or judge by marginal initials at the time of filing.

d. Pre–Punching and Attachments. All documents presented for filing or lodging in paper format must be pre-punched with two (2) normal-size holes (approximately ¼″ diameter), centered 2¾ inches apart, ½ to ⅝ inches from the top edge of the document. No pages of any document should have any attachment affixed thereto. All pages must be firmly bound at the top.

e. Exhibits. Except where compliance is impracticable, exhibits must be paged in consecutive numerical order and each page must show the exhibit number either immediately above or below the page number. Unless the physical nature of the exhibit renders it impracticable, exhibits must be attached to the documents to which they belong and must be readable without detaching the exhibit from the accompanying document.

Each document containing exhibits must have, as a cover page to the exhibits, a table of contents indicating the page number of each of the succeeding exhibits. If exhibits are tabbed, the tabs must be at the bottom and not at the sides.

f. Compliance. Unless a waiver is first obtained from the Court, the Clerk must not file any document which does not comply with the requirements of these rules. Said document will be endorsed "lodged" until approved by the Court.

g. Adversary Proceeding. The Clerk must refuse to accept for filing any complaint, petition or any other pleading in a civil case, other than a Petition for Limitation of Liability under Rule F of the Admiralty and Maritime Rules, unless it is entitled as an adversary proceeding naming the defendant or respondent.

h. Party Filing Document. Except as provided in the federal rules, or by leave of court, no document will be filed in any case by any person not a party thereto.

i. Copies:

1. The original of all documents, including exhibits attached thereto, must be filed together with one legible conformed copy for the Court's use, except motions filed under Criminal Local Rule 47.1.b.1.

2. The original and three copies must be filed in a three judge case.

3. In a consolidated proceeding the original and one copy will be filed in the low-numbered case or the lead case as may be designated by the Court. The case number of each consolidated case must appear on each pleading following the lead case number.

4. If parties presenting documents for filing request the Clerk to return a conformed copy by U.S. Mail, an extra copy must be submitted for this purpose and must be accompanied by a self-addressed envelope bearing sufficient postage.

5. The original and two copies of all substitutions of attorneys must be filed.

j. Title Page. The first page of every document must contain the following information which may be single spaced:

1. The name, address and telephone number of the attorney appearing for a party or of an individual appearing pro se, must be printed or typewritten in the space to the left of the page's center and beginning at line one. Attorneys appearing pro hac vice and attorneys employed or retrained by the United States or its agencies and authorized to practice in this court pursuant to Civil Local Rule 83.3.c.3, will list their bar numbers for the states of which they are active members. Attorneys appearing for a party must also include their California State Bar Number. The space to the right of the page's center must be reserved for the Clerk's filing stamp.

2. The title of the Court must commence at or below line eight of the first page.

3. Below and to the left of the title of the Court, the title of the action must be inserted. In the event the parties are too numerous for all to be named on the first page, the names of the parties may be carried onto the successive page(s).

In the space to the right of center the following will appear: The number of the action, a brief designation of the document's nature, mention of any motion or affidavits or memorandum in support and "Demand for Jury Trial", if any.

4. The following information must appear on the cover page of each motion, and any opposition and reply, in the space opposite the caption below the case number: name of judicial officer, courtroom number and the date and time of hearing.

5. Names must be typed below signatures on document.

k. Paragraphing Pleadings. Averments in any pleading which seeks relief must be made in numbered paragraphs, each of which must be limited, as far as is practicable, to a statement of a single set of circumstances. Responsive pleadings must contain numbered paragraphs, each of which corresponds to the paragraph to which it is directed.

l. Citations. When citing Acts of Congress or sections of them, counsel must include the corresponding appropriate U.S.C. citations. When counsel cite regulations, counsel must supply the appropriate citations to the Code of Federal Regulations, including code number, page, section and the date of the regulation's promulgation.

m. Captions. All documents submitted for filing must be filed and captioned separately. Sentencing memoranda may be filed together with motions for departure, or may be filed separately from motions for departure. Objections to presentence reports must be filed separately. Sentencing summary charts must be filed. Double captions are required for cross- and counter-complaints, third party complaints, and their responses.

[Effective August 18, 1997. Amended effective April 6, 1998; August 10, 1999; November 19, 2001; October 25, 2004; December 1, 2009; February 8, 2013; March 22, 2013; January 1, 2014; February 2, 2015; January 30, 2016; December 1, 2018; June 25, 2019.]

CIVIL RULE 5.2   PROOF OF SERVICE

Proof of service of all papers required or permitted to be served, other than those for which a particular method of proof is prescribed in the Fed. R. Civ. P., must be filed in the Clerk's Office promptly and in any event before action is to be taken thereon by the Court or the parties. No proof of service is required when a paper is served by filing it with the Court's Electronic Filing System. Where required, the proof must show the day and manner of service and may be (1) written acknowledgment of service, on the original of the copy served, by the attorney or person in charge of his office receiving a copy thereof, or (2) by certificate of a member of the bar of this court; (3) by affidavit of the person who mailed or otherwise served the papers, or (4) by any other proof satisfactory to the Court.

If an affidavit of mailing or of service is attached to the original pleading, it must be attached underneath the same so that the character of the pleading is easily discernible.

Failure to make the proof of service required by this subdivision does not affect the validity of the service; and the Court may at any time allow the proof of service to be amended or supplied unless it clearly appears that to do so would result in material prejudice to the substantial rights of any party.

[Effective August 18, 1997. Amended effective October 25, 2004; December 1, 2009; December 1, 2018.]

CIVIL RULE 5.3   FACSIMILE FILINGS

a. Method of Filing. A fax filing agency will file all fax transmitted pleadings on behalf of the parties or their counsel. NO DOCUMENTS MAY BE TRANSMITTED DIRECTLY TO THE CLERK BY FAX FOR FILING. ANY DOCUMENTS SO TRANSMITTED MUST BE REJECTED AND NOT FILED.

1. The fax filing agency acts as the agent of the filing party and not as agent of the Court. A document will be deemed filed when it is submitted by the fax filing agency, received in the Clerk's Office, and filed by the Clerk. Mere transmission to or receipt by the fax filing agency will not be construed as filing.

2. The fax filing agency must meet all technical requirements under Civil Local Rule 5.1.

3. Counsel or parties utilizing a fax filing agency will ensure that additional copies necessary for filing will be reproduced by the fax filing agency, and any applicable filing fees are submitted at the time of filing.

b. When Filed. Electronic transmission of a document via facsimile machine does not constitute filing; filing is complete when the document is filed with the Clerk.

c. Form, Paper, Legibility. Only plain paper (no thermal paper) facsimile machines may be used. All documents must be on size 8½″ x 11″ bond. All copies must be clear, clean and legible, and comply with Civil Local Rule 5.1.

d. Original Signature. The image of the original manual signature on the fax copy will constitute an original signature for all court purposes. The original signed document must not be substituted except by court order. The original signed document must be maintained by the attorney of record or the party originating the document, for a period no less than the maximum allowable time to complete the appellate process. Upon request, the original document must be provided to other parties for review.

e. Transmission Record. The sending party is required to maintain a transmission record in the event fax filing late becomes an issue. A transmission record means the document printed by the sending facsimile machine stating the telephone number of the receiving machine, the number of pages sent, the transmission time, and an indication of errors in transmission.

[Effective August 18, 1997. Amended effective December 1, 2009.]

CIVIL RULE 5.4   ELECTRONIC CASE FILING

a. Scope of Electronic Case Filing. Except as prescribed by local rule, order, or other procedure, the Court has designated all cases to be assigned to the Electronic Filing System. Unless otherwise expressly provided in the Court's Electronic Case Filing Administrative Policies and Procedures Manual, the Court's Local Rules, or in exceptional circumstances preventing a registered user from filing electronically, as of November 1, 2006 all petitions, motions, memoranda of law, or other pleadings and documents to be filed with the Court by a registered user in connection with a case assigned to the Electronic Filing System must be electronically filed. Unless otherwise ordered by the Court, all attorneys admitted to practice before the Southern District of California must register for Electronic Case Filing.

b. Consequences of Electronic Filing. Electronic transmission of a document to the Electronic Filing System in the manner prescribed by the Court's Administrative Policies and Procedures Manual, together with the transmission of an NEF from the Court, constitutes filing of the document for all purposes of the Federal Rules of Civil Procedure and the Local Rules of this court, and constitutes entry of the document on the docket kept by the Clerk in accordance with Fed. R. Civ. P. 58 and 79.

c. Service of Pleadings and Documents Filed Electronically. The NEF that is automatically generated by the Court's Electronic Filing System constitutes service of the filed document on Filing Users. Parties who are not Filing Users must be served with a copy of any pleading or other document filed electronically in accordance with the Federal

Rules of Civil Procedure and these Local Rules. A certificate of service is not required when a party electronically files a document on other Filing Users with the Court's Electronic Filing System, but, as set forth in Civ. L.R. 5.2, a certificate of service is required for service on any parties who are not Filing Users.

d. Consent to Electronic Service. Registration as a Filing User constitutes consent to Electronic Service of all documents as provided in this General Order and in accordance with the Federal Rules of Civil Procedures and Federal Rules of Criminal Procedure.

e. Official Court Record. The official court record will be the electronic file maintained on the Court's servers. This includes information transmitted to the Court in electronic format, as well as documents filed in paper form, scanned, and made a part of the electronic record to the extent permitted by the Court's policies. The official record will also include any documents or exhibits that may be impractical to scan. The electronic file maintained on the Court's servers must contain a reference to any such documents filed with the Court. For cases initiated prior to the implementation of the Electronic Filing System, the official court record will include both the pre-implementation paper file maintained by the Clerk, as well as the post-implementation electronic files maintained on the Court's servers. The Clerk's Office must not maintain a paper court file in any case initiated on or after the effective date of these procedures except as otherwise provided in these procedures.

f. Electronic Filing Policies and Procedures. The Court's CM/ECF Administrative Policies and Procedures Manual, which may be obtained on the Court's website or upon request from the Clerk, sets forth the guidelines parties must follow to file documents electronically. The Court may direct the Clerk to strike from the record any document which fails to comply with the requirements for electronic filing set forth in the Administrative Policies and Procedures Manual.

[Effective May 1, 2006. Amended effective July 16, 2007; December 1, 2009; December 1, 2018.]

CIVIL RULE 7.1 MOTION PRACTICE, EXTENSIONS, ENLARGEMENTS OR SHORTENING OF TIME, SUBMISSION OF ORDERS

a. Scope of Rule. Unless otherwise ordered by a judge of this district, or unless contrary to statute or in conflict with a provision of the Fed.R.Civ.P., the provisions of this rule will apply to motions, applications and orders to show cause, or other request for ruling by the Court. Such matters include motions to withdraw the reference from the bankruptcy court, appeals of orders by the bankruptcy court, and objections to magistrate judge's orders pursuant to Rule 72.a, Fed. R. Civ. P.

b. Motion Hearing Dates. All hearing dates for any matters on which a ruling is required must be obtained from the Clerk of the judge to whom the case is assigned.

c. Computation of Time. All legal holidays and computation of time must be as provided in Rule 6, Fed.R.Civ.P.

d. Argument and Submission.

1. *Written and Oral Argument.* Motions must be determined upon the moving papers referred to herein and oral argument. A judge may, in the judge's discretion, decide a motion without oral argument.

2. *Argument by Telephonic Conference.* At the discretion of the Court, argument concerning a noticed motion may be conducted through the use of a telephone conference call to be arranged, initiated and paid for by the party proposing this method of oral argument. If such telephonic argument is approved by the Court, the matter may be taken off the regular motion hearing calendar, and reset for a date and/or time more convenient to the Court and the parties.

e. Time for Hearing and Schedule for Filing Papers.

1. *Twenty–Eight (28) Day Rule—Setting Time for Hearing.* When there has been an adverse appearance, a written notice of a matter requiring the Court's ruling is necessary, unless otherwise provided by rule or court order. Pursuant to the provisions of Civil Local Rule 7.1.b all hearing dates for any motion must be obtained from the law clerk of the judge to whom the case is assigned. Unless the Court shortens time and except as otherwise specified in Civil Local Rule 7.1.e.6, any motion, application or notice of other matter requiring the Court's ruling, plus all necessary supporting documents, will require a minimum filing date of twenty-eight (28) days prior to the date for which the matter is noticed. (For example, the motion and supporting documents for a motion to be heard on a Monday must be filed and served no later than the fourth (4th) Monday prior to the Monday hearing. If the fourth Monday prior to the Monday hearing is a holiday, however, then the motion and supporting documents would be due five (5) Fridays before the hearing.)

2. *Time for Filing Opposition.* Except as otherwise specified in Civil Local Rule 7.1.e.1, each party opposing a motion, application or order to show cause must file that opposition or statement of non-opposition with the Clerk and serve the movant or the movant's attorney not later than fourteen (14) calendar days prior to the noticed hearing. (For example, for a motion to be heard on a Monday, the opposition papers must be filed and served no later than two Mondays prior to the noticed hearing.)

3. *Reply Memorandum of Points and Authorities.* Except as otherwise specified in Civil Local Rule 7.1.e.1, any reply memorandum must be filed and served not later than seven (7) days prior to the date for which the matter is noticed. (For example, for a hearing, the reply papers must be filed and served no later than by the Monday prior to the hearing. If the Monday prior to the hearing is a holiday, however, then the reply papers would be due two (2) Fridays prior to the hearing.) See Fed. R. Civ. P. 6(e).

4. *Service of Motions and Opposition by Mail.* For those parties not required or authorized by the Court to file and serve motions and oppositions electronically using the Case Management/Electronic Case Filing System, unless otherwise provided by order of the Court, the sixty, (60) twenty-eight (28) and fourteen (14) day periods of notice set forth in Civil Local Rules 7.1.e.1, 7.1.e.2 and 7.1.e.6 are increased for purposes of mail service upon opposing parties of counsel by three (3) days. The extension of time for service does not extend

court filing deadlines. Federal Rule of Civil Procedure 6(d), extending the time within which an act may or must, be done, does not apply to the notice periods governed by this section. Any motion, or opposition, and supporting documentation will not be accepted for filing unless accompanied by proof of service demonstrating either hand-delivery or compliance with this section's mailing provisions.

5. *Applications for Orders Shortening Time.* All applications for orders shortening time under these rules must be submitted ex parte, be accompanied by a proposed order, and be served on all opposing parties.

6. *Social Security Cases.*

a) Applicability. This rule will apply to actions for judicial review that are filed by a single plaintiff solely against the Commissioner of Social Security Administration, and that raise claims pursuant to 42 U.S.C. § 405(g) only.

b) Use of First Name and Last Initial in Opinions. Opinions by the Court in these cases will refer to any non-government parties by using only their first name and last initial.

c) Inclusion of Last Four Digits of Social Security Number in Complaint. All complaints filed pursuant to this rule will state the last four digits of plaintiff's Social Security number. If the plaintiff's application for Social Security benefits was filed on another person's wage-record, the last four digits of that person's Social Security number will also be included in the Complaint.

d) Response to Complaint. The certified administrative record filed by the Social Security Administration will suffice as the agency's answer to the complaint, and will be due sixty (60) days after service of the summons and complaint, unless a motion to dismiss is filed.

e) Merits Briefing. Unless, otherwise ordered by the Court, the parties will adhere to the following briefing schedule with respect to the merits of the case:

1. Plaintiff's merits brief will be due within 35 days of the filing of the administrative record.

2. The Social Security Administration's opposition is due 35 days after Plaintiff's brief is filed.

3. Plaintiff's reply brief, if any, will be due 14 days after defendant's brief is filed.

No other briefs or motions are required to be filed for the Court to dispose of the case on its merits.

f) Oral Argument. No oral argument in cases that fall within the scope of this rule is authorized unless otherwise ordered by the Court.

g) Other Motions. This rule is not intended to prevent parties from making any other appropriate motions under the Federal Rules of Civil Procedure.

7. *Untimely Motions.* The Clerk's Office is directed not to file untimely motions and responses thereto without the consent of the judicial officer assigned to the case.

8. *Special Briefing Schedules.* All documents to be filed in response to a special briefing schedule must contain the language 'special briefing schedule ordered' directly below the designation of the document's nature.

f. Contents of Papers Filed.

1. *Motions, Notices, Statement of Facts.* Each motion or other request for ruling by the Court must include within it a Memorandum of Points and Authorities in support of the motion and a caption listing the nature of the motion, hearing date and time, and the judge who will hear the motion. Where appropriate, a separate or a joint statement of material facts, required declarations or affidavits, or exhibits, must be supplied.

2. *Movant.*

a) In addition to the affidavits required or permitted by Fed. R. Civ. P. 6(d) and 56, copies of all documentary evidence which the movant intends to submit in support of the motion, or other request for ruling by the Court, must be served and filed with the motion.

b) Waiver. A movant's failure to file any papers required under the local rules may be deemed as a waiver of the motion, or other request for ruling by the Court.

3. *Opposing Party.*

a) Unless otherwise provided by rule or court order, a party opposing a motion, or other request for ruling by the Court must file a written opposition. If such party chooses not to oppose the motion, the party must file a written statement that the party does not oppose the motion or other request for ruling by the Court.

b) Opposing Party's Papers and Contents. Documentary evidence and points and authorities—The opposition must contain a brief and complete statement of all reasons in opposition to the position taken by the movant, an answering memorandum of points and authorities, and copies of all documentary evidence upon which the party in opposition relies.

c. Waiver. If an opposing party fails to file the papers in the manner required by Civil Local Rule 7.1.e.2, that failure may constitute a consent to the granting of a motion or other request for ruling by the Court.

g. Withdrawal, Continuance, Failure to Appear.

1. *Withdrawal.* Any movant who does not intend to proceed with a motion or other request for ruling by the Court must notify opposing counsel and the judge before whom the matter is pending as soon as possible.

2. *Continuances.* Any request for continuance of a noticed matter must be made as soon as possible to the judge to whom the matter is assigned. Prior to seeking such continuance, the party seeking the continuance must contact all opposing parties or their counsel to determine whether they would agree to such continuance.

3. *Failure to Appear.* If no one appears to oppose a motion or other request for ruling, the movant must relate the matter's material elements and the Court may render its decision.

h. Length of Brief in Support of or in Opposition to Motions. Briefs or memoranda in support of or in opposition to all motions noticed for the same motion day must not exceed a total of twenty-five (25) pages in length, per party, for all such motions without leave of the judge who will hear the motion. No reply memorandum will exceed ten (10) pages without leave of the judge. Briefs and memoranda exceeding ten (10) pages in length must have a table of contents and a table of authorities cited.

i. Applications for Reconsideration.

1. Whenever any motion or any application or petition for any order or other relief has been made to any judge and has been refused in whole or in part, or has been granted conditionally or on terms, and a subsequent motion or application or petition is made for the same relief in whole or in part upon the same or any alleged different state of facts, it will be the continuing duty of each party and attorney seeking such relief to present to the judge to whom any subsequent application is made an affidavit of a party or witness or certified statement of an attorney setting forth the material facts and circumstances surrounding each prior application, including inter alia: (1) when and to what judge the application was made, (2) what ruling or decision or order was made thereon, and (3) what new or different facts and circumstances are claimed to exist which did not exist, or were not shown, upon such prior application.

2. Except as may be allowed under Rules 59 and 60 of the Federal Rules of Civil Procedure, any motion or application for reconsideration must be filed within twenty-eight (28) days after the entry of the ruling, order or judgment sought to be reconsidered.

j. Joinders in Motions.

1. The Clerk must refuse to accept for filing any joinder in motions if there are no pending motions on file.

2. Each joinder must specifically identify the party(s) and the particular motion(s) to which the joinder applies.

[Effective August 18, 1997. Amended effective August 10, 1999; November 19, 2001; October 25, 2004; October 25, 2004; July 16, 2007; December 1, 2009; February 2, 2015; January 30, 2016; June 4, 2019; June 25, 2019.]

CIVIL RULE 7.2 STIPULATIONS/JOINT MOTIONS

a. Except as otherwise provided, stipulations must be recognized as binding on the Court only when approved by the judge.

b. Any stipulation for which court approval is sought must first be filed as a "joint motion." Parties are not required to obtain a hearing date for the motion, and are not required to file a separate points and authorities or declaration unless required by the nature of the motion or requested by the assigned judicial officer.

c. Upon the filing of a joint motion, the filing party must also submit a proposed order to the assigned judicial officer. The proposed order must be a document separate from the joint motion.

[Effective August 18, 1997. Amended effective April 6, 1998; July 16, 2007; December 1, 2009.]

CIVIL RULE 8.2 CIVIL RIGHTS ACT (42 U.S.C. § 1983)

a. Complaint by Prisoners. Complaints by prisoners under the Civil Rights Act, 42 U.S.C. § 1983, must be legibly written or typewritten on forms supplied by the Court and signed by the plaintiff complainant. The forms must be completed in accordance with the instructions provided with the forms. The complaint must contain a short and plain statement of the claim and each averment must be simple, concise, and direct. Additional pages not to exceed fifteen (15) in number may be included with the Court approved form complaint, provided the form is completely filled in to the extent applicable in the particular case. The Court approved form and any additional pages submitted must be written or typed on only one side of a page and the writing or typewriting must be no smaller in size than standard elite type. Complaints tendered to the Clerk for filing which do not comply with this rule may be returned by the Clerk, together with a copy of this rule, to the person tendering said complaint.

b. Forma Pauperis. All actions sought to be filed in forma pauperis pursuant to 28 U.S.C. § 1915 must comply with Civil Local Rule 3.2.

[Effective August 18, 1997. Amended effective December 1, 2009.]

CIVIL RULE 9.2 THREE–JUDGE COURT

a. In any action or proceeding which a party believes is required to be heard by a three-judge District Court, the words "Three–Judge District Court Requested" or the equivalent must be included immediately following the title of the first pleading in which the cause of action requiring a three-judge court is pleaded. Unless the basis for the request is apparent from the pleading, it must be set forth in the pleading or in a brief statement attached thereto. The words "Three–Judge District Court Requested" or the equivalent on a pleading is a sufficient request under 28 U.S.C. § 2284.

b. In any action or proceeding in which a three-judge court is requested, parties must file the original and three copies of every pleading, motion, notice, or other document with the Clerk until it is determined either that a three-judge court will not be convened or that the three-judge court has been convened and dissolved, and the case remanded to a single judge. The parties may be permitted to file fewer copies by order of the Court.

c. A failure to comply with this local rule is not a ground for failing to convene or for dissolving a three-judge court.

d. The Clerk must forthwith notify the assigned judge of such filing.

[Effective August 18, 1997. Amended effective December 1, 2009.]

CIVIL RULE 12.1 EXTENSION OF TIME TO ANSWER

Extensions of time for answering, or moving to dismiss a complaint will only be secured by obtaining the approval of a judicial officer, who will base the decision on a showing of good cause.

[Effective August 18, 1997.]

CIVIL RULE 15.1   AMENDED PLEADINGS

a. Amended Pleadings. Every pleading to which an amendment is permitted as a matter of right or has been allowed by court order, must be complete in itself without reference to the superseded pleading. All amended pleadings must contain copies of all exhibits referred to in such amended pleadings. Permission may be obtained from the Court, if desired, for the removal of any exhibit or exhibits attached to prior pleadings, in order that the same may be attached to the amended pleading. Each amended pleading must be designated successively as first amended, second amended, etc.

b. Motions to Amend. Any motion to amend a pleading must be accompanied by: (1) a copy of the proposed amended pleading, and (2) a version of the proposed amended pleading that shows—through redlining, underlining, strikeouts, or other similarly effective typographic methods—how the proposed amended pleading differs from the operative pleading. If the Court grants the motion, the moving party must file and serve the amended pleading.

c. Amended Pleadings Filed After Motions to Dismiss or Strike. Any amended pleading filed after the granting of a motion to dismiss or motion to strike with leave to amend, must be accompanied by a version of that pleading that shows—through redlining, underlining, strikeouts, or other similarly effective typographic methods—how that pleading differs from the previously dismissed pleading.

d. Pro Se Parties in Custody. Parties who are in custody and appearing pro se are exempted from complying with the requirements of Civil Local Rule 15.1.b. to provide a version of the proposed amended pleading that shows how that pleading differs from the operating pleading. Pro se parties in custody are also exempted from the requirements of Civil Local Rule 15.1.c.

[Effective August 18, 1997. Amended effective April 6, 1998; February 2, 2015.]

CIVIL RULE 16.1   PRETRIAL AND SETTING FOR TRIAL

a. Application of This Rule.

1. Pretrial proceedings and setting of cases for trial must be governed by Fed.R.Civ.P. 16 and this rule, and by such orders as are issued pursuant thereto. The timing of the Federal Rule 16(b) scheduling order is adjusted to accommodate the Early Neutral Evaluation Conference, as allowed under Fed. R. Civ P. 1.

2. All civil and admiralty cases must be pre-tried unless a pre-trial is waived by order of the Court.

b. Counsel's Duty of Diligence. All counsel and parties, if they are proceeding pro se, must proceed with diligence to take all steps necessary to bring an action to readiness for trial. In doing so they should be mindful of the requirements of Rule 16(c), Fed.R.Civ.P., following subparagraph (11) there-

to, and the sanctions contained in Rule 16(f) Fed.R.Civ.P., for failure to prepare for and participate in good faith in the pretrial conference process.

c. Early Neutral Evaluation ("ENE") Conference.

1. Within forty-five (45) days of the filing of an answer, counsel and the parties must appear before the assigned judicial officer supervising discovery for an early neutral evaluation conference; this appearance must be made with authority to discuss and enter into settlement.

At any time after the filing of a complaint and before an answer has been filed, counsel for any party may make a request in writing to the judicial officer assigned to supervise discovery in the case to hold an early neutral evaluation conference, discovery conference or status/case management conference. Copies of the request must be sent to counsel for the parties and the parties whose addresses are known to the requesting counsel. Upon receiving such request, the judicial officer will examine the circumstances of the case and the reasons for the request and determine whether any such conference would assist in the reduction of expense and delay the case. The judicial officer will hold such conferences as he or she deems appropriate.

    a) At the ENE conference, the judicial officer and the parties will discuss the claims and defenses and seek to settle the case.

    b) The ENE conference will be informal, off the record, privileged, and confidential.

    c) Attendance may be excused only for good cause shown and by permission of the Court. Sanctions may be appropriate for an unexcused failure to attend.

2. If no settlement is reached at the ENE conference, the judicial officer may do one of the following:

    a) Discuss the parties' willingness to agree to non-binding arbitration or mediation within forty-five (45) days (1) in any case where the judicial officer believes arbitration or mediation, might result in a cost-effective resolution of the lawsuit, or (2) in any case where the parties have indicated an interest in arbitration or mediation. Additionally, a case management conference will be set in these cases approximately sixty (60) days after the ENE conference.

    b) Where no arbitration or mediation is agreed upon, the judicial officer must hold a case management conference within thirty (30) days after the ENE conference. The case management conference may be held at the conclusion of the ENE conference.

d. Case Management Conference. The parties who have responsibility over the litigation and the counsel who is responsible for the case, will be present at the case management conference. The judicial officer may approve attendance of a party or counsel by telephonic conference call. At a reasonable time *before* this conference all counsel will discuss discovery and endeavor to resolve any disputes.

1. At the conference, the judicial officer will (1) discuss the complexity of the case; (2) encourage a cooperative discovery schedule; (3) discuss the likelihood for further motions; (4) discuss the number of anticipated percipient and expert witnesses; (5) evaluate the case and the need for early supervi-

sion of settlement discussions; (6) discuss the availability of ADR alternatives; and (7) discuss any other special factors applicable to the progress of the case.

2. At the end of the conference the judicial officer must prepare a case management order which will:

a) Include a discovery schedule;

b) Set a time for a further case management conference, if necessary;

c) If appropriate, set a time for the proponent of each issue to identify expert witnesses; set a time for the responding party to identify expert witnesses in reply; set a time for the depositions of experts; set a time for the supplementation of such expert designation depending on the circumstances;

d) Set a deadline for filing pretrial motions.

e) Set a date for a pretrial hearing before the district judge who will try the case. The date for such hearing will be approved by the trial judge.

3. *Setting of Dates.*

a) At the case management or pre-trial conference a trial date will be set by the magistrate judge if directed by the district judge assigned to the case.

b) Senior district judges who have not referred the case to a magistrate judge will set all dates themselves.

c) The trial date must be firm and all requests for continuances of trial and motions dates will be granted only for good cause shown.

d) No trial date will be continued except by written order approved by the trial judge.

4. At the case management conference, the judicial officer will set a date for a mandatory settlement conference unless it is determined that such a conference should be excused.

e. **Cases in Which Status Conferences Are Not Required.** At the discretion of a judge assigned to the case, ENE and case management conferences need not be set in the following categories of cases:

1. Habeas corpus cases;

2. Cases reviewing administrative rulings;

3. Social Security Cases;

4. Default proceedings;

5. Cases in which a substantial number of defendants have not answered;

6. Actions to enforce judgments;

7. Bankruptcy appeals;

8. ENE conferences will not be set in Section 1983 cases.

f. **Pretrial.**

1. *Postponement of Pretrial Proceeding.*

a) By Stipulation. If additional time is required in which to comply with this rule, the parties may contact the Court's staff and submit a timely stipulation which sets forth the reasons for their request for a continuance.

b) By Motion. If counsel is unable to obtain the stipulation provided by the Civil Local Rule 7.2 a motion to continue or to be relieved from compliance with any requirement of Civil Local Rule 7.1.g.1 may, upon seven (7) days written notice, be presented on the Court's motion calendar.

2. *Memorandum of Contentions of Fact and Law.*

a) General. Unless the Court specifies otherwise, no later than 5:00 p.m. twenty-eight (28) days prior to the pretrial hearing, each party must serve on each other party and file with the Clerk a "Memorandum of Contentions of Fact and Law" which contains a concise statement of the material facts and the points of law claimed by such party and cites the authorities upon which the party intends to rely at trial.

b) Abandoned Issues. Each party must set forth a statement of any issues raised by the pleadings which have been abandoned.

c) Exhibits. Each party must set forth a list of all exhibits such party expects to offer at the trial other than those to be used for impeachment with a description of each exhibit sufficient for identification, the list being substantially in the following form:

Case Title: ＿＿＿＿＿＿ Case No. ＿＿＿＿
List of ＿＿＿＿＿＿＿＿＿ Exhibits

NUMBER	DATE MARKED	DATE ADMITTED	DESCRIPTION

Each party must place the case caption at the top as shown, and show "Plaintiff's" or "Defendant's" before the word "Exhibits" and, below that, only the spaces labeled "Number" and "Description" are required to be filled in prior to trial.

Plaintiff must number plaintiff's exhibits numerically and defendant's by alphabetic letters as follows: A to Z; then AA to AZ; then BA to BZ, etc. So far as is possible, exhibits must be numbered in the order in which they will be presented and offered at trial.

The parties are to consult the judge's courtroom clerk concerning problems as to the numbering of exhibits.

d) Witnesses. Each party must set forth the names and addresses of all prospective witnesses, except impeaching witnesses, and, in the case of expert witnesses, a brief narrative statement of qualifications of such witness and the substance of the testimony which such witness is expected to give. Only witnesses so listed will be permitted to testify at the trial except for good cause shown.

3. *Memorandum of Contentions of Fact and Law: Specific Situations.* In negligence, wrongful death, contract, eminent domain and patent cases the memorandum must particularize items set forth below.

a) Negligence Cases. The plaintiff must set forth: acts of negligence claimed, specific laws and regulations alleged to have been violated, a statement as to whether the doctrine of res ipsa loquitur is relied upon, and the basis for such reliance, a detailed list of personal injuries claimed, a detailed list of permanent personal injuries claimed including the nature and extent thereof, the age of the plaintiff, the life and work expectancy of the plaintiff if permanent injury is claimed, an itemized statement of all special damages to date, such as medical, hospital, nursing, etc., expenses, with the amount and to whom paid, a detailed statement of loss of earnings claimed and a detailed list of any property damage.

The defendant must set forth any acts of comparative or contributory negligence claimed in addition to any other defense he intends to interpose.

b) Wrongful Death Cases. In addition to the information required by Civil Local Rule 16.1.f.3.a, the plaintiff must set forth further information as follows: decedent's date of birth, marital status, including age of surviving spouse; employment for five years before date of death; work expectancy; reasonable probability of promotion; rate of earnings for five years before date of death; life expectancy under the mortality tables; general physical condition immediately prior to date of death; the names, dates of birth, and relationship of decedent's children and relatives; a detailed list of injuries claimed by said relatives and children; a list of decedent's dependents; the amounts of monetary contributions or their equivalent made to each of such dependents by decedent for a five-year period prior to date of death; a statement of the decedent's personal expenses and a fair allocation of the usual family expenses for decedent's living expenses for a period of at least three years prior to the date of death; and the amount claimed for care, advice, nurture, guidance, training, etc., by the deceased, if a parent, during the minority of any dependent.

The defendant must set forth any acts of comparative or contributory negligence claimed, in addition to any other defenses the defendant intends to interpose.

c) Contract Cases. The parties must set forth: whether the contract relied on was oral or in writing, specifying the writing, the date thereof and the parties thereto, the terms of the contract which are relied on by the party, any collateral oral agreement, if claimed, and the terms thereof, any specific breach of contract claimed, any misrepresentations of fact alleged, an itemized statement of damages claimed to have resulted from any alleged breach, the source of such information, how computed, and any books or records available to sustain such damage claim, whether modification of the contract or waiver of covenant is claimed, and if so, what modification or waiver and how accomplished.

d) Eminent Domain Cases. Disclosure in addition to that contained within Civil Local Rule 16.1.f.2 must be made as follows: Not later than seven (7) days in advance of pretrial hearing, each party appearing must file with the trial judge in camera a summary "Statement of Comparable Transactions" which contains: relevant facts as to each sale or other transaction to be relied upon as comparable to the taking, including the alleged date of such transaction, the names of all of the parties to the transaction, the consideration paid and the date of recordation, and the book, page or other identification of any record of such transaction. Such statements must be in a form and content suitable to be present-

ed to the jury as a summary of evidence on the subject. The judge may, thereafter, release the list of comparables to opposing counsel.

At least seven (7) days prior to trial each party appearing must serve and file a "Statement as to Just Compensation" setting forth a brief schedule of contentions as to the fair market value in cash, at the time of taking, of the estate or interest taken, the maximum amount of any benefit proximately resulting from the taking, and the amount of any claimed damage proximately resulting from severance.

e) Patent Cases. The parties and attorneys must comply with the following:

1. Each party must set forth a short specific statement of the party's contentions as to the teaching of the claims in the patents where it is contended the patent or patents are invalid;

2. The party asserting the validity of the patent must set forth a short specific statement of plaintiff's contentions as to how the patent or patents are infringed;

3. The party contesting the validity of the patent must set forth a short specific statement of defendant's contentions as to why the patent or patents are not infringed.

4. *Meetings of Counsel.*

a) Timing and Purpose of Meeting. At least twenty-one (21) days in advance of the pretrial hearing, and after each party has filed and served its memorandum of contentions of fact and law, the attorneys for the parties must convene at a suitable time and place. The purpose of the meeting is to arrive at stipulations and agreements resulting in simplification of the triable issues and to confer concerning the content of the pretrial order. Counsel for the plaintiff has the duty of arranging for meetings and for preparation of the Pretrial Order mandated by Civil Local Rule 16.1.f.6.c.

b) Exchanges Between Counsel. At the meeting, all exhibits other than those to be used for impeachment must be displayed or exchanged.

c) Content of Exhibits Exchanged. Each photograph, map, drawing and the like must contain a legend on its face or reverse side. The legend must state by date the relevant matters of fact as to what the party offering such an exhibit claims is fairly duplicate.

d) Failure to Display and/or Exchange Exhibits. Failure to display and/or exchange exhibits to or with opposing counsel will permit the Court to decline admission of same into evidence.

5. *Conduct of the Pretrial Hearing.* At the pretrial hearing the Court will consider:

a) Pleadings and Other Documents. The pleadings, proposed amendments to the pleadings and papers and exhibits then on file including stipulations, statements and memoranda filed pursuant to Civil Local Rule 16.1.f.2 and f.3 and all matters referred to in Fed.R.Civ.P. 16.

b) Motions. All motions and other proceedings then pending.

c) Settlement and Simplification. The possibilities for settlement of the case and other matters which may be presented concerning parties, process, pleading or proof with a view to simplifying issues and bringing about a just, speedy and inexpensive determination of the matter.

d) Future Proceedings. Future and additional pretrial meetings where required and, upon termination of the final pretrial hearing, the date upon which the case will be set for trial.

e) Consent to a Magistrate Judge. Whether the parties will consent to a magistrate judge to conduct the trial.

6. *Pretrial Order.*

a) Responsibility of Plaintiff's Counsel. Counsel for the plaintiff will be responsible for preparing the pretrial order and arranging the meetings of counsel pursuant to this rule. Not less than fourteen (14) days in advance of the pretrial hearing, plaintiff's counsel must provide opposing counsel with the proposed pretrial order for review and approval. Opposing counsel must communicate promptly with plaintiff's attorney concerning any objections to form or content of the pretrial order, and both parties should attempt promptly to resolve their differences, if any, concerning the order.

b) Lodging with the Judge's Chambers. No later than seven (7) days prior to the pretrial hearing, plaintiff will lodge a Pretrial Order with the judge's chambers.

c) Format. Attorneys for all parties appearing in the case must have approved the Pretrial Order as to form and substance. The Pretrial Order will contain the following unless the Court orders otherwise:

1. A statement to be read to the jury, not in excess of one page, of the nature of the case and the claims and defenses.

2. A list of the causes of action to be tried, referenced to the Complaint [and Counterclaim if applicable]. For each cause of action, the order must succinctly list the elements of the claim, damages and any defenses. A cause of action in the Complaint [and/or Counterclaim] which is not listed will be dismissed with prejudice.

3.(a) A list of each witness counsel actually expect to call at trial with a brief statement not exceeding four sentences, of the substance of the witnesses' testimony.

(b) A list of each expert witness counsel actually expects to call at trial with a brief statement, not exceeding four sentences, of the substance of the expert witnesses' testimony.

(c) A list of additional witnesses, including experts, counsel do not expect to call at this time but reserve the right to call along with a brief statement, not to exceed four sentences, of the substance of the witnesses' testimony.

4.(a) A list of all exhibits that counsel actually expect to offer at trial with a one-sentence description of the exhibit.

(b) A list of all other exhibits that counsel do not expect to offer at this time but reserve the right to offer if necessary at trial with a one-sentence description of the exhibit.

5. A statement of all facts to which the parties stipulate. This statement must be on a separate page and will be read to and provided to the jury. The parties are directed to meet with the assigned magistrate judge to work out as many stipulations of fact as possible.

6. A list of all deposition transcripts by page and line, or videotape depositions by section that will be offered at trial.

7. In addition to filing proposed jury instructions in accordance with Fed. R. Civ. P. 51 and CivLR 51.1, the parties must e-mail the proposed instructions in Word or Wordperfect form to Chambers. If a party disagrees with a particular instruction, the party must submit an alternate instruction.

8. This case will be tried by (jury) (by the Court without a jury).

9. Time estimated for trial is ( ) days.

7. *Trial Counsel to Be Present.* Unless otherwise ordered by the Court, counsel who will conduct the trial will appear at the pretrial hearing.

8. *Penalties: Pretrial.* Failure of counsel for any party to appear before the Court at pretrial proceedings or to complete the necessary preparations therefor may be considered an abandonment or failure to prosecute or defend diligently, and judgment may be entered against the defaulting party either with respect to a specific issue or on the entire case.

9. *Preparations for Trial.* Unless otherwise ordered, the parties must, not less than seven (7) calendar days prior to the date on which the trial is scheduled to commence:

a) Serve and file briefs on all significant disputed issues of the law, including foreseeable procedural and evidentiary issues, setting forth briefly the party's position and the supporting arguments and authorities;

b) In jury cases, serve and file proposed voir dire questions, jury instructions and forms of verdict which must conform to Civil Local Rule 51.1; and (2) in court cases, serve and file proposed findings of fact and conclusions of law;

c) Exchange copies of all exhibits to be offered that were not already provided under Civil Local Rule 16.1.f.4.b and all schedules, summaries, diagrams and charts to be used at the trial other than for impeachment or rebuttal. Each proposed exhibit must be pre-marked for identification in a manner clearly distinguishing plaintiff's from defendant's exhibits. Upon request, a party must make the original or the underlying documents of any exhibit available for inspection and copying. Nothing in this rule will excuse a failure to comply in good faith with the time for exchanging exhibits under Civil Local Rule 16.1.f.4.b.

[Effective August 18, 1997. Amended effective March 2, 1998; January 1, 2000; January 1, 2001; November 19, 2001; October 25, 2004; December 1, 2009; January 1, 2014; February 2, 2015; January 30, 2016; April 24, 2017.]

CIVIL RULE 16.2 STATUS AND SCHEDULING CONFERENCES

Magistrate judges may hold status conference and issue scheduling orders in any case which has been referred to the magistrate judge by the district judge for that purpose.

[Effective August 18, 1997.]

CIVIL RULE 16.3 SETTLEMENT CONFERENCES AND PROCEEDINGS

a. Mandatory Settlement Conference. In each civil action, a mandatory settlement conference must be scheduled before the assigned magistrate judge or such other judicial officer as the assigned district judge may direct. If the judicial officer assigned to conduct the settlement conference determines that a case is ready for a settlement conference prior to the scheduled date, the judge may order the parties and counsel to appear for such a conference.

b. Attendance of Parties. The judge conducting the settlement conference may require the parties or representatives of a party other than counsel, who have authority to negotiate and enter into a binding settlement, to be present at the settlement conference.

c. Disqualification of Judge. The judge conducting the settlement conference will be disqualified from trying the case unless there is an agreement by all the parties to waive this restriction.

d. In Camera Communications. The judge conducting the settlement conference may receive in camera communications from each party and its counsel, and must maintain such in confidence unless there is a stipulation to the contrary.

e. Follow–Up Settlement Conference. The judge conducting the settlement conference may schedule as many follow-up settlement conferences as the judge finds appropriate in light of the complexity of the matter or any circumstances in the case.

f. Alternative Settlement Procedures. A district or magistrate judge may order a non-binding mini-trial or summary jury trial in all cases the judge finds, after a hearing with an opportunity to be heard, that (1) the potential judgment does not exceed $250,000 and (2) that the use of this procedure will probably resolve the case. In determining whether to order a mini-trial or summary jury trial, the judge must also consider the costs of the procedure and the costs that may be saved by ordering such a non-binding trial. After considering the above and any other relevant factors, the judge may order the parties to participate in a non-binding mini-trial or summary jury trial notwithstanding that one or more of the parties has objected thereto. A district and magistrate judge may also order a non-binding mini-trial or summary jury trial in all other cases where the parties have consented to such procedure.

g. Post–Verdict Settlement Conferences. In the event that a civil case is tried before the Court or a jury and a verdict is returned, the trial judge may order the case referred to the assigned magistrate judge or such other judge the

parties mutually agree upon for the purpose of scheduling a settlement conference. The settlement judge will immediately schedule the settlement conference and order the parties and counsel to be present. This conference must be held before the judgment becomes final.

h. The settlement conference will be off the record, privileged and confidential, unless otherwise ordered by the Court.

[Effective August 18, 1997. Amended effective March 2, 1998; November 19, 2001; December 1, 2009.]

CIVIL RULE 16.4 ASSESSMENT OF JURY COSTS

If for any reason attributable to counsel or parties, including settlement, the Court is unable to commence a jury trial as scheduled, where a panel of prospective jurors have reported for voir dire, the Court may assess against counsel or parties responsible all or part of the cost of the panel.

[Effective August 18, 1997.]

CIVIL RULE 17.1 ACTIONS INVOLVING MINORS OR INCOMPETENTS

a. Order of Judgment Required. No action by or on behalf of a minor or incompetent, or in which a minor or incompetent has an interest, will be settled, compromised, voluntarily discontinued, dismissed or terminated without court order or judgment. All settlements and compromises must be reviewed by a magistrate judge before any order of approval will issue. The parties may, with district judge approval consent to magistrate judge jurisdiction under 28 U.S.C. § 636(c) for entry of an order approving the entire settlement or compromise.

b. Payment and Disbursement of Funds.

1. Money or property recovered by a minor or incompetent California resident by settlement or judgment must be paid and disbursed in accordance with California Probate Code Section 3600, et seq. If the recipient of the money or property is not a California resident, disbursement must occur pursuant to court restrictions which are similar to those of Section 3600, et seq.

2. Should a guardian be necessary a certified copy of guardianship letters and a State Court certificate must be filed with the Clerk prior to any distribution to the guardian unless otherwise ordered by the Court. The certificate will verify that the guardian has filed a surety bond in an amount to be determined by the Court.

3. Should money or property be held in a trust for a minor or an incompetent, the proposed trust instrument must be submitted to a magistrate judge on an ex parte petition for review and approval before the settlement is approved or the judgment is entered. The magistrate judge may require approval of the form of the documents by an appropriate state judge in the jurisdiction where the minor or incompetent resides. The parties may also consent to magistrate judge jurisdiction to approve the entire settlement under 28 U.S.C. § 636(c). Where the parties consent to magistrate judge jurisdiction to approve the entire settlement, the approval of

the trust documents and the settlement may be consolidated in one properly noticed hearing.

4. Any withdrawals or disbursements from the trust must be made in accordance with the procedures and applicable laws of the state.

a) The Ex Parte Petition For Approval of Terms of Trust should generally contain the following information:

1. Identity of the petitioner;

2. The terms and total amount of the settlement and the amount to go into the trust;

3. The circumstances giving rise to the settlement or judgment and a general description of the plaintiff's injuries and needs;

4. Suggested amount of bond;

5. If for a Special Needs Trust, the petition should make the allegations to support the determinations required under California Probate Code § 3600(b) for the establishment of the trust; and,

6. Any other information that may be required.

b) A Proposed Order must be submitted by the attorney for the petitioner and must comply with the requirements of this rule and California Probate Code § 3600, et seq. and include the following:

1. An order for the appropriate bond;

2. An order that the first accounting, if required, be filed within one year of the establishment of the trust with the San Diego Superior Court. If the recipient of the money or property is not a California resident, the accounting must be made to the appropriate court in the jurisdiction where the minor or incompetent resides;

3. If the order is for the approval of the terms of a Special Needs Trust, it should contain:

(a) A statement that the petitioner will provide that all liens have been satisfied prior to the establishment of the trust by the Court; and,

(b) A statement that the "court makes no specific finding or order with respect to whether the Special Needs Trust for the Benefit of _____ satisfies or complies with applicable federal laws or regulations."

4. The order will provide that the terms of the trust are approved and those terms will be fully set forth within said Order, not as an attachment. The parties are further directed to proceed with settlement approval hearings or the entry of judgment as appropriate.

c) A copy of the executed trust document, as approved pursuant to this rule, along with a certification by the trustee that any court ordered surety bond is in force, must be filed with the Court prior to any distribution to the trust.

[Effective August 18, 1997. Amended effective August 16, 1999; December 1, 2009; February 2, 2015.]

CIVIL RULE 23.1   CLASS ACTIONS

In any action sought to be maintained as a class action:

a. The complaint, or other pleading asserting a class action must bear the legend "Class Action" below the docket number; and

b. The complaint must include a statement describing the class or classes on behalf of which the action is sought to be maintained.

[Effective August 18, 1997. Amended, effective April 6, 1998; December 1, 2009.]

CIVIL RULE 26.1   DEPOSITION AND DISCOVERY

a. **Conference Required.** The Court will entertain no motion pursuant to Rules 26 through 37, Fed.R.Civ.P., unless counsel will have previously met and conferred concerning all disputed issues. If counsel for the moving party seeks to arrange such a conference and counsel for the party against whom the motion is made willfully refuses or fails to meet and confer, the judge (in absence of a prior order dispensing good cause with such a meeting) may order a payment of reasonable expenses, including attorney's fees, pursuant to Rule 37, Fed. R.Civ.P. and Civil Local Rule 83.1. If counsel have offices in the same county, they are to meet in person. If counsel have offices in different counties, they are to confer by telephone. Under no circumstances may the parties satisfy the meet and confer requirement by exchanging written correspondence.

b. **Certificate of Compliance.** At the time of filing any motion with respect to Rules 26 through 37, Fed.R.Civ.P., counsel for the moving party must serve and file a certificate of compliance with this rule.

c. **Protective Order.** Any party or non-party against whom a motion under Rule 37(a) or Rule 45(d)(1), Fed.R.Civ. P., is being made may notice for hearing at the same time a motion for protective order under Rule 26(c), Fed.R.Civ.P.

d. **Principles Controlling Dispositions of Motions.** In the disposition of any motion made under Rules 37(a) or 26(c), Fed.R.Civ.P., the Court will be guided by the rule of construction contained in Civil Local Rule 1.1.c. to secure the just, efficient and economical determination of every action and proceeding.

e. **Discovery Motion.** All motions to compel discovery are referred to the magistrate judge assigned to the case. The magistrate judge maintains discretion to waive all or part of the requirements of Civil Local Rule 7.1.f. in deciding discovery motions.

[Effective August 18, 1997. Amended effective January 1, 2000; January 1, 2001; October 25, 2004; December 1, 2009.]

CIVIL RULE 30.1   DEPOSITIONS

a. **Transcripts/Record Cost.** The deposing party must assume the cost of the record or transcription unless, upon motion or the parties' agreement, the Court orders a waiver of transcription or a different apportionment of cost.

b. **Court Copy.** Whenever a deposition or any part thereof is to be read in Court, counsel using same must furnish a copy to the judge, which copy must be in addition to the original filed with the Court.

[Effective August 18, 1997. Amended effective January 1, 2001; October 25, 2004; December 1, 2009.]

CIVIL RULE 33.1   INTERROGATORIES

a.   **Limitation on Number of Interrogatories.**   No party will serve on any other party interrogatories which, including discrete subparts, number more than twenty-five interrogatories without leave of Court.   Any party desiring to serve additional interrogatories must submit to the Court a written motion setting forth the proposed additional interrogatories and the reasons establishing good cause for their use.

b.   **Answers and Objections to Interrogatories.**   Answers and objections to interrogatories, objections to answers to interrogatories or motions for more definite answers pursuant to Rule 37(a), Fed.R.Civ.P. must identify and quote each interrogatory in full immediately preceding the statement of any answer or objection thereto.

c.   **Filing.**   Unless filing is ordered by the Court on motion of a party or upon its own motion, interrogatories, requests for production and the answers thereto need not be filed unless and until they are used in the proceedings.

[Effective August 18, 1997. Amended effective January 1, 2001; October 25, 2004; July 16, 2007; December 1, 2009.]

CIVIL RULE 36.1   REQUESTS FOR ADMISSION

a.   **Limitation on Number of Requests for Admission.**   No party will serve on any other party requests for admission which, including subparagraphs, number more than twenty-five requests for admission without leave of Court.   Any party desiring to serve additional requests for admission must submit to the Court a written memorandum setting forth the proposed additional requests for admission and the reasons establishing good cause for their use.

b.   **Answers and Objections to Requests for Admission.**   Responses and objections to requests for admission or answers thereto pursuant to Rule 36, Fed.R.Civ.P. must identify and quote each request for admission in full immediately preceding the statement of any answer or objection thereto.

c.   **Filing.**   Unless filing is ordered by the Court on motion of a party or upon its own motion, requests for admission, and requests for production and the answers thereto need not be filed unless and until they are used in the proceedings.

[Effective August 18, 1997. Amended effective January 1, 2001; October 25, 2004; December 1, 2009.]

CIVIL RULE 38.1   JURY DEMAND

Where demand is made for a jury trial, it must appear immediately following the title of the complaint, petition or answer containing the demand, or on such other pleading as may be permitted under Rule 38(b), Fed.R.Civ.P.

Any other notation on the civil cover sheet, such as those described in Civil Local Rule 3.1, will not constitute a demand for jury trial under these rules.

[Effective August 18, 1997. Amended, effective October 25, 2004; December 1, 2009.]

CIVIL RULE 40.1   ASSIGNMENT OF CIVIL CASES

a.   **Assignment of Civil Cases.**   All actions and proceedings of a civil nature must be numbered consecutively upon the filing of the first document in each such action or proceeding, and the judges will, from time to time, determine, and indicate by formal order to the Clerk, the method by which each action or proceeding will be assigned to a particular judge, to the end that over a period of time each judge must be assigned substantially equal amounts of work.   Neither the Clerk nor any deputy will have any discretion in determining the judge to whom any matter is assigned, the action of the Clerk being ministerial only.   The method of assignment chosen by the judges will be such that the judge to whom any particular matter is to be assigned, in accordance with this rule, must not be known by or disclosed to the Clerk, or any member of the staff, or to any other person, until after such action or proceeding has been filed and numbered.   The judge to whom a case is assigned, or the Chief Judge of the district, may transfer such a case at any time to a consenting judge in the interest of efficient administration of the judicial business of the district.

b.   **Assignments to New Judges.**   Upon the induction of a new judge or judges, the Court will assign the new judge(s) a portion of the existing civil case load from the dockets of the active judges.   The Clerk will then indicate to each active judge the number of cases to be transferred to the new judge.

The Court will enter an order designating the number of such cases to be selected by the transferring judge and the number to be chosen randomly by the Clerk.   The transferring judge may decline to transfer a case and then another case will be randomly selected.

The new judge may refuse to accept any such transfer when there are grounds for recusal, in which instance another case will be selected.

The Clerk will then add the name of the new judge to the random selection system that governs the assignment of new cases to active judges.

c.   **Assignments to Senior Judges.**   Senior District Judges may, in their discretion, direct the reassignment of any case pending before them to another randomly selected District Judge.

d.   **Temporary Designation.**   Absent an order to the contrary, all the judges sitting in this District are designated to handle any matters requiring action on cases assigned to a judge who is unavailable.

e.   **Low Number Rule, Criteria.**   The Clerk must promptly examine the original complaint or petition in each civil action and proceeding hereafter filed and ascertain whether any one or more civil actions or proceedings pending or any one or more currently filed appear (1) to arise from the same or substantially identical transactions, happenings, or events; or (2) involve the same or substantially the same parties or property, or (3) involve the same patent or the same trademark; or (4) call for determination of the same or substantially identical questions of law; or (5) where a case is refiled within one year of having previously been terminated by the Court; or (6) for other reasons would entail substantial duplication of labor if heard by different judges.

f. Notice of Related Case, Duties of Counsel. Whenever counsel has reason to believe that a pending action or proceeding on file or about to be filed is related to another pending action or proceeding on file in this or any other federal or State Court (whether pending, dismissed, or otherwise terminated), counsel must promptly file and serve on all known parties to each related action or proceeding a notice of related case, stating the title, number and filing date of each action or proceeding believed to be related, together with a brief statement of their relationship and the reasons why assignment to a single district judge is or is not likely to effect a saving of judicial effort and other economies. The Clerk will promptly notify the Court of such filing. This is a continuing duty that applies not only when counsel files a case with knowledge of a related action or proceeding but also applies after the date of filing whenever counsel learns of a related action or proceeding.

g. Definition of Related Action. An action or proceeding is related to another action or proceeding where both of them:

1. Involve some of the same parties and are based on the same or similar claims, or

2. Involve the same property, transaction, patent, trademark, or event, or

3. Involve substantially the same facts and the same questions of law.

h. Duties of Clerk. Whenever it appears to the Clerk that any one or more of the above circumstances set forth in Civil Local Rule 40.1.e exist, it will be the duty of the Clerk to report the cases in question to the judges concerned at the earliest date practicable.

The Clerk's report must set forth, as to each action or proceeding listed therein: (1) the case number, (2) the fullest practicable statement of the names of all parties, (3) a brief statement of the nature of the case and the relief sought, (4) the name of the attorney for plaintiff or petitioning party, and (5) such other information as will, in the opinion of the Clerk, assist in determining whether a case should be transferred under this "low-number" rule. The Clerk's report must be accompanied by an appropriate order for the signature of the judges concerned with the proposed transfer.

i. Assignments and Transfers. In order to avoid unnecessary duplication of judicial effort, all pending civil actions and proceedings, which are determined to be related to any other pending civil action or proceeding pursuant to the criteria set forth in Civil Local Rule 40.1.e will be assigned to the district and magistrate judge to whom the lowest numbered case was assigned, or the magistrate judge, if the parties consent, and the magistrate judge is handling the lower numbered case by consent. Orders for transfers of cases subject to this "low-numbered" rule must be made and entered at the earliest practicable date following commencement of the action or proceedings.

j. Transfer Limitation. No single series of cases comprising more than ten in number may be transferred to a single judge pursuant to this order without the consent of the transferee judge.

[Effective August 18, 1997. Amended effective November 10, 1997; January 1, 2000; October 25, 2004; August 11, 2005; May 1, 2006; December 1, 2009; November 1, 2011; February 2, 2015; January 30, 2016; July 5, 2021.]

CIVIL RULE 40.2 NOTICE OF PARTY WITH FINANCIAL INTEREST

Any non-governmental corporate party to an action in this court must file a "Corporate Disclosure Statement" identifying all its parent corporations and listing any publicly held company that owns 10% or more of the party's stock. A party will file a separate statement entitled "Notice of Party with Financial Interest" with its initial appearance in the Court and will supplement the statement within a reasonable time of any change in the information.

[Effective March 2, 2000. Amended effective December 1, 2009; December 1, 2018.]

CIVIL RULE 41.1 DISMISSAL FOR WANT OF PROSECUTION AND FOR FAILURE TO COMPLY WITH LOCAL RULES

a. Actions or proceedings which have been pending in this court for more than six months, without any proceeding or discovery having been taken therein during such period, may, after notice, be dismissed by the Court for want of prosecution, at the calling of a calendar prepared for that purpose by the Clerk. Such a dismissal must be without prejudice, unless otherwise ordered.

b. Failure to comply with the provisions of the local rules of this court may also be grounds for dismissal under this rule.

[Effective August 18, 1997. Amended effective December 1, 2009.]

CIVIL RULE 47.1 EXAMINATION OF JURORS

Unless otherwise ordered, the examination of trial jurors will be conducted by the judge. Counsel will submit any questions which they desire to be propounded to the jurors in accordance with Civil Local Rule 16.1.f.9.b.

[Effective August 18, 1997. Amended, effective October 25, 2004; December 1, 2009.]

CIVIL RULE 51.1 FILING, SERVICE AND FORM OF PROPOSED INSTRUCTIONS

a. Filing. Jury instructions must be filed in accordance with Rule 51, Fed.R.Civ.P. The judge may in the judge's discretion, receive additional requests for instructions at any time prior to the commencement of argument to the jury.

b. Style. Each proposed instruction must be concise, cover only one subject which must be indicated in the caption, set forth the identity of the party submitting it, be written in full on a separate page, be consecutively numbered, and set forth citations to the authorities supporting it.

c. Objections. Objections to proposed instructions may be made in writing or orally, as time permits. Such objections should normally be accompanied by citations of supporting authority. Prior to argument of counsel to the jury, the Court must inform counsel of the instructions which will be given.

d. Instructions. If an instruction is submitted from a recognized book of instructions, it must be from the latest edition thereof (so noted at the bottom of the instruction); and if modified in any way, deleted material must be shown in parentheses and additions must be underscored.

[Effective August 18, 1997. Amended, effective October 25, 2004; December 1, 2009.]

CIVIL RULE 53.1   SPECIAL MASTER REPORTS (28 U.S.C. § 636(b)(2))

Any party may seek review of, or action on, a special master's report filed by a magistrate judge in accordance with the provisions of Rule 53(e) of the Fed.R.Civ.P.

[Effective August 18, 1997. Amended, effective October 25, 2004.]

CIVIL RULE 54.1   COSTS

a. In General. See 28 U.S.C. §§ 1920 and 1923; Rule 54(d), Fed. R. Civ. P. Unless otherwise ordered by the Court, or stipulated by the parties, the prevailing party is entitled to costs. Within fourteen (14) days after entry of judgment, the party in whose favor a judgment for costs is awarded or allowed by law, and who claims costs, must file with the Clerk the bill of costs, together with a notice of when the Clerk will hear the application. Unless otherwise ordered by the Court, the filing of a motion under Fed. R. Civ. P. 59 or 60 does not extend the time to file the bill of costs. Prevailing party may elect to hold a telephonic hearing upon notice to the Clerk and the attorney for the adverse party. It will be the responsibility of the prevailing party to initiate the conference call.

The bill of costs must itemize the costs claimed and must be supported by a memorandum of costs, an affidavit of counsel that the costs claimed are allowable by law, are correctly stated, and were necessarily incurred, and copies of the invoices for requested costs. Cost bill forms must be made available by the Clerk's office upon request.

The notice must specify the hour and date when application to the Clerk to tax the costs will be made, which must not be less than fourteen (14) nor more than twenty-one (21) days from the date of the notice. Any opposition or memorandum by the opposing party must be filed at a time specified by the Clerk prior to the hearing indicated on the bill of costs.

b. Items Taxable as Costs. It is the custom of the Court to allow certain items of costs not otherwise allowed or prohibited by statute or by specific order, as follows:

1. *Fees for Service of Process.* Fees for service of process (whether served by the United States Marshal or other persons authorized by Fed. R. Civ. P. 4) are allowable. Fees for expedited service are allowable only if the Court ordered service to be effected on an expedited basis. Costs for service of subpoenas are taxable as well as service of summonses and complaints.

2. *Fees Incident to Transcripts—Trial Transcripts.* Except as provided below, the cost of transcripts is not normally allowable unless, before it is incurred, it is approved by a judge or stipulated to be recoverable by counsel.

a) The cost of the original and one (1) copy of a trial transcript, a daily transcript and of a transcript of matters prior or subsequent to trial, furnished the Court is taxable, when either requested by the Court, or prepared pursuant to stipulation. Mere acceptance by the Court does not constitute a request. Copies of transcripts for counsel's own use are not taxable in the absence of a special order of the Court.

b) The cost of transcripts necessarily obtained for appeal is allowable.

c) The cost of a transcript of a statement by a judge from the bench which is to be reduced to a formal order prepared by counsel is allowable.

3. *Depositions.* Costs incurred in connection with taking depositions, including:

a) The cost of an original and one copy of any deposition (including videotaped depositions) necessarily obtained for use in the case is allowable. Depositions need not be introduced in evidence or used at trial to be taxable so long as at the time it was taken it could reasonably be expected that the deposition would be used for trial preparation, rather than mere discovery. Counsel's copies (whether paper or electronic), in excess of the original and one copy are not taxable, regardless of which party took the deposition.

b) If both video and stenographic depositions are taken, they both will be allowed as costs only if the video deposition is used at trial. The cost of electronic versions is recoverable.

c) The reasonable expenses of the deposition reporter, and the notary or other official presiding at the taking of the depositions are recoverable, including travel and subsistence.

d) Postage cost, including registry, for sending the original deposition to the Clerk for filing is recoverable.

e) Counsel's fees, expenses in arranging for taking and expenses in attending the taking of a deposition are not recoverable, except as provided by statute or by the Fed. R. Civ. P.

f) Fees for the witness at the taking of a deposition are taxable at the same rate as for attendance at trial. The witness need not be under subpoena.

g) A reasonable fee for a necessary interpreter at the taking of a deposition is recoverable.

h) The attendance fee of a reporter when a witness fails to appear is allowable if the claimant made use of available process to compel the attendance of the witness.

4. *Witness Fees.* Fees paid to witnesses, including:

a) Per diem, mileage, subsistence and attendance fees as provided in 28 U.S.C. § 1821 paid to witnesses subpoenaed and/or actually attending the proceeding, if the witness is served with the subpoena within California or as otherwise authorized by Fed. R. Civ. P. 45(b)(2).

1. Such fees are taxable even though the witness does not take the stand, provided the witness necessarily attends the Court.

2. Such fees are taxable even though the witness attends voluntarily upon request and is not under subpoena.

3. If the witness comes from outside the district, the transportation expenses taxable must be based on the most direct route, and on the most economical rate reasonably available, for means of the transportation used by the witness, subject to the additional provisions of the Fed. R. Civ. P.

4. Witness fees and subsistence are taxable only for the reasonable period during which the witness is within the district.

5. If a witness appears on the same date in related cases requiring appearance in the same court, one set of fees is taxable, the single set as taxed to be divided equally among the related cases.

b) Witness fees for a party if required to attend by opposing party; and

c) Witness fees for officers and employees of a corporation if they are not parties in their individual capacities.

d) Unless otherwise provided by law, fees for expert witnesses are not taxable in a greater amount than that statutorily allowable for ordinary witnesses.

e) The reasonable fee of a competent interpreter is taxable, if the fee of the witness involved is taxable. The reasonable fee of a competent translator is taxable if the document translated is necessarily filed, or admitted into evidence.

5. *Compensation of Court–Appointed Experts.* Compensation of court-appointed experts, compensation for interpreters, and salaries, fees, expenses and costs of special interpretation services (28 U.S.C. §§ 1828 and 1920(6)) are allowable.

6. *Exemplification and Copies of Papers.*

a) The cost of copies necessarily obtained for use in the case are taxable if one or more of the following criteria are met:

1. copies were provided either to the Court or to opposing counsel either by court order, or rule or statute.

2. copies were used as court exhibits, either admitted into evidence, or attached to a motion.

3. The fee of an official for certification, or proof regarding nonexistence of a document is taxable.

4. The reasonable fee of a competent translated is taxable if the document translated is taxable.

5. Notary fees are taxable if actually incurred, but only for documents which are required to be notarized and which are necessarily filed.

6. The cost of patent file wrappers and prior art patents are taxable at the rate charged by the patent office. Expenses for service of persons checking patent office records to determine what should be ordered are not taxable.

b) The following copy costs are not taxable:

1. The cost of copies submitted in lieu of originals because of the convenience of offering counsel or client are not taxable.

2. The cost of reproducing copies of motions, pleadings, notices and other routine case papers is not allowable.

3. The cost of copies obtained for counsel's own use is not taxable.

c) Procedure regarding copy and electronic conversion costs:

The party seeking recovery must present documentary evidence in the form of affidavits describing the documents copied or converted, to whom they were provided, the number of pages copied or converted, and the cost per page or per hour, and the use of or intended purpose for the items copied or converted. If documents were provided only to the party seeking recovery, that party must specify the purpose of acquisition and photocopying or for conversion of the documents served. In the absence of a specific showing, recovery must be denied.

7. *Maps, Charts, Models, Photographs, Summaries, Computations, and Statistical Summaries.*

a) The cost of preparing charts, diagrams, videotapes and other visual aids to be used as exhibits is taxable if such exhibits are reasonably necessary to assist the jury or the Court in understanding the issues at the trial. An explanation of how the above related to a material issue in the case will be provided.

b) The cost of photographs, 16″ × 20″ in size or less, is taxable if admitted into evidence, the cost of photographs attached to documents required to be filed and served on opposing counsel is limited to 8″ × 10″. Enlargements greater than 16″ × 20″ are not taxable except by order of the Court.

c) The cost of models is not taxable except by order of the Court.

d) The cost of compiling summaries, computations, and statistical comparisons is not taxable, except by prior approval by the Court.

e) The cost of preparing material for electronic retrieval and demonstrations (i.e. CD ROM and VHS tape) is taxable only as it relates to exhibits admitted in evidence, the cost to rent the equipment for court is not taxable.

8. *Fees to Masters, Receivers and Commissioners.* Fees to masters, receivers, and commissioners are taxable as costs, unless otherwise ordered by the Court.

9. *Premiums on Undertakings, Bonds or Security Stipulations.* The party entitled to recover costs will ordinarily be allowed premiums paid on undertakings, bonds or security stipulations, where the same have been furnished by reason of

express requirement of the law, or on order of the Court or a judge thereof, or where the same is necessarily required to enable the party to secure some right accorded him in the action or proceeding.

10. *Removed Cases.* In a case removed from the State Court, costs incurred in the State Court prior to removal must be recovered by the prevailing party in federal court to the extent they are covered in this rule or otherwise permitted by state law.

11. *Admiralty.* Fees for compensation, as set by general order, for keepers of boats, vessels and other property attached or libeled are taxable as costs.

12. *Appeals.* Costs incurred on appeal as allowed by the Federal Rules of Appellate Procedure.

c. Costs Not Allowed. Unless a party must substantiate the claim by reference to statutes or decisions for the following costs, the following will not ordinarily be allowed: (1) accountant's fees incurred for investigation, (2) the purchase of infringing devices in patent cases, (3) the physical examination of on opposing party, (4) courtesy copies of exhibits furnished to opposing counsel without request, and (5) rental of equipment for use at court hearings or trial.

d. Costs Where Offer of Judgment Filed. (See Rule 68, Fed. R. Civ. P.) If the defendant offers a judgment in a certain sum which is rejected by the plaintiff, and the case thereafter goes to trial with the resulting recovery (plus any authorized pre-offer costs and attorney's fees) of only the amount previously offered by the defendant, or less, then the defendant is the prevailing party. No costs will be allowed to either party if the Court is unable to clearly determine the prevailing party.

e. Costs Against the Government. (See 28 U.S.C. § 2412)

f. Party Entitled to Costs. The determination of the prevailing party will be within the discretion of the Court in all cases except where such determination is inconsistent with statute or the Fed. R. Civ. P. or the rules of the appellate courts. If each side recovers in part, ordinarily the party recovering the larger sum will be considered the prevailing party. The defendant is the prevailing party upon any termination of the case without judgment for the plaintiff except a voluntary dismissal under Fed. R. Civ. P. 41(a).

g. Method of Taxation of Costs.

1. At the time specified in the notice, the party objecting to any item of costs contained in the bill of costs must file the objections in writing, specifying each item to which objection is made and the ground of the objection, and file any affidavit or present facts relied on which may be rebutted by the opposing party.

2. The Clerk will thereupon proceed to tax the costs, and must allow such items specified in said bill of costs as are properly chargeable as costs. The Clerk must make an insertion of the costs in the docket.

3. The taxation of costs made by the Clerk must be final, unless modified on review as provided in Local Rule 54.1.h.

4. Notice of the Clerk's taxation of costs must be given by mailing a copy of the bill as approved by the Clerk to all parties in accordance with Rule 5, Fed. R. Civ. P.

5. Except as otherwise provided by law, costs will be taxed on the date set notwithstanding the fact that an appeal may have been filed.

h. Review of Costs. A review of the decision of the Clerk in the taxation of costs may be taken to the Court on motion to re-tax by any party in accordance with Rule 54(d), Fed. R. Civ. P., and Civil Local Rule 7.1.

1. A motion to retax must be served and filed within seven (7) days after receipt of the notice provided for in Civil Local Rule 54.1.g or unless within the seven (7) day period the Court permits the motion to be made orally.

2. A motion to retax must particularly specify the ruling of the Clerk excepted to and no others will be considered at the hearing, except that the opposing party may, within (3) days of service of the motion to retax, file a cross-motion to retax.

i. Writ of Execution for Costs. The Clerk will, upon request, issue a writ of execution to recover costs or attorney's fees included in the judgment:

1. Upon presentation of a certified copy of the final judgment in the District Court; or

2. Upon presentation of a mandate of the Court of Appeals to recover costs taxed by the appellate court.

[Effective August 18, 1997. Amended effective August 10, 1999; November 19, 2001; October 25, 2004; December 1, 2009; December 1, 2018.]

CIVIL RULE 55.1 DEFAULT JUDGMENTS

If plaintiff(s) fail(s) to move for default judgment within thirty (30) days of the entry of a default, the Clerk will prepare, with notice, an order to show cause why the complaint against the defaulted party should not be dismissed.

[Effective August 18, 1997. Amended, effective March 2, 1998; April 6, 1998; August 10, 1999; December 1, 2009.]

CIVIL RULE 58.1 ENTRY OF COURT–ISSUED DOCUMENT

All orders, decrees, judgments, and proceedings of the Court will be filed in the Electronic Filing System, which will constitute entry on the docket kept by the Clerk under Fed.R.Civ.P. 58 and 79. Any order or other court-issued document filed electronically without the original signature of a judge or clerk has the same force and effect as if the judge or clerk had signed a paper copy of the order and it had been entered on the docket in a conventional manner. Orders may also be issued as "text-only" entries on the docket, without an attached document. Such orders are official and binding.

[Effective May 1, 2006. Amended effective July 16, 2007.]

CIVIL RULE 65.1.2 BONDS AND SURETIES

a. When Required. A judge may, upon demand of any party, where authorized by law and for good cause shown, require any party to furnish security for costs which may be awarded against such party in an amount and on such terms as are appropriate.

b. Qualifications of Surety. Every bond must have as surety either: (1) a corporation authorized by the Secretary of the Treasury of the United States to act as surety on official bonds under 31 U.S.C. §§ 9301—9306; (2) a corporation authorized to act as surety under the law of the State of California; (3) two individual residents in the district, each of whom owns real or personal property within the district of value sufficient to justify the full amount of the suretyship; or (4) a cash deposit of the required amount, made with the Clerk and filed with a bond signed by the principals. An individual who executes a bond as a surety pursuant to this subsection will attach an affidavit which gives the full name, occupation, residence and business address and demonstrations that the individual owns real or personal property within the district. After excluding property exempt from execution and deducing liabilities (including those which have arisen by virtue of suretyship on other bonds or undertakings), the real or personal property must be valued at no less than twice the amount of the bond.

When real property is listed in a proposed surety's affidavit, or a trust deed on real property is proposed to be posted as security for a bond required under this rule, the prospective surety must provide either a title report showing title in the name of the surety; or an opinion letter by an attorney that the legal description on the deed of trust is accurate, and that the surety has title. The value of all real property or personal property listed in a proposed surety's affidavit or otherwise posted as security must first be approved by the magistrate judge or district judge.

c. Court Officers as Sureties. No Clerk, marshal or other employee of the Court, nor any member of the bar representing a party in the particular action or proceeding will be accepted as surety on any bond or other undertaking in any action or proceeding in this court. Cash deposits on bonds may be made by members of the bar on certification that the funds are the property of a specified person who has signed as surety on the bond. Upon exoneration of the bond, such monies must be returned to the owner and not to the attorney.

Trust deeds accepted by the Court must be recorded in the county where the real property is located. The trust deed must show in the upper-left hand corner the name of the attorney of record, address of this court, name of the party, and case number. The trust deed must show the United States of America as Beneficiary. Once recorded, the trust deed must be forwarded to the Clerk of Court. When exonerating a bond to release a trust deed and to reconvey it to the surety, releasing a passport, automobile title, or other real property, the order must be clearly entitled "order to exonerate a bond." A sample order is available from the Clerk's Office.

d. Examination of Sureties. Any party may apply for an order requiring any opposing party to show cause why it should not be required to furnish further or different security, or to require the justification of personal sureties.

e. Approval of Bonds by Attorney and Clerk (or Judge).

1. *Attorney.* Every recognizance, bond, stipulation or undertaking hereinafter presented to the Clerk or a judge of the Court for approval, where approval by the Court is required, must have appended thereto a certificate of the attorney for the party for whom the bond is being filed substantially in the following form:

This bond has been examined and recommended for approval as provided in Civil Local Rule 65.1.2, and the within bond (is)(is not) required by law to be approved by a judge.

Dated this _____ day of _____, 20 _____

_____

Attorney

Such endorsement by the attorney will signify to the Court that said attorney has carefully examined the said recognizance, bond, stipulation or undertaking, and that the attorney knows the contents thereof; and the purposes for which it is executed; that in the attorney's opinion the same is in due form, that the attorney believes the affidavits of qualification to be true and has determined whether the bond is required to be approved by a judge.

2. *Clerk (or Judge)* A recognizance, bond, stipulation or undertaking must further have appended thereto a statement of approval by the Clerk or judge, if approval by the judge is required, substantially as follows:

I hereby approve the foregoing bond.

Dated: _____, 20 _____

_____

Clerk (or United States District Judge or Magistrate Judge)

f. Bonds or Other Security.

1. *Approval, Filing and Service.* If eligible under Civil Local Rule 65.1.2, the bond or other security may be approved and filed by the Clerk. A copy of the bond or other security plus notice of filing must be served on all affected parties promptly.

2. *Objections.* The Court must determine objections to the form of the bond or other security or sufficiency of the surety.

3. *Execution.* Except where otherwise provided by Fed. R. Civ. P. 62, or order of the Court, execution may issue after thirty (30) days from entry of a judgment unless a bond or other security has been approved by the Clerk.

g. Summary Judgment Against Sureties.

1. *The Judgment.* Every bond within the scope of Civil Local Rule 65.1.2 will contain the surety or sureties' consent that in case of the principal's, surety or sureties' default, upon notice of not less than twenty-eight (28) days the Court may proceed summarily and render judgment against them and award execution.

2. *Service.* Any indemnitee or party in interest who seeks the judgment provided by Civil Local Rule 65.1.2.g will proceed by motion and with respect to personal sureties and corporate sureties will make the service provided by Fed. R. Civ. P. 5(b) or 31 U.S.C. Section 9306, respectively.

h. Filing.

1. *Filing of Security.* Upon application of any party, and for good cause shown, the Court may require any plaintiff, any nonresident removing defendant, or any nonresident party to a civil action transferred to this court from another district to file security for costs.

2. *Form of Security.* The security for costs must consist of a bond in the sum of $250.00 or such other amount as the Court may order. It must secure the payment of all costs of the action which a party may ultimately be directed to pay to any other party.

3. *By Other Parties.* Upon good cause, the Court may order original or additional security to be given by any part.

[Effective August 18, 1997. Amended effective August 10, 1999; November 19, 2001; October 25, 2004; December 1, 2009; April 30, 2018; December 1, 2018.]

CIVIL RULE 66.1   RECEIVERS

a. Appointment of Receivers. Application for the appointment of a receiver may be made after the complaint has been filed and the summons issued.

1. *Temporary Receivers.* A temporary receiver may be appointed without notice to the party sought to be subjected to a receivership in accordance with the requirements and limitations of Rule 65(b), Fed.R.Civ.P.

2. *Permanent Receivers.* A permanent receiver may be appointed after notice and hearing upon an order to show cause. This order will be issued by a judge upon appointment of a temporary receiver or upon application of the plaintiff and must be served on all parties. The defendant must provide the temporary receiver (or, if there is no temporary receiver, the plaintiff) within seven (7) days a list of the defendant's creditors, and their addresses. Not less than seven (7) days before the hearing, the temporary receiver (or, if none, the plaintiff) must mail to the creditors listed the notice of the hearing and file the proof of mailing.

3. *Bond.* A judge may require any receiver appointed to furnish a bond in such amount as deemed reasonable.

b. Employment of Experts. The receiver must not employ an attorney, accountant or investigator without an order of a judge. The compensation of all such employees must be fixed by the Court.

c. Application for Fees. All applications for fees for services rendered in connection with a receivership must be made by petition setting forth in reasonable detail the nature of the services and must be heard in open court.

d. Deposit of Funds. A receiver must deposit all funds received in a depository designated by a judge, entitling the account with the name and number of the action. At the end of each month, the receiver must deliver to the Clerk a statement of account and the canceled checks.

e. Reports. Within thirty (30) days of appointment, a permanent receiver must file with the Court a verified report and petition for instructions, which must be heard on fourteen (14) days' notice to all known creditors and parties. The report must contain a summary of the operations of the receiver, an inventory of the assets and their appraised value, a schedule of all receipts and disbursements, and a list of all creditors, their addresses and the amounts of their claims. The petition must contain the receiver's recommendation as to the continuance of the receivership and the receiver's reasons. At the hearing, the judge will determine whether the receivership should be continued and, if so, will fix the time for future reports of the receiver.

f. Notice of Hearings. The receiver must give all interested parties at least fourteen (14) days' notice of the time and place of all pertinent hearings of all:

1. Petitions for the payment of dividends to creditors;

2. Petitions for confirmation of sales of property;

3. Reports of the receiver;

4. Applications for fees of the receiver or of any attorney, accountant or investigator, the notice to state the services performed and the fee requested; and,

5. Applications for discharge of the receiver.

[Effective August 18, 1997. Amended effective October 25, 2004; December 1, 2009.]

CIVIL RULE 67.1   DEPOSIT AND DISBURSEMENTS OF REGISTRY FUNDS

a. Receipt of Funds.

1. No money will be sent to the Court or its officers for deposit in the Court's registry without a court order signed by the presiding district or magistrate judge in the case or proceeding.

2. The party making the deposit or transferring funds to the Court's registry will serve the order permitting the deposit or transfer on the Clerk of Court.

3. Unless provided for elsewhere in this Local Rule, all monies ordered to be paid to the Court or received by its officers in any case pending or adjudicated will be deposited with the Treasurer of the United States in the name and to the credit of this court pursuant to 28 U.S.C. § 2041 through depositories designated by the Treasury to accept such deposit on its behalf.

b. Investment of Registry Funds.

1. Unless otherwise ordered by a district judge, all funds deposited in the registry of the Court in which the principal equals or exceeds $5000 are to be placed in an interest-bearing account. The Court Registry Investment System ("CRIS"), administered by the Administrative Office of the United States Courts under 28 U.S.C. § 2045, will be the only investment mechanism authorized.

2. The Director of the Administrative Office of the United States Courts is designated as custodian for CRIS. The Director or the Director's designee will perform the duties of

custodian. Funds held in the CRIS remain subject to the control and jurisdiction of the Court.

3. Money from each case deposited in the CRIS will be "pooled" together with those on deposit with the Treasury to the credit of other courts in the CRIS and used to purchase Government Account Securities through the Bureau of Public Debt, which will be held at the Treasury, in an account in the name and to the credit of the Director of the Administrative Office of the United States Courts. The pooled funds will be invested in accordance with the principals of the CRIS Investment Policy as approved by the Registry Monitoring Group.

4. An account for each case will be established in the CRIS titled in the name of the case giving rise to the investment of the fund. Income generated from fund investments will be distributed to each case based on the ratio each account's principal and earnings has to the aggregate principal and income total in the fund. Reports showing the interest earned and the principal amounts contributed in each case will be prepared and distributed to each court participating in the CRIS and made available to litigants and/or their counsel.

c. Deduction of Fees.

1. The custodian is authorized and directed by this Local Rule to deduct the investment services fee for the management of investments in the CRIS and the registry fee for maintaining accounts deposited with the Court.

2. The investment services fee is assessed from interest earnings to the pool and is to be assessed before a pro rata distribution of earnings to court cases.

3. The registry fee is assessed by the custodian from each case's pro rata distribution of the earnings and is to be determined on the basis of the rates published by the Director of the Administrative Office of the United States Courts as approved by the Judicial Conference of the United States.

d. Disbursement of Registry Funds.

1. Upon the entry of a judgment, funds, if any, on deposit in the registry of the Court will be disbursed only by order of the Court after the time for appeal has expired, or upon written stipulation by all parties approved by the Court.

2. Each order directing the Clerk to disburse funds must be clearly entitled "order to disburse funds" and must be without conditions to be met prior to disbursement of said funds. It must indicate which parties are entitled to principal and any accrued interest.

The order must also contain the name and mailing address of the party entitled to said funds, unless forbidden elsewhere in these rules of the Court's General Order, in which case the information may be redacted and/or provided directly to the Clerk's Financial Office.

Taxpayer identification numbers for the check payees must be delivered directly to the Clerk's Financial Office prior to disbursement.

3. A sample order is available from the Clerk's Office.

[Effective August 18, 1997. Amended effective December 1, 2009; February 2, 2015.]

CIVIL RULE 69.1 PROCEEDINGS TO ENFORCE JUDGMENTS (IN DISTRICT AND OUT OF DISTRICT)

a. All motions for Judgment Debtor examinations made in connection with a civil or criminal judgment obtained in this district must be filed with the magistrate judge assigned to the case. All motions for Judgment Debtor examinations made in connection with an out-of-district judgment registered in this district must be filed with the magistrate judge handling CVB duty. All motions for Judgment Debtor examinations are heard weekly on Wednesday mornings on the CVB calendar.

b. All other motions concerning execution of a judgment must be made to the assigned district judge, unless the motion relates to the post-judgment discovery, in which case the motion must be made to the assigned magistrate judge. If no judge has been previously assigned, the case will be randomly assigned to a district judge and a magistrate judge under a new Civil Number (CV).

[Effective February 15, 2018.]

CIVIL RULE 72.1 UNITED STATES MAGISTRATE JUDGES

a. **Jurisdiction Under 28 U.S.C. § 636(a).** Each United States magistrate judge of this court is authorized to perform the duties prescribed by 28 U.S.C. § 636(a), and may administer oaths and affirmations and take acknowledgments, affidavits and depositions.

b. **Determination of Non–Dispositive Pretrial Matters—28 U.S.C. § 636(b)(1)(A).** Pursuant to 28 U.S.C. § 636(b)(1)(A) a magistrate judge will hear and determine any pretrial motions, including discovery motions, other than the dispositive motions which are specified in 28 U.S.C. § 636(b)(1)(A).

c. **Proposed Orders Regarding Case–Dispositive Motions—28 U.S.C. § 636(b)(1)(B).**

1. Upon the designation by district judge, a magistrate judge may submit to a district judge a proposed order containing findings of fact and recommendations for disposition by the district judge of the following pretrial motions in civil cases:

a) Motions for injunctive relief, including temporary restraining orders and preliminary and permanent injunctions;

b) Motions for judgment on the pleadings;

c) Motions for summary judgment;

d) Motions to dismiss or permit the maintenance of a class action;

e) Motions to dismiss for failure to state a claim upon which relief may be granted;

f) Motions to involuntarily dismiss an action;

2. A district judge may designate a magistrate judge to conduct hearings, including evidentiary hearings, and submit proposed findings of fact and the recommendations for the disposition by the district judge of prisoner petitions challenging the conditions of confinement.

3. A magistrate judge may determine any preliminary matters and conduct any necessary evidentiary hearing or other proceeding arising in the exercise of the authority conferred by this subsection.

d. Prisoner Cases Under 28 U.S.C. § 2254 Not Involving the Death Penalty. Unless the district judge chooses to retain a case which does not involve the death penalty, the assigned magistrate judge is hereby designated to perform any and all of the duties specified in § 2254, Rule 8.b. and the rules governing proceedings in the United States District Courts under § 2254 of Title 28, U.S.C., and must:

1. Receive a copy of all filings and other items submitted concerning the matter;

2. Conduct all preliminary matters and issue any preliminary orders as deemed necessary;

3. Conduct any necessary evidentiary hearing, pursuant to Rule 8 of the rules governing proceedings in the United States courts under § 2254 of Title 28, U.S.C., or other appropriate proceedings; and

4. Submit to a district judge of the Court a report containing proposed findings of fact and recommendations for disposition of the petition by the district judge. Any order disposing of the petition on its merits may only be made by a district judge of the Court.

e. Prisoner Cases Under 28 U.S.C. §§ 2254 Involving the Death Penalty and 2255. Upon designation by a district judge, a magistrate judge may perform the duties specified in § 2254, Rule 8.b. and the rules governing proceedings in the United States District Courts under § 2254 (involving the death penalty) and § 2255 of Title 28, U.S.C. Any order disposing of the petition may only be made by a district judge.

f. Special Master References. A magistrate judge may be designated by a judge to serve as a special master in appropriate civil cases in accordance with 28 U.S.C. § 636(b)(2) and Rule 53 of the Fed.R.Civ.P. Upon the consent of the parties, a magistrate judge may be designated by a judge to serve as a special master in any civil case, notwithstanding the limitations of Rule 53.b of Fed.R.Civ.P.

g. Conduct of Trials and Disposition of Civil Cases Upon Consent of the Parties—28 U.S.C. § 636(c). Upon the written consent of the parties, a full-time magistrate judge may conduct any or all proceedings in any civil case which is filed in this court, including the conduct of a jury or non-jury trial, and may order the entry of a final judgment, in accordance with 28 U.S.C. § 636(c). In the course of conducting such proceedings upon consent of the parties, a magistrate judge may hear and determine any and all pretrial and post trial motions which are filed by the parties, including case-dispositive motions.

h. Other Duties. A magistrate judge is also authorized to:

1. Exercise general supervision of civil calendars, conduct calendar and status calls, and determine motions to expedite or postpone the trial of cases for the district judge;

2. Conduct pretrial conferences, settlement conferences and related pretrial proceedings in civil cases, and conduct summary trials or alternative dispute resolution proceedings in civil cases;

3. Conduct voir dire and select petit juries for the Court in civil cases with the consent of the parties;

4. Accept petit jury verdicts in civil cases in the absence of a district judge;

5. Issue subpoenas, writs of habeas corpus ad testificandum or habeas corpus ad prosequendum or other orders necessary to obtain the presence of parties, witnesses or evidence needed for court proceedings;

6. Order the exoneration of forfeiture bonds;

7. Conduct proceedings for the collection of civil penalties of not more than $200 assessed under the Federal Boat Safety Act of 1971, in accordance with 46 U.S.C.;

8. Conduct examinations of judgment debtors in accordance with Rule 69 of the Fed.R.Civ.P.;

9. Conduct naturalization hearings. (All orders from any naturalization hearing must be submitted to a district judge of this court for approval.)

10. Perform any additional duty not inconsistent with the Constitution and laws of the United States.*

[Effective August 18, 1997. Amended effective January 1, 2000; October 25, 2004; December 1, 2009.]

* [**Publisher's Note:** *See also* General Order 635, *post.*]

CIVIL RULE 72.2 ASSIGNMENT AND DESIGNATION PROCEDURES

a. Order of Designation and Assignment. A matter assigned to the magistrate judges either as a matter of course by the Clerk of the United States District Court or by an order of special designation by a district judge of the Court under 28 U.S.C. § 636(b) or (c), precisely stating the nature of the matter, will be assigned to a specific magistrate judge as follows:

b. Civil Matters. The Clerk must assign civil matters by lot as described in Civil Local Rule 40.1. In civil matters where reference to a magistrate judge is dependent upon the consent of the parties, such as trials, the district judge may assign the matter to a particular magistrate judge selected by the parties.

c. Upon filing, civil cases must be assigned by the Clerk to a magistrate judge. The magistrate judge must hear and determine Civil Local Rule 72.1.b pretrial motions.

d. Where designated by a judge the magistrate judge may conduct additional pre-trial conferences and hear motions and perform the duties set forth in Civil Local Rule 72.1.c.

e. Each magistrate judge will be designated to perform the duties set forth in Civil Local Rule 72.1.d.

f. Where the parties consent to trial and disposition of a case by a magistrate judge under Civil Local Rule 72.1.f of these rules, such case must be set before the magistrate judge for the conduct of all further proceedings and the entry of judgment.

g. Notice of Hearing. A magistrate judge assigned a matter must set the time of hearing, notify all parties and make any further necessary orders consistent with the requirements of the Local Rules of Court for the Southern District.

h. Nothing in these rules preclude the Court, or a district judge from reserving any proceedings for conduct by a district judge, rather than a magistrate judge. The Court, moreover, may by general order modify the method of assigning proceedings to a magistrate judge as changing conditions may warrant.

[Effective August 18, 1997. Amended effective October 25, 2004; December 1, 2009.]

CIVIL RULE 72.3 ASSIGNMENT OF § 1983 PRISONER CIVIL CASES TO UNITED STATES MAGISTRATE JUDGES

a. In all of the District's civil § 1983 prisoner cases, a magistrate judge will be assigned to hear and conduct proceedings designated by 28 U.S.C. § 636(b)(1), unless the district judge orders otherwise.

b. The Clerk will give the parties written notice of their opportunity to consent to magistrate judge jurisdiction under 28 U.S.C. § 636(c) pursuant to Fed.R.Civ.P. 73(b)(1) at the time a summons is issued or, when each defendant first responds to the complaint, if notice could not have been provided earlier.

c. Pursuant to Fed.R.Civ.P. 73(b)(2), the assigned district judge, magistrate judge, or the Clerk may thereafter remind the parties of the magistrate judge's availability by issuing a Notice, Consent, and Reference of the civil action to the magistrate judge pursuant to 28 U.S.C. § 636(c)(1). That Notice will advise the parties that they are free to withhold consent without adverse substantive consequences. If all the parties decide to consent, all parties will submit the jointly signed Notice as a proposed Order consenting to the referral, or each will separately submit his or her signed Notice consenting to the referral to the Clerk in paper format via U.S. Mail. Pursuant to Fed.R.Civ.P.73(b)(1), and in order to protect the voluntariness of the parties' consent pursuant to 28 U.S.C. § 636(c)(2), the district judge or magistrate judge will be informed of a party's response to this Notice only if all parties have submitted written consent to the referral.

d. Upon the written consent of all parties, the case will be referred to the magistrate judge to conduct all proceedings, including a jury or nonjury trial, and order entry of a final judgment in accordance with 28 U.S.C. § 636(c), Fed.R.Civ. P.73 and Local Civil Rule 73.1.

e. In the absence of written consent of all parties, the magistrate judge will conduct all necessary hearings and submit proposed findings of fact and recommendations for the disposition of all motions excepted from the magistrate judge's jurisdiction by 28 U.S.C. § 636(b)(1)(A), unless the district judge orders otherwise.

f. All hearing dates for any pretrial matter excepted by 28 U.S.C. § 636(b)(1)(A) must be obtained from the law clerk of the magistrate judge to whom the case has been referred either on a consent basis pursuant to 28 U.S.C. § 636(c), or for proposed findings of fact and recommendations for the disposi-

tion by the assigned district judge pursuant to 28 U.S.C. § 636(b)(1)(B) and Local Civil Rule 7.1. Unless all parties have consented, or the district judge deems them unnecessary, the magistrate judge will file his or her findings and recommendations with the Court and set dates for the filing of written objections pursuant to 28 U.S.C. § 636(b)(1). Written objections, if any, must be directed to the district judge assigned to the case pursuant to 28 U.S.C. § 636(b)(1)(C).

g. All cases will be set for a Case Management Conference as soon as practicable following the filing of the first answer. Early Neutral Evaluation Conferences will not be set in these matters pursuant to Local Civil Rule 16.1.e.8; however, settlement conferences may be set when the case is determined ready for settlement by a judicial officer.

[Effective August 18, 1997. Amended effective March 2, 1998; June 28, 1999; December 1, 2009; June 1, 2020.]

CIVIL RULE 73.1 SPECIAL PROVISION FOR THE DISPOSITION OF CIVIL CASES BY A MAGISTRATE JUDGE ON CONSENT OF THE PARTIES 28 U.S.C. § 636(c)(2)

a. Notice. The Clerk must notify the parties in all civil cases that they may consent to have a magistrate judge conduct any or all proceedings in the case and order the entry of a final judgment. Such notice must be handed or mailed to the plaintiff or plaintiff's representative at the time an action is filed and to other parties as attachments to copies of the complaint and summons when served. Additional notices may be furnished to the parties at later stages of the proceedings, and may be included with pretrial notices and instructions.

b. Execution of Consent. The Clerk must not accept a consent form unless it has been signed by all the parties in a case. The plaintiff must be responsible for securing the execution of a consent form by the parties and for filing such form with the Clerk. No consent form will be made available, nor will its contents be made known to any judicial officer, unless all parties have consented to the reference to a magistrate judge. A district or magistrate judge may advise the parties of the availability of a magistrate judge to try a civil case or hear a civil motion by consent. However, no action must be taken to effect the voluntariness of the parties to consent or lack of consent to the magistrate judge. The district judge must also advise the parties that they are free to withhold consent without adverse substantive consequences.

[Effective August 18, 1997. Amended effective December 1, 2009.]

CIVIL RULE 77.1 LOCATION AND HOURS OF THE CLERK

The Office of the Clerk of this Court will be in the Federal Office Building at United States Courthouse Annex at 333 W. Broadway, San Diego. The office will be open to the bar and public between the hours of 8:30 a.m. and 4:30 p.m. each day except Saturdays, Sundays and court holidays. A drop-off box for filings and pleadings will be available at the 4th Floor of the United States Courthouse Annex at 333 W. Broadway, outside Room 420. Documents deposited in the drop-off box must be in a sealed envelope. Filings and pleadings deposited in the drop-off box prior to 6:00 p.m., Monday through Friday, except court holidays, will reflect the date of deposit. The United States Courthouse Annex closes promptly at 6:00 p.m., Monday through Friday, and is closed all day on weekends and court holidays. Matters requiring immediate judicial attention should never be placed in the drop-off box.

[Effective August 18, 1997. Amended effective December 1, 2009; February 8, 2013.]

CIVIL RULE 77.2 ORDERS GRANTABLE BY CLERK

The Clerk is authorized to sign and enter orders specifically allowed to be signed by the Clerk under the Fed.R.Civ.P. and is, in addition, authorized to sign and enter the following orders without further direction of a judge:

a. Orders specifically appointing persons to serve process in accordance with Rule 4, Fed.R.Civ.P.

b. Orders on consent noting satisfaction of a judgment, providing for the payment of money, withdrawing stipulations, annulling bonds, exonerating sureties or setting aside a default.

c. Orders of dismissal on consent, with or without prejudice, except in cases to which Rules 23, 23.1 or 66, Fed.R.Civ.P. apply.

d. Orders entering default for failure to plead or otherwise defend in accordance with Fed.R.Civ.P. 55(b)(1);

e. Any other orders which pursuant to Fed.R.Civ.P. 77(c) do not require direction by the Court.

[Effective August 18, 1997. Amended, effective October 25, 2004.]

CIVIL RULE 77.3 NOTICE OF COURT ORDERS AND JUDGMENTS

Immediately upon the entry of an order or judgment in an action within the Electronic Filing System, the Clerk will transmit to filing users a Notice of Electronic Filing. Electronic transmission of the NEF constitutes the Notice required by Fed.R.Civ.P. 77(d). The Clerk must give notice in a paper form to a person who has not consented to electronic services in accordance with the Federal Rules of Civil Procedures.

[Effective May 1, 2006.]

CIVIL RULE 77.4 SESSIONS OF COURT

The Court must be in continuous session in San Diego.

[Effective August 18, 1997. Amended effective December 1, 2009.]

CIVIL RULE 77.6 COURT LIBRARY

The Court maintains a law library for the primary use of judges and personnel of the Court. In addition, attorneys admitted to practice in this Court may use the library while actively engaged in actions or proceedings pending in the Court. The library is operated in accordance with such rules and regulations as the Court may from time to time adopt.

[Effective August 18, 1997.]

CIVIL RULE 79.1 CUSTODY AND DISPOSITION OF EXHIBITS AND TRANSCRIPTS

a. Presentation of Evidence. Unless otherwise ordered, where possible evidence must be presented in electronic format through use of the presentation technology available in the courtroom to display evidence to the jury and the Court. Requirements for courtroom technology and the format of exhibits can be found on the District Court's website at www.casd.uscourts.gov.

b. Custody With Clerk of Court. Unless otherwise directed by the Court, or except as provided in Section c, all trial exhibits admitted into evidence in criminal and civil actions will be placed in the custody of the Clerk of Court.

c. Custody With the Offering Party. All exhibits received in evidence that are in the nature of narcotic drugs, legal or counterfeit money, firearms, sensitive materials or contraband of any kind will be entrusted to the custody of the arresting or investigative agency of the Government pending disposition of the action and for any appeal period thereafter.

d. Disposition of Exhibits, Sealed Documents and Filed Depositions by Clerk of Court. Unless otherwise ordered by the Court, every exhibit marked for identification or introduced in evidence and all depositions and transcripts must be returned to the party who produced them at the conclusion of the trial or hearing. It will be counsel's responsibility to produce any and all exhibits for the Court of Appeals, when requested by that court, if an appeal is taken, or to this court when requested.

e. Courts Discretion to Provide Supplemental Copies. Nothing in this rule limits the discretion of the Court to provide supplemental hard copies of the exhibits to the jury to facilitate their review.

[Effective August 18, 1997. Amended effective December 1, 2009; December 1, 2018.]

CIVIL RULE 79.2 BOOKS AND RECORDS OF THE CLERK

a. Files, Custody, and Withdrawal. All files of the Court must remain in the custody of the Clerk and no record or paper belonging to the files of the Court will be taken from the custody of the Clerk without special order of a judge and a proper receipt signed by the person obtaining the record or paper. No such order will be made except in extraordinary circumstances.

b. Sealed Documents. Documents filed under seal in civil actions will be returned to the party submitting them upon entry of the final judgment or termination of the appeal, if any, unless otherwise ordered by the Court.

c. Sealing Orders. Documents that are to be filed under seal must be accompanied by an order sealing them. If the order is also to be filed under seal, it must so state.

[Effective August 18, 1997. Amended, effective August 10, 1999.]

CIVIL RULE 83.1 SANCTIONS FOR NONCOMPLIANCE WITH RULES

a. Failure of counsel, or of any party, to comply with these rules, with the Federal Rules of Civil or Criminal Procedure, or with any order of the Court may be grounds for imposition by the Court of any and all sanctions authorized by statute or rule or within the inherent power of the Court, including, without limitation, dismissal of any actions, entry of default, finding of contempt, imposition of monetary sanctions or attorneys' fees and costs, and other lesser sanctions.

b. For violations of these Local Rules or of a specific court order, the Court may, in imposing monetary sanctions, order that the monetary sanctions be paid to the Miscellaneous Fines, Penalties and Forfeitures, Not Otherwise Classified, fund of the United States Treasury.

[Effective August 18, 1997. Amended effective February 2, 2015; January 30, 2016.]

CIVIL RULE 83.2 SECURITY OF THE COURT

The Court, or any judge, may from time to time make such orders or impose such requirements as may be reasonably necessary to assure the security of the Court and all persons in attendance.

[Effective August 18, 1997. Amended effective December 1, 2009.]

CIVIL RULE 83.3 ATTORNEYS—ADMISSION TO PRACTICE, STANDARDS OF CONDUCT—DUTIES

a. Definitions. For convenience, attorneys, proctors, advocates, solicitors, and counselors of this court will be referred to in these rules by the designation, "attorneys."

b. Practice. Only a member of the bar of this court may enter appearances for a party, sign stipulations or receive payment or enter satisfaction of judgment, decree or order.

c. Admission of Attorneys to Practice.

1. *Requirements and Procedures.*

a) Admission to the Bar of this Court. Admission to and continuing membership in the bar of this court is limited to attorneys of good moral character who are active members in good standing of the State Bar of California.

b) Procedure for Admission. Each applicant for admission must present to the Clerk a written petition for admission, on the form supplied by the Court, stating the applicant's residence and/or office address, the applicant's email address, and California State Bar Number, and by what courts the applicant has been admitted to practice and the respective dates of admission to those courts.

The petition must be signed, certifying that the attorney is a member in good standing of the State Bar of California.

Upon qualification, the applicant may be admitted, upon oral motion or without appearing, as determined by the Court, by signing the prescribed oath and paying the prescribed fee, together with any required assessment, which the Clerk will place to the credit of the Court non-appropriated funds.

c) Each attorney admitted to this Court must adhere to the Code of Conduct set forth in Civ. L.R. 2.1 and Crim. L.R. 2.1, respectively.

2. *Practice in This Court.* Except as herein otherwise provided, only members of the bar of this court will practice in this court.

3. *Attorneys for the United States.* An attorney who is not eligible for admission under Civil Local Rule 83.3.c.1.a hereof, but who is a member in good standing of, and eligible to practice before, the bar of any United States Court or of the highest court of any state, or of any territory or insular possession of the United States, may practice in this court in any matter in which the attorney is employed or retained by the United States or its agencies. Attorneys so permitted to practice in this court are subject to the jurisdiction of the court with respect to their conduct to the same extent as members of the bar of this court.

4. *Pro Hac Vice.* An attorney not eligible for admission under Civil Local Rule 83.3.c hereof, but who is a member in good standing of, and eligible to practice before, the bar of any United States Court or of the highest court of any state or of any territory or insular possession of the United States, who is of good moral character, and who has been retained to appear in this court, and who agrees to adhere to this court's rules, including without limitation, the Court's Code of Conduct under Civ. L.R. 2.1 and Crim. L.R. 2.1, may, upon written application and in the discretion of the Court, be permitted to appear and participate in a particular case. Unless authorized by the Constitution of the United States or acts of Congress, an attorney is not eligible to practice pursuant to this local rule if any one or more of the following apply to the attorney: (1) resides in California, (2) is regularly employed in California, or (3) is regularly engaged in business, professional, or other activities in California.

The pro hac vice application must be presented to the Clerk, along with an admission fee in the amount set by the judges of this court by general order. The fees must be deposited in the non-appropriated funds of the Court and divided between the library fund and the pro-bono fund in the manner designated by such general order. The application must state under penalty of perjury (1) the attorney's city and state of residence and office address, (2) by what court(s) the attorney has been admitted to practice and the date(s) of admission, (3) that the attorney is in good standing and eligible to practice in said court, (4) that the attorney is not currently suspended or disbarred in any other court, (5) if the attorney has concurrently or within one year preceding the current application made any pro hac vice application to this court, the title and the number of each matter wherein the application was made, and the date of application, and whether or not the application was granted and (6) that the attorney has read, understands and agrees to adhere to each of this Court's Rules, including, without limitation, the Court's Code of Conduct under Civ. L.R.2.1 Na Crim. L.R. 2.1. The attorney must also designate in the application a member of the bar of this court with whom the Court and opposing counsel may readily communicate regarding the conduct of the case and upon whom papers will be served. The attorney must file with such application the address, telephone number and written consent of such designee.

5. *Designation of Local Counsel.* A judge to whom a case is assigned may in that case, in the judge's discretion, require an attorney appearing in this court pursuant to the provisions of this rule and who maintains an office outside of this district to designate a member of the bar of this court who does maintain an office within this district as co-counsel with the authority to act as attorney of record for all purposes. The attorney must file with such designation the address, telephone number and written consent of such designee.

6. *Yuma Criminal Defense Attorneys.* Attorneys in good standing at the bar of the United States District Court for the District of Arizona who are employed by the Federal Public Defender of Arizona or who are members of the Criminal Justice Act Panel of that court, will be deemed admitted to the bar of the United States District Court for the Southern District of California for the limited purpose of providing legal services to defendants in the Southern District of California criminal proceedings heard by judicial officers at the District of Arizona Yuma point of holding court.

d. Notice of Change of Status. An attorney who is a member of the bar of this court, or who has been permitted to practice in this court under Civil Local Rule 83.3.c, must promptly notify the court of any change in status in another jurisdiction which would make the attorney ineligible for membership in the bar of this court under Civil Local Rule 83.3.c, or ineligible to practice in this court under Civil Local Rule 83.3.c hereof. In the event the attorney is no longer eligible to practice in another jurisdiction by reason of suspension for nonpayment of fees or enrollment as an inactive member, the attorney will immediately be suspended from practice before this court without any order of court and until the attorney becomes eligible to practice in such other jurisdiction. Any attorney seeking reinstatement may file a petition with the Clerk of Court with supporting documentation showing that he or she meets the requirements of 83.3.c.1.a, for determination by the Chief Judge.

e. Notice of Change of Address or Facsimile Number or Email Address. An attorney who is a member of the bar of this court, or who has been permitted to practice in this court under Civil Local Rule 83.3.c must promptly notify the Court of any change of address. If the attorney has a facsimile authorization or email address on file and, if any of the information changes, the attorney must promptly notify the Court.

f. Appearances, Substitutions and Withdrawal of Attorneys.

1. *Appearances.* Whenever a party has appeared by an attorney, the party may not afterwards appear or act in the party's own behalf in the action, or take any step in that action, unless an order of substitution has first have been made by the Court, after notice to the attorney of such party, and to the opposite party; provided, that the Court may in its discretion hear a party in open court, notwithstanding the fact that the party has appeared, or is represented by an attorney.

2. *Substitutions.* When an attorney of record for any person ceases to act for a party, such party must appear in person or appoint another attorney by a written substitution of attorney signed by the party, the attorney ceasing to act, and the newly appointed attorney, or by a written designation filed in the case and served upon the attorney ceasing to act, unless attorney is deceased, in which event the designation of a new attorney will so state. Until such substitution is approved by the Court, the authority of the attorney of record will continue for all proper purposes.

3. *Withdrawals.*

   a) A motion to withdraw as attorney of record must be served on the adverse party and on the moving attorney's client.

   b) A declaration pertaining to such service must be filed. Failure to make serve as required by this section or to file the required declaration of service will result in a denial of the motion.

4. *Special Appearances.* An attorney may make a special appearance for a limited proceeding only with the permission of the Court.

g. Ex Parte Motions and Orders.

1. All motions to a judge of this court for ex parte orders must be made by a party appearing in propria persona or by an attorney of this court.

2. A motion for an order must not be made ex parte unless it appears by affidavit or declaration (1) that within a reasonable time before the motion the party informed the opposing party or the opposing party's attorney when and where the motion would be made; or (2) that the party in good faith attempted to inform the opposing party and the opposing party's attorney but was unable to do so, specifying the efforts made to inform them; or (3) that for reasons specified the party should not be required to inform the opposing party or the opposing party's attorney.

h. Penalty for Unauthorized Practice. The Court may order any person who practices before it in violation of Civil Local Rule 83.3 to pay an appropriate penalty which upon payment the Clerk must credit to the Court Library or Pro Bono Fund as designated by the Court. Payment of such sum must be an additional condition of admission or reinstatement to the bar of this court or to practice in this court.

i. Fees. The admission fee required of all admitted to practice before this court will be designated by general order and made payable to the Clerk. The amount mandated by law must be deposited into the Treasury, and the remainder will be (1) deposited in the non-appropriated funds of the Court, and (2) divided between the library fund and the pro-bono fund as the judges so designate by general order. Each application provided in Civil Local Rule 83.3.c must be accompanied by a receipt verifying payment to the Clerk of the designated fee and assessments.

j. Appearances by Corporations. Only natural persons representing their individual interests in propria persona may appear in court without representation by an attorney permitted to practice pursuant to Civil Local Rule 83.3. All other parties, including corporations, partnerships and other legal entities, may appear in court only through an attorney permitted to practice pursuant to Civil Local Rule 83.3.

[Effective August 18, 1997. Amended effective August 10, 1999; November 15, 1999; March 2, 2000; May 24, 2004; July 16, 2007; December 1, 2009; January 1, 2011; November 1, 2011; February 2, 2015; April 24, 2017; December 1, 2018; June 25, 2019; March 18, 2020.]

CIVIL RULE 83.6 GRATUITIES

No person must directly or indirectly give or offer to give, nor must any judge, employee, or attache of this court accept, any gift or gratuity directly or indirectly related to services performed by or for the Court.

[Effective August 18, 1997. Amended effective December 1, 2009.]

CIVIL RULE 83.7 FREE PRESS— FAIR TRIAL PROVISIONS

a. Official Newspapers. The "San Diego Daily Transcript" of San Diego (published by the "Daily Journal Corporation"), being a newspaper of general circulation within the County of San Diego and within above district, and the "Imperial Valley Press" of El Centro, California, being a newspaper of general circulation in the County of Imperial and within the above district, are designated as the official newspapers for publication of all notices required to be published by law or order of this court.

The Court may, in any case for the convenience of the parties in interest or in the interest of justice, designate any other newspaper for publication of notices as the Court may determine.

b. Publicity. Courthouse supporting personnel, including, among others, marshals, clerks and deputies, law clerks, messengers and court reporters, will not disclose to any person information relating to any pending criminal or civil proceeding that is not part of the public records of the Court without specific authorization of the Court, nor will any such personnel discuss with the public the merits of such proceeding while it is pending before the Court.

c. Photographs, Broadcasts, Video Tapes and Tape Recordings Prohibited. All forms, means and manner of taking photographs, tape recordings, videotaping, broadcasting, or televising are prohibited in the United States Courthouse Building during the course of, or in connection with, any judicial proceedings, whether the Court is actually in session or not. This rule will not prohibit recordings by a court reporter provided, however, no court reporter or any other person will use or permit to be used any part of any recording of a court proceeding on, or in connection with, any radio, video tape or television broadcast of any kind. The Court may permit photographs of exhibits to be taken by or under direction of counsel. The Court, on motion, may permit the video taping of depositions in rooms other than courtrooms to be used for court proceedings.

d. Publicity in Criminal Cases. In criminal cases or proceedings before any judge of this court, prosecuting attorneys and defense counsel, as officers of this court, and their associates, assistants, agents, enforcement officers and investigators, must refrain from making, or advising or encouraging others to make to, for, or in the press, or on radio, television or other news media, statements concerning the parties, witnesses, merits of cases, probable evidence, or other matters which are likely to prejudice the ability of either the government or the defendant to obtain a fair trial.

[Effective August 18, 1997. Amended effective December 1, 2009; February 8, 2013; April 4, 2016.]

CIVIL RULE 83.8 NON–APPROPRIATED FUNDS—PLAN FOR ADMINISTRATION OF THE COURT LIBRARY FUND AND PRO BONO FUND

Pursuant to the "Guidelines for Non-Appropriated Funds Maintained by the Courts of the United States" issued by the Director of the Administrative Office of the United States Courts on October 1, 1981, the United States District Court for the Southern District of California has adopted the following plan for the administration and operation of the funds derived from attorney admission fees. These funds will be held by the Court in appropriate depositories, separate from other monies received by the Court. They will be expended at the direction of the Chief Judge, or in accordance with guidelines set forth in Section A of this plan, below, and in subsequent orders of the Court. Unreasonable accumulations to both funds must be avoided.

a. Guidelines for Use.

1. *Library Fund.* Consistent with Judicial Conference Guidelines, the fund must be used for purposes approved by the District Court judges for expenses that inure to the benefit of members of the bench and the bar of the Court, including, but not limited to the following:

a) Expenses of the Court Library for which appropriated funds are not available at the time the expense is incurred (such as payment for publications and periodicals, filing services, temporary assistance with special projects and the computerization of library catalog);

b) Expenses related to attorney admission proceedings;

c) Expenses related to attorney discipline enforcement and proceedings;

d) Lawyer lounge and other courthouse facilities benefitting the bar;

e) Equipment and materials to assist attorneys in the courtroom;

f) Expenses for printing court rules, manuals on practice and procedure, a slip opinion index, and other documents related to court operations given to attorneys upon admission to the bar;

g) Attorney expenses for court committee meetings;

h) Expenses in connection with court memorial and commendation services;

i) Court projects and programs that interest or benefit the bar or which enhance the quality of advocacy in the Court;

j) Expenses of the collection and preservation of court records;

k) Expenses for the development of historical and educational materials describing the Court for use by the bar, including, but not limited to, the Annual Reports;

l) Costs of special projects or acquisitions to further the administration of justice in the courts;

m) If appropriated funds are not available, training and professional dues for Court Library personnel designed to enhance the administration of justice and to benefit the bar;

n) Fees for services rendered by outside auditors in auditing the fund, in accordance with Section 4 below;

o) Costs of the annual Southern District of California Conference, and costs associated with the Court's participation in the Ninth Circuit Judicial Conference.

2. *Pro Bono Fund.*

a) The Pro Bono Fund must be used for reimbursement of out-of-pocket expenses, necessarily incurred by court-appointed attorneys representing indigents pro bono in civil cases not covered by the Criminal Justice Act, provided that approval for such expenses is first obtained from the magistrate judge assigned the case, or if for any reason the magistrate judge is unavailable, or if the total expenses in the case exceed $1,000.00, the district judge assigned the case. In the event of a showing of extraordinary circumstances, the requirement of prior approval may be waived by the magistrate judge or the district judge. Further, funds may be used to help defray or reimburse administrative costs in screening applicants referred by the Court. Application for such funds must be approved by the Court. Additionally, the funds may be used for purposes which enhance the purpose and goal of creating, supporting, and maintaining a group of volunteer lawyers who will assist the Court in representing indigents pro bono in civil cases. Application for such funds must be approved by the Court.

In the event the party represented recovers costs, the out-of-pocket expenses allowed under this section must be redeposited into the fund.

b) The funds must not be used to pay for materials or supplies available from statutory appropriations nor to supplement the salary of any court officer or employee.

c) The funds may be used as a revolving account to pay for expenses for which the Fund will be entirely reimbursed.

b. **Custodian of the Fund.**

1. The Clerk will act as custodian of the funds and will be responsible for receiving payment of attorney admission fees and for safeguarding, depositing, disbursing and accounting for all assets of the funds. Monies paid into the funds must be kept separate and distinct from any other monies received by the Court.

In particular, the custodian must:

a) Make payments from the funds for purposes authorized in accordance with Section a;

b) Establish an appropriate accounting system for the funds and maintain proper records of receipts and disbursements;

c) Prepare and submit to the Court a quarterly report on funds activities, setting forth the balance, receipts, disbursements in accordance with the fiscal plan;

d) Invest funds in accordance with the guidelines set forth in Section C, below, and;

e) Perform such other duties as the Court may direct.

2. Upon appointment by the Court of a successor custodian, the outgoing custodian must prepare and sign the following statements in conjunction with the exit audit or inspection conducted by an auditor or disinterested inspector as designated by the Court;

a) A statement of assets and liabilities;

b) A statement of operations or of receipts and disbursements since the end of the period covered by the last statement of operations and net worth; and

c) A statement of the balance in any Fund accounts as of the date of transfer to the successor custodian.

The successor custodian must execute a receipt for all funds after being satisfied as to the accuracy of the statements and records provided by the outgoing custodian. Acceptance may be conditioned upon audit and verification when the circumstances warrant.

c. **Management of Fund.** The District Court judges will act as the advisory committee supervising the fund. Duties specified below as those of the Clerk and Chief Judge apply also to the Clerk's designee or acting chief.

1. *Library Fund.* The judges delegate to the Clerk authority to authorize expenditures totaling $500 per month. If any expenditures exceed that amount, the Clerk will refer the request to the Chief Judge who will have the authority to approve individual expenditures not exceeding $2,500. A Library Fund Committee, consisting of the current Chief Judge, the immediate former Chief Judge, and the next Chief Judge, will have the authority to approve individual expenditures not exceeding $5,000. In the absence of the immediate former Chief Judge, the current Chief Judge will designate another district judge to the Library Fund Committee. Approval by a majority of the district judges is needed to authorize individual expenditures in excess of $5,000. For any check in excess of $500, the signature of the Chief Judge as well as the Clerk is required.

2. *Pro Bono Fund.* Disbursements from the pro bono fund must be made according to the provisions of Section a.2. Approval by the District Court judges is needed to authorize general expenditures not related to a specific case in excess of $500 per month. Furthermore, for any check in excess of $500, the signature of the Chief Judge as well as the Clerk is required.

3. *Report.* The Clerk of Court will distribute the quarterly report required in Section b.1.C to the Chief Judge who will distribute it to the District Court judges for review. Further, any other reports, such as those required in Section b.2 or Section d will be distributed by the Chief Judge to all District Court judges for review.

d. **Audits and Inspections.** Funds are subject to audit by the Administrative Office of the United States Courts. The

Court may appoint an outside auditor or disinterested inspector (who may be a government employee) to conduct such additional audits as the Court determines may be necessary or appropriate. The written results of each such audit or inspection must be provided to the Court. Reasonable compensation may be provided from fund assets if the auditor or inspector is not a government employee acting in an official capacity.

A terminal audit or inspection must be performed prior to the dissolution of the funds and a written accounting rendered to the Court.

e. Protection of the Fund. All receipts must be deposited only in federally insured banks or savings institutions and whenever practical and feasible, all substantial sums must be placed in interest bearing accounts or certificates of deposit that are insured by the FDIC, in government securities, or in money market funds invested in government obligations, at the direction of the Court. Efforts must be made to maximize the return on investments consistent with requirements of convenience and safety.

f. Dissolution of the Fund. The Court may dissolve the funds or any portion of those funds whenever considered appropriate. Care must be taken to ensure that all outstanding obligations are liquidated prior to dissolution of the funds, including any expense resulting from the required terminal audit or inspection. In addition, efforts must be made to dispose of the assets of the funds in ways which fulfill the purposes of the funds, as set forth in Section a.1 and 2, above.

[Effective August 18, 1997. Amended effective November 19, 2001; October 25, 2004; December 1, 2009; February 8, 2013; February 2, 2015; April 30, 2018.]

CIVIL RULE 83.9 CORRESPONDENCE AND COMMUNICATIONS WITH THE JUDGE

Except as otherwise provided by law, attorneys or parties to any action or proceeding must refrain from writing letters to the judge, or otherwise communicating with the judge unless opposing counsel is present. All matters to be called to a judge's attention should be formally submitted as hereinafter provided. Except as authorized by the judge, attorneys must not send copies to the judge of letters sent to others.

[Effective August 18, 1997. Amended effective December 1, 2009.]

CIVIL RULE 83.11 PERSONS APPEARING WITHOUT AN ATTORNEY IN PROPRIA PERSONA

a. Any person who is appearing propria persona, (without an attorney) (i.e. pro se) must appear personally for such purpose and may not delegate that duty to any other person, including husband or wife, or another party on the same side appearing without an attorney. Any person appearing propria persona is bound by these rules of court and by the Fed. R.Civ.P. or Fed.R.Crim.P., as appropriate. Failure to comply therewith may be ground for dismissal or judgment by default.

b. A party proceeding pro se must keep the Court and opposing parties advised as to current address. If mail directed to a pro se plaintiff by the Clerk at the plaintiff's last designated address is returned by the Post Office, and if such plaintiff fails to notify the Court and opposing parties within 60 days thereafter of the plaintiff's current address, the Court may dismiss the action without prejudice for failure to prosecute.

[Effective August 18, 1997. Amended effective December 1, 2009.]

[HABEAS CORPUS RULES]

CIVIL RULE HC.1   HABEAS CORPUS PROCEEDINGS—VENUE

The provisions of 28 U.S.C. § 2241(d) provide for the filing of petitions in more than one judicial district. However, this court will make an independent determination of whether venue is appropriate in this district.

[Effective August 18, 1997.]

CIVIL RULE HC.2   HABEAS CORPUS PROCEEDINGS (28 U.S.C. § 2254)—PETITIONS NOT INVOLVING THE DEATH PENALTY

a. Assignment to Judges. The petition will be assigned to a district judge and a magistrate judge. In accordance with Local Rule 72.1.d. and 28 U.S.C. § 636(b), the magistrate judge must conduct any and all of the duties specified in Rule 8 of the Rules Governing § 2254 Cases. If a petitioner has previously sought relief in this district with respect to the same conviction, the petition, if possible, will be assigned to the district judge who was assigned to the prior petition.

b. Form of the Petition. Pursuant to Rule 2(d) of the Rules Governing § 2254 Cases, the form of the petition must substantially follow the form prescribed by this court. The Clerk will make this form available to petitioners without charge.

c. Procedures for Considering the Petition.

1. Written requests for enlargement must be made before the expiration of the time period to be extended and must show good cause for the extension. The request for an enlargement of time must be served on the opposing party and a proof of service filed.

2. To assist the Court in exercising its duties under Rule 8 of the rules governing § 2254 cases, a party may make a request for an evidentiary hearing. The request must include a specification of which factual issues require a hearing and a summary of the evidence the party proposes to offer. Any opposition to the request for an evidentiary hearing must be made within fourteen (14) days from the service of the request.

d. Evidentiary Hearing. If an evidentiary hearing is held, the Court may order the preparation of a transcript of the hearing. Upon the preparation of the transcript, the Court may establish a reasonable schedule for further briefing and argument of the issues considered at the hearing.

e. Dispositive Rulings on the Merits.

1. In accordance with Civil Local Rule 72.1 and 28 U.S.C. § 636(b), the magistrate judge must submit to a district judge proposed findings of fact and recommendations for disposition. The magistrate judge must file proposed findings and recommendations with the Court and a copy must be mailed to all parties. Within the time period set forth in the magistrate judge's report and recommendation, but not less than fourteen (14) days, any party may serve and file written objections to the proposed findings and recommendations by timely filing an original and one (1) copy of the objections and a proof of service showing that the objections were served on the opposing party. The district judge must make a de novo determination of those portions of the report or specified proposed findings or recommendations to which an objection is made. A district judge may accept, reject, seek clarification or modify in whole or in part any findings or recommendations made by the magistrate judge.

2. The district judge may also issue a separate written opinion which will be filed or state an oral opinion on the record in open court, which must be promptly transcribed and filed.

[Effective August 18, 1997. Amended effective April 6, 1998; January 1, 2000; October 25, 2004; April 15, 2005; December 1, 2009.]

CIVIL RULE HC.3   HABEAS CORPUS PROCEEDINGS (28 U.S.C. § 2254)—PETITIONS INVOLVING DEATH PENALTY

a. Applicability. This rule will govern the procedures for a first petition for a writ of habeas corpus filed pursuant to 28 U.S.C. § 2254 in which a petitioner seeks relief from a judgment imposing the penalty of death. A subsequent filing may be deemed a first petition under these rules to a particular petition if the original filing was not dismissed on the merits. The application of this rule may be modified by the judge to whom the petition is assigned. These rules will supplement the Rules Governing § 2254 Cases and do not in any regard alter or supplant those rules.

b. Notices From California Attorney General. The California Attorney General will send the following reports:

1. *Report Upon Setting of Execution Date.* Whenever an execution date is set, the California Attorney General must send prompt notice to the Clerk of this Court and Chief Judge of this District Court, within seven (7) days; and

2. *Semi–Annual Report.* The California Attorney General must electronically send to the Chief Judge of this District Court and designated recipients a semi-annual report that lists:

   a) All scheduled executions in California;

   b) All capital cases, pending on direct appeal before the California Supreme Court;

   c) All capital cases affirmed on direct appeal and pending before the California Supreme Court on first state habeas corpus petitions; and

   d) The county of conviction for each case.

c. Notice From Petitioner's Counsel. Whenever counsel determines that a petition will be filed in this court, counsel must promptly file with the Clerk of this court and send to the California Attorney General a written notice of intention to file a petition. The notice must state the name of the petitioner, the district in which petitioner was convicted, the place of petitioner's incarceration, and the status of petitioner's State Court proceedings. The notice is for the information of the

Court only, and the failure to file the notice will not preclude the filing of the petition.

d. Counsel.

1. *Appointment of Counsel.* Each indigent petitioner must be represented by counsel unless petitioner has clearly elected to represent himself and the court is satisfied, after hearing, that petitioner's election is intelligent and voluntary. Unless petitioner is represented by retained counsel, counsel must be appointed in every such case at the earliest practicable time. A panel of attorneys qualified for appointment in death penalty cases will be certified by a selection board appointed by the Chief Judge of the district. This board will consist of a federal defender, a member of the California Appellate Project (CAP), a member of the state bar, and a representative of the state public defender.

When a death judgment is affirmed by the California Supreme Court and any subsequent proceedings in the State Courts have concluded, California Appellate Project will forward to the selection board the name of state appellate counsel and, if counsel is willing to continue representation on federal habeas corpus, California Appellate Project's evaluation of counsel's performance in the State Courts and recommendation on whether counsel should be appointed in federal court.

If state appellate counsel is available to continue representation into federal courts, and is deemed qualified to do so by the selection board, there is a presumption in favor of continued representation except when state appellate counsel was also counsel at trial.

In light of this presumption, it is expected that appointed counsel who is willing to continue representation and who has been certified by the selection board as qualified to do so would ordinarily file a motion for appointment of counsel on behalf of the client together with the client's federal habeas corpus petition. If, however, counsel for any reason wishes to confirm the appointment before preparing the petition, counsel may move for appointment, as described above, before filing the petition.

If state appellate counsel is not available to represent petitioner on federal habeas corpus or if appointment of state appellate counsel would be inappropriate for any reason, the Court must appoint counsel upon application of petitioner. The Clerk of Court must have available forms for such application. Counsel may be appointed from the panel of qualified attorneys certified by the selection board, or the Court may appoint any other attorney under 18 U.S.C. § 3599. Either California Appellate Project or the selection board may suggest one or more counsel for appointment. The Court may also request suggestion of one or more counsel from California Appellate Project or the selection board. If application for appointed counsel is made before a petition has been filed, the application must be assigned to a district judge in the same manner that a petition would be assigned, and counsel must be appointed by the assigned judge. The judge so assigned must be the judge assigned when counsel files a petition for writ of habeas corpus.

2. *Second Counsel.* Appointment and compensation of second counsel will be governed by § 2.11 of Volume VII of the Guide to Judiciary Policies and Procedures, Appointment of Counsel in Criminal Cases.

e. Assignment to Judges. Notwithstanding the general assignment plan of this court, petitions must be assigned to judges of the Court as follows:

1. The Clerk of the Court must establish a separate category for these petitions, to be designated with the title "Capital case".

2. All active or combination of active and senior judges of this court must participate in the assignments without regard to intra district venue.

3. Petitions in the capital case category must be assigned blindly and randomly by the Clerk of the Court to each of the active or combination of active and senior judges of the Court.

4. If the assigned judge has filed a certificate of unavailability with the Clerk of the Court which is in effect on the date of assignment, a new random assignment will be made to another judge immediately.

5. If a petitioner has previously sought relief in this court with respect to the same conviction, the petition will be assigned to the judge who was assigned to the prior proceeding.

6. Pursuant to 28 U.S.C. § 636(b)(1)(B), and not inconsistent with law, magistrate judges may be designated by the Court to perform all duties under these rules, including evidentiary hearings.

f. Transfer of Venue. Subject to the provisions of 28 U.S.C. § 2241(d), it is the policy of this court that a petition should be heard in the district in which petitioner was convicted, rather than in the district of petitioner's present confinement.

If an order for the transfer of venue is made, the judge will order a stay of execution which must continue until such time as the transferee court acts upon the petition or the order of stay.

g. Stays of Execution.

1. *Stay Pending Final Disposition.* Upon the filing of a habeas corpus petition, unless the petition is patently frivolous, the District Court must issue a stay of execution pending final disposition of the matter.

2. *Temporary Stay for Appointment of Counsel.* Where counsel in State Court proceedings withdraws at the conclusion of the State Court proceedings or is otherwise not available or qualified to proceed, the selection panel will designate an attorney from the panel who will assist an indigent petitioner in filing pro se applications for appointment of counsel and for temporary stay of execution. Upon the filing of this application the District Court must issue a temporary stay of execution and appoint counsel from the panel of attorneys certified for appointment. The temporary stay will remain in effect for forty-five (45) days unless extended by the Court.

3. *Temporary Stay for Preparation of the Petition.* Where counsel new to the case is appointed, upon counsel's application for a temporary stay of execution accompanied by a specification of nonfrivolous issues to be raised in the petition, the District Court must issue a temporary stay of

execution unless no nonfrivolous issues are presented. The temporary stay will remain in effect for one hundred twenty (120) days to allow newly appointed counsel to prepare and file the petition. The temporary stay may be extended by the Court upon a subsequent showing of good cause.

4. *Temporary Stay for Transfer of Venue.* (See paragraph f.)

5. *Temporary Stay for Unexhausted Claims.* If the petition indicates that there are unexhausted claims from which the State Court remedy is still available, petitioner may be granted a thirty (30) day period in which to commence litigation on the unexhausted claims in State Court. During the proceedings in State Court, the proceedings on the petition will be stayed. After the State Court proceedings have been completed, petitioner may amend the petition with respect to the newly exhausted claims.

6. *Stay Pending Appeal.* If the petition is denied and a certificate of probable cause for appeal is issued, the Court will grant a stay of execution which will continue in effect until the Court of Appeals acts upon the appeal of the order of stay.

7. *Notice of Stay.* Upon the granting of any stay of execution, the Clerk of the Court will immediately notify the warden of San Quentin Prison and the California Attorney General. The California Attorney General must assure that the Clerk of the Court has a twenty-four-hour telephone number to the warden.

h. Procedures for Considering the Petition. Unless the judge summarily dismisses the petition under Rule 4 of the Rules Governing § 2254 Cases, the following schedule and procedures must apply, subject to modification by the judge. Requests for enlargement of any time period in this rule must comply with the applicable local rules of the Court.

1. Respondent must as soon as practicable, but in any event on or before twenty-one (21) days from the date of service of the petition, lodge with the Court the following:

a) Transcripts of the state trial court proceedings.

b) Appellant's and respondent's briefs on direct appeal to the California Supreme Court, and the opinion or orders of that court.

c) Petitioner's and respondent's briefs in any State Court habeas corpus proceedings, and all opinions, orders and transcripts of such proceedings.

d) Copies of all pleadings, opinions and orders in any previous federal habeas corpus proceeding filed by petitioner which arose from the same conviction.

e) An index of all materials described in paragraphs (A) through (D) above. Such materials are to be marked and numbered so that they can be uniformly cited. Respondent must serve this index upon counsel for petitioner.

If any items identified in paragraphs (A) through (D) above are not available, respondent must state when, if at all, such missing material can be filed.

2. If counsel for petitioner claims that respondent has not complied with the requirements of paragraph (a),* or if counsel for petitioner does not have copies of all the documents lodged with the Court by respondent, counsel for petitioner must immediately notify the Court in writing, with a copy to respondent. Copies of any missing documents will be provided to counsel for petitioner by the Court.

3. Respondent must file an answer to the petition with accompanying points and authorities within thirty (30) days from the date of service of the petition. Respondent must include in the answer the matters defined in Rule 5 of the Rules Governing § 2254 Cases and must attach any other relevant documents not already filed.

4. No discovery will be had without leave of the Court.

5. Unless extended by the Court at any time, a request for an evidentiary hearing by either party must be made within fourteen (14) days from the filing of the answer to the petition. The request must include specification of which factual issues require a hearing and a summary of what evidence petitioner proposes to offer. Any opposition to the request for an evidentiary hearing must be made within fourteen (14) days from the filing of the request. The Court will then give due consideration to whether an evidentiary hearing will be held.

i. Evidentiary Hearing. If an evidentiary hearing is held, the Court will order the preparation of a transcript of the hearing, which is to be immediately provided to petitioner and respondent for use in briefing and argument. Upon the preparation of the transcript, the Court may establish a reasonable schedule for further briefing and argument of the issues considered at the hearing.

j. Rulings. The Court's rulings may be in the form of a written opinion which will be filed, or in the form of an oral opinion on the record in an open court, which must be promptly transcribed and filed.

The Clerk of the Court will immediately notify the warden of San Quentin Prison and the California Attorney General whenever relief is granted on a petition.

The Clerk of the Court will immediately notify the Clerk of the United States Court of Appeals for the Ninth Circuit by telephone of (a) the issuance of a final order denying or dismissing a petition without a certificate of probable cause for appeal, or (b) the denial of a stay of execution.

When a notice of appeal is filed, the Clerk of the Court will transmit the available records to the Court of Appeals immediately.

[Effective August 18, 1997. Amended effective October 25, 2004; December 1, 2009.]

* [**Publisher's Note:** So in original.]

[ADMIRALTY AND MARITIME RULES]

CIVIL RULE A.1 SCOPE OF RULES FOR ADMIRALTY AND MARITIME CLAIMS

Application. These rules apply to claims governed by the Supplemental Rules for Certain Admiralty and Maritime Claims of the Fed.R.Civ.P., which are referred to within these rules as Rules A through F.

[Effective August 18, 1997. Amended effective January 1, 2000; October 25, 2004; December 1, 2009.]

CIVIL RULE B.1 ATTACHMENT AND GARNISHMENT PROVISIONS

a. Attachment and Garnishment. The verification of a complaint containing a prayer for process under Rule B, if made by plaintiff's attorney or other agent not having personal knowledge or knowledge acquired in the ordinary course of business of the facts alleged in the complaint as grounds of the claim, must state the circumstances making it necessary for such attorney or other agent to make the verification and the sources of the information.

b. Affidavit of Defendant's Absence. The affidavit of plaintiff or plaintiff's attorney that defendant cannot be found within the district, required by Rule B, must state with particularity the efforts made to locate the defendant in the district.

c. Judicial Authorization for Issuance of Writ. Before the Clerk will issue process of attachment and garnishment in accordance with Rule B, the verified complaint and affidavit required by Rule B must be reviewed by a district judge or magistrate judge and, if probable cause be found to exist under Rule B, an order so stating and authorizing issuance of process must issue. Alias process may thereafter be issued by the Clerk upon application without further order of the Court.

d. Hearing and Summary Release of Property. Except in actions by the United States for forfeitures based upon federal statutory violations and actions by seamen for wages, whenever property is attached, any person claiming an interest in the property will be entitled to a prompt hearing before a district or magistrate judge upon written notice to plaintiff, and to an order vacating the attachment immediately and granting other appropriate relief unless plaintiff shows cause at the hearing why such an order should not issue.

[Effective August 18, 1997. Amended effective April 6, 1998; December 1, 2009.]

CIVIL RULE C.1 ACTIONS IN REM

a. Actions In Rem. If, before or after commencement of suit, plaintiff accepts any written undertaking to respond on behalf of the vessel or other property sued in return for foregoing the arrest or stipulating to the release of such vessel or other property, the undertaking will become a defendant in place of the vessel or other property sued and be deemed referred to under the name of the vessel or other property in any pleading, order or judgment in the action referred to in the undertaking. The preceding must apply to any such undertaking, subject to its own terms and whether or not it complies with Civil Local Rule 65.1.2 and has been approved by a judge or clerk.

b. Publication of Notice of Action and Arrest. Plaintiff will cause the notice required by Rule C(4) to be published once in the official newspaper of the Court. The notice must contain the title and number of the action or proceeding, the date of the arrest, the identity of the property arrested, the name of the marshal, and the name and address of the attorney for plaintiff. It must also contain a statement that claims of persons entitled to possession must be filed with the District Court and served upon the attorney for plaintiff within fourteen (14) days after publication; that answers to the complaint must be filed and served within twenty-one (21) days after the filing of the claim, or within such additional time as may be allowed by a judge; that in lieu of an answer, default may be noted and condemnation ordered; and that applications for intervention under Rule 24, Fed.R.Civ.P., by persons claiming maritime liens or other interests, may be untimely if not filed within the time allowed for claims to possession.

c. Intangible Property; Summons Under Rules C(3) and E(4)(c). The summons issued pursuant to Rule C(3) must direct the person having control of funds (consisting of freight, the proceeds of property sold, or other intangible property that is the subject of the action) to show cause why such funds or property should not be delivered to the Court to abide the judgment. This showing may be made by filing with the Clerk and serving on the attorney for plaintiff (1) within fourteen (14) days after the date of publication of notice of action and arrest or within such additional time as may be allowed, a claim under Rule C(6); and (2) within twenty-one (21) days after filing of the claim, an answer to the complaint. If claim and answer are not to be interposed, such person must deliver or pay over to the marshal the property or funds claimed by plaintiff with interest and costs. Service of such summons will have the effect of an arrest of the property and will bring it within the control of the Court.

[Effective August 18, 1997. Amended effective October 25, 2004; December 1, 2009.]

CIVIL RULE E.1 ACTIONS IN REM AND QUASI IN REM

a. Judgment by Default.

1. No default judgment will be entered by the Clerk in any Admiralty proceeding, unless ordered by the Court.

2. On the expiration of the time to answer, if no answer or exceptions have been filed, the plaintiff or petitioner may have an ex parte hearing of the cause and a judgment without notice, except that;

3. If the claimant has appeared by attorney, seven (7) days' notice of the hearing must be given. In actions by the United States for forfeitures based upon federal statutory violations,

the notice to an owner or other known potential claimants must be by certified or registered mail with return service to the last known mailing address.

4. If there has been no appearance by the owner of arrested or attached property, final judgment must not enter against such owner or property until it is shown by affidavit that notice of the suit has been given pursuant to Fed.R.Civ.P. Supp. B(2) and to:

a) The owner of the property (other than a vessel) if known to the plaintiff or petitioner, and otherwise the owner's agent, if known;

b) The owner, or managing owner, if more than one, of the vessel arrested or attached if known, and the owner or managing owner, if more than one, recorded as such in the records of the United States Coast Guard, in the case of a documented vessel of the United States or in the records of the California Department of Motor Vehicles, in a case where it has issued a certificate of ownership, and if notice cannot be given to such owner, the agent of the vessel, if any be known, within the district;

5. Any holder of a security interest in the vessel arrested or attached whose interest is recorded as described in (b) above.

The notice to an owner or agent must be by personal service within the district, or if that cannot be done, by first class mail with return service, if available, to the mailing address of record, or in the absence of a recorded address, to the last known address. Notice to others may be by either of the foregoing methods. Failure to give notice as provided by this rule will be grounds for setting aside default under applicable rules, but will not affect the title to property sold under a judgment.

b. Security for Costs and Marshal's Fees and Expenses; Forfeiture Actions Brought by the United States.

1. *Costs.* In an action covered by Rule E, a party may serve upon an adverse party and file notice to post security for costs and expenses. Unless otherwise ordered by a judge, the amount of the security will be $500.00. The party notified must post security within five days after service, unless exempted by law or by order of a judge upon good cause shown. Should the party fail to do so, it may neither file additional papers nor participate further in proceedings, except for the purpose of seeking relief from this Rule. In actions by the United States for forfeitures for federal statutory violations, security for costs must be paid pursuant to the procedures established in the customs laws, 19 U.S.C. §§ 1607 and 1608.

2. *Marshal's Fees and Expenses.* The marshal is not required to execute process in an action within Rule E unless deposit has been made covering fees and expenses of seizing and keeping the property arrested or attached for a minimum of fourteen (14) days. The party requesting execution of process must advance any additional fees and expenses from time to time as the marshal requests until the property is released or disposed of pursuant to Rule E.

c. Execution of Process; Custody of Property.

1. *Property in Custody of an Officer of the United States.* Where property in the custody of an officer or employee of the United States is to be arrested or attached, the marshal must deliver a copy of the complaint and warrant for arrest or summons and process of attachment to such officer or employee, or if the officer or employee is not found within the district, then to the custodian of the property within the district, and must notify such officer, employee or custodian not to relinquish such property from custody, except to the marshal, subject to further order of a judge.

2. *Custody of Vessels; Keepers; Security; Expenses.* Upon arrest or attachment of a vessel under process issued by the Court, the marshal must place one or more keepers thereon who must remain aboard until the vessel is released or disposed of pursuant to Rule E, unless otherwise ordered.

On motion of any party, made after notice to the marshal and all parties who have appeared, a judge may order that custody of the vessel be given to the operator of a marina or similar facility, repair yard, or company regularly carrying on the business of ship's agent, if a judge finds that such firm or person can and will safely keep the vessel and has in effect adequate insurance to cover any liability for failure to do so. If the vessel must be moved to the place where custody will be maintained, a judge may also require insurance or other security to protect those having an interest in the vessel, as well as those claiming against her, from loss of or damage to the res, or liability of the vessel, incurred during the movement. The order allowing such custody must fix fees to be charged therefor and for any other services to be rendered the vessel and must provide for their payment to the marshal in advance. The provisions of this rule requiring insurance or security do not apply to the United States or to an officer, employee or agent thereof.

3. *Vessel Operations.* The marshal, deputies and keepers of a vessel arrested or attached must not interfere with the conduct of cargo and other operations normal to a vessel in berth, repair work, dry-docking or undry-docking (in the case of a vessel in a shipyard) unless a judge so orders. Neither the United States nor the marshal will be liable for the consequences of the continuation of any such activities during the arrest or attachment. Upon motion of any interested party (which may be made ex parte when the urgency of the matter requires) and for good cause shown, a judge may order the marshal to prevent or require the conduct of any operations of a vessel under arrest or attachment.

d. Appraisement of Property for Purpose of Bonding. Orders for the appraisement of arrested or attached property for the purpose of bonding and sale may be entered as a matter of course by the Clerk of the District Court at the request of any interested party. If the parties do not agree in writing upon an appraiser, the Clerk will name one. Any party having a claim to the property may appeal immediately to the judge from such appointment. The appraiser must be sworn to the faithful and impartial discharge of duties before any federal or state officer authorized by law to administer oaths. The appraiser must give one day's notice of the time and place of making the appraisement to the attorneys of record in the proceeding, and must file the appraisement, when made, with the Clerk of the District Court.

e. **Sales.**

1. *Notice.* Notice of a sale of arrested or attached property must be in accordance with 28 U.S.C. §§ 2001–2004. Unless otherwise ordered by a judge upon a showing of urgency or impracticality, notice of the sale of property must be published daily for at least seven (7) days immediately before the date of sale.

2. *Confirmation.* Unless otherwise provided in the order, in all public auction sales by the marshal under orders of sale in admiralty and maritime claims, the marshal must require of the last and highest bidder at the sale a minimum deposit in cash, certified check or cashier's check, of the full purchase price not to exceed $500, and otherwise $500 or ten percent of the bid, whichever is greater. The balance, if any, of the purchase price must be paid in cash, certified check or cashier's check before confirmation of the sale or within three days of dismissal of any filed opposition. When the Court determines on the merits that a plaintiff or plaintiff in intervention has a valid claim senior in priority to all other parties, that plaintiff in intervention foreclosing a properly recorded and endorsed preferred mortgage on, or other valid security interest in the vessel may bid, without payment of cash, certified check or cashier's check, up to the total amount of the secured indebtedness as established by affidavit filed and served on all other parties no later than seven (7) days prior to the date of sale.

At the conclusion of the sale, the marshal must forthwith file a written report to the judge of the fact of sale, the price obtained and the name and address of the buyer. The Clerk of the District Court must endorse upon such report the time and date of its filing. If within three days, exclusive of Saturdays, Sundays, and legal holidays, no written objection is filed, the sale will stand confirmed as of course, without the necessity of any affirmative action thereon by a judge; except that no sale will stand confirmed until the buyer has complied fully with the terms of the purchase. If no opposition to the sale is filed, the expenses of keeping the property pending confirmation of sale must be charged against the party bearing expenses before the sale (subject to taxation as costs), except that if confirmation is delayed by the purchaser's failure to pay any balance which is due on the price, the cost of keeping the property subsequent to the three-day period hereinabove specified must be borne by the purchaser. A party filing an opposition to the sale, whether seeking the reception of a higher bid or a new public sale by the marshal, must give prompt notice to all other parties and to the purchaser. Such party must also, prior to filing an opposition, secure the marshal's endorsement upon it acknowledging deposit with the marshal of the necessary expense of keeping the property for at least five days. Pending the judge's determination of the opposition, such party must also advance any further expense at such times and in such amounts as the marshal will request, or as a judge orders upon application of the marshal or the opposing party. Such expense may later be subject to taxation as costs. In the event of failure to make such advance, the opposition must fail without necessity for affirmative action thereon by a judge. If the opposition fails, the expense of keeping the property during its pendency must be borne by the party filing the opposition.

3. *Sale of Forfeited Property.* In actions by the United States for forfeitures based upon federal statutory violations, the United States marshal must sell or dispose of forfeited property or property to be sold pursuant to an order for interlocutory sale, in a commercially reasonable manner and in accordance with law unless otherwise provided in the order.

[Effective August 18, 1997. Amended effective April 6, 1998; January 1, 2000; October 25, 2004; December 1, 2009.]

CIVIL RULE F.1   LIMITATION OF LIABILITY

Limitation of Liability—Security for Costs. Unless otherwise ordered by a judge, the amount of the security for costs required to be filed in an action for limitation of liability under Rule F(1) is $500. In such an action, the security for costs may be combined with the security for value and interest.

[Effective August 18, 1997.]

PATENT LOCAL RULES

1. SCOPE OF RULES

1.1 TITLE

These are the Local Rules of Practice for Patent Cases before the United States District Court for the Southern District of California. They should be cited as "Patent L.R. ___."

[Effective April 3, 2006.]

1.2 EFFECTIVE DATE

These Patent Local Rules take effect on December 1, 2009, and will apply to any case filed thereafter.

[Effective April 3, 2006. Amended effective December 1, 2009.]

1.3 SCOPE AND CONSTRUCTION

These Patent Local Rules apply to all civil actions filed in or transferred to this court which allege infringement of a utility patent in a complaint, counterclaim, cross-claim or third party claim, or which seek a declaratory judgment that a utility patent is not infringed, is invalid or is unenforceable. The Court may accelerate, extend, eliminate, or modify the obligations or deadlines set forth in these Patent Local Rules based on the Court's schedule or the circumstances of any particular case, including, without limitation, the complexity of the case or the number of patents, claims, products, or parties involved. If any motion filed prior to the Claim Construction Hearing provided for in Patent L.R. 4.5 raises claim construc-

tion issues, the Court may, for good cause shown, defer the motion until after completion of the disclosures, filings, or ruling following the Claim Construction Hearing.

The Civil Local Rules of this court also apply to these actions, except to the extent they are inconsistent with these Patent Local Rules.

[Effective April 3, 2006.]

1.4 APPLICATION OF RULES WHEN NO SPECIFIED TRIGGERING EVENT

If the filings or actions in a case do not trigger the application of these Patent Local Rules, as soon as any party ascertains that circumstances exist to make application of these Patent Local Rules appropriate to the case, that party should notify the assigned magistrate judge so the matter may be scheduled for a Case Management Conference.

[Effective April 3, 2006.]

1.5 NOTICE OF RELATED PATENT CASE

Civil Local Rule 40.1 applies to patent cases. The parties must notify the Court of any other cases in the district involving the same patent.

[Effective January 30, 2016.]

2. GENERAL PROVISIONS

2.1 GOVERNING PROCEDURE

a. Early Neutral Evaluation ("ENE") Conference. Within sixty (60) days of a defendant making its first appearance in the case, counsel and the parties will appear before the assigned magistrate judge for an ENE conference pursuant to Civ.L.R. 16.1.c.1. No later than twenty-one (21) days before the ENE, the parties will meet and confer pursuant to Fed. R.Civ.P. 26(f).

If no settlement is reached at the ENE Conference, the magistrate judge will proceed with the Initial Case Management Conference. At the end of the conference, the magistrate judge must prepare a case management order which will include:

1. A discovery schedule, including an initial date for the substantial completion of document discovery including electronically stored information ("ESI"), and a later date for the completion of all fact discovery;

2. A date for the Claim Construction Hearing within nine (9) months of the date of a defendant's first appearance;

3. A trial date within eighteen (18) months of the date the complaint was filed, if practicable, for "standard" cases (defined as typically having one or two defendants and one or two

patents); and, within twenty-four (24) months for complex cases, if practicable;

4. A dispositive motion filing cutoff date to include any motions addressing any *Daubert* issues;

5. A date for the Mandatory Settlement Conference; and

6. All other pretrial dates, as required in Civ.L.R. 16.1.d.2, as appropriate.

b. Initial Case Management Conference. When the parties confer with each other pursuant to Fed.R.Civ.P. 26(f), in addition to matters covered by Fed.R.Civ.P. 26, the parties must discuss and address in the Joint Discovery Plan filed pursuant to Fed.R.Civ.P. 26(f), the following topics:

1. Proposed modification of the deadlines provided for in these Patent Local Rules, and the effect of any such modification on the date and time of the Claim Construction Hearing, if any;

2. The need for and specific limits on discovery relating to claim construction, including depositions of percipient and expert witnesses; and

3. The need, if any, to phase damage discovery.

c. Settlement Conferences.

1. The judge conducting the settlement conference may require the parties or representatives of a party other than counsel, who have authority to negotiate and enter into a binding settlement, be present at the settlement conference.

2. When ordered to appear, each party, claims adjusters for insured defendants, in addition to any other representatives with "full authority" to enter into a binding settlement, as well as the principal attorney(s) responsible for the litigation, must be present and legally and factually prepared to discuss and resolve the case at the Settlement Conference. Any variation from this Rule or special arrangements desired in cases must be proposed no later than twenty-one (21) days in advance of the settlement conference to the settlement judge.

3. "Full authority" means that the individuals at the settlement conference be authorized to fully negotiate settlement terms and to agree at that time to any settlement terms acceptable to the parties, and to bind the party, without the need to call others not present at the conference for authority or approval.

4. No later than fourteen (14) days before the settlement conference, each party will designate in writing to all other parties, the person(s) and their title(s) or position(s) with the party who will attend and have settlement authority at the conference.

[Effective April 3, 2006. Amended effective February 8, 2013; January 1, 2014.]

2.2 CONFIDENTIALITY

If any document or information produced under these Patent Local Rules is deemed confidential by the producing party and if the Court has not entered a protective order, until a protective order is issued by the Court, the document will be marked "Confidential" or with some other confidential designation (such as "Confidential—Outside Attorneys Eyes Only") by the disclosing party and disclosure of the confidential document or information will be limited to each party's outside attorney(s) of record and the employees of such outside attorney(s). An approved model form of protective order is available on the Court's website (www.casd.uscourts.gov) and may be amended by the Court over time as deemed appropriate.

If a party is not represented by an outside attorney, disclosure of the confidential document or information will be limited to a designated "in house" attorney, whose identity and job functions will be disclosed to the producing party five court days prior to any such disclosure. The person(s) to whom disclosure of a confidential document or information is made under this Patent Local Rule will keep it confidential and use it only for purposes of litigating the case.

A document may not be filed under seal unless authorized by an order entered by the judge before whom the hearing or proceeding related to the proposed sealed document will take place.

[Effective April 3, 2006. Amended effective February 8, 2013.]

2.3 CERTIFICATION OF INITIAL DISCLOSURES.

All statements, disclosures, or charts filed or served in accordance with these Patent Local Rules must be dated and signed by counsel of record. Counsel's signature will constitute a certification that to the best of his or her knowledge, information and belief, formed after an inquiry that is reasonable under the circumstances, that information contained in the statement, disclosure, or chart is complete and correct at the time it is made.

[Effective April 3, 2006.]

2.4 ADMISSIBILITY OF DISCLOSURES.

Statements, disclosures, or charts governed by these Patent Local Rules are admissible to the extent permitted by the Federal Rules of Evidence or Federal Rules of Civil Procedure. However, the statements or disclosures provided for in Patent Local Rules 4.1 and 4.2 are not admissible for any purpose other than in connection with motions seeking an extension or modification of the time periods within which actions contemplated by these Patent Local Rules must be taken.

[Effective April 3, 2006.]

2.5 RELATIONSHIP TO FEDERAL RULES OF CIVIL PROCEDURE.

Except as provided in this paragraph or as otherwise ordered, it will not be a legitimate ground for objecting to an opposing party's discovery request (*e.g.*, interrogatory, document request, request for admission, deposition question), or declining to provide information otherwise required to be disclosed pursuant to Fed.R.Civ.P. 26(a)(1), that the discovery request or disclosure requirement is premature in light of, or otherwise conflicts with, these Patent Local Rules. A party may object, however, to responding to the following categories of discovery requests on the ground that they are premature in light of the timetable provided in the Patent Local Rules:

a. Requests seeking to elicit a party's claim construction position;

b. Requests seeking to elicit from the patent claimant a comparison of the asserted claims and the accused apparatus, product, device, process, method, act, or other instrumentality;

c. Requests seeking to elicit from an accused infringer a comparison of the asserted claims and the prior art; and

d. Requests seeking to elicit an opinion of counsel, and related documents, upon which a party intends to rely for any patent-related claim or defense.

Where a party properly objects to a discovery request as set forth above, that party must provide the requested information on the date on which it is required to provide, the requested information to an opposing party under these Patent Local Rules, unless another legitimate ground for objection exists.

[Effective April 3, 2006. Amended effective December 1, 2009; February 8, 2013.]

3. PATENT DISCLOSURES

3.1 DISCLOSURE OF ASSERTED CLAIMS AND INFRINGEMENT CONTENTIONS.

Not later than fourteen (14) days after the Initial Case Management Conference, a party claiming patent infringement must serve on all parties a "Disclosure of Asserted Claims and Infringement Contentions." Separately for each opposing party, the "Disclosure of Asserted Claims and Infringement Contentions" must contain the following information:

a. Each claim of each patent in suit that is allegedly infringed by each opposing party;

b. Separately for each asserted claim, each accused apparatus, product, device, process, method, act, or other instrumentality ("Accused Instrumentality") of each opposing party of which the party is aware. This identification must be as specific as possible. Each product, device and apparatus must be identified by name or model number, if known. Each method or process must be identified by name, if known, or by any product, device, or apparatus which, when used, allegedly results in the practice of the claimed method or process;

c. A chart identifying specifically where each element of each asserted claim is found within each Accused Instrumentality, including for each element that such party contends is governed by 35 U.S.C. § 112(6), the identity of the structure(s), act(s), or material(s) in the Accused Instrumentality that performs the claimed function;

d. For each claim which is alleged to have been indirectly infringed, an identification of any direct infringement and a description of the acts of the alleged indirect infringer that contribute to or are inducing that direct infringement. Insofar as alleged direct infringement is based on joint acts of multiple parties, the role of each such party in the direct infringement must be described.

e. Whether each element of each asserted claim is claimed to be literally present and/or present under the doctrine of equivalents in the Accused Instrumentality;

f. For any patent that claims priority to an earlier application, the priority date to which each asserted claim allegedly is entitled;

g. If a party claiming patent infringement asserts or wishes to preserve the right to rely, for any purpose, on the assertion that its own apparatus, product, device, process, method, act, or other instrumentality practices the claimed invention, the party must identify, separately for each asserted claim, each such apparatus, product, device, process, method, act, or other instrumentality that incorporates or reflects that particular claim; and

h. If a party claiming infringement alleges willful infringement, the basis for such allegation.

[Effective April 3, 2006. Amended effective December 1, 2009; February 8, 2013.]

3.2 DOCUMENT PRODUCTION ACCOMPANYING DISCLOSURE.

With the "Disclosure of Asserted Claims and Infringement Contentions," the party claiming patent infringement must produce to each opposing party or make available for inspection and copying, the following documents in the possession, custody or control of that party:

a. Documents (e.g., contracts, purchase orders, invoices, advertisements, marketing materials, offer letters, beta site testing agreements, and third party or joint development agreements) sufficient to evidence each discussion with, disclosure to, or other manner of providing to a third party, or sale of or offer to sell, the claimed invention prior to the date of application for the patent in suit. A party's production of a document as required within these rules does not constitute an admission that such document evidences or is prior art under 35 U.S.C. § 102;

b. All documents evidencing the conception, reduction to practice, design and development of each claimed invention, which were created on or before the date of application for the patent in suit or the priority date identified pursuant to Patent L.R. 3.1.e, whichever is earlier;

c. A copy of the file history for each patent in suit and each application to which a claim for priority is made under Patent L.R. 3.1.e;

d. Documents sufficient to evidence ownership of the patent rights by the party asserting patent infringement; and

e. If a party identifies instrumentalities pursuant to Patent L.R. 3.1.g, documents sufficient to show the operation of any aspects or elements of such instrumentalities the patent claimant relies upon as embodying any asserted claims.

The producing party must separately identify by production number which documents correspond to each category. If the documents identified above are not in the possession, custody or control of the party charged with production, that party must use its best efforts to obtain all responsive documents and make a timely disclosure.

[Effective April 3, 2006. Amended effective December 1, 2009; February 8, 2013.]

3.3 INVALIDITY CONTENTIONS.

Not later than sixty (60) days after service upon it of the "Disclosure of Asserted Claims and Infringement Contentions," each party opposing a claim of patent infringement must serve on all parties its "Invalidity Contentions," which must contain the following information:

a. The identity of each item of prior art that allegedly anticipates each asserted claim or renders it obvious. This includes information about any alleged knowledge or use of the invention in this country prior to the date of invention of the patent. Each prior art patent must be identified by its number, country of origin, and date of issue. Each prior art publication must be identified by its title, date of publication, and where feasible, author and publisher. Prior art under 35 U.S.C. § 102(b) must be identified by specifying the item offered for sale or publicly used or known, the date the offer or use took place or the information became known, and the identity of the person or entity that made the use or that made and received the offer, or the person or entity that made the information known or to whom it was made known. Prior art under 35 U.S.C. § 102(f) must be identified by providing the name of the person(s) from whom and the circumstances under which the invention or any part of it was derived. Prior art under 35 U.S.C. § 102(g) must be identified by providing the identities of the person(s) or entities involved in and the circumstances surrounding the making of the invention before the patent applicant(s);

b. Whether each item of prior art anticipates each asserted claim or renders it obvious. If obviousness is alleged, an explanation of why the prior art renders the asserted claim obvious, including an identification of any combinations of prior art showing obviousness;

c. A chart identifying where specifically in each alleged item of prior art each element of each asserted claim is found, including for each element that such party contends is governed by 35 U.S.C. § 112(6), the identity of the structure(s), act(s), or material(s) in each item of prior art that performs the claimed function;

d. Any grounds of invalidity based on indefiniteness under 35 U.S.C. § 112(2) of any of the asserted claims;

e. Any grounds of invalidity based on lack of written description, lack of enabling disclosure, or failure to describe the best mode under 35 U.S.C. § 112(1).

[Effective April 3, 2006. Amended effective July 16, 2007; December 1, 2009; February 8, 2013.]

3.4 DOCUMENT PRODUCTION ACCOMPANYING INVALIDITY CONTENTIONS

With the "Invalidity Contentions," the party opposing a claim of patent infringement must produce or make available for inspection and copying:

a. Source code, specifications, schematics, flow charts, artwork, formulas, or other documentation sufficient to show the operation of any aspects or elements of any Accused Instrumentality identified by the patent claimant in its Patent L.R. 3.1.c chart; and

b. A copy of each item of prior art identified pursuant to Patent L.R. 3.3.a which does not appear in the file history of the patent(s) at issue. To the extent any such item is not in English, an English translation of the portion(s) relied upon must be produced.

[Effective April 3, 2006. Amended effective February 8, 2013.]

3.5 DISCLOSURE REQUIREMENTS IN PATENT CASES FOR DECLARATORY RELIEF.

a. Invalidity Contentions If No Claim of Infringement. In all cases in which a party files a complaint or other pleading seeking a declaratory judgment that a patent is not infringed, is invalid, or is unenforceable, Patent Local Rules 3.1 and 3.2 will not apply unless and until a claim for patent infringement is made by a party. If the defendant does not assert a claim for patent infringement in answer to the complaint, no later than fourteen (14) days after the Initial Case Management Conference the party seeking a declaratory judgment must serve upon each opposing party Invalidity Contentions that conform to Patent L.R. 3.3 and produce or make available for inspection and copying the documents described in Patent L.R. 3.4.

b. Inapplicability of Rule. This Patent L.R. 3.5 does not apply to cases in which a request for declaratory judgment that a patent is not infringed, is invalid, or is unenforceable, is filed in response to a complaint for infringement of the same patent.

[Effective April 3, 2006. Amended effective December 1, 2009; February 8, 2013.]

3.6 AMENDED AND FINAL CONTENTIONS.

a. As a matter of right, a party asserting infringement may serve Amended Infringement Contentions no later than the filing of the parties' Joint Claim Construction Chart. Thereafter, absent undue prejudice to the opposing party, a party asserting infringement may only amend its infringement contentions:

1. If, not later than thirty (30) days after service of the Court's Claim Construction Ruling, the party asserting infringement believes in good faith that amendment is necessitated by a claim construction that differs from that proposed by such party; or

2. Upon a timely motion showing good cause.

b. As a matter of right, a party opposing a claim of patent infringement may serve "Amended Invalidity Contentions" no later than the completion of claim construction discovery. Thereafter, absent undue prejudice to the opposing party, a party opposing infringement may only amend its validity contentions:

1. If a party claiming patent infringement has served "Amended Infringement Contentions," and the party opposing a claim of patent infringement believes in good faith that the Amended Infringement Contentions so require;

2. If, not later than fifty (50) days after service of the Court's Claim Construction Ruling, the party opposing infringement believes in good faith that amendment is necessitated by a claim construction that differs from that proposed by such party; or

3. Upon a timely motion showing good cause.

This rule does not relieve any party from its obligations under Fed.R.Civ.P. 26 to timely supplement disclosures and discovery responses.

[Effective April 3, 2006. Amended effective December 1, 2009; February 8, 2013; April 30, 2018.]

3.7 ADVICE OF COUNSEL

Not later than thirty (30) days after filing of the Claim Construction Order, each party relying upon advice of counsel as part of a patent-related claim or defense for any reason must:

a. Produce or make available for inspection and copying the opinion(s) and any other documentation relating to the opinion(s) as to which that party agrees the attorney-client or work product protection has been waived; and

b. Provide a written summary of any oral advice and produce or make available for inspection and copying that summary and documents related thereto for which the attorney-client and work product protection have been waived; and

c. Serve a privilege log identifying any other documents, except those authored by counsel acting solely as trial counsel, relating to the subject matter of the opinion(s) which the party is withholding on the grounds of attorney-client privilege or work product protection.

A party who does not comply with the requirements of Patent L.R. 3.7 will not be permitted to rely on advice of counsel for any purpose, absent a stipulation of all parties or by order of the Court, which will be entered only upon showing of good cause.

[Effective April 3, 2006. Former Rule 3.8 redesignated as Rule 3.7 and amended effective February 8, 2013.]

3.8 WILLFULNESS [DELETED EFFECTIVE FEBRUARY 8, 2013]

4. CLAIM CONSTRUCTION PROCEEDINGS

4.1 EXCHANGE OF PRELIMINARY CLAIM CONSTRUCTION AND EXTRINSIC EVIDENCE.

a. Not later than fourteen (14) days after the service of the "Invalidity Contentions" pursuant to Patent L.R. 3.3, the parties will simultaneously exchange a preliminary proposed construction of each claim term, phrase, or clause which the parties have identified for claim construction purposes. Each such "Preliminary Claim Constructions" will also, for each element which any party contends is governed by 35 U.S.C. § 112(6), identify the structure(s), act(s), or material(s) described in the specification corresponding to that element.

b. Simultaneously with exchange of the "Preliminary Claim Constructions," the parties must also provide a preliminary identification of extrinsic evidence, including without limitation, dictionary definitions, citations to learned treatises and prior art, and testimony of percipient and expert witnesses they contend support their respective claim constructions. The parties must identify each such item of extrinsic evidence by production number or produce a copy of any such item not previously produced. With respect to any such witness, percipient or expert, the parties must also provide a brief description of the substance of that witness's proposed testimony.

c. Not later than fourteen (14) days after the service of the "Preliminary Claim Constructions" pursuant to Patent L.R. 4.1.a, the parties will simultaneously exchange "Responsive Claim Constructions" identifying whether the responding party agrees with the other party's proposed construction, or identifying an alternate construction in the responding party's preliminary construction, or setting forth the responding party's alternate construction.

d. Simultaneous with exchange of the "Responsive Claim Constructions" pursuant to Patent L.R. 4.1.c, the parties must also provide a preliminary identification of extrinsic evidence, including without limitation, dictionary definitions, citations to learned treatises and prior art, and testimony of percipient and expert witnesses they contend support any responsive claim constructions. The parties must identify each such item of extrinsic evidence by production number or produce a copy of any such item not previously produced. With respect to any such witness, percipient or expert, the parties must also provide a brief description of the substance of that witness's proposed testimony.

e. The parties must thereafter meet and confer for the purposes of narrowing the issues and finalizing preparation of a Joint Claim Construction Chart, Worksheet and Hearing Statement.

[Effective April 3, 2006. Amended effective December 1, 2009; February 8, 2013.]

4.2 JOINT CLAIM CONSTRUCTION CHART, WORKSHEET AND HEARING STATEMENT.

Not later than fourteen (14) days after service of the "Responsive Claim Constructions" pursuant to Patent L.R. 4.1.c, the parties must complete and file a Joint Claim Construction Chart, Joint Claim Construction Worksheet and Joint Hearing Statement.

a. The Joint Hearing Statement must include an identification of the terms whose construction will be most significant to the resolution of the case up to a maximum of ten (10) terms. The parties must also identify any term among the ten (10) whose construction will be case or claim dispositive. If the parties cannot agree on the ten (10) most significant terms, the parties must identify the ones which they do agree are most significant and then they may evenly divide the remainder with each party identifying what it believes are the remaining most significant terms. However, the total terms identified by all parties as most significant cannot exceed ten (10). For example, in a case involving two (2) parties, if the parties agree upon the identification of five (5) terms as most significant, each may only identify two (2) additional terms as most significant; if the parties agree upon eight (8) such terms, each party may only identify only one (1) additional term as most significant.

b. The Joint Claim Construction Chart must have a column listing complete language of disputed claims with the disputed terms in bold type and separate columns for each party's proposed construction of each disputed term. Each party's proposed construction of each disputed claim term, phrase, or clause, must identify all references from the specification or prosecution history that support that construction, and identify any extrinsic evidence known to the party on which it intends to rely either to support its proposed construction of the claim or to oppose any party's proposed construction of the claim, including, but not limited to, as permitted by law, dictionary definitions, citations to learned treatises and prior art, and testimony of percipient and expert witnesses. For every claim with a disputed term, each party must identify with specificity the impact of the proposed constructions on the merits of the case.

c. The parties' Joint Claim Construction Worksheet must be in the format set forth in Appendix A and include any proposed constructions to which the parties agree, as well as those in dispute. The parties must jointly submit the Joint Claim Construction Worksheet on computer disk in both Word and WordPerfect format or in such other format as the Court may direct.

d. The Joint Hearing Statement must include:

1. The anticipated length of time necessary for the Claim Construction Hearing;

2. Whether any party proposes to call one or more witnesses, including experts, at the Claim Construction Hearing, the identity of each such witness, and for each expert, a summary of each opinion to be offered in sufficient detail to permit a meaningful deposition of that expert; and

3. The order of presentation at the Claim Construction Hearing.

e. At the Court's discretion, within seven (7) days of the submission of the Joint Claim Construction Chart, Joint Claim Construction Worksheet and Joint Hearing Statement, the Court will hold a status conference with the parties, in person or by telephone, to discuss scheduling, witnesses and any other matters regarding the Claim Construction Hearing.

[Effective April 3, 2006. Amended effective December 1, 2009; February 8, 2013. Technical amendment effective January 1, 2014. Amended effective April 24, 2017.]

4.3 COMPLETION OF CLAIM CONSTRUCTION DISCOVERY.

Not later than twenty-eight (28) days after service and filing of the Joint Claim Construction Chart, Joint Claim Construc-

tion Worksheet and Joint Hearing Statement, the parties must complete all discovery, including depositions of any percipient or expert witnesses that they intend to use in the Claim Construction Hearing. Fed.R.Civ.P. 30 applies to depositions taken pursuant to Patent L.R. 4.3, except as to experts. An expert witness identified in a party's Joint Hearing Statement pursuant to Patent L.R. 4.2.c, may be deposed on claim construction issues. The identification of an expert witness in the Joint Hearing Statement may be deemed good cause for a further deposition on all substantive issues.

[Effective April 3, 2006. Amended effective December 1, 2009.]

4.4 CLAIM CONSTRUCTION BRIEFS.

a. Not later than fourteen (14) days after close of claim construction discovery, the parties will simultaneously file and serve opening briefs and any evidence supporting their claim construction.

b. Not later than fourteen (14) days after service of the opening briefs, the parties will simultaneously file and serve briefs responsive to the opposing party's opening brief and any evidence directly rebutting the supporting evidence contained in the opposing party's opening brief.

c. Absent leave of Court, the provisions of Civ.L.R. 7.1.h for length of briefs for supporting and reply memoranda will apply to the length of opening and responsive claim construction briefs.

[Effective April 3, 2006. Amended effective December 1, 2009; February 8, 2013; April 24, 2017.]

4.5 CLAIM CONSTRUCTION HEARING.

Not later than twenty-eight (28) days after service of responsive briefs and subject to the convenience of the Court's calendar, the Court will conduct a Claim Construction Hearing, if the Court believes a hearing is necessary for construction of the claims at issue. The Court may also order in its discretion a tutorial hearing, to occur before, or on the date of, the Claim Construction Hearing.

Attached as Appendix B is a time line illustrating the exchange and filing deadlines set forth in these Patent Local Rules.

[Effective April 3, 2006. Amended effective December 1, 2009; February 8, 2013.]

APPENDIX A. APPROVED FORM OF JOINT
CLAIM CONSTRUCTION WORKSHEET

JOINT CLAIM CONSTRUCTION WORKSHEET

PATENT CLAIM	AGREED PROPOSED CONSTRUCTION	PLAINTIFF'S PROPOSED CONSTRUCTION	DEFENDANT'S PROPOSED CONSTRUCTION	COURT'S CONSTRUCTION
1. Claim language as it appears in the patent with terms and phrases to be construed in bold.	Proposed construction if the parties agree.	Plaintiff's proposed construction if parties disagree.	Defendant's proposed construction if parties disagree.	Blank column for Court to enter its construction.
2. Claim language as it appears in the patent with terms and phrases to be construed in bold.	Proposed construction if the parties agree.	Plaintiff's proposed construction if parties disagree.	Defendant's proposed construction if parties disagree.	Blank column for Court to enter its construction.
3. Claim language as it appears in the patent with terms and phrases to be construed in bold.	Proposed construction in the parties agree.	Plaintiff's proposed construction if parties disagree.	Defendant's proposed construction if parties disagree.	Blank column for Court to enter its construction

[Effective April 3, 2006. Amended effective December 21, 2009; February 8, 2013.]

APPENDIX B.   TIME LINE OF EXCHANGE AND FILING DATES

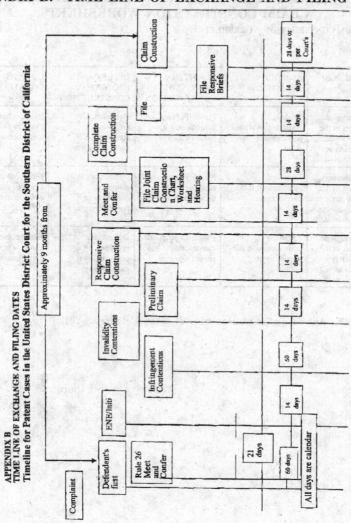

APPENDIX B
TIME LINE OF EXCHANGE AND FILING DATES
Timeline for Patent Cases in the United States District Court for the Southern District of California

[Effective April 3, 2006.   Amended effective February 8, 2013.]

866

MODEL PROTECTIVE ORDER

Plaintiff,   CASE NO. 00cv0000

Plaintiff,   PROTECTIVE ORDER

vs.

Defendant,

Defendant.

The Court recognizes that at least some of the documents and information ("materials") being sought through discovery in the above-captioned action are, for competitive reasons, normally kept confidential by the parties. The parties have agreed to be bound by the terms of this Protective Order ("Order") in this action.

The materials to be exchanged throughout the course of the litigation between the parties may contain trade secret or other confidential research, technical, cost, price, marketing or other commercial information, as is contemplated by Federal Rule of Civil Procedure 26(c)(1)(G). The purpose of this Order is to protect the confidentiality of such materials as much as practical during the litigation. THEREFORE:

DEFINITIONS

1. The term "confidential information" will mean and include information contained or disclosed in any materials, including documents, portions of documents, answers to interrogatories, responses to requests for admissions, trial testimony, deposition testimony, and transcripts of trial testimony and depositions, including data, summaries, and compilations derived therefrom that is deemed to be Confidential Information by any party to which it belongs.

2. The term "materials" will include, but is not be limited to: documents; correspondence; memoranda; bulletins; blueprints; specifications; customer lists or other material that identify customers or potential customers; price lists or schedules or other matter identifying pricing; minutes; telegrams; letters; statements; cancelled checks; contracts; invoices; drafts; books of account; worksheets; notes of conversations; desk diaries; appointment books; expense accounts; recordings; photographs; motion pictures; compilations from which information can be obtained and translated into reasonably usable form through detection devices; sketches; drawings; notes (including laboratory notebooks and records); reports; instructions; disclosures; other writings; models and prototypes and other physical objects.

3. The term "Counsel" will mean outside counsel of record, and other attorneys, paralegals, secretaries, and other support staff employed in the law firms identified below: _____ ["Counsel" also includes _____, in-house attorneys for [Plaintiff] and _____, in-house attorneys for [Defendant].]

GENERAL RULES

4. Each party to this litigation that produces or discloses any materials, answers to interrogatories, responses to requests for admission, trial testimony, deposition testimony, and transcripts of trial testimony and depositions, or information that the producing party believes should be subject to this Protective Order may designate the same as "CONFIDENTIAL" or "CONFIDENTIAL—FOR COUNSEL ONLY".

a. *Designation as "CONFIDENTIAL"*: Any party may designate information as "CONFIDEN-TIAL" only if, in the good faith belief of such party and its counsel, the unrestricted disclosure of such information could be potentially prejudicial to the business or operations of such party.

b. *Designation as "CONFIDENTIAL—FOR COUNSEL ONLY"*: Any party may designate information as "CONFIDENTIAL—FOR COUNSEL ONLY" only if, in the good faith belief of such party and its counsel, the information is among that considered to be most sensitive by the party, including but not limited to trade secret or other confidential research, development, financial or other commercial information.

5. In the event the producing party elects to produce materials for inspection, no marking need be made by the producing party in advance of the initial inspection. For purposes of the initial inspection, all materials produced will be considered as "CONFIDENTIAL—FOR COUNSEL ONLY", and must be treated as such pursuant to the terms of this Order. Thereafter, upon selection of specified materials for copying by the inspecting party, the producing party must, within a reasonable time prior to producing those materials to the inspecting party, mark the copies of those materials that contain Confidential Information with the appropriate confidentiality marking.

6. Whenever a deposition taken on behalf of any party involves a disclosure of Confidential Information of any party:

   a. the deposition or portions of the deposition must be designated as containing Confidential Information subject to the provisions of this Order; such designation must be made on the record whenever possible, but a party may designate portions of depositions as containing Confidential Information after transcription of the proceedings; [A] party will have until fourteen (14) days after receipt of the deposition transcript to inform the other party or parties to the action of the portions of the transcript to be designated "CONFIDENTIAL" or "CONFIDENTIAL—FOR COUNSEL ONLY".

   b. the disclosing party will have the right to exclude from attendance at the deposition, during such time as the Confidential Information is to be disclosed, any person other than the deponent, counsel (including their staff and associates), the Court reporter, and the person(s) agreed upon pursuant to paragraph 8 below; and

   c. the originals of the deposition transcripts and all copies of the deposition must bear the legend "CONFIDENTIAL" or "CONFIDENTIAL—FOR COUNSEL ONLY", as appropriate, and the original or any copy ultimately presented to a court for filing must not be filed unless it can be accomplished under seal, identified as being subject to this Order, and protected from being opened except by order of this court.

7. All Confidential Information designated as "CONFIDENTIAL" or "CONFIDENTIAL—FOR COUNSEL ONLY" must not be disclosed by the receiving party to anyone other than those persons designated within this order and must be handled in the manner set forth below and, in any event, must not be used for any purpose other than in connection with this litigation, unless and until such designation is removed either by agreement of the parties, or by order of the Court.

8. Information designated "CONFIDENTIAL—FOR COUNSEL ONLY" must be viewed only by counsel (as defined in paragraph 3) of the receiving party, and by independent experts under the conditions set forth in this Paragraph. The right of any independent expert to receive any Confidential Information will be subject to the advance approval of such expert by the producing party or by permission of the Court. The party seeking approval of an independent expert must provide the producing party with the name and curriculum vitae of the proposed independent expert, and an executed copy of the form attached hereto as Exhibit A, in advance of providing any Confidential Information of the producing party to the expert. Any objection by the producing party to an independent expert receiving Confidential Information must be made in writing within fourteen (14) days following receipt of the identification of the proposed expert. Confidential Information may be disclosed to an independent expert if the fourteen (14) day period has passed and no objection has been made. The approval of independent experts must not be unreasonably withheld.

9. Information designated "confidential" must be viewed only by counsel (as defined in paragraph 3) of the receiving party, by independent experts (pursuant to the terms of paragraph 8), by court personnel, and by the additional individuals listed below, provided each such individual has read this Order in advance of disclosure and has agreed in writing to be bound by its terms:

   (a) Executives who are required to participate in policy decisions with reference to this action;

   (b) Technical personnel of the parties with whom Counsel for the parties find it necessary to consult, in the discretion of such counsel, in preparation for trial of this action; and

   (c) Stenographic and clerical employees associated with the individuals identified above.

10. With respect to material designated "CONFIDENTIAL" or "CONFIDENTIAL—FOR COUNSEL ONLY", any person indicated on the face of the document to be its originator, author or a recipient of a copy of the document, may be shown the same.

11. All information which has been designated as "CONFIDENTIAL" or "CONFIDENTIAL— FOR COUNSEL ONLY" by the producing or disclosing party, and any and all reproductions of that information, must be retained in the custody of the counsel for the receiving party identified in paragraph 3, except that independent experts authorized to view such information under the terms of this Order may retain custody of copies such as are necessary for their participation in this litigation.

12. Before any materials produced in discovery, answers to interrogatories, responses to requests for admissions, deposition transcripts, or other documents which are designated as Confidential Information are filed with the Court for any purpose, the party seeking to file such material must seek permission of the Court to file the material under seal.

13. At any stage of these proceedings, any party may object to a designation of the materials as Confidential Information. The party objecting to confidentiality must notify, in writing, counsel for the designating party of the objected-to materials and the grounds for the objection. If the dispute is not resolved consensually between the parties within seven (7) days of receipt of such a notice of objections, the objecting party may move the Court for a ruling on the objection. The materials at issue must be treated as Confidential Information, as designated by the designating party, until the Court has ruled on the objection or the matter has been otherwise resolved.

14. All Confidential Information must be held in confidence by those inspecting or receiving it, and must be used only for purposes of this action. Counsel for each party, and each person receiving Confidential Information must take reasonable precautions to prevent the unauthorized or inadvertent disclosure of such information. If Confidential Information is disclosed to any person other than a person authorized by this Order, the party responsible for the unauthorized disclosure must immediately bring all pertinent facts relating to the unauthorized disclosure to the attention of the other parties and, without prejudice to any rights and remedies of the other parties, make every effort to prevent further disclosure by the party and by the person(s) receiving the unauthorized disclosure.

15. No party will be responsible to another party for disclosure of Confidential Information under this Order if the information in question is not labeled or otherwise identified as such in accordance with this Order.

16. If a party, through inadvertence, produces any Confidential Information without labeling or marking or otherwise designating it as such in accordance with this Order, the designating party may give written notice to the receiving party that the document or thing produced is deemed Confidential Information, and that the document or thing produced should be treated as such in accordance with that designation under this Order. The receiving party must treat the materials as confidential, once the designating party so notifies the receiving party. If the receiving party has disclosed the materials before receiving the designation, the receiving party must notify the designating party in writing of each such disclosure. Counsel for the parties will agree on a mutually acceptable manner of labeling or marking the inadvertently produced materials as "CONFIDENTIAL" or "CONFI- DENTIAL—FOR COUNSEL ONLY"—SUBJECT TO PROTECTIVE ORDER.

17. Nothing within this order will prejudice the right of any party to object to the production of any discovery material on the grounds that the material is protected as privileged or as attorney work product.

18. Nothing in this Order will bar counsel from rendering advice to their clients with respect to this litigation and, in the course thereof, relying upon any information designated as Confidential Information, provided that the contents of the information must not be disclosed.

19. This Order will be without prejudice to the right of any party to oppose production of any information for lack of relevance or any other ground other than the mere presence of Confidential Information. The existence of this Order must not be used by either party as a basis for discovery that is otherwise improper under the Federal Rules of Civil Procedure.

20. Nothing within this order will be construed to prevent disclosure of Confidential Information if such disclosure is required by law or by order of the Court.

21. Upon final termination of this action, including any and all appeals, counsel for each party must, upon request of the producing party, return all Confidential Information to the party that produced the information, including any copies, excerpts, and summaries of that information, or must destroy same at the option of the receiving party, and must purge all such information from all machine-readable media on which it resides. Notwithstanding the foregoing, counsel for each party may retain all pleadings, briefs, memoranda, motions, and other documents filed with the Court that refer to or incorporate Confidential Information, and will continue to be bound by this Order with

respect to all such retained information. Further, attorney work product materials that contain Confidential Information need not be destroyed, but, if they are not destroyed, the person in possession of the attorney work product will continue to be bound by this Order with respect to all such retained information.

22. The restrictions and obligations set forth within this order will not apply to any information that: (a) the parties agree should not be designated Confidential Information; (b) the parties agree, or the Court rules, is already public knowledge; (c) the parties agree, or the Court rules, has become public knowledge other than as a result of disclosure by the receiving party, its employees, or its agents in violation of this Order; or (d) has come or will come into the receiving party s legitimate knowledge independently of the production by the designating party. Prior knowledge must be established by pre-production documentation.

23. The restrictions and obligations within this order will not be deemed to prohibit discussions of any Confidential Information with anyone if that person already has or obtains legitimate possession of that information.

24. Transmission by email or some other currently utilized method of transmission is acceptable for all notification purposes within this Order.

25. This Order may be modified by agreement of the parties, subject to approval by the Court.

26. The Court may modify the terms and conditions of this Order for good cause, or in the interest of justice, or on its own order at any time in these proceedings. The parties prefer that the Court provide them with notice of the Courts intent to modify the Order and the content of those modifications, prior to entry of such an order.

IT IS SO ORDERED this _____ day of _____, ___

_____
Judge, United States District Court

UNITED STATES DISTRICT COURT
SOUTHERN DISTRICT OF CALIFORNIA

```
    +                          )
                               )
            Plaintiffs,        )    AGREEMENT TO BE BOUND
      v.                       )    BY PROTECTIVE ORDER
                               )
                               )
                               )
            Defendant.         )
    _____)
```

I, _____, declare and say that:

1.   I am employed as _____ by _____.

2.   I have read the Protective Order entered in _____ v. _____, Case No. ___, and have received a copy of the Protective Order.

3.   I promise that I will use any and all "Confidential" or "Confidential—For Counsel Only" information, as defined in the Protective Order, given to me only in a manner authorized by the Protective Order, and only to assist counsel in the litigation of this matter.

4.   I promise that I will not disclose or discuss such "Confidential" or "Confidential—For Counsel Only" information with anyone other than the persons described in paragraphs 3, 8 and 9 of the Protective Order.

5.   I acknowledge that, by signing this agreement, I am subjecting myself to the jurisdiction of the United States District Court for the Southern District of California with respect to enforcement of the Protective Order.

6.   I understand that any disclosure or use of "Confidential" or "Confidential—For Counsel Only" information in any manner contrary to the provisions of the Protective Order may subject me to sanctions for contempt of court.

I declare under penalty of perjury that the foregoing is true and correct.

Date: _____

_____

[Former Appendix A effective April 3, 2006. Amended effective December 21, 2009. Redesignated as an undesignated attachment and amended effective February 8, 2013. Amended effective May 29, 2014; February 15, 2018.]

CRIMINAL RULES

CRIMINAL RULE 1.1   SCOPE AND AVAILABILITY OF RULES

a. Title and Citation. These are the Local Rules of Practice in Criminal proceedings before the United States District Court for the Southern District of California. They may be cited as "CrimLR____."

b. Effective Date. These Rules become effective on December 1, 2009.

c. Scope of Rules; Construction, Definitions. The rules under this title govern criminal proceedings in the United States District Court for the Southern District of California. The rules under this title, issued pursuant to Rule 57, Fed. R.Crim.P., supplement the Federal Rules of Criminal Procedure and must be construed in harmony with the Federal Rules.

d. Waiver of Rules. A judge may on application, in any case for the convenience of the parties in interest, or in the interest of justice, waive the applicability of these rules.

e. Applicable Civil Rules. The provisions of the following Civil Local Rules will apply to all criminal actions and proceedings, except where they may be inconsistent with the Federal Rules of Criminal Procedure or provisions of law specifically applicable to criminal cases:

1. Rule 1.1 Scope and Availability of Local Rules

2. Rule 1.2 Availability of Local Rules

3. Rule 3.2 Actions in Forma Pauperis

4. Rule 4.5 Fee Schedule

5. Rule 5.1 Form, Paper, Legibility; Nature of Documents to be Filed

6. Rule 5.3 Fax Filings

7. Rule 5.4 Electronic Case Filings

8. Rule 7.2 Stipulations

9. Rule 15.1 Amended Pleadings

10. Rule 16.4 Assessment of Jury Costs

11. Rule 40.1.c Assignments to Senior Judges and Rule 40.1.d Temporary Designation

12. Rule 47.1 Examination of Jurors

13. Rule 51.1 Filing, Service and Form of Proposed Jury Instructions

14. Rule 67.1 Disbursement of Registry funds

15. Rule 77.1 Location and Hours of Clerk

16. Rule 77.4 Sessions of Court

17. Rule 77.6 Court Library

18. Rule 79.1 Custody and disposition of Exhibits and Transcripts

19. Rule 79.2 Books and Records of the Clerk

20. Rule 83.2 Security of Court

21. Rule 83.3 Attorney Admissions, Standards

22. Rule 83.6 Gratuities

23. Rule 83.7 Free Press, Fair Trial

24. Rule 83.8 Non-appropriated Funds

25. Rule 83.9 Correspondence and Communications with the Judge

[Effective August 18, 1997. Amended effective August 10, 1999; January 1, 2000; November 19, 2001; October 25, 2004; May 1, 2006; July 16, 2007; December 1, 2009; January 30, 2016; July 5, 2021.]

CRIMINAL RULE 2.1   PROFESSIONALISM

The provisions of Civil Local Rule 2.1 (Professionalism) are incorporated herein by reference in their entirety and will govern the conduct of all participants in all criminal cases and proceedings pending in this court.

[Effective March 18, 2020.]

CRIMINAL RULE 2.2   DISCIPLINE

The provisions of Civil Local Rule 2.2 (Discipline) are incorporated herein by reference in their entirety and will govern the conduct of all participants in all criminal cases and proceedings pending in this court.

[Effective March 18, 2020.]

CRIMINAL RULE 10.1   ARRAIGNMENTS

Except where otherwise ordered by a district judge, all arraignments in criminal cases must be conducted by the magistrate judge assigned to the case.

[Effective August 18, 1997. Amended effective April 6, 1998; December 1, 2009.]

CRIMINAL RULE 11.1   REFERRAL OF FELONY CASES TO MAGISTRATE JUDGES FOR TAKING OF GUILTY PLEAS

All guilty pleas in felony cases may be referred to the assigned magistrate judge to administer the allocution pursuant to Rule 11 of the Federal Rules of Criminal Procedure.

a. Consent or Report and Recommendation. The magistrate judge will proceed with the taking of the guilty plea upon such referral from the district judge with the written consent of the defendant, the defendant's attorney, and the Assistant U.S. Attorney, or upon referral from the District Court for a report and recommendation.

b. Findings. The magistrate judge must make written findings as to each of the subjects set forth in Rule 11 of the Federal Rules of Criminal Procedure, the voluntariness of the guilty plea and the sufficiency of the factual basis establishing each of the essential elements of the offense. In a prosecution under 8 U.S.C. § 1326, the magistrate judge must also make a written finding as to whether the defendant admitted being deported and removed subsequent to the date set forth in the indictment or information.

c. Recommendation. The magistrate judge must make a recommendation, in writing, to the assigned district judge as to whether or not the district judge should accept the defendant's plea of guilty.

d. Objections. Objections to the magistrate judge's findings and recommendation must be filed within fourteen (14) days of the entry of the magistrate judge's findings and recommendation.

e. Sentencing. The magistrate judge must set the sentencing hearing on the calendar of the assigned district judge.

f. Transcripts. The Clerk may order a transcript of the Rule 11 allocation and provide the district judge with a copy of the transcript at least seven (7) days before sentencing hearing if requested by the district judge.

[Effective August 18, 1997. Amended effective January 1, 2000; November 19, 2001; December 17, 2001; October 8, 2007. Renumbered and amended effective December 1, 2009.]

CRIMINAL RULE 12.1   RULE 12 MOTIONS

Motions under Rule 12, Fed.R.Crim.P., must not be made prior to entry of a not guilty plea at initial arraignment.

[Effective August 18, 1997. Amended effective October 25, 2004; December 1, 2009.]

CRIMINAL RULE 16.1A   MEET AND CONFER REQUIREMENT

Not later than fourteen calendar days after the arraignment on an Indictment or Information, the attorney for the defendant(s) and the attorney for the government must confer and attempt to agree on a timetable and procedures for the pretrial disclosure of materials set forth in Federal Rule of Criminal Procedure 16. Generally, this conference should be in person; however, in early disposition (fast track) cases or when it is impractical to meet in person, the conference may be conducted via telephone or email.

During the conference, or as soon as practicable thereafter considering the size and complexity of the case, the parties should consider ways in which to ensure the elimination of unjustifiable expense and delay and the expeditious government production of electronically stored information ("ESI") and other voluminous discovery. If discovery includes ESI, the parties must discuss the appropriate form and format of the production of materials containing ESI. To the extent practicable, this material should be produced in a searchable and reasonably usable format.

Not later than seven calendar days prior to the first motion hearing, the parties must inform the Court in writing of the agreed upon timetable for the production of discovery, including the Alien Registration File, body-port-or remote cam video, car/vehicle inspection, DEA drug reports, cell phone extraction data, and/or ESI where applicable, and any areas of disagreement.

[Effective June 1, 2020.]

CRIMINAL RULE 16.1B   PLEADINGS AND MOTIONS BEFORE TRIAL DEFENSES AND OBJECTIONS

Discovery Motions. All criminal discovery motions must be made to the assigned district judge. The district judge may refer a discovery motion to a magistrate judge for determination. A magistrate judge may hear motions to preserve evidence before a case is assigned to a district judge, and thereafter as requested by the assigned district judge. A magistrate judge may order discovery when necessarily incident to any hearing the judge is conducting.

[Former Rule 16.1 effective August 18, 1997. Amended effective December 1, 2009; January 30, 2016. Renumbered effective June 1, 2020.]

CRIMINAL RULE 17.1   SUBPOENAS

a. Payment of Costs. As authorized by Rule 17(b), Fed. R.Crim.P., the Court orders that the cost incurred for the service of process and witness fees for each witness subpoenaed by defense counsel appointed under the Criminal Justice Act must be paid in the same manner in which similar costs and fees are paid in case of witnesses subpoenaed in behalf of the government. All subpoenas issued under this rule must bear the name of defense counsel who will cause to be placed thereon after counsel's name the words: "appointed under Criminal Justice Act".

b. Production. No subpoena in a criminal case may require the production of books, papers, documents or other objects at a date and time or place other than the date, time and place at which the trial, hearing or proceeding at which these items are to be offered in evidence is scheduled to take place, unless the Court has entered an order under Rule 17(c) of the Federal Rules of Criminal Procedure authorizing the issuance of such subpoena. Any motion for the issuance of a subpoena under Rule 17(c) must be made to the magistrate judge assigned to criminal duty at the time of the filing of the motion, unless otherwise ordered by a district judge assigned to the case, and must be returnable in no less than seven (7) days from the filing of the motion. Except for good cause shown, all motions for a subpoena duces tecum under Rule 17(c) must be served on all parties who may file an opposition or response not less than seventy-two (72) hours prior to the return date of the motion. Motions seeking subpoenas duces tecum under this subsection must be supported by an affidavit or declaration establishing that: (1) the documents or objects sought are evidentiary and relevant; (2) that the documents or objects sought are not otherwise reasonably procurable in advance of the trial, hearing or proceeding by exercise of due diligence; (3) that the moving party cannot properly prepare for trial without such production and inspection in advance of trial and the failure to obtain such inspection may tend unreasonably to delay the trial, and (4) that the application is made in good faith and is not intended for the purpose of general discovery. Any subpoena duces tecum issued under this subsection must be returnable and the items sought thereunder must be produced before the magistrate judge. The Clerk must maintain the items produced pursuant to such subpoenas but must make them available for the inspection of the parties and the attorneys.

[Effective August 18, 1997. Amended effective October 25, 2004; December 1, 2009.]

CRIMINAL RULE 23.1 TRIAL BRIEFS

Unless otherwise ordered by the Court, counsel for the government and for each defendant may file a trial brief prior to commencement of trial. Copies must be provided for the trial judge and adverse counsel. The brief should set forth any reasonably foreseeable point of law bearing on the issues upon which either party relies that are unusual or which otherwise require support, with citation of relevant statutes, ordinances, rules, cases and other authorities.

[Effective August 18, 1997. Amended effective December 1, 2009.]

CRIMINAL RULE 28.1 INTERPRETERS

a. Courtroom Proceedings. Only officially designated interpreters may interpret official courtroom proceedings. Regardless of the presence of a private interpreter, such official interpreter must interpret all proceedings in the courtroom.

b. Out–of–Court Interpreting.

1. *Interviews.* Official interpreters must also be available when needed to interpret at interviews between the attorney and the non-English speaking client and witnesses outside of court.

2. *Compensation for Out–of–Court Interpreters.* Compensation for such interpreting must be at the rate listed in the miscellaneous fee schedule. In court-appointed cases, the interpreter must submit a separate CJA Form 21 (or CJA Form 31 in federal capital prosecutions and in death penalty federal habeas corpus proceedings) for payment in each case.

[Effective August 18, 1997. Amended effective April 6, 1998. Redesignated and amended effective October 19, 1999. Amended effective March 24, 2000; October 25, 2004; December 1, 2009.]

CRIMINAL RULE 30.1 JURY INSTRUCTIONS

a. Proposed Instructions. In all jury trials, counsel for the government and for each defendant must serve and file proposed written instructions prior to the beginning of trial. Copies must be provided for the trial judge and adverse counsel. Each requested instruction must be numbered, indicate which party presents it, and cite the source of the instruction together with additional supporting authority.

b. Source Identification. If an instruction is submitted from a recognized book of instructions it must be from the latest edition of the book of instructions (so noted at the bottom of the instructions); and if modified in any way, deleted material must be shown in parentheses and additions must be underscored.

c. Objections. Objections to requested instructions may be made either in writing or orally as time permits. Such objections should normally be accompanied by citation of supporting authority.

d. Additional Instructions. Additional requested instructions and objections may be received by the Court, in its discretion, at any time prior to counsels' arguments to the jury. The Court must in accordance with Rule 30, Fed. R.Crim.P., inform counsel of its proposed action upon the requests prior to their argument.

[Effective August 18, 1997. Amended effective October 25, 2005; December 1, 2009.]

CRIMINAL RULE 32.1 SENTENCE, JUDGMENT AND PROBATION

a. Presentence Reports.

1. *Time for Hearing.* Probation and sentencing hearings will normally be scheduled seventy-seven (77) days (that is, eleven (11) weeks) following the conviction if the conviction occurs on a Monday, or seventy-seven (77) days following the Monday subsequent to the conviction should the conviction not occur on a Monday. If an evidentiary hearing is necessary, a subsequent date and time may be fixed by the sentencing judge. Counsel should check with the trial judge as to whether counsel should have witnesses available on the scheduled sentencing date.

2. *Modification of Schedule.* For good cause shown, the Court may modify the time schedule for sentencing hearing or the filing requirements.

3. *Presentence Report.* The presentence report is to be completed, filed with the Court, and mailed (or made available to defense counsel who make pickup arrangements) thirty-five (35) days (that is, five weeks) prior to the date fixed for the sentencing hearing. It must include the sentencing summary chart following this rule.

4. *Review.* Defense counsel must review the presentence report with the defendant prior to and sufficiently in advance of the time for filing objections and requests for departure other than United States Sentencing Commission, Guidelines Manual, § 5K1.1 (5K1.1), if any, so as to meet the deadlines set forth below. In cases where the defendant is acting as his/her own counsel (pro per), service is to be made by mailing a copy of the presentence report to an out-of-custody defendant, with a specific notice attached advising the individual defendant of the filing dates for the filings described in this order which must be filed and served on the Court, U.S. Attorney and Probation Office.

5. *Objections.* Fourteen (14) days prior to the date fixed for the sentencing hearing, all objections, if any, to the presentence report must be filed and served by the government and counsel for the defendant. If the presentence report is not timely filed—that is, thirty-five (35) days prior to the scheduled sentencing date—then the defendant and the government must have seventeen (17) days following the actual date on which the presentence report is filed within which to file and serve. Objections should not include arguments for aggravation or leniency, unless based on claimed errors in the presentence report.

6. *Motions for Departure.* Unless otherwise ordered by the Court, any motions for departure (other than 5K1.1) must be filed and served by the moving party no less than fourteen

(14) days before the sentencing hearing. The departure motion and supporting memorandum must set forth a summary of the factual and legal bases for the requested departure. Opposition to motions for departure must be filed and served no less than seven (7) days before the sentencing hearing. If no opposition is filed, the departure motion will be deemed unopposed.

7. *Other Matters.* Matters other than objections, motions for departure, and responses to those objections & motions may be addressed in a sentencing memorandum filed and served no less than seven (7) days before the sentencing hearing date. If the parties have executed a written plea agreement, it must be summarized in a sentencing memorandum, and filed no less than seven (7) days *before* the sentencing hearing.

8. *Sentencing Summary Chart.** Counsel must file their completed sentencing summary charts no later than seven (7) days before the sentencing hearing. If the district judge assigned to the case is a district judge from another district sitting in this court by designation, the parties must clearly indicate the name of the visiting judge on their respective sentencing summary chart and file it with the Clerk's Office. The sentencing summary chart must contain all pertinent calculations to summarize counsel's requested analysis of the guidelines application in the case. The Court may promulgate

by general order a sentencing summary chart form that it deems appropriate.

9. *Addendum Addressing Objections.* No less than seven (7) days before the scheduled sentencing hearing, the Probation Department must file and serve an addendum addressing all objections, if any, which have been timely filed by any party. Such report may additionally address any departure requests where probation is able to assist the Court further.

10. *Form.* The sentencing date and time must appear on the cover page of any objections, and replies to those objections, to the presentence report, and any sentencing memoranda, in the space opposite the caption below the file number.

11. *Time Line Chart.* Following this rule is a schematic diagram of the procedure delineated in this rule. The purpose of the diagram is to provide pictorial assistance to those involved in the sentencing process. The actual procedures, however, are those specified in the narrative of the Rule, not the diagram.

12. *Late Filings Unacceptable.* All counsel are advised that the filing dates set forth in this rule are critical. *Absent a showing of good cause, any late filings by counsel will not be considered by the Court.* Log these dates and comply.

[Effective August 18, 1997. Amended effective April 6, 1998; July 26, 2002; October 25, 2004; December 1, 2009; February 15, 2018.]

* [**Publisher's Note:** *See also* General Order 567, *post.*]

SENTENCING SUMMARY CHART

USPO _____
AUSA _____
DEF _____

Defendant's Name: _____   Docket No. _____
Attorney's Name: _____   Phone No.: _____
Guideline Manual Used: _____   Agree With USPO Calc.: _____
Base Offense Level: (Drug Quantity, if Applicable): _____
Special Offense Characteristics:

_____   _____
_____   _____
_____   _____
_____ /

Victim Related Adjustment: _____
Adjustment for Role in the Offense: _____
Adjustment for Obstruction of Justice: _____
Adjustment for Reckless Endangerment During Flight: _____
Adjusted Offense Level: _____
☐ Combined   ☐ Career Off.   ☐ Armed Career
   (Mult. Counts)   Crim.
Adjustment for Acceptance of Responsibility: _____
Total Offense Level: _____
Criminal History Score: _____
Criminal History Category: _____
☐ Career Offender ☐ Armed Career Criminal
Guideline Range:
(Range limited by: ☐ minimum mandatory ☐ statutory maximum)

from _____ months
to   _____ months

Departures: _____   _____
            _____

Resulting Guideline Range: Adjusted Offense Level _____   from _____ months
                                                                      to   _____ months

Recommendation: _____

[Effective August 18, 1997. Amended effective July 26, 2002.]

TIME LINE FOR U.S. DISTRICT COURT SOUTHERN DISTRICT

LOCAL RULE RE: SENTENCING GUIDELINES

```
1 _____ 77 DAYS TOTAL _____
2 _____ 35 days before sentencing _____
3 _____ 14 days before sentencing _____
4 _____ 14 days before sentencing _____
5 _____ 7 days before sentencing _____
```

	2) 35 Days before Sentencing	3) 14 Days before sentencing	4) 14 Days before sentencing	5) 7 Days before sentencing
1 CONVICTION DATE VERDICT OR GUILTY PLEA PSR IS ASSIGNED TO PROBATION OFFICER (P.O.)	**2** PSR FILED WITH COURT BY P.O. SERVED ON/(DISCLOSED TO) AUSA AND DEFENSE COUNSEL 35 DAYS BEFORE SENTENCING	**3** OBJECTIONS FILED WITH COURT AND SERVED ON OPPOSING COUNSEL AND PROBATION 14 DAYS AFTER FILING OF PSR	**4** MOTION TO DEPART FILED BY GOVERNMENT AND DEFENSE WITH SUPPORTING MEMORANDUM	**5** PSR ADDENDUM, PLEA AGREEMENT, SUMMARIES, SENTENCING MEMORANDUM, LETTERS, FILED AND SERVED 7 DAYS BEFORE SENTENCING, 5K FURNISHED
				SENTENCING HEARINGS ON DISPUTED POINTS (EXCEPT EVIDENTIARY HEARINGS) ARGUMENTS AND OBJECTIONS TO DEPARTURE, ETC.

NOTES:

1. Except for the filing of objections, days are counted back from the sentencing date, i.e., the PSR is to be filed 35 days before the date for sentencing, replies, 7 days before.

2. Defense counsel must review PSR with defendant. In pro se cases, service must be made on defendant.

3. Objections should not include arguments for aggravation, lenience, or departures, unless based on errors in the PSR and are to be filed 14 days before sentencing.

4. Sentencing memos, reference letters, plea agreement summaries, 5K materials, etc., must be received no less than 7 days before sentencing.

5. Evidentiary hearings on contested matters will generally not be conducted on the sentencing date, but will be scheduled at a later time.

[Effective August 18, 1997. Amended effective December 1, 2009.]

CRIMINAL RULE 44.1   RIGHT TO AND ASSIGNMENT OF COUNSEL

a. Right to and Appointment of Counsel. If a defendant, appearing without counsel in a criminal proceeding, desires to obtain retained counsel, a reasonable continuance for arraignment, not to exceed seven (7) days at any one time, will be granted for that purpose. If the defendant requests appointment of counsel by the Court, or fails for an unreasonable time to appear with retained counsel, the assigned district judge or magistrate judge must, subject to the applicable financial eligibility requirements, appoint counsel, unless the defendant elects to proceed without counsel and signs and files the court-approved form of waiver of right to counsel. In that case the judge or magistrate judge must nevertheless designate counsel to advise and assist defendant to the extent defendant might thereafter desire. Appointment of counsel must be made in accordance with the plan of this court adopted pursuant to the Criminal Justice Act of 1964 and on file with the Clerk.

b. Appearance and Withdrawal of Counsel. An attorney appearing for a defendant in a criminal case, whether retained or appointed, must promptly file with the Clerk a written appearance. An attorney who has appeared may thereafter withdraw only upon notice to the defendant and all parties to the case, and an order of Court finding that good cause exists and granting leave to withdraw. Failure of defendant to pay agreed compensation must not be deemed good cause for withdrawal. If an attorney seeks to withdraw after the arraignment, such application must be made to the assigned district judge. No magistrate judge will relieve counsel after arraignment unless the district judge has specifically referred the application to withdraw to the magistrate judge.

Unless such leave is granted, the attorney must continue to represent the defendant until the case is dismissed, the defendant is acquitted or convicted, or the time for making post-trial motions and for filing notice of appeal, as specified in Rule 4(b) Fed.R.App.P., has expired. If an appeal is taken, the attorney must continue to serve until leave to withdraw is granted by the Court having jurisdiction of the case or until other counsel is appointed by that court as provided in 18 U.S.C. § 3006A and in "Provisions for the Representation on Appeal of Defendants Financially Unable to Obtain Representation" as adopted by the Judicial Council of the Ninth Circuit.

c. No attorney appointed by the Court to represent a defendant under the Criminal Justice Act will retain or hire any person related to that attorney by blood or marriage within the degree of first cousin including the relatives described in 5 U.S.C. § 3110(a)(3), as an interpreter, investigator, paralegal, associate attorney, expert or other person to be compensated under the Criminal Justice Act. The Court will not approve any compensation under the Criminal Justice Act for the services of any such person.

[Effective August 18, 1997. Amended effective May 14, 2002; October 25, 2004; December 1, 2009.]

CRIMINAL RULE 46.1   RELEASE FROM CUSTODY

a. Bail, Conditions of Release.

1. *Release.* In all criminal cases where a defendant is ordered released, other than on defendant's own recognizance, the district or magistrate judge setting the condition of release must enter a written order setting forth the conditions of the defendant's release. A judge ordering a defendant's release may refer the case to a magistrate judge to prepare the Order of Conditions for Release. A copy of the order must be provided to the defendant by the Clerk.

2. *Posting Bail.* A defendant posting bail in a criminal case must have the following documents delivered to the Clerk:

a) Personal Appearance Bonds

1. Properly completed personal appearance bond on the form designated by the Court;

2. A copy of the order of conditions for release signed by the judge setting bail;

3. The advice of penalties and sanctions form signed by the defendant;

4. Any cash or other collateral required by the Court to be posted;

5. Properly completed bail and surety information sheets approved by an Assistant United States Attorney on the forms designated by the Court; and

6. If real property is to be posted as a security for the bond then the defendant must deliver to the Clerk:

Either a title report showing title in the name of sureties; or an opinion letter by an attorney that the legal description on the deed of trust is accurate, and the sureties have title;

A copy of a properly recorded deed of trust signed by all owners of the property.

The value of real property to be posted as security must first be approved by the judge setting conditions of release.

b) Corporate Surety Bonds.

1. A properly executed surety bond on the form approved by the Court from a surety accepted by the Clerk.

2. A properly completed bail information sheet approved by an Assistant United States Attorney, on the form designated by the Court; and

3. An advice of penalties and sanctions form signed by the defendant.

3. *Approval.* The required bail documents must be reviewed by both the counsel for the defendant and the government and if in compliance with the rules they must place their initials in the upper right corner of the bond. Upon receipt of the above documents fully completed and in proper form, the Clerk must initial the bond and transmit it to the judge for approval. Upon approval, the Clerk must issue a release.

For good cause shown, a judge may waive any requirement of this rule by specific order.

b. Motions to Modify Bail. Except as otherwise ordered by a district judge, magistrate judges must, subject to the provisions of 18 U.S.C. §§ 3141 et. seq., hear and determine all motions to modify bail.

c. Posting Security. When the release of a defendant is conditioned upon the deposit of cash or other security with the Court, such deposit must be made with the Clerk.

d. Bail Review. A magistrate judge must hear the first bail review, including bail review after indictment unless bail was previously set in open court by a district judge after hearing. If bail is set by a district judge after an adversary hearing, the magistrate judge must be specifically authorized by that district judge to thereafter hear a bail review. If the conditions of release are not amended at the review hearing, the magistrate judge must set forth in writing the reasons for continuing the requirements if requested by either party. Further review by a district judge must be heard upon the record of the reasons for the bail set forth in writing by the magistrate judge, together with additional information that may be presented. All bail reviews will be determined promptly. If no district judge has been assigned to the case, the Clerk will randomly assign a district judge to hear the matter. Upon assignment of a district judge to the case, the assigned district judge will hear all bail reviews, including those pending.

e. Approval of Bonds and Sureties. A judge must approve all bail bonds prior to the release of a defendant. The signatures of sureties on personal appearance bonds must be witnessed by counsel for the defendant, a defense investigator, a notary, a deputy clerk, or any attorney admitted to practice law before the courts of the State of California.

f. Bonds on Appeal. Except as otherwise ordered by a judge of the Court, all bonds on appeal must be approved by a judge.

g. Exoneration of Bond and Release of Collateral. When the judicial officer has exonerated a bond involving collateral of any kind, the defense attorney must file with the Court a proposed order for release and/or reconveyance of the collateral. All motions for release of collateral will be handled by the magistrate judge who set the bond unless the bond was set by the district judge or if the district judge orders otherwise. When a defendant moves for release of collateral, and the Assistant United States Attorney does not object, the parties will file a joint motion and proposed order for release and/or reconveyance of the collateral with the assigned magistrate judge. If the Assistant United States Attorney does object, then the defense attorney will file a noticed motion for release and/or reconveyance of the collateral. If the assigned magistrate judge is no longer with the,* then such motions will be filed with the presiding magistrate judge. Any proposed order releasing and/or reconveying property will identify with specificity the collateral involved.

[Effective August 18, 1997. Amended effective August 25, 1999; October 25, 2004; December 1, 2009; February 2, 2015; December 6, 2019.]

* So in original. Probably should say "the court".

CRIMINAL RULE 47.1 MOTIONS

a. Motions Before Judge. All hearing dates for any motions must be obtained from the courtroom deputy of the judge to whom the case is assigned.

b. Filing Moving Papers.

1. *Filing.* The original of all motions, including all attached exhibits, on behalf of any defendant, or on behalf of any moving party except the United States, must be filed with the Clerk at least fourteen (14) days prior to the date for which the motion is noticed unless the Court, for good cause and by order only, shortens that time. The noticed hearing date and time must appear on the cover page of each motion, and any opposition, in the space opposite the caption, below the file number.

2. *Service.* Other criminal motions must be served upon the adverse party, or the party's attorney, and filed with the Clerk at least fourteen (14) days prior to the date for which the motion is noticed unless the Court, for good cause and by order only, shortens such time.

3. *Accompaniments.* Each motion or other request for ruling by the Court must include within it a Memorandum of Points and Authorities in support of the motion and a caption listing the nature of the motion, hearing date and time, and the judge who will hear the motion. Where appropriate a separate or a joint statement of material facts, required declarations or affidavits or exhibits, must be supplied.

4. *Untimely Motions.* The Clerk's Office is directed not to file untimely motions and responses thereto without the consent of the judicial officer assigned to the case.

c. Time for Filing Opposition. Each party opposing the motion must not later than seven (7) days prior to the hearing, serve upon the adverse party, or the party's attorney, and file with the Clerk either an opposition containing a brief and complete statement of all reasons in opposition to the position taken by the movant, an answering memorandum of points and authorities and copies of all documentary evidence upon which the party in opposition relies; or, a written statement that the party will not oppose the motion.

d. Joinders in Motions.

1. The Clerk must refuse to accept for filing any joinder in motions if there are no pending motions on file.

2. Each joinder must specifically identify the particular motion(s) to which the joinder applies and the basis for the defendant's standing to raise such motion, where necessary.

e. Length of Brief in Support of or in Opposition to Motions. Briefs of memoranda in support of or in opposition to all motions noticed for the same motion day must not exceed twenty-five (25) pages in length total for all such motions without leave of a district judge.

f. Disposition After Motions Are Calendared. Any time a case is calendared for motions and counsel for either side knows that a disposition is to take place, counsel has a duty to call the court clerk of the appropriate judge at the earliest available time to inform the Court of the disposition.

g. Declarations in Support of and in Opposition to Criminal Motions.

1. *When Declarations Required.* Criminal motions requiring a predicate factual finding must be supported by declaration(s). When an opposing party contests a representation of fact contained in a moving declaration, opposition must likewise be supported by a declaration which places that represen-

tation into dispute. When an opposing party does not contest such a representation, but argues instead that additional facts render that representation moot or immaterial, the opposing party must support its argument with declaration(s) setting forth such additional facts. The Court need not grant an evidentiary hearing where either party fails to properly support its motion or opposition.

2. *Contents of Declarations.* Each declaration must set forth, under penalty of perjury, all facts then known and upon which it is contended the motion should be granted or denied. Each declaration must show affirmatively that the declarant is competent to testify to the matter stated therein, must avoid argument and conclusions of law and must in all other respects contain only such representations as would be admissible under the Federal Rules of Evidence.

3. *Timely Filing of Declarations.* Declarations submitted in support of and in opposition to criminal motions must be filed in a timely manner in accordance with the filing deadlines set forth in Criminal Local Rules 47.1.b and 47.1.c.

4. *Availability of Declarants.* Each declarant in support of and in opposition to criminal motions must be made available for cross-examination at the hearing of the motion, unless the opposing party does not dispute the facts contained in the declaration.

[Effective August 18, 1997. Amended effective August 10, 1999; December 1, 2009; January 1, 2014; June 25, 2019.]

CRIMINAL RULE 57.1 SANCTIONS FOR NONCOMPLIANCE WITH RULES

a.   Failure of counsel or of any party to comply with these rules, with the Federal Rules of Criminal Procedure, or with any order of the Court may be grounds for imposition by the Court of any and all sanctions authorized by statute or rule or within the inherent power of the Court.

b.   Failure to comply with these local rules governing criminal proceedings in this court will not be ground for dismissal of charges against the defendant.

c.   For violations of these Local Rules or of a specific court order, the Court may, in imposing monetary sanctions, order that the monetary sanctions be paid to the Miscellaneous Fines, Penalties and Forfeitures, Not Otherwise Classified, fund of the United States Treasury.

[Effective August 18, 1997. Amended effective October 25, 2004; December 1, 2009; February 2, 2015.]

CRIMINAL RULE 57.2 ASSIGNMENT

a.   Criminal cases must be numbered consecutively upon the filing of the indictment or information in each such action or proceeding. The judges will, from time to time, determine, and indicate by formal order to the Clerk the method by which each action or proceeding will be assigned to a particular judge, to the end that over a period of time each judge must be assigned substantially an equal amount of work. Neither the Clerk nor any deputy clerk or magistrate judge will have any discretion in determining the judge to whom any matter is assigned, the action of the Clerk being ministerial only. The method of assignment chosen by the judges must be such that

the judge to whom any particular matter is to be assigned, in accordance with this rule, must not be known by or disclosed to the Clerk or magistrate judge or any member of their staff, or to any other person, until after such action or proceeding has been assigned.

b.   The judge to whom a case is assigned or the Chief Judge of the district, may transfer such case at any time to a consenting judge in the interest of efficient administration of the judicial business of the district.

[Effective August 18, 1997. Amended effective October 25, 2004; July 16, 2007; March 16, 2009; December 1, 2009.]

CRIMINAL RULE 57.2.1 RELATED CASES

a.   Definition of Related Action.

1.   Criminal cases are deemed related when (a) all of the defendants named in each of the cases are the same and none of the cases include defendants not named in any of the other cases, or (b) prosecution against different defendants arises from (i) a common wiretap, (ii) a common search warrant, or (iii) activities that are part of the same alleged criminal event or transaction, that is, the cases involve substantially the same facts and the same questions of law.

2.   If a civil forfeiture proceeding is filed concerning a criminal defendant, or a defendant is charged in a criminal case while a civil forfeiture proceeding is pending concerning that defendant, the civil and criminal cases are to be deemed related.

3.   Criminal cases are also deemed related when a case is dismissed, with or without prejudice, and a subsequent case involving the same parties and related to the same subject matter is filed within one year of having been previously terminated by the Court.

4.   A case is considered "pending" until one year after all named defendants have been sentenced. A case is also considered pending if it is one of the cases listed in paragraphs 5, 6, or 7 herein.

5.   If a defendant is serving a term of probation or supervised release on a case in this district and the defendant is charged with a new offense in this district, the new case is deemed related to the case in which the defendant is on such term of probation or supervised release if the defendant is the sole defendant in the new case.

6.   If a defendant is accused of an offense charged in this district and is on probation or supervised release in another district, and that district transfers jurisdiction over the supervision to this district, any revocation proceedings will be deemed related to the new case pending in this district.

7.   If a defendant is charged with escape under 18 U.S.C. § 751 from a sentence imposed by a judge of this court, the escape charge will be deemed related to the case in which the sentence from which the defendant allegedly escaped was imposed.

b.   **Form.**   At the time of returning an indictment or filing of an information, the United States Attorney must, on a form submitted to the Clerk, file a Notice of Related Case, indicating the name(s) and docket number(s) of any related cases pending in this Court, and certifying the particular reason(s) for the case-related designation.

c. Assignment. Related cases must be assigned in the following manner: The Clerk must assign the new case to the judge to whom the oldest, pending related case is assigned. If a judge who is assigned a case under this procedure determines that the cases in question are not related to one of the judge's pending cases, the judge may transfer the new case to the Clerk for reassignment. A senior judge may elect to decline the assignment of a new related case.

[Effective March 16, 2009. Amended effective December 1, 2009; February 8, 2013; February 2, 2015; April 16, 2018.]

CRIMINAL RULE 57.3 ASSIGNMENT AND DESIGNATION PROCEDURES MATTERS TO MAGISTRATE JUDGES

Order of Designation and Assignment. A matter assigned to the magistrate judges either as a matter of course by the Clerk of the United States District Court or by an order of special designation by a district judge of the Court under 28 U.S.C. § 636(b) or (c), precisely stating the nature of the matter, must be assigned to a specific magistrate judge as follows:

a. *Criminal Cases.*

1. Criminal Matters. Where the case has previously been assigned to a specific magistrate judge during the course of criminal complaint duty, the matter will be referred to that magistrate judge.

2. Misdemeanor Cases. All misdemeanor cases must be assigned, upon the filing of an information, complaint or violation notice, or the return of an indictment, to a magistrate judge, who will proceed in accordance with the provisions of 18 U.S.C. § 3401 and Rule 58 of the Federal Rules of Criminal Procedure.

3. Felony Cases. Upon the return of an indictment or the filing of an information, all felony cases must be assigned to a magistrate judge for the conduct of an arraignment and such other pretrial proceedings, or hearings as the assigned district judge will designate.

4. Proceedings. Magistrate judges must conduct all proceedings under Rules 3, 4, 5, and 4.1 of the Federal Rules of Criminal Procedure.

5. Notice of Hearing. A magistrate judge assigned a matter must set the time of hearing, notify all parties and make any further necessary orders consistent with the requirements for the local rules of the Court for the Southern District.

6. Appointment of Counsel. Magistrate judges must appoint counsel for indigent defendants. A magistrate judge may not relieve counsel for a defendant once the case has been set on the calendar of a district judge unless the district judge has specifically referred the matter to the magistrate judge for consideration of relieving counsel and appointing new counsel.

7. Other than—

a) Modifying or revoking conditions of release or other applications relating to release;

b) Applications to allow persons assisting counsel to enter the facility where the defendant is confined;

c) Applications for writs of habeas corpus ad testificandum, and applications under Criminal Local Rule 17.1;

A magistrate judge will not hear any application or motion in a criminal case on a district judge's calendar unless the district judge refers such application or matter to the magistrate judge for disposition.

b. *General.* Nothing in these rules will preclude the Court, or a district judge from reserving any proceedings for conduct by a district judge, rather than a magistrate judge. The Court, moreover, may by general order modify the method of assigning proceedings to a magistrate judge as changing conditions may warrant.

[Effective August 18, 1997. Amended effective December 1, 2009.]

CRIMINAL RULE 57.4 UNITED STATES MAGISTRATE JUDGES

a. Jurisdiction Under 28 U.S.C. § 636(a). Each United States magistrate judge of this court is authorized to perform the duties prescribed by 28 U.S.C. § 636(a), and may:

1. Exercise all the powers and duties conferred or imposed on United States magistrate judges by law and the Federal Rules of Criminal Procedure;

2. Administer oaths and affirmations, impose conditions of release or orders of detention under 18 U.S.C. § 3141 et seq. and take acknowledgments, affidavits, and depositions;

3. Conduct extradition proceedings, in accordance with 18 U.S.C. § 3184.

b. Proposed Orders Regarding Case–Dispositive Motions—28 U.S.C. § 636(b)(1)(B).

1. Upon designation by a district judge, a magistrate judge may submit to a district judge a proposed order containing findings of fact and recommendations for disposition by the district judge of the following pretrial motions in criminal cases:

a) Motions to dismiss or quash an indictment or information made by a defendant; and

b) Motions to suppress evidence in a criminal case.

2. A magistrate judge may determine any preliminary matters and conduct any necessary evidentiary hearing or other proceeding arising in the exercise of the authority conferred by this subsection.

c. Other Duties. A magistrate judge is also authorized to:

1. Conduct arraignments in criminal cases not triable by the magistrate judge and take not guilty pleas in such cases;

2. Receive grand jury returns in accordance with Rule 6(f) of Fed.R.Crim.P.;

3. Accept waivers of indictment, pursuant to Rule 7(b) of Fed.R.Crim.P.;

4.   Conduct necessary proceedings leading to the potential revocation of probation or supervised release;

5.   Issue subpoenas, writs of habeas corpus ad testificandum or habeas corpus ad prosequendum, or other orders necessary to obtain the presence of parties, witnesses or evidence needed for court proceedings;

6.   Order the exoneration of appearance bonds and the release and/or reconveyance of collateral;

7.   Conduct proceedings for initial commitment of narcotic addicts under Title III of the Narcotic Addict Rehabilitation Act;

8.   Perform the functions specified in 18 U.S.C. §§ 4107, 4108 and 4109, regarding proceedings for verification of consent by offenders to transfer to or from the United States and the appointment of counsel for those proceedings;

9.   Hear motions and enter orders for examinations to determine mental competency under 18 U.S.C. § 4241;

10. Grant motions to dismiss in criminal cases when made by the United States attorney or at any other time when authorized by statute or rule and when such dismissal is within the jurisdiction of the magistrate judge or pursuant to a plea agreement entered into before the magistrate judge;

11. Perform any additional duty not inconsistent with the Constitution and laws of the United States.

[Effective August 18, 1997. Amended effective October 25, 2004; December 1, 2009; February 2, 2015.]

CRIMINAL RULE 57.5   PROCEDURE IN IMPERIAL COUNTY CASES

a.   Initial Appearance. The magistrate judge in Imperial County will conduct the initial appearance under Rule 5, Fed.R.Crim.P., of each defendant brought before him charged with a felony criminal offense.

b.   Further Proceedings. The magistrate judge in Imperial County will conduct such duties as are assigned by the Court.

c.   Transfer of File. Upon completion of the proceedings before the magistrate judge in Imperial County, California, the complete magistrate judge's file will be forwarded to the Clerk's Office.

[Effective August 18, 1997. Amended effective August 10, 1999; November 19, 2001; October 25, 2004; December 1, 2009.]

CRIMINAL RULE 58.1   MISDEMEANORS

a.   Designation of Magistrate Judges. Subject to the limitation of 18 U.S.C. § 3401, magistrate judges are specially designated to try persons accused of, and sentence persons convicted of misdemeanor offenses committed within this district. In addition, magistrate judges may dispose of misdemeanor offenses which are transferred to this district under Rule 20, Fed.R.Crim.P. A magistrate judge may direct the probation office to conduct a presentence investigation of any person convicted of a misdemeanor offense and to render a

report to the magistrate judge prior to the imposition of sentence.

b.   Appeal From Conviction by Magistrate Judge.

1.   *Notice of Appeal.* Pursuant to Rule 58(g), Federal Rules of Criminal Procedure, a defendant who has been convicted by a magistrate judge may appeal to a judge by filing a timely notice of appeal.

2.   *Record.* A transcript, if desired, must be ordered except that, in the absence of a reporter, the transcript must be ordered as directed by the Clerk of Court. Applications for orders pertaining to a transcript must be made to the magistrate judge.

Within thirty (30) days after a transcript has been ordered, the original and one copy must be filed with the magistrate judge and all recordings must be returned to the Clerk of Court. If not ordered within fourteen (14) days.* If not ordered within fourteen (14) days after the notice of appeal is filed, the record on appeal will be deemed complete.

3.   *Notice of Hearing.* The Clerk must assign the appeal to a district judge and notify the parties of the time set for oral argument. Argument must be scheduled not less than sixty nor more than ninety (90) days after the date of the notice. However, an earlier date may be set upon application of a party for good cause to the judge to whom the appeal has been assigned.

4.   *Time for Serving and Filing Briefs.* The appellant must serve and file the brief within twenty-one (21) days after the notice of hearing. The appellee must serve and file the brief within twenty-one (21) days after service of the brief of the appellant. The appellant may serve and file a reply brief within seven days after service of the brief of the appellee. These periods may be altered by order of the assigned judge.

c.   Orders and Judgments in Misdemeanor Cases. Any party may seek review or appeal of a decision by a magistrate judge in a misdemeanor case pursuant to Rule 58(g) of the Federal Rules of Criminal Procedure.

[Effective August 18, 1997. Amended effective December 1, 2009.]

* So in original.

CRIMINAL RULE 58.2   DISPOSITION OF MISDEMEANOR CASES—18 U.S.C. § 3401

A magistrate judge may:

a.   Try persons accused of, and sentence persons convicted of, misdemeanors committed within this district in accordance with 18 U.S.C. § 3401;

b.   Direct the probation office of the Court to conduct a presentence investigation in any misdemeanor case; and

c.   Conduct a jury trial in any misdemeanor case where the defendant so requests and is entitled to trial by jury under the Constitution and laws of the United States.

[Effective August 18, 1997. Amended effective December 1, 2009; January 30, 2016.]

ELECTRONIC CASE FILING

Section 1: The Electronic Filing System

a. Authorization for Electronic Filing. Pursuant to General Order No. 550, beginning on November 1, 2006, the U.S. District Court for the Southern District of California will require attorneys and others who have obtained permission of the court in civil and criminal cases to file documents with the court electronically, over the Internet, through its Case Management/Electronic Case Filing (CM/ECF) system. The court expects all attorneys practicing in this District to participate in electronic filing to the extent practicable.

Electronic transmission of a document to the CM/ECF system, together with the transmission of a Notice of Electronic Filing from the court, constitutes filing of the document for purposes of Rule 5(d) of the Federal Rules of Civil Procedure and Rule 49(d) of the Federal Rules of Criminal Procedure, and constitutes entry of the document on the docket kept by the Clerk of Court under Rules 58 and 79 of the Federal Rules of Civil Procedure. The following court policies govern electronic filing in this district unless, due to extraordinary circumstances, in a particular case, a judicial officer determines that these policies should be modified in the interest of justice.

b. Scope of Electronic Filing. Except as prescribed by local rule, order, or other procedure, the court has designated all cases to be assigned to the Electronic Filing System. Unless otherwise expressly provided in these rules or in exceptional circumstances preventing a registered user from filing electronically, all petitions, motions, memoranda of law, or other pleadings and documents required to be filed with the court by a registered user in connection with a case assigned to the Electronic Filing System must be electronically filed.

Case initiating documents in civil cases, including but not limited to the civil Complaint and Notice of Removal, must be filed electronically. All sealed case initiating documents in civil cases must be filed in paper format. All case initiating documents in criminal cases, including the criminal Complaint, Information, Indictment and Superseding Information or Indictment, must be filed in paper format at the Clerk's Office. All subsequent documents must be filed by registered users electronically except as provided in these rules or as ordered by the court.

c. The Official Record and Maintenance of Original Paper Documents. The official court record will be the electronic file maintained on the court's servers. This includes information transmitted to the Court in electronic format, as well as documents filed in paper form, scanned, and made a part of the electronic record to the extent permitted by the court's policies. The official record will also include any documents or exhibits that may be impractical to scan. The electronic file maintained on the court's servers must contain a reference to any such documents filed with the court. For cases initiated prior to the implementation of the Electronic Filing System, the official court record will include both the pre-implementation paper file maintained by the Clerk, as well as the post-implementation electronic files maintained on the court's servers. The Clerk's Office will not maintain a paper court file in any case initiated on or after the effective date of these procedures except as otherwise provided in these procedures.

If an original pleading has some intrinsic value, the filing party must retain the original paper document for a period of five years from the date the document is signed, or for one year after the expiration of all time periods for appeal, whichever period is greater, and must provide the original paper document to the court upon request.

d. Definitions

CASE MANAGEMENT/ELECTRONIC CASE FILING SYSTEM, referred to in these procedures as the system or CM/ECF, means the Internet-based system for filing documents and maintaining court case files in the United States District Court for the Southern District of California.

DOCUMENT means pleadings, motions, exhibits, declarations, affidavits, memoranda, papers, orders, notices, and any other filing by or with the court.

ELECTRONIC FILING means uploading a document directly from the registered user's computer in "Portable Document Format" (.pdf), using the CM/ECF system to file that document in the court's case file. Individual .pdf documents must not exceed thirty-five (35) megabytes (MB) in size. Pacific Time applies to all filings. Sending a document or pleading to the court via e-mail other than as described below does not constitute "electronic filing."

NOTICE OF ELECTRONIC FILING, referred to in these procedures as NEF, is a notice automatically generated by the CM/ECF system at the time a document is filed with the court. The notice sets forth the time of filing, the name of the attorney and/or party filing the document, the type of document, the text of the docket entry, the name of the party and/or attorney receiving the notice, and an electronic link (hyperlink) to the filed document which allows recipients to retrieve the document automatically.

.pdf refers to Portable Document Format, a proprietary file format developed by Adobe Systems, Inc. A document file created with a word processor, or a paper document which has been scanned, must be converted to Portable Document Format to be electronically filed with the court. Converted files contain the extension ".pdf". Documents which exist only in paper form may be scanned into .pdf for electronic filing. The Court recommends scanner settings at 400 pixels per inch (ppi). Electronic documents must be converted to .pdf directly from a word processing program (e.g., Microsoft Word® or Corel WordPerfect®).

REGISTERED USER is an individual who has been issued a login and password by the court to electronically file documents.

PACER (Public Access to Court Electronic Records) is an automated system that allows a subscriber to view, print and download court case file information over the Internet for a fee.

    e. System Availability. The CM/ECF system is designed to provide service 24 hours a day. The parties, however, are encouraged to file documents in advance of filing deadlines and during normal business hours. The Clerk's Office has established a Help Desk (866–233–7983) to respond to questions regarding CM/ECF and the registration process. The Help Desk will be staffed business days from 8:30 a.m. to 4:30 p.m. Information can also be obtained on the court web site at www.casd. uscourts.gov.

    f. Registration and Attorney Responsibilities. Registration in the CM/ECF system for the purpose of electronic service of pleadings and other papers is mandatory for attorneys.

    All attorneys in good standing must register for access to the CM/ECF system. To submit an electronic application for admission/registration, an attorney must have an individual upgraded PACER account. For additional information on how to register for an individual PACER account, please visit https://www.casd.uscourts.gov/cmecf/nextgen.aspx. Once an individual PACER account has been obtained, visit www.pacer.gov and select Manage My Account > Maintenance > Attorney Admissions / E–File Registration. Any questions may be emailed to the CASD CM/ECF helpdesk at ecfhelp@casd.uscourts.gov.

    Registration constitutes consent to electronic service of documents by e-mail, as provided by the Federal Rules of Civil, Criminal and Appellate Procedure. An attorney may register up to two (2) additional e-mail addresses.

    An attorney whose e-mail address, mailing address, telephone or fax number has changed must update the information through the PACER website and file a timely notification of the changes. Attorneys employed by federal, state, and local government agencies are responsible for updating their attorney information upon their appointment and separation from their respective agency.

    Electronic filing through CM/ECF is required for all attorneys beginning November 1, 2006, except as otherwise provided herein.

    A filing party must maintain an electronic mailbox of sufficient capacity, with the appropriate e-mail permissions, to receive electronic notice of case-related transmissions.

    If an attorney fails to file electronically and does so without leave of court, he or she must also file a "Notice of Non–Compliance with Mandatory Electronic Filing" setting forth the reason(s) for filing in non-electronic form.

    After leave to appear pro hac vice has been granted, attorneys will have five (5) days to register for electronic filing.

    An attorney may apply to the court for permission to file documents in paper form. Effective November 1, 2006, attorneys must show good cause to file and serve using non-electronic filing. Permission for non-electronic filing may be withdrawn at any time by the court and the attorney may be required to file documents using the CM/ECF system.

    g. Logins and Passwords. Documents filed under an attorney's login and password will constitute that attorney's signature for purposes of the Local Rules and Federal Rules of Civil and

Criminal Procedure, including Rule 11 of the Federal Rules of Civil Procedure. The attorney is responsible for all documents filed with his or her password.

If a registered user believes the security of an existing password has been compromised, the user must immediately change the password through PACER.

h. Privacy. Unless otherwise ordered by the court, parties must refrain from including, or must partially redact where inclusion is necessary, the following personal data identifiers from all pleadings and documents filed with the court, including exhibits thereto:

1. *Social Security Numbers.* If an individual's Social Security number must be included in a pleading, only the last four digits of that number should be used.

2. *Names of Minor Children.* If the involvement of a minor child must be mentioned, only the initials of that child should be used.

3. *Dates of Birth.* If an individual's date of birth must be included in a pleading, only the year should be used.

4. *Financial Account Numbers.* If the financial account numbers are relevant, only the last four digits of these numbers should be used.

5. In criminal cases, the home address of any individual (e.g., victims).

The responsibility for redacting personal identifiers rests solely with the parties. The Clerk's Office will not review each document for compliance with this rule. A party filing a redacted document must retain the complete unredacted document for the duration of the case, including any period of appeal, unless instructed by the Court to file the complete unredacted document under seal.

Pursuant to General Order 514–E, Social Security cases will be excluded from electronic public access except for access by judiciary employees, the United States Attorney or its representatives and the litigants in those cases.

Without a court order, the court will not provide public electronic access to the following documents:

a. Sealed documents (e.g., motions for downward departure for substantial assistance, plea agreements indicating cooperation).

b. Unexecuted warrants of any kind and associated petitions for warrants (e.g., arrest warrants, search warrants).

c. Pretrial bail reports and bond supporting documents.

d. Pre–Sentence reports and the statement of reasons related to the judgment of conviction.

e. Juvenile records.

f. Magistrate information sheets and financial affidavits filed in seeking representation pursuant to the Criminal Justice Act.

g. Pleadings and reports related to the competency or mental health of a defendant.

h. Civil settlement documents that contain information in section one above. It shall be the attorney's obligation to obtain an order sealing such documents.

i. Ex parte requests for authorization of investigative, expert or other services pursuant to the Criminal Justice Act.

j. Documents in criminal cases containing identifying information about jurors or potential jurors.

k. Any other documents the court concludes is good cause to exclude from electronic access.

i. Technical Specifications. Current technical specifications for CM/ECF can be found at the court's official web site, www.casd.uscourts.gov. Specifications may change periodically. Registered users may refer to the web site for the most current requirements.

Section 2: Electronic Filing and Service of Documents

a. Filing. Electronically filed documents must meet the requirements of Fed. R. Civ. P. 10 (Form of Pleadings), and Local Civil Rule 5.1, as if they had been submitted on paper. Documents filed electronically are also subject to any page limitations set forth by Court order or by Local Civil Rule 7.1, Local Civil Rule 8.2, and Local Criminal Rule 47.1.

Unless otherwise expressly provided in these rules or in exceptional circumstances preventing a registered user from filing electronically, all applications, motions, memoranda of law, or other pleadings and documents required to be filed with the Court by a registered user in connection with a case assigned to the Electronic Filing System must be electronically filed.

Unless otherwise authorized by the court, E-mailing a document to the Clerk's Office or to the assigned judge does not constitute "filing" of the document.

The court may, upon the motion of a party or upon its own motion, strike any inappropriately filed document.

b. Pro Se Litigants. Unless otherwise authorized by the court, all documents submitted for filing to the Clerk's Office by parties appearing without an attorney must be in legible, paper form. The Clerk's Office will scan and electronically file the document.

A pro se party seeking leave to electronically file documents must file a motion and demonstrate the means to do so properly by stating their equipment and software capabilities in addition to agreeing to follow all rules and policies in the CM/ECF Administrative Policies and Procedures Manual. If granted leave to electronically file, the pro se party must register as a user with the Clerk's Office and as a subscriber to PACER within five (5) days.

A pro se party must seek leave to electronically file documents in each case filed. If an attorney enters an appearance on behalf of a pro se party, the attorney must advise the Clerk's Office to terminate the login and password for the pro se party.

c. Case Initiating Documents. Case initiating documents in civil cases, including but not limited to the civil Complaint and Notice of Removal, must be filed electronically. All sealed case initiating documents in civil cases must be filed in paper format. All case initiating documents in criminal cases, including but not limited to the criminal Complaint, Information, and Superseding Information, must be filed in paper format at the Clerk's Office. Indictments and all sealed case initiating documents in criminal cases must be filed in paper format.

d. Service.

1. *Summons.* The Clerk's Office will issue each summons, and the service of a summons must be effected pursuant to Rule 4 of the Federal Rules of Civil Procedure and the Federal Rules of Criminal Procedure.

After a summons has been served, or a waiver of service via summons has been received, the serving registered user must promptly scan the return of service or waiver and electronically file it. Non-registered filers may file the return of service or waiver with the Clerk's Office.

2. *Service of Documents.* Whenever a document is electronically filed in accordance with these procedures, the CM/ECF system will generate a "Notice of Electronic Filing" (NEF) to the filing party, the assigned judge and any registered user in the case. The NEF will constitute service of the document for purposes of the Federal Rules of Civil, Criminal and Appellate Procedure. Registration as a CM/ECF user constitutes consent to electronic service through the court's transmission facilities.

Each registered user of the CM/ECF system is responsible for assuring that the user's e-mail account is monitored regularly, and that e-mail notices are opened in a timely manner.

A certificate of service is not required when a party electronically files a document in the court's electronic filing system. If a certificate of service is required, the certificate must state the manner in which service or notice was accomplished on each party. If the certificate of service is signed by someone other than a registered user, the filing party must scan and electronically file the original signed document as set forth in Section 2.f.2 below.

Any document that is not filed electronically through the court's electronic filing system must be served as a paper copy, pursuant to the Federal Rules of Civil, Criminal and Appellate Procedure.

A party who is not a registered participant of CM/ECF is entitled to service of a paper copy of any electronically filed document. The filing party must serve the non-registered party with the document according to the Federal Rules of Civil, Criminal and Appellate Procedure.

A non-registered filing party who files document(s) with the Clerk's Office for scanning and entry to CM/ECF must serve paper copies on all non-registered parties to the case. There will be some delay in the scanning, electronic filing and subsequent electronic noticing to registered users. If time is an issue, non-registered filers must provide a paper copy of the document(s) to all parties.

e. Courtesy Copies for Judicial Officers. Unless otherwise ordered by the court, parties must deliver to the Clerk's Office or mail directly to the judge's chambers, within 24 hours after filing, any criminal or civil case filing which exceeds 20 pages in length including attachments and exhibits. In addition, where a party makes multiple filings in a case on the same day, and those filings cumulatively exceed 20 pages, a courtesy copy must be provided to the assigned judicial officer. If the nature of the filing is such that the need for a judge's immediate attention is anticipated or desired, a courtesy copy must be delivered on the same day as the filing. A copy of the Notice of Electronic Filing must precede the first page of the courtesy copy. Courtesy copies are to be addressed to the attention of the assigned judicial officer.

f. Signatures.

1. *Registered Users.* The registered user log-in and password required to submit documents to the CM/ECF system will serve as that registered user's signature for purposes of Rule 11 of the Federal Rules of Civil Procedure and for all other purposes under the Federal Rules of Civil, Criminal and Appellate Procedure and the Local Rules of this court. The name of the CM/ECF registered user under whose log-in and password the document is submitted must be preceded by a "s/" and typed in the space where the signature would otherwise appear. The correct format for an attorney signature is as follows:

> s/Adam Attorney
> Attorney for (Plaintiff/Defendant)
> E-mail: adam_attorney@lawfirm.com

2. *Non–Registered Signatories.* If the original document requires the signature of a non-registered signatory, the filing party must scan and electronically file the original document. The electronically filed document maintained on the court's servers will constitute the official version of that record. The filing party must retain the original document for a period of five years from the date the document is signed, or for one year after the expiration of all time periods for appeal, whichever period is greater, and must provide the original paper document to the Court upon request.

3. *Criminal Defendants.* A document required to be filed electronically which contains the signature of a defendant in a criminal case must be electronically filed as a scanned document in .pdf. The filing party is required to verify the legibility of the scanned document before electronically filing it with the court. The filing party must retain the original paper document for a period of five years from the date the document is signed, or for one year after the expiration of all time periods for appeal, whichever period is greater, and must provide the original paper document to the Court upon request.

4. *Stipulations and Other Documents Requiring Multiple Signatures.* All stipulations must be filed as joint motions. The filer of a joint motion need not obtain a hearing date prior to filing the joint motion. At the time a joint motion is filed, the filer must e-mail a proposed order to the e-mail address of the assigned judicial officer pursuant to the procedures set forth in section 2.h below.

The filer of any joint motion or other document requiring more than one signature must certify that the content of the document is acceptable to all persons required to sign the document by obtaining either physical signatures or authorization for the electronic signatures of all parties on the document. Physical, facsimile or electronic signatures are permitted. The filer must electronically file the document indicating the signatories as "s/Jane Doe," "s/John Smith," etc., for each electronic signature.

Except as otherwise ordered, parties will have one business day to file an Objection to Electronic Filing if they object to contents of the joint motion or document that contains their signature. The assigned judicial officer will prepare an order, or enter a text order on the docket, following the filing of a joint motion.

g. Motions, Applications, or Other Requests for Ruling by the Court.

1. Pursuant to Local Civil Rule 7.1.b and Local Civil Rule 7.1.e, all hearing dates for any motion, application, or other requests for ruling by the Court must be obtained from the law clerk of the judge to whom the case is assigned before any motion, application, or other requests for ruling by the Court are filed electronically.

2. Any supporting memorandum of points and authorities, declarations, and exhibits associated with motions, applications, or other requests for ruling by the Court, must be filed as attachments to the motion in the CM/ECF system.

3. Civil and criminal motions, and responses thereto, must be filed according to the deadlines set forth in Local Civil Rule 7.1 and Local Criminal Rule 47.1.

4. A party wishing to file a motion or response on shortened time must file a motion for an order shortening time as required by the Local Rules. Counsel must e-mail a proposed order to the assigned judicial officer at the address indicated in section 2.h below.

5. The Court may, upon its own motion, strike any inappropriately filed document.

h. Proposed Orders and Orders. Registered users SHOULD NOT FILE OR SUBMIT proposed orders within the electronic filing system. At the time of filing any joint motion, motion for continuance or extension of time, motion for an order shortening time, or similar non-dispositive procedural motion, the filer must also e-mail a separate proposed order to the assigned judicial officer at the e-mail address provided below, with a copy of the e-mail and proposed order also being sent to opposing counsel.

The proposed order must be in editable word processing format (i.e. Microsoft Word), and not in .pdf format. The proposed order should not contain the name and law firm information of the filing party, and should not contain the word "proposed" in the caption.

The e-mail subject line should include the case number, followed by a short description of the attachment (i.e., 10cv1234—Order Granting Motion for Continuance). **These e-mail addresses are not to be utilized to communicate with the Court unless otherwise permitted or when communications are solicited by the Court.** Opposing counsel will have one business day to e-mail chambers any objections to the proposed order.

U.S. District Judges

efile_sabraw@casd.uscourts.gov   efile_miller@casd.uscourts.gov

efile_hayes@casd.uscourts.gov   efile_whelan@casd.uscourts.gov

efile_sammartino@casd.uscourts.gov   efile_lorenz@casd.uscourts.gov

efile_bencivengo@casd.uscourts.gov   efile_burns@casd.uscourts.gov

efile_curiel@casd.uscourts.gov   efile_houston@casd.uscourts.gov

efile_bashant@casd.uscourts.gov   efile_benitez@casd.uscourts.gov

efile_robinson@casd.uscourts.gov   efile_anello@casd.uscourts.gov

efile_huff@casd.uscourts.gov   efile_battaglia@casd.uscourts.gov

efile_moskowitz@casd.uscourts.gov

U.S. Magistrate Judges

efile_gallo@casd.uscourts.gov   efile_montenegro@casd.uscourts.gov

efile_major@casd.uscourts.gov   efile_lopez@casd.uscourts.gov

efile_skomal@casd.uscourts.gov   efile_berg@casd.uscourts.gov

efile_dembin@casd.uscourts.gov   efile_goddard@casd.uscourts.gov

efile_crawford@casd.uscourts.gov   efile_butcher@casd.uscourts.gov

efile_burkhardt@casd.uscourts.gov   efile_brooks@casd.uscourts.gov

efile_schopler@casd.uscourts.gov   efile_stormes@casd.uscourts.gov

i. *Ex Parte* Documents. Ordinary Ex Parte motions, for which notice is to be provided to all parties, should be filed electronically. Ex Parte documents for which no notice is to be provided to opposing parties should be filed in paper format under seal. Ex Parte documents filed in the system will be served on all parties.

j. Sealed and Juvenile Documents. All sealed documents in criminal cases and cases involving juveniles must be filed and served in paper format. Sealed documents in civil cases are to be filed electronically in CM/ECF and served in paper format.

Any document submitted for filing under seal in civil cases must be accompanied by a motion authorizing such filing. In civil cases the motion to seal will be filed as a public document using the appropriate CM/ECF event located under the "Sealed Documents" category. The proposed document to be filed under seal must be lodged electronically using the "Sealed Lodged Proposed Document" event located under the "Sealed Documents" category.

If the motion to seal is granted, the judge will issue an order authorizing the electronic filing by the Clerk's Office of the lodged proposed document under seal. If the motion to seal is denied, the document will remain lodged under seal without further consideration absent contrary direction from the Court.

Electronic filing is not permitted in sealed cases. Documents intended for filing in sealed cases must be submitted in paper format. Ex Parte documents for which no notice is to be provided to opposing parties should be filed in paper format under seal.

1. *Procedures for E–Filing Sealed Documents in Civil Cases.*

a. To e-file any sealed document in a civil case, including motions, responses, replies, declarations, etc., a filer must first e-file a motion to seal using the "Motion to File Document(s) Under Seal" event located in the civil events menu under "Sealed Documents." The motion will be a public entry on the docket and the document will be available to the public. All parties in the case will receive notice of the electronic filing. The proposed sealed documents should not be attached to this public filing.

b. After filing the Motion to File Document(s) Under Seal, the filer shall immediately submit the proposed sealed documents in CM/ECF using the "Sealed Lodged Proposed Document" event located under the "Sealed Documents" category. The proposed document must include the notation "UNDER SEAL" in the caption. The proposed sealed documents will be unavailable for viewing by any attorney or member of the public. However, the docket text associated with the entry will be available for viewing by attorneys and the public. The docket entry will not contain specific information identifying the nature of the proposed sealed document. All parties in the case will receive notice of the electronic filing, however, the document itself will be unavailable. Counsel must serve copies on opposing counsel in a conventional manner.

c. Counsel must e-mail a separate proposed order in word processing format to the assigned judicial officer at the e-mail address provided above in Section 2.h. If the order is also to be filed under seal, it must so state.

d. If counsel believes the motion for leave to file documents under seal itself should be filed under seal, counsel shall follow the same process to obtain leave to file that motion under seal.

k. Exhibits. Exhibits must be submitted electronically in CM/ECF as attachments. If the entire exhibit exceeds thirty-five (35) megabytes, it must be submitted in multiple segments, not to exceed thirty-five (35) megabytes each.

Pursuant to Local Civil Rule 5.1.e, except where compliance is impracticable, exhibits must be paged in consecutive numerical order. Each document containing exhibits must have, as a cover page to the exhibits, a table of contents indicating the page number of each of the succeeding exhibits.

The filing party is required to verify the legibility of the scanned exhibits prior to electronically filing them with the court. Parties should scan documents in black and white, unless color is a critical feature of the information.

Original exhibits must be retained by the submitting party for the duration of the case, including any period of appeal.

A party may seek leave of the court to allow the non-electronic filing of exhibits when they are not convertible to electronic form (e.g. videotapes, maps, etc.). If leave is granted, the filing party must prepare a cover page in pleading format to be submitted with the exhibits. The cover page must contain a table of contents indicating the page number of each of the succeeding exhibits. The caption will state what document, if any, the exhibits are supporting. The actual exhibits must be tabbed and bound if appropriate.

Evidentiary and trial exhibits must be submitted directly to the appropriate courtroom deputy clerk and will not be filed with the court.

l.   Hyperlinks. In order to preserve the integrity of the court record, attorneys wishing to insert hyperlinks in court filings should continue to use the traditional citation method for the cited authority, in addition to the hyperlink. The Judiciary's policy on hyperlinks is that a hyperlink contained in a filing is no more than a convenient mechanism for accessing material cited in the document. A hyperlink reference is extraneous to any filed document and is not part of the court's record.

m.   Technical Failures. A registered user whose filing is made untimely as the result of a technical failure may seek appropriate relief from the court.

n.   Correcting Filing or Docket Errors.

1.   Once a document is submitted and becomes part of the case docket, corrections to the docket may be made only by the Clerk's Office. The CM/ECF system will not permit the filing party to make changes to the document or docket entry once the transaction has been accepted.

2.   The filing party should not attempt to re-file an incorrectly filed document.

3.   The filing party must contact the Clerk's Office CM/ECF Help Desk as soon as an error has been discovered and provide the case number and document number. If appropriate, the Clerk's Office will make a docket entry indicating the document was filed in error. The filing party will be advised if the document needs to be re-filed.

4.   If the Clerk's Office discovers filing or docketing errors, the filer will be advised of what further action, if any, is required to address the error. However, if the error is minor, the Clerk's Office may correct the error, with or without notifying the parties.

5.   In the event it appears a document has been filed in the wrong case, the Clerk's Office will docket an entry indicating this possible error and notify the filing party. If it is confirmed as an error, the party will be directed to re-file the document in the correct case. The Clerk's Office will not delete any documents filed by a party unless ordered by the court.

o.   Transcripts. The Judicial Conference has adopted a policy regarding electronic access to court transcripts. The following procedures apply as to transcripts:

Transcripts filed by contract court reporters or official transcribers will be submitted to the Clerk's Office in .pdf through e-mail to a designated e-mail address. The e-mail address for contract court reporters and official transcribers is ecftranscripts@casd.uscourts.gov.

Transcripts will be electronically filed and available for viewing at the Clerk's Office public terminal, but may NOT be copied or reproduced by the Clerk's Office for a period of 90 days. Registered users who have purchased the transcript during the 90 day period will be provided remote electronic access to the transcript in CM/ECF. The court reporter or official transcriber will notify the Clerk's Office when a registered user in a case has purchased the transcript so that access to the transcript can be given to the purchaser through the court's CM/ECF system.

Within 7 calendar days of the filing of the official transcript in CM/ECF, each party wishing to redact a transcript must electronically file a "Notice of Intent to Request Redaction." If no such notice is filed within the allotted time, the court will assume redaction of personal data identifiers from the transcript is not necessary. If redaction is requested, within 21 calendar days from the e-filing of the transcript with the Clerk, or longer by order of the Court, the parties must submit to the court reporter or official transcriber a redaction request statement indicating by page and line where personal identifiers appear in the transcript and how they are to be redacted. The responsibility for redacting personal identifiers rests solely with counsel and the parties. Personal identifiers are Social Security numbers, financial account numbers, names of minor children, dates of birth, and in criminal cases, home addresses.

p.   Exceptions to Electronic Filing. The following documents must be submitted in paper form:

1.   Sealed Documents in Criminal Cases and Cases Involving Juveniles

2.   Sealed Civil Complaint and Sealed Notice of Removal

3.   Indictment

4.   Financial Affidavit in Support of Request for Appointment of Counsel

5. Bond Documents

6. Writs Issued

7. Reports of Medical or Mental Evaluations of Criminal Case Defendants

8. Letter to Sentencing Judge Recommending Downward Departure Under USSG § 5K1.1

9. Stipulation of Fact and Joint Motion for Release of Material Witnesses (in Alien Smuggling Cases)

10. Grand Jury Matters, including:

a. Grand Jury Returns

b. Voting Slips

c. Grand Jury Transcripts

11. Consent/Declination Form (Pursuant to General Order No. 707)

12. Consent of a Civil Action to a Magistrate Judge (Pursuant to Civil Local Rule 73.1.b)

12. Civil Miscellaneous Cases Filed by Unregistered Attorneys

13. Any other document or filing that the court orders not to be electronically filed, imaged or maintained in the CM/ECF system.

[Adopted effective May 15, 2008. Amended effective April 2, 2012; October 4, 2012; November 26, 2012; May 6, 2013; November 18, 2013; May 9, 2014; January 15, 2015; November 9, 2016; January 20, 2017; January 2, 2018; February 6, 2018; March 2, 2018; September 24, 2018; October 29, 2018; November 6, 2018; December 27, 2018; January 22, 2019; August 1, 2019; June 1, 2020; September 15, 2020; March 3, 2021; March 31, 2021.]

SELECTED GENERAL ORDERS
GENERAL ORDER NO. 70–I. IN THE MATTER OF TRANSCRIPT RATES

Pursuant to Title 28, United States Code, Section 753, the following transcript rates per page are prescribed by the Court and are effective this date:

	Original	First Copy to each party	Each Additional Copy to Same Party
Ordinary Transcript	$3.65	$.90	$.60
14–Day Transcript	$4.25	$.90	$.60
Expedited Transcript	$4.85	$.90	$.60
Daily Transcript	$6.05	$1.20	$.90
Hourly Transcript	$7.25	$1.20	$.90
Realtime Transcript	One feed, $3.05 per page; two to four feeds, $2.10 per page; five or more feeds, $1.50 per page.		

(A realtime "feed" is the electronic data flow from the court reporter to the computer of each person or party ordering and receiving the realtime transcription in the courtroom.)

[Dated: April 22, 2011.]

GENERAL ORDER NO.147–J. IN THE MATTER OF ADOPTION OF A JURY SELECTION PLAN (AS AMENDED) AND PROPOSED LOCAL RULE CHANGE

Pursuant to 28 U.S.C. §§ 1861 through 1869, as amended, the following Jury Selection Plan ("Plan") is hereby adopted by this Court. The Plan was approved by the Judicial Council of the Ninth Circuit on March 12, 2021. The Plan supersedes General Orders 147—147–H, General Orders 626—626B, and Civil Local Rule 83.10. Civil Local Rule 83.10 will be repealed and removed from the Court's Local Rules.

The adoption of this Plan follows the public comment period established in General Order 147–I, the Court's consideration of the comments received, and consultation with members of the community who provided the comments. The Court has incorporated many of the suggestions offered by the community, in an effort to go beyond the legal requirements and to reach more people in the community who may be eligible for jury service.

The Plan will expand the source lists to include California Driver's Licenses and Identification Cards. The Plan also states affirmatively its historical use of the National Change of Address Database, and the addition of zip code replacement for juror qualification forms returned as "undeliverable" or to which no timely response has been received.

This Plan will be in effect on a pilot basis for two years from the date of this Order. At that time, the Court will consider whether the Plan will require further amendment.

UNITED STATES DISTRICT COURT FOR THE SOUTHERN DISTRICT OF CALIFORNIA
JURY PLAN
(Approved by the Ninth Circuit Judicial Council on March 12, 2021)

CHAPTER ONE

General Matters

Section 1.01 Authority. This Jury Plan is adopted by the United States District Court for the Southern District of California, which consists of the counties of San Diego and Imperial, in accordance with the provisions of the Jury Selection and Service Act of 1968 (Public Law 90–274), as amended and codified in 28 U.S.C. § 1861 *et seq.*

Section 1.02 Application. This Jury Plan will take effect after approval by a reviewing panel of the United States Court of Appeals for the Ninth Circuit pursuant to 28 U.S.C. § 1863(a). The prior Jury Plan will be superseded as of the effective date of this revised Plan. A copy of the revised Plan, as approved by the reviewing panel, will be provided to the Administrative Office of the United States Courts and the Attorney General of the United States.

Section 1.03 Definitions. For purposes of this Plan:

"Jury Selection Process" will be deemed to include all activities associated with the master and qualified jury wheels relating to the random selection, qualification, summoning, and service of grand and petit jurors.

"Chief Judge" means the Chief Judge of this District, or any supervising "Jury Judge" appointed by the Chief Judge.

"Clerk" and "Clerk of Court" means the Clerk of this District Court, any authorized deputy clerk, or any other person authorized by the Chief Judge or by this Plan to assist the Clerk in the performance of duties under this Plan.

Section 1.04 Policy. It is the policy of the Court that all litigants in this Court, entitled to trial by jury, have the right to grand and petit juries selected at random from a fair cross section of the community in the district wherein the Court convenes. It is also the policy of the Court that all citizens in the district have the opportunity to be considered for service on grand and petit juries, and have an obligation to serve as jurors when summoned for that purpose.

Section 1.05 Discrimination Prohibited. No citizen will be excluded from service as a grand or petit juror on account of race, color, religion, sex, national origin, or economic status.

Section 1.06 Management Responsibilities. In accordance with 28 U.S.C. § 1863(b)(*l*), the Clerk of Court will manage the Jury Selection Process under the supervision and control of the Chief Judge, or of such other judge of the District Court as the Chief Judge designates.

The Court finds that electronic data processing methods can be advantageously used for managing this Plan. Therefore, a properly programmed electronic data processing system or a combination system employing both manual and electronic machine methods, may be used for all randomized drawings and to perform other clerical and recordkeeping jury functions.

In the event of an emergency, computer malfunction, or any overt or obvious deviation from this Plan caused by automation, the Clerk, with the approval of the Chief Judge or Jury Judge, will manually, or by alternative electronic methods, proceed from the last step correctly implemented to manage the Plan.

Section 1.07 Delegation of the Clerk's Management Responsibilities. In accordance with 28 U.S.C. §§ 1863(b)(*l*) and 1869(a), the Clerk of Court may delegate responsibility for the day-to-day operation of the Jury Selection Process to any authorized deputy clerk.

The Clerk may use the services of non-court personnel to assist in the Jury Selection Process. For purposes of this plan, the phrase "non-court personnel" may include, but is not limited to:

(a) County or State officials, and their employees or agents, who are responsible for custody and maintenance of the source lists identified in Section 2.01 of this Plan.

(b) Owners, employees, operators and/or agents of computer or data processing centers, barcoding facilities, mail handling centers, document reproduction facilities, and optical scanning facilities, and similar facilities whose services are requested or employed by the Clerk to support the Jury Selection Process.

(c) Other non-court administrative or clerical persons whose services are requested or employed by the Clerk to select, process, and/or mail the various documents and records involved in the Jury Selection Process.

When requests for names to build the master wheel are issued to non-court personnel (e.g., computer personnel, local or state officials), the work must be conducted pursuant to detailed instructions by the Clerk of Court. Once such selection is completed, the non-court personnel must certify that the selection was completed pursuant to the instructions of the Clerk of Court.

Section 1.08 Emptying and Refilling the District Master Jury Wheel. The Clerk of Court will create and maintain a master jury wheel. In accordance with 28 U.S.C. § 1863(b)(4), the Clerk is directed to empty and refill the master jury wheel by the thirtieth of June every two years after the general national elections. When the master jury wheel is emptied, the existing qualified jury wheel will continue to be used until the Clerk determines that an adequate number of persons from the new master jury wheel have been qualified. At that time, the old qualified jury wheel will be emptied and new qualified jury wheel created. Summoned jurors from the previous qualified jury wheel may serve at the same time with jurors selected from a later qualified jury wheel. If additional time is needed to empty and refill the master jury wheel, permission must be obtained from the Chief Judge of the Circuit.

Section 1.09 Method and Manner of the Random Selection of Jurors. The randomized selection procedures set forth in this Plan must ensure that the names chosen will represent all segments of the source lists from which drawn, that the mathematical odds of any single name being picked are substantially equal.

(a) The selection of names from the complete source list databases in electronic media for the master jury wheel may be accomplished by a purely randomized process through a properly programmed electronic data processing system. Similarly, at the option of the Clerk and after consultation with the Chief Judge or Jury Judge, a properly programmed electronic data processing system for purely randomized selection may be used to select names from the master wheel for the purpose of determining qualification for jury service, from the qualified wheel for summoning persons to serve as grand or petit jurors, from the pool of jurors to serve as a panel, and from the panel of jurors to serve as a jury. Such random selections of names from the source lists for inclusion in the master wheel by data computer personnel must ensure that each county within the district is substantially proportionally represented in the master jury wheel in accordance with 28 U.S.C. § 1863(b)(3). The purely randomized selection procedure may be used for all drawings. (*See* Section 2.03 herein for the procedures to ensure proper proportional county representation in the district master jury wheel.)

(b) *Manual Randomized Selection of Jury Panels and Petit Juries.* After the jurors have been summoned, the clerk has the option, after consultation with the Chief Judge or Jury Judge, to randomly select jurors manually for petit or grand jury panels and for petit juries for specific cases by:

(1) preserving the computer prepared random sequence of the names of jurors summoned and assigning jurors to panels in the order listed; or preserving the computer prepared random sequence of the names of jurors impaneled and assigning jurors to petit juries in the order listed; or

(2) drawing names at random from a box, jury wheel, or similar container containing the names of the present pool or panel of jurors.

Section 1.10 General Notice. In accordance with 28 U.S.C. § 1864(a), the Clerk will post a general notice for public review in the Clerk's Office and on the Court's public website explaining the process by which names are periodically and randomly drawn from the source list and the master and qualified wheels.

Section 1.11 Protection of Jurors' Employment. No employer can discharge, threaten to discharge, intimidate, or coerce any permanent employee over such employee's jury service, or the attendance or scheduled attendance in connection with such jury service. Any employer who violates the provisions of this section will be subject to penalties specified by 28 U.S.C. § 1875.

Section 1.12 Modifications. Modifications to this Plan may be made from time to time by this Court, upon approval of the Ninth Circuit Reviewing Panel of the Judicial Council and must be made when so directed by the Reviewing Panel.

CHAPTER TWO

Source Lists, Initial Random Selection, and the Master Jury Wheel

Section 2.01 Source Lists (*See* 28 U.S.C. §§ 1861 and 1863(b)(2) and (3)). The Court finds that county voter registration lists, supplemented by the California driver's license for non–AB60 licenses and state ID information, will be used for the creation of the master jury wheel. The court finds this "multiple-source list" represents a fair cross section of the citizens residing in the district.

Section 2.02 Size of the Master Jury Wheel (*See* 28 U.S.C. § 1863(b)(4)). In no event should the quantity of names placed in the master jury wheel be less than one-half of one percent of the total number of names on registered voter lists.

The Chief Judge or Jury Judge may order additional names to be placed in the master jury wheels from time to time as necessary.

Section 2.03 Substantial Proportional Representation and the Master Jury Wheel. When selecting names from the source list, specific and detailed procedures will be followed to ensure the random selection of a fair cross section of the persons residing in the community in the district where the court convenes. Such random selection of names from the source list for inclusion in the master wheel will be designed to ensure that each county within the district is substantially proportionately represented in the master jury wheels.

Section 2.04 Filling the Master Jury Wheel. The master wheel will be obtained as follows: The Clerk must ascertain the total number of registered voters in both counties and divide that number by the number of names to be selected for the master jury wheel. For instance, if there are 500,000 registered voters and 20,000 names are needed, 500,000 will be divided by 20,000 producing a quotient of 25. Then the Clerk must draw by lot a number, between zero and 26, and the name corresponding to that number from the source lists of each county, along with each 25th name corresponding to that number thereafter to the end of the source list.

The master wheel must maintain a division for each county between jurors who reside in each county. Jurors may be selected for service in one county, or both as the Court may direct.

CHAPTER THREE

Drawing Names from the Master Jury Wheel, Juror Qualification, and the Qualified Jury Wheel

Section 3.01 Drawing Names from the Master Jury Wheel. From time to time as required, the Clerk must draw at random from the master jury wheel the names of as many persons as may be required for jury service. 28 U.S.C. § 1864(a).

Section 3.02 Juror Qualification Questionnaires. The Clerk will mail a juror qualification questionnaire notice to every person randomly selected pursuant to Section 3.01 of this plan. 28 U.S.C. § 1864(a). The notice will direct the juror to complete a juror qualification questionnaire through the Court's internet website within ten (10) days. If a juror does not complete the juror qualification questionnaire online, a paper copy of the questionnaire will be mailed with instructions to complete and return the questionnaire to the Clerk by mail within ten (10) days of receipt.

For each juror qualification form returned to the court as "undeliverable" and those to which no timely response has been received, the Clerk will randomly draw the name of another person residing in the same zip code and mail a new juror qualification notice to that person.

National Change of Address (NCOA) Database: When mailing juror qualification questionnaires, the Clerk will submit names on the Master Jury Wheel to be updated and corrected through the national change-of-address system of the United States Postal Service.

Section 3.03 Failure to Submit a Juror Qualification Questionnaire or Appear. If a person fails to submit a completed juror qualification questionnaire, the Clerk may issue a summons to the person directing them to appear in the Clerk's Office to complete the qualification questionnaire. 28 U.S.C. § 1864(a). No juror fees or costs for this appearance will be paid, unless otherwise ordered by the Court. 28 U.S.C § 1864(b) lists the penalties that may be imposed by the court.

Section 3.04 Determining Juror Qualification Status. The Court, or the Clerk of Court or designee, under the supervision of the Court, will determine solely on the basis of information provided on the juror qualification questionnaire and other competent evidence whether a person is unqualified for, exempt, or to be excused from jury service. 28 U.S.C. § 1865(a). The Clerk must enter such determination on the questionnaire or in the jury management database.

(a) *Disqualification from Jury Service.* In accordance with 28 U.S.C. § 1865(b), any person will be deemed qualified to serve on grand and petit juries in this district unless such person:

(1) is not a citizen of the United States, is less than 18 years old, or has not resided for a period of one year within the judicial district;

(2) is unable to read, write, and understand the English language with a degree of proficiency sufficient to satisfactorily fill out the juror qualification questionnaire;

(3) is unable to speak the English language;

(4) is incapable, by reason of mental or physical infirmity, to render satisfactory jury service; or

(5) has a charge pending against him for the commission of, or has been convicted in a State or Federal court of record of, a crime punishable by imprisonment for more than one year and his civil rights have not been restored.

The Clerk of Court or his designee will submit to the designated Jury Judge any returned juror qualification questionnaires containing information that suggests doubt as to the individual's English skills so that the Jury Judge may determine whether the individual is qualified to serve as a juror.

(b) *Exemption from Jury Service.* In accordance with 28 U.S.C. § 1863(b)(6), the following persons are barred from jury service on the grounds that they are exempt:

(1) members in active service in the Armed Forces of the United States;

(2) members of the fire or police departments of any municipality, county or district; and

(3) public officers in the executive, legislative, or judicial branches of the Government of the United States, or any state, district, territory, possession or subdivision thereof, who are actively engaged in the performance of their official duties. A "public officer" means a person who is elected to public office or who is directly appointed by a person elected to public office.

(c) *Excuses from Jury Service on Individual Request.*

(1) Permanent Excuse. In accordance with 28 U.S.C. § 1863(b)(5)(A) and (B), the Court finds that jury service by members of the following occupational classes or groups of persons would entail undue hardship or extreme inconvenience to the members thereof, and the excuse of such members would not be inconsistent with §§ 1861 and 1862 of 28 U.S.C, and will be granted upon individual written request to those:

(A) persons age 70 years or older;

(B) Any person having active care and custody of a child or children under 10 years of age whose health and/or safety would be jeopardized by absence of such person for jury service; or a person who is essential to the care of aged or infirm persons;

(C) persons who have served as grand or petit jurors in a federal court within the past two years; or

(D) volunteer safety personnel. For purposes of this subparagraph, the term "volunteer safety personnel" means individuals serving a public agency (as defined in Section 1203(6) of Title I of the Omnibus Crime Control and Safe Streets Act of 1968) in an official capacity, without compensation, as firefighters or members of a rescue squad or ambulance crew.

(2) Temporary Excuse. Upon application showing undue hardship or extreme inconvenience, any qualified juror may be temporarily excused from jury service for such period as the Clerk deems necessary. Unless otherwise directed by the Court, those individuals temporarily excused from jury service should either be summoned again for jury service with their pool if it is deferred, or their names should be reinserted into their respective qualified jury wheel for possible future selection.

Section 3.05 Qualified Jury Wheel. The Clerk must maintain a qualified jury wheel for this district and will place in said wheel the names of all persons randomly selected from their respective master jury wheel who are determined to be qualified to serve as jurors and are not exempt or excused from service pursuant to this Plan.

CHAPTER FOUR

Selection of Grand and Petit Jurors

Section 4.01 Selection and Impanelment of Grand and Petit Jurors (See 28 U.S.C. § 1866(a)). The Clerk will draw at random from the qualified jury wheel the names of as many persons as may be required for assignment to grand and petit jury panels in the District. Grand jurors will be randomly drawn from both counties maintaining the proportional relationship between the two counties. From those summoned for grand jury, 23 names will be chosen at random in the presence of a judge of the Court on the day when said jurors report in response to summons. These must serve as members of a grand jury.

Section 4.02 Summoning Grand and/or Petit Jurors (See 28 U.S.C. § 1866(b)). The Clerk will issue and serve personally or send by first class mail summonses to the persons whose names are so drawn.

Section 4.03 Petit Jury Term—One Day Appearance/One Trial. It is the policy of the Southern District of California that all prospective petit jurors serve "one day" or "one trial" during a two week "on call" term of service. Petit jurors appearing in the United States District Court for the Southern District of California may, upon completion of their "one day" or "one trial" service, be released from further jury service obligations for a period of not less than two years. The Court reserves the right to modify the provisions of this petit jury policy when the interests of justice so require.

Section 4.04 Disclosure of Petit Juror Information. Names drawn from the qualified jury wheel must not be made public except by order of Court. The Clerk must provide copies of the information cards respecting the petit jury panel members who are selected for service in this court to the U.S. Attorney, and to Federal Defenders of San Diego, and to the District Court Library for the use of civil and other criminal practitioners. The cards will have the jurors' Social Security Numbers, addresses and telephone numbers blocked out. The Clerk must provide copies of information cards to the U.S. Attorney of grand jurors who are selected for service. When the Clerk has assigned a venire panel to a particular trial, the list of names so assigned may be furnished to the attorneys for the parties and any parties appearing *pro se* in said trial at a time in advance, if allowed by standing order of the Court or otherwise ordered by the trial judge. Notwithstanding this general policy, any trial judge may order the Clerk to keep jurors names confidential until the morning of trial in any case where the interests of justice so require.

Section 4.05 Grand Jury Impanelment (See 28 U.S.C. § 1863(b)(8)). One or more grand juries will be impaneled for this district in accordance with court orders issued by the Chief Judge or Jury Judge. The impanelment of every grand jury will not be conducted in open court or within public view.

Section 4.06 Term of Grand Jury. Each grand jury will serve until discharged by the Court, but no regular grand jury will serve more than 18 months unless the Court extends the service of the grand jury upon a determination that such extension is in the public interest, in accordance with Rule 6(g) of the Federal Rules of Criminal Procedure.

Section 4.07 Alternate Grand Jurors. The Court may direct that alternate grand jurors be selected at the same time a grand jury is selected. Alternate grand jurors, in the order in which they were selected, may thereafter be impaneled to replace excused grand jurors. Alternate grand jurors will be drawn in the same manner and must have the same qualifications as the regular grand jurors, and if impaneled, must be subject to the same challenges, will take the same oath and have the same authority as the regular grand jurors.

Section 4.08 Disclosure of Grand Juror Information (See 28 U.S.C. § 1863(b)(7)). Except as authorized by written order of the Court, the names and information relating to any summoned or serving grand juror or grand jury panel will be confidential and not disclosed to any litigant or member of the public. Applications for disclosure of grand juror information must be made by motion to the Chief Judge or his designee and must set forth why disclosure should be allowed.

CHAPTER FIVE

Exclusion or Excuse from Jury Service

Section 5.01 Exclusion or Excuse from Jury Service. Except as provided elsewhere in this Plan, no person or class of persons will be disqualified, excluded, excused, or exempted from service as jurors; provided, however, that any person summoned for jury service may be:

(a) excluded by the Court on the grounds that such person may be unable to render impartial jury service or that his service as a juror would be likely to disrupt the proceedings;

(b) excluded upon peremptory challenge as provided by law;

(c) excluded pursuant to the procedure specified by law upon a challenge by any party for good cause shown;

(d) excluded upon determination of the Court, after hearing in open court, that service as a juror would be likely to threaten the secrecy of the proceedings, or otherwise adversely affect the integrity of jury deliberations, and that exclusion of such person will not be inconsistent with the policy stated in 28 U.S.C. §§ 1861 and 1862.

Section 5.02 Jury Service Limit. In any two (2) year period, no person will be required to:

(a) serve or attend court for prospective service as a petit juror for a total of more than thirty (30) days, except when necessary to complete service in a particular case, or

(b) serve on more than one grand jury, or

(c) serve as both a grand and petit juror.

Section 5.03 Permanent Exclusion or Excuse from Jury Service. Whenever a person is permanently excluded or excused from jury service under this Chapter, the Clerk will note the same on the questionnaire or in the jury management database.

CHAPTER SIX

Disclosure and Retention of Jury Selection Records

Section 6.01 Release of Jury Plan Information. The Clerk is authorized to provide a copy of this Jury Plan to any person requesting information about the jury selection process, and may post the Plan to the court's public website. All other requests for information about the Jury Selection Process must be submitted in writing to the Clerk of Court, who will confer with the Chief Judge or Jury Judge prior to releasing any information.

Section 6.02 Release of Juror Records (*See* 28 U.S.C. § 1867(f)) The contents of records and papers used in the Jury Selection Process will not be disclosed, except upon written order of the Court. Applications for disclosure of records related to the Jury Selection Process must be made by motion to the judge presiding in the case in which the application is made, or if not in a pending case, to the Chief Judge or Jury Judge. Any such motion must set forth why disclosure should be allowed.

Section 6.03 Retention of Juror Records. In accordance with 28 U.S.C. § 1868, the Clerk will keep all records and papers relating to the Jury Selection Process for four years following the emptying and refilling of the master jury wheels and the completion of service of all jurors selected from those master jury wheels, or for such longer periods of time as the Court may require. Such records may then be destroyed, providing the means used ensures the privacy of their contents.

Section 6.04 Request to Inspect Juror Records (See 28 U.S.C. § 1868). Applications to inspect Jury Selection Process records to determine the validity of the selection of any jury must be made by motion to the Chief Judge and must set forth why disclosure should be allowed.

Section 6.05 Report on Operation of the Jury Selection Plan. The Clerk of Court or his designee will complete and submit an AO–12 Report on Operation of the Jury Selection Plan to the Chief Judge and designated Jury Judge one year after the first mailing of juror qualification forms from the Master Jury Wheel.

[Dated: March 24, 2021. Amended May 3, 2021.]

GENERAL ORDER NO. 301–J. IN THE MATTER OF ADMISSION FEE ALLOCATION OF ADMISSION FEE

Effective January 1, 2021, the admission fee required of all admitted to practice before this Court will be two hundred and thirteen dollars ($213.00). Of the admission fee, one hundred and eighty-eight dollars ($188.00) must be deposited into the Treasury as mandated by law. The Court hereby designates that the remaining twenty-five dollars ($25.00) must be allocated to the Court's Library Fund, unless otherwise ordered by the Court.

[Dated: December 22, 2020.]

GENERAL ORDER NO. 370–B. ATTORNEY FEES ALLOWABLE IN FEDERAL CAPITAL PROSECUTIONS AND HABEAS CORPUS DEATH PENALTY CASES UNDER THE CRIMINAL JUSTICE ACT

General Order No. 370–A filed on April 18, 2005, is vacated and replaced by this order.

Effective for work performed on or after January 1, 2006, the maximum rate of compensation for counsel for a defendant in a federal capital prosecution or for a petitioner in a federal death penalty habeas corpus case shall be as follows:

(1) For federal capital prosecutions a maximum rate allowed as set by the Annual Fiscal Year Defendant Services Appropriation.

(2) For federal death penalty habeas corpus cases—maximum as have been authorized and approved by the Judicial Council for the Ninth Circuit. Such rates appear in the Capital Case Budget and Management Policy of the Judicial Council of the Ninth Circuit at paragraph 3.

[Dated: January 31, 2006.]

GENERAL ORDER NO. 499–F. IN THE MATTER OF PLAN OF THE UNITED STATES DISTRICT COURT FOR THE SOUTHERN DISTRICT OF CALIFORNIA PURSUANT TO THE CRIMINAL JUSTICE ACT

Pursuant to the provision of the Criminal Justice Act, the judges of the United States District Court for the Southern District of California have adopted the following amended Plan for the adequate representation of any person otherwise financially unable to obtain adequate representation.

CRIMINAL JUSTICE ACT PLAN

I. AUTHORITY

Pursuant to the Criminal Justice Act of 1964 as amended (CJA), Section 3006A of Title 18, United States Code, Volume VII, the judges of the United States District Court for the Southern District of California, have adopted this Plan for any person financially unable to obtain adequate representation in connection with a criminal matter.

A. Pursuant to the Criminal Justice Act ("CJA") of 1964, as amended, 18 U.S.C. § 3006A, the Judicial Council of the Ninth Circuit Model Plan for the Implementation and Administration of the CJA; and the Guidelines for Administering the CJA and Related Statutes, Volume 7A, Guide to Judiciary Policy ("CJA Guidelines"), the judges of the United States District Court for the Southern District of California have adopted this CJA Plan ("Plan") for any person financially unable to obtain adequate representation in connection with a criminal matter.

II. STATEMENT OF POLICY

A. This Plan provides for the furnishing of representational and other services by Federal Defenders of San Diego, Inc. ("Federal Defender"), and private attorneys compensated under the CJA and related statutes.

B. This Plan must be administered so that those accused of a crime, or otherwise eligible for services under the CJA, will not be deprived of the right to counsel, or any element of representation necessary to an effective defense, due to lack of financial resources.

III. OBJECTIVES OF THIS CJA PLAN ARE:

A. To attain the goal of equal justice under the law;

B. To provide all eligible persons with timely appointed counsel services that are consistent with the best practices of the legal profession and commensurate with those services rendered when counsel is privately retained;

C. To provide cost-effective services that also protect the independence of the defense function so that the rights of individual defendants are safeguarded and enforced;

D. To engage in recruitment efforts to establish a diverse CJA panel and ensure that all qualified attorneys are encouraged to participate in the furnishing of representation in CJA cases; and

E. To particularize the requirements of the CJA, the USA Patriot Improvement and Reauthorization Act of 2005 (re-codified at 18 U.S.C. § 3599), and the CJA Guidelines in a manner that meets the needs of this district.

IV. COMPLIANCE

A. The Court, its Clerk of Court ("Clerk"), the Federal Defender and private attorneys appointed pursuant to the CJA must comply with this Plan.

B. The Court will ensure that a current copy of the CJA Plan and any appendices are made available on the Court's website and provided to panel members upon designation as a member of one of the CJA panels for the Southern District of California (collectively, "CJA panel").

V. DEFINITIONS

A. "Appointed attorney" includes an attorney designated to represent a financially eligible person under the CJA and this Plan. Such attorneys include private attorneys that are members of the CJA panel ("CJA attorneys" or "panel members") and the Federal Defender and its staff attorneys.

B. "CJA Panel" or "panel" refers to the panels identified in Section X.A of this Plan that, collectively, constitute the CJA Panel, unless otherwise indicated.

C. "Representation services" includes services rendered by appointed counsel, investigators, experts, interpreters, other service providers, including litigation support vendors and expenses.

D. "Federal Defender" includes the Executive Director of Federal Defenders of San Diego, Incorporated, and his or her staff attorneys.

E. "Appropriate Resource Counsel" are experts who may assist the Court in the selection and appointment of counsel in capital cases. See Appendix D, Section III.

F. "Court" refers to the United States District Court for the Southern District of California or the judge presiding over a particular matter.

G. "CJA Supervising Attorney" is an employee designated by the Clerk to assist the Court in the administration of this Plan.

H. "Panel Attorney District Representative" ("PADR") is a member of the CJA Panel who is selected by the Chief Judge to serve as a district representative on the circuit's CJA Panel for the Defender Services, CJA PADR program and local CJA committees.

VI. ADMINISTRATIVE COMPONENTS OF THIS PLAN

A. The Court will administer this Plan, with aspects of this Plan delegated and/or assigned to the Clerk, the CJA Committee, the CJA Criminal Advisory Committee, the CJA Material Witness Advisory Committee, the Criminal Appellate Committee and the CJA Death Penalty Committee as provided herein.

B. The Clerk.

1. The Clerk is delegated and assigned the tasks of managing CJA assignments and duty schedules, as required; maintaining the records of the CJA Plan and implementing its operational procedures and processes, including but not limited to billing policies and procedures and voucher review operations. The Clerk will collaborate with the CJA Committee, the CJA Criminal Advisory Committee, the CJA Material Witness Advisory Committee, and the Federal Defender to ensure the effective and timely provision of representational services to the accused.

2. The Clerk will develop and recommend cost-effective measures for the Court to consider relating to the provision of services in a manner that does not interfere with the panel members' independent function of providing quality representation.

3. The Clerk will maintain current lists of all panel members, their current office addresses, email or other electronic addresses, and telephone numbers, along with records relating to qualifications (including any foreign language proficiency), panel experience, allegations of misconduct, and the Court's action on the same.

4. *The CJA Supervising Attorney.* The CJA Supervising Attorney, through the Clerk of Court, will assist the Clerk and Court in the administration of this Plan. The CJA Supervising Attorney's duties and responsibilities will include: reviewing CJA vouchers and funding requests; processing vouchers and funding requests through delegation by judicial officers; coordinating and collaborating

with the Ninth Circuit CJA Case Budgeting Attorney ("CBA") and/or the National Litigation Support Team Attorney ("NLSTA") regarding case budgeting, preliminary discovery review and any other matters subject to voucher review in multi-defendant and other significant noncapital cases as appropriate; and coordinating and collaborating with the Court's Death Penalty Law Clerk, in addition to consulting with the CBA and/or the NLSTA and assisting the appointed counsel in capital cases regarding case budgeting, preliminary discovery and any other matters subject to voucher review in capital cases; and providing and/or participating in panel training.

C. The CJA Committee.

1. The Chief Judge has appointed a committee consisting of district judges and magistrate judges known as the CJA Committee.

2. One member will be selected by the Chief Judge to serve as its Chair at the discretion of the Chief Judge.

3. The CJA Committee will recommend to the full Court the appointment of attorneys to the CJA Panel, the removal of non-performing panel members, amendments to this Plan that will provide improved representation to the accused, and cost-effective representation and management measures.

4. The district judges will vote on the appointment of attorneys to the CJA panel, the removal of attorneys from the CJA Panel and amendments to this Plan.

5. The Committee will also collaborate and coordinate on matters relating to the implementation of this Plan with the Clerk, the CJA Supervising Attorney, the CJA Criminal Advisory Committee, the CJA Material Witness Advisory Committee, and the Federal Defender as appropriate or as directed by the Chief Judge of the Court.

D. CJA Criminal Defense Advisory Committee.

1. The CJA Criminal Defense Advisory Committee (previously known as the CJA Advisory Committee) has been established by the Court. The Criminal Defense Advisory Committee will be composed of seven experienced CJA panel members selected by the Court, one of whom will be designated by the Court as its Chair.

2. The Court should make a diligent effort to ensure that the composition of this advisory committee reflects the ethnic, racial, gender, and geographic diversity of this district.

3. The CJA Criminal Defense Advisory Committee members will serve a minimum term of four years. The Court may stagger the terms to ensure continuity of experience on the committee.

4. The CJA Criminal Defense Advisory Committee will review and recommend applicants for selection to the CJA Criminal Panel as requested by the CJA Committee and/or the Court.

5. The CJA Criminal Defense Advisory Committee will meet at least twice a year, and at any time the Court requests the committee to consider any issue relating to the administration of the Plan.

6. The CJA Criminal Defense Advisory Committee will collaborate with the Court and the Clerk, through the CJA Supervising Attorney, on appointment protocols, case assignments, and any other matter that will improve the administration of the panel.

7. The CJA Criminal Defense Advisory Committee will coordinate training and continuing education with the Material Witness Advisory Committee, the Federal Defender, the CJA Committee, and the CJA Supervisory Attorney as directed by the Court.

8. The CJA Criminal Defense Advisory Committee will administer a mentor program as directed by the Court and with the assistance of the CJA Supervising Attorney.

E. CJA Material Witness Defense Advisory Committee.

1. The CJA Material Witness Defense Advisory Committee is hereby established by the Court. The Material Witness Advisory Committee will consist of at least three experienced material witness panel members selected by the Court, one of whom will be designated by the Court as its Chair.

2. The Court should make a diligent effort to ensure that the composition of the Material Witness Defense Advisory Committee reflects the ethnic, racial, gender, and geographic diversity of this district.

3. The Material Witness Defense Advisory Committee members will serve a minimum term of two years. The Court may stagger the terms to ensure continuity of experience on the committee.

4. The Material Witness Defense Advisory Committee will review and recommend applicants for selection to the CJA Material Witness Panel as requested by the CJA Committee and/or the Court.

5. The Material Witness Defense Advisory Committee will meet at least twice a year, and at any time the Court requests the committee to consider any issue relating to the administration of the Plan.

6. The Material Witness Defense Advisory Committee will collaborate with the Court and the Clerk, through the CJA Supervising Attorney, on appointment protocols, case assignments, and any other matter that will improve the administration of the Plan.

7. The Material Witness Defense Advisory Committee will coordinate and conduct material witness-specific training with the CJA Committee and the CJA Supervisory Attorney as directed by the Court and attend and participate in continuing legal education training provided by the Federal Defender and the CJA Criminal Advisory Committee as directed by the Court.

F. Criminal Appellate Panel Committee.

1. This Committee is composed of the Federal Defender or designee, the Presiding Magistrate Judge and a District Court Judge.

2. Notices for applications for the panel are published by the Clerk.

3. The Committee will review the applications and present its recommendations for panel selection to the Ninth Circuit Coordinator for Appellate Counsel who makes the final selection of appellate panel members.

G. Capital Case Committee.

1. The Capital Case Committee is composed of the Federal Defender and the appropriate Resource Counsel ("Resource Counsel") and will be activated only when necessary to assist the Court with the appointment of qualified counsel in a capital case.

2. Selection procedures and Counsel Qualifications are contained in Appendix D.

3. Selected panel members will represent defendants charged with or who have received notice that he/she may be charged with, or convicted of, a capital offense but only on the case to which he/she is specifically appointed. See Section X.A.6.

VII. DETERMINATION OF ELIGIBILITY FOR CJA REPRESENTATION

A. Subject Matter Eligibility.

1. *Mandatory:* Representation must be provided for any financially eligible person who:

a. is charged with a felony or with a Class A misdemeanor;

b. is a juvenile alleged to have committed an act of juvenile delinquency as defined in 18 U.S.C. § 5031;

c. is charged with a violation of probation, or faces a revocation, modification or enlargement of a condition, extension, or other adverse change of a term of probation;

d. is charged with a violation of supervised release or faces a revocation, modification, or enlargement of a condition, extension or other adverse change of a term of supervised release;

e. is under arrest, when such representation is required by law;

f. is entitled to appointed counsel in parole proceedings;

g. is subject to a mental condition hearing under Chapter 313 of Title 18, United States Code;

h. is in custody as a material witness;

i. is seeking to set aside or vacate a death sentence or when an evidentiary hearing is warranted in a non-capital proceeding under 28 U.S.C. §§ 2254 or 2255;

j. is entitled to appointment of counsel in verification of consent proceedings pursuant to a transfer of an offender to or from the United States for the execution of penal sentence under 18 U.S.C. § 4109;

k. is otherwise entitled to appointment of counsel under the Sixth Amendment to the Constitution;

l.   is seeking early termination of probation or supervised release; or

m.   faces loss of liberty in a case and federal law requires the appointment of counsel.

2.   *Discretionary.*   Whenever a district judge or magistrate judge determines that the interests of justice so require, representation may be provided for any financially eligible person who:

a.   is charged with a petty offense (Class B or C misdemeanor or an infraction) for which a sentence of confinement is authorized;

b.   is seeking relief under 28 U.S.C. §§ 2241, 2254, 2255 other than to set aside or vacate a death sentence, unless an evidentiary hearing is warranted (see Section VII.A.1.i, *supra*);

c.   is charged with civil or criminal contempt and faces loss of liberty;

d.   has been called as a witness before a grand jury, a court, the Congress, or a federal agency or commission which has the power to compel testimony, and there is reason to believe, either prior to or during testimony, that the witness could be subject to a criminal prosecution, a civil or criminal contempt proceeding or face loss of liberty;

e.   has been advised by the United States Attorney or a law enforcement officer that they are the target of a grand jury investigation;

f.   is proposed by the United States attorney for processing under a pretrial diversion program; or

g.   is held for international extradition under chapter 209 of Title 18, United States Code.

B.   Ancillary Matters.

1.   Representation may also be provided for financially eligible persons in ancillary matters appropriate to the criminal proceedings under 18 U.S.C. § 3006A(c).   In determining whether representation in an ancillary matter is appropriate to the criminal proceedings, the Court should consider whether such representation is reasonably necessary to:

a.   protect a constitutional right;

b.   contribute in some significant way to the defense of the principal criminal charge;

c.   aid in preparation for the trial or disposition of the principal criminal charge;

d.   enforce the terms of a plea agreement in the principal criminal charge;

e.   preserve the claim of the CJA client to an interest in real or personal property subject to civil forfeiture proceeding under 18 U.S.C. § 983, 19 U.S.C. § 1602, 21 U.S.C. § 881, or similar statutes, which property, if recovered by the client, may be considered for reimbursement under 18 U.S.C. § 3006A(f); or

f.   effectuate the return of real or personal property belonging to the CJA client, which may be subject to a motion for return of property under Fed. R. Crim. P. 41(g), which property, if recovered by the client, may be considered for reimbursement under 18 U.S.C. § 3006A(f).

C.   Presentation of Accused for Financial Eligibility Determination—Duties of the Federal Defender.

1.   In cases in which the Federal Defender may be appointed, the office will:

a.   immediately investigate and determine whether an actual or potential conflict exists; and

b.   in the event of an actual or potential conflict, promptly notify the Court to facilitate the timely appointment of other counsel.

2.   When practicable, the Federal Defender will discuss the right to be appointed counsel with the person indicating financial eligibility and, if appointment of counsel seems likely, assist in the completion of a financial affidavit (Form CJA–23) and arrange to have the person promptly presented before a magistrate judge or district judge for determination of financial eligibility and appointment of counsel.

D.   Determination of Financial Eligibility.

1.   In every case where appointment of counsel is authorized under 18 U.S.C. § 3006A(a) and related statutes, the Court must advise the person that he or she has a right to be represented by counsel throughout the case and that, if so desired, counsel will be appointed to represent the person if he or she is financially unable to obtain counsel.

2.   The determination of eligibility for representation under the CJA is a judicial function to be performed by the Court after making appropriate inquiries concerning the person's financial eligibility. Other employees of the Court may be designated to obtain or verify the facts relevant to the financial eligibility determination.

3.   In determining whether a person is "financially unable to obtain counsel," consideration should be given to the cost of providing the person and his or her dependents with the necessities of life, the cost of securing pretrial release, asset encumbrance, and the likely cost of retained counsel.

4.   The initial determination of eligibility must be made without regard to the financial ability of the person's family to retain counsel unless the family indicates a willingness and ability to do so promptly.

5.   Any doubts about a person's eligibility should be resolved in the person's favor. Erroneous determinations of eligibility may be corrected at a later time.

6.   Relevant information bearing on the person's financial eligibility should be reflected on a financial eligibility affidavit approved by the Court (Form CJA–23).

7.   If at any time after appointment of the Federal Defender or panel member, the district judge or magistrate judge finds that the accused is financially able to obtain an attorney, in whole or in part, for legal or other provider services in connection with the representation, the judge may terminate the appointment of the Federal Defender or panel member, order that any funds available to the accused be paid as provided in 18 U.S.C. § 3006A(f), or take other appropriate action including permitting the Federal Defender or panel member to continue to represent the client and order that the client reimburse part or all of the cost of representation to the Government.

8.   If at any stage of the proceedings a judge finds that a person is no longer financially able to pay retained counsel or other representation costs, the judge has discretion, pursuant to 18 U.S.C. § 3006A(c), to authorize appointment and payment for previously retained counsel under the CJA.

   a.   In deciding whether to authorize the appointment, the Court may consider whether retained counsel is a panel member or one who regularly practices in federal court.

   b.   Regarding payment, the Court may inquire into the fees already paid to the retained attorney. Such inquiry may include requiring retained counsel to provide copies of the retainer agreement, billing statements, and a statement of funds actually received from or on behalf of the client.

   c.   The Court may find it appropriate to allow the retained attorney to begin billing under the CJA upon appointment. Alternatively, the Court may appoint the retained attorney Nunc pro tunc to the start of counsel's representation. In the latter scenario, the Court may order that any funds paid to retained counsel be attributed to work performed and costs incurred at the applicable CJA hourly rate until the funds are deemed exhausted. Other equitable arrangements may be appropriate. Once exhausted, counsel and service providers may begin billing under the CJA.

VIII.   TIMELY APPOINTMENT

A.   Appointed counsel must be provided to eligible persons as soon as feasible in the following circumstances, whichever occurs earliest:

1.   after the accused is taken into custody; or

2.   when the accused appears before a magistrate or district court judge; or

3.   when the accused is formally charged or notified of charges if formal charges are sealed; or

4.   when a person receives a target letter; or

5.   when a magistrate or district court judge otherwise considers appointment of counsel appropriate under the CJA or this Plan.

B.   The Court may utilize an "on call" or "duty day" appointment process. CJA attorneys may be appointed to be on call or may be assigned duty days to advise persons who are in custody, or who otherwise may be entitled to counsel, prior to their first appearance.

C.   When practicable, Pretrial Services will provide to the Court information on matters relating to bail.

D. Appointment of counsel may be made retroactive to include representation provided prior to appointment.

E. A person deemed entitled to representation under the CJA will not have the right to select his or her appointed counsel from the attorneys employed by the Federal Defender, the CJA panel, or otherwise.

IX. FEDERAL DEFENDERS OF SAN DIEGO, INC.

A. The Federal Defender, established in this district pursuant to the CJA, is hereby recognized as the Defender Community Organization responsible for rendering defense services upon appointment throughout this district.

B. The Federal Defender should be capable of providing legal services throughout the district and shall maintain offices in San Diego, California and El Centro, California.

C. The Executive Director will be responsible for the supervision and management of the Federal Defender organization. Accordingly, cases assigned to the Federal Defender may be further reassigned, at his/her discretion, to staff attorneys.

D. The Federal Defender must provide high-quality representation consistent with the best practices of the legal profession and commensurate with those services rendered when counsel is privately retained.

E. The Federal Defender will continually monitor the workloads of its staff to ensure high quality representation for all clients.

F. The Federal Defender must conform to the highest standards of professional conduct, including but not limited to the American Bar Association's Model Rules of Professional Conduct, Code of Conduct for Federal Public Defender Employees, Model Code of Conduct for Federal Community Defender Employees, Rules of Professional Conduct for the Bar of the State of California, and this Court's Local Rules.

G. Neither the Federal Defender nor any staff attorney may engage in the private practice of law except as authorized by the Model Code of Conduct for Federal Community Defender Employees.

H. The Federal Defender will continually assess the training needs of his/her staff and, in collaboration and coordination with the Chairs of the CJA Criminal Defense Advisory Committee, the CJA Material Witness Defense Advisory Committee, and the CJA Committee, assess training needs and provide training opportunities and other educational resources to CJA panel members and potential applicants to the panel.

X. ESTABLISHMENT OF THE CJA PANEL

A. The following identified panels are established and will collectively constitute the CJA Panel in this district. Unless otherwise indicated, the use of the word "panel" in this Plan applies to all panel members.

1. *The Criminal Defense Panel.* The panel members will be appointed by the Court to handle misdemeanor cases originating in the San Diego Sector and felony cases in the district.

2. *The El Centro Criminal Defense Panel.* The panel members will be appointed by the Court to handle misdemeanor cases and handle as co-counsel felony cases originating in the El Centro Sector. See Appendix C.

3. *The Material Witness ("MW") Defense Panel.* The panel members will be appointed by the Court to handle all MWs involved in felony cases originating in the District.

4. *The Central Violations Bureau ("CVB") Defense Panel.* The panel members will be appointed by the Court to handle CVB cases originating in the District.

5. *The Criminal Appellate Panel.* Panel members will be appointed to handle all non-capital criminal appeals, except where the pre-conviction panel member has no apparent conflict, has not been granted leave to withdraw or has not been otherwise relieved by the Court. Panel members will not be appointed to handle post-conviction collateral proceedings.

6. *Capital Case Panel.* Counsel appointed to represent defendants charged with, received notice that he/she may be charged with, or convicted of, a capital offense will comprise the Capital Case Panel. The nature and duration of an appointment to this panel is distinguished from an appointment made in noncapital cases. The selection as appointed counsel in a capital case is case-specific. Accordingly, these panel members are not selected for a period of time or for multiple appointments or multiple case assignments, but only for the duration of the case to which he/she is appointed. Once the assigned matter is resolved, the panel member is no longer a panel member and no longer subject to the rules contained in this Plan

B. Size of CJA Panel.

1. The size of the CJA panel will be determined by the Court upon the recommendation of the CJA Committee and in collaboration with the Chairs of the CJA Criminal Defense Advisory Committee and the CJA MW Defense Advisory Committee based on the caseload of panel members and other demands that may negatively impact effective representation.

2. The CJA panel must be large enough to provide a sufficient number of experienced attorneys to handle the CJA caseload, yet small enough so that CJA panel members will receive an adequate number of appointments to maintain their proficiency in federal criminal defense work, thereby enabling them to provide high-quality representation consistent with the best practices of the legal profession.

XI. APPLICATIONS AND QUALIFICATIONS FOR MEMBERSHIP ON THE NONCAPITAL CJA PANELS

A. Application forms for membership on the CJA panels will be available from the Court upon publication of notice regarding the relevant application period, which will be at least once per year. The Court may consider appointment of attorneys to supplement the CJA panel at any time.

B. Qualifications for appointment are set forth in Appendix A.

XII. QUALIFICATIONS FOR APPOINTMENT ON CAPITAL CASES

Qualifications and appointment of counsel to represent defendants that have been charged with, received notice that he/she may be charged with, or been convicted of a capital offense are contained in Appendix D.

XIII. COMPENSATION FOR CJA PANEL MEMBERS

A. Fair compensation to appointed counsel is a critical component of the administration of justice. CJA panel attorneys must be compensated for time expended in court and time reasonably expended out of court and reimbursed for expenses reasonably incurred.

B. The Court will set the compensation rate for panel members at an amount not to exceed compensation limits set by the Judicial Conference and reported in the Guide, Vol. 7A, § 620.60. Compensation rates will be available on the Clerk's website.

C. Unless otherwise provided in this Plan, claims for compensation and other voucher requests must be submitted as provided in Appendices E and F.

XIV. ACCESS TO INVESTIGATIVE, INTERPRETER/TRANSLATOR, EXPERT, AND OTHER REPRESENTATIONAL SERVICES

A. Panel members and the accused will have reasonable access to investigator, interpreter/translator, expert, and other services necessary for an adequate, independent defense.

B. Guidelines for the use of associate and contract counsel deemed necessary for the panel member to provide an adequate and independent defense, and compensation of associate and contract counsel are contained in Appendix B.

C. Unless otherwise provided, requests for authorization of funds for investigative, expert, and other necessary services must be submitted as provided in this Plan. See Appendices E and F.

D. The hourly rates and statutory maximums per case for investigators, interpreters/translators, experts, and all other service providers deemed necessary for an adequate and independent defense will be set by the Court based upon the availability of resources and skills set of similar provider-types within the district and based upon the needs of this district. The compensation may be subject to future adjustments by the Court. Compensation rates will be available on the Clerk's website.

XV. APPOINTMENT AND CASE ASSIGNMENT IN NON–CAPITAL CASES

A. Panel Membership Is a Privilege—Not a Right. The appointment of applicants to the CJA panel, their subsequent case assignments, and the procedures and responsibilities contained in this Plan do not create a property interest in being a member of or remaining on the CJA panel. Appointment to the panel is a matter of privilege and not of right, and the Court may remove a panel member at any time.

B. Appointment Procedures.

1. The Court, through the Clerk, is responsible for overseeing the appointment of cases to panel members and the Federal Defender. The Court will maintain a record of panel member appointments and, as deemed appropriate, data reflecting the apportionment of appointments between the Federal Defender and panel members.

2. The appointment of cases to panel members and the Federal Defender will ordinarily be made on a rotational basis. In a complex or otherwise difficult case, the Court may appoint counsel outside the normal rotation to ensure the defendant has sufficiently experienced counsel.

3. In addition to the rotational appointment process, the Court may utilize at its discretion an "on call" or "duty day" assignment/appointment process based upon the needs of the district.

4. The Court has the discretion to determine the manner and means of appointing newly selected panel members in the CJA rotation.

C. Number of Counsel in a Non–Capital Case.

1. In most cases, only one panel attorney will be appointed to represent a client.

2. The Court may appoint more than one attorney to represent a single client based upon (1) the nature of the charges brought or contemplated against an accused, (2) the geographic location of the accused within the Southern District, and/or (3) other considerations making the case extremely difficult as determined by the Court.

D. Apportionment of Cases.

1. Where practical, the assignment of cases will be apportioned between the panel members the Federal Defender as determined by the Court upon consultation with the Federal Defender and the CJA Criminal Defense Committee.

2. The Court may exercise discretion to permit an individual panel member, upon request, be appointed to less than a proportional number of cases than otherwise assigned to panel members.

XVI. REAPPOINTMENT OF CJA PANEL MEMBERS IN NON–CAPITAL CASES

A. A panel member who wishes to be considered for reappointment must apply for appointment to an additional term prior to the expiration of his or her current term. Applicants seeking reappointment will compete with all applicants for selection.

B. Panel members must satisfy the applicable duties and responsibilities set forth in Section XX and the training requirements and conditions set forth in Section XXI of this Plan.

C. The CJA Committee will solicit recommendations from the CJA Supervising Attorney, the CJA Criminal Defense Advisory Committee and the CJA MW Defense Advisory Committee concerning the quality of representation and performance of lawyers seeking reappointment.

XVII. TERMS OF CJA PANEL MEMBERS IN NON–CAPITAL CASES

A. Panel members will serve a term of two years, generally beginning with appointments on or after December each year, with the opportunity to reapply for successive terms. Such service shall at all times be at the pleasure of the Court.

B. The terms of panel members may be staggered to facilitate continuity of high-quality and experienced representation on the panel.

XVIII. REMOVAL OR SUSPENSION FROM THE CJA PANEL

A. By the Court. Notwithstanding the provisions in Section XIX, a panel member may be suspended or removed from the panel prior to expiration of his or her term whenever the Court so determines it is clear the representation is resulting in immediate harm to a client or otherwise necessary to ensure the effective representation of accused persons.

B. Mandatory Removal. Any panel member who is suspended or disbarred from the practice of law by the state court before whom such member is admitted, the bar of this Court, or any federal court will be removed from the CJA panel immediately.

C. Automatic Disciplinary Review. The CJA Committee will conduct an automatic disciplinary review of any CJA panel member against whom any licensing authority, grievance committee, or administrative body has taken any adverse action, including but not limited to contempt, sanction, or a reprimand against the panel member. The panel member will receive notice and have an opportunity to be heard. The CJA Committee will recommend appropriate action to the full Court.

D. Notification. The panel member, the CJA Criminal Defense Advisory Committee or the CJA MW Defense Advisory Committee, as appropriate, and the Clerk of Court will be immediately notified when a panel member is removed or suspended.

E. Removal from a Case. A panel member may be removed from an individual case if the judge presiding over the matter deems it necessary in the interest of justice.

XIX. COMPLAINTS

A. Purpose. To ensure the proper administration of justice, civility and the adherence to the Standards and Professional Conduct referred to in Section XX.A, *infra*, the Court adopts the following procedures to provide a clear avenue of redress relating to allegations of misconduct and/or unprofessional conduct associated with the performance of duties proscribed in this Plan.

B. Initiation. A complaint concerning performance or misconduct of a panel member, an attorney employed by the Federal Defender, associate or contract counsel (hereafter, "the attorney") may be initiated by any concerned individual and should be directed to the Chair of the CJA Committee. Complaints must be in writing and state the alleged misconduct or deficiency with specificity. The CJA Committee will determine whether further investigation is necessary.

C. Concerned individuals include clients, family members of clients, judges, prosecutors, fellow panel members and staff members of the USAO, the Federal Defender, U.S. Pretrial Services, U.S. Probation, the United States Marshal Service, any detention facility, the Clerk or the Court's staff.

D. Notice. Upon receiving a written complaint, the CJA Committee will notify the attorney and the Chief District Judge of the specific allegations and will advise the attorney whether it has commenced an investigation or dismissed the complaint. Written complaints alleging deficient performance or misconduct against an attorney employed by the Federal Defender will be referred to the Federal Defender for investigation and all follow-up actions.

E. Response. An attorney under review may be asked to respond in writing and appear before the CJA Committee or may request to do so.

F. Protective Action. Prior to deciding the matter, the CJA Committee may recommend the attorney's suspension or removal from any pending case, or removal from the CJA Panel, and may take any other protective action that is in the best interest of the attorney's clients, individuals involved or the administration of this Plan.

G. Investigation. Any investigation undertaken by the CJA Committee will be concluded within forty-five days (45) days of receiving the initial complaint. Should the investigation need to continue beyond this prescribed period, the CJA Committee must notify both the attorney and the Chief District Judge in writing.

H. The CJA Committee may in its discretion delegate the responsibility of conducting the investigation to the CJA Criminal Defense Committee or CJA MW Defense Committee, as appropriate. The CJA Committee will make every effort to avoid conflicts of interests.

I. Review and Recommendation. After investigation and review, the CJA Committee may recommend closing the matter with no further action or may recommend appropriate remedial action, including:

1. removing the attorney from the panel permanently or temporarily;

2. limiting the attorney's participation to certain categories of cases;

3. directing the attorney to complete specific training requirements before receiving further panel appointments;

4. limiting the attorney's participation to handling cases that are directly supervised or overseen by another panel member or other experienced practitioner or assigning a mentor;

5. directing the attorney to attend counseling for substance abuse issues; or

6. any other appropriate remedial action.

J. Oversight of Remedial Action. Should the CJA Committee recommend any remedial action on the part of the attorney, the CJA Committee will establish, in its recommendation to the Chief District Judge, a plan for overseeing completion of conditions for full panel reinstatement.

K. Final Disposition by the Court. The CJA Committee will forward its recommendation to the Chief District Judge for consideration and final disposition. The Chief District Judge will communicate a final disposition in writing to the attorney, the CJA Committee, and the CJA Criminal Defense Committee or CJA Material Witness Defense Committee, as appropriate.

L. Confidentiality. Information acquired concerning complaints and potential disciplinary action will remain confidential unless otherwise directed by the Court or required by applicable ethical standards.

M. The Clerk will retain records, under seal, of complaints against attorneys and actions thereon for a period of five years, unless otherwise ordered by the Court.

XX.   PANEL MEMBER DUTIES

A.   Standards and Professional Conduct.

1. Panel members must provide high-quality representation consistent with the best practices of the legal profession.

2. Panel members must conform to the highest standards of professional conduct, including but not limited to the local rules and general orders of this Court, the California Rules of Professional Conduct, and other standards for professional conduct adopted by the Court. Such conduct includes being accessible to clients and exercising civility in interactions with the client, opposing parties, and the Court.

3. Within ten days, panel members must notify the Chair of the CJA Committee and the CJA Supervising Attorney when any state or federal court, licensing authority, grievance committee, or administrative body has taken action against the panel member by issuing a finding of contempt, sanction, or reprimand.

B. Waiver of All Claims. Except for claims that may be permitted by the Federal Tort Claims Act, panel members will waive and hold harmless all claims against the United States, its officers, employees, and the court-appointed members of any committee identified in this Plan resulting from participation in the administration of the provisions of this Plan.

C. Discovery Produced Via Protective Order. Panel members will return to the government or the judge presiding over the case all discovery produced by stipulation and/or protective order pursuant to the terms of said stipulation or order unless otherwise ordered by the Court. Where the panel member reasonably believes that certain requested discovery material must be maintained by counsel after the conclusion of the case, the matter should be brought to the court's attention at the time of the request for such material.

D.   Use of Qualified Service Providers.

1. Panel members will engage only qualified service providers.

2. Panel members have a duty to ensure the service provider is certified or licensed as required by his/her trade or profession and is otherwise in good standing with the certification or licensing agency.

3. Panel members should carefully review and revise the service providers' bills and records to ensure that the amount billed is accurate and reasonable.

E. Record Keeping. Panel members must maintain contemporaneous time and expense records for all work performed by associates, contract lawyers, paralegals, support staff, and other service providers in a manner consistent with Appendix H. Such records may be subject to audit and must be maintained for three years after approval of the final voucher.

F. Case Budgeting. In non-capital representations that involve unusual complexity and/or voluminous discovery and are likely to become extraordinary in terms of cost, panel members should consult with the CJA Supervising Attorney and/or the CBA and comply with budgeting directives in a manner consistent with in Appendix F.

G. Adherence to the Rules Supporting this Plan. Panel members are bound by the provisions of this Plan and any and all revisions and appendices to this Plan.

H. Material Breach. The Court's decision that there has been a material breach of a duty or other provision of this Plan may result in suspension or removal from the CJA panel.

XXI. TRAINING AND CONTINUING LEGAL EDUCATION (CLE)

A. The Court may require panel members with limited federal criminal practice to attend post-selection training conducted by the Federal Defender, the CJA Criminal Defense Advisory Committee and/or the CJA MW Defense Advisory Committee on federal criminal law and procedure, including related areas of law such as immigration law, as a condition to the receipt of case assignments/appointments. The training must be completed according to the timeframe and any other conditions set by the Court.

B. Appointed counsel is expected to remain current with developments in federal criminal law, practice, and procedure, along with the Recommendations for Electronically Stored Information Discovery Production in Federal Criminal Cases ("ESI Protocol").

C. Appointed counsel is expected to attend training sponsored by the Federal Defender as otherwise required by the Court.

D. Appointed counsel must participate annually in at least five hours of CLE relevant to federal criminal practice, including but not limited to federal criminal procedure and practice, federal sentencing law and procedure, and immigration consequences relating to federal criminal practice.

E. CLE must be completed by August 1 of each calendar year. Evidence of annual written CLE certification(s) must be submitted by each panel member to the Chair of the CJA Committee, through the Clerk of Court, by November 15 of each calendar year. Panel members must include evidence of compliance within an application to be re-appointed to the CJA Panel.

XXII. MENTOR PROGRAM

Newly appointed panel members may be required to participate in a mentor program directed or approved by the Court. Experienced panel members will be selected to serve as mentors to newly appointed panel members for a period of time determined by the Court.

XXIII. NO DUAL ENGAGEMENTS

No appointed counsel may require, request, or accept any payment, promise of payment or other consideration for the representation of a defendant for whom he/she is appointed, unless such payment is approved by order of the Court.

APPENDIX A

QUALIFICATIONS FOR APPOINTMENT (NON–CAPITAL CJA PANELS)

I. Applicants for the CJA panel must be members in good standing with the State Bar of California, United States District Court for the Southern District of California, and the Ninth Circuit Court of Appeals.

II. Applicants must maintain a primary or satellite office in the Southern District of California.

III. Applicants must demonstrate strong litigation skills and experience representing persons charged with serious criminal offenses and demonstrate a commitment to the defense of individuals who lack the financial means to hire an attorney, AND

A. Applicants for the CJA Criminal Defense Panel must:

1. Have practiced felony criminal law at least four (4) years in the United States District Court and demonstrated strong litigation skills and proficiency with the Federal Sentencing Guidelines, Bail Reform Act, Federal Rules of Criminal Procedure, and Federal Rules of Evidence; OR

2. Have for the last two (2) preceding years practiced for and been employed by either:

(a) The criminal division of the Office of the United States Attorney in any federal judicial district; or

(b) Federal Defenders of San Diego, Inc. or another federal community or public defender office in any federal judicial district; OR

3. Have practiced criminal law at least four (4) years in a court of competent jurisdiction; and in the last two (2) years have second-chaired an attorney in the United States District Court in:

(a) Two felony trials; and

(b) Four sentencing hearings in which the United States Sentencing Guidelines were applied; OR

4. Have for the last four (4) preceding years, the last two (2) years of which involved the prosecution or defense of felony cases, been employed by either:

(a) A county or state district attorney's office or other prosecutor's office in any state, or

(b) A county or state public defender's office in any state, and

(c) Have demonstrated that his/her criminal practice involved significant immigration-related consequences that impacted litigation strategy, disposition, and/or sentencing; OR

5. Have practiced criminal law for at least four (4) years in a court of competent jurisdiction; and

(a) Have for the last two (2) preceding years attained and maintained at least a Level III criminal attorney certification/eligibility rating, as established by the San Diego County District Attorney, the San Diego County Public Defender, the San Diego Office of the Alternate Public Defender, or equivalent, and

(b) Have demonstrated that his/her criminal practice involved significant immigration-related consequences that impacted litigation strategy, disposition, and/or sentencing.

B. Applicants for the CJA Material Witness Defense Panel must:

1. Have at least two (2) years of experience in the prosecution and/or defense of felony criminal cases;

2. Have demonstrated that his/her criminal practice involved immigration-related consequences that impacted litigation strategy, disposition, and/or sentencing; and

3. Have demonstrated that he/she has practice experience with the deposition practice in civil or criminal court.

C. Applicants for the CJA Central Violations Bureau (CVB) Panel must:

1. Have at least two (2) years of experience in the prosecution and/or defense of misdemeanor cases; OR

2. Have at least two (2) years as a Commissioned Officer, a Non–Commissioned Officer, or service in the military police or criminal investigation personnel in the U.S. Armed Services.

IV. Applicants who do not possess the above experience but believe they have other equivalent experience are encouraged to apply and provide in writing the details of that experience for the Court's consideration.

V. The Court may authorize limited exceptions to the qualification provisions of this Plan in a manner that fits the needs of this district, provides effective delivery of representation services while protecting the independence of the defense function, and gives due consideration to the unique nature of criminal litigation in this district or particular representation type.

VI.   Post-selection training and practice requirements will be imposed for selectees having limited federal experience.   See Section XXI.A of the Plan.

APPENDIX B

ASSOCIATE AND CONTRACT COUNSEL (USE AND COMPENSATION)

I.   The Court expends considerable effort in identifying and selecting experienced, qualified attorneys to provide quality representation to federal indigent defendants.   To that end, the Court has a vested interest in ensuring associate and contract counsel can adequately assist panel members in providing quality representation to clients.

II.   An "associate counsel" is defined as an attorney who is a partner in or employee of the panel member's law firm.   A "contract attorney" is defined as an attorney who is not a partner or employee of the panel member's law firm.

III.   Panel members are encouraged to use associate and contract attorneys who are not panel members to reduce costs where the panel members' expertise is not required, such as for legal research and docket review, preliminary discovery review, or non-substantive court appearances. However, the panel members' expertise is required relative to all substantive work, including in-court hearings (except for status hearings or requests to continue); plea negotiations; advisement relating to a plea offer; and handling the plea hearing, the probation interview, the safety valve/substantial assistance interview, and sentencing.

IV.   Prior authorization is required for use of associate and contract counsel as provided in Appendix E.   The panel member should present sufficient information to permit the court to consider the necessity of the service, the work to be assigned, the proposed attorney's experience, and an appropriate hourly rate.

V.   The panel member should develop a plan to divide responsibilities among the contract or associate counsel and panel member so that each is performing duties effectively and efficiently, thereby avoiding unnecessary duplication of effort.

   A.   While meetings may be needed to effectively divide responsibilities and to coordinate efforts, the panel member should also avoid unnecessary conferences.   In–person meetings are compensable if the frequency and time billed are reasonable given the needs of a case, but the panel member should always assess the need for a meeting in advance and consider whether the purpose of the meeting could be served equally by a conference call or other electronic transmission.

   B.   The associate and contract counsel may be compensated for reasonable time conferring with the panel member.

   C.   Prior approval must be obtained from the judge presiding over the case for an associate or contract counsel to appear in Court as a compensated second chair.   Reasonable notice must be provided to allow the court to rule on the necessity of the associate or contract counsel's participation without delaying the proceeding.

VI.   The compensatory services of associate and contract counsel and that of the panel member, in combination, may not exceed the maximum case-related rate for the case or the amount preauthorized as provided in the Plan.

VII.   The compensatory services of associate and contract counsel may not be billed as an expense of the panel member.   eVoucher forms CJA–20 and CJA–30 should be used to bill these services. Such vouchers must be submitted at the same time as the panel member for the same billing period.

VIII.   The Court will set the compensation for associate counsel and contract counsel pursuant to an experience-based, hourly rate schedule that will be subject to proportionate adjustment based upon any future change to the hourly rates of panel members.   Compensation rates will be available on the Clerk's website.

IX.   An associate or contract attorney who is also a panel member may be engaged to perform substantive work, as described herein, and will be permitted to bill at the normal CJA panel rate.

APPENDIX C

PROCEDURES FOR CRIMINAL CASES IN THE EL CENTRO SECTOR

The following procedures will apply in connection with the appointment of CJA counsel and the Federal Defender in criminal cases originating in the El Centro sector of this District:

I.   CJA CRIMINAL DEFENSE COUNSEL

A.   On the first appearance of a defendant charged with a misdemeanor and a felony or with a felony offense or offenses in the El Centro United States District Courthouse, in cases where the Federal Defender is not appointed, the magistrate judge will appoint both CJA Lead Counsel from the San Diego sector ("Lead Counsel") and CJA Co-counsel from the El Centro sector ("Co–counsel") to represent the defendant. Lead Counsel with work cooperatively with Co-counsel on these cases.

B.   It will be the responsibility of Lead Counsel to evaluate the charges and evidence against the defendant, advise the defendant regarding the case, and counsel the defendant regarding any plea offer. While the case is pending in El Centro, Lead Counsel is strongly encouraged to avoid travel to El Centro in connection with these responsibilities or other preliminary court proceeding.

C.   Following the defendant's first appearance, Lead Counsel is strongly encouraged to delegate to Co-counsel all preliminary appearances on behalf of the defendant in the El Centro United States District Courthouse, including but not limited to the preliminary hearing, a hearing to waive indictment or to arraign the defendant on the indictment, any bail, status, or detention hearing, and any change of plea hearing. Lead Counsel is also strongly encouraged to communicate with the defendant by video conference and telephone where feasible, with Co-counsel physically visiting the client in Lead Counsel's stead, when the defendant is not housed in San Diego County.

D.   Lead counsel may not utilize contract or in-house associates to travel to El Centro but must instead utilize Co-counsel for any work in El Centro not performed directly by Lead Counsel.

E.   Lead Counsel will continue to represent the defendant and make all appearances on behalf of the defendant upon the transfer of the defendant's case to the San Diego United States District Courthouse. Co–counsel will have limited ongoing involvement upon transfer of the defendant's case to the San Diego United States District Courthouse.

F.   For a defendant charged only with a misdemeanor offense in the El Centro sector of this District, the magistrate judge will appoint counsel from the El Centro sector or the Federal Defender to represent the defendant as the defendant's sole counsel.

II.   INTERPRETERS AND OTHER SERVICE PROVIDERS

A.   To minimize travel costs, panel members (CJA Criminal Defense Counsel and CJA MW Counsel) must make reasonable efforts to retain the services of interpreters and other service providers from the El Centro sector where the proposed services are to be performed, if such providers are reasonably available. It is anticipated that interpreters or other service providers will not travel to El Centro in connection with any interview, investigation, or other proceeding.

B.   Interpreters and other service providers will not be reimbursed for travel to El Centro without prior approval by the CJA Supervising Attorney, upon a showing of good cause. To the extent such travel is approved, the travel rate shall be no more than fifty dollars ($50) an hour.

APPENDIX D

APPOINTMENT OF COUNSEL AND CASE MANAGEMENT IN CAPITAL CASES

I.   CAPITAL CASES.

For purposes of this plan, "capital cases" are those involving the death penalty and include: (1) prosecutions under any provision of federal law carrying a potential penalty of death; (2) direct appeals from cases wherein the death penalty was imposed by a federal court; (3) post-conviction proceedings in which an individual sentenced to death by a federal court is seeking to set aside or vacate the conviction or sentence under 28 U.S.C. § 2255; and (4) habeas corpus proceedings in which an individual sentenced to death by a state court is seeking to set aside or vacate the conviction or sentence under 28 U.S.C. § 2254. As such, the provisions of this Appendix apply to all capital cases whether originating in state court or a United States District Court.

II. APPLICABLE LEGAL AUTHORITY

The appointment and compensation of counsel in capital cases and the authorization and payment of persons providing investigative, expert, and other services are governed by 18 U.S.C. §§ 3005, 3006A, and 3599; the CJA Guidelines, Ch. 6; the Ninth Circuit CJA Policies and Procedures and CivLR HC. 3(d).

III. UTILIZATION OF THE DEATH PENALTY RESOURCE COUNSEL PROJECTS

A. For assistance with the selection and appointment of counsel, case budgeting, and legal, practical and other matters arising in federal capital cases, the Court will rely on the death penalty expert services available through the Administrative Office of United States Courts Defender Services Death Penalty Resource Counsel projects. The resource counsel projects include: 1) Federal Death Penalty Resource Counsel and Capital Resource Counsel Projects (for federal capital trials); 2) Federal Capital Appellate Resource Counsel Project; 3) Federal Capital Habeas Section 2255 Project; and 4) National and Regional Habeas Assistance and Training Counsel Projects (Section 2254).

B. The appropriate resource counsel to be consulted depends upon the nature of the case or representation-type. As such, the appropriate resource counsel project will be involved in a given case.

C. Pursuant to Section VI.G of the Plan, the appropriate resource counsel project will be a member of the Capital Case Committee to assist the Court with the particular appointment.

IV. COUNSEL QUALIFICATIONS

A. The Court should ensure that all attorneys appointed in federal death penalty cases must:

1. be well qualified as demonstrated by their training, commitment to the defense of capital cases, and distinguished prior criminal defense experience;

2. meet the minimum experience standards set forth in 18 U.S.C. § 3599(b)–(d), 18 U.S.C. § 3005, and other applicable laws as well as any applicable Ninth Circuit rules;

3. have sufficient time and resources to devote to the representation, considering their current caseload and the extraordinary demands of a capital case; and

4. meet all applicable guidelines adopted by the American Bar Association and other legal organizations regarding the quality of legal representation in capital cases;

B. In trial-level capital cases requiring the appointment of "learned counsel," such counsel must meet the minimum standards in 18 U.S.C. §§ 3005 and 3599(b) or (d). Learned counsel should have distinguished prior criminal defense experience in the trial, appeal, or post-conviction review of federal or state death-penalty cases that, in combination with co-counsel, will assure high-quality representation.

C. In direct appeals and post-conviction proceedings under 18 U.S.C. §§ 2254 or 2255, appointed counsel must meet the minimum standards required by 18 U.S.C. § 3599(c) or (d) and should have distinguished prior criminal defense experience in federal criminal appeals, capital appeals, federal post- conviction proceedings, or capital post-conviction proceedings.

D. Out–of–district counsel, including a Federal Defender, who possess the requisite expertise may be considered for appointment in capital cases to achieve high-quality representation.

E. An attorney furnished by a state or local public defender organization or a private, non-profit organization to represent a person charged with a capital crime or seeking federal capital habeas corpus relief may be appointed if the attorney is a fully qualified Federal Defender, CJA panel attorney or an attorney appointed pro hac vice. See 18 U.S.C. § 3006A(a)(3).

F. "Distinguished prior criminal defense experience" contemplates excellence, not simply prior experience.

V. APPOINTMENT OF COUNSEL

A. Recommendation of Capital Case Committee

1. When appointing counsel, the Court must consider the recommendation of the Capital Case Committee relating to qualified counsel.

2. The Capital Case Committee will submit a Report and Recommendation ("Report") providing the nature and extent of the search effort, the candidates' experience, the candidates' availability to handle the matter and other distinct reasons supporting the recommendations. The Report will be filed under seal for the Court's review.

3. When practicable, given the high demand for qualified counsel, the Report should contain at least two qualified candidates.

4. The Court should consider and give due weight to the recommendations made in the Report of vetted, qualified counsel and articulate reasons for not doing so.

5. The Court may consider other qualified candidates having the requisite experience and availability to handle the matter. Under 18 U.S.C. § 3599(d), the Court, for good cause, may appoint an attorney who may not qualify under 18 U.S.C. § 3599(b) or (c) but who has the background, knowledge, and experience necessary to represent the defendant properly in a capital case, giving due consideration to the seriousness of the possible penalty and the unique and complex nature of the litigation. Such appointments should be made after consultation with the Capital Case Committee.

B. Trial Counsel

1. The appointment of qualified capital trial counsel must occur as soon as practicable after a defendant is charged with a federal criminal offense where the penalty of death is possible.

2. To protect the rights of an individual who, although not charged, is the subject of an investigation in a federal death-eligible case, the Court may appoint capitally qualified counsel upon request, consistent with these provisions.

3. At the outset of every capital case, the Court must appoint two attorneys, at least one of whom meets the qualifications for "learned counsel" as described above.

C. Direct Appeals

1. Counsel representing a death-sentenced federal appellant should include at least one attorney who did not represent the appellant at trial.

2. Each trial counsel who withdraws should be replaced with similarly qualified counsel to represent the defendant on appeal.

3. Out–of–district counsel, including a Federal Defender, who possess the requisite expertise may be considered for appointment in capital appeals to achieve high quality representation together with other efficiencies.

4. Appellate counsel, between them, should have distinguished prior experience in federal criminal appeals.

5. At least one of the attorneys appointed must have the requisite background, knowledge, and experience required by 18 USC § 3599(c) or (d).

D. Post–Conviction Proceedings

1. In any post-conviction proceeding under 18 U.S.C. §§ 2255 or 2254, the Court must appoint at least one qualified attorney and may consider appointing at least two attorneys given the complex, demanding, and protracted nature of death penalty proceedings.

2. For § 2255 proceedings, appointment should take place, if possible, prior to denial of certiorari on direct appeal by the United States Supreme Court.

3. For § 2254 proceedings, appointment should take place at the earliest time permissible by law to permit federal counsel to avail themselves of the full statute-of-limitations period to prepare a petition.

VI. APPOINTMENT EXTENDS THROUGH ALL PROCEEDINGS

A. The appointment of counsel in capital cases extends "throughout every subsequent stage of judicial proceedings" as defined in 18 U.S.C. § 3599(e) and the Guide, Vol. 7A, § 620.70

B.   Appointed Counsel in a capital case will be considered a member of the Capital Case Panel in the district during the course of the appointment.

VII.   DISCRETION TO APPOINT THE FEDERAL DEFENDER.

Notwithstanding any provision herein and absent a conflict of interest, the Court is not precluded from the consideration and the appointment of an otherwise qualified Federal Defender.

VIII.   COMPENSATION

A.   Statutory maxima do not apply in the defense of capital cases.

B.   The Court will set the compensation rate at an amount not to exceed compensation limits set by the Judicial Conference and reported in the Guide, Vol. 7A, § 620.60.   In the interest of justice and in furtherance of relevant statutory provisions regarding qualifications of counsel in capital cases, the Court should compensate counsel at a rate sufficient to ensure adequate compensation.

IX.   BUDGETING AND SERVICE PROVIDER RESOURCES

A.   All capital cases, unless staffed only by a Federal Defender, must be budgeted.

B.   As early as practicable after appointment, the Court, CJA Supervisory Attorney, CBA and/or the NLSTA must discuss with appointed counsel the preparation and submission of a budget that will be subject to modification in light of facts and developments that emerge as the case proceeds.

C.   The budget should be prepared with the assistance of the CJA Supervisory Attorney, the CBA and/or NLSTA.

D.   Appointed Counsel will consult regularly with the district's CJA Supervising Attorney, the CBA and the appropriate Resource Counsel.

E.   Questions concerning the appointment and compensation of additional counsel and the authorization and payment of investigative, expert, and other service providers in capital cases may be directed to The CJA Supervisory Attorney, CBA and/or NLSLTA, or to the appropriate Federal Resource Counsel or the AO Defender Services Office, Legal and Policy Division Duty Attorney.

F.   The budgeting process should be guided by § III of the Criminal Justice Act Policies and Procedures adopted by the Judicial Council of the Ninth Circuit and those set forth in the Guide, Vol. 7A, §§ 640.20–40.

X.   OTHER PROVISIONS APPLY

Any and all provisions of the Plan, not specifically designated as applicable to non-capital CJA only, applies to appointed counsel in capital cases.

APPENDIX E
VOUCHER AUTHORIZATION ADMINISTRATION AND REVIEW
I.   eVOUCHER REQUIRED.

All claims for compensation should be submitted electronically through the CJA eVoucher system on the appropriate CJA eVoucher form.   Counsel's requests for preauthorization, claims for compensation, and supporting documentation, as well as the Court's approval, modification, or rejection of the same should be entered and maintained on eVoucher to facilitate transparency of all eVoucher-related operations, procedures, and decisions.

II.   PREAUTHORIZATION OF ATTORNEY FEES

A.   Panel members must utilize the CJA–26 form in eVoucher to request preauthorization of attorney fees in cases anticipated to exceed the statutory maximum and cases subject to budgeting.

To aid district court and circuit review of a preauthorization request, panel members should utilize the Clerk's Request for Excess Compensation ("REC") form to be attached to the CJA–26 that will include documentation to support the request.

B.   Associate and contract attorney services anticipated to be in excess of eight hours require prior authorization.   In seeking prior authorization, counsel should utilize the Clerk's REC form to be attached to the CJA–26 that will include the nature of and the necessity for the service, the experience level of the attorney, the hourly rate requested, and the estimated number of hours to complete the anticipated task.

III.   PREAUTHORIZATION OF SERVICE PROVIDER FEES

A.   Title 18 U.S.C., Section 3006A(e)(2) and Ninth Circuit policy requires preauthorization of service provider fees in excess of the statutory maximum.   In the rare instance preauthorization is not feasible, counsel must attach supporting justification to the voucher to aid circuit review of nunc pro tunc requests.

B.   Panel attorneys must utilize the eVoucher AUTH form to request preauthorization of fees for any service provider type anticipated to exceed the statutory maximum.

C.   When seeking prior approval, counsel must indicate the necessity for the service, the hourly rate requested for the provider, and the estimated number of hours to complete the anticipated task.

D.   To aid circuit review of a preauthorization request, counsel should utilize the Clerk's Service Provider Funding Request form ("AUTH form") to be attached to the AUTH in eVoucher that will include a resume/CV, any applicable license and case budgeting documentation to support the request.

IV.   PREAUTHORIZATION OF SERVICES PERFORMED BY RELATIVES.

Panel attorneys must utilize the AUTH form in eVoucher to request preauthorization of fees for service providers who are relatives and who are not associates in counsel's law firm.   When seeking such approval, counsel must indicate the nature of the relationship, the necessity for the services of the provider, the experience of the provider, the hourly rate charged, and the estimated number of hours to complete the anticipated task.

V.   WHEN PRIOR APPROVED HOURS ARE CONSIDERED INSUFFICIENT TO COMPLETE THE ASSIGNED TASK

A.   If counsel obtains preauthorization and it later becomes apparent that the cost will exceed the initially approved amount, requests for additional compensation must be authorized by the Court before any further service is provided.

B.   Nunc pro tunc requests will be considered only upon good cause, such as when a task not previously contemplated required immediate action.

VI.   PREAUTHORIZATION FOR INTERIM VOUCHERS

A.   Panel members must utilize the CJA–26 form in eVoucher to request preauthorization to submit interim vouchers in extended or complex representations.   The Court may authorize the submission of interim vouchers upon good cause as to the unique particulars of the case.   Interim vouchers may also be authorized via a budget prepared with the Ninth Circuit CJA Case Budgeting Attorney ("CBA").

B.   The Court will review for approval all interim vouchers requesting payment of fees in excess of the statutory maximum for cases in which the circuit reviewing judge or designee has approved a budget, a request to exceed the statutory maximum for attorney fees (CJA–26), or a preauthorization for service provider fees.   Only the final payment voucher will be submitted for review and approval by the circuit reviewing judge or designee.

C.   Interim vouchers that do not exceed the preauthorized maximum will not be sent to the circuit for review unless otherwise directed by the circuit reviewing judge or designee.

D. In cases where the circuit reviewing judge or designee has not approved a preauthorization request to exceed the case compensation maximum for attorney fees, the Court will submit all approved interim payment vouchers to the circuit for review once the statutory maximum is exceeded. To aid district court and circuit review, counsel should utilize the Clerk's REC form to be attached to the CJA–26 that will justify the excess costs.

VII. DEADLINE FOR VOUCHER SUBMISSION

A. Final vouchers should be submitted no later than 90 days after the filing of the judgment and commitment order or other disposition. Counsel is required to submit associate counsel vouchers on the same CJA–20 form. Counsel is required to submit contract counsel vouchers on a separate CJA–20 at the same time as his or her own voucher. Counsel is encouraged, but not required, to submit service providers at the same time as his or her own voucher. Counsel is responsible for advising and encouraging service providers to abide by this voucher submission requirement.

B. Given that panel members handle a significant volume of criminal matters in this district, vouchers submitted up to one year after the case terminates may be approved if good cause is shown.

C. Counsel must obtain prior court authorization before submitting a voucher over one year after the case terminates. Counsel should submit a motion and declaration attached to the CJA–26 that demonstrates good cause for the untimely submission. The Court will make the decision on the request. In the event the Court approves the request, counsel can submit the CJA–20 voucher. When submitting such a request, counsel undertakes a serious risk of not being paid for the representation.

VIII. VOUCHER REVIEW

A. The Clerk's Voucher Review Staff ("VRS") will review all voucher submissions for mathematical accuracy and technical compliance with the CJA Guidelines and the Ninth Circuit CJA Policies and Procedures as adopted in this Plan. The VRS may reduce or increase the amount payable to reflect a correction to a mathematical or technical error.

B. Authority to approve vouchers submitted to the Court for payment pursuant to 18 U.S.C. §§ 3006A(d)(5) and 3599(a)1), (f) and (g), including those submitted for investigator, interpreter, expert, or other provider services, is delegated to the VRS subject to the following restrictions:

1. The VRS should not reduce or increase the amount payable for any reason other than to reflect a correction to a mathematical or technical error.

2. The total attorney fees claimed for a panel member's representation including associate or contract counsel must be equal to or less than $3,500.00 per criminal representation or $1,000.00 per material witness, supervised release, and/or Central Violations Bureau ("CVB") representation.

3. The total amount claimed for investigator, interpreter, expert, or other service provider types must be equal to or less than $1,600.00, excluding expenses, per provider type (not per provider).

4. The Court, upon periodic review of the delegated threshold amounts contained herein, may exercise its discretion to increase the delegated threshold amounts for the purpose of enhancing efficiencies, considering the caseload, staff resources and other demands that negatively impact effective monitoring and review of vouchers.

C. The CJA Supervising Attorney is delegated the authority to:

1. Review, approve, reduce, or deny any voucher or request for panel member compensation and/or any service provider services submitted in which

a. the VRS identifies a reasonableness or other question on matters within its delegated authority, or

b. the claimed amount exceeds the thresholds identified in Section VIII.B, *supra*.

2. Review, approve, reduce, or deny any requests for preauthorization required by this Plan, including but not limited to requests for interim vouchers; funding for service providers exceeding the current statutory maximum; funding for associate and contract counsel; and/or funding for non-attorney relatives.

3. Coordinate and collaborate with the CBA and/or NLST regarding case budgeting, preliminary discovery review, and any other matters subject to voucher review in complex, multi-defendant and other potential high-cost cases.

4. Coordinate and collaborate with the Court's Death Penalty Law Clerk, in addition to consulting with the CA and/or the NLSTA regarding case budgeting, preliminary discovery and any other matters subject to voucher review in capital cases.

D. The judge presiding over a case may elect to opt out of all or any portion of this delegation based upon the unique nature of the case or the service provider type.

IX. PROCEDURES FOR VOUCHER REDUCTION

A. Voucher review and/or reduction should not occur due to concerns relating to the diminishing of CJA program funds caused by the government's adverse financial conditions.

B. In the event the CJA Supervising Attorney determines any voucher claims or preauthorization requests should be reduced or denied:

1. The CJA Supervising Attorney will notify the panel member of the reason for the proposed voucher reduction or denial of a request for preauthorization, identifying the proposed amount of the reduction, explain the reason(s) for it, and require counsel's response to the notice and advise counsel of the option to submit a written request for reconsideration. The request for reconsideration must address reasons for reduction established by the CJA Supervising Attorney and the propriety and reasonableness of the voucher or preauthorization request. A response must be submitted to the CJA Supervising Attorney within 14 calendar days of notification of the proposed reduction or denial unless good cause is shown.

2. The CJA Supervising Attorney will review a timely submitted request for reconsideration and may grant it in full, in part, or not at all. The CJA Supervising Attorney's decision and supporting rationale for the denial of any part of a request for reconsideration shall be communicated to the panel member. Within ten calendar days of such notice, the panel member may appeal the denial of reconsideration to the judge presiding over the case. The appeal should be filed with the CJA Supervising Attorney who shall immediately refer the matter for decision, together with the complete voucher file, to the judge who presided over the case. The judge's decision on appeal shall be final.

C. Review by Judge Opting–Out of the Delegation to the CJA Supervising Attorney on a Particular Case

1. Authority to Opt–Out. A judge presiding over a case may "opt-out" of all or any portion of the delegation of authority provided in this section.

2. Notice and Order. When a judge opting out of the delegation of authority determines that any voucher or series of vouchers, or pre-authorization request, or a portion(s) thereof, should be reduced or denied based upon failing to conform to the Court's billing guidelines, unreasonableness, or is otherwise inaccurate or improper, the judge shall do the following:

a. Issue an order to the panel member or service provider to show cause.

b. Identify the issue(s) concerning to the Court along with the proposed amount of the reduction or denial, explain the reason(s) therefor, require a response by the panel member or service provider, and advise of the option to request independent review.

3. Response by counsel. The panel member or service provider should respond to the show cause with a written explanation addressing the identified issue(s) and supporting the reasonableness of the request within 14 days of receipt and elect one of the following options:

a. Accept the proposed reduction or denial;

b. Contest the proposed reduction or denial and waive independent review; or

c. Contest the proposed reduction or denial and request independent review.

4. Judge's Options. The judge will review counsel's response.

a. If the panel member or service provider fails to timely respond, the judge will make a final decision and authorize the reduced payment;

b. If the panel member or service provider accepts the proposed reduction or denial, the judge will make a final decision and authorize the reduced payment;

c. If the panel member or service provider contests the proposed reduction or denial and waives independent review, the court will consider the response of the panel member or service provider, and make a final decision and authorize payment, as appropriate;

d. If the panel member or service provider contests the proposed reduction or denial, requests an alternative payment amount in his/her response, and requests independent review, and the judge determines the requested alternative payment amount is reasonable and otherwise appropriate based upon the explanation(s) in the response, the judge may make a final decision approving the alternative payment, and authorize the alternative payment; or

e. If the panel member or service provider contests the proposed reduction or denial, and requests independent review, and (d) does not apply, the judge will forward the matter to a reviewing judge. The reviewing judge will be selected by a way of a computer-assisted random selection or a duty judge-based system to ensure independent review.

5. Independent Review and Recommendation

a. The reviewing judge will conduct a review and investigation to determine whether the voucher of the panel member or service provider conforms to the Court's billing guidelines, is reasonable considering a funding authorization and/or the circumstances of the case and is otherwise accurate or proper.

b. The investigation may include a review of the explanation(s) of the panel member or service provider, vouchers submitted by other panel members or service providers in the same or similar cases, a review of court records, records of detention facilities, and/or interviews of court staff, panel members or service providers including the individual whose voucher is being reviewed.

c. No provision of this section will be construed as permitting disclosure to the panel member or service provider of information from which they may infer the source, and no information shall be disclosed to the panel member or service provider or be obtained by any process which would jeopardize the confidentiality of communications of persons whose opinion have been sought in the investigation.

d. The reviewing judge will determine whether the voucher complies with the Court's billing guidelines, is reasonable or is not otherwise accurate or proper, specifying the reasons therefor. The reviewing judge shall make a recommendation regarding whether no reduction, the proposed reduction or any other reduction is appropriate.

e. A copy of the recommendation will be provided to the panel member or service provider, the CJA Supervising Attorney, and the judge presiding over the matter.

6. Finality

a. The presiding judge will give significant weight to the reviewing judge's recommendation in making a final decision.

b. Whether or not the presiding judge adopts the reviewing judge's recommendation, the judge's decision is final and there is no additional right of review or further appeal.

D. Any determination that a voucher should be considered for reduction or reduced under Sections IX.B and/or C, above, does not necessarily constitute a finding of wrongdoing.

X. All information gathered pertaining to a panel member or service provider during any voucher review becomes the property of the United States District Court for the Southern District of California and is to be treated as confidential.

XI. All matters relating to the preauthorization and voucher review process, including all initial and final decisions by the CJA Supervising Attorney, all requests by panel members and service providers for reconsideration or independent review relating to voucher reduction or denial of any request, will be maintained within eVoucher to ensure a transparent account and record of all exchanges between the panel member, service provider, reviewers and the final decision of the Court.

APPENDIX F
BILLING, TIMESHEETS, RECORD KEEPING, AND EXPENSES
I. TIMESHEETS AND RECORDKEEPING

A. Specificity in Timesheets. Actual time billing must be in tenths of an hour. Each entry in the timesheet of the panel member or service provider must reflect discrete individual tasks as to actual time spent. Time spent should not be bundled (except for tasks requiring less than six minutes, as explained below), especially tasks billable to different voucher categories. For example, if in one day counsel spent two hours conducting research, three hours reviewing discovery, 30 minutes on phone calls, and one hour drafting correspondence, counsel must create four separate entries in eVoucher for that day, with each task corresponding to its appropriate category. This requirement also applies to service providers.

Information must be provided in detail sufficient to permit meaningful review, without violating the canons of ethics or disclosing client confidences, so that reviewers may determine that the amount sought in the voucher provides fair compensation for the services rendered. In particular:

1. Describe division of work between panel member and associate/contract attorney or any other service provider;

2. Describe witness interviews with sufficient information to distinguish between individuals (*e.g.*, "Witness 1" or "W1" or "Witness A.K.");

3. Identify the person(s) involved in telephone conversations or conferences and general topic of discussion (using descriptors or initials where confidentiality is needed);

4. Generally, describe any issue being researched or drafted; and

5. When preparing or reviewing a court filing, identify the document by name or ECF number.

B. Record and Discovery Review

1. Counsel should include all discovery review and all docket filing review on the voucher.

2. The information should:

a. Provide specificity by describing the type of discovery review; (transcripts, reports, medical records, photos, audio recordings, etc.);

b. List bates number ranges or approximate number of pages;

c. Describe the length of audio or video recordings, as applicable; and

d. Describe docket entry review in ECF and note docket number.

C. Aggregate Time. Multiple tasks in one day of less than 0.1 hour (six minutes) each (*e.g.*, reviewing ECF documents, reviewing and sending brief emails, leaving phone messages) must be quantified together at no more than the total actual time expended on all tasks.

D. Excess Hours in One Day. If billing more than eight (8) hours in a single day when not in trial, counsel must ensure that sufficient justification is provided to explain the necessity for the excessive time. Without such justification, the voucher may be questioned or rejected with a request to provide additional information.

E. Multiple Vouchers When Representing Multiple Clients. When multiple vouchers are submitted due to representing multiple clients in a given case or proceeding, and when an entry is replicated on multiple vouchers—for example, pre-disposition preparation, video preparation and depositions, deferred prosecution matters, or CVB matters—the panel member should specify in each voucher whether there were multiple, separate meetings or whether there was one meeting and the total time was split across the various voucher submittal.

F. Delays Outside of the Control of Panel Member or Service Provider

1. Any compensable claims resulting from delay caused by factors outside of the control of the panel member or service provider must be specifically documented.

2. Examples of delays outside of the control of the panel members or service providers include jail processing time, jail lock-downs, court wait times and wait times relating to the production of a defendant or material witness or the arrival of opposing counsel to hearings, interviews or depositions.

3. Voucher time entries must clearly and separately account for such delays.

G. Further Guidance. Further guidance regarding specificity for timesheets is provided on the CJA page of the Court's website. When clarification is needed, counsel should consult with the VRS and/or CJA Supervising Attorney regarding the level of specificity required in the supporting documentation.

II. COMPENSABLE AND NON–COMPENSABLE SERVICES

A. Budgeting and Voucher Preparation. Time spent preparing a CJA–20 or CJA–30 (attorney payment voucher in a capital case) is not compensable. Time spent reviewing and certifying expert and service provider vouchers as required by this Plan is compensable, but the act of creating or submitting a CJA–21 or CJA–31 in eVoucher is not. Additionally, time spent preparing a budget, a CJA–26 or an AUTH is compensable because it requires counsel to plan for litigation by preliminarily reviewing records, sorting through discovery, initiating contact with experts and other service providers, and assessing overall case needs.

B. Making Travel Arrangements. Time spent making travel arrangements, whether undertaken by an attorney, paralegal, or other staff member, is not compensable. Time spent preparing a request for travel authorization is compensable.

C. Travel—Appointed Counsel

1. Appointed counsel will be compensated for travel time and expenses reasonably incurred, subject to the prevailing limitations placed upon travel and subsistence expenses of federal judiciary employees in accordance with existing government travel regulations. Counsel should consult with the district's CJA Committee, the VRS, or the Clerk's CJA Supervising Attorney for those regulations.

2. Advance approval by the Court is required in two circumstances: (1) out-of-district travel and (2) overnight travel. When feasible, counsel is expected to perform case-related work while traveling. Counsel should not perform non–CJA–related work while traveling if such travel time is billed to the CJA representation.

D. Travel—Service Providers

1. Unless otherwise provided in this Plan, service providers must be compensated for travel time and expenses reasonably incurred. However, advance approval by the Court is required in these circumstances: (1) out-of-district travel, and (2) overnight travel.

2. Interpreters, as service providers, are also entitled to travel expenses.

a. However, due to the availability of Spanish speaking interpreters in the El Centro Sector (consult with VRS for list), interpreter/translator travel time to the El Centro Sector is limited to $50 an hour, unless prior approval is obtained. Any rate in excess of the approved hourly range requires a supporting statement establishing the necessity of the higher rate and should be preauthorized as provided in this Plan prior to any travel undertaken.

b. The USAO and appointed counsel should make every effort to avoid less than 24 hours' notice of a cancelled interpreter appointment. Should that occur, the interpreter may bill for any actual out-of-pocket expenses and for the time required to get to and from the appointment.

E. Negotiating Hourly Rates. Counsel are encouraged to negotiate with service providers, especially higher-cost specialists, for lower hourly rate for travel time. If the service provider bills travel at a reduced rate, time spent performing case-related work while traveling is not "travel time" and should be compensated at the full (i.e., not reduced) hourly rate. Case-related work is work relevant to the responsibilities or duties assigned to the service provider by the panel member.

F. Non–Compensable Administrative Work

1. Filing court documents (CM/ECF);

2. Downloading, reviewing, renaming, saving, printing, or forwarding a Notice of Electronic Filing ("NEF") unless NEF is text-only entry unaccompanied by ECF document;

3. Mailing, faxing, copying;

4. Preparing correspondence by either drafting from general instructions or typing in prescribed format;

5. Transcribing dictation, editing and proofreading initial drafts, general word processing;

6. Receiving, screening, and referring telephone and in-person callers;

7. Answering/obtaining general inquiries/information about the attorney's office;

8. Setting up meetings and conferences and informing participants of dates, times, locations, etc., and maintaining office calendar;

9. Setting up and booking travel arrangements for counsel, clients, or expert service providers;

10. Notifying clients of dates and times of court appearances and appointments with counsel, interpreters, and other experts;

11. Opening and closing case files; and

12. Preparing attorney or expert billing.

G. Discovery Organization and Review

1. Preliminary Case Review and Expenditure Plan. As soon as practical after receiving discovery, panel members are encouraged to consider defense strategy and the anticipated time for services needed from associate/contract counsel, interpreters, investigators, or other service providers and submit a "Preliminary Defense Expenditure Plan" attached to a CJA–26.

2. Complex Cases

a. After the Court pronounces the criminal case complex and/or the case is determined to involve voluminous discovery, panel member(s), should confer with the Ninth Circuit's CJA Case Budgeting Attorney ("CBA"), the CJA Supervising Attorney, or a member of the National Litigation Support Team ("NLST") in the Defender Services Office and/or the judge presiding over the case.

b. In any case where counsel is contracting for discovery-related services in excess of $10,000 or seeking to purchase computer hardware or software in excess of $800, counsel must confer with the CBA or the NLST and CJA Supervising Attorney. CJA Guidelines § 320.70.40(a)(2).

H. Potential High–Cost Cases. At the onset of a case that has the potential for budgeting due to the nature of the case or discovery, the appointed counsel and the United States Attorney should meet and confer about the nature, volume, and mechanics of producing discovery. See Fed. R. Crim. P. 16.1. Appointed counsel should then present a preliminary budget detailing an efficient and cost-effective method to process, distribute, and organize discovery. This may include the use of an eDiscovery vendor, case management software, and/or use of paralegals and investigators. If the Court appoints consultants or attorneys skilled in electronic discovery to assist appointed counsel in developing a budget and discovery plan, the time associated with preparing the budget is compensable and should be included in the panel member's budget.

I. Multi–Defendant Cases. In multi-defendant cases, appointed counsel should meet and confer about the nature, volume, and organization of discovery review. Appointed counsel must make every effort to collaborate and share discovery management resources with co-counsel involved in the case to the extent conflicts can be avoided. Conflicts related to collaborating and sharing discovery resources should be brought to the attention of the district judge and the CBA/NLST and the CJA Supervising Attorney.

J. Discovery Document Budgeting

1. To reduce extraordinary expenses associated with record review of cases with voluminous documents, a two-stage approach should be employed for review of discovery materials. Use of a paralegal is strongly encouraged.

a. In the first stage, the Court approves a reasonable amount for a paralegal to assess the available materials and prepare an inventory or index, including a general description of each box. Original documents that have potential use as exhibits should be preserved and copies made as needed for the paralegal or attorney to use during substantive review. The paralegal(s) may be supervised by an associate or contract attorney.

b. In the second stage, counsel should know the types and volume of documents that need careful review (*e.g.*, police reports with handwritten notes) (core materials) and those that may need less detailed attention (non–core materials). Accordingly, counsel should be in a position to prepare a detailed and more accurate budget proposal for review of the core and non-core materials.

c. The budget may include time for preliminary review and organization of materials by a paralegal, supervising associate, or contract attorney prior to attorney review.

III. EXPENSES

A. Prior approval of the Court is required for any non-travel, case-related expense in excess of $900, out-of-district or overnight travel, and travel to El Centro by an interpreter.

B. The use of couriers, messengers, and other premium delivery services such as Federal Express, and United Parcel Service is discouraged unless there is a genuine necessity for the service or unless the cost of the premium service does not exceed United States Postal Service express mail rates. Explanations and receipts for all such services are required.

C. Counsel should use the most fiscally responsible method for discovery duplication. In some instances, this will require coordination among co-counsel, a "meet and confer" with the AUSA, or use of an outside vendor.

D. In–house copying is strongly encouraged and is reimbursable at a rate not to exceed fifteen cents ($0.15) per page and twenty-five cents per page for color copies. If in-house duplication is neither feasible nor cost effective, panel members are expected to negotiate the lowest rate possible from an outside vendor. Counsel should utilize the special rates made available to the U.S. Courts by contract.

E. Panel members' office overhead and items or services of a personal nature including but not limited to flat-fee computerized research plans unless itemized by client, land and cellular telephone maintenance fees, books and publications, office supplies and equipment, all costs related to educational seminars, and items of a personal nature (*i.e.*, clothing, haircuts, or meals for the defendant) are non-reimbursable expenses. The cost of use by panel members of computer-assisted legal research (*e.g.*, Westlaw) may be allowed as a reimbursable out-of-pocket expense provided the research pertains to the case and the amount claimed is reasonable and properly documented. Counsel are encouraged to copy relevant material from computer-assisted legal research aids in lieu of extended periods of reviewing and digesting material online.

F. Transcript requests must be submitted on the CJA–24 form. Except during trial, expedited or daily transcripts are discouraged. Transcript orders from magistrate case proceedings (where no court reporter was present) should be electronically filed in CM/ECF using the Transcript Order Form available on the Court's website. The form should be electronically filed after receipt of notice that the CJA–24 voucher has been approved.

G. Any requests for expedited or daily transcripts must be justified and preapproved by the Court.

H. Non–travel expenses that exceed $50 require receipts that should be attached in the "Documents" tab of a payment voucher in eVoucher; all travel expenses for meals, lodging, and transportation (except mileage) require itemized receipts.

I. As stated elsewhere herein, the services of non-appointed counsel (associate and contract counsel) <u>may not</u> be billed as an expense of the panel member even if the attorney is an employee or partner of the panel member's firm. Contract counsel (non–employee or partner of the panel member) are required to use separate voucher forms (CJA–20 and CJA–30) to bill those services. Such vouchers must be submitted at the same time as the panel member's voucher for the same billing period and be certified by the panel member, as directed by the CJA Supervising Attorney. Compensation for non-appointed counsel is included in the calculation of the case maximum.

IV. MAINTAINING RECORDS

A. Panel members are responsible for keeping track and must maintain contemporaneous time and attendance records for all work performed, including work performed by associates, partners, contract lawyers, and support staff, as well as expense records. This record-keeping requirement includes all information entered into eVoucher timesheets, provided the information is entered as soon as feasible after performing the work described or based upon contemporaneous notes. These records may be subject to audit and must be retained for at least three years after approval of the final voucher for any appointment.

B. Counsel should advise all investigative, expert, and other service providers that they must maintain contemporaneous time and attendance records for all work billed by them as well as expense records. These records are subject to audit and must be maintained for at least three years after approval of the service provider's or appointed counsel's final voucher, whichever is later.

[Dated: July 15, 2020.]

GENERAL ORDER NO. 514–E.   IN THE MATTER OF ADOPTING A POLICY ON PRIVACY AND PUBLIC ACCESS TO ELECTRONIC CASE FILES

In compliance with the policy of the Judicial Conference of the United States, and the E–Government Act of 2002, and in order to promote electronic access to case files while also protecting personal privacy and other legitimate interests, parties shall refrain from including or shall partially redact where inclusion is necessary, the following personal data identifiers from all pleadings filed with the court, including exhibits thereto, whether filed electronically or in paper, unless otherwise ordered by the Court, or excluded from public access as in sections 1 and 2, infra.

a.   Social Security Numbers. If an individual's Social Security number must be included in a pleading, only the last four digits of that number should be used.

b.   Names of Minor Children. If the involvement of a minor child must be mentioned, only the initials of that child should be used.

c.   Dates of Birth. If an individual's date of birth must be included in a pleading, only the year should be used.

d.   Financial Account Numbers. If the financial account numbers are relevant, only the last four digits of these numbers should be used.

e.   In criminal cases, the home address of any individual (e.g., victims).

In compliance with the E–Government Act of 2002, a party wishing to file a document containing the personal data identifiers listed above may file an unredacted document under seal. This document shall be retained by the court as part of the record. The court may, however, still require the party to file a redacted copy for the public file. In criminal cases, if the government needs to include in an indictment or government counsel or defense counsel need to include in a pleading the personal identifiers listed above, counsel will file the material under seal and file a redacted copy within five (5) days.

1.   Social Security cases shall be excluded from remote electronic public access except for access by judiciary employees, the United States Attorney or its representatives and the litigants in those cases. For these persons, access to these cases through the Internet will be allowed only through a login and password system.

2.   Without a court order, the following documents will not be included in the public case file and will not be made available to the public at the courthouse or via remote electronic access:

a.   Sealed documents (e.g., motions for downward departure for substantial assistance, plea agreements indicating cooperation).

b.   Unexecuted warrants of any kind and associated petitions for warrants (e.g., arrest warrants, search warrants).

c.   Pretrial bail reports and bond supporting documents.

d.   Pre–Sentence reports and the statement of reasons related to the judgment of conviction.

e.   Juvenile records.

f.   Magistrate information sheets and financial affidavits filed in seeking representation pursuant to the Criminal Justice Act.

g.   Pleadings and reports related to the competency or mental health of a defendant.

h.   Civil settlement documents that contain information in section one above. It shall be the attorney's obligation to obtain an order sealing such documents.

i.   Ex parte requests for authorization of investigative, expert or other services pursuant to the Criminal Justice Act.

j.   Documents in criminal cases containing identifying information about jurors or potential jurors.

k.   Any other documents the court concludes is good cause to exclude from electronic access.

[Dated: December 22, 2020.]

GENERAL ORDER NO. 550. IN THE MATTER OF PROCEDURAL
RULES FOR ELECTRONIC CASE FILING

Federal Rules of Civil Procedure 5 and 83, and Federal Rules of Criminal Procedure 57, authorize courts to establish practices and procedures for filing, signing, and verifying documents by electronic means. This Court intends to implement an Electronic Case Filing ("ECF") System in the fall of 2006. This system will provide for the creation, retention, and storage of court records and service of notice and court orders by electronic means. With certain defined exceptions, the Court shall require all documents in civil and criminal cases to be filed within the ECF system beginning on November 1, 2006. The purpose of this Order is to authorize the implementation of the ECF System. Both this Order and the Court's Administrative Policies and Procedures Manual governing the use of the ECF system shall be made available to the public on the Court's web site.

IT IS THEREFORE ORDERED AS FOLLOWS:

I. Definitions.

1. *Case Management/Electronic Case Filing System,* or CM/ECF, means the Internet-based system for filing documents and maintaining court case files in the United States District Court for the Southern District of California.

2. *Electronic Filing* means uploading a document directly from the registered user's computer in "Portable Document Format" (.pdf), using the CM/ECF system to file that document in the Court's case file.

3. *Registered User* or *Filing User* is an individual who is registered to use CM/ECF in the Southern District of California and has been issued a login and password by the Court.

4. *".pdf"* refers to Portable Document Format, a proprietary file format developed by Adobe Systems, Inc. A document filed created with a word processor, or a paper document which has been scanned, must be converted to Portable Document Format to be electronically filed with the Court.

5. *Notice of Electronic Filing* or NEF, is a notice automatically generated by the CM/ECF system at the time a document is filed with the Court. The notice sets forth the time of filing, the name of the attorney and/or party filing the document, the type of document, the text of the docket entry, the name of the party and/or attorney receiving the notice, and an electronic link (hyperlink) to the filed document which allows recipients to retrieve the document automatically.

II. Scope of Electronic Filing.

1. Except as prescribed by local rule, order, or other procedure, the Court has designated all cases to be assigned to the Electronic Case Filing ("ECF") System.

2. Registered users will be permitted to electronically file documents beginning on September 18, 2006. With certain defined exceptions, the Court shall require all documents in civil and criminal cases to be filed within the ECF System beginning on November 1, 2006.

3. Attorneys wishing to obtain an ECF exemption may seek relief in the manner set forth in the Court's Administrative Policies and Procedures Manual.

4. The electronic filing of petitions, pleadings, motions, or other documents by an attorney who is a registered participant in the Electronic Case Filing System, using the registered attorney's login and password, shall constitute the signature of that attorney under Federal Rule of Civil Procedure 11.

5. No attorney shall knowingly permit or cause his/her password to be utilized by anyone other than an authorized employee of the law firm or organization.

6. No person shall knowingly utilize or cause another person to utilize the password of a registered attorney unless such person is an authorized employee of the law firm or organization.

7. The electronic filing of pleadings or other documents in accordance with the Electronic Case Filing Procedures shall constitute entry of that pleading or other document on the docket kept by the Clerk under Federal Rule of Civil Procedure 79.

8. The Office of the Clerk shall enter all orders, decrees, judgments, and proceedings of the Court in accordance with the Electronic Case Filing Procedures, which shall constitute entry of the order, decree, judgment, or proceeding on the docket kept by the Clerk under Federal Rule of Civil Procedure 58 and Federal Rule of Criminal Procedure 55.

9. The NEF that is automatically generated by the Court's Electronic Filing System constitutes service of the filed document on Filing Users. A certificate of service is required to be filed and must state the manner in which service or notice was accomplished on each party.

10. Participation in the Electronic Case Filing System by receipt of a password from the Court shall constitute a request for service and notice electronically pursuant to Federal Rule of Civil Procedure 5(b)(2)(D) and Federal Rule of Criminal Procedure 49. Participants in the Electronic Case Filing System, by receiving a password from the Court, agree to receive service by electronic means.

III. Amendments to the Local Rules.

[Publisher's Note: For the text of Local Civil Rules 5.4, 58.1, and 77.2, and Local Criminal Rules 1.1 and 49.1, see ante.]

The period for public comment shall be until August 11, 2006. Absent further order of this Court, the effective date of the Rule changes is September 5, 2006. Any comments should be submitted to the Clerk, U.S. District Court, at 880 Front Street, Room 4290, San Diego, California 92101–8900. Please note on the envelope: In re: Electronic Case Filing.
[Dated: May 22, 2006.]

GENERAL ORDER NO. 552A. U.S. PRETRIAL SERVICES INTERVIEWS

Pursuant to the Court's policy of promoting early, prompt, and efficient judicial evaluation for eligibility of bond and the setting of conditions of release for arrested individuals facing charges:

The United States Marshal's Service shall continue to make arrested persons in their custody available for initial interviews by Pretrial Services Officers at the earliest practicable time during days the Court is in session. Pretrial Services Officers shall be given a reasonable period of time within which to interview arrested persons obtaining only information identified on the attached Interview Sheet. Thereafter, attorneys from Federal Defenders of San Diego, Inc. or other defense counsel shall be given a reasonable period of time within which to interview arrested persons. This procedure shall go into effect with the filing of this General Order.
[Dated: April 2, 2007.]

U.S. Pretrial Services Interview

Defendant Name: _____ *Citizenship: _____

Date & Place of Birth: _____

Present Address: _____ Time at Address: _____

Phone: _____

Prior Address: _____

Family/Surety Information:

Name	Relationship	Present Address & Phone	Serve as Surety?

Marital Status: _____   Name & Number of Spouse: _____

Children: _____

Educational Background: _____

Employment: _____

Military Service: _____

Health: _____

* This question will not be asked of individuals charged with Title 8 U.S.C., sections 1325 and/or 1326.

GENERAL ORDER NO. 567. IN THE MATTER OF THE FILING OF SENTENCING SUMMARY CHARTS

IT IS HEREBY ORDERED, pursuant to Local Criminal Rule 32.1.a.9, that sentencing summary charts must be filed electronically, through the Court's CM/ECF system. Counsel is not required to deliver a copy of the sentencing summary chart to chambers.

[Dated: January 16, 2008.]

GENERAL ORDER NO. 598–D. IN THE MATTER OF THE ASSIGNMENT OF PATENT AND PLANT VARIETY PROTECTION CASES

In August 2011, the judges of the Court elected to participate in the Patent and Plant Variety Protection Pilot Project established pursuant to Pub. L. No. 111–349, 124 Stat. 3674, 28 U.S.C. § 137 ("Patent Pilot Project"). The Court's participation in the Patent Pilot Project is subject to the statutorily promulgated procedures of the Patent Pilot Project. This Order amends and supercedes the prior versions of General Order 598. The following additional procedures apply to the Patent Pilot Project:

1. A judge of this Court wishing to participate in the Patent Pilot Project ("patent judge") must notify the chief judge.

2. Newly filed patent and plant variety protection cases ("patent cases") are initially assigned randomly pursuant to Civil Local Rule 40.1(a). In accordance with Civil Local Rule 40.1(b), newly filed patent cases, other than "false marking" cases under 35 U.S.C. § 292, are assigned pursuant to the provisions of this order.

3. Where a newly filed patent case is randomly assigned to a judge who is not participating in the Patent Pilot Project ("non–participating judge"), the non-participating judge may, within twenty-eight (28) days of the filing of the case, decline the assignment and ask that the case be reassigned to one of the patent judges. Where the case is randomly assigned and the initially assigned judge recuses, the next assigned non-participating judge will have fourteen (14) days from that reassignment to decline the case under this General Order. The case will remain on the docket of the assigned non-participating judge unless the assignment is declined as stated in this General Order.

4. If a non-participating judge declines the random assignment, and all of the patent judges recuse thereafter, the case will be assigned back to the first assigned non-participating judge who did not recuse.

5. The Clerk of Court will maintain a separate assignment deck ("Patent Pilot Project deck") for use in the reassignment of cases to patent judges, and each patent judge's name will appear in this deck an equal number of times. Reassignments made using the Patent Pilot Project deck must be made randomly in accordance with Civil Local Rule 40.1(a). When a non-participating judge declines a case assignment, the docket will state that the assigned judge has declined assignment pursuant to General Order 598.

6. The Clerk of Court will maintain a method for the equalization in the assignment of cases between patent judges and non-participating judges, to the end that over a period of time each judge is assigned substantially equal amounts of work. Such method is subject to the approval of the district judges.

7. Civil Local Rule 40.1 applies to patent cases. The parties must notify the Court of any other cases in the district involving the same patent.

8. If a patent judge declines assignment or recuses from any case involving the same patent currently pending before the judge, the judge is not required to decline assignment or recuse from all related cases involving the patent, unless required by law.

9. The following judges are currently designated as patent judges: The Honorable Marilyn L. Huff; The Honorable Dana M. Sabraw; The Honorable Roger T. Benitez; The Honorable Janis L. Sammartino; and The Honorable Cathy Ann Bencivengo.

[Dated: December 2, 2015.]

GENERAL ORDER NO. 602. IN THE MATTER OF USE OF ASSOCIATES AND CONTRACT ATTORNEYS ON CJA CASES

Whereas the Judicial Council of the Ninth Circuit has promulgated a Criminal Justice Act and Budgeting Policy in which "[a]ppointed counsel are encouraged to use lower-billing associates, contract lawyers, paralegals or other means to minimize costs where lead attorney expertise may not be required," IT IS THEREFORE ORDERED AS FOLLOWS:

In non-capital cases, the Court approves use of associate attorneys for tasks in which lead attorney expertise is not required, in all cases in which the total fees for CJA counsel do not exceed the statutory maximum.

In non-capital cases, the Court also approves use of contract attorneys for tasks in which lead attorney expertise is not required, up to a maximum of 8 hours in any one case, without further approval of the Court.

For purposes of this Order, "associate attorney" is defined as an attorney who is a partner or employee of the CJA attorney's law firm. "Contract attorney" is be defined as an attorney who is not a partner or employee of the CJA attorney's law firm.

The rates of compensation for associate and contract attorneys shall be as follows, subject to proportionate adjustment based on any future changes to the hourly rate for CJA attorneys:

- Attorneys with less than 3 years of experience shall be permitted to bill at the rate of $75 per hour.
- Attorneys with 3 to 6 years of experience shall be permitted to bill at the rate of $100 per hour.
- Attorneys with more than 6 years of experience shall be permitted to bill at the rate of $115 per hour.

An attorney who is also a member of the CJA panel, however, shall be permitted to bill at the normal CJA rate.

Nothing in this Order shall limit an individual District Judge's discretion to regulate attorney appearances and rates of compensation in his or her own cases.

[Dated: March 1, 2014.]

GENERAL ORDER NO. 607. IN THE MATTER OF THE ASSIGNMENT OF DISTRICT JUDGES TO DETERMINE THE MENTAL COMPETENCY OF DEFENDANTS

Pursuant to Local Criminal Rule 57.4.c.9, magistrate judges are authorized to order examinations to determine mental competency under 18 U.S.C. § 4241.

If a district judge is already assigned to the case, the hearing to determine mental competency will be placed on that district judge's calendar.

If a district judge has not been assigned to the case because there is no information or indictment, the Clerk will randomly assign a district judge to the case to hold the hearing to determine mental competency. Any information or indictment that is later filed will be assigned to the same district judge who determined mental competency in that case.

A district judge may designate a magistrate judge to conduct the competency hearing and to submit proposed findings of fact and recommendations.

[Dated: February 22, 2012.]

GENERAL ORDER NO. 613–A. IN THE MATTER OF OBTAINING CJA SERVICES WITHOUT PRIOR AUTHORIZATION

Pursuant to 18 U.S.C. § 3006A(e)(2), prior approval is required for investigative, expert, and other services if the total cost of those services exceeds $900.00. Because the CJA representations in this District routinely require use of the services of investigators and interpreters, and the cost of those services combined may ordinarily exceed $900.00, to avoid the necessity of CJA defense counsel having to expend the time necessary in hundreds of cases each year to make application to exceed the $900.00 total maximum, the Court hereby authorizes CJA defense counsel to utilize the services of interpreters and investigators up to $900.00 for each such service without further order of the Court.

CJA defense counsel and service providers will otherwise comply with 18 U.S.C. § 3006A(e)(2).

[Dated: March 2, 2021.]

GENERAL ORDER NO. 614. IN THE MATTER OF CJA VOUCHERS IN PRETRIAL DIVERSION CASES

Criminal Justice Act ("CJA") vouchers submitted by defense counsel and other service providers in all pretrial diversion cases monitored by a Magistrate Judge, including the Alternative to Prison Solutions (APS) diversion program, are referred to the Magistrate Judge handling the case.

The Magistrate Judge is authorized to resolve all CJA vouchers in pretrial diversion cases and to modify, if appropriate, the intervals at which defense counsel must submit vouchers. Absent an order to the contrary, defense counsel appointed to a diversion case monitored by a Magistrate Judge must submit an interim voucher, which will cover all work performed up to the date of submission, within 60 days of the defendant's entry into the diversion program.

The final voucher must be submitted within 30 days after the defendant successfully completes the diversion program or is unsuccessfully terminated from the diversion program. The final voucher will cover all work performed after the submission of the interim voucher through completion of the diversion program.

If the defendant is unsuccessfully terminated from the diversion program and additional court proceedings occur before a District Judge, another voucher must be submitted to the presiding District Judge and will cover all work performed after diversion termination through final resolution of the criminal case.

[Dated: September 12, 2012.]

GENERAL ORDER NO. 623. IN THE MATTER OF CAMERAS AND RECORDING DEVICES PROHIBITED IN THE UNITED STATES COURTHOUSE BUILDINGS

Pursuant to Civil Local Rule 83.7.c, cameras and recording devices that are solely cameras and/or recording devices can not be brought into the United States Courthouse Buildings. Devices that have cameras and recording devices as accessories (such as cell phones, I-pads, etc.) are permitted in the United States Courthouse Buildings. However, the use of cameras and recorders contained in those devices is prohibited as provided in Civil Local Rule 83.7.c. A judge may permit cameras to be brought into the United States Courthouse Buildings in connection with a matter or ceremony before them.

[Dated: January 14, 2013.]

GENERAL ORDER NO. 627. IN THE MATTER OF MOTIONS CONCERNING PRETRIAL RELEASE

When a defendant or the attorney for the Government makes a motion under 18 U.S.C. § 3145(a) and (b) to amend conditions of release, revoke an order of release, or revoke or amend an order of detention, and the indictment or information has not yet been filed against the defendant, and this Court has original jurisdiction over the offense, the Clerk will randomly assign the matter to a district judge to hear the motion.

[Dated: February 25, 2013.]

GENERAL ORDER NO. 635. IN THE MATTER OF MOTIONS IN CRIMINAL CASES TO RELEASE AND/OR RECONVEY COLLATERAL FOR BAIL

Pursuant to Civil Local Rule 72.1.h.10, all motions in a criminal case to release and/or reconvey collateral for bail under Criminal Local Rule 46.1.g, will be made before the Magistrate Judge who set the conditions of release, or in their absence, the Presiding Magistrate Judge.

[Dated: February 6, 2014.]

GENERAL ORDER NO. 644D. IN THE MATTER OF STUDENT PRACTICE IN THE SOUTHERN DISTRICT OF CALIFORNIA

A. Except as set forth herein, an eligible law student acting under the supervision of a member of the bar of this Court may speak or appear on behalf of a client in criminal or civil matters, if the client has filed a written consent with the Court, and subject to the restrictions set forth below.

B. Student Eligibility.

1. The student must be enrolled and in good standing in a law school accredited by the American Bar Association or the State Bar of California;

2. The student must have completed one (1) full academic year of study;

3. The student must have completed or be enrolled in a course in evidence. For civil cases, an eligible law student must have also completed a course in civil procedure. For criminal cases, an eligible law student must have also completed or be enrolled in courses in criminal law and criminal procedure. An eligible law student must also have knowledge of and be familiar with the Federal Rules of Civil and Criminal Procedure as well as the Federal Rules of Evidence, the Rules of Professional Conduct of the State Bar of California, and applicable statutory rules, and rules of this Court;

4. The student must be certified by the dean of a law school as being adequately trained to fulfill all responsibilities as a legal intern in compliance with this Order;

5. The student cannot accept compensation for his or her legal services either directly or indirectly from a client;

6. The student must file with the Clerk of this Court any and all documents required to comply with this Order.

C. Supervising Attorney.

1. The Supervising Attorney must be a member of this Court for no less than five years, and have such substantial litigation experience as to satisfy the Court of his or her ability to supervise the student;

2. The Supervising Attorney must be registered for the Court's CM/ECF System;

3. The Supervising Attorney must file with the Clerk of the Court a "Request to Undertake the Supervision of an Eligible Law Student" for each case in which an eligible student may participate. The undertaking, if approved by the Court, may be withdrawn by the supervising attorney by filing a written notice with the Clerk of the Court and by giving notice of such withdrawal to the affected student;

4.   The Supervising Attorney must appear with the student in any oral presentations before this Court;

5.   The Supervising Attorney must read, approve and sign all documents filed with this Court;

6.   The Supervising Attorney must assume personal professional responsibility for the student's work in matters before this Court;

7.   The Supervising Attorney must assist and counsel the student in the preparation of the student's work in matters before this Court;

8.   The Supervising Attorney must be responsible to supplement oral or written work of the student as necessary to assure proper representation of the client. All written work will be filed over the signature of the supervising attorney.

D.   Law School Dean's Certification.

1.   The Certification must be filed with the Clerk of the Court and may remain in effect for one year, subject to renewal;

2.   The Certification must state that the Dean knows of no reason which would render the law student ineligible under this Order;

3.   The Certification may be withdrawn for good cause by the dean with notice to the Court and to the student. Such cause must be stated in the notice filed with the Court.

E.   Acts in Which Eligible Students May Engage. An Eligible Student may engage in the following acts under supervision of the Supervising Attorney and with the written consent of the client and the consent of the Court on the record:

In Criminal Cases:

1.   Orally present matters in Central Violations Bureau cases before Magistrate Judges.

2.   Orally participate in initial appearances, arraignments, and bail hearings before a Magistrate Judge, with the specific authorization of the Magistrate Judge;

3.   Argue sentencing matters before a Magistrate Judge, only with the specific authorization of the Magistrate Judge;

4.   Assist in any other proceedings before a Magistrate Judge, with the specific authorization of the Magistrate Judge;

5.   Argue or otherwise participate in any proceeding before a District Judge if expressly authorized by that judge;

6.   Have his or her name appear under that of the Supervising Attorney on pleadings the student co-wrote, with the approval of the Magistrate Judge or District Judge.

In Civil Cases:

1.   Argue or otherwise participate in any proceeding before a District Judge or Magistrate Judge if expressly authorized by that judge;

2.   Have his or her name appear under that of the Supervising Attorney on pleadings the student co-wrote, with the approval of the Magistrate Judge or District Judge;

3.   Participate in depositions with the acquiescence of all parties.

F.   Opt–Out Provision. Any District Judge or Magistrate Judge may opt out of the provisions of this General Order and decline to allow student participation in any proceedings.

G.   This Order will allow eligible students to engage in acts in criminal cases as set forth in section E, only if the Supervising Attorney is employed by the United States Attorney's Office or Federal Defenders of San Diego.

[Dated: October 25, 2018.]

GENERAL ORDER NO. 731.   IN THE MATTER OF PRO HAC VICE ADMISSION FEE (ALLOCATION OF FEE)

Effective March 1, 2021, the pro hac vice admission fee required by Civil Local Rule 83.3.c.4 will be two hundred and thirteen dollars ($213.00), such fee to be deposited in the non-appropriated funds of the court.   Of the fee, one hundred and eighty-three dollars ($183.00) will be deposited into the library fund, and the remaining thirty dollars ($30.00) will be allocated to the court's pro bono fund, unless otherwise ordered by the Court.

[Dated: February 23, 2021.]

INDEX TO
UNITED STATES DISTRICT COURT
FOR THE SOUTHERN DISTRICT OF CALIFORNIA

RULES OF PROCEDURE OF THE JUDICIAL PANEL ON MULTIDISTRICT LITIGATION

Renumbered and Amended Effective November 2, 1998

Including Amendments Effective
October 4, 2016

I. RULES FOR MULTIDISTRICT LITIGATION UNDER 28 U.S.C. § 1407

RULE 1.1 DEFINITIONS

(a) "Panel" means the members of the United States Judicial Panel on Multidistrict Litigation appointed by the Chief Justice of the United States pursuant to 28 U.S.C. § 1407.

(b) "Chair" means the Chair of the Panel appointed by the Chief Justice of the United States pursuant to Section 1407, or the member of the Panel properly designated to act as Chair.

(c) "Clerk of the Panel" means the official that the Panel appoints to that position. The Clerk of the Panel shall perform such duties that the Panel or the Panel Executive delegates.

(d) "Electronic Case Filing (ECF)" refers to the Panel's automated system that receives and stores documents filed in electronic form. All attorneys filing pleadings with the Panel must do so using ECF. All pro se individuals are non-ECF users, unless the Panel orders otherwise.

(e) "MDL" means a multidistrict litigation docket which the Panel is either considering or has created by transferring cases to a transferee district for coordinated or consolidated pretrial proceedings pursuant to Section 1407.

(f) "Panel Executive" means the official appointed to act as the Panel's Chief Executive and Legal Officer. The Panel Executive may appoint, with the approval of the Panel, necessary deputies, clerical assistants and other employees to perform or assist in the performance of the duties of the Panel Executive. The Panel Executive, with the approval of the Panel, may make such delegations of authority as are necessary for the Panel's efficient operation.

(g) "Pleadings" means all papers, motions, responses, or replies of any kind filed with the Panel, including exhibits attached thereto, as well as all orders and notices that the Panel issues.

(h) "Tag-along action" refers to a civil action pending in a district court which involves common questions of fact with either (1) actions on a pending motion to transfer to create an MDL or (2) actions previously transferred to an existing MDL, and which the Panel would consider transferring under Section 1407.

(i) "Transferee district" is the federal district court to which the Panel transfers an action pursuant to Section 1407, for inclusion in an MDL.

(j) "Transferor district" is the federal district court where an action was pending prior to its transfer pursuant to Section 1407, for inclusion in an MDL, and where the Panel may remand that action at or before the conclusion of pretrial proceedings.

[Former Rule 1 adopted May 3, 1993, effective July 1, 1993. Renumbered Rule 1.1 September 1, 1998, effective November 2, 1998. Amended September 8, 2010, effective October 4, 2010.]

RULE 2.1 RULES AND PRACTICE

(a) Customary Practice. The Panel's customary practice shall govern, unless otherwise fixed by statute or these Rules.

(b) Failure to Comply With Rules. When a pleading does not comply with these Rules, the Clerk of the Panel may advise counsel of the deficiencies and set a date for full compliance. If counsel does not fully comply within the established time, the Clerk of the Panel shall file the non-complying pleading, but the Chair may thereafter order it stricken.

(c) Admission to Practice Before the Panel. Every member in good standing of the Bar of any district court of the United States is entitled to practice before the Panel, provided, however, that he or she has established and maintains a CM/ECF account with any United States federal court. Any attorney of record in any action transferred under Section 1407 may continue to represent his or her client in any district court of the United States to which such action is transferred. Parties are not required to obtain local counsel.

(d) Pendency of Motion or Conditional Order. The pendency of a motion, order to show cause, conditional transfer order or conditional remand order before the Panel pursuant to 28 U.S.C. § 1407 does not affect or suspend orders and pretrial proceedings in any pending federal district court action and does not limit the pretrial jurisdiction of that court. An order to transfer or remand pursuant to 28 U.S.C. § 1407 shall be effective only upon its filing with the clerk of the transferee district court.

(e) Reassignment. If for any reason the transferee judge is unable to continue those responsibilities, the Panel shall make the reassignment of a new transferee judge.

[Former Rule 5 adopted May 3, 1993, effective July 1, 1993. Renumbered Rule 1.2 September 1, 1998, effective November 2, 1998. Former Rule 4 adopted May 3, 1993, effective July 1, 1993. Renumbered Rule 1.3 and amended September 1, 1998, effective November 2, 1998. Former Rule 6 adopted May 3, 1993, effective July 1, 1993. Renumbered Rule 1.4 September 1, 1998, effective November 2, 1998. Former Rule 18 adopted May 3, 1993, effective July 1, 1993. Renumbered Rule 1.5 September 1, 1998, effective November 2, 1998. Former Rules 1.2, 1.3, 1.4, and 1.5 redesignated and amended September 8, 2010, effective October 4, 2010.]

RULE 3.1 ELECTRONIC RECORDS AND FILES; COPY FEES

(a) Electronic Record. Effective October 4, 2010, the official Panel record shall be the electronic file maintained on the Panel's servers. This record includes, but is not limited to, Panel pleadings, documents filed in paper and then scanned and made part of the electronic record, and Panel orders and notices filed. The official record also includes any documents or exhibits that may be impractical to scan. These documents and exhibits shall be kept in the Panel offices.

(b) Maintaining Records. Records and files generated prior to October 4, 2010, may be (i) maintained at the Panel offices, (ii) temporarily or permanently removed to such places at such times as the Clerk of the Panel or the Chair shall direct, or (iii) transferred whenever appropriate to the Federal Records Center.

(c) Fees. The Clerk of the Panel may charge fees for duplicating records and files, as prescribed by the Judicial Conference of the United States.

[Former Rule 2 adopted May 3, 1993, effective July 1, 1993. Renumbered Rule 5.1 and amended September 1, 1998, effective November 2, 1998. Former Rule 5.1 redesignated and amended September 8, 2010, effective October 4, 2010.]

RULE 3.2 ECF USERS: FILING REQUIREMENTS

(a) Form of Pleadings. This Rule applies to pleadings that ECF users file with the Panel.

(i) Each pleading shall bear the heading "Before the United States Judicial Panel on Multidistrict Litigation," the identification "MDL No.___" and the descriptive title designated by the Panel. If the Panel has not yet designated a title, counsel shall use an appropriate description.

(ii) The final page of each pleading shall contain the name, address, telephone number, fax number and email address of the attorney or party designated to receive service of pleadings in the case, and the name of each party represented.

(iii) Each brief submitted with a motion and any response to it shall not exceed 20 pages, exclusive of exhibits. Each reply shall not exceed 10 pages and shall address arguments raised in the response(s). Absent exceptional circumstances and those set forth in Rule 6.1(d), the Panel will not grant motions to exceed page limits.

(iv) Each pleading shall be typed in size 12 point font (for both text and footnotes), double spaced (text only), in a letter size document (8½ × 11 inch) with sequentially numbered pages.

(v) Each exhibit shall be separately numbered and clearly identified.

(vi) Proposed Panel orders shall not be submitted.

(b) Place of Filing. Counsel shall sign and verify all pleadings electronically in accordance with these Rules and the Panel's Administrative Policies and Procedures for Electronic Case Filing found at www.jpml.uscourts.gov. A pleading filed electronically constitutes a written document for the purpose of these Rules and the Federal Rules of Civil Procedure and is deemed the electronically signed original thereof. All pleadings, except by pro se litigants, shall conform with this Rule beginning on October 4, 2010.

(i)* Pleadings shall not be transmitted directly to any Panel member.

(c) Attorney Registration. Only attorneys identified, or to be identified, pursuant to Rule 4.1, shall file pleadings. Each of these attorneys must register as a Panel CM/ECF user through www.jpml.uscourts.gov. Registration/possession of a CM/ECF account with any United States federal court shall be deemed consent to receive electronic service of all Panel orders and notices as well as electronic service of pleadings from other parties before the Panel.

(d) Courtesy Copy of Specified Pleadings. Counsel shall serve the Clerk of the Panel, for delivery within 1 business day of filing, with a courtesy paper copy of any of the following pleadings: (i) a motion to transfer and its supporting brief; (ii) a response to a show cause order; (iii) a motion to vacate a conditional transfer order or a conditional remand order; and (iv) any response, reply, supplemental information or interested party response related to the pleadings listed in (i), (ii) and (iii). No courtesy copies of any other pleadings are required. Courtesy copies of pleadings totaling 10 pages or less (including any attachments) may be faxed to the Panel. The courtesy copy shall include all exhibits, shall be clearly marked "Courtesy Copy–Do Not File," shall contain the CM/ECF pleading number (if known), and shall be mailed or delivered to:

> Clerk of the Panel
> United States Judicial Panel on Multidistrict Litigation
> Thurgood Marshall Federal Judiciary Building
> One Columbus Circle, NE, Room G–255, North Lobby
> Washington, DC 20002–8041

(e) Privacy Protections. The privacy protections contained in Rule 5.2 of the Federal Rules of Civil Procedure shall apply to all Panel filings.

[Former Rule 3 adopted May 3, 1993, effective July 1, 1993. Renumbered Rule 5.11 and amended September 1, 1998, effective November 2, 1998; renumbered Rule 5.1.1 and amended March 25, 2010, effective April 1, 2010. Former Rule 7 adopted May 3, 1993, effective July 1, 1993. Renumbered Rule 5.12 and amended September 1, 1998, effective November 2, 1998. Amended April 2, 2001, effective April 2, 2001; paragraph (a) suspended in part by Order filed April 19, 2005; renumbered Rule 5.1.2 and amended March 25, 2010, effective April 1, 2010. Former Rule 9 adopted May 3, 1993, effective July 1, 1993. Renumbered Rule 7.1 and amended September 1, 1998, effective November 2, 1998. Amended April 2, 2001, effective April 2, 2001. Former Rules 5.1.1, 5.1.2, and 7.1 redesignated in part and amended September 8, 2010, effective October 4, 2010. Amended effective July 6, 2011; October 4, 2016.]

* **[Publisher's Note:** So in original. No subdivision (ii) promulgated.]

RULE 3.3 NON–ECF USERS: FILING REQUIREMENTS

(a) Definition of Non–ECF Users. Non–ECF users are all pro se individuals, unless the Panel orders otherwise. This Rule shall apply to all motions, responses and replies that non-ECF users file with the Panel.

(b) Form of Pleadings. Unless otherwise set forth in this Rule, the provisions of Rule 3.2 shall apply to non-ECF users.

(i) Each pleading shall be flat and unfolded; plainly written or typed in size 12 point font (for both text and footnotes), double spaced (text only), and printed single-sided on letter size (8 ½ × 11 inch) white paper with sequentially numbered pages; and fastened at the top-left corner without side binding or front or back covers.

(ii) Each exhibit shall be separately numbered and clearly identified. Any exhibits exceeding a cumulative total of 50 pages shall be bound separately.

(c) Place of Filing. File an original and one copy of all pleadings with the Clerk of the Panel by mailing or delivering to:

> Clerk of the Panel
> United States Judicial Panel on Multidistrict Litigation
> Thurgood Marshall Federal Judiciary Building
> One Columbus Circle, NE,
> Room G–255, North Lobby
> Washington, DC 20002–8041

(i) Pleadings not exceeding a total of 10 pages, including exhibits, may be faxed to the Panel office.

(ii) The Clerk of the Panel shall endorse the date for filing on all pleadings submitted for filing.

[Former Rule 3 adopted May 3, 1993, effective July 1, 1993. Renumbered Rule 5.11 and amended September 1, 1998, effective November 2, 1998; renumbered Rule 5.1.1 and amended March 25, 2010, effective April 1, 2010. Former Rule 7 adopted May 3, 1993, effective July 1, 1993. Renumbered Rule 5.12 and amended September 1, 1998, effective November 2, 1998. Amended April 2, 2001, effective April 2, 2001; paragraph (a) suspended in part by Order filed April 19, 2005; renumbered Rule 5.1.2 and amended March 25, 2010, effective April 1, 2010. Former Rule 9 adopted May 3, 1993, effective July 1, 1993. Renumbered Rule 7.1 and amended September 1, 1998, effective November 2, 1998. Amended April 2, 2001, effective April 2, 2001. Former Rules 5.1.1, 5.1.2, and 7.1 redesignated in part and amended September 8, 2010, effective October 4, 2010.]

RULE 4.1 SERVICE OF PLEADINGS

(a) Proof of Service. The Panel's notice of electronic filing shall constitute service of pleadings. Registration/possession by counsel of a CM/ECF account with any United States federal court shall be deemed consent to receive electronic service of all pleadings. All pleadings shall contain a proof of service on all other parties in all involved actions. The proof of service shall indicate the name and manner of service. If a party is not represented by counsel, the proof of service shall indicate the name of the party and the party's last known address. The proof of service shall indicate why any person named as a party in a constituent complaint was not served with the Section 1407 pleading.

(b) Service Upon Transferor Court. The proof of service pertaining to motions for a transfer or remand pursuant to 28 U.S.C. § 1407 shall certify that counsel has transmitted a copy of the motion for filing to the clerk of each district court where an affected action is pending.

(c) Notice of Appearance. Within 14 days after the issuance of a (i) notice of filing of a motion to initiate transfer under Rule 6.2, (ii) notice of filed opposition to a CTO under Rule 7.1, (iii) a show cause order under Rules* 8.1, (iv) notice of filed opposition to a CRO under Rule 10.2, or (v) notice of filing of a motion to remand under Rule 10.3, each party or designated attorney as required hereinafter shall file a Notice of Appearance notifying the Clerk of the Panel of the name, address and email address of the attorney designated to file and receive service of all pleadings. Each party shall designate only one attorney. Any party not represented by counsel shall be served by mailing such pleadings to the party's last known address. Except in extraordinary circumstances, the Panel will not grant requests for an extension of time to file the Notice of Appearance.

(d) Liaison Counsel. If the transferee district court appoints liaison counsel, this Rule shall be satisfied by serving each party in each affected action and all liaison counsel. Liaison counsel shall receive copies of all Panel orders concerning their particular litigation and shall be responsible for distribution to the parties for whom he or she serves as liaison counsel.

[Former Rule 8 adopted May 3, 1993, effective July 1, 1993. Renumbered Rule 5.2 and amended September 1, 1998, effective November 2, 1998; March 26, 2009, effective December 1, 2009. Former Rule 5.2 redesignated and amended September 8, 2010, effective October 4, 2010. Technical revisions effective July 6, 2011.]

* [**Publisher's Note:** So in original.]

RULE 5.1   CORPORATE DISCLOSURE STATEMENT

(a) Requirements. A nongovernmental corporate party must file a disclosure statement that: (1) identifies any parent corporation and any publicly held corporation owning 10% or more of its stock; or (2) states that there is no such corporation.

(b) Deadline. A party shall file the corporate disclosure statement within 14 days after issuance of a notice of the filing of a motion to transfer or remand, an order to show cause, or a motion to vacate a conditional transfer order or a conditional remand order.

(c) Updating. Each party must update its corporate disclosure statement to reflect any change in the information therein (i) until the matter before the Panel is decided, and (ii) within 14 days after issuance of a notice of the filing of any subsequent motion to transfer or remand, order to show cause, or motion to vacate a conditional transfer order or a conditional remand order in that docket.

[Former Rule 2 adopted May 3, 1993, effective July 1, 1993. Renumbered Rule 5.1 and amended September 1, 1998, effective November 2, 1998. Former Rule 5.3 redesignated and amended September 8, 2010, effective October 4, 2010. Amended effective July 6, 2011.]

RULE 5.1.3   FILING OF PAPERS: COMPUTER GENERATED DISK REQUIRED [DELETED SEPT. 8, 2010, EFF. OCT. 4, 2010]

[Added May 22, 2000, effective June 1, 2000. And amended July 30, 2007, effective July 30, 2007; renumbered Rule 5.1.3 and amended March 25, 2010, effective April 1, 2010. Deleted September 8, 2010, effective October 4, 2010.]

RULE 6.1   MOTION PRACTICE

(a) Application. This Rule governs all motions requesting Panel action generally. More specific provisions may apply to motions to transfer (Rule 6.2), miscellaneous motions (Rule 6.3), conditional transfer orders (Rule 7.1), show cause orders (Rule 8.1), conditional remand orders (Rule 10.2) and motions to remand (Rule 10.3).

(b) Form of Motions. All motions shall briefly describe the action or relief sought and shall include:

(i) a brief which concisely states the background of the litigation and movant's factual and legal contentions;

(ii) a numbered schedule providing

(A) the complete name of each action involved, listing the full name of each party included as such on the district court's docket sheet, not shortened by the use of references such as "et al." or "etc.";

(B) the district court and division where each action is pending;

(C) the civil action number of each action; and

(D) the name of the judge assigned each action, if known;

(iii) a proof of service providing

(A) a service list listing the full name of each party included on the district court's docket sheet and the complaint, including opt-in plaintiffs not listed on the docket sheet; and

(B) in actions where there are 25 or more plaintiffs listed on the docket sheet, list the first named plaintiff with the reference "et al." if all the plaintiffs are represented by the same attorney(s);

(iv) a copy of all complaints and docket sheets for all actions listed on the Schedule; and

(v) exhibits, if any, identified by number or letter and a descriptive title.

(c) Responses and Joinders. Any other party may file a response within 21 days after filing of a motion. Failure to respond to a motion shall be treated as that party's acquiescence to it. A joinder in a motion shall not add any action to that motion.

(d) Replies. The movant may file a reply within 7 days after the lapse of the time period for filing a response. Where a movant is replying to more than one response in opposition, the movant may file a consolidated reply with a limit of 20 pages.

(e) Alteration of Time Periods. The Clerk of the Panel has the discretion to shorten or enlarge the time periods set forth in this Rule as necessary.

(f) Notification of Developments. Counsel shall promptly notify the Clerk of the Panel of any development that would partially or completely moot any Panel matter.

[Former Rule 10 adopted May 3, 1993, effective July 1, 1993. Renumbered Rule 7.2 and amended September 1, 1998, effective November 2, 1998. Amended April 2, 2001, effective April 2, 2001; March 26, 2009, December 1, 2009. Former Rule 7.2 redesignated in part and amended September 8, 2010, effective October 4, 2010.]

RULE 6.2 MOTIONS TO TRANSFER FOR COORDINATED OR CONSOLIDATED PRETRIAL PROCEEDINGS

(a) Initiation of Transfer. A party to an action may initiate proceedings to transfer under Section 1407 by filing a motion in accordance with these Rules. A copy of the motion shall be filed in each district court where the motion affects a pending action.

(b) Notice of Filing of Motion to Transfer. Upon receipt of a motion, the Clerk of the Panel shall issue a "Notice of Filing of Motion to Transfer" to the service list recipients. The Notice shall contain the following: the filing date of the motion, caption, MDL docket number, briefing schedule and pertinent Panel policies. After a motion is filed, the Clerk of the Panel shall consider any other pleading to be a response unless the pleading adds an action. The Clerk of the Panel may designate such a pleading as a motion, and distribute a briefing schedule applicable to all or some of the parties, as appropriate.

(c) Notice of Appearance. Within 14 days of issuance of a "Notice of the Filing of a Motion to Transfer," each party or designated attorney shall file a Notice of Appearance in accordance with Rule 4.1(c).

(d) Notice of Potential Tag-along Actions. Any party or counsel in a new group of actions under consideration for transfer under Section 1407 shall promptly notify the Clerk of the Panel of any potential tag-along actions in which that party is also named or in which that counsel appears.

(e) Interested Party Responses. Any party or counsel in one or more potential tag-along actions as well as amicus curiae may file a response to a pending motion to transfer. Such a pleading shall be deemed an Interested Party Response.

(f) Amendment to a Motion. Before amending a motion to transfer, a party shall first contact the Clerk of the Panel to ascertain whether such amendment is feasible and permissible considering the Panel's hearing schedule. Any such amendment shall be entitled "Amendment to Motion for Transfer," and shall clearly and specifically identify and describe the nature of the amendment.

(i) Where the amended motion includes new civil actions, the amending party shall file a "Schedule of Additional Actions" and a revised Proof of Service.

(ii) The Proof of Service shall state (A) that all new counsel have been served with a copy of the amendment and all previously-filed motion papers, and (B) that all counsel previously served with the original motion have been served with a copy of the amendment.

(iii) The Clerk of the Panel may designate the amendment with a different denomination (*e.g.*, a notice of potential tag-along action(s)) and treatment.

(h) Oral Argument*. The Panel shall schedule oral arguments as needed and as set forth in Rule 11.1.

[Former Rule 10 adopted May 3, 1993, effective July 1, 1993. Renumbered Rule 7.2 and amended September 1, 1998, effective November 2, 1998. Amended April 2, 2001, effective April 2, 2001; March 26, 2009, December 1, 2009. Former Rule 15 adopted May 3, 1993, effective July 1, 1993. Renumbered Rule 6.2 and amended September 1, 1998, effective November 2, 1998. Former Rule 7.2 redesignated in part and amended September 8, 2010, effective October 4, 2010. Technical revisions effective July 6, 2011.]

* [Publisher's Note: So in original.]

RULE 6.3 MOTIONS FOR MISCELLANEOUS RELIEF

(a) Definition. Motions for miscellaneous relief include, but are not limited to, requests for extensions of time, exemption from ECF requirements, page limit extensions, or expedited consideration of any motion.

(b) Panel Action. The Panel, through the Clerk, may act upon any motion for miscellaneous relief, at any time, without waiting for a response. A motion for extension of time to file a pleading or perform an act under these Rules must state specifically the revised date sought and must be filed before the deadline for filing the pleading or performing the act. Any party aggrieved by the Clerk of the Panel's action may file objections for consideration. Absent exceptional circumstances, the Panel will not grant any extensions of time to file a notice of opposition to either a conditional transfer order or a conditional remand order.

[Former Rule 15 adopted May 3, 1993, effective July 1, 1993. Renumbered Rule 6.2 and amended September 1, 1998, effective November 2, 1998. Former Rule 6.2 redesignated and amended September 8, 2010, effective October 4, 2010.]

RULE 7.1 CONDITIONAL TRANSFER ORDERS (CTO) FOR TAG–ALONG ACTIONS

(a) Notice of Potential Tag-along Actions. Any party or counsel in actions previously transferred under Section 1407 shall promptly notify the Clerk of the Panel of any potential tag-along actions in which that party is also named or in which that counsel appears. The Panel has several options: (i) filing a CTO under Rule 7.1, (ii) filing a show cause order under Rule 8.1, or (iii) declining to act (Rule 7.1(b)(i)).

(b) Initiation of CTO. Upon learning of the pendency of a potential tag-along action, the Clerk of the Panel may enter a conditional order transferring that action to the previously designated transferee district court for the reasons expressed in the Panel's previous opinions and orders. The Clerk of the Panel shall serve this order on each party to the litigation but shall not send the order to the clerk of the transferee district court until 7 days after its entry.

(i)* If the Clerk of the Panel determines that a potential tag-along action is not appropriate for inclusion in an MDL proceeding and does not enter a CTO, an involved party may move for its transfer pursuant to Rule 6.1.

(c) Notice of Opposition to CTO. Any party opposing the transfer shall file a notice of opposition with the Clerk of the Panel within the 7–day period. In such event, the Clerk of the Panel shall not transmit the transfer order to the clerk of the transferee district court, but shall notify the parties of the briefing schedule.

(d) Failure to Respond. Failure to respond to a CTO shall be treated as that party's acquiescence to it.

(e) Notice of Appearance. Within 14 days after the issuance of a "Notice of Filed Opposition" to a CTO, each opposing party or designated attorney shall file a Notice of Appearance in accordance with Rule 4.1(c).

(f) Motion to Vacate CTO. Within 14 days of the filing of its notice of opposition, the party opposing transfer shall file a motion to vacate the CTO and brief in support thereof. The Clerk of the Panel shall set the motion for the next appropriate hearing session. Failure to file and serve a motion and brief shall be treated as withdrawal of the opposition and the Clerk of the Panel shall forthwith transmit the order to the clerk of the transferee district court.

(g) Notification of Developments. Parties to an action subject to a CTO shall notify the Clerk of the Panel if that action is no longer pending in its transferor district court.

(h) Effective Date of CTO. CTOs are effective when filed with the clerk of the transferee district court.

[Former Rule 12 adopted May 3, 1993, effective July 1, 1993. Renumbered Rule 7.4 and amended September 1, 1998, effective November 2, 1998. Amended April 2, 2001, effective April 2, 2001; March 26, 2009, December 1, 2009. Former Rule 7.4 redesignated and amended September 8, 2010, effective October 4, 2010. Technical revisions effective July 6, 2011.]

* [**Publisher's Note:** So in original. No (b)(ii) promulgated.]

RULE 7.2 MISCELLANEOUS PROVISIONS CONCERNING TAG–ALONG ACTIONS

(a) Potential Tag-alongs in Transferee Court. Potential tag-along actions filed in the transferee district do not require Panel action. A party should request assignment of such actions to the Section 1407 transferee judge in accordance with applicable local rules.

(b) Failure to Serve. Failure to serve one or more of the defendants in a potential tag-along action with the complaint and summons as required by Rule 4 of the Federal Rules of Civil Procedure does not preclude transfer of such action under Section 1407. Such failure, however, may constitute grounds for denying the proposed transfer where prejudice can be shown. The failure of the Clerk of the Panel to serve a CTO on all plaintiffs or defendants or their counsel may constitute grounds for the Clerk to reinstate the CTO or for the aggrieved party to seek § 1407(c) remand.

[Former Rule 13 adopted May 3, 1993, effective July 1, 1993. Renumbered Rule 7.5 and amended September 1, 1998, effective November 2, 1998. Amended April 2, 2001, effective April 2, 2001. Former Rule 7.5 redesignated and amended September 8, 2010, effective October 4, 2010. Amended effective July 6, 2011.]

RULE 8.1 SHOW CAUSE ORDERS

(a) Entry of Show Cause Order. When transfer of multidistrict litigation is being considered on the initiative of the Panel pursuant to 28 U.S.C. § 1407(c)(i), the Clerk of the Panel may enter an order directing the parties to show cause why a certain civil action or actions should not be transferred for coordinated or consolidated pretrial proceedings. Any party shall also promptly notify the Clerk of the Panel whenever they learn of any other federal district court actions which are similar to those which the show cause order encompasses.

(b) Notice of Appearance. Within 14 days of the issuance of an order to show cause, each party or designated attorney shall file a Notice of Appearance in accordance with Rule 4.1(c).

(c) Responses. Unless otherwise provided by order, any party may file a response within 21 days of the filing of the show cause order. Failure to respond to a show cause order shall be treated as that party's acquiescence to the Panel action.

(d) Replies. Within 7 days after the lapse of the time period for filing a response, any party may file a reply.

(e) Notification of Developments. Counsel shall promptly notify the Clerk of the Panel of any development that would partially or completely moot any matter subject to a show cause order.

[Former Rule 7.3 adopted May 3, 1993, effective July 1, 1993. Renumbered Rule 7.3 and amended September 1, 1998, effective November 2, 1998; March 26, 2009, effective December 1, 2009. Former Rule 7.3 redesignated and amended September 8, 2010, effective October 4, 2010.]

RULE 9.1 TRANSFER OF FILES; NOTIFICATION REQUIREMENTS

(a) Notice to Transferee Court Clerk. The Clerk of the Panel, via a notice of electronic filing, will notify the clerk of the transferee district whenever a Panel transfer order should be filed in the transferee district court. Upon receipt of an electronically certified copy of a Panel transfer order from the clerk of the transferee district, the clerk of the transferor district shall transmit the record of each transferred action to the transferee district and then, unless Rule 9.1(b) applies, close the transferred action in the transferor district.

(b) Retention of Claims. If the transfer order provides for the separation and simultaneous remand of any claim, cross-claim, counterclaim, or third-party claim, the clerk of the transferor district shall retain jurisdiction over any such claim and shall not close the action.

(c) Notice to Clerk of Panel. The clerk of the transferee district shall promptly provide the Clerk of the Panel with the civil action numbers assigned to all transferred actions and the identity of liaison counsel, if or when designated. The clerk of the transferee district shall also promptly notify the Clerk of the Panel of any dispositive ruling that terminates a transferred action.

[Former Rule 19 adopted May 3, 1993, effective July 1, 1993. Renumbered Rule 1.6 and amended September 1, 1998, effective November 2, 1998. Former Rule 1.6 redesignated in part and amended September 8, 2010, effective October 4, 2010.]

RULE 10.1 TERMINATION AND REMAND

(a) Termination. Where the transferee district court terminates an action by valid order, including but not limited to summary judgment, judgment of dismissal and judgment upon stipulation, the transferee district court clerk shall transmit a copy of that order to the Clerk of the Panel. The terminated action shall not be remanded to the transferor court and the transferee court shall retain the original files and records unless the transferee judge or the Panel directs otherwise.

(b) Initiation of Remand. Typically, the transferee judge recommends remand of an action, or a part of it, to the transferor court at any time by filing a suggestion of remand with the Panel. However, the Panel may remand an action or any separable claim, cross-claim, counterclaim or third-party claim within it, upon

(i) the transferee court's suggestion of remand,

(ii) the Panel's own initiative by entry of an order to show cause, a conditional remand order or other appropriate order, or

(iii) motion of any party.

[Former Rule 14 adopted May 3, 1993, effective July 1, 1993. Renumbered Rule 7.6 and amended September 1, 1998, effective November 2, 1998. Amended April 2, 2001, effective April 2, 2001; March 26, 2009, effective December 1, 2009. Former Rule 7.6 redesignated in part and amended September 8, 2010, effective October 4, 2010.]

RULE 10.2 CONDITIONAL REMAND ORDERS (CRO)

(a) Entering a CRO. Upon the suggestion of the transferee judge or the Panel's own initiative, the Clerk of the Panel shall enter a conditional order remanding the action or actions to the transferor district court. The Clerk of the Panel shall serve this order on each party to the litigation but shall not send the order to the clerk of the transferee district court for 7 days from the entry thereof.

(i)* The Panel may, on its own initiative, also enter an order that the parties show cause why a matter should not be remanded. Rule 8.1 applies to responses and replies with respect to such a show cause order.

(b) Notice of Opposition. Any party opposing the CRO shall file a notice of opposition with the Clerk of the Panel within the 7–day period. In such event, the Clerk of the Panel shall not transmit the remand order to the clerk of the transferee district court and shall notify the parties of the briefing schedule.

(c) Failure to Respond. Failure to respond to a CRO shall be treated as that party's acquiescence to it.

(d) Notice of Appearance. Within 14 days after the issuance of a "Notice of Filed Opposition" to a CRO, each opposing party or designated attorney shall file a Notice of Appearance in accordance with Rule 4.1(c).

(e) Motion to Vacate CRO. Within 14 days of the filing of its notice of opposition, the party opposing remand shall file a motion to vacate the CRO and brief in support thereof. The Clerk of the Panel shall set the motion for the next appropriate Panel hearing session. Failure to file and serve a motion and brief shall be treated as a withdrawal of the opposition and the Clerk of the Panel shall forthwith transmit the order to the clerk of the transferee district court.

(f) Effective Date of CRO. CROs are not effective until filed with the clerk of the transferee district court.

[Former Rule 14 adopted May 3, 1993, effective July 1, 1993. Renumbered Rule 7.6 and amended September 1, 1998, effective November 2, 1998. Amended April 2, 2001, effective April 2, 2001; March 26, 2009, effective December 1, 2009. Former Rule 7.6 redesignated in part and amended September 8, 2010, effective October 4, 2010. Technical revisions effective July 6, 2011.]

* [**Publisher's Note:** So in original. No (a)(ii) promulgated.]

RULE 10.3 MOTION TO REMAND

(a) Requirements of the Motion. If the Clerk of the Panel does not enter a CRO, a party may file a motion to remand to the transferor court pursuant to these Rules. Because the Panel is reluctant to order a remand absent the suggestion of the transferee judge, the motion must include:

(i) An affidavit reciting whether the movant has requested a suggestion of remand and the judge's response, whether the parties have completed common discovery and other pretrial proceedings, and whether the parties have complied with all transferee court orders.

(ii) A copy of the transferee district court's final pretrial order, if entered.

(b) Filing Copy of Motion. Counsel shall file a copy of the motion to remand in the affected transferee district court.

(c) Notice of Appearance. Within 14 days of the issuance of a "Notice of Filing" of a motion to remand, each party or designated attorney shall file a Notice of Appearance in accordance with Rule 4.1(c).

[Former Rule 14 adopted May 3, 1993, effective July 1, 1993. Renumbered Rule 7.6 and amended September 1, 1998, effective November 2, 1998. Amended April 2, 2001, effective April 2, 2001; March 26, 2009, effective December 1, 2009. Former Rule 7.6 redesignated in part and amended September 8, 2010, effective October 4, 2010. Technical revisions effective July 6, 2011.]

RULE 10.4 TRANSFER OF FILES ON REMAND

(a) Designating the Record. Upon receipt of an order to remand from the Clerk of the Panel, the parties shall furnish forthwith to the transferee district clerk a stipulation or designation of the contents of the record or part thereof to be remanded.

(b) Transfer of Files. Upon receipt of an order to remand from the Clerk of the Panel, the transferee district shall transmit to the clerk of the transferor district the following concerning each remanded action:

(i) a copy of the individual docket sheet for each action remanded;

(ii) a copy of the master docket sheet, if applicable;

(iii) the entire file for each action remanded, as originally received from the transferor district and augmented as set out in this Rule;

(iv) a copy of the final pretrial order, if applicable; and

(v) a "record on remand" as designated by the parties in accordance with 10.4(a).

[Former Rule 19 adopted May 3, 1993, effective July 1, 1993. Renumbered Rule 1.6 and amended September 1, 1998, effective November 2, 1998. Former Rule 1.6 redesignated in part and amended September 8, 2010, effective October 4, 2010.]

RULE 11.1 HEARING SESSIONS AND ORAL ARGUMENT

(a) Schedule. The Panel shall schedule sessions for oral argument and consideration of other matters as desirable or necessary. The Chair shall determine the time, place and agenda for each hearing session. The Clerk of the Panel shall give appropriate notice to counsel for all parties. The Panel may continue its consideration of any scheduled matters.

(b) Oral Argument Statement. Any party affected by a motion may file a separate statement setting forth reasons why oral argument should, or need not, be heard. Such statements shall be captioned "Reasons Why Oral Argument Should [Need Not] Be Heard" and shall be limited to 2 pages.

(i)* The parties affected by a motion to transfer may agree to waive oral argument. The Panel will take this into consideration in determining the need for oral argument.

(c) Hearing Session. The Panel shall not consider transfer or remand of any action pending in a federal district court when any party timely opposes such transfer or remand without first holding a hearing session for the presentation of oral argument. The Panel may dispense with oral argument if it determines that:

(i) the dispositive issue(s) have been authoritatively decided; or

(ii) the facts and legal arguments are adequately presented and oral argument would not significantly aid the decisional process.

Unless otherwise ordered, the Panel shall consider all other matters, such as a motion for reconsideration, upon the basis of the pleadings.

(d) Notification of Oral Argument. The Panel shall promptly notify counsel of those matters in which oral argument is scheduled, as well as those matters that the Panel will consider on the pleadings. The Clerk of the Panel shall require counsel to file and serve notice of their intent to either

make or waive oral argument. Failure to do so shall be deemed a waiver of oral argument. If counsel does not attend oral argument, the matter shall not be rescheduled and that party's position shall be treated as submitted for decision on the basis of the pleadings filed.

(i) Absent Panel approval and for good cause shown, only those parties to actions who have filed a motion or written response to a motion or order shall be permitted to present oral argument.

(ii) The Panel will not receive oral testimony except upon notice, motion and an order expressly providing for it.

(e) Duty to Confer. Counsel in an action set for oral argument shall confer separately prior to that argument for the purpose of organizing their arguments and selecting representatives to present all views without duplication. Oral argument is a means for counsel to emphasize the key points of their arguments, and to update the Panel on any events since the conclusion of briefing.

(f) Time Limit for Oral Argument. Barring exceptional circumstances, the Panel shall allot a maximum of 20 minutes for oral argument in each matter. The time shall be divided among those with varying viewpoints. Counsel for the moving party or parties shall generally be heard first.

[Former Rule 16 adopted May 3, 1998, effective July 1, 1993. Renumbered Rule 16.1 and amended September 1, 1998, effective November 2, 1998. Amended April 2, 2001, effective April 2, 2001. Former Rule 16.1 redesignated and amended September 8, 2010, effective October 4, 2010.]

* [**Publisher's Note:** So in original. No (b)(ii) promulgated.]

RULES 12 TO 15. [RESERVED]

II. RULES FOR MULTICIRCUIT PETITIONS FOR REVIEW UNDER 28 U.S.C. § 2112(a)(3)

RULE 25.1 DEFINITIONS

The Panel promulgates these Rules pursuant to its authority under 28 U.S.C. § 2112(a)(3) to provide a means for the random selection of one circuit court of appeals to hear consolidated petitions for review of agency decisions.

An "Agency" means an agency, board, commission or officer of the United States government, that has received two or more petitions for review in a circuit court of appeals to enjoin, set aside, suspend, modify or otherwise review or enforce an action.

[Former Rule 20 adopted May 3, 1993, effective July 1, 1993. Renumbered Rule 25.1 and amended September 1, 1998, effective November 2, 1998. Amended September 8, 2010, effective October 4, 2010.]

RULE 25.2 FILING OF NOTICES

(a) Submitting Notice. An affected agency shall submit a notice of multicircuit petitions for review pursuant to 28 U.S.C. § 2112(a)(3) to the Clerk of the Panel by electronic means in the manner these Rules require and in accordance with the Panel's Administrative Policies and Procedures for Electronic

Case Filing, except that the portion of Rule 3.2(d) requiring a courtesy copy is suspended in its entirety.

(b) Accompaniments to Notices. All notices of multicircuit petitions for review shall include:

(i) a copy of each involved petition for review as the petition for review is defined in 28 U.S.C. § 2112(a)(2);

(ii) a schedule giving

(A) the date of the relevant agency order;

(B) the case name of each petition for review involved;

(C) the circuit court of appeals in which each petition for review is pending;

(D) the appellate docket number of each petition for review;

(E) the date of filing by the court of appeals of each petition for review; and

(F) the date of receipt by the agency of each petition for review; and

(iii) proof of service (*see* Rule 25.3).

(c) Scope of Notice. All notices of multicircuit petitions for review shall embrace exclusively petitions for review filed in the courts of appeals within 10 days after issuance of an agency order and received by the affected agency from the petitioners within that 10–day period.

(d) Filing at the Panel. The Clerk of the Panel shall file the notice of multicircuit petitions for review and endorse thereon the date of filing.

(e) Filing With Each Circuit Clerk. The affected agency shall file copies of notices of multicircuit petitions for review with the clerk of each circuit court of appeals in which a petition for review is pending.

[Former Rule 21 adopted May 3, 1993, effective July 1, 1993. Renumbered Rule 25.2 and amended September 1, 1998, effective November 2, 1998. Amended September 8, 2010, effective October 4, 2010. Technical revisions effective July 6, 2011.]

RULE 25.3   SERVICE OF NOTICES

(a) Proof of Service. Notices of multicircuit petitions for review shall include proof of service on all other parties in the petitions for review included in the notice. Rule 25 of the Federal Rules of Appellate Procedure governs service and proof of service. The proof of service shall state the name, address and email address of each person served and shall indicate the party represented by each and the manner in which service was accomplished on each party. If a party is not represented by counsel, the proof of service shall indicate the name of the party and his or her last known address. The affected party shall submit proof of service for filing with the Clerk of the Panel and shall send copies thereof to each person included within the proof of service.

(b) Service on Clerk of Circuit. The proof of service pertaining to notices of multicircuit petitions for review shall certify the affected party has mailed or delivered copies of the notices to the clerk of each circuit court of appeals in which a petition for review is pending that is included in the notice. The Clerk shall file the notice with the circuit court.

[Former Rule 22 adopted May 3, 1993, effective July 1, 1993. Renumbered Rule 25.3 September 1, 1998, effective November 2, 1998. Amended September 8, 2010, effective October 4, 2010.]

RULE 25.4   FORM OF NOTICES; PLACE OF FILING

(a) Unless otherwise provided here, Rule 3.2 governs the form of a notice of multicircuit petitions for review. Each notice shall bear the heading "Notice to the United States Judicial Panel on Multidistrict Litigation of Multicircuit Petitions for Review," followed by a brief caption identifying the involved agency, the relevant agency order, and the date of the order.

(b) Rule 3.2(b) and (c) govern the manner of filing a notice of multicircuit petitions for review.

[Former Rule 23 adopted May 3, 1993, effective July 1, 1993. Renumbered Rule 25.4 and amended September 1, 1998, effective November 2, 1998. Amended September 8, 2010, effective October 4, 2010.]

RULE 25.5   RANDOM SELECTION

(a) Selection Process. Upon filing a notice of multicircuit petitions for review, the Clerk of the Panel shall randomly select a circuit court of appeals from a drum containing an entry for each circuit wherein a constituent petition for review is pending. Multiple petitions for review pending in a single circuit shall be allotted only a single entry in the drum. A designated deputy other than the random selector shall witness the random selection. Thereafter, an order on behalf of the Panel shall be issued, signed by the random selector and the witness,

(i) consolidating the petitions for review in the court of appeals for the circuit that was randomly selected; and

(ii) designating that circuit as the one in which the record is to be filed pursuant to Rules 16 and 17 of the Federal Rules of Appellate Procedure.

(b) Effective Date. A consolidation of petitions for review shall be effective when the Clerk of the Panel enters the consolidation order.

[Former Rule 24 adopted May 3, 1993, effective July 1, 1993. Renumbered Rule 17.1 September 1, 1998, effective November 2, 1998. Former Rule 17.1 redesignated and amended September 8, 2010, effective October 4, 2010.]

RULE 25.6   SERVICE OF PANEL CONSOLIDATION ORDER

(a) The Clerk of the Panel shall serve the Panel's consolidation order on the affected agency through the individual or individuals, as identified in Rule 25.2(a), who submitted the notice of multicircuit petitions for review on behalf of the agency.

(b) That individual or individuals, or anyone else designated by the agency, shall promptly serve the Panel's consolidation order on all other parties in all petitions for review included in the Panel's consolidation order, and shall promptly submit a proof of that service to the Clerk of the Panel. Rule 25.3 governs service.

(c) The Clerk of the Panel shall serve the Panel's consolidation order on the clerks of all circuit courts of appeals that were among the candidates for the Panel's random selection.

[Former Rule 25 adopted May 3, 1993, effective July 1, 1993. Renumbered Rule 25.5 and amended September 1, 1998, effective November 2, 1998. Former Rule 25.5 redesignated and amended September 8, 2010, effective October 4, 2010.]

III. CONVERSION TABLE

New to Old:

New Rule / Previous Rule		New Rule / Previous Rule	
1.1	1.1	9.1	1.6
2.1	1.2, 1.3, 1.4, 1.5	10.1	7.6
3.1	5.1	10.2	7.6
3.2	5.1.1, 5.1.2, 7.1	10.3	7.6
3.3	5.1.1, 5.1.2, 7.1	10.4	1.6
4.1	5.2	11.1	16.1
5.1	5.3	25.1	25.1
6.1	7.2	25.2	25.1, 25.2
6.2	7.2	25.3	25.3
6.3	6.2	25.4	25.1, 25.4
7.1	7.4	25.5	17.1
7.2	7.5	25.6	25.5
8.1	7.3		

Old to New:

Previous Rule / New Rule		Previous Rule / New Rule	
1.1	1.1	7.1	3.2, 3.3
1.2	2.1	7.2	6.1
1.3	2.1	7.3	8.1
1.4	2.1	7.4	7.1
1.5	2.1	7.5	7.2
1.6	10.4	7.6	10.1
5.1	3.1	16.1	11.1
5.1.1	3.2, 3.3	17.1	25.5
5.1.2	3.2, 3.3	25.1	25.1, 25.2, 25.4
5.1.3	-	25.2	25.2
5.2	4.1	25.3	25.3
5.3	5.1	25.4	25.4
6.2	6.3	25.5	25.6

[October 2010.]

ELECTRONIC CASE FILING ADMINISTRATIVE POLICIES AND PROCEDURES

1. DEFINITIONS.

1.1 **"ELECTRONIC FILING SYSTEM" (ECF)** refers to the United States Judicial Panel on Multidistrict Litigation's (the Panel's) automated system that receives and stores documents filed in electronic form. The program is part of the CM/ECF (Case Management/Electronic Case Files) software which was developed for the Federal Judiciary by the Administrative Office of the United States Courts.

1.2 **"CLERK OF THE PANEL"** means the official appointed by the Panel to act as Clerk of the Panel and shall include those deputized by the Clerk of the Panel to perform or assist in the performance of the duties of the Clerk of the Panel.

1.3 **"FILING USER"** is an individual who has a Panel-issued login and password to file documents electronically. In accordance with Rule 1.4 of the Rules of Procedure of the United States Judicial Panel on Multidistrict Litigation (the Panel Rules), every member in good standing of the Bar of any district court of the United States is entitled to practice before the Judicial Panel on Multidistrict Litigation.

1.4 **"NOTICE OF ELECTRONIC FILING" (NEF)** is a notice automatically generated by the Electronic Filing System at the time a document is filed with the system, setting forth the time of filing, the date the document is entered on the docket, the name of the party and attorney filing the document, the type of document, the text of the docket entry, the name of the party and/or attorney receiving the notice, and an electronic link (hyperlink) to the filed document, which allows recipients to retrieve the document automatically. A document shall not be considered filed for the purposes of the Panel's Rules until the filing party receives a system generated Notice of Electronic Filing with a hyperlink to the electronically filed document.

1.5 **"PACER" (Public Access to Court Electronic Records)** is an automated system that allows an individual to view, print and download Panel docket information over the Internet.

1.6 **"PDF" (Portable Document Format).** A document file created with a word processor, or a paper document which has been scanned, must be converted to portable document format to be filed electronically with the Panel. Converted files contain the extension ".pdf".

1.7 **"TECHNICAL FAILURE"** is defined as a failure of Panel owned/leased hardware, software, and/or telecommunications facility which results in the inability of a Filing User to submit a filing electronically. Technical failure does not include malfunctioning of a Filing User's equipment.

2. SCOPE OF ELECTRONIC FILING.

(a) All multidistrict litigation matters (MDLs) brought before the Panel under 28 U.S.C. § 1407 shall be assigned to the Electronic Filing System. Effective October 1, 2010, all MDLs, proceedings, motions, memoranda of law and other pleadings or documents filed with the Panel in new and existing dockets must be filed using CM/ECF unless otherwise specified herein.

(b) The filing of all MDL papers shall be accomplished electronically under procedures outlined in the Panel's CM/ECF User Manual.

(c) A party proceeding pro se shall not file electronically, unless otherwise permitted by the Panel. Pro se filers shall file paper originals of all documents. The clerk's office will scan these original documents into the JPML's electronic system, unless otherwise sealed.

3. ELIGIBILITY, REGISTRATION, PASSWORDS.

(a) Any attorney admitted to the Bar of any United States district court is eligible to practice before the Panel. Unless otherwise exempt as set forth herein, to become a Filing User, an attorney must register as a Filing User by completing the prescribed registration form and submitting it to the Clerk of the Panel.

(b) Registration as a Filing User constitutes consent to electronic service of all documents filed with or issued by the Panel in accordance with the Panel Rules.

(c) By submitting the online registration form, the Filing Users certify that they have read and are familiar with the Panel Rules and these administrative policies and procedures governing electronic filing and the method of training in the System used prior to becoming a Filing User. Filing users must also have a PACER account. An individual may register more than one Internet email address. The clerk's office will email the login and password to the attorney.

(d) Once the registration is processed by the clerk, the Filing User shall protect the security of the User password and immediately notify the clerk if the Filing User learns that the password has been compromised. Filing Users may be subject to sanctions for failure to comply with this provision. After registering, attorneys may change their passwords. If an attorney comes to believe that the security of an existing password has been compromised and that a threat to the System exists, the attorney must change his or her password immediately.

(e) Exemptions from mandatory electronic filing may be granted upon submission of a written request to the clerk. The written request shall include a supporting affidavit showing a substantial undue hardship. Final authority to grant such request is vested in the Clerk of the Panel or his/her designee.

(f)(1) Each attorney is responsible for keeping his/her contact information up to date. If an attorney is leaving a law firm and is the attorney of record on an existing case and representation in the case will remain with the law firm, withdrawal and substitution of counsel must be made prior to the attorney's termination in the law firm, for the following reason:

The attorney leaving the firm has an email address with the law firm he or she is leaving on record with the Panel. This email address may be disabled by the law firm as soon as the attorney terminates his/her employment. The electronic notices in CM/ECF will continue to go to the terminated attorney's email address at the former firm. If the email address is disabled at the law firm, the attorney will not receive the electronic notice. If a withdrawal/substitution of counsel has not been filed prior to the attorney leaving the firm, the law firm should not disable the email account of the attorney leaving the firm until another attorney in the firm enters his/her appearance. The law firm should designate someone in the firm to check this email account for CM/ECF notices until substitution of counsel has been filed with the Panel.

(2) If the attorney leaving the firm is taking active cases from the firm, the attorney needs to change his/her email address as soon as possible, otherwise the attorney will not receive electronic notices from CM/ECF. The email will continue to be sent to the former law firm's email address still on record. Procedures for changing an email address may be found in the Panel's CM/ECF User Manual.

4. ELECTRONIC FILING AND SERVICE OF DOCUMENTS.

(a) Electronic transmission of a document to the Electronic Filing System in accordance with these procedures, together with the transmission of a (System) Notice of Electronic Filing from the Panel with a hyperlink to the electronically filed document, constitutes filing of the document for all purposes of the Panel Rules of Procedure.

(b) Emailing a document to the clerk's office does not constitute filing the document. A document shall not be considered filed until the System generates a Notice of Electronic Filing (NEF) with a hyperlink to the electronically filed document.

(c) Before filing a scanned document with the court, a Filing User must verify its legibility.

(d) When a document has been filed electronically, the official record of that document is the electronic recording as stored by the Panel and the filing party is bound by the document as filed. A document filed electronically is deemed filed on the date and time stated on the Notice of Electronic Filing (NEF) from the Panel.

(e) Filing a document electronically does not alter the filing deadline for that document. Filing must be completed before midnight, **EASTERN TIME**, in order to be considered timely filed that day. However, if time of day is of the essence, the Clerk of the Panel may order a document filed by a certain time.

(f) Upon the filing of a document, a docket entry will be created using the information provided by the Filing User. The clerk will, where necessary and appropriate, modify the docket entry description to comply with quality control standards. In the event a Filing User electronically files a document in the wrong MDL or associated civil action, or the incorrect PDF document is attached, the Clerk of the Panel, or his/her designee, shall be authorized to strike the document from the record. A notice of the action striking a document from the record shall be served on all parties in the case.

(g) By participating in the electronic filing process, the parties consent to the electronic service of all documents, and shall make available electronic mail addresses for service. Upon the filing of a document by a Filing User, a Notice of Electronic Filing (NEF), with a hyperlink to the electronic document and an email message will be automatically generated by the electronic filing system, and sent via electronic mail to the email addresses of all parties who have registered in the MDL. In addition to receiving email notifications of filing activity, the Filing User is strongly encouraged to sign on to the electronic filing system at regular intervals to check the docket in his/her MDL and/or civil action.

(h) If the filing of an electronically submitted document requires leave of the Panel, such as a request to file out-of-time, the attorney shall attach the proposed document as an attachment to the motion requesting leave to file. If the Clerk of the Panel grants the motion, the document will be electronically filed without further action by the Filing User.

(i) A certificate of service must be included with all documents filed electronically. Such certificate shall indicate that service was accomplished pursuant to the Panel's electronic filing procedures. Service by electronic mail shall constitute service pursuant to Panel Rule 5.2.

A party who is not a registered CM/ECF participant with any United States federal court is entitled to a paper copy of any electronically filed pleading, document, or order pursuant to Panel Rule 5.1.1.(b). The filing party must therefore provide the non-registered attorney or party, including a terminated party or attorney, if appropriate, with the pleading, document, or order pursuant to Panel Rule 5.2. Under the Rule, they can be served with a paper copy of the electronically filed document, or they can consent in writing to service by any other method, including other forms of electronic service such as fax or direct email.

The following is a suggested certificate of service for electronic filing:

CERTIFICATE OF SERVICE

On [Date], I electronically filed this document through the CM/ECF system, which will send a notice of electronic filing to: [Attorney Name (attach list if necessary)]; and I [mailed] [hand delivered] [faxed] this document and the notice of electronic filing to: [Attorney/Party Name], [Address], [Parties Represented], [Civil Action(s)] (attach list if necessary).

> /s/ [typed name of attorney]
> Attorney's name
> Law Firm Name (if applicable)
> Address
> Phone Number
> Fax Number
> Attorney's Email address
> Attorney for:

5. ENTRY OF PANEL DOCUMENTS.

(a) A document entered or issued by the Panel will be filed in accordance with these procedures and such filing shall constitute entry on the docket kept by the Clerk.

(b) All signed orders will be electronically filed or entered. An order containing the electronic signature of a Panel Judge or the Clerk of the Panel shall have the same force and effect as if the Panel Judge or Clerk of the Panel had affixed a signature to a paper copy of the order and the order had been entered on the docket in a conventional manner.

(c) Orders may also be issued as "text-only" entries on the docket, without an attached document. Such orders are official and binding.

6. NOTICE OF PANEL ORDERS AND NOTICES.

Immediately upon the entry of an order or notice by the Panel, the clerk will transmit to Filing Users in affected cases in the MDL, in electronic form, a Notice of Electronic Filing (NEF), with a hyperlink to the electronic document. Electronic transmission of the NEF, along with a hyperlink to the electronic document, constitutes the notice required by Panel Rule 5.2. The clerk must give notice in paper form to a pro se party or an attorney who is not a Filing User to the extent notice is required.

7. ATTACHMENTS AND EXHIBITS.

Documents referenced as exhibits or attachments shall be filed in accordance with these administrative policies and procedures and the Panel's CM/ECF User Manual, unless otherwise ordered by the Panel. A Filing User shall submit as exhibits or attachments only those excerpts of the referenced documents that are directly germane to the matter under consideration by the Panel. Excerpted material must be clearly and prominently identified as such. Filing Users who file excerpts of documents as exhibits or attachments under these procedures do so without prejudice to their right to file timely additional excerpts or the complete document. Responding parties may timely file additional excerpts or the complete document that they believe are directly germane. The Panel may require parties to file additional excerpts or the complete document.

8. SEALED DOCUMENTS.

To ensure proper storage of a document, a document subject to a sealing order must be filed with the Panel on paper in a sealed envelope marked "sealed", citing thereon the MDL docket number and title and the associated case caption and case number; or by attaching thereto a paper copy of the Panel's order sealing the document or a copy of the NEF citing the entry of the court's order sealing the document. The clerk may require the document to be accompanied by a disk or CD–ROM containing the document in .pdf format. Only a motion to file a document under seal may be filed electronically, unless prohibited by law. The order of the Panel authorizing the filing of documents under seal may be filed electronically, unless prohibited by law or otherwise directed by the Panel. If a document is filed under seal pursuant to the E–Government Act of 2002, the filing party is nevertheless required to file a redacted copy for the public record along with the unredacted sealed document.

9. SPECIAL FILING REQUIREMENTS AND EXCEPTIONS.

9.1 Special Filing Requirements

The documents listed below shall be presented for filing on paper. The clerk may require the document be accompanied by a disk or CD–ROM containing the document in .pdf format:

> Sealed
>
> MDL dockets involving Qui Tam Cases (under seal)

9.2 Exceptions

All documents shall be filed electronically unless otherwise ordered by the Panel or specifically exempt herein.

10. RETENTION REQUIREMENTS.

(a) A document that is electronically filed and requires an original signature other than that of the Filing User must be maintained in paper form by counsel and/or the firm representing the party on whose behalf the document was filed until one year after all periods for appeals expire. On request of the Panel, said counsel must provide the original document for review.

(b) The clerk's office may choose to discard certain documents brought to the clerk's office for filing in paper form after those documents are scanned and uploaded to the System (to include pro se filings). Therefore, counsel and pro se filers shall provide the Panel with a copy of the original documents with intrinsic value for scanning and maintain the original signature in accordance with 10(a).

11. SIGNATURES.

(a) The user login and password required to submit documents to the Electronic Filing System serve as the Filing User signature on all electronic documents filed with the court. They serve as a signature for purposes of the Panel Rules and any other purpose for which a signature is required in connection with proceedings before the Panel.

(b) Each document filed electronically must indicate in the caption that it has been electronically filed. An electronically filed document must include a signature block in compliance with Panel Rule 7.1(e), and must set forth the name, address, telephone number, fax number, and email address. In addition, the name of the Filing User under whose login and password the document is submitted must be preceded by an "/s/" and typed in the space where the signature would otherwise appear. No Filing User or other person may knowingly permit or cause to permit a Filing User password to be used by anyone other than an authorized agent of the Filing User.

(c) A document requiring signatures of more than one party must be filed either by:

(1) electronically filing a scanned document containing all necessary signatures; or

(2) representing the consent of the other parties on the document; or

(3) identifying on the document the party whose signature is required and by the submission of a notice of endorsement by the other parties no later than three (3) business days after filing; or

(4) any other manner approved by the Panel.

(d) A non-filing signatory or party who disputes the authenticity of an electronically filed document with a non-attorney signature, or the authenticity of the signature on that document; or the authenticity of an electronically filed document containing multiple signatures or the authenticity of the signature themselves, must file an objection to the document within fourteen (14) days of service of the document.

(e) Any party challenging the authenticity of an electronically filed document or the attorney's signature on that document must file an objection to the document within fourteen (14) days of service of the document.

(f) If a party wishes to challenge the authenticity of an electronically filed document or signature after the fourteen (14) day period, the party shall file a motion to seek a ruling from the Panel.

12. SERVICE OF DOCUMENTS BY ELECTRONIC MEANS.

12.1 Service

12.1.1 Filing User

Upon the electronic filing of a pleading or other document, the Panel's Electronic Case Filing System will automatically generate and send a Notice of Electronic Filing (NEF) to all Filing Users associated with that MDL and/or associated cases, along with a hyperlink to the electronic document. Transmission of the Notice of Electronic Filing with a hyperlink to the electronic document constitutes service of the filed document.

The NEF must include the time of filing, the date the document was entered on the docket, the name of the party and attorney filing the document, the type of document, the text of the docket entry, and an electronic link (hyperlink) to the filed document, allowing anyone receiving the notice by email to retrieve the document automatically. If the Filing User becomes aware that the NEF was not transmitted successfully to a party, or that the notice is deficient, *i.e.*, the electronic link to the document is defective, the filer shall serve the electronically filed document by email, hand, facsimile, or by first-class mail postage prepaid immediately upon notification of the NEF deficiency.

12.1.2 Individual who is not a Filing User

A non-registered participant is entitled to receive a paper copy of any electronically filed document from the party making such filing. Service of such paper copy must be made according to the Panel Rules.

13. TECHNICAL FAILURES.

(a) If the site is unable to accept filings continuously or intermittently for more than one (1) hour occurring after 12:00 noon Eastern Time that day, the Clerk of the Panel shall deem the Panel's Electronic Case Filing web site to be subject to a technical failure.

(b) If a Filing User experiences a technical failure as defined herein, the Filing User may submit the document to the Clerk of the Panel, provided that the document is accompanied by a certification, signed by the Filing User, that the Filing User has attempted to file the document electronically at least twice, with those unsuccessful attempts occurring at least one (1) hour apart after 12:00 noon Eastern Time that day. The Clerk may require the document to be accompanied by a disk or CD–ROM which contains the document in .pdf format.

(c) The initial point of contact for a Filing User experiencing technical difficulty filing a document electronically will be the Panel's CM/ECF Help Desk at the numbers listed on the Panel's web site and in the CM/ECF User Manual.

(d) A Filing User who suffers prejudice as a result of a technical failure as defined herein or a Filing User who cannot file a time-sensitive document electronically due to unforeseen technical difficulties, such as the malfunctioning of a Filing User's equipment, may seek relief from the Clerk of the Panel.

14. PUBLIC ACCESS.

14.1   (a) A person may receive information from the Electronic Filing System at the Panel's Internet site by obtaining a PACER login and password.   A person who has PACER access may retrieve docket sheets and documents (unless otherwise sealed or restricted) in MDL dockets and associated civil cases.   Any case or document under seal shall not be available electronically or through any other means.

(b) If a case or document has been restricted, a PACER user may retrieve the docket sheet over the Internet, but only a Filing User who is counsel of record may retrieve restricted documents electronically.   However, a restricted case or document will be available for viewing by the public at the clerk's office.

(c) Electronic access to electronic docket sheets and all documents filed in the System, unless sealed, is available to the public for viewing at no charge during regular business hours at the clerk's office.   A copy fee for an electronic reproduction is required in accordance with 28 U.S.C. § 1932.

(d) Conventional copies and certified copies of electronically filed documents may be purchased at the clerk's office.   The fee for copying and certifying will be in accordance with 28 U.S.C. § 1932.

14.2   Sensitive Information

Since the public may access certain case information over the Internet through the Panel's Electronic Filing System, sensitive information should not be included in any document filed with the court unless such inclusion is necessary and relevant.   In accordance with these Administrative Policies and Procedures, if sensitive information must be included, certain personal and identifying information such as Social Security numbers, financial account numbers, dates of birth and names of minor children shall be redacted from the pleading, whether it is filed electronically or on paper.

The Panel recognizes that parties may need to include in the record a document containing information such as driver's license number; medical records, treatment and diagnosis; employment history; individual financial information; and proprietary or trade secret information.

To avoid unnecessary disclosure of private, personal or financial information, a party may:

(a) **RESTRICTED MDL DOCKETS OR DOCUMENTS.**

File a "Motion to Seal" or "Motion to Seal Document".   The motion must state the reason and show good cause for restricting remote access to the case.   If the motion is granted, remote access to documents will be limited to Filing Users who are counsel of record.   However, the MDL docket sheet and/or documents will be available for viewing by the public at the clerk's office.

(b) **EXHIBITS.**

File an exhibit containing private, personal or financial information as an attachment to a pleading entitled "Notice of Filing Restricted Exhibit".   The notice and the attached exhibit shall be filed as a separate docket entry, rather than as an attachment to the pleading supported by the exhibit.   Remote public access to the notice and exhibit will be limited to Filing Users who are counsel of record.   The notice and exhibit will, however, be available for viewing by the public at the clerk's office.

(c) **DOCUMENTS UNDER SEAL.**

(1) File a redacted copy of a pleading or exhibit containing private, personal or financial information, whether electronically or on paper, while concurrently filing an unredacted copy under seal.   This document shall be retained by the Panel as part of the record.

OR

(2) File a reference list under seal.   The reference list shall contain the complete personal data identifier(s) and the redacted identifier(s) used in its (their) place in the filing.   All references in the case to the redacted identifier(s) included in the reference list will be construed to refer to the corresponding complete identifier.   The reference list must be filed under seal, and may be amended as of right.   It shall be retained by the Panel as part of the record.

(d) **MOTION TO SEAL.**

File a motion to seal the document or MDL associated case.   The motion must state the reason and show good cause for sealing the document or MDL associated case.   If the motion to seal is granted, the document or case under seal will not be available electronically or through any other means.

It is the sole responsibility of counsel and the parties to ensure that all documents filed with the Panel comply with these Administrative Policies and Procedures, regarding public access to electronic case files. The Clerk will not review any document for redaction.

Counsel are strongly urged to share this information with all clients so that an informed decision about the inclusion, redaction, and/or exclusion of certain materials may be made.

[Effective May 2010.]

SELECTED ORDERS AND NOTICES

MISCELLANEOUS ORDER 20–01.   IN RE: SUSPENSION OF PANEL RULES 3.2(d) AND 3.3(c)(i) [COVID–19]

The United States Judicial Panel on Multidistrict Litigation continues to monitor the most current statements from the Centers for Disease Control and Prevention (CDC), as well as all communications disseminated by the Administrative Office of the U.S. Courts (AO), regarding the COVID–19 virus (coronavirus). In light of these recommendations, as well as those by local public health authorities, Panel staff are teleworking until further notice. Panel staff remain available during regular business hours. Parties and other members of the public needing assistance should contact the Panel's office via telephone or email. During this period, Panel operations will continue as normal to the extent possible. Some modifications to Panel operations, though, are necessary. Therefore, it is:

ORDERED that the Panel office is closed to in-person filings until further order of the Panel. Filings with the Panel should be made using another method, such as electronic filing using CM/ECF or via facsimile, as set forth in the Panel Rules;

IT IS FURTHER ORDERED that Rule 3.2(d)—requiring counsel to serve the Clerk of the Panel, for delivery within one business day of filing, courtesy copies of specified pleadings-is suspended until further order of the Panel; and

IT IS FURTHER ORDERED that Rule 3.3(c)(i)—limiting pleadings filed via facsimile to ten pages-is suspended until further order of the Panel.

[Effective March 16, 2020.]

FEDERAL COURTS MISCELLANEOUS FEE SCHEDULES
COURT OF APPEALS FEE SCHEDULE
(Effective December 1, 2020)

The fees included in the Court of Appeals Miscellaneous Fee Schedule[1] are to be charged for services provided by the courts of appeals, including relevant services[2] provided by the bankruptcy appellate panels established under 28 U.S.C. § 158(b)(1).

- The United States should not be charged fees under this schedule, except as prescribed in Items 2, 4, and 5 when the information requested is available through remote electronic access.

- Federal agencies or programs that are funded from judiciary appropriations (agencies, organizations, and individuals providing services authorized by the Criminal Justice Act, 18 U.S.C. § 3006A, and bankruptcy administrators) should not be charged any fees under this schedule.

(1) For docketing a case on appeal or review, or docketing any other proceeding, $500.

- Each party filing a notice of appeal pays a separate fee to the district court, but parties filing a joint notice of appeal pay only one fee.

- There is no docketing fee for an application for an interlocutory appeal under 28 U.S.C. § 1292(b) or other petition for permission to appeal under Fed. R. App. P. 5, unless the appeal is allowed.

- There is no docketing fee for a direct bankruptcy appeal or a direct bankruptcy cross appeal, when the fee has been collected by the bankruptcy court in accordance with item 14 of the Bankruptcy Court Miscellaneous Fee Schedule.

- This fee is collected in addition to the statutory fee of $5 that is collected under 28 U.S.C. § 1917.

(2) For conducting a search of the court of appeals or bankruptcy appellate panel records, $32 per name or item searched. This fee applies to services rendered on behalf of the United States if the information requested is available through remote electronic access.

(3) For certification of any document, $11. For the issuance of an apostille, $47.

(4)

a. For reproducing any document and providing a copy in paper form, $.50 per page. This fee applies to services rendered on behalf of the United States if the document requested is available through remote electronic access.

b. For reproducing and transmitting in any manner a copy of an electronic record stored outside of the court's electronic case management system, including but not limited to, document files, audio and video recordings (other than a recording of a court proceeding), $31 per record provided.

(5) For reproducing recordings of proceedings, regardless of the medium, $32, including the cost of materials. This fee applies to services rendered on behalf of the United States if the recording is available through remote electronic access.

(6) For reproducing the record in any appeal in which the court of appeals does not require an appendix pursuant to Fed. R. App. P. 30(f), (or, in appeals before a bankruptcy appellate panel, pursuant to Fed. R. Bankr. P. 8018(e)), $89.

(7) For retrieval of one box of records from a Federal Records Center, National Archives, or other storage location removed from the place of business of the court, $64. For retrievals involving multiple boxes, $39 for each additional box. For electronic retrievals, $10 plus any charges assessed by the Federal Records Center, National Archives, or other storage location removed from the place of business of the courts.

(8) For any payment returned or denied for insufficient funds, or reversed due to a chargeback, $53.

(9) For copies of opinions, a fee commensurate with the cost of printing, as fixed by each court of appeals.

(10) For copies of the local rules of court, a fee commensurate with the cost of distributing the copies. The court may also distribute copies of the local rules without charge.

(11) For filing:

- Any separate or joint notice of appeal or application for appeal from the bankruptcy appellate panel, $5;

- A notice of the allowance of an appeal from the bankruptcy appellate panel, $5.

(12) For counsel's requested use of the court's videoconferencing equipment in connection with each oral argument, the court may charge and collect a fee of $200 per remote location.

(13) For original admission of attorney to practice, including a certificate of admission, $188. For a duplicate certificate of admission or certificate of good standing, $20.

1 Issued in accordance with 28 U.S.C. § 1913.

2 Item 13 does not apply to bankruptcy appellate panels.

DISTRICT COURT FEE SCHEDULE

(Effective December 1, 2020)

The fees included in the District Court Miscellaneous Fee Schedule[1] are to be charged for services provided by the district courts.

- The United States should not be charged fees under this schedule, with the exception of those specifically prescribed in Items 2, 4 and 5, when the information requested is available through remote electronic access.

- Federal agencies or programs that are funded from judiciary appropriations (agencies, organizations, and individuals providing services authorized by the Criminal Justice Act, 18 U.S.C. § 3006 and bankruptcy administrators) should not be charged any fees under this schedule.

1. For filing any document that is not related to a pending case or proceeding, $49.

2. For conducting a search of the district court records, $32 per name or item searched. This fee applies to services rendered on behalf of the United States if the information requested is available through electronic access.

3. For certification of any document, $11. For exemplification of any document, $23. For the issuance of an apostille, $47.

4.

a. For reproducing any record and providing a copy in paper form, $.50 per page. This fee shall apply to paper copies made from either: (1) original documents; or (2) microfiche or microfilm reproductions of the original records. This fee shall apply to services rendered on behalf of the United States if the record requested is available through electronic access.

b. For reproducing and transmitting in any manner a copy of an electronic record stored outside of the court's electronic case management system, including but not limited to, document files, audio recordings, and video recordings, $31 per record provided. Audio recordings of court proceedings continue to be governed by a separate fee in item 5 of this schedule.

5. For reproduction of an audio recording of a court proceeding, $32. This fee applies to services rendered on behalf of the United States, if the recording is available electronically.

6. For each microfiche sheet of film or microfilm jacket copy of any court record, where available, $6.

7. For retrieval of one box of records from a Federal Records Center, National Archives, or other storage location removed from the place of business of the court, $64. For retrievals involving multiple boxes, $39 for each additional box. For electronic retrievals, $10 plus any charges assessed by the Federal Records Center, National Archives, or other storage location removed from the place of business of the courts.

8. For any payment returned or denied for insufficient funds, or reversed due to a chargeback, $53.

9. For an appeal to a district judge from a judgment of conviction by a magistrate judge in a misdemeanor case, $39.

10. For original admission of attorneys to practice, $188 each, including a certificate of admission. For a duplicate certificate of admission or certificate of good standing, $20.

11. The court may charge and collect fees commensurate with the cost of providing copies of the local rules of court. The court may also distribute copies of the local rules without charge.

12.

- For handling registry funds deposited with and held by the court, the clerk shall assess a charge from interest earnings, in accordance with the detailed fee schedule issued by the Director of the Administrative Office of the United States Courts.

- For management of registry funds invested through the Court Registry Investment System, a fee at an annual rate of 10 basis points of assets on deposit shall be assessed from interest earnings, excluding registry funds from disputed ownership interpleader cases deposited under 28 U.S.C. § 1335 and held in a Court Registry Investment System Disputed Ownership Fund.

- For management of funds deposited under 28 U.S.C. § 1335 and invested in a Disputed Ownership Fund through the Court Registry Investment System, a fee at an annual rate of 20 basis points of assets on deposit shall be assessed from interest earnings.

- The Director of the Administrative Office has the authority to waive these fees for cause.

13. For filing an action brought under Title III of the Cuban Liberty and Democratic Solidarity (LIBERTAD) Act of 1996, P.L. 104–114, 110 Stat. § 785 (1996), $6,800. (This fee is in addition to the filing fee prescribed in 28 U.S.C. § 1914(a) for instituting any civil action other than a writ of habeas corpus.)

14. Administrative fee for filing a civil action, suit, or proceeding in a district court, $52. This fee does not apply to applications for a writ of habeas corpus or to persons granted in forma pauperis status under 28 U.S.C. § 1915.

15. Processing fee for an offense charged on a federal violation notice, $30.

1 Issued in accordance with 28 U.S.C. § 1914.

BANKRUPTCY COURT FEE SCHEDULE

(Effective December 1, 2020)

The fees included in the Bankruptcy Court Miscellaneous Fee Schedule[1] are to be charged for services provided by the bankruptcy courts.

- The United States should not be charged fees under this schedule, with the exception of those specifically prescribed in Items 1, 3 and 5 when the information requested is available through remote electronic access.

- Federal agencies or programs that are funded from judiciary appropriations (agencies, organizations, and individuals providing services authorized by the Criminal Justice Act, 18 U.S.C. § 3006A, and bankruptcy administrators) should not be charged any fees under this schedule.

1.   a.   For reproducing any document and providing a copy in paper form, $.50 per page. This fee applies to services rendered on behalf of the United States if the document requested is available through electronic access.

b.   For reproducing and transmitting in any manner a copy of an electronic record stored outside of the court's electronic case management system, including but not limited to, document files, audio recordings, and video recordings, $31 per record provided. Audio recordings of court proceedings continue to be governed by a separate fee under item 3 of this schedule.

2.   For certification of any document, $11. For exemplification of any document, $23.

3.   For reproduction of an audio recording of a court proceeding, $32. This fee applies to services rendered on behalf of the United States if the recording is available electronically.

4.   For filing an amendment to the debtor's schedules of creditors, lists of creditors, or mailing list, $32, except:

- The bankruptcy judge may, for good cause, waive the charge in any case.

- This fee must not be charged if -

  - the amendment is to change the address of a creditor or an attorney for a creditor listed on the schedules; or

  - the amendment is to add the name and address of an attorney for a creditor listed on the schedules.

5.   For conducting a search of the bankruptcy court records, $32 per name or item searched. This fee applies to services rendered on behalf of the United States if the information requested is available through electronic access.

6.   For filing a complaint, $350, except:

- If the trustee or debtor-in-possession files the complaint, the fee must be paid only by the estate, to the extent there is an estate.

- This fee must not be charged if -

  - the debtor is the plaintiff; or

  - a child support creditor or representative files the complaint and submits the form required by § 304(g) of the Bankruptcy Reform Act of 1994.

7.   For filing any document that is not related to a pending case or proceeding, $49.

8.   Administrative fee:

- For filing a petition under Chapter 7, 12, or 13, $78.

- For filing a petition under Chapter 9, 11, or 15, $571.

- When a motion to divide a joint case under Chapter 7, 12, or 13 is filed, $78.

- When a motion to divide a joint case under Chapter 11 is filed, $571.

9.   For payment to trustees pursuant to 11 U.S.C. § 330(b)(2), a $15 fee applies in the following circumstances:

- For filing a petition under Chapter 7.

- For filing a notice of conversion to a Chapter 7 case.
- For filing a motion to convert a case to a Chapter 7 case.
- For filing a motion to divide a joint Chapter 7 case.
- For filing a motion to reopen a Chapter 7 case.

10.   In addition to any fees imposed under Item 9, above, the following fees must be collected:

- For filing a motion to convert a Chapter 12 case to a Chapter 7 case or a notice of conversion pursuant to 11 U.S.C. § 1208(a), $45.
- For filing a motion to convert a Chapter 13 case to a Chapter 7 case or a notice of conversion pursuant to 11 U.S.C. § 1307(a), $10.

The fee amounts in this item are derived from the fees prescribed in 28 U.S.C. § 1930(a).

If the trustee files the motion to convert, the fee is payable only from the estate that exists prior to conversion.

If the filing fee for the chapter to which the case is requested to be converted is less than the fee paid at the commencement of the case, no refund may be provided.

11.   For filing a motion to reopen, the following fees apply:

- For filing a motion to reopen a Chapter 7 case, $245.
- For filing a motion to reopen a Chapter 9 case, $1167.
- For filing a motion to reopen a Chapter 11 case, $1167.
- For filing a motion to reopen a Chapter 12 case, $200.
- For filing a motion to reopen a Chapter 13 case, $235.
- For filing a motion to reopen a Chapter 15 case, $1167.

The fee amounts in this item are derived from the fees prescribed in 28 U.S.C. § 1930(a).

The reopening fee must be charged when a case has been closed without a discharge being entered.

The court may waive this fee under appropriate circumstances or may defer payment of the fee from trustees pending discovery of additional assets. If payment is deferred, the fee should be waived if no additional assets are discovered.

The reopening fee must not be charged in the following situations:

- to permit a party to file a complaint to obtain a determination under Rule 4007(b); or
- when a debtor files a motion to reopen a case based upon an alleged violation of the terms of the discharge under 11 U.S.C. § 524; or
- when the reopening is to correct an administrative error; or
- to redact a record already filed in a case, pursuant to Fed. R. Bankr. P. 9037, if redaction is the only reason for reopening; or
- when a party files a motion to reopen a case to request to withdraw unclaimed funds, unless the court orders otherwise.

12.   For retrieval of one box of records from a Federal Records Center, National Archives, or other storage location removed from the place of business of the court, $64. For retrievals involving multiple boxes, $39 for each additional box. For electronic retrievals, $10 plus any charges assessed by the Federal Records Center, National Archives, or other storage location removed from the place of business of the courts.

13.   For any payment returned or denied for insufficient funds, or reversed due to a chargeback, $53.

14.   For filing an appeal or cross appeal from a judgment, order, or decree, $293.

This fee is collected in addition to the statutory fee of $5 that is collected under 28 U.S.C. § 1930(c) when a notice of appeal is filed.

Parties filing a joint notice of appeal should pay only one fee.

If a trustee or debtor-in-possession is the appellant, the fee must be paid only by the estate, to the extent there is an estate.

Upon notice from the court of appeals that a direct appeal or direct cross-appeal has been authorized, an additional fee of $207 must be collected.

15.   For filing a case under Chapter 15 of the Bankruptcy Code, $1167.

This fee is derived from and equal to the fee prescribed in 28 U.S.C. § 1930(a)(3) for filing a case commenced under Chapter 11 of Title 11.

16.   The court may charge and collect fees commensurate with the cost of providing copies of the local rules of court. The court may also distribute copies of the local rules without charge.

17.

- For handling registry funds deposited with and held by the court, the clerk shall assess a charge from interest earnings, in accordance with the detailed fee schedule issued by the Director of the Administrative Office of the United States Courts.

- For management of registry funds invested through the Court Registry Investment System, a fee at an annual rate of 10 basis points of assets on deposit shall be assessed from interest earnings, excluding registry funds from disputed ownership interpleader cases deposited under 28 U.S.C. § 1335 and held in a Court Registry Investment System Disputed Ownership Fund.

- For management of funds deposited under 28 U.S.C. § 1335 and invested in a Disputed Ownership Fund through the Court Registry Investment System, a fee at an annual rate of 20 basis points of assets on deposit shall be assessed from interest earnings.

- The Director of the Administrative Office has the authority to waive these fees for cause.

18.   For a motion filed by the debtor to divide a joint case filed under 11 U.S.C. § 302, the following fees apply:

- For filing a motion to divide a joint Chapter 7 case, $245.

- For filing a motion to divide a joint Chapter 11 case, $1167.

- For filing a motion to divide a joint Chapter 12 case, $200.

- For filing a motion to divide a joint Chapter 13 case, $235.

These fees are derived from and equal to the filing fees prescribed in 28 U.S.C. § 1930(a).

19.   For filing the following motions, $188:

- To terminate, annul, modify or condition the automatic stay;

- To compel abandonment of property of the estate pursuant to Rule 6007(b) of the Federal Rules of Bankruptcy Procedure;

- To withdraw the reference of a case or proceeding under 28 U.S.C. § 157(d); or

- To sell property of the estate free and clear of liens under 11 U.S.C. § 363(f).

This fee must not be collected in the following situations:

- For a motion for relief from the co-debtor stay;

- For a stipulation for court approval of an agreement for relief from a stay; or

- For a motion filed by a child support creditor or its representative, if the form required by § 304(g) of the Bankruptcy Reform Act of 1994 is filed.

20.   For filing a transfer of claim, $26 per claim transferred.

21.   For filing a motion to redact a record, $26 per affected case. The court may waive this fee under appropriate circumstances.

1 Issued in accordance with 28 U.S.C. § 1930.

JUDICIAL PANEL ON MULTIDISTRICT LITIGATION FEE SCHEDULE

(Effective December 1, 2020)

Following are fees to be charged for services to be performed by the clerk of the Judicial Panel on Multidistrict Litigation[1].

No fees are to be charged for services rendered on behalf of the United States, with the exception of those specifically prescribed in items 1 and 3. No fees under this schedule shall be charged to federal agencies or programs which are funded from judiciary appropriations, including, but not limited to, agencies, organizations, and individuals providing services authorized by the Criminal Justice Act, 18 U.S.C. § 3006A.

(1) For every search of the records of the court conducted by the clerk of the court or a deputy clerk, $32 per name or item searched. This fee shall apply to services rendered on behalf of the United States if the information requested is available through electronic access.

(2) For certification of any document or paper, whether the certification is made directly on the document or by separate instrument, $11.

(3)

a. For reproducing any record and providing a copy in paper form, $.50 per page. This fee shall apply to paper copies made from either: (1) original documents; or (2) microfiche or microfilm reproductions of the original records. This fee shall apply to services rendered on behalf of the United States if the record requested is available through electronic access.

b. For reproducing and transmitting in any manner a copy of an electronic record stored outside of the court's electronic case management system, including but not limited to, document files, audio recordings, and video recordings, $31 per record provided.

(4) For retrieval of one box of records from a Federal Records Center, National Archives, or other storage location removed from the place of business of the court, $64. For retrievals involving multiple boxes, $39 for each additional box. For electronic retrievals, the fee is $19.90 which includes the Judiciary Administrative Fee and the Federal Records Center electronic retrieval flat rate fee.

(5) For any payment returned or denied for insufficient funds, or reversed due to a chargeback, $53.

[1] Issued in accordance with 28 U.S.C. § 1932.

ELECTRONIC PUBLIC ACCESS FEE SCHEDULE

(Issued in accordance with 28 U.S.C. §§ 1913, 1914, 1926, 1930, 1932)

(Effective January 1, 2020)

The fees included in the Electronic Public Access Fee Schedule are to be charged for providing electronic public access to court records.

Fees for Public Access to Court Electronic Records (PACER)

1. Except as provided below, for electronic access to any case document, docket sheet, or case-specific report via PACER: $0.10 per page, not to exceed the fee for thirty pages.

2. For electronic access to transcripts and non-case specific reports via PACER (such as reports obtained from the PACER Case Locator or docket activity reports): $0.10 per page.

3. For electronic access to an audio file of a court hearing via PACER: $2.40 per audio file.

Fees for Courthouse Electronic Access

4. For printing copies of any record or document accessed electronically at a public terminal in a courthouse: $0.10 per page.

PACER Service Center Fees

5. For every search of court records conducted by the PACER Service Center, $30 per name or item searched.

6. For the PACER Service Center to reproduce on paper any record pertaining to a PACER account, if this information is remotely available through electronic access: $0.50 per page.

7. For any payment returned or denied for insufficient funds, $53.

Free Access and Exemptions

8. Automatic Fee Exemptions:

- No fee is owed for electronic access to court data or audio files via PACER until an account holder accrues charges of more than $30.00 in a quarterly billing cycle.

- Parties in a case (including *pro se* litigants) and attorneys of record receive one free electronic copy, via the notice of electronic filing or notice of docket activity, of all documents filed electronically, if receipt is required by law or directed by the filer.

- No fee is charged for access to judicial opinions.

- No fee is charged for viewing case information or documents at courthouse public access terminals.

- No fee is charged for Chapter 13 bankruptcy trustees to download quarterly (i.e., once every 90 days) a list of the trustee's cases from the PACER Case Locator.

9. Discretionary Fee Exemptions:

- Courts may exempt certain persons or classes of persons from payment of the user access fee. Examples of individuals and groups that a court may consider exempting include: indigents, bankruptcy case trustees, pro bono attorneys, pro bono alternative dispute resolution neutrals, Section 501(c)(3) not-for-profit organizations, and individual researchers associated with educational institutions. Courts should not, however, exempt individuals or groups that have the ability to pay the statutorily established access fee. Examples of individuals and groups that a court should not exempt include: local, state or federal government agencies, members of the media, privately paid attorneys or others who have the ability to pay the fee.

- In considering granting an exemption, courts must find:

  - that those seeking an exemption have demonstrated that an exemption is necessary in order to avoid unreasonable burdens and to promote public access to information;

  - that individual researchers requesting an exemption have shown that the defined research project is intended for scholarly research, that it is limited in scope, and that it is not intended for redistribution on the internet or for commercial purposes. A request is limited in scope if the amount of exempt access requested is narrowly tailored to meet the needs of the defined research project.

- If the court grants an exemption:
  - the user receiving the exemption must agree not to sell the data obtained as a result, and must not transfer any data obtained as the result of a fee exemption, unless expressly authorized by the court; and
  - the exemption should be granted for a definite period of time, should be limited in scope, and may be revoked at the discretion of the court granting the exemption.
- Courts may provide local court information at no cost (e.g., local rules, court forms, news items, court calendars, and other information) to benefit the public.

Applicability to the United States and State and Local Governments

10. Unless otherwise authorized by the Judicial Conference, these fees must be charged to the United States, except to federal agencies or programs that are funded from judiciary appropriations (including, but not limited to, agencies, organizations, and individuals providing services authorized by the Criminal Justice Act [18 U.S.C. § 3006A], and bankruptcy administrators).

11. The fee for printing copies of any record or document accessed electronically at a public terminal ($0.10 per page) described in (4) above does not apply to services rendered on behalf of the United States if the record requested is not remotely available through electronic access.

12. The fee for local, state, and federal government entities, shall be $0.08 per page until April 1, 2015, after which time, the fee shall be $0.10 per page.

JUDICIAL CONFERENCE POLICY NOTES

The Electronic Public Access (EPA) fee and its exemptions are directly related to the requirement that the judiciary charge user-based fees for the development and maintenance of electronic public access services. The fee schedule provides examples of users that may not be able to afford reasonable user fees (such as indigents, bankruptcy case trustees, individual researchers associated with educational institutions, 501(c)(3) not-for-profit organizations, and court-appointed pro bono attorneys), but requires those seeking an exemption to demonstrate that an exemption is limited in scope and is necessary in order to avoid an unreasonable burden. In addition, the fee schedule includes examples of other entities that courts should not exempt from the fee (such as local, state or federal government agencies, members of the media, and attorneys). The goal is to provide courts with guidance in evaluating a requestor's ability to pay the fee.

Judicial Conference policy also limits exemptions in other ways. First, it requires exempted users to agree not to sell the data they receive through an exemption (unless expressly authorized by the court). This prohibition is not intended to bar a quote or reference to information received as a result of a fee exemption in a scholarly or other similar work. Second, it permits courts to grant exemptions for a definite period of time, to limit the scope of the exemptions, and to revoke exemptions. Third, it cautions that exemptions should be granted as the exception, not the rule, and prohibits courts from exempting all users from EPA fees.